From Plato to Wittgenstein

From Plato to Wittgenstein

The Historical Foundations of Mind

Daniel Kolak, Editor
William Paterson College

Wadsworth Publishing Company

Belmont, California
A Division of Wadsworth, Inc.

Philosophy Editor: Tammy Goldfeld
Editorial Assistant: Kristina Pappas
Production Service Coordinator: Deborah T. Kramer
Production Editor: Sara Hunsaker/*Ex Libris*
Print Buyer: Karen Hunt
Permissions Editor: Bob Kauser
Designer: Vargas/Williams/Design
Proof Reader: Elliot Simon
Cover: Harry Voigt
Compositor: Kachina Typesetting
Printer: Arcata Graphics/Fairfield

 This book is printed on acid-free recycled paper.

International Thomson Publishing
The trademark ITP is used under license

1 2 3 4 5 6 7 8 9 10—98 97 96 95 94

Library of Congress Cataloging-in-Publication Data

Kolak, Daniel.
    From Plato to Wittgenstein : the historical foundations of mind / Daniel Kolak.
       p.   cm.
    ISBN 0-534-21420-7
    1. Philosophy of mind—History—Sources. 2. Philosophy of mind.
I. Title.
BD418.3.K65   1994
128'.2—dc20   93-27324
                                             CIP

For David Goloff

Preface

Recent developments in philosophy, in general, and philosophy of mind, in particular, are so difficult to understand and so technical that, without first exploring the rich history leading up to them, students are simply unprepared to understand contemporary material. Yet most professors are forced either into altogether ignoring most of the historical developments, which would make contemporary work coherent to the student, or else using many original sources published separately, which tend to be prohibitive in cost.

From Plato to Wittgenstein: The Historical Foundations of Mind solves the problem by offering all the important original sources, in most cases complete and unabridged, in one volume. It is a dozen books rolled into one. Organized chronologically, it lets students experience the development of ideas and concepts gradually, at their own pace, and within their own minds. Instead of the dialectical, point counterpoint approach, students get a sense of the historical evolution of the mind, the concepts of mind, and the philosophy of mind. The key philosophers are allowed to speak for themselves; students join in the great conversation. By having a complete and full assemblage of the masterwork texts under one roof, the professor can choose the appropriate contemporary sources knowing the student will be prepared.

The sense in which we do not directly experience the objective, mind-independent world "out there," except through our own minds, is one of the most difficult insights for students to grasp. The representational nature of perception, the interpretive elements in our experience, and the functional relationship between concepts and percepts are so closely interwoven and ever present that it even may be difficult to realize why we need a theory of mind. The gradual awakening to the presence and workings of our own minds and the contributions our thoughts and concepts make to the world we experience required centuries of gradual development. Giving just the "philosophical results" outside of the context, without working through their historical development, tends to remove the philosophical power of the very realizations about the mind that have been involved in the progress of philosophy from its beginning. The material in this book does not have to be put into context because it comes with its own context. The works of the great philosophers are followed by more works of great philosophers who are building upon the previous works; in nearly each case the subsequent philosopher directly comments on the previous philosopher. The effect is cumulative. By the end of the book the student is ready to tackle the most sophisticated contemporary literature.

Instead of the usual detour of encapsulated interpretations, I have tried to bridge the gap between today's student and the primary texts with extensive, detailed reading questions. The step-by-step companion study guide, *One Thousand and One Questions*, designed to be used alongside *From Plato to Wittgenstein*, focuses the reader's attention directly, paragraph by paragraph, to the action on the page.

I thank Garrett Thomson, Philip Turetzky, John Peterman, and John O'Connor for their help with this project. Thanks also to the reviewers: John Bickle, East Carolina University; Mary Ann Carroll, Appalachian State University; Robert Klee, Ithaca College; Glenn Ross, Franklin and Marshall College; Paul Sagal, New Mexico State University; and especially Jack Furlong, Transylvania University, for his superb insights and encouragement.

Daniel Kolak

Contents

Introduction

OFTEN STUDENTS ARE INTRODUCED to philosophy of mind as if it were simply another subject matter, and they are presented with various tidbits that illustrate the "issues" and the "problems," in the hope that they will gain some abstract idea about what philosophy itself is. But, divorced from a specific field of knowledge, philosophy taught in this manner tends to produce merely a vague, general feeling of skepticism and relativism about knowledge. For this reason, this book is centered around a broad but specific topic: the human mind. Each of the original selections, while touching upon many central philosophical issues, has been pivotal in the discovery, development, and enhancement of philosophy. You will be not just reading about philosophy of mind but also doing philosophy.

When we explore the history of the philosophy of mind, time becomes a landscape through which the ever-elusive truth, though never seen and never attained at any moment, leaves a distinct trail. The purpose of this book is to get you out of the epistemic myopia of the present by providing a peripheral vision that spans from Plato to Wittgenstein. You will then be ready to look at the rich and varied present without being blinded by its current verisimilitudes and vicissitudes.

This anthology is a sourcebook of those aspects of the historical development of the mind, the concept of mind, and the philosophy of mind most essential to understanding with wisdom some of the current philosophical "revolutions": artificial intelligence and machine models, linguistic models, neuroscience, and cognitive science. "Understanding" is meant here in the philosophical sense: seeing not just the picture but where the picture ends, seeing the frame holding the picture—that is, understanding what the theory solves and what it does not solve and why. Otherwise, one is likely to forget that any conceptual framework is just that—a conceptual framework, subject to its own paradigms, limited, and ultimately likely to be discarded into the graveyard of the 10,000 theories and the 10,000 gods.

Starting from the background of Plato and Aristotle, the readings present the original, classical sources of the conceptual evolution that began with the moderns (Descartes, Locke, Berkeley, Hume, Leibniz, Kant, etc.) and their 19th- and 20th-century critics (James and Russell) and continues to the advent of the mathematical/logical and linguistic innovations of Russell and Wittgenstein. It is, after all, this last stage of development that has led to our ability to literally build a mind from scratch by placing logic and mathematics into a machine.

I
Plato

BORN IN ATHENS IN ABOUT 427 B.C. to a prominent Greek family, Plato became one of the greatest and most influential thinkers in history. He wrote philosophy, poetry, and drama; he also worked as a politician and was even a champion fighter. At the age of 40, he founded the world's first university, The Academy, a center for philosophical inquiry that lasted over a thousand years.

Like his famous teacher Socrates, Plato pursued and communicated wisdom not by writing or reading but by thinking out loud with others—that is, through direct contact among living minds. This process involves not just speaking and listening but *conversing,* which means, literally, "the action of moving about, living." By engaging in philosophical conversation, we're not merely thinking out loud for the purpose of agreeing or disagreeing with this or that thought; in philosophy, "What do you think?" is not the same as "Do you agree or disagree with this idea?" Ordinary thinking is to philosophical thought what painting by numbers is to painting, what reading books is to writing, what playing music by notes is to composing. And insofar as philosophy according to Socrates and Plato is a group activity, it requires moving thoughts and ideas around to see them from all sides, until together we arrive at the truth. The purpose is not to build a system of answers, an orthodoxy, in which the philosopher then settles. The Socratic philosopher is not a settler at all but an explorer, a guide who must forever continue on.

Socrates wrote nothing. He insisted that to write thoughts down and then pass them off as philosophy would not just be antithetical to philosophy but would destroy it. Philosophy books, he claimed, would make it possible for nonphilosophers to pretend to be teaching philosophy; humanity would then forget what true philosophy is. Ironically, the only reason we know he said this is that his greatest pupil, Plato, wrote those words down!

Unlike Socrates, Plato left many written works. Most, however, like *The Republic* (from which the first reading is taken), were intended for nonphilosophers who hadn't had the benefit of attending the Academy. Even there, Plato writes:

> . . . philosophy, the noblest pursuit of all, is not likely to be much esteemed by those of the opposite faction; not that the greatest and most lasting injury is done to her by her opponents, but by her own professing followers. . . . the greater number of them are arrant rogues, and the best are useless.

In other words, he thought most professing philosophers are notorious, shameful swindlers—at best pleasantly mischievous. So we should not emulate them. Those few shining stars who are true philosophers might blind us, so we shouldn't emulate them either. Philosophers, of either the good or the bad variety, are to the serious would-be philosopher useless.

What, then, should we do? Ignore the philosophers and follow our own whims, think any thoughts? Then we would count ourselves among the most ignorant of all: the cave dwellers who live in the dark, seduced by mere shadows and images, prisoners of their own ignorance. Should we instead forget about examining philosophical questions? In that case, we are not even living a miserable life of illusion; according to Socrates, our lives would be absolutely worthless and we would be as good as dead. Well, what is the would-be philosopher to do? You don't know? Good!

The Socratic state of unknowing is sometimes confused with mere ignorance, sometimes with religious or poetic mysticism. It is neither. Ignorance means, literally, ignoring the truth through false knowledge by attachment to lies, deceptions, and illusion. Mysticism is the denial of rational knowledge. There is a big difference between, on the one hand, being ignorant or blinding oneself to the known and, on the other, knowing the unknown.

True wisdom, according to Socrates, means knowing the unknown. To see the profound difference, consider what it means when an amnesiac asks, perplexed, "Who am I?" Something has gone wrong, and the person has forgotten; the problem is pathological. When, on the other hand, the philosopher asks "Who am I?" the problem is not one of ignorance or memory loss. Rather, this person is remembering not to be blinded by what seems most obvious. The problem is that the philosopher sees more, not less.

Through Plato's direction, the Academy spawned a slew of scientific and mathematical innovations, linking 5th-century-B.C. Pythagorean mathematics with Egyptian geometry and arithmetic done in Alexandria. Plato's student Theaetetus invented solid geometry and did the first work ever on conic sections. Eudoxus, author of the theory of proportions found in Euclid's *Elements*, who had moved his own school to Athens to collaborate with Plato, invented the method of finding the areas and volumes of curvilinear figures by exhaustion, a precursor to calculus; he also designed the astronomical scheme of concentric spheres, later revised by Aristotle. Another pupil, Archytas, began what later would become mechanical science. Plato's Academy also led in the development of jurisprudence and political philosophy, concerning itself with ethical and moral issues, especially those relating to how to make a better society. Plato's most famous pupil, Aristotle, developed a system of both ethics and logic, originating the experimental method in physics and biology.

With regard to Plato's own work, the 20th-century philosopher Alfred Whitehead describes the entire subsequent 24 centuries of philosophy as "a series of footnotes to Plato." In "The Sun, the Divided Line, and the Cave," it is easy to see why. These are some of Plato's most famous passages: the allegory of the cave, the simile of the sun, and the divided line from *The Republic*, a work Plato kept revising all his life. Here you will find all the major philosophical themes: true knowledge, ignorance, wisdom, the nature of the human soul, a discourse on philosophical thinking. Written in dialogue form, the narrator and main character is Socrates, Plato's famous teacher and mentor.

About 20 years before Plato began writing *The Republic*, Socrates was put to death for "corrupting the youth and raising doubts about the accepted Gods." The first dialogue describes a conversation that supposedly took place ten or so years before Socrates' fateful drinking of the hemlock, during a pause in the Peloponnesian War (between Athens and Sparta), while Athens was still a democracy. The characters are the narrator, Socrates, and Plato's brothers, Glaucon and Adeimantus.

The second dialogue, "Phaedo," takes place in the prison of Socrates. The narrator, Phaedo, tells of his final conversation with Socrates before Socrates drank the hemlock and died. Socrates explains that, instead of fearing death, he looks forward to the liberation of the soul, which during life is in bondage through its own self-deception. He says:

> The soul is fastened and glued to the body—until philosophy received her, she could only view real existence through the bars of a prison, not in and through herself; she was wallowing in the mire of every sort of ignorance, and by reason of lust had become the principal accomplice in her own captivity. This was her original state; and then . . . philosophy, seeing how terrible was her confinement, of which she was to herself the cause, received and gently comforted her and sought to release her, pointing out that the eye and the ear and the other senses are full of deception, and persuading her to retire from them, and abstain from all but the necessary use of them, and be gathered up and collected into herself, bidding her trust in herself and her own pure apprehension of pure existence, and to mistrust whatever comes to her through other channels and is subject to variation; for such things are visible and tangible, but what she sees in her own nature is intelligible and invisible. And the soul of the true philosopher thinks that she ought not to resist this deliverance . . . (*Phaedo* §82–83).

The Sun, the Divided Line, and the Cave

Plato

The many, as we say, are seen but not known, and the ideas are known but not seen.

Exactly.

And what is the organ with which we see the visible things?

The sight, he said.

And with the hearing, I said, we hear, and with the other senses perceive the other objects of sense?

True.

But have you remarked that sight is by far the most costly and complex piece of workmanship which the artificer of the senses ever contrived?

No, I never have, he said.

Then reflect: has the ear or voice need of any third or additional nature in order that the one may be able to hear and the other to be heard?

Nothing of the sort.

No, indeed, I replied; and the same is true of most, if not all, the other senses—you would not say that any of them requires such an addition?

Certainly not.

But you see that without the addition of some other nature there is no seeing or being seen?

How do you mean?

Sight being, as I conceive, in the eyes, and he who has eyes wanting to see; colour being also present in them, still unless there be a third nature specially adapted to the purpose, the owner of the eyes will see nothing and the colours will be invisible.

Of what nature are you speaking?

Of that which you term light, I replied.

True, he said.

Noble, then, is the bond which links together sight and visibility, and great beyond other bonds by no small difference of nature; for light is their bond, and light is no ignoble thing?

Nay, he said, the reverse of ignoble.

And which, I said, of the gods in heaven would you say was the lord of this element? Whose is that light which makes the eye to see perfectly and the visible to appear?

You mean the sun, as you and all mankind say.

May not the relation of sight to this deity be described as follows?

How?

Neither sight nor the eye in which sight resides is the sun?

No.

Yet of all the organs of sense the eye is the most like the sun?

By far the most like.

And the power which the eye possesses is a sort of effluence which is dispensed from the sun?

Exactly.

Then the sun is not sight, but the author of sight who is recognised by sight.

True, he said.

And this is he whom I call the child of the good, whom the good begat in his own likeness, to be in the visible world, in relation to sight and the things of sight, what the good is in the intellectual world in relation to mind and the things of mind.

Will you be a little more explicit? he said.

Why, you know, I said, that the eyes, when a person directs them towards objects on which the light of day is no longer shining, but the moon and stars only, see dimly, and are nearly blind; they seem to have no clearness of vision in them?

Very true.

But when they are directed towards objects on which the sun shines, they see clearly and there is sight in them?

SOURCE: *The Dialogues of Plato* translated by Benjamin Jowett (London: The Clarendon Press, 1892).

Certainly.

And the soul is like the eye: When resting upon that on which truth and being shine, the soul perceives and understands and is radiant with intelligence; but when turned towards the twilight of becoming and perishing, then she has opinion only, and goes blinking about, and is first of one opinion and then of another, and seems to have no intelligence?

Just so.

Now, that which imparts truth to the known and the power of knowing to the knower is what I would have you term the idea of good, and this you will deem to be the cause of science, and of truth in so far as the latter becomes the subject of knowledge; beautiful too, as are both truth and knowledge, you will be right in esteeming this other nature as more beautiful than either; and, as in the previous instance, light and sight may be truly said to be like the sun, and yet not to be the sun, so in this other sphere, science and truth may be deemed to be like the good, but not the good; the good has a place of honour yet higher.

What a wonder of beauty that must be, he said, which is the author of science and truth, and yet surpasses them in beauty; for you surely cannot mean to say that pleasure is the good?

God forbid, I replied, but may I ask you to consider the image in another point of view?

In what point of view?

You would say, would you not, that the sun is not only the author of visibility in all visible things, but of generation and nourishment and growth, though he himself is not generation?

Certainly.

In like manner the good may be said to be not only the author of knowledge to all things known, but of their being and essence, and yet the good is not essence, but far exceeds essence in dignity and power.

Glaucon said, with a ludicrous earnestness: By the light of heaven, how amazing!

Yes, I said, and the exaggeration may be set down to you; for you made me utter my fancies.

And pray continue to utter them; at any rate let us hear if there is anything more to be said about the similitude of the sun.

Yes, I said, there is a great deal more.

Then omit nothing, however slight.

I will do my best, I said, but I should think that a great deal will have to be omitted.

You have to imagine, then, that there are two ruling powers, and that one of them is set over the intellectual world, the other over the visible. I do not say heaven, lest you should fancy that I am playing upon the name. . . . May I suppose that you have this distinction of the visible and intelligible fixed in your mind?

I have.

Now take a line which has been cut into two unequal parts, and divide each of them again in the same proportion, and supppose the two main divisions to answer, one to the visible and the other to the intelligible, and then compare the subdivisions in respect of their clearness and want of clearness, and you will find that the first section in the sphere of the visible consists of images. And by images I mean, in the first place, shadows, and in the second place, reflections in water and in solid, smooth and polished bodies and the like: Do you understand?

Yes, I understand.

Imagine, now, the other section, of which this is only the resemblance, to include the animals which we see, and everything that grows or is made.

Very good.

Would you not admit that both the sections of this division have different degrees of truth, and that the copy is to the original as the sphere of opinion is to the sphere of knowledge?

Most undoubtedly.

Next proceed to consider the manner in which the sphere of the intellectual is to be divided.

In what manner?

Thus:—There are two subdivisions, in the lower of which the soul uses the figures given by the former division as images; the enquiry can only be hypothetical, and instead of going upwards to a principle descends to the other end; in the higher of the two, the soul passes out of hypotheses, and goes up to a principle which is above hypotheses, making no use of images as in the former case, but proceeding only in and through the ideas themselves.

I do not quite understand your meaning, he said.

Then I will try again; you will understand me better when I have made some preliminary remarks. You are aware that students of geometry, arithmetic, and the kindred sciences assume the odd and the even and the figures and three kinds of angles and the like in their several branches of science; these are their hypotheses, which they and every body are supposed to know, and therefore they do not deign to give any account of them either to themselves or others; but they begin with them, and go on until they arrive at last, and in a consistent manner, at their conclusion?

Yes, he said, I know.

And do you not know also that although they make use of the visible forms and reason about them, they are thinking not of these, but of the ideals which they resemble; not of the figures which they draw, but of the absolute square and the absolute diameter, and so on— the forms which they draw or make, and which have shadows and reflections in water of their own, are converted by them into images, but they are really seeking to behold the things themselves, which can only be seen with the eye of the mind?

This is true.

And of this kind I spoke as the intelligible, although in the search after it the soul is compelled to use hypotheses; not ascending to a first principle, because she is unable to rise above the region of hypothesis, but employing the objects of which the shadows below are resemblances in their turn as images, they having in relation to the shadows and reflections of them a greater distinctness, and therefore a higher value.

I understand, he said, that you are speaking of the province of geometry and the sister arts.

And when I speak of the other division of the intelligible, you will understand me to speak of that other sort of knowledge which reason herself attains by the power of dialectic, using the hypotheses not as first principles, but only as hypotheses—that is to say, as steps and points of departure into a world which is above hypotheses, in order that she may soar beyond them to the first principle of the whole; and clinging to this and then to that which depends on this, by successive steps she descends again without the aid of any sensible object, from ideas, through ideas, and in ideas she ends.

I understand you, he replied, not perfectly, for you seem to me to be describing a task which is really tremendous; but, at any rate, I understand you to say that knowledge and being, which the science of dialectic contemplates, are clearer than the notions of the arts, as they are termed, which proceed from hypotheses only: these are also contemplated by the understanding, and not by the senses: yet, because they start from hypotheses and do not ascend to a principle, those who contemplate them appear to you not to exercise the higher reason upon them, although when a first principle is added to them they are cognizable by the higher reason. And the habit which is concerned with geometry and the cognate sciences I suppose that you would term understanding and not reason, as being intermediate between opinion and reason.

You have quite conceived my meaning, I said; and now, corresponding to these four divisions, let there be four faculties in the soul—reason answering to the highest, understanding to the second, faith (or conviction) to the third, and perception of shadows to the last—and let there be a scale of them, and let us suppose that the several faculties have clearness in the same degree that their objects have truth.

I understand, he replied, and give my assent, and accept your arrangement.

And now, I said, let me show in a figure how far our nature is enlightened or unenlightened: Behold! human beings living in an underground den, which has a mouth open towards the light and reaching all along the den; here they have been from their childhood, and have their legs and necks chained so that they cannot move, and can only see before them, being prevented by the chains from turning round their heads. Above and behind them a fire is blazing at a distance, and between the fire and the prisoners there is a raised way; and you will see, if you look, a low wall built along the way, like the screen which marionette players have in front of them, over which they show the puppets.

I see.

And do you see, I said, men passing along the wall carrying all sorts of vessels, and statues and figures of animals made of wood and stone and various materials, which appear over the wall? Some of them are talking, others silent.

You have shown me a strange image, and they are strange prisoners.

Like ourselves, I replied, and they see only their own shadows, or the shadows of one another, which the fire throws on the opposite wall of the cave?

True, he said, how could they see anything but the shadows if they were never allowed to move their heads?

And of the objects which are being carried in like manner they would only see the shadows?

Yes, he said.

And if they were able to converse with one another, would they not suppose that they were naming what was actually before them?

Very true.

And suppose further that the prison had an echo which came from the other side, would they not be sure to fancy when one of the passers-by spoke that the voice which they heard came from the passing shadow?

No question, he replied.

To them, I said, the truth would be literally nothing but the shadows of the images.

That is certain.

And now look again, and see what will naturally follow if the prisoners are released and disabused of their error. At first, when any of them is liberated and compelled suddenly to stand up and turn his neck round and walk and look towards the light, he will suffer sharp pains; the glare will distress him, and he will be unable to see the realities of which in his former state he had seen the shadows; and then conceive some one saying to him, that what he saw before was an illusion, but that now, when he is approaching nearer to being and his eye is turned towards more real existence, he has a clearer vision—what will be his reply? And you may further imagine that his instructor is pointing to the objects as they pass and requiring him to name them—will he not be perplexed? Will he not fancy that the shadows which he formerly saw are truer than the objects which are now shown to him?

Far truer.

And if he is compelled to look straight at the light, will he not have a pain in his eyes which will make him turn away to take refuge in the objects of vision which he can see, and which he will conceive to be in reality clearer than the things which are now being shown to him?

True, he said.

And suppose once more, that he is reluctantly dragged up a steep and rugged ascent, and held fast until he is forced into the presence of the sun himself, is he not likely to be pained and irritated? When he approaches the light his eyes will be dazzled, and he will not be able to see anything at all of what are now called realities.

Not all in a moment, he said.

He will require to grow accustomed to the sight of the upper world. And first he will see the shadows best, next the reflections of men and other objects in the water, and then the objects themselves; then he will gaze upon the light of the moon and the stars and the spangled heaven; and he will see the sky and the stars by night better than the sun or the light of the sun by day?

Certainly.

Last of all he will be able to see the sun, and not mere reflections of him in the water; but he will see him in his own proper place, and not in another; and he will contemplate him as he is.

Certainly.

He will then proceed to argue that this is he who gives the season and the years, and is the guardian of all that is in the visible world, and in a certain way the cause of all things which he and his fellows have been accustomed to behold?

Clearly, he said, he would first see the sun and then reason about him.

And when he remembered his old habitation, and the wisdom of the den and his fellow-prisoners, do you not suppose that he would felicitate himself on the change, and pity them?

Certainly, he would.

And if they were in the habit of conferring honours among themselves on those who were quickest to observe the passing shadows and to remark which of them went before, and which followed after, and which were together, and who were therefore best able to draw conclusions as to the future, do you think that he would care for such honours and glories, or envy the possessors of them? Would he not say with Homer,

'Better to be the poor servant of a poor master,'

and to endure anything, rather than think as they do and live after their manner?

Yes, he said, I think that he would rather suffer anything than entertain these false notions and live in this miserable manner.

Imagine once more, I said, such an one coming suddenly out of the sun to be replaced in his old situation; would he not be certain to have his eyes full of darkness?

To be sure, he said.

And if there were a contest, and he had to compete in measuring the shadows with the prisoners who had never moved out of the den, while his sight was still weak, and before his eyes had become steady (and the time which would be needed to acquire this new habit of sight might be very considerable), would he not be ridiculous? Men would say of him that up he went and down he came without his eyes; and that it was better not even to think of ascending; and if anyone tried to loose another and lead him up to the light, let them only catch the offender, and they would put him to death.

No question, he said.

The entire allegory, I said, you may now append, dear Glaucon, to the previous argument; the prison-house is the world of sight, the light of the fire is the sun, and you will not misapprehend me if you interpret the journey upwards to be the ascent of the soul into the intellectual world according to my poor belief, which, at your desire, I have ex-pressed—whether rightly or wrongly God knows. But, whether true or false, my opinion is that in the world of knowledge the idea of good appears last of all, and is seen only with an effort; and, when seen, is also inferred to be the universal author of all things beautiful and right, parent of light and of the lord of light in this visible world, and the immediate source of reason and truth in the intellectual; and that this is the power upon which he who would act rationally either in public or private life must have his eye fixed.

I agree, he said, as far as I am able to understand you.

Moreover, I said, you must not wonder that those who attain to this beatific vision are unwilling to descend to human affairs; for their souls are ever hastening into the upper world where they desire to dwell; which desire of theirs is very natural, if our allegory may be trusted.

Yes, very natural.

And is there anything surprising in one who passes from divine contemplations to the evil state of man, misbehaving himself in a ridiculous manner; if, while his eyes are blinking and before he has become accustomed to the surrounding darkness, he is compelled to fight in courts of law, or in other places, about the images or the shadows of images of justice, and is endeavouring to meet the conceptions of those who have never yet seen absolute justice?

Anything but surprising, he replied.

Any one who has common sense will remember that the bewilderments of the eyes are of two kinds, and arise from two causes, either from coming out of the light or from going into the light, which is true of the mind's eye, quite as much as of the bodily eye; and he who remembers this when he sees any one whose vision is perplexed and weak, will not be too ready to laugh; he will first ask whether that soul of man has come out of the brighter life and is unable to see because unaccustomed to the dark, or having turned from darkness to the day is dazzled by excess of light. And he will count the one happy in his condition and state of being, and he will pity the other; or, if he have a mind to laugh at the soul which comes from below into the light, there will be more reason in this than in the laugh which greets him who returns from above out of the light into the den.

That, he said, is a very just distinction.

But then, if I am right, certain professors of education must be wrong when they say that they can put a knowledge into the soul which was not there before, like sight into blind eyes.

They undoubtedly say this, he replied.

Whereas, our argument shows that the power and capacity of learning exists in the soul already; and that just as the eye was unable to turn from darkness to light without the whole body, so too the instrument of knowledge can only by the movement of the whole soul be turned from the world of becoming into that of being, and learn by degrees to endure the sight of being, and of the brightest and best of being, or in other words, of the good.

Very true.

And must there not be some art which will effect conversion in the easiest and quickest manner; not implanting the faculty of sight, for that exists already, but has been turned in the wrong direction and is looking away from the truth?

Yes, he said, such an art may be presumed.

And whereas the other so-called virtues of the soul seem to be akin to bodily qualities, for even when they are not originally innate they can be implanted later by habit and exercise, the virtue of wisdom more than anything else contains a divine element which always remains and by this conversion is rendered useful and profitable, or, on the other hand, hurtful and useless.

Phaedo

Plato

Your favourite doctrine, Socrates, that knowledge is simply recollection, if true, also necessarily implies a previous time in which we have learned that which we now recollect. But this would be impossible unless our soul had been in some place before existing in the form of man; here then is another proof of the soul's immortality.

But tell me, Cebes, said Simmias, interposing, what arguments are urged in favour of this doctrine of recollection. I am not very sure at the moment that I remember them.

One excellent proof, said Cebes, is afforded by questions. If you put a question to a person in a right way, he will give a true answer of himself, but how could he do this unless there were knowledge and right reason already in him? And this is most clearly shown when he is taken to a diagram or to anything of that sort.

But if, said Socrates, you are still incredulous, Simmias, I would ask you whether you may not agree with me when you look at the matter in another way;—I mean, if you are still incredulous as to whether knowledge is recollection?

Incredulous I am not, said Simmias, but I want to have this doctrine of recollection brought to my own recollection, and, from what Cebes has said, I am beginning to recollect and be convinced: But I should still like to hear what you were going to say.

This is what I would say, he replied:—We should agree, if I am not mistaken, that what a man recollects he must have known at some previous time.

Very true.

And what is the nature of this knowledge or recollection? I mean to ask: Whether a person who, having seen or heard or in any way perceived anything, knows not only that, but has a

SOURCE: *The Dialogues of Plato* translated by Benjamin Jowett (London: The Clarendon Press, 1892).

conception of something else which is the subject, not of the same but of some other kind of knowledge, may not be fairly said to recollect that of which he has the conception?

What do you mean?

I mean what I may illustrate by the following instance:—The knowledge of a lyre is not the same as the knowledge of a man?

True.

And yet what is the feeling of lovers when they recognize a lyre, or a garment, or anything else which the beloved has been in the habit of using? Do not they, from knowing the lyre, form in the mind's eye an image of the youth to whom the lyre belongs? And this is recollection. In like manner any one who sees Simmias may remember Cebes; and there are endless examples of the same thing.

Endless, indeed, replied Simmias.

And recollection is most commonly a process of recovering that which has been already forgotten through time and inattention.

Very true, he said.

Well; and may you not also from seeing the picture of a house or a lyre remember a man? and from the picture of Simmias, you may be led to remember Cebes;

True.

Or you may also be led to the recollection of Simmias himself?

Quite so.

And in all these cases, the recollection may be derived from things either like or unlike?

It may be.

And when the recollection is derived from like things, then another consideration is sure to arise, which is—whether the likeness in any degree falls short or not of that which is recollected?

Very true, he said.

And shall we proceed a step further, and affirm that there is such a thing as equality, not of one piece of wood or stone with another, but that, over and above this, there is absolute equality? Shall we say so?

Say so, yes, replied Simmias, and swear to it, with all the confidence in life.

And do we know the nature of this absolute essence?

To be sure, he said.

And whence did we obtain our knowledge?

Did we not see equalities of material things, such as pieces of wood and stones, and gather from them the idea of an equality which is different from them? For you will acknowledge that there is a difference. Or look at the matter in another way:—Do not the same pieces of wood or stone appear at one time equal, and at another time unequal?

That is certain.

But are real equals ever equal? or is the idea of equality the same as of inequality?

Impossible, Socrates.

Then these (so-called) equals are not the same with the idea of equality?

I should say, clearly not, Socrates.

And yet from these equals, although differing from the idea of equality, you conceived and attained that idea?

Very true, he said.

Which might be like, or might be unlike them?

Yes.

But that makes no difference: Whenever from seeing one thing you conceived another, whether like or unlike, there must surely have been an act of recollection?

Very true.

But what would you say of equal portions of wood and stone, or other material equals? and what is the impression produced by them? Are they equals in the same sense in which absolute equality is equal? or do they fall short of this perfect equality in a measure?

Yes, he said, in a very great measure too.

And must we not allow, that when I or any one, looking at any object, observes that the thing which he sees aims at being some other thing, but falls short of, and cannot be, that other thing, but is inferior, he who makes this observation must have had a previous knowledge of that to which the other, although similar, was inferior.

Certainly.

And has not this been our own case in the matter of equals and of absolute equality?

Precisely.

Then we must have known equality previously to the time when we first saw the material equals, and reflected that all these apparent equals strive to attain absolute equality, but fall short of it?

Very true.

And we recognize also that this absolute equality has only been known, and can only be known, through the medium of sight or touch, or of some other of the senses, which are all alike in this respect?

Yes, Socrates, as far as the argument is concerned, one of them is the same as the other.

From the senses then is derived the knowledge that all sensible things aim at an absolute equality of which they fall short?

Yes.

Then before we began to see or hear or perceive in any way, we must have had a knowledge of absolute equality, or we could not have referred to that standard the equals which are derived from the senses?—for to that they all aspire, and of that they fall short.

No other inference can be drawn from the previous statements.

And did we not see and hear and have the use of our other senses as soon as we were born?

Certainly.

Then we must have acquired the knowledge of equality at some previous time?

Yes.

That is to say, before we were born, I suppose?

True.

And if we acquired this knowledge before we were born, and were born having the use of it, then we also knew before we were born and at the instant of birth not only the equal or the greater or the less, but all other ideas; for we are not speaking only of equality, but of beauty, goodness, justice, holiness, and of all which we stamp with the name of essence in the dialectical process, both when we ask and when we answer questions. Of all this we may certainly affirm that we acquired the knowledge before birth?

We may.

But if, after having acquired, we have not forgotten what in each case we acquired, then we must always have come into life having knowledge, and shall always continue to know as long as life lasts—for knowing is the acquiring and retaining knowledge and not forgetting. Is not forgetting, Simmias, just the losing of knowledge?

Quite true, Socrates.

But if the knowledge which we acquired before birth was lost by us at birth, and if afterwards by the use of the senses we recovered what we previously knew, will not the process which we call learning be a recovering of the knowledge which is natural to us, and may not this be rightly termed recollection?

Very true.

So much is clear—that when we perceive something, either by the help of sight, or hearing, or some other sense, from that perception we are able to obtain a notion of some other thing like or unlike which is associated with it but has been forgotten. Whence, as I was saying, one of two alternatives follows:—either we had this knowledge at birth, and continued to know through life; or, after birth, those who are said to learn only remember, and learning is simply recollection.

Yes, that is quite true, Socrates.

And which alternative, Simmias, do you prefer? Had we the knowledge at our birth, or did we recollect the things which we knew previously to our birth?

I cannot decide at the moment.

At any rate you can decide whether he who has knowledge will or will not be able to render an account of his knowledge? What do you say?

Certainly, he will.

But do you think that every man is able to give an account of these very matters about which we are speaking?

Would that they could, Socrates, but I rather fear that to-morrow, at this time, there will no longer be any one alive who is able to give an account of them such as ought to be given.

Then you are not of opinion, Simmias, that all men know these things?

Certainly not.

They are in process of recollecting that which they learned before?

Certainly.

But when did our souls acquire this knowledge?—not since we were born as men?

Certainly not.

And therefore, previously?

Yes.

Then, Simmias, our souls must also have

existed without bodies before they were in the form of man, and must have had intelligence.

Unless indeed you suppose, Socrates, that these notions are given us at the very moment of birth; for this is the only time which remains.

Yes, my friend, but if so, when do we lose them? for they are not in us when we are born—that is admitted. Do we lose them at the moment of receiving them, or if not at what other time?

No, Socrates, I perceive that I was unconsciously talking non-sense.

Then may we not say, Simmias, that if, as we are always repeating, there is an absolute beauty, and goodness, and an absolute essence of all things; and if to this, which is now discovered to have existed in our former state, we refer all our sensations, and with this compare them, finding these ideas to be pre-existent and our inborn possession—then our souls must have had a prior existence, but if not, there would be no force in the argument? There is the same proof that these ideas must have existed before we were born, as that our souls existed before we were born; and if not the ideas, then not the souls. . . .

[N]ow let us return to the previous discussion. Is that idea or essence, which in the dialectical process we define as essence or true existence—whether essence of equality, beauty, or anything else—are these essences, I say, liable at times to some degree of change? or are they each of them always what they are, having the same simple self-existent and unchanging forms, not admitting of variation at all, or in any way, or at any time?

They must be always the same, Socrates, replied Cebes.

And what would you say of the many beautiful—whether men or horses or garments or any other things which are named by the same names and may be called equal or beautiful—are they all unchanging and the same always, or quite the reverse? May they not rather be described as almost always changing and hardly ever the same, either with themselves or with one another?

The latter, replied Cebes, they are always in a state of change.

And these you can touch and see and perceive with the senses, but the unchanging things you can only perceive with the mind—they are invisible and are not seen?

That is very true, he said.

Well then, added Socrates, let us suppose that there are two sorts of existences—one seen, the other unseen.

Let us suppose them.

The seen is the changing, and the unseen is the unchanging?

That may be also supposed.

And, further, is not one part of us body, another part soul?

To be sure.

And to which class is the body more alike and akin?

Clearly to the seen—no one can doubt that.

And is the soul seen or not seen?

Not by man, Socrates.

And what we mean by 'seen' and 'not seen' is that which is or is not visible to the eye of man?

Yes, to the eye of man.

And is the soul seen or not seen?

Not seen.

Unseen then?

Yes.

Then the soul is more like to the unseen, and the body to the seen?

That follows necessarily, Socrates.

And were we not saying long ago that the soul when using the body as an instrument of perception, that is to say, when using the sense of sight or hearing or some other sense (for the meaning of perceiving through the body is perceiving through the senses)—were we not saying that the soul too is then dragged by the body into the region of the changeable, and wanders and is confused; the world spins round her, and she is like a drunkard, when she touches change?

Very true.

But when returning into herself she reflects, then she passes into the other world, the region of purity, and eternity, and immortality, and unchangeableness, which are her kindred, and with them she ever lives, when she is by herself and is not let or hindered; then she ceases from her erring ways, and being in communion with the unchanging is unchanging. And this state of the soul is called wisdom?

That is well and truly said, Socrates, he replied.

And to which class is the soul more nearly alike and akin, as far as may be inferred from this argument, as well as from the preceding one?

I think, Socrates, that, in the opinion of every one who follows the argument, the soul will be infinitely more like the unchangeable—even the most stupid person will not deny that.

And the body is more like the changing?

Yes.

Yet once more consider the matter in another light: When the soul and the body are united, then nature orders the soul to rule and govern, and the body to obey and serve. Now which of these two functions is akin to the divine? and which to the mortal? Does not the divine appear to you to be that which naturally orders and rules, and the mortal to be that which is subject and servant?

True.

And which does the soul resemble?

The soul resembles the divine, and the body the mortal—there can be no doubt of that, Socrates.

Then reflect, Cebes: of all which has been said is not this the conclusion?—that the soul is in the very likeness of the divine, and immortal, and intellectual, and uniform, and indissoluble, and unchangeable; and that the body is in the very likeness of the human, and mortal, and unintellectual, and multiform, and dissoluble, and changeable. Can this, my dear Cebes, be denied?

It cannot. . . .

Very good, Socrates, said Simmias, then I will tell you my difficulty, and Cebes will tell you his. I feel myself (and I daresay that you have the same feeling), how hard or rather impossible is the attainment of any certainty about questions such as these in the present life. And yet I should deem him a coward who did not prove what is said about them to the uttermost, or whose heart failed him before he had examined them on every side. For he should persevere until he has achieved one of two things: either he should discover, or be taught the truth about them; or, if this be impossible, I would have him take the best and most irrefragable of human theories, and let this be the raft upon which he sails through life—not without risk, as I admit, if he cannot find some word of God which will more surely and safely carry him. And now, as you bid me, I will venture to question you, and then I shall not have to reproach myself hereafter with not having said at the time what I think. For when I consider the matter, either alone or with Cebes, the argument does certainly appear to me, Socrates, to be not sufficient.

Socrates answered: I dare say, my friend, that you may be right, but I should like to know in what respect the argument is insufficient.

In this respect, replied Simmias:—Suppose a person to use the same argument about harmony and the lyre—might he not say that harmony is a thing invisible, incorporeal, perfect, divine, existing in the lyre which is harmonized, but that the lyre and the strings are matter and material, composite, earthy, and akin to mortality? And when someone breaks the lyre, or cuts and rends the strings, then he who takes this view would argue as you do, and on the same analogy, that the harmony survives and has not perished—you cannot imagine, he would say, that the lyre without the strings, and the broken strings themselves which are mortal remain, and yet that the harmony, which is of heavenly and immortal nature and kindred, has perished—perished before the mortal. The harmony must still be somewhere, and the wood and strings will decay before anything can happen to that. The thought, Socrates, must have occurred to your own mind that such is our conception of the soul; and that when the body is in a manner strung and held together by the elements of hot and cold, wet and dry, then the soul is the harmony or due proportionate admixture of them. But if so, whenever the strings of the body are unduly loosened or overstrained through disease or other injury, then the soul, though most divine, like other harmonies of music or of works of art, of course perishes at once; although the material remains of the body may last for a considerable time, until they are either decayed or burnt. And if any one maintains that the soul, being the harmony of the elements of the body, is first to perish in that which is called death, how shall we answer him?

Socrates looked fixedly at us as his manner was, and said with a smile: Simmias has reason on his side; and why does not some one of you who is better able than myself answer him? for there is force in his attack upon me. But perhaps, before we answer him, we had better also hear what Cebes has to say that we may gain time for reflection, and when they have both spoken, we may either assent to them, if there is truth in what they say, or if not, we will maintain our position. Please to tell me then, Cebes, he said, what was the difficulty which troubled you?

Cebes said: I will tell you. My feeling is that the argument is where it was, and open to the same objections which were urged before; for I am ready to admit that the existence of the soul before entering into the bodily form has been very ingeniously, and, if I may say so, quite sufficiently proven; but the existence of the soul after death is still, in my judgment, unproven. Now my objection is not the same as that of Simmias; for I am not disposed to deny that the soul is stronger and more lasting than the body, being of opinion that in all such respects the soul very far excels the body. Well then, says the argument to me, why do you remain unconvinced? When you see that the weaker continues in existence after the man is dead, will you not admit that the more lasting must also survive during the same period of time? Now I will ask you to consider whether the objection, which, like Simmias, I will express in a figure, is of any weight. The analogy which I will adduce is that of an old weaver, who dies, and after his death somebody says:—He is not dead, he must be alive;—see, there is the coat which he himself wove and wore, and which remains whole and undecayed. And then he proceeds to ask of some one who is incredulous, whether a man lasts longer, or the coat which is in use and wear; and when he is answered that a man lasts far longer, thinks that he has thus certainly demonstrated the survival of the man, who is the more lasting, because the less lasting remains. But that, Simmias, as I would beg you to remark, is a mistake; any one can see that he

who talks thus is talking nonsense. For the truth is, that the weaver aforesaid, having woven and worn many such coats, outlived several of them; and was outlived by the last; but a man is not therefore proved to be slighter and weaker than a coat. Now the relation of the body to the soul may be expressed in a similar figure; and any one may very fairly say in like manner that the soul is lasting, and the body weak and shortlived in comparison. He may argue in like manner that every soul wears out many bodies, especially if a man live many years. While he is alive the body deliquesces and decays, and the soul always weaves another garment and repairs the waste. But of course, whenever the soul perishes, she must have on her last garment, and this will survive her; and then at length, when the soul is dead, the body will show its native weakness, and quickly decompose and pass away. I would therefore rather not rely on the argument from superior strength to prove the continued existence of the soul after death. For granting even more than you affirm to be possible, and acknowledging not only that the soul existed before birth, but also that the souls of some exist, and will continue to exist after death, and will be born and die again, and that there is a natural strength in the soul which will hold out and born many times—nevertheless, we may be still inclined to think that she will weary in the labours of successive births, and may at last succumb in one of her deaths and utterly perish; and this death and dissolution of the body which brings destruction to the soul may be unknown to any of us, for no one of us can have had any experience of it: And if so, then I maintain that he who is confident about death has but a foolish confidence, unless he is able to prove that the soul is altogether immortal and imperishable. But if he cannot prove the soul's immortality, he who is about to die will always have reason to fear that when the body is disunited, the soul also may utterly perish.

All of us, as we afterwards remarked to one another, had an unpleasant feeling at hearing what they said. When we had been so firmly convinced before, now to have our faith shaken seemed to introduce a confusion and uncertainty, not only into the previous argument, but into any future one; either we were incapable of forming a judgment, or there were no grounds of belief. . . .

Socrates paused awhile, and seemed to be absorbed in reflection. At length he said: You are raising a tremendous question, Cebes, involving the whole nature of generation and corruption, about which, if you like, I will give you my own experience; and if anything which I say is likely to avail towards the solution of your difficulty you may make use of it.

I should very much like, said Cebes, to hear what you have to say.

Then I will tell you, said Socrates. When I was young, Cebes, I had a prodigious desire to know that department of philosophy which is called the investigation of nature; to know the causes of things, and why a thing is and is created or destroyed appeared to me to be a lofty profession; and I was always agitating myself with the consideration of questions such as these:—Is the growth of animals the result of some decay which the hot and cold principle contracts, as some have said? Is the blood the element with which we think, or the air, or the fire? or perhaps nothing of the kind—but the brain may be the originating power of the perceptions of hearing and sight and smell, and memory and opinion may come from them, and science may be based on memory and opinion when they have attained fixity. And then I went on to examine the corruption of them, and then to the things of heaven and earth, and at last I concluded myself to be utterly and absolutely incapable of these enquiries, as I will satisfactorily prove to you. For I was fascinated by them to such a degree that my eyes grew blind to things which I had seemed to myself, and also to others, to know quite well; I forgot what I had before thought self-evident truths; e.g. such a fact as that the growth of man is the result of eating and drinking; for when by the digestion of food flesh is added to flesh and bone to bone, and whenever there is an aggregation of congenial elements, the lesser bulk becomes larger and the small man great. Was not that a reasonable notion?

Yes, said Cebes, I think so.

Well; but let me tell you something more.

There was a time when I thought that I understood the meaning of greater and less pretty well; and when I saw a great man standing by a little one, I fancied that one was taller than the other by a head; or one horse would appear to be greater than another horse; and still more clearly did I seem to perceive that ten is two more than eight, and that two cubits are more than one, because two is the double of one.

And what is now your notion of such matters? said Cebes.

I should be far enough from imagining, he replied, that I knew the cause of any of them, by heaven I should; for I cannot satisfy myself that, when one is added to one, the one to which the addition is made becomes two, or that the two units added together make two by reason of the addition. I cannot understand how, when separated from the other, each of them was one and not two, and now, when they are brought together, the mere juxtaposition or meeting of them should be the cause of their becoming two: neither can I understand how the division of one is the way to make two; for then a different cause would produce the same effect,—as in the former instance the addition and juxtaposition of one to one was the cause of two, in this the separation and subtraction of one from the other would be the cause. Nor am I any longer satisfied that I understand the reason why one or anything else is either generated or destroyed or is at all, but I have in my mind some confused notion of a new method, and can never admit the other.

Then I heard some one reading, as he said, from a book of Anaxagoras, that mind was the disposer and cause of all, and I was delighted at this notion, which appeared quite admirable, and I said to myself: If mind is the disposer, mind will dispose all for the best, and put each particular in the best place; and I argued that if any one desired to find out the cause of the generation or destruction or existence of anything, he must find out what state of being or doing or suffering was best for that thing, and therefore a man had only to consider the best for himself and others, and then he would also know the worse, since the same science comprehended both. And I rejoiced to think that I had found in Anaxagoras a teacher of the causes of existence such as I desired, and I imagined that he would tell me first whether the earth is flat or round; and whichever was true, he would proceed to explain the cause and the necessity of this being so, and then he would teach me the nature of the best and show that this was best; and if he said that the earth was in the centre, he would further explain that this position was the best, and I should be satisfied with the explanation given, and not want any other sort of cause. And I thought that I would then go on and ask him about the sun and moon and stars, and that he would explain to me their comparative swiftness, and their returnings and various states, active and passive, and how all of them were for the best. For I could not imagine that when he spoke of mind as the disposer of them, he would give any other account of their being as they are, except that this was best; and I thought that when he had explained to me in detail the cause of each and the cause of all, he would go on to explain to me what was best for each and what was good for all. These hopes I would not have sold for a large sum of money, and I seized the books and read them as fast as I could in my eagerness to know the better and the worse.

What expectations I had formed, and how grievously was I disappointed! As I proceeded, I found my philosopher altogether forsaking mind or any other principle of order, but having recourse to air, and ether, and water, and other eccentricities. I might compare him to a person who began by maintaining generally that mind is the cause of the actions of Socrates, but who, when he endeavoured to explain the causes of my several actions in detail, went on to show that I sit here because my body is made up of bones and muscles; and the bones, as he would say, are hard and have joints which divide them, and the muscles are elastic, and they cover the bones, which have also a covering or environment of flesh and skin which contains them; and as the bones are lifted at their joints by the contraction or relaxation of the muscles, I am able to bend my limbs, and this is why I am sitting here in a curved posture—that is what he would say; and he would have a similar explanation of my talking to you, which he would attribute to sound, and air, and hearing, and he would assign ten thousand other causes of the same sort, forgetting to mention the true cause, which is, that the Athenians have thought fit to condemn me, and accordingly I have thought it better and more right to remain here and undergo my sentence; for I am inclined to think that these muscles and bones of mine would have gone off long ago to Megara or Boeotia—by the dog, they would, if they had been moved only by their own idea of what was best, and if I had not chosen the better and nobler part, instead of playing truant and running away, of enduring any punishment which the state inflicts. There is surely a strange confusion of causes and conditions in all this. It may be said, indeed, that without bones and muscles and the other parts of the body I cannot execute my purposes. But to say that I do as I do because of them, and that this is the way in which mind acts, and not from the choice of the best, is a very careless and idle mode of speaking. I wonder that they cannot distinguish the cause from the condition, which the many, feeling about in the dark, are always mistaking and misnaming. And thus one man makes a vortex all round and steadies the earth by the heaven; another gives the air as a support to the earth, which is a sort of broad trough. Any power which in arranging them as they are arranges them for the best never enters into their minds; and instead of finding any superior strength in it, they rather expect to discover another Atlas of the world who is stronger and more everlasting and more containing than the good; —of the obligatory and containing power of the good they think nothing; and yet this is the principle which I would fain learn if any one would teach me. But as I have failed either to discover myself, or to learn of any one else, the nature of the best, I will exhibit to you, if you like, what I have found to be the second best mode of enquiring into the cause.

I should very much like to hear, he replied.

Socrates proceeded:—I thought that as I had failed in the contemplation of true existence, I ought to be careful that I did not lose the eye of my soul; as people may injure their bodily eye by observing and gazing on the sun during an eclipse, unless they take the precaution of only looking at the image reflected in the water, or in some similar medium. So in my own case, I was afraid that my soul might be blinded altogether if I looked at things with my eyes or tried to apprehend them by the help of the senses. And I thought that I had better have recourse to the world of mind and seek there the truth of existence.

II
Aristotle

ARISTOTLE (384–322 B.C.), the son of Nichomachus, a doctor, was born in Stagira, a greek colonial town settled by the Ionians, whose philosophers had been the first to investigate nature. At age 17, Aristotle entered Plato's Academy as a student. Plato called him "the Brain" and "Bookworm." Aristotle quickly became his most prodigious pupil. Aristotle stayed for 20 years at the Academy, where he went from being a student to becoming one its greatest investigators and teachers. Besides absorbing Plato's comprehensive world view, Aristotle systematized all areas of knowledge and wrote on virtually every subject, including physics, astronomy, meteorology, taxonomy, psychology, biology, ethics, politics, aesthetics, metaphysics, and logic.

When Aristotle entered the Academy, Plato, who was then 60, was involved in the division of "ideas" further and further down until the *infima species,* the final unit of division—the indivisible—could be reached. This endeavor influenced Aristotle's early work, especially his development of logic and metaphysics. But whereas Plato considered the senses as illusory, seeking knowledge through pure reason, which could be communicated only abstractly (through myths, allegories, and similes such as the Sun, the Divided Line, and the Cave), Aristotle became convinced that the senses, though not sufficient in themselves, were the true road to wisdom. Although the two thinkers maintained a deep friendship until Plato's death, at age 81, philosophically they were divided over whether reason or experience was primary, and over the nature of ideas and the forms. Plato's development of ideas was based on geometrical forms, the abstract rules of numbers, and a love of mathematics; Aristotle's classifications of genera and species led him away from pure mathematics and toward natural science, especially organic biology and physiology.

At 42, Aristotle accepted an invitation from King Philip II of Macedonia to become private tutor to his 13-year-old crown prince, Alexander. Less than six years later, Alexander became Alexander the Great, conqueror of the known world. According to legend, as Alexander moved eastward, conquering the Persian Empire and Asia, he would at each new place gather exotic flowers and send them back to Aristotle, who had returned to Athens to set up his own school, the Lyceum. It lasted 800 years. Whereas Plato's Academy led in the development of mathematics and geometry, the Lyceum focused on applied scientific research, especially in the natural sciences.

Not being a citizen, Aristotle had to rent the Athenian land the Lyceum occupied. Although he was highly regarded as one of the greatest minds of the time, many Athenians resented him for having trained the Macedonian who had become their conqueror. So, when in 323 B.C. Alexander suddenly died and the Macedonians were ousted from power, Athens turned against Aristotle. Ironically, Plato's greatest pupil, like Plato's teacher Socrates, ended up being arrested by the Athenian government and charged with the crimes of atheism and impiety! Sentenced to death or exile, Aristotle—unlike Socrates—chose exile. A year later, he died on the island of Euboea.

Metaphysics

Aristotle

All men by nature desire to know. An indication of this is the delight we take in our senses; for even apart from their usefulness they are loved for themselves; and above all others the sense of sight. For not only with a view to action, but even when we are not going to do anything, we prefer seeing (one might say) to everything else. The reason is that this, most of all the senses, makes us know and brings to light many differences between things.

By nature animals are born with the faculty of sensation, and from sensation memory is produced in some of them, though not in others. And therefore the former are more intelligent and apt at learning than those which cannot remember; those which are incapable of hearing sounds are intelligent though they cannot be taught, e.g. the bee, and any other race of animals that may be like it; and those which besides memory have this sense of hearing can be taught.

The animals other than man live by appearances and memories, and have but little of connected experience; but the human race lives also by art and reasonings. Now from memory experience is produced in men; for the several memories of the same thing produce finally the capacity for a single experience. And experience seems pretty much like science and art, but really science and art come to men *through* experience; for 'experience made art,' as Polus says, 'but inexperience luck.' Now art arises when from many notions gained by experience one universal judgement about a class of objects is produced. For to have a judgement that when Callias was ill of this disease this did him good, and similarly in the case of Socrates and in many individual cases, is a matter of experience; but to judge that it has done good to all persons of a certain

constitution, marked off in one class, when they were ill of this diease, e.g. to phlegmatic or bilious people when burning with fever,— this is a matter of art.

With a view to action experience seems in no respect inferior to art, and men of experience succeed even better than those who have theory without experience. (The reason is that experience is knowledge of individuals, art of universals, and actions and productions are all concerned with the individual; for the physician does not cure *man*, except in an incidental way, but Callias or Socrates or some other called by some such individual name, who happens to be a man. If, then, a man has the theory without the experience, and recognizes the universal but does not know the individual included in this, he will often fail to cure; for it is the individual that is to be cured.) But yet we think that *knowledge* and *understanding* belong to art rather than to experience, and we suppose artists to be wiser than men of experience (which implies that Wisdom depends in all cases rather on knowledge); and this because the former know the cause, but the latter do not. For men of experience know that the thing is so, but do not know why, while the others know the 'why' and the cause. Hence we think also that the master-workers in each craft are more honourable and know in a truer sense and are wiser than the manual workers, because they know the causes of the things that are done (we think the manual workers are like certain lifeless things which act indeed, but act without knowing what they do as fire burns,—but while the lifeless things perform each of their functions by a natural tendency, the labourers perform them through habit); thus we view them as being wiser not in virtue of being able to act, but of having the theory for themselves and knowing the causes. And in general it is a sign of the man who knows and of the man who does not know, that the

SOURCE: *Metaphysics* by Aristotle, translated by W. D. Ross (Oxford University Press, 1908).

former can teach, and therefore we think art more truly knowledge than experience is; for artists can teach, and men of mere experience cannot.

Again, we do not regard any of the senses as Wisdom; yet surely these give the most authoritative knowledge of particulars. But they do not tell us the 'why' of anything—e.g. why fire is hot; they only say *that* it is hot.

At first he who invented any art whatever that went beyond the common perceptions of man was naturally admired by men, not only because there was something useful in the inventions, but because he was thought wise and superior to the rest. But as more arts were invented, and some were directed to the necessities of life, others to recreation, the inventors of the latter were naturally always regarded as wiser than the inventors of the former, because their branches of knowledge did not aim at utility. Hence when all such inventions were already established, the science which do not aim at giving pleasure or at the necessities of life were discovered, and first in the places where men first began to have leisure. This is why the mathematical arts were founded in Egypt; for there the priestly caste was allowed to be at leisure.

We have said in the *Ethics* what the difference is between art and science and the other kindred faculties; but the point of our present discussion is this, that all men suppose what is called Wisdom to deal with the first causes and the principles of things; so that, as has been said before, the man of experience is thought to be wiser than the possessors of any sense-perception whatever, the artist wiser than the men of experience, the master-worker than the mechanic, and the theoretical kinds of knowledge to be more of the nature of Wisdom than the productive. Clearly then Wisdom is knowledge about certain principles and causes.

Since we are seeking this knowledge, we must inquire of what kind are the causes and the principles, the knowledge of which is Wisdom. If one were to take the notions we have about the wise man, this might perhaps make the answer more evident. We suppose first, then, that the wise man knows all things, as far as possible, although he has not knowledge of each of them in detail; secondly, that he who can learn things that are difficult, and not easy for man to know, is wise (sense-perception is common to all, and therefore easy and no mark of Wisdom); again, that he who is more exact and more capable of teaching the causes is wiser, in every branch of knowledge; and that of the sciences, also, that which is desirable on its own account and for the sake of knowing it is more of the nature of Wisdom than that which is desirable on account of its results, and the superior science is more of the nature of Wisdom than the ancillary; for the wise man must not be ordered but must order, and he must not obey another, but the less wise must obey *him*.

Such and so many are the notions, then, which we have about Wisdom and the wise. Now of these characteristics that of knowing all things must belong to him who has in the highest degree universal knowledge; for he knows in a sense all the instances that fall under the universal. And these things, the most universal, are on the whole the hardest for men to know; for they are farthest from the senses. And the most exact of the sciences are those which deal most with first principles; for those which involve fewer principles are more exact than those which involve additional principles, e.g. arithmetic than geometry. But the science which investigates causes is also *instructive*, in a higher degree, for the people who instruct us are those who tell the causes of each thing. And understanding and knowledge pursued for their own sake are found most in the knowledge of that which is most knowable (for he who chooses to know for the sake of knowing will choose most readily that which is most truly knowledge, and such is the knowledge of that which is most knowable); and the first principles and the causes are most knowable; for by reason of these, and from these, all other things come to be known, and not these by means of the things subordinate to them. And the science which knows to what end each thing mist be done is the most authoritative of the sciences, and more authoritative than any ancillary science; and this end is the good of that thing, and in general the supreme good in the whole of nature.

Judged by all the tests we have mentioned, then, the name in question falls to the same science; this must be a science that investigates the first principles and causes; for the good, i.e. the end, is one of the causes.

That it is not a science of production is clear even from the history of the earliest philosophers. For it is owing to their wonder that men both now begin and at first began to philosophize; they wondered originally at the obvious difficulties, then advanced little by little and stated difficulties about the greater matters, e.g. about the phenomena of the moon and those of the sun and of the stars, and about the genesis of the universe. And a man who is puzzled and wonders thinks himself ignorant (whence even the lover of myth is in a sense a lover of Wisdom, for the myth is composed of wonders); therefore since they philosophized in order to escape from ignorance, evidently they were pursuing science in order to know, and not for any utilitarian end. And this is confirmed by the facts; for it was when almost all the necessities of life and the things that make for comfort and recreation had been secured, that such knowledge began to be sought. Evidently then we do not seek it for the sake of any other advantage; but as the man is free, we say, who exists for his own sake and not for another's, so we pursue this as the only free science, for it alone exists for its own sake.

Hence also the possession of it might be justly regarded as beyond human power; for in many ways human nature is in bondage, so that according to Simonides 'God alone can have this privilege,' and it is unfitting that man should not be content to seek the knowledge that is suited to him. If, then, there is something in what the poets say, and jealousy is natural to the divine power, it would probably occur in this case above all, and all who excelled in this knowledge would be unfortunate. But the divine power cannot be jealous (nay, according to the proverb 'bards tell many a lie'), nor should any other science be thought more honourable than one of this sort. For the most divine science is also most honourable; and this science alone must be, in two ways, most divine. For the science which it would be most meet for God to have is a divine science, and so is any science that deals with divine objects; and this science alone has both these qualities; for (1) God is thought to be among the causes of all things and to be a first principle, and (2) such a science either God alone can have, or God above all others. All the sciences, indeed, are more necessary than this, but none is better.

Yet the acquisition of it must in a sense end in something which is the opposite of our original inquiries. For all men begin, as we said, by wondering that things are as they are, as they do about self-moving marionettes, or about the solstices or the incommensurability of the diagonal of a square with the side; for it seems wonderful to all who have not yet seen the reason, that there is a thing which cannot be measured even by the smallest unit. But we must end in the contrary and, according to the proverb, the better state, as is the case in these instances too when men learn the cause; for there is nothing which would surprise a geometer so much as if the diagonal turned out to be commensurable.

We have stated, then, what is the nature of the science we are searching for, and what is the mark which our search and our whole investigation must reach.

Evidently we have to acquire knowledge of the original causes (for we say we know each thing only when we think we recognize its first cause), and causes are spoken of in four senses. In one of these we mean the substance, i.e. the essence (for the "why' is reducible finally to the definition, and the ultimate 'why' is a cause and principle); in another the matter or substratum, in a third the source of the change, and in a fourth the cause opposed to this, the purpose and the good (for this is the end of all generation and change). We have studied these causes sufficiently in our work on nature, but yet let us call to our aid those who have attacked the investigation of being and philosophized about reality before us. For obviously they too speak of certain principles and causes; to go over their views, then, will be of profit to the present inquiry, for we shall either find another kind of cause, or be more convinced of the correctness of those which we now maintain.

Of the first philosophers, then, most thought the principles which were of the nature of matter were the only principles of all things. That of which all things that are consist, the first from which they come to be, the last into which they are resolved (the substance remaining, but changing in its modifications), this they say is the element and this the principle of things, and therefore they think nothing is either generated or destroyed, since this sort of entity is always conserved, as we say Socrates neither comes to be absolutely when he comes to be beautiful or musical, nor ceases to be when he loses these characteristics, because the substratum, Socrates himself, remains. Just so they say nothing else comes to be or ceases to be; for there must be some entity— either one or more than one—from which all other things come to be, it being conserved.

Yet they do not all agree as to the number and the nature of these principles. Thales, the founder of this type of philosophy, says the principle is water (for which reason he declared that the earth rests on water), getting the notion perhaps from seeing that the nutriment of all things is moist, and that heat itself is generated from the moist and kept alive by it (and that from which they come to be is a principle of all things). He got his notion from this fact, and from the fact that the seeds of all things have a moist nature, and that water is the origin of the nature of moist things.

Some think that even the ancients who lived long before the present generation, and first framed accounts of the gods, had a similar view of nature; for they made Ocean and Tethys the parents of creation, and described the oath of the gods as being by water, to which they give the name of Styx; for what is oldest is most honourable, and the most honourable thing is that by which one swears. It may perhaps be uncertain whether this opinion about nature is primitive and ancient, but Thales at any rate is said to have declared himself thus about the first cause. Hippo no one would think fit to include among these thinkers, because of the paltriness of his thought.

Anaximenes and Diogenes make air prior to water, and the most primary of the simple bodies, while Hippasus of Metapontium and Heraclitus of Ephesus say this of fire, and Empedocles says it of the four elements (adding a fourth—earth—to those which have been named); for these, he says, always remain and do not come to be, except that they come to be more or fewer, being aggregated into one and segregated out of one.

Anaxagoras of Clazomenae, who, though older than Empedocles, was later in his philosophical activity, says the principles are infinite in number; for he says almost all the things that are made of parts like themselves, in the manner of water or fire, are generated and destroyed in this way, only by aggregation and segregation, and are not in any other sense generated or destroyed, but remain eternally.

From these facts one might think that the only cause is the so-called material cause; but as men thus advanced, the very facts opened the way for them and joined in forcing them to investigate the subject. However true it may be that all generation and destruction proceed from some one or (for that matter) from more elements, why does this happen and what is the cause? For at least the substratum itself does not make itself change; e.g. neither the wood nor the bronze causes the change of either of them, nor does the wood manufacture a bed and the bromze a statue, but something else is the cause of the change. And to seek this is to seek the second cause, as *we* should say,—that from which comes the beginning of the movement. Now those who at the very beginning set themselves to this kind of inquiry, and said the substratum was one, were not at all dissatisfied with themselves; but some at least of those who maintain it to be one—as though defeated by this search for the second cause—say the one and nature as a whole is unchangeable not only in respect of generation and destruction (for this is a primitive belief, and all agreed in it), but also of all other change; and this view is peculiar to them. Of those who said the universe was one, then, none succeeded in discovering a cause of this sort, except perhaps Parmenides, and he only inasmuch as he supposes that there is not only one but also in some sense two causes. But for those who make more elements it is more possible to state the second cause, e.g. for those who make hot and cold, or fire and earth, the elements; for they treat fire as having a nature which fits it to move things, and water and earth and such things they treat in the contrary way.

When these men and the principles of this kind had had their day, as the latter were found inadequate to generate the nature of things men were again forced by the truth itself, as we said, to inquire into the next kind of cause. For it is not likely either that fire or earth or any such element should be the reason why things manifest goodness and beauty both in their being and in their coming to be, or that those thinkers should have supposed it was; nor again could it be right to entrust so great a matter to spontaneity and chance. When one man said, then, that reason was present—as in animals, so throughout nature—as the cause of order and of all arrangement, he seemed like a sober man in contrast with the random talk of his predecessors. We know that Anazagoras certainly adopted these views, but Hermotimus of Clazomenae is credited with expressing them earlier. Those who thought thus stated that there is a principle of things which is at the same time the cause of beauty, and that sort of cause from which things acquire movement.

One might suspect that Hesiod was the first to look for such a thing—or some one else who put love or desire among existing things as a principle, as Parmenides, too, does; for he, in constructing the genesis of the universe, says:—

Love first of all the Gods she planned.

And Hesiod says:—

First of all things as chaos made, and then
Broad-breasted earth, . . .
And love, 'mid all the gods pre-eminent

which implies that among existing things there must be from the first a cause which will move things and bring them together. How these thinkers should be arranged with regard to priority of discovery let us be allowed to decide later; but since the contraries of the various forms of good were also perceived to be present in nature—not only order and the beautiful, but also disorder and the ugly, and

bad things in greater number than good, and ignoble things than beautiful—therefore another thinker introduced friendship and strife, each of the two the cause of one of these two sets of qualities. For if we were to follow out the view of Empedocles, and interpret it according to its meaning and not to its lisping expression, we should find that friendship is the cause of good things, and strife of bad. Therefore, if we said that Empedocles in a sense both mentions, and is the first to mention, the bad and the good as principles, we should perhaps be right, since the cause of all goods is the good itself.

These thinkers, as we say, evidently grasped, and to this extent, two of the causes which we distinguished in our work on nature—the matter and the source of the movement—vaguely, however, and with no clearness, but as untrained men behave in fights; for they go round their opponents and often strike fine blows, but they do not fight on scientific principles, and so too these thinkers do not seem to know what they say; for it is evident that, as a rule, they make no use of their causes except to a small extent. For Anaxagoras uses reason as a *deus ex machina* for the making of the world, and when he is at a loss to tell from what cause something necessarily is, then he drags reason in, but in all other cases ascribes events to anything rather than to reason. And Empedocles, though he uses the causes to a greater extent than this, neither does so sufficiently nor attains consistency in their use. At least, in many cases he makes love segregate things, and strife aggregate them. For whenever the universe is dissolved into its elements by strife, fire is aggregated into one, and so is each of the other elements; but whenever again under the influence of love they come together into one, the parts must again be segregated out of each element.

Empedocles, then, in contrast with his predecessors, was the first to introduce the dividing of this cause, not positing one source of movement, but different and contrary sources. Again, he was the first to speak of four material elements; yet he does not *use* four, but treats them as two only; he treats fire by itself, and its opposites—earth, air, and water—as one kind of thing. We may learn this by study of his verses.

This philosopher then, as we say, has spoken of the principles in this way, and made them of this number. Leucippus and his associate Democritus say that the full and the empty are the elements, calling the one being and the other non-being—the full and solid being being, the empty non-being (whence they say being no more is than non-being, because the solid no more is than the empty); and they make these the material causes of things. And as those who make the underlying substance one generate all other things by its modifications, supposing the rare and the dense to be the sources of the modifications, in the same way these philosophers say the differences in the elements are the causes of all other qualities. These differences, they say, are three—shape and order and position. For they say the real is differentiated only by 'rhythm' and 'inter-contact' and 'turning'; and of these rhythm is shape, inter-contact is order, and turning is position; for A differs from N in shape, AN from NA in order, Ⅎ from H in position. The question of movement—whence or how it is to belong to things—these thinkers, like the others, lazily neglected.

Regarding the two causes, then, as we say, the inquiry seems to have been pushed thus far by the early philosophers.

Contemporaneously with these philosophers and before them, the so-called Pythagoreans, who were the first to take up mathematics, not only advanced this study, but also having been brought up in it they thought its principles were the principles of all things. Since of these principles numbers are by nature the first, and in numbers they seemed to see many resemblances to the things that exist and come into being—more than in fire and earth and water (such and such a modification of numbers being justice, another being soul and reason, another being opportunity—and similarly almost all other things being numerically expressible); since, again, they saw that the modifications and the ratios of the musical scales were expressible in numbers;—since then, all other things seemed in their whole nature to be modelled on numbers, and numbers seemed to be the first things in the whole of nature, they supposed the elements of numbers to be the elements of all things, and the whole heaven to be a musical scale and a number. And all the properties of numbers and scales which they could show to agree with the attributes and parts and the whole arrangement of the heavens, they collected and fitted into their scheme; and if there was a gap anywhere, they readily made additions so as to make their whole theory coherent. E.g. as the number 10 is thought to be perfect and to comprise the whole nature of numbers, they say that the bodies which move through the heavens are ten, but as the visible bodies are only nine, to meet this they invent a tenth—the 'counter-earth'. We have discussed these matters more exactly elsewhere.

But the object of our review is that we may learn from these philosophers also what they suppose to be the principles and how these fall under the causes we have named. Evidently, then, these thinkers also consider that number is the principle both as matter for things and as forming both their modifications and their permanent states, and hold that the elements of number are the even and the odd, and that of these the latter is limited, and the former unlimited; and that the One proceeds from both of these (for it is both even and odd), and number from the One; and that the whole heaven, as has been said, is numbers.

Other members of this same school say there are ten principles, which they arrange in two columns of cognates—limited and unlimited, odd and even, one and plurality, right and left, male and female, resting and moving, straight and curved, light and darkness, good and bad, square and oblong. In this way Alcmaeon of Croton seems also to have conceived the matter, and either he got this view from them or they got it from him; for he expressed himself similarly to them. For he says most human affairs go in pairs, meaning not definite contrarieties such as the Pythagoreans speak of, but any chance contrarieties, e.g. white and black, sweet and bitter, good and bad, great and small. He threw out indefinite suggestions about the other contrarieties, but the Pythagoreans declared both how many and which their contrarieties are.

From both these schools, then, we can learn this much, that the contraries are the principles of things; and how many these principles are and which they are, we can learn from one of the two schools. But how these principles can be brought together under the causes we have named has not been clearly and articulately stated by them; they seem, however, to range the elements under the head of matter; for out of these as immanent parts they say substance is composed and moulded.

From these facts we may sufficiently perceive the meaning of the ancients who said the elements of nature were more than one; but there are some who spoke of the universe as if it were one entity, though they were not all alike either in the excellence of their statement or in its conformity to the facts of nature. The discussion of them is in no way appropriate to our present investigation of causes, for they do not, like some of the natural philosophers, assume being to be one and yet generate it out of the one as out of matter, but they speak in another way; those others add change, since they generate the universe, but these thinkers say the universe is unchangeable. Yet *this* much is germane to the present inquiry: Parmenides seems to fasten on that which is one in definition, Melissus on that which is one in matter, for which reason the former says that it is limited, the latter that it is unlimited; while Xenophanes, the first of these partisans of the One (for Parmenides is said to have been his pupil), gave no clear statement, nor does he seem to have grasped the nature of either of these causes, but with reference to the whole material universe he says the One is God. Now these thinkers, as we said, must be neglected for the purposes of the present inquiry—two of them entirely, as being a little too naive, viz. Xenophanes and Melissus; but Parmenides seems in places to speak with more insight. For, claiming that, besides the existent, nothing non-existent exists, he thinks that of necessity one thing exists, viz. the existent and nothing else (on this we have spoken more clearly in our work on nature), but being forced to follow the observed facts, and supposing the existence of that which is one in definition, but more than one according to our

sensations, he now posits two causes and two principles, calling them hot and cold, i.e. fire and earth; and of these he ranges the hot with the existent, and the other with the non-existent.

From what has been said, then, and from the wise men who have now sat in council with us, we have got thus much—on the one hand from the earliest philosophers, who regard the first principle as corporeal (for water and fire and such things are bodies), and of whom some suppose that there is one corporeal principle, others that there are more than one, but both put these under the head of matter; and on the other hand from some who posit both this cause and besides this the source of movement, which we have got from some as single and from others as twofold.

Down to the Italian school, then, and apart from it, philosophers have treated these subjects rather obscurely, except that, as we said, they have in fact used two kinds of cause, and one of these—the source of movement—some treat as one and others as two. But the Pythagoreans have said in the same way that there are two principles, but added this much, which is peculiar to them, that they thought that finitude and infinity were not attributes of certain other things, e.g. of fire or earth or anything else of this kind, but that infinity itself and unity itself were the substance of the things of which they are predicated. This is why number was the substance of all things. On this subject, then, they expressed themselves thus; and regarding the question of essence they began to make statements and definitions, but treated the matter too simply. For they both defined superficially and thought that the first subject of which a given definition was predicable was the substance of the thing defined, as if one supposed that 'double' and '2' were the same, because 2 is the first thing of which 'double' is predicable. But surely to be double and to be 2 are not the same; if they are, one thing will be many—a consequence which they actually drew. From the earlier philosophers, then, and from their successors we can learn thus much.

After the systems we have named came the philosophy of Plato, which in most respects followed these thinkers, but had peculiarities that distinguished it from the philosophy of the Italians. For, having in his youth first become familiar with Cratylus and with the Heraclitean doctrines (that all sensible things are ever in a state of flux and there is no knowledge about them), these views he held even in later years. Socrates, however, was busying himself about ethical matters and neglecting the world of nature as a whole but seeking the universal in these ethical matters, and fixed thought for the first time on definitions; Plato accepted his teaching, but held that the problem applied not to sensible things but to entities of another kind—for this reason, that the common definition could not be a definition of any sensible thing, as they were always changing. Things of this other sort, then, he called Ideas, and sensible things, he said, were all named after these, and in virtue of a relation to these; for the many existed by participation in the Ideas that have the same name as they. Only the name 'participation' was new; for the Pythagoreans say that things exist by 'imitation' of numbers, and Plato says they exist by participation, changing the name. But what the participation or the imitation of the Forms could be they left an open question.

Further, besides sensible things and Forms he says there are the objects of mathematics, which occupy an intermediate position, differing from sensible things in being eternal and unchangeable, from Forms in that there are many alike, while the Form itself is in each case unique.

Since the Forms were the causes of all other things, he thought their elements were the elements of all things. As matter, the great and the small were principles; as essential reality, the One; for from the great and the small, by participation in the One, come the Numbers.

But he agreed with the Pythagoreans in saying that the One is substance and not a predicate of something else; and in saying that the Numbers are the causes of the reality of other things he agreed with them; but positing a dyad and constructing the infinite out of great and small, instead of treating the infinite as one, is peculiar to him; and so is his view that the Numbers exist apart from sensible

things, while *they* say that the things themselves are Numbers, and do not place the objects of mathematics between Forms and sensible things. His divergence from the Pythagoreans in making the One and the Numbers separate from things, and his introduction of the Forms, were due to his inquiries in the region of definitions (for the earlier thinkers had no tincture of dialectic), and his making the other entity besides the One a dyad was due to the belief that the numbers, except those which were prime, could be neatly produced out of the dyad as out of some plastic material.

Yet what *happens* is the contrary; the theory is not a reasonable one. For they make many things out of the matter, and the form generates only once, but what we observe is that one table is made from one matter, while the man who applies the form, though he is one, makes many tables. And the relation of the male to the female is similar; for the latter is impregnated by one copulation, but the male impregnates many females; yet these are analogues of those first principles.

Plato, then, declared himself thus on the points in question; it is evident from what has been said that he has used only two causes, that of the essence and the material cause (for the Forms are the causes of the essence of all other things, and the One is the cause of the essence of the Forms); and it is evident what the underlying matter is, of which the Forms are predicated in the case of sensible things, and the One in the case of Forms, viz. that this is a dyad, the great and the small. Further, he has assigned the cause of good and that of evil to the elements, one to each of the two, as we say some of his predecessors sought to do, e.g. Empedocles and Anaxagoras.

Our review of those who have spoken about first principles and reality and of the way in which they have spoken, has been concise and summary; but yet we have learnt *this* much from them, that of those who speak about 'principle' and 'cause' no one has mentioned any principle except those which have been distinguished in our work on nature, but all evidently have some inkling of *them*, though only vaguely. For some speak of the first principle as matter, whether they suppose one or more first principles, and whether they suppose this to be a body or to be incorporeal; e.g. Plato spoke of the great and the small, the Italians of the infinite, Empedocles of fire, earth, water, and air, Anaxagoras of the infinity of things composed of similar parts. These, then, have all had a notion of this kind of cause, and so have all who speak of air or fire or water, or something denser than fire and rarer than air; for some have said the prime element is of this kind.

These thinkers grasped this cause only; but certain others have mentioned the source of movement, e.g. those who make friendship and strife, or reason, or love, a principle.

The essence, i.e. the substantial reality, no one has expressed distinctly. It is hinted at chiefly by those who believe in the Forms; for they do not suppose either that the Forms are the matter of sensible things, and the One the matter of the Forms, or that they are the source of movement (for they say these are causes rather of immobility and of being at rest), but they furnish the Forms as the essence of every other thing, and the One as the essence of the Forms.

That for whose sake actions and changes and movements take place, they assert to be a cause in a way, but not in this way, i.e. not in the way in which it is its *nature* to be a cause. For those who speak of reason or friendship class these causes as goods; they do not speak, however, as if anything that exists either existed or came into being for the sake of these, but as if movements started from these. In the same way those who say the One or the existent is the good, say that it is the cause of substance, but not that substance either is or comes to be for the sake of this. Therefore it turns out that in a sense they both say and do not say the good is a cause; for they do not call it a cause *qua* good but only incidentally.

All these thinkers, then, as they cannot pitch on another cause, seem to testify that we have determined rightly both how many and of what sort the causes are. Besides this it is plain that when the causes are being looked for, either all four must be sought thus or they must be sought in one of these four ways. Let

us next discuss the possible difficulties with regard to the way in which each of these thinkers has spoken, and with regard to his situation relatively to the first principles.

Those, then, who say the universe is one and posit one kind of thing as matter, and as corporeal matter which has spatial magnitude, evidently go astray in many ways. For they posit the elements of bodies only, not of incorporeal things, though there are also incorporeal things. And in trying to state the causes of generation and destruction, and in giving a physical account of all things, they do away with the cause of movement. Further, they err in not positing the substance, i.e. the essence, as the cause of anything, and besides this in lightly calling any of the simple bodies except earth the first principle, without inquiring how they are produced out of one another,—I mean fire, water, earth, and air. For some things are produced out of each other by combination, others by separation, and this makes the greatest difference to their priority and posteriority. For (1) in a way the property of being most elementary of all would seem to belong to the first thing from which they are produced by combination, and *this* property would belong to the most fine-grained and subtle of bodies. For this reason those who make fire the principle would be most in agreement with this argument. But each of the other thinkers agrees that the element of corporeal things is of this sort. At least none of those who named one element claimed that earth was the element, evidently because of the coarseness of its grain. (Of the other three elements each has found some judge on its side; for some maintain that fire, others that water, others that air is the element. Yet why, after all, do they not name earth also, as most men do? For people say all things are earth. And Hesiod says earth was produced first of corporeal things; so primitive and popular has the opinion been.) According to this argument, then, no one would be right who either says the first principle is any of the elements other than fire, or supposes it to be denser than air but rarer than water. But (2) if that which is later in generation is prior in nature, and that which is concocted and compounded is later in generation, the contrary of what we have been saying must be true—water must be prior to air, and earth to water.

So much, then, for those who posit one cause such as we mentioned; but the same is true if one supposes more of these, as Empedocles says the matter of things is four bodies. For he too is confronted by consequences some of which are the same as have been mentioned, while others are peculiar to him. For we see these bodies produced from one another, which implies that the same body does not always remain fire or earth (we have spoken about this in our works on nature); and regarding the cause of movement and the question whether we must posit one or two, he must be thought to have spoken neither correctly nor altogether plausibly. And in general, change of quality is necessarily done away with for those who speak thus, for on their view cold will not come from hot nor hot from cold. For if it did there would be something that accepted the contraries themselves, and there would be some one entity that became fire and water, which Empedocles denies.

As regards Anaxagoras, if one were to suppose that he said there were two elements, the supposition would accord thoroughly with an argument which Anaxagoras himself did not state articulately, but which he must have accepted if any one had led him on to it. True, to say that in the beginning all things were mixed is absurd both on other grounds and because it follows that they must have existed before in an unmixed form, and because nature does not allow any chance thing to be mixed with any chance thing, and also because on this view modifications and accidents could be separated from substances (for the same things which are mixed can be separated); yet if one were to follow him up, piecing together what he means, he would perhaps be seen to be somewhat modern in his views. For when nothing was separated out, evidently nothing could be truly asserted of the substance that then existed. I mean, e.g., that it was neither white nor black, nor grey nor any other colour, but of necessity colourless; for if it had been coloured, it would have had one of these colours. And similarly, by this same argument,

it was flavourless, nor had it any similar attribute; for it could not be either of any quality or of any size, nor could it be any definite kind of thing. For if it were, one of the particular forms would have belonged to it, and this is impossible, since all were mixed together; for the particular form would necessarily have been already separated out, but he says all were mixed except reason, and this alone was unmixed and pure. From this it follows, then, that he must say the principles are the One (for this is simple and unmixed) and the Other, which is of such a nature as we suppose the indefinite to be before it is defined and partakes of some form. Therefore, while expressing himself neither rightly nor clearly, he means something like what the later thinkers say and what is now more clearly seen to be the case.

But these thinkers are, after all, at home only in arguments about generation and destruction and movement; for it is practically only of this sort of substance that they seek the principles and the causes. But those who extend their vision to all things that exist, and of existing things suppose some to be perceptible and others not perceptible, evidently study both classes, which is all the more reason why one should devote some time to seeing what is good in their views and what bad from the standpoint of the inquiry we have now before us.

The 'Pythagoreans' treat of principles and elements stranger than those of the physical philosophers (the reason is that they got the principles from non-sensible things, for the objects of mathematics, except those of astronomy, are of the class of things without movement); yet their discussions and investigations are all about nature; for they generate the heavens, and with regard to their parts and attributes and functions they observe the phenomena, and use up the principles and the causes in explaining these, which implies that they agree with the others, the physical philosophers, that the *real* is just all that which is perceptible and contained by the so-called 'heavens'. But the causes and the principles which they mention are, as we said, sufficient to act as steps even up to the higher realms of reality, and are more suited to these than to theories about nature. They do not tell us at all, however, how there can be movement if limit and unlimited and odd and even are the only things assumed, or how without movement and change there can be generation and destruction, or the bodies that move through the heavens can do what they do.

Further, if one either granted them that spatial magnitude consists of these elements, or this were proved, still how would some bodies be light and others have weight? To judge from what they assume and maintain they are speaking no more of mathematical bodies than of perceptible; hence they have said nothing whatever about fire or earth or the other bodies of this sort, I suppose because they have nothing to say which applies *peculiarly* to perceptible things.

Further, how are we to combine the beliefs that the attributes of number, and number itself, are causes of what exists and happens in the heavens both from the beginning and now, and that there is no other number than this number out of which the world is composed? When in one particular region they place opinion and opportunity, and, a little above or below, injustice and decision or mixture, and allege, as proof, that each of these is a number, and that there happens to be already in this place a plurality of the extended bodies composed of numbers, because these attributes of number attach to the various places,—this being so, is this number, which we must suppose each of these abstractions to be, the same number which is exhibited in the material universe, or is it another than this? Plato says it is different; yet even he thinks that both these bodies and their causes are numbers, but that the *intelligible* numbers are causes, while the others are *sensible*.

Let us leave the Pythagoreans for the present; for it is enough to have touched on them as much as we have done. But as for those who posit the Ideas as causes, firstly, in seeking to grasp the causes of the things around us, they introduced others equal in number to these, as if a man who wanted to count things thought he would not be able to do it while they were few, but tried to count them when he had added to their number. For the Forms are practically equal to—or not fewer than—the things, in trying to explain which these thinkers proceeded from them to the Forms. For to each thing there answers an entity which has the same name and exists apart from the substances, and so also in the case of all other groups there is a one over many, whether the many are in this world or are eternal.

Further, of the ways in which we prove that the Forms exist, none is convincing; for from some no inference necessarily follows, and from some arise Forms even of things of which we think there are no Forms. For according to the arguments from the existence of the sciences there will be Forms of all things of which there are sciences and according to the 'one over many' argument there will be Forms even of negations, and according to the argument that there is an object for thought even when the thing has perished, there will be Forms of perishable things; for we have an image of these. Further, of the more accurate arguments, some lead to Ideas of relations, of which we say there is no independent class, and others introduce the 'third man.'

And in general the arguments for the Forms destroy the things for whose existence we are more zealous than for the existence of the Ideas; for it follows that not the dyad but number is first, i.e. that the relative is prior to the absolute,—besides all the other points on which certain people by following out the opinions held about the Ideas have come into conflict with the principles of the theory.

Further, according to the assumption on which our belief in the Ideas rests, there will be Forms not only of substances but also of many other things (for the concept is single not only in the case of substances but also in the other cases, and there are sciences not only of substance but also of other things, and a thousand other such difficulties confront them). But according to the necessities of the case and the opinions held about the Forms, if Forms can be shared in there must be Ideas of substances only. For they are not shared in incidentally, but a thing must share in its Form as in something not predicated of a subject (by 'being shared in incidentally' I mean that e.g. if a thing shares in 'double itself', it shares also in 'eternal', but incidentally; for 'eternal' hap-

pens to be predicable of the 'double'). Therefore the Forms will be substance; but the same
terms indicate substance in this and in the
ideal world (or what will be the meaning of
saying that there is something apart from the
particulars—the one over many?). And if the
Ideas and the particulars that share in them
have the same form, there will be something
common to these; for why should '2' be one
and the same in the perishable 2's or in those
which are many but eternal, and not the same
in the '2 itself' as in the particular 2? But if
they have not the same form, they must have
only the name in common, and it is as if one
were to call both Callias and a wooden image a
'man,' without observing any community between them.

Above all one might discuss the question
what on earth the Forms contribute to sensible
things, either to those that are eternal or to
those that come into being and cease to be. For
they cause neither movement nor any change
in them. But again they help in no wise either
towards the knowledge of the other things (for
they are not even the substance of these, else
they would have been in them), or towards
their being, if they are not *in* the particulars
which share in them; though if they were, they
might be thought to be causes, as white causes
whiteness in a white object by entering into its
composition. But this argument, which first
Anaxagoras and later Eudoxus and certain
others used, is very easily upset; for it is not
difficult to collect many insuperable objections
to such a view.

But, further, all other things cannot come
from the Forms in any of the usual senses of
'from'. And to say that they are patterns and
the other things share in them is to use empty
words and poetical metaphors. For what is it
that works, looking to the Ideas? And anything can either be, or become, like another
without being copied from it, so that whether
Socrates exists or not a man like Socrates
might come to be; and evidently this might be
so even if Socrates were eternal. And there will
be several patterns of the same thing, and
therefore several Forms; e.g., 'animal' and
'two-footed' and also 'man himself' will be
Forms of man. Again, the Forms are patterns
not only of sensible things, but of Forms them-

selves also; i.e. the genus, as genus of various
species, will be so; therefore the same thing
will be pattern and copy.

Again, it would seem impossible that the
substance and that of which it is the substance
should exist apart; how, therefore, could the
Ideas, being the substances of things, exist
apart? In the *Phaedo* the case is stated in this
way—that the Forms are causes both of being
and of becoming, yet when the Forms exist,
still the things that share in them do not come
into being, unless there is something to originate movement; and many other things come
into being (e.g. a house or a ring) of which we
say there are no Forms. Clearly, therefore,
even the other things can both be and come
into being owing to such causes as produce the
things just mentioned.

Again, if the Forms are numbers, how can
they be causes? Is it because existing things are
other numbers, e.g. one number is man, another is Socrates, another Callias? Why then
are the one set of numbers causes of the other
set? It will not make any difference even if the
former are eternal and the latter are not. But
if it is because things in this sensible world (e.g.
harmony) are ratios of numbers, evidently the
things between which they are ratios are some
one class of things. If, then, this—the matter—
is some definite thing, evidently the numbers
themselves too will be ratios of something to
something else, e.g. if Callias is a numerical
ratio between fire and earth and water and air,
his Idea also will be a number of certain other
underlying things; and man-himself, whether
it is a number in a sense or not, will still be
a numerical ratio of certain things and
not a number proper, nor will it be a kind
of number merely because it is a numerical
ratio.

Again, from many numbers one number is
produced, but how can one Form come from
many Forms? And if the number comes not
from the many numbers themselves but from
the units in them, e.g. in 10,000, how is it with
the units? If they are specifically alike, numerous absurdities will follow, and also if they are
not alike (neither the units in one number
being themselves like one another nor those in
other numbers being all like to all); for in what
will they differ, as they are without quality?

This is not a plausible view, nor is it consistent with our thought on the matter.

Further, they must set up a second kind of number (with which arithmetic deals), and all the objects which are called 'intermediate' by some thinkers; and how do these exist or from what principles do they proceed? Or why must they be intermediate between the things in this sensible world and the things-themselves?

Further, the units in 2 must each come from a prior 2; but this is impossible.

Further, why is a number, when taken all together, one?

Again, besides what has been said, if the units are *diverse* the Platonists should have spoken like those who say there are four, or two, elements; for each of these thinkers gives the name of element not to that which is common, e.g. to body, but to fire and earth, whether there is something common to them, viz. body, or not. But in fact the Platonists speak as if the One were *homogeneous* like fire or water; and if this is so, the numbers will not be substances. Evidently, if there is a One-itself and this is a first principle, 'one' is being used in more than one sense; for otherwise the theory is impossible.

When we wish to reduce substances to their principles, we state that lines come from the short and long (i.e. from a kind of small and great), and the plane from the broad and narrow, and body from the deep and shallow. Yet how then can either the plane contain a line, or the solid a line or a plane? For the broad and narrow is a different class from the deep and shallow. Therefore, just as number is not present in these, because the many and few are different from these, evidently no other of the higher classes will be present in the lower. But again the broad is not a genus which includes the deep, for then the solid would have been a species of plane. Further, from what principle will the presence of the *points* in the line be derived? Plato even used to object to this class of things as being a geometrical fiction. He gave the name of principle of the line—and this he often posited—to the indivisible lines. Yet these must have a limit; therefore the argument from which the existence of the line follows proves also the existence of the point.

In general, though philosophy seeks the cause of perceptible things, we have given this up (for we say nothing of the cause from which change takes its start), but while we fancy we are stating the substance of perceptible things, we assert the existence of a second class of substances, while our account of the way in which they are the substances of perceptible things is empty talk; for 'sharing', as we said before, means nothing.

Nor have the Forms any connexion with what we see to be the cause in the case of the arts, that for whose sake both all mind and the whole of nature are operative,—with this cause which we assert to be one of the first principles; but mathematics has come to be identical with philosophy for modern thinkers, though they say that it should be studied for the sake of other things.

Further, one might suppose that the substance which according to them underlies as matter is too mathematical, and is a predicate and differentia of the substance, i.e. of the matter, rather than matter itself; i.e. the great and the small are like the rare and the dense which the physical philosophers speak of, calling these the primary differentiae of the substratum; for these are a kind of excess and defect. And regarding movement, if the great and the small are to *be* movement, evidently the Forms will be moved; but if they are not to be movement, whence did movement come? The whole study of nature has been annihilated.

And what is thought to be easy—to show that all things are one—is not done; for what is proved by the method of setting out instances is not that all things are one but that there is a One itself,—if we grant all the assumptions. And not even this follows, if we do not grant that the universal is a genus; and this in some cases it cannot be.

Nor can it be explained either how the lines and planes and solids that come after the numbers exist or can exist, or what significance they have; for these can neither be Forms (for they are not numbers), nor the intermediates (for those are the objects of mathematics), nor the perishable things. This is evidently a distinct fourth class.

In general, if we search for the elements of

existing things without distinguishing the many senses in which things are said to exist, we cannot find them, especially if the search for the elements of which things are made is conducted in this manner. For it is surely impossible to discover what 'acting' or 'being acted on', or 'the straight', is made of, but if elements can be discovered at all, it is only the elements of substances; therefore either to seek the elements of all existing things or to think one has them is incorrect.

And how could we *learn* the elements of all things? Evidently we cannot start by knowing anything before. For as he who is learning geometry, though he may know other things before, knows none of the things with which the science deals and about which he is to learn, so is it in all other cases. Therefore if there is a science of all things, such as some assert to exist, he who is learning this will know nothing before. Yet all learning is by means of premisses which are (either all or some of them) known before,—whether the learning be by demonstration or by definitions; for the elements of the definition must be known before and be familiar; and learning by induction proceeds similarly. But again, if the science were actually innate, it were strange that we are unaware of our possession of the greatest of sciences.

Again, how is one to *come to know* what all things are made of, and how is this to be made *evident*? This also affords a difficulty; for there might be a conflict of opinion, as there is about certain syllables; some say *za* is made out of *s* and *d* and *a*, while others say it is a distinct sound and none of those that are familiar.

Further, how could we know the objects of sense without having the sense in question? Yet we ought to, if the elements of which all things consist, as complex sounds consist of the elements proper to sound, are the same.

It is evident, then, even from what we have said before, that all men seem to seek the causes named in the *Physics*, and that we cannot name any beyond these; but they seek these vaguely; and though in a sense they have all been described before, in a sense they have not been described at all. For the earliest philosophy is, on all subjects, like one who

lisps, since it is young and in its beginnings. For even Empedocles says bone exists by virtue of the ratio in it. Now this is the essence and the substance of the thing. But it is similarly necessary that flesh and each of the other tissues should be the ratio of its elements, or that not one of them should; for it is on account of this that both flesh and bone and everything else will exist, and not on account of the matter, which *he* names,—fire and earth and water and air. But while he would necessarily have agreed if another had said this, he has not said it clearly.

On these questions our views have been expressed before; but let us return to enumerate the difficulties that might be raised on these same points; for perhaps we may get from them some help towards our later difficulties.

Book α

The investigation of the truth is in one way hard, in another easy. An indication of this is found in the fact that no one is able to attain the truth adequately, while, on the other hand, we do not collectively fail, but every one says something true about the nature of things, and while individually we contribute little or nothing to the truth, by the union of all a considerable amount is amassed. Therefore, since the truth seems to be like the proverbial door, which no one can fail to hit, in this respect it must be easy, but the fact that we can have a whole truth and not the particular part we aim at shows the difficulty of it.

Perhaps, too, as difficulties are of two kinds, the cause of the present difficulty is not in the facts but in us. For as the eyes of bats are to the blaze of day, so is the reason in our soul to the things which are by nature most evident of all.

It is just that we should be grateful, not only to those with whose views we may agree, but also to those who have expressed more superficial views; for these also contributed something, by developing before us the powers of thought. It is true that if there had been no

Timotheus we should have been without much of our lyric poetry; but if there had been no Phrynis there would have been no Timotheus. The same holds good of those who have expressed views about the truth; for from some thinkers we have inherited certain opinions, while the others have been responsible for the appearance of the former.

It is right also that philosophy should be called knowledge of the truth. For the end of theoretical knowledge is truth, while that of practical knowledge is action (for even if they consider how things are, practical men do not study the eternal, but what is relative and in the present). Now we do not know a truth without its cause; and a thing has a quality in a higher degree than other things if in virtue of it the similar quality belongs to the other things as well (e.g. fire is the hottest of things; for it is the cause of the heat of all other things); so that that which causes derivative truths to be true is most true. Hence the principles of eternal things must be always most true (for they are not merely sometimes true, nor is there any cause of their being, but they themselves are the cause of the being of other things), so that as each thing is in respect of being, so is it in respect of truth.

But evidently there *is* a first principle, and the causes of things are neither an infinite series nor infinitely various in kind. For (1) neither can one thing proceed from another, as from matter, *ad infinitum* (e.g. flesh from earth, earth from air, air from fire, and so on without stopping), nor can the source of movement form an endless series (man for instance being acted on by air, air by the sun, the sun by Strife, and so on without limit). Similarly the final causes cannot go on *ad infinitum*,—walking being for the sake of health, this for the sake of happiness, happiness for the sake of something else, and so one thing always for the sake of another. And the case of the essence is similar. For in the case of intermediates, which have a last term and a term prior to them, the prior must be the cause of the later terms, For if we had to say which of the three is the cause, we should say the first; surely not the last, for the final term is the cause of none; nor even the intermediate, for

it is the cause only of one. (It makes no difference whether there is one intermediate or more, nor whether they are infinite or finite in number.) But of series which are infinite in this way, and of the infinite in general, all the parts down to that now present are alike intermediates; so that if there is no first there is no cause at all.

Nor can there be an infinite process downwards, with a beginning in the upward direction, so that water should proceed from fire, earth from water, and so always some other kind should be produced. For one thing comes *from* another in two ways—not in the sense in which 'from' means 'after' (as we say 'from the Isthmian games come the Olympian'), but either (i) as the man comes from the boy, by the boy's changing, or (ii) as air comes from water. By 'as the man comes from the boy' we mean 'as that which has come to be from that which is coming to be, or as that which is finished from that which is being achieved' (for as becoming is between being and not being, so that which is becoming is always between that which is and that which is not; for the learner is a man of science in the making, and this is what is meant when we say that *from* a learner a man of science is being made); on the other hand, coming from another thing as water comes from air implies the destruction of the other thing. This is why changes of the former kind are not reversible, and the boy does not come from the man (for it is not that which comes to be something that comes to be as a result of coming to be, but that which exists after the coming to be; for it is thus that the day, too, comes from the morning—in the sense that it comes after the morning; which is the reason why the morning cannot come from the day); but changes of the other kind are reversible. But in both cases it is impossible that the number of terms should be infinite. For terms of the former kind, being intermediates, must have an end, and terms of the latter kind change back into *one another*; for the destruction of either is the generation of the other.

At the same time it is impossible that the first cause, being eternal, should be destroyed; for since the process of becoming is not infinite in the upward direction, that which is the first thing by whose destruction something came to be must be non-eternal.

Further, the *final cause* is an end, and that sort of end which is not for the sake of something else, but for whose sake everything else is; so that if there is to be a last term of this sort, the process will not be infinite; but if there is no such term, there will be no final cause, but those who maintain the infinite series eliminate the Good without knowing it (yet no one would try to do anything if he were not going to come to a limit); nor would there be reason in the world; the reasonable man, at least, always acts for a purpose, and this is a limit; for the end is a limit.

But the *essence,* also, cannot be reduced to another definition which is fuller in expression. For the original definition is always more of a definition, and not the later one; and in a series in which the first term has not the required character, the next has not it either.—Further, those who speak thus destroy science; for it is not possible to have this till one comes to the unanalysable terms. And knowledge becomes impossible; for how can one apprehend things that are infinite in this way? For this is not like the case of the line, to whose divisibility there is no stop, but which we cannot think if we do not make a stop (for which reason one who is tracing the infinitely divisible line cannot be counting the possibilities of section), but the whole line also must be apprehended by something in us that does not move from part to part.—Again, nothing infinite can exist; and if it could, at least the notion of infinity is not infinite.

But (2) if the *kinds* of causes had been infinite in number, then also knowledge would have been impossible; for we think we know, only when we have ascertained the causes, but that which is infinite by addition cannot be gone through in a finite time.

The effect which lectures produce on a hearer depends on his habits; for we demand the language we are accustomed to, and that which is different from this seems not in keeping but somewhat unintelligible and foreign because of its unwontedness. For it is the customary that is intelligible. The force of habit is shown by the laws, in which the legendary and childish elements prevail over our knowledge about them, owing to habit. Thus some people do not listen to a speaker unless he speaks mathematically, others unless he gives instances, while others expect him to cite a poet as witness. And some want to have everything done accurately, while others are annoyed by accuracy, either because they cannot follow the connexion of thought or because they regard it as pettifoggery. For accuracy has something of this character, so that as in trade so in argument some people think it mean. Hence one must be already trained to know how to take each sort of argument, since it is absurd to seek at the same time knowledge and the way of attaining knowledge; and it is not easy to get even one of the two.

The minute accuracy of mathematics is not to be demanded in all cases, but only in the case of things which have no matter. Hence its method is not that of natural science; for presumably the whole of nature has matter. Hence we must inquire first what nature is: for thus we shall also see what natural science treats of. . . .

III

René Descartes

RENÉ DESCARTES (1596–1650) was born in La Haye in Touraine, France. His father, a councillor of the *parlement* of Rennes in Brittany, entered him at age 8 in the celebrated Jesuit college La Flèche. After studying philosophy, science, and literature, he took a degree in law, only to turn to gambling, fencing, and horsemanship. He even fought a duel over a love affair; had he lost, philosophy and mathematics would both no doubt have turned out quite differently.

Though a citizen of France, Descartes served as a soldier in three armies: in the Netherlands, Bavaria, and in Hungary. When he turned 33, having grown disillusioned with "the book of the world," he moved to Holland. After a dream in which he says he experienced a mystical vision and "discovered the foundations of a marvellous science," he began developing his iconoclastic philosophy. Over the next 20 years he published four books, and his reputation as an original and profound thinker quickly grew. By the time he invented analytic geometry and the Cartesian Coordinate System, he had become famous throughout Europe.

Because Descartes turned from basing knowledge on accepted authority to basing it on one's own rational intuitions, he is often called the founder of modern philosophy. His *Meditations on the First Philosophy* is a radical criticism of all previous philosophy and science. Many philosophers objected furiously to it; others praised it as a great achievement. In *The World* he supported the radical Copernican geocentric view of the solar system; after hearing about Galileo's troubles with the Catholic Church, however, he stopped its publication. A few years later the president of the University of Utrecht nonetheless labeled Descartes an atheist and condemned him to the local magistrates.

In his profound and original philosophical works, Descartes rejects Aristotelianism in favor of a return to a type of Platonism, formulating a new system of universal knowledge founded on undoubtable premises and then, as in mathematics, proceeding with straightforward deductions in which each step is as clear as the starting proposition. He attempted to construct a "universal mathematics," a complete system of absolute validity regarding not just the nature of numbers and figures but the whole world, linking for the first time geometry and algebra and thereby inventing analytic geometry. In discovering that geometrical representations could be represented algebraically, Descartes became convinced that all aspects of reality ultimately were mathematical and therefore accessible—perfectly, clearly, and distinctly—to the mind. Since size, shape, volume, and so on—representations of the objects we find in nature—are geometrical representations that, by Descartes' method, can be purely mathematically represented, it should be possible for us to understand everything.

Although the first selection, written in 1628, is one of his earliest works, it was not published until 1701, more than half a century after Descartes' death. In it he formulates the rules for philosophical thought that leads to clear and distinct ideas via a method modeled after the precision of mathematical thought. The goal was not mathematical theory in the form of mathematics but a perfect understanding of ourselves and the world.

In the second reading, his six famous *Meditations,* Descartes raises the question of whether knowledge is attained through rational intuition or through sensory experience—a major preoccupation for later philosophers such as Locke, Berkeley, and Hume and an issue that has continued to perplex 20th-century thinkers. Here Descartes is clearly a forerunner of Kant's critique of dogmatic metaphysics, planting the seeds of idealism with his argument that we know our own minds more immediately than we know our bodies and the physical world.

Rules for the Direction of the Mind

René Descartes

Rule I

The end of study should be to direct the mind towards the enunciation of sound and correct judgments on all matters that come before it.

Whenever men notice some similarity between two things, they are wont to ascribe to each, even in those respects in which the two differ, what they have found to be true of the other. Thus they erroneously compare the sciences, which entirely consist in the cognitive exercise of the mind, with the arts, which depend upon an exercise and disposition of the body. They see that not all the arts can be acquired by the same man, but that he who restricts himself to one, most readily becomes the best executant, since it is not so easy for the same hand to adapt itself both to agricultural operations and to harp-playing, or to the performance of several such tasks as to one alone. Hence they have held the same to be true of the sciences also, and distinguishing them from one another according to their subject matter, they have imagined that they ought to be studied separately, each in isolation from all the rest. But this is certainly wrong. For since the sciences taken all together are identical with human wisdom, which always remains one and the same, however applied to different subjects, and suffers no more differentiation proceeding from them than the light of the sun experiences from the variety of the things which it illumines, there is no need for minds to be confined at all within limits; for neither does the knowing of one truth have an effect like that of the acquisition of one art and

SOURCE: *Rules for the Direction of the Mind* by René Descartes, translated by Elizabeth S. Haldane and G. R. T. Ross (Cambridge: Cambridge University Press, 1911).

prevent us from finding out another, it rather aids us to do so. Certainly it appears to me strange that so many people should investigate human customs with such care, the virtues of plants, the motions of the stars, the transmutations of metals, and the objects of similar sciences, while at the same time practically none bethink themselves about good understanding, or universal Wisdom, though nevertheless all other studies are to be esteemed not so much for their own value as because they contribute something to this. Consequently we are justified in bringing forward this as the first rule of all, since there is nothing more prone to turn us aside from the correct way of seeking out truth than this directing of our inquiries, not towards their general end, but towards certain special investigations. I do not here refer to perverse and censurable pursuits like empty glory or base gain; obviously counterfeit reasonings and quibbles suited to vulgar understanding open up a much more direct route to such a goal than does a sound apprehension of the truth. But I have in view even honourable and laudable pursuits, because these mislead us in a more subtle fashion. For example take our investigations of those sciences conducive to the conveniences of life or which yield that pleasure which is found in the contemplation of truth, practically the only joy in life that is complete and untroubled with any pain. There we may indeed expect to receive the legitimate fruits of scientific inquiry; but if, in the course of our study, we think of them, they frequently cause us to omit many facts which are necessary to the understanding of other matters, because they seem to be either of slight value or of little interest. Hence we must believe that all the sciences are so inter-connected, that it is much easier to study them all together than to isolate one from all the others. If, therefore, anyone wishes to search out the truth of things in serious earnest, he ought not to select one special science; for all the sciences are conjoined with each other and interdependent: he ought rather to think how to increase the natural light of reason, not for the purpose of resolving this or that difficulty of scholastic type, but in order that his understanding may light his will to its proper choice in all the contingencies of life. In a short time he will see with amazement that he has made much more progress than those who are eager about particular ends, and that he has not only obtained all that they desire, but even higher results than fall within his expectation.

Rule II

Only those objects should engage our attention, to the sure and indubitable knowledge of which our mental powers seem to be adequate.

Science in its entirety is true and evident cognition. He is no more learned who has doubts on many matters than the man who has never thought of him; nay he appears to be less learned if he has formed wrong opinions on any particulars. Hence it were better not to study at all than to occupy one's self with objects of such difficulty, that, owing to our inability to distinguish true from false, we are forced to regard the doubtful as certain; for in those matters any hope of augmenting our knowledge is exceeded by the risk of diminishing it. Thus in accordance with the above maxim we reject all such merely probable knowledge and make it a rule to trust only what is completely known and incapable of being doubted. No doubt men of education may persuade themselves that there is but little of such certain knowledge, because, forsooth, a common failing of human nature has made them deem it too easy and open to everyone, and so led them to neglect to think upon such truths; but I nevertheless announce that there are more of these than they think—truths which suffice to give a rigorous demonstration of innumerable propositions, the discussion of which they have hitherto been unable to free from the element of probability. Further, because they have believed that it was unbecoming for a man of education to confess ignorance on any point, they have so accustomed themselves to trick out their fabricated explanations, that they have ended by gradually imposing on themselves and thus have issued them to the public as genuine.

But if we adhere closely to this rule we shall find left but few objects of legitimate study. For there is scarce any question occurring in the sciences about which talented men have not disagreed. But whenever two men come to opposite decisions about the same matter one of them at least must certainly be in the wrong, and apparently there is not even one of them who knows; for if the reasoning of the second was sound and clear he would be able so to lay it before the other as finally to succeed in convincing *his* understanding also. Hence apparently we cannot attain to a perfect knowledge in any such case of probable opinion, for it would be rashness to hope for more than others have attained to. Consequently if we reckon correctly, of the sciences already discovered, Arithmetic and Geometry alone are left, to which the observance of this rule reduces us.

Yet we do not therefore condemn that method of philosophizing which others have already discovered and those weapons of the schoolmen, probable syllogisms, which are so well suited for polemics. They indeed give practice to the wits of youths and, producing emulation among them, act as a stimulus; and it is much better for their minds to be moulded by opinions of this sort, uncertain though they appear, as being objects of controversy among the learned, than to be left entirely to their own devices. For thus through lack of guidance they might stray into some abyss; but as long as they follow in their masters' footsteps, though they may diverge at times from the truth, they will yet certainly find a path which is at least in this respect safer, that it has been approved of by more prudent people. We ourselves rejoice that we in earlier years experienced this scholastic training; but now, being released from that oath of allegiance which bound us to our old masters, and since, as becomes our riper years, we are no longer subject to the ferule, if we wish in earnest to establish for ourselves those rules which shall aid us in scaling the heights of human knowledge, we must admit assuredly among the primary members of our catalogue that maxim which forbids us to abuse our leisure as many do, who neglect all easy quests and take up their time only with difficult matters; for they, though certainly making all sorts of subtle conjectures and elaborating most plausible arguments with great ingenuity, frequently find too late that after all their labours they have only increased the multitude of their doubts, without acquiring any knowledge whatsoever.

But now let us proceed to explain more carefully our reasons for saying, as we did a little while ago, that of all the sciences known as yet, Arithmetic and Geometry alone are free from any taint of falsity or uncertainty. We must note then that there are two ways by which we arrive at the knowledge of facts, viz. by experience and by deduction. We must further observe that while our inferences from experience are frequently fallacious, deduction, or the pure illation of one thing from another, though it may be passed over, if it is not seen through, cannot be erroneous when performed by an understanding that is in the least degree rational. And it seems to me that the operation is profited but little by those constraining bonds by means of which the Dialecticians claim to control human reason, though I do not deny that that discipline may be serviceable for other purposes. My reason for saying so is that none of the mistakes which men can make (men, I say, not beasts) are due to faulty inference; they are caused merely by the fact that we found upon a basis of poorly comprehended experiences, or that propositions are posited which are hasty and groundless.

This furnishes us with an evident explanation of the great superiority in certitude of Arithmetic and Geometry to other sciences. The former alone deal with an object so pure and uncomplicated, that they need make no assumptions at all which experience renders uncertain, but wholly consist in the rational deduction of consequences. They are on that account much the easiest and clearest of all, and possess an object such as we require, for in them it is scarce humanly possible for anyone

to err except by inadvertence. And yet we should not be surprised to find that plenty of people of their own accord prefer to apply their intelligence to other studies, or to Philosophy. The reason for this is that every person permits himself the liberty of making guesses in the matter of an obscure subject with more confidence than in one which is clear, and that it is much easier to have some vague notion about any subject, no matter what, than to arrive at the real truth about a single question however simple that may be.

But one conclusion now emerges out of these considerations, viz. not, indeed, that Arithmetic and Geometry are the sole sciences to be studied, but only that in our search for the direct road towards truth we should busy ourselves with no object about which we cannot attain a certitude equal to that of the demonstrations of Arithmetic and Geometry.

Rule III

In the subjects we propose to investigate, our inquiries should be directed, not to what others have thought, nor to what we ourselves conjecture, but to what we can clearly and perspicuously behold and with certainty deduce; for knowledge is not won in any other way.

To study the writings of the ancients is right, because it is a great boon for us to be able to make use of the labours of so many men; and we should do so, both in order to discover what they have correctly made out in previous ages, and also that we may inform ourselves as to what in the various sciences is still left for investigation. But yet there is a great danger lest in a too absorbed study of these works we should become infected with their errors, guard against them as we may. For it is the way of writers, whenever they have allowed themselves rashly and credulously to take up a position in any controverted matter, to try with the subtlest of arguments to compel us to go along with them. But when, on the contrary, they have happily come upon something certain and evident, in displaying it they never fail to surround it with ambiguities, fearing, it would seem, lest the simplicity of their explanation should make us respect their discovery less, or because they grudge us an open vision of the truth.

Further, supposing now that all were wholly open and candid, and never thrust upon us doubtful opinions as true, but expounded every matter in good faith, yet since scarce anything has been asserted by any one man the contrary of which has not been alleged by another, we should be eternally uncertain which of the two to believe. It would be no use to total up the testimonies in favour of each, meaning to follow that opinion which was supported by the greater number of authors; for if it is a question of difficulty that is in dispute, it is more likely that the truth would have been discovered by few than by many. But even though all these men agreed among themselves, what they teach us would not suffice for us. For we shall not, e.g. all turn out to be mathematicians though we know by heart all the proofs that others have elaborated, unless we have an intellectual talent that fits us to resolve difficulties of any kind. Neither, though we have mastered all the arguments of Plato and Aristotle, if yet we have not the capacity for passing a solid judgment on these matters, shall we become Philosophers; we should have acquired the knowledge not of a science, but of history.

I lay down the rule also, that we must wholly refrain from ever mixing up conjectures with our pronouncements on the truth of things. This warning is of no little importance. There is no stronger reason for our finding nothing in the current. Philosophy which is so evident and certain as not to be capable of being controverted, than the fact that the learned, not content with the recognition of what is clear and certain, in the first instance hazard the assertion of obscure and ill-comprehended theories, at which they have arrived merely by probable conjecture. Then afterwards they gradually attach complete credence to them, and mingling them promiscuously with what is true and evident, they finish by being unable to deduce any conclusion which does not appear to depend upon some proposition of the doubtful sort, and hence is not uncertain.

But lest we in turn should slip into the same error, we shall here take note of all those mental operations by which we are able, wholly without fear of illusion, to arrive at the knowledge of things. Now I admit only two, viz. intuition and induction.

By *intuition* I understand, not the fluctuating testimony of the senses, nor the misleading judgment that proceeds from the blundering constructions of imagination, but the conception which an unclouded and attentive mind gives us so readily and distinctly that we are wholly freed from doubt about that which we understand. Or, what comes to the same thing, *intuition* is the undoubting conception of an unclouded and attentive mind, and springs from the light of reason alone; it is more certain than deduction itself, in that it is simpler, though deduction, as we have noted above, cannot by us be erroneously conducted. Thus each individual can mentally have intuition of the fact that he exists, and that he thinks; that the triangle is bounded by three lines only, the sphere by a single superficies, and so on. Facts of such a kind are far more numerous than many people think, disdaining as they do to direct their attention upon such simple matters.

But in case anyone may be put out by this new use of the term intuition and of other terms which in the following pages I am similarly compelled to dissever from their current meaning, I here make the general announcement that I pay no attention to the way in which particular terms have of late been employed in the schools, because it would have been difficult to employ the same terminology while my theory was wholly different. All that I take note of is the meaning of the Latin of each word, when, in cases where an appropriate term is lacking, I wish to transfer to the vocabulary that expresses my own meaning those that I deem most suitable.

This evidence and certitude, however, which belongs to intuition, is required not only in the enunciation of propositions, but also in discursive reasoning of whatever sort. For example consider this consequence: 2 and 2 amount to the same as 3 and 1. Now we need to see intuitively not only that 2 and 2 make 4, and that likewise 3 and 1 make 4, but further that the third of the above statements is a necessary conclusion from these two.

Hence now we are in a position to raise the question as to why we have, besides intuition, given this supplementary method of knowing, viz. knowing by *deduction,* by which we understand all necessary inference from other facts that are known with certainty. This, however, we could not avoid, because many things are known with certainty, though not by themselves evident, but only deduced from true and known principles by the continuous and uninterrupted action of a mind that has a clear vision of each step in the process. It is in a similar way that we know that the last link in a long chain is connected with the first, even though we do not take in by means of one and the same act of vision all the intermediate links on which that connection depends, but only remember that we have taken them successively under review and that each single one is united to its neighbour, from the first even to the last. Hence we distinguish this mental intuition from deduction by the fact that into the conception of the latter there enters a certain movement or succession, into that of the former there does not. Further deduction does not require an immediately presented evidence such as intuition possesses; its certitude is rather conferred upon it in some way by memory. The upshot of the matter is that it is possible to say that those propositions indeed which are immediately deduced from first principles are known now by intuition, now by deduction, i.e. in a way that differs according to our point of view. But the first principles themselves are given by intuition alone, while, on the contrary, the remote conclusions are furnished only by deduction.

These two methods are the most certain routes to knowledge, and the mind should admit no others. All the rest should be rejected as suspect of error and dangerous. But this does not prevent us from believing matters that have been divinely revealed as being more certain than our surest knowledge, since belief in these things, as all faith in obscure matters, is an action not of our intelligence, but of our will. They should be heeded also since, if they have any basis in our understanding, they can and ought to be, more than all things else,

discovered by one or other of the ways above-mentioned, as we hope perhaps to show at greater length on some future opportunity.

Rule IV

There is need of a method for finding out the truth.

So blind is the curiosity by which mortals are possessed, that they often conduct their minds along unexplored routes, having no reason to hope for success, but merely being willing to risk the experiment of finding whether the truth they seek lies there. As well might a man burning with an unintelligent desire to find treasure, continuously roam the streets, seeking to find something that a passer by might have chanced to drop. This is the way in which most Chemists, many Geometricians, and Philosophers not a few prosecute their studies. I do not deny that sometimes in these wanderings they are lucky enough to find something true. But I do not allow that this argues greater industry on their part, but only better luck. But however that may be, it were far better never to think of investigating truth at all, than to do so without a method. For it is very certain that unregulated inquiries and confused reflections of this kind only confound the natural light and blind our mental powers. Those who so become accustomed to walk in darkness weaken their eye-sight so much that aferwards they cannot bear the light of day. This is confirmed by experience; for how often do we not see that those who have never taken to letters, give a sounder and clearer decision about obvious matters than those who have spent all their time in the schools? Moreover by a method I mean certain and simple rules, such that, if a man observe them accurately, he shall never assume what is false as true, and will never spend his mental efforts to no purpose, but will always gradually increase his knowledge and so arrive at a true understanding of all that does not surpass his powers.

These two points must be carefully noted, viz. never to assume what is false as true, and to arrive at a knowledge which takes in all things. For, if we are without the knowledge of any of the things which we are capable of understanding, that is only because we have never perceived any way to bring us to this knowledge, or because we have fallen into the contrary error. But if our method rightly explains how our mental vision should be used, so as not to fall into the contrary error, and how deduction should be discovered in order that we may arrive at the knowledge of all things, I do not see what else is needed to make it complete; for I have already said that no science is acquired except by mental intuition or deduction. There is besides no question of extending it further in order to show how these said operations ought to be effected, because they are the most simple and primary of all. Consequently, unless our understanding were already able to employ them, it could comprehend none of the precepts of that very method, not even the simplest. But as for the other mental operations, which Dialectic does its best to direct by making use of these prior ones, they are quite useless here; rather they are to be accounted impediments, because nothing can be added to the pure light of reason which does not in some way obscure it.

Since then the usefulness of this method is so great that without it study seems to be harmful rather than profitable, I am quite ready to believe that the greater minds of former ages had some knowledge of it, nature even conducting them to it. For the human mind has in it something that we may call divine, wherein are scattered the first germs of useful modes of thought. Consequently it often happens that however much neglected and choked by interfering studies they bear fruit of their own accord. Arithmetic and Geometry, the simplest sciences, give us an instance of this; for we have sufficient evidence that the ancient Geometricians made use of a certain analysis which they extended to the resolution of all problems, though they grudged the secret to posterity. At the present day also there flourishes a certain kind of Arithmetic, called Algebra, which designs to effect, when dealing with numbers, what the ancients achieved in the matter of figures.

These two methods are nothing else than the spontaneous fruit sprung from the inborn principles of the discipline here in question; and I do not wonder that these sciences with their very simple subject matter should have yielded results so much more satisfactory than others in which greater obstructions choke all growth. But even in the latter case, if only we take care to cultivate them assiduously, fruits will certainly be able to come to full maturity.

This is the chief result which I have had in view in writing this treatise. For I should not think much of these rules, if they had no utility save for the solution of the empty problems with which Logicians and Geometers have been wont to beguile their leisure; my only achievement thus would have seemed to be an ability to argue about trifles more subtly than others. Further, though much mention is here made of numbers and figures, because no other sciences furnish us with illustrations of such self-evidence and certainty, the reader who follows my drift with sufficient attention will easily see that nothing is less in my mind than ordinary Mathematics, and that I am expounding quite another science, of which these illustrations are rather the outer husk than the constituents. Such a science should contain the primary rudiments of human reason, and its province ought to extend to the eliciting of true results in every subject. To speak freely, I am convinced that it is a more powerful instrument of knowledge than any other that has been bequeathed to us by human agency, as being the source of all others. But as for the outer covering I mentioned, I mean not to employ it to cover up and conceal my method for the purpose of warding off the vulgar; rather I hope so to clothe and embellish it that I may make it more suitable for presentation to the human mind.

When first I applied my mind to Mathematics I read straight away most of what is usually given by the mathematical writers, and I paid special attention to Arithmetic and Geometry, because they were said to be the simplest and so to speak the way to all the rest. But in neither case did I then meet with authors who fully satisfied me. I did indeed learn in their works many propositions about numbers which I found on calculation to be true. As to figures, they in a sense exhibited to my eyes a great number of truths and drew conclusions from certain consequences. But they did not seem to make it sufficiently plain to the mind itself why those things are so, and how they discovered them. Consequently I was not surprised that many people, even of talent and scholarship, should, after glancing at these sciences, have either given them up as being empty and childish or, taking them to be very difficult and intricate, been deterred at the very outset from learning them. For really there is nothing more futile than to busy one's self with bare numbers and imaginary figures in such a way as to appear to rest content with such trifles, and so to resort to those superficial demonstrations, which are discovered more frequently by chance than by skill, and are a matter more of the eyes and the imagination than of the understanding, that in a sense one ceases to make use of one's reason. I might add that there is no more intricate task than that of solving by this method of proof new difficulties that arise, involved as they are with numerical confusions. But when I afterwards bethought myself how it could be that the earliest pioneers of Philosophy in bygone ages refused to admit to the study of wisdom any one who was not versed in Mathematics, evidently believing that this was the easiest and most indispensable mental exercise and preparation for laying hold of other more important sciences, I was confirmed in my suspicion that they had knowledge of a species of Mathematics very different from that which passes current in our time. I do not indeed imagine that they had a perfect knowledge of it, for they plainly show how little advanced they were by the insensate rejoicings they display and the pompous thanksgivings they offer for the most trifling discoveries. I am not shaken in my opinion by the fact that historians make a great deal of certain machines of theirs. Possibly these machines were quite simple, and yet the ignorant and wonder-loving multitude might easily have lauded them as miraculous. But I am convinced that certain primary germs of truth implanted by nature in human minds—though in our case the daily reading and hearing of innumerable diverse errors stifle them—had a very great vitality in that rude and unsophisticated age of the ancient world. Thus the same mental illumination which let them see that virtue was to be preferred to pleasure, and honour to utility, although they knew not why this was so, made them recognize true notions in Philosophy and Mathematics, although they were not yet able thoroughly to grasp these sciences. Indeed I seem to recognize certain traces of this true Mathematics in Pappus and Diophantus, who though not belonging to the earliest age, yet lived many centuries before our own times. But my opinion is that these writers then with a sort of low cunning, deplorable indeed, suppressed this knowledge. Possibly they acted just as many inventors are known to have done in the case of their discoveries, i.e. they feared that their method being so easy and simple would become cheapened on being divulged, and they preferred to exhibit in its place certain barren truths, deductively demonstrated with show enough of ingenuity, as the results of their art, in order to win from us our admiration for these achievements, rather than to disclose to us that method itself which would have wholly annulled the admiration accorded. Finally there have been certain men of talent who in the present age have tried to revive this same art. For it seems to be precisely that science known by the barbarous name Algebra, if only we could extricate it from that vast array of numbers and inexplicable figures by which it is overwhelmed, so that it might display the clearness and simplicity which, we imagine, ought to exist in a genuine Mathematics. It was these reflections that recalled me from the particular studies of Arithmetic and Geometry to a general investigation of Mathematics, and thereupon I sought to determine what precisely was universally meant by that term, and why not only the above mentioned sciences, but also Astronomy, Music, Optics, Mechanics and several others are styled parts of Mathematics. Here indeed it is not enough to look to the origin of the word; for since the name 'Mathematics' means exactly the same thing as 'scientific study,' these other branches could, with as much right as Geometry itself, be called Mathematics. Yet we see that almost anyone who has had the slightest schooling, can easily distinguish what relates to Mathematics in any question from that which belongs to the other sciences. But as I considered the matter carefully it gradually came to light that all those matters only were referred to Mathematics in which order and measurement are investigated, and that it makes no difference whether it be in numbers, figures, stars, sounds or any other object that the question of measurement arises. I saw consequently that there must be some general science to explain that element as a whole which gives rise to problems about order and measurement, restricted as these are to no special subject matter. This, I perceived, was called 'Universal Mathematics,' not a far fetched designation, but one of long standing which has passed into current use, because in this science is contained everything on account of which the others are called parts of Mathematics. We can see how much it excels in utility and simplicity the sciences subordinate to it, by the fact that it can deal with all the objects of which they have cognizance and many more besides, and that any difficulties it contains are found in them as well, added to the fact that in them fresh difficulties arise due to their special subject matter which in it do not exist. But now how comes it that though everyone knows the name of this science and understands what is its province even without studying it attentively, so many people laboriously pursue the other dependent sciences, and no one cares to master this one? I should marvel indeed were I not aware that everyone thinks it to be so very easy, and had I not long since observed that the human mind passes over what it thinks it can easily accomplish, and hastens straight away to new and more imposing occupations.

I, however, conscious as I am of my inadequacy, have resolved that in my investigation into truth I shall follow obstinately such an order as will require me first to start with what is simplest and easiest, and never permit me to proceed farther until in the first sphere there seems to be nothing further to be done. This is why up to the present time to the best of my ability I have made a study of this universal Mathematics; consequently I believe that when I go on to deal in their turn with more profound sciences, as I hope to do soon,

my efforts will not be premature. But before I make this transition I shall try to bring together and arrange in an orderly manner, the facts which in my previous studies I have noted as being more worthy of attention. Thus I hope both that at a future date, when through advancing years my memory is enfeebled, I shall, if need be, conveniently be able to recall them by looking in this little book, and that having now disburdened my memory of them I may be free to concentrate my mind on my future studies.

Rule V

Method consists entirely in the order and disposition of the objects towards which our mental vision must be directed if we would find out any truth. We shall comply with it exactly if we reduce involved and obscure propositions step by step to those that are simpler, and then starting with the intuitive apprehension of all those that are absolutely simple, attempt to ascend to the knowledge of all others by precisely similar steps.

In this alone lies the sum of all human endeavor, and he who would approach the investigation of truth must hold to this rule as closely as he who enters the labyrinth must follow the thread which guided Theseus. But many people either do not reflect on the precept at all, or ignore it altogether, or presume not to need it. Consequently they often investigate the most difficult questions with so little regard to order, that, to my mind, they act like a man who should attempt to leap with one bound from the base to the summit of a house, either making no account of the ladders provided for his ascent or not noticing them. It is thus that all Astrologers behave, who, though in ignorance of the nature of the heavens, and even without having made proper observations of the movements of the heavenly bodies, expect to be able to indicate their effects. This is also what many do who study Mechanics apart from Physics, and rashly set about devising new instruments for producing motion. Along with them go also those Philosophers who, neglecting experience, imagine that truth will spring from their brain like Pallas from the head of Zeus.

Now it is obvious that all such people violate the present rule. But since the order here required is often so obscure and intricate that not everyone can make it out, they can scarcely avoid error unless they diligently observe what is laid down in the following proposition.

Rule VI

In order to separate out what is quite simple from what is complex, and to arrange these matters methodically, we ought, in the case of every series in which we have deduced certain facts the one from the other, to notice which fact is simpe, and to mark the interval, greater, less, or equal, which separates all the others from this.

Although this proposition seems to teach nothing very new, it contains, nevertheless, the chief secret of method, and none in the whole of this treatise is of greater utility. For it tells us that all facts can be arranged in certain series, not indeed in the sense of being referred to some ontological genus such as the categories employed by Philosophers in their classification, but in so far as certain truths can be known from others; and thus, whenever a difficulty occurs we are able at once to perceive whether it will be profitable to examine certain others first, and which, and in what order.

Further, in order to do that correctly, we must note first that for the purpose of our procedure, which does not regard things as isolated realities, but compares them with one another in order to discover the dependence in knowledge of one upon the other, all things can be said to be either absolute or relative.

I call that absolute which contains within itself the pure and simple essence of which we are in quest. Thus the term will be applicable to whatever is considered as being independent, or a cause, or simple, universal, one, equal, like, straight, and so forth; and the absolute I call the simplest and the easiest of all, so that we can make use of it in the solution of questions.

But the relative is that which, while partici-

pating in the same nature, or at least sharing in it to some degree which enables us to relate it to the absolute and to deduce it from that by a chain of operations, involves in addition something else in its concept which I call relativity. Examples of this are found in whatever is said to be dependent, or an effect, composite, particular, many, unequal, unlike, oblique, etc. These relatives are the further removed from the absolute, in proportion as they contain more elements of relativity subordinate the one to the other. We state in this rule that these should all be distinguished and their correlative connection and natural order so observed, that we may be able by traversing all the intermediate steps to proceed from the most remote to that which is in the highest degree absolute.

Herein lies the secret of this whole method, that in all things we should diligently mark that which is most absolute. For some things are from one point of view more absolute than others, but from a different standpoint are more relative. Thus though the universal is more absolute than the particular because its essence is simpler, yet it can be held to be more relative than the latter, because it depends upon individuals for its existence, and so on. Certain things likewise are truly more absolute than others, but yet are not the most absolute of all. Thus relatively to individuals, species is something absolute, but contrasted with genus it is relative. So too, among things that can be measured, extension is something absolute, but among the various aspects of extension it is length that is absolute, and so on. Finally also, in order to bring out more clearly that we are considering here not the nature of each thing taken in isolation, but the series involved in knowing them, we have purposely enumerated cause and equality among our absolutes, though the nature of these terms is really relative. For though Philosophers make cause and effect correlative, we find that here even, if we ask what the effect is, we must first know the cause and not conversely. Equals too mutually imply one another, but we can know unequals only by comparing them with equals and not *per contra*.

Secondly we must note that there are but few pure and simple essences, which either our experiences or some sort of light innate in us enable us to behold as primary and existing *per se*, not as depending on any others. These we say should be carefully noticed, for they are just those facts which we have called the simplest in any single series. All the others can only be perceived as deductions from these, either immediate and proximate, or not to be attained save by two or three or more acts of inference. The number of these acts should be noted in order that we may perceive whether the facts are separated from the primary and simplest proposition by a greater or smaller number of steps. And so pronounced is everywhere the inter-connecton of ground and consequence, which gives rise, in the objects to be examined, to those series to which every inquiry must be reduced, that it can be investigated by a sure method. But because it is not easy to make a review of them all, and besides, since they have not so much to be kept in the memory as to be detected by a sort of mental penetration, we must seek for something which will so mould our intelligence as to let it perceive these connected sequences immediately whenever it needs to do so. For this purpose I have found nothing so effectual as to accustom ourselves to turn our attention with a sort of penetrative insight on the very minutest of the facts which we have already discovered.

Finally we must in the third place note that our inquiry ought not to start with the investigation of difficult matters. Rather, before setting out to attack any definite problem, it behoves us first, without making any selection, to assemble those truths that are obvious as they present themselves to us, and afterwards, proceeding step by step, to inquire whether any others can be deduced from these, and again any others from these conclusions and so on, in order. This done, we should attentively think over the truths we have discovered and mark with diligence the reasons why we have been able to detect some more easily than others, and which these are. Thus, when we come to attack some definite problem we shall be able to judge what previous questions it were best to settle first. For example, if it comes into my thought that the number 6 is twice 3, I may then ask what is twice 6, viz. 12;

again, perhaps I seek for the double of this, viz. 24, and again of this, viz. 48. Thus I may easily deduce that there is the same proportion between 3 and 6, as between 6 and 12, and likewise 12 and 24, and so on, and hence that the numbers 3, 6, 12, 24, 48, etc. are in continued proportion. But though these facts are all so clear as to seem almost childish, I am now able by attentive reflection to understand what is the form involved by all questions that can be propounded about the proportions or relations of things, and the order in which they should be investigated; and this discovery embraces the sum of the entire science of Pure Mathematics.

For first I perceive that it was not more difficult to discover the double of six than that of three; and that equally in all cases, when we have found a proportion between any two magnitudes, we can find innumerable others which have the same proportion between them. So too there is no increase of difficulty, if three, or four, or more of such magnitudes are sought for, because each has to be found separately and without any relation to the others. But next I notice that though, when the magnitudes 3 and 6 are given, one can easily find a third in continued proportion, viz. 12, it is yet not equally easy, when the two extremes, 3 and 12, are given, to find the mean proportional, viz. 6. When we look into the reason for this, it is clear that here we have a type of difficulty quite different from the former; for, in order to find the mean proportional, we must at the same time attend to the two extremes and to the proportion which exists between these two in order to discover a new ratio by dividing the previous one; and this is a very different thing from finding a third term in continued proportion with two given numbers. I go forward likewise and examine whether, when the numbers 3 and 24 were given, it would have been equally easy to determine one of the two intermediate proportionals, viz. 6 and 12. But here still another sort of difficulty arises more involved than the previous ones, for on this occasion we have to attend not to one or two things only but to three, in order to discover the fourth. We may go still further and inquire whether if only 3 and 48 had been given it would have been still more difficult to discover one of the three mean proportionals, viz. 6, 12, and 24. At the first blush this indeed appears to be so; but immediately afterwards it comes to mind that this difficulty can be split up and lessened, if first of all we ask only for the mean proportional between 3 and 48, viz. 12, and then seek for the other mean proportional between 3 and 12, viz. 6, and the other between 12 and 48, viz. 24. Thus we have reduced the problem to the difficulty of the second type shown above.

These illustrations further lead me to note that the quest for knowledge about the same thing can traverse different routes, the one much more difficult and obscure than the other. Thus to find these four continued proportionals, 3, 6, 12, and 24, if two consecutive numbers be assumed, e.g. 3 and 6, or 6 and 12, or 12 and 24, in order that we may discover the others, our task will be easy. In this case we shall say that the proposition to be discovered is directly examined. But if the two numbers given are alternates, like 3 and 12, or 6 and 24, which are to lead us to the discovery of the others, then we shall call this an indirect investigation of the first mode. Likewise if we are given two extremes like 3 and 24, in order to find out from these the intermediates 6 and 12, the investigation will be indirect and of the second mode. Thus I should be able to proceed further and deduce many other results from this example; but these will be sufficient, if the reader follows my meaning when I say that a proposition is directly deduced, or indirectly, and will reflect that from a knowledge of each of these matters that are simplest and primary, much may be discovered in other sciences by those who bring to them attentive thought and a power of sagacious analysis.

Rule VII

If we wish our science to be complete, those matters which promote the end we have in view must one and all be scrutinized by a movement of thought which is continuous and nowhere interrupted; they must also be included in an enumeration which is both adequate and methodical.

It is necessary to obey the injunctions of this rule if we hope to gain admission among the certain truths for those which, we have declared above, are not immediate deductions from primary and self-evident principles. For this deduction frequently involves such a long series of transitions from ground to consequent that when we come to the conclusion we have difficulty in recalling the whole of the route by which we have arrived at it. This is why I say that there must be a continuous movement of thought to make good this weakness of the memory. Thus, e.g. if I have first found out by separate mental operations what the relation is between the magnitudes A and B, then what between B and C, between C and D, and finally between D and E, that does not entail my seeing what the relation is between A and E, nor can the truths previously learnt give me a precise knowledge of it unless I recall them all. To remedy this I would run them over from time to time, keeping the imagination moving continuously in such a way that while it is intuitively perceiving each fact it simultaneously passes on to the next; and this I would do until I had learned to pass from the first to the last so quickly, that no stage in the process was left to the care of the memory, but I seemed to have the whole in intuition before me at the same time. This method will both relieve the memory, diminish the sluggishness of our thinking, and definitely enlarge our mental capacity.

But we must add that this movement should nowhere be interrupted. Often people who attempt to deduce a conclusion too quickly and from remote principles do not trace the whole chain of intermediate conclusions with sufficient accuracy to prevent them from passing over many steps without due consideration. But it is certain that wherever the smallest link is left out the chain is broken and the whole of the certainty of the conclusion falls to the ground.

Here we maintain that an enumeration [of the steps in a proof] is required as well, if we wish to make our science complete. For resolving most problems other precepts are profitable, but enumeration alone will secure our always passing a true and certain judgment on whatsoever engages our attention; by means of it nothing at all will escape us, but we shall evidently have some knowledge of every step.

This enumeration or induction is thus a review or inventory of all those matters that have a bearing on the problem raised, which is so thorough and accurate that by its means we can clearly and with confidence conclude that we have omitted nothing by mistake. Consequently as often as we have employed it, if the problem defies us, we shall at least be wiser in this respect, viz. that we are quite certain that we know of no way of resolving it. If it chance, as often it does, that we have been able to scan all the routes leading to it which lie open to the human intelligence, we shall be entitled boldly to assert that the solution of the problem lies outside the reach of human knowledge.

Furthermore we must note that by adequate enumeration or induction is only meant that method by which we may attain surer conclusions than by any other type of proof, with the exception of simple intuition. But when the knowledge of some matter cannot be reduced to this, we must cast aside all syllogistic fetters and employ induction, the only method left us, but one in which all confidence should be reposed. For whenever single facts have been immediately deduced the one from the other, they have been already reduced, if the inference was evident, to a true intuition. But if we infer any single thing from various and disconnected facts, often our intellectual capacity is not so great as to be able to embrace them all in a single intuition; in which case our mind should be content with the certitude attaching to this operation. It is in precisely similar fashion that though we cannot with one single gaze distinguish all the links of a lengthy chain, yet if we have seen the connection of each with its neighbour, we shall be entitled to say that we have seen how the first is connected with the last.

I have declared that this operation ought to be adequate, because it is often in danger of being defective and consequently exposed to error. For sometimes, even though in our enumeration we scrutinize many facts which are highly evident, yet if we omit the smallest step the chain is broken and the whole of the certitude of the conclusion falls to the ground. Sometimes also, even though all the facts are included in an accurate enumeration, the single steps are not distinguished from one another, and our knowledge of them all is thus only confused.

Further, while now the enumeration ought to be complete, now distinct, there are times when it need have neither of these characters; it was for this reason that I said only that it should be adequate. For if I want to prove by enumeration how many genera there are of corporeal things, or of those that in any way fall under the senses, I shall not assert that they are just so many and no more, unless I previously have become aware that I have included them all in my enumeration, and have distinguished them each separately from all the others. But if in the same way I wish to prove that the rational soul is not corporeal, I do not need a complete enumeration; it will be sufficient to include all bodies in certain collections in such a way as to be able to demonstrate that the rational soul has nothing to do with any of these. If, finally, I wish to show by enumeration that the area of a circle is greater than the area of all other figures whose perimeter is equal, there is no need for me to call in review all other figures; it is enough to demonstrate this of certain others in particular, in order to get thence by induction the same conclusion about all the others.

I added also that the enumeration ought to be methodical. This is both because we have no more serviceable remedy for the defects already instanced, than to scan all things in an orderly manner; and also because it often happens that if each single matter which concerns the quest in hand were to be investigated separately, no man's life would be long enough for the purpose, whether because they are far too many, or because it would chance that the same things had to be repeated too often. But if all these facts are arranged in the best order, they will for the most part be reduced to determinate classes, out of which it will be sufficient to take one example for exact inspection, or some one feature in a single case, or certain things rather than others, or at least we shall never have to waste our time in traversing the same ground twice. The advantage of this course is so great that often many particulars can, owing to a well devised arrangement, be gone over in a short space of time and with little trouble, though at first view the matter looked immense.

But this order which we employ in our enumerations can for the most part be varied and depends upon each man's judgment. For this reason, if we would elaborate it in our thought with greater penetration, we must remember what was said in our fifth proposition. There are also many of the trivial things of man's devising, in the discovery of which the whole method lies in the disposal of this order. Thus if you wish to construct a perfect anagram by the transposition of the letters of a name, there is no need to pass from the easy to the difficult, nor to distinguish absolute from relative. Here there is no place for these operations; it will be sufficient to adopt an order to be followed in the transpositions of the letters which we are to examine, such that the same arrangements are never handled twice over. The total number of transpositions should, e.g. be split up into definite classes, so that it may immediately appear in which there is the best hope of finding what is sought. In this way the task is often not tedious but merely child's play.

However, these three propositions should not be separated, because for the most part we have to think of them together, and all equally tend towards the perfecting of our method. There was no great reason for treating one before the other, and we have expounded them but briefly here. The reason for this is that in the rest of the treatise we have practically nothing else left for consideration. Therefore we shall then exhibit in detail what here we have brought together in a general way.

Rule VIII

If in the matters to be examined we come to a step in the series of which our understanding is not sufficiently well able to have an intuitive cognition, we must stop short there. We must make no attempt to examine what follows; thus we shall spare ourselves superfluous labour.

The three preceding rules prescribe and explain the order to be followed. The present rule, on the other hand, shows when it is wholly necessary and when it is merely useful. Thus it is necessary to examine whatever constitutes a single step in that series, by which we pass from relative to absolute, or conversely, before discussing what follows from it. But if, as often happens, many things pertain to the same step, though it is indeed always profitable to review them in order, in this case we are not forced to apply our method of observation so strictly and rigidly. Frequently it is permissible to proceed farther, even though we have not clear knowledge of all the facts it involves, but know only a few or a single one of them.

This rule is a necessary consequence of the reasons brought forward in support of the second. But it must not be thought that the present rule contributes nothing fresh towards the advancement of learning, though it seems only to bid us refrain from further discussion, and apparently does not unfold any truth. For beginners, indeed, it has no further value than to teach them how not to waste time, and it employs nearly the same arguments in doing so as Rule II. But it shows those who have perfectly mastered the seven preceding maxims, how in the pursuit of any science so to satisfy themselves as not to desire anything further. For the man who faithfully complies with the former rules in the solution of any difficulty, and yet by the present rule is bidden desist at a certain point, will then know for certainty that no amount of application will enable him to attain to the knowledge desired, and that not owing to a defect in his intelligence, but because the nature of the problem itself, or the fact that he is human, prevents him. But this knowledge is not the less science than that which reveals the nature of the thing itself; in fact he would seem to have some mental defect who should extend his curiosity farther.

But what we have been saying must be illustrated by one or two examples. If, for example, one who studies only Mathematics were to seek to find that curve which in dioptrics is called the anaclastic, that from which parallel rays are so refracted that after the refraction they all meet in one point,—it will be easy to see, by applying Rules V and VI, that the determination of this line depends upon the relation which the angles of refraction bear to the angles of incidence. But because he is unable to discover this, since it is a matter not of Mathematics but of Physics, he is here forced to pause at the threshold. Nor will it avail him to try and learn this from the Philosophers or to gather it from experience; for this would be to break Rule III. Furthermore this proposition is both composite and relative; but in the proper place we shall show that experience is unambiguous only when dealing with the wholly simple and absolute. Again, it will be vain for him to assume some relation or other as being that which prevails between such angles, and conjecture that this is the truest to fact; for in that case he would be on the track not of the anaclastic, but merely of that curve which could be deduced from his assumption.

If, however, a man who does not confine his studies to Mathematics, but, in accordance with the first rule, tries to discover the truth on all points, meets with the same difficulty, he will find in addition that this ratio between the angles of incidence and of refraction depends upon changes in their relation produced by varying the medium. Again these changes depend upon the manner in which the ray of light traverses the whole transparent body; while the knowledge of the way in which the light thus passes through presupposes a knowledge of the nature of the action of light, to understand which finally we must know what a natural potency is in general, this last being the most absolute term in the whole series in question. When, therefore, by a mental intuition he has clearly comprehended the nature of this, he will, in compliance with Rule V, proceed backwards by the same steps. And if when he comes to the second step he is unable straightway to determine the nature of light, he will, in accordance with the seventh rule, enumerate all the other natural potencies, in order that the knowledge of some other of them may help him, at least by analogy (of which more anon), to understand this. This done, he will ask how the ray traverses the whole of the transparent body, and will so follow out the other points methodically, that

at last he will arrive at the anaclastic itself. Though this has long defied the efforts of many inquirers, I see no reason why a man who fully carried out our method should fail to arrive at a convincing knowledge of the matter.

But let us give the most splendid example of all. If a man proposes to himself the problem of examining all the truths for the knowledge of which human reason suffices—and I think that this is a task which should be undertaken once at least in his life by every person who seriously endeavours to attain equilibrium of thought—, he will, by the rules given above, certainly discover that nothing can be known prior to the understanding, since the knowledge of all things else depends upon this and not conversely. Then, when he has clearly grasped all those things which follow proximately on the knowledge of the naked understanding, he will enumerate among other things whatever instruments of thought we have other than the understanding; and these are only two, viz. imagination and sense. He will therefore devote all his energies to the distinguishing and examining of these three modes of cognition, and seeing that in the strict sense truth and falsity can be a matter of the understanding alone, though often it derives its origin from the other two faculties, he will attend carefully to every source of deception in order that he may be on his guard. He will also enumerate exactly all the ways leading to truth which lie open to us, in order that he may follow the right way. They are not so many that they cannot all be easily discovered and embraced in an adequate enumeration. And though this will seem marvellous and incredible to the inexpert, as soon as in each matter he has distinguished those cognitions which only fill and embellish the memory, from those which cause one to be deemed really more instructed, which it will be easy for him to do . . . ; he will feel assured that any absence of further knowledge is not due to lack of intelligence or of skill, and that nothing at all can be known by anyone else which he is not capable of knowing, provided only that he gives to it his utmost mental application. And though many problems may present themselves, from the solution of which this rule prohibits him, yet because he will clearly perceive that they pass the limits of human intelligence, he will deem that he is not the more ignorant on that account; rather, if he is reasonable, this very knowledge, that the solution can be discovered by no, will abundantly satisfy his curiosity.

But lest we should always be uncertain as to the powers of the mind, and in order that we may not labour wrongly and at random before we set ourselves to think out things in detail, we ought once in our life to inquire diligently what the thoughts are of which the human mind is capable. In order the better to attain this end we ought, when two sets of inquiries are equally simple, to choose the more useful.

This method of ours resembles indeed those devices employed by the mechanical crafts, which do not need the aid of anything outside of them, but themselves supply the directions for making their own instruments. Thus if a man wished to practise any one of them, e.g. the craft of a smith, and were destitute of all instruments, he would be forced to use at first a hard stone or a rough lump of iron as an anvil, take a piece of rock in place of a hammer, make pieces of wood serve as tongs, and provide himself with other such tools as necessity required. Thus equipped, he would not then at once attempt to forge swords or helmets or any manufactured article of iron for others to use. He would first of all fashion hammer, anvil, tongs, and the other tools useful for himself. This example teaches us that, since thus at the outset we have been able to discover only some rough precepts, apparently the innate possession of our mind, rather than the product of technical skill, we should not forthwith attempt to settle the controversies of Philosophers, or solve the puzzles of the Mathematicians, by their help. We must first employ them for searching out with our utmost attention all the other things that are more urgently required in the investigation of truth. And this since there is no reason why it should appear more difficult to discover these than any of the answers which the problems propounded by Geometry or Physics or the other sciences are wont to demand.

Now no more useful inquiry can be proposed than that which seeks to determine the nature and the scope of human knowledge. This is why we state this very problem succinctly in the single question, which we deem should be answered at the very outset with the aid of the rules which we have already laid down. This investigation should be undertaken once at least in his life by anyone who has the slightest regard for truth, since in pursuing it the true instruments of knowledge and the whole method of inquiry come to light. But nothing seems to me more futile than the conduct of those who boldly dispute about the secrets of nature, the influence of the heavens on these lower regions, the predicting of future events and similar matters, as many do, without yet having ever asked even whether human reason is adequate to the solution of these problems. Neither ought it to seem such a toilsome and difficult matter to define the limits of that understanding of which we are directly aware as being within us, when we often have no hesitation in passing judgment even on things that are without us and quite foreign to us. Neither is it such an immense task to attempt to grasp in thought all the objects comprised within this whole of things, in order to discover how they singly fall under our mental scrutiny. For nothing can prove to be so complex or so vague as to defeat the efforts of the method of enumeration above described, directed towards restraining it within certain limits or arranging it under certain categories. But to put this to the test in the matter of the question above propounded, we first of all divide the whole problem relative to it into two parts; for it ought either to relate to us who are capable of knowledge, or to the things themselves which can be known; and these two factors we discuss separately.

In ourselves we notice that while it is the understanding alone which is capable of knowing, it yet is either helped or hindered by three other faculties, namely imagination, sense, and memory. We must therefore examine these faculties in order, with a view to finding out where each may prove to be an impediment, so that we may be on our guard; or where it may profit us, so that we may use to the full the resources of these powers. This first part of our problem will accordingly be discussed with the aid of a sufficient enumeration, as will be shown in the succeeding proposition.

We come secondly to the things themselves which must be considered only in so far as they are the objects of the understanding. From this point of view we divide them into the class (1) of those whose nature is of the extremest simplicity and (2) of the complex and composite. Simple natures must be either spiritual or corporeal or at once spiritual and corporeal. Finally among the composites there are some which the understanding realises to be complex before it judges that it can determine anything about them; but there are also others which it itself puts together. All these matters will be expounded at greater length in the twelfth proposition, where it will be shown that there can be no falsity save in the last class—that of the compounds made by the understanding itself. This is why we further subdivide these into the class of those which are deducible from natures which are of the maximum simplicity and are known *per se*, of which we shall treat in the whole of the succeeding book; and into those which presuppose the existence of others which the facts themselves show us to be composite. To the exposition of these we destine the whole of the third book.

But we shall indeed attempt in the whole of this treatise to follow so accurately the paths which conduct men to the knowledge of the truth and to make them so easy, that anyone who has perfectly learned the whole of this method, however moderate may be his talent, may see that no avenue to the truth is closed to him from which everyone else is not also excluded, and that his ignorance is due neither to a deficiency in his capacity nor to his method of procedure. But as often as he applies his mind to the understanding of some matter, he will either be entirely successful, or he will realise that success depends upon a certain experiment which he is unable to perform, and in that case he will not blame his mental capacity although he is compelled to stop short there. Or finally he may show that the knowledge desired wholly exceeds the limits of the human intelligence; and consequently he will believe that he is none the more ignorant on that account. For to have

discovered this is knowledge in no less degree than the knowledge of anything else.

Rule IX

We ought to give the whole of our attention to the most insignificant and most easily mastered facts, and remain a long time in contemplation of them until we are accustomed to behold the truth clearly and distinctly.

We have now indicated the two operations of our understanding, intuition and deduction, on which alone we have said we must rely in the acquisition of knowledge. Let us therefore in this and in the following proposition proceed to explain how we can render ourselves more skilful in employing them, and at the same time cultivate the two principal faculties of the mind, to wit perspicacity, by viewing single objects distinctly, and sagacity, by the skilful deduction of certain facts from others.

Truly we shall learn how to employ our mental intuition from comparing it with the way in which we employ our eyes. For he who attempts to view a multitude of objects with one and the same glance, sees none of them distinctly; and similarly the man who is wont to attend to many things at the same time by means of a single act of thought is confused in mind. But just as workmen, who are employed in very fine and delicate operations and are accustomed to direct their eyesight attentively to separate points, by practice have acquired a capacity for distinguishing objects of extreme minuteness and subtlety; so likewise do people who do not allow their thought to be distracted by various objects at the same time, but always concentrate it in attending to the simplest and easiest particulars, are clear-headed.

But it is a common failing of mortals to deem the more difficult the fairer; and they often think that they have learned nothing when they see a very clear and simple cause for a fact, while at the same time they are lost in admiration of certain sublime and profound philosophical explanations, even though these for the most part are based upon foundations which no one has adequately surveyed—a mental disorder which prizes the darkness higher than the light. But it is notable that those who have real knowledge discern the truth with equal facility whether they evolve it from matter that is simple or that is obscure; they grasp each fact by an act of thought that is similar, single, and distinct, after they have once arrived at the point in question. The whole of the difference between the apprehension of the simple and of the obscure lies in the route taken, which certainly ought to be longer if it conducts us from our initial and most absolute principles to a truth that is somewhat remote.

Everyone ought therefore to accustom himself to grasp in his thought at the same time facts that are at once so few and so simple, that he shall never believe that he has knowledge of anything which he does not mentally behold with a distinctness equal to that of the objects which he knows most distinctly of all. It is true that some men are born with a much greater aptitude for such discernment than others, but the mind can be made much more expert at such work by art and exercise. But there is one fact which I should here emphasize above all others; and that is that everyone should firmly persuade himself that none of the sciences, however abstruse, is to be deduced from lofty and obscure matters, but that they all proceed only from what is easy and more readily understood.

For example if I wish to examine whether it is possible for a natural force to pass at one and the same moment to a spot at a distance and yet to traverse the whole space in between, I shall not begin to study the force of magnetism or the influence of the stars, not even the speed of light, in order to discover whether actions such as these occur instantaneously; for the solution of this question would be more difficult than the problem proposed. I should rather bethink myself of the spatial motions of bodies, because nothing in the sphere of motion can be found more obvious to sense than this. I shall observe that while a stone cannot pass to another place in one and the same moment, because it is a body, yet a force similar to that which moves the stone is communicated exactly instantaneously if it passes unencumbered from one object to another. For instance, if I move one end of a stick of whatever length, I easily understand that the power by which that part of the stick is moved necessarily moves also all its other parts at the same moment, because then the force passes unencumbered and is not imprisoned in any body, e.g. a stone, which bears it along.

In the same way if I wish to understand how one and the same simple cause can produce contrary effects at the same time, I shall not cite the drugs of the doctors which expel certain humours and retain others; nor shall I romance about the moon's power of warming with its light and chilling by means of some occult power. I shall rather cast my eyes upon the balance in which the same weight raises one arm at the same time as it depresses the other, or take some other familiar instance.

Rule X

In order that it may acquire sagacity the mind should be exercised in pursuing just those inquiries of which the solution has already been found by others; and it ought to traverse in a systematic way even the most trifling of men's inventions, though those ought to be preferred in which order is explained or implied.

I confess that my natural disposition is such that I have always found, not the following of the arguments of others, but the discovery of reasons by my own proper efforts, to yield me the highest intellectual satisfaction. It was this alone that attracted me, when I was still a young man, to the study of science. And whenever any book by its title promised some new discovery, before I read further, I tried whether I could achieve something similar by means of some inborn faculty of invention, and I was careful lest a premature perusal of the book might deprive me of this harmless pleasure. So often was I successful that at length I perceived that I no longer came upon the truth by proceeding as others commonly do, viz. by pursuing vague and blind inquiries and relying more on good fortune than on skill. I saw that by long experience I had discovered certain rules which are of no little help in this inquiry, and which I used afterwards in devising further rules. Thus it was that I diligently elaborated the whole of this method and came to the conclusion that I had followed that plan of study which was the most fruitful of all.

But because not all minds are so much inclined to puzzle things out unaided, this proposition announces that we ought not immediately to occupy ourselves with the more difficult and arduous problems, but first should discuss those disciplines which are easiest and simplest, and those above all in which order most prevails. Such are the arts of the craftsmen who weave webs and tapestry, or of women who embroider or use in the same work threads with infinite modification of texture. With these are ranked all play with numbers and everything that belongs to Arithmetic, and the like. It is wonderful how all these studies discipline our mental powers, provided that we do not know the solutions from others, but invent them ourselves. For since nothing in these arts remains hidden, and they are wholly adjusted to the capacity of human cognition, they reveal to us with the greatest distinctness innumerable orderly systems, all different from each other, but none the less conforming to rule, in the proper observance of which systems of order consists the whole of human sagacity.

It was for this reason that we insisted that method must be employed in studying those matters; and this in those arts of less importance consists wholly in the close observation of the order which is found in the object studied, whether that be an order existing in the thing itself, or due to subtle human devising. Thus if we wish to make out some writing in which the meaning is disguised by the use of a cypher, though the order here fails to present itself, we yet make up an imaginary one, for the purpose both of testing all the conjectures we may make about single letters, words or sentences, and in order to arrange them so that when we sum them up we shall be able to tell all the inferences that we can deduce from them. We must principally beware of wasting our time in such cases by proceeding at random and unmethodically; for even though the solution can often be found without method, and by lucky people sometimes quicker, yet such procedure is likely to enfeeble the faculties and to make people accustomed to the trifling and the childish, so that for the future their minds will stick on the surface of things, incapable of penetrating beyond it. But meanwhile we must not fall into the error of those who, having devoted themselves solely to what is lofty and serious, find that after many years of toil they have acquired, not the profound knowledge they hoped for, but only mental confusion. Hence we must give ourselves practice first in those easier disciplines, but methodically, so that by open and familiar ways we may ceaselessly accustom ourselves to penetrate as easily as though we were at play into the very heart of these subjects. For by this means we shall afterwards gradually feel (and in a space of time shorter than we could at all hope for) that we are in a position with equal facility to deduce from evident first principles many propositions which at first sight are highly intricate and difficult.

It may perhaps strike some with surprise that here, where we are discussing how to improve our power of deducing one truth from another, we have omitted all the precepts of the dialecticians, by which they think to control the human reason. They prescribe certain formulae of argument, which lead to a conclusion with such necessity that, if the reason commits itself to their trust, even though it slackens its interest and no longer pays a heedful and close attention to the very proposition inferred, it can nevertheless at the same time come to a sure conclusion by virtue of the form of the argument alone. Exactly so; the fact is that frequently we notice that often the truth escapes away out of these imprisoning bonds, while the people themselves who have used them in order to capture it remain entangled in them. Other people are not so frequently entrapped; and it is a matter of experience that the most ingenious sophisms hardly ever impose on anyone who uses his unaided reason, while they are wont to deceive the sophists themselves.

Wherefore as we wish here to be particularly careful lest our reason should go on holiday while we are examining the truth of any matter, we reject those formulae as being opposed to our project, and look out rather for all the aids by which our thought may be kept attentive, as will be shown in the sequel. But, to say a few words more, that it may appear still more evident that this style of argument contributes nothing at all to the discovery of the truth, we must note that the Dialecticians are unable to devise any syllogism which has a true conclusion, unless they have first secured the material out of which to construct it, i.e. unless they have already ascertained the very truth which is deduced in that syllogism. Whence it is clear that from a formula of this kind they can gather nothing that is new, and hence the ordinary Dialectic is quite valueless for those who desire to investigate the truth of things. Its only possible use is to serve to explain at times more easily to others the truths we have already ascertained; hence it should be transferred from Philosophy to Rhetoric.

Rule XI

If, after we have recognized intuitively a number of simple truths, we wish to draw any inference from them, it is useful to run them over in a continuous and uninterrupted act of thought, to reflect upon their relations to one another, and to grasp together distinctly a number of these propositions so far as is possible at the same time. For this is a way of making our knowledge much more certain, and of greatly increasing the power of the mind.

Here we have an opportunity of expounding more clearly what has been already said of mental intuition in the third and seventh rules. In one passage we opposed it to deduction, while in the other we distinguished it from enumeration only, which we defined as an inference drawn from many and diverse things. But the simple deduction of one thing from another, we said in the same passage, was effected by intuition.

It was necessary to do this, because two things are requisite for mental intuition. Firstly the proposition intuited must be clear and distinct; secondly it must be grasped in its totality at the same time and not successively. As for deduction, if we are thinking of how the process works, as we were in Rule III, it appears not to occur all at the same time, but involves a sort of movement on the part of our mind when it infers one thing from another. We were justified therefore in distinguishing deduction in that rule from intuition. But if we wish to consider deduction as an accomplished fact, as we did in what we said relatively to the seventh rule, then it no longer designates a movement, but rather the completion of a movement, and therefore we suppose that it is presented to us by intuition when it is simple and clear, but not when it is complex and involved. When this is the case we give it the name of enumeration or induction, because it cannot then be grasped as a whole at the same time by the mind, and its certainty depends to some extent on the memory, in which our judgments about the various matters enumerated must be retained, if from their assemblage a single fact is to be inferred.

All these distinctions had to be made if we were to elucidate this rule. We treated of mental intuition solely in Rule IX; the tenth dealt with enumeration alone; but now the present rule explains how these two operations aid and complete each other. In doing so they seem to grow into a single process by virtue of a sort of motion of thought which has an attentive and vision-like knowledge of one fact and yet can pass at the very same moment to another.

Now to this co-operation we assign a two-fold advantage. Firstly it promotes a more certain knowledge of the conclusion with which we are concerned, and secondly it makes the mind readier to discover fresh truths. In fact the memory, on which we have said depends the certainty of the conclusions which embrace more than we can grasp in a single act of intuition, though weak and liable to fail us, can be renewed and made stronger by this continuous and constantly repeated process of thought. Thus if diverse mental acts have led me to know what is the relation between a first and a second magnitude, next between the second and a third, then between the third and a fourth, and finally the fourth and a fifth, that need not lead me to see what is the relation between the first and the fifth, nor can I deduce it from what I already know, unless I remember all the other relations. Hence what I have to do is to run over them all repeatedly in my mind, until I pass so quickly from the first to the last that practically no step is left to the memory, and I seem to view the whole all at the same time.

Everyone must see that this plan does much to counteract the slowness of the mind and to enlarge its capacity. But in addition we must note that the greatest advantage of this rule consists in the fact that, by reflecting on the mutual dependence of two propositions, we acquire the habit of distinguishing at a glance what is more or less relative, and what the steps are by which a relative fact is related to something absolute. For example, if I run over a number of magnitudes that are in continued proportion, I shall reflect upon all the following facts: viz. that the mental act is entirely similar—and not easier in the one case, more difficult in another—by which I grasp the relation between the first and the second, the second and third, third and fourth, and so on; while yet it is more difficult for me to conceive what the relation of the second is to the first and to the third at the same time, and much more difficult still to tell its relation to the first and fourth, and so on. These considerations then lead me to see why, if the first and second alone are given, I can easily find the third and fourth, and all the others; the reason being that this process requires only single and distinct acts of thought. But if only the first and the third are given, it is not so easy to recognize the mean, because this can only be accomplished by means of a mental operation in which two of the previous acts are involved. If the first and the fourth magnitudes alone are given, it is still more difficult to present to ourselves the two means, because here three acts of thought come in simultaneously. It would seem likely as a consequence that it would be even more difficult to discover the three means between the first and the fifth. The reason why this is not so is due to a fresh fact; viz. even though here four mental acts come together they can yet be disjoined, since four can be divided by another number. Thus I can discover the third by itself from the first and fifth, then the second from the first and third, and so on. If one accustoms one's self to reflect on these and similar problems, as often as a new question arises, at once one recognizes what produces its special difficulty, and what is the simplest method of dealing with all cases; and to be able to do so is a valuable aid to the discovery of the truth.

Rule XII

Finally we ought to employ all the aids of understanding, imagination, sense and memory, first for the purpose of having a distinct intuition of simple propositions; partly also in order to compare the propositions to be proved with those we know already, so that we may be able to recognize their truth; partly also in order to discover the truths, which should be compared with each other so that nothing may be left lacking on which human industry may exercise itself.

This rule states the conclusion of all that we said before, and shows in general outline what had to be explained in detail, in this wise.

In the matter of the cognition of facts two things alone have to be considered, ourselves who know and the objects themselves which are to be known. Within us there are four faculties only which we can use for this purpose, viz. understanding, imagination, sense and memory. The understanding is indeed alone capable of perceiving the truth, but yet it ought to be aided by imagination, sense and memory, lest perchance we omit any expedient that lies within our power. On the side of the facts to be known it is enough to examine three things; first that which presents itself spontaneously, secondly how we learn one thing by means of another, and thirdly what (truths) are deduced from what. This enumeration appears to me to be complete, and to omit nothing to which our human powers can apply.

I should have liked therefore to have turned to the first point and to have explained in this passage, what the human mind is, what body, and how it is 'informed' by mind; what the faculties in the complex whole are which serve the attainment of knowledge, and what the agency of each is. But this place seems hardly to give me sufficient room to take in all the matters which must be premised before the truth in this subject can become clear to all. For my desire is in all that I write to assert nothing controversial unless I have already stated the very reasons which have brought me to that conclusion, and by which I think that others also may be convinced.

But because at present I am prevented from doing this, it will suffice me to explain as briefly as possible that mode of viewing everything within us which is directed towards the discovery of truth, which most promotes my purpose. You need not believe that the facts are so unless you like. But what prevents us following these suppositions, if it appears that they do no harm to the truth, but only render it all much clearer? In Geometry you do precisely the same thing when you make certain assumptions about a quantity which do not in any way weaken the force of your arguments, though often our experience of its nature in Physics makes us judge of it quite otherwise.

Let us then conceive of the matter as follows:—all our external senses, in so far as they are part of the body, and despite the fact that we direct them towards objects, so manifesting activity, viz. a movement in space, nevertheless properly speaking perceive in virtue of passivity alone, just in the way that wax receives an impression from a seal. And it should not be thought that all we mean to assert is an analogy between the two. We ought to believe that the way is entirely the same in which the exterior figure of the sentient body is really modified by the object, as that in which the shape of the surface of the wax is altered by the seal. This has to be admitted not only in the case of the figure, hardness, roughness, etc. of a body which we perceive by touch, but even when we are aware of heat, cold, and the like qualities. It is likewise with the other senses. The first opaque structure in the eye receives the figure impressed upon it by the light with its various colours; and the first membrane in the ears, the nose, and the tongue that resists the further passage of the object, thus also acquires a new figure from the sound, the odour, and the savour, as the case may be.

It is exceedingly helpful to conceive all those matters thus, for nothing falls more readily under sense than figure, which can be touched and seen. Moreover that nothing false issues from this supposition more than from any other, is proved by the fact that the concept of figure is so common and simple that it is involved in every object of sense. Thus whatever you suppose colour to be, you cannot deny that it is extended and in consequence possessed of figure. Is there then any disadvantage, if, while taking care not to admit any new entity uselessly, or rashly to imagine that it exists, and not denying indeed the beliefs of others concerning colour, but merely abstracting from every other feature except that it possesses the nature of figure, we conceive the diversity existing between white, blue, and red, etc., as being like the difference between the following similar figures?

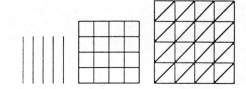

The same argument applies to all cases; for it is certain that the infinitude of figures suffices to express all the differences in sensible things.

Secondly we must believe that while the external sense is stimulated by the object, the figure which is conveyed to it is carried off to some other part of the body, that part called the common sense, in the very same instant and without the passage of any real entity from one to the other. It is in exactly the same manner that now when I write I recognize that at the very moment when the separate characters are being written down on the paper, not only is the lower end of the pen moved, but every motion in that part is simultaneously shared by the whole pen. All these diverse motions are traced by the upper end of the pen likewise in the air, although I do not conceive of anything real passing from the one extremity to the other. Now who imagines that the connection between the different parts of the human body is slighter than that between the ends of a pen, and what simpler way of expressing this could be found?

Thirdly we must believe that the common sense has a function like that of a seal, and impresses on the fancy or imagination, as though on wax, those very figures and ideas which come uncontaminated and without bodily admixture from the external senses. But this fancy is a genuine part of the body, of sufficient size to allow its different parts to assume various figures in distinctness from each other and to let those parts acquire the practice of retaining the impressions for some time. In the latter case we give the faculty the name of memory.

In the fourth place we must conceive that the motor force or the nerves themselves derive their origin from the brain, in which the fancy is located, and that the fancy moves them in various ways, just as the external senses act on the common sense, or the lower extremity of the pen moves the whole pen. This example also shows how the fancy can be the cause of many motions in the nerves, motions of which, however, it does not have the images stamped upon it, possessing only certain other images from which these latter follow. Just so the whole pen does not move exactly in the way in which its lower end does; nay the greater part seems to have a motion that is quite different from and contrary to that of the other. This lets us understand how all the motions of the other animals can come about, though we can ascribe to them no knowledge at all, but only fancy of a purely corporeal kind. We can explain also how in ourselves all those operations occur which we perform without any aid from the reason.

Finally and in the fifth place, we must think that that power by which we are properly said to know things, is purely spiritual, and not less distinct from every part of the body than blood from bone, or hand from eye. It is a single agency, whether it receives impressions from the common sense simultaneously with the fancy, or applies itself to those that are preserved in the memory, or forms new ones. Often the imagination is so beset by these impressions that it is unable at the same time to receive ideas from the common sense, or to transfer them to the motor mechanism in the way befitting its purely corporeal character. In all these operations this cognitive power is at one time passive, at another active, and resembles now the seal and now the wax. But the resemblance on this occasion is only one of analogy, for among corporeal things there is nothing wholly similar to this faculty. It is one and the same agency which, when applying itself along with the imagination to the common sense, is said to see, touch, etc.; if applying itself to the imagination alone in so far as that is endowed with diverse impressions, it is said to remember; if it turn to the imagination in order to create fresh impressions, it is said to imagine or conceive; finally if it act alone it is said to understand. How this latter function takes place I shall explain at greater length in the proper place. Now it is the same faculty that in correspondence with those various functions is called either pure understanding, or imagination, or memory, or sense. It is properly called mind when it either forms new ideas in the fancy, or attends to those already formed. We consider it as capable of the above various operations, and this distinction between those terms must in the sequel be borne in mind. But after having grasped these facts the attentive reader will gather what help is to be expected from each particular faculty, and discover how far human effort can avail to supplement the deficiencies of our mental powers.

For, since the understanding can be stimulated by the imagination, or on the contrary act on it; and seeing that the imagination can act on the senses by means of the motor power applying them to objects, while they on the contrary can act on it, depicting on it the images of bodies; considering on the other hand that the memory, at least that which is corporeal and similar to that of the brutes, is in no respect distinct from the imagination; we come to the sure conclusion that, if the understanding deal with matters in which there is nothing corporeal or similar to the corporeal, it cannot be helped by those faculties, but that, on the contrary, to prevent their hampering it, the senses must be banished and the imagination as far as possible divested of every distinct impression. But if the understanding proposes to examine something that can be referred to the body, we must form the idea of that thing as distinctly as possible in the imagination; and in order to effect this with greater ease, the thing itself which this idea is to represent must be exhibited to the external senses. Now when the understanding wishes to have a distinct intuition of particular facts a multitude of objects is of no use to it. But if it wishes to deduce one thing from a number of objects, as often has to be done, we must banish from the ideas of the objects presented whatsoever does not require present attention, in order that the remainder may be the more readily retained in memory. In the same way it is not on those occasions that the objects themselves ought to be presented to the external senses, but rather certain compendious abbreviations which, provided they guard the memory against lapse, are the handier the shorter they are. Whosoever observes all these recommendations, will, in my opinion, omit nothing that relates to the first part of our rule.

Now we must approach the second part of our task. That was to distinguish accurately the notions of simple things from those which are built up out of them; to see in both cases where falsity might come in, so that we might be on our guard and give our attention to those matters only in which certainty was possible. But here, as before, we must make certain assumptions which probably are not agreed on by all. It matters little, however, though they are not believed to be more real than those imaginary circles by means of which Astronomers describe their phenomena, provided that you employ them to aid you in discerning in each particular case what sort of knowledge is true and what false.

Finally, then, we assert that relatively to our knowledge single things should be taken in an order different from that in which we should regard them when considered in their more real nature. Thus, for example, if we consider a body as having extension and figure, we shall indeed admit that from the point of view of the thing itself it is one and simple. For we

cannot from that point of view regard it as compounded of corporeal nature, extension and figure, since these elements have never existed in isolation from each other. But relatively to our understanding we call it a compound constructed out of these three natures, because we have thought of them separately before we were able to judge that all three were found in one and the same subject. Hence here we shall treat of things only in relation to our understanding's awareness of them, and shall call those only simple, the cognition of which is so clear and so distinct that they cannot be analysed by the mind into others more distinctly known. Such are figure, extension, motion, etc.; all others we conceive to be in some way compounded out of these. This principle must be taken so universally as not even to leave out those objects which we sometimes obtain by abstraction from the simple natures themselves. This we do, for example, when we say that figure is the limit of an extended thing, conceiving by the term limit something more universal than by the term figure, since we can talk of a limit of duration, a limit of motion, and so on. But our contention is right, for then, even though we find the meaning of limit by abstracting it from figure, nevertheless it should not for that reason seem simpler than figure. Rather, since it is predicated of other things, as for example of the extreme bounds of a space of time or of a motion, etc., things which are wholly different from figure, it must be abstracted from those natures also; consequently it is something compounded out of a number of natures wholly diverse, of which it can be only ambiguously predicated.

Our second assertion is that those things which relatively to our understanding are called simple, are either purely intellectual or purely material, or else common both to intellect and to matter. Those are purely intellectual which our understanding apprehends by means of a certain inborn light, and without the aid of any corporeal image. That a number of such things exist is certain; and it is impossible to construct any corporeal idea which shall represent to us what the act of knowing is, what doubt is, what ignorance, and likewise what the action of the will is which it is possible to term volition, and so with other things. Yet we have a genuine knowledge of all these things, and know them so easily that in order to recognize them it is enough to be endowed with reason. Those things are purely material which we discern only in bodies; e.g. figure, extension, motion, etc. Finally those must be styled common which are ascribed now to corporeal things, now to spirits, without distinction. Such are existence, unity, duration and the like. To this group also we must ascribe those common notions which are, as it were, bonds for connecting together the other simple natures, and on whose evidence all the inferences which we obtain by reasoning depend. The following are examples:— things that are the same as a third thing are the same as one another. So too:—things which do not bear the same relation to a third thing, have some diversity from each other, etc. As a matter of fact these common notions can be discerned by the understanding either unaided or when it is aware of the images of material things.

But among these simple natures we must rank the privative and negative terms corresponding to them in so far as our intelligence grasps them. For it is quite as genuinely an act of knowledge by which I am intuitively aware of what nothing is, or an instant, or rest, as that by which I know what existence is, or lapse of time, or motion. This way of viewing the matter will be helpful in enabling us henceforth to say that all the rest of what we know is formed by composition out of these simple natures. Thus, for example, if I pronounce the judgment that some figure is not moving, I shall say that in a certain sense my idea is a complex of figure and rest; and so in other cases.

Thirdly we assert that all these simple natures are known *per se* and are wholly free from falsity. It will be easy to show this, provided we distinguish that faculty of our understanding by which it has intuitive awareness of things and knows them, from that by which it judges, making use of affirmation and denial. For we may imagine ourselves to be ignorant of things which we really know, for example on such occasions as when we believe that in such things, over and above what we have present to us or attain to by thinking, there is something else hidden from us, and when this belief of ours is false. Whence it is evident that we are in error if we judge that any one of these simple natures is not completely known by us. For if our mind attains to the least acquaintance with it, as must be the case, since we are assumed to pass some judgment on it, this fact alone makes us infer that we know it completely. For otherwise it could not be said to be simple, but must be complex—a compound of that which is present in our perception of it, and that of which we think we are ignorant.

In the fourth place we point out that the union of these things one with another is either necessary or contingent. It is necessary when one is so implied in the concept of another in a confused sort of way that we cannot conceive either distinctly, if our thought assigns to them separateness from each other. Thus figure is conjoined with extension, motion with duration or time, and so on, because it is impossible to conceive of a figure that has no extension, nor of a motion that has no duration. Thus likewise if I say 'four and three are seven,' this union is necessary. For we do not conceive the number seven distinctly unless we include in it the numbers three and four in some confused way. In the same way whatever is demonstrated of figures or numbers is necessarily united with that of which it is affirmed. Further, this necessity is not restricted to the field of sensible matters alone. The conclusion is necessary also in such a case—If Socrates says he doubts everything, it follows necessarily that he knows this at least— that he doubts. Likewise he knows that something can be either true or false, and so on, for all those consequences necessarily attach to the nature of doubt. The union, however, is contingent in those cases where the things are conjoined by no inseparable bond. Thus when we say a body is animate, a man is clothed, etc. Likewise many things are often necessarily united with one another, though most people, not noticing what their true relation is, reckons them among those that are contingently connected. As example, I give the following propositions:—'I exist, therefore God exists': also 'I know, therefore I have a mind distinct from my body,' etc. Finally we must note that very many necessary propositions become contingent when converted. Thus though from the fact that I exist I may infallibly conclude that God exists, it is not for that reason allowable to affirm that because God exists I also exist.

Fifthly we remark that no knowledge is at any time possible of anything beyond those simple natures and what may be called their intermixture or combination with each other. Indeed it is often easier to be aware of several of them in union with each other, than to separate one of them from the others. For, to illustrate, I am able to know what a triangle is, though I have never thought that in that knowledge was contained the knowledge of an angle, a line, the number three, figure, extension, etc. But that does not prevent me from saying that the nature of the triangle is composed of all these natures, and that they are better known than the triangle since they are the elements which we comprehend in it. It is possible also that in the triangle many other features are involved which escape our notice, such as the magnitude of the angles, which are equal to two right angles, and the innumerable relations which exist between the sides and the angles, or the size of the area, etc.

Sixthly, we say that those natures which we call composite are known by us, either because experience shows us what they are, or because we ourselves are responsible for their composition. Matter of experience consists of what we perceive by sense, what we hear from the lips of others, and generally whatever reaches our understanding either from external sources or from that contemplation which our mind directs backwards on itself. Here it must be noted that no direct experience can ever deceive the understanding if it restrict its attention accurately to the object presented to it, just as it is given to it either at firsthand or by means of an image, and if it moreover refrain from judging that the imagination faithfully reports the objects of the senses, or that the senses take on the true forms of things, or in fine that external things always are as they appear to be; for in all these judgments we are exposed to error. This happens, for example, when we believe as fact what is

merely a story that someone has told us; or when one who is ill with jaundice judges everything to be yellow because his eye is tinged with yellow. So finally, too, when the imagination is diseased, as in cases of melancholia, and a man thinks that his own disorderly fancies represent real things. But the understanding of a wise man will not be deceived by these fancies, since he will judge that whatever comes to him from his imagination is really depicted in it, but yet will never assert that the object has passed complete and without any alteration from the external world to his senses, and from his senses to his imagination, unless he has some previous ground for believing this. Moreover we ourselves are responsible for the composition of the things present to our understanding when we believe that there is something in them which our mind never experiences when exercising direct perception. Thus if a man suffering from jaundice persuades himself that the things he sees are yellow, this thought of his will be composite, consisting partly of what his imagination represents to him, and partly of what he assumes on his own account, namely that the colour looks yellow not owing to the defect in his eye, but because the things he sees really are yellow. Whence the conclusion comes that we can go wrong only when the things we believe are in some way compounded by ourselves.

Seventhly, this compounding can come about in other ways, namely by impulse, by conjecture, or by deduction. Impulse sways the formation of judgments about things on the part of those whom their own initiative constrains to believe something, though they can assign no reason for their belief, but are merely determined either by some higher Power, or by their own free will, or by their fanciful disposition. The first cause is never a source of error, the second rarely, the third almost always. But a consideration of the first does not concern us here because it does not fall within the province of human skill. The working of conjecture is shown, for example, in this: water which is at a greater distance from the centre of the globe than earth, is likewise less dense substance, and likewise the air which is above the water, is still rarer;

hence we hazard the guess that above the air nothing exists but a very pure aether, which is much rarer than air itself. Moreover nothing that we construct in this way really deceives us, if we merely judge it to be probable and never affirm it to be true; in fact it makes us better instructed.

Deduction is thus left to us as the only means of putting things together so as to be sure of their truth. Yet in it too there may be many defects. Thus if, in this space which is full of air, there is nothing to be perceived either by sight, touch, or any other sense, we conclude that the space is empty, we are in error, and our synthesis of the nature of a vacuum with that of this space is wrong. This is the result as often as we judge that we can deduce anything universal and necessary from a particular or contingent fact. But it is within our power to avoid this error, if, for example, we never interconnect any objects unless we are directly aware that the conjunction of the one with the other is wholly necessary. Thus we are justified if we deduce that nothing can have figure which has not extension, from the fact that figure and extension are necessarily conjoined.

From all these considerations we conclude firstly—that we have shown distinctly and, as we judge, by an adequate enumeration, what we were originally able to express only confusedly and in a rough and ready way. This was that mankind has no road towards certain knowledge open to it, save those of self-evident intuition and necessary deduction; further, that we have shown what those simple natures are of which we spoke in the eighth proposition. It is also quite clear that this mental vision extends both to all those simple natures, and to the knowledge of the necessary connections between them, and finally to everything else which the understanding accurately experiences either at first hand or in the imagination. Deduction, however, will be further treated in what follows.

Our second conclusion is that in order to know these simple natures no pains need be taken, because they are of themselves sufficiently well known. Application comes in only in isolating them from each other and scrutinizing them separately with steadfast mental gaze. There is no one whose intelligence is so dull as not to perceive that when he is seated he in some way differs from what he is when standing. But not everyone separates with equal distinctness the nature of position from the other elements contained in the cognition in question, or is able to assert that in this case nothing alters save the position. Now it is not without reason that we call attention to the above doctrine; for the learned have a way of being so clever as to contrive to render themselves blind to things that are in their own nature evident, and known by the simplest peasant. This happens when they try to explain by something more evident those things that are self-evident. For what they do is either to explain something else, or nothing at all. Who, for instance, does not perfectly see what that is, whatsoever it may be, in respect of which alteration occurs when we change position? But is there anyone who would grasp that very thing when he was told that *place is the surface of the body surrounding us?* This would be strange seeing that that surface can change though I stay still and do not change my place, or that, on the contrary, it can so move along with me that, although it continues to surround me, I am nevertheless no longer in the same place. Do not these people really seem to use magic words which have a hidden force that eludes the grasp of human apprehension? They define *motion*, a fact with which everyone is quite familiar, as *the actualisation of what exists in potentiality, in so far as it is potential!* Now who understands these words? And who at the same time does not know what motion is? Will not everyone admit that those philosophers have been trying to find a knot in a bulrush? We must therefore maintain that no definitions are to be used in explaining things of this kind lest we should take what is complex in place of what is simple. We must be content to isolate them from each other, and to give them, each of us, our individual attention, studying them with that degree of mental illumination which each of us possesses.

Our third conclusion is that the whole of human knowledge consists in a distinct perception of the way in which those simple natures combine in order to build up other objects. It is important to note this; because whenever some difficulty is brought forward for examination, almost everyone is brought to a standstill at the very outset, being in doubt as to the nature of the notions he ought to call to mind, and believing that he has to search for some new kind of fact previously unknown to him. Thus, if the question is, 'what is the nature of the magnet?' people like that at once prognosticate difficulty and toil in the inquiry, and dismissing from mind every well-known fact, fasten on whatsoever is most difficult, vaguely hoping that by ranging over the fruitless field where multifarious causes lie, they will find something fresh. But he who reflects that there can be nothing to know in the magnet which does not consist of certain simple natures evident in themselves, will have no doubt how to proceed. He will first collect all the observations with which experience can supply him about this stone, and from these he will next try to deduce the character of that inter-mixture of simple natures which is necessary to produce all those effects which he has seen to take place in connection with the magnet. This achieved, he can boldly assert that he has discovered the real nature of the magnet in so far as human intelligence and the given experimental observations can supply him with this knowledge.

Finally, it follows fourthly from what has been said that we must not fancy that one kind of knowledge is more obscure than another, since all knowledge is of the same nature throughout, and consists solely in combining what is self-evident. This is a fact recognized by very few. People have their minds already occupied by the contrary opinion, and the more bold among them, indeed, allow themselves to uphold their private conjectures as though they were sound demonstrations, and in matters of which they are wholly ignorant feel premonitions of the vision of truths which seem to present themselves through a cloud. These they have no hesitation in propounding, attaching to their concepts certain words by means of which they are wont to carry on long and reasoned out discussions, but which in reality neither they nor their audience understand. On the other hand more diffident people often refrain from many investigations that are quite easy and are in the first degree necessary to life, merely because they think themselves unequal to the task. They believe that these matters can be discovered by others who are endowed with better mental faculties, and embrace the opinion of those in whose authority they have most confidence.

We assert fifthly that by deduction we can get only things from words, cause from effect, or effect from cause, like from like, or parts or the whole itself from the parts. . . .

For the rest, in order that there may be no want of coherence in our series of precepts, we divide the whole matter of knowledge into simple propositions and 'questions.' In connection with simple propositions the only precepts we give are those which prepare our cognitive faculties for fixing distinctly before them any objects, whatsoever they are, and scrutinizing them with keen intelligence, since propositions of this type do not arise as the result of inquiry, but present themselves to us spontaneously. This part of our task we have undertaken in the first twelve rules, in which, we believe, we have displayed everything which, in our opinion, can facilitate the exercise of our reason. But as to 'questions' some of them can be perfectly well comprehended, even though we are ignorant of their solution; these we shall treat by themselves in the next twelve rules, Finally there are others, whose meaning is not quite clear, and these we reserve for the last twelve. This division has been made advisedly, both in order to avoid mentioning anything which presupposes an acquaintance with what follows, and also for the purpose of unfolding first what we feel to be most important first to inculcate in cultivating the mental powers. Among the 'questions' whose meaning is quite plain, we must to begin with note that we place those only in which we perceive three things distinctly; to wit, the marks by which we can identify what we are looking for when it occurs; what precisely the fact is from which our answer ought to be deduced; and how it is to be proved that these (the ground and its consequence) so depend one on another that it is impossible for either to change while the other remains unchanged. In this way we shall have all the premises we require, and the only thing remaining to be shown will be how to discover the conclusion. This will not be a matter of deducing some one fact from a single simple matter (we have already said that we can do this without the help of rules), but of disentangling so skilfully some one fact that is conditioned by a number of others which all involve one another, that in recognizing it there shall be no need to call upon a higher degree of mental power than in making the simplest inference. 'Questions' of this kind, being highly abstract and occurring almost exclusively in Arithmetic and Geometry, seem to the inexperienced of little value. But I warn them that people ought to busy and exercise themselves a long time in learning this art, who desire to master the subsequent portions of this method, in which all the other types of 'question' are treated.

Rule XIII

Once a 'question' is perfectly understood, we must free it of every conception superfluous to its meaning, state it in its simplest terms, and, having recourse to an enumeration, split it up into the various sections beyond which analysis cannot go in minuteness.

This is the only respect in which we imitate the Dialecticians; just as they, in teaching their doctrine of the forms of syllogism, assume that the terms or matter of their syllogisms are already known, so also we on this occasion lay it down as a prerequisite that the question to be solved should be perfectly understood. But we do not, as they, distinguish two extremes and a middle term. The following is the way in which we look at the whole matter. Firstly, in every 'question' there must be something of which we are ignorant; otherwise there is no use asking the question. Secondly, this very matter must be designated in some way or other; otherwise there would be nothing to determine us to investigate it rather than anything else. Thirdly, it can only be so designated by the aid of something else which is already known. All three conditions are realised even in questions that are not fully understood. Thus if the problem be the nature of

the magnet, we already know what is meant by the two words 'magnet' and 'nature,' and this knowledge determines us to seek one sort of answer rather than another, and so on. But over and above this, if the question is to be perfectly stated, we require that it should be wholly determinate, so that we shall have nothing more to seek for than what can be inferred from the data. For example some one might set me the question, what is to be inferred about the nature of the magnet from that set of experiments precisely which Gilbert asserts he has performed, be they trustworthy or not. So again the question may be, what my conclusion is as to the nature of sound, founding my judgment merely on the precise fact that the three strings A, B, and C give out an identical sound, when by hypothesis B, though twice as thick as A, but not longer, is kept in tension by a weight that is twice as heavy; while C, though no thicker than A, but merely twice as long, is nevertheless kept in tension by a weight four times as heavy. Other illustrations might be given; but they all make it quite clear how all imperfectly expressed 'questions' may be reduced to others whose meaning is quite clear, as I shall show at greater length in the proper place. We see also how it is possible to follow this rule in divesting any difficulty, where the problem is properly realised, of every superfluous conception, and in reducing it to a form in which we no longer deem that we are treating of this or that special matter, but are dealing only in a general way with certain magnitudes which have to be fitted together. Thus, to illustrate, after we have limited ourselves to the consideration of this or that set of experiments merely relative to the magnet, there is no difficulty in dismissing from view all other aspects of the case.

We add also that the problem ought to be reduced to its simplest statement in accordance with Rules V and VI, and resolved into parts in accordance with Rule VII. Thus if I employ a number of experiments in investigating the magnet, I shall run them over successively, taking each by itself. Again if my inquiry is about sound, as in the case above, I shall separately consider the relation between strings A and B, then that between A and C, and so on, so that afterwards my enumeration of results may be sufficient, and may embrace every case. These three rules are the only ones which the pure understanding need observe in dealing with the terms of any proposition before approaching its ultimate solution, though that requires us to employ the following eleven rules. The third part of this Treatise will show us more clearly how to apply them. Further by a 'question' we understand everything in which either truth or falsity is found; and we must enumerate the different types of 'question' in order to determine what we are able to accomplish in each case.

We have already said that there can be no falsity in the mere intuition of things, whether they are simple or united together. So conceived these are not called 'questions,' but they acquire that designation so soon as we prepare to pass some determinate judgment about them. Neither do we limit the title to those questions which are set us by other people. His own ignorance, or more correctly his own doubt, presented a subject of inquiry to Socrates when first he began to study it and to inquire whether it was true that he doubted everything, and maintained that such was indeed the case.

Moreover in our 'questions' we seek to derive either things from words, or causes from effects, or effects from causes, or the whole or other parts from parts, or to infer several of these simultaneously.

We are said to seek to derive things from words when the difficulty consists merely in the obscurity of the language employed. To this class we refer firstly all riddles, like that of the Sphinx about the animal which to begin with is four-footed, then two-footed, and finally three-footed. A similar instance is that of the fishers who, standing on the bank with rods and hooks ready for the capture of fish, said that they no longer possessed those creatures which they had caught, but on the other hand had those which they had not yet been able to catch. So in other cases; but besides these, in the majority of matters on which the learned dispute, the question is almost always one of names. We ought not to judge so ill of our great thinkers as to imagine that they conceive the objects themselves wrongly, in cases where they do not employ fit words in explaining

them. Thus when people call *place* the *surface of the surrounding body,* there is no real error in their conception; they merely employ wrongly the word *place,* which by common use signifies that simple and self-evident nature in virtue of which a thing is said to be here or there. This consists wholly in a certain relation of the thing said to be in the place towards the parts of the space external to it, and is a feature which certain writers, seeing that the name place was reserved for the surface of the surrounding body, have improperly called the thing's *intrinsic position.* So it is in other cases; indeed these verbal questions are of such frequent occurrence, that almost all controversy would be removed from among Philosophers, if they were always to agree as to the meaning of words.

We seek to derive causes from effects when we ask concerning anything, whether it exists or what it is. . . .

Since, however, when a 'question' is propounded for solution we are frequently unable at once to discern its type, or to determine whether the problem is to derive things from words, or causes from effects, etc., for this reason it seems to be superfluous to say more here in detail about these matters. It will occupy less space and consists, in order that, by separating it out from all complicating circumstances, we may solve it the more easily. But over and above this we must attend to the various separate problems involved in it, in order that if there are any which are easy to resolve we may omit them; when these are removed, only that will remain of which we are still in ignorance. Thus in that instance of the vessel which was described a short time ago, it is indeed quite easy to see how the vessel should be made; a column must be fixed in its centre, a bird must be painted on it. But all these things will be set aside as not touching the essential point; thus we are left with the difficulty by itself, consisting in the fact that the whole of the water, which had previously remained in the vessel, after reaching a certain height, flows out. It is for this that we have to seek a reason.

Here therefore we maintain that what is worth while doing is simply this—to explore in an orderly way all the data furnished by the proposition, to set aside everything which we see is clearly immaterial, to retain what is necessarily bound up with the problem, and to reserve what is doubtful for a more careful examination.

Rule XIV

The same rule is to be applied also to the real extension of bodies. It must be set before the imagination by means of mere figures, for this is the best way to make it clear to the understanding.

But in proposing to make use of the imagination as an aid to our thinking, we must note that whenever one unknown fact is deduced from another that is already known, that does not show that we discover any new kind of entity, but merely that this whole mass of knowledge is extended in such a way that we perceive that the matter sought for participates in one way or another in the nature of the data given in the proposition. For example if a man has been blind from his birth it is not to be expected that we shall be able by any train of reasoning to make him perceive the true ideas of the colours which we have derived from our senses. But if a man has indeed once perceived the primary colours, though he has never seen the intermediate or mixed tints, it is possible for him to construct the images of those which he has not seen from their likeness to the others, by a sort of deduction. Similarly if in the magnet there be any sort of nature the like of which our mind has never yet known, it is hopeless to expect that reasoning will ever make us grasp it; we should have to be furnished either with some new sense or with a divine intellect. But we shall believe ourselves to have attained whatever in this matter can be achieved by our human faculties, if we discern with all possible distinctness that mixture of entities or natures already known which produced just those effects which we notice in the magnet.

Indeed all these previously known entities, viz. extension, figure, motion and the like, the enumeration of which does not belong to this place, are recognized by means of an idea which is one and the same in the various subject matters. The figure of a silver crown which we imagine, is just the same as that of one that is golden. Further this common idea is transferred from one subject to another, merely by means of the simple comparison by which we affirm that the object sought for is in this or that respect like, or identical with, or equal to a particular datum. Consequently in every train of reasoning it is by comparison merely that we attain to a precise knowledge of the truth. Here is an example:—all *A* is *B*, all *B* is *C*, therefore all *A* is *C*. Here we compare with one another a *quaesitum* and a *datum*, viz. *A* and *C*, in respect of the fact that each is *B*, and so on. But because, as we have often announced, the syllogistic forms are of no aid in perceiving the truth about objects, it will be for the reader's profit to reject them altogether and to conceive that all knowledge whatsoever, other than that which consists in the simple and naked intuition of single independent objects, is a matter of the comparison of two things or more, with each other. In fact practically the whole of the task set the human reason consists in preparing for this operation; for when it is open and simple, we need no aid from art, but are bound to rely upon the light of nature alone, in beholding the truth which comparison gives us.

We must further mark that comparison should be simple and open, only as often as *quaesitum* and *datum* participate equally in a certain nature. Note that the only reason why preparation is required for comparison that is not of this nature is the fact that the common nature we spoke of does not exist equally in both, but is complicated with certain other relations or ratios. The chief part of our human industry consists merely in so transmuting these ratios as to show clearly a uniformity between the matter sought for and something else already known.

Next we must mark that nothing can be reduced to this uniformity, save that which admits of a greater and a less, and that all such matter is included under the term magnitude. Consequently when, in conformity with the previous rule, we have freed the terms of the problem from any reference to a particular subject, we shall discover that all we have left to deal with consists of magnitudes in general.

We shall, however, even in this case make use of our imagination, employing not the naked understanding but the intellect as aided by images of particulars depicted on the fancy. Finally we must note that nothing can be asserted of magnitudes in general that cannot also be ascribed to any particular instance.

This lets us easily conclude that there will be no slight profit in transferring whatsoever we find asserted of magnitudes in general to that particular species of magnitude which is most easily and distinctly depicted in our imagination. But it follows from what we stated about the twelfth rule that this must be the real extension of body abstracted from everything else except the fact that it has figure; for in that place we represented the imagination itself along with the ideas it contains as nothing more than a really material body possessing extention and figure. This is also itself evident; for no other subject displays more distinctly differences in ratio of whatsoever kind. Though one thing can be said to be more or less white than another, or a sound sharper or flatter, and so on, it is yet impossible to determine exactly whether the greater exceeds the less in the proportion two to one, or three to one, etc., unless we treat the quantity as being in a certain way analogous to the extension of a body possessing figure. Let us then take it as fixed and certain that perfectly definite 'questions' are almost free from difficulty other than that of transmuting ratios so that they may be stated as equations. Let us agree too that everything in which we discover precisely this difficulty, can be easily, and ought to be, disengaged from reference to every other subject, and immediately stated in terms of extension and figure. It is about these alone that we shall for this reason henceforth treat, up to and as far as the twenty-fifth rule, omitting the consideration of everything else.

My desire is that here I may find a reader who is an eager student of Arithmetic and Geometry, though indeed I should prefer him to have had no practice in these arts, rather than to be an adept after the ordinary standard. For the employment of the rules which I here unfold is much easier in the study of Arithmetic and Geometry (and it is all that is needed in learning them) than in inquiries of any other kind. Further its usefulness as a means towards the attainment of a profounder knowledge is so great, that I have no hesitation in saying that it was not the case that this part of our method was invented for the purpose of dealing with mathematical problems, but rather that mathematics should be studied almost solely for the purpose of training us in this method. I shall presume no knowledge of anything in mathematics except perhaps such facts as are self-evident and obvious to everyone. But the way in which people ordinarily think about them, even though not vitiated by any glaring errors, yet obscures our knowledge with many ambiguous and ill-conceived principles, which we shall try incidentally to correct in the following pages.

By extension we understand whatever has length, breadth, and depth, not inquiring whether it be a real body or merely space; nor does it appear to require further explanation, since there is nothing more easily perceived by our imagination. Yet the learned frequently employ distinctions so subtle that the light of nature is dissipated in attending to them, and even those matters of which no peasant is ever in doubt become invested in obscurity. Hence we announce that by extension we do not here mean anything distinct and separate from the extended object itself; and we make it a rule not to recognize those metaphysical entities which really cannot be presented to the imagination. For even though someone could persuade himself, for example, that supposing every extended object in the universe were annihilated, that would not prevent extension in itself alone existing, this conception of his would not involve the use of any corporeal image, but would be based on a false judgment of the intellect working by itself. He will admit this himself, if he reflect attentively on this very image of extension when, as will then happen, he tries to construct it in his imagination. For he will notice that, as he perceives it, it is not divested of a reference to every object, but that his imagination of it is quite different from his judgment about it. Consequently, whatever our understanding may believe as to the truth of the matter, those abstract entities are never given to our imagination as separate from the objects in which they inhere.

But since henceforth we are to attempt nothing without the aid of the imagination, it will be worth our while to distinguish carefully the ideas which in each separate case are to convey to the understanding the meaning of the words we employ. To this end we submit for consideration these three forms of expression:—*extension occupies place, body possesses extension,* and *extension is not body.*

The first statement shows how extension may be substituted for that which is extended. My conception is entirely the same if I say *extension occupies place,* as when I say *that which is extended occupies place.* Yet that is no reason why, in order to avoid ambiguity, it should be better to use the term *that which is extended;* for that does not indicate so distinctly our precise meaning, which is, that a subject occupies place owing to the fact that it is extended. Someone might interpret the expression to mean merely *that which is extended is an object occupying place,* just in the same way as if I had said *that which is animate occupies place.* This explains why we announced that here we would treat of extension, preferring that to 'the extended,' although we believe that there is no difference in the conception of the two.

Let us now take up these words: *body possesses extension.* Here the meaning of *extension* is not identical with that of body, yet we do not construct two distinct ideas in our imagination, one of body, the other of extension, but merely a single image of extended body; and from the point of view of the thing it is exactly as if I had said: *body is extended,* or better, *the extended is extended.* This is a peculiarity of those entities which have their being merely in something else, and can never be conceived without the subject in which they exist. How different is it with those matters which are really distinct from the subjects of which they are predicated. If, for example, I say *Peter has wealth,* my idea of Peter is quite different from that of wealth. So if I say *Paul is wealthy,* my image is quite different from that which I should have if I said *the wealthy man is wealthy.* Failure to distinguish the diversity between these two cases is the cause of the error of those numerous people who believe that extension contains

something distinct from that which is extended, in the same way as Paul's wealth is something different from Paul himself.

Finally, take the expression: *extension is not body.* Here the term extension is taken quite otherwise than as above. When we give it this meaning there is no special idea corresponding to it in the imagination. In fact this entire assertion is the work of the naked understanding, which alone has the power of separating out abstract entities of this type. But this is a stumbling-block for many, who, not perceiving that extension so taken, cannot be grasped by the imagination, represent it to themselves by means of a genuine image. Now such an idea necessarily involves the concept of body, and if they say that extension so conceived is not body, their heedlessness involves them in the contradiction of saying that *the same thing is at the same time body and not body.* It is likewise of great moment to distinguish the meaning of the enunciations in which such names as *extension, figure, number, superficies, line, point, unity,* etc. are used in so restricted a way as to exclude matters from which they are not really distinct. Thus when we say: *extension* or *figure is not body; number is not the thing that is counted; a superficies is the boundary of a body; the line the limit of a surface, the point of a line; unity is not a quantity,* etc.; all these and similar propositions must be taken altogether outside the bounds of the imagination, if they are to be true. Consequently we shall not discuss them in the sequel.

But we should carefully note that in all other propositions in which these terms, though retaining the same signification and employed in abstraction from their subject matter, do not exclude or deny anything from which they are not really distinct, it is both possible and necessary to use the imagination as an aid. The reason is that even though the understanding in the strict sense attends merely to what is signified by the name, the imagination nevertheless ought to fashion a correct image of the object, in order that the very understanding itself may be able to fix upon other features belonging to it that are not expressed by the name in question, whenever there is occasion to do so, and may never imprudently believe that they have been excluded. Thus, if number be the question, we imagine an object which we can measure by summing a plurality of units. Now though it is allowable for the understanding to confine its attention for the present solely to the multiplicity displayed by the object, we must be on our guard nevertheless not on that account afterwards to come to any conclusion which implies that the object which we have described numerically has been excluded from our concept. But this is what those people do who ascribe mysterious properties to number, empty inanities in which they certainly would not believe so strongly, unless they conceived that number was something distinct from the things we number. In the same way, if we are dealing with figure, let us remember that we are concerned with an extended subject, though we restrict ourselves to conceiving it merely as possessing figure. When body is the object let us reflect that we are dealing with the very same thing, taken as possessing length, breadth and depth. Where superficies comes in, our object will still be the same though we conceive it as having length and breadth, and we shall leave out the element of depth, without denying it. The line will be considered as having length merely, while in the case of the point the object, though still the same, will be divested in our thought of every characteristic save that of being something existent.

In spite of the way in which I have dwelt on this topic, I fear that men's minds are so dominated by prejudice that very few are free from the danger of losing their way here, and that, notwithstanding the length of my discourse, I shall be found to have explained myself too briefly. Those very disciplines Arithmetic and Geometry, though the most certain of all the sciences, nevertheless lead us astray here. For is there a single Arithmetician who does not believe that the numbers with which he deals are not merely held in abstraction from any subject matter by the understanding, but are really distinct objects of the imagination? Does not your Geometrician obscure the clearness of his subject by employing irreconcileable principles? He tells you that lines have no breadth, surfaces no depth; yet he subsequently wishes to generate the one out of the other, not noticing that a line, the

movement of which is conceived to create a surface, is really a body; or that, on the other hand, the line which has no breadth, is merely a mode of body. But, not to take more time in going over these matters, it will be more expeditious for us to expound the way in which we assume our object should be taken, in order that we may most easily give a proof of whatsoever is true in Arithmetic and Geometry.

Here therefore we deal with an extended object, considering nothing at all involved in it save extension, and purposely refraining from using the word quantity, because there are certain Philosophers so subtle as to distinguish it also from extension. We assume such a simplification of our problems as to leave nothing else to be inquired about except the determination of a certain extension by comparing it with a certain other extension that is already determinately known. For here we do not look to discover any new sort of fact; we merely wish to make a simplification of ratios, be they ever so involved, such that we may discover some equation between what is unknown and something known. Since this is so, it is certain that whatsoever differences in ratio exist in these subjects can be found to prevail also between two or more extensions. Hence our purpose is sufficiently served if in extension itself we consider everything that can aid us in setting out differences in ratio; but there are only three such features, viz. dimension, unity and figure.

By dimension I understand nothing but the mode and aspect according to which a subject is considered to be measurable. Thus it is not merely the case that length, breadth and depth are dimensions; but weight also is a dimension in terms of which the heaviness of objects is estimated. So, too, speed is a dimension of motion, and there are an infinite number of similar instances. For that very division of the whole into a number of parts of identical nature, whether it exist in the real order of things or be merely the work of the understanding, gives us exactly that dimension in terms of which we apply number to objects. Again that mode which constitutes number is properly said to be a species of dimension, though there is not an absolute identity between the meaning of the two terms. For if we proceed by taking part after part until we reach the whole, the operation is then said to be counting, whereas if conversely we look upon the whole as something split up into parts, it is an object which we measure. Thus we measure centuries by years, days, hours and moments, while if we count up moments, hours, days and years, we shall finish with a total of centuries.

It clearly follows that there may be an infinite number of dimensions in the same subject, which make no addition at all to the objects which possess them, but have the same meaning whether they are based on anything real in the objects themselves, or are the arbitrary inventions of our own mind. Weight is indeed something real existing in a body, and the speed of motion is a reality, and so with the division of a century into years and days. But it is otherwise with the division of the day into hours and moments, etc. Yet all these subdivisions are exactly similar if considered merely from the point of view of dimension, as we ought to regard them both here and in the science of Mathematics. It falls rather to Physics to inquire whether they are founded on anything real.

Recognition of this fact throws much light on Geometry, since in that science almost everyone goes wrong in conceiving that quantity has three species, the line, the superficies, and the solid. But we have already stated that the line and the superficies are not conceived as being really distinct from solid body, or from one another. Moreover if they are taken in their bare essence as abstractions of the understanding, they are no more diverse species of quantity than the 'animal' and 'living creature' in man are diverse species of substance. Incidentally also we have to note that the three dimensions of body, length, breadth and depth, are only in name distinct from one another. For there is nothing to prevent us, in any solid body with which we are dealing, from taking any of the extensions it presents as the length, or any other as its depth, and so on. And though these three dimensions have a real basis in every extended object quâ extended, we have nevertheless no special concern in this science with them more than with

countless others, which are either mental creations or have some other ground in objects. For example in the case of the triangle, if we wish to measure it exactly, we must acquaint ourselves with three features of its existence, viz. either its three sides, or two sides and an angle, or two angles and its area, and so forth. Now these can all be styled dimensions. Similarly in a trapezium five facts have to be noted, in a tetrahedron six, and so on. But if we wish to choose here those dimensions which shall give most aid to our imagination, we shall never attend at the same time to more than one or two of those depicted in our imagination, even though we know that in the matter set before us with which we are dealing several others are involved. For the art of our method consists in distinguishing as many elements as possible, so that though we attend to only a few simultaneously, we shall yet cover them all in time, taking one after the other.

The unit is that common element in which, as above remarked, all the things compared with each other should equally participate. If this be not already settled in our problems, we can represent it by one of the magnitudes already presented to us, or by any other magnitude we like, and it will be the common measure of all the others. We shall understand that in it there exists every dimension found in those very widely sundered facts which are to be compared with each other, and we shall conceive it either (1) merely as something extended, omitting every other more precise determination—and then it will be identical with the point of Geometry, considered as generating a line by its movement; or (2) we shall conceive it as a line, or (3) as a square.

To come to figures, we have already shown above how it is they alone that give us a means of constructing the images of all objects whatsoever. It remains to give notice in this place, that of the innumerable diverse species of figure, we shall employ only those which most readily express differences of relation or proportion. Moreover there are two sorts of objects only which are compared with each other, viz. numerical assemblages and magnitudes. Now there are also two sorts of figures by means of which these may be presented to our conception. For example we have the points which represent a triangular number, or again the 'tree' which illustrates genealogical relation as in such a case—

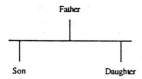

So in similar instances. Now these are figures designed to express numerical assemblages; but those which are continuous and undivided like the triangle, the square, etc..

explain the nature of magnitudes.

But in order that we may point out which of all these figures we are going to use, it ought to be known that all the relations which can exist between things of this kind, must be referred to two heads, viz. either to order or to measurement.

We must further realise that while the discovery of an order is no light task, as may be seen throughout this treatise, which makes this practically its sole subject, yet once the order has been discovered there is no difficulty at all in knowing it. The seventh rule shows us how we may easily review in sequence mentally the separate elements which have been arranged in order, for the reason that in this class of relation the bond between the terms is a direct one involving nothing but the terms themselves, and not requiring mediation by means of a third term, as is the case in measurement. The unfolding of relations of measurement will therefore be all that we shall treat of here. For I recognize the order in which A and B stand, without considering anything except these two—the extreme terms of the relation. But I can recognize the ratio of the magnitude of two to that of three, only by considering some third thing, namely unity, which is the common measure of both.

We must likewise bear in mind that, by the help of the unit we have assumed, continuous magnitudes can sometimes be reduced in their entirety to numerical expressions, and that this can always be partly realised. Further it is possible to arrange our assemblage of units in such an order that the problem which previously was one requiring the solution of a question in measurement, is now a matter merely involving an inspection of order. Now our method helps us greatly in making the progress which this transformation effects.

Finally remember that of the dimensions of continuous magnitude none are more distinctly conceived than length and breadth, and that we ought not to attend to more than these two simultaneously in the same figure, if we are to compare two diverse things with each other. The reason is, that when we have more than two diverse things to compare with each other, our method consists in reviewing them successively and attending only to two of them at the same time.

Observation of these facts leads us easily to our conclusion. This is that there is no less reason for abstracting our propositions from those figures of which Geometry treats, if the inquiry is one involving them, than from any other subject matter. Further, in doing so we need retain nothing but rectilinear and rectangular superficies, or else straight lines, which we also call figures, because they serve quite as well as surfaces in aiding us to imagine an object which actually has extension, as we have already said. Finally those same figures have to represent for us now continuous magnitudes, again a plurality of units or number also. Human ingenuity can devise nothing simpler for the complete expression of differences of relation.

Rule XV

It is likewise very often helpful to draw these figures and display them to the external senses, in order thus to facilitate the continued fixation of our attention.

The way in which these figures should be depicted so that, in being displayed before our eyes, the images may be the more distinctly formed in our imagination is quite self-evident. To begin with we represent unity in three ways, viz. by a square, □, if we consider our unit as having length and breadth, or secondly by a line, ——, if we take it merely as having length, or lastly by a point, •, if we think only of the fact that it is by aid of which we construct a numerical assemblage. But however it is depicted and conceived, we shall always remember that the unit is an object extended in every direction, and admitting of countless dimensions. So also the terms of our proposition, in cases where we have to attend at the same time to two different magnitudes belonging to them, will be represented by a rectangle whose two sides will be the two magnitudes in question. Where they are incommensurable with our unit we shall employ the following figure,

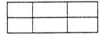

but where they are commensurable we shall use this

or this

and nothing more is needed save where it is a question of a numerical assemblage of units. Finally if we attend only to one of the magnitudes of the terms employed, we shall portray that either as a rectangle, of which one side is the magnitude considered and the other is unity, thus [   ] —and this will happen whenever the magnitude has to be compared with some surface. Or we shall employ a line alone, in this fashion, ——, if we take it as an incommensurable length; or thus, • • • • •, if it be a number.

Rule XVI

When we come across matters which do not require our present attention, it is better, even though they are necessary to our conclusion, to represent them by highly abbreviated symbols, rather than by complete figures. This guards against error due to defect of memory on the one hand, and, on the other, prevents that distraction of thought which an effort to keep those matters in mind while attending to other inferences would cause.

But because our maxim is that not more than two different dimensions out of the countless number that can be depicted in our imagination ought to be the object either of our bodily or of our mental vision, it is of importance so to retain all those outside the range of present attention that they may easily come up to mind as often as need requires. Now memory seems to be a faculty created by nature for this very purpose. But since it is liable to fail us, and in order to obviate the need of expending any part of our attention in refreshing it, while we are engaged with other thoughts, art has most opportunely invented the device of writing. Relying on the help this gives us, we leave nothing whatsoever to memory, but keep our imagination wholly free to receive the ideas which are immediately occupying us, and set down on paper whatever ought to be preserved. In doing so we employ the very briefest symbols, in order that, after distinctly examining each point in accordance with Rule IX, we may be able, as Rule XI bids us do, to traverse them all with an extremely rapid motion of our thought and include as many as possible in a single intuitive glance.

Everything, therefore, which is to be looked upon as single from the point of view of the solution of our problem, will be represented by a single symbol which can be constructed in any way we please. But to make things easier we shall employ the characters *a, b, c,* etc. for expressing magnitudes already known, and *A, B, C,* etc. for symbolising those that are unknown. To these we shall often prefix the numerical symbols, 1, 2, 3, 4, etc., for the purpose of making clear their number, and again we shall append those symbols to the former when we want to indicate the number of the relations which are to be remarked in them. Thus if I employ the formula $2a$ that will be the equivalent of the words 'the double of the magnitude which is symbolised by the letter a, and which contains three relations.' By this device not only shall we economize our words, but, which is the chief thing, display the terms of our problem in such a detached and un-encumbered way that, even though it is so full as to omit nothing, there will nevertheless be nothing superfluous to be discovered in our symbols, or anything to exercise our mental powers to no purpose, by requiring the mind to grasp a number of things at the same time.

In order that all this may be more clearly understood, we must note first, that while Arithmeticians have been wont to designate undivided magnitudes by groups of units, or else by some number, we on the other hand abstract at this point from numbers themselves no less than from Geometrical figures or any-thing else, as we did a little time ago. Our reason for doing this is partly to avoid the tedium of a long and superfluous calculation, but chiefly that those portions of the matter considered which are relevant to the problem may always remain distinct, and may not be entangled with numbers that are of no help to us at all. Thus if we are trying to find the hypotenuse of the right-angled triangle whose sides are 9 and 12, the Arithmetician will tell us that it is $\sqrt{225}$, i.e. 15. But we shall write a and b in place of 9 and 12, and shall find the hypotenuse to be $\sqrt{a^2 + b^2}$; and the two members of the expression a^2 and b^2 will re-main distinct, whereas the number confuses them altogether.

Note further that by the number of rela-tions attaching to a quantity I mean a sequence of ratios in continued proportion, such as the Algebra now in vogue attempts to express by sundry dimensions and figures. It calls the first of these the radix, the second the square, the third the cube, the fourth the biquadratic, and so on. I confess that for a long time I myself was imposed upon by these names. For, after the straight line and the square there was nothing which seemed to be capable of being placed more clearly before my imagination

than the cube and the other figures of the same type; and with their aid I succeeded in solving not a few difficulties. But at last, after testing the matter well, I discovered that I had never found out anything by their means which I could not have recognized more easily and distinctly without employing their aid. I saw that this whole nomenclature must be abandoned, if our conceptions are not to be-come confused; for that very magnitude which goes by the name of the cube or the biquadrat-ic, is nevertheless never to be presented to the imagination otherwise than as a line or a sur-face, in accordance with the previous rule. We must therefore be very clear about the fact that the radix, the square, the cube, etc., are merely magnitudes in continued proportion, which always imply the previous assumption of that arbitrarily chosen unit of which we spoke above. Now the first proportional is re-lated to this unit directly and by a single ratio. But the second proportional requires the mediation of the first, and consequently is re-lated to the unit by a pair of ratios. The third, being mediated by the first and second, has a triple relation to the standard unit, and so on. Therefore we shall henceforth call that magni-tude, which in Algebra is styled the radix, the first proportional; that called the square we shall term the second proportional, and so in other cases.

Finally it must be noticed that even though here, in order to examine the nature of a diffi-culty, we abstract the terms involved from cer-tain numerical complications, it yet often hap-pens that a simpler solution will be found by employing the given numbers than if we ab-stract from them. This is due to the double function of numbers, already pointed out, which use the same symbols to express now order, and now measure. Hence, after seeking a solution in general terms for our problem, we ought to transform its terms by substituting for them the given numbers, in order to see whether these supply us with any simpler solu-tion. Thus, to illustrate, after seeing that the hypotenuse of the right-angled triangle whose sides are a and b is $\sqrt{a^2 + b^2}$, we should sub-stitute 81 for a^2, and 144 for b^2. These added together give 225, the root of which, or mean proportional between unity and 225, is 15.

This will let us see that a hypotenuse whose length is 15 is commensurable with sides whose lengths are 9 and 12, quite apart from the general law that it is the hypotenuse of a right-angled triangle whose sides are as 3 to 4. We, whose object is to discover a knowledge of things which shall be evident and distinct, insist on all those distinctions. It is quite otherwise with Arithmeticians, who, if the result required turns up, are quite content even though they do not perceive how it depends upon the data, though it is really in knowledge of this kind alone that science properly consists.

Moreover, it must be observed that, as a general rule, nothing that does not require to be continuously borne in mind ought to be committed to memory, if we can set it down on paper. This is to prevent that waste of our powers which occurs if some part of our attention is taken up with the presence of an object in our thought which it is superfluous to bear in mind. What we ought to do is to make a reference-table and set down in it the terms of the problem as they are first stated. Then we should state the way in which the abstract formulation is to be made and the symbols to be employed, in order that, when the solution has been obtained in terms of these symbols, we may easily apply it, without calling in the aid of memory at all, to the particular case we are considering: for it is only in passing from a lesser to a greater degree of generality that abstraction has any *raison d'etre*. What I should write therefore would be something like this:—

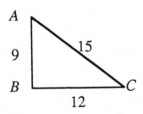

In the right-angled triangle *ABC* to find the hypotenuse *AC* (stating the problem abstractly, in order that the derivation of the length of the hypotenuse from the lengths of the sides may be quite general). Then for *AB*, which is

equal to 9, I shall substitute *a*; for *BC*, equal to 12, I put *b*, and similarly in other cases.

To conclude, we draw attention to the fact that these four rules will be further employed in the third part of this Treatise, though we shall conceive them somewhat more generally than we have been doing. But all this will be explained in its proper place.

Rule XVII

When a problem is proposed for discussion we should run it over, taking a direct course, and for this reason neglecting the fact that some of its terms are known, others unknown. To follow the true connection, when presenting to mind the dependence of separate items on one another, will also aid us to do this.

The four previous rules showed us how, when the problems are determinate and fully comprehended, we may abstract them from their subject matter and so transform them that nothing remains to be investigated save how to discover certain magnitudes, from the fact that they bear such and such a relation to certain other magnitudes already given. But in the five following rules we shall now explain how these same problems are to be treated in such a way that though a single proposition contains ever so many unknown magnitudes they may all be subordinated to one another; the second will stand to the first, as the first to unity, and so too the third to the second, and the fourth to the third, and so in succession, making, however numerous, a total magnitude equal to a certain known magnitude. In doing this our method will be so sure that we may safely affirm that it passes the wit of man to reduce our terms to anything simpler.

For the present, however, I remark that in every inquiry that is to be solved by deduction there is one way that is plain and direct, by which we may more easily than by any other pass from one set of terms to another, while all other routes are more difficult and indirect. In order to understand this we must remember what was said relative to the eleventh rule, where we expounded the nature of that chain of propositions, a comparison of the neighbouring members of which enables us to see how the first is related to the last, even though it is not so easy to deduce the intermediate terms from the extremes. Now therefore if we fix our attention on the interdependence of the various links, without ever interrupting the order, so that we may thence infer how the last depends upon the first, we review the problem in a direct manner. But, on the other hand, if, from the fact that we know the first and the last to be connected with each other in a certain way, we should want to deduce the nature of the middle terms which connect them, we should then be following an order that was wholly indirect and upside down. But because here we are considering only involved inquiries, in which the problem is, given certain extremes, to find certain intermediates by the inverse process of reasoning, the whole of the device here disclosed will consist in treating the unknown as though they were known, and thus being able to adopt the easy and direct method of investigation even in problems involving any amount of intricacy. There is nothing to prevent us always achieving this result, since we have assumed from the commencement of this section of our work that we recognize the dependence of the unknown terms in the inquiry on those that are known to be such that the former are determined by the latter. This determination also is such that if, recognizing it, we consider the terms which first present themselves and reckon them even though unknown among the known, and thus deduce from them step by step and by a true connection all the other terms, even those which are known, treating them as though they were unknown, we shall fully realise the purpose of this rule. Illustrations of this doctrine, as of the most of what is immediately to follow, will be reserved until the twenty-fourth rule, since it will be more convenient to expound them there.

Rule XVIII

To this end only four operations are required, addition, subtraction, multiplication and division. Of these the two latter are often to be dispensed with here, both in order to avoid any unforeseen complication, and because it will be easier to deal with them at a later stage.

It is often from lack of experience on the part of the teacher that the multiplicity of rules proceeds; and matters that might have been reduced to one general rule are less clear if distributed among many particular statements. Wherefore we propose to reduce the whole of the operations which it is advisable to employ in going through our inquiry, i.e. in deducing certain magnitudes from others, to as few as four heads. It will become clear when we come to explain these how it is that they suffice for the purpose.

This is how we proceed. If we arrive at the knowledge of one magnitude owing to the fact that we already know the parts of which it is composed, the process is one of addition. If we discover the part because we already know the whole and the excess of the whole over this part, it is division. Further it is impossible to derive a magnitude from others that are determinately fixed, and in which it is in any way contained, by any other methods. But if we have to derive a magnitude from others from which it is wholly diverse and in which it is in nowise contained, we must find some other way of relating it to them. Now if we trace out this connection or relation directly we must employ multiplication; if indirectly, division.

In explaining clearly these latter two operations the fact must be grasped that the unit of which we spoke before is here the basis and foundation of all the relations, and has the first place in the series of magnitudes in continued proportion. Further, remember that the given magnitudes occupy the second position, while those to be discovered stand at the third, the fourth and the remaining points in the series, if the proportion be direct. If, however, the proportion be indirect, the magnitude to be discovered occupies the second position or the other intermediate points, and that which is given, the last.

Thus if it is stated that as unity is to *a,* say to 5, which is given, so is *b,* i.e. 7, to the magnitude to be found, which is *ab,* i.e. 35, then *a* and *b* are at the second position, and *ab,* their product, at the third. So too if we are further told that as 1 is to *c*, say 9, so is *ab*, say 35, to the magnitude we are seeking, i.e. 315, then *abc* is in the fourth position, and is the product of two multiplications among the terms *a*, *b* and *c*, which are at the second position; so it is in other cases. Likewise as 1 is to *a*, say 5, so *a*, i.e. 5, is to a^2, i.e. 25. Again, as unity is to *a*, i.e. 5, so is a^2, i.e. 25, to a^3, i.e. 125; and finally as unity is to *a*, i.e. 5, so is a^3, i.e. 125, to a^4, i.e. 625, and so on. For the multiplication is performed in precisely the same way, whether the magnitude is multiplied by itself or by some other quite different number.

But if we now are told that, as unity is to *a*, say 5, the given divisor, so is *B*, say 7, *the quaesitum*, to *ab*, i.e. 35, the given dividend, we have on this occasion an example of the indirect or inverted order. For the only way to discover *B*, the *quaesitum*, is to divide the given *ab* by *a*, which is also given. The case is the same if the proposition is, 'as unity is to *A*, say 5, the *quaesitum*, so is this *A* to a^2, i.e. 25, which is given'; or again, 'as unity is to *A*, i.e. 5, the *quaesitum*, so is A^2, i.e. 25, which we also have to discover, to a^3, i.e. 125, which is given'; similarly in other cases. All these processes fall under the title 'division,' although we must note that these latter specimens of the process contain more difficulty than the former, because the magnitude to be found comes in a greater number of times in them, and consequently it involves a greater number of relations in such problems. For on such occasions the meaning is the same as if the enunciation were, 'extract the square root of a^2, i.e. 25,' or 'extract the cube root of a^3, i.e. 125,' and so on in other cases. This then is the way in which Arithmeticians commonly put the matter. But alternatively we may explain the problems in the terms employed by Geometricians: it comes to the same thing if we say, 'find a mean proportional between that assumed magnitude, which we call unity, and that indicated by a^2,' or 'find two mean proportionals between unity and a^3,' and so in other cases.

From these considerations it is easy to infer how these two operations suffice for the discovery of any magnitudes whatsoever which are to be deduced from others in virtue of some relation. And now that we have grasped them, the next thing to do is to show how these operations are to be brought before the scrutiny of the imagination and how presented to our actual vision, in order that we may explain how they may be used or practised.

In addition or subtraction we conceive our object under the aspect of a line, or of some extended magnitude in which length is alone to be considered. For if we are to add line *a* to line *b*,

we add the one to the other in the following way *ab*,

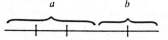

and get as a result *c*.

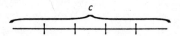

But if the smaller has to be taken from the larger, viz. *b* from *a*,

we place the one above the other thus,

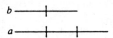

and this will give us that part of the larger which the smaller cannot cover, viz. ——.

In multiplication we also conceive the given magnitudes as lines. But we imagine a rectangle to be constructed out of them; for, if we multiply *a* by *b*,

we fit them together at right angles in the following way,

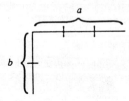

and so make the rectangle

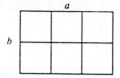

Again, if we wish to multiply *ab* by *c*,

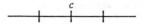

we ought to conceive *ab* as a line, viz. *ab*,

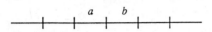

in order that to represent *abc* we may obtain the following figure:

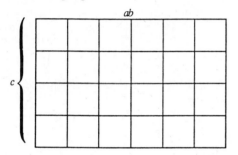

Finally in a division in which the divisor is given, we imagine the magnitude to be divided to be a rectangle, one side of which is the divisor and the other the quotient. Thus if the rectangle *ab* is to be divided by *a*,

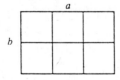

we take away from it the breadth *a* and are left with *b* for quotient:

On the contrary if this rectangle is divided by *b*, we take away the height *b*, and the quotient will be *a*,

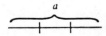

But in those divisions in which the divisor is not given, but only indicated by some relation, as when we are bidden extract the square or cube root, then we must note that the term to be divided and all the others must be always conceived as lines in continued proportion, of which the first is unity, the last the magnitude to be divided. The way in which any number of mean proportionals between this and unity may be discovered will be disclosed in its proper place. At present it is sufficient to have pointed out that according to our hypothesis those operations have not yet been fully dealt with here, since to be carried out they require an indirect and reverse movement on the part of the imagination; and at present we are treating only of questions in which the movement of thought is to be direct.

As for the other operations, they can be carried out with the greatest ease in the way in which we have stated they are to be conceived. Nevertheless it remains for us to show how the terms employed in them are to be constructed. For even though on our first taking up some problem we are free to conceive the terms involved as lines or as rectangles, without introducing any other figures, as was said in reference to the fourteenth rule, nevertheless it is frequently the case that, in the course of the solution, what was a rectangle, constructed by the multiplication of two lines, must presently be conceived as a line, for the purpose of some further operation. Or it may be the case that the same rectangle, or a line formed by some addition or subtraction, has next to be conceived as some other rectangle drawn upon the line by which it is to be divided.

It is therefore worth our while here to expound how every rectangle may be transformed into a line, and conversely how a line or even a rectangle may be turned into another rectangle of which the side is indicated. This is the easiest thing in the world for Geometricians to do, provided they recognize that whenever we compare lines with some rectangle, as here, we always conceive those lines as rectangles, one side of which is the length that we took to represent our unit. For if we do so the whole matter resolves itself into the following proposition: Given a rectangle, to construct another rectangle equal to it upon a given side.

Now though this problem is one familiar to a mere beginner in Geometry, I wish to explain it, lest I should seem to have omitted something.

Rule XIX

Employing this method of reasoning we have to find out as many magnitudes as we have unknown terms, treated as though they were known, for the purpose of handling the problem in the direct way; and these must be expressed in the two different ways. For this will give us as many equations as there are unknowns.

Rule XX

Having got our equations, we must proceed to carry out such operations as we have neglected, taking care never to multiply where we can divide.

Rule XXI

If there are several equations of this kind, we should reduce them all to a single one, viz. that the terms of which do not occupy so many places in the series of magnitudes that are in continued proportion. The terms of the equation should then be themselves arranged in the order which this series follows.

THE END

Meditations on the First Philosophy

In Which the Existence of God, and the Real Distinction of Mind and Body, Are Demonstrated

René Descartes

Preface to the Reader

I have already slightly touched upon the questions respecting the existence of God and the nature of the human soul, in the "Discourse on the Method of Rightly Conducting the Reason, and Seeking Truth in the Sciences," published in French in the year 1637; not, however, with the design of there treating of them fully, but only, as it were, in passing, that I might learn from the judgments of my readers in what way I should afterwards handle them: for these questions appeared to me to be of such moment as to be worthy of being considered more than once, and the path which I follow in discussing them is so little trodden, and so remote from the ordinary route, that I thought it would not be expedient to illustrate

SOURCE: *Meditations on the First Philosophy* by René Descartes, translated by John Veitch (Open Court, 1901).

it at greater length in French, and in a discourse that might be read by all, lest even the more feeble minds should believe that this path might be entered upon by them.

But, as in the Discourse on Method, I had requested all who might find aught meriting censure in my writings, to do me the favour of pointing it out to me, I may state that no objections worthy of remark have been alleged against what I then said on these questions, except two, to which I will here briefly reply, before undertaking their more detailed discussion.

The first objection is that though, while the human mind reflects on itself, it does not perceive that it is any other than a thinking thing, it does not follow that its nature or essence consists only in its being a thing which thinks; so that the word *only* shall exclude all other things which might also perhaps be said to pertain to the nature of the mind.

To this objection I reply, that it was not my intention in that place to exclude these according to the order of truth in the matter (of which I did not then treat), but only according to the order of thought; so that my meaning was, that I clearly apprehended nothing, so far as I was conscious, as belonging to my essence, except that I was a thinking thing, or a thing possessing in itself the faculty of thinking. But I will show hereafter how, from the consciousness that nothing besides thinking belongs to the essence of the mind, it follows that nothing else does in truth belong to it.

The second objection is that it does not follow, from my possessing the idea of a thing more perfect than I am, that the idea itself is more perfect than myself, and much less that what is represented by the idea exists.

But I reply that in the term *idea* there is here something equivocal; for it may be taken either materially for an act of the understanding, and in this sense it cannot be said to be more perfect than I, or objectively, for the thing represented by that act, which, although it be not supposed to exist out of my understanding, may, nevertheless, be more perfect than myself, by reason of its essence. But, in the sequel of this treatise I will show more amply how, from my possessing the idea of a

thing more perfect than myself, it follows that this thing really exists.

Besides these two objections, I have seen, indeed, two treatises of sufficient length relating to the present matter. In these, however, my conclusions, much more than my premises, were impugned, and that by arguments borrowed from the commonplaces of the atheists. But, as arguments of this sort can make no impression on the minds of those who shall rightly understand my reasonings, and as the judgments of many are so irrational and weak that they are persuaded rather by the opinions on a subject that are first presented to them, however false and opposed to reason they may be, than by a true and solid, but subsequently received, refutation of them, I am unwilling here to reply to these strictures from a dread of being, in the first instance, obliged to state them.

I will only say, in general, that all which the atheists commonly allege in favour of the non-existence of God, arises continually from one or other of these two things, namely, either the ascription of human affections to Deity, or the undue attribution to our minds of so much vigour and wisdom that we may essay to determine and comprehend both what God can and ought to do; hence all that is alleged by them will occasion us no difficulty, provided only we keep in remembrance that our minds must be considered finite, while Deity is incomprehensible and infinite.

Now that I have once, in some measure, made proof of the opinions of men regarding my work, I again undertake to treat of God and the human soul, and at the same time to discuss the principles of the entire First Philosophy, without, however, expecting any commendation from the crowd for my endeavours, or a wide circle of readers. On the contrary, I would advise none to read this work, unless such as are able and willing to meditate with me in earnest, to detach their minds from commerce with the senses, and likewise to deliver themselves from all prejudice; and individuals of this character are, I well know, remarkably rare. But with regard to those who, without caring to comprehend the order and connection of the reasonings, shall study only detached clauses for the purpose of small but noisy criticism, as is the custom with many, I may say that such persons will not profit greatly by the reading of this treatise; and although perhaps they may find opportunity for cavilling in several places, they will yet hardly start any pressing objections, or such as shall be deserving of reply.

But since, indeed, I do not promise to satisfy others on all these subjects at first sight, nor arrogate so much to myself as to believe that I have been able to foresee all that may be the source of difficulty to each one, I shall expound, first of all, in the *Meditations,* those considerations by which I feel persuaded that I have arrived at a certain and evident knowledge of truth, in order that I may ascertain whether the reasonings which have prevailed with myself will also be effectual in convincing others. I will then reply to the objections of some men, illustrious for their genius and learning, to whom these Meditations were sent for criticism before they were committed to the press; for these objections are so numerous and varied that I venture to anticipate that nothing, at least nothing of any moment, will readily occur to any mind which has not been touched upon in them.

Hence it is that I earnestly entreat my readers not to come to any judgment on the questions raised in the Meditations until they have taken care to read the whole of the Objections, with the relative Replies.

Synopsis of the Six Following Meditations

In the First Meditation I expound the grounds on which we may doubt in general of all things, and especially of material objects, so long, at least, as we have no other foundations for the sciences than those we have hitherto possessed. Now, although the utility of a doubt so general may not be manifest at first sight, it is nevertheless of the greatest, since it delivers us from all prejudice, and affords the easiest pathway by which the mind may withdraw itself from the senses; and, finally, makes it impossible for us to doubt wherever we afterwards discover truth.

In the Second, the mind which, in the exercise of the freedom peculiar to itself, supposes that no object is, of the existence of which it has even the slighest doubt, finds that, meanwhile, it must itself exist. And this point is likewise of the highest moment, for the mind is thus enabled easily to distinguish what pertains to itself, that is, to the intellectual nature, from what is to be referred to the body. But since some, perhaps, will expect, at this stage of our progress, a statement of the reasons which establish the doctrine of the immortality of the soul, I think it proper here to make such aware, that it was my aim to write nothing of which I could not give exact demonstration, and that I therefore felt myself obliged to adopt an order similar to that in use among the geometers, viz., to premise all upon which the proposition in question depends, before coming to any conclusion respecting it. Now, the first and chief prerequisite for the knowledge of the immortality of the soul is our being able to form the clearest possible conception of the soul itself, and such as shall be absolutely distinct from all our notions of body; and how this is to be accomplished is there shown. There is required, besides this, the assurance that all objects which we clearly and distinctly think are true in that very mode in which we think them; and this could not be established previously to the Fourth Meditation. Father, it is necessary, for the same purpose, that we possess a distinct conception of corporeal nature, which is given partly in the Second and partly in the Fifth and Sixth Meditations. And, finally, on these grounds, we are necessitated to conclude, that all those objects which are clearly and distinctly conceived to be diverse substances, as mind and body, are substances really reciprocally distinct; and this inference is made in the Sixth Meditation. The absolute distinction of mind and body is, besides, confirmed in this Second Meditation, by showing that we cannot conceive body unless as divisible; while, on the other hand, mind cannot be conceived unless as indivisible. For we are not able to conceive the half of a mind, as we can of any body, however small, so that the natures of these two substances are to be held, not only as diverse, but even in some measure as contraries. I have not, however, pursued this discussion further in the present treatise, as well for the reason that these considerations are sufficient to show that the destruction of the mind does not follow from the corruption of the body, and thus to afford to men the hope of a future life, as also because the premises from which it is competent for us to infer the immortality of the soul, involve an explication of the whole principles of Physics: in order to establish, in the first place, that generally all substances, that is, all things which can exist only in consequence of having been created by God, are in their own nature incorruptible, and can never cease to be, unless God himself, by refusing his concurrence to them, reduce them to nothing; and, in the second place, that body, taken generally, is a substance, and therefore can never perish, but that the human body, in as far as it differs from other bodies, is constituted only by a certain configuration of members, and by other accidents of this sort, while the human mind is not made up of accidents, but is a pure substance. For although all the accidents of the mind be changed—although, for example, it think certain things, will others, and perceive others, the mind itself does not vary with these changes; while, on the contrary, the human body is no longer the same if a change take place in the form of any of its parts: from which it follows that the body may, indeed, without difficulty perish, but that the mind is in its own nature immortal.

In the Third Meditation, I have unfolded at sufficient length, as appears to me, my chief argument for the existence of God. But yet, since I was there desirous to avoid the use of comparisons taken from material objects, that I might withdraw, as far as possible, the minds of my readers from the senses, numerous obscurities perhaps remain, which, however, will, I trust, be afterwards entirely removed in the Replies to the Objections: thus, among other things, it may be difficult to understand how the idea of a being absolutely perfect, which is found in our minds, possesses so much objective reality that it must be held to arise from a cause absolutely perfect. This is illustrated in the Replies by the comparison of a highly perfect machine, the idea of which exists in the mind of some workman; for as the objective perfection of this idea must have some cause, viz., either the science of the workman, or of some other person from whom he has received the idea, in the same way the idea of God, which is found in us, demands God himself for its cause.

In the Fourth, it is shown that all which we clearly and distinctly perceive is true; and, at the same time, is explained wherein consists the nature of error; points that require to be known as well for confirming the preceding truths, as for the better understanding of those that are to follow. But, meanwhile, it must be observed, that I do not at all there treat of Sin, that is, of error committed in the pursuit of good and evil, but of that sort alone which arises in the determination of the true and the false. Nor do I refer to matters of faith, or to the conduct of life, but only to what regards speculative truths, and such as are known by means of the natural light alone.

In the Fifth, besides the illustration of corporeal nature, taken generically, a new demonstration is given of the existence of God, not free, perhaps, any more than the former, from certain difficulties, but of these the solution will be found in the Replies to the Objections. I further show, in what sense it is true that the certitude of geometrical demonstrations themselves is dependent on the knowledge of God.

Finally, in the Sixth, the act of the understanding is distinguished from that of the imagination; the marks of this distinction are described; the human mind is shown to be really distinct from the body, and, nevertheless, to be so closely conjoined therewith, as together to form, as it were, a unity. The whole of the errors which arise from the senses are brought under review, while the means of avoiding them are pointed out; and, finally, all the grounds are adduced from which the existence of material objects may be inferred; not, however, because I deemed them of great utility in establishing what they prove, viz., that there is in reality a world, that men are possessed of bodies, and the like, the truth of which no one of sound mind ever seriously doubted; but because, from a close consideration of them, it is perceived that they are neither so strong nor clear as the reasonings which conduct us to the knowledge of our mind and of God; so that the latter are, of all which come under human knowledge, the most certain and manifest—a conclusion which it was my single aim in these Meditations to establish; on which account I here omit mention of the various other questions which, in the course of the discussion, I had occasion likewise to consider.

Meditation I:
Of the Things of Which We May Doubt

Several years have now elapsed since I first became aware that I had accepted, even from my youth, many false opinions for true, and that consequently what I afterwards based on such principles was highly doubtful; and from that time I was convinced of the necessity of undertaking once in my life to rid myself of all the opinions I had adopted, and of commencing anew the work of building from the foundation, if I desired to establish a firm and abiding superstructure in the sciences. But as this enterprise appeared to me to be one of great magnitude, I waited until I had attained an age so mature as to leave me no hope that at any stage of life more advanced I should be better able to execute my design. On this account, I have delayed so long that I should henceforth consider I was doing wrong were I still to consume in deliberation any of the time that now remains for action. To-day, then, since I have opportunely freed my mind from all cares, . . . and since I am in the secure possession of leisure in a peaceable retirement, I will at length apply myself earnestly and freely to the general overthrow of all my former opinions. But, to this end, it will not be necessary for me to show that the whole of these are false—a point, perhaps, which I shall never reach; but as even now my reason convinces me that I ought not the less carefully to withhold belief from what is not entirely certain and indubitable, than from what is manifestly false, it will be sufficient to justify the rejection of the whole if I shall find in each

some ground for doubt. Nor for this purpose will it be necessary even to deal with each belief individually, which would be truly an endless labour; but, as the removal from below of the foundation necessarily involves the downfall of the whole edifice, I will at once approach the criticism of the principles on which all my former beliefs rested.

All that I have, up to this moment, accepted as possessed of the highest truth and certainty, I received either from or through the senses. I observed, however, that these sometimes misled us; and it is the part of prudence not to place absolute confidence in that by which we have even once been deceived.

But it may be said, perhaps, that, although the senses occasionally mislead us respecting minute objects, and such as are so far removed from us as to be beyond the reach of close observation, there are yet many other of their informations, of the truth of which it is manifestly impossible to doubt; as for example, that I am in this place, seated by the fire, clothed in a winter dressing-gown, that I hold in my hands this piece of paper, with other intimations of the same nature. But how could I deny that I possess these hands and this body, and withal escape being classed with persons in a state of insanity, whose brains are so disordered and clouded by dark bilious vapours as to cause them pertinaciously to assert that they are monarchs when they are in the greatest poverty; or clothed [in gold] and purple when destitute of any covering; or that their head is made of clay, their body of glass, or that they are gourds? I should certainly be not less insane than they, were I to regulate my procedure according to examples so extravagant.

Though this be true, I must nevertheless here consider that I am a man, and that, consequently, I am in the habit of sleeping, and representing to myself in dreams those same things, or even sometimes others less probable, which the insane think are presented to them in their waking moments. How often have I dreamt that I was in these familiar circumstances,—that I was dressed, and occupied this place by the fire, when I was lying undressed in bed? At the present moment, however, I certainly look upon this paper with eyes wide awake; the head which I now move is not asleep; I extend this hand consciously and with express purpose, and I perceive it; the occurrences in sleep are not so distinct as all this. But I cannot forget that, at other times, I have been deceived in sleep by similar illusions; and, attentively considering those cases, I perceive so clearly that there exist no certain marks by which the state of waking can ever be distinguished from sleep, that I feel greatly astonished; and in amazement I almost persuade myself that I am now dreaming.

Let us suppose, then, that we are dreaming, and that all these particulars—namely, the opening of the eyes, the motion of the head, the forth-putting of the hands—are merely illusions; and even that we really possess neither an entire body nor hands such as we see. Nevertheless, it must be admitted at least that the objects which appear to us in sleep are, as it were, painted representations which could not have been formed unless in the likeness of realities; and, therefore, that those general objects, at all events,—namely, eyes, a head, hands, and an entire body—are not simply imaginary, but really existent. For, in truth, painters themselves, even when they study to represent sirens and satyrs by forms the most fantastic and extraordinary, cannot bestow upon them natures absolutely new, but can only make a certain medley of the members of different animals; or if they chance to imagine something so novel that nothing at all similar has ever been seen before, and such as is, therefore, purely fictitious and absolutely false, it is at least certain that the colours of which this is composed are real.

And on the same principle, although these general objects, viz., eyes, a head, hands, and the like, be imaginary, we are nevertheless absolutely necessitated to admit the reality at least of some other objects still more simple and universal than these, of which, just as of certain real colours, all those images of things, whether true and real, or false and fantastic, that are found in our consciousness, are formed.

To this class of objects seem to belong corporeal nature in general and its extension; the figure of extended things, their quantity or magnitude, and their number, as also the

place in, and the time during, which they exist, and other things of the same sort. We will not, therefore, perhaps reason illegitimately if we conclude from this that Physics, Astronomy, Medicine, and all the other sciences that have for their end the consideration of composite objects, are indeed of a doubtful character; but that Arithmetic, Geometry, and the other sciences of the same class, which regard merely the simplest and most general objects, and scarcely inquire whether or not these are really existent, contain somewhat that is certain and indubitable: for whether I am awake or dreaming, it remains true that two and three make five, and that a square has but four sides; nor does it seem possible that truths so apparent can ever fall under a suspicion of falsity.

Nevertheless, the belief that there is a God who is all-powerful, and who created me, such as I am, has, for a long time, obtained steady possession of my mind. How, then, do I know that he has not arranged that there should be neither earth, nor sky, nor any extended thing, nor figure, nor magnitude, nor place, providing at the same time, however, for [the rise in me of the perceptions of all these objects, and] the persuasion that these do not exist otherwise than as I perceive them? And further, as I sometimes think that others are in error respecting matters of which they believe themselves to possess a perfect knowledge, how do I know that I am not also deceived each time I add together two and three, or number the sides of a square, or form some judgment still more simple, if more simple indeed can be imagined? But perhaps Deity has not been willing that I should be thus deceived, for He is said to be supremely good. If, however, it were repugnant to the goodness of Deity to have created me subject to constant deception, it would seem likewise to be contrary to his goodness to allow me to be occasionally deceived, and yet it is clear that this is permitted. Some, indeed, might perhaps be found who would be disposed rather to deny the existence of a Being so powerful than to believe that there is nothing certain. But let us for the present refrain from opposing this opinion, and grant that all which is here said of a Deity is fabulous: nevertheless in whatever way it be supposed that I reached the state in which I exist, whether by fate, or chance, or by an endless series of antecedents and consequents, or by any other means, it is clear that the probability of my being so imperfect as to be the constant victim of deception, will be increased exactly in proportion as the power possessed by the cause, to which they assign my origin, is lessened. To these reasonings I have assuredly nothing to reply, but am constrained at last to avow that there is nothing of all that I formerly believed to be true of which it is impossible to doubt, and that not through thoughtlessness or levity, but from cogent and maturely considered reasons; so that henceforward, if I desire to discover anything certain, I ought not the less carefully to refrain from assenting to those same opinions than to what might be shown to be manifestly false.

But it is not sufficient to have made these observations; care must be taken likewise to keep them in remembrance. For those old and customary opinions perpetually recur—long and familiar usage giving them the right of occupying my mind, even almost against my will, and subduing my belief; nor will I lose the habit of deferring to them and confiding in them so long as I shall consider them to be what in truth they are, viz., opinions to some extent doubtful, as I have already shown, but still highly probable, and such as it is much more reasonable to believe than deny. It is for this reason I am persuaded that I shall not be doing wrong, if, taking an opposite judgment of deliberate design, I become my own deceiver, by supposing, for a time, that all those opinions are entirely false and imaginary, until at length, having thus balanced my old by my new prejudices, my judgment shall no longer be turned aside by perverted usage from the path that may conduct to the perception of truth. For I am assured that, meanwhile, there will arise neither peril nor error from this course, and that I cannot for the present yield too much to distrust, since the end I now seek is not action but knowledge.

I will suppose, then, not that Deity, who is sovereignly good and the fountain of truth, but that some malignant demon, who is at once exceedingly potent and deceitful, has employed all his artifice to deceive me; I will suppose that the sky, the air, the earth, colours, figures, sounds, and all external things, are nothing better than the illusions of dreams, by means of which this being has laid snares for my credulity; I will consider myself as without hands, eyes, flesh, blood, or any of the senses, and as falsely believing that I am possessed of these; I will continue resolutely fixed in this belief, and if indeed by this means it be not in my power to arrive at the knowledge of truth, I shall at least do what is in my power, . . . and guard with settled purpose against giving my assent to what is false, and being imposed upon by this deceiver, whatever be his power and artifice.

But this undertaking is arduous, and a certain indolence insensibly leads me back to my ordinary course of life; and just as the captive, who, perchance, was enjoying in his dreams an imaginary liberty, when he begins to suspect that it is but a vision, dreads awakening, and conspires with the agreeable illusions that the deception may be prolonged; so I, of my own accord, fall back into the train of my former beliefs, and fear to arouse myself from my slumber, lest the time of laborious wakefulness that would succeed this quiet rest, in place of bringing any light of day, should prove inadequate to dispel the darkness that will arise from the difficulties that have now been raised.

Meditation II: Of the Nature of the Human Mind and That It Is More Easily Known Than the Body

The Meditation of yesterday has filled my mind with so many doubts, that it is no longer in my power to forget them. Nor do I see, meanwhile, any principle on which they can be resolved; and, just as if I had fallen all of a sudden into very deep water, I am so greatly disconcerted as to be unable either to plant my feet firmly on the bottom or sustain myself by swimming on the surface. I will, nevertheless, make an effort, and try anew the same path on which I had entered yesterday, that is, proceed by casting aside all that admits of the slightest doubt, not less than if I had discovered it to be absolutely false; and I will continue always in this track until I shall find something that is certain, or at least, if I can do nothing more, until I shall know with certainty that there is nothing certain. Archimedes, that he might transport the entire globe from the place it occupied to another, demanded only a point that was firm and immoveable; so also, I shall be entitled to entertain the highest expectations, if I am fortunate enough to discover only one thing that is certain and indubitable.

I suppose, accordingly, that all the things which I see are false; I believe that none of those objects which my fallacious memory represents ever existed; I suppose that I possess no senses; I believe that body, figure, extension, motion, and place are merely fictions of my mind. What is there, then, that can be esteemed true? Perhaps this only, that there is absolutely nothing certain.

But how do I know that there is not something different altogether from the objects I have now enumerated, of which it is impossible to entertain the slightest doubt? Is there not a God, or some being, by whatever name I may designate him, who causes these thoughts to arise in my mind? But why suppose such a being, for it may be I myself am capable of producing them? Am I, then, at least not something? But I before denied that I possessed senses or a body; I hesitate, however, for what follows from that? Am I so dependent on the body and the senses that without these I cannot exist? But I had the persuasion that there was absolutely nothing in the world, that there was no sky and no earth, neither minds nor bodies; was I not, therefore, at the same time, persuaded that I did not exist? Far from it; I assuredly existed, since I was persuaded. But there is I know not what being, who is possessed at once of the highest power and the deepest cunning, who is constantly employing all his ingenuity in deceiving me. Doubtless, then, I exist, since I am deceived; and let him deceive me as he may, he can never bring it about that I am nothing, so long as I shall be conscious that I am something. So that it must, in fine, be maintained, all things being maturely and carefully considered, that this proposition I am, I exist, is necessarily true each time it is expressed by me, or conceived in my mind.

But I do not yet know with sufficient clearness what I am, though assured that I am; and hence, in the next place, I must take care, lest perchance I inconsiderately substitute some other object in room of what is properly myself, and thus wander from truth, even in that knowledge which I hold to be of all others the most certain and evident. For this reason, I will now consider anew what I formerly believed myself to be, before I entered on the present train of thought; and of my previous opinion I will retrench all that can in the least be invalidated by the grounds of doubt I have adduced, in order that there may at length remain nothing but what is certain and indubitable. What then did I formerly think I was? Undoubtedly I judged that I was a man. But what is a man? Shall I say a rational animal? Assuredly not; for it would be necessary forthwith to inquire into what is meant by animal, and what by rational, and thus, from a single question, I should insensibly glide into others, and these more difficult than the first; nor do I now possess enough of leisure to warrant me in wasting my time amid subtleties of this sort. I prefer here to attend to the thoughts that sprung up of themselves in my mind, and were inspired by my own nature alone, when I applied myself to the consideration of what I was. In the first place, then, I thought that I possessed a countenance, hands, arms, and all the fabric of members that appears in a corpse, and which I called by the name of body. It further occurred to me that I was nourished, that I walked, perceived, and thought, and all those actions I referred to the soul; but what the soul itself was I either did not stay to consider, or, if I did, I imagined that it was something extremely rare and subtile, like wind, or flame, or ether, spread through my grosser parts. As regarded the body, I did not even doubt of its nature, but thought I distinctly knew it, and if I had wished to describe it according to the notions I then entertained, I should have explained myself in this manner: By body I understand all that can be terminated by a certain figure; that can be comprised in a certain place, and so fill a certain space as therefrom to exclude every other body; that can be perceived either by touch, sight, hearing, taste, or smell; that can be moved in different ways, not indeed of itself, but by something foreign to it by which it is touched; for the power of self-motion, as likewise that of perceiving and thinking, I held as by no means pertaining to the nature of body; on the contrary, I was somewhat astonished to find such faculties existing in some bodies.

But, since I suppose there exists an extremely powerful, and, if I may so speak, malignant being, whose whole endeavours are directed towards deceiving me? Can I affirm that I possess any one of all those attributes of which I have lately spoken as belonging to the nature of body? After attentively considering them in my own mind, I find none of them that can properly be said to belong to myself. To recount them were idle and tedious. Let us pass, then, to the attributes of the soul. The first mentioned were the powers of nutrition and walking; but, if it be true that I have no body, it is true likewise that I am capable neither of walking nor of being nourished. Perception is another attribute of the soul; but perception too is impossible without the body: besides, I have frequently, during sleep, believed that I perceived objects which I afterwards observed I did not in reality perceive. Thinking is another attribute of the soul; and here I discover what properly belongs to myself. This alone is inseparable from me. I am — I exist: This is certain; but how often? As often as I think; for perhaps it would even happen, if I should wholly cease to think, that I should at the same time altogether cease to be. I now admit nothing that is not necessarily true: I am therefore, precisely speaking, only a thinking thing, that is, a mind, understanding, or reason, — terms whose signification was before unknown to me. I am, however, a real thing, and really existent; but what thing? The answer was, a thinking thing. The question now arises, am I aught besides? I will stimulate my imagination with a view to discover whether I am not still something more than a thinking being. Now it is plain I am not the assemblage of members called the human body; I am not a thin and penetrating air

diffused through all these members, or wind, or flame, or vapour, or breath, or any of all the things I can imagine; for I supposed that all these were not, and, without changing the supposition, I find that I still feel assured of my existence.

But it is true, perhaps, that those very things which I suppose to be non-existent, because they are unknown to me, are not in truth different from myself whom I know. This is a point I cannot determine, and do not now enter into any dispute regarding it. I can only judge of things that are known to me: I am conscious that I exist, and I who know that I exist inquire into what I am. It is, however, perfectly certain that the knowledge of my existence, thus precisely taken, is not dependent on things, the existence of which is as yet unknown to me: and consequently it is not dependent on any of the things I can feign in imagination. Moreover, the phrase itself, I frame an image, reminds me of my error; for I should in truth frame one if I were to imagine myself to be anything, since to imagine is nothing more than to contemplate the figure or image of a corporeal thing; but I already know that I exist, and that it is possible at the same time that all those images, and in general all that relates to the nature of body, are merely dreams [or chimeras]. From this I discover that it is not more reasonable to say, I will excite my imagination that I may know more distinctly what I am, than to express myself as follows: I am now awake, and perceive something real; but because my perception is not sufficiently clear, I will of express purpose go to sleep that my dreams may represent to me the object of my perception with more truth and clearness. And, therefore, I know that nothing of all that I can embrace in imagination belongs to the knowledge which I have of myself, and that there is need to recall with the utmost care the mind from this mode of thinking, that it may be able to know its own nature with perfect distinctness.

But what, then, am I? A thinking thing, it has been said. But what is a thinking thing? It is a thing that doubts, understands, affirms, denies, wills, refuses, that imagines also, and perceives. Assuredly it is not little, if all these properties belong to my nature. But why should they not belong to it? Am I not that very being who now doubts of almost everything; who, for all that, understands and conceives certain things; who affirms one alone as true, and denies the others; who desires to know more of them, and does not wish to be deceived; who imagines many things, sometimes even despite his will; and is likewise percipient of many, as if through the medium of the senses. Is there nothing of all this as true as that I am, even although I should be always dreaming, and although he who gave me being employed all his ingenuity to deceive me? Is there also any one of these attributes that can be properly distinguished from my thought, or that can be said to be separate from myself? For it is of itself so evident that it is I who doubt, I who understand, and I who desire, that it is here unnecessary to add anything by way of rendering it more clear. And I am as certainly the same being who imagines; for, although it may be that nothing I imagine is true, still the power of imagination does not cease really to exist in me and to form part of my thought. In fine, I am the same being who perceives, that is, who apprehends certain objects as by the organs of sense, since, in truth, I see light, hear a noise, and feel heat. But it will be said that these presentations are false, and that I am dreaming. Let it be so. At all events it is certain that I seem to see light, hear a noise, and feel heat; this cannot be false, and this is what in me is properly called perceiving, which is nothing else than thinking. From this I begin to know what I am with somewhat greater clearness and distinctness than heretofore.

But, nevertheless, it still seems to me, and I cannot help believing, that corporeal things, whose images are formed by thought, and are examined by the same, are known with much greater distinctness than that I know not what part of myself which is not imaginable; although, in truth, it may seem strange to say that I know and comprehend with greater distinctness things whose existence appears to me doubtful, that are unknown, and do not belong to me, than others of whose reality I am persuaded, that are known to me, and appertain to my proper nature; in a word, than myself. But I see clearly what is the state of the case. My mind is apt to wander, and will not yet submit to be restrained within the limits of truth. Let us therefore leave the mind to itself once more, and, according to it every kind of liberty, in order that, having afterwards withdrawn it from these gently and opportunely, it may then be the more easily controlled.

Let us now accordingly consider the objects that are commonly thought to be the most distinctly known, viz., the bodies we touch and see; not, indeed, bodies in general, for these general notions are usually somewhat more confused, but one body in particular. Take, for example, this piece of wax; it is quite fresh, having been but recently taken from the beehive; it has not yet lost the sweetness of the honey it contained; it still retains somewhat of the odour of the flowers from which it was gathered; its colour, figure, size, are apparent; it is hard, cold, easily handled; and sounds when struck upon with the finger. In fine, all that contributes to make a body as distinctly known as possible, is found in the one before us. But, while I am speaking, let it be placed near the fire—what remained of the taste exhales, the smell evaporates, the colour changes, its figure is destroyed, its size increases, it becomes liquid, it grows hot, it can hardly be handled, and, although struck upon, it emits no sound. Does the same wax still remain after this change? It must be admitted that it does remain; no one doubts it, or judges otherwise. What, then, was it I knew with so much distinctness in the piece of wax? Assuredly, it could be nothing of all that I observed by means of the senses, since all the things that fell under taste, smell, sight, touch, and hearing are changed, and yet the same wax remains. It was perhaps what I now think, viz., that this wax was neither the sweetness of honey, the pleasant odour of flowers, the whiteness, the figure, nor the sound, but only a body that a little before appeared to me conspicuous under these forms, and which is now perceived under others. But, to speak precisely, what is it that I imagine when I think of it in this way? Let it be attentively considered, and, retrenching all that does not belong to the wax, let us see what remains. There certainly remains nothing, except something extended, flexible, and movable. But what is meant by flexible and movable? Is it not that I imagine that the piece of wax, being round, is capable of becoming square, or of passing from a square into a triangular figure? Assuredly such is not the case, because I conceive that it admits of an infinity of similar changes; and I am, moreover, unable to compass this infinity by imagination, and consequently this conception which I have of the wax is not the product of the faculty of imagination. But what now is this extension? Is it not also unknown? for it becomes greater when the wax is melted, greater when it is boiled, and greater still when the heat increases; and I should not conceive according to truth, the wax as it is, if I did not suppose that the piece we are considering admitted even of a wider variety of extension than I ever imagined. I must, therefore, admit that I cannot even comprehend by imagination what the piece of wax is, and that it is the mind alone which perceives it. I speak of one piece in particular; for, as to wax in general, this is still more evident. But what is the piece of wax that can be perceived only by the mind? It is certainly the same which I see, touch, imagine; and, in fine, it is the same which, from the beginning, I believed it to be. But the perception of it is neither an act of sight, of touch, nor of imagination, and never was either of these, though it might formerly seem so, but is simply an intuition of the mind, which may be imperfect and confused, as it formerly was, or very clear and distinct, as it is at present, according as the attention is more or less directed to the elements which it contains, and of which it is composed.

But, meanwhile, I feel greatly astonished when I observe its proneness to error. For although, without at all giving expression to what I think, I consider all this in my own mind, words yet occasionally impede my progress, and I am almost led into error by the terms of ordinary language. We say, for example, that we see the same wax when it is before us, and not that we judge it to be the same from its retaining the same colour and figure: whence I should forthwith be disposed to conclude that the wax is known by the act of sight, and not by the intuition of the mind alone, were it not for the analogous instance of

human beings passing on in the street below, as observed from a window. In this case I do not fail to say that I see the men themselves, just as I say that I see the wax; and yet what do I see from the window beyond hats and cloaks that might cover artificial machines, whose motions might be determined by springs? But I judge that there are human beings from these appearances, and thus I comprehend, by the faculty of judgment alone which is in the mind, what I believed I saw with my eyes.

The man who makes it his aim to rise to knowledge superior to the common, ought to be ashamed to seek occasions of doubting from the vulgar forms of speech: instead, therefore, of doing this, I shall proceed with the matter in hand, and inquire whether I had a clearer and more perfect perception of the piece of wax when I first saw it, and when I thought I knew it by means of the external sense itself, or, at all events, by the common sense as it is called, that is, by the imaginative faculty; or whether I rather apprehend it more clearly at present, after having examined with greater care, both what it is, and in what way it can be known. It would certainly be ridiculous to entertain any doubt on this point. For what, in that first perception, was there distinct? What did I perceive which any animal might not have perceived? But when I distinguish the wax from its exterior forms, and when, as if I had stripped it of its vestments, I consider it quite naked, it is certain, although some error may still be found in my judgment, that I cannot, nevertheless, thus apprehend it without possessing a human mind.

But, finally, what shall I say of the mind itself, that is, of myself? for as yet I do not admit that I am anything but mind. What, then! I who seem to possess so distinct an apprehension of the piece of wax,—do I not know myself, both with greater truth and certitude, and also much more distinctly and clearly? For if I judge that the wax exists because I see it, it assuredly follows, much more evidently, that I myself am or exist, for the same reason: for it is possible that what I see may not in truth be wax, and that I do not even possess eyes with which to see anything; but it cannot be that when I see, or, which comes to the same thing, when I think I see, I myself who think am nothing. So likewise, if I judge that the wax exists because I touch it, it will still also follow that I am; and if I determine that my imagination, or any other cause, whatever it be, persuades me of the existence of the wax, I will still draw the same conclusion. And what is here remarked of the piece of wax, is applicable to all the other things that are external to me. And further, if the perception of wax appeared to me more precise and distinct, after that not only sight and touch, but many other causes besides, rendered it manifest to my apprehension, with how much greater distinctness must I now know myself, since all the reasons that contribute to the knowledge of the nature of wax, or of any body whatever, manifest still better the nature of my mind? And there are besides so many other things in the mind itself that contribute to the illustration of its nature, that those dependent on the body, to which I have here referred, scarcely merit to be taken into account.

But, in conclusion, I find I have insensibly reverted to the point I desired; for, since it is now manifest to me that bodies themselves are not properly perceived by the senses nor by the faculty of imagination, but by the intellect alone; and since they are not perceived because they are seen and touched, but only because they are understood, I readily discover that there is nothing more easily or clearly apprehended than my own mind. But because it is difficult to rid one's self so promptly of an opinion to which one has been long accustomed, it will be desirable to tarry for some time at this stage, that, by long continued meditation, I may more deeply impress upon my memory this new knowledge.

Meditation III: Of God—That He Exists

I will now close my eyes, I will stop my ears, I will turn away my senses from their objects, I will even efface from my consciousness all the images of corporeal things; or at least, because this can hardly be accomplished, I will consider them as empty and false; and thus, holding converse only with myself, and closely examining my nature, I will endeavour to obtain by degrees a more intimate and familiar knowledge of myself. I am a thinking thing, that is, a being who doubts, affirms, denies, knows a few objects, and is ignorant of many,—wills, refuses,—who imagines likewise, and perceives; for, as I before remarked, although the things which I perceive or imagine are perhaps nothing at all apart from me [and in themselves], I am nevertheless assured that those modes of consciousness which I call perceptions and imaginations, in as far only as they are modes of consciousness, exist in me. And in the little I have said I think I have summed up all that I really know, or at least all that up to this time I was aware I knew. Now, as I am endeavouring to extend my knowledge more widely, I will use circumspection, and consider with care whether I can still discover in myself anything further which I have not yet hitherto observed. I am certain that I am a thinking thing; but do I not therefore likewise know what is required to render me certain of a truth? In this first knowledge, doubtless, there is nothing that gives me assurance of its truth except the clear and distinct perception of what I affirm, which would not indeed be sufficient to give me the assurance that what I say is true, if it could ever happen that anything I thus clearly and distinctly perceived should prove false; and accordingly it seems to me that I may now take as a general rule, that all that is very clearly and distinctly apprehended is true.

Nevertheless I before received and admitted many things as wholly certain and manifest, which yet I afterwards found to be doubtful. What, then, were those? They were the earth, the sky, the stars, and all the other objects which I was in the habit of perceiving by the senses. But what was it that I clearly perceived in them? Nothing more than that the ideas and the thoughts of those objects were presented to my mind. And even now I do not deny that these ideas are found in my mind. But there was yet another thing which I affirmed, and which, from having been accustomed to believe it, I thought I clearly perceived, although, in truth, I did not perceive it at all; I mean the existence of objects external to me, from which those ideas proceeded, and to which they had a perfect resemblance; and it was here I was mistaken, or if I judged correctly, this assuredly was not to be traced to any knowledge I possessed.

But when I considered any matter in arithmetic and geometry, that was very simple and easy, as, for example, that two and three added together make five, and things of this sort, did I not view them with at least sufficient clearness to warrant me in affirming their truth? Indeed, if I afterwards judged that we ought to doubt of these things, it was for no other reason than because it occurred to me that a God might perhaps have given me such a nature as that I should be deceived, even respecting the matters that appeared to me the most evidently true. But as often as this pre-conceived opinion of the sovereign power of a God presents itself to my mind, I am constrained to admit that it is easy for him, if he wishes it, to cause me to err, even in matters where I think I possess the highest evidence; and, on the other hand, as often as I direct my attention to things which I think I apprehend with great clearness, I am so persuaded of their truth that I naturally break out into expressions such as these: Deceive me who may, no one will yet ever be able to bring it about that I am not, so long as I shall be conscious that I am, or at any future time cause it to be true that I have never been, it being now true that I am, or make two and three more or less than five, in supposing which, and other like absurdities, I discover a manifest contradiction.

And in truth, as I have no ground for believing that Deity is deceitful, and as, indeed, I have not even considered the reasons by which the existence of a Deity of any kind is established, the ground of doubt that rests only on this supposition is very slight, and, so to speak, metaphysical. But, that I may be able wholly to remove it, I must inquire whether there is a God, as soon as an opportunity of doing so shall present itself; and if I find that there is a God, I must examine likewise whether he can be a deceiver: for, without the knowledge of these two truths, I do not see that I can ever be certain of anything. And that I may be enabled to examine this without

interrupting the order of meditation I have proposed to myself, it is necessary at this stage to divide all my thoughts into certain classes, and to consider in which of these classes truth and error are, strictly speaking, to be found.

Of my thoughts some are, as it were, images of things, and to these alone properly belongs the name *idea;* as when I think a man, a chimera, the sky, an angel, or God. Others, again, have certain other forms; as when I will, fear, affirm, or deny, I always, indeed, apprehend something as the object of my thought, but I also embrace in thought something more than the representation of the object; and of this class of thoughts some are called volitions or affections, and others judgments.

Now, with respect to ideas, if these are considered only in themselves, and are not referred to any object beyond them, they cannot, properly speaking, be false; for, whether I imagine a goat or a chimera, it is not less true that I imagine the one than the other. Nor need we fear that falsity may exist in the will or affections; for although I may desire objects that are wrong, and even that never existed, it is still true that I desire them. There thus only remain our judgments, in which we must take diligent heed that we be not deceived. But the chief and most ordinary error that arises in them consists in judging that the ideas which are in us are like or conformed to the things that are external to us; for assuredly, if we but considered the ideas themselves as certain modes of our thought, without referring them to anything beyond, they would hardly afford any occasion of error.

But, among these ideas, some appear to me to be innate, others adventitious, and others to be made by myself; for, as I have the power of conceiving what is called a thing, or a truth, or a thought, it seems to me that I hold this power from no other source than my own nature; but if I now hear a noise, if I see the sun, or if I feel heat, I have all along judged that these sensations proceeded from certain objects existing out of myself; and, in fine, it appears to me that sirens, hippogryphs, and the like, are inventions of my own mind. But I may even perhaps come to be of opinion that all my ideas are of the class which I call adventitious, or that they are all innate, or that they are all factitious, for I have not yet clearly discovered their true origin; and what I have here principally to do is to consider, with reference to those that appear to come from certain objects without me, what grounds there are for thinking them like these objects.

The first of these grounds is that it seems to me I am so taught by nature; and the second that I am conscious that those ideas are not dependent on my will, and therefore not on myself, for they are frequently presented to me against my will,—as at present, whether I will or not, I feel heat; and I am thus persuaded that this sensation or idea of heat is produced in me by something different from myself, viz., by the heat of the fire by which I sit. And it is very reasonable to suppose that this object impresses me with its own likeness rather than any other thing.

But I must consider whether these reasons are sufficiently strong and convincing. When I speak of being taught by nature in this matter, I understand by the word nature only a certain spontaneous impetus that impels me to believe in a resemblance between ideas and their objects, and not a natural light that affords a knowledge of its truth. But these two things are widely different; for what the natural light shows to be true can be in no degree doubtful, as, for example, that I am because I doubt, and other truths of the like kind: inasmuch as I possess no other faculty whereby to distinguish truth from error, which can teach me the falsity of what the natural light declares to be true, and which is equally trustworthy; but with respect to natural impulses, I have observed, when the question related to the choice of right or wrong in action, that they frequently led me to take the worse part; nor do I see that I have any better ground for following them in what relates to truth and error. Then, with respect to the other reason, which is that because these ideas do not depend on my will, they must arise from objects existing without me, I do not find it more convincing than the former; for, just as those natural impulses, of which I have lately spoken, are found in me, notwithstanding that they are not always in harmony with my will, so likewise it may be that I possess some power

not sufficiently known to myself capable of producing ideas without the aid of external objects, and, indeed, it has always hitherto appeared to me that they are formed during sleep, by some power of this nature, without the aid of aught external. And, in fine, although I should grant that they proceeded from those objects, it is not a necessary consequence that they must be like them. On the contrary, I have observed, in a number of instances, that there was a great difference between the object and its idea. Thus, for example, I find in my mind two wholly diverse ideas of the sun; the one, by which it appears to me extremely small, draws its origin from the senses, and should be placed in the class of adventitious ideas; the other, by which it seems to be many times larger than the whole earth, is taken up on astronomical grounds, that is, elicited from certain notions born with me, or is framed by myself in some other manner. These two ideas cannot certainly both resemble the same sun; and reason teaches me that the one which seems to have immediately emanated from it is the most unlike. And these things sufficiently prove that hitherto it has not been from a certain and deliberate judgment, but only from a sort of blind impulse, that I believed in the existence of certain things different from myself, which, by the organs of sense, or by whatever other means it might be, conveyed their ideas or images into my mind.

But there is still another way of inquiring whether, of the objects whose ideas are in my mind, there are any that exist out of me. If ideas are taken in so far only as they are certain modes of consciousness, I do not remark any difference or inequality among them, and all seem, in the same manner, to proceed from myself; but, considering them as images, of which one represents one thing and another a different, it is evident that a great diversity obtains among them. For, without doubt, those that represent substances are something more, and contain in themselves, so to speak, more objective reality, than those that represent only modes or accidents; and again, the idea by which I conceive a God, eternal, infinite, all-knowing, all-powerful, and the creator of all things that are out of himself,—

this, I say, has certainly in it more objective reality than those ideas by which finite substances are represented.

Now, it is manifest by the natural light that there must at least be as much reality in the efficient and total cause as in its effect; for whence can the effect draw its reality if not from its cause? and how could the cause communicate to it this reality unless it possessed it in itself? And hence it follows, not only that what is cannot be produced by what is not, but likewise that the more perfect,—in other words, that which contains in itself more reality,—cannot be the effect of the less perfect: and this is not only evidently true of those effects, whose reality is actual or formal, but likewise of ideas, whose reality is only considered as objective. Thus, for example, the stone that is not yet in existence, not only cannot now commence to be, unless it be produced by that which possesses in itself, formally or eminently, all that enters into its composition; and heat can only be produced in a subject that was before devoid of it, by a cause that is of an order, at least as perfect as heat; and so of the others. But further, even the idea of the heat, or of the stone, cannot exist in me unless it be put there by a cause that contains, at least, as much reality as I conceive existent in the heat or in the stone: for, although that cause may not transmit into my idea anything of its actual or formal reality, we ought not on this account to imagine that it is less real; but we ought to consider that, its nature is such as of itself to demand no other formal reality than that which it borrows from our consciousness, of which it is but a mode. But in order that an idea may contain this objective reality rather than that, it must doubtless derive it from some cause in which is found at least as much formal reality as the idea contains of objective; for, if we suppose that there is found in an idea anything which was not in its cause, it must of course derive this from nothing. But, however imperfect may be the mode of existence by which a thing is objectively in the understanding by its idea, we certainly cannot, for all that, allege that this mode of existence is nothing, nor, consequently, that the idea owes its origin to nothing. Nor must it be imagined that, since the reality which is considered in

these ideas is only objective, the same reality need not be formally in the causes of these ideas, but only objectively: for, just as the mode of existing objectively belongs to ideas by their peculiar nature, so likewise the mode of existing formally appertains to the causes of these ideas, by their peculiar nature. And although an idea may give rise to another idea, this regress cannot, nevertheless, be infinite; we must in the end reach a first idea, the cause of which is, as it were, the archetype in which all the reality that is found objectively in these ideas is contained formally. I am thus clearly taught by the natural light that ideas exist in me as pictures or images, which may in truth readily fall short of the perfection of the objects from which they are taken, but can never contain anything greater or more perfect.

And in proportion to the time and care with which I examine all those matters, the conviction of their truth brightens and becomes distinct. But, to sum up, what conclusion shall I draw from it all? It is this;—if the objective reality of any one of my ideas be such as clearly to convince me, that this same reality exists in me neither formally nor eminently, and if, as follows from this, I myself cannot be the cause of it, it is a necessary consequence that I am not alone in the world, but that there is besides myself some other being who exists as the cause of that idea; while, on the contrary, if no such idea be found in my mind, I shall have no sufficient ground of assurance of the existence of any other being besides myself; for, after a most careful search, I have, up to this moment, been unable to discover any other ground.

But, among these my ideas, besides that which represents myself, respecting which there can be here no difficulty, there is one that represents a God; others that represent corporeal and inanimate things; others angels; others animals; and, finally, there are some that represent men like myself. But with respect to the ideas that represent other men, or animals, or angels, I can easily suppose that they were formed by the mingling and composition of the other ideas which I have of myself, of corporeal things, and of God, although there were, apart from myself, neither men, animals, nor angels. And with regard to the ideas of corporeal objects, I never discovered in them anything so great or excellent which I myself did not appear capable of originating; for, by considering these ideas closely and scrutinising them individually, in the same way that I yesterday examined the idea of wax, I find that there is but little in them that is clearly and distinctly perceived. As belonging to the class of things that are clearly apprehended, I recognise the following, viz., magnitude or extension in length, breadth, and depth; figure, which results from the termination of extension; situation, which bodies of diverse figures preserve with reference to each other; and motion or the change of situation; to which may be added substance, duration, and number. But with regard to light, colours, sounds, odours, tastes, heat, cold, and the other tactile qualities, they are thought with so much obscurity and confusion, that I cannot determine even whether they are true or false; in other words, whether or not the ideas I have of these qualities are in truth the ideas of real objects. For although I before remarked that it is only in judgments that formal falsity, or falsity properly so called, can be met with, there may nevertheless be found in ideas a certain material falsity, which arises when they represent what is nothing as if it were something. Thus, for example, the ideas I have of cold and heat are so far from being clear and distinct, that I am unable from them to discover whether cold is only the privation of heat, or heat the privation of cold; or whether they are not real qualities: and since, ideas being as it were images, there can be none that does not seem to us to represent some object, the idea which represents cold as something real and positive will not improperly be called false, if it be correct to say that cold is nothing but a privation of heat; and so in other cases. To ideas of this kind, indeed, it is not necessary that I should assign any author besides myself: for if they are false, that is, represent objects that are unreal, the natural light teaches me that they proceed from nothing; in other words, that they are in me only because something is wanting to the perfection of my nature; but if these ideas are true, yet because they exhibit to me so little reality that I cannot even distinguish the object

represented from non-being, I do not see why I should not be the author of them.

With reference to those ideas of corporeal things that are clear and distinct, there are some which, as appears to me, might have been taken from the idea I have of myself, as those of substance, duration, number, and the like. For when I think that a stone is a substance, or a thing capable of existing of itself, and that I am likewise a substance, although I conceive that I am a thinking and non-extended thing, and that the stone, on the contrary, is extended and unconscious, there being thus the greatest diversity between the two concepts,—yet these two ideas seem to have this in common that they both represent substances. In the same way, when I think of myself as now existing, and recollect besides that I existed some time ago, and when I am conscious of various thoughts whose number I know, I then acquire the ideas of duration and number, which I can afterwards transfer to as many objects as I please. With respect to the other qualities that go to make up the ideas of corporeal objects, viz., extension, figure, situation, and motion, it is true that they are not formally in me, since I am merely a thinking being; but because they are only certain modes of substance, and because I myself am a substance, it seems possible that they may be contained in me eminently.

There only remains, therefore, the idea of God, in which I must consider whether there is anything that cannot be supposed to originate with myself. By the name God, I understand a substance infinite, independent, all-knowing, all-powerful, and by which I myself, and every other thing that exists, if any such there be, were created. But these properties are so great and excellent, that the more attentively I consider them the less I feel persuaded that the idea I have of them owes its origin to myself alone. And thus it is absolutely necessary to conclude, from all that I have before said, that God exists: for though the idea of substance be in my mind owing to this, that I myself am a substance, I should not, however, have the idea of an infinite substance, seeing I am a finite being, unless it were given me by some substance in reality infinite.

And I must not imagine that I do not

apprehend the infinite by a true idea, but only by the negation of the finite, in the same way that I comprehend repose and darkness by the negation of motion and light: since, on the contrary, I clearly perceive that there is more reality in the infinite substance than in the finite, and therefore that in some way I possess the perception of the infinite before that of the finite, that is, the perception of God before that of myself, for how could I know that I doubt, desire, or that something is wanting to me, and that I am not wholly perfect, if I possessed no idea of a being more perfect than myself, by comparison of which I knew the deficiencies of my nature?

And it cannot be said that this idea of God is perhaps materially false, and consequently that it may have arisen from nothing, as I before said of the ideas of heat and cold, and the like: for, on the contrary, as this idea is very clear and distinct, and contains in itself more objective reality than any other, there can be no one of itself more true, or less open to the suspicion of falsity.

The idea, I say, of a being supremely perfect, and infinite, is in the highest degree true; for although, perhaps, we may imagine that such a being does not exist, we cannot, nevertheless, suppose that his idea represents nothing real, as I have already said of the idea of cold. It is likewise clear and distinct in the highest degree, since whatever the mind clearly and distinctly conceives as real or true, and as implying any perfection, is contained entire in this idea. And this is true, nevertheless, although I do not comprehend the infinite, and although there may be in God an infinity of things that I cannot comprehend, nor perhaps even compass by thought in any way; for it is of the nature of the infinite that it should not be comprehended by the finite; and it is enough that I rightly understand this, and judge that all which I clearly perceive, and in which I know there is some perfection, and perhaps also an infinity of properties of which I am ignorant, are formally or eminently in God, in order that the idea I have of him may become the most true, clear, and distinct of all the ideas in my mind.

But perhaps I am something more than I suppose myself to be, and it may be that all those perfections which I attribute to God, in some way exist potentially in me, although they do not yet show themselves, and are not reduced to act. Indeed, I am already conscious that my knowledge is being increased by degrees; and I see nothing to prevent it from thus gradually increasing to infinity, nor any reason why, after such increase and perfection, I should not be able thereby to acquire all the other perfections of the Divine nature; nor, in fine, why the power I possess of acquiring those perfections, if it really now exist in me, should not be sufficient to produce the ideas of them. Yet, on looking more closely into the matter, I discover that this cannot be; for, in the first place, although it were true that my knowledge daily acquired new degrees of perfection, and although there were potentially in my nature much that was not as yet actually in it, still all these excellences make not the slightest approach to the idea I have of the Deity, in whom there is no perfection merely potentially existent; for it is even an unmistakeable token of imperfection in my knowledge, that it is augmented by degrees. Further, although my knowledge increase more and more, nevertheless I am not, therefore, induced to think that it will ever be actually infinite, since it can never reach that point beyond which it shall be incapable of further increase. But I conceive God as actually infinite, so that nothing can be added to his perfection. And, in fine, I readily perceive that the objective being of an idea cannot be produced by a being that is merely potentially existent, which, properly speaking, is nothing, but only by a being existing formally or actually.

And, truly, I see nothing in all that I have now said which it is not easy for any one, who shall carefully consider it, to discern by the natural light; but when I allow my attention in some degree to relax, the vision of my mind being obscured, and, as it were, blinded by the images of sensible objects, I do not readily remember the reason why the idea of a being more perfect than myself, must of necessity have proceeded from a being in reality more perfect. On this account I am here desirous to inquire further, whether I, who possess this idea of God, could exist supposing there were no God. And I ask, from whom could I, in that case, derive my existence? Perhaps from myself, or from my parents, or from some other causes less perfect than God; for anything more perfect, or even equal to God, cannot be thought or imagined. But if I were myself the author of my being, I should doubt of nothing, I should desire nothing, and, in fine, no perfection would be awanting to me; for I should have bestowed upon myself every perfection of which I possess the idea, and I should thus be God. And it must not be imagined that what is now wanting to me is perhaps of more difficult acquisition than that of which I am already possessed; for, on the contrary, it is quite manifest that it was a matter of much higher difficulty that I, a thinking being, should arise from nothing, than it would be for me to acquire the knowledge of many things of which I am ignorant, and which are merely the accidents of a thinking substance; and certainly, if I possessed of myself the greater perfection of which I have now spoken, I would not at least have denied to myself things that may be more easily obtained. I could not, indeed, have denied to myself any property which I perceive is contained in the idea of God, because there is none of these that seems to me to be more difficult to make or acquire; and if there were any that should happen to be more difficult to acquire, they would certainly appear so to me, because I should discover in them a limit to my power. And though I were to suppose that I always was as I now am, I should not, on this ground, escape the force of these reasonings, since it would not follow, even on this supposition, that no author of my existence needed to be sought after. For the whole time of my life may be divided into an infinity of parts, each of which is in no way dependent on any other; and, accordingly, because I was in existence a short time ago, it does not follow that I must now exist, unless in this moment some cause create me anew as it were,—that is, conserve me. In truth, it is perfectly clear and evident to all who will attentively consider the nature of duration, that the conservation of a substance, in each moment of its duration, requires the same power and act that would be necessary to create it, supposing it were not yet in ex-

istence; so that it is manifestly a dictate of the natural light that conservation and creation differ merely in respect of our mode of thinking. All that is here required, therefore, is that I interrogate myself to discover whether I possess any power by means of which I can bring it about that I, who now am, shall exist a moment afterwards; for, since I am merely a thinking thing, if such a power resided in me, I should, without doubt, be conscious of it; but I am conscious of no such power, and thereby I manifestly know that I am dependent upon some being different from myself.

But perhaps the being upon whom I am dependent, is not God, and I have been produced either by my parents, or by some causes less perfect than Deity. This cannot be: for, as I before said, it is perfectly evident that there must at least be as much reality in the cause as in its effect; and accordingly, since I am a thinking thing, and possess in myself an idea of God, whatever in the end be the cause of my existence, it must of necessity be admitted that it is likewise a thinking being, and that it possesses in itself the idea and all the perfections I attribute to Deity. Then it may again be inquired whether this cause owes its origin and existence to itself, or to some other cause. For if it be self-existent, it follows, from what I have before laid down, that this cause is God; for, since it possesses the perfection of self-existence, it must likewise, without doubt, have the power of actually possessing every perfection of which it has the idea—in other words, all the perfections I conceive to belong to God. But if it owe its existence to another cause than itself, we demand again, for a similar reason, whether this second cause exists of itself or through some other, until, from stage to stage, we at length arrive at an ultimate cause, which will be God. And it is quite manifest that in this matter there can be no infinite regress of causes, seeing that the question raised respects not so much the cause which once produced me, as that by which I am at this present moment conserved.

Nor can it be supposed that several causes concurred in my production, and that from one I received the idea of one of the perfections I attribute to Deity, and from another the idea of some other, and thus that all those perfections are indeed found somewhere in the universe, but do not all exist together in a single being who is God; for, on the contrary, the unity, the simplicity or inseparability of all the properties of Deity, is one of the chief perfections I conceive him to possess; and the idea of this unity of all the perfections of Deity could certainly not be put into my mind by any cause from which I did not likewise receive the ideas of all the other perfections; for no power could enable me to embrace them in an inseparable unity, without at the same time giving me the knowledge of what they were.

Finally, with regard to my parents, although all that I believed respecting them be true, it does not, nevertheless, follow that I am conserved by them, or even that I was produced by them, in so far as I am a thinking being. All that, at the most, they contributed to my origin was the giving of certain dispositions to the matter in which I have hitherto judged that I or my mind, which is what alone I now consider to be myself, is enclosed; and thus there can here be no difficulty with respect to them, and it is absolutely necessary to conclude from this alone that I am, and possess the idea of a being absolutely perfect, that is, of God, that his existence is most clearly demonstrated.

There remains only the inquiry as to the way in which I received this idea from God; for I have not drawn it from the senses, nor is it even presented to me unexpectedly, as is usual with the ideas of sensible objects, when these are presented or appear to be presented to the external organs of the senses; it is not even a pure production or fiction of my mind, for it is not in my power to take from or add to it; and consequently there but remains the alternative that it is innate, in the same way as is the idea of myself. And, in truth, it is not to be wondered at that God, at my creation, implanted this idea in me, that it might serve, as it were, for the mark of the workman impressed on his work; and it is not also necessary that the mark should be something different from the work itself; but considering only that God is my creator, it is highly probable that he in some way fashioned me after his own image and likeness, and that I perceive this likeness, in which is contained the idea of

God, by the same faculty by which I apprehend myself,—in other words, when I make myself the object of reflection, I not only find that I am an incomplete, and dependent being, and one who unceasingly aspires after something better and greater than he is; but, at the same time, I am assured likewise that he upon whom I am dependent possesses in himself all the goods after which I aspire, and that not merely indefinitely and potentially, but infinitely and actually, and that he is thus God. And the whole force of the argument of which I have here availed myself to establish the existence of God, consists in this, that I perceive I could not possibly be of such a nature as I am, and yet have in my mind the idea of a God, if God did not in reality exist,—this same God, I say, whose idea is in my mind—that is, a being who possesses all those lofty perfections, of which the mind may have some slight conception, without, however, being able fully to comprehend them—and who is wholly superior to all defect: whence it is sufficiently manifest that he cannot be a deceiver, since it is a dictate of the natural light that all fraud and deception spring from some defect.

But before I examine this with more attention, and pass on to the consideration of other truths that may be evolved out of it, I think it proper to remain here for some time in the contemplation of God himself—that I may ponder at leisure his marvellous attributes— and behold, admire, and adore the beauty of this light so unspeakably great, as far, at least, as the strength of my mind, which is to some degree dazzled by the sight, will permit. For just as we learn by faith that the supreme felicity of another life consists in the contemplation of the Divine majesty alone, so even now we learn from experience that a like meditation, though incomparably less perfect, is the source of the highest satisfaction of which we are susceptible in this life.

Meditation IV:
Of Truth and Error

I have been habituated these bygone days to detach my mind from the senses, and I have accurately observed that there is exceedingly little which is known with certainty respecting corporeal objects,—that we know much more of the human mind, and still more of God himself. I am thus able now without difficulty to abstract my mind from the contemplation of imaginable objects, and apply it to those which, as disengaged from all matter, are purely intelligible. And certainly the idea I have of the human mind in so far as it is a thinking thing, and not extended in length, breadth, and depth, and participating in none of the properties of body, is incomparably more distinct than the idea of any corporeal object; and when I consider that I doubt, in other words, that I am an incomplete and depending being, the idea of a complete and independent being, that is to say of God, occurs to my mind with so much clearness and distinctness,—and from the fact alone that this idea is found in me, or that I who possess it exist, the conclusions that God exists, and that my own existence, each moment of its continuance, is absolutely dependent upon him, are so manifest,—as to lead me to believe it impossible that the human mind can know anything with more clearness and certitude. And now I seem to discover a path that will conduct us from the contemplation of the true God, in whom are contained all the treasures of science and wisdom, to the knowledge of the other things in the universe.

For, in the first place, I discover that it is impossible for him ever to deceive me, for in all fraud and deceit there is a certain imperfection: and although it may seem that the ability to deceive is a mark of subtlety or power, yet the will testifies without doubt of malice and weakness; and such, accordingly, cannot be found in God. In the next place, I am conscious that I possess a certain faculty of judging, which I doubtless received from God, along with whatever else is mine; and since it is impossible that he should will to deceive me, it is likewise certain that he has not given me a faculty that will ever lead me into error, provided I use it aright.

And there would remain no doubt on this head, did it not seem to follow from this, that I can never therefore be deceived; for if all I possess be from God, and if he planted in me

no faculty that is deceitful, it seems to follow that I can never fall into error. Accordingly, it is true that when I think only of God, and turn wholly to him, I discover no cause of error or falsity: but immediately thereafter, recurring to myself, experience assures me that I am nevertheless subject to innumerable errors. When I come to inquire into the cause of these, I observe that there is not only present to my consciousness a real and positive idea of God, or of a being supremely perfect, but also, so to speak, a certain negative idea of nothing,—in other words, of that which is at an infinite distance from every sort of perfection, and that I am, as it were, a mean between God and nothing, or placed in such a way between absolute existence and non-existence, that there is in truth nothing in me to lead me into error, in so far as an absolute being is my creator; but that, on the other hand, as I thus likewise participate in some degree of nothing or of non-being, in other words, as I am not myself the supreme Being, and as I am wanting in many perfections, it is not surprising I should fall into error. And I hence discern that error, so far as error is not something real, which depends for its existence on God, but is simply defect; and therefore that, in order to fall into it, it is not necessary God should have given me a faculty expressly for this end, but that my being deceived arises from the circumstance that the power which God has given me of discerning truth from error is not infinite.

Nevertheless this is not yet quite satisfactory; for error is not a pure negation, but the privation or want of some knowledge which it would seem I ought to possess. But, on considering the nature of God, it seems impossible that he should have planted in his creature any faculty not perfect in its kind, that is, wanting in some perfection due to it: for if it be true, that in proportion to the skill of the maker the perfection of his work is greater, what thing can have been produced by the supreme Creator of the universe that is not absolutely perfect in all its parts? And assuredly there is no doubt that God could have created me such as that I should never be deceived; it is certain, likewise, that he always wills what is best; is it better, then, that I should be capable of being deceived than that I should not?

Considering this more attentively, the first thing that occurs to me is the reflection that I must not be surprised if I am not always capable of comprehending the reasons why God acts as he does; nor must I doubt of his existence because I find, perhaps, that there are several other things besides the present respecting which I understand neither why nor how they were created by him; for, knowing already that my nature is extremely weak and limited, and that the nature of God, on the other hand, is immense, incomprehensible, and infinite, I have no longer any difficulty in discerning that there is an infinity of things in his power whose causes transcend the grasp of my mind: and this consideration alone is sufficient to convince me, that the whole class of final causes is of no avail in physical things; for it appears to me that I cannot, without exposing myself to the charge of temerity, seek to discover the ends of Deity.

It further occurs to me that we must not consider only one creature apart from the others, if we wish to determine the perfection of the works of Deity, but generally all his creatures together; for the same object that might perhaps, with some show of reason, be deemed highly imperfect if it were alone in the world, may for all that be the most perfect possible, considered as forming part of the whole universe: and although, as it was my purpose to doubt of everything, I only as yet know with certainty my own existence and that of God, nevertheless, after having remarked the infinite power of Deity, I cannot deny that he may have produced many other objects, or at least that he is able to produce them, so that I may occupy a place in the relation of a part to the great whole of his creatures.

Whereupon, regarding myself more closely, and considering what my errors are, I observe that these depend on the concurrence of two causes, viz., the faculty of cognition which I possess, and that of election or the power of free choice,—in other words, the understanding and the will. For by the understanding alone, I merely apprehend the ideas regarding which I may form a judgment; nor is any error, properly so called, found in it

thus accurately taken. And although there are perhaps innumerable objects in the world of which I have no idea in my understanding, it cannot, on that account, be said that I am deprived of those ideas, but simply that I do not possess them, because, in truth, there is no ground to prove that Deity ought to have endowed me with a larger faculty of cognition than he has actually bestowed upon me; and however skilful a workman I suppose him to be, I have no reason, on that account, to think that it was obligatory on him to give to each of his works all the perfections he is able to bestow upon some. Nor, moreover, can I complain that God has not given me freedom of choice, or a will sufficiently ample and perfect, since, in truth, I am conscious of will so ample and extended as to be superior to all limits. And what appears to me here to be highly remarkable is that, of all the other properties I possess, there is none so great and perfect as that I do not clearly discern it could be still greater and more perfect. For, to take an example, if I consider the faculty of understanding which I possess, I find that it is of very small extent, and greatly limited, and at the same time I form the idea of another faculty of the same nature, much more ample and even infinite; and seeing that I can frame the idea of it, I discover, from this circumstance alone, that it pertains to the nature of God. In the same way, if I examine the faculty of memory or imagination, or any other faculty I possess, I find none that is not small and circumscribed, and in God immense. It is the faculty of will only, or freedom of choice, which I experience to be so great that I am unable to conceive the idea of another that shall be more ample and extended; so that it is chiefly my will which leads me to discern that I bear a certain image and similitude of Deity. For although the faculty of will is incomparably greater in God than in myself, as well in respect of the knowledge and power that are conjoined with it, and that render it stronger and more efficacious, as in respect of the object, since in him it extends to a greater number of things, it does not, nevertheless, appear to me greater, considered in itself formally and precisely: for the power of will consists only in this, that we are able to do or not to do the same thing, or rather in this alone, that in affirming or denying, pursuing or shunning, what is proposed to us by the understanding, we so act that we are not conscious of being determined to a particular action by any external force. For, to the possession of freedom, it is not necessary that I be alike indifferent towards each of two contraries; but, on the contrary, the more I am inclined towards the one, whether because I clearly know that in it there is the reason of truth and goodness, or because God thus internally disposes my thought, the more freely do I choose and embrace it; and assuredly divine grace and natural knowledge, very far from diminishing liberty, rather augment and fortify it. But the indifference of which I am conscious when I am not impelled to one side rather than to another for want of a reason, is the lowest grade of liberty, and manifests defect or negation of knowledge rather than perfection of will; for if I always clearly knew what was true and good, I should never have any difficulty in determining what judgment I ought to come to, and what choice I ought to make, and I should thus be entirely free without ever being indifferent.

From all this I discover, however, that neither the power of willing, which I have received from God, is of itself the source of my errors, for it is exceedingly ample and perfect in its kind; nor even the power of understanding, for as I conceive no object unless by means of the faculty that God bestowed upon me, all that I conceive is doubtless rightly conceived by me, and it is impossible for me to be deceived in it.

Whence, then, spring my errors? They arise from this cause alone, that I do not restrain the will, which is of much wider range than the understanding, within the same limits, but extend it even to things I do not understand, and as the will is of itself indifferent to such, it readily falls into error and sin by choosing the false in room of the true, and evil instead of good.

For example, when I lately considered whether aught really existed in the world, and found that because I considered this question, it very manifestly followed that I myself existed, I could not but judge that what I so clearly conceived was true, not that I was forced to this judgment by any external cause, but simply because great clearness of the understanding was succeeded by strong inclination in the will; and I believed this the more freely and spontaneously in proportion as I was less indifferent with respect to it. But now I not only know that I exist, in so far as I am a thinking being, but there is likewise presented to my mind a certain idea of corporeal nature; hence I am in doubt as to whether the thinking nature which is in me, or rather which I myself am, is different from that corporeal nature, or whether both are merely one and the same thing, and I here suppose that I am as yet ignorant if any reason that would determine me to adopt the one belief in preference to the other — whence it happens that it is a matter of perfect indifference to me which of the two suppositions I affirm or deny, or whether I form any judgment at all in the matter.

This indifference, moreover, extends not only to things of which the understanding has no knowledge at all, but in general also to all those which it does not discover with perfect clearness at the moment the will is deliberating upon them; for, however probable the conjectures may be that dispose me to form a judgment in a particular matter, the simple knowledge that these are merely conjectures, and not certain and indubitable reasons, is sufficient to lead me to form one that is directly the opposite. Of this I lately had abundant experience, when I laid aside as false all that I had before held for true, on the single ground that I could in some degree doubt of it. But if I abstain from judging of a thing when I do not conceive it with sufficient clearness and distinctness, it is plain that I act rightly, and am not deceived; but if I resolve to deny or affirm, I then do not make a right use of my free will; and if I affirm what is false, it is evident that I am deceived: moreover, even although I judge according to truth, I stumble upon it by chance, and do not therefore escape the imputation of a wrong use of my freedom; for it is a dictate of the natural light, that the knowledge of the understanding ought always to precede the determination of the will.

And it is this wrong use of the freedom of the will in which is found the privation that constitutes the form of error. Privation, I say, is found in the act, in so far as it proceeds from myself, but it does not exist in the faculty which I received from God, nor even in the act, in so far as it depends on him; for I have assuredly no reason to complain that God has not given me a greater power of intelligence or more perfect natural light than he has actually bestowed, since it is of the nature of a finite understanding not to comprehend many things, and of the nature of a created understanding to be finite; on the contrary, I have every reason to render thanks to God, who owed me nothing, for having given me all the perfections I possess, and I should be far from thinking that he has unjustly deprived me of, or kept back, the other perfections which he has not bestowed upon me.

I have no reason, moreover, to complain because he has given me a will more ample than my understanding, since, as the will consists only of a single element, and that indivisible, it would appear that this faculty is of such a nature that nothing could be taken from it [without destroying it]: and certainly, the more extensive it is, the more cause I have to thank the goodness of him who bestowed it upon me.

And, finally, I ought not also to complain that God concurs with me in forming the acts of this will, or the judgments in which I am deceived, because those acts are wholly true and good, in so far as they depend on God; and the ability to form them is a higher degree of perfection in my nature than the want of it would be. With regard to privation, in which alone consists the formal reason of error and sin, this does not require the concurrence of Deity, because it is not a thing and if it be referred to God as to its cause, it ought not to be called privation, but negation. For in truth it is no imperfection in Deity that he has accorded to me the power of giving or withholding my assent from certain things of which he has not put a clear and distinct knowledge in my understanding; but it is doubtless an imperfection in me that I do not use my freedom aright, and readily give my judgment on matters which I only obscurely and confusedly conceive.

I perceive, nevertheless, that it was easy for Deity so to have constituted me as that I should never be deceived, although I still remained free and possessed of a limited knowledge, viz., by implanting in my understanding a clear and distinct knowledge of all the objects respecting which I should ever have to deliberate; or simply by so deeply engraving on my memory the resolution to judge of nothing without previously possessing a clear and distinct conception of it, that I should never forget it. And I easily understand that, in so far as I consider myself as a single whole, without reference to any other being in the universe, I should have been much more perfect than I now am, had Deity created me superior to error; but I cannot therefore deny that it is not somehow a greater perfection in the universe, that certain of its parts are not exempt from defect, as others are, than if they were all perfectly alike.

And I have no right to complain because God, who placed me in the world, was not willing that I should sustain that character which of all others is the chief and most perfect; I have even good reason to remain satisfied on the ground that, if he has not given me the perfection of being superior to error by the first means I have pointed out above, which depends on a clear and evident knowledge of all the matters regarding which I can deliberate, he has at least left in my power the other means, which is, firmly to retain the resolution never to judge where the truth is not clearly known to me: for, although I am conscious of the weakness of not being able to keep my mind continually fixed on the same thought, I can nevertheless, by attentive and oft-repeated meditation, impress it so strongly on my memory that I shall never fail to recollect it as often as I require it, and I can acquire in this way the habitude of not erring; and since it is in being superior to error that the highest and chief perfection of man consists, I deem that I have not gained little by this day's meditation, in having discovered the source of error and falsity.

And certainly this can be no other than what I have now explained: for as often as I so restrain my will within the limits of my knowledge, that it forms no judgment except regarding objects which are clearly and distinctly represented to it by the understanding, I can never be deceived; because every clear and distinct conception is doubtless something, and as such cannot owe its origin to nothing, but must of necessity have God for its author—God, I say, who, as supremely perfect, cannot, without a contradiction, be the cause of any error; and consequently it is necessary to conclude that every such conception is true. Nor have I merely learned to-day what I must avoid to escape error, but also what I must do to arrive at the knowledge of truth; for I will assuredly reach truth if I only fix my attention sufficiently on all the things I conceive perfectly, and separate these from others which I conceive more confusedly and obscurely: to which for the future I shall give diligent heed.

Meditation V: Of the Essence of Material Things and, Again, of God—That He Exists

Several other questions remain for consideration respecting the attributes of God and my own nature or mind. I will, however, on some other occasion perhaps resume the investigation of these. Meanwhile, as I have discovered what must be done and what avoided to arrive at the knowledge of truth, what I have chiefly to do is to essay to emerge from the state of doubt in which I have for some time been, and to discover whether anything can be known with certainty regarding material objects. But before considering whether such objects as I conceive exist without me, I must examine their ideas in so far as these are to be found in my consciousness, and discover which of them are distinct and which confused.

In the first place, I distinctly imagine that quantity which the philosophers commonly call continuous, or the extension in length, breadth, and depth that is in this quantity, or rather in the object to which it is attributed. Further, I can enumerate in it many diverse parts, and attribute to each of these all sorts of sizes, figures, situations, and local motions;

and, in fine, I can assign to each of these motions all degrees of duration. And I not only distinctly know these things when I thus consider them in general; but besides, by a little attention, I discover innumerable particulars respecting figures, numbers, motion, and the like, which are so evidently true, and so accordant with my nature, that when I now discover them I do not so much appear to learn anything new, as to call to remembrance what I before knew, or for the first time to remark what was before in my mind, but to which I had not hitherto directed my attention. And what I here find of most importance is, that I discover in my mind innumerable ideas of certain objects, which cannot be esteemed pure negations, although perhaps they possess no reality beyond my thought, and which are not framed by me though it may be in my power to think, or not to think them, but possess true and immutable natures of their own. As, for example, when I imagine a triangle, although there is not perhaps and never was in any place in the universe apart from my thought one such figure, it remains true nevertheless that this figure possesses a certain determinate nature, form, or essence, which is immutable and eternal, and not framed by me, nor in any degree dependent on my thought; as appears from the circumstance, that diverse properties of the triangle may be demonstrated, viz., that its three angles are equal to two right, that its greatest side is subtended by its greatest angle, and the like, which, whether I will or not, I now clearly discern to belong to it, although before I did not at all think of them, when, for the first time, I imagined a triangle, and which accordingly cannot be said to have been invented by me. Nor is it a valid objection to allege, that perhaps this idea of a triangle came into my mind by the medium of the senses, through my having seen bodies of a triangular figure; for I am able to form in thought an innumerable variety of figures with regard to which it cannot be supposed that they were ever objects of sense, and I can nevertheless demonstrate diverse properties of their nature no less than of the triangle, all of which are assuredly true since I clearly conceive them: and they are therefore something, and not mere negations;

for it is highly evident that all that is true is something; and I have already fully shown the truth of the principle, that whatever is clearly and distinctly known is true. And although this had not been demonstrated, yet the nature of my mind is such as to compel me to assent to what I clearly conceive while I so conceive it; and I recollect that even when I still strongly adhered to the objects of sense, I reckoned among the number of the most certain truths those I clearly conceived relating to figures, numbers, and other matters that pertain to arithmetic and geometry, and in general to the pure mathematics.

But now if because I can draw from my thought the idea of an object, it follows that all I clearly and distinctly apprehend to pertain to this object, does in truth belong to it, may I not from this derive an argument for the existence of God? It is certain that I no less find the idea of a God in my consciousness, that is, the idea of a being supremely perfect, than that of any figure or number whatever: and I know with not less clearness and distinctness that an [actual and] eternal existence pertains to his nature than that all which is demonstrable of any figure or number really belongs to the nature of that figure or number; and, therefore, although all the conclusions of the preceding Meditations were false, the existence of God would pass with me for a truth at least as certain as I ever judged any truth of mathematics to be, although indeed such a doctrine may at first sight appear to contain more sophistry than truth. For, as I have been accustomed in every other matter to distinguish between existence and essence, I easily believe that the existence can be separated from the essence of God, and that thus God may be conceived as not actually existing. But, nevertheless, when I think of it more attentively, it appears that the existence can no more be separated from the essence of God, than the idea of a mountain from that of a valley, or the equality of its three angles to two right angles, from the essence of a triangle; so that it is not less impossible to conceive a God, that is, a being supremely perfect, to whom existence is awanting, or who is devoid of a certain perfection, than to conceive a mountain without a valley.

But though, in truth, I cannot conceive a God unless as existing, any more than I can a mountain without a valley, yet, just as it does not follow that there is any mountain in the world merely because I conceive a mountain with a valley, so likewise, though I conceive God as existing, it does not seem to follow on that account that God exists; for my thought imposes no necessity on things; and as I may imagine a winged horse, though there be none such, so I could perhaps attribute existence to God, though no God existed. But the cases are not analogous, and a fallacy lurks under the semblance of this objection: for because I cannot conceive a mountain without a valley, it does not follow that there is any mountain or valley in existence, but simply that the mountain or valley, whether they do or do not exist, are inseparable from each other; whereas, on the other hand, because I cannot conceive God unless as existing, it follows that existence is inseparable from him, and therefore that he really exists: not that this is brought about by my thought, or that it imposes any necessity on things, but, on the contrary, the necessity which lies in the thing itself, that is, the necessity of the existence of God, determines me to think in this way: for it is not in my power to conceive a God without existence, that is, a being supremely perfect, and yet devoid of an absolute perfection, as I am free to imagine a horse with or without wings.

Nor must it be alleged here as an objection, that it is in truth necessary to admit that God exists, after having supposed him to possess all perfections, since existence is one of them, but that my original supposition was not necessary; just as it is not necessary to think that all quadrilateral figures can be inscribed in the circle, since, if I supposed this, I should be constrained to admit that the rhombus, being a figure of four sides, can be therein inscribed, which, however, is manifestly false. This objection is, I say, incompetent; for although it may not be necessary that I shall at any time entertain the notion of Deity, yet each time I happen to think of a first and sovereign being, and to draw, so to speak, the idea of him from the storehouse of the mind, I am necessitated to attribute to him all kinds of perfections, though I may not then enumerate them all, nor think of each of them in particular. And this necessity is sufficient, as soon as I discover that existence is a perfection, to cause me to infer the existence of this first and sovereign being: just as it is not necessary that I should ever imagine any triangle, but whenever I am desirous of considering a rectilineal figure composed of only three angles, it is absolutely necessary to attribute those properties to it from which it is correctly inferred that its three angles are not greater than two right angles, although perhaps I may not then advert to this relation in particular. But when I consider what figures are capable of being inscribed in the circle, it is by no means necessary to hold that all quadrilateral figures are of this number; on the contrary, I cannot even imagine such to be the case, so long as I shall be unwilling to accept in thought aught that I do not clearly and distinctly conceive: and consequently there is a vast difference between false suppositions, as is the one in question, and the true ideas that were born with me, the first and chief of which is the idea of God. For indeed I discern on many grounds that this idea is not factitious, depending simply on my thought, but that it is the representation of a true and immutable nature: in the first place, because I can conceive no other being, except God, to whose essence existence pertains; in the second, because it is impossible to conceive two or more gods of this kind; and it being supposed that one such God exists, I clearly see that he must have existed from all eternity, and will exist to all eternity; and finally, because I apprehend many other properties in God, none of which I can either diminish or change.

But, indeed, whatever mode of probation I in the end adopt, it always returns to this, that it is only the things I clearly and distinctly conceive which have the power of completely persuading me. And although, of the objects I conceive in this manner, some, indeed, are obvious to every one, while others are only discovered after close and careful investigation; nevertheless, after they are once discovered, the latter are not esteemed less certain than the former. Thus, for example, to take the case of a right-angled triangle, although it is not so manifest at first that the square of the base is equal to the squares of the other two sides, as that the base is opposite to the greatest angle; nevertheless, after it is once apprehended, we are as firmly persuaded of the truth of the former as of the latter. And, with respect to God, if I were not pre-occupied by prejudices, and my thought beset on all sides by the continual presence of the images of sensible objects, I should know nothing sooner or more easily than the fact of his being. For is there any truth more clear than the existence of a Supreme Being, or of God, seeing it is to his essence alone that existence pertains? And although the right conception of this truth has cost me much close thinking, nevertheless at present I feel not only as assured of it as of what I deem most certain, but I remark further that the certitude of all other truths is so absolutely dependent on it, that without this knowledge it is impossible ever to know anything perfectly.

For although I am of such a nature as to be unable, while I possess a very clear and distinct apprehension of a matter, to resist the conviction of its truth, yet because my constitution is also such as to incapacitate me from keeping my mind continually fixed on the same object, and as I frequently recollect a past judgment without at the same time being able to recall the grounds of it, it may happen meanwhile that other reasons are presented to me which would readily cause me to change my opinion, if I did not know that God existed; and thus I should possess no true and certain knowledge, but merely vague and vacillating opinions. Thus, for example, when I consider the nature of the triangle, it most clearly appears to me, who have been instructed in the principles of geometry, that its three angles are equal to two right angles, and I find it impossible to believe otherwise, while I apply my mind to the demonstration; but as soon as I cease from attending to the process of proof, although I still remember that I had a clear comprehension of it, yet I may readily come to doubt of the truth demonstrated, if I do not know that there is a God: for I may persuade myself that I have been so constituted by nature as to be sometimes deceived, even in matters which I think I apprehend with the greatest evidence and certitude, especially when I recollect that I frequently considered many things to be true and certain which other reasons afterwards constrained me to reckon as wholly false.

But after I have discovered that God exists, seeing I also at the same time observed that all things depend on him, and that he is no deceiver, and thence inferred that all which I clearly and distinctly perceive is of necessity true; although I no longer attend to the grounds of a judgment, no opposite reason can be alleged sufficient to lead me to doubt of its truth, provided only I remember that I once possessed a clear and distinct comprehension of it. My knowledge of it thus becomes true and certain. And this same knowledge extends likewise to whatever I remember to have formerly demonstrated, as the truths of geometry and the like: for what can be alleged against them to lead me to doubt of them? Will it be that my nature is such that I may be frequently deceived? But I already know that I cannot be deceived in judgments of the grounds of which I possess a clear knowledge. Will it be that I formerly deemed things to be true and certain which I afterwards discovered to be false? But I had no clear and distinct knowledge of any of those things, and, being as yet ignorant of the rule by which I am assured of the truth of a judgment, I was led to give my assent to them on grounds which I afterwards discovered were less strong than at the time I imagined them to be. What further objection, then, is there? Will it be said that perhaps I am dreaming, or that all the thoughts of which I am now conscious have no more truth than the reveries of my dreams? But although, in truth, I should be dreaming, the rule still holds that all which is clearly presented to my intellect is indisputably true.

And thus I very clearly see that the certitude and truth of all science depends on the knowledge alone of the true God, insomuch that, before I knew him, I could have no perfect knowledge of any other thing. And now that I know him, I possess the means of acquiring a perfect knowledge respecting innumerable matters, as well relative to God himself and other intellectual objects as to corporeal nature, in so far as it is the object of pure mathematics.

Meditation VI: Of the Existence of Material Things and of the Real Distinction Between the Mind and Body of Man

There now only remains the inquiry as to whether material things exist. With regard to this question, I at least know with certainty that such things may exist, in as far as they constitute the object of the pure mathematics, since, regarding them in this aspect, I can conceive them clearly and distinctly. For there can be no doubt that God possesses the power of producing all the objects I am able distinctly to conceive, and I never considered anything impossible to him, unless when I experienced a contradiction in the attempt to conceive it aright. Further, the faculty of imagination which I possess, and of which I am conscious that I make use when I apply myself to the consideration of material things, is sufficient to persuade me of their existence: for, when I attentively consider what imagination is, I find that it is simply a certain application of the cognitive faculty to a body which is immediately present to it, and which therefore exists.

And to render this quite clear, I remark, in the first place, the difference that subsists between imagination and pure intellection. For example, when I imagine a triangle I not only conceive that it is a figure comprehended by three lines, but at the same time also I look upon these three lines as present by the power and internal application of my mind, and this is what I call imagining. But if I desire to think of a chiliogon, I indeed rightly conceive that it is a figure composed of a thousand sides, as easily as I conceive that a triangle is a figure composed of only three sides; but I cannot imagine the thousand sides of a chiliogon as I do the three sides of a triangle, nor, so to speak, view them as present. And although, in accordance with the habit I have of always imagining something when I think of corporeal things, it may happen that, in conceiving a chiliogon, I confusedly represent some figure to myself, yet it is quite evident that this is not a chiliogon, since it in no wise differs from that which I would represent to myself, if I were to think of a myriogon, or any other figure of many sides; nor would this representation be of any use in discovering and unfolding the properties that constitute the difference between a chiliogon and other polygons. But if the question turns on a pentagon, it is quite true that I can conceive its figure, as well as that of a chiliogon, without the aid of imagination; but I can likewise imagine it by applying the attention of my mind to its five sides, and at the same time to the area which they contain. Thus I observe that a special effort of mind is necessary to the act of imagination, which is not required to conceiving or understanding; and this special exertion of mind clearly shows the difference between imagination and pure intellection. I remark, besides, that this power of imagination which I possess, in as far as it differs from the power of conceiving, is in no way necessary to my essence, that is, to the essence of my mind; for although I did not possess it, I should still remain the same that I now am, from which it seems we may conclude that it depends on something different from the mind. And I easily understand that, if some body exists, with which my mind is so conjoined and united as to be able, as it were, to consider it when it chooses, it may thus imagine corporeal objects; so that this mode of thinking differs from pure intellection only in this respect, that the mind in conceiving turns in some way upon itself, and considers some one of the ideas it possesses within itself; but in imagining it turns towards the body, and contemplates in it some object conformed to the idea which it either of itself conceived or apprehended by sense. I easily understand, I say, that imagination may be thus formed, if it is true that there are bodies; and because I find no other obvious mode of explaining it, I thence, with probability, conjecture that they exist, but only with probability; and although I carefully examine all things, nevertheless I do not find that, from the distinct idea of corporeal nature I have in my imagination, I can necessarily infer the existence of any body.

But I am accustomed to imagine many other objects besides that corporeal nature which is the object of the pure mathematics, as, for example, colours, sounds, tastes, pain, and the like, although with less distinctness; and, inasmuch as I perceive these objects much better by the senses, through the medium of which and of memory, they seem to have reached the imagination, I believe that, in order the more advantageously to examine them, it is proper I should at the same time examine what sense-perception is, and inquire whether from those ideas that are apprehended by this mode of thinking, I cannot obtain a certain proof of the existence of corporeal objects.

And, in the first place, I will recall to my mind the things I have hitherto held as true, because perceived by the senses, and the foundations upon which my belief in their truth rested; I will, in the second place, examine the reasons that afterwards constrained me to doubt of them; and, finally, I will consider what of them I ought now to believe.

Firstly, then, I perceived that I had a head, hands, feet, and other members composing that body which I considered as part, or perhaps even as a whole, of myself. I perceived further, that that body was placed among many others, by which it was capable of being affected in diverse ways, both beneficial and hurtful; and what was beneficial I remarked by a certain sensation of pleasure, and what was hurtful by a sensation of pain. And, besides this pleasure and pain, I was likewise conscious of hunger, thirst, and other appetites, as well as certain corporeal inclinations towards joy, sadness, anger, and similar passions. And, out of myself, besides the extension, figure, and motions of bodies, I likewise perceived in them hardness, heat, and the other tactile qualities, and, in addition, light, colours, odours, tastes, and sounds, the variety of which gave me the means of distinguishing the sky, the earth, the sea, and generally all the other bodies, from one another. And certainly, considering the ideas of all these qualities, which were presented to my mind, and which alone I properly and immediately perceived, it was not without reason that I thought I perceived certain objects wholly different from my thought, namely, bodies from which those ideas proceeded; for I was conscious that the ideas were presented to me without my consent being required, so that I could not perceive any object, however desirous I might be, unless it were present to the organ of sense; and it was wholly out of my power not to perceive it when it was thus present. And because the ideas I perceived by the senses were much more lively and clear, and even, in their own way, more distinct than any of those I could of myself frame by meditation, or which I found impressed on my memory, it seemed that they could not have proceeded from myself, and must therefore have been caused in me by some other objects; and as of those objects I had no knowledge beyond what the ideas themselves gave me, nothing was so likely to occur to my mind as the supposition that the objects were similar to the ideas which they caused. And because I recollected also that I had formerly trusted to the senses, rather than to reason, and that the ideas which I myself formed were not so clear as those I perceived by sense, and that they were even for the most part composed of parts of the latter, I was readily persuaded that I had no idea in my intellect which had not formerly passed through the senses. Nor was I altogether wrong in likewise believing that that body which, by a special right, I called my own, pertained to me more properly and strictly than any of the others; for in truth, I could never be separated from it as from other bodies: I felt in it and on account of it all my appetites and affections, and in fine I was affected in its parts by pain and the titillation of pleasure, and not in the parts of the other bodies that were separated from it. But when I inquired into the reason why, from this I know not what sensation of pain, sadness of mind should follow, and why from the sensation of pleasure joy should arise, or why this indescribable twitching of the stomach, which I call hunger, should put me in mind of taking food, and the parchedness of the throat of drink, and so in other cases, I was unable to give any explanation, unless that I was so taught by nature; for there is assuredly no affinity, at least none that I am able to comprehend, between this irritation of the stomach and the desire of food, any more than

between the perception of an object that causes pain and the consciousness of sadness which springs from the perception. And in the same way it seemed to me that all the other judgments I had formed regarding the objects of sense, were dictates of nature; because I remarked that those judgments were formed in me, before I had leisure to weigh and consider the reasons that might constrain me to form them.

But, afterwards, a wide experience by degrees sapped the faith I had reposed in my senses; for I frequently observed that towers, which at a distance seemed round, appeared square when more closely viewed, and that colossal figures, raised on the summits of these towers, looked like small statues, when viewed from the bottom of them; and, in other instances without number, I also discovered error in judgments founded on the external senses; and not only in those founded on the external, but even in those that rested on the internal senses; for is there aught more internal than pain? and yet I have sometimes been informed by parties whose arm or leg had been amputated, that they still occasionally seemed to feel pain in that part of the body which they had lost,—a circumstance that led me to think that I could not be quite certain even that any one of my members was affected when I felt pain in it. And to these grounds of doubt I shortly afterwards also added two others of very wide generality: the first of them was that I believed I never perceived anything when awake which I could not occasionally think I also perceived when asleep, and as I do not believe that the ideas I seem to perceive in my sleep proceed from objects external to me, I did not any more observe any ground for believing this of such as I seem to perceive when awake; the second was that since I was as yet ignorant of the author of my being, or at least supposed myself to be so, I saw nothing to prevent my having been so constituted by nature as that I should be deceived even in matters that appeared to me to possess the greatest truth. And, with respect to the grounds on which I had before been persuaded of the existence of sensible objects, I had no great difficulty in finding suitable answers to them; for as nature seemed to incline me to many things from which reason made me averse, I thought that I ought not to confide much in its teachings. And although the perceptions of the senses were not dependent on my will, I did not think that I ought on that ground to conclude that they proceeded from things different from myself, since perhaps there might be found in me some faculty, though hitherto unknown to me, which produced them.

But now that I begin to know myself better, and to discover more clearly the author of my being, I do not, indeed, think that I ought rashly to admit all which the senses seem to teach, nor, on the other hand, is it my conviction that I ought to doubt in general of their teachings.

And, firstly, because I know that all which I clearly and distinctly conceive can be produced by God exactly as I conceive it, it is sufficient that I am able clearly and distinctly to conceive one thing apart from another, in order to be certain that the one is different from the other, seeing they may at least be made to exist separately, by the omnipotence of God; and it matters not by what power this separation is made, in order to be compelled to judge them different; and, therefore, merely because I know with certitude that I exist, and because, in the meantime, I do not observe that aught necessarily belongs to my nature or essence beyond my being a thinking thing, I rightly conclude that my essence consists only in my being a thinking thing, [or a substance whose whole essence or nature is merely thinking]. And although I may, or rather, as I will shortly say, although I certainly do possess a body with which I am very closely conjoined; nevertheless, because, on the one hand, I have a clear and distinct idea of myself, in as far as I am only a thinking and unextended thing, and as, on the other hand, I possess a distinct idea of body, in as far as it is only an extended and unthinking thing, it is certain that I, [that is, my mind, by which I am what I am], is entirely and truly distinct from my body, and may exist without it.

Moreover, I find in myself diverse faculties of thinking that have each their special mode: for example, I find I possess the faculties of imagining and perceiving, without which I can

indeed clearly and distinctly conceive myself as entire, but I cannot reciprocally conceive them without conceiving myself, that is to say, without an intelligent substance in which they reside, for [in the notion we have of them, or to use the terms of the schools] in their formal concept, they comprise some sort of intellection; whence I perceive that they are distinct from myself as modes are from things. I remark likewise certain other faculties, as the power of changing place, of assuming diverse figures, and the like, that cannot be conceived and cannot therefore exist, any more than the preceding, apart from a substance in which they inhere. It is very evident, however, that these faculties, if they really exist, must belong to some corporeal or extended substance, since in their clear and distinct concept there is contained some sort of extension, but no intellection at all. Farther, I cannot doubt but that there is in me a certain passive faculty of perception, that is, of receiving and taking knowledge of the ideas of sensible things; but this would be useless to me, if there did not also exist in me, or in some other thing, another active faculty capable of forming and producing those ideas. But this active faculty cannot be in me [in as far as I am but a thinking thing], seeing that it does not presuppose thought, and also that those ideas are frequently produced in my mind without my contributing to it in any way, and even frequently contrary to my will. This faculty must therefore exist in some substance different from me, in which all the objective reality of the ideas that are produced by this faculty, is contained formally or eminently, as I before remarked; and this substance is either a body, that is to say, a corporeal nature in which is contained formally [and in effect] all that is objectively [and by representation] in those ideas; or it is God himself, or some other creature, of a rank superior to body, in which the same is contained eminently. But as God is no deceiver, it is manifest that he does not of himself and immediately communicate those ideas to me, nor even by the intervention of any creature in which their objective reality is not formally, but only eminently, contained. For as he has given me no faculty whereby I can discover this to be the case, but, on the contrary, a very strong inclination to believe that those ideas arise from corporeal objects, I do not see how he could be vindicated from the charge of deceit, if in truth they proceeded from any other source, or were produced by other causes than corporeal things: and accordingly it must be concluded, that corporeal objects exist. Nevertheless they are not perhaps exactly such as we perceive by the senses, for their comprehension by the senses is, in many instances, very obscure and confused; but it is at least necessary to admit that all which I clearly and distinctly conceive as in them, that is, generally speaking, all that is comprehended in the object of speculative geometry, really exists external to me.

But with respect to other things which are either only particular, as, for example, that the sun is of such a size and figure, etc., or are conceived with less clearness and distinctness, as light, sound, pain, and the like, although they are highly dubious and uncertain, nevertheless on the ground alone that God is no deceiver, and that consequently he has permitted no falsity in my opinions which he has not likewise given me a faculty of correcting, I think I may with safety conclude that I possess in myself the means of arriving at the truth. And, in the first place, it cannot be doubted that in each of the dictates of nature there is some truth: for by nature, considered in general, I now understand nothing more than God himself, or the order and disposition established by God in created things; and by my nature in particular I understand the assemblage of all that God has given me.

But there is nothing which that nature teaches me more expressly [or more sensibly] than that I have a body which is ill affected when I feel pain, and stands in need of food and drink when I experience the sensations of hunger and thirst, etc. And therefore I ought not to doubt but that there is some truth in these informations.

Nature likewise teaches me by these sensations of pain, hunger, thirst, etc., that I am not only lodged in my body as a pilot in a vessel, but that I am besides so intimately conjoined, and as it were intermixed with it, that my mind and body compose a certain unity. For if this were not the case, I should not feel pain when my body is hurt, seeing I am merely a thinking thing, but should perceive the wound by the understanding alone, just as a pilot perceives by sight when any part of his vessel is damaged; and when my body has need of food or drink, I should have a clear knowledge of this, and not be made aware of it by the confused sensations of hunger and thirst; for, in truth, all these sensations of hunger, thirst, pain, etc., are nothing more than certain confused modes of thinking, arising from the union and apparent fusion of mind and body.

Besides this, nature teaches me that my own body is surrounded by many other bodies, some of which I have to seek after, and others to shun. And indeed, as I perceive different sorts of colours, sounds, odours, tastes, heat, hardness, etc., I safely conclude that there are in the bodies from which the diverse perceptions of the senses proceed, certain varieties corresponding to them, although, perhaps, not in reality like them; and since, among these diverse perceptions of the senses, some are agreeable, and others disagreeable, there can be no doubt that my body, or rather my entire self, in as far as I am composed of body and mind, may be variously affected, both beneficially and hurtfully, by surrounding bodies.

But there are many other beliefs which, though seemingly the teaching of nature, are not in reality so, but which obtained a place in my mind through a habit of judging inconsiderately of things. It may thus easily happen that such judgments shall contain error: thus, for example, the opinion I have that all space in which there is nothing to affect my senses is void; that in a hot body there is something in every respect similar to the idea of heat in my mind; that in a white or green body there is the same whiteness or greenness which I perceive; that in a bitter or sweet body there is the same taste, and so in other instances; that the stars, towers, and all distant bodies, are of the same size and figure as they appear to our eyes, etc. But that I may avoid everything like indistinctness of conception, I must accurately define what I properly understand by being taught by nature. For nature is here taken in a narrower sense than when it signifies the sum of all the things which God has given me; seeing that in that meaning the notion comprehends much that belongs only to the mind [to which I am not here to be understood as referring when I use the term nature]; as, for example, the notion I have of the truth, that what is done cannot be undone, and all the other truths I discern by the natural light; and seeing that it comprehends likewise much besides that belongs only to body, and is not here any more contained under the name nature, as the quality of heaviness, and the like, of which I do not speak,—the term being reserved exclusively to designate the things which God has given to me as a being composed of mind and body. But nature, taking the term in the sense explained, teaches me to shun what causes in me the sensation of pain, and to pursue what affords me the sensation of pleasure, and other things of this sort; but I do not discover that it teaches me, in addition to this, from these diverse perceptions of the senses, to draw any conclusions respecting external objects without a previous consideration of them by the mind; for it is, as appears to me, the office of the mind alone, and not of the composite whole of mind and body, to discern the truth in those matters. Thus, although the impression a star makes on my eye is not larger than that from the flame of a candle, I do not, nevertheless, experience any real or positive impulse determining me to believe that the star is not greater than the flame; the true account of the matter being merely that I have so judged from my youth without any rational ground. And, though on approaching the fire I feel heat, and even pain on approaching it too closely, I have, however, from this no ground for holding that something resembling the heat I feel is in the fire, any more than that there is something similar to the pain; all that I have ground for believing is, that there is something in it, whatever it may be, which excites in me those sensations of heat or pain. So also, although there are spaces in which I find nothing to excite and affect my senses, I must not therefore conclude that those spaces contain in them no body; for I see that in this, as in many other similar matters, I have been accustomed to pervert the order of nature, because these perceptions of the senses, although given me by nature merely to signify to my mind what things are beneficial and hurtful to the composite whole of which it is a part, and being sufficiently clear and distinct for that purpose, are nevertheless used by me as infallible rules by which to determine immediately the essence of the bodies that exist out of me, of which they can of course afford me only the most obscure and confused knowledge.

But I have already sufficiently considered how it happens that, notwithstanding the supreme goodness of God, there is falsity in my judgments. A difficulty, however, here presents itself, respecting the things which I am taught by nature must be pursued or avoided, and also respecting the internal sensations in which I seem to have occasionally detected error: Thus, for example, I may be so deceived by the agreeable taste of some viand with which poison has been mixed, as to be induced to take the poison. In this case, however, nature may be excused, for it simply leads me to desire the viand for its agreeable taste, and not the poison, which is unknown to it; and thus we can infer nothing from this circumstance beyond that our nature is not omniscient; at which there is assuredly no ground for surprise, since, man being of a finite nature, his knowledge must likewise be of limited perfection. But we also not unfrequently err in that to which we are directly impelled by nature, as is the case with invalids who desire drink or food that would be hurtful to them. It will here, perhaps, be alleged that the reason why such persons are deceived is that their nature is corrupted; but this leaves the difficulty untouched, for a sick man is not less really the creature of God than a man who is in full health; and therefore it is as repugnant to the goodness of God that the nature of the former should be deceitful as it is for that of the latter to be so. And, as a clock, composed of wheels and counter weights, observes not the less accurately all the laws of nature when it is ill made, and points out the hours incorrectly, than when it satisfies the desire of the maker in every respect; so likewise if the body of man be considered as a kind of machine, so made up and composed of bones, nerves, muscles, veins, blood, and skin, that although there were in it no mind, it would still exhibit the same motions which it at present manifests involuntarily, and therefore without the aid of the mind, I easily discern that it would also be as natural for such a body, supposing it dropsical, for example, to experience the parchedness of the throat that is usually accompanied in the mind by the sensation of thirst, and to be disposed by this parchedness to move its nerves and its other parts in the way required for drinking, and thus increase its malady and do itself harm, as it is natural for it, when it is not indisposed to be stimulated to drink for its good by a similar cause; and although looking to the use for which a clock was destined by its maker, I may say that it is deflected from its proper nature when it incorrectly indicates the hours, and on the same principle, considering the machine of the human body as having been formed by God for the sake of the motions which it usually manifests, although I may likewise have ground for thinking that it does not follow the order of its nature when the throat is parched and drink does not tend to its preservation, nevertheless I yet plainly discern that this latter acceptation of the term nature is very different from the other; for this is nothing more than a certain denomination, depending entirely on my thought, and hence called extrinsic, by which I compare a sick man and an imperfectly constructed clock with the idea I have of a man in good health and a well made clock; while by the other acceptation of nature is understood something which is truly found in things, and therefore possessed of some truth.

But certainly, although in respect of a dropsical body, it is only by way of exterior denomination that we say its nature is corrupted, when, without requiring drink, the throat is parched; yet, in respect of the composite whole, that is, of the mind in its union with the body, it is not a pure denomination, but really an error of nature, for it to feel thirst when drink would be hurtful to it: and, accordingly, it still remains to be considered why it is that the goodness of God does not prevent the nature of man thus taken from being fallacious.

To commence this examination accordingly, I here remark, in the first place, that there is a vast difference between mind and body, in respect that body, from its nature, is always divisible, and that mind is entirely indivisible. For in truth, when I consider the mind, that is, when I consider myself in so far only as I am a thinking thing, I can distinguish in myself no parts, but I very clearly discern that I am somewhat absolutely one and entire; and although the whole mind seems to be united to the whole body, yet, when a foot, an arm, or any other part is cut off, I am conscious that nothing has been taken from my mind; nor can the faculties of willing, perceiving, conceiving, etc., properly be called its parts, for it is the same mind that is exercised [all entire] in willing, in perceiving, and in conceiving, etc. But quite the opposite holds in corporeal or extended things; for I cannot imagine any one of them [how small soever it may be], which I cannot easily sunder in thought, and which, therefore, I do not know to be divisible. This would be sufficient to teach me that the mind or soul of man is entirely different from the body, if I had not already been apprised of it on other grounds.

I remark, in the next place, that the mind does not immediately receive the impression from all the parts of the body, but only from the brain, or perhaps even from one small part of it, viz., that in which the common sense is said to be, which as often as it is affected in the same way, gives rise to the same perception in the mind, although meanwhile the other parts of the body may be diversely disposed, as is proved by innumerable experiments, which it is unnecessary here to enumerate.

I remark, besides, that the nature of body is such that none of its parts can be moved by another part a little removed from the other, which cannot likewise be moved in the same way by any one of the parts that lie between those two, although the most remote part does not act at all. As, for example, in the cord A, B, C, D, if its last part D, be pulled, the first part A, will not be moved in a different way than it would be were one of the intermediate parts B or C to be pulled, and the last part D meanwhile to remain fixed. And in the same way, when I feel pain in the foot, the science of physics teaches me that this sensation is experienced by means of the nerves dispersed over the foot, which, extending like cords from it to the brain, when they are contracted in the foot, contract at the same time the inmost parts of the brain in which they have their origin, and excite in these parts a certain motion appointed by nature to cause in the mind a sensation of pain, as if existing in the foot: but as these nerves must pass through the tibia, the leg, the loins, the back, and neck, in order to reach the brain, it may happen that although their extremities in the foot are not affected, but only certain of their parts that pass through the loins or neck, the same movements, nevertheless, are excited in the brain by this motion as would have been caused there by a hurt received in the foot, and hence the mind will necessarily feel pain in the foot, just as if it had been hurt; and the same is true of all the other perceptions of our senses.

I remark, finally, that as each of the movements that are made in the part of the brain by which the mind is immediately affected, impresses it with but a single sensation, the most likely supposition in the circumstances is, that this movement causes the mind to experience, among all the sensations which it is capable of impressing upon it, that one which is the best fitted, and generally the most useful for the preservation of the human body when it is in full health. But experience shows us that all the perceptions which nature has given us are of such a kind as I have mentioned; and accordingly, there is nothing found in them that does not manifest the power and goodness of God. Thus, for example, when the nerves of the foot are violently or more than usually shaken, the motion passing through the medulla of the spine to the innermost parts of the brain affords a sign to the mind on which it experiences a sensation, viz., of pain, as if it were in the foot, by which the mind is admonished and excited to do its utmost to remove the cause of it as dangerous and hurtful to the foot. It is true that God could have so constituted the nature of man as that the same motion in the brain would have informed the mind of something altogether different: the motion might, for example, have been the occasion on which the mind became conscious of itself, in so far as it is in the brain, or in so far as it is in some place intermediate between the

foot and the brain, or, finally, the occasion on which it perceived some other object quite different; whatever that might be; but nothing of all this would have so well contributed to the preservation of the body as that which the mind actually feels. In the same way, when we stand in need of drink, there arises from this want a certain parchedness in the throat that moves its nerves, and by means of them the internal parts of the brain; and this movement affects the mind with the sensation of thirst, because there is nothing on that occasion which is more useful for us than to be made aware that we have need of drink for the preservation of our health; and so in other instances.

Whence it is quite manifest that, notwithstanding the sovereign goodness of God, the nature of man, in so far as it is composed of mind and body, cannot but be sometimes fallacious. For, if there is any cause which excites, not in the foot, but in some one of the parts of the nerves that stretch from the foot to the brain, or even in the brain itself, the same movement that is ordinarily created when the foot is ill affected, pain will be felt, as it were, in the foot, and the sense will thus be naturally deceived; for as the same movement in the brain can but impress the mind with the same sensation, and as this sensation is much more frequently excited by a cause which hurts the foot than by one acting in a different quarter, it is reasonable that it should lead the mind to feel pain in the foot rather than in any other part of the body. And if it sometimes happens that the parchedness of the throat does not arise, as is usual, from drink being necessary for the health of the body, but from quite the opposite cause, as is the case with the dropsical, yet it is much better that it should be deceitful in that instance, than if, on the contrary, it were continually fallacious when the body is well-disposed; and the same holds true in other cases.

And certainly this consideration is of great service, not only in enabling me to recognize the errors to which my nature is liable, but likewise in rendering it more easy to avoid or correct them: for, knowing that all my senses more usually indicate to me what is true than what is false, in matters relating to the advantage of the body, and being able almost always to make use of more than a single sense in examining the same object, and besides this, being able to use my memory in connecting present with past knowledge, and my understanding which has already discovered all the causes of my errors, I ought no longer to fear that falsity may be met with in what is daily presented to me by the senses. And I ought to reject all the doubts of those bygone days, as hyperbolical and ridiculous, especially the general uncertainty respecting sleep, which I could not distinguish from the waking state: for I now find a very marked difference between the two states, in respect that our memory can never connect our dreams with each other and with the course of life, in the way it is in the habit of doing with events that occur when we are awake. And, in truth, if some one, when I am awake, appeared to me all of a sudden and as suddenly disappeared, as do the images I see in sleep, so that I could not observe either whence he came or whither he went, I should not without reason esteem it either a spectre or phantom formed in my brain, rather than a real man. But when I perceive objects with regard to which I can distinctly determine both the place whence they come, and that in which they are, and the time at which they appear to me, and when, without interruption, I can connect the perception I have of them with the whole of the other parts of my life, I am perfectly sure that what I thus perceive occurs while I am awake and not during sleep. And I ought not in the least degree to doubt of the truth of those presentations, if, after having called together all my senses, my memory, and my understanding for the purpose of examining them, no deliverance is given by any one of these faculties which is repugnant to that of any other: for since God is no deceiver, it necessarily follows that I am not herein deceived. But because the necessities of action frequently oblige us to come to a determination before we have had leisure for so careful an examination, it must be confessed that the life of man is frequently obnoxious to error with respect to individual objects; and we must, in conclusion, acknowledge the weakness of our nature.

IV
Thomas Hobbes

THOMAS HOBBES (1588–1679) decided to become a philosopher when, one day in the library, he came across the Pythagorean Theorem, studied it, and—in a flash of insight—was seduced by geometry and the power of reason into spending the rest of his life trying to understand the world. Educated at Oxford University, Hobbes fled the country when England was torn by civil strife. He went to France, where he ended up reading Descartes' *Meditations* before its publication. The work looked to him so derivative of Plato that his first response was to say "I am sorry that so excellent an author of new speculations should publish this old stuff." Descartes published all of Hobbes' objections, along with his own rebuttals.

Ten years later, in 1651, Hobbes published his own masterwork, *Leviathan*. Like Descartes, he developed a method of inquiry, but his ran along a different path. Hobbes called his method, which was influenced not only by Descartes but also by Galileo, *resolution and composition*. Like Descartes' second rule for the direction of the mind, which itself is based on Plato's division of ideas, *resolution* involves analysis of complex wholes into simpler elements. Like Descartes' third rule, *composition consists in synthesis*, or putting back together the parts into a whole. But the similarities end there. Whereas Descartes argued that the mind is something completely separate and distinct from the body, and not reducible to physical elements, Hobbes maintained that the mind is not separate from the body; rather, like the body, it is itself a purely physical thing.

In the first reading, each of Hobbes' objections is followed, in italics, by Descartes' response. As was his style, Descartes does not mention Hobbes directly by name. The second selection is from Hobbes' *Leviathan*, in which he distinguishes two different functions of the mind: (1) sense, imagination, and the movements arising from them; (2) ratiocination—calculation, using words, of the causes of phenomena. The former is natural, and the latter is artificial in that it depends on the manipulation of language and the naming of things. Philosophy's main concern is with the latter.

Objections to Descartes' *Meditations*

Thomas Hobbes

First Objection

(In reference to the first Meditation: *Concerning those matters that may be brought within the sphere of the doubtful.*)

It is sufficiently obvious from what is said in this Meditation, that we have no criterion for distinguishing dreaming from waking and from what the senses truly tell us; and that hence the images present to us when we are awake and using our senses are not accidents inhering in external objects, and fail to prove that such external objects do as a fact exist. And therefore, if we follow our senses without using any train of reasoning, we shall be justified in doubting whether or not anything exists. Hence we acknowledge the truth of this Meditation. But, since Plato and other ancient Philosophers have talked about this want of certitude in the matters of sense, and since the difficulty in distinguishing the waking state from dreams is a matter of common observation, I should have been glad if our author, so distinguished in the handling of modern speculations, had refrained from publishing those matters of ancient lore.

Reply

The reasons for doubt here admitted as true by this Philosopher were propounded by me only as possessing verisimilitude, and my reason for employing them was not that I might retail them as new, but partly that I might prepare my readers' minds for the study of

SOURCE: *Objections to Descartes'* Meditations by Thomas Hobbes, translated by Elizabeth S. Haldane and G. R. T. Ross (Cambridge: Cambridge University Press, 1911).

intellectual matters and for distinguishing them from matters corporeal, a purpose for which such arguments seem wholly necessary; in part also because I intended to reply to these very arguments in the subsequent Meditations; and partly in order to show the strength of the truths I afterwards propound, by the fact that such metaphysical doubts cannot shake them. Hence, while I have sought no praise from their rehearsal, I believe that it was impossible for me to omit them, as impossible as it would be for a medical writer to omit the description of a disease when trying to teach the method of curing it.

Objection II

(In opposition to the second Meditation: *Concerning the nature of the Human Mind.*)

I am a thing that thinks; *quite correct. From the fact that I think, or have an image, whether sleeping or waking, it is inferred that I am exercising thought; for* I think and I am exercising thought *mean the same thing. From the fact that I am exercising thought it follows that* I am, *since that which thinks is not nothing. But, where it is added,* this is the mind, the spirit, the understanding, the reason, *a doubt arises. For it does not seem to be good reasoning to say:* I am exercising thought, *hence* I am thought; *or* I am using my intellect, *hence* I am intellect. *For in the same way I might say,* I am walking; *hence* I am the walking. *It is hence an assumption on the part of M. Descartes that that which understands is the same as the exercise of understanding which is an act of that which understands, or, at least, that that which understands is the same as the understanding, which is a power possessed by that which thinks. Yet all Philosophers distinguish a subject from its faculties and activities, i.e. from its properties and essences; for the* entity *itself is one thing, its* essence *another. Hence it is possible for a thing that thinks to be the subject of the mind, reason, or understanding, and hence to be something corporeal; and the opposite of this has been assumed, not proved. Yet this inference is the basis of the conclusion that M. Descartes seems to wish to establish.*

In the same place he says, I know that I exist; the question is, who am I—the being that I know? *It is certain that the knowledge of this being thus accurately determined does not depend on those things which I do not yet know to exist.*

It is quite certain that the knowledge of this proposition, I exist, *depends upon that other one,* I think, *as he has himself correctly shown us. But whence comes our knowledge of this proposition,* I think? *Certainly from that fact alone, that we can conceive no activity whatsoever apart from its subject, e.g. we cannot think of leaping apart from that which leaps, of knowing apart from a knower, or of thinking without a thinker.*

And hence it seems to follow that that which thinks is something corporeal; for, as it appears, the subjects of all activities can be conceived only after a corporeal fashion, or as a material guise, as M. Descartes himself afterwards shows, when he illustrates by means of wax, this wax was understood to be always the same thing, i.e. the identical matter underlying the many successive changes, though its colour, consistency, figure, and other activities were altered. Moreover it is not by another thought that I infer that I think; for though anyone may think that he has thought (to think so is precisely the same as remembering), yet we cannot think that we are thinking, nor similarly know that we know. For this would entail the repetition of the question an infinite number of times: whence do you know, that you know, that you know, that you know?

Hence, since the knowledge of this proposition, I exist, *depends upon the knowledge of that other,* I think, *and the knowledge of it upon the fact that we cannot separate thought from a matter that thinks, the proper inference seems to be that that which thinks is material rather than immaterial.*

Reply

Where I have said, *this is the mind, the spirit, the intellect, or the reason,* I understood by these names not merely faculties, but rather what is endowed with the faculty of thinking; and this sense the two former terms commonly, the latter frequently bear. But I used them in this sense so expressly and in so may places that I cannot see what occasion there was for any doubt about their meaning.

Further, there is here no parity between walking and thinking; for walking is usually held to refer only to that action itself, while thinking applies now to the action, now to the faculty of thinking, and again to that in which the faculty exists.

Again I do not assert that that which understands and the activity of understanding are the same thing, nor indeed do I mean that the thing that understands and the understanding are the same, if the term understanding be taken to refer to the faculty of understanding; they are identical only when the understanding means the thing itself that understands. I admit also quite gladly that, in order to designate that thing or substance, which I wished to strip of everything that did not belong to it, I employed the most highly abstract terms I could; just as, on the contrary this Philosopher uses terms that are as concrete as possible, e.g. *subject, matter, body,* to signify that which thinks, fearing to let it be sundered from the body.

But I have no fear of anyone thinking that his method of coupling diverse things together is better adapted to the discovery of the truth than mine, that gives the greatest possible distinctness to every single thing. But, dropping the verbal controversy, let us look to the facts in dispute.

A thing that thinks, he says, *may be something corporeal; and the opposite of this has been assumed; not proved.* But really I did not assume the opposite, neither did I use it as a basis for my argument; I left it wholly undetermined until Meditation VI, in which its proof is given.

Next he quite correctly says, that *we cannot conceive any activity apart from its subject,* e.g. thought apart from that which thinks, since that which thinks is not nothing. But, wholly without any reason, and in opposition to the ordinary use of language and good Logic, he adds, *hence it seems to follow that that which thinks is something corporeal; for the subjects of all activi-*

ties are indeed *understood as falling within the sphere of substance* (or even, if you care, *as wearing the guise of matter,* viz. metaphysical matter), but not on that account are they to be defined as bodies.

On the other hand both logicians and as a rule all men are wont to say that substances are of two kinds, spiritual and corporeal. And all that I proved, when I took wax as an example, was that its colour, hardness, and figure did not belong to the formal nature of the wax itself. I did not there treat either of the formal nature of the mind, or even of the formal nature of body.

Again it is irrelevant to say, as this Philosopher here does, that one thought cannot be the subject of another thought. Who, except my antagonist himself, even imagined that it could? But now, for a brief explanation of the matter,—it is certain that no thought can exist apart from a thing that thinks; no activity, no accident can be without a substance in which to exist. Moreover, since we do not apprehend the substance itself immediately through itself, but by means only of the fact that it is the subject of certain activities, it is highly rational, and a requirement forced on us by custom, to give diverse names to those substances that we recognize to be the subjects of clearly diverse activities or accidents, and afterwards to inquire whether those diverse names refer to one and the same or to diverse things. But there are *certain* activities, which we call *corporeal,* e.g. magnitude, figure, motion, and all those that cannot be thought of apart from extension in space; and the substance in which they exist is called *body.* It cannot be pretended that the substance that is the subject of figure is different from that which is the subject of spatial motion, etc., since all these activities agree in presupposing extension. Further, there are other activities, which we call *thinking* activities, e.g. understanding, willing, imagining, feeling, etc., which agree in falling under the description of thought, perception, or consciousness. The substance in which they reside we call a *thinking thing* or *the mind,* or any other name we care, provided only we do not confound it with corporeal substance, since thinking activities have no affinity with corporeal activities, and thought, which is the common

nature in which the former agree, is totally different from extension, the common term for describing the latter.

But after we have formed two distinct concepts of those two substances, it is easy, from what has been said in the sixth Meditation, to determine whether they are one and the same or distinct.

Objection III

What then is there distinct from my thought? What can be said to be separate from me myself?

Perchance some one will answer the question thus—I, the very self that thinks, am held to be distinct from my own thought; and, though it is not really separate from me, my thought is held to be diverse from me, just in the way (as has been said before) that leaping is distinguished from the leaper. But if M. Descartes shows that he who understands and the understanding are identical we shall lapse back into the scholastic mode of speaking. The understanding understands, the vision sees, will wills, and by exact analogy, walking, or at least the faculty of walking will walk. Now all this is obscure, incorrect, and quite unworthy of M. Descartes' wonted clearness.

Reply

I do not deny that I, the thinker, am distinct from my own thought, in the way in which a thing is distinct from its mode. But when I ask, *what then is there distinct from my thought,* this is to be taken to refer to the various modes of thought there recounted, not to my substance; and when I add, *what can be said to be separate from me myself,* I mean only that these modes of thinking exist entirely in me. I cannot see on what pretext the imputation here of doubt and obscurity rests.

Objection IV

Hence it is left for me to concede that I do not even understand by the imagination what this wax is, but conceive it by the mind alone.

There is a great difference between imagining, i.e. having some idea, and conceiving with the mind, i.e. inferring, as the result of a train of reasoning, that something is, or exists. But M. Descartes has not explained to us the sense in which they differ. The ancient peripatetics also have taught clearly enough that substance is not perceived by the senses, but is known as a result of reasoning.

But what shall we now say, if reasoning chance to be nothing more than the uniting and stringing together of names or designations by the word is? It will be a consequence of this that reason gives us no conclusion about the nature of things, but only about the terms that designate them, whether, indeed, or not there is a convention (arbitrarily made about their meanings) according to which we join these names together. If this be so, as is possible, reasoning will depend on names, names on the imagination, and imagination, perchance, as I think, on the motion of the corporeal organs. Thus mind will be nothing but the motions in certain parts of an organic body.

Reply

I have here explained the difference between imagination and a pure mental concept, as when in my illustration I enumerated the features in wax that were given by the imagination and those solely due to a conception of the mind. But elsewhere also I have explained how it is that one and the same thing, e.g. a pentagon, is one way an object of the understanding, in another way of the imagination. Moreover, in reasoning we unite not names but the things signified by the names; and I marvel that the opposite can occur to anyone. For who doubts whether a Frenchman and a German are able to reason in exactly the same way about the same things, though they yet conceive the words in an entirely diverse way? And has not my opponent condemned himself in talking of conventions arbitrarily made about the meanings of words? For, if he admits that words signify anything, why will he not allow our reasonings to refer to this something that is signified, rather than to the words alone? But, really, it will be as correct to infer that earth is heaven or anything else that is desired, as to conclude that mind is motion.

Objection V

In reference to the third Meditation—concerning God—some of these (thoughts of man) are, so to speak, images of things, and to these alone is the title 'idea' properly applied; examples are my thought of a man, or of a Chimera, of Heavens, of an Angel, or of God.

When I think of a man, I recognize an idea, or image, with figure and colour as its constituents; and concerning this I can raise the question whether or not it is the likeness of a man. So it is also when I think of the heavens. When I think of the chimera, I recognize an idea or image, being able at the same time to doubt whether or not it is the likeness of an animal, which, though it does not exist, may yet exist or has at some other time existed.

But, when one thinks of an Angel, what is noticed in the mind is now the image of a flame, now that of a fair winged child, and this, I may be sure, has no likeness to an Angel, and hence is not the idea of an Angel. But believing that created beings exist that are the ministers of God, invisible and immaterial, we give the name of Angel to this object of belief, this supposed being, though the idea used in imagining an Angel is, nevertheless, constructed out of the ideas of visible things.

It is the same way with the most holy name of God; we have no image, no idea corresponding to it. Hence we are forbidden to worship God in the form of an image, lest we should think we could conceive Him who is inconceivable.

Hence it appears that we have no idea of God. But just as one born blind who has frequently been brought close to a fire and has felt himself growing warm, recognizes that there is something which made him warm, and, if he hears it called fire, concludes that fire exists, though he has no acquaintance with its shape or colour, and has no idea of fire nor image that he can discover in his mind; so a man, recognizing that there must be some cause of his images and ideas, and another previous cause of this cause and so on continuously, is finally carried on to a conclusion, or to the supposition of some eternal cause, which, never having begun to be, can have no cause prior to it: and hence he necessarily concludes that something eternal exists. But nevertheless he has no idea that he can assert to be that of this eternal being, and he merely gives a name to the object of his faith or reasoning and calls it God.

Since now it is from this position, viz. that there is an idea of God in our soul, that M. Descartes proceeds to prove the theorem that God (an all-powerful, all-wise Being, the creator of the world) exists, he should have explained this idea of God better, and he should have deduced from it not only God's existence, but also the creation of the world.

Reply

Here the meaning assigned to the term idea is merely that of images depicted in the corporeal imagination; and, that being agreed on, it is easy for my critic to prove that there is no proper idea of Angel or of God. But I have, everywhere, from time to time, and principally in this place, shown that I take the term idea to stand for whatever the mind directly perceives; and so when I will or when I fear, since at the same time I perceive that I will and fear, that very volition and apprehension are ranked among my ideas. I employed this term because it was the term currently used by Philosophers for the forms of perception of the Divine mind, though we can discover no imagery in God; besides I had no other more suitable term. But I think I have sufficiently well explained what the idea of God is for those who care to follow my meaning; those who prefer to wrest my words from the sense I give them, I can never satisfy. The objection that here follows, relative to the creation of the world, is plainly irrelevant.

Objection VI

But other *(thoughts)* possess other forms as well. For example, in willing, fearing, affirming, denying, though I always perceive something as the subject of my thought, yet in my thought I embrace something more than the similitude of that thing; and, of the thoughts of this kind, some are called volitions or affections, and others judgments.

When a man wills or fears, he has indeed an image of the thing he fears or of the action he wills;

but no explanation is given of what is further embraced in the thought of him who wills or fears. If indeed fearing be thinking, I fail to see how it can be anything other than the thought of the thing feared. In what respect does the fear produced by the onrush of a lion differ from the idea of the lion as it rushes on us, together with its effect (produced by such an idea in the heart), which impels the fearful man towards that animal motion we call flight? Now this motion of flight is not thought; whence we are left to infer that in fearing, there is no thinking save that which consists in the representation of the thing feared. The same account holds true of volition.

Further you do not have affirmation and negation without words and names; consequently brute creatures cannot affirm or deny, not even in thought, and hence are likewise unable to judge. Yet a man and a beast may have similar thoughts. For, when we assert that a man runs, our thought does not differ from that which a dog has when it sees its master running. Hence neither affirmation nor negation add anything to the bare thought, unless that increment be our thinking that the names of which the affirmation consists are the names of the same thing in him who affirms. But this does not mean that anything more is contained in our thought than the representation of the thing, but merely that that representation is there twice over.

Reply

It is self-evident that seeing a lion and fearing it at the same time is different from merely seeing it. So, too, it is one thing to see a man running, another thing to affirm to oneself that one sees it, an act that needs no language. I can see nothing here that needs an answer.

Objection VII

It remains for me to examine in what way I have received that idea from God. I have neither derived it from the senses; nor has it ever come to me contrary to my expectation, as the ideas of sensible things are wont to do, when these very things present themselves to the external organs of sense or seem to do so. Neither also has it been constructed as a fictitious idea by me, for I can take nothing from it and am quite unable to add to it. Hence the conclusion is left that it is innate in me, just as the idea of my own self is innate in me.

If there is no idea of God (now it has not been proved that it exists), as seems to be the case, the whole of this argument collapses. Further (if it is my body that is being considered) the idea of my own self proceeds from sight; but (if it is a question of the soul) there is no idea of the soul. We only infer by means of the reason that there is something internal in the human body, which imparts to it its animal motion, and by means of which it feels and moves; and this, whatever it be, we name the soul, without employing any idea.

Reply

If there is an idea of God (as it is manifest there is), the whole of this objection collapses. When it is said further that we have no idea of the soul but that we arrive at it by an inference of reason, that is the same as saying that there is no image of the soul depicted in the imagination, but that that which I have called its idea does, nevertheless, exist.

Objection VIII

But the other idea of the sun is derived from astronomical reasonings, i.e. is elicited from certain notions that are innate in me.

It seems that at one and the same time the idea of the sun must be single whether it is beheld by the eyes, or is given by our intelligence as many times larger than it appears. For this latter thought is not an idea of the sun, but an inference by argument that the idea of the sun would be many times larger if we viewed the sun from a much nearer distance.

But at different times the ideas of the sun may differ, e.g. when one looks at it with the naked eye and through a telescope. But astronomical reasonings do not increase or decrease the idea of the sun; rather they show that the sensible idea is misleading.

Reply

Here too what is said not to be an idea of the sun, but is, nevertheless, described, is exactly what I call an idea.

Objection IX

For without doubt those ideas, which reveal substance to me, are something greater, and, so to speak, contain within them more objective reality than those which represent only modes or accidents. And again, that by means of which I apprehend a supreme God who is eternal, infinite, omniscient, all-powerful, and the creator of all else there is besides, assuredly possesses more objective reality than those ideas that reveal to us finite substances.

I have frequently remarked above that there is no idea either of God or of the soul; I now add that there is no idea of substance. For substance (the substance that is a material, subject to accidents and changes) is perceived and demonstrated by the reason alone, without yet being conceived by us, or furnishing us with any idea. If that is true, how can it be maintained that the ideas which reveal substance to me are anything greater or possess more objective reality than those revealing accidents to us? Further I pray M. Descartes to investigate the meaning of more reality. Does reality admit of more and less? Of, if he thinks that one thing can be more a thing than another, let him see how he is to explain it to our intelligence with the clearness called for in demonstration, and such as he himself has at other times employed.

Reply

I have frequently remarked that I give the name idea to that with which reason makes us acquainted just as I also do to anything else that is in any way perceived by us. I have likewise explained how reality admits of more and less; viz. in the way in which substance is greater than mode; and if there be real qualities or incomplete substances, they are things to a greater extent then modes are, but less than complete substances. Finally, if there be an infinite and independent substance, it is more a thing than a substance that is finite and dependent. Now all this is quite self-evident.

Objection X

Hence there remains alone the idea of God, concerning which we must consider whether it is not something that is capable of proceeding from me myself. By the name of God I understand a substance that is infinite, independent, all-knowing, all-powerful, and by which both I myself and everything else, if anything else does exist, have been created. Now all these characteristics are such that, the more diligently I attend to them, the less do they appear capable of proceeding from me alone; hence, from what has been already said, we must conclude that God necessarily exists.

When I consider the attributes of God, in order to gather thence the idea of God, and see whether there is anything contained in it that cannot proceed from ourselves, I find, unless I am mistaken, that what we assign in thought to the name of God neither proceeds from ourselves nor needs to come from any other source than external objects. For by the word God I mean a substance, i.e. I understand that God exists (not by means of an idea but by reasoning). This substance is infinite (i.e. I can neither conceive nor imagine its boundaries or extreme parts, without imagining further parts beyond them); whence it follows that corresponding to the term infinite there arises an idea not of the Divine infinity, but of my own bounds or limitations. It is also independent, i.e. I have no conception of a cause from which God originates; whence it is evident that I have no idea corresponding to the term independent, save the memory of my own ideas with their commencement at divers times and their consequent dependence.

Wherefore to say that God is independent, is merely to say that God is to be reckoned among the number of those things, of the origin of which we have no image. Similarly to say that God is infinite, is identical with saying that He is among those objects of the limits of which we have no conception. Thus any idea of God is ruled out; for what sort of idea is that which has neither origin nor termination?

Take the term all-knowing. Here I ask: What idea does M. Descartes employ in apprehending the intellectual activity of God?

All powerful. *So too, what is the idea by which we apprehend power, which is relative to that which lies in the future, i.e. does not exist? I certainly understand what power is by means of an image, or memory of past events, inferring it in this wise— Thus did He, hence thus was He able to do; therefore as long as the same agent exists He will be able to act so again, i.e. He has the power of acting. Now these are all ideas that can arise from external objects.*

Creator of everything that exists. *Of creation some image can be constructed by me out of the objects I behold, e.g. the birth of a human being or its growth from something small as a point to the size and figure it now possesses. We have no other idea than this corresponding to the term creator. But in order to prove creation it is not enough to be able to imagine the creation of the world. Hence although it had been demonstrated that an infinite, independent, all-powerful, etc. being exists, nevertheless it does not follow that a creator exists. Unless anyone thinks that it is correct to infer, from the fact that there is a being which we believe to have created everything, that hence the world was at some time created by Him.*

Further, when M. Descartes says that the idea of God and that of the soul are innate in us, I should like to know whether the minds of those who are in a profound and dreamless sleep yet think. If not, they have at that time no ideas. Whence no idea is innate, for what is innate is always present.

Reply

Nothing that we attribute to God can come from external objects as a copy proceeds from its exemplar, because in God there is nothing similar to what is found in external things, i.e. in corporeal objects. But whatever is unlike them in our thought must come manifestly not from them, but from the cause of that diversity existing in our thought.

Further I ask how my critic derives the intellectual comprehension of God from external things. But I can easily explain the idea which I have of it, by saying that by idea I mean whatever is the form of any perception.

For does anyone who understands something not perceive that he does so? and hence does he not possess that form or idea of mental action? It is by extending this indefinitely that we form the idea of the intellectual activity of God; similarly also with God's other attributes.

But since we have employed the idea of God existing in us for the purpose of proving His existence, and such mighty power is comprised in this idea, that we comprehend that it would be contradictory, if God exists, for anything besides Him to exist, unless it were created by Him; it clearly follows, from the fact that His existence has been demonstrated, that it has been also proved that the whole world, or whatever things other than God exist, have been created by Him.

Finally when I say that an idea is innate in us, I do not mean that it is always present to us. This would make no idea innate. I mean merely that we possess the faculty of summoning up this idea.

Objection XI

The whole force of the argument lies in this—that I know I could not exist, and possess the nature I have, that nature which puts me in possession of the idea of God, unless God did really exist, the God, I repeat, the idea of whom is found in me.

Since, then, it has not been proved that we possess an idea of God, and the Christian religion obliges us to believe that God is inconceivable, which amounts, in my opinion, to saying that we have no idea of Him, it follows that no proof of His existence has been effected, much less of His work of creation.

Reply

When it is said that we cannot conceive God, to conceive means to comprehend adequately. For the rest, I am tired of repeating how it is that we can have an idea of God. There is nothing in these objections that invalidates my demonstrations.

Objection XII

(Directed against the fourth Meditation, *Concerning the true and the false.*)

And thus I am quite sure that error, in so far as it is error, is nothing real, but merely defect. Hence in order to go astray, it is not necessary for me to have a faculty specially assigned to me by God for this purpose.

It is true that ignorance is merely a defect, and that we stand in need of no special positive faculty in order to be ignorant; but about error the case is not so clear. For it appears that stones and inanimate things are unable to err solely because they have no faculty of reasoning, or imagining. Hence it is a very direct inference that, in order to err, a faculty of reasoning, or at least of imagination is required; now both of these are positive faculties with which all beings that err, and only beings that err, have been endowed.

Further, M. Descartes says—I perceive that they *(viz. my mistakes)* depend upon the cooperation of two causes, viz. my faculty of cognition, and my faculty of choice, or the freedom of my will. *But this seems to be contradictory to what went before. And we must note here also that the freedom of the will has been assumed without proof, and in opposition to the opinion of the Calvinists.*

Reply

Although in order to err the faculty of reasoning (or rather of judging, or affirming and denying) is required, because error is a lack of this power it does not hence follow that this defect is anything real, just as it does not follow that blindness is anything real, although stones are not said to be blind merely because they are incapable of vision. I marvel that in these objections I have as yet found nothing that is properly argued out. Further I made no assumption concerning freedom which is not a matter of universal experience; our natural light makes this most evident and I cannot make out why it is said to be contradictory to previous statements.

But though there are many who, looking to the Divine foreordination, cannot conceive how that is compatible with liberty on our part, nevertheless no one, when he considers himself alone, fails to experience the fact that to will and to be free are the same thing [or rather that there is no difference between what is voluntary and what is free]. But this is no place for examining other people's opinions about this matter.

Objection XIII

For example, whilst I, during these days, sought to discuss whether anything at all existed, and noted that, from the very fact that I raised this question, it was an evident consequence that I myself existed, I could not indeed refrain from judging that what I understood so clearly was true; this was not owing to compulsion by some external force, but because the consequence of the great mental illumination was a strong inclination of the will, and I believed the above truth the more willingly and freely, the less indifferent I was towards it.

This term, great mental illumination, *is metaphorical, and consequently is not adapted to the purposes of argument. Moreover everyone who is free from doubt claims to possess a similar illumination, and in his will there is the same inclination to believe that of which he does not doubt, as in that of the one who truly knows. Hence while this illumination may be the cause that makes a man obstinately defend or hold some opinion, it is not the cause of his knowing it to be true.*

Further, not only to know a thing to be true, but also to believe it or give assent to it, have nothing to do with the will. For, what is proved by valid argument or is recounted as credible, is believed by us whether we will or no. It is true that affirming and denying, maintaining or refuting propositions, are acts of will; but it does not follow on that account that internal assent depends upon the will.

Therefore the demonstration of truth that follows is not adequate—and it is in this misuse of our free-will, that this privation consists that constitutes the form of error.

Reply

It does not at all matter whether or not the term *great illumination* is proper to argument, so long as it is serviceable for explanation, as in fact it is. For no one can be unaware that by mental illumination is meant clearness of cognition, which perhaps is not possessed by everyone who thinks he possesses it. But this does not prevent it from being very different from a bigoted opinion, to the formation of which there goes no perceptual evidence.

Moreover when it is here said that when a thing is clearly perceived we give our assent whether we will or no, that is the same as saying that we desire what we clearly know to be good whether willing or unwilling; for the word *unwilling* finds no entrance in such circumstances, implying as it does that we will and do not will the same thing.

Objection XIV

(To the fifth Meditation, On the essence of material things.)

As, for example, when I imagine a triangle, though perhaps such a figure does not exist at all outside my thought, or never has existed, it has nevertheless a determinate nature, or essence, or immutable and eternal form, which is not a fiction of my construction, and does not depend on my mind, as is evident from the fact that various properties of that triangle may be demonstrated.

If the triangle exists nowhere at all, I do not understand how it can have any nature; for that which exists nowhere does not exist. Hence it has no existence or nature. The triangle in the mind comes from the triangle we have seen, or from one imaginatively constructed out of triangles we have beheld. Now when we have once culled the thing (from which we think that the idea of triangle originates) by the name triangle, although the triangle itself perishes, yet the name remains. In the same way if, in our thought, we have once conceived that the angles of a triangle are together all equal to two right angles, and have given this other name to the trian-

*gle—possessed of three angles equal to two
right angles—although there were no angle at all
in existence, yet the name would remain; and the
truth of this proposition will be of eternal duration—*
a triangle is possessed of three angles equal to
two right angles. *But the nature of the triangle
will not be of eternal duration, if it should chance
that triangle perished.*

In like manner the proposition, man is animal,
*will be eternally true, because the names it employs
are eternal, but if the human race were to perish
there would no longer be a human nature.*

*Whence it is evident that essence in so far as it is
distinguished from existence is nothing else than a
union of names by means of the verb is. And thus
essence without existence is a fiction of our mind.
And it appears that as the image of a man in the
mind is to the man so is essence to existence; or that
the essence of Socrates bears to his existence the
relation that this proposition,* Socrates is a man, *to
this other,* Socrates is *or* exists. *Now the proposition,* Socrates is a man, *means, when Socrates does
not exist, merely the connection of its terms; and* is,
or to be, has underlying it the image of the unity of a
thing designated by two names.*

Reply

The distinction between essence and existence
is known to all; and all that is here said about
eternal names in place of concepts or ideas of
an eternal truth, has been already satisfactorily
refuted.

Objection XV

(Directed against the sixth Meditation—
Concerning the existence of material things.)

For since God has evidently given me no
faculty by which to know this (*whether or not our
ideas proceed from bodies*), but on the contrary
has given me a strong propensity towards the
belief that they do proceed from corporeal
things, I fail to see how it could be made out
that He is not a deceiver, if our ideas proceeded from some other source than corporeal things. Consequently corporeal objects
must exist.

*It is the common belief that no fault is committed
by medical men who deceive sick people for their
health's sake, nor by parents who mislead their children for their good; and that the evil in deception lies
not in the falsity of what is said, but in the bad intent
of those who practice it. M. Descartes must therefore
look to this proposition,* God can in no case deceive us, *taken universally, and see whether it is
true; for if it is not true, thus universally taken, the
conclusion,* hence corporeal things exist, *does
not follow.*

Reply

For the security of my conclusion we do not
need to assume that we can never be deceived
(for I have gladly admitted that we are often
deceived), but that we are not deceived when
that error of ours would argue an intention to
deceive on the part of God, an intention it is
contradictory to impute to Him. Once more
this is bad reasoning on my critic's part.

Final Objection

For now I perceive how great the difference is
between the two (i.e. between waking and
dreaming) from the fact that our dreams are
never conjoined by our memory with the
whole of the rest of our life's action.

*I ask whether it is really the case that one, who
dreams he doubts whether he dreams or no, is unable
to dream that his dream is connected with the idea of
a long series of past events. If he can, those things
which to the dreamer appear to be the actions of his
past life may be regarded as true just as though he
had been awake. Besides, since, as M. Descartes
himself asserts, all certitude and truth in knowledge
depend alone upon our knowing the true God, either
it will be impossible for an Atheist to infer from the
memory of his previous life that he wakes, or it will be
possible for a man to know that he is awake, apart
from knowledge of the true God.*

Reply

One who dreams cannot effect a real connection between what he dreams and the ideas of

past events, though he can dream that he does connect them. For who denies that in his sleep a man may be deceived? But yet when he has awakened he will easily detect his error.

But an Atheist is able to infer from the memory of his past life that he is awake; still he cannot know that this sign is sufficient to give him the certainty that he is not in error, unless he knows that it has been created by a God who does not deceive.

Leviathan

Thomas Hobbes

Chapter 1: Of Sense

Sense. Concerning the thoughts of man, I will consider them first singly, and afterwards in train, or dependence upon one another. Singly, they are every one a *representation* or *appearance,* of some quality, or other accident of a body without us, which is commonly called an *object.* Which object worketh on the eyes, ears, and other parts of a man's body; and by diversity of working, produceth diversity of appearances.

The original of them all, is that which we call SENSE, for there is no conception in a man's mind, which hath not at first, totally, or by parts, been begotten upon the organs of sense. The rest are derived from that original.

To know the natural cause of sense, is not very necessary to the business now in hand; and I have elsewhere written of the same at large. Nevertheless, to fill each part of my present method, I will briefly deliver the same in this place.

The cause of sense, is the external body, or object, which presseth the organ proper to each sense, either immediately, as in the taste and touch; or mediately, as in seeing, hearing, and smelling; which pressure, by the mediation of the nerves, and other strings and membranes of the body, continued inwards to the brain and heart, causeth there a resistance, or counter-pressure, or endeavour of the heart to deliver itself, which endeavour, because *outward,* seemeth to be some matter without. And this *seeming,* or *fancy,* is that which men call *sense;* and consisteth, as to the eye, in a *light,* or *colour figured;* to the ear, in a *sound;* to the nostrils in an *odour;* to the tongue and palate, in a *savour;* and to the rest of the body, in *heat, cold, hardness, softness,* and such other qualities as we discern by *feeling.* All which qualities, called *sensible,* are in the object, that causeth them, but so many several motions of the matter, by which it presseth our organs diversely. Neither in us that are pressed, are they any thing else, but divers motions; for motion produceth nothing but motion. But their appearance to us is fancy, the same waking, that dreaming. And as pressing, rubbing, or striking the eye, makes us fancy a light; and pressing the ear, produceth a din; so do the bodies also we see, or hear, produce the same by their strong, though unobserved action. For if these colours and sounds were in the bodies, or objects that cause them, they could not be severed from them, as by glasses, and in echoes by reflection, we see they are; where we know the thing we see is in one place, the appearance in another. And though at some certain distance, the real and very object seem invested with the fancy it begets in us; yet the

SOURCE: *The English Works of Thomas Hobbes of Malmesbury,* collected and edited by Sir William Molesworth, (London: John Bohn, 1839).

object is one thing, the image or fancy is another. So that sense, in all cases, is nothing else but original fancy, caused, as I have said, by the pressure, that is, by the motion, of external things upon our eyes, ears, and other organs thereunto ordained.

But the philosophy-schools, through all the universities of Christendom, grounded upon certain texts of Aristotle, teach another doctrine, and say, for the cause of *vision*, that the thing seen, sendeth forth on every side a *visible species*, in English, a *visible show, apparition*, or *aspect*, or *a being seen;* the receiving whereof into the eye, is *seeing*. And for the cause of *hearing*, that the thing heard, sendeth forth an *audible species*, that is an *audible aspect*, or *audible being seen;* which entering at the ear, maketh *hearing*. Nay, for the cause of *understanding* also, they say the thing understood, sendeth forth an *intelligible species*, that is, an *intelligible being seen;* which, coming into the understanding, makes us understand. I say not this, as disproving the use of universities; but because I am to speak hereafter of their office in a commonwealth, I must let you see on all occasions by the way, what things would be amended in them; amongst which the frequency of insignificant speech is one.

Chapter 2: Of Imagination

Imagination. That when a thing lies still, unless somewhat else stir it, it will lie still for ever, is a truth that no man doubts of. But that when a thing is in motion, it will eternally be in motion, unless somewhat else stay it, though the reason be the same, namely, that nothing can change itself, is not so easily assented to. For men measure, not only other men, but all other things, by themselves; and because they find themselves subject after motion to pain, and lassitude, think every thing else grows weary of motion, and seeks repose of its own accord; little considering, whether it be not some other motion, wherein that desire of rest they find in themselves, consisteth. From hence it is, that the schools say, heavy bodies fall downwards, out of an appetite to rest,

and to conserve their nature in that place which is most proper for them; ascribing appetite, and knowledge of what is good for their conservation, which is more than man has, to things inanimate, absurdly.

When a body is once in motion, it moveth, unless something else hinder it, eternally; and whatsoever hindreth it, cannot in an instant, but in time, and by degrees, quite extinguish it; and as we see in the water, though the wind cease, the waves give not over rolling for a long time after: so also it happeneth in that motion, which is made in the internal parts of a man, then, when he sees, dreams, &c. For after the object is removed, or the eye shut, we still retain an image of the thing seen, though more obscure than when we see it. And this is it, the Latins call *imagination*, from the image made in seeing; and apply the same, though improperly, to all the other senses. But the Greeks call it *fancy;* which signifies *appearance*, and is as proper to one sense, as to another. IMAGINATION therefore is nothing but *decaying sense;* and is found in men, and many other living creatures, as well sleeping, as waking.

The decay of sense in men waking, is not the decay of the motion made in sense; but an obscuring of it, in such manner as the light of the sun obscureth the light of the stars; which stars do no less exercise their virtue, by which they are visible, in the day than in the night. But because amongst many strokes, which our eyes, ears, and other organs receive from external bodies, the predominant only is sensible; therefore, the light of the sun being predominant, we are not affected with the action of the stars. And any object being removed from our eyes, though the impression it made in us remain, yet other objects more present succeeding, and working on us, the imagination of the past is obscured, and made weak, as the voice of a man is in the noise of the day. From whence it followeth, that the longer the time is, after the sight or sense of any object, the weaker is the imagination. For the continual change of man's body destroys in time the parts which in sense were moved: so that distance of time, and of place, hath one and the same effect in us. For as at a great distance of place, that which we look at appears dim, and without distinction of the smaller parts; and as voices grow weak, and inarticulate; so also, after great distance of time, our imagination of the past is weak; and we lose, for example, of cities we have seen, many particular streets, and of actions, many particular circumstances. This *decaying sense,* when we would express the thing itself, I mean *fancy* itself, we call *imagination,* as I said before: but when we would express the decay, and signify that the sense is fading, old, and past, it is called *memory.* So that imagination and memory are but one thing, which for divers considerations hath divers names.

Much memory, or memory of many things, is called *experience.* Again, imagination being only of those things which have been formerly perceived by sense, either all at once, or by parts at several times; the former, which is the imagining the whole object as it was presented to the sense, is *simple* imagination, as when one imagineth a man, or horse, which he hath seen before. The other is *compounded;* as when, from the sight of a man at one time, and of a horse at another, we conceive in our mind a Centaur. So when a man compoundeth the image of his own person with the image of the actions of another man, as when a man imagines himself a Hercules or an Alexander, which happeneth often to them that are much taken with reading of romances, it is a compound imagination, and properly but a fiction of the mind. There be also other imaginations that rise in men, though waking, from the great impression made in sense: as from gazing upon the sun, the impression leaves an image of the sun before our eyes a long time after; and from being long and vehemently attent upon geometrical figures, a man shall in the dark, though awake, have the images of lines and angles before his eyes; which kind of fancy hath no particular name, as being a thing that doth not commonly fall into men's discourse.

The imaginations of them that sleep, are those we call *dreams.* And these also (as all other imaginations) have been before, either totally, or by parcels in the sense. And because in sense, the brain, and nerves, which are the necessary organs of sense, are so benumbed in sleep, as not easily to be moved by the action of *external objects,* there can happen in sleep, no imagination; and therefore no dream, but what proceeds from the agitation of the inward parts of man's body; which inward parts, for the connexion they have with the brain, and other organs, when they be distempered, do keep the same in motion; whereby the imaginations there formerly made, appear as if a man were waking; saving that the *organs of sense* being now benumbed, so as there is no new object, which can master and obscure them with a more vigorous impression, a dream must needs be more clear, in this silence of sense, than are our waking thoughts. And hence it cometh to pass, that it is a hard matter, and by many thought impossible to distinguish exactly between *sense* and *dreaming.* For my part, when I consider, that in dreams, I do not often, nor constantly think of the same persons, places, objects, and actions that I do waking; nor remember so long a train of coherent thoughts, dreaming, as at other times; and because waking I often observe the absurdity of dreams, but never dream of the absurdities of my waking thoughts; I am well satisfied, that being awake, I know I dream not; though when I dream, I think my self awake.

And seeing dreams are caused by the distemper of some of the inward parts of the body; diverse distempers must needs cause different dreams. And hence it is, that lying cold breedeth dreams of fear, and raiseth the thought and image of some fearful object (the motion from the brain to the inner parts, and from the inner parts to the brain being reciprocal:) And that as anger causeth heat in some parts of the body, when we are awake; so when we sleep, the over heating of the same parts causeth anger, and raiseth up in the brain the imagination of an enemy. In the same manner; as natural kindness, when we are awake causeth desire; and desire makes heat in certain other parts of the body; so also, too much heat in those parts, while we sleep, raiseth in the brain an imagination of some kindness shown. In sum, our dreams are the reverse of our waking imaginations; the motion when we are awake, beginning at one end; and when we dream, at another. . . .

Chapter 3: Of the Consequence or Train of Imaginations

By *consequence,* or TRAIN of thoughts, I understand that succession of one thought to another, which is called, to distinguish it from discourse in words, *mental discourse.*

When a man thinketh on any thing whatsoever, his next thought after, is not altogether so casual as it seems to be. Not every thought to every thought succeeds indifferently. But as we have no imagination, whereof we have not formerly had sense, in whole, or in parts; so we have no transition from one imagination to another, whereof we never had the like before in our senses. The reason whereof is this. All fancies are motions within us, relics of those made in the sense: and those motions that immediately succeeded one another in the sense, continue also together after sense: insomuch as the former coming again to take place, and be predominant, the latter followeth, by coherence of the matter moved, in such manner, as water upon a plane table is drawn which way any one part of it is guided by the finger. But because in sense, to one and the same thing perceived, sometimes one thing, sometimes another succeedeth, it comes to pass in time, that in the imagining of any thing, there is no certainly what we shall imagine next; only this is certain, it shall be something that succeeded the same before, at one time or another.

Train of Thoughts Unguided. This train of thoughts, or mental discourse, is of two sorts. The first is *unguided, without design,* and inconstant; wherein there is no passionate thought, to govern and direct those that follow, to itself, as the end and scope of some desire, or other passion: in which case the thoughts are said to wander, and seem impertinent one to another, as in a dream. Such are commonly the thoughts of men, that are not only without company, but also without care of any thing; though even then their thoughts are as busy as at other times, but without harmony; as the sound which a lute out of tune would yield to any man; or in tune,

to one that could not play. And yet in this wild ranging of the mind, a man may oft-times perceive the way of it, and the dependence of one thought upon another. For in a discourse of our present civil war, what could seem more impertinent, than to ask, as one did, what was the value of a Roman penny? Yet the coherence to me was manifest enough. For the thought of the war, introduced the thought of the delivering up the king to his enemies; the thought of that, brought in the thought of the delivering up of Christ; and that again the thought of the thirty pence, which was the price of that treason; and thence easily followed that malicious question, and all this is a moment of time; for thought is quick.

Train of Thoughts Regulated. The second is more constant; as being *regulated* by some desire, and design. For the impression made by such things as we desire, or fear, is strong, and permanent, or, if it cease for a time, of quick return: so strong it is sometimes, as to hinder and break our sleep. From desire, ariseth the thought of some means we have seen produce the like of that which we aim at; and from the thought of that, the thought of means to that mean; and so continually, till we come to some beginning within our own power. And because the end, by the greatness of the impression, comes often to mind, in case our thoughts begin to wander, they are quickly again reduced into the way: which observed by one of the seven wise men, made him give men this precept, which is now worn out, *Respice finem;* that is to say, in all your actions, look often upon what you would have, as the thing that directs all your thoughts in the way to attain it.

The train of regulated thoughts is of two kinds: One, when of an effect imagined, we seek the causes, or means that produce it: and this is common to man and beast. The other is, when imagining any thing whatsoever, we seek all the possible effects, that can by it be produced; that is to say, we imagine what we can do with it, when we have it. Of which I have not at any time seen any sign, but in man only; for this is a curiosity hardly incident to the nature of any where, and when he had it; that is to say, to find some certain, and limited time and place, in which to begin a method of seeking. Again, from thence, his thoughts run over the same places and times, to find what action, or other occasion might make him lose it. This we call *remembrance,* or calling to mind: the Latins call it *reminiscentia,* as it were a *re-conning* of our former actions. . . .

There is no other act of man's mind, that I can remember, naturally planted in him, so as to need no other thing, to the exercise of it, but to be born a man, and live with the use of his five senses. Those other faculties, of which I shall speak by and by, and which seem proper to man only, are acquired and increased by study and industry; and of most men learned by instruction, and discipline; and proceed all from the invention of words, and speech. For besides sense, and thoughts, and the train of thoughts, the mind of man has no other motion; though by the help of speech, and method, the same faculties may be improved to such a height, as to distinguish men from all other living creatures. . . .

Chapter 4: Of Speech

The invention of *printing,* though ingenious, compared with the invention of *letters,* is no great matter. But who was the first that found the use of letters, is not known. He that first brought them into Greece, men say was Cadmus, the son of Agenor, king of Phoenicia. A profitable invention for continuing the memory of time passed, and the conjunction of mankind, dispersed into so many, and distant regions of the earth; and withal difficult, as proceeding from a watchful observation of the divers motions of the tongue, palate, lips, and other organs of speech; whereby to make as many differences of characters, to remember them. But the most noble and profitable invention of all other, was that of SPEECH, consisting of *names* or *appellations,* and their connexion; whereby men register their thoughts; recall them when they are past; and also declare them one to another for mutual utility and conversation; without which, there had been amongst men, neither commonwealth, nor society, nor contract, nor peace, no more

than amongst lions, bears, and wolves. The first author of *speech* was God himself, that instructed Adam how to name such creatures as he presented to his sight; for the Scripture goeth no further in this matter. But this was sufficient to direct him to add more names, as the experience and use of the creatures should give him occasion; and to join them in such manner by degrees, as to make himself understood; and so by succession of time, so much language might be gotten, as he had found use for; though not so copious, as an orator or philosopher has need of: for I do not find anything in the Scripture, out of which, directly or by consequence, can be gathered, that Adam was taught the names of all figures, numbers, measures, colours, sounds, fancies, relations; much less the names of words and speech, as *general, special, affirmative, negative, interrogative, optative, infinitive,* all which are useful; and least of all, of *entity, intentionality, quiddity,* and other insignificant words of the school.

But all this language gotten, and augmented by Adam and his posterity, was again lost at the Tower of Babel, when, by the hand of God, every man was stricken, for his rebellion, with an oblivion of his former language. And being hereby forced to disperse themselves into several parts of the world, it must needs be, that the diversity of tongues that now is, proceeded by degrees from them, in such manner, as need, the mother of all inventions, taught them; and in tract of time grew everywhere more copious.

The general use of speech, is to transfer our mental discourse, into verbal: or the train of our thoughts, into a train of words; and that for two commodities, whereof one is the registering of the consequences of our thoughts; which being apt to slip out of our memory and put us to a new labour, may again be recalled, by such words as they were marked by. So that the first use of names is to serve for *marks,* or *notes* of remembrance. Another is, when many use the same words, to signify, by their connexion and order, one to another, what they conceive, or think of each matter; and also what they desire, fear, or have any other passion for. And for this use they are called *signs.* Special uses of speech are these: first, to register, what by cogitation, we find to be the cause of anything, present or past; and what we find things present or past may produce, or effect; which in sum, is acquiring of arts. Secondly; to show to others that knowledge which we have attained, which is, to counsel and teach one another. Thirdly, to make known to others our wills and purposes, that we may have the mutual help of one another. Fourthly, to please and delight ourselves and others, by playing with our words, for pleasure or ornament, innocently.

To these uses, there are also four correspondent abuses. First, when men register their thoughts wrong, by the inconstancy of the signification of their words; by which they register for their conception, that which they never conceived, and so deceive themselves. Secondly, when they use words metaphorically; that is, in other sense than that they are ordained for; and thereby deceive others. Thirdly, by words, when they declare that to be their will, which is not. Fourthly, when they use them to grieve one another; for seeing nature hath armed living creatures, some with teeth, some with horns, and some with hands, to grieve an enemy, it is but an abuse of speech, to grieve him with the tongue, unless it be one whom we are obliged to govern; and then it is not to grieve, but to correct and amend.

The manner how speech serveth to the remembrance of the consequence of causes and effects, consisteth in the imposing of *names,* and the *connexion* of them.

Of names, some are *proper,* and singular to one only thing, as *Peter, John, this man, this tree;* and some are *common* to many things, as *man, horse, tree;* every of which, though but one name, is nevertheless the name of divers particular things; in respect of all which together, it is called an *universal;* there being nothing in the world universal but names; for the things named are every one of them individual and singular.

One universal name is imposed on many things, for their similitude in some quality, or other accident; and whereas a proper name bringeth to mind one thing only, universals recall any one of those many.

And of names universal, some are of more,

and some of less extent; the larger comprehending the less large; and some again of equal extent, comprehending each other reciprocally. As for example; the name *body* is of larger signification than the word *man,* and comprehendeth it; and the names *man* and *rational,* are of equal extent, comprehending mutually one another. But here we must take notice, that by a name is not always understood, as in grammar, one only word; but sometimes, by circumlocution, many words together. For all these words, *he that in his actions observeth the laws of his country,* make but one name, equivalent to this one word, *just.*

By this imposition of names, some of larger, some of stricter signification, we turn the reckoning of the consequences of things imagined in the mind, into a reckoning of the consequences of appellations. For example: a man that hath no use of speech at all, such as is born and remains perfectly deaf and dumb, if he set before his eyes a triangle, and by it two right angles, such as are the corners of a square figure, he may, by meditation, compare and find, that the three angles of that triangle, are equal to those two right angles that stand by it. But if another triangle be shown him, different in shape from the former, he cannot know, without a new labour, whether the three angles of that also be equal to the same. But he that hath the use of words, when he observes, that such quality was consequent, not to the length of the sides, nor to any other particular thing in his triangle; but only to this, that the sides were straight, and the angles three; and that that was all, for which he named it a triangle; will boldly conclude universally, that such equality of angles is in all triangles whatsoever; and register his invention in these general terms, *every triangle hath its three angles equal to two right angles.* And thus the consequence found in one particular, comes to be registered and remembered, as a universal rule, and discharges our mental reckoning, of time and place, and delivers us from all labour of the mind, saving the first, and makes that which was found true *here,* and *now,* to be true in *all times* and *places.*

But the use of words in registering our thoughts is in nothing so evident as in numbering. A natural fool that could never learn by heart the order of numeral words, as *one, two,* and *three,* may observe every stroke of the clock, and nod to it, or say *one, one, one,* but can never know what hour it strikes. And it seems, there was a time when those names of number were not in use; and men were fain to apply their fingers of one or both hands, to those things they desired to keep account of; and that thence it proceeded, that now our numeral words are but ten, in any nation, and in some but five; and then they begin again. And he that can tell ten, if he recite them out of order, will lose himself, and not know when he has done. Much less will he be able to add, and subtract, and perform all other operations of arithmetic. So that without words there is no possibility of reckoning of numbers; much less of magnitudes, of swiftness, of force, and other things, the reckonings whereof are necessary to the being, or well-being of mankind.

When two names are joined together into a consequence, or affirmation, as thus, *a man is a living creature;* or thus, *if he be a man, he is a living creature;* if the latter name, *living creature,* signify all that the former name *man* signifieth, then the affirmation, or consequence, is *true;* otherwise *false.* For *true* and *false* are attributes of speech, not of things. And where speech is not, there is neither *truth* nor *falsehood; error* there may be, as when we expect that which shall not be, or suspect what has not been; but in neither case can a man be charged with untruth.

Seeing then that truth consisteth in the right ordering of names in our affirmations, a man that seeketh precise truth had need to remember what every name he uses stands for, and to place it accordingly, or else he will find himself entangled in words, as a bird in lime twigs, the more he struggles the more belimed. And therefore in geometry, which is the only science that it hath pleased God hitherto to bestow on mankind, men begin at settling the significations of their words; which settling of significations they call *definitions,* and place them in the beginning of their reckoning.

By this it appears how necessary it is for any man that aspires to true knowledge, to examine the definitions of former authors; and either to correct them, where they are negligently set down, or to make them himself. For the errors of definitions multiply themselves according as the reckoning proceeds, and lead men into absurdities, which at last they see, but cannot avoid, without reckoning anew from the beginning, in which lies the foundation of their errors. From whence it happens, that they which trust to books do as they that cast up many little sums into a greater, without considering whether those little sums were rightly cast up or not; and at last finding the error visible, and not mistrusting their first grounds, know not which way to clear themselves, but spend time in fluttering over their books; as birds that entering by the chimney, and finding themselves enclosed in a chamber, flutter at the false light of a glass window, for want of wit to consider which way they came in. So that in the right definition of names lies the first use of speech; which is the acquisition of science: and in wrong, or no definitions, lies the first abuse; from which proceed all false and senseless tenets; which make those men that take their instruction from the authority of books, and not from their own meditation, to be as much below the condition of ignorant men, as men endued with true science are above it. For between true science and erroneous doctrines, ignorance is in the middle. Natural sense and imagination are not subject to absurdity. Nature itself cannot err; and as men abound in copiousness of language, so they become more wise, or more mad than ordinary. Nor is it possible without letters for any man to become either excellently wise, or, unless his memory be hurt by disease or ill constitution of organs, excellently foolish. For words are wise men's counters, they do but reckon by them; but they are the money of fools, that value them by the authority of an Aristotle, a Cicero, or a Thomas, or any other doctor whatsoever, if but a man,

Subject to names, is whatsoever can enter into or be considered in an account, and be added one to another to make a sum, or subtracted one from another and leave a remainder. The Latins called accounts of money *rationes,* and accounting *ratiocinatio;* and that which we in bills or books of account call *items,* they call *nomina,* that is *names;* and thence it seems to proceed, that they extended the word *ratio* to the faculty of reckoning in all other things. The Greeks have but one word, λόγος for both *speech* and *reason;* not that they thought there was no speech without reason, but no reasoning without speech: and the act of reasoning they called *syllogism,* which signifieth summing up of the consequences of one saying to another. And because the same thing may enter into account for divers accidents, their names are, to show that diversity, diversely wrested and diversified. This diversity of names may be reduced to four general heads.

First, a thing may enter into account for *matter* or *body;* as *living, sensible, rational, hot, cold, moved, quiet;* with all which names the word *matter,* or *body,* is understood; all such being names of matter.

Secondly, it may enter into account, or be considered, for some accident or quality which we conceive to be in it; as for *being moved,* for *being so long,* for *being hot,* &c.; and then, of the name of the thing itself, by a little change or wresting, we make a name for that accident, which we consider; and for *living* put into the account *life;* for *moved, motion;* for *hot, heat;* for *long, length;* and the like: and all such names are the names of the accidents and properties by which one matter and body is distinguished from another. These are called *names abstract,* because severed, not from matter, but from the account of matter.

Thirdly, we bring into account the properties of our own bodies whereby we make such distinction; as when anything is seen by us, we reckon not the thing itself, but the sight, the colour, the idea of it in the fancy: and when anything is heard, we reckon it not, but the hearing or sound only, which is our fancy or conception of it by the ear; and such are names of fancies.

Fourthly, we bring into account, consider, and give names, to *names* themselves, and to *speech:* for *general, universal, special, equivocal,* are names of names. And *affirmation, interrogation, commandment, narration, syllogism, sermon, oration,* and many other such, are names of speeches. And this is all the variety of names *positive;* which are put to mark somewhat which is in nature, or may be feigned by the

mind of man, as bodies that are, or may be conceived to be; or of bodies, the properties that are, or may be feigned to be; or words and speech.

There be also other names, called *negative,* which are notes to signify that a word is not the name of the thing in question, as these words, *nothing, no man, infinite, indocible, three want four,* and the like; which are nevertheless of use in reckoning, or in correcting of reckoning, and call to mind our past cogitations, though they be not names of anything, because they make us refuse to admit of names not rightly used.

All other names are but insignificant sounds; and those of two sorts. One when they are new, and yet their meaning not explained by definition; whereof there have been abundance coined by schoolmen, and puzzled philosophers.

Another, when men make a name of two names, whose significations are contradictory and inconsistent; as this name, an *incorporeal body,* or, which is all one, an *incorporeal substance,* and a great number more. For whensoever any affirmation is false, the two names of which it is composed, put together and made one, signify nothing at all. For example, if it be a false affirmation to say *a quadrangle is round,* the word *round quadrangle* signifies nothing, but is a mere sound. So likewise, if it be false to say that virtue can be poured, or blown up and down, the words *impoured virtue, inblown virtue,* are as absurd and insignificant as a *round quadrangle.* And therefore you shall hardly meet with a senseless and insignificant word, that is not made up of some Latin or Greek names. A Frenchman seldom hears our Saviour called by the name of *parole,* but by the name of *verbe* often; yet *verbe* and *parole* differ no more, but that one is Latin and the other French.

When a man, upon the hearing of any speech, hath those thoughts which the words of that speech and their connexion were ordained and constituted to signify, then he is said to understand it; *understanding* being nothing else but conception caused by speech. And therefore if speech be peculiar to man, as for ought I know it is, then is understanding peculiar to him also. And therefore of absurd and false affirmations, in case they be universal, there can be no understanding; though many think they understand then, when they do but repeat the words softly, or con them in their mind.

What kinds of speeches signify the appetites, aversions, and passions of man's mind; and of their use and abuse, I shall speak when I have spoken of the passions.

The names of such things as affect us, that is, which please and displease us, because all men be not alike affected with the same thing, nor the same man at all times, are in the common discourses of men of *inconstant* signification. For seeing all names are imposed to signify our conceptions, and all our affections are but conceptions, when we conceive the same things differently, we can hardly avoid different naming of them. For though the nature of that we conceive, be the same; yet the diversity of our reception of it, in respect of different constitutions of body, and prejudices of opinion, gives every thing a tincture of our different passions. And therefore in reasoning a man must take heed of words; which besides the signification of what we imagine of their nature, have a signification also of the nature, disposition, and interest of the speaker; such as are the names of virtues and vices; for one man calleth *wisdom*, what another calleth *fear;* and one *cruelty*, what another *justice;* one *prodigality*, what another *magnanimity;* and one *gravity*, what another *stupidity*, &c. And therefore such names can never be true grounds of any ratiocination. No more can metaphors, and tropes of speech; but these are less dangerous, because they profess their inconstancy; which the other do not.

Chapter 5: Of Reason and Science

When a man *reasoneth*, he does nothing else but conceive a sum total, from *addition* of parcels; or conceive a remainder, from *subtraction* of one sum from another; which, if it be done by words, is conceiving of the consequence of the names of all the parts, to the name of the whole; or from the names of the whole and one part, to the name of the other part. And though in some things, as in numbers, besides adding and subtracting, men name other operations, as *multiplying* and *dividing*, yet they are the same; for multiplication, is but adding together of things equal; and division, but subtracting of one thing, as often as we can. These operations are not incident to numbers only, but to all manner of things that can be added together, and taken one out of another. For as arithmeticians teach to add and subtract in *numbers;* so the geometricians teach the same in *lines, figures,* solid and superficial, *angles, proportions, times,* degrees of *swiftness, force, power,* and the like; the logicians teach the same in *consequences of words;* adding together two *names* to make an *affirmation,* and two *affirmations* to make a *syllogism;* and *many syllogisms* to make a *demonstration;* and from the *sum,* or *conclusion* of a *syllogism,* they subtract one *proposition* to find the other. Writers of politics add together *pactions* to find men's *duties;* and lawyers, *laws* and *facts,* to find what is *right* and *wrong* in the actions of private men. In sum, in what matter soever there is place for *addition* and *subtraction,* there also is place for *reason;* and where these have no place, there *reason* has nothing at all to do.

Out of all which we may define, that is to say determine, what that is, which is meant by this word *reason*, when we reckon it amongst the faculties of the mind. For REASON, in this sense, is nothing but *reckoning*, that is adding and subtracting, of the consequences of general names agreed upon for the *marking* and *signifying* of our thoughts; I say *marking* them when we reckon by ourselves, and *signifying*, when we demonstrate or approve our reckonings to other men.

And, as in arithmetic, unpractised men must, and professors themselves may often, err, and cast up false; so also in any other subject of reasoning, the ablest, most attentive, and most practised men may deceive themselves, and infer false conclusions; not but that reason itself is always right reason, as well as arithmetic is a certain and infallible art: but no one man's reason, nor the reason of any one number of men, makes the certainty; no more than an account is therefore well cast up, because a great many men have unanimously approved it. And therefore, as when there is a controversy in an account, the parties must by their own accord, set up, for right reason, the reason of some arbitrator, or judge, to whose sentence they will both stand, or their controversy must either come to blows, or be undecided, for want of a right reason constituted by nature; so it is also in all debates of what kind so-ever. And when men that think themselves wiser than all others, clamour and demand right reason for judge, yet seek no more, but that things should be determined, by no other men's reason but their own, it is as intolerable in the society of men, as it is in play after trump is turned, to use for trump on every occasion, that suite whereof they have most in their hand. For they do nothing else, that will have every of their passions, as it comes to bear sway in them, to be taken for right reason, and that in their own controversies: bewraying their want of right reason, by the claim they lay to it.

The use and end of reason, is not the finding of the sum and truth of one, or a few consequences, remote from the first definitions, and settled significations of names, but to begin at these, and proceed from one consequence to another. For there can be no certainty of the last conclusion, without a certainty of all those affirmations and negations, on which it was grounded and inferred. As when a master of a family, in taking an account, casteth up the sums of all the bills of expense into one sum, and not regarding how each bill is summed up, by those that give them in account; nor what it is he pays for; he advantages himself no more, than if he allowed the account in gross, trusting to every of the accountants' skill and honesty: so also in reasoning of all other things, he that takes up conclusions on the trust of authors, and doth not fetch them from the first items in every reckoning, which are the significations of names settled by definitions, loses his labour; and does not know anything, but only believeth.

When a man reckons without the use of words, which may be done in particular things, as when upon the sight of any one thing, we conjecture what was likely to have preceded, or is likely to follow upon it; if that which he thought likely to follows, not, or that which he thought likely to have preceded it, hath not preceded it, this is called *error;* to which even the most prudent men are subject. But when we reason in words of general signification, and fall upon a general inference which is false, though it be commonly called *error,* it is indeed an *absurdity,* or senseless speech. For error is but a deception, in presuming that somewhat is passed, or to come; of which, though it were not past, or not to come, yet there was no impossibility discoverable. But when we make a general assertion, unless it be a true one, the possibility of it is inconceivable. And words whereby we conceive nothing but the sound, are those we call *absurd, insignificant,* and *nonsense.* And therefore if a man should talk to me of a *round quadrangle;* or, *accidents of bread in cheese;* or *immaterial substances;* or of *a free subject; a free will;* or any *free,* but free from being hindered by opposition, I should not say he were in an error, but that his words were without meaning, that is to say, absurd.

I have said before, in the second chapter, that a man did excel all other animals in this faculty, that when he conceived any thing whatsoever, he was apt to enquire the consequences of it, and what effects he could do with it. And now I add this other degree of the same excellence, that he can by words reduce the consequences he finds to general rules, called *theorems,* or *aphorisms;* that is, he can reason, or reckon, not only in number, but in all other things, whereof one may be added unto, or subtracted from another.

But this privilege is allayed by another; and that is, by the privilege of absurdity; to which no living creature is subject, but man only. And of men, those are of all most subject to it, that profess philosophy. For it is most true that Cicero saith of them somewhere; that there can be nothing so absurd, but may be found in the books of philosophers. And the reason is manifest. For there is not one of them that begins his ratiocination from the defintions, or explications of the names they are to use; which is a method that hath been used only in geometry; whose conclusions have thereby been made indisputable.

I. The first cause of absurd conclusions I

ascribe to the want of method; in that they begin not their ratiocination from definitions; that is, from settled significations of their words: as if they could cast account, without knowing the value of the numeral words, *one, two,* and *three.*

And whereas all bodies enter into account upon divers considerations, which I have mentioned in the precedent chapter; these considerations being diversely named, divers absurdities proceed from the confusion, and unfit connexion of their names into assertions. And therefore,

II. The second cause of absurd assertions, I ascribe to the giving of names of *bodies* to *accidents;* or of *accidents* to *bodies;* as they do, that say, *faith is infused,* or *inspired;* when nothing can be *poured,* or *breathed* into anything, but body; and that, *extension* is *body;* that *phantasms* are *spirits,* &c.

III. The third I ascribe to the giving of the names of the *accidents* of *bodies without us,* to the *accidents* of our *own bodies;* as they do that say, the *colour is in the body; the sound is in the air,* &c.

IV. The fourth, to the giving of the names of *bodies* to *names,* or *speeches;* as they do that say, that *there be things universal;* that *a living creature is genus,* or *a general thing,* &c.

V. The fifth, to the giving of the names of *accidents* to *names* and *speeches;* as they do that say, *the nature of a thing is its definition; a man's command is his will;* and the like.

VI. The sixth, to the use of metaphors, tropes, and other rhetorical figures, instead of words proper. For though it be lawful to say, for example, in common speech, *the way goeth, or leadeth hither, or thither; the proverb says this or that,* whereas ways cannot go, nor proverbs speak; yet in reckoning, and seeking of truth, such speeches are not to be admitted.

VII. The seventh, to names that signify nothing; but are taken up, and learned by rote from the schools, as *hypostatical, transubstantiate, consubstantiate, eternal-now,* and the like canting of schoolmen.

To him that can avoid these things it is not easy to fall into any absurdity, unless it be by the length of an account; wherein he may perhaps forget what went before. For all men by nature reason alike, and well, when they have good principles. For who is so stupid, as both

to mistake in geometry, and also to persist in it, when another detects his error to him?

By this it appears that reason is not, as sense and memory, born with us; nor gotten by experience only, as prudence is; but attained by industry; first in apt imposing of names; and secondly by getting a good and orderly method in proceeding from the elements, which are names, to assertions made by connexion of one of them to another; and so to syllogisms, which are the connexions of one assertion to another, till we come to a knowledge of all the consequences of names appertaining to the subject in hand; and that is it, men call SCIENCE. And whereas sense and memory are but knowledge of fact, which is a thing past and irrevocable. *Science* is the knowledge of consequences, and dependence of one fact upon another: by which, out of that we can presently do, we know how to do something else when we will, or the like another time; because when we see how anything comes about, upon what causes, and by what manner; when the like causes come into our power, we see how to make it produce the like effects.

Children therefore are not endued with reason at all, till they have attained the use of speech; but are called reasonable creatures, for the possibility apparent of having the use of reason in time to come. And the most part of men, though they have the use of reasoning a little way, as in numbering to some degree; yet it serves them to little use in common life; in which they govern themselves, some better, some worse, according to their differences of experience, quickness of memory, and inclinations to several ends; but specially according to good or evil fortune, and the errors of one another. For as for *science,* or certain rules of their actions, they are so far from it, they know not what it is. Geometry they have thought conjuring; but for other sciences, they who have not been taught the beginnings and some progress in them, that they may see how they be acquired and generated, are in this point like children, that having no thought of generation, are made believe by the women that their brothers and sisters are not born, but found in the garden.

But yet they that have no *science,* are in

better, and nobler condition, with their natural prudence; than men, that by misreasoning, or by trusting them that reason wrong, fall upon false and absurd general rules. For ignorance of causes, and of rules, does not set men so far out of their way, as relying on false rules, and taking for causes of what they aspire to, those that are not so, but rather causes of the contrary.

To conclude, the light of human minds is perspicuous words, but by exact definitions first snuffed, and purged from ambiguity; *reason* is the *pace;* increase of *science,* the *way;* and the benefit of mankind, the *end.* And, on the contrary, metaphors, and senseless and ambiguous words, are like *ignes fatui;** and reasoning upon them is wandering amongst innumerable absurdities; and their end, contention and sedition, or contempt.

As, much experience, is *prudence;* so, is much science, *sapience.* For though we usually have one name of wisdom for them both; yet the Latins did always distinguish between *prudentia* and *sapientia;* ascribing the former to experience, the later to science. But to make their difference appear more clearly, let us suppose one man endowed with an excellent natural use, and dexterity in handling his arms; and another to have added to that dexterity, an acquired science, of where he can offend, or be offended by his adversary, in every possible posture, or guard: The ability of the former, would be to the ability of the later, as *prudence* to *sapience;* both useful; but the later infallible. But they that trusting only to the authority of books, follow the blind blindly, are like him that trusting to the false rules of a master of fence, ventures presumptuously upon an adversary, that either kills, or disgraces him.

The signs of science, are some, certain and infallible; some, uncertain. Certain, when he that pretendeth the science of any thing, can teach the same; that is to say, demonstrate the truth thereof perspicuously to another: Uncertain, when only some particular events answer to his pretense, and upon many occasions prove so as he says they must. Signs of prudence are all uncertain; because to observe by

*ignitors of foolishness

experience, and remember all circumstances that may alter the success, is impossible. But in any business, whereof a man has not infallible science to proceed by; to forsake his own natural judgement, and be guided by general sentences read in authors, and subject to many exceptions, is a sign of folly, and generally scorned by the name of *pedantry.* And even of those men themselves that in Councils of the Common-wealth, love to show their reading of politics and history, very few do it in their domestic affairs, where their particular interest is concerned; having prudence enough for their private affairs, but in public they study more the reputation of their own wit, than the success of another's business. . . .

Chapter 6: Of the Interior Beginnings of Voluntary Motions, Commonly Called the Passions, and the Speeches by Which They Are Expressed

There be in animals, two sorts of *motions* peculiar to them: one called *vital;* begun in generation, and continued without interruption through their whole life; such as are the *course* of the *blood,* the *pulse,* the *breathing,* the *concoction, nutrition, excretion,* &c., to which motions there needs no help of imagination: the other is *animal motion,* otherwise called *voluntary motion;* as to *go,* to *speak,* to *move* any of our limbs, in such manner as is first fancied in our minds. That sense is motion in the organs and interior parts of man's body caused by the action of the things we see, hear, &c.; and that fancy is but the relics of the same motion, remaining after sense, has been already said in the first and second chapters. And because *going, speaking,* and the like voluntary motions, depend always upon a precedent thought of *whither, which way,* and *what;* it is evident, that the imagination is the first internal beginning of all voluntary motion. And although unstudied men do not conceive any motion at all to be there, where the thing moved is invisible; or the space it is moved in is, for the shortness of it, insensible; yet that doth not hinder, but that such motions are. For let a space be never so little, that which is moved over a greater space, whereof that little one is part, must first be moved over that. These small beginnings of motion, within the body of man, before they appear in walking, speaking, striking, and other visible actions, are commonly called EN-DEAVOUR.

This endeavour, when it is toward something which causes it, is called APPETITE, or DESIRE; the latter, being the general name; and the other oftentimes restrained to signify the desire of food, namely *hunger* and *thirst*. And when the endeavour is fromward something, it is generally called AVERSION. These words, *appetite* and *aversion*, we have from the Latins; and they both of them signify the motions, one of approaching, the other of retiring. So also do the Greek words for the same, which are ὀρμή and ἀφορμή. For nature itself does often press upon men those truths, which afterwards, when they look for somewhat beyond nature, they stumble at. For the Schools find in mere appetite to go, or move, no actual motion at all: but because some motion they must acknowledge, they call it metaphorical motion; which is but an absurd speech: for though words may be called metaphorical; bodies and motions can not.

That which men desire, they are also said to LOVE: and to HATE those things for which they have aversion. So that desire and love are the same thing; save that by desire, we always signify the absence of the object; by love, most commonly the presence of the same. So also by aversion, we signify the absence; and by hate, the presence of the object.

Of appetites and aversions, some are born with men; as appetite of food, appetite of excretion, and exoneration, which may also and more properly be called aversions, from somewhat they feel in their bodies; and some other appetites, not many. The rest, which are appetites of particular things, proceed from experience, and trial of their effects upon themselves or other men. For of things we know not at all, or believe not to be, we can have no further desire, than to taste and try. But aversion we have for things, not only which we know have hurt us, but also that we do not know whether they will hurt us, or not.

Those things which we neither desire, nor hate, we are said to *contemn;* CONTEMPT being nothing else but an immobility, or contumacy of the heart, in resisting the action of certain things; and proceeding from that the heart is already moved otherwise, by other more potent objects; or from want of experience of them.

And because the constitution of a man's body is in continual mutation, it is impossible that all the same things should always cause in him the same appetites, and aversions: much less can all men consent, in the desire of almost any one and the same object.

But whatsoever is the object of any man's appetite or desire, that is it which he for his part calleth *good:* and the object of his hate and aversion, evil; and of his contempt, *vile* and *inconsiderable.* For these words of good, evil, and contemptible, are ever used with relation to the person that useth them: there being nothing simply and absolutely so; nor any common rule of good and evil, to be taken from the nature of the objects themselves; but from the person of the man, where there is no commonwealth; or, in a commonwealth, from the person that representeth it; or from an arbitrator or judge, whom men disagreeing shall by consent set up, and make his sentence the rule thereof.

The Latin tongue has two words, whose significations approach to those of good and evil; but are not precisely the same; and those are *pulchrum* and *turpe.* Whereof the former signifies that, which by some apparent signs promiseth good; and the latter, that which promiseth evil. But in our tongue we have not so general names to express them by. But for *pulchrum* we say in some things, *fair;* in others, *beautiful,* or *handsome,* or *gallant,* or *honourable,* or *comely,* or *amiable;* and for *turpe, foul, deformed, ugly, base, nauseous,* and the like, as the subject shall require; all which words, in their proper places, signify nothing else but the *mien,* or countenance, that promiseth good and evil. So that of good there be three kinds; good in the promise, that is *pulchrum;* good in effect, as the end desired, which is called *jucundum, delightful;* and good as the means, which is called *utile, profitable;* and as many of evil: For *evil* in promise, is that they call *turpe;* evil in effect, and end, is *molestum, unpleasant, troublesome;* and evil in the means, *inutile, unprofitable, hurtful.*

As, in sense, that which is really within us, is, as I have said before, only motion, caused by the action of external objects, but in apparence; to the sight, light and colour; to the ear, sound; to the nostril, odour, &c.: so, when the action of the same object is continued from the eyes, ears, and other organs to the heart, the real effect there is nothing but motion, or endeavour; which consisteth in appetite, or aversion, to or from the object moving. But the apparence, or sense of that motion, is that we either call *delight,* or *trouble of mind.*

This motion, which is called appetite, and for the apparence of it *delight,* and *pleasure,* seemeth to be a corroboration of vital motion, and a help thereunto; and therefore such things as caused delight, were not improperly called *jucunda, a juvando,* from helping or fortifying; and the contrary, *molesta, offensive,* from hindering, and troubling the motion vital.

Pleasure therefore, or *delight,* is the appearence, or sense of good; and *molestation,* or *displeasure,* the appearence, or sense of evil. And consequently all appetite, desire, and love, is accompanied with some delight more or less; and all hatred and aversion, with more or less displeasure and offence.

Of pleasures or delights, some arise from the sense of an object present; and those may be called *pleasure of sense;* the word *sensual,* as it is used by those only that condemn them, having no place till there be laws. Of this kind are all onerations and exonerations of the body; as also all that is pleasant, in the *sight, hearing, smell, taste,* or *touch.* Others arise from the expectation, that proceeds from foresight of the end, or consequence of things; whether those things in the sense please or displease. And these are *pleasures of the mind* of him that draweth those consequences, and are generally called JOY. In the like manner, displeasures are some in the sense, and called PAIN; others in the expectation of consequences, and are called GRIEF.

These simple passions called *appetite, desire, love, aversion, hate, joy,* and *grief,* have their names for divers considerations diversified. As first, when they one succeed another, they are diversely called from the opinion men have of the likelihood of attaining what they desire. Secondly, from the object loved or hated. Thirdly, from the consideration of many of them together. Fourthly, from the alteration or succession itself.

For *appetite,* with an opinion of attaining, is called HOPE.

The same, without such opinion, DESPAIR.

Aversion, with opinion of HURT from the object, FEAR. . . .

Fear of power invisible, feigned by the mind, or imagined from tales publicly allowed, RELIGION; not allowed, SUPERSTITION. And when the power imagined, is truly such as we imagine, TRUE RELIGION.

Fear, without the apprehension of why, or what, PANIC TERROR, called so from the fables, that makes Pan the author of them; whereas, in truth, there is always in him that so feareth first, some apprehension of the cause, though the rest run away by example, every one supposing his fellow to know why. And therefore this passion happens to none but in a throng, or multitude of people.

Joy, from apprehension of novelty, ADMIRATION; proper to man, because it excites the appetite of knowing the cause.

Joy, arising from imagination of a man's own power and ability, is that exultation of the mind which is called GLORYING: which if grounded upon the experience of his own former actions, is the same with *confidence:* but if grounded on the flattery of others; or only supposed by himself, for delight in the consequences of it, is called VAIN-GLORY: which name is properly given; because a well grounded *confidence* begetteth attempt; whereas the supposing of power does not, and is therefore rightly called *vain.* . . .

When in the mind of man, appetites, and aversions, hopes, and fears, concerning one and the same thing, arise alternately; and divers good and evil consequences of the doing, or omitting the thing propounded, come successively into our thoughts; so that sometimes we have an appetite to it; sometimes an aversion from it; sometimes hope to be able to do it; sometimes despair, or fear to attempt it; the whole sum of desires, aversions, hopes and fears continued till the thing be either done, or thought impossible, is that we call DELIBERA-TION.

Therefore of things past, there is no *deliberation;* because manifestly impossible to be changed: nor of things known to be impossible, or thought so; because men know, or think such deliberation vain. But of things impossible, which we think possible, we may deliberate; not knowing it is in vain. And it is called *deliberation;* because it is a putting an end to the *liberty* we had of doing, or omitting, according to our own appetite, or aversion.

This alternate succession of appetites, aversions, hopes and fears, is no less in other living creatures than in man: and therefore beasts also deliberate.

Every *deliberation* is then said to *end,* when that whereof they deliberate, is either done, or thought impossible; because till then we retain the liberty of doing, or omitting; according to our appetite, or aversion.

In *deliberation,* the last appetite, or aversion, immediately adhering to the action, or to the omission thereof, is that we call the WILL; the act, not the faculty, of *willing.* And beasts that have *deliberation,* must necessarily also have *will.* The definition of the *will,* given commonly by the Schools, that it is a *rational appetite,* is not good. For if it were, then could there be no voluntary act against reason. For a *voluntary act* is that, which proceedeth from the *will,* and no other. But if instead of a rational appetite, we shall say an appetite resulting from a precedent deliberation, then the definition is the same that I have given here. *Will,* therefore, *is the last appetite in deliberating.* And though we say in common discourse, a man had a will once to do a thing, that nevertheless he forbore to do; yet that is properly but an inclination, which makes no action voluntary; because the action depends not of it, but of the last inclination, or appetite. For if the intervenient appetites, make any action voluntary; then by the same reason all intervenient aversions, should make the same action involuntary; and so one and the same action, should be both voluntary and involuntary.

By this it is manifest, that not only actions that have their beginning from covetousness, ambition, lust, or other appetites to the thing propounded; but also those that have their beginning from aversion, or fear of those consequences that follow the omission, are *voluntary actions. . . .*

V

John Locke

JOHN LOCKE (1632–1704), one of the greatest of all British philosophers, studied at Oxford University, which at the time was still under the influence of medieval scholasticism. He became deeply interested in philosophy after reading Descartes' *Meditations*, especially in terms of his attempt to work out a method that could accommodate the progress being made in the newly emerging sciences. But whereas Descartes was a rationalist who argued that the mind gains knowledge through reason, Locke was an empiricist who argued that the mind learns almost everything through sensory experiences. He agreed with Descartes, however, that the mind and our ideas—or sense-contents—are better and more directly known than physical objects, which are known only indirectly through our ideas.

In many ways, Locke's *Essay Concerning Human Understanding* is a critical response to, and further development of, the views of Descartes. Locke attacks the idea of innate knowledge, arguing that all ideas in the mind can be accounted for through experience—either via sensation (mental events derived from the outer senses) or via reflection (mental events evoked through introspection). He further differentiates simple ideas (like *red*, *cold*, and *salty*), which are atomic in that they cannot be fractured or divided, from complex compound ideas, put together by the mind, which do not correspond to the real world (such as fictional objects). He tries to explain the origin of all our ideas by analysis of complex ideas into simpler ones.

In Book I, Locke paved the way for his account of the nature and origin of the mind and of ideas provided in Book II by criticizing established opinion, particularly that of innate ideas. At birth, the mind, according to Locke, is a blank slate, knowing nothing, ready to learn anything and everything—which it can do only through experience. All our ideas—about substance, identity, quantity, and even God—are derived from experience. In the second book he gives an account of the history and origin of our ideas, the phenomena of existence, on which our understanding of ourselves and the world is based.

Essay Concerning Human Understanding

Book II

John Locke

Introduction

1. Since it is the *understanding* that sets man above the rest of sensible beings, and gives him all the advantage and dominion which he has over them; it is certainly a subject, even for its nobleness, worth our labour to inquire into. The understanding, like the eye, whilst it makes us see and perceive all other things, takes no notice of itself; and it requires art and pains to set it at a distance and make it its own object. But whatever be the difficulties that lie in the way of this inquiry; whatever it be that keeps us so much in the dark to ourselves; sure I am that all the light we can let in upon our minds, all the acquaintance we can make with our own understandings, will not only be very pleasant, but bring us great advantage, in directing our thoughts in the search of other things.

2. This, therefore, being my purpose—to inquire into the original, certainty, and extent of *human knowledge,* together with the grounds and degrees of *belief, opinion,* and *assent;*—I shall not at present meddle with the physical consideration of the mind; or trouble myself to examine wherein its essence consists; or by what motions of our spirits or alterations of our bodies we come to have any *sensation* by our organs, or any *ideas* in our understandings; and whether those ideas do in their formation, any or all of them, depend on matter or not. These are speculations which, however curious and entertaining, I shall de-

SOURCE: *Essay Concerning Human Understanding,* Book II, by John Locke. First published in 1690.

cline, as lying out of my way in the design I am now upon. It shall suffice to my present purpose, to consider the discerning faculties of a man, as they are employed about the objects which they have to do with. And I shall imagine I have not wholly misemployed myself in the thoughts I shall have on this occasion, if, in this historical, plain method, I can give any account of the ways whereby our understandings come to attain those notions of things we have; and can set down any measures of the certainty of our knowledge; or the grounds of those persuasions which are to be found amongst men, so various, different, and wholly contradictory; and yet asserted somewhere or other with such assurance and confidence, that he that shall take a view of the opinions of mankind, observe their opposition, and at the same time consider the fondness and devotion wherewith they are embraced, the resolution and eagerness wherewith they are maintained, may perhaps have reason to suspect, that either there is no such thing as truth at all, or that mankind hath no sufficient means to attain a certain knowledge of it.

3. It is therefore worth while to search out the bounds between opinion and knowledge; and examine by what measures, in things whereof we have no certain knowledge, we ought to regulate our assent and moderate our persuasion. In order whereunto I shall pursue this following method:—

First, I shall inquire into the original of those *ideas,* notions, or whatever else you please to call them, which a man observes, and is conscious to himself he has in his mind; and the ways whereby the understanding comes to be furnished with them.

Secondly, I shall endeavor to show what *knowledge* the understanding hath by those ideas; and the certainty, evidence, and extent of it.

Thirdly, I shall make some inquiry into the nature and grounds of *faith* or *opinion:* whereby I mean that assent which we give to any proposition as true, of whose truth yet we have no certain knowledge. And here we shall have occasion to examine the reasons and degrees of *assent.*

4. If by this inquiry into the nature of the understanding, I can discover the powers thereof; how far they reach; to what things they are in any degree proportionate; and where they fail us, I suppose it may be of use to prevail with the busy mind of man to be more cautious in meddling with things exceeding its comprehension; to stop when it is at the utmost extent of its tether; and to sit down in a quiet ignorance of those things which, upon examination, are found to be beyond the reach of our capacities. We should not then perhaps be so forward, out of an affectation of an universal knowledge, to raise questions, and perplex ourselves and others with disputes about things to which our understandings are not suited; and of which we cannot frame in our minds any clear or distinct perceptions, or whereof (as it has perhaps too often happened) we have not any notions at all. If we can find out how far the understanding can extend its view; how far it has faculties to attain certainty; and in what cases it can only judge and guess, we may learn to content ourselves with what is attainable by us in this state.

5. For though the comprehension of our understandings comes exceeding short of the vast extent of things, yet we shall have cause enough to magnify the bountiful Author of our being, for that proportion and degree of knowledge he has bestowed on us, so far above all the rest of the inhabitants of this our mansion. Men have reason to be well satisfied with what God hath thought fit for them, since he hath given them (as St. Peter says) πάντα πρὸς ζωὴν καί εὐσέβειαν, whatsoever is necessary for the conveniences of life and information of virtue; and has put within the reach of their discovery, the comfortable provision for this life, and the way that leads to a better. How short soever their knowledge may come of an universal or perfect comprehension of whatsoever is, it yet secures their great concernments, that they have light enough to lead them to the knowledge of their Maker, and the sight of their own duties. Men may find matter sufficient to busy their heads, and employ their hands with variety, delight, and satisfaction, if they will not boldly quarrel with their own constitution, and throw away the blessings their hands are filled with, because they are not big enough to grasp everything. We shall not have much reason to complain of the narrowness of our minds, if we will not employ them about what may be of use to us; for of that they are very capable. And it will be an unpardonable, as well as childish peevishness, if we undervalue the advantages of our knowledge, and neglect to improve it to the ends for which it was given us, because there are some things that are set out of the reach of it. It will be no excuse to an idle and untoward servant, who would not attend his business by candle light, to plead that he had not broad sunshine. The Candle that is set up in us shines bright enough for all our purposes. The discoveries we can make with this ought to satisfy us; and we shall then use our understandings right, when we entertain all objects in that way and proportion that they are suited to our faculties, and upon those grounds they are capable of being proposed to us; and not peremptorily or intemperately require demonstration, and demand certainty, where probability only is to be had, and which is sufficient to govern all our concernments. If we will disbelieve everything, because we cannot certainly know all things, we shall do muchwhat as wisely as he who would not use his legs, but sit still and perish, because he had no wings to fly.

6. When we know our own strength, we shall the better know what to undertake with hopes of success; and when we have well surveyed the *powers* of our own minds, and made some estimate what we may expect from them, we shall not be inclined either to sit still, and not set our thoughts on work at all, in despair of knowing anything; nor on the other side, question everything, and disclaim all knowledge, because some things are not to be un-

derstood. It is of great use to the sailor to know the length of his line, though he cannot with it fathom all the depths of the ocean. It is well he knows that it is long enough to reach the bottom, at such places as are necessary to direct his voyage, and caution him against running upon shoals that may ruin him. Our business here is not to know all things, but those which concern our conduct. If we can find out those measures, whereby a rational creature, put in that state in which man is in this world, may and ought to govern his opinions, and actions depending thereon, we need not to be troubled that some other things escape our knowledge.

7. This was that which gave the first rise to this *Essay* concerning the understanding. For I thought that the first step towards satisfying several inquiries the mind of man was very apt to run into, was, to take a survey of our own understandings, examine our own powers, and see to what things they were adapted. Till that was done I suspected we began at the wrong end, and in vain sought for satisfaction in a quiet and sure possession of truths that most concerned us, whilst we let loose our thoughts into the vast ocean of Being; as if all that boundless extent were the natural and undoubted possession of our understandings, wherein there was nothing exempt from its decisions, or that escaped its comprehensions. Thus men, extending their inquiries beyond their capacities, and letting their thoughts wander into those depths where they can find no sure footing, it is no wonder that they raise questions and multiply disputes, which, never coming to any clear resolution, are proper only to continue and increase their doubts, and to confirm them at last in perfect scepticism. Whereas, were the capacities of our understandings well considered, the extent of our knowledge once discovered, and the horizon found which sets the bounds between the enlightened and dark parts of things; between what is and what is not comprehensible by us, men would perhaps with less scruple acquiesce in the avowed ignorance of the one, and employ their thoughts and discourse with more advantage and satisfaction in the other.

8. Thus much I thought necessary to say concerning the occasion of this Inquiry into

[H]uman Understanding. But, before I proceed on to what I have thought on this subject, I must here in the entrance beg pardon of my reader for the frequent use of the word *idea*, which he will find in the following treatise. It being that term which, I think, serves best to stand for whatsoever is the *object* of the understanding when a man thinks, I have used it to express whatever is meant by *phantasm, notion, species*, or *whatever it is which the mind can be employed about in thinking;* and I could not avoid frequently using it.

I presume it will be easily granted me, that there are such *ideas* in men's minds: every one is conscious of them in himself; and men's words and actions will satisfy him that they are in others.

Our first inquiry then shall be,—how they come into the mind.

Chapter I: Of Ideas in General and Their Original

1. Every man being conscious to himself that he thinks; and that which his mind is applied about whilst thinking being the *ideas* that are there, it is past doubt that men have in their minds several ideas,—such as are those expressed by the words *whiteness, hardness, sweetness, thinking, motion, man, elephant, army, drunkenness*, and others: it is in the first place then to be inquired, *How he comes by them?*

I know it is a received doctrine, that men have native ideas, and original characters, stamped upon their minds in their very first being. This opinion I have at large examined already; and, I suppose what I have said in the foregoing Book will be much more easily admitted, when I have shown whence the understanding may get all the ideas it has; and by what ways and degrees they may come into the mind;—for which I shall appeal to every one's own observation and experience.

2. Let us then suppose the mind to be, as we say, white paper, void of all characters, without any ideas:—How comes it to be furnished? Whence comes it by that vast store which the busy and boundless fancy of man

has painted on it with an almost endless variety? Whence has it all the *materials* of reason and knowledge? To this I answer, in one word, from EXPERIENCE. In that all our knowledge is founded; and from that it ultimately derives itself. Our observation employed either, about external sensible objects, or about the internal operations of our minds perceived and reflected on by ourselves, is that which supplies our understandings with all the *materials* of thinking. These two are the fountains of knowledge, from whence all the ideas we have, or can naturally have, do spring.

3. First, our Senses, conversant about particular sensible objects, do convey into the mind several distinct perceptions of things, according to those various ways wherein those objects do affect them. And thus we come by those *ideas* we have of *yellow, white, heat, cold, soft, hard, bitter, sweet,* and all those which we call sensible qualities; which when I say the senses convey into the mind, I mean, they from external objects convey into the mind what produces there those perceptions. This great source of most of the ideas we have, depending wholly upon our senses, and derived by them to the understanding, I call SENSATION.

4. Secondly, the other fountain from which experience furnisheth the understanding with ideas is,—the perception of, the operations of our own mind within us, as it is employed; about the ideas it has got;—which operations, when the soul comes to reflect on and consider, do furnish the understanding with another set of ideas, which could not be had from things without. And such are *perception, thinking, doubting, believing, reasoning, knowing, willing,* and all the different actings of our own minds;—which we being conscious of, and observing in ourselves, do from these receive into our understandings as distinct ideas as we do from bodies affecting our senses. This source of ideas every man has wholly in himself; and though it be not sense, as having nothing to do with external objects, yet it is very like it, and might properly enough be called *internal sense.* But as I call the other Sensation, so I call this REFLECTION, the ideas it affords being such only as the mind gets by reflecting on its own operations within itself. By reflection then, in the following part of this discourse, I would be understood to mean, that notice which the mind takes of its own operations, and the manner of them, by reason whereof there come to be ideas of these operations in the understanding. These two, I say, viz. external material things, as the objects of SENSATION, and the operations of our own minds within, as the objects of REFLECTION, are to me the only originals from whence all our ideas take their beginnings. The term *operations* here I use in a large sense, as comprehending not barely the actions of the mind about its ideas, but some sort of passions arising sometimes from them, such as is the satisfaction or uneasiness arising from any thought.

5. The understanding seems to me not to have the least glimmering of any ideas which it doth not receive from one of these two. *External objects* furnish the mind with the ideas of sensible qualities, which are all those different perceptions they produce in us; and *the mind* furnishes the understanding with ideas of its own operations.

These, when we have taken a full survey of them, and their several modes, [combinations, and relations,] we shall find to contain all our whole stock of ideas; and that we have nothing in our minds which did not come in one of these two ways. Let any one examine his own thoughts, and thoroughly search into his understanding; and then let him tell me, whether all the original ideas he has there, are any other than of the objects of his senses, or of the operations of his mind, considered as objects of his reflection. And how great a mass of knowledge soever he imagines to be lodged there, he will, upon taking a strict view, see that he has not any idea in his mind but what one of these two have imprinted;—though perhaps, with infinite variety compounded and enlarged by the understanding, as we shall see hereafter.

6. He that attentively considers the state of a child, at his first coming into the world, will have little reason to think him stored with plenty of ideas, that are to be the matter of his future knowledge. It is *by degrees* he comes to be furnished with them. And though the ideas

of obvious and familiar qualities imprint themselves before the memory begins to keep a register of time or order, yet it is often so late before some unusual qualities come in the way, that there are few men that cannot recollect the beginning of their acquaintance with them. And if it were worth while, no doubt a child might be so ordered as to have but a very few, even of the ordinary ideas, till he were grown up to a man. But all that are born into the world, being surrounded with bodies that perpetually and diversely affect them, variety of ideas, whether care be taken of it or not, are imprinted on the minds of children. Light and colours are busy at hand everywhere, when the eye is but open; sounds and some tangible qualities fail not to solicit their proper senses, and force an entrance to the mind;—but yet, I think, it will be granted easily, that if a child were kept in a place where he never saw any other but black and white till he were a man, he would have no more ideas of scarlet or green, than he that from his childhood never tasted an oyster, or a pine-apple, has of those particular relishes.

7. Men then come to be furnished with fewer or more simple ideas from without according as the objects they converse with afford greater or less variety; and from the operations of their minds within, according as they more or less reflect on them. For, though he that contemplates the operations of his mind, cannot but have plain and clear ideas of them; yet, unless he turn his thoughts that way, and considerrs them *attentively* he will no more have clear and distinct ideas of all the operations of his mind, and all that may be observed therein, than he will have all the particular ideas of any landscape, or of the parts and motions of a clock, who will not turn his eyes to it, and with attention heed all the parts of it. The picture, or clock may be so placed, that they may come in this way every day; but yet he will have but a confused idea of all the parts they are made up of, till he applies himself with attention, to consider them each in particular.

8. And hence we see the reason why it is pretty late before most children get ideas of the operations of their own minds; and some have not any very clear or perfect ideas of the greatest part of them all their lives. Because, though they pass there continually, yet, like floating visions, they make not deep impressions enough to leave in their mind clear, distinct, lasting ideas, till the understanding turns inward upon itself, reflects on its own operations, and makes them the objects of its own contemplation. Children when they come first into it, are surrounded with a world of new things, which, by a constant solicitation of their senses, draw the mind constantly to them; forward to take notice of new, and apt to be delighted with the variety of changing objects. Thus the first years are usually employed and diverted in looking abroad. Men's business in them is to acquaint themselves with what is to be found without; and so growing up in a constant attention to outward sensations, seldom make any considerable reflection on what passes within them, till they come to be of riper years; and some scarce ever at all.

9. To ask, at what *time* a man has first any ideas, is to ask, when he begins to perceive;—*having ideas,* and *perception,* being the same thing. I know it is an opinion, that the soul always thinks, and that it has the actual perception of ideas in itself constantly, as long as it exists; and that actual thinking is as inseparable from the soul as actual extension is from the body; which if true, to inquire after the beginning of a man's ideas is the same as to inquire after the beginning of his soul. For, by this account, soul and its ideas, as body and its extension, will begin to exist both at the same time.

10. But whether the soul be supposed to exist, antecedent to, or coeval with, or some time after the first rudiments of organization, or the beginnings of life in the body, I leave to be disputed by those who have better thought of that matter. I confess myself to have one of those dull souls, that doth not perceive itself always to contemplate ideas; nor can conceive it any more necessary for the soul always to think, than for the body always to move: the perception of ideas being (as I conceive) to the soul, what motion is to the body; not its essence, but one of its operations. And therefore, though thinking be supposed never so much the proper action of the soul, yet it is not necessary to suppose that it should be always

thinking, always in action. That, perhaps, is the privilege of the infinite Author and Preserver of all things, who 'never slumbers nor sleeps'; but is not competent to any finite being, at least not to the soul of man. We know certainly, by experience, that we *sometimes* think; and thence draw this infallible consequence,—that there is something in us that has a power to think. But whether that substance *perpetually* thinks or no, we can be no further assured than experience informs us. For, to say that actual thinking is essential to the soul, and inseparable from it, is to beg what is in question, and not to prove it by reason;—which is necessary to be done, if it be not a self-evident proposition. But whether this, 'That the soul always thinks,' be a self-evident proposition, that everybody assents to at first hearing, I appeal to mankind. It is doubted whether I thought at all last night or no. The question being about a matter of fact, it is begging it to bring, as a proof for it, an hypothesis, which is the very thing in dispute: by which way one may prove anything, and it is but supposing that all watches, whilst the balance beats, think, and it is sufficiently proved, and past doubt, that my watch thought all last night. But he that would not deceive himself, ought to build his hypothesis on matter of fact, and make it out by sensible experience, and not presume on matter of fact, because of his hypothesis, that is, because he supposes it to be so; which way of proving amounts to this, that I must necessarily think all last night, because another supposes I always think, though I myself cannot perceive that I always do so.

But men in love with their opinions may not only suppose what is in question, but allege wrong matter of fact. How else could any one make it an inference of mine, that a thing is not, because we are not sensible of it in our sleep? I do not say there is no *soul* in a man, because he is not sensible of it in his sleep; but I do say, he cannot *think* at any time, waking or sleeping, without being sensible of it. Our being sensible of it is not necessary to anything but to our thoughts; and to them it is; and to them it always will be necessary, till we can think without being conscious of it.

11. I grant that the soul, in a waking man, is never without thought, because it is the condition of being awake. But whether sleeping without dreaming be not an affection of the whole man, mind as well as body, may be worth a waking man's consideration; it being hard to conceive that anything should think and not be conscious of it. If the soul doth think in a sleeping man without being conscious of it, I ask whether, during such thinking, it has any pleasure or pain, or be capable of happiness or misery? I am sure the man is not; no more than the bed or earth he lies on. For to be happy or miserable without being conscious of it, seems to me utterly inconsistent and impossible. Or if it be possible that the *soul* can, whilst the body is sleeping, have its thinking, enjoyments, and concerns, its pleasures or pain, apart, which the *man* is not conscious of nor partakes in,—it is certain that Socrates asleep and Socrates awake is not the same person; but his soul when he sleeps, and Socrates the man, consisting of body and soul, when he is waking, are two persons: since waking Socrates has no knowledge of, or concernment for that happiness or misery of his soul, which it enjoys alone by itself whilst he sleeps, without perceiving anything of it; no more than he has for the happiness or misery of a man in the Indies, whom he knows not. For, if we take wholly away all consciousness of our actions and sensations, especially of pleasure and pain, and the concernment that accompanies it, it will be hard to know wherein to place personal identity.

12. The soul, during sound sleep, thinks, say these men. Whilst it thinks and perceives, it is capable certainly of those of delight or trouble, as well as any other perceptions; and *it* must necessarily be *conscious* of its own perceptions. But it has all this apart: the sleeping *man*, it is plain, is conscious of nothing of all this. Let us suppose, then, the soul of Castor, while he is sleeping, retired from his body; which is no impossible supposition for the men I have here to do with, who so liberally allow life, without a thinking soul, to all other animals. These men cannot then judge it impossible, or a contradiction, that the body should live without the soul; nor that the soul should subsist and think, or have perception even perception, of happiness or misery, without

the body. Let us then, I say, suppose the soul of Castor separated during his sleep from his body, to think apart. Let us suppose, too, that it chooses for its scene of thinking the body of another man, v.g. Pollux, who is sleeping without a soul. For, if Castor's soul can think, whilst Castor is asleep, what Castor is never conscious of, it is no matter what *place* it chooses to think in. We have here, then, the bodies of two men with only one soul between them, which we will suppose to sleep and wake by turns; and the soul still thinking in the waking man, whereof the sleeping man is never conscious, has never the least perception. I ask, then whether Castor, and Pollux, thus with only one soul between them, which thinks and perceives in one what the other is never conscious of, nor is concerned for, are not two as distinct *persons* as Castor and Hercules, or as Socrates and Plato were? And whether one of them might not be very happy, and the other very miserable? Just by the same reason, they make the soul and the man two persons, who make the soul think apart what the man is not conscious of. For, I suppose nobody will make identity of persons to consist in the soul's being united to the very same numerical particles of matter. For if that be necessary to identity, it will be impossible, in that constant flux of the particles of our bodies, that any man should be the same person two days, or two moments, together.

13. Thus, methinks, every drowsy nod shakes their doctrine, who teach that the soul is always thinking. Those, at least, who do at any time *sleep without dreaming*, can never be convinced that their thoughts are sometimes for four hours busy without their knowing of it; and if they are taken in the very act, waked in the middle of that sleeping contemplation, can give no manner of account of it.

14. It will perhaps be said,—That the soul thinks even in the soundest sleep, but the *memory* retains it not. That the soul in a sleeping man should be this moment busy a thinking, and the next moment in a waking man not remember nor be able to recollect one jot of all those thoughts, is very hard to be conceived, and would need some better proof than bare assertion to make it be believed. For who can without any more ado, but being barely told

so, imagine that the greatest part of men do, during all their lives, for several hours every day, think of something, which if they were asked, even in the middle of these thoughts, they could remember nothing at all of? Most men, I think, pass a great part of their sleep without dreaming. I once knew a man that was bred a scholar, and had no bad memory, who told me he had never dreamed in his life, till he had that fever he was then newly recovered of, which was about the five or six and twentieth year of his age. I suppose the world affords more such instances: at least every one's acquaintance will furnish him with examples enough of such as pass most of their nights without dreaming.

15. To think often, and never to retain it so much as one moment, is a very useless sort of thinking; and the soul, in such a state of thinking, does very little, if at all, excel that of a looking-glass, which constantly receives variety of images, or ideas, but retains none; they disappear and vanish, and there remain no footsteps of them; the looking-glass is never the better for such ideas, nor the soul for such thoughts. Perhaps it will be said, that in a waking *man* the materials of the body are employed, and made use of, in thinking; and that the memory of thoughts is retained by the impressions that are made on the brain, and the traces there left after such thinking; but that in the thinking of the *soul,* which is not perceived in a sleeping man, there the soul thinks apart, and making no use of the organs of the body, leaves no impressions on it, and consequently no memory of such thoughts. Not to mention again the absurdity of two distinct persons, which follows from this supposition, I answer, further,—That whatever ideas the mind can receive and contemplate without the help of the body, it is reasonable to conclude it can retain without the help of the body too; or else the soul, or any separate spirit, will have but little advantage by thinking. If it has no memory of its own thoughts; if it cannot lay them up for its own use, and be able to recall them upon occasion; if it cannot reflect upon what is past, and make use of its former experiences, reasonings, and contemplations, to what purpose does it think? They who make the soul a thinking thing, at

this rate, will not make it a much more noble being than those do whom they condemn, for allowing it to be nothing but the subtilist parts of matter. Characters drawn on dust, that the first breath of wind effaces; or impressions made on a heap of atoms, or animal spirits, are altogether as useful, and render the subject as noble, as the thoughts of a soul that perish in thinking; that, once out of sight, are gone for ever, and leave no memory of themselves behind them. Nature never makes excellent things for mean or no uses: and it is hardly to be conceived that our infinitely wise Creator should make so admirable a faculty as the power of thinking, that faculty which comes nearest the excellency of his own incomprehensible being, to be so idly and uselessly employed, at least a fourth part of its time here, as to think constantly, without remembering any of those thoughts, without doing any good to itself or others, or being any way useful to any other part of the creation. If we will examine it, we shall not find, I suppose, the motion of dull and senseless matter, any where in the universe, made so little use of and so wholly thrown away.

16. It is true, we have sometimes instances of perception whilst we are asleep, and retain the memory of those thoughts: but how extravagant and incoherent for the most part they are; how little conformable to the perfection and order of a rational being, those who are acquainted with dreams need not be told. This I would willingly be satisfied in,— whether the soul, when it thinks thus apart, and as it were separate from the body, acts less rationally than when conjointly with it, or no. If its separate thoughts be less rational, then these men must say, that the soul owes the perfection of rational thinking to the body: if it does not, it is a wonder that our dreams should be, for the most part, so frivolous and irrational; and that the soul should retain none of its more rational soliloquies and meditations.

17. Those who so confidently tell us that the soul always actually thinks, I would they would also tell us, what those ideas are that are in the soul of a child, before or just at the union with the body, before it hath received any by sensation. The dreams of sleeping men are, as I take it, all made up of the waking man's ideas; though for the most part oddly put together. It is strange, if the soul has ideas of its own that it derived not from sensation or reflection, (as it must have, if it thought before it received any impressions from the body,) that it should never, in its private thinking, (so private, that the man himself perceives it not,) retain any of them the very moment it wakes out of them, and then make the man glad with new discoveries. Who can find it reason that the soul should, in its retirement during sleep, have so many hours' thoughts, and yet never light on any of those ideas it borrowed not from sensation or reflection; or at least preserve the memory of none but such, which, being occasioned from the body, must needs be less natural to a spirit? It is strange the soul should never once in a man's whole life recall over any of its pure native thoughts, and those ideas it had before it borrowed anything from the body; never bring into the waking man's view any other ideas but what have a tang of the cask, and manifestly derive their original from that union. If it always thinks, and so had ideas before it was united, or before it received any from the body, it is not to be supposed but that during sleep it recollects its native ideas; and during that retirement from communicating with the body, whilst it thinks by itself, the ideas it is busied about should be, sometimes at least, those more natural and congenial ones which it had in itself, underived from the body, or its own operations about them: which, since the waking man never remembers, we must from this hypothesis conclude either that the soul remembers something that the man does not; or else that memory belongs only to such ideas as are derived from the body, or the mind's operations about them.

18. I would be glad also to learn from these men who so confidently pronounce that the human soul, or, which is all one, that a man always thinks, how they come to know it; nay, how they come to know that they themselves think, when they themselves do not perceive it. This, I am afraid, is to be sure without proofs, and to know without perceiving. It is, I suspect, a confused notion, taken up to serve an hypothesis; and none of those clear truths, but either their own evidence forces us to admit,

or common experience makes it impudence to deny. For the most that can be said of it is, that it is possible the soul may always think, but not always retain it in memory. And I say, it is as possible that the soul may not always think; and much more probable that it should sometimes not think, than that it should often think, and that a long while together, and not be conscious to itself, the next moment after, that it had thought.

19. To suppose the soul to think, and the man not to perceive it, is, as has been said, to make two persons in one man. And if one considers well these men's way of speaking, one should be led into a suspicion that they do so. For they who tell us that the *soul* always thinks, do never, that I remember, say that a *man* always thinks. Can the soul think, and not the man? Or a man think, and not be conscious of it? This, perhaps, would be suspected of jargon in others. If they say the man thinks always, but is not always conscious of it, they may as well say his body is extended without having parts. For it is altogether as intelligible to say that a body is extended without parts, as that anything thinks without being conscious of it, or perceiving that it does so. They who talk thus may, with as much reason, if it be necessary to their hypothesis, say that a man is always hungry, but that he does not always feel it; whereas hunger consists in that very sensation, as thinking consists in being conscious that one thinks. If they say that a man is always conscious to himself of thinking, I ask, How they know it? Consciousness is the perception of what passes in a man's own mind. Can another man perceive that I am conscious of anything, when I perceive it not myself? No man's knowledge here can go beyond his experience. Wake a man out of a sound sleep, and ask him what he was that moment thinking of. If he himself be conscious of nothing he then thought on, he must be a notable diviner of thoughts that can assure him that he was thinking. May he not, with more reason, assure him he was not asleep? This is something beyond philosophy; and it cannot be less than revelation, that discovers to another thoughts in my mind, when I can find none there myself. And they must needs have a penetrating sight who can certainly see that I

think, when I cannot perceive it myself, and when I declare that I do not; and yet can see that dogs or elephants do not think, when they give all the demonstration of it imaginable, except only telling us that they do so. This some may suspect to be a step beyond the Rosicrucians; it seeming easier to make one's self invisible to others, than to make another's thoughts visible to me, which are not visible to himself. But it is but defining the soul to be 'a substance that always thinks,' and the business is done. If such definition be of any authority, I know not what it can serve for but to make many men suspect that they have no souls at all; since they find a good part of their lives pass away without thinking. For no definitions that I know, no suppositions of any sect, are of force enough to destroy constant experience; and perhaps it is the affectation of knowing beyond what we perceive, that makes so much useless dispute and noise in the world.

20. I see no reason, therefore, to believe that the soul thinks before the senses have furnished it with ideas to think on; and as those are increased and retained, so it comes, by exercise, to improve its faculty of thinking in the several parts of it; as well as, afterwards, by compounding those ideas, and reflecting on its own operations, it increases its stock, as well as facility in remembering, imagining, reasoning, and other modes of thinking.

21. He that will suffer himself to be informed by observation and experience, and not make his own hypothesis the rule of nature, will find few signs of a soul accustomed to much thinking in a new-born child, and much fewer of any reasoning at all. And yet it is hard to imagine that the rational soul should think so much, and not reason at all. And he that will consider that infants newly come into the world spend the greatest part of their time in sleep, and are seldom awake but when either hunger calls for the teat, or some pain (the most importunate of all sensations), or some other violent impression on the body, forces the mind to perceive and attend to it;— he, I say, who considers this, will perhaps find reason to imagine that a *fœtus* in the mother's womb differs not much from the state of a vegetable, but passes the greatest part of its time without perception or thought; doing

very little but sleep in a place where it needs not seek for food, and is surrounded with liquor, always equally soft, and near of the same temper; where the eyes have no light, and the ears so shut up are not very susceptible of sounds; and where there is little or no variety, or change of objects, to move the senses.

22. Follow a child from its birth, and observe the alterations that time makes, and you shall find, as the mind by the senses comes more and more to be furnished with ideas, it comes to be more and more awake; thinks more, the more it has matter to think on. After some time it begins to know the objects which, being most familiar with it, have made lasting impressions. Thus it comes by degrees to know the persons it daily converses with, and distinguishes them from strangers; which are instances and effects of its coming to retain and distinguish the ideas the senses convey to it. And so we may observe how the mind, *by degrees,* improves in these; and *advances* to the exercise of those other faculties of enlarging, compounding, and abstracting its ideas, and of reasoning about them, and reflecting upon all these; of which I shall have occasion to speak more hereafter.

23. If it shall be demanded then, *when* a man *begins* to have any ideas, I think the true answer is,—*when he first has any sensation.* For, since there appear not to be any ideas in the mind before the senses have conveyed any in, I conceive that ideas in the understanding are coeval with *sensation; which is such an impression or motion made in some part of the body, as [produces some perception] in the understanding.* It is about these impressions made on our senses by outward objects that the mind seems *first* to employ itself, in such operations as we call perception, remembering, consideration, reasoning, &c.

24. In time the mind comes to reflect on its own operations about the ideas got by sensation, and thereby stores itself with a new set of ideas, which I call ideas of reflection. These are the impressions that are made on our senses by outward objects that are extrinsical to the mind; and its own operations, proceeding from powers intrinsical and proper to itself, which, when reflected on by itself, become also objects of its contemplation—are, as

I have said, the original of all knowledge. Thus the first capacity of human intellect is,— that the mind is fitted to receive the impressions made on it; either through the senses by outward objects, or by its own operations when it reflects on them. This is the first step a man makes towards the discovery of anything, and the groundwork whereon to build all those notions which ever he shall have naturally in this world. All those sublime thoughts which tower above the clouds, and reach as high as heaven itself, take their rise and footing here: in all that great extent wherein the mind wanders, in those remote speculations it may seem to be elevated with, it stirs not one jot beyond those ideas which *sense* or *reflection* have offered for its contemplation.

25. In this part the understanding is merely passive; and whether or no it will have these beginnings, and as it were materials of knowledge, is not in its own power. For the objects of our senses do, many of them, obtrude their particular ideas upon our minds whether we will or not; and the operations of our minds will not let us be without, at least, some obscure notions of them. No man can be wholly ignorant of what he does when he thinks. These simple ideas, when offered to the mind, the understanding can no more refuse to have, nor alter when they are imprinted, nor blot them out and make new ones itself, than a mirror can refuse, alter, or obliterate the images or ideas which the objects set before it do therein produce. As the bodies that surround us do diversely affect our organs, the mind is forced to receive the impressions; and cannot avoid the perception of those ideas that are annexed to them.

Chapter II: Of Simple Ideas

1. The better to understand the nature, manner, and extent of our knowledge, one thing is carefully to be observed concerning the ideas we have; and that is, that some of them are *simple* and some *complex.*

Though the qualities that affect our senses are, in the things themselves, so united and blended, that there is no separation, no distance between them; yet it is plain, the ideas they produce in the mind enter by the senses simple and unmixed. For, though the sight and touch often take in from the same object, at the same time, different ideas;—as a man sees at once motion and colour; the hand feels softness and warmth in the same piece of wax: yet the simple ideas thus united in the same subject, are as perfectly distinct as those that come in by different senses. The coldness and hardness which a man feels in a piece of ice being as distinct ideas in the mind as the smell and whiteness of a lily; or as the taste of sugar, and smell of a rose. And there is nothing can be plainer to a man than the clear and distinct perception he has of those simple ideas; which, being each in itself uncompounded, contains in it nothing but *one uniform appearance, or conception of the mind,* and is not distinguishable into different ideas.

2. These simple ideas, the materials of all our knowledge, are suggested and furnished to the mind only by those two ways above mentioned, viz. sensation and reflection. When the understanding is once stored with these simple ideas, it has the power to repeat, compare, and unite them, even to an almost infinite variety, and so can make at pleasure new complex ideas. But it is not in the power of the most exaulted wit, or enlarged understanding, by any quickness or variety of thought, to *invent* or *frame* one new simple idea in the mind, not taken in by the ways before mentioned: nor can any force of the understanding *destroy* those that are there. The dominion of man, in this little world of his own understanding being muchwhat the same as it is in the great world of visible things; wherein his power, however managed by art and skill, reaches no farther than to compound and divide the materials that are made to his hand; but can do nothing towards the making the least particle of new matter, or destroying one atom of what is already in being. The same inability will every one find in himself, who shall go about to fashion in his understanding one simple idea, not received in by his senses from external objects, or by reflection from the operations of his own mind about them. I would have any one try to fancy any taste which had never affected his palate; or frame the idea of a scent he had never smelt: and when he can do this, I will also conclude that a blind man hath ideas of colours, and a deaf man true distinct notions of sounds.

3. This is the reason why—though we cannot believe it impossible to God to make a creature with other organs, and more ways to convey into the understanding the notice of corporeal things than those five, as they are usually counted, which he has given to man— yet I think it is not possible for any *man* to imagine any other qualities in bodies, howsoever constituted, whereby they can be taken notice of, besides sounds, tastes, smells, visible and tangible qualities. And had mankind been made but with four senses, the qualities then which are the objects of the fifth sense had been as far from our notice, imagination, and conception, as now any belonging to a sixth, seventh, or eighth sense can possibly be;— which, whether yet some other creatures, in some other parts of this vast and stupendous universe, may not have, will be a great presumption to deny. He that will not set himself proudly at the top of all things, but will consider the immensity of this fabric, and the great variety that is to be found in this little and inconsiderable part of it which he has to do with, may be apt to think that, in other mansions of it, there may be other and different intelligent beings, of whose faculties he has as little knowledge or apprehension as a worm shut up in one drawer of a cabinet hath of the senses or understanding of a man; such variety and excellency being suitable to the wisdom and power of the Maker. I have here followed the common opinion of man's having but five senses; though, perhaps, there may be justly counted more;—but either supposition serves equally to my present purpose.

Chapter III: Of Simple Ideas of Sense

1. The better to conceive the ideas we receive from sensation, it may not be amiss for us to consider them, in reference to the different

ways whereby they make their approaches to our minds, and make themselves perceivable by us.

First, then, There are some which come into our minds *by one sense only.*

Secondly, There are others that convey themselves into the mind *by more senses than one.*

Thirdly, Others that are had from *reflection only.*

Fourthly, There are some that make themselves way, and are suggested to the mind *by all the ways of sensation and reflection.*

We shall consider them apart under these several heads.

There are some ideas which have admittance only through one sense, which is peculiarly adapted to receive them. Thus light and colours, as white, red, yellow, blue; with their several degrees or shades and mixtures, as green, scarlet, purple, sea-green, and the rest, come in only by the eyes. All kinds of noises, sounds, and tones, only by the ears. The several tastes and smells, by the nose and palate. And if these organs, or the nerves which are the conduits to convey them from without to their audience in the brain,—the mind's presence-room (as I may so call it)—are any of them so disordered as not to perform their functions, they have no postern to be admitted by; no other way to bring themselves into view, and be perceived by the understanding.

The most considerable of those belonging to the touch, are heat and cold, and solidity: all the rest, consisting almost wholly in the sensible configuration, as smooth and rough; or else, more or less firm adhesion of the parts, as hard and soft, tough and brittle, are obvious enough.

2. I think it will be needless to enumerate all the particular simple ideas belonging to each sense. Nor indeed is it possible if we would; there being a great many more of them belonging to most of the senses than we have names for. This variety of smells, which are as many almost, if not more, than species of bodies in the world, do most of them want names. Sweet and stinking commonly serve our turn for these ideas, which in effect is little more than to call them pleasing or displeasing; though the smell of a rose and violet, both

sweet, are certainly very distinct ideas. Nor are the different tastes, that by our palates we receive ideas of, much better provided with names. Sweet, bitter, sour, harsh, and salt are almost all the epithets we have to denominate that numberless variety of relishes, which are to be found distinct, not only in almost every sort of creatures, but in the different parts of the same plant, fruit, or animal. The same may be said of colours and sounds. I shall, therefore, in the account of simple ideas I am here giving, content myself to set down only such as are most material to our present purpose, or are in themselves less apt to be taken notice of though they are very frequently the ingredients of our complex ideas; amongst which, I think, I may well account solidity, which therefore I shall treat of in the next chapter.

Chapter IV: Idea of Solidity

---

1. The idea of *solidity* we receive by our touch: and it arises from the resistance which we find in body to the entrance of any other body into the place it possesses, till it has left it. There is no idea which we receive more constantly from sensation than solidity. Whether we move or rest, in what posture soever we are, we always feel something under us that supports us, and hinders our further sinking downwards; and the bodies which we daily handle make us perceive that, whilst they remain between them, they do, by an insurmountable force, hinder the approach of the parts of our hands that press them. *That which thus hinders the approach of two bodies, when they are moved one towards another, I call solidity.* I will not dispute whether this acceptation of the word solid be nearer to its original signification than that which mathematicians use it in. It suffices that I think the common notion of solidity will allow, if not justify, this use of it; but if any one think it better to call it *impenetrability,* he has my consent. Only I have thought the term solidity the more proper to express this idea, not only because of its vulgar use in that sense, but also because it carries something more of positive in it than impenetrability; which is negative, and is perhaps

more a consequence of solidity, than solidity itself. This, of all other, seems the idea most intimately connected with, and essential to body; so as nowhere else to be found or imagined, but only in matter. And though our senses take no notice of it, but in masses of matter, of a bulk sufficient to cause a sensation in us: yet the mind, having once got this idea from such grosser sensible bodies, traces it further, and considers it, as well as figure, in the minutest particle of matter that can exist; and finds it inseparably inherent in body, wherever or however modified.

2. This is the idea which belongs to body, whereby we conceive it to fill space. The idea of which filling of space is,—that where we imagine any space taken up by a solid substance, we conceive it so to possess it, that it excludes all other solid substances; and will for ever hinder any other two bodies, that move towards one another in a straight line, from coming to touch one another, unless it removes from between them in a line not parallel to that which they move in. This idea of it, the bodies which we oridnarily handle sufficiently furnish us with.

3. This resistance, whereby it keeps other bodies out of the space which it possesses, is so great, that no force, how great soever, can surmount it. All the bodies in the world, pressing a drop of water on all sides, will never be able to overcome the resistance which it will make, soft as it is, to their approaching one another, till it be removed out of their way: whereby our idea of solidity is distinguished both from pure space, which is capable neither of resistance nor motion; and from the ordinary idea of hardness. For a man may conceive two bodies at a distance, so as they may approach one another, without touching or displacing any solid thing, till their superficies come to meet; whereby, I think, we have the clear idea of space without solidity. For (not to go so far as annihilation of any particular body) I ask, whether a man cannot have the idea of the motion of one single body alone, without any other succeeding immediately into its place? I think it is evident he can: the idea of motion in one body no more including the idea of motion in another, than the idea of a square figure in one body includes the idea of a square figure in another. I do not ask,

whether bodies do so *exist,* that the motion of one body cannot really be without the motion of another. To determine this either way, is to beg the question for or against a *vacuum.* But my question is,—whether one cannot have the *idea* of one body moved, whilst others are at rest? And I think this no one will deny. If so, then the place it deserted gives us the idea of pure space without solidity; whereinto any other body may enter, without either resistance or protrusion of anytl.ing. When the sucker in a pump is drawn, the space it filled in the tube is certainly the same whether any other body follows the motion of the sucker or not: nor does it imply a contradiction that, upon the motion of one body, another that is only contiguous to it should not follow it. The necessity of such a motion is built only on the supposition that the world is full; but not on the distinct *ideas* of space and solidity, which are as different as resistance and not resistance, protrusion and not protrusion. And that men have ideas of space without a body, their very disputes about a vacuum plainly demonstrate, as is shown in another place.

4. Solidity is hereby also differences from hardness, in that solidity consists in repletion, and so an utter exclusion of other bodies out of the space it possesses: but hardness, in a firm cohesion of the parts of matter, making up masses of a sensible bulk, so that the whole does not easily change its figure. And indeed, hard and soft are names that we give to things only in relation to the constitutions of our own bodies; that being generally called hard by us, which will put us to pain sooner than change figure by the pressure of any part of our bodies; and that, on the contrary, soft, which changes the situation of its parts upon an easy and unpainful touch.

But this difficulty of changing the situation of the sensible parts amongst themselves, or of the figure of the whole, gives no more solidity to the hardest body in the world than to the softest; nor is an adamant one jot more solid than water. For, though the two flat sides of two pieces of marble will more easily approach each other, between which there is nothing but water or air, then if there be a diamond between them; yet it is not that the parts of the diamond are more solid than those of water, or resist more; but because the parts of water, being more easily separable from each other, they will, by a side motion, be more easily removed, and give way to the approach of the two pieces of marble. But if they could be kept from making place by that side motion, they would eternally hinder the approach of these two pieces of marble, as much as the diamond; and it would be as impossible by any force to surmount their resistance, as to surmount the resistance of the parts of a diamond. The softest body in the world will as invincibly resist the coming together of any other two bodies, if it be not put out of the way, but remain between them, as the hardest that can be found or imagined. He that shall fill a yielding soft body well with air or water, will quickly find its resistance. And he that thinks that nothing but bodies that are hard can keep his hands from approaching one another, may be pleased to make a trial, with the air inclosed in a football. The experiment, I have been told, was made at Florence, with a hollow globe of gold filled with water, and exactly closed; which further shows the solidity of so soft a body as water. For the golden globe thus filled, being put into a press, which was driven by the extreme force of screws, the water made itself way through the pores of that very close metal, and finding no room for a nearer approach of its particles within, got to the outside, where it rose like a dew, and so fell in drops, before the sides of the globe could be made to yield to the violent compression of the engine that squeezed it.

By this idea of solidity is the extension of body distinguished from the extension of space:—the extension of body being nothing but the cohesion or continuity of solid, separable, movable parts; and the extension of space, the continuity of unsolid, inseparable, and immovable parts. Upon the solidity of bodies also depend their mutual impulse, resistance, and protrusion. Of pure space then, and solidity, there are several (amongst which I confess myself one) who persuade themselves they have clear and distinct ideas; and that they can think on space, without anything in it that resists or is protruded by body. This is the idea of pure space, which they think they have as clear as any idea they can have of the extension of body: the idea of the distance between the opposite parts of a concave superficies being equally as clear without as with the idea of

any solid parts between: and on the other side, they persuade themselves that they have, distinct from that of pure space, the idea of *something that fills space,* that can be protruded by the impulse of other bodies, or resist their motion. If there be others that have not these two ideas distinct, but confound them, and make but one of them, I know not how men, who have the same idea under different names, or different ideas under the same name, can in that case talk with one another; any more than a man who, not being blind or deaf, has distinct ideas of the colour of scarlet and the sound of a trumpet, could discourse concerning scarlet colour with the blind man I mentioned in another place, who fancied that the idea of scarlet was like the sound of a trumpet.

If any one asks me, *What this solidity is,* I send him to his senses to inform him. Let him put a flint or a football between his hands, and then endeavor to join them, and he will know. If he thinks this not a sufficient explication of solidity, what it is, and wherein it consists; I promise to tell him what it is, and wherein it consists, when he tells me what thinking is, or wherein it consists; or explains to me what extension or motion is, which perhaps seems much easier. The simple ideas we have, are such as experience teaches them us; but if, beyond that, we endeavor by words to make them clearer in the mind, we shall succeed no better than if we went about to clear up the darkness of a blind man's mind by talking; and to discourse into him the ideas of light and colours. The reason of this I shall show in another place.

Chapter V: Of Simple Ideas of Divers Senses

The ideas we get by more than one sense are, of *space* or *extension, figure, rest,* and *motion.* For these make perceivable impressions, both on the eyes and touch; and we can receive and convey into our minds the ideas of the extension, figure, motion, and rest of bodies, both by seeing and feeling. But having occasion to speak more at large of these in another place, I here only enumerate them.

Chapter VI: Of Simple Ideas of Reflection

The mind receiving the ideas mentioned in the foregoing chapters from without, when it turns its view inward upon itself, and observes its own actions about those ideas it has, takes from thence other ideas, which are as capable to be the objects of its contemplation as any of those it received from foreign things.

The two great and principal actions of the mind, which are most frequently considered, and which are so frequent that every one that pleases may take notice of them in himself, are these two: —

Perception, or *Thinking;* and *Volition*, or *Willing.*

The power of thinking is called the *Understanding*, and the power of volition is called the *Will;* and these two powers or abilities in the mind are denominated faculties.

Of some of the *modes* of these simple ideas of reflection, such as are *remembrance, discerning, reasoning, judging, knowledge, faith*, &c., I shall have occasion to speak hereafter.

Chapter VII: Of Simple Ideas of Both Sensation and Reflection

1. There be other simple ideas which convey themselves into the mind by all the ways of sensation and reflection, viz. *pleasure* or *delight*, and its opposite, *pain*, or *uneasiness; power; existence; unity.*

2. Delight or uneasiness, one or other of them, join themselves to almost all our ideas both of sensation and reflection; and there is scarce any affection of our senses from without, any retired thought of our mind within, which is not able to produce in us pleasure or pain. By pleasure and pain, I would be understood to signify, whatsoever delights or molests us; whether it arises from the thoughts of our minds, or anything operating on our bodies. For, whether we call it satisfaction, delight, pleasure, happiness, &c., on the one side, or uneasiness, trouble, pain, torment, anguish, misery, &c., on the other, they are still but different degrees of the same thing, and belong to the ideas of pleasure and pain, delight or uneasiness; which are the names I shall most commonly use for those two sorts of ideas.

3. The infinite wise Author of our being, having given us the power over several parts of our bodies, to move or keep them at rest as we think fit; and also, by the motion of them, to move ourselves and other contiguous bodies, in which consist all the actions of our body: having also given a power to our minds, in several instances, to choose, amongst its ideas, which it will think on, and to pursue the inquiry of this or that subject with consideration and attention, to excite us to these actions of thinking and motion that we are capable of, — has been pleased to join to several thoughts, and several sensations a perception of delight. If this were wholly separated from all our outward sensations, and inward thoughts, we should have no reason to prefer one thought or action to another; negligence to attention, or motion to rest. And so we should neither stir our bodies, nor employ our minds, but let our thoughts (if I may so call it) run adrift, without any direction or design, and suffer the ideas of our minds, like unregarded shadows, to make their appearances there, as it happened, without attending to them. In which state man, however furnished with the faculties of understanding and will, would be a very idle, inactive creature, and pass his time only in a lazy, lethargic dream. It has therefore pleased our wise Creator to annex to several objects, and the ideas which we receive from them, as also to several of our thoughts, a concomitant pleasure, and that in several objects, to several degrees, that those faculties which he had endowed us with might not remain wholly idle and unemployed by us.

4. Pain has the same efficacy and use to set us on work that pleasure has, we being as ready to employ our faculties to avoid that, as to pursue this: only this is worth our consideration, that pain is often produced by the same objects and ideas that produce pleasure in us. This their near conjunction, which makes us often feel pain in the sensations

where we expected pleasure, gives us new occasion of admiring the wisdom and goodness of our Maker, who, designing the preservation of our being, has annexed pain to the application of many things to our bodies, to warn us of the harm that they will do, and as advices to withdraw from them. But he, not designing our preservation barely, but the preservation of every part and organ in its perfection, hath in many cases annexed pain to those very ideas which delight us. Thus heat, that is very agreeable to us in one degree, by a little greater increase of it proves no ordinary torment; and the most pleasant of all sensible objects, light itself, if there be too much of it, if increased beyond a due proportion to our eyes, causes a very painful sensation. Which is wisely and favourably so ordered by nature, that when any object does, by the vehemency of its operation, disorder the instruments of sensation, whose structures cannot but be very nice and delicate, we might, by the pain, be warned to withdraw, before the organ be quite put out of order, and so be unfitted for its proper function for the future. The consideration of those objects that produce it may well persuade us, that this is the end or use of pain. For, though great light be insufferable to our eyes, yet the highest degree of darkness does not at all disease them: because that, causing no disorderly motion in it, leaves that curious organ unarmed in its natural state. But yet excess of cold as well as heat pains us: because it is equally destructive to that temper which is necessary to the preservation of life, and the exercise of the several functions of the body, and which consists in a moderate degree of warmth; or, if you please, a motion of the insensible parts of our bodies, confined within certain bounds.

5. Beyond all this, we may find another reason why God hath scattered up and down several degrees of pleasure and pain, in all the things that environ and affect us; and blended them together in almost all that our thoughts and senses have to do with;—that we, finding imperfection, dissatisfaction, and want of complete happiness, in all the enjoyments which the creatures can afford us, might be led to seek it in the enjoyment of Him with whom there is fullness of joy, and at whose right hand are pleasures for evermore.

6. Though what I have here said may not, perhaps, make the ideas of pleasure and pain clearer to us than our own experience does, which is the only way that we are capable of having them; yet the consideration of the reason why they are annexed to so many other ideas, serving to give us due sentiments of the wisdom and goodness of the Sovereign Disposer of all things, may not be unsuitable to the main end of these inquiries: the knowledge and veneration of him being the chief end of all our thoughts, and the proper business of all understandings.

7. *Existence* and *Unity* are two other ideas that are suggested to the understanding by every object without, and every idea within. When ideas are in our minds, we consider them as being actually there, as well as we consider things to be actually without us; which is, that they exist, or have existence. And whatever we can consider as one thing, whether a real being or idea, suggests to the understanding the idea of unity.

8. *Power* also is another of those simple ideas which we receive from sensation and reflection. For, observing in ourselves that we do and can think, and that we can at pleasure move several parts of our bodies which were at rest; the effects, also, that natural bodies are able to produce in one another, occurring every moment to our senses,—we both these ways get the idea of power.

9. Besides these there is another idea, which, though suggested by our senses, yet is more constantly offered to us by what passes in our minds; and that is the idea of *succession*. For if we look immediately into ourselves, and reflect on what is observable there, we shall find our ideas always, whilst we are awake, or have any thought, passing in train, one going and another coming, without intermission.

10. These, if they are not all, are at least (as I think) the most considerable of those simple ideas which the mind has, and out of which is made all its other knowledge; all which it receives only by the two forementioned ways of sensation and reflection.

Nor let any one think these too narrow bounds for the capacious mind of man to expatiate in, which takes its flight further than the stars, and cannot be confined by the limits of the world; that extends its thoughts often even beyond the utmost expansion of Matter, and makes excursions into that incomprehensible Inane. I grant all this, but desire any one to assign any *simple idea* which is not received from one of those inlets before mentioned, or any *complex idea* not made out of those simple ones. Nor will it be so strange to think these few simple ideas sufficient to employ the quickest thought, or largest capacity; and to furnish the materials of all that various knowledge, and more various fancies and opinions of all mankind, if we consider how many words may be made out of the various composition of twenty-four letters; or if, going one step further, we will but reflect on the variety of combinations that may be made with barely one of the above-mentioned ideas, viz. number, whose stock is inexhaustible and truly infinite: and what a large and immense field doth extension alone afford the mathematicians?

Chapter VIII: Some Further Considerations Concerning Our Simple Ideas of Sensation

1. Concerning the simple ideas of Sensation, it is to be considered,—that whatsoever is so constituted in nature as to be able, by affecting our senses, to cause any perception in the mind, doth thereby produce in the understanding a simple idea; which, whatever be the external cause of it, when it comes to be taken notice of by our discerning faculty, it is by the mind looked on and considered there to be a real positive idea in the understanding, as much as any other whatsoever; though, perhaps, the cause of it be but a privation of the subject.

2. Thus the ideas of heat and cold, light and darkness, white and black, motion and rest, are equally clear and positive ideas in the mind; though, perhaps, some of the causes which produce them are barely privations, in those subjects from whence our senses derive those ideas. These the understanding, in its view of them, considers all as distinct positive ideas, without taking notice of the causes that produce them: which is an inquiry not belonging to the idea, as it is in the understanding,

but to the nature of the things existing without us. These are two very different things, and carefully to be distinguished; it being one thing to perceive and know the idea of white or black, and quite another to examine what kind of particles they must be, and how ranged in the superficies, to make any object appear white or black.

3. A painter or dyer who never inquired into their causes hath the ideas of white and black, and other colours, as clearly, perfectly, and distinctly in his understanding, and perhaps more distinctly, than the philosopher who hath busied himself in considering their natures, and thinks he knows how far either of them is, in its cause, positive or privative; and the idea of black is no less positive in his mind than that of white, however the cause of that colour in the external object may be only a privation.

4. If it were the design of my present undertaking to inquire into the natural causes and manner of perception, I should offer this as a reason why a privative cause might, in some cases at least, produce a positive idea; viz. that all sensation being produced in us only by different degrees and modes of motion in our animal spirits, variously agitated by external objects, the abatement of any former motion must as necessarily produce a new sensation as the variation or increase of it; and so introduce a new idea, which depends only on a different motion of the animal spirits in that organ.

5. But whether this be so or not I will not here determine, but appeal to every one's own experience, whether the shadow of a man, though it consists of nothing but the absence of light (and the more the absence of light is, the more discernible is the shadow) does not, when a man looks on it, cause as clear and positive idea in his mind, as a man himself, though covered over with clear sunshine? And the picture of a shadow is a positive thing. Indeed, we have negative names, which stand not directly for positive ideas, but for their absence, such as *insipid, silence, nihil*, &c.; which words denote positive ideas, v.g. *taste, sound, being*, with a signification of their absence.

6. And thus one may truly be said to see darkness. For, supposing a hole perfectly dark, from whence no light is reflected, it is

certain one may see the figure of it, or it may be painted; or whether the ink I write with makes any other idea, is a question. The privative causes I have here assigned of positive ideas are according to the common opinion; but, in truth, it will be hard to determine whether there be really any ideas from a privative cause, till it be determined, whether rest be any more a privation than motion.

7. To discover the nature of our *ideas* the better, and to discourse of them intelligibly, it will be convenient to distinguish them *as they are ideas or perceptions in our minds; and as they are modifications of matter in the bodies that cause such perceptions in us:* that so we may not think (as perhaps usually is done) that they are exactly the images and resemblances of something inherent in the subject; most of those of sensation being in the mind no more the likeness of something existing without us, than the names that stand for them are the likeness of our ideas, which yet upon hearing they are apt to excite in us.

8. Whatsoever the mind perceives *in itself,* or is the immediate object of perception, thought, or understanding, that I call *idea; and* the power to produce any idea in our mind, I call *quality* of the subject wherein that power is. Thus a snowball having the power to produce in us the ideas of white, cold, and round,—the power to produce those ideas in us, as they are in the snowball, I call qualities; and as they are sensations or perceptions in our understandings, I call them ideas; which *ideas,* if I speak of sometimes as in the things themselves, I would be understood to mean those qualities in the objects which produce them in us.

9. Qualities thus considered in bodies are, *First,* such as are utterly inseparable from the body, in what state soever it be; and such as in all the alterations and changes it suffers, all the force can be used upon it, it constantly keeps; and such as sense constantly finds in every particle of matter which has bulk enough to be perceived; and the mind finds inseparable from every particle of matter, though less than to make itself singly be perceived by our senses: v.g. Take a grain of wheat, divide it into two parts; each part has still solidity, extension, figure, and mobility: divide it again, and it retains still the same qualities; and so

divide it on, till the parts become insensible; they must retain still each of them all those qualities. For division (which is all that a mill, or pestle, or any other body, does upon another, in reducing it to insensible parts) can never take away either solidity, extension, figure, or mobility from any body, but only makes two or more distinct separate masses of matter, of that which was but one before; all which distinct masses, reckoned as so many distinct bodies, after division, make a certain number. These I call *original* or *primary qualities* of body, which I think we may observe to produce simple ideas in us, viz. solidity, extension, figure, motion or rest, and number.

10. *Secondly,* such qualities which in truth are nothing in the objects themselves but powers to produce various sensations in us by their primary qualities, i.e. by the bulk, figure, texture, and motion of their insensible parts, as colours, sounds, tastes, &c. These I call *secondary qualities.* To these might be added a *third* sort, which are allowed to be barely powers; though they are as much real qualities in the subject as those which I, to comply with the common way of speaking, call qualities, but for distinction, secondary qualities. For the power in fire to produce a new colour, or consistency, in *wax* or *clay,*—by its primary qualities, is as much a quality in fire, as the power it has to produce in *me* a new idea or sensation of warmth or burning, which I felt not before,—by the same primary qualities, viz. the bulk, texture, and motion of its insensible parts.

11. The next thing to be considered is, how bodies produce ideas in us; and that is manifestly by impulse, the only way which we can conceive bodies to operate in.

12. If then external objects be not united to our minds when they produce ideas therein; and yet we perceive these *original* qualities in such of them as singly fall under our senses, it is evident that some motion must be thence continued by our nerves, or animal spirits, by some parts of our bodies, to the brains or the seat of sensation, there to produce in our minds the particular ideas we have of them. And since the extension, figure, number, and motion of bodies of an observable bigness, may be perceived at a distance by the sight, it is evident some singly imperceptible bodies must

come from them to the eyes, and thereby convey to the brain some motion; which produces these ideas which we have of them in us.

13. After the same manner that the ideas of these original qualities are produced in us, we may conceive that the ideas of *secondary* qualities are also produced, viz. by the operation of insensible particles on our senses. For, it being manifest that there are bodies and good store of bodies, each whereof are so small, that we cannot by any of our senses discover either their bulk, figure, or motion,—as is evident in the particles of the air and water, and others extremely smaller than those; perhaps as much smaller than the particles of air and water, as the particles of air and water are smaller than peas or hail-stones;—let us suppose at present that the different motions and figures, bulk and number, of such particles, affecting the several organs of our senses, produce in us those different sensations which we have from the colours and smells of bodies; v.g. that a violet, by the impulse of such insensible particles of matter, of peculiar figures and bulks, and in different degrees and modifications of their motions, causes the ideas of the blue colour, and sweet scent of that flower to be produced in our minds. It being no more impossible to conceive that God should annex such ideas to such motions, with which they have no similitude, than that he should annex the idea of pain to the motion of a piece of steel dividing our flesh, with which that idea hath no resemblance.

14. What I have said concerning colours and smells may be understood also of tastes and sounds, and other the like sensible qualities; which, whatever reality we by mistake attribute to them, are in truth nothing in the objects themselves, but powers to produce various sensations in us; and depend on those primary qualities, viz. bulk, figure, texture, and motion of parts as I have said.

15. From whence I think it easy to draw this observation,—that the ideas of primary qualities of bodies are resemblances of them, and their patterns do really exist in the bodies themselves, but the ideas produced in us by these secondary qualities have no resemblance of them at all. There is nothing like our ideas, existing in the bodies themselves. They are, in

the bodies we denominate from them, only a power to produce those sensations in us: and what is sweet, blue, or warm in idea, is but the certain bulk, figure, and motion of the insensible parts, in the bodies themselves, which we call so.

16. Flame is denominated hot and light; snow, white and cold; and manna, white and sweet, from the ideas they produce in us. Which qualities are commonly thought to be the same in those bodies that those ideas are in us, the one the perfect resemblance of the other, as they are in a mirror, and it would by most men be judged very extravagant if one should say otherwise. And yet he that will consider that the same fire that, at one distance produces in us the sensation of warmth, does, at a nearer approach, produce in us the far different sensation of pain, ought to bethink himself what reason he has to say—that this idea of warmth, which was produced in him by the fire, is *actually in the fire;* and his idea of pain, which the same fire produced in him the same way, is *not* in the fire. Why are whiteness and coldness in snow, and pain not, when it produces the one and the other idea in us; and can do neither, but by the bulk, figure, number, and motion of its solid parts?

17. The particular bulk, number, figure, and motion of the parts of fire or snow are really in them,—whether any one's senses perceive them or no: and therefore they may be called *real* qualities, because they really exist in those bodies. But light, heat, whiteness, or coldness, are no more really in them than sickness or pain is in manna. Take away the sensation of them; let not the eyes see light or colours, nor the ears hear sounds; let the palate not taste, nor the nose smell, and all colours, tastes, odours, and sounds, *as they are such particular ideas,* vanish and cease, and are reduced to their causes, i.e. bulk, figure, and motion of parts.

18. A piece of manna of a sensible bulk is able to produce in us the idea of a round or square figure; and by being removed from one place to another, the idea of motion. This idea of motion represents it as it really is in manna moving: a circle or square are the same, whether in idea or existence, in the mind or in the manna. And this, both motion

and figure, are really in the manna, whether we take notice of them or no: this everybody is ready to agree to. Besides, manna, by the bulk, figure, texture, and motion of its parts, has a power to produce the sensations of sickness, and sometimes of acute pains or gripings in us. That these ideas of sickness and pain are *not* in the manna, but effects of its operations on us, and are nowhere when we feel them not; this also every one readily agrees to. And yet men are hardly to be brought to think that sweetness and whiteness are not really in manna; which are but the effects of the operations of manna, by the motion, size, and figure of its particles, on the eyes and palate: as the pain and sickness caused by manna are confessedly nothing but the effects of its operations on the stomach and guts, by the size, motion, and figure of its insensible parts, (for by nothing else can a body operate, as has been proved): as if it could not operate on the eyes and palate, and thereby produce in the mind particular distinct ideas, which in itself it has not, as well as we allow it can operate on the guts and stomach, and thereby produce distinct ideas, which in itself it has not. These ideas, being all effects of the operations of manna on several parts of our bodies, by the size, figure, number, and motion of its parts;—why those produced by the eyes and palate should rather be thought to be really in the manna, than those produced by the stomach and guts; or why the pain and sickness, ideas that are the effect of manna, should be thought to be nowhere when they are not felt; and yet the sweetness and whiteness, effects of the same manna on other parts of the body, by ways equally as unknown, should be thought to exist in the manna, when they are not seen or tasted, would need some reason to explain.

19. Let us consider the red and white colours in porphyry. Hinder light from striking on it, and its colours vanish; it no longer produces any such ideas in us: upon the return of light it produces these appearances on us again. Can any one think any real alterations are made in the porphyry by the presence or absence of light; and that those ideas of whiteness and redness are really in porphyry in the light, when it is plain *it has no colour in the dark?*

It has, indeed, such a configuration of particles, both night and day, as are apt, by the rays of light rebounding from some parts of that hard stone, to produce in us the idea of redness, and from others the idea of whiteness; but whiteness or redness are not in it at any time, but such a texture that hath the power to produce such a sensation in us.

20. Pound an almond, and the clear white colour will be altered into a dirty one, and the sweet taste into an oily one. What real alteration can the beating of the pestle make in any body, but an alteration of the texture of it?

21. Ideas being thus distinguished and understood, we may be able to give an account how the same water, at the same time, may produce the idea of cold by one hand and of heat by the other: whereas it is impossible that the same water, if those ideas were really in it, should at the same time be both hot and cold. For, if we imagine *warmth,* as it is in our hands, to be nothing but a certain sort and degree of motion in the minute particles of our nerves or animal spirits, we may understand how it is possible that the same water may, at the same time, produce the sensations of heat in one hand and cold in the other; which yet *figure* never does, that never producing the idea of a square by one hand which has produced the idea of a globe by another. But if the sensation of heat and cold be nothing but the increase or diminution of the motion of the minute parts of our bodies, caused by the corpuscles of any other body, it is easy to be understood, that if that motion be greater in one hand than in the other; if a body be applied to the two hands, which has in its minute particles a greater motion than in those of one of the hands, and a less than in those of the other, it will increase the motion of the one hand and lessen it in the other; and so cause the different sensations of heat and cold that depend thereon.

22. I have in what just goes before been engaged in physical inquiries a little further than perhaps I intended. But, it being necessary to make the nature of sensation a little understood; and to make the difference between the *qualities* in bodies, and the *ideas* produced by them in the mind, to be distinctly conceived, without which it were impossible to

discourse intelligibly of them;—I hope I shall be pardoned this little excursion into natural philosophy; it being necessary in our present inquiry to distinguish the *primary* and *real* qualities of bodies, which are always in them (viz. solidity, extension, figure, number, and motion, or rest, and are sometimes perceived by us, viz. when the bodies they are in are big enough singly to be discerned), from those *secondary* and *imputed* qualities, which are but the powers of several combinations of those primary ones, when they operate without being distinctly discerned;—whereby we may also come to know what ideas are, and what are not, resemblances of something really existing in the bodies we denominate from them.

23. The qualities, then, that are in bodies, rightly considered, are of three sorts:—

First, The bulk, figure, number, situation, and motion or rest of their solid parts. Those are in them, whether we perceive them or not; and when they are of that size that we can discover them, we have by these an idea of the thing as it is in itself; as is plain in artificial things. These I call *primary qualities.*

Secondly, The power that is in any body, by reason of its insensible primary qualities, to operate after a peculiar manner on any of our senses, and thereby produce in *us* the different ideas of several colours, sounds, smells, tastes, &c. These are usually called *sensible qualities.*

Thirdly, The power that is in any body, by reason of the particular constitution of its primary qualities, to make such a change in the bulk, figure, texture, and motion of *another body,* as to make it operate on our senses differently from what it did before. Thus the sun has a power to make wax white, and fire to make lead fluid. These are usually called *powers.*

The first of these, as has been said, I think may be properly called real, original, or primary qualities; because they are in the things themselves, whether they are perceived or not; and upon their different modifications it is that the secondary qualities depend.

The other two are only powers to act differently upon other things: which powers result from the different modifications of those primary qualities.

24. But, though the two latter sorts of qualities are powers barely, and nothing but powers, relating to several other bodies, and resulting from the different modifications of the original qualities, yet they are generally otherwise thought of. For the *second* sort, viz. the powers to produce several ideas in us, by our senses, are looked upon as real qualities in the things thus affecting us: but the *third* sort are called and esteemed barely powers. v.g. The idea of heat or light, which we receive by our eyes, or touch, from the sun, are commonly thought real qualities existing in the sun, and something more than mere powers in it. But when we consider the sun in reference to wax, which it melts or blanches, we look on the whiteness and softness produced in the wax, not as qualities in the sun, but effects produced by powers in it. Whereas, if rightly considered, these qualities of light and warmth, which are perceptions in me when I am warmed or enlightened by the sun, are no otherwise in the sun, than the changes made in the wax, when it is blanched or melted, are in the sun. They are all of them equally *powers in the sun, depending on its primary qualities;* whereby it is able, in the one case, so to alter the bulk, figure, texture, or motion of some of the insensible parts of my eyes or hands, as thereby to produce in me the idea of light or heat; and in the other, it is able so to alter the bulk, figure, texture, or motion of the insensible parts of the wax, as to make them fit to produce in me the distinct ideas of white and fluid.

25. The reason why the one are ordinarily taken for real qualities, and the other only for bare powers, seems to be, because the ideas we have of distinct colours, sounds, &c., containing nothing at all in them of bulk, figure, or motion, we are not apt to think them the effects of these primary qualities; which appear not, to our senses, to operate in their production, and with which they have not any apparent congruity or conceivable connexion. Hence it is that we are so forward to imagine, that those ideas are the resemblances of something really existing in the objects themselves: since sensation discovers nothing of bulk, figure, or motion of parts in their production;

nor can reason show how bodies, *by their bulk, figure, and motion,* should produce in the mind the ideas of blue or yellow, &c. But, in the other case, in the operations of bodies changing the qualities one of another, we plainly discover that the quality produced hath commonly no resemblance with anything in the thing producing it; wherefore we look on it as a bare effect of power. For, though receiving the idea of heat or light from the sun, we are apt to think *it* is a perception and resemblance of such a quality in the sun; yet when we see wax, or a fair face, receive change of colour from the sun, we cannot imagine *that* to be the reception or resemblance of anything in the sun, because we find not those different colours in the sun itself. For, our senses being able to observe a likeness or unlikeness of sensible qualities in two different external objects, we forwardly enough conclude the production of any sensible quality in any subject to be an effect of bare power, and not the communication of any quality which was really in the efficient, when we find no such sensible quality in the thing that produced it. But our senses, not being able to discover any unlikeness between the idea produced in us, and the quality of the object producing it, we are apt to imagine that our ideas are resemblances of something in the objects, and not the effects of certain powers placed in the modification of their primary qualities, with which primary qualities the ideas produced in us have no resemblance.

26. To conclude. Beside those before-mentioned primary qualities in bodies, viz. bulk, figure, extension, number, and motion of their solid parts; all the rest, whereby we take notice of bodies, and distinguish them one from another, are nothing else but several powers in them, depending on those primary qualities; whereby they are fitted, either by immediately operating on our bodies to produce several different ideas in us; or else, by operating on other bodies, so to change their primary qualities as to render them capable of producing ideas in us different from what before they did. The former of these, I think, may be called secondary qualities *immediately perceivable:* the later, secondary qualities, *mediately perceivable.*

Chapter IX: Of Perception

1. Perception, as it is the first faculty of the mind exercised about our ideas; so it is the first and simplest idea we have from reflection, and is by some called thinking in general. Though thinking, in the propriety of the English tongue, signifies that sort of operation in the mind about its ideas, wherein the mind is active; where it, with some degree of voluntary attention, considers anything. *For in bare naked perception, the mind is, for the most part, only passive; and what it perceives, it cannot avoid perceiving.*

2. What perception is, every one will know better by reflecting on what he does himself, when he sees, hears, feels, &c., or thinks, than by any discourse of mine. Whoever reflects on what passes in his own mind cannot miss it. And if he does not reflect, all the words in the world cannot make him have any notion of it.

3. This is certain, that whatever alterations are made in the body, if they reach not the mind; whatever impressions are made on the outward parts, if they are not taken notice of within, there is no perception. Fire may burn our bodies with no other effect than it does a billet, unless the motion be continued to the brain, and there the sense of heat, or idea of pain, be produced in the mind; wherein consists actual perception.

4. How often may a man observe in himself, that whilst his mind is intently employed in the contemplation of some objects, and curiously surveying some ideas that are there, it takes no notice of impressions of sounding bodies made upon the organ of hearing, with the same alteration that uses to be for the producing the idea of sound? A sufficient impulse there may be on the organ; but it not reaching the observation of the mind, there follows no perception: and though the motion that uses to produce the idea of sound be made in the ear, yet no sound is heard. Want of sensation, in this case, is not through any defect in the organ, or that the man's ears are less affected than at other times when he does hear: but that which uses to produce the idea, though conveyed in by the usual organ, not being

taken notice of in the understanding, and so imprinting no idea in the mind, there follows no sensation. So that wherever there is sense or perception, there some idea is actually produced, and present in the understanding.

5. Therefore I doubt not but children, by the exercise of their senses about objects that affect them in the womb, receive some few ideas before they are born, as the unavoidable effects, either of the bodies that environ them, or else of those wants or diseases they suffer; amongst which (if one may conjecture concerning things not very capable of examination) I think the ideas of hunger and warmth are two: which probably are some of the first that children have, and which they scarce ever part with again.

6. But though it be reasonable to imagine that children receive some ideas before they come into the world, yet these simple ideas are far from those *innate principles* which some contend for, and we, above, have rejected. These here mentioned, being the effects of sensation, are only from some affections of the body, which happen to them there, and so depend on something exterior to the mind; no otherwise differing in their manner of production from other ideas derived from sense, but only in the precedency of time. Whereas those innate principles are supposed to be quite of another nature; not coming into the mind by any accidental alterations in, or operations on the body; but, as it were, original characters impressed upon it, in the very first moment of its being and constitution.

7. As there are some ideas which we may reasonably suppose may be introduced into the minds of children in the womb, subservient to the necessities of their life and being there: so, after they are born, those ideas are the earliest imprinted which happen to be the sensible qualities which first occur to them; amongst which light is not the least considerable, nor of the weakest efficacy. And how covetous the mind is to be furnished with all such ideas as have no pain accompanying them, may be a little guessed by what is observable in children new-born; who always turn their eyes to that part from whence the light comes, lay them how you please. But the ideas that are most familiar at first, being various

according to the divers circumstances of children's first entertainment in the world, the order wherein the several ideas come at first into the mind is very various, and uncertain also; neither is it much material to know it.

8. We are further to consider concerning perception, that the ideas we receive by sensation are often, in grown people, altered by the judgment, without our taking notice of it. When we set before our eyes a round globe of any uniform colour, v.g. gold, alabaster, or jet, it is certain that the idea thereby imprinted on our mind is of a flat circle, variously shadowed, with several degrees of light and brightness coming to our eyes. But we having, by use, been accustomed to perceive what kind of appearance convex bodies are wont to make in us; what alterations are made in the reflections of light by the difference of the sensible figures of bodies;—the judgment presently, by an habitual custom, alters the appearances into their causes. So that from that which is truly variety of shadow or colour, collecting the figure, it makes it pass for a mark of figure, and frames to itself the perception of a convex figure and an uniform colour; when the idea we receive from thence is only a plane variously coloured, as is evident in painting. To which purpose I shall here insert a problem of that very ingenious and studious promoter of real knowledge, the learned and worthy Mr. Molineux, which he was pleased to send me in a letter some months since; and it is this:—'Suppose a man *born* blind, and now adult, and taught by his *touch* to distinguish between a cube and a sphere of the same metal, and nighly of the same bigness, so as to tell, when he felt one and the other, which is the cube, which the sphere. Suppose then the cube and sphere placed on a table, and the blind man be made to see: *quære*, whether *by his sight, before he touched them*, he could now distinguish and tell which is the globe, which the cube?' To which the acute and judicious proposer answers, 'Not. For, though he has obtained the experience of how a globe, how a cube affects his touch, yet he has not yet obtained the experience, that what affects his touch so or so, must affect his sight so or so; or that a protuberant angle in the cube, that pressed his hand unequally, shall appear to his eye as it

does in the cube.'—I agree with this thinking gentleman, whom I am proud to call my friend, in his answer to this problem; and am of opinion that the blind man, at first sight, would not be able with certainty to say which was the globe, which the cube, whilst he only saw them; though he could unerringly name them by his touch, and certainly distinguish them by the difference of their figures felt. This I have set down, and leave with my reader, as an occasion for him to consider how much he may be beholden to experience, improvement, and acquired notions, where he thinks he had not the least use of, or help from them. And the rather, because this observing gentleman further adds, that 'having, upon the occasion of my book, proposed this to divers very ingenious men, he hardly ever met with one that at first gave the answer to it which he thinks true, till by hearing his reasons they were convinced.'

9. But this is not, I think, usual in any of our ideas, but those received by sight. Because sight, the most comprehensive of all our senses, conveying to our minds the ideas of light and colours, which are peculiar only to that sense; and also the far different ideas of space, figure, and motion, the several varieties whereof change the appearances of its proper object, viz. light and colours; we bring ourselves by use to judge of the one by the other. This, in many cases by a settled habit,—in things whereof we have frequent experience, is performed so constantly and so quick, that we take that for the perception of our sensation which is an idea formed by our judgment; so that one, viz. that of sensation, serves only to excite the other, and is scarce taken notice of itself;—as a man who reads or hears with attention and understanding, takes little notice of the characters or sounds, but of the ideas that are excited in him by them.

10. Nor need we wonder that this is done with so little notice, if we consider how quick the actions of the mind are performed. For, as itself is thought to take up no space, to have no extension; so its actions seem to require no time, but many of them seem to be crowded into an instant. I speak this in comparison to the actions of the body. Any one may easily observe this in his own thoughts, who will take

the pains to reflect on them. How, as it were in an instant, do our minds, with one glance, see all the parts of a demonstration, which may very well be called a long one, if we consider the time it will require to put it into words, and step by step show it another? Secondly, we shall not be so much surprised that this is done in us with so little notice, if we consider how the facility which we get of doing things, by a custom of doing, makes them often pass in us without our notice. Habits, especially such as are begun very early, come at last to produce actions in us, which often escape our observation. How frequently do we, in a day, cover our eyes with our eyelids, without perceiving that we are at all in the dark! Men that, by custom, have got the use of a by-word, do almost in every sentence pronounce sounds which, though taken notice of by others, they themselves neither hear nor observe. And therefore it is not so strange, that our mind should often change the idea of its sensation into that of its judgment, and make one serve only to excite the other, without our taking notice of it.

11. This faculty of perception seems to me to be, that which puts the distinction betwixt the animal kingdom and the inferior parts of nature. For, however, vegetables have, many of them, some degrees of motion, and upon the different application of other bodies to them, do very briskly alter their figures and motions, and so have obtained the name of sensitive plants, from a motion which has some resemblance to that which in animals follows upon sensation: yet I suppose it is all bare *mechanism;* and no otherwise produced than the turning of a wild oat-beard, by the insinuation of the particles of moisture, or the shortening of a rope, by the affusion of water. All which is done without any sensation in the subject, or the having or receiving any ideas.

12. Perception, I believe, is, in some degree, in all sorts of animals; though in some possibly the avenues provided by nature for the reception of sensations are so few, and the perception they are received with so obscure and dull, that it comes extremely short of the quickness and variety of sensation which is in other animals; but yet it is sufficient for, and wisely adapted to, the state and condition of

that sort of animals who are thus made. So that the wisdom and goodness of the Maker plainly appear in all the parts of this stupendous fabric, and all the several degrees and ranks of creatures in it.

13. We may, I think, from the make of an oyster or cockle, reasonably conclude that it has not so many, nor so quick senses as a man, or several other animals; nor if it had, would it, in that state and incapacity of transferring itself from one place to another, be bettered by them. What good would sight and hearing do to a creature that cannot move itself to or from the objects wherein at a distance it perceives good or evil? And would not quickness of sensation be an inconvenience to an animal that must lie still where chance has once placed it, and there receive the afflux of colder or warmer, clean or foul water, as it happens to come to it?

14. But yet I cannot but think there is some small dull perception, whereby they are distinguished from perfect insensibility. And that this may be so, we have plain instances, even in mankind itself. Take one in whom decrepit old age has blotted out the memory of his past knowledge, and clearly wiped out the ideas his mind was formerly stored with, and has, by destroying his sight, hearing, and smell quite, and his taste to a great degree, stopped up almost all the passages for new ones to enter; or if there be some of the inlets yet half open, the impressions made are scarcely perceived, or not at all retained. How far such an one (notwithstanding all that is boasted of innate principles) is in his knowledge and intellectual faculties above the condition of a cockle or an oyster, I leave to be considered. And if a man had passed sixty years in such a state, as it is possible he might, as well as three days, I wonder what difference there would be, in any intellectual perfections, between him and the lowest degree of animals.

15. Perception then being the *first* step and degree towards knowledge, and the inlet of all the materials of it; the fewer senses any man, as well as any other creature, hath; and the fewer and duller the impressions are that are made by them; and the duller the faculties are that are employed about them,—the more remote are they from that knowledge which is to

be found in some men. But this being in great variety of degrees (as may be perceived amongst men) cannot certainly be discovered in the several species of animals, much less in their particular individuals. It suffices me only to have remarked here,—that perception is the first operation of all our intellectual faculties, and the inlet of all knowledge in our minds. And I am apt too to imagine, that it is perception, in the lowest degree of it, which puts the boundaries between animals and the inferior ranks of creatures. But this I mention only as my conjecture by the by; it being indifferent to the matter in hand which way the learned shall determine of it.

Chapter X: Of Retention

1. The next faculty of the mind, whereby it makes a further progress towards knowledge, is that which I call *retention;* or the keeping of those simple ideas which from sensation or reflection it hath received. This is done two ways.

First, by keeping the idea which is brought into it, for some time actually in view, which is called *contemplation.*

2. The other way of retention is, the power to revive again in our minds those ideas which, after imprinting, have disappeared, or have been as it were laid aside out of sight. And thus we do, when we conceive heat or light, yellow or sweet,—the object being removed. This is *memory,* which is as it were the storehouse of our ideas. For, the narrow mind of man not being capable of having many ideas under view and consideration at once, it was necessary to have a repository, to lay up those ideas which, at another time, it might have use of. But, our *ideas* being nothing but actual perceptions in the mind, which cease to be anything when there is no perception of them; this laying up of our ideas in the repository of the memory signifies no more but this,—that the mind has a power in many cases to revive perceptions which it has once had, with this additional perception annexed to them, that *it has had them before.* And in this sense it is that

our ideas are said to be in our memories, when indeed they are actually nowhere;—but only there is an ability in the mind when it will to revive them again, and as it were paint them anew on itself, though some with more, some with less difficulty; some more lively, and others more obscurely. And thus it is, by the assistance of this faculty, that we are said to have all those ideas in our understandings which, though we do not actually contemplate, yet we *can* bring in sight, and make appear again, and be the objects of our thoughts, without the help of those sensible qualities which first imprinted them there.

3. Attention and repetition help much to the fixing any ideas in the memory. But those which naturally at first make the deepest and most lasting impressions, are those which are accompanied with pleasure or pain. The great business of the senses being, to make us take notice of what hurts or advantages the body, it is wisely ordered by nature, as has been shown, that pain should accompany the reception of several ideas; which, supplying the place of consideration and reasoning in children, and acting quicker than consideration in grown men, makes both the old and young avoid painful objects with that haste which is necessary for their preservation; and in both settles in the memory a caution for the future.

4. Concerning the several degrees of lasting, wherewith ideas are imprinted on the memory, we may observe,—that some of them have been produced in the understanding by an object affecting the senses once only, and no more than once; others, that have more than once offered themselves to the senses, have yet been little taken notice of: the mind, either heedless, as in children, or otherwise employed, as in men intent only on one thing; not setting the stamp deep into itself. And in some, where they are set on with care and repeated impressions, either through the temper of the body, or some other fault, the memory is very weak. In all these cases, ideas in the mind quickly fade, and often vanish quite out of the understanding, leaving no more footsteps or remaining characters of themselves than shadows do flying over fields of corn, and the mind is as void of them as if they had never been there.

5. Thus many of those ideas which were produced in the minds of children, in the beginning of their sensation, (some of which perhaps, as of some pleasures and pains, were before they were born, and others in their infancy,) if in the future course of their lives they are not repeated again, are quite lost, without the least glimpse remaining of them. This may be observed in those who by some mischance have lost their sight when they were very young; in whom the ideas of colours having been but slightly taken notice of, and ceasing to be repeated, do quite wear out; so that some years after, there is no more notion nor memory of colours left in their minds, than in those of people born blind. The memory of some men, it is true, is very tenacious, even to a miracle. But yet there seems to be a constant decay of all our ideas, even of those which are struck deepest, and in minds the most retentive; so that if they be not sometimes renewed, by repeated exercise of the senses, or reflection on those kinds of objects which at first occasioned them, the print wears out, and at last there remains nothing to be seen. Thus the ideas, as well as children, of our youth, often die before us: and our minds represent to us those tombs to which we are approaching; where, though the brass and marble remain, yet the inscriptions are effaced by time, and the imagery moulders away. The pictures drawn in our minds are laid in fading colours; and if not sometimes refreshed, vanish and disappear. How much the constitution of our bodies and the make of our animal spirits are concerned in this; and whether the temper of the brain makes this difference, that in some it retains the characters drawn on it like marble, in others like freestone, and in others little better than sand, I shall not here inquire; though it may seem probable that the constitution of the body does sometimes influence the memory, since we oftentimes find a disease quite strip the mind of all its ideas, and the flames of a fever in a few days calcine all those images to dust and confusion, which seemed to be as lasting as if graved in marble.

6. But concerning the ideas themselves, it is easy to remark, that those that are oftenest refreshed (amongst which are those that are conveyed into the mind by more ways than

one) by a frequent return of the objects or actions that produce them, fix themselves best in the memory, and remain clearest and longest there; and therefore those which are of the original qualities of bodies, viz. solidity, extension, figure, motion, and rest; and those that almost constantly affect our bodies, as heat and cold; and those which are the affections of all kinds of beings, as existence, duration, and number, which almost every object that affects our senses, every thought which employs our minds, bring along with them;—these, I say, and the like ideas, are seldom quite lost, whilst the mind retains any ideas at all.

7. In this secondary perception, as I may so call it, or viewing again the ideas that are lodged in the memory, the mind is oftentimes more than barely passive; the appearance of those dormant pictures depending sometimes on the *will*. The mind very often sets itself on work in search of some hidden idea, and turns as it were the eye of the soul upon it; though sometimes too they start up in our minds of their own accord, and offer themselves to the understanding; and very often are roused and tumbled out of their dark cells into open daylight, by turbulent and tempestuous passions; our affections bringing ideas to our memory, which had otherwise lain quiet and unregarded. This further is to be observed, concerning ideas lodged in the memory, and upon occasion revived by the mind, that they are not only (as the word *revive* imports) none of them new ones, but also that the mind takes notice of them as of a former impression, and renews its acquaintance with them, as with ideas it had known before. So that though ideas formerly imprinted are not all constantly in view, yet in remembrance they are constantly known to be such as have been formerly imprinted; i.e. in view, and taken notice of before, by the understanding.

8. Memory, in an intellectual creature, is necessary in the next degree to perception. It is of so great moment, that, where it is wanting, all the rest of our faculties are in a great measure useless. And we in our thoughts, reasonings, and knowledge, could not proceed beyond present objects, were it not for the assistance of our memories; wherein there may be two defects:—

First, That it loses the idea quite, and so far it produces perfect ignorance. For, since we can know nothing further than we have the idea of it, when that is gone, we are in perfect ignorance.

Secondly, That it moves slowly, and retrieves not the ideas that it has, and are laid up in store, quick enough to serve the mind upon occasion. This, if it be to a great degree, is stupidity; and he who, through this default in his memory, has not the ideas that are really preserved there, ready at hand when need and occasion calls for them, were almost as good be without them quite, since they serve him to little purpose. The dull man, who loses the opportunity, whilst he is seeking in his mind for those ideas that should serve his turn, is not much more happy in his knowledge than one that is perfectly ignorant. It is the business therefore of the memory to furnish to the mind those dormant ideas which it has present occasion for; in the having them ready at hand on all occasions, consists that which we call invention, fancy, and quickness of parts.

9. These are defects we may observe in the memory of one man compared with another. There is another defect which we may conceive to be in the memory of man in general;—compared with some superior created intellectual beings, which in this faculty may so far excel man, that they may have *constantly* in view the whole scene of all their former actions, wherein no one of the thoughts they have ever had may slip out of their sight. The omniscience of God, who knows all things, past, present, and to come, and to whom the thoughts of men's hearts always lie open, may satisfy us of the possibility of this. For who can doubt but God may communicate to those glorious spirits, his immediate attendants, any of his perfections; in what proportions he pleases, as far as created finite beings can be capable? It is reported of that prodigy of parts, Monsieur Pascal, that till the decay of his health had impaired his memory, he forgot nothing of what he had done, read, or thought, in any part of his rational age. This is a privilege so little known to most men, that it seems almost incredible to those who, after the ordinary way, measure all others by themselves; but yet, when considered, may help us

to enlarge our thoughts towards greater per-fections of it, in superior ranks of spirits. For this of Monsieur Pascal was still with the nar-rowness that human minds are confined to here,—of having great variety of ideas only by succession, not all at once. Whereas the several degrees of angels may probably have larger views; and some of them be endowed with capacities able to retain together, and con-stantly set before them, as in one picture, all their past knowledge at once. This, we may conceive, would be no small advantage to the knowledge of a thinking man,—if all his past thoughts and reasonings could be *always* present to him. And therefore we may sup-pose it one of those ways, wherein the knowl-edge of separate spirits may exceedingly sur-pass ours.

10. This faculty of laying up and retaining the ideas that are brought into the mind, several other animals seem to have to a great degree, as well as man. For, to pass by other instances, birds learning of tunes, and the en-deavours one may observe in them to hit the notes right, put it past doubt with me, that they have perception, and retain ideas in their memories, and use them for patterns. For it seems to me impossible that they should en-deavour to conform their voices to notes (as it is plain they do) of which they had no ideas. For, though I should grant sound may me-chanically cause a certain motion of the animal spirits in the brains of those birds, whilst the tune is actually playing; and that motion may be continued on to the muscles of the wings, and so the bird mechanically be driven away by certain noises, because this may tend to the bird's preservation; yet that can never be sup-posed a reason why it should cause mechani-cally—either whilst the tune is playing, much less after it has ceased—such a motion of the organs in the bird's voice as should conform it to the notes of a foreign sound, which imita-tion can be of no use to the bird's preservation. But, which is more, it cannot with any appear-ance of reason be supposed (much less proved) that birds, without sense and memory, can approach their notes nearer and nearer by degrees to a tune played yesterday; which if they have no idea of in their memory, is now nowhere, nor can be a pattern for them to

imitate, or which any repeated essays can bring them nearer to. Since there is no reason why the sound of a pipe should leave traces in their brains, which, not at first, but by their after-endeavours, should produce the like sounds; and why the sounds they make them-selves, should not make traces which they should follow, as well as those of the pipe, is impossible to conceive.

Chapter XI: Of Discerning and Other Operations of the Mind

1. Another faculty we may take notice of in our minds is that of *discerning* and *distinguish-ing* between the several ideas it has. It is not enough to have a confused perception of something in general. Unless the mind had a distinct perception of different objects and their qualities, it would be capable of very little knowledge, though the bodies that affect us were as busy about us as they are now, and the mind were continually employed in thinking. On this faculty of distinguishing one thing from another depends the evidence and cer-tainty of several, even very general, proposi-tions, which have passed for innate truths;—because men, overlooking the true cause why those propositions find universal assent, im-pute it wholly to native uniform impressions; whereas it in truth depends upon this clear discerning faculty of the mind, whereby it *per-ceives* two ideas to be the same, or different. But of this more hereafter.

2. How much the imperfection of accurate-ly discriminating ideas one from another lies, either in the dulness or faults of the organs of sense; or want of acuteness, exercise, or atten-tion in the understanding; or hastiness and precipitancy, natural to some tempers, I will not here examine: it suffices to take notice, that this is one of the operations that the mind may reflect on and observe in itself. It is of that consequence to its other knowledge, that so far as this faculty is in itself dull, or not rightly made use of, for the distinguishing one thing from another,—so far our notions are con-fused, and our reason and judgment dis-

turbed or misled. If in having our ideas in the memory ready at hand consists quickness of parts; in this, of having them unconfused, and being able nicely to distinguish one thing from another, where there is but the least difference, consists, in a great measure, the exactness of judgment, and clearness of reason, which is to be observed in one man above another. And hence perhaps may be given some reason of that common observation,—that men who have a great deal of wit, and prompt memories, have not always the clearest judgment or deepest reason. For *wit* lying most in the assemblage of ideas, and putting those together with quickness and variety, wherein can be found any resemblance or congruity, thereby to make up pleasant pictures and agreeable visions in the fancy; *judgment,* on the contrary, lies quite on the other side, in separating carefully, one from another, ideas wherein can be found the least difference, thereby to avoid being misled by similitude, and by affinity to take one thing for another. This is a way of proceeding quite contrary to metaphor and allusion; wherein for the most part lies that entertainment and pleasantry of wit, which strikes so lively on the fancy, and therefore is so acceptable to all people, because its beauty appears at first sight, and there is required no labour of thought to examine what truth or reason there is in it. The mind, without looking any further, rests satisfied with the agreeableness of the picture and the gaiety of the fancy. And it is a kind of affront to go about to examine it, by the severe rules of truth and good reason; whereby it appears that it consists in something that is not perfectly conformable to them.

3. To the well distinguishing our ideas, it chiefly contributes that they be *clear* and *determinate.* And when they are so, it will not breed any confusion or mistake about them, though the senses should (as sometimes they do) convey them from the same object differently on different occasions, and so seem to err. For, though a man in a fever should from sugar have a bitter taste, which at another time would produce a sweet one, yet the idea of bitter in that man's mind would be as clear and distinct from the idea of sweet as if he had tasted only gall. Nor does it make any more confusion between the two ideas of sweet and bitter, that the same sort of body produces at one time one, and at another time another idea by the taste, than it makes a confusion in two ideas of white and sweet, or white and round, that the same piece of sugar produces them both in the mind at the same time. And the ideas of orange-colour and azure, that are produced in the mind by the same parcel of the infusion of *lignum nephriticum,* are no less distinct ideas than those of the same colours taken from two very different bodies.

4. The COMPARING them one with another, in respect of extent, degrees, time, place, or any other circumstances, is another operation of the mind about its ideas, and is that upon which depends all that large tribe of ideas comprehended under *relation;* which, of how vast an extent it is, I shall have occasion to consider hereafter.

5. How far brutes partake in this faculty, is not easy to determine. I imagine they have it not in any great degree: for, though they probably have several ideas distinct enough, yet it seems to me to be the prerogative of human understanding, when it has sufficiently distinguished any ideas, so as to perceive them to be perfectly different, and so consequently two, to cast about and consider in what circumstances they are capable to be compared. And therefore, I think, beasts compare not their ideas further than some sensible circumstances annexed to the objects themselves. The other power of comparing, which may be observed in men, belonging to general ideas, and useful only to abstract reasonings, we may probably conjecture beasts have not.

6. The next operation we may observe in the mind about its ideas is COMPOSITION; whereby it puts together several of those simple ones it has received from sensation and reflection, and combines them into complex ones. Under this of composition may be reckoned also that of *enlarging,* wherein, though the composition does not so much appear as in more complex ones, yet it is nevertheless a putting several ideas together, though of the same kind. Thus, by adding several units together, we make the idea of a dozen; and putting together the repeated ideas of several perches, we frame that of a furlong.

7. In this also, I suppose, brutes come far short of man. For, though they take in, and retain together, several combinations of simple ideas, as possibly the shape, smell, and voice of his master make up the complex idea a dog has of him, or rather are so many distinct marks whereby he knows him; yet I do not think they do of themselves ever compound them, and make complex ideas. And perhaps even where we think they have complex ideas, it is only one simple one that directs them in the knowledge of several things, which possibly they distinguish less by their sight than we imagine. For I have been credibly informed that a bitch will nurse, play with, and be fond of young foxes, as much as, and in place of her puppies, if you can but get them once to suck her so long that her milk may go through them. And those animals which have a numerous brood of young ones at once, appear not to have any knowledge of their number; for though they are mightily concerned for any of their young that are taken from them whilst they are in sight or hearing, yet if one or two of them be stolen from them in their absence, or without noise, they appear not to miss them, or to have any sense that their number is lessened.

8. When children have, by repeated sensations, got ideas fixed in their memories, they begin by degrees to learn the use of signs. And when they have got the skill to apply the organs of speech to the framing of articulate sounds, they begin to make use of words, to signify their ideas to others. These verbal signs they sometimes borrow from others, and sometimes make themselves, as one may observe among the new and unusual names children often give to things in the first use of language.

9. The use of words then being to stand as outward marks of our internal ideas, and those ideas being taken from particular things, if every particular idea that we take in should have a distinct name, names must be endless. To prevent this, the mind makes the particular ideas received from particular objects to become general; which is done by considering them as they are in the mind such appearances,—separate from all other existences, and the circumstances of real existence, as time, place, or any other concomitant ideas. This is called ABSTRACTION, whereby ideas taken from particular beings become general representatives of all of the same kind; and their names general names, applicable to whatever exists conformable to such abstract ideas. Such precise, naked appearances in the mind, without considering how, whence, or with what others they came there, the understanding lays up (with names commonly annexed to them) as the standards to rank real existences into sorts, as they agree with these patterns, and to denominate them accordingly. Thus the same colour being observed to-day in chalk or snow, which the mind yesterday received from milk, it considers that appearance alone, makes it a representative of all of that kind; and having given it the name *whiteness*, it by that sound signifies the same quality wheresoever to be imagined or met with; and thus universals, whether ideas or terms, are made.

10. If it may be doubted whether beasts compound and enlarge their ideas that way to any degree; this, I think I may be positive in,—that the power of abstracting is not at all in them; and that the having of general ideas is that which puts a perfect distinction betwixt man and brutes, and is an excellency which the faculties of brutes do by no means attain to. For it is evident we observe no footsteps in them of making use of general signs for universal ideas; from which we have reason to imagine that they have not the faculty of abstracting, or making general ideas, since they have no use of words, or any other general signs.

11. Nor can it be imputed to their want to fit organs to frame articulate sounds, that they have no use or knowledge of general words; since many of them, we find, can fashion such sounds, and pronounce words distinctly enough, but never with any such application. And, on the other side, men who, through some defect in the organs, want words, yet fail not to express their universal ideas by signs, which serve them instead of general words, a faculty which we see beasts come short in. And, therefore, I think, we may suppose, that

it is in this that the species of brutes are discriminated from man: and it is that proper difference wherein they are wholly separated, and which at last widens to so vast a distance. For if they have any ideas at all, and are not bare machines, (as some would have them,) we cannot deny them to have some reason. It seems as evident to me, that they do [some of them in certain instances] reason, as that they have sense; but it is only in particular ideas, just as they received them from their senses. They are the best of them tied up within those narrow bounds, and have not (as I think) the faculty to enlarge them by any kind of abstraction.

12. How far idiots are concerned in the want or weakness of any, or all of the foregoing faculties, an exact observation of their several ways of faultering would no doubt discover. For those who either perceive but dully, or retain the ideas that come into their minds but ill, who cannot readily excite or compound them, will have little matter to think on. Those who cannot distinguish, compare, and abstract, would hardly be able to understand and make use of language, or judge or reason to any tolerable degree; but only a little and imperfectly about things present, and very familiar to their senses. And indeed any of the forementioned faculties, if wanting, or out of order, produce suitable defects in men's understandings and knowledge.

13. In fine, the defect in naturals seems to proceed from want of quickness, activity, and motion in the intellectual faculties, whereby they are deprived of reason; whereas madmen, on the other side, seem to suffer by the other extreme. For they do not appear to me to have lost the faculty of reasoning, but having joined together some ideas very wrongly, they mistake them for truths; and they err as men do that argue right from wrong principles. For, by the violence of their imaginations, having taken their fancies for realities, they make right deductions from them. Thus you shall find a distracted man fancying himself a king, with a right inference require suitable attendance, respect, and obedience: others who have thought themselves made of glass, have used the caution necessary to preserve

such brittle bodies. Hence it comes to pass that a man who is very sober, and of a right understanding in all other things, may in one particular be as frantic as any in Bedlam; if either by any sudden very strong impression, or long fixing his fancy upon one sort of thoughts, incoherent ideas have been cemented together so powerfully, as to remain united. But there are degrees of madness, as of folly; the disorderly jumbling ideas together is in some more, and some less. In short, herein seems to lie the difference between idiots and madmen: that madmen put wrong ideas together, and so make wrong propositions, but argue and reason right from them; but idiots make very few or no propositions, and reason scarce at all.

14. These, I think, are the first faculties and operations of the mind, which it makes use of in understanding; and though they are exercised about all its ideas in general, yet the instances I have hitherto given have been chiefly in simple ideas. And I have subjoined the explication of these faculties of the mind to that of simple ideas, before I come to what I have to say concerning complex ones, for these following reasons:—

First, Because several of these faculties being exercised at first principally about simple ideas, we might, by following nature in its ordinary method, trace and discover them, in their rise, progress, and gradual improvements.

Secondly, Because observing the faculties of the mind, how they operate about simple ideas,—which are usually, in most men's minds, much more clear, precise, and distinct than complex ones,—we may the better examine and learn how the mind extracts, denominates, compares, and exercises, in its other operations about those which are complex, wherein we are much more liable to mistake.

Thirdly, Because these very operations of the mind about ideas received from sensations, are themselves, when reflected on, another set of ideas, derived from that other source of our knowledge, which I call reflection; and therefore fit to be considered in this place after the simple ideas of sensation. Of compounding, comparing, abstracting, &c., I have but just spoken, having occasion to treat of them more at large in other places.

15. And thus I have given a short, and, I think, true *history of the first beginnings of human knowledge;*—whence the mind has its first objects; and by what steps it makes its progress to the laying in and storing up those ideas; out of which is to be framed all the knowledge it is capable of: wherein I must appeal to experience and observation whether I am in the right: the best way to come to truth being to examine things as really they are, and not to conclude they are, as we fancy of ourselves, or have been taught by others to imagine.

16. To deal truly, this is the only way that I can discover, whereby the *ideas of things* are brought into the understanding. If other men have either innate ideas or infused principles, they have reason to enjoy them; and if they are sure of it, it is impossible for others to deny them the privilege that they have above their neighbours. I can speak but of what I find in myself, and is agreeable to those notions, which, if we will examine the whole course of men in their several ages, countries, and educations, seem to depend on those foundations which I have laid, and to correspond with this method in all the parts and degrees thereof.

17. I pretend not to teach, but to inquire; and therefore cannot but confess here again,—that external and internal sensation are the only passages I can find of knowledge to the understanding. These alone, as far as I can discover, are the windows by which light is let into this *dark room.* For, methinks, the understanding is not much unlike a closet wholly shut from light, with only some little openings left, to let in external visible resemblances, or ideas of things without: [would the pictures coming into such a dark room but stay there], and lie so orderly as to be found upon occasion, it would very much resemble the understanding of a man, in reference to all objects of sight, and the ideas of them.

These are my guesses concerning the means whereby the understanding comes to have and retain simple ideas, and the modes of them, with some other operations about them.

I proceed now to examine some of these simple ideas and their modes a little more particularly.

Chapter XII: Of Complex Ideas

1. We have hitherto considered those ideas, in the reception whereof the mind is only passive, which are those simple ones received from sensation and reflection before mentioned, whereof the mind cannot make one to itself, nor have any idea which does not wholly consist of them. But as the mind is wholly passive in the reception of all its simple ideas, so it exerts several acts of its own, whereby out of its simple ideas, as the materials and foundations of the rest, the others are framed. The acts of the mind, wherein it exerts its power over its simple ideas, are chiefly these three: (1) Combining several simple ideas into one compound one; and thus all *complex ideas* are made. (2) The second is bringing two ideas, whether simple or complex, together, and setting them by one another, so as to take a view of them at once, without uniting them into one; by which way it gets all its *ideas of relations.* (3) The third is separating them from all other ideas that accompany them in their real existence: this is called abstraction: and thus all its *general ideas* are made. This shows man's power, and its ways of operation, to be much the same in the material and intellectual world. For the materials in both being such as he has no power over, either to make or destroy, all that man can do is either to unite them together, or to set them by one another, or wholly separate them. I shall here begin with the first of these in the consideration of complex ideas, and come to the other two in their due places. As simple ideas are observed to exist in several combinations united together, so the mind has a power to consider several of them united together as one idea; and that not only as they are united in external objects, but as itself has joined them together. Ideas thus made up of several simple ones put together, I call *complex;*—such as are beauty, gratitude, a man, an army, the universe; which, though complicated of various simple ideas, or com-

plex ideas made up of simple ones, yet are, when the mind pleases, considered each by itself, as one entire thing, and signified by one name.

2. In this faculty of repeating and joining together its ideas, the mind has great power in varying and multiplying the objects of its thoughts, infinitely beyond what sensation or reflection furnished it with: but all this still confined to those simple ideas which it received from those two sources, and which are the ultimate materials of all its compositions. For simple ideas are all from things themselves, and of these the mind *can* have no more, nor other than what are suggested to it. It can have no other ideas of sensible qualities than what come from without by the senses; nor any ideas of other kind of operations of a thinking substance, than what it finds in itself. But when it has once got these simple ideas, it is not confined barely to observation, and what offers itself from without; it can, by its own power, put together those ideas it has, and make new complex ones, which it never received so united.

3. *Complex ideas,* however, compounded and decompounded, though their number be infinite, and the variety endless, wherewith they fill and entertain the thoughts of men; yet I think they may be all reduced under these three heads:—

1. MODES.
2. SUBSTANCES.
3. RELATIONS.

4. First, *Modes* I call such complex ideas which, however compounded, contain not in them the supposition of subsisting by themselves, but are considered as dependences on, or affections of substances;—such as are the ideas signified by the words triangle, gratitude, murder, &c. And if in this I use the word mode in somewhat a different sense from its ordinary signification, I beg pardon; it being unavoidable in discourses, differing from the ordinary received notions, either to make new words, or to use old words in somewhat a new signification; the later whereof, in our present case, is perhaps the more tolerable of the two.

5. Of these *modes,* there are two sorts which deserve distinct consideration:—

First, there are some which are only variations, or different combinations of the same simple idea, without the mixture of any other;—as a dozen, or score; which are nothing but the ideas of so many distinct units added together, and these I call *simple modes* as being contained within the bounds of one simple idea.

Secondly, there are others compounded of simple ideas of several kinds, put together to make one complex one;—v.g. beauty, consisting of a certain composition of colour and figure, causing delight to the beholder; theft, which being the concealed change of the possession of anything, without the consent of the proprietor, contains, as is visible, a combination of several ideas of several kinds: and these I call *mixed modes.*

6. Secondly, the ideas of *substances* are such combinations of simple ideas as are taken to represent distinct *particular* things subsisting by themselves; in which the supposed or confused idea of substance, such as it is, is always the first and chief. Thus if to substance be joined the simple idea of a certain dull whitish colour, with certain degrees of weight, hardness, ductility, and fusibility, we have the idea of lead; and a combination of the ideas of a certain sort of figure, with the powers of motion, thought and reasoning, joined to substance, make the ordinary idea of a man. Now of substances also, there are two sorts of ideas: one of *single* substances, as they exist separately, as of a man or a sheep; the other of several of those put together, as an army of men, or flock of sheep—which *collective* ideas of several substances thus put together are as much each of them one single idea as that of a man or an unit.

7. Thirdly, the last sort of complex ideas is that we call *relation,* which consists in the consideration and comparing one idea with another.

Of these several kinds we shall treat in their order.

8. If we trace the progress of our minds, and with attention observe how it repeats, adds together, and unites its simple ideas received from sensation or reflection, it will lead us further than at first perhaps we should have imagined. And, I believe, we shall find, if

we warily observe the originals of our notions, that *even the most abstruse ideas,* how remote soever they may seem from sense, or from any operations of our own minds, are yet only such as the understanding frames to itself, by repeating and joining together ideas that it had either from objects of sense, or from its own operations about them: so that those even large and abstract ideas are derived from sensation or reflection, being no other than what the mind, by the ordinary use of its own faculties, employed about ideas received from objects of sense, or from the operations it observes in itself about them, may, and does, attain unto.

This I shall endeavour to show in the ideas we have of space, time, and infinity, and some few others that seem the most remote, from those originals.

Chapter XIII: Complex Ideas of Simple Modes—and, First, of the Simple Modes of Idea of Space

---

1. Though in the foregoing part I have often mentioned simple ideas, which are truly the materials of all our knowledge; yet having treated of them there, rather in the way that they come into the mind, than as distinguished from others more compounded, it will not be perhaps amiss to take a view of some of them again under this consideration, and examine those different modifications of the *same* idea; which the mind either finds in things existing, or is able to make within itself without the help of any extrinsical object, or an foreign suggestion.

Those modifications of any *one* simple idea (which, as has been said, I call *simple modes*) are as perfectly different and distinct ideas in the mind as those of the greatest distance or contrariety. For the idea of two is as distinct from that of one, as blueness from heat, or either of them from any number: and yet it is made up only of that simple idea of an unit repeated; and repetitions of this kind joined together

make those distinct simple modes, of a dozen, a gross, a million.

2. I shall begin with the simple idea of *space.* I have showed above, chap. 4, that we get the idea of space, both by our sight and touch; which, I think, is so evident, that it would be as needless to go to prove that men perceive, by their sight, a distance between bodies of different colours, or between the parts of the same body, as that they see colours themselves; nor is it less obvious, that they can do so in the dark by feeling and touch.

3. This space, considered barely in length between any two beings, without considering anything else between them, is called *distance:* if considered in length, breadth, and thickness, I think it may be called *capacity.* The term *extension* is usually applied to it in what manner soever considered.

4. Each different distance is a different modification of space; and each idea of any different distance, or space, is a *simple mode* of this idea. Men, for the use and by the custom of measuring, settle in their minds the ideas of certain stated lengths,—such as are an inch, foot, yard, fathom, mile, diameter of the earth, &c., which are so many distinct ideas made up only of space. When any such stated lengths or measures of space are made familiar to men's thoughts, they can, in their minds, repeat them as often as they will, without mixing or joining to them the idea of body, or anything else; and frame to themselves the ideas of long, square, or cubic feet, yards or fathoms, here amongst the bodies of the universe, or else beyond the utmost bounds of all bodies; and, by adding these still one to another, enlarge their ideas of space as much as they please. The power of repeating or doubling any idea we have of any distance, and adding it to the former as often as we will, without being ever able to come to any stop or stint, let us enlarge it as much as we will, is that which gives us the idea of *immensity.*

5. There is another modification of this idea, which is nothing but the relation which the parts of the termination of extension, or circumscribed space, have amongst themselves. This the touch discovers in sensible bodies, whose extremities come within our reach; and the eye takes both from bodies and

colours, whose boundaries are within its view: where, observing how the extremities terminate,—either in straight lines which meet at discernible angles, or in crooked lines wherein no angles can be perceived; by considering these as they relate to one another, in all parts of the extremities of any body or space, it has that idea we call *figure,* which affords to the mind infinite variety. For, besides the vast number of different figures that do really exist in the coherent masses of matter, the stock that the mind has in its power, by varying the idea of space, and thereby making still new compositions, by repeating its own ideas, and joining them as it pleases, is perfectly inexhaustible. And so it can multiply figures *in infinitum.*

6. For the mind having a power to repeat the idea of any length directly stretched out, and join it to another in the same direction, which is to double the length of that straight line; or else join another with what inclination it thinks fit, and so make what sort of angle it pleases: and being able also to shorten any line it imagines, by taking from it one half, one fourth, or what part it pleases, without being able to come to an end of any such divisions, it can make an angle of any bigness. So also the lines that are its sides, of what length it pleases, which joining again to other lines, of different lengths, and at different angles till it has wholly enclosed any space, it is evident that it can multiply figures, both in their shape and capacity, *in infinitum;* all which are but so many different simple modes of space.

The same that it can do with straight lines, it can also do with crooked, or crooked and straight together; and the same it can do in lines, it can also in superficies; by which we may be led into farther thoughts of the endless variety of figures that the mind has a power to make, and thereby to multiply the simple modes of space.

7. Another idea coming under this head, and belonging to this tribe, is that we call *place.* As in simple space, we consider the relation of distance between any two bodies or points; so in our idea of place, we consider the relation of distance betwixt anything, and any two or more points, which are considered as keeping the same distance one with another, and so

considered as at rest. For when we find anything at the same distance now which it was yesterday, from any two or more points, which have not since changed their distance one with another, and with which we then compared it, we say it hath kept the same place: but if it hath sensibly altered its distance with either of those points, we say it hath changed its place: though, vulgarly speaking, in the common notion of place, we do not always exactly observe the distance from these precise points, but from larger portions of sensible objects, to which we consider the thing placed to bear relation, and its distance from which we have some reason to observe.

8. Thus, a company of chess-men, standing on the same squares of the chess-board where we left them, we say they are all in the *same* place, or unmoved, though perhaps the chess-board hath been in the mean time carried out of one room into another; because we compared them only to the parts of the chess-board, which keep the same distance one with another. The chess-board, we also say, is in the same place it was, if it remain in the same part of the cabin, though perhaps the ship which it is in sails all the while. And the ship is said to be in the same place, supposing it kept the same distance with the parts of the neighbouring land; though perhaps the earth hath turned round, and so both chess-men, and board, and ship, have every one changed place, in respect of remoter bodies, which have kept the same distance one with another. But yet the distance from certain parts of the board being that which determines the place of the chess-men; and the distance from the fixed parts of the cabin (with which we made the comparison) being that which determined the place of the chess-board; and the fixed parts of the earth that by which we determined the place of the ship,—these things may be said to be in the same place in those respects: though their distance from some other things, which in this matter we did not consider, being varied, they have undoubtedly changed place in that respect; and we ourselves shall think so, when we have occasion to compare them with those other.

9. But this modification of distance we call place, being made by men for their common

use, that by it they might be able to design the particular position of things, where they had occasion for such designation; men consider and determine of this place by reference to those adjacent things which best served to their present purpose, without considering other things which, to another purpose, would better determine the place of the same thing. Thus in the chess-board, the use of the designation of the place of each chess-man being determined only within that chequered piece of wood, it would cross that purpose to measure it by anything else; but when these very chess-men are put up in a bag, if any one should ask where the black king is, it would be proper to determine the place by the part of the room it was in, and not by the chess-board; there being another use of designing the place it is now in, than when in play it was on the chess-board, and so must be determined by other bodies. So if any one should ask, in what place are the verses which report the story of Nisus and Euryalus, it would be very improper to determine this place, by saying, they were in such a part of the earth, or in Bodley's library: but the right designation of the place would be by the parts of Virgil's works; and the proper answer would be, that these verses were about the middle of the ninth book of his Æneids, and that they have been always constantly in the same place ever since Virgil was printed: which is true, though the book itself hath moved a thousand times, the use of the idea of place here being, to know in what part of the book that story is, that so, upon occasion, we may know where to find it, and have recourse to it for use.

10. That our idea of place is nothing else but such a relative position of anything as I have before mentioned, I think is plain, and will be easily admitted, when we consider that we can have no idea of the place of the universe, though we can of all the parts of it; because beyond that we have not the idea of any fixed, distinct, particular beings, in reference to which we can imagine it to have any relation of distance; but all beyond it is one uniform space or expansion, wherein the mind finds no variety, no marks. For to say that the world is somewhere, means no more than that it does exist; this, though a phrase

borrowed from place, signifying only its existence, not location; and when one can find out, and frame in his mind, clearly and distinctly, the place of the universe, he will be able to tell us whether it moves or stands still in the undistinguishable inane of infinite space: though it be true that the word place has sometimes a more confused sense, and stands for that space which anybody takes up; and so the universe is in a place.

The idea, therefore, of place we have by the same means that we get the idea of space, (whereof this is but a particular limited consideration,) viz. by our sight and touch; by either of which we receive into our minds the ideas of extension or distance.

11. There are some that would persuade us, that body and extension are the same thing, who either change the signification of words, which I would not suspect them of,—they having so severely condemned the philosophy of others, because it hath been too much placed in the uncertain meaning, or deceitful obscurity of doubtful or insignificant terms. If, therefore, they mean by body and extension the same that other people do, viz. by *body* something that is solid and extended, whose parts are separable and movable different ways; and by *extension,* only the space that lies between the extremities of those solid coherent parts, and which is possessed by them,—they confound very different ideas one with another; for I appeal to every man's own thoughts, whether the idea of space be not as distinct from that of solidity, as it is from the idea of scarlet colour? It is true, solidity cannot exist without extension, neither can scarlet colour exist without extension, but this hinders not, but that they are distinct ideas. Many ideas require others, as necessary to their existence or conception, which yet are very distinct ideas. Motion can neither be, nor be conceived, without space; and yet motion is not space, nor space motion; space can exist without it, and they are very distinct ideas; and so, I think, are those of space and solidity. Solidity is so inseparable an idea from body, that upon that depends its filling of space, its contact, impulse, and communication of motion upon impulse. And if it be a reason to prove that spirit is different from body, because thinking

includes not the idea of extension in it; the same reason will be as valid, I suppose, to prove that space is not body, because it includes not the idea of solidity in it; *space* and *solidity* being as distinct ideas as *thinking* and *extension,* and as wholly separable in the mind one from another. Body then and extension, it is evident, are two distinct ideas. For,

12. First, Extension includes no solidity, nor resistance to the motion of body, as body does.

13. Secondly, The parts of pure space are inseparable one from the other; so that the continuity cannot be separated, neither really nor mentally. For I demand of any one to remove any part of it from another, with which it is continued, even so much as in thought. To divide and separate actually is, as I think, by removing the parts one from another, to make two superficies, where before there was a continuity: and to divide mentally is, to make in the mind two superficies, where before there was a continuity, and consider them as removed one from the other; which can only be done in things considered by the mind as capable of being separated; and by separation, of acquiring new distinct superficies, which they then have not, but are capable of. But neither of these ways of separation, whether real of mental, is, as I think, compatible to pure space.

It is true, a man may consider so much of such a space as is answerable or commensurate to a foot, without considering the rest, which is, indeed, a partial consideration, but not so much as mental separation or division; since a man can no more mentally divide, without considering two superficies separate one from the other, than he can actually divide, without making two superficies disjoined one from the other: but a partial consideration is not separating. A man may consider light in the sun without its heat, or mobility in body without its extension, without thinking of their separation. One is only a partial consideration, terminating in one alone; and the other is a consideration of both, as existing separately.

14. Thirdly, The parts of pure space are immovable, which follows from their inseparability; motion being nothing but change of distance between any two things; but this cannot be between parts that are inseparable,

which, therefore, must needs be at perpetual rest one amongst another.

Thus the determined idea of simple space distinguishes it plainly and sufficiently from body; since its parts are inseparable, immovable, and without resistance to the motion of body.

15. If any one ask me *what* this space I speak of *is,* I will tell him when he tells me what his extension is. For to say, as is usually done, that extension is to have *partes extra partes,* is to say only, that extension is extension. For what am I the better informed in the nature of extension, when I am told that extension is to have parts that are extended, exterior to parts that are extended, i.e. extension consists of extended parts? As if one, asking what a fibre was, I should answer him,—that it was a thing made up of several fibres. Would he thereby be enabled to understand what a fibre was better than he did before? Or rather, would he not have reason to think that my design was to make sport with him, rather than seriously to instruct him?

16. Those who contend that space and body are the same, bring this dilemma:—either this space is something or nothing; if nothing be between two bodies, they must necessarily touch; if it be allowed to be something, they ask, Whether it be body or spirit? To which I answer by another question, Who told them that there was, or could be, nothing but *solid beings, which could not think,* and *thinking beings that were not extended?*—which is all they mean by the terms *body* and *spirit.*

17. If it be demanded (as usually it is) whether this space, void of body, be *substance* or *accident,* I shall readily answer I know not; nor shall be ashamed to own my ignorance, till they that ask show me a clear distinct idea of substance.

18. I endeavour as much as I can to deliver myself from those fallacies which we are apt to put upon ourselves, by taking words for things. It helps not our ignorance to feign a knowledge where we have none, by making a noise with sounds, without clear and distinct significations. Names made at pleasure, neither alter the nature of things, nor make us understand them, but as they are signs of and stand for determined ideas. And I desire those

who lay so much stress on the sound of these two syllables, *substance,* to consider whether applying it, as they do, to the infinite, incomprehensible God, to finite spirits, and to body, it be in the same sense; and whether it stands for the same idea, when each of those three so different beings are called substances. If so, whether it will thence follow—that God, spirits, and body, agreeing in the same common nature of substance, differ not any otherwise than in a bare different *modification* of that substance; as a tree and a pebble, being in the same sense body, and agreeing in the common nature of body, differ only in a bare modification of that common matter, which will be a very harsh doctrine. If they say, that they apply it to God, finite spirit, and matter, in three different significations and that it stands for one idea when God is said to be a substance; for another when the soul is called substance; and for a third when body is called so;—if the name substance stands for three several distinct ideas, they would do well to make known those distinct ideas, or at least to give three distinct names to them, to prevent in so important a notion the confusion and errors that will naturally follow from the promiscuous use of so doubtful a term; which is so far from being suspected to have three distinct, that in ordinary use it has scarce one clear distinct signification. And if they can thus make three distinct ideas of substance, what hinders why another may not make a fourth?

19. They who first ran into the notion of *accidents,* as a sort of real beings that needed something to inhere in, were forced to find out the word *substance* to support them. Had the poor Indian philosopher (who imagined that the earth also wanted something to bear it up) but thought of this word substance, he needed not to have been at the trouble to find an elephant to support it, and a tortoise to support his elephant: the word substance would have done it effectually. And he that inquired might have taken it for as good an answer from an Indian philosopher,—that substance, without knowing what it is, is that which supports the earth, as we take it for a sufficient answer and good doctrine from our European philosophers,—that substance, without knowing what it is, is that which supports accidents. So that of substance, we have no idea of what it is, but only a confused, obscure one of what it does.

20. Whatever a learned man may do here, an intelligent American, who inquired into the nature of things, would scarce take it for a satisfactory account, if, desiring to learn our architecture, he should be told that a pillar is a thing supported by a basis, and a basis something that supported a pillar. Would he not think himself mocked, instead of taught, with such an account as this? And a stranger to them would be very liberally instructed in the nature of books, and the things they contained, if he should be told that all learned books consisted of paper and letters, and that letters were things inhering in paper, and paper a thing that held forth letters: a notable way of having clear ideas of letters and paper. But were the Latin words, *inhaerentia* and *substantio,* put into the plain English ones that answer them, and were called *sticking on* and *under-propping,* they would better discover to us the very great clearness there is in the doctrine of substance and accidents, and show of what use they are in deciding of questions in philosophy.

21. But to return to our idea of space. If body be not supposed infinite, (which I think no one will affirm,) I would ask, whether, if God placed a man at the extremity of corporeal beings, he could not stretch his hand beyond his body? If he could, then he would put his arm where there was before space without body; and if there he spread his fingers, there would still be space between them without body. If he could not stretch out his hand, it must be because of some external hindrance; (for we suppose him alive, with such a power of moving the parts of his body that he hath now, which is not in itself impossible, if God so pleased to have it; or at least it is not impossible for God so to move him:) and then I ask,—whether that which hinders his hand from moving outwards be substance or accident, something or nothing? And when they have resolved that, they will be able to resolve themselves,—what that is, which is or may be between two bodies at a distance, that is not body, and has no solidity. In the mean

time, the argument is at least as good, that, where nothing hinders, (as beyond the utmost bounds of all bodies) a body put in motion may move on, as where there is nothing between, there two bodies must necessarily touch. For pure space between is sufficient to take away the necessity of mutual contact; but bare space in the way is not sufficient to stop motion. The truth is, these men must either own that they think body infinite, though they are loth to speak it out, or else affirm that space is not body. For I would fain meet with that thinking man that can in his thoughts set any bounds to space, more than he can to duration; or by thinking hope to arrive at the end of either. And therefore, if his idea of eternity be infinite, so is his idea of immensity; they are both finite or infinite alike.

22. Farther, those who assert the impossibility of space existing without matter, must not only make body infinite, but must also deny a power in God to annihilate any part of matter. No one, I suppose, will deny that God can put an end to all motion that is in matter, and fix all the bodies of the universe in a perfect quiet and rest, and continue them so long as he pleases. Whoever then will allow that God can, during such a general rest, *annihilate* either this book or the body of him that reads it, must necessarily admit the possibility of a vacuum. For, it is evident that the space that was filled by the parts of the annihilated body will still remain, and be a space without body. For the circumambient bodies being in perfect rest, are a wall of adamant, and in that state make it a perfect impossibility for any other body to get into that space. And indeed the necessary motion of one particle of matter into the place from whence another particle of matter is removed, is but a consequence from the supposition of plenitude; which will therefore need some better proof than a supposed matter of fact, which experiment can never make out;— our own clear and distinct ideas plainly satisfying us, that there is no necessary connexion between space and solidity, since we can conceive the one without the other. And those who dispute for or against a vacuum, do thereby confess they have distinct *ideas* of vacuum and plenum, i.e. that they have an idea of extension void of solidity, though they deny its

existence; or else they dispute about nothing at all. For they who so much alter the signification of words, as to call extension body, and consequently make the whole essence of body to be nothing but pure extension without solidity, must talk absurdly whenever they speak of *vacuum;* since it is impossible for extension to be without extension. For *vacuum,* whether we affirm or deny its existence, signifies space without body; whose very existence no one can deny to be possible, who will not make matter infinite, and take from God a power to annihilate any particle of it.

23. But not to go so far as beyond the utmost bounds of body in the universe, nor appeal to God's omnipotency to find a *vacuum,* the motion of bodies that are in our view and neighbourhood seems to me plainly to evince it. For I desire any one so to divide a solid body, of any dimension he pleases, as to make it possible for the solid parts to move up and down freely every way within the bounds of that superficies, if there be not left in it a void space as big as the least part into which he had divided the said solid body. And if, where the least particle of the body divided is as big as a mustard-seed, a void space equal to the bulk of a mustard-seed be requisite to make room for the free motion of the parts of the divided body within the bounds of its superficies, where the particles of matter are 100,000,000 less than a mustard-seed, there must also be a space void of solid matter as big as 100,000,000 part of a mustard-seed; for if it hold in the one it will hold in the other, and so on *in infinitum.* And let this void space be as little as it will, it destroys the hypothesis of plenitude. For if there can be a space void of body equal to the smallest separate particle of matter now existing in nature, it is still space without body; and makes as great a difference between space and body as if it were $\mu\acute{\epsilon}\gamma\alpha$ $\chi\acute{\alpha}\sigma\mu\alpha$, a distance as wide as any in nature. And therefore, if we suppose not the void space necessary to motion equal to the least parcel of the divided solid matter, but to $\frac{1}{10}$ or $\frac{1}{1000}$ of it, the same consequence will always follow of space without matter.

24. But the question being here,—Whether the idea of space or extension be the same with the idea of body? it is not necessary to prove

the real existence of a *vacuum*, but the idea of it; which it is plain men have when they inquire and dispute whether there be a *vacuum* or no. For if they had not the idea of space without body, they could not make a question about its existence: and if their idea of body did not include in it something more than the bare idea of space, they could have no doubt about the plenitude of the world; and it would be as absurd to demand, whether there were space without body, as whether there were space without space, or body without body, since these were but different names of the same idea.

25. It is true, the idea of extension joins itself so inseparably with all visible, and most tangible qualities, that it suffers us to *see* no one, or *feel* very few external objects, without taking in impressions of extension too. This readiness of extension to make itself be taken notice of so constantly with other ideas, has been the occasion, I guess, that some have made the whole essence of body to consist in extension; which is not much to be wondered at, since some have had their minds, by their eyes and touch, (the busiest of all our senses,) so filled with the idea of extension, and, as it were, wholly possessed with it, that they allowed no existence to anything that had not extension. I shall not now argue with those men, who take the measure and possibility of all being only from their narrow and gross imaginations: but having here to do only with those who conclude the essence of body to be extension, because they say they cannot imagine any sensible quality of any body without extension,—I shall desire them to consider, that, had they reflected on their ideas of tastes and smells as much as on those of sight and touch; nay, had they examined their ideas of hunger and thirst, and several other pains, they would have found that *they* included in them no idea of extension at all, which is but an affection of body, as well as the rest, discoverable by our senses, which are scarce acute enough to look into the pure essences of things.

26. If those ideas which are constantly joined to all others, must therefore be concluded to be the essence of those things which have constantly those ideas joined to them, and are inseparable from them; then unity is without doubt the essence of everything. For there is not any object of sensation or reflection which does not carry with it the idea of one: but the weakness of this kind of argument we have already shown sufficiently.

27. To conclude: whatever men shall think concerning the existence of a *vacuum*, this is plain to me—that we have as clear an idea of space distinct from solidity, as we have of solidity distinct from motion, or motion from space. We have not any two more distinct ideas; and we can as easily conceive space without solidity, as we can conceive body or space without motion, though it be never so certain that neither body nor motion can exist without space. But whether any one will take space to be only a *relation* resulting from the existence of other beings at a distance; or whether they will think the words of the most knowing King Solomon, 'The heaven, and the heaven of heavens, cannot contain thee;' or those more emphatical ones of the inspired philosopher St. Paul, 'In him we live, move, and have our being,' are to be understood in a literal sense, I leave every one to consider: only our idea of space is, I think, such as I have mentioned, and distinct from that of body. For, whether we consider, in matter itself, the distance of its coherent solid parts, and call it, in respect of those solid parts, extension; or whether, considering it as lying between the extremities of any body in its several dimensions, we call it length, breadth, and thickness; or else, considering it as lying between any two bodies or positive beings, without any consideration whether there be any matter or not between, we call it distance;—however named or considered, it is always the same uniform simple idea of space, taken from objects about which our senses have been conversant; whereof, having settled ideas in our minds, we can revive, repeat, and add them one to another as often as we will, and consider the space or distance so imagined, either as filled with solid parts, so that another body cannot come there without displacing and thrusting out the body that was there before; or else as void of solidity, so that a body of equal dimensions to that empty or

pure space may be placed in it, without the removing or expulsion of anything that was there. But, to avoid confusion in discourses concerning this matter, it were possibly to be wished that the name *extension* were applied only to matter, or the distance of the extremities of particular bodies; and the term *expansion* to space in general, with or without solid matter possessing it,—so as to say space is expanded and body extended. But in this everyone has his liberty: I propose it only for the more clear and distinct way of speaking.

28. The knowing precisely what our words stand for, would, I imagine, in this as well as a great many other cases, quickly end the dispute. For I am apt to think that men, when they come to examine them, find their simple ideas all generally to agree, though in discourse with one another they perhaps confound one another with different names. I imagine that men who abstract their thoughts, and do well examine the ideas of their own minds; cannot much differ in thinking; however they may perplex themselves with words, according to the way of speaking of the several schools or sects they have been bred up in: though amongst unthinking men, who examine not scrupulously and carefully their own ideas, and strip them not from the marks men use for them, but confound them with words, there must be endless dispute, wrangling, and jargon; especially if they be learned, bookish men, devoted to some sect, and accustomed to the language of it, and have learned to talk after others. But if it should happen that any two thinking men should really have different ideas, I do not see how they could discourse or argue one with another. Here I must not be mistaken, to think that every floating imagination in men's brains is presently of that sort of ideas I speak of. It is not easy for the mind to put off those confused notions and prejudices it has imbibed from custom, inadvertency, and common conversation. It requires pains and assiduity to examine its ideas, till it resolves them into those clear and distinct simple ones, out of which they are compounded; and to see which, amongst its simple ones, have or have not a *necessary* connexion and dependence one upon another.

Till a man doth this in the primary and original notions of things, he builds upon floating and uncertain principles, and will often find himself at a loss.

Chapter XIV: Idea of Duration and Its Simple Modes

1. There is another sort of distance, or length the idea whereof we get not from the permanent parts of space, but from the fleeting and perpetually perishing parts of succession. This we call *duration;* the simple modes whereof are any different lengths of it whereof we have distinct ideas, as *hours, days, years,* &c., *time* and *eternity.*

2. The answer of a great man, to one who asked what time was: *Si non rogas intelligo,* (which amounts to this; The more I set myself to think of it, the less I understand it,) might perhaps persuade one that time, which reveals all other things, is itself not to be discovered. Duration, time, and eternity, are, not without reason, thought to have something very abstruse in their nature. But however remote these may seem from our comprehension, yet if we trace them right to their originals, I doubt not but one of those sources of all our knowledge, viz. sensation and reflection, will be able to furnish us with these ideas, as clear and distinct as many others which are thought much less obscure; and we shall find that the idea of eternity itself is derived from the same common original with the rest of our ideas.

3. To understand *time* and *eternity* aright, we ought with attention to consider what idea it is we have of *duration,* and how we came by it. It is evident to any one who will but observe what passes in his own mind, that there is a train of ideas which constantly succeed one another in his understanding, as long as he is awake. Reflection on these appearances of several ideas one after another in our minds, is that which furnishes us with the idea of *succession:* and the distance between any parts of that succession, or between the appearance of any two ideas in our minds, is that we call *duration.*

For whilst we are thinking, or whilst we receive successively several ideas in our minds, we know that we do exist; and so we call the existence, or the continuation of the existence of ourselves, or anything else, commensurate to the succession of any ideas in our minds, the duration of ourselves, or any such other thing co-existent with our thinking.

4. That we have our notion of succession and duration from this original, viz. from reflection on the train of ideas, which we find to appear one after another in our own minds, seems plain to me, in that we have no perception of duration but by considering the train of ideas that take their turns in our understandings. When that succession of ideas ceases, our perception of duration ceases with it; which every one clearly experiments in himself, whilst he sleeps soundly, whether an hour or a day, a month or a year; of which duration of things, while he sleeps or thinks not, he has no perception at all, but it is quite lost to him; and the moment wherein he leaves off to think till the moment he begins to think again, seems to him to have no distance. And so I doubt not it would be to a waking man, if it were possible for him to keep *only one* idea in his mind, without variation and the succession of others. And we see, that one who fixes his thoughts very intently on one thing, so as to take but little notice of the succession of ideas that pass in his mind, whilst he is taken up with that earnest contemplation, lets slip out of his account a good part of that duration, and thinks that time shorter than it is. But if sleep commonly unites the distant parts of duration, it is because during that time we have no succession of ideas in our minds. For if a man, during his sleep, dreams, and variety of ideas make themselves perceptible in his mind one after another, he hath then, during such dreaming, a sense of duration, and of the length of it. By which it is to me very clear, that men derive their ideas of duration from their reflections on the train of the ideas they observe to succeed one another in their own understandings; without which observation they can have no notion of duration, whatever may happen in the world.

5. Indeed a man having, from reflecting on the succession and number of his own thoughts, got the notion or idea of duration, he can apply that notion to things which exist while he does not think; as he that has got the idea of extension from bodies by his sight or touch, can apply it to distances, where no body is seen or felt. And therefore, though a man has no perception of the length of duration which passed whilst he slept or thought not; yet, having observed the revolution of days and nights, and found the length of their duration to be in appearance regular and constant, he can, upon the supposition that that revolution has proceeded after the same manner whilst he was asleep or thought not, as it used to do at other times, he can, I say, imagine and make allowance for the length of duration whilst he slept. But if Adam and Eve, (when they were alone in the world,) instead of their ordinary night's sleep, had passed the whole twenty-four hours in one continued sleep, the duration of that twenty-four hours had been irrecoverably lost to them, and been for ever left out of their account of time.

6. Thus by reflecting on the appearing of various ideas one after another in our understandings, we get the notion of succession; which, if any one should think we did rather get from our observation of motion by our senses, he will perhaps be of my mind when he considers, that even motion produces in his mind an idea of succession no otherwise than as it produces there a continued train of distinguishable ideas. For a man looking upon a body really moving, perceives yet no motion at all unless that motion produces a constant train of successive ideas: v.g. a man becalmed at sea, out of sight of land, in a fair day, may look on the sun, or sea, or ship, a whole hour together, and perceive no motion at all in either; though it be certain that two, and perhaps all of them, have moved during that time a great way. But as soon as he perceives either of them to have changed distance with some other body, as soon as this motion produces any new idea in him, then he perceives that there has been motion. But wherever a man is, with all things at rest about him, without perceiving any motion at all,—if during this hour of quiet he has been thinking, he will perceive the various ideas of his own thoughts in his own mind, appearing one after another, and

thereby observe and find succession where he could observe no motion.

7. And this, I think, is the reason why motions very slow, though they are constant, are not perceived by us; because in their remove from one sensible part towards another, their change of distance is so slow, that it causes no new ideas in us, but a good while one after another. And so not causing a constant train of new ideas to follow one another immediately in our minds, we have no perception of motion; which consisting in a constant succession, we cannot perceive that succession without a constant succession of varying ideas arising from it.

8. On the contrary, things that move so swift as not to affect the senses distinctly with several distinguishable distances of their motion, and so cause not any train of ideas in the mind, are not also perceived. For anything that moves round about in a circle, in less times than our ideas are wont to succeed one another in our minds, is not perceived to move; but seems to be a perfect entire circle of that matter or colour, and not a part of a circle in motion.

9. Hence I leave it to others to judge, whether it be not probable that our ideas do, whilst we are awake, succeed one another in our minds at certain distances; not much unlike the images in the inside of a lantern, turned round by the heat of a candle. This appearance of theirs in train, though perhaps it may be sometimes faster and sometimes slower, yet, I guess, varies not very much in a waking man: there seem to be certain bounds to the quickness and slowness of the succession of those ideas one to another in our minds, beyond which they can neither delay nor hasten.

10. The reason I have for this odd conjecture is, from observing that, in the impressions made upon any of our senses, we can but to a certain degree perceive any succession; which, if exceeding quick, the sense of succession is lost, even in cases where it is evident that there is a real succession. Let a cannon-bullet pass through a room, and in its way take with it any limb, or fleshy parts of a man, it is as clear as any demonstration can be, that it must strike successively the two sides of the room: it is also evident, that it must touch one part of the flesh first, and another after, and so in succession: and yet, I believe, nobody who ever felt the pain of such a shot, or heard the blow against the two distant walls, could perceive any succession either in the pain or sound of so swift a stroke. Such a part of duration as this, wherein we perceive no succession, is that which we call an *instant,* and is that which takes up the time of only one idea in our minds, without the succession of another; wherein, therefore, we perceive no succession at all.

11. This also happens where the motion is so slow as not to supply a constant train of fresh ideas to the senses, as fast as the mind is capable of receiving new ones into it; and so other ideas of our own thoughts, having room to come into our minds between those offered to our senses by the moving body, there the sense of motion is lost; and the body, though it really moves, yet, not changing perceivable distance with some other bodies as fast as the ideas of our own minds do naturally follow one another in train, the thing seems to stand still; as is evident in the hands of clocks, and shadows of sun-dials, and other constant but slow motions, where, though, after certain intervals, we perceive, by the change of distance, that it hath moved, yet the motion itself we perceive not.

12. So that to me it seems, that the constant and regular succession of *ideas* in a waking man, is, as it were, the measure and standard of all other successions. Whereof, if any one either exceeds the pace of our ideas, as where two sounds or pains, &c., take up in their succession the duration of but one idea; or else where any motion or succession is so slow, as that it keeps not pace with the ideas in our minds, or the quickness in which they take their turns, as when any one or more ideas in their ordinary course come into our mind, between those which are offered to the sight by the different perceptible distances of a body in motion, or between sounds or smells following one another,—there also the sense of a constant continued succession is lost, and we perceive it not, but with certain gaps of rest between.

13. If it be so, that the ideas of our minds,

whilst we have any there, do constantly change and shift in a continual succession, it would be impossible, may any one say, for a man to think long of any one thing. By which, if it be meant that a man may have one self-same single idea a long time alone in his mind, without any variation at all, I think, in matter of fact, it is not possible. For which (not knowing how the ideas of our minds are framed, of what materials they are made, whence they have their light, and how they come to make their appearances) I can give no other reason but experience: and I would have any one try, whether he can keep one unvaried single idea in his mind, without any other, for any considerable time together.

14. For trial, let him take any figure, any degree of light or whiteness, or what other he pleases, and he will, I suppose, find it difficult to keep all other ideas out of his mind; but that some, either of another kind, or various considerations of that idea, (each of which considerations is a new idea,) will constantly succeed one another in his thoughts, let him be as wary as he can.

15. All that is in a man's power in this case, I think, is only to mind and observe what the ideas are that take their turns in his understanding; or else to direct the sort, and call in such as he hath a desire or use of: but hinder the constant succession of fresh ones, I think he cannot, though he may commonly choose whether he will heedfully observe and consider them.

16. Whether these several ideas in a man's mind be made by certain motions, I will not here dispute; but this I am sure, that they include no idea of motion in their appearance; and if a man had not the idea of motion otherwise, I think he would have none at all, which is enough to my present purpose; and sufficiently shows that the notice we take of the ideas of our own minds, appearing there one after another, is that which gives us the idea of succession and duration, without which we should have no such ideas at all. It is not then *motion*, but the constant train of *ideas* in our minds whilst we are waking, that furnishes us with the idea of duration; whereof motion no otherwise gives us any perception than as it causes in our minds a constant succession of

ideas, as I have before showed: and we have as clear an idea of succession and duration, by the train of other ideas succeeding one another in our minds, without the idea of any motion, as by the train of ideas caused by the uninterrupted sensible change of distance between two bodies, which we have from motion; and therefore we should as well have the idea of duration were there no sense of motion at all.

17. Having thus got the idea of duration, the next thing natural for the mind to do, is to get some *measure* of this common duration, whereby it might judge of its different lengths, and consider the distinct order wherein several things exist; without which a great part of our knowledge would be confused, and a great part of history be rendered very useless. This consideration of duration, as set out by certain periods, and marked by certain measures or epochs, is that, I think, which most properly we call *time*.

18. In the measuring of extension, there is nothing more required but the application of the standard or measure we make use of to the thing of whose extension we would be informed. But in the measuring of duration this cannot be done, because no two different parts of succession can be put together to measure one another. And nothing being a measure of duration but duration, as nothing is of extension but extension, we cannot keep by us any standing, unvarying measure of duration, which consists in a constant fleeting succession, as we can of certain lengths of extension, as inches, feet, yards, &c., marked out in permanent parcels of matter. Nothing then could serve well for a convenient measure of time, but what has divided the whole length of its duration into apparently equal portions, by constantly repeated periods. What portions of duration are not distinguished, or considered as distinguished and measured, by such periods, come not so properly under the notion of time; as appears by such phrases as these, viz. 'Before all time,' and 'When time shall be no more.'

19. The diurnal and annual revolutions of the sun, as having been, from the beginning of nature, constant, regular, and universally observable by all mankind, and supposed

equal to one another, have been with reason made use of for the measure of duration. But the distinction of days and years having depended on the motion of the sun, it has brought this mistake with it, that it has been thought that motion and duration were the measure one of another. For men, in the measuring of the length of time, having been accustomed to the ideas of minutes, hours, days, months, years, &c., which they found themselves upon any mention of time or duration presently to think on, all which portions of time were measured out by the motion of those heavenly bodies, they were apt to confound time and motion; or at least to think that they had a necessary connexion one with another. Whereas any constant periodical equidistant spaces of duration, if constant and universally appearance, or alteration of ideas, in seemingly observable, would have as well distinguished the intervals of time, as those that have been made use of. For, supposing the sun, which some have taken to be a fire, had been lighted up at the same distance of time that it now every day comes about to the same meridian, and then gone out again about twelve hours after, and that in the space of an annual revolution it had sensibly increased in brightness and heat, and so decreased again,—would not such regular appearances serve to measure out the distances of duration to all that could observe it, as well without as with motion? For if the appearances were constant, universally observable, in equidistant periods, they would serve mankind for measure of time as well were the motion away.

20. For the freezing of water, or the blowing of a plant, returning at equidistant periods in all parts of the earth, would as well serve men to reckon their years by, as the motions of the sun: and in effect we see, that some people in America counted their years by the coming of certain birds amongst them at their certain seasons, and leaving them at others. For a fit of an ague; the sense of hunger or thirst; a smell or a taste; or any other idea returning constantly at equidistant periods, and making itself universally be taken notice of, would not fail to measure out the course of succession, and distinguish the distances of time. Thus we see that men born blind count time well enough by years, whose revolutions yet they cannot distinguish by motions that they perceive not. And I ask whether a blind man, who distinguished his years either by the heat of summer, or cold of winter; by the smell of any flower of the spring, or taste of any fruit of the autumn, would not have a better measure of time than the Romans had before the reformation of their calendar by Julius Cæsar, or many other people, whose years, notwithstanding the motion of the sun, which they pretended to make use of, are very irregular? And it adds no small difficulty to chronology, that the exact lengths of the years that several nations counted by, are hard to be known, they differing very much one from another, and I think I may say all of them from the precise motion of the sun. And if the sun moved from the creation to the flood constantly in the equator, and so equally dispersed its light and heat to all the habitable parts of the earth, in days all of the same length, without its annual variations to the tropics, as a late ingenious author supposes, I do not think it very easy to imagine, that (notwithstanding the motion of the sun) men should in the antediluvian world, from the beginning, count by years, or measure their time by periods that had no sensible marks very obvious to distinguish them by.

21. But perhaps it will be said,—without a regular motion, such as of the sun, or some other, how could it ever be known that such periods were equal? To which I answer,—the equality of any other returning appearances might be known by the same way that that of days was known, or presumed to be so at first; which was only by judging of them by the train of ideas which had passed in men's minds in the intervals; by which train of ideas discovering inequality in the natural days, but none in the artificial days, the artificial days, or νυχθήμερα, were guessed to be equal, which was sufficient to make them serve for a measure; though exacter search has since discovered inequality in the diurnal revolutions of the sun, and we know not whether the annual also be not unequal. These yet, by their presumed and apparent equality, serve as well to reckon time by (though not to measure the parts of duration exactly) as if they could be

proved to be exactly equal. We must, therefore, carefully distinguish betwixt duration itself, and the measures we make use of to judge of its length. Duration, in itself, is to be considered as going on in one constant, equal, uniform course: but none of the measures of it which we make use of can be *known* to do so, nor can we be assured that their assigned parts or periods are equal in duration one to another; for two successive lengths of duration, however measured, can never be demonstrated to be equal. The motion of the sun, which the world used so long and so confidently for an exact measure of duration, has, as I said, been found in its several parts unequal. And though men have, of late, made use of a pendulum, as a more steady and regular motion than that of the sun, or, (to speak more truly,) of the earth;—yet if any one should be asked how he certainly knows that the two successive swings of a pendulum are equal, it would be very hard to satisfy him that they are infallibly so; since we cannot be sure that the cause of that motion, which is unknown to us, shall always operate equally; and we are sure that the medium in which the pendulum moves is not constantly the same: either of which varying, may alter the equality of such periods, and thereby destroy the certainty and exactness of the measure by motion, as well as any other periods of other appearances; the notion of duration still remaining clear, though our measures of it cannot (any of them) be demonstrated to be exact. Since then no two portions of succession can be brought together, it is impossible ever certainly to know their equality. All that we can do for a measure of time is, to take such as have continual successive appearances at seemingly equidistant periods; of which seeming equality we have no other measure, but such as the train of our own ideas have lodged in our memories, with the concurrence of other *probable* reasons, to persuade us of their equality.

22. One thing seems strange to me,—that whilst all men manifestly measured time by the motion of the great and visible bodies of the world, time yet should be defined to be the 'measure of motion': whereas it is obvious to every one who reflects ever so little on it, that to measure motion, space is as necessary to be considered as time; and those who look a little farther will find also the bulk of the thing moved necessary to be taken into the computation, by any one who will estimate or measure motion so as to judge right of it. Nor indeed does motion any otherwise conduce to the measuring of duration, than as it constantly brings about the return of certain sensible ideas, in seeming equidistant periods. For if the motion of the sun were as unequal as of a ship driven by unsteady winds, sometimes very slow, and at others irregularly very swift; or if, being constantly equally swift, it yet was not circular, and produced not the same appearances,—it would not at all help us to measure time, any more than the seeming unequal motion of a comet does.

23. Minutes, hours, days, and years are, then, no more necessary to time or duration, than inches, feet, yards, and miles, marked out in any matter, are to extension. For, though we in this part of the universe, by the constant use of them, as of periods set out by the revolutions of the sun, or as known parts of such periods, have fixed the ideas of such lengths of duration in our minds, which we apply to all parts of time whose lengths we would consider; yet there may be other parts of the universe, where they no more use these measures of ours, than in Japan they do our inches, feet, or miles; but yet something analogous to them there must be. For without some regular periodical returns, we could not measure ourselves, or signify to others, the length of any duration; though at the same time the world were as full of motion as it is now, but no part of it disposed into regular and apparently equidistant revolutions. But the different measures that may be made use of for the account of time, do not at all alter the notion of duration, which is the thing to be measured; no more than the different standards of a foot and a cubit alter the notion of extension to those who make use of those different measures.

24. The mind having once got such a measure of time as the annual revolution of the sun, can apply that measure to duration wherein that measure itself did not exist, and with which, in the reality of its being, it had nothing to do. For should one say, that Abraham was born in the two thousand seven hun-

dred and twelfth year of the Julian period, it is altogether as intelligible as reckoning from the beginning of the world, though there were so far back no motion of the sun, nor any motion at all. For, though the Julian period be supposed to begin several hundred years before there were really either days, nights, or years, marked out by any revolutions of the sun,— yet we reckon as right, and thereby measure durations as well, as if really at that time the sun had existed, and kept the same ordinary motion it doth now. The idea of duration equal to an annual revolution of the sun, is as easily *applicable* in our thoughts to duration, where no sun or motion was, as the idea of a foot or yard, taken from bodies here, can be applied in our thoughts to duration, where no sun or motion was, as the idea of a foot or yard, taken from bodies here, can be applied in our thoughts to distances beyond the confines of the world, where are no bodies at all.

25. For supposing it were 5639 miles, or millions of miles, from this place to the remotest body of the universe, (for, being finite, it must be at a certain distance,) as we suppose it to be 5639 years from this time to the first existence of any body in the beginning of the world;—we can, in our thoughts, apply this measure of a year to duration before the creation, or beyond the duration of bodies or motion, as we can this measure of a mile to space beyond the utmost bodies; and by the one measure duration, where there was no motion, as well as by the other measure space in our thoughts, where there is no body.

26. If it be objected to me here, that, in this way of explaining of time, I have begged what I should not, viz. that the world is neither eternal nor infinite; I answer, That to my present purpose it is not needful, in this place, to make use of arguments to evince the world to be finite both in duration and extension. But it being at least as conceivable as the contrary, I have certainly the liberty to suppose it, as well as any one hath to suppose the contrary; and I doubt not, but that every one that will go about it, may easily conceive in his mind the beginning of motion, though not of all duration, and so may come to a step and *non ultra* in his consideration of motion. So also, in his thoughts, he may set limits to body, and the extension belonging to it; but not to space,

where no body is, the utmost bounds of space and duration being beyond the reach of thought, as well as the utmost bounds of number are beyond the largest comprehension of the mind; and all for the same reason, as we shall see in another place.

27. By th same means, therefore, and from the same original that we come to have the idea of time, we have also that idea which we call Eternity; viz. having got the idea of succession and duration, by reflecting on the train of our own ideas, caused in us either by the natural appearances of those ideas coming constantly of themselves into our waking thoughts, or else caused by external objects successively affecting our senses; and having from the revolutions of the sun got the ideas of certain lengths of duration,—we can in our thoughts add such lengths of duration to one another, as often as we please, and apply them, so added, to durations past or to come. And this we can continue to do on, without bounds or limits, and proceed *in infinitum,* and apply thus the length of the annual motion of the sun to duration, supposed before the sun's or any other motion had its being; which is no more difficult or absurd, than to apply the notion I have of the moving of a shadow one hour to-day upon the sun-dial to the duration of something last night, v.g. the burning of a candle, which is not absolutely separate from all actual motion; and it is as impossible for the duration of that flame for an hour last night to co-exist with any motion that now is, or for ever shall be, as for any part of duration, that was before the beginning of the world, to co-exist with the motion of the sun now. But yet this hinders not but that, having the *idea* of the length of the motion of the shadow on a dial between the marks of two hours, I can as distinctly measure in my thoughts the duration of that candle-light last night, as I can the duration of anything that does now exist: and it is no more than to think, that, had the sun shone then on the dial, and moved after the same rate it doth now, the shadow on the dial would have passed from one hour-line to another whilst that flame of the candle lasted.

28. The notion of an hour, day, or year, being only the idea I have of the length of certain periodical regular motions, neither of which motions do ever all at once exist, but

only in the ideas I have of them in my memory derived from my senses or reflection; I can with the same ease, and for the same reason, apply it in my thoughts to duration antecedent to all manner of motion, as well as to anything that is but a minute or a day antecedent to the motion that at this very moment the sun is in. All things past are equally and perfectly at rest; and to this way of consideration of them are all one, whether they were before the beginning of the world, or but yesterday: the measuring of any duration by some motion depending not at all on the *real* co-existence of that thing to that motion, or any other periods of revolution, but the having a clear *idea* of the length of some periodical known motion, or other interval of duration, in my mind, and applying that to the duration of the thing I would measure.

29. Hence we see that some men imagine the duration of the world, from its first existence to this present year 1689, to have been 5639 years, or equal to 5639 annual revolutions of the sun, and others a great deal more; as the Egyptians of old, who in the time of Alexander counted 23,000 years from the reign of the sun; and the Chinese now, who account the world 3,269,000 years old, or more; which longer duration of the world according to their computation, though I should not believe to be true, yet I can equally imagine it with them, and as truly understand, and say one is longer than the other, as I understand, that Methusalem's life was longer than Enoch's. And if the common reckoning of 5639 should be true, (as it may be as well as any other assigned,) it hinders not at all my imagining what others mean, when they make the world one thousand years older, since every one may with the same facility imagine (I do not say believe) the world to be 50,000 years old, as 5639; and may as well conceive the duration of 50,000 years as 5639. Whereby it appears that, to the measuring the duration of anything by time, it is not requisite that that thing should be co-existent to the motion we measure by, or any other periodical revolution; but it suffices to this purpose, that we have the idea of the length of *any* regular periodical appearances, which we can in our minds apply to duration, with which the motion or appearance never co-existed.

30. For, as in the history of the creation delivered by Moses, I can imagine that light existed three days before the sun was, or had any motion, barely by thinking that the duration of light before the sun was created was so long as (*if* the sun had moved then as it doth now) would have been equal to three of his diurnal revolutions; so by the same way I can have an idea of the chaos, or angels, being created before there was either light or any continued motion, a minute, an hour, a day, a year, or one thousand years. For, if I can but consider duration equal to one minute, before either the being or motion of any body, I can add one minute more till I come to sixty; and by the same way of adding minutes, hours, or years (i.e. such or such parts of the sun's revolutions, or any other period whereof I have the idea) proceed *in infinitum,* and suppose a duration exceeding as many such periods as I can reckon, let me add whilst I will, which I think is the notion we have of eternity; of whose infinity we have no other notion than we have of the infinity of number, to which we can add for ever without end.

31. And thus I think it is plain, that from those two fountains of all knowledge before mentioned, viz. reflection and sensation, we got the ideas of duration, and the measures of it.

For, First, by observing what passes in our minds, how our ideas there in train constantly some vanish and others begin to appear, we come by the idea of *succession*.

Secondly, by observing a distance in the parts of this succession, we get the idea of *duration*.

Thirdly, by sensation observing certain appearances, at certain regular and seeming equidistant periods, we get the ideas of certain *lengths or measures of duration*, as minutes, hours, days, years, &c.

Fourthly, by being able to repeat those measures of time, or ideas of stated length of duration, in our minds, as often as we will, we can come to imagine *duration, where nothing does really endure or exist;* and thus we imagine tomorrow, next year, or seven years hence.

Fifthly, by being able to repeat ideas of any length of time, as of a minute, a year, or an age, as often as we will in our own thoughts, and adding them one to another, without ever coming to the end of such addition, any nearer than we can to the end of number, to which we can always add; we come by the idea of *eternity*, as the future eternal duration of our souls, as well as the eternity of that infinite Being which must necessarily have always existed.

Sixthly, by considering any part of infinite duration, as set out by periodical measures, we come by the idea of what we call *time* in general. . . .

Chapter XVI: Idea of Number

---

1. Amongst all the ideas we have, as there is none suggested to the mind by more ways, so there is none more simple, than that of *unity*, or one: it has no shadow of variety or composition in it: every object our senses are employed about; every idea in our understandings; every thought of our minds, brings this idea along with it. And therefore it is the most intimate to our thoughts, as well as it is, in its agreement to all other things, *the most universal idea we have*. For number applies itself to men, angels, actions, thoughts; everything that either doth exist, or can be imagined.

2. By repeating this idea in our minds, and adding the repetitions together, we come by the *complex* ideas of the *modes* of it. Thus, by adding one to one, we have the complex idea of a couple; by putting twelve units together, we have the complex idea of a dozen; and so of a score, or a million, or any other number.

3. The *simple modes* of *number* are of all other the most distinct; every the least variation, which is an unit, making each combination as clearly different from that which approacheth nearest to it, as the most remote; two being as distinct from one, as two hundred; and the idea of two as distinct from the idea of three, as the magnitude of the whole earth is from that of a mite. This is not so in other simple modes, in which it is not so easy, nor perhaps possible for us to distinguish betwixt two approaching ideas, which yet are really different. For who will undertake to find a difference between the white of this paper and that of the next degree to it: or can form distinct ideas of every the least excess in extension?

4. The clearness and distinctness of each mode of number from all others, even those that approach nearest, makes me apt to think that demonstrations in numbers, if they are not more evident and exact than in extension, yet they are more general in their use, and more determinate in their application. Because the ideas of numbers are more precise and distinguishable than in extension; where every equality and excess are not so easy to be observed or measured; because our thoughts cannot in space arrive at any determined smallness beyond which it cannot go, as an unit; and therefore the quantity or proportion of any the least excess cannot be discovered; which is clear otherwise in number, where, as has been said, 91 is as distinguishable from 90 as from 9000, though 91 be the next immediate excess to 90. But it is not so in extension, where, whatsoever is more than just a foot or an inch, is not distinguishable from the standard of a foot or an inch; and in lines which appear of an equal length, one may be longer than the other by innumerable parts: nor can any one assign an angle, which shall be the next biggest to a right one.

5. By the repeating, as has been said, the idea of an unit, and joining it to another unit, we make thereof one collective idea, marked by the name two. And whatsoever can do this, and proceed on, still adding one more to the last collective idea which he had of any number, and gave a name to it, may count, or have ideas, for several collections of units, distinguished one from another, as far as he hath a series of names for following numbers, and a memory to retain that series, with their several names: all numeration being but still the adding of one unit more, and giving to the whole together, as comprehended in one idea, a new or distinct name or sign, whereby to know it from those before and after, and distinguish it from every smaller or greater multitude of units. So that he that can add one to one, and so to two, and so go on with his tale, taking still with him the distinct names belonging to every progression; and so again, by subtracting an unit from each collection, retreat and lessen them, is capable of all the ideas of numbers within the compass of his language, or for which he hath names, though not perhaps of more. For, the several simple modes of num-

bers being in our minds but so many combinations of units, which have no variety, nor are capable of any other difference but more or less, names or marks for each distinct combination seem more necessary than in any other sort of ideas. For, without such names or marks, we can hardly well make use of numbers in reckoning, especially where the combination is made up of any great multitude of units; which put together, without a name or mark to distinguish that precise collection, will hardly be kept from being a heap in confusion.

6. This I think to be the reason why some Americans I have spoken with (who were otherwise quick and rational parts enough,) could not, as we do, by any means count to 1000; nor had any distinct idea of that number, though they could reckon very well to 20. Because their language being scanty, and accommodated only to the few necessaries of a needy, simple life, unacquainted either with trade or mathematics, had no words in it to stand for 1000; so that when they were discoursed with of those greater numbers, they would show the hairs of their head, to express a great multitude, which they could not number; which inability, I suppose, proceeded from their want of names.* The *Tououpinambos* had no names for numbers above 5; any number beyond that they made out by showing their fingers, and the fingers of others who were present. And I doubt not but we ourselves might distinctly number in words a great deal further than we usually do, would we find out but some fit denominations to signify them by; whereas, in the way we take now to name them, by millions of millions of millions, &c., it is hard to go beyond eighteen, or at most, four and twenty, decimal progressions without confusion. But to show how much distinct names conduce to our well reckoning, or having useful ideas of numbers, let us see all these following figures in one continued line, as the marks of one number: v.g.

The ordinary way of naming this number in English, will be the often repeating of millions, of millions, of millions, of millions, of millions, of millions, of millions, of millions, (which is the denomination of the second six figures. In which way, it will be very hard to have any distinguishing notions of this number. But whether, by giving every six figures a new and orderly denomination, these, and perhaps a great many more figures in progression, might not easily be counted distinctly, and ideas of them both got more easily to ourselves, and more plainly signified to others, I leave it to be considered. This I mention only to show how necessary distinct names are to numbering, without pretending to introduce new ones of my invention.

7. Thus children, either for want of names to mark the several progressions of numbers, or not having yet the faculty to collect scattered ideas into complex ones, and range them in a regular order, and so retain them in their memories, as is necessary to reckoning, do not begin to number very early, nor proceed in it very far or steadily, till a good while after they are well furnished with good store of other ideas: and one may often observe them discourse and reason pretty well, and have very clear conceptions of several other things, before they can tell twenty. And some, through the default of their memories, who cannot retain the several combinations of numbers, with their names, annexed in their distinct orders, and the dependence of so long a train of numeral progressions, and their relation one to another, are not able all their lifetime to reckon, or regularly go over any moderate series of numbers. For he that will count twenty, or have any idea of that number, must know that nineteen went before, with the distinct name or sign of every one of them, as they stand marked in their order; for wherever this fails, a gap is made, the chain breaks, and the progress in numbering can go no

Nonillions	Octillions	Septillions	Sextillions	Quintrillions	Quartrillions	Trillions	Billions	Millions	Units
857324	162486	345896	437918	423147	248106	235421	261734	368149	623137

*Let us hope he was talking about the Native Americans of the time, who did not have the benefit of education.

further. So that to reckon right, it is required, (1) That the mind distinguish carefully two ideas, which are different one from another only by the addition or subtraction of *one* unit: (2) That it retain in memory the names or marks of the several combinations, from an unit to that number; and that not confusedly, and at random, but in that exact order that the numbers follow one another. In either of which, if it trips, the whole business of numbering will be disturbed, and there will remain only the confused idea of multitide, but the ideas necessary to distinct numeration will not be attained to.

8. This further is observable in number, that it is that which the mind makes use of in measuring all things that by us are measurable, which principally are *expansion* and *duration;* and our idea of infinity, even when applied to those, seems to be nothing but the infinity of number. For what else are our ideas of Eternity and Immensity, but the repeated additions of certain ideas of imagined parts of duration and expansion, with the infinity of number; in which we can come to no end of addition? For such an inexhaustible stock, number (of all other our ideas) most clearly furnishes us with, as is obvious to every one. For let a man collect into one sum as great a number as he pleases, this multitude, how great soever, lessens not one jot the power of adding to it, or brings him any nearer the end of the inexhaustible stock of number; where still there remains as much to be added, as if none were taken out. And this *endless addition* or *addibility* (if any one like the word better) of numbers, so apparent to the mind, is that, I think, which gives us the clearest and most distinct idea of infinity: of which more in the following chapter.

Chapter XVII: Of Infinity

1. He that would know what kind of idea it is to which we give the name of *infinity,* cannot do it better than by considering to what infinity is by the mind more immediately attributed; and then how the mind comes to frame it.

Finite and *infinite* seem to me to be looked upon by the mind as the *modes of quantity,* and to be attributed primarily in their first designation only to those things which have parts, and are capable of increase or diminution by the addition or subtraction of any the least part: and such are the ideas of space, duration, and number, which we have considered in the foregoing chapters. It is true, that we cannot but be assured, that the great God, of whom and from whom are all things, is incomprehensibly infinite: but yet, when we apply to that first and supreme Being our idea of infinite, in our weak and narrow thoughts, we do it primarily in respect to his duration and ubiquity; and, I think, more figuratively to his power, wisdom, and goodness, and other attributes, which are properly inexhaustible and incomprehensible, &c. For, when we call *them* infinite, we have no other idea of this infinity but what carries with it some reflection on, and imitation of, that number or extent of the acts or objects of God's power, wisdom, and goodness, which can never be supposed so great, or so many, which these attitudes will not always surmount and exceed, let us multiply them in our thoughts as far as we can, with all the infinity of endless number. I do not pretend to say how these attributes are in God, who is infinitely beyond the reach of our narrow capacities: they do, without doubt, contain in them all possible perfection: but this, I say, is our way of conceiving them, and these our ideas of their infinity.

2. Finite then, and infinite, being by the mind looked on as *modifications* of expansion and duration, the next thing to be considered is, — *How the mind comes by them.* As for the idea of finite, there is no great difficulty. The obvious portions of extension that affect our senses, carry with them into the mind the idea of finite: and the ordinary periods of succession, whereby we measure time and duration, as hours, days, and years, are bounded lengths. The difficulty is, how we come by those *boundless ideas* of eternity and immensity; since the objects we converse with come so much short of any approach or proportion to that largeness.

3. Every one that has any idea of any stated lengths of space, as a foot, finds that he can repeat that idea; and joining it to the former,

make the idea of two feet; and by the addition of a third, three feet; and so on, without ever coming to an end of his additions, whether of the same idea of a foot, or, if he pleases, of doubling it, or any other idea he has of any length, as a mile, or diameter of the earth, or of the *orbis magnus:* for whichever of these he takes, and how often soever he doubles, or any otherwise multiplies it, he finds, that, after he has continued his doubling in his thoughts, and enlarged his idea as much as he pleases, he has no more reason to stop, nor is one jot nearer the end of such addition, than he was at first setting out: the power of enlarging his idea of space by further additions remaining still the same, he hence takes the idea of infinite space.

4. This, I think, is the way whereby the mind gets the *idea* of infinite space. It is a quite different consideration, to examine whether the mind has the idea of such a boundless space *actually existing;* since our ideas are not always proofs of the existence of things: but yet, since this comes here in our way, I suppose I may say, that we are *apt to think* that space in itself is actually boundless, to which imagination the idea of space or expansion of itself naturally leads us. For, it being considered by us, either as the extension of body, or as existing by itself, without any solid matter taking it up, (for of such a void space we have not only the idea, but I have proved, as I think, from the motion of body, its necessary existence,) it is impossible the mind should be ever able to find or suppose any end of it, or be stopped anywhere in its progress in this space, how far soever it extends its thoughts. Any bounds made with body, even adamantine walls, are so far from putting a stop to the mind in its further progress in space and extension that it rather facilitates and enlarges it. For so far as that body reaches, so far no one can doubt of extension; and when we are come to the utmost extremity of body, what is there that can there put a stop, and satisfy the mind that it is at the end of space, when it perceives that it is not; nay, when it is satisfied that body itself can move into it? For, if it be necessary for the motion of body, that there should be an empty space, though ever so little, here amongst bodies; and if it be possible for body

to move in or through that empty space;—nay, it is impossible for any particle of matter to move but into an empty space; the same possibility of a body's moving into a void space, beyond the utmost bounds of body, as well as into a void space interspersed amongst bodies, will always remain clear and evident: the idea of empty pure space, whether within or beyond the confines of all bodies, being exactly the same, differing not in nature, though in bulk; and there being nothing to hinder body from moving into it. So that wherever the mind places itself by any thought, either amongst, or remote from all bodies, it can, in this uniform idea of space, nowhere find any bounds, any end; and so must necessarily conclude it, by the very nature and idea of each part of it, to be actually infinite.

5. As, by the power we find in ourselves of repeating, as often as we will, any idea of space, we get the idea of *immensity;* so, by being able to repeat the idea of any length of duration we have in our minds, with all the endless addition of number, we come by the idea of *eternity.* For we find in ourselves, we can no more come to an end of such repeated ideas than we can come to the end of number; which every one perceives he cannot. But here again it is another question, quite different from our having an *idea* of eternity, to know whether there were *any real being,* whose duration has been eternal. And as to this, I say, he that considers something now existing, must necessarily come to Something eternal. But having spoke of this in another place, I shall say here no more of it, but proceed on to some other considerations of our idea of infinity.

6. If it be so, that our idea of infinity be got from the power we observe in ourselves of repeating, without end, our own ideas, it may be demanded,—Why we do not attribute infinity to other ideas, as well as those of space and duration; since they may be as easily, and as often, repeated in our minds as the other: and yet nobody ever thinks of infinite sweetness, or infinite whiteness, though he can repeat the idea of sweet or white, as frequently as those of a yard or a day? To which I answer,—All the ideas that are considered as having parts, and are capable of increase by the addition of any equal or less parts, afford

us, by their repetition, the idea of infinity; because, with this endless repetition, there is continued an enlargement of which there *can* be no end. But in other ideas it is not so. For to the largest idea of extension or duration that I at present have, the addition of any the least part makes an increase; but to the perfectest idea I have of the whitest whiteness, if I add another of a less or equal whiteness, (and of a whiter than I have, I cannot add the idea,) it makes no increase, and enlarges not my idea at all; and therefore the different ideas of whiteness, &c. are called degrees. For those ideas that consist of parts are capable of being augmented by every addition of the least part; but it you take the idea of white, which one parcel of snow yielded yesterday to our sight, and another idea of white from another parcel of snow you see to-day, and put them together in your mind, they embody, as it were, and run into one, and the idea of whiteness is not at all increased; and if we add a less degree of whiteness to a greater, we are so far from increasing, that we diminish it. Those ideas that consist not of parts cannot be augmented to what proportion men please, or be stretched beyond what they have received by their senses; but space, duration, and number, being capable of increase by repetition, leave in the mind an idea of endless room for more; not can we conceive anywhere a stop to a further addition or progression: and so those ideas *alone* lead our minds towards the thought of infinity.

7. Though our idea of infinity arise from the contemplation of quantity, and the endless increase the mind is able to make in quantity, by the repeated additions of what portions thereof it pleases; yet I guess we cause great confusion in our thoughts, when we join infinity to any supposed idea of quantity the mind can be thought to have, and so discourse or reason about an infinite quantity, as an infinite space, or an infinite duration. For, as our idea of infinity being, as I think, *an endless growing idea, but the idea* of any quantity the mind has, being at that time *terminated* in that idea, (for be it as great as it will, it can be no greater than it is,)—to join infinity to it, is to adjust a standing measure to a growing bulk; and therefore I think it is not an insignificant subtilty, if I say,

that we are carefully to distinguish between the idea of the infinity of space, and the idea of a space infinite. The first is nothing but a supposed endless progression of the mind, over what repeated ideas of space it pleases; but to have actually in the mind the idea of a space infinite, is to suppose the mind already passed over, and actually to have a view of *all* those repeated ideas of space which an *endless* repetition can never totally represent to it; which carries in it a plain contradiction.

8. This, perhaps, will be a little plainer, if we consider it in numbers. The infinity of numbers, to the end of whose addition every one perceives there is no approach, easily appears to any one that reflects on it. But, how clear soever this idea of the infinity of number be, there is nothing yet more evident than the absurdity of the actual idea of an infinite number. Whatsoever *positive* ideas we have in our minds of any space, duration, or number, let them be ever so great, they are still finite; but when we suppose an inexhaustible remainder, from which we remove all bounds, and wherein we allow the mind an endless progression of thought, without ever completing the idea, there we have our idea of infinity: which, though it seems to be pretty clear when we consider nothing else in it but the negation of an end, yet, when we would frame in our minds the idea of an infinite space or duration, that idea is very obscure and confused, because it is made up of two parts, very different, if not inconsistent. For, let a man frame in his mind an idea of any space or number, as great as he will; it is plain the mind *rests and terminates* in that idea, which is contrary to the idea of infinity, which *consists in a supposed endless progression.* And therefore I think it is that we are so easily confounded, when we come to argue and reason about infinite space or duration, &c. Beause the parts of such an idea not being perceived to be, as they are, inconsistent, the one side or other always perplexes, whatever consequences we draw from the other; as an idea of motion not passing on would perplex any one who should argue from such an idea, which is not better than an idea of motion at rest. And such another seems to me to be the idea of a space, or (which is the same thing) a number infinite, i.e. of a space or

number which the mind actually has, and so views and terminates in; and of a space or number, which, in a constant and endless enlarging and progression, it can in thought never attain to. For, how large soever an idea of space I have in my mind, it is no larger than it is that instant that I have it, though I be capable the next instant to double it, and so on *in infinitum;* for that alone is infinite which has no bounds; and that the idea of infinity, in which our thoughts can find none.

9. But of all other ideas, it is number, as I have said, which I think furnishes us with the clearest and most distinct idea of infinity we are capable of. For, even in space and duration, when the mind pursues the idea of infinity, it there makes use of the ideas and repetitions of numbers, as of millions and millions of miles, or years, which are so many distinct ideas,—kept best by number from running into a confused heap, wherein the mind loses itself; and when it has added together as many millions, &c., as it pleases, of known lengths of space or duration, the clearest idea it can get of infinity, is the confused, incomprehensible remainder of endless addible numbers, which affords no prospect of stop or boundary.

10. It will, perhaps, give us a little further light into the idea we have of infinity, and discover to us, that it is *nothing but the infinity of number applied to determinate parts, of which we have in our minds, the distinct ideas,* if we consider that number is not generally thought by us infinite, whereas duration and extension are apt to be so; which arises from hence,—that in number we are at one end, as it were: for there being in number nothing *less* than an unit, we there stop, and are at an end; but in addition, or increase of number, we can set no bounds: and so it is like a line, whereof one end terminating with us, the other is extended still forwards, beyond all that we can conceive. But in space and duration it is otherwise. For in duration we consider it as if this line of number were extended *both* ways—to an inconceivable, undeterminate, and infinite length; which is evident to any one that will but reflect on what consideration he hath of Eternity; which, I suppose, will find to be nothing else but the turning this infinity of number both ways, *à parte ante,* and *à parte post,* as they

speak. For, when we would consider eternity, *à parte ante,* what do we but, beginning from ourselves and the present time we are in, repeat in our minds the ideas of years, or ages, or any other assignable portion of duration past, with a prospect of proceeding in such addition with all the infinity of number: and when we would consider eternity, *à parte post,* we just after the same rate begin from ourselves, and reckon by multiplied periods yet to come, still extending that line of number as before. And these two being put together, are that infinite duration we call *Eternity:* which, as we turn our view either way, forwards or backwards, appears infinite, because we still turn that way the infinite end of number, i.e. the power still of adding more.

11. The same happens also in space, wherein, conceiving ourselves to be, as it were, in the centre, we do on all sides pursue those indeterminable lines of number; and reckoning any way from ourselves, a yard, mile, diameter of the earth, or *orbis magnus,*— by the infinity of number, we add others to them, as often as we will. And having no more reason to set apparent infinity to us also in that, which has the infinity also of number; but with this difference,—that, in the former considerations of the infinity of space and duration, we only use addition of numbers; whereas this is like the division of an unit into its fractions, wherein the mind also can proceed *in infinitum,* as well as in the former additions; it being indeed but the addition still of new numbers: though in the addition of the one, we can have no more the *positive* idea of a space infinitely great, than, in the division of the other, we can have the [positive] idea of a body infinitely little;—our idea of infinity being, as I may say, a growing or fugitive idea, still in a boundless progression, that can stop nowhere.

13. Though it be hard, I think, to find any-one so absurd as to say he has the *positive* idea of an actual infinite number; the infinity whereof lies only in a power still of adding any combination of units to any former number, and that as long and as much as one will; the like also being in the infinity of space and duration, which power leaves always to the mind room for endless additions;—yet there be those who imagine they have *positive* ideas

of infinite duration and space. It would, I think, be enough to destroy any such positive idea of infinite, to ask him that has it,— whether he could add to it or no; which would easily show the mistake of such a positive idea. We can, I think, have no positive idea of any space or duration which is not made up of, and commensurate to, repeated numbers of feet or yards, or days and years; which are the common measures, whereof we have the ideas in our minds, and whereby we judge of the greatness of this sort of quantities. And therefore, since an infinite idea of space or duration must needs be made up of infinite parts, it can have no other infinity than that of number *capable* still of further addition; but not an actual positive idea of a number infinite. For, I think it is evident, that the addition of finite things together (as are all lengths whereof we have the positive ideas) can never otherwise produce the idea of infinite than as number does; which, consisting of additions of finite units one to another, suggests the idea of infinite, only by a power we find we have of still increasing the sum, and adding more of the same kind; without coming one jot nearer the end of such progression.

14. They who would prove their idea of infinite to be positive, seem to me to do it by a pleasant argument, taken from the negation of an end; which being negative, the negation of it is positive. He that considers that the end is, in body, but the extremity or superficies of that body, will not perhaps be forward to grant that the end is a bare negative: and he that perceives the end of his pen is black or white, will be apt to think that the end is something more than a pure negation. Nor is it, when applied to duration, the bare negation of existence, but more properly the last moment of it. But if they will have the end to be nothing but the bare negation of existence, I am sure they cannot deny but the beginning is the first instant of being, and is not by any body conceived to be a bare negation; and therefore, by their own argument, the idea of eternal, *à parte ante,* or of a duration without a beginning, is but a negative idea.

15. The idea of infinite has, I confess, something of positive in all those things we apply to it. When we would think of infinite space or duration, we at first step usually make some very large idea, as perhaps of millions of ages, or miles, which possibly we double and multiply several times. All that we thus amass together in our thoughts is positive, and the assemblage of a great number of positive ideas of space or duration. But what still remains beyond this we have no more a positive distinct notion of than a mariner has of the depth of the sea; where, having let down a large portion of his sounding-line, he reaches no bottom. Whereby he knows the depth to be so many fathoms, and more; but how much the more is, he hath no distinct notion at all: and could he always supply new line, and find the plummet always sink, without ever stopping, he would be something in the posture of the mind reaching after a complete and positive idea of infinity. In which case, let this line be ten, or ten thousand fathoms long, it equally discovers what is beyond it, and gives only this confused and comparative idea, that this is not all, but one may yet go farther. So much as the mind comprehends of any space, it has a positive idea of: but in endeavouring to make it infinite,—it being always enlarging, always advancing,—the idea is still imperfect and incomplete. So much space as the mind takes a view of in its contemplation of greatness, is a clear picture, and positive in the understanding: but infinite is still greater. 1. Then the idea of *so much* is positive and clear. 2. The idea of *greater* is also clear; but it is but a comparative idea, the idea of *so much greater as cannot be comprehended.* 3. And this is plainly negative: not positive. For he has no positive clear idea of the largeness of any extension, (which is that sought for in the idea of infinite), that has not a comprehensive idea of the dimensions of it: and such, nobody, I think, pretends to in what is infinite. For to say a man has a positive clear idea of any quantity, without knowing how great it is, is as reasonable as to say, he has the positive clear idea of the number of the sands on the sea-shore, who knows not how many there be, but only that they are more than twenty. For just such a perfect and positive idea has he of an infinite space or duration, who says it is *larger than* the extent or duration of ten, one hundred, one thousand, or any other number of miles, or

years, whereof he has or can have a positive idea; which is all the idea, I think, we have of infinite. So that what lies beyond our positive idea *towards* infinity, lies in obscurity, and has the indeterminate confusion of a negative idea, wherein I know I neither do nor can comprehend all I would, it being too large for a finite and narrow capacity. And that cannot but be very far from a positive complete idea, wherein the greatest part of what I would comprehend is left out, under the undeterminate intimation of being still greater. For to say, that, having in any quantity measured so much, or gone so far, you are not yet at the end, is only to say that that quantity is greater. So that the negation of an end in any quantity is, in other words, only to say that it is bigger; and a total negation of an end is but carrying this bigger still with you, in all the progressions your thoughts shall make in quantity; and adding this *idea of still greater* to *all* the ideas you have, or can be supposed to have, of quantity. Now, whether such an idea as that be positive, I leave any one to consider.

16. I ask those who say they have a positive idea of eternity, whether their idea of duration includes in it succession, or not? If it does not, they ought to show the difference of their notion of duration, when applied to an eternal Being, and to a finite; since, perhaps, there may be others as well as I, who will own to them their weakness of understanding in this point, and acknowledge that the notion they have of duration forces them to conceive, that whatever has duration, is of a longer continuance to-day than it was yesterday. If, to avoid succession in external existence, they return to the *punctum stans* of the schools, I suppose they will thereby very little mend the matter, or help us to a more clear and positive idea of infinite duration; there being nothing more inconceivable to me than duration without succession. Besides, that *punctum stans*, if it signify anything, being not *quantum*, finite or infinite cannot belong to it. But, if our weak apprehensions cannot separate succession from any duration whatsoever, our idea of eternity can be nothing but of *infinite succession of moments of duration wherein anything does exist;* and whether any one has, or can have, a positive idea of an actual infinite number, I leave him to consider, till his infinite number be so great that he himself can add no more to it; and as long as he can increase it, I doubt he himself will think the idea he hath of it a little too scanty for positive infinity.

17. I think it unavoidable for every considering, rational creature, that will but examine his own or any other existence, to have the notion of an eternal, wise Being, who had no beginning: and such an idea of infinite duration I am sure I have. But this negation of a beginning, being but the negation of a positive thing, scarce gives me a positive idea of infinity; which, whenever I endeavour to extend my thoughts to, I confess myself at a loss, and I find I cannot attain any clear comprehension of it.

18. He that thinks he has a positive idea of infinite space, will, when he considers it, find that he can no more have a positive idea of the greatest, than he has of the least space. For in this latter, which seems the easier of the two, and more within our comprehension, we are capable only of a comparative idea of smallness, which will always be less than any one whereof we have the positive idea. All our *positive* ideas of any quantity, whether great or little, have always bounds, though our *comparative* idea, whereby we can always add to the one, and take from the other, hath no bounds. For that which remains, either great or little, not being comprehended in that positive idea which we have, lies in obscurity; and we have no other idea of it, but of the power of enlarging the one and diminishing the other, *without ceasing.* A pestle and mortar will as soon bring any particle of matter to indivisibility, as the acutest thought of a mathematician; and a surveyor may as soon with his chain measure out infinite space, as a philosopher by the quickest flight of mind reach it, or by thinking comprehend it; which is to have a positive idea of it. He that thinks on a cube of an inch diameter, has a clear and positive idea of it in his mind, and so can frame one of ½, ¼, ⅛, and so on, till he has the idea in his thoughts of something very little; but yet reaches not the idea of that incomprehensible littleness which division can produce. What remains of smallness is as far from his thoughts as when he first began; and therefore he never comes at all to

have a clear and positive idea of that smallness which is consequent to infinite divisibility.

19. Every one that looks towards infinity does, as I have said, at first glance make some very large idea of that which he applies it to, let it be space or duration; and possibly he wearies his thoughts, by multiplying in his mind that first large idea: but yet by that he comes no nearer to the having a positive clear idea of what remains to make up a positive infinite, than the country fellow had of the water which was yet to come, and pass the channel of the river where he stood:

'Rusticus expectat dum defluat amnis, at ille
Labitur, et labetur in omne volubilis ævum.'

20. There are some I have met that put so much difference between infinite duration and infinite space, that they persuade themselves that they have a positive idea of eternity, but that they have not, nor can have any idea of infinite space. The reason of which mistake I suppose to be this—that finding, by a due contemplation of causes and effects, that it is necessary to admit some Eternal Being, and so to consider the real existence of that Being as taken up and commensurate to their idea of eternity; but, on the other side, not finding it necessary, but, on the contrary, apparently absurd, that body should be infinite, they forwardly conclude that they can have no idea of infinite space, because they can have no idea of infinite matter. Which consequence, I conceive, is very ill collected, because the existence of matter is no ways necessary to the existence of space, no more than the existence of motion, or the sun, is necessary to duration, though duration uses to be measured by it. And I doubt not but that a man may have the idea of ten thousand miles square, without any body so big, as well as the idea of ten thousand years, without any body so old. It seems as easy to me to have the idea of space empty of body, as to think of the capacity of a bushel without corn, or the hollow of a nut-shell without a kernel in it: it being no more necessary that there should be existing a solid body, infinitely extended, because we have an idea of the infinity of space, than it is necessary that the world should be eternal, because we have an idea of infinite duration. And why should we

think our idea of infinite space requires the real existence of matter to support it, when we find that we have as clear an idea of an infinite duration to come, as we have of infinite duration past? Though I suppose nobody thinks it conceivable that anything does or has existed in that future duration. Nor is it possible to join our idea of future duration with present or past existence, any more than it is possible to make the ideas of yesterday, to-day, and to-morrow to be the same; or bring ages past and future together, and make them contemporary. But if these men are of the mind, that they have clearer ideas of infinite duration than of infinite space, because it is past doubt that God has existed from all eternity, but there is no real matter co-extended with infinite space; yet those philosophers who are of opinion that infinite space is possessed by God's infinite omnipresence, as well as infinite duration by his eternal existence, must be allowed to have as clear an idea of infinite space as of infinite duration; though neither of them, I think, has any positive idea of infinity in either case. For whatsoever positive ideas a man has in his mind of any quantity, he can repeat it, and add it to the former, as easy as he can add together the ideas of two days, or two paces, which are positive ideas of lengths he has in his mind, and so on as long as he pleases: whereby, if a man had a positive idea of infinite, either duration or space, he could add two infinities together; nay, make one infinite infinitely bigger than another—absurdities too gross to be confuted.

21. But yet if after all this, there be men who persuade themselves that they have clear positive comprehensive ideas of infinity, it is fit they enjoy their privilege: and I should be very glad (with some others that I know, who acknowledge they have none such) to be better informed by their communication. For I have been hitherto apt to think that the great and inextricable difficulties which perpetually involve all discourses concerning infinity,— whether of space, duration, or divisibility, have been the certain marks of a defect in our ideas of infinity, and the disproportion the nature thereof has to the comprehension of our narrow capacities. For, whilst men talk and dispute of infinite space or duration, as if

they had as complete and positive ideas of them as they have of the names they use for them, or as they have of a yard, or an hour, or any other determinate quantity; it is no wonder if the incomprehensible nature of the thing they discourse of, or reason about, leads them into perplexities and contradictions, and their minds be overlaid by an object too large and mighty to be surveyed and managed by them.

22. If I have dwelt pretty long on the consideration of duration, space, and number, and what arises from the contemplation of them,—Infinity, it is possibly no more than the matter requires; there being few simple ideas whose *modes* give more exercise to the thoughts of men than those do. I pretend not to treat of them in their full latitude. It suffices to my design to show how the mind receives them, such as they are, from sensation and reflection; and how even the idea we have of infinity, how remote soever it may seem to be from any object of sense, or operation of our mind, has, nevertheless, as all our other ideas, its original there. Some mathematicians perhaps, of advanced speculations, may have other ways to introduce into their minds ideas of infinity. But this hinders not but that they themselves, as well as all other men, got the first ideas which they had of infinity from sensation and reflection, in the method we have here set down. . . .

Chapter XXVII: Of Identity and Diversity

---

1. Another occasion the mind often takes of comparing, is the very being of things, when, considering *anything as existing at any determined time and place*, we compare it with *itself existing at another time*, and thereon form the ideas of *identity* and *diversity*. When we see anything to be in any place in any instant of time, we are sure (be it what it will) that it is that very thing, and not another which at that same time exists in another place, how like and undistinguishable soever it may be in all other respects: and in this consists *identity*, when the ideas it is

attributed to vary not at all from what they were that moment wherein we consider their former existence, and to which we compare the present. For we never finding, nor conceiving it possible, that two things of the same kind should exist in the same place at the same time, we rightly conclude, that, whatever exists anywhere at any time, excludes all of the same kind, and is there itself alone. When therefore we demand whether anything be the *same* or no, it refers always to something that existed such a time in such a place, which it was certain, at that instant, was the same with itself, and no other. From whence it follows, that one thing cannot have two beginnings of existence, nor two things one beginning; it being impossible for two things of the same kind to be or exist in the same instant, in the very same place; or one and the same thing in different places. That, therefore, that had one beginning, is the same thing; and that which had a different beginning in time and place from that, is not the same, but diverse. That which has made the difficulty about this relation has been the little care and attention used in having precise notions of the things to which it is attributed.

2. We have the ideas but of three sorts of substances:

1. *God.*
2. *Finite intelligences.*
3. *Bodies.*

First, *God* is without beginning, eternal, unalterable, and everywhere, and therefore concerning his identity there can be no doubt.

Secondly, *Finite spirits* having had each its determinate time and place of beginning to exist, the relation to that time and place will always determine to each of them its identity, as long as it exists.

Thirdly, The same will hold of every *particle of matter*, to which no addition or subtraction of matter being made, it is the same. For, though these three sorts of substances, as we term them, do not exclude one another out of the same place, yet we cannot conceive but that they must necessarily each of them exclude any of the same kind out of the same place: or else the notions and names of identity and diversity would be in vain, and there could be no such distinctions of substances, or anything else one from another. For example: could two bodies be in the same place at the same time; then those two parcels of matter must be one and the same, take them great or little; nay, all bodies must be one and the same. For, by the same reason that two particles of matter may be in one place, all bodies may be in one place: which, when it can be supposed, takes away the distinction of identity and diversity of one and more, and renders it ridiculous. But it being a contradiction that two or more should be one, identity and diversity are relations and ways of comparing well founded, and of use to the understanding.

3. All other things being but modes or relations ultimately terminated in substances, the identity and diversity of each particular existence of them too will be by the same way determined: only as to things whose existence is in succession, such as are the actions of finite beings, v.g. *motion* and *thought,* both which consist in a continued train of succession, concerning *their* diversity there can be no question: because each perishing the moment it begins, they cannot exist in different times, or in different places, as permanent beings can at different times exist in distant places; and therefore no motion or thought, considered as at different times, can be the same, each part thereof having a different beginning of existence.

4. From what has been said, it is easy to discover what is so much inquired after, the *principium individuationis;* and that, it is plain, is existence itself; which determines a being of any sort to a particular time and place, incommunicable to two beings of the same kind. This, though it seems easier to conceive in simple substances or modes; yet, when reflected on, is not more difficult in compound ones, if care be taken to what it is applied: v.g. let us suppose an atom, i.e. a continued body under one immutable superficies, existing in a determined time and place; it is evident, that, considered in any instant of its existence, it is in that instant the same with itself. For, being at that instant what it is, and nothing else, it is the same, and so must continue as long as its existence is continued; for so long it will be the

same, and no other. In like manner, if two or more atoms be joined together into the same mass, every one of those atoms will be the same, by the foregoing rule: and whilst they exist united together, the mass, consisting of the same atoms, must be the same mass, or the same body, let the parts be ever so differently jumbled. But if one of these atoms be taken away, or one new one added, it is no longer the same mass or the same body. In the state of living creatures, their identity depends not on a mass of the same particles, but on something else. For in them the variation of great parcels of matter alters not the identity; an oak growing from a plant to a great tree, and then lopped, is still the same oak; and a colt grown up to a horse, sometimes fat, sometimes lean, is all the while the same horse: though, in both these cases, there may be a manifest change of the parts; so that truly they are not either of them the same masses of matter, though they be truly one of them the same oak, and the other the same horse. The reason whereof is, that, in these two cases—a *mass of matter* and a *living body*—identity is not applied to the same thing.

5. We must therefore consider wherein an oak differs from a mass of matter, and that seems to me to be in this, that the one is only the cohesion of particles of matter any how united, the other such a disposition of them as constitutes the parts of an oak; and such an organization of those parts as is fit to receive and distribute nourishment, so as to continue and frame the wood, bark, and leaves, &c., of an oak, in which consists the vegetable life. That being then one plant which has such an organization of parts in one coherent body, partaking of one common life, it continues to be the same plant as long as it partakes of the same life, though that life be communicated to new particles of matter vitally united to the living plant, in a like continued organization conformable to that sort of plants. For this organization, being at any one instant in any one collection of matter, is in that particular concrete distinguished from all other, and *is* that individual life, which existing constantly from that moment both forwards and backwards, in the same continuity of insensibly succeeding parts united to the living body of the

plant, it has that identity which makes the same plant, and all the parts of it, parts of the same plant, during all the time that they exist united in that continued organization, which is fit to convey that common life to all the parts so united.

6. The case is not so much different in *brutes* but that any one may hence see what makes an animal and continues it the same. Something we have like this in machines, and may serve to illustrate it. For example, what is a watch? It is plain it is nothing but a fit organization or construction of parts to a certain end, which, when a sufficient force is added to it, it is capable to attain. If we would suppose this machine one continued body, all whose organized parts were repaired, increased, or diminished by a constant addition or separation of insensible parts, with one common life, we should have something very much like the body of an animal; with this difference, That, in an animal the fitness of the organization, and the motion wherein life exists, begin together, the motion coming from within; but in machines the force coming sensibly from without, is often away when the organ is in order, and well fitted to receive it.

7. This also shows wherein the identity of the same *man* consists; viz. in nothing but a participation of the same continued life, by constantly fleeting particles of matter, in succession vitally united to the same organized body. He that shall place the identity of man in anything else, but, like that of other animals, in one fitly organized body, taken in any one instant, and from thence continued, under one organization of life, in several successively fleeting particles of matter united to it will find it hard to make an embryo, one of years, mad and sober, the *same* man, by any supposition, that will not make it possible for Seth, Ismael, Socrates, Pilate, St. Austin, and Caesar Borgia, to be the same man. For if the identity of *soul alone* makes the same *man;* and there be nothing in the nature of matter why the same individual spirit may not be united to different bodies, it will be possible that those men, living in distant ages, and of different tempers, may have been the same man: which way of speaking must be from a very strange use of the word man, applied to an idea out of which

body and shape are excluded. And that way of speaking would agree yet worse with the notions of those philosophers who allow of transmigration, and are of opinion that the souls of men may, for their miscarriages, be detruded into the bodies of beasts, as fit habitations, with organs suited to the satisfaction of the brutal inclinations. But yet I think nobody, could he be sure that the *soul* of Heliogabalus were in one of his hogs, would yet say that hog were a *man* or *Heliogabalus*.

8. It is not therefore unity of substance that comprehends all sorts of identity, or will determine it in every case; but to conceive and judge of it aright, we must consider what idea the word it is applied to stands for: it being one thing to be the same *substance*, another the same *man*, and a third the same *person*, if *person, man,* and *substance,* are three names standing for three different ideas;—for such as is the idea belonging to that name, such must be the identity; which, if it had been a little more carefully attended to, would possibly have prevented a great deal of that confusion which often occurs about this matter, with no small seeming difficulties, especially concerning *personal* identity, which therefore we shall in the next place a little consider.

9. An animal is a living organized body; and consequently the same animal, as we have observed, is the same continued *life* communicated to different particles of matter, as they happen successively to be united to that organized living body. And whatever is talked of other definitions, ingenious observation puts it past doubt, that the idea in our minds, of which the sound man in our mouths is the sign, is nothing else but of an animal of such a certain form. Since I think I may be confident, that, whoever should see a creature of his own shape or make, though it had no more reason all its life than a cat or a parrot, would call him still a *man;* or whoever should hear a cat or a parrot discourse, reason, and philosophize, would call or think it nothing but a *cat* or a *parrot;* and say, the one was a dull irrational man, and the other is a very intelligent rational parrot. A relation we have in an author of great note, is sufficient to countenance the supposition of a rational parrot. His words are:

'I had a mind to know, from Prince Maurice's own mouth, the account of a common, but much credited story, that I had heard so often from many others, of an old parrot he had in Brazil, during his government there, that spoke, and asked, and answered common questions, like a reasonable creature: so that those of his train there generally concluded it to be witchery or possession; and one of his chaplains, who lived long afterwards in Holland, would never from that time endure a parrot, but said they all had a devil in them. I had heard many particulars of this story, and assevered by people hard to be discredited, which made me ask Prince Maurice what there was of it. He said, with his usual plainness and dryness in talk, there was something true, but a great deal false of what had been reported. I desired to know of him what there was of the first. He told me short and coldly, that he had heard of such an old parrot when he had been at Brazil; and though he believed nothing of it, and it was a good way off, yet he had so much curiosity as to send for it: that it was a very great and a very old one; and when it came first into the room where the prince was, with a great many Dutchmen about him, it said presently, *What a company of white men are here!* They asked it, what it thought that man was, pointing to the prince. It answered, *Some General or other.* When they brought it close to him, he asked it, *D'où venez-vous?* It answered, *De Marinnan.* The Prince, *À qui estes-vous?* The parrot, *À un Portugais.* The Prince, *Que fais-tu là?* Parrot, *Fe garde les poulles.* The Prince laughed, and said, *Vous gardez les poulles?* The parrot answered, *Oui, moi; et je sçai bien faire*;* and made the chuck four or five times that people use to make to chickens when they call them. I set down the words of this worthy dialogue in French, just as Prince Maurice said them to me. I asked him in what language the parrot spoke, and he said in Brazilian. I asked whether he understood Brazilian; he said No, but he had

taken care to have two interpreters by him, the one a Dutchman that spoke Brazilian, and the other a Brazilian that spoke Dutch; that he asked them separately and privately, and both of them agreed in telling him just the same thing that the parrot had said. I could not but tell this odd story, because it is so much out of the way, and from the first hand, and what may pass for a good one; for I dare say this Prince at least believed himself in all he told me, having ever passed for a very honest and pious man: I leave it to naturalists to reason, and to other men to believe, as they please upon it; however, it is not, perhaps, amiss to relieve or enliven a busy scene sometimes with such digressions, whether to the purpose or no.'

10. I have taken care that the reader should have the story at large in the author's own words, because he seems to me not to have thought it incredible; for it cannot be imagined that so able a man as he, who had sufficiency enough to warrant all the testimonies he gives of himself, should take so much pains, in a place where it had nothing to do, to pin so close, not only a man whom he mentions as his friend, but on a Prince in whom he acknowledges very great honesty and piety, a story which, if he himself thought incredible, he could not but also think ridiculous. The Prince, it is plain, who vouches this story, and our author, who relates it from him, both of them call this talker a parrot: and I ask any one else who thinks such a story fit to be told, whether, if this parrot, and all of its kind, had always talked, as we have a prince's word for it this one did,—whether, I say, they would not have passed for a race of *rational animals;* but yet, whether, for all that, they would have been allowed to be men, and not *parrots?* For I presume it is not the idea of a thinking or rational being alone that makes the *idea of a man* in most people's sense: but of a body, so and so shaped, joined to it; and if that be the idea of a man, the same successive body not shifted all at once, must, as well as the same immaterial spirit, go to the making of the same man.

11. This being premised, to find wherein personal identity consists, we must consider what *person* stands for;—which, I think, is a thinking intelligent being, that has reason and

*(. . . he asked it, "Where are you from?" It answered, "From Marinnan." The Prince, "To whom do you belong?" Parrot, "To a Portugese." The Prince, "What do you do?" Parrot, "I guard the chickens." The Prince laughed, and said, "You look after the chickens?" The parrot answered, "Yes, I do; and I do it very well.")

reflection, and can consider itself as itself, the same thinking thing, in different times and places; which it does only by that consciousness which is inseparable from thinking, and, as it seems to me, essential to it: it being impossible for any one to perceive without *perceiving* that he does perceive. When we see, hear, smell, taste, feel, meditate, or will anything, we know that we do so. Thus it is always as to our present sensations and perceptions: and by this every one is to himself that which he calls *self:*—it not being considered, in this case, whether the same self be continued in the same or divers substances. For, since consciousness always accompanies thinking, and it is that which makes every one to be what he calls self, and thereby distinguishes himself from all other thinking things, in this alone consists personal identity, i.e. the sameness of a rational being: and as far as this consciousness can be extended backwards to any past action or thought, so far reaches the identity of that person; it is the same self now it was then; and it is by the same self with this present one that now reflects on it, that that action was done.

12. But it is further inquired, whether it be the same identical substance. This few would think they had reason to doubt of, if these perceptions, with their consciousness, always remained present in the mind, whereby the same thinking thing would be always consciously present, and, as would be thought, evidently the same to itself. But that which seems to make the difficulty is this, that this consciousness being interrupted always by forgetfulness, there being no moment of our lives wherein we have the whole train of all our past actions before our eyes in one view, but even the best memories losing the sight of one part whilst they are viewing another; and we sometimes, and that the greatest part of our lives, not reflecting on our past selves, being intent on our present thoughts, and in sound sleep having no thoughts at all, or at least none with that consciousness which remarks our waking thoughts,—I say, in all these cases, our consciousness being interrupted, and we losing the sight of our past selves, doubts are raised whether we are the same thinking thing, i.e. the same *substance* or no. Which,

however reasonable or unreasonable, concerns not *personal* identity at all. The question being what makes the same person; and not whether it be the same identical substance, which always thinks in the same person, which, in this case, matters not at all: different substances, by the same consciousness (where they do partake in it) being united into one person, as well as different bodies by the same life are united into one animal, whose identity is preserved in that change of substances by the unity of one continued life. For, it being the same consciousness that makes a man be himself to himself, personal identity depends on that only, whether it be annexed solely to one individual substance, or can be continued in a succession of several substances. For as far as any intelligent being *can* repeat the idea of any past action with the same consciousness it had of it at first, and with the same consciousness it has of any present action; so far it is the same personal self. For it is by the consciousness it has of its present thoughts and actions, that it is *self to itself* now, and so will be the same self, as far as the same consciousness can extend to actions past or to come; and would be by distance of time, or change of substance, no more two persons, than a man be two men by wearing other clothes to-day than he did yesterday, with a long or a short sleep between: the same consciousness uniting those distant actions into the same person, whatever substances contributed to their production.

13. That this is so, we have some kind of evidence in our very bodies, all whose particles, whilst vitally united to this same thinking conscious self, so that *we feel* when they are touched, and are affected by, and conscious of good or harm that happens to them, are a part of ourselves; i.e. of our thinking conscious self. Thus, the limbs of his body are to every one a part of himself; he sympathizes and is concerned for them. Cut off a hand, and thereby separate it from that consciousness he had of its heat, cold, and other affections, and it is then no longer a part of that which is himself, any more than the remotest part of matter. Thus, we see the *substance* whereof personal self consisted at one time may be varied at another, without the change of personal identity; there being no question about the same

person, though the limbs which but now were a part of it, be cut off.

14. But the question is, Whether if the same substance which thinks be changed, it can be the same person; or, remaining the same, it can be different persons?

And to this I answer: First, This can be no question at all to those who place thought in a purely material animal constitution, void of an immaterial substance. For, whether their supposition be true or no, it is plain they conceive personal identity preserved in something else than identity of substance; as animal identity is preserved in identity of life, and not of substance. And therefore those who place thinking in an immaterial substance only, before they can come to deal with these men, must show why personal identity cannot be preserved in the change of immaterial substances, or variety of particular immaterial substances, as well as animal identity is preserved in the change of material substances, or variety of particular bodies: unless they will say, it is one immaterial spirit that makes the same life in brutes, as it is one immaterial spirit that makes the same person in men; which the Cartesians at least will not admit, for fear of making brutes thinking things too.

15. But next, as to the first part of the question, Whether, if the same thinking substance (supposing immaterial substances only to think) be changed, it can be the same person? I answer, that cannot be resolved but by those who know what kind of substances they are that do think; and whether the consciousness of past actions can be transferred from one thinking substance to another. I grant were the same consciousness the same individual action it could not: but it being a present representation of a past action, why it may not be possible, that they may be represented to the mind to have been which really never was, will remain to be shown. And therefore how far the consciousness of past actions is annexed to any individual agent, so that another cannot possibly have it, will be hard for us to determine, till we know what kind of action it is that cannot be done without a reflex act of perception accompanying it, and how performed by thinking substances, who cannot think without being conscious of it. But

that which we call the same consciousness, not being the same individual act, why one intellectual substance may not have represented to it, as done by itself, what *it* never did, and was perhaps done by some other agent—why I say, such a representation may not possibly be without reality of matter of fact, as well as several representations in dreams are, which yet whilst dreaming we take for true—will be difficult to conclude from the nature of things. And that it never is so, will by us, till we have clearer views of the nature of thinking substances, be best resolved into the goodness of God; who, as far as the happiness or misery of any of his sensible creatures is concerned in it, will not, by a fatal error of theirs, transfer from one to another that consciousness which draws reward or punishment with it. How far this may be an argument against those who would place thinking in a system of fleeting animal spirits, I leave to be considered. But yet, to return to the question before us, it must be allowed, that, if the same consciousness (which, as has been shown, is quite a different thing from the same numerical figure or motion in body) can be transferred from one thinking substance to another, it will be possible that two thinking substances may make but one person. For the same consciousness being preserved, whether in the same or different substances, the personal identity is preserved.

16. As to the second part of the question, Whether the same immaterial substance remaining, there may be two distinct persons; which question seems to me to be built on this,—Whether the same immaterial being, being conscious of the action of its past duration, may be wholly stripped of all the consciousness of its past existence, and lose it beyond the power of ever retrieving it again: and so as it were beginning a new account from a new period, have a consciousness that *cannot* reach beyond this new state. All those who hold preexistence are evidently of this mind; since they allow the soul to have no remaining consciousness of what it did in that pre-existent state, either wholly separate from body, or informing any other body; and if they should not, it is plain experience would be against them. So that personal identity, reaching no further than consciousness reaches, a pre-existent

spirit not having continued so many ages in a state of silence, must needs make different persons. Suppose a Christian Platonist or a Pythagorean should, upon God's having ended all his works of creation the seventh day, think his soul hath existed ever since; and should imagine it has revolved in several human bodies; as I once met with one, who was persuaded his had been the *soul* of Socrates (how reasonably I will not dispute; this I know, that in the post he filled, which was no inconsiderable one, he passed for a very rational man, and the press has shown that he wanted not parts or learning;)—would any one say, that he, being not conscious of any of Socrates's actions or thoughts, could be the same *person* with Socrates? Let any one reflect upon himself, and conclude that he has in himself an immaterial spirit, which is that which thinks in him, and, in the constant change of his body keeps him the same: and is that which he calls *himself:* let him also suppose it to be the same soul that was in Nestor or Thersites, at the siege of Troy, (for souls being, as far as we know anything of them, in their nature indifferent to any parcel of matter, the supposition has no apparent absurdity in it,) which it may have been, as well as it is now the soul of any other man: but he now having no consciousness of any of the actions either of Nestor or Thersites, does or can he conceive himself the same person with either of them? Can he be concerned in either of their action's? attribute them to himself, or think them his own, more than the actions of any other men that ever existed? So that this consciousness, not reaching to any of the actions of either of those men, he is no more one *self* with either of them than if the soul or immaterial spirit that now informs him had been created, and began to exist, when it began to inform his present body; though it were never so true, that the same *spirit* that informed Nestor's or Thersites' body were numerically the same that now inform his. For this would no more make him the same person with Nestor, than if some of the particles of matter that were once a part of Nestor were now a part of this man; the same immaterial substance, without the same consciousness, no more making the same person, by being united to any body, than the same

particle of matter, without consciousness, united to any body, makes the same person. But let him once find himself conscious of any of the actions of Nestor, he then finds himself the same person with Nestor.

17. And thus may we be able, without any difficulty, to conceive the same person at the resurrection, though in a body not exactly in make or parts the same which he had here,—the same consciousness going along with the soul that inhabits it. But yet the soul alone, in the change of bodies, would scarce to any one but to him that makes the soul the man, be enough to make the same man. For should the soul of a prince, carrying with it the consciousness of the prince's past life, enter and inform the body of a cobbler, as soon as deserted by his own soul, every one sees he would be the same *person* with the prince, accountable only for the prince's actions: but who would say it was the same *man?* The body too goes to the making the man, and would, I guess, to everybody determine the man in this case, wherein the soul, with all its princely thoughts about it, would not make another man: but he would be the same cobbler to every one besides himself. I know that, in the ordinary way of speaking, the same person, and the same man, stand for one and the same thing. And indeed every one will always have a liberty to speak as he pleases, and to apply what articulate sounds to what ideas he thinks fit, and change them as often as he pleases. But yet, when we will inquire what makes the same *spirit, man,* or *person,* we must fix the ideas of spirit, man, or person in our minds; and having resolved with ourselves what we mean by them, it will not be hard to determine, in either of them, or the like, when it is the same, and when not.

18. But though the same immaterial substance or soul does not alone, wherever it be, and in whatsoever state, make the same *man;* yet it is plain, consciousness, as far as ever it can be extended—should it be to ages past—unites existences and actions very remote in time into the same *person,* as well as it does the existences and actions of the immediately preceding moment: so that whatever has the consciousness of present and past actions, is the same person to whom they both belong. Had I the same consciousness that I saw the ark and

Noah's flood, as that I saw an overflowing of the Thames last winter, or as that I write now, I could no more doubt that I who write this now, that saw the Thames overflowed last winter, and that viewed the flood at the general deluge, was the same *self*,—place that self in what *substance* you please—than that I who write this am the same *myself* now whilst I write (whether I consist of all the same substance, material or immaterial, or no) that I was yesterday. For as to this point of being the same self, it matters not whether this present self be made up of the same or other substances—I being as much concerned, and as justly accountable for any action that was done a thousand years since, appropriated to me now by this self-consciousness, as I am for what I did the last moment.

19. *Self* is that conscious thinking thing,—whatever substance made up of, (whether spiritual or material, simple or compounded, it matters not)—which is sensible or conscious of pleasure and pain, capable of happiness or misery, and so is concerned for itself, as far as that consciousness extends. Thus every one finds that, whilst comprehended under that consciousness, the little finger is as much a part of himself as what is most so. Upon separation of this little finger, should this consciousness go along with the little finger, and leave the rest of the body, it is evident the little finger would be the person, the same person; and self then would have nothing to do with the rest of the body. As in this case it is the consciousness that goes along with the substance, when one part is separate from another, which makes the same person, and constitutes this inseparable self: so it is in reference to substances remote in time. That with which the consciousness of this present thinking thing *can* join itself, makes the same person, and is one self with it, and with nothing else; and so attributes to itself, and owns all the actions of that thing, as its own, as far as that consciousness reaches, and no further; as every one who reflects will perceive.

20. In this personal identity is founded all the right and justice of reward and punishment; happiness and misery being that for which every one is concerned for *himself*, and not mattering what becomes of any *substance*,

not joined to, or affected with that consciousness. For, as it is evident in the instance I gave but now, if the consciousness went along with the little finger when it was cut off, that would be the same self which was concerned for the whole body yesterday, as making part of itself, whose actions then it cannot but admit as its own now. Though, if the same body should still live, and immediately from the separation of the little finger have its own peculiar consciousness, whereof the little finger knew nothing, it would not at all be concerned for it, as a part of itself, or could own any of its actions, or have any of them imputed to him.

21. This may show us wherein personal identity consists: not in the identity of substance, but, as I have said, in the identity of consciousness, wherein if Socrates and the present mayor of Queinborough agree, they are the same person: if the same Socrates waking and sleeping do not partake of the same consciousness, Socrates waking and sleeping is not the same person. And to punish Socrates waking for what sleeping Socrates thought, and waking Socrates was never conscious of, would be no more of right, than to punish one twin for what his brother-twin did, whereof he knew nothing, because their outsides were so like, that they could not be distinguished; for such twins have been seen.

22. But yet possibly it will still be objected,—Suppose I wholly lose the memory of some parts of my life, beyond a possibility of retrieving them, so that perhaps I shall never be conscious of them again; yet am I not the same person that did those actions, had those thoughts that I once was conscious of, though I have now forgot them? To which I answer, that we must here take notice what the word *I* is applied to; which, in this case, is the *man* only. And the same man being presumed to be the same person, I is easily here supposed to stand also for the same person. But if it be possible for the same man to have distinct incommunicable consciousness at different times, it is past doubt the same man would at different times make different persons; which, we see, is the sense of mankind in the solemnest declaration of their opinions, human laws not punishing the mad man for the sober man's actions, nor the sober man for what the

mad man did,—thereby making them two persons: which is somewhat explained by our way of speaking in English when we say such an one is 'not himself,' or is 'beside himself'; in which phrases it is insinuated, as if those who now, or at least first used them, thought that self was changed; the self-same person was no longer in that man.

23. But yet it is hard to conceive that Socrates, the same individual man, should be two persons. To help us a little in this, we must consider what is meant by Socrates, or the same individual *man.*

First, it must be either the same individual, immaterial, thinking substance; in short, the same numerical soul, and nothing else.

Secondly, or the same animal, without any regard to an immaterial soul.

Thirdly, or the same immaterial spirit united to the same animal.

Now, take which of these suppositions you please, it is impossible to make personal identity to consist in anything but consciousness; or reach any further than that does.

For, by the first of them, it must be allowed possible that a man born of different women, and in distant times, may be the same man. A way of speaking which, whoever admits, must allow it possible for the same man to be two distinct persons, as any two that have lived in different ages without the knowledge of one another's thoughts.

By the second and third, Socrates, in this life and after it, cannot be the same man any way, but by the same consciousness; and so making human identity to consist in the same thing wherein we place personal identity, there will be no difficulty to allow the same man to be the same person. But then they who place human identity in consciousness only, and not in something else, must consider how they will make the infant Socrates the same man with Socrates after the resurrection. But whatsoever to some men makes a man, and consequently the same individual man, wherein perhaps few are agreed, personal identity can by us be placed in nothing but consciousness, (which is that alone which makes what we call *self,*) without involving us in great absurdities.

24. But is not a man drunk and sober the same person? why else is he punished for the fact he commits when drunk, though he be never afterwards conscious of it? Just as much the same person as a man that walks, and does other things in his sleep, is the same person, and is answerable for any mischief he shall do in it. Human laws punish both, with a justice suitable to *their* way of knowledge;—because, in these cases, they cannot distinguish certainly what is real, what counterfeit: and so the ignorance in drunkenness or sleep is not admitted as a plea. [For, though punishment be annexed to personality, and personality to consciousness, and the drunkard perhaps be not conscious of what he did, yet human judicatures justly punish him; because the fact is proved against him, but want of consciousness cannot be proved for him.] But in the Great Day, wherein the secrets of all hearts shall be laid open, it may be reasonable to think, no one shall be made to answer for what he knows nothing of; but shall receive his doom, his conscience accusing or excusing him.

25. Nothing but consciousness can unite remote existences into the same person: the identity of substance will not do it; for whatever substance there is, however framed, without consciousness there is no person: and a carcass may be a person, as well as any sort of substance be so, without consciousness.

Could we suppose two distinct incommunicable consciousnesses acting the same body, the one constantly by day, the other by night; and, on the other side, the same consciousness, acting by intervals, two distinct bodies: I ask, in the first case, whether the day and the night—man would not be two as distinct persons as Socrates and Plato? And whether, in the second case, there would not be one person in two distinct bodies, as much as one man is the same in two distinct clothings? Nor is it at all material to say, that this same, and this distinct consciousness, in the cases above mentioned, is owing to the same and distinct immaterial substances, bringing it with them to those bodies; which, whether true or no, alters not the case: since it is evident the personal identity would equally be determined by the consciousness, whether that consciousness were annexed to some individual immaterial substance or no. For, granting that the thinking substance in man must be necessarily supposed immaterial, it is evident that immaterial thinking thing may sometimes part with its past consciousness, and be restored to it again: as appears in the forgetfulness men often have of their past actions; and the mind many times recovers the memory of a past consciousness, which it had lost for twenty years together. Make these intervals of memory and forgetfulness to take their turns regularly by day and night, and you have two persons with the same immaterial spirit, as much as in the former instance two persons with the same body. So that self is not determined by identity or diversity of substance, which it cannot be sure of, but only by identity of consciousness.

26. Indeed it may conceive the substance whereof it is now made up to have existed formerly, united in the same conscious being: but, consciousness removed, that substance is no more itself, or makes no more a part of it, than any other substance; as is evident in the instance we have already given of a limb cut off, of whose heat, or cold, or other affections, having no longer any consciousness, it is no more of a man's self than any other matter of the universe. In like manner it will be in reference to any immaterial substance, which is void of that consciousness whereby I am myself to myself: [if there be any part of its existence which] I cannot upon recollection join with that present consciousness whereby I am now myself, it is, in that part of its existence, no more *myself* than any other immaterial being. For, whatsoever any substance has thought or done, which I cannot recollect, and by my consciousness make my own thought and action, it will no more belong to me, whether a part of me thought or did it, than if it had been thought or done by any other immaterial being anywhere existing.

27. I agree, the more probable opinion is, that this consciousness is annexed to, and the affection of, one individual immaterial substance.

But let men, according to their diverse hypotheses, resolve of that as they please. This every intelligent being, sensible of happiness or misery must grant—that there is something that is *himself*, that he is concerned for, and would have happy; that this self has existed in a continued duration more than one instant, and therefore it is possible may exist, as it has done, months and years to come, without any certain bounds to be set to its duration; and may be the same self, by the same consciousness continued on for the future. And thus, by this consciousness he finds himself to be the same self which did such and such an action some years since, by which he comes to be happy or miserable now. In all which account of self, the same numerical *substance* is not considered as making the same self; but the same continued *consciousness*, in which several substances may have been united, and again separated from it, which, whilst they continued in a vital union with that wherein this consciousness then resided, made a part of that same self. Thus any part of our bodies, vitally united to that which is conscious in us, makes a part of ourselves: but upon separation from the vital union by which that consciousness is communicated, that which a moment since was part of ourselves, is now no more so than a part of another man's self is a part of me: and it is not impossible but in a little time may become a real part of another person. And so we have the same numerical substance become a part of two different persons; and the same person preserved under the change of various substances. Could we suppose any spirit wholly stripped of all its memory or consciousness of past actions, as we find our minds always are of a great part of ours, and sometimes of them all; the union or separation of such a spiritual substance would make no variation of personal identity, any more than that of any particle of matter does. Any substance vitally united to the present thinking being is a part of that very same self which now is; anything united to it by a consciousness of former actions, makes also a part of the same self, which is the same both then and now.

28. *Person*, as I take it, is the name for this self. Wherever a man finds what he calls himself, there, I think, another may say is the same person. It is a forensic term, appropriating actions and their merit; and so belongs only to intelligent agents, capable of a law, and happiness, and misery. This personality extends itself beyond present existence to what is past, only by consciousness,—whereby it becomes

concerned and accountable; owns and imputes to itself past actions, just upon the same ground and for the same reason as it does the present. All which is founded in a concern for happiness, the unavoidable concomitant of consciousness; that which is conscious of pleasure and pain, desiring that that self that is conscious should be happy. And therefore whatever past actions it cannot reconcile or *appropriate* to that present self by consciousness, it can be no more concerned in than if they had never been done: and to receive pleasure or pain, i.e. reward or punishment, on the account of any such action, is all one as to be made happy or miserable in its first being, without any demerit at all. For, supposing a *man* punished now for what he had done in another life, whereof he could be made to have no consciousness at all, what difference is there between that punishment and being *created* miserable? And therefore, conformable to this, the apostle tells us, that, at the great day, when every one shall 'receive according to his doings, the secrets of all hearts shall be laid open.' The sentence shall be justified by the consciousness all persons shall have, that *they themselves,* in what bodies soever they appear, or what substances soever that consciousness adheres to, are the *same* that committed those actions, and deserve that punishment for them.

29. I am apt enough to think I have, in treating of this subject, made some suppositions that will look strange to some readers, and possibly they are so in themselves. But yet, I think they are such as are pardonable, in this ignorance we are in of the nature of that thinking thing that is in us, and which we look on as *ourselves.* Did we know what it was; or how it was tied to a certain system of fleeting animal spirits; or whether it could or could not perform its operations of thinking and memory out of a body organized as ours is; and whether it has pleased God that no one such spirit shall ever be united to any but one such body, upon the right constitution of whose organs its memory should depend; we might see the absurdity of some of those suppositions I have made. But taking, as we ordinarily now do (in the dark concerning these matters,) the

soul of a man for an immaterial substance, independent from matter, and indifferent alike to it all; there can, from the nature of things, be no absurdity at all to suppose that the same *soul* may at different times be united to different *bodies,* and with them make up for that time one *man:* as well as we suppose a part of a sheep's body yesterday should be a part of a man's body to-morrow, and in that union make a vital part of Melibœus himself, as well as it did of his ram.

30. To conclude: Whatever substance begins to exist, it must, during its existence, necessarily be the same: whatever compositions of substances begin to exist, during the union of those substances, the concrete must be the same: whatsoever mode begins to exist, during its existence it is the same: and so if the composition be of distinct substances and different modes, the same rule holds. Whereby it will appear, that the difficulty or obscurity that has been about this matter rather rises from the names ill-used, than from any obscurity in things themselves. For whatever makes the specific idea to which the name is applied, if that idea be steadily kept to, the distinction of anything into the same and divers will easily be conceived, and there can arise no doubt about it.

31. For, supposing a rational spirit be the idea of a *man,* it is easy to know what is the same man, viz. the same spirit—whether separate or in a body—will be the *same man.* Supposing a rational spirit vitally united to a body of a certain conformation of parts to make a man; whilst that rational spirit, with that vital conformation of parts, though continued in a fleeting successive body, remains, it will be the *same man.* But if to any one the idea of a man be but the vital union of parts in a certain shape; as long as that vital union and shape remain in a concrete, no otherwise the same but by a continued succession of fleeting particles, it will be the *same man.* For, whatever be the composition whereof the complex idea is made, whenever existence makes it one particular thing under any denomination, *the same existence continued* preserves it the *same* individual under the same denomination.

VI
George Berkeley

GEORGE BERKELEY (1695–1753) was born in Kilkenny, Ireland. At the age of 15 he entered Trinity College, Dublin, where he studied the writings of the luminaries of the time—Locke, Newton, and Melebranche—as well as those of previous masters, such as Bacon, Descartes, Hobbes, and Leibniz. Berkeley learned mathematics, physics, and optics from the works of Kepler, Descartes, and Newton, but his greatest influence was Plato. Deeply critical of both Descartes and Newton, Berkeley saw the scientific revolution of his day as symptomatic of the decline of the philosophical mind, on its way toward being seduced away from real inquiry, being blinded by its own knowledge to the awe and mystery of existence. He argued vehemently that science and mathematics were both ultimately on par with religion with regard to not being able to dispell the mystery; in his criticism of the calculus of Newton and Leibniz, he wrote: "He who can digest a second or third fluxion . . . need not, methinks, be squeamish about any point in divinity." In pointing out the presence of insoluble paradoxes at the center of scientific and mathematical thought, showing them ultimately on a par with religious thought, he was being not so much a skeptic as a true philosopher—highlighting the holes in the conceptual framework not for the purpose of destroying it but for improving and revising it.

Berkeley remained at Trinity for 13 years, producing his most important works there: *Essays Towards a New Theory of Vision* (1709), *Three Dialogues Between Hylas and Philonous* (1713), and *A Treatise Concerning Human Knowlege* (1710), which was written when he was only 25. All three works, however, were either ignored or vehemently disliked, mostly because they were completely misunderstood. He was labeled a skeptic, even though he tried to refute skepticism, and his views were generally regarded as patently absurd.

His books having, in his eyes, failed, Berkeley journeyed to the American Colonies with the idea of founding a new university styled after Plato's Academy. There he hoped to be an educator, not a reeducator, as he saw himself in England. "The savage Americans," he wrote, "if they are in a state purely natural and unimproved by education, they are also unencumbered with all that rubbish of superstition and prejudice, which is the effect of a wrong one." He lived in Newport, Rhode Island, while awaiting the monetary support he had been promised in order to begin building his would-be academy in Bermuda. The money never came, forcing him to give up the project and return to London, where he stayed for three years until he received a position as Bishop of Cloyne. He continued to write, but his books fell mostly on deaf ears during his lifetime. Subsequent philosophers, however, have held him in great esteem. David Hume called Berkeley's pioneering work on the nature of the mind, particularly the complex, bundled nature of our ideas, "one of the greatest and most valuable discoveries that has been made of late years in the republic of letters."American idealists considered Berkeley their founder, including Josiah Royce (1855–1916) at Harvard, who developed his own brand of absolute idealism. The great American pragmatist Charles Sanders Pierce (1839–1914) claimed that it was Berkeley who paved the way toward pragmatism. Immanuel Kant, though supposedly a critic of Berkeley's idealism, seems to have relied very heavily on Berkeley's views, especially Berkeley's criticism of materialism; Kant's transcendental idealism incorporates Berkeley's famous dictum *esse est percipi* ("to be is to be perceived"), tailored in Berkeley's own unique way. Arthur Schopenhauer credits Berkeley as being the first to put forth the view that the world is a *representation,* an idea in the mind. Ernst Mach, influential in both physics and philosophy, was guided in his criticisms of absolute space, time, and motion by the work of Berkeley, leading to the development of the revolutionary idea in physics of the fundamental role that the conscious observer plays in the making of reality; indeed, not just Einsteinian relativity, but also contemporary quantum mechanics, can be viewed as the ultimate vindication of Berkeley's ideas.

A Treatise Concerning the Principles of Human Knowledge

Wherein the Chief Causes of Error and Difficulty in the Sciences, with the Grounds of Skepticism, Atheism, and Irreligion, Are Inquired Into

George Berkeley

Preface

What I here make public has, after a long and scrupulous inquiry, seemed to me evidently true and not unuseful to be known—particularly to those who are tainted with skepticism or want a demonstration of the existence and immateriality of God or the natural immortality of the soul. Whether it be so or no, I am content the reader should impartially examine, since I do not think myself any further concerned for the success of what I have written than as it is agreeable to truth. But to the end this may not suffer I make it my request that the reader suspend his judgment till he has once at least read the whole through with that degree of attention and thought which the subject matter shall seem to deserve. For as there are some passages that, taken by themselves, are very liable (nor could it be remedied) to gross misinterpretation, and to be charged with most absurd consequences which, nevertheless, upon an entire perusal will appear not to follow from them, so likewise, though the whole should be read over, yet, if this be done transiently, it is very probable my sense may be mistaken; but to a thinking reader, I flatter myself, it will be throughout clear and obvious. As for the characters of novelty and singularity which some of the following notions may seem to bear, it is, I hope, needless to make any apology on that account. He must surely be either very weak or

SOURCE: *The Works of George Berkeley* edited by A. C. Fraser (London, 1871).

very little acquainted with the sciences who shall reject a truth that is capable of demonstration for no other reason but because it is newly known and contrary to the prejudices of mankind. Thus much I thought fit to premise in order to prevent, if possible, the hasty censures of a sort of men who are too apt to condemn an opinion before they rightly comprehend it.

Introduction

1. Philosophy being nothing else but the study of wisdom and truth, it may with reason be expected that those who have spent most time and pains in it should enjoy a greater calm and serenity of mind, a greater clearness and evidence of knowledge, and be less disturbed with doubts and difficulties than other men. Yet so it is, we see the illiterate bulk of mankind that walk the high road of plain common sense, and are governed by the dictates of nature, for the most part easy and undisturbed. To them nothing that is familiar appears unaccountable or difficult to comprehend. They complain not of any want of evidence in their senses, and are out of all danger of becoming skeptics. But no sooner do we depart from sense and instinct to follow the light of a superior principle, to reason, meditate, and reflect on the nature of things, but a thousand scruples spring up in our minds concerning those things which before we seemed fully to comprehend. Prejudices and errors of sense do from all parts discover themselves to our view; and, endeavoring to

correct these by reason, we are insensibly drawn into uncouth paradoxes, difficulties, and inconsistencies, which multiply and grow upon us as we advance in speculation, till at length, having wandered through many intricate mazes, we find ourselves just where we were, or, which is worse, sit down in a forlorn skepticism.

2. The cause of this is thought to be the obscurity of things, or the natural weakness and imperfection of our understandings. It is said the faculties we have are few and those designed by nature for the support and comfort of life, and not to penetrate into the inward essence and constitution of things. Besides, the mind of man being finite, when it treats of things which partake of infinity it is not to be wondered at if it run into absurdities and contradictions, out of which it is impossible it should ever extricate itself, it being of the nature of infinite not to be comprehended by that which is finite.

3. But, perhaps, we may be too partial to ourselves in placing the fault originally in our faculties and not rather in the wrong use we make of them. It is a hard thing to suppose that right deductions from true principles should ever end in conseqences which cannot be maintained or made consistent. We should believe that God has dealt more bountifully with the sons of men than to give them a strong desire for that knowledge which he had placed quite out of their reach. This were not agreeable to the wonted, indulgent methods of Providence, which, whatever appetites it may have implanted in the creatures, does usually furnish them with such means as, if rightly made use of, will not fail to satisfy them. Upon the whole, I am inclined to think that the far greater part, if not all, of those difficulties which have hitherto amused philosophers and blocked up the way to knowledge, are entirely owing to ourselves—that we have first raised a dust and then complain we cannot see.

4. My purpose therefore is to try if I can discover what those principles are which have introduced all that doubtfulness and uncertainty, those absurdities and contradictions, into the several sects of philosophy—insomuch that the wisest men have thought our ignorance incurable, conceiving it to arise from the natural dullness and limitation of our faculties. And surely it is a work well deserving our pains to make a strict inquiry concerning the first principles of human knowledge, to sift and examine them on all sides, especially since there may be some grounds to suspect that those lets and difficulties which stay and embarrass the mind in its search after truth do not spring from any darkness and intricacy in the objects or natural defect in the understanding so much as from false principles which have been insisted on, and might have been avoided.

5. How difficult and discouraging soever this attempt may seem when I consider how many great and extraordinary men have gone before me in the same designs, yet I am not without some hopes—upon the consideration that the largest views are not always the clearest, and that he who is shortsighted will be obliged to draw the object nearer, and may, perhaps, by a close and narrow survey discern that which had escaped far better eyes.

6. In order to prepare the mind of the reader for the easier conceiving what follows, it is proper to premise somewhat, by way of introduction, concerning the nature and abuse of language. But the unraveling this matter leads me in some measure to anticipate my design by taking notice of what seems to have had a chief part in rendering speculation intricate and perplexed and to have occasioned innumerable errors and difficulties in almost all parts of knowledge. And that is the opinion that the mind has a power of framing *abstract ideas* or notions of things. He who is not a perfect stranger to the writings and disputes of philosophers must needs acknowledge that no small part of them are spent about abstract ideas. These are in a more especial manner thought to be the object of those sciences which go by the name of logic and metaphysics, and of all that which passes under the notion of the most abstracted and sublime learning, in all which one shall scarce find any question handled in such a manner as does not suppose their existence in the mind, and that it is well acquainted with them.

7. It is agreed on all hands that the qualities or modes of things do never really exist each of them apart by itself and separated from

all others, but are mixed, as it were, and blended together, several in the same object. But we are told the mind, being able to consider each quality singly, or abstracted from those other qualities with which it is united, does by that means frame to itself abstract ideas. For example, there is perceived by sight an object extended, colored, and moved: this mixed or compound idea the mind, resolving into its simple, constituent parts and viewing each by itself, exclusive of the rest, does frame the abstract ideas of extension, color, and motion. Not that it is possible for color or motion to exist without extension, but only that the mind can frame to itself by *abstraction* the idea of color exclusive of extension, and of motion exclusive of both color and extension.

8. Again, the mind having observed that in the particular extensions perceived by sense there is something common and alike in all, and some other things peculiar, as this or that figure or magnitude, which distinguish them one from another, it considers apart or singles out by itself that which is common, making thereof a most abstract idea of extension, which is neither line, surface, nor solid, nor has any figure or magnitude, but is an idea entirely prescinded from all these. So likewise the mind, by leaving out of the particular colors perceived by sense that which distinguishes them one from another, and retaining that only which is common to all, makes an idea of color in abstract, which is neither red, nor blue, nor white, nor any other determinate color. And, in like manner, by considering motion abstractedly not only from the body moved, but likewise from the figure it describes, and all particular directions and velocities, the abstract idea of motion is framed, which equally corresponds to all particular motions whatsoever that may be perceived by sense.

9. And as the mind frames to itself abstract ideas of qualities or modes, so does it, by the same precision or mental separation, attain abstract ideas of the more compounded beings which include several coexistent qualities. For example, the mind, having observed that Peter, James, and John resemble each other in certain common agreements of shape and other qualities, leaves out of the complex or compounded idea it has of Peter, James, and any other particular man that which is peculiar to each, retaining only what is common to all, and so makes an abstract idea wherein all the particulars equally partake—abstracting entirely from and cutting off all those circumstances and differences which might determine it to any particular existence. And after this manner it is said we come by the abstract idea of *man* or, if you please, humanity, or human nature; wherein it is true there is included color, because there is no man but has some color, but then it can be neither white, nor black, nor any particular color, because there is no one particular color wherein all men partake. So likewise there is included stature, but then it is neither tall stature, nor low stature, nor yet middle stature, but something abstracted from all these. And so of the rest. Moeover, there being a great variety of other creatures that partake in some parts, but not all, of the complex idea of man, the mind, leaving out those parts which are peculiar to men, and retaining those only which are common to all the living creatures, frames the idea of *animal*, which abstracts not only from all particular men, but also all birds, beasts, fishes, and insects. The constitutent parts of the abstract idea of animal are body, life, sense, and spontaneous motion. By "body" is meant body without any particular shape or figure, there being no one shape or figure common to all animals, without covering, either of hair, or feathers, or scales, etc., nor yet naked: hair, feathers, scales, and nakedness being the distinguishing properties of particular animals, and for that reason left out of the *abstract idea*. Upon the same account the spontaneous motion must be neither walking, nor flying, nor creeping; it is nevertheless a motion, but what that motion is it is not easy to conceive.

10. Whether others have this wonderful faculty of abstracting their ideas, they best can tell; for myself I find indeed I have a faculty of imagining, or representing to myself, the ideas of those particular things I have perceived, and of variously compounding and dividing them. I can imagine a man with two heads, or the upper parts of a man joined to the body of a horse. I can consider the hand, the eye, the

nose, each by itself abstracted or separated from the rest of the body. But then whatever hand or eye I imagine, it must have some particular shape and color. Likewise the idea of man that I frame to myself must be either of a white, or a black, or a tawny, a straight, or a crooked, a tall, or a low, or a middle-sized man. I cannot by any effort of thought conceive the abstract idea above described. And it is equally impossible for me to form the abstract idea of motion distinct from the body moving, and which is neither swift nor slow, curvilinear nor rectilinear; and the like may be said of all other abstract general ideal whatsoever. To be plain, I own myself able to abstract in one sense, as when I consider some particular parts or qualities separated from others, with which, though they are united in some object, yet it is possible they may really exist without them. But I deny that I can abstract one from another, or conceive separately, those qualities which it is impossible should exist so separated; or that I can frame a general notion by abstracting from particulars in the manner aforesaid—which two last are the two proper acceptations of "abstraction." And there are grounds to think most men will acknowledge themselves to be in my case. The generality of men which are simple and illiterate never pretend to abstract notions. It is said they are difficult and not to be attained without pains and study; we may therefore reasonably conclude that, if such there be, they are confined only to the learned.

11. I proceed to examine what can be alleged in defense of the doctrine of abstraction, and try if I can discover what it is that inclines the men of speculation to embrace an opinion so remote from common sense as that seems to be. There has been a late, deservedly esteemed philosopher* who, no doubt, has given it very much countenance by seeming to think the having abstract general ideas is what puts the widest difference in point of understanding betwixt man and beast.—

> The having of general ideas [he says] is that which puts a perfect distinction betwixt man and brutes, and is an excellency which the faculties of brutes do by no means attain unto.

*John Locke

For, it is evident we observe no footsteps in them of making use of general signs for universal ideas; from which we have reason to imagine that they have not the faculty of abstracting, or making general ideas, since they have no use of words or any other general signs.

And a little after:

> Therefore, I think, we may suppose that it is in this that the species of brutes are discriminated from men, and it is that proper difference wherein they are wholly separated, and which at last widens to so wide a distance. For, if they have any ideas at all, and are not bare machines (as some would have them), we cannot deny them to have some reason. It seems as evident to me that they do, some of them, in certain instances reason as that they have sense; but it is only in particular ideas, just as they receive them from their senses. They are the best of them tied up within those narrow bounds, and have not (as I think) the faculty to enlarge them by any kind of abstraction.—John Locke, *Essay on Human Understanding*, Bk. II, chap. 11, secs. 10f.

I readily agree with this learned author that the faculties of brutes can by no means attain to abstraction. But then if this be made the distinguishing property of that sort of animals, I fear a great many of those that pass for men must be reckoned into their number. The reason that is here assigned why we have no grounds to think brutes have abstract general ideas is that we observe in them no use of words or any other general signs; which is built on this supposition—that the making use of words implies the having general ideas. From which it follows that men who use language are able to abstract or generalize their ideas. That this is the sense and arguing of the author will further appear by his answering the question he in another place puts: "Since all things that exist are only particulars, how come we by general terms?" His answer is: "Words become general by being made the signs of general ideas."—(*Essay on Human Understanding*, Bk. III, chap. 3, sec. 6.) But it seems that a word becomes general by being made the sign, not of an abstract general idea, but of several particular ideas, any one of which it indifferently suggests to the mind.

For example, when it is said, "the change of motion is proportional to the impressed force," or that, "whatever has extension is divisible," these propositions are to be understood of motion and extension in general; and nevertheless it will not follow that they suggest to my thoughts an idea of motion without a body moved, or any determinate direction and velocity, or that I must conceive an abstract general idea of extension which is neither line, surface, nor solid, neither great nor small, black, white, nor red, nor of any other determinate color. It is only implied that whatever motion I consider, whether it be swift or slow, perpendicular, horizontal, or oblique, or in whatever object, the axiom concerning it holds equally true. As does the other of every particular extension, it matters not whether line, surface, or solid, whether of this or that magnitude or figure.

12. By observing how ideas become general we may the better judge how words are made so. And here it is to be noted that I do not deny absolutely there are general ideas, but only that there are any *abstract* general ideas; for, in the passages above quoted, wherein there is mention of general ideas, it is always supposed that they are formed by abstraction, after the manner set forth in sections 8 and 9. Now, if we will annex a meaning to our words and speak only of what we can conceive, I believe we shall acknowledge that an idea which, considered in itself, is particular, becomes general by being made to represent or stand for all other particular ideas of the same sort. To make this plain by an example, suppose a geometrician is demonstrating the method of cutting a line in two equal parts. He draws, for instance, a black line of an inch in length: this, which in itself is a particular line, is nevertheless with regard to its signification general, since, as it is there used, it represents all particular lines whatsoever; for that which is demonstrated of it is demonstrated of all lines or, in other words, of a line in general. And, as that *particular* line becomes general by being made a sign, so the *name* "line," which taken absolutely is particular, by being a sign is made general. And as the former owes its generality not to its being the sign of an abstract or general line, but of all

particular right lines that may possibly exist, so the latter must be thought to derive its generality from the same cause, namely, the various particular lines which it indifferently denotes.

13. To give the reader a yet clearer view of the nature of abstract ideas, and the uses they are thought necessary to, I shall add one more passage out of the *Essay on Human Understanding,* which is as follows:

> Abstract ideas are not so obvious or easy to children or the yet unexercised mind as particular ones. If they seem so to grown men it is only because by constant and familiar use they are made so. For, when we nicely reflect upon them, we shall find that general ideas are fictions and contrivances of the mind, that carry difficulty with them, and do not so easily offer themselves as we are apt to imagine. For example, does it not require some pains and skill to form the general idea of a triangle (which is yet none of the most abstract, comprehensive, and difficult); for it must be neither oblique nor rectangle, neither equilateral, equicrural, nor scalenon, but *all and none* of these at once? In effect, it is something imperfect that cannot exist, an idea wherein some parts of several different and *inconsistent* ideas are put together. It is true the mind in this imperfect state has need of such ideas and makes all the haste to them it can, for the convenience of communication and enlargement of knowledge to both which it is naturally very much inclined. But yet one has reason to suspect such ideas are marks of our imperfection. At least this is enough to show that the most abstract and general ideas are not those that the mind is first and most easily acquainted with, nor such as its earliest knowledge is conversant about.—Bk. IV, chap. 7, sec. 9.

If any man has the faculty of framing in his mind such an idea of a triangle as is here described, it is in vain to pretend to dispute him out of it, nor would I go about it. All I desire is that the reader would fully and certainly inform himself whether he has such an idea or no. And this, methinks, can be no hard task for anyone to perform. What more easy than for anyone to look a little into his own thoughts, and there try whether he has, or can attain to have, an idea that shall correspond with the description that is here given of the general idea of a triangle, which is "neither oblique nor rectangle, equilateral, equicrural nor scalenon, but all and none of these at once"?

14. Much is here said of the difficulty that abstract ideas carry with them, and the pains and skill requisite to the forming them. And it is on all hands agreed that there is need of great toil and labor of the mind to emancipate our thoughts from particular objects and raise them to those sublime speculations that are conversant about abstract ideas. From all which the natural consequence should seem to be, that so difficult a thing as the forming abstract ideas was not necessary for *communication,* which is so easy and familiar to all sorts of men. But, we are told, if they seem obvious and easy to grown men, "it is only because by constant and familiar use they are made so." Now, I would fain know at what time it is men are employed in surmounting that difficulty and furnishing themselves with those necessary helps for discourse. It cannot be when they are grown up, for then it seems they are not conscious of any such painstaking; it remains, therefore, to be the business of their childhood. And surely the great and multiplied labor of framing abstract notions will be found a hard task for that tender age. Is it not a hard thing to imagine that a couple of children cannot prate together of their sugar plums and rattles and the rest of their little trinkets till they have first tacked together numberless inconsistencies and so framed in their minds abstract general ideas and annexed them to every common name they make use of?

15. Nor do I think them a whit more needful for the *enlargement of knowledge* than for *communication.* It is, I know, a point much insisted on, that all knowledge and demonstration are about universal notions, to which I fully agree; but then it does not appear to me that those notions are formed by abstraction in the manner premised—*universality,* so far as I can comprehend, not consisting in the absolute, positive nature or conception of any thing, but in the relation it bears to the particulars signified or represented by it; by virtue whereof it is that things, names, or notions, being in their own nature *particular,* are rendered *universal.* Thus, when I demonstrate any proposition concerning triangles, it is to be supposed that I have in view the universal idea of a triangle, which ought not to be understood as if I could frame an idea of a triangle which was neither equilateral, nor scalenon, nor equicrural, but only that the particular triangle I consider, whether of this or that sort it matters not, does equally stand for and represent all rectilinear triangles whatsoever, and is in that sense *universal.* All which seems very plain and not to include any difficulty in it.

16. But here it will be demanded how we can know any proposition to be true of all particular triangles, except we have first seen it demonstrated of the abstract idea of a triangle which equally agrees to all? For, because a property may be demonstrated to agree to some one particular triangle, it will not thence follow that it equally belongs to any other triangle which in all respects is not the same with it. For example, having demonstrated that the three angles of an isosceles rectangular triangle are equal to two right ones, I cannot therefore conclude this affection agrees to all other triangles which have neither a right angle nor two equal sides. It seems therefore that, to be certain this proposition is universally true, we must either make a particular demonstration for every particular triangle, which is impossible, or once for all demonstrate it of the abstract idea of a triangle in which all the particulars do indifferently partake and by which they are all equally represented. To which I answer that, though the idea I have in view whilst I make the demonstration be, for instance, that of an isosceles rectangular triangle whose sides are of a determinate length, I may nevertheless be certain it extends to all other rectilinear triangles, of what sort or bigness soever. And that because neither the right angle, nor the equality, nor determinate length of the sides are at all concerned in the demonstration. It is true the diagram I have in view includes all these particulars, but then there is not the least mention made of them in the proof of the proposition. It is not said the three angles are equal to two right ones, because one of them is a right angle, or because the sides comprehending it are

of the same length. Which sufficiently shows that the right angle might have been oblique, and the sides unequal, and for all that the demonstration have held good. And for this reason it is that I conclude that to be true of any obliquangular or scalenon which I had demonstrated of a particular right-angled equicrural traingle, and not because I demonstrated the proposition of the abstract idea of a triangle.

17. It were an endless as well as a useless thing to trace the Schoolmen, those great masters of abstraction, through all the manifold, inextricable labyrinths of error and dispute which their doctrine of abstract natures and notions seems to have led them into. What bickerings and controversies, and what a learned dust have been raised about those matters, and what mighty advantage has been from thence derived to mankind, are things at this day too clearly known to need being insisted on. And it had been well if the ill effects of that doctrine were confined to those only who make the most avowed profession of it. When men consider the great pains, industry, and parts that have for so many ages been laid out on the cultivation and advancement of the sciences, and that notwithstanding all this the far greater part of them remains full of darkness and uncertainty, and disputes that are like never to have an end, and even those that are thought to be supported by the most clear and cogent demonstrations, contain in them paradoxes which are perfectly irreconcilable to the understandings of men, and that, taking all together, a small portion of them does supply any real benefit to mankind, otherwise than by being an innocent diversion and amusement—I say the consideration of all this is apt to throw them into a despondency and perfect contempt of all study. But this may, perhaps, cease upon a view of the false principles that have obtained in the world, amongst all which there is none, methinks, has a more wide influence over the thoughts of speculative men than this of *abstract* general ideas.

18. I come now to consider the *source* of this prevailing notion, and that seems to me to be language. And surely nothing of less extent than reason itself could have been the source of an opinion so universally received. The truth of this appears, as from other reasons, so also from the plain confession of the ablest patrons of abstract ideas, who acknowledge that they are made in order to naming; from which it is a clear consequence that if there had been no such thing as speech or universal signs there never had been any thought of abstraction. See Bk. III, chap. 6, sec. 39, and elsewhere of the *Essay on Human Understanding*. Let us examine the manner wherein words have contributed to the origin of that mistake: First then, it is thought that every name has, or ought to have, one only precise and settled signification, which inclines men to think there are certain abstract, determinate ideas which constitute the true and only immediate signification of each general name; and that it is by the mediation of these abstract ideas that a general name comes to signify any particular thing. Whereas, in truth, there is no such thing as one precise and definite signification annexed to any general name, they all signifying indifferently a great number of particular ideas. All which does evidently follow from what has been already said, and will clearly appear to anyone by a little reflection. To this it will be objected that every name that has a definition is thereby restrained to one certain signification. For example, a "triangle" is defined to be "a plane surface comprehended by three right lines," by which that name is limited to denote one certain idea and no other. To which I answer that in the definition it is not said whether the surface be great or small, black or white, nor whether the sides are long or short, equal or unequal, nor with what angles they are inclined to each other; in all which there may be great variety, and consequently there is no one settled idea which limits the signification of the word "triangle." It is one thing for to keep a name constantly to the same definition, and another to make it stand everywhere for the same idea; the one is necessary, the other useless and impracticable.

19. But, to give a further account how words came to produce the doctrine of abstract ideas, it must be observed that it is a received opinion that language has no other end but the communicating ideas, and that every significant name stands for an idea. This

being so, and it being withal certain that names which yet are not thought altogether insignificant do not always mark out particular conceivable ideas, it is straightway concluded that they stand for abstract notions. That there are many names in use amongst speculative men which do not always suggest to others determinate, particular ideas is what nobody will deny. And a little attention will discover that it is not necessary (even in the strictest reasonings) that significant names which stand for ideas should, every time they are used, excite in the understanding the ideas they are made to stand for—in reading and discoursing, names being for the most part used as letters are in algebra, in which, though a particular quantity be marked by each letter, yet to proceed right it is not requisite that in every step each letter suggest to your thoughts that particular quantity it was appointed to stand for.

20. Besides, the communicating of ideas marked by words is not the chief and only end of language, as is commonly supposed. There are other ends, as the raising of some passion, the exciting to or deterring from an action, the putting the mind in some particular disposition—to which the former is in many cases barely subservient, and sometimes entirely omitted, when these can be obtained without it, as I think does not unfrequently happen in the familiar use of language. I entreat the reader to reflect with himself and see if it does not often happen, either in hearing or reading a discourse, that the passions of fear, love, hatred, admiration, disdain, and the like, arise immediately in his mind upon the perception of certain words, without any ideas coming between. At first, indeed, the words might have occasioned ideas that were fit to produce those emotions; but, if I mistake not, it will be found that, when language is once grown familiar, the hearing of the sounds or sight of the characters is oft immediately attended with those passions which at first were wont to be produced by the intervention of ideas that are now quite omitted. May we not, for example, be affected with the promise of a *good thing,* though we have not an idea of what it is? Or is not the being threatened with danger sufficient to excite a dread, though we think not

of any particular evil likely to befall us, nor yet frame to ourselves an idea of danger in abstract? If anyone shall join ever so little reflection of his own to what has been said, I believe that it will evidently appear to him that general names are often used in the propriety of language without the speaker's designing them for marks of ideas in his own, which he would have them raise in the mind of the hearer. Even proper names themselves do not seem always spoken with a design to bring into our view the ideas of those individuals that are supposed to be marked by them. For example, when a Schoolman tells me, "Aristotle has said it," all I conceive he means by it is to dispose me to embrace his opinion with the deference and submission which custom has annexed to that name. And this effect may be so instantly produced in the minds of those who are accustomed to resign their judgment to the authority of that philosopher, as it is impossible any idea either of his person, writings, or reputation should go before. Innumerable examples of this kind may be given, but why should I insist on those things which everyone's experience will, I doubt not, plentifully suggest unto him?

21. We have, I think, shown the impossibility of abstract ideas. We have considered what has been said for them by their ablest patrons, and endeavored to show they are of no use for those ends to which they are thought necessary. And lastly, we have traced them to the source from whence they flow, which appears to be language.—It cannot be denied that words are of excellent use in that by their means all that stock of knowledge which has been purchased by the joint labors of inquisitive men in all ages and nations may be drawn into the view and made the possession of one single person. But at the same time it must be owned that most parts of knowledge have been strangely perplexed and darkened by the abuse of words, and general ways of speech wherein they are delivered. Since therefore words are so apt to impose on the understanding, whatever ideas I consider, I shall endeavor to take them bare and naked into my view, keeping out of my thoughts so far as I am able those names which long and constant use has so strictly united with them;

from which I may expect to derive the following advantages:

22. *First,* I shall be sure to get clear of all controversies purely verbal—the springing up of which weeds in almost all the sciences has been a main hindrance to the growth of true and sound knowledge. *Secondly,* this seems to be a sure way to extricate myself out of that fine and subtle net of *abstract ideas* which has so miserably perplexed and entangled the minds of men; and that with this peculiar circumstance, that by how much the finer and more curious was the wit of any man, by so much the deeper was he likely to be ensnared and faster held therein. *Thirdly,* so long as I confine my thoughts to my own ideas divested of words, I do not see how I can easily be mistaken. The objects I consider I clearly and adequately know. I cannot be deceived in thinking I have an idea which I have not. It is not possible for me to imagine that any of my own ideas are alike or unlike that are not truly so. To discern the agreements or disagreements there are between my ideas, to see what ideas are included in any compound idea and what not, there is nothing more requisite than an attentive perception of what passes in my own understanding.

23. But the attainment of all these advantages does presuppose an entire deliverance from the deception of words, which I dare hardly promise myself—so difficult a thing it is to dissolve a union so early begun and confirmed by so long a habit as that betwixt words and ideas. Which difficulty seems to have been very much increased by the doctine of *abstraction.* For so long as men thought abstract ideas were annexed to their words, it does not seem strange that they should use words for ideas—it being found an impracticable thing to lay aside the word and retain the *abstract* idea in the mind, which in itself was perfectly inconceivable. This seems to me the principal cause why those men who have so emphatically recommended to others the laying aside all use of words in their meditations, and contemplating their bare ideas, have yet failed to perform it themselves. Of late many have been very sensible of the absurd opinions and insignificant disputes which grow out of the abuse of words. And, in order to remedy these evils, they advise well that we attend to the ideas signified and draw off our attention from the words which signify them. But, how good soever this advice may be they have given others, it is plain they could not have a due regard to it themselves so long as they thought the only immediate use of words was to signify ideas, and that the immediate signification of every general name was a determinate abstract idea.

24. But, these being known to be mistakes, a man may with greater ease prevent his being imposed on by words. He that knows he has no other than *particular* ideas will not puzzle himself in vain to find out and conceive the *abstract* idea annexed to any name. And he that knows names do not always stand for ideas will spare himself the labor of looking for ideas where there are none to be had. It were, therefore, to be wished that everyone would use his utmost endeavors to obtain a clear view of the ideas he would consider, separating from them all that dress and encumbrance of words which so much contribute to blind the judgment and divide the attention. In vain do we extend our view into the heavens and pry into the entrails of the earth, in vain do we consult the writings of learned men and trace the dark footsteps of antiquity—we need only draw the curtain of words, to behold the fairest tree of knowledge, whose fruit is excellent and within the reach of our hand.

25. Unless we take care to clear the first principles of knowledge from the embarrassment and delusion of words, we may make infinite reasonings upon them to no purpose; we may make infinite reasonings upon them to no purpose; we may draw consequences from consequences, and be never the wiser. The further we go, we shall only lose ourselves the more irrecoverably, and be the deeper entangled in difficulties and mistakes. Whoever, therefore, designs to read the following sheets, I entreat him to make my words the occasion of his own thinking and endeavor to attain the same train of thoughts in reading that I had in writing them. By this means it will be easy for him to discover the truth or falsity of what I say. He will be out of all danger of being deceived by my words, and I do not see how he can be led into an error by considering his own naked, undisguised ideas.

Of the Principles of Human Knowledge

It is evident to anyone who takes a survey of the *objects* of human knowledge that they are either ideas actually imprinted on the senses, or else such as are perceived by attending to the passions and operations of the mind, or lastly, ideas formed by help of memory and imagination—either compounding, dividing, or barely representing those originally perceived in the aforesaid ways. By sight I have the ideas of light and colors, with their several degrees and variations. By touch I perceive, for example, hard and soft, heat and cold, motion and resistance, and of all these more and less either as to quantity or degree. Smelling furnishes me with odors, the palate with tastes, and hearing conveys sounds to the mind in all their variety of tone and composition. And as several of these are observed to accompany each other, they come to be marked by one name, and so to be reputed as one thing. Thus, for example, a certain color, taste, smell, figure, and consistence having been observed to go together, are accounted one distinct thing signified by the name "apple"; other collections of ideas constitute a stone, a tree, a book, and the like sensible things—which as they are pleasing or disagreeable excite the passions of love, hatred, joy, grief, and so forth.

2. But, besides all that endless variety of ideas or objects of knowledge, there is likewise something which knows or perceives them and exercises divers operations, as willing, imagining, remembering, about them. This perceiving, active being is what I call "mind," "spirit," "soul," or "myself." By which words I do not denote any one of my ideas, but a thing entirely distinct from them, wherein they exist or, which is the same thing, whereby they are perceived—for the existence of an idea consists in being perceived.

3. That neither our thoughts, nor passions, nor ideas formed by the imagination exist without the mind is what everybody will allow. And it seems no less evident that the various sensations or ideas imprinted on the sense, however blended or combined together (that is, whatever objects they compose), cannot exist otherwise than in a mind perceiving them.—I think an intuitive knowledge may be obtained of this by anyone that shall attend to what is meant by the term "exist" when applied to sensible things. The table I write on I say exists, that is, I see and feel it; and if I were out of my study I should say it existed—meaning thereby that if I was in my study I might perceive it, or that some other spirit actually does perceive it. There was an odor, that is, it was smelled, there was a sound, that is to say, it was heard; a color or figure, and it was perceived by sight or touch. This is all that I can understand by these and the like expressions. For as to what is said of the absolute existence of unthinking things without any relation to their being perceived, that seems perfectly unintelligible. Their *esse* is *percipi*, nor is it possible they should have any existence out of the minds or thinking things which perceive them.

4. It is indeed an opinion strangely prevailing amongst men that houses, mountains, rivers, and, in a word, all sensible objects have an existence, natural or real, distinct from their being perceived by the understanding. But with how great an assurance and acquiescence soever this principle may be entertained in the world, yet whoever shall find in his heart to call it in question may, if I mistake not, perceive it to involve a manifest contradiction. For what are the forementioned objects but the things we perceive by sense? And what do we perceive besides our own ideas or sensations? And is it not plainly repugnant that any one of these, or any combination of them, should exist unperceived?

5. If we thoroughly examine this tenet it will, perhaps, be found at bottom to depend on the doctrine of *abstract ideas*. For can there be a nicer strain of abstraction than to distinguish the existence of sensible objects from their being perceived, so as to conceive them existing unperceived? Light and colors, heat and cold, extension and figures—in a word, the things we see and feel—what are they but so many sensations, notions, ideas, or impressions on the sense? And is it possible to

separate, even in thought, any of these from perception? For my part, I might as easily divide a thing from itself. I may, indeed, divide in my thoughts, or conceive apart from each other, those things which, perhaps, I never perceived by sense so divided. Thus I imagine the trunk of a human body without the limbs, or conceive the smell of a rose without thinking on the rose itself. So far, I will not deny, I can abstract—if that may properly be called "abstraction" which extends only to the conceiving separately such objects as it is possible may really exist or be actually perceived asunder. But my conceiving or imagining power does not extend beyond the possibility of real existence or perception. Hence, as it is impossible for me to see or feel anything without an actual sensation of that thing, so it is impossible for me to conceive in my thoughts any sensible thing or object distinct from the sensation or perception of it.

6. Some truths there are so near and obvious to the mind that a man need only open his eyes to see them. Such I take this important one to be, to wit, that all the choir of heaven and furniture of the earth, in a word, all those bodies which compose the mighty frame of the world, have not any subsistence without a mind—that their *being* is to be perceived or known, that, consequently so long as they are not actually perceived by me or do not exist in my mind or that of any other created spirit, they must either have no existence at all or else subsist in the mind of some eternal spirit—it being perfectly unintelligible, and involving all the absurdity of abstraction, to attribute to any single part of them an existence independent of a spirit. To be convinced of which, the reader need only reflect, and try to separate in his own thoughts, the *being* of a sensible thing from its *being perceived*.

7. From what has been said it follows there is not any other substance than *spirit,* or that which perceives. But, for the fuller proof of this point, let it be considered the sensible qualities are color, figure, motion, smell, taste, and such like—that is, the ideas perceived by sense. Now, for an idea to exist in an unperceiving thing is a manifest contradiction, for to have an idea is all one as to perceive; that, therefore, wherein color, figure, and the like qualities exist must perceive them; hence it is clear there can be no unthinkng substance or *substratum* of those ideas.

8. But, say you, though the ideas themselves do not exist without the mind, yet there may be things like them, whereof they are copies or resemblances, which things exist without the mind in an unthinking substance. I answer, an idea can be like nothing but an idea; a color or figure can be like nothing but another color or figure. If we look but ever so little into our thoughts, we shall find it impossible for us to conceive a likeness except only between our ideas. Again, I ask whether those supposed originals or external things, of which our ideas are the pictures or representations, be themselves perceivable or no? If they are, then they are ideas and we have gained our point; but if you say they are not, I appeal to anyone whether it be sense to assert a color is like something which is invisible; hard or soft, like something which is intangible; and so of the rest.

9. Some there are who make a distinction betwixt *primary* and *secondary* qualities. By the former they mean extension, figure, motion, rest, solidity or impenetrability, and number; by the latter they denote all other sensible qualities, as colors, sounds, tastes, and so forth. The ideas we have of these they acknowledge not to be the resemblances of anything existing without the mind, or unperceived, but they will have our ideas of the primary qualities to be patterns or images of things which exist without the mind, in an unthinking substance which they call "matter." By "matter," therefore, we are to understand an inert, senseless substance, in which extension, figure, and motion do actually subsist. But it is evident from what we have already shown that extension, figure, and motion are only ideas existing in the mind, and that an idea can be like nothing but another idea, and that consequently neither they nor their archetypes can exist in an unperceiving substance. Hence it is plain that the very notion of what is called "matter" or "corporeal substance" involves a contradiction in it.

10. They who assert that figure, motion, and the rest of the primary or original qualities do exist without the mind in unthinking

substances do at the same time acknowledge that colors, sounds, heat, cold, and suchlike secondary qualities do not—which they tell us are sensations existing in the mind alone, that depend on and are occasioned by the different size, texture, and motion of the minute particles of matter. This they take for an undoubted truth which they can demonstrate beyond all exception. Now, if it be certain that those original qualities are inseparably united with the other sensible qualities, and not, even in thought, capable of being abstracted from them, it plainly follows that they exist only in the mind. But I desire anyone to reflect and try whether he can, by any abstraction of thought, conceive the extension and motion of a body without all other sensible qualities. For my own part, I see evidently that it is not in my power to frame an idea of a body extended and moved, but I must withal give it some color or other sensible quality which is acknowledged to exist only in the mind. In short, extension, figure, and motion, abstracted from all other qualities, are inconceivable. Where therefore the other sensible qualities are, there must these be also, to wit, in the mind and nowhere else.

11. Again, *great* and *small, swift* and *slow* are allowed to exist nowhere without the mind, being entirely relative, and changing as the frame or position of the organs of sense varies. The extension, therefore, which exists without the mind is neither great nor small, the motion neither swift nor slow; that is, they are nothing at all. But, say you, they are extension in general, and motion in general: thus we see how much the tenet of extended movable substances existing without the mind depends on that strange doctrine of *abstract ideas*. And here I cannot but remark how nearly the vague and indeterminate description of matter or corporeal substance, which the modern philosophers are run into by their own principles, resembles that antiquated and so much ridiculed notion of *materia prima*, to be met with in Aristotle and his followers. Without extension, solidity cannot be conceived; since, therefore, it has been shown that extension exists not in an unthinking substance, the same must also be true of solidity.

12. That number is entirely the creature of the mind, even though the other qualities be allowed to exist without, will be evident to whoever considers that the same thing bears a different denomination of number as the mind views it with different respects. Thus the same extension is one, or three, or thirty-six, according as the mind considers it with reference to a yard, a foot, or an inch. Number is so visibly relative and dependent on men's understanding that it is strange to think how anyone should give it an absolute existence without the mind. We say one book, one page, one line; all these are equally units, though some contain several of the others. And in each instance it is plain the unit relates to some particular combination of ideas arbitrarily put together by the mind.

13. Unity I know some will have to be a simple or uncompounded idea accompanying all other ideas into the mind. That I have any such idea answering the word "unity" I do not find; and if I had, methinks I could not miss finding it; on the contrary, it should be the most familiar to my understanding, since it is said to accompany all other ideas and to be perceived by all the ways of sensation and reflection. To say no more, it is an *abstract idea.*

14. I shall further and that, after the same manner as modern philosophers prove certain sensible qualities to have no existence in matter, or without the mind, the same thing may be likewise proved of all other sensible qualities whatsoever. Thus, for instance, it is said that heat and cold are affections only of the mind, and not at all patterns of real beings existing in the corporeal substances which excite them. For that the same body which appears cold to one hand seems warm to another. Now, why may we not as well argue that figure and extension are not patterns or resemblances of qualities existing in matter, because to the same eye at different stations, or eyes of a different texture at the same station, they appear various and cannot, therefore, be the images of anything settled and determinate without the mind? Again, it is proved that sweetness is not really in the sapid thing, because, the thing remaining unaltered, the sweetness is changed into bitter, as in case of a fever or otherwise vitiated palate. Is it not as reasonable to say that motion is not without

the mind, since if the succession of ideas in the mind become swifter, the motion, it is acknowledged, shall appear slower without any alteration in any external object?

15. In short, let anyone consider those arguments which are thought manifestly to prove that colors and tastes exist only in the mind, and he shall find they may with equal force be brought to prove the same thing of extension, figure, and motion. Though it must be confessed this method of arguing does not so much prove that there is no extension or color in an outward object as that we do not know by sense which is the true extension or color of the object. But the arguments foregoing plainly show it to be impossible that any color or extension at all, or other sensible quality whatsoever, should exist in an unthinking subject without the mind, or, in truth, that there should be any such thing as an outward object.

16. But let us examine a little the received opinion.—It is said extension is a mode or accident of matter, and that matter is the *substratum* that supports it. Now I desire that you would explain what is meant by matter's "supporting" extension. Say you, I have no idea of matter and, therefore, cannot explain it. I answer, though you have no positive, yet, if you have any meaning at all, you must at least have a relative idea of matter; though you know not what it is, yet you must be supposed to know what relation it bears to accidents, and what is meant by its supporting them. It is evident "support" cannot here be taken in its usual or literal sense—as when we say that pillars support a building; in what sense therefore must it be taken?

17. If we inquire into what the most accurate philosophers declare themselves to mean by "material substance," we shall find them acknowledge they have no other meaning annexed to those sounds but the idea of being in general together with the relative notion of its supporting accidents. The general idea of being appears to me the most abstract and incomprehensible of all other; and as for its supporting accidents, this, as we have just now observed, cannot be understood in the common sense of those words; it must, therefore, be taken in some other sense, but what that is

they do not explain. So that when I consider the two parts or branches which make the signification of the words "material substance," I am convinced there is no distinct meaning annexed to them. But why should we trouble ourselves any further in discussing this material *substratum* or support of figure and motion and other sensible qualities? Does it not suppose they have an existence without the mind? And is not this a direct repugnancy and altogether inconceivable?

18. But, though it were possible that solid, figured, movable substances may exist without the mind, corresponding to the ideas we have of bodies, yet how is it possible for us to know this? Either we must know it by sense or by reason. As for our senses, by them we have the knowledge only of our sensations, ideas, or those things that are immediately perceived by sense, call them what you will; but they do not inform us that things exist without the mind, or unperceived, like to those which are perceived. This the materialists themselves acknowledge. It remains therefore that if we have any knowledge at all of external things, it must be by reason, inferring their existence from what is immediately perceived by sense. But what reason can induce us to believe the existence of bodies without the mind, from what we perceive, since the very patrons of matter themselves do not pretend there is any necessary connection betwixt them and our ideas? I say it is granted on all hands (and what happens in dreams, frenzies, and the like, puts it beyond dispute) that it is possible we might be affected with all the ideas we have now, though no bodies existed without resembling them. Hence it is evident the supposition of external bodies is not necessary for the producing our ideas; since it is granted they are produced sometimes, and might possibly be produced always in the same order we see them in at present, without their concurrence.

19. But though we might possibly have all our sensations without them, yet perhaps it may be thought easier to conceive and explain the manner of their production by supposing external bodies in their likeness rather than otherwise; and so it might be at least probable there are such things as bodies that excite their ideas in our minds. But neither can this be

said, for, though we give the materialists their external bodies, they by their own confession are never the nearer knowing how our ideas are produced, since they own themselves unable to comprehend in what manner body can act upon spirit, or how it is possible it should imprint any idea in the mind. Hence it is evident the production of ideas or sensations in our minds can be no reason why we should suppose matter or corporeal substances, since that is acknowledged to remain equally inexplicable with or without this supposition. If therefore it were possible for bodies to exist without the mind, yet to hold they do so must needs be a very precarious opinion, since it is to suppose, without any reason at all, that God has created innumerable beings that are entirely useless and serve to no manner of purpose.

20. In short, if there were external bodies, it is impossible we should ever come to know it; and if there were not, we might have the very same reasons to think there were that we have now. Suppose—what no one can deny possible—an intelligence without the help of external bodies, to be affected with the same train of sensations or ideas that you are, imprinted in the same order and with like vividness in his mind. I ask whether that intelligence has not all the reason to believe the existence of corporeal substances, represented by his ideas and exciting them in his mind, that you can possibly have for believing the same thing? Of this there can be no question—which one consideration is enough to make any reasonable person suspect the strength of whatever arguments he may think himself to have for the existence of bodies without the mind.

21. Were it necessary to add any further proof against the existence of matter after what has been said, I could instance several of those errors and difficulties (not to mention impieties) which have sprung from that tenet. It has occasioned numberless controversies and disputes in philosophy, and not a few of far greater moment in religion. But I shall not enter into the detail of them in this place as well because I think arguments a posteriori are unnecessary for confirming what has been, if I mistake not, sufficiently demonstrated a

priori, as because I shall hereafter find occasion to speak somewhat of them.

22. I am afraid I have given cause to think me needlessly prolix in handling this subject. For to what purpose is it to dilate on that which may be demonstrated with the utmost evidence in a line or two to anyone that is capable of the least reflection? It is but looking into your own thoughts, and so trying whether you can conceive it possible for a sound, or figure, or motion, or color to exist without the mind or unperceived. This easy trial may make you see that what you contend for is a downright contradiction. Insomuch that I am content to put the whole upon this issue: if you can but conceive it possible for one extended movable substance, or, in general, for any one idea, or anything like an idea, to exist otherwise than in a mind perceiving it, I shall readily give up the cause. And, as for all that compages of external bodies which you contend for, I shall grant you its existence, though you cannot either give me any reason why you believe it exists, or assign any use to it when it is supposed to exist. I say the bare possibility of your opinion's being true shall pass for an argument that it is so.

23. But, say you, surely there is nothing easier than to imagine trees, for instance, in a park, or books existing in a closet, and nobody by to perceive them. I answer you may so, there is no difficulty in it; but what is all this, I beseech you, more than framing in your mind certain ideas which you call books and trees, and at the same time omitting to frame the idea of anyone that may perceive them? But do not you yourself perceive or think of them all the while? This therefore is nothing to the purpose; it only shows you have the power of imagining or forming ideas in your mind; but it does not show that you can conceive it possible the objects of your thought may exist without the mind. To make out this, it is necessary that you conceive them existing unconceived or unthought of, which is a manifest repugnancy. When we do our utmost to conceive the existence of external bodies, we are all the while only contemplating our own ideas. But the mind, taking no notice of itself, is deluded to think it can and does conceive bodies existing unthought of or without the mind, though at the same time they

are apprehended by or exist in itself. A little attention will discover to anyone the truth and evidence of what is here said, and make it unnecessary to insist on any other proofs against the existence of *material substance*.

24. It is very obvious, upon the least inquiry into our own thoughts, to know whether it be possible for us to understand what is meant by "the absolute existence of sensible objects in themselves, or without the mind." To me it is evident those words mark out either a direct contradiction or else nothing at all. And to convince others of this, I know no readier or fairer way than to entreat they would calmly attend to their own thoughts; and if by this attention the emptiness or repugnancy of those expressions does appear, surely nothing more is requisite for their conviction. It is on this, therefore, that I insist, to wit, that "the absolute existence of unthinking things" are words without a meaning, or which include a contradiction. This is what I repeat and inculcate, and earnestly recommend to the attentive thoughts of the reader.

25. All our ideas, sensations, or the things which we perceive, by whatsoever names they may be distinguished, are visibly inactive—there is nothing of power or agency included in them. So that one idea or object of thought cannot produce or make any alteration in another. To be satisfied of the truth of this, there is nothing else requisite but a bare observation of our ideas. For since they and every part of them exist only in the mind, it follows that there is nothing in them but what is perceived; but whoever shall attend to his ideas, whether of sense or reflection, will not perceive in them any power or activity; there is, therefore, no such thing contained in them. A little attention will discover to us that the very being of an idea implies passiveness and inertness in it, insomuch that it is impossible for an idea to do anything or, strictly speaking, to be the cause of anything; neither can it be the resemblance or pattern of any active being, as is evident from sec. 8. Whence it plainly follows that extension, figure, and motion cannot be the cause of our sensations. To say, therefore, that these are the effects of powers resulting from the configuration, number, motion, and size of corpuscles must certainly be false.

26. We perceive a continual succession of ideas, some are anew excited, others are changed or totally disappear. There is, therefore, some cause of these ideas, whereon they depend and which produces and changes them. That this cause cannot be any quality or idea or combination of ideas is clear from the preceding section. It must therefore be a substance; but it has been shown that there is no corporeal or material substance: it remains, therefore, that the cause of ideas is an incorporeal, active substance or spirit.

27. A spirit is one simple, undivided, active being—as it perceives ideas it is called "the understanding," and as it produces or otherwise operates about them it is called "the will." Hence there can be no *idea* formed of a soul or spirit; for all ideas whatever, being passive and inert (*vide* sec. 25), they cannot represent unto us, by way of image or likeness, that which acts. A little attention will make it plain to anyone that to have an idea which shall be like that active principle of motion and change of ideas is absolutely impossible. Such is the nature of *spirit*, or that which acts, that it cannot be of itself perceived, but only by the effects which it produces. If any man shall doubt of the truth of what is here delivered, let him but reflect and try if he can frame the idea of any power or active being, and whether he has ideas of two principal powers marked by the names "will" and "understanding," distinct from each other as well as from a third idea of substance or being in general, with a relative notion of its supporting or being the subject of the aforesaid powers—which is signified by the name "soul" or "spirit." This is what some hold; but, so far as I can see, the words "will," "soul," "spirit" do not stand for different ideas or, in truth, for any idea at all, but for something which is very different from ideas, and which, being an agent, cannot be like unto, or represented by, any idea whatsoever. [Though it must be owned at the same time that we have some notion of soul, spirit, and the operations of the mind, such as willing, loving, hating—in as much as we know or understand the meaning of those words.]

28. I find I can excite ideas in my mind at pleasure, and vary and shift the scene as oft as I think fit. It is no more than willing, and

straightway this or that idea arises in my fancy; and by the same power it is obliterated and makes way for another. This making and unmaking of ideas does very properly denominate the mind active. Thus much is certain and grounded on experience; but when we talk of unthinking agents or of exciting ideas exclusive of volition, we only amuse ourselves with words.

29. But, whatever power I may have over my own thoughts, I find the ideas actually perceived by sense have not a like dependence on my will. When in broad daylight I open my eyes, it is not in my power to choose whether I shall see or no, or to determine what particular objects shall present themselves to my view; and so likewise as to the hearing and other senses; the ideas imprinted on them are not creatures of my will. There is therefore some *other* will or spirit that produces them.

30. The ideas of sense are more strong, lively, and distinct than those of the imagination; they have likewise a steadiness, order, and coherence, and are not excited at random, as those which are the effects of human wills often are, but in a regular train or series, the admirable connection whereof sufficiently testifies the wisdom and benevolence of its Author. Now the set rules or established methods wherein the mind we depend on excites in us the ideas of sense are called "the laws of nature"; and these we learn by experience, which teaches us that such and such ideas are attended with such and such other ideas in the ordinary course of things.

31. This gives us a sort of foresight which enables us to regulate our actions for the benefit of life. And without this we should be eternally at a loss; we could not know how to act anything that might procure us the least pleasure or remove the least pain of sense. That food nourishes, sleep refreshes, and fire warms us; that to sow in the seedtime is the way to reap in the harvest; and in general that to obtain such or such ends, such or such means are conducive—all this we know, not by discovering any necessary connection between our ideas, but only by the observation of the settled laws of nature, without which we should be all in uncertainty and confusion, and a grown man no more know how to manage himself in the affairs of life than an infant just born.

32. And yet this consistent, uniform working which so evidently displays the goodness and wisdom of that Governing Spirit whose Will constitutes the laws of nature, is so far from leading our thoughts to Him that it rather sends them awandering after second causes. For when we perceive certain ideas of sense constantly followed by other ideas, and we know this is not of our own doing, we forthwith attribute power and agency to the ideas themselves and make one the cause of another, than which nothing can be more absurd and unintelligible. Thus, for example, having observed that when we perceive by sight a certain round, luminous figure, we at the same time perceive by touch the idea or sensation called "heat," we do from thence conclude the sun to be the cause of heat. And in like manner perceiving the motion and collision of bodies to be attended with sound, we are inclined to think the latter an effect of the former.

33. The ideas imprinted on the senses by the Author of Nature are called "real things"; and those excited in the imagination, being less regular, vivid, and constant, are more properly termed "ideas" or "images of things" which they copy and represent. But then our sensations, be they never so vivid and distinct, are nevertheless ideas, that is, they exist in the mind, or are perceived by it, as truly as the ideas of its own framing. The ideas of sense are allowed to have more reality in them, that is, to be more strong, orderly, and coherent than the creatures of the mind; but this is no argument that they exist without the mind. They are also less dependent on the spirit, or thinking substance which perceives them, in that they are excited by the will of another and more powerful spirit; yet still they are *ideas;* and certainly no idea, whether faint or strong, can exist otherwise than in a mind perceiving it.

34. Before we proceed any further it is necessary to spend some time in answering objections which may probably be made against the principles hitherto laid down. In doing of which, if I seem too prolix to those of quick apprehensions, I hope it may be par-

doned, since all men do not equally apprehend things of this nature, and I am willing to be understood by everyone.

First, then, it will be objected that by the foregoing principles all that is real and substantial in nature is banished out of the world, and instead thereof a chimerical scheme of *ideas* takes place. All things that exist, exist only in the mind, that is, they are purely notional. What therefore becomes of the sun, moon, and stars? What must we think of houses, rivers, mountains, trees, stones, nay, even of our own bodies? Are all these but so many chimeras and illusions on the fancy? To all which, and whatever else of the same sort may be objected, I answer that by the principles premised we are not deprived of any one thing in nature. Whatever we see, feel, hear, or anywise conceive or understand remains as secure as ever, and is as real as ever. There is a *rerum natura,* and the distinction between realities and chimeras retains its full force. This is evident from secs. 29, 30, and 33, where we have shown what is meant by "real things" in opposition to "chimeras" or ideas of our own framing; but then they both equally exist in the mind, and in that sense they are alike *ideas.*

35. I do not argue against the existence of any one thing that we can apprehend either by sense or reflection. That the things I see with my eyes and touch with my hands do exist, really exist, I make not the least question. The only thing whose existence we deny is that which philosophers call matter or corporeal substance. And in doing of this there is no damage done to the rest of mankind, who, I dare say, will never miss it. The atheist indeed will want the color of an empty name to support his impiety; and the philosophers may possibly find they have lost a great handle for trifling and disputation.

36. If any man thinks this detracts from the existence or reality of things, he is very far from understanding what has been premised in the plainest terms I could think of. Take here an abstract of what has been said: there are spiritual substances, minds, or human souls, which will or excite ideas in themselves at pleasure, but these are faint, weak, and unsteady in respect of others they perceive by sense—which, being impressed upon them according to certain rules or laws of nature, speak themselves the effects of a mind more powerful and wise than human spirits. These latter are said to have more *reality* in them than the former—by which is meant that they are more affecting, orderly, and distinct, and that they are not fictions of the mind perceiving them. And in this sense the sun that I see by day is the real sun, and that which I imagine by night is the idea of the former. In the sense here given of "reality" it is evident that every vegetable, star, mineral, and in general each part of the mundane system, is as much a *real being* by our principles as by any other. Whether others mean anything by the term "reality" different from what I do, I entreat them to look into their own thoughts and see.

37. It will be urged that this much at least is true, to wit, that we take away all corporeal substances. To this my answer is that if the word "substance" be taken in the vulgar sense—for a combination of sensible qualities, such as extension, solidity, weight, and the like—this we cannot be accused of taking away; but if it be taken in a philosophic sense—for the support of accidents or qualities without the mind—then indeed I acknowledge that we take it away, if one may be said to take away that which never had any existence, not even in the imagination.

38. But, say you, it sounds very harsh to say we eat and drink ideas, and are clothed with ideas. I acknowledge it does so—the word "idea" not being used in common discourse to signify the several combinations of sensible qualities which are called "things"; and it is certain that any expression which varies from the familiar use of language will seem harsh and ridiculous. But this does not concern the truth of the proposition which, in other words, is no more than to say we are fed and clothed with those things which we perceive immediately by our senses. The hardness or softness, the color, taste, warmth, figure, and suchlike qualities, which combined together constitute the several sorts of victuals and apparel, have been shown to exist only in the mind that perceives them; and this is all that is meant by calling them "ideas," which word if it was as ordinarily used as "thing," would sound

no harsher nor more ridiculous than it. I am not for disputing about the propriety, but the truth of the expression. If therefore you agree with me that we eat and drink and are clad with the immediate objects of sense, which cannot exist unperceived or without the mind, I shall readily grant it is more proper or conformable to custom that they should be called "things" rather than "ideas."

39. If it be demanded why I make use of the word "idea," and do not rather in compliance with custom call them "things," I answer I do it for two reasons; first, because the term "thing" in contradistinction to "idea" is generally supposed to denote somewhat existing without the mind; secondly, because "thing" has a more comprehensive signification than "idea," including spirits or thinking things as well as ideas. Since therefore the objects of sense exist only in the mind and are withal thoughtless and inactive, I chose to mark them by the word "idea," which implies those properties.

40. But, say what we can, someone perhaps may be apt to reply he will still believe his senses, and never suffer any arguments, how plausible soever, to prevail over the certainty of them. Be it so; assert the evidence of sense as high as you please, we are willing to do the same. That what I see, hear, and feel does exist—that is to say, is perceived by me—I no more doubt than I do of my own being. But I do not see how the testimony of sense can be alleged as a proof for the existence of anything which is not perceived by sense. We are not for having any man turn skeptic and disbelieve his senses; on the contrary, we give them all the stress and assurance imaginable; nor are there any principles more opposite to skepticism than those we have laid down, as shall be hereafter clearly shown.

41. *Secondly,* it will be objected that there is a great difference betwixt real fire, for instance, and the idea of fire, betwixt dreaming or imagining oneself burned, and actually being so. This and the like may be urged in opposition to our tenets. To all which the answer is evident from what has been already said; and I shall only add in this place that if real fire be very different from the idea of fire, so also is the real pain that it occasions very

different from the idea of the same pain, and yet nobody will pretend that real pain either is, or can possibly be, in an unperceiving thing, or without the mind, any more than its idea.

42. *Thirdly,* it will be objected that we see things actually without or at a distance from us, and which, consequently, do not exist in the mind, it being absurd that those things which are seen at the distance of several miles should be as near to us as our own thoughts. In answer to this I desire it may be considered that in a dream we do oft perceive things as existing at a great distance off, and yet for all that those things are acknowledged to have their existence only in the mind.

43. But for the fuller clearing of this point it may be worth while to consider how it is that we perceive distance and things placed at a distance by sight. For that we should in truth see external space, and bodies actually existing in it, some nearer, others farther off, seems to carry with it some opposition to what has been said of their existing nowhere without the mind. The consideration of this difficulty it was that gave birth to my *Essay Towards a New Theory of Vision,* which was published not long since, wherein it is shown that distance or outness is neither immediately of itself perceived by sight, nor yet apprehended or judged of by lines and angles, or anything that has a necessary connection with it; but that it is only suggested to our thoughts by certain visible ideas and sensations attending vision, which in their own nature have no manner of similitude or relation either with distance or things placed at a distance; but by a connection taught us by experience they come to signify and suggest them to us after the same manner that words of any language suggest the ideas they are made to stand for; insomuch that a man born blind and afterwards made to see would not, at first sight, think the things he saw to be without his mind or at any distance from him. See sec. 41 of the forementioned treatise.

44. The ideas of sight and touch make two species entirely distinct and heterogeneous. The former are marks and prognostics of the latter. That the proper objects of sight neither exist without mind, nor are the images of external things, was shown even in that treatise. Though throughout the same the

contrary be supposed true of tangible objects—not that to suppose that vulgar error was necessary for establishing the notion therein laid down, but because it was beside my purpose to examine and refute it in a discourse concerning *vision*. So that in strict truth the ideas of sight, when we apprehend by them distance and things placed at a distance, do not suggest or mark out to us things actually existing at a distance, but only admonish us what ideas of touch will be imprinted in our minds at such and such distances of time, and in consequence of such and such actions. It is, I say, evident from what has been said in the foregoing parts of this treatise, and in sec. 147 and elsewhere of the *Essay Concerning Vision,* that visible ideas are the language whereby the Governing Spirit on whom we depend informs us what tangible ideas he is about to imprint upon us in case we excite this or that motion in our own bodies. But for a fuller information in this point I refer to the *Essay* itself.

45. *Fourthly,* it will be objected that from the foregoing principles it follows things are every moment annihilated and created anew. The objects of sense exist only when they are perceived; the trees, therefore, are in the garden, or the chairs in the parlor, no longer than while there is somebody by to perceive them. Upon shutting my eyes all the furniture in the room is reduced to nothing, and barely upon opening them it is again created. In answer to all which I refer the reader to what has been said in secs. 3, 4, etc., and desire he will consider whether he means anything by the actual existence of an idea distinct from its being perceived. For my part, after the nicest inquiry I could make, I am not able to discover that anything else is meant by those words; and I once more entreat the reader to sound his own thoughts and not suffer himself to be imposed on by words. If he can conceive it possible either for his ideas or their archetypes to exist without being perceived, then I give up the cause; but if he cannot, he will acknowledge it is unreasonable for him to stand up in defense of he knows not what and pretend to charge on me as an absurdity the not assenting to those propositions which at bottom have no meaning in them.

46. It will not be amiss to observe how far the received principles of philosophy are themselves chargeable with those pretended absurdities. It is thought strangely absurd that upon closing my eyelids all the visible objects around me should be reduced to nothing; and yet is not this what philosophers commonly acknowledge when they agree on all hands that light and colors, which alone are the proper and immediate objects of sight, are mere sensations that exist no longer than they are perceived? Again, it may to some, perhaps, seem very incredible that things should be every moment creating, yet this very notion is commonly taught in the Schools. For the Schoolmen, though they acknowledge the existence of matter, and that the whole mundane fabric is framed out of it, are nevertheless of opinion that it cannot subsist without the divine conservation, which by them is expounded to be a continual creation.

47. Further, a little thought will discover to us that though we allow the existence of matter or corporeal substance, yet it will unavoidably follow, from the principles which are now generally admitted, that the particular bodies of what kind soever do none of them exist whilst they are not perceived. For it is evident from sec. 11 and the following sections that the matter philosophers contend for is an incomprehensible somewhat, which has none of those particular qualities whereby the bodies falling under our senses are distinguished one from another. But, to make this more plain, it must be remarked that the infinite divisibility of matter is now universally allowed, at least by the most approved and considerable philosophers, who on the received principles demonstrate it beyond all exception. Hence it follows that there is an infinite number of parts in each particle of matter which are not perceived by sense. The reason, therefore, that any particular body seems to be of a finite magnitude, or exhibits only a finite number of parts to sense, is not because it contains no more, since in itself it contains an infinite number of parts, but because the sense is not acute enough to discern them. In proportion, therefore, as the sense is rendered more acute, it perceives a greater number of parts in the object; that is, the object appears greater, and its figure varies,

those parts in its extremities which were before unperceivable appearing now to bound it in very different lines and angles from those perceived by an obtuser sense. And at length, after various changes of size and shape, when the sense becomes infinitely acute, the body shall seem infinite. During all which there is no alteration in the body, but only in the sense. Each body, therefore, considered in itself, is infinitely extended, and consequently void of all shape or figure. From which it follows that, though we should grant the existence of matter to be ever so certain, yet it is withal as certain—the materialists themselves are by their own principles forced to acknowledge—that neither the particular bodies perceived by sense, nor anything like them, exists without the mind. Matter, I say, and each particle thereof, is according to them infinite and shapeless, and it is the mind that frames all that variety of bodies which compose the visible world, any one whereof does not exist longer than it is perceived.

48. If we consider it, the objection proposed in sec. 45 will not be found reasonably charged on the principles we have premised, so as in truth to make any objection at all against our notions. For though we hold indeed the objects of sense to be nothing else but ideas which cannot exist unperceived, yet we may not hence conclude they have no existence except only while they are perceived by us, since there may be some other spirit that perceives them, though we do not. Wherever bodies are said to have no existence without the mind, I would not be understood to mean this or that particular mind, but all minds whatsoever. It does not therefore follow from the foregoing principles that bodies are annihilated and created every moment or exist not at all during the intervals between our perception of them.

49. *Fifthly,* it may perhaps be objected that if extension and figure exist only in the mind, it follows that the mind is extended and figured, since extension is a mode or attribute which (to speak with the Schools) is predicated of the subject in which it exists. I answer, those qualities are in the mind only as they are perceived by it—that is, not by way of *mode* or *attribute,* but only by way of *idea;* and it no more follows that the soul or mind is extended, because extension exists in it alone, than it does that it is red or blue, because those colors are on all hands acknowledged to exist in it, and nowhere else. As to what philosophers say of subject and mode, that seems very groundless and unintelligible. For instance, in this proposition "a die is hard, extended, and square," they will have it that the word "die" denotes a subject or substance distinct from the hardness, extension, and figure which are predicated of it, and in which they exist. This I cannot comprehend; to me a die seems to be nothing distinct from those things which are termed its modes or accidents. And to say a die is hard, extended, and square is not to attribute those qualities to a subject distinct from and supporting them, but only an explication of the meaning of the word "die."

50. *Sixthly,* you will say there have been a great many things explained by matter and motion; take away these and you destroy the whole corpuscular philosophy and undermine those mechanical principles which have been applied with so much success to account for the phenomena. In short, whatever advances have been made, either by ancient or modern philosophers, in the study of nature do all proceed on the supposition that corporeal substance or matter does really exist. To this I answer that there is not any one phenomenon explained on that supposition which may not as well be explained without it, as might easily be made appear by an induction of particulars. To explain the phenomena is all one as to show why, upon such and such occasions, we are affected with such and such ideas. But how matter should operate on a spirit, or produce any idea in it, is what no philosopher will pretend to explain; it is therefore evident there can be no use of matter in natural philosophy. Besides, they who attempt to account for things do it not by corporeal substance, but by figure, motion, and other qualities, which are in truth no more than mere ideas and, therefore, cannot be the cause of anything, as has been already shown. See sec. 25.

51. *Seventhly,* it will upon this be demanded whether it does not seem absurd to take away natural causes and ascribe everything to the immediate operation of spirits?

We must no longer say, upon these principles, that fire heats, or water cools, but that a spirit heats, and so forth. Would not a man be deservedly laughed at who should talk after this manner? I answer, he would so; in such things we ought to "think with the learned and speak with the vulgar." They who by demonstration are convinced of the truth of the Copernican system do nevertheless say, "the sun rises," "the sun sets," or "comes to the meridian"; and if they affected a contrary style in common talk it would without doubt appear very ridiculous. A little reflection on what is here said will make it manifest that the common use of language would receive no manner of alteration or disturbance from the admission of our tenets.

52. In the ordinary affairs of life, any phrases may be retained so long as they excite in us proper sentiments or dispositions to act in such a manner as is necessary for our well-being, how false soever they may be if taken in a strict and speculative sense. Nay, this is unavoidable, since, propriety being regulated by custom, language is suited to the received opinions, which are not always the truest. Hence it is impossible, even in the most rigid, philosophic reasonings, so far to alter the bent and genius of the tongue we speak, as never to give a handle for cavilers to pretend difficulties and inconsistencies. But a fair and ingenuous reader will collect the sense from the scope and tenor and connection of a discourse, making allowances for those inaccurate modes of speech which use has made inevitable.

53. As to the opinion that there are no corporeal causes, this has been heretofore maintained by some of the Schoolmen, as it is of late by others among the modern philosophers who, though they allow matter to exist, yet will have God alone to be the immediate efficient cause of all things. These men saw that amongst all the objects of sense there was none which had any power or activity included in it, and that by consequence this was likewise true of whatever bodies they supposed to exist without the mind, like unto the immediate objects of sense. But then, that they should suppose an innumerable multitude of created beings which they acknowledge are not capable of producing any one effect in

nature, and which therefore are made to no manner of purpose, since God might have done everything as well without them—this I say, though we should allow it possible, must yet be a very unaccountable and extravagant supposition.

54. In the *eighth* place, the universal concurrent assent of mankind may be thought by some an invincible argument in behalf of matter, or the existence of external things. Must we suppose the whole world to be mistaken? And if so, what cause can be assigned of so widespread and predominant an error? I answer, first, that, upon a narrow inquiry, it will not perhaps be found so many as is imagined do really believe the existence of matter or things without the mind. Strictly speaking, to believe that which involves a contradiction, or has no meaning in it, is impossible; and whether the foregoing expressions are not of that sort, I refer it to the impartial examination of the reader. In one sense, indeed, men may be said to believe that matter exists, that is, they act as if the immediate cause of their sensations, which affects them every moment and is so nearly present to them, were some senseless unthinking being. But that they should clearly apprehend any meaning marked by those words, and form thereof a settled speculative opinion, is what I am not able to conceive. This is not the only instance wherein men impose upon themselves, by imagining they believe those propositions they have often heard, though at bottom they have no meaning in them.

55. But secondly, though we should grant a notion to be ever so universally and steadfastly adhered to, yet this is but a weak argument of its truth to whoever considers what a vast number of prejudices and false opinions are everywhere embraced with the utmost tenaciousness by the unreflecting (which are the far greater) part of mankind. There was a time when the antipodes and motion of the earth were looked upon as monstrous absurdities even by men of learning; and if it be considered what a small proportion they bear to the rest of mankind, we shall find that at this day those notions have gained but a very inconsiderable footing in the world.

56. But it is demanded that we assign a

cause of this prejudice and account for its obtaining in the world. To this I answer that men, knowing they perceived several ideas whereof they themselves were not the authors—as not being excited from within nor depending on the operation of their wills—this made them maintain those ideas, or objects of perception, had an existence independent of and without the mind, without ever dreaming that a contradiction was involved in those words. But philosophers having plainly seen that the immediate objects of perception do not exist without the mind, they in some degree corrected the mistake of the vulgar, but at the same time run into another which seems no less absurd, to wit, that there are certain objects really existing without the mind or having a subsistence distinct from being perceived, of which our ideas are only images or resemblances, imprinted by those objects on the mind. And this notion of the philosophers owes its origin to the same cause with the former, namely, their being conscious that they were not the authors of their own sensations, which they evidently knew were imprinted from without, and which therefore must have some cause distinct from the minds on which they are imprinted.

57. But why they should suppose the ideas of sense to be excited in us by things in their likeness, and not rather have recourse to *spirit* which alone can act, may be accounted for, first because they were not aware of the repugnancy there is, as well in supposing things like unto our ideas existing without, as in attributing to them power or activity. Secondly, because the supreme spirit which excites those ideas in our minds is not marked out and limited to our view by any particular finite collection of sensible ideas, as human agents are by their size, complexion, limbs, and motions. And thirdly, because His operations are regular and uniform. Whenever the course of nature is interrupted by a miracle, men are ready to own the presence of a superior agent. But when we see things go on in the ordinary course, they do not excite in us any reflection; their order and concatenation, though it be an argument of the greatest wisdom, power, and goodness in their Creator, is yet so constant and familiar to us that we do

not think them the immediate effects of a *free spirit,* especially since inconstancy and mutability in acting, though it be an imperfection, is looked on as a mark of *freedom.*

58. *Tenthly,* it will be objected that the notions we advance are inconsistent with several sound truths in philosophy and mathematics. For example, the motion of the earth is now universally admitted by astronomers as a truth grounded on the clearest and most convincing reasons. But on the foregoing principles there can be no such thing. For motion being only an idea, it follows that if it be not perceived it exists not; but the motion of the earth is not perceived by sense. I answer, that tenet, if rightly understood, will be found to agree with the principles we have premised, for the question whether the earth moves or no amounts in reality to no more than this, to wit, whether we have reason to conclude, from what has been observed by astronomers, that if we were placed in such and such circumstances, and such or such a position and distance both from the earth and sun, we should perceive the former to move among the choir of the planets, and appearing in all respects like one of them; and this, by the established rules of nature which we have no reason to mistrust, is reasonably collected from the phenomena.

59. We may, from the experience we have had of the train and succession of ideas in our minds, often make, I will not say uncertain conjectures, but sure and well-grounded predictions concerning the ideas we shall be affected with pursuant to a great train of actions, and be enabled to pass a right judgment of what would have appeared to us in case we were placed in circumstances very different from those we are in at preent. Herein consists the knowledge of nature, which may preserve its use and certainty very consistently with what has been said. It will be easy to apply this to whatever objections of the like sort may be drawn from the magnitude of the stars or any other discoveries in astronomy or nature.

60. In the *eleventh* place, it will be demanded to what purpose serves that curious organization of plants and the admirable mechanism in the parts of animals; might not vegetables grow and shoot forth leaves and blossoms, and animals perform all their mo-

tions as well without as with all that variety of internal parts so elegantly contrived and put together; which, being ideas, have nothing powerful or operative in them, nor have any necessary connection with the effects ascribed to them? If it be a spirit that immediately produces every effect by a fiat or act of his will, we must think all that is fine and artificial in the works, whether of man or nature, to be made in vain. By this doctrine, though an artist has made the spring and wheels, and every movement of a watch, and adjusted them in such a manner as he knew would produce the motions he designed, yet he must think all this done to no purpose, and that it is an Intelligence which directs the index and points to the hour of the day. If so, why may not the Intelligence do it, without his being at the pains of making the movements and putting them together? Why does not an empty case serve as well as another? And how comes it to pass that whenever there is any fault in the going of a watch, there is some corresponding disorder to be found in the movements, which being mended by a skillful hand all is right again? The like may be said of all the clockwork of nature, great part whereof is so wonderfully fine and subtle as scarce to be discerned by the best microscope. In short, it will be asked how, upon our principles, any tolerable account can be given, or any final cause assigned, of an innumerable multitude of bodies and machines, framed with the most exquisite art, which in the common philosophy have very apposite uses assigned them and serve to explain abundance of phenomena?

61. To all which I answer, first, that though there were some difficulties relating to the administration of Providence, and the uses by it assigned to the several parts of nature which I could not solve by the foregoing principles, yet this objection could be of small weight against the truth and certainty of those things which may be proved a priori with the utmost evidence. Secondly, but neither are the received principles free from the like difficulties, for it may still be demanded to what end God should take those roundabout methods of effecting things by instruments and machines which no one can deny might have been effected by the mere command of His will

without all that apparatus; nay, if we narrowly consider it, we shall find the objection may be retorted with greater force on those who hold the existence of those machines without the mind, for it has been made evident that solidity, bulk, figure, motion, and the like have no *activity* or *efficacy* in them so as to be capable of producing any one effect in nature. See sec. 25. Whoever, therefore, supposes them to exist (allowing the supposition possible) when they are not perceived does it manifestly to no purpose, since the only use that is assigned to them, as they exist unperceived, is that they produce those perceivable effects which in truth cannot be ascribed to anything but spirit.

62. But, to come nearer the difficulty, it must be observed that though the fabrication of all those parts and organs be not absolutely necessary to the producing any effect, yet it is necessary to the producing of things in a constant regular way according to the laws of nature. There are certain general laws that run through the whole chain of natural effects; these are learned by the observation and study of nature and are by men applied as well to the framing artificial things for the use and ornament of life as to the explaining the various phenomena—which explication consists only in showing the conformity any particular phenomen has to the general laws of nature or, which is the same thing, in discovering the *uniformity* there is in the production of natural effects, as will be evident to whoever shall attend to the several instances wherein philosophers pretend to account for appearances. That there is a great and conspicuous use in these regular, constant methods of working observed by the Supreme Agent has been shown in sec. 31. And it is no less visible that a particular size, figure, motion, and disposition of parts are necessary, though not absolutely, to the producing any effect, yet to the producing it according to the standing mechanical laws of nature. Thus, for instance, it cannot be denied that God, or the Intelligence which sustains and rules the ordinary course of things, might, if He were minded to produce a miracle, cause all the motions on the dial-plate of a watch, though nobody had ever made the movements and put them in it; but yet, if He will act agreeably

to the rules of mechanism by Him for wise ends established and maintained in the Creation, it is necessary that those actions of the watchmaker, whereby he makes the movements and rightly adjusts them, precede the production of the aforesaid motions, as also that any disorder in them be attended with the perception of some corresponding disorder in the movements, which, being once corrected, all is right again.

63. It may indeed on some occasions be necessary that the Author of Nature display His overruling power in producing some appearance out of the ordinary series of things. Such exceptions from the general rules of nature are proper to surprise and awe men into an acknowledgment of the Divine Being; but then they are to be used but seldom, otherwise there is a plain reason why they should fail of that effect. Besides, God seems to choose the convincing our reason of His attributes by the works of nature, which discover so much harmony and contrivance in their make and are such plain indications of wisdom and benficence in their Author rather than to astonish us into a belief of His being by anomalous and surprising events.

64. To set this matter in a yet clearer light, I shall observe that what has been objected in sec. 60 amounts in reality to no more than this: ideas are not anyhow and at random produced, there being a certain order and connection between them, like to that of cause and effect; there are also several combinations of them made in a very regular and artificial manner, which seem like so many instruments in the hand of nature that, being hidden, as it were, behind the scenes, have a secret operation in producing those appearances which are seen on the theater of the world, being themselves discernible only to the curious eye of the philosopher. But, since one idea cannot be the cause of another, to what purpose is that connection? And, since those instruments, being barely *inefficacious perceptions* in the mind, are not subservient to the production of natural effects, it is demanded why they are made, or, in other words, what reason can be assigned why God should make us, upon a close inspection into His works, behold so great variety of ideas so artfully laid together, and so much

according to rule, it not being credible that He would be at the expense (if one may so speak) of all that art and regularity to no purpose.

65. To all which my answer is, first, that the connection of ideas does not imply the relation of *cause* and *effect,* but only of a mark or *sign* with the thing *signified.* The fire which I see is not the cause of the pain I suffer upon my approaching it, but the mark that forewarns me of it. In like manner, the noise that I hear is not the effect of this or that motion or collision of the ambient bodies, but the sign thereof. Secondly, the reason why ideas are formed into machines, that is, artificial and regular combinations, is the same with that for combining letters into words. That a few original ideas may be made to signify a great number of effects and actions, it is necessary they be variously combined together. And, to the end their use be permanent and universal, these combinations must be made by *rule* and with *wise contrivance.* By this means abundance of information is conveyed unto us concerning what we are to expect from such and such actions and what methods are proper to be taken for the exciting such and such ideas, which in effect is all that I conceive to be distinctly meant when it is said that, by discerning the figure, texture, and mechanism of the inward parts of bodies, whether natural or artificial, we may attain to know the several uses and properties depending thereon, or the nature of the thing.

66. Hence it is evident that those things which, under the notion of a cause cooperating or concurring to the production of effects, are altogether inexplicable and run us into great absurdities may be very naturally explained and have a proper and obvious use assigned to them when they are considered only as marks or signs for our information. And it is the searching after and endeavoring to understand [those signs instituted by] the Author of Nature that ought to be the employment of the natural philosopher, and not the pretending to explain things by corporeal causes, which doctrine seems to have too much estranged the minds of men from that active principle, that supreme and wise Spirit "in whom we live, move, and have our being."

67. In the *twelfth* place, it may perhaps be

objected that—though it be clear from what has been said that there can be no such thing as an inert, senseless, extended, solid, figured, movable substance existing without the mind, such as philosophers describe matter—yet, if any man shall leave out of his idea of *matter* the positive ideas of extension, figure, solidity, and motion and say that he means only by that word an inert, senseless substance that exists without the mind or unperceived, which is the occasion of our ideas, or at the presence whereof God is pleased to excite ideas in us—it does not appear but that matter taken in this sense may possibly exist. In answer to which I say, first, that it seems no less absurd to suppose a substance without accidents than it is to suppose accidents without a substance. But secondly, though we should grant this unknown substance may possibly exist, yet where can it be supposed to be? That it exists not in the mind is agreed; and that it exists not in place is no less certain—since all extension exists only in the mind, as has been already proved. It remains therefore that it exists nowhere at all.

68. Let us examine a little the description that is here given us of *matter*. It neither acts, nor perceives, nor is perceived, for this is all that is meant by saying it is an inert, senseless, unknown substance; which is a definition entirely made up of negatives, excepting only the relative notion of its standing under or supporting. But then it must be observed that it supports nothing at all, and how nearly this comes to the description of a *nonentity* I desire may be considered. But, say you, it is the *unknown occasion* at the presence of which ideas are excited in us by the will of God. Now I would fain know how anything can be present to us which is neither perceivable by sense nor reflection, nor capable of producing any idea in our minds, nor is at all extended, nor has any form, nor exists in any place. The words "to be present," when thus applied, must needs be taken in some abstract and strange meaning, and which I am not able to comprehend.

69. Again, let us examine what is meant by "occasion." So far as I can gather from the common use of language, that word signifies either the agent which produces any effect or else something that is observed to accompany or go before it in the ordinary course of things. But when it is applied to matter as above described, it can be taken in neither of those senses, for matter is said to be passive and inert, and so cannot be an agent or efficient cause. It is also unperceivable, as being devoid of all sensible qualities, and so cannot be the occasion of our perceptions in the latter sense, as when the burning my finger is said to be the occasion of the pain that attends it. What therefore can be meant by calling matter an "occasion"? This term is either used in no sense at all or else in some sense very distant from its received signification.

70. You will perhaps say that matter, though it be not perceived by us, is nevertheless perceived by God, to whom it is the occasion of exciting ideas in our minds. For, say you, since we observe our sensations to be imprinted in an orderly and constant manner, it is but reasonable to suppose there are certain constant and regular occasions of their being produced. That is to say, that there are certain permanent and distinct parcels of matter, corresponding to our ideas, which, though they do not excite them in our minds or anyways immediately affect us, as being altogether passive and unperceivable to us, they are nevertheless to God, by whom they are perceived, as it were, so many occasions to remind Him when and what ideas to imprint on our minds that so things may go on in a constant uniform manner.

71. In answer to this I observe that, as the notion of matter is here stated, the question is no longer concerning the existence of a thing distinct from *spirit* and *idea,* from perceiving and being perceived, but whether there are not certain ideas of I know not what sort in the mind of God which are so many marks or notes that direct Him how to produce sensations in our minds in a constant and regular method—much after the same manner as a musician is directed by the notes of music to produce that harmonious train and composition of sound which is called a "tune," though they who hear the music do not perceive the notes and may be entirely ignorant of them. But this notion of matter seems too extravagant to deserve a confutation. Besides, it

is in effect no objection against what we have advanced, to wit, that there is no senseless, unperceived substance.

72. If we follow the light of reason we shall, from the constant uniform method of our sensations, collect the goodness and wisdom of the spirit who excites them in our minds; but this is all that I can see reasonably concluded from thence. To me, I say, it is evident that the being of a spirit infinitely wise, good, and powerful is abundantly sufficient to explain all the appearances of nature. But, as for *inert, senseless matter,* nothing that I perceive has any the least connection with it or leads to the thoughts of it. And I would fain see anyone explain any the meanest phenomenon in nature by it or show any manner of reason, though in the lowest rank of probability, that he can have for its existence, or even make any tolerable sense or meaning of that supposition. For as to its being an occasion we have, I think, evidently shown that with regard to us it is no occasion. It remains therefore that it must be, if at all, the occasion to God of exciting ideas in us, and what this amounts to we have just now seen.

73. It is worth while to reflect a little on the motives which induced men to suppose the existence of *material substance;* that so having observed the gradual ceasing and expiration of those motives or reasons, we may proportionably withdraw the assent that was grounded on them. First, therefore, it was thought that color, figure, motion, and the rest of the sensible qualities or accidents did really exist without the mind; and for this reason it seemed needful to suppose some unthinking *substratum* or substance wherein they did exist, since they could not be conceived to exist by themselves. Afterwards, in process of time, men being convinced that colors, sounds, and the rest of the sensible, secondary qualities had no existence without the mind, they stripped this *substratum* or material substance of those qualities, leaving only the primary ones, figure, motion, and suchlike, which they still conceived to exist without the mind, and consequently to stand in need of a material support. But it having been shown that none even of these can possibly exist otherwise than in a spirit or mind which perceives them, it

follows that we have no longer any reason to suppose the being of matter; nay, that it is utterly impossible there should be any such thing so long as that word is taken to denote an *unthinking substratum* of qualities or accidents wherein they exist without the mind.

74. But though it be allowed by the materialists themselves that matter was thought of only for the sake of supporting accidents, and, the reason entirely ceasing, one might expect the mind should naturally, and without any reluctance at all, quit the belief of what was solely grounded thereon, yet the prejudice is riveted so deeply in our thoughts that we can scarce tell how to part with it, and are therefore inclined, since the *thing* itself is indefensible, at least to retain the *name,* which we apply to I know not what abstracted and indefinite notions of being, or occasion, though without any show of reason, at least so far as I can see. For what is there on our part, or what do we perceive among all the ideas, sensations, notions which are imprinted on our minds, either by sense or reflection, from whence may be inferred the existence of an inert, thoughtless, unperceived occasion? And, on the other hand, on the part of an all-sufficient Spirit, what can there be that should make us believe or even suspect He is directed by an inert occasion to excite ideas in our minds?

75. It is a very extraordinary instance of the force of prejudice, and much to be lamented, that the mind of man retains so great a fondness, against all the evidence of reason, for a stupid, thoughtless *somewhat,* by the interposition whereof it would as it were screen itself from the Providence of God and remove him farther off from the affairs of the world. But though we do the utmost we can to secure the belief of matter, though, when reason forsakes us, we endeavor to support our opinion on the bare possibility of the thing, and though we indulge ourselves in the full scope of an imagination not regulated by reason to make out that poor possibility, yet the upshot of all is that there are certain *unknown ideas* in the mind of God; for this, if anything, is all that I conceive to be meant by "occasion" with regard to God. And this at the bottom is no longer contending for the thing, but for the name.

76. Whether, therefore, there are such ideas in the mind of God, and whether they may be called by the name "matter," I shall not dispute. But if you stick to the notion of an unthinking substance or support of extension, motion, and other sensible qualities, then to me it is most evidently impossible there should be any such thing, since it is a plain repugnancy that those qualities should exist in or be supported by an unperceiving substance.

77. But, say you, though it be granted that there is no thoughtless support of extension and the other qualities or accidents which we perceive, yet there may, perhaps, be some inert, unperceiving substance or *substratum* of some other qualities, as incomprehensible to us as colors are to a man born blind, because we have not a sense adapted to them. But if we had a new sense, we should possibly no more doubt of their existence than a blind man made to see does of the existence of light and colors. I answer, first, if what you mean by the word "matter" be only the unknown support of unknown qualities, it is no matter whether there is such a thing or no, since it no way concerns us; and I do not see the advantage there is in disputing about we know not *what*, and we know not *why*.

78. But, secondly, if we had a new sense, it could only furnish us with new ideas or sensations; and then we should have the same reason against their existing in an unperceiving substance that has been already offered with relation to figure, motion, color, and the like. Qualities, as has been shown, are nothing else but *sensations* or *ideas*, which exist only in a *mind* perceiving them; and this is true not only of the ideas we are acquainted with at present, but likewise of all possible ideas whatsoever.

79. But, you will insist, what if I have no reason to believe the existence of matter? What if I cannot assign any use to it or explain anything by it, or even conceive what is meant by that word? Yet still it is no contradiction to say that matter exists, and that this matter is in general a *substance*, or *occasion of ideas*, though, indeed, to go about to unfold the meaning or adhere to any particular explication of those words may be attended with great difficulties. I answer, when words are used without a meaning, you may put them together as you please without danger of running into a contradiction. You may say, for example, the twice two is equal to seven, so long as you declare you do not take the words of that proposition in their usual acceptation but for marks of you know not what. And, by the same reason, you may say there is an inert, thoughtless substance without accidents which is the occasion of our ideas. And we shall understand just as much by one proposition as the other.

80. In the *last* place, you will say, What if we give up the cause of material substance and assert that matter is an unknown *somewhat*—neither substance nor accident, spirit nor idea, inert, thoughtless, indivisible, immovable, unextended, existing in no place? For, say you, whatever may be urged against *substance* or *occasion*, or any other positive or relative notion of matter, has no place at all so long as this *negative* definition of matter is adhered to. I answer, You may, if so it shall seem good, use the word "matter" in the same sense as other men use "nothing," and so make those terms convertible in your style. For, after all, this is what appears to me to be the result of that definition, the parts whereof, when I consider with attention, either collectively or separate from each other, I do not find there is any kind of effect or impression made on my mind different from what is excited by the term "nothing."

81. You will reply, perhaps, that in the foresaid definition is included what does sufficiently distinguish it from nothing—the positive, abstract idea of *quiddity, entity,* or *existence.* I own, indeed, that those who pretend to the faculty of framing abstract general ideas do talk as if they had such an idea, which is, say they, the most abstract and general notion of all; that is, to me, the most incomprehensible of all others. That there are a great variety of spirits of different orders and capacities whose faculties both in number and extent are far exceeding those the Author of my being has bestowed on me, I see no reason to deny. And for me to pretend to determine by my own few, stinted, narrow inlets of perception what ideas the inexhaustible power of the Supreme Spirit may imprint upon them were certainly the utmost folly and presumption—since there

may be, for aught that I know, innumerable sorts of ideas or sensations, as different from one another, and from all that I have perceived, as colors are from sounds. But how ready soever I may be to acknowledge the scantiness of my comprehension with regard to the endless variety of spirits and ideas that might possibly exist, yet for anyone to pretend to a notion of entity or existence, *abstracted* from *spirit* and *idea,* from perceiving and being perceived is, I suspect, a downright repugnancy and trifling with words.—It remains that we consider the objections which may possibly be made on the part of religion.

82. Some there are who think that, though the arguments for the real existence of bodies which are drawn from reason be allowed not to amount to demonstration, yet the Holy Scriptures are so clear in the point as will sufficiently convince every good Christian that bodies do really exist, and are something more than mere ideas, there being in Holy Writ innumerable facts related which evidently suppose the reality of timber and stone, mountains and rivers, and cities, and human bodies. To which I answer that no sort of writings whatever, sacred or profane, which use those and the like words in the vulgar acceptation, or so as to have a meaning in them, are in danger of having their truth called in question by our doctrine. That all those things do really exist, that there are bodies, even corporeal substances, when taken in the vulgar sense, has been shown to be agreeable to our principles; and the difference betwixt *things* and *ideas, realities* and *chimeras* has been distinctly explained. See secs. 29, 30, 33, 36, etc. And I do not think that either what philosophers call "matter," or the existence of objects without the mind, is anywhere mentioned in Scripture.

83. Again, whether there be or be not external things, it is agreed on all hands that the proper use of words is the marking out conceptions, or things only as they are known and perceived by us; whence it plainly follows that in the tenets we have laid down there is nothing inconsistent with the right use and significance of *language,* and that discourse, of what kind soever, so far as it is intelligible, remains undisturbed. But all this seems so very manifest, from what has been set forth in the premises, that it is needless to insist any further on it.

84. But it will be urged that miracles do, at least, lose much of their stress and import by our principles. What must we think of Moses' rod? Was it not *really* turned into a serpent, or was there only a change of *ideas* in the minds of the spectators? And can it be supposed that our Saviour did no more at the marriage-feast in Cana than impose on the sight and smell and taste of the guests, so as to create in them the appearance or idea only of wine? The same may be said of all other miracles, which, in consequence of the foregoing principles, must be looked upon only as so many cheats or illusions of fancy. To this I reply that the rod was changed into a real serpent, and the water into real wine. That this does not in the least contradict what I have elsewhere said will be evident from secs. 34 and 35. But this business of *real* and *imaginary* has been already so plainly and fully explained, and so often referred to, and the difficulties about it are so easily answered from what has gone before, that it were an affront to the reader's understanding to resume the explication of it in this place. I shall only observe that if at table all who were present should see, and smell, and taste, and drink wine, and find the effects of it, with me there could be no doubt of its reality, so that at bottom the scruple concerning real miracles has no place at all on ours, but only on the received principles, and consequently makes rather for than against what has been said.

85. Having done with the objections, which I endeavored to propose in the clearest light, and gave them all the force and weight I could, we proceed in the next place to take a view of our tenets in their consequences. Some of these appear at first sight—as that several difficult and obscure questions, on which abundance of speculation has been thrown away, are entirely banished from philosophy: whether corporeal substance can think; whether matter be infinitely divisible; and how it operates on spirit—these and the like inquiries have given infinite amusement to philosophers in all ages, but, depending on the existence of matter, they have no longer any place on our principles. Many other advan-

tages there are, as well with regard to religion as the sciences, which it is easy for anyone to deduce from what has been premised; but this will appear more plainly in the sequel.

86. From the principles we have laid down it follows human knowledge may naturally be reduced to two heads—that of *ideas* and that of *spirits*. Of each of these I shall treat in order.

And, *first*, as to ideas or unthinking things. Our knowledge of these has been very much obscured and confounded, and we have been led into very dangerous errors, by supposing a twofold existence of the objects of sense—the one *intelligible* or in the mind, the other *real* and without the mind, whereby unthinking things are thought to have a natural subsistence of their own distinct from being perceived by spirits. This, which, if I mistake not, has been shown to be a most groundless and absurd notion, is the very root of skepticism, for so long as men thought that real things subsisted without the mind, and that their knowledge was only as far forth *real* as it was conformable to *real things,* it follows they could not be certain they had any real knowledge at all. For how can it be known that the things which are perceived are conformable to those which are not perceived or exist without the mind?

87. Color, figure, motion, extension, and the like, considered only as so many *sensations* in the mind, are perfectly known, there being nothing in them which is not perceived. But if they are looked on as notes or images, referred to *things* or *archetypes* existing without the mind, then are we involved all in skepticism. We see only the appearances, and not the real qualities of things. What may be the entension, figure, or motion of anything really and absolutely, or in itself, it is impossible for us to know, but only the proportion or the relation they bear to our senses. Things remaining the same, our ideas vary, and which of them, or even whether any of them at all, represent the true quality really existing in the thing, it is out of our reach to determine. So that, for aught we know, all we see, hear, and feel may be only phantom and vain chimera, and not at all agree with the real things existing in *rerum natura.* All this skepticism follows

from our supposing a difference between *things* and *ideas,* and that the former have a subsistence without the mind or unperceived. It were easy to dilate on this subject and show how the arguments urged by skeptics in all ages depend on the supposition of external objects.

88. So long as we attribute a real existence to unthinking things, distinct from their being perceived, it is not only impossible for us to know with evidence the nature of any real unthinking being, but even that it exists. Hence it is that we see philosophers distrust their senses and doubt of the existence of heaven and earth, of everything they see or feel, even of their own bodies. And after all their labor and struggle of thought, they are forced to own we cannot attain to any self-evident or demonstrative knowledge of the existence of sensible things. But all this doubtfulness which so bewilders and confounds the mind and makes philosophy ridiculous in the eyes of the world vanishes if we annex a meaning to our words and do not amuse ourselves with the terms "absolute," "external," "exist," and suchlike, signifying we know not what. I can as well doubt of my own being as of the being of those things which I actually perceive by sense; it being a manifest contradiction that any sensible object should be immediately perceived by sight or touch and at the same time have no existence in nature, since the very *existence* of an unthinking being consists in *being perceived.*

89. Nothing seems of more importance toward erecting a firm system of sound and real knowledge, which may be proof against the assaults of skepticism, than to lay the beginning in a distinct explication of what is meant by "thing," "reality," "existence"; for in vain shall we dispute concerning the real existence of things or pretend to any knowledge thereof, so long as we have not fixed the meaning of those words. "Thing" or "being" is the most general name of all; it comprehends under it two kinds entirely distinct and heterogenous, and which have nothing common but the name, to wit, *spirits* and *ideas.* The former are active, indivisible substances; the latter are inert, fleeting, dependent beings which subsist not by themselves, but are sup-

ported by or exist in minds or spiritual substances.

90. Ideas imprinted on the senses are real things, or do really exist—this we do not deny, but we deny they can subsist without the minds which perceive them, or that they are resemblances of any archetypes existing without the mind, since the very being of a sensation or idea consists in being perceived, and an idea can be like nothing but an idea. Again, the things perceived by sense may be termed "external" with regard to their origin—in that they are not generated from within by the mind itself, but imprinted by a spirit distinct from that which perceives them. Sensible objects may likewise be said to be "without the mind" in another sense, namely, when they exist in some other mind; thus, when I shut my eyes, the things I saw may still exist, but it must be in another mind.

91. It were a mistake to think that what is here said derogates in the least from the reality of things. It is acknowledged, on the received principles, that extension, motion, and, in a word, all sensible qualities have need of a support, as not being able to subsist by themselves. But the objects perceived by sense are allowed to be nothing but combinations of those qualities, and consequently cannot subsist by themselves. Thus far, it is agreed on all hands. So that in denying the things perceived by sense an existence independent of a substance or support wherein they may exist, we detract nothing from the received opinion of their *reality,* and are guilty of no innovation in that respect. All the difference is that, according to us, the unthinking beings perceived by sense have no existence distinct from being perceived, and cannot therefore exist in any other substances than those unextended indivisible substances or *spirits* which act and think and perceive them; whereas philosophers vulgarly hold that the sensible qualities exist in an inert, extended, unperceiving substance which they call "matter," to which they attribute a natural subsistence, exterior to all thinking beings, or distinct from being perceived by any mind whatsoever, even the eternal mind of the Creator, wherein they suppose only ideas of the corporeal substances created by him, if indeed they allow them to be at all created.

92. For as we have shown the doctrine of matter or corporeal substance to have been the main pillar and support of skepticism, so likewise, upon the same foundation, have been raised all the impious schemes of atheism and irreligion. Nay, so great a difficulty has it been thought to conceive matter produced out of nothing that the most celebrated among the ancient philosophers, even of these who maintained the being of a God, have thought matter to be uncreated and coeternal with Him. How great a friend *material substance* has been to atheists in all ages were needless to relate. All their monstrous systems have so visible and necessary a dependence on it that, when this cornerstone is once removed, the whole fabric cannot choose but fall to the ground, insomuch that it is no longer worth while to bestow a particular consideration on the absurdities of every wretched sect of atheists.

93. That impious and profane persons should readily fall in with those systems which favor their inclinations by deriding immaterial substance and supposing the soul to be divisible and subject to corruption as the body, which exclude all freedom, intelligence, and design from the formation of things, and instead thereof make a self-existent, stupid, unthinking substance the root and origin of all beings; that they should hearken to those who deny a Providence, or inspection of a Superior Mind over the affairs of the world, attributing the whole series of events either to blind chance or fatal necessity arising from the impulse of one body or another—all this is very natural. And, on the other hand, when men of better principles observe the enemies of religion lay so great a stress on *unthinking matter,* and all of them use so much industry and artifice to reduce everything to it, methinks they should rejoice to see them deprived to their grand support and driven from that only fortress without which your Epicureans, Hobbists, and the like, have not even the shadow of a pretense, but become the most cheap and easy triumph in the world.

94. The existence of matter, or bodies unperceived, has not only been the main support of atheists and fatalists, but on the same principle does idolatry likewise in all its various forms depend. Did men but consider that the sun, moon, and stars, and every other object of

the senses are only so many sensations in their minds, which have no other existence but barely being perceived, doubtless they would never fall down and worship their own *ideas,* but rather address their homage to that Eternal Invisible Mind which produces and sustains all things.

95. The same absurd principle, by mingling itself with the articles of our faith, has occasioned no small difficulties to Christians. For example, about the resurrection, how many scruples and objections have been raised by Socinians[14] and others? But do not the most plausible of them depend on the supposition that a body is denominated "the same," with regard not to the form or that which is perceived by sense, but the material substance, which remains the same under several forms? Take away this *material substance,* about the identity whereof all the dispute is, and mean by "body" what every plain, ordinary person means by that word, to wit, that which is immediately seen and felt, which is only a combination of sensible qualities or ideas, and then their most unanswerable objections come to nothing.

96. Matter being once expelled out of nature drags with it so many skeptical and impious notions, such an incredible number of disputes and puzzling questions, which have been thorns in the sides of divines as well as philosophers and made so much fruitless work for mankind, that if the arguments we have produced against it are not found equal to demonstration (as to me they evidently seem), yet I am sure all friends to knowledge, peace, and religion have reason to wish they were.

97. Beside the external existence of the objects of perception, another great source of errors and difficulties with regard to ideal knowledge is the doctrine of *abstract ideas,* such as it has been set forth in the Introduction. The plainest things in the world, those we are most intimately acquainted with and perfectly know, when they are considered in an abstract way, appear strangely difficult and incomprehensible. Time, place, and motion, taken in particular or concrete, are what everybody knows, but, having passed through the hands of a metaphysician, they become too abstract and fine to be apprehended by men of ordinary sense. Bid your servant meet you at

such a *time* in such a *place,* and he shall never stay to deliberate on the meaning of those words; in conceiving that particular time and place, or the motion by which he is to get thither, he finds not the least difficulty. But if *time* be taken exclusive of all those particular actions and ideas that diversify the day, merely for the continuation of existence or duration in abstract, then it will perhaps gravel even a philosopher to comprehend it.

98. Whenever I attempt to frame a simple idea of *time,* abstracted from the succession of ideas in my mind, which flows uniformly and is participated by all beings, I am lost and embrangled in inextricable difficulties. I have no notion of it at all, only I hear others say it is infinitely divisible, and speak of it in such a manner as leads me to entertain odd thoughts of my existence; since that doctrine lays one under an absolute necessity of thinking, either that he passes away innumerable ages without a thought or else that he is annihilated every moment of his life, both which seem equally absurd. Time therefore being nothing, abstracted from the succession of ideas in our minds, it follows that the duration of any finite spirit must be estimated by the number of ideas or actions succeeding each other in that same spirit or mind. Hence, it is a plain consequence that the soul always thinks; and in truth whoever shall go about to divide in his thoughts or abstract the *existence* of a spirit from its *cogitation* will, I believe, find it no easy task.

99. So likewise when we attempt to abstract extension and motion from all other qualities, and consider them by themselves, we presently lose sight of them, and run into great extravagances. All which depend on a twofold abstraction; first, it is supposed that extension, for example, may be abstracted from all other sensible qualities; and secondly, that the entity of extension may be abstracted from its being perceived. But whoever shall reflect, and take care to understand what he says, will, if I mistake not, acknowledge that all sensible qualities are alike *sensations* and alike *real;* that where the extension is, there is the color, too, to wit, in his mind, and that their archetypes can exist only in some other *mind;* and that the objects of sense are nothing but those sensations combined, blended, or (if one

may so speak) concreted together; none of all which can be supposed to exist unperceived.

100. What it is for a man to be happy, or an object good, everyone may think he knows. But to frame an abstract idea of happiness, prescinded from all particular pleasure, or of goodness from everything that is good, this is what few can pretend to. So likewise a man may be just and virtuous without having precise ideas of justice and virtue. The opinion that those and the like words stand for general notions, abstracted from all particular persons and actions, seems to have rendered morality difficult, and the study thereof of less use to mankind. And in effect the doctrine of *abstraction* has not a little contributed toward spoiling the most useful parts of knowledge.

101. The two great provinces of speculative science conversant about ideas received from sense and their relations are natural philosophy and mathematics; with regard to each of these I shall make some observations. And first I shall say somewhat of natural philosophy. On this subject it is that the skeptics triumph. All that stock of arguments they produce to depreciate our faculties and make mankind appear ignorant and low are drawn principally from this head, to wit, that we are under an invincible blindness as to the *true* and *real* nature of things. This they exaggerate, and love to enlarge on. We are miserably bantered, say they, by our senses, and amused only with the outside and show of things. The real essence, the internal qualities and constitution of every the meanest object, is hidden from our view; something there is in every drop of water, every grain of sand, which it is beyond the power of human understanding to fathom or comprehend. But it is evident from what has been shown that all this complaint is groundless, and that we are influenced by false principles to that degree as to mistrust our senses and think we know nothing of those things which we perfectly comprehend.

102. One great inducement to our pronouncing ourselves ignorant of the nature of things is the current opinion that everything includes within itself the cause of its properties; or that there is in each object an inward essence which is the source whence its discernible qualities flow, and whereon they depend.

Some have pretended to account for appearances by occult qualities, but of late they are mostly resolved into mechanical causes, to wit, the figure, motion, weight, and suchlike qualities of insensible particles; whereas, in truth, there is no other agent or efficient cause than *spirit,* it being evident that motion, as well as all other *ideas,* is perfectly inert. See sec. 25. Hence, to endeavor to explain the production of colors or sounds by figure, motion, magnitude, and the like, must needs be labor in vain. And accordingly we see the attempts of that kind are not at all satisfactory. Which may be said in general of those instances wherein one idea or quality is assigned for the cause of another. I need not say how many hypotheses and speculations are left out, and how much the study of nature is abridged by this doctrine.

103. The great mechanical principle now in vogue is *attraction.* That a stone falls to the earth, or the sea swells toward the moon, may to some appear sufficiently explained thereby. But how are we enlightened by being told this is done by attraction? Is it that that word signifies the manner of the tendency, and that it is by the mutual drawing of bodies instead of their being impelled or protruded toward each other? But nothing is determined of the manner or action, and it may as truly (for aught we know) be termed "impulse," or "protrusion," as "attraction." Again, the parts of steel we see cohere firmly together, and this also is accounted for by attraction; but, in this as in the other instances, I do not perceive that anything is signified besides the effect itself; for as to the manner of the action whereby it is produced, or the cause which produces it, these are not so much as aimed at.

104. Indeed, if we take a view of the several phenomena and compare them together, we may observe some likeness and conformity between them. For example, in the falling of a stone to the ground, in the rising of the sea toward the moon, in cohesion and crystallization, there is something alike, namely, a union or mutual approach of bodies. So that any one of these or the like phenomena may not seem strange or surprising to a man who has nicely observed and compared the effects of nature. For that only is thought so which is un-

common, or a thing by itself, and out of the ordinary course of our observation. That bodies should tend toward the center of the earth is not thought strange, because it is what we perceive every moment of our lives. But, that they should have a like gravitation toward the center of the moon may seem odd and unaccountable to most men, because it is discerned only in the tides. But a philosopher, whose thoughts take in a larger compass of nature, having observed a certain similitude of appearances, as well in the heavens as the earth, that argue innumerable bodies to have a mutual tendency toward each other, which he denotes by the general name "attraction," whatever can be reduced to that he thinks justly accounted for. Thus he explains the tides by the attraction of the terraqueous globe toward the moon, which to him does not appear odd or anomalous, but only a particular example of a general rule or law of nature.

105. If therefore we consider the difference there is betwixt natural philosophers and other men with regard to their knowledge of the phenomena, we shall find it consists not in an exacter knowledge of the efficient cause that produces them—for that can be no other than the *will of a spirit*—but only in a greater largeness of comprehension, whereby analogies, harmonies, and agreements are discovered in the works of nature, and the particular effects explained, that is, reduced to general rules, see sec. 62, which rules, grounded on the analogy and uniformness observed in the production of natural effects, are most agreeable and sought after by the mind; for that they extend our prospect beyond what is present and near to us, and enable us to make very probable conjectures touching things that may have happened at very great distances of time and place, as well as to predict things to come; which sort of endeavor toward omniscience is much affected by the mind.

106. But we should proceed warily in such things, for we are apt to lay too great a stress on analogies, and, to the prejudice of truth, humor that eagerness of the mind whereby it is carried to extend its knowledge into general theorems. For example, gravitation or mutual attraction, because it appears in many instances, some are straightway for pronouncing "universal"; and that to attract and be attracted by every other body is an essential quality inherent in all bodies whatsoever. Whereas it appears the fixed stars have no such tendency toward each other; and so far is that gravitation from being *essential* to bodies that in some instances a quite contrary principle seems to show itself; as in the perpendicular growth of plants, and the elasticity of the air. There is nothing necessary or essential in the case, but it depends entirely on the will of the governing spirit, who causes certain bodies to cleave together or tend toward each other according to various laws, whilst he keeps others at a fixed distance; and to some he gives a quite contrary tendency to fly asunder just as he sees convenient.

107. After what has been premised, I think we may lay down the following conclusions. First, it is plain philosophers amuse themselves in vain when they inquire for any natural efficient cause distinct from a *mind* or *spirit*. Secondly, considering the whole creation is the workmanship of a *wise and good agent,* it should seem to become philosophers to employ their thoughts (contrary to what some hold) about the final causes of things; and I must confess I see no reason why pointing out the various ends to which natural things are adapted, and for which they were originally with unspeakable wisdom contrived, should not be thought one good way of accounting for them, and altogether worthy a philosopher. Thirdly, from what has been premised no reason can be drawn why the history of nature should not still be studied, and observations and experiments made; which, that they are of use to mankind, and enable us to draw any general conclusions, is not the result of any immutable habitudes or relations between things themselves, but only of God's goodness and kindness to men in the administration of the world. See secs. 30 and 31. Fourthly, by a diligent observation of the phenomena within our view, we may discover the general laws of nature, and from them deduce the other phenomena; I do not say "demonstrate," for all deductions of that kind depend on a supposition that the Author of Nature always operates uniformly and in a constant observance of

those rules we take for principles, which we cannot evidently know.

108. Those men who frame general rules from the phenomena and afterwards derive the phenomena from those rules seem to consider signs rather than causes. A man may well understand natural signs without knowing their analogy, or being able to say by what rule a thing is so or so. And, as it is very possible to write improperly, through too strict an observance of general grammar rules; so, in arguing from general rules of nature, it is not impossible we may extend the analogy too far, and by that means run into mistakes.

109. As, in reading other books, a wise man will choose to fix his thoughts on the sense and apply it to use, rather than lay them out in grammatical remarks on the language, so, in perusing the volume of nature, it seems beneath the dignity of the mind to affect an exactness in reducing each particular phenomenon to general rules, or showing how it follows from them. We should propose to ourselves nobler views, such as to recreate and exalt the mind with a prospect of the beauty, order, extent, and variety of natural things: hence, by proper inferences, to enlarge our notions of the grandeur, wisdom, and beneficence of the Creator; and lastly, to make the several parts of the Creation, so far as in us lies, subservient to the ends they were designed for—God's glory and the sustentation and comfort of ourselves and fellow creatures.

110. The best key for the aforesaid analogy or natural science will be easily acknowledged to be a certain celebrated treatise of *mechanics.** In the entrance of which justly admired treatise, time, space, and motion are distinguished into *absolute* and *relative, true* and *apparent, mathematical* and *vulgar;* which distinction, as it is at large explained by the author, does suppose these quantities to have an existence without the mind; and that they are ordinarily conceived with relation to sensible things, to which nevertheless in their own nature they bear no relation at all.

111. As for "time," as it is there taken in an absolute or abstracted sense, for the duration or perseverance of the existence of things, I have nothing more to add concerning it after what has been already said on that subject. Secs. 97 and 98. For the rest, this celebrated author holds there is an *absolute space,* which, being unperceivable to sense, remains in itself similar and immovable; and relative space to be the measure thereof, which, being movable and defined by its situation in respect of sensible bodies, is vulgarly taken for immovable space. "Place" he defines to be that part of space which is occupied by any body; and according as the space is absolute or relative, so also is the place. "Absolute motion" is said to be the translation of a body from absolute place to absolute place, as relative motion is from one relative place to another. And, because the parts of absolute space do not fall under our senses, instead of them we are obliged to use their sensible measures, and so define both place and motion with respect to bodies which we regard as immovable. But it is said in philosophical matters we must abstract from our senses, since it may be that none of those bodies which seem to be quiescent are truly so, and the same thing which is moved relatively may be really at rest; as likewise one and the same body may be in relative rest and motion, or even moved with contrary relative motions at the same time, according as its place is variously defined. All which ambiguity is to be found in the apparent motions, but not at all in the true or absolute, which should therefore be alone regarded in philosophy. And the true we are told are distinguished from apparent or relative motions by the following properties.—First, in true or absolute motion all parts which preserve the same position with respect to the whole partake of the motions of the whole. Secondly, the place being moved, that which is placed therein is also moved; so that a body moving in a place which is in motion does participate in the motion of its place. Thirdly, true motion is never generated or changed otherwise than by force impressed on the body itself. Fourthly, true motion is always changed by force impressed on the body moved. Fifthly, in circular motion, barely relative, there is no centrifugal force which, nevertheless, in that which is true or absolute, is proportional to the quantity of motion.

*Isaac Newton, *Philosophiae Naturalis Principia Mathematica* (London, 1687). [ed.]

112. But, notwithstanding what has been said, it does not appear to me that there can be any motion other than *relative;* so that to conceive motion there must be at least conceived two bodies, whereof the distance or position in regard to each other is varied. Hence, if there was one only body in being it could not possibly be moved. This seems evident, in that the idea I have of motion does necessarily include relation.

113. But, though in every motion it be necessary to conceive more bodies than one, yet it may be that one only is moved, namely, that on which the force causing the change of distance is impressed, or, in other words, that to which the action is applied. For, however some may define relative motion, so as to term that body "moved" which changes its distance from some other body, whether the force or action causing that change were applied to it or no, yet as relative motion is that which is perceived by sense, and regarded in the ordinary affairs of life, it should seem that every man of common sense knows what it is as well as the best philosopher. Now I ask anyone whether, in his sense of motion as he walks along the streets, the stones he passes over may be said to *move*, because they change distance with his feet? To me it seems that though motion includes a relation of one thing to another, yet it is not necessary that each term of the relation be denominated from it. As a man may think of somewhat which does not think, so a body may be moved to or from another body which is not therefore itself in motion.

114. As the place happens to be variously defined, the motion which is related to it varies. A man in a ship may be said to be quiescent with relation to the sides of the vessel, and yet move with relation to the land. Or he may move eastward in respect of the one, and westward in respect of the other. In the common affairs of life, men never go beyond the earth to define the place of any body; and what is quiescent in respect of that is accounted *absolutely* to be so. But philosophers, who have a great extent of thought, and juster notions of the system of things, discover even the earth itself to be moved. In order therefore to fix their notions, they seem to conceive the corporeal world as finite, and the utmost un-

moved walls or shell thereof to be the place whereby they estimate true motions. If we sound our own conceptions, I believe we may find all the absolute motion we can frame an idea of to be at bottom no other than relative motion thus defined. For, as has been already observed, absolute motion, exclusive of all external relation, is incomprehensible; and to this kind of relative motion all the above-mentioned properties, causes, and effects ascribed to absolute motion will, if I mistake not, be found to agree. As to what is said of the centrifugal force, that it does not at all belong to circular relative motion, I do not see how this follows from the experiment which is brought to prove it. See *Philosophiae Naturalis Principia Mathematica, in Schol. Def. VIII.* For the water in the vessel at that time wherein it is said to have the greatest relative circular motion, has, I think, no motion at all; as is plain from the foregoing section.

115. For, to denominate a body "moved" it is requisite, first, that it change its distance or situation with regard to some other body; and secondly, that the force or action occasioning that change be applied to it. If either of these be wanting, I do not think that, agreeably to the sense of mankind, or the propriety of language, a body can be said to be in motion. I grant indeed that it is possible for us to think a body which we see change its distance from some other to be moved, though it have no force applied to it (in which sense there may be apparent motion), but then it is because the force causing the change of distance is imagined by us to be applied or impressed on that body thought to move; which indeed shows we are capable of mistaking a thing to be in motion which is not, and that is all.

116. From what has been said, it follows that the philosophic consideration of motion does not imply the being of an *absolute space*, distinct from that which is perceived by sense and related to bodies, which that it cannot exist without the mind is clear upon the same principles that demonstrate the like of all other objects of sense. And perhaps, if we inquire narrowly, we shall find we cannot even frame an idea of *pure space* exclusive of all body. This I must confess seems impossible, as being a most abstract idea. When I excite a

motion in some part of my body, if it be free or without resistance, I say there is *space;* but if I find a resistance, then I say there is *body;* and in proportion as the resistance to motion is lesser or greater, I say the space is more or less *pure.* So that when I speak of pure or empty space, it is not to be supposed that the word "space" stands for an idea distinct from or conceivable without body and motion— though indeed we are apt to think every noun substantive stands for a distinct idea that may be separated from all others; which has occasioned infinite mistakes. When, therefore, supposing all the world to be annihilated besides my own body, I say there still remains *pure space,* thereby nothing else is meant but only that I conceive it possible for the limbs of my body to be moved on all sides without the least resistance; but if that, too, were annihilated, then there could be no motion, and consequently no space. Some, perhaps, may think the sense of seeing does furnish them with the idea of pure space; but it is plain from what we have elsewhere shown, that the ideas of space and distance are not obtained by that sense. See the *Essay Concerning Vision.*

117. What is here laid down seems to put an end to all those disputes and difficulties that have sprung up amongst the learned concerning the nature of *pure space.* But the chief advantage arising from it is that we are freed from that dangerous dilemma to which several who have employed their thoughts on this subject imagine themselves reduced, to wit, of thinking either the real space is God, or else that there is something besides God which is eternal, uncreated, infinite, indivisible, immutable. Both which may justly be thought pernicious and absurd notions. It is certain that not a few divines, as well as philosophers of great note, have, from the difficulty they found in conceiving either limits or annihilation of space, concluded it must be divine. And some of late have set themselves particularly to show that the incommunicable attributes of God agree to it. Which doctrine, how unworthy soever it may seem of the Divine Nature, yet I do not see how we can get clear of it so long as we adhere to the received opinions.

118. Hitherto of natural philosophy: we come now to make some inquiry concerning the other great branch of speculative knowledge, to wit, mathematics. These, how celebrated soever they may be for their clearness and certainty of demonstration, which is hardly anywhere else to be found, cannot nevertheless be supposed altogether free from mistakes, if in their principles there lurks some secret error which is common to the professors of those sciences with the rest of mankind. Mathematicians, though they deduce their theorems from a great height of evidence, yet their first principles are limited by the consideration of quantity; and they do not ascend into any inquiry concerning those transcendental maxims which influence all the particular sciences, each part whereof, mathematics not excepted, does consequently participate of the errors involved in them. That the principles laid down by mathematicians are true, and their way of deduction from those principles clear and incontestable, we do not deny; but we hold there may be certain erroneous maxims of greater extent than the object of mathematics, and for that reason not expressly mentioned, though tacitly supposed throughout the whole progress of that science; and that the ill effects of those secret, unexamined errors are diffused through all the branches thereof. To be plain, we suspect the mathematicians are as well as other men concerned in the errors arising from the doctrine of abstract general ideas and the existence of objects without the mind.

119. Arithmetic has been thought to have for its object abstract ideas of *number;* of which to understand the properties and mutual habitudes is supposed no mean part of speculative knowledge. The opinion of the pure and intellectual nature of numbers in abstract has made them in esteem with those philosophers who seem to have affected an uncommon fineness and elevation of thought. It has set a price on the most trifling numerical speculations which in practice are of no use but serve only for amusement, and has therefore so far infected the minds of some that they have dreamed of mighty mysteries involved in numbers and attempted the explication of natural things by them. But, if we inquire into our own thoughts and consider what has been premised, we may perhaps entertain a low opin-

ion of those high flights and abstractions, and look on all inquiries about numbers only as so many *difficiles nugae,* so far as they are not subservient to practice and promote the benefit of life.

120. Unity in abstract we have before considered in sec. 13, from which and what has been said in the Introduction, it plainly follows there is not any such idea. But, number being defined a "collection of units," we may conclude that, if there be no such thing as unity or unit in abstract, there are no ideas of number in abstract denoted by the numerical names and figures. The theories therefore in arithmetic, if they are abstracted from the names and figures, as likewise from all use and practice, as well as from the particular things numbered, can be supposed to have nothing at all for their object; hence we may see how entirely the science of numbers is subordinate to practice, and how jejune and trifling it becomes when considered as a matter of mere speculation.

121. However, since there may be some who, deluded by the specious show of discovering abstracted verities, waste their time in arithmetical theorems and problems which have not any use, it will not be amiss if we more fully consider and expose the vanity of that pretense; and this will plainly appear by taking a view of arithmetic in its infancy, and observing what it was that originally put men on the study of that science, and to what scope they directed it. It is natural to think that at first, men, for ease of memory and help of computation, made use of counters, or in writing of single strokes, points, or the like, each whereof was made to signify a unit, that is, some one thing of whatever kind they had occasion to reckon. Afterwards they found out the more compendious ways of making one character stand in place of several strokes or points. And, lastly, the notation of the Arabians or Indians came into use, wherein, by the repetition of a few characters or figures, and varying the signification of each figure according to the place it obtains, all numbers may be most aptly expressed; which seems to have been done in imitation of language, so that an exact analogy is observed betwixt the notation by figures and names, the nine simple

figures answering the nine first numeral names and places in the former, corresponding to denominations in the latter. And agreeably to those conditions of the simple and local value of figures were contrived methods of finding, from the given figures or marks of the parts, what figures and how placed are proper to denote the whole, or vice versa. And having found the sought figures, the same rule or analogy being observed throughout, it is easy to read them into words; and so the number becomes perfectly known. For then the number of any particular things is said to be known, when we know the name or figures (with their due arrangement) that according to the standing analogy belong to them. For, these signs being known, we can by the operations of arithmetic know the signs of any part of the particular sums signified by them; and, thus computing in signs (because of the connection established betwixt them and the distinct multitudes of things whereof one is taken for a unit), we may be able rightly to sum up, divide, and proportion the things themselves that we intend to number.

122. In arithmetic, therefore, we regard not the *things,* but the *signs,* which nevertheless are not regarded for their own sake, but because they direct us how to act with relation to things, and dispose rightly of them. Now, agreeable to what we have before observed of words in general (sec. 19, Introd.) it happens here likewise that abstract ideas are thought to be signified by numeral names or characters, while they do not suggest ideas of particular things to our minds. I shall not at present enter into a more particular dissertation on this subject, but only observe that it is evident from what has been said, those things which pass for abstract truths and theorems concerning numbers are in reality conversant about no object distinct from particular numerable things, except only names and characters which originally came to be considered on no other account but their being signs, or capable to represent aptly whatever particular things men had need to compute. Whence it follows that to study them for their own sake would be just as wise, and to as good purpose as if a man, neglecting the true use or original intention and subservience of language, should

spend his time in impertinent criticisms upon words, or reasonings and controversies purely verbal.

123. From numbers we proceed to speak of *extension,* which, considered as relative, is the object of geometry. The *infinite* divisibility of *finite* extension, though it is not expressly laid down either as an axiom or theorem in the elements of that science, yet is throughout the same everywhere supposed and thought to have so inseparable and essential a connection with the principles and demonstrations in geometry that mathematicians never admit it into doubt, or make the least question of it. And, as this notion is the source from whence do spring all those amusing geometrical paradoxes which have such a direct repugnancy to the plain common sense of mankind, and are admitted with so much reluctance into a mind not yet debauched by learning; so is it the principal occasion of all that nice and extreme subtlety which renders the study of mathematics so difficult and tedious. Hence, if we can make it appear that no finite extension contains innumerable parts, or is infinitely divisible, it follows that we shall at once clear the science of geometry from a great number of difficulties and contradictions which have ever been esteemed a reproach to human reason, and withal make the attainment thereof a business of much less time and pains than it hitherto has been.

124. Every particular finite extension which may possibly be the object of our thought is an *idea* existing only in the mind, and consequently each part thereof must be perceived. If, therefore, I cannot perceive innumerable parts in any finite extension that I consider, it is certain they are not contained in it; but it is evident that I cannot distinguish innumerable parts in any particular line, surface, or solid, which I either perceive by sense, or figure to myself in my mind: wherefore I conclude they are not contained in it. Nothing can be plainer to me than that the extensions I have in view are no other than my own ideas; and it is no less plain that I cannot resolve any one of my ideas into an infinite number of other ideas, that is, that they are not infinitely divisible. If by "finite extension" be meant something distinct from a finite idea, I declare

I do not know what that is, and so cannot affirm or deny anything of it. But if the terms "extension," "parts," and the like, are taken in any sense conceivable, that is, for ideas, then to say a finite quantity or extension consists of parts infinite in number is so manifest a contradiction that everyone at first sight acknowledges it to be so; and it is impossible it should ever gain the assent of any reasonable creature who is not brought to it by gentle and slow degrees, as a converted gentile to the belief of transubstantiation. Ancient and rooted prejudices do often pass into principles; and those propositions which once obtain the force and credit of a *principle* are not only themselves, but likewise whatever is deducible from them, thought privileged from all examination. And there is no absurdity so gross which, by this means, the mind of man may not be prepared to swallow.

125. He whose understanding is prepossessed with the doctrine of abstract general ideas may be persuaded that (whatever be thought of the ideas of sense) extension in *abstract* is infinitely divisible. And one who thinks the objects of sense exist without the mind will perhaps in virtue thereof be brought to admit that a line but an inch long may contain innumerable parts—really existing, though too small to be discerned. These errors are grafted as well in the minds of geometricians as of other men, and have a like influence on their reasonings; and it were no difficult thing to show how the arguments from geometry made use of to support the infinite divisibility of extension are bottomed on them. At present we shall only observe in general whence it is that the mathematicians are all so fond and tenacious of this doctrine.

126. It has been observed in another place that the theorems and demonstrations in geometry are conversant about universal ideas (sec. 15, Introd.); where it is explained in what sense this ought to be understood, to wit, that the particular lines and figures included in the diagram are supposed to stand for innumerable others of different sizes; or, in other words, the geometer considers them abstracting from their magnitude—which does not imply that he forms an abstract idea, but only that he cares not what the particular magni-

tude is, whether great or small, but looks on that as a thing indifferent to the demonstration. Hence it follows that a line in the scheme but an inch long must be spoken of as though it contained ten thousand parts, since it is regarded not in itself, but as it is universal; and it is universal only in its signification, whereby it represents innumerable lines greater than itself, in which may be distinguished ten thousand parts or more, though there may not be above an inch in it. After this manner, the properties of the lines signified are (by a very usual figure) transferred to the sign, and thence, through mistake, thought to appertain to it considered in its own nature.

127. Because there is no number of parts so great but it is possible there may be a line containing more, the inch-line is said to contain parts more than any assignable number; which is true, not of the inch taken absolutely, but only for the things signified by it. But men, not retaining that distinction in their thoughts, slide into a belief that the small particular line described in paper contains in itself parts innumerable. There is no such thing as the ten thousandth part of an inch; but there is of a mile or diameter of the earth, which may be signified by that inch. When therefore I delineate a triangle on paper, and take one side not above an inch, for example, in length to be the radius, this I consider as divided into ten thousand or one hundred thousand parts or more; for, though the ten thousandth part of that line considered in itself is nothing at all, and consequently may be neglected without any error or inconvenience, yet these described lines, being only marks standing for greater quantities, whereof it may be the ten thousandth part is very considerable, it follows that, to prevent notable errors in practice, the radius must be taken of ten thousand parts or more.

128. From what has been said the reason is plain why, to the end any theorem may become universal in its use, It is necessary we speak of the lines described on paper as though they contained parts which really they do not. In doing of which, if we examine the matter thoroughly, we shall perhaps discover that we cannot conceive an inch itself as consisting of, or being divisible into, a thousand parts, but only some other line which is far greater than an inch, and represented by it; and that when we say a line is "infinitely divisible" we must mean a line which is infinitely great. What we have here observed seems to be the chief cause why to suppose the infinite divisibility of finite extension has been thought necessary in geometry.

129. The several absurdities and contradictions which flowed from this false principle might, one would think, have been esteemed so many demonstrations against it. But, by I know not what logic, it is held that proofs a posteriori are not to be admitted against propositions relating to infinity, as though it were not impossible even for an infinite mind to reconcile contradictions; or as if anything absurd and repugnant could have a necessary connection with truth or flow from it. But whoever considers the weakness of this pretense will think it was contrived on purpose to humor the laziness of the mind which had rather acquiese in an indolent skepticism than be at the pains to go through with a severe examination of those principles it has ever embraced for true.

130. Of late the speculations about infinites have run so high, and grown to such strange notions, as have occasioned no small scruples and disputes among the geometers of the present age. Some there are of great note who, not content with holding that finite lines may be divided into an infinite number of parts, do yet further maintain that each of those infinitesimals is itself subdivisible into an infinity of other parts or infinitesimals of a second order, and so on ad infinitum. These, I say, assert there are infinitesimals of infinitesimals of infinitesimals, without ever coming to an end: so that according to them an inch does not barely contain an infinite number of parts, but an infinity of an infinity of an infinity ad infinitum of parts. Others there be who hold all orders of infinitesimals below the first to be nothing at all; thinking it with good reason absurd to imagine there is any positive quantity or part of extension which, though multiplied infinitely, can ever equal the smallest given extension. And yet on the other hand it seems no less absurd to think the square, cube, or other power of a positive

real root should itself be nothing at all; which they who hold infinitesimals of the first order, denying all of the subsequent orders, are obliged to maintain.

131. Have we not therefore reason to conclude that they are *both* in the wrong, and that there is in effect no such thing as parts infinitely small, or an infinite number of parts contained in any finite quantity? But you will say that if this doctrine obtains it will follow that the very foundations of geometry are destroyed, and those great men who have raised that science to so astonishing a height have been all the while building a castle in the air. To this it may be replied that whatever is useful in geometry and promotes the benefit of human life does still remain firm and unshaken on our principles; that science considered as practical will rather receive advantage than any prejudice from what has been said. But to set this in a due light may be the suject of a distinct inquiry. For the rest, though it should follow that some of the more intricate and subtle parts of speculative mathematics may be pared off without any prejudice to truth, yet I do not see what damage will be thence derived to mankind. On the contrary, it were highly to be wished that men of great abilities and obstinate application would draw off their thoughts from those amusements, and employ them in the study of such things as lie nearer the concerns of life, or have a more direct influence on the manners.

132. If it be said that several theorems undoubtedly true are discovered by methods in which infinitesimals are made use of, which could never have been if their existence included a contradiction in it, I answer that upon a thorough examination it will not be found that in any instance it is necessary to make use of or conceive infinitesimal parts of finite lines, or even quantities less than the *minimum sensible;* nay, it will be evident this is never done, it being impossible.

133. By what we have premised it is plain that very numerous and important errors have taken their rise from those false principles which were impugned in the foregoing parts of this treatise; and the opposites of those erroneous tenets at the same time appear to be most fruitful principles, from whence do flow innumerable consequences highly advantageous to true philosophy, as well as to religion. Particularly *matter,* or *the absolute existence of corporeal objects,* has been shown to be that wherein the most avowed and pernicious enemies of all knowledge, whether human or divine, have ever placed their chief strength and confidence. And surely, if by distinguishing the real existence of unthinking things from their being perceived, and allowing them a subsistence of their own out of the minds of spirits, no one thing is explained in nature, but, on the contrary, a great many inexplicble difficulties arise; if the supposition of matter is barely precarious, as not being grounded on so much as one single reason; if its consequences cannot endure the light of examination and free inquiry, but screen themselves under the dark and general pretense of "infinites being incomprehensible"; if withal the removal of this *matter* be not attended with the least evil consequence; if it be not even missed in the world, but everything as well, nay, much easier conceived without it; if, lastly, both skeptics and atheists are forever silenced upon supposing only spirits and ideas, and this scheme of things is perfectly agreeable both to reason and religion: methinks we may expect it should be admitted and firmly embraced, though it were proposed only as a *hypothesis,* and the existence of matter had been allowed possible, which yet I think we have evidently demonstrated that it is not.

134. True it is that, in consequence of the foregoing principles, several disputes and speculations which are esteemed no mean parts of learning are rejected as useless. But, how great a prejudice soever against our notions this may give to those who have already been deeply engaged and made large advances in studies of that nature, yet by others we hope it will not be thought any just ground of dislike to the principles and tenets herein laid down that they abridge the labor of study, and make human sciences more clear, compendious, and attainable than they were before.

135. Having dispatched what we intended to say concerning the knowledge of *ideas,* the method we proposed leads us in the next place to treat of *spirits*—with regard to which, per-

haps, human knowledge is not so deficient as is vulgarly imagined. The great reason that is assigned for our being thought ignorant of the nature of spirits is our not having an *idea* of it. But surely it ought not to be looked on as a defect in a human understanding that it does not perceive the idea of spirit if it is manifestly impossible there should be any such idea. And this, if I mistake not, has been demonstrated in section 27; to which I shall here add that a spirit has been shown to be the only substance or support wherein the unthinking beings or ideas can exist; but that this *substance* which supports or perceives ideas should itself be an idea or like an idea is evidently absurd.

136. It will perhaps be said that we want a sense (as some have imagined) proper to know substances withal, which, if we had, we might know our own soul as we do a triangle. To this I answer, that, in case we had a new sense bestowed upon us, we could only receive thereby some new sensations or ideas of sense. But I believe nobody will say that what he means by the terms "soul" and "substance" is only some particular sort of idea or sensation. We may therefore infer, that all things duly considered, it is not more reasonable to think our faculties defective in that they do not furnish us with an idea of spirit or active thinking substance than it would be if we should blame them for not being able to comprehend a *round square*.

137. From the opinion that spirits are to be known after the manner of an idea or sensation have risen many absurd and heterodox tenets, and much skepticism about the nature of the soul. It is even probable that this opinion may have produced a doubt in some whether they had any soul at all distinct from their body, since upon inquiry they could not find they had an idea of it. That an *idea* which is inactive, and the existence whereof consists in being perceived, should be the image or likeness of an agent subsisting by itself seems to need no other refutation than barely attending to what is meant by those words. But perhaps you will say that though an idea cannot resemble a spirit in its thinking, acting, or subsisting by itself, yet it may in some other respects; and it is not necessary that an idea or image be in all respects like the original.

138. I answer, if it does not in those mentioned, it is impossible it should represent it in any other thing. Do but leave out the power of willing, thinking, and perceiving ideas, and there remains nothing else wherein the idea can be like a spirit. For by the word "spirit" we mean only that which thinks, wills, and perceives; this, and this alone, constitutes the signification of that term. If therefore it is impossible that any degree of those powers should be represented in an idea, it is evident there can be no idea of a spirit.

139. But it will be objected that, if there is no idea signified by the terms "soul," "spirit," and "substance," they are wholly insignificant or have no meaning in them. I answer, those words do mean or signify a real thing, which is neither an idea nor like an idea, but that which perceives ideas, and wills, and reasons about them. What I am myself, that which I denote by the term "I," is the same with what is meant by "soul," or "spiritual substance." If it be said that this is only quarreling at a word, and that, since the immediate significations of other names are by common consent called "ideas," no reason can be assigned why that which is signified by the name "spirit" or "soul" may not partake in the same appellation. I answer, all the unthinking objects of the mind agree in that they are entirely passive, and their existence consists only in being perceived; whereas a soul or spirit is an active being whose existence consists, not in being perceived, but in perceiving ideas and thinking. It is therefore necessary, in order to prevent equivocation and confounding natures perfectly disagreeing and unlike, that we distinguish between *spirit* and *idea*. See sec. 27.

140. In a large sense, indeed, we may be said to have an idea [or rather a notion] of *spirit;* that is, we understand the meaning of the word, otherwise we could not affirm or deny anything of it. Moreover, as we conceive the ideas that are in the minds of other spirits by means of our own, which we suppose to be resemblances of them, so we know other spirits by means of our own soul—which in that sense is the image or idea of them; it having a like respect to other spirits that blueness or heat by me perceived has to those ideas perceived by another.

141. It must not be supposed that they who assert the natural immortality of the soul are of opinion that it is absolutely incapable of annihilation even by the infinite power of the Creator who first gave it being, but only that it is not liable to be broken or dissolved by the ordinary laws of nature or motion. They indeed who hold the soul of man to be only a thin vital flame, or system of animal spirits, make it perishing and corruptible as the body; since there is nothing more easily dissipated than such a being, which it is naturally impossible should survive the ruin of the tabernacle wherein it is enclosed. And this notion has been greedily embraced and cherished by the worst part of mankind, as the most effectual antidote against all impressions of virtue and religion. But it has been made evident that bodies, of what frame or texture soever, are barely passive ideas in the mind, which is more distant and heterogeneous from them than light is from darkness. We have shown that the soul is indivisible, incorporeal, unextended, and it is consequently incorruptible. Nothing can be plainer than that the motions, changes, decays, and dissolutions which we hourly see befall natural bodies (and which is what we mean by "the course of nature") cannot possibly affect an active, simple, uncompounded substance; such a being therefore is indissoluble by the force of nature; that is to say, the soul of man is naturally immortal.

142. After what has been said, it is, I suppose, plain that our souls are not to be known in the same manner as senseless, inactive objects, or by way of *idea*. *Spirits* and *ideas* are things so wholly different that when we say "they exist," "they are known," or the like, these words must not be thought to signify anything common to both natures. There is nothing alike or common in them; and to expect that by any multiplication or enlargement of our faculties we may be enabled to know a spirit as we do a triangle seems as absurd as if we should hope to see a sound. This is inculcated because I imagine it may be of moment toward clearing several important questions and preventing some very dangerous errors concerning the nature of the soul. We may not, I think, strictly be said to have an *idea*

of an active being, or of an action, although we may be said to have a *notion* of them. I have some knowledge or notion of my mind, and its acts about ideas, inasmuch as I know or understand what is meant by those words. What I know, that I have some notion of. I will not say that the terms "idea" and "notion" may not be used convertibly, if the world will have it so; but yet it conduces to clearness and propriety that we distinguish things very different by different names. It is also to be remarked that, all relations including an act of the mind, we cannot so properly be said to have an idea, but rather a notion of the relations or habitudes between things. But if, in the modern way, the word "idea" is extended to spirits, and relations, and acts, this is, after all, an affair of verbal concern.

143. It will not be amiss to add that the doctrine of *abstract ideas* has had no small share in rendering those sciences intricate and obscure which are particularly conversant about spiritual things. Men have imagined they could frame abstract notions of the powers and acts of the mind and consider them prescinded as well from the mind or spirit itself as from their respective objects and effects. Hence a great number of dark and ambiguous terms, presumed to stand for abstract notions, have been introduced into metaphysics and morality, and from these have grown infinite distractions and disputes amongst the learned.

144. But nothing seems more to have contributed toward engaging men in controversies and mistakes with regard to the nature and operations of the mind than the being used to speak of those things in terms borrowed from sensible ideas. For example, the will is termed "the motion of the soul": this infuses a belief that the mind of man is as a ball in motion, impelled and determined by the objects of sense, as necessarily as that is by the stroke of a racket. Hence arise endless scruples and errors of dangerous consequence in morality. All which, I doubt not, may be cleared, and truth appear plain, uniform, and consistent, could but philosophers be prevailed on to retire into themselves, and attentively consider their own meaning.

145. From what has been said it is plain that we cannot know the existence of other spirits otherwise than by their operations, or the ideas by them excited in us. I perceive several motions, changes, and combinations of ideas that inform me there are certain particular agents, like myself, which accompany them and concur in their production. Hence, the knowledge I have of other spirits is not immediate, as is the knowledge of my ideas, but depending on the intervention of ideas, by me referred to agents or spirits distinct from myself, as effects or concomitant signs.

146. But though there be some things which convince us human agents are concerned in producing them, yet it is evident to everyone that those things which are called "the works of nature," that is, the far greater part of the ideas or sensations perceived by us, are not produced by, or dependent on, the wills of men. There is therefore some other spirit that causes them; since it is repugnant that they should subsist by themselves. See sec. 29. But, if we attentively consider the constant regularity, order, and concatenation of natural things, the surprising magnificence, beauty, and perfection of the larger, and the exquisite contrivance of the smaller parts of the creation, together with the exact harmony and correspondence of the whole, but above all the never-enough-admired laws of pain and pleasure, and the instincts or natural inclinations, appetites, and passions of animals; I say if we consider all these things, and at the same time attend to the meaning and import of the attributes: one, eternal, infinitely wise, good, and perfect, we shall clearly perceive that they belong to the aforesaid spirit, "who works all in all," and "by whom all things consist."

147. Hence it is evident that God is known as certainly and immediately as any other mind or spirit whatsoever distinct from ourselves. We may even assert that the existence of God is far more evidently perceived than the existence of men; because the effects of nature are infinitely more numerous and considerable than those ascribed to human agents. There is not any one mark that denotes a man, or effect produced by him, which does not more strongly evince the being of that spirit who is the Author of Nature. For it is evident that in affecting other persons the will of man has no other object than barely the motion of the limbs of his body; but that such a motion should be attended by, or excite any idea in the mind of another, depends wholly on the will of the Creator. He alone it is who, "upholding all things by the word of his power," maintains that intercourse between spirits whereby they are able to perceive the existence of each other. And yet this pure and clear light which enlightens everyone is itself invisible.

148. It seems to be a general pretense of the unthinking herd that they cannot *see* God. Could we but see him, say they, as we see a man, we should believe that he is, and, believing, obey his commands. But alas, we need only open our eyes to see the sovereign Lord of all things, with a more full and clear view than we do any one of our fellow creatures. Not that I imagine we see God (as some will have it) by a direct and immediate view; or see corporeal things, not by themselves, but by seeing that which represents them in the essence of God, which doctrine is, I must confess, to me incomprehensible. But I shall explain my meaning: a human spirit or person is not perceived by sense, as not being an idea; when therefore we see the color, size, figure, and motions of a man, we perceive only certain sensations or ideas excited in our own minds; and these being exhibited to our view in sundry distinct collections, serve to mark out onto us the existence of finite and created spirits like ourselves. Hence it is plain we do not see a man—if by "man" is meant that which lives, moves, perceives, and thinks as we do—but only such a certain collection of ideas as directs us to think there is a distinct principle of thought and motion, like to ourselves, accompanying and represented by it. And after the same manner we see God: all the difference is that, whereas some one finite and narrow assemblage of ideas denotes a particular human mind, whithersoever we direct our view, we do at all times and in all places perceive manifest tokens of the divinity: everything we see, hear, feel, or anywise perceive by sense, being a sign or effect of the power

of God; as is our perception of those very motions which are produced by men.

149. It is therefore plain that nothing can be more evident to anyone that is capable of the least reflection than of existence of God, or a spirit who is intimately present to our minds, producing in them all that variety of ideas or sensations which continually affect us, on whom we have an absolute and entire dependence, in short "in whom we live, and move, and have our being." That the discovery of this great truth, which lies so near and obvious to the mind, should be attained to by the reason of so very few, is a sad instance of the stupidity and inattention of men who, though they are surrounded with such clear manifestations of the Deity, are yet so little affected by them that they seem, as it were, blinded with excess of light.

150. But you will say, has nature no share in the production of natural things, and must they be all ascribed to the immediate and sole operation of God? I answer, if by "nature" is meant only the visible *series* of effects or sensations imprinted on our minds, according to certain fixed and general laws, then it is plain that nature, taken in this sense, cannot produce anything at all. But, if by "nature" is meant some being distinct from God, as well as from the laws of nature, and things perceived by sense, I must confess that word is to me an empty sound without any intelligible meaning annexed to it. Nature, in this acceptation, is a vain chimera, introduced by these heathens who had not just notions of the omnipresence and infinite perfection of God. But it is more unaccountable that it should be received among Christians, professing belief in the Holy Scriptures, which constantly ascribe those effects to the immediate hand of God that heathen philosophers are wont to impute to nature. "The Lord he causeth the vapours to ascend; he maketh lightnings with rain; he bringeth forth the wind out of his treasures." Jerem. 10:13. "He turneth the shadow of death into the morning, and maketh the day dark with night." Amos 5:8. "He visiteth the earth, and maketh it soft with showers: He blesseth the springing thereof, and crowneth the year with his goodness; so that the pastures are clothed with flocks, and the valleys are covered over with corn." See Psalm 65. But notwithstanding that this is the constant language of Scripture, yet we have I know not what aversion from believing that God concerns himself so nearly in our affairs. Fain would we suppose him at a great distance off, and substitute some blind, unthinking deputy in his stead, though (if we may believe Saint Paul) "he be not far from every one of us."

151. It will, I doubt not, be objected that the slow and gradual methods observed in the production of natural things do not seem to have for their cause the immediate hand of an Almighty Agent. Besides, monsters, untimely births, fruits blasted in the blossom, rains failing in desert places, miseries incident to human life, and the like, are so many arguments that the whole frame of nature is not immediately actuated and superintended by a spirit of infinite wisdom and goodness. But the answer to this objection is in a good measure plain from sec. 62; it being visible that the aforesaid methods of nature are absolutely necessary, in order to working by the most simple and general rules, and after a steady and consistent manner; which argues both the wisdom and goodness of God. Such is the artificial contrivance of this mighty machine of nature that, whilst its motions and various phenomena strike on our senses, the hand which actuates the whole is itself unperceivable to men of flesh and blood. "Verily" (says the prophet) "thou art a God that hidest thyself." Isiah 45:15. But, though God conceal himself from the eyes of the sensual and lazy, who will not be at the least expense of thought, yet to be an unbiased and attentive mind nothing can be more plainly legible than the intimate presence of an all-wise Spirit, who fashions, regulates, and sustains the whole system of being. It is clear, from what we have elsewhere observed, that the operating according to general and stated laws is so necessary for our guidance in the affairs of life, and letting us into the secret of nature, that without it all reach and compass of thought, all human sagacity and design, could serve to no manner of purpose; it were even impossible there should be any such faculties or powers in

the mind. See sec. 31. Which one consideration abundantly outbalances whatever particular inconveniences may thence arise.

152. We should further consider that the very blemishes and defects of nature are not without their use, in that they make an agreeable sort of variety and augment the beauty of the rest of the creation, as shades in a picture serve to set off the brighter and more enlightened parts. We would likewise do well to examine whether our taxing the waste of seeds and embryos, and accidental destruction of plants and animals, before they come to full maturity, as an imprudence in the Author of Nature, be not the effect of prejudice contracted by our familiarity with impotent and saving mortals. In man indeed a thrifty management of those things which he cannot procure without much pains and industry may be esteemed wisdom. But we must not imagine that the inexplicably fine machine of an animal or vegetable costs the great Creator any more pains or trouble in its production than a pebble does; nothing being more evident than that an ominipotent spirit can indifferently produce everything by a mere fiat or act of his will. Hence, it is plain that the splendid profusion of natural things should not be interpreted weakness or prodigality in the agent who produces them, but rather be looked on as an argument of the riches of his power.

153. As for the mixture of pain or uneasiness which is in the world, pursuant to the general laws of nature, and the actions of finite, imperfect spirits, this, in the state we are in at present, is indispensably necessary to our well-being. But our prospects are too narrow. We take, for instance, the idea of some one particular pain into our thoughts, and account it *evil;* whereas, if we enlarge our view, so as to comprehend the various ends, connections, and dependencies of things, on what occasions and in what proportions we are affected with pain and pleasure, the nature of human freedom, and the design with which we are put into the world; we shall be forced to acknowledge that those particular things which, considered in themselves, appear to be evil, have the nature of good, when considered as linked with the whole system of beings.

154. From what has been said, it will be manifest to any considering person, that it is merely for want of attention and comprehensiveness of mind that there are any favorers of atheism or the Manichaean heresy* to be found. Little and unreflecting souls may indeed burlesque the works of Providence the beauty and order whereof they have not capacity, or will not be at the pains to comprehend; but those who are masters of any justness and extent of thought, and are withal used to reflect, can never sufficiently admire the divine traces of wisdom and goodness that shine throughout the economy of nature. But what truth is there which shines so strongly on the mind that by an aversion of thought, a willful shutting of the eyes, we may not escape seeing it? Is it therefore to be wondered at if the generality of men, who are ever intent on business or pleasure, and little used to fix or open the eye of their mind, should not have all that conviction and evidence of the being of God which might be expected in reasonable creatures?

155. We should rather wonder that men can be found so stupid as to neglect, than that neglecting they should be unconvinced of such an evident and momentous truth. And yet it is to be feared that too many of parts and leisure, who live in Christian countries, are, merely through a supine and dreadful negligence, sunk into a sort of atheism. Since it is downright impossible that a soul pierced and enlightened with a thorough sense of the omnipresence, holiness, and justice of that Almighty Spirit should persist in a remorseless violation of his laws. We ought, therefore, earnestly to meditate and dwell on those important points; that so we may attain convic-

*A great religious movement, named after its founder, Mani of Persia, "the apostle of God," who lived 216–276 A.D. Not really a heretical movement within Christianity, but a separate religion that blended Zoroastrian, Buddhist, and Christian doctrine. Mani held that the universe is a struggle between two equal powers: light and good, versus dark and evil. Manichaeans professed themselves to be on the side of light, fighting, through asceticism, for freedom. Among its adherents were St. Augustine (in his youth) and the Albigenses in France. [ed.]

tion without all scruple "that the eyes of the Lord are in every place beholding the evil and the good; that he is with us and keepth us in alll places whither we go, and giveth us bread to eat and raiment to put on"; and that he is present and conscious to our innermost thoughts; and that we have a most absolute and immediate dependence on him. A clear view of which great truths cannot choose but fill our hearts with an awful circumspection and holy fear, which is the strongest incentive to *virtue* and the best guard against *vice*.

156. For, after all, what deserves the first place in our studies is the consideration of God and our duty; which to promote, as it was the main drift and design of my labors, so shall I esteem them altogether useless and ineffectual if, by what I have said, I cannot inspire my readers with a pious sense of the presence of God; and, having shown the falseness or vanity of those barren speculations which make the chief employment of learned men, the better dispose them to reverence and embrace the salutary truths of the Gospel, which to know and to practice is the highest perfection of human nature.

VII
David Hume

DAVID HUME (1711–1776) was born in Scotland. His family pushed him to study law, but he hated it, finding solace only in reading and writing philosophy. At the age of 28 he suffered a "nervous breakdown." After his recuperation he worked in a merchant's office in Bristol, England, but, not liking that work either, he moved to France. He spent most of his time in the same place where Descartes had gone to school, La Fleche, and there he wrote *A Treatise of Human Nature*. Three years later Hume returned to England to publish his masterpiece, but it was largely ignored. When he tried to get a teaching position in philosophy nobody would hire him; he was accused of heresy and atheism because of what he had written in the *Treatise*. So he supported himself as a tutor to a mad marquess and as a secretary, first to a general and then to an ambassador. After failing yet again in 1752 to get hired as a philosopher in Glasgow, he secured a job as head librarian at the Advocates' Library in Edinburgh. In his late forties, Hume began receiving a wider audience for his writings. By 1762, James Boswell had declared him to be "the greatest writer in Britain."

Hume had a tremendous influence on all the philosophers who came after him. Immanuel Kant said it was Hume who had awakened him from his "dogmatic slumbers." Hume influenced Auguste Compte in his development of positivism, the antitheological and antimetaphysical system of scientific knowledge, as well as Jeremy Bentham and John Stuart Mill. Hume has probably had more influence on 20th-century philosophy than any other modern philosopher.

Hume developed the empirical philosophy of Locke and Berkeley to its logical conclusion. Whereas Locke's views were tempered by common sense, often inconsistently, and Berkeley made an exception to his empiricist principles to save his notion of the self, Hume refused to make his philosophy bow to common sense and developed the first truly consistent view of empiricism. A sympathetic critic of Hume once remarked that, by making empirical philosophy self-consistent, Hume "made it incredible." Indeed, in many ways Hume is not just a skeptic but a philosophical extremist. He not only denies the existence of the self, but he provides devastating empirical analyses of many difficult concepts—such as causation, morality, space, time, and freedom—formulating skeptical objections to all inferences that go beyond immediate experience. In doing so, he argues that even impressions of the "external" senses exist only in the sensing mind, and he rejects all attempts to argue from the senses to the existence of continuing physical substances outside the mind. In pushing Berkeley's criticism of abstract ideas and general entities to their extreme, Hume dissolves the idea of a continuously existing mental substance, replacing the notion with the famous "bundle theory" of the mind. According to Hume, the mind is an aggregate, or bundle, of discrete and discontinuous experiences; the mind only seems continuous because imagination smooths out the borders, bumps, and ceaseless changes.

A Treatise of Human Nature

Book I: Of the Understanding

David Hume

Part I:
Of Ideas, Their Origin, Composition, Connexion, Abstraction, &c.

Section I:
Of the Origin of Our Ideas

All the perceptions of the human mind resolve themselves into two distinct kinds, which I shall call IMPRESSIONS and IDEAS. The difference betwixt these consists in the degrees of force and liveliness with which they strike upon the mind, and make their way into our thought or consciousness. Those perceptions, which enter with most force and violence, we may name *impressions;* and under this name I comprehend all our sensations, passions and emotions, as they make their first appearance in the soul. By *ideas* I mean the faint images of these in thinking and reasoning; such as, for instance, are all the perceptions excited by the present discourse, excepting only, those which arise from the sight and touch, and excepting the immediate pleasure or uneasiness it may occasion. I believe it will not be very necessary to employ many words in explaining this distinction. Every one of himself will readily perceive the difference betwixt feeling and thinking. The common degrees of these are easily distinguished; tho' it is not impossible but in particular instances they may very nearly approach to each other. Thus in sleep, in a fever, in madness, or in any very violent emotions of soul, our ideas may approach to our impressions: As on the other hand it sometimes happens, that our impressions are so faint and low, that we cannot distinguish them from our ideas. But notwithstanding this near resemblance in a few instances, they are in general so very different, that no-one can make a scruple to rank them under distinct heads, and assign to each a peculiar name to mark the difference.[1]

There is another division of our perceptions, which it will be convenient to observe, and which extends itself both to our impressions and ideas. This division is into SIMPLE and COMPLEX. Simple perceptions or impressions and ideas are such as admit of no distinction nor separation. The complex are the contrary to these, and may be distinguished into parts. Tho' a particular colour, taste, and smell are qualities all united together in this apple, 'tis easy to perceive they are not the same, but are at least distinguishable from each other.

Having by these divisions given an order and arrangement to our objects, we may now apply ourselves to consider with the more accuracy their qualities and relations. The first circumstance, that strikes my eye, is the great resemblance betwixt our impressions and ideas in every other particular, except their degree of force and vivacity. The one seem to be in a manner the reflexion of the other; so

---

[1] I here make use of these terms, *impression and idea*, in a sense different from what is usual, and I hope this liberty will be allowed me. Perhaps I rather restore the word, idea, to its original sense, from which Mr. *Locke* had perverted it, in making it stand for all our perceptions. By the term of impression I would not be understood to express the manner, in which our lively perceptions are produced in the soul, but merely the perceptions themselves; for which there is no particular name either in the *English* or any other language, that I know of.

SOURCE: David Hume, *A Treatise of Human Nature*. First published in 1738.

that all the perceptions of the mind are double, and appear both as impressions and ideas. When I shut my eyes and think of my chamber, the ideas I form are exact representations of the impressions I felt; nor is there any circumstance of the one, which is not to be found in the other. In running over my other perceptions, I find still the same resemblance and representation. Ideas and impressions appear always to correspond to each other. This circumstance seems to me remarkable, and engages my attention for a moment.

Upon a more accurate survey I find I have been carried away too far by the first appearance, and that I must make use of the distinction of perceptions into *simple and complex,* to limit this general decision, *that all our ideas and impressions are resembling.* I observe, that many of our complex ideas never had impressions, that corresponded to them, and that many of our complex impressions never are exactly copied in ideas. I can imagine to myself such a city as the *New Jerusalem,* whose pavement is gold and walls are rubies, tho' I never saw any such. I have seen *Paris;* but shall I affirm I can form such an idea of that city, as will perfectly represent all its streets and houses in their real and just proportions?

I perceive, therefore, that tho' there is in general a great resemblance betwixt our *complex* impressions and ideas, yet the rule is not universally true, that they are exact copies of each other. We may next consider how the case stands with our *simple* perceptions. After the most accurate examination, of which I am capable, I venture to affirm, that the rule here holds without any exception, and that every simple idea has a simple impression, which resembles it; and every simple impression a correspondent idea. That idea of red, which we form in the dark, and that impression, which strikes our eyes in sun-shine, differ only in degree, not in nature. That the case is the same with all our simple impressions and ideas, 'tis impossible to prove by a particular enumeration of them. Every one may satisfy himself in this point by running over as many as he pleases. But if any one should deny this universal resemblance, I know no way of convincing him, but by desiring him to shew a simple impression, that has not a correspondent idea, or a simple idea, that has not a correspondent impression. If he does not answer this challenge, as 'tis certain he cannot, we may from his silence and our own observation establish our conclusion.

Thus we find, that all simple ideas and impressions resemble each other; and as the complex are formed from them, we may affirm in general, that these two species of perception are exactly correspondent. Having discover'd this relation, which requires no farther examination, I am curious to find some other of their qualities. Let us consider how they stand with regard to their existence, and which of the impressions and ideas are causes, and which effects.

The *full* examination of this question is the subject of the present treatise; and therefore we shall here content ourselves with establishing one general proposition, *That all our simple ideas in their first appearance are deriv'd from simple impressions, which are correspondent to them, and which they exactly represent.*

In seeking for phænomena to prove this proposition, I find only those of two kinds; but in each kind the phænomena are obvious, numerous, and conclusive. I first make myself certain, by a new review, of what I have already asserted, that every simple impression is attended with a correspondent idea, and every simple idea with a correspondent impression. From this constant conjunction of resembling perceptions I immediately conclude, that there is a great connexion betwixt our correspondent impressions and ideas, and that the existence of the one has a considerable influence upon that of the other. Such a constant conjunction, in such an infinite number of instances, can never arise from chance; but clearly proves a dependence of the impressions on the ideas, or of the ideas on the impressions. That I may know on which side this dependence lies, I consider the order of their *first appearance;* and find by constant experience, that the simple impressions always take the precedence of their correspondent ideas, but never appear in the contrary order. To give a child an idea of scarlet or orange, of sweet or bitter, I present the objects, or in other words, convey to him these impressions; but proceed not so absurdly, as to endeavour to produce the impressions by exciting the ideas. Our ideas upon their appearance produce not their correspondent impressions, nor do we perceive any colour, or feel any sensation merely upon thinking of them. On the other hand we find, that any impressions either of the mind or body is constantly followed by an idea, which resembles it, and is only different in the degrees of force and liveliness. The constant conjunction of our resembling perceptions, is a convincing proof, that the one are the causes of the other; and this priority of the impressions is an equal proof, that our impressions are the causes of our ideas, not our ideas of our impressions.

To confirm this I consider another plain and convincing phænomenon; which is, that where-ever by any accident the faculties, which give rise to any impressions, are obstructed in their operations, as when one is born blind or deaf; not only the impressions are lost, but also their correspondent ideas; so that there never appear in the mind the least traces of either of them. Nor is this only true, where the organs of sensation are entirely destroy'd, but likewise where they have never been put in action to produce a particular impression. We cannot form to ourselves a just idea of the taste of a pine-apple, without having actually tasted it.

There is however one contradictory phænomenon, which may prove, that 'tis not absolutely impossible for ideas to go before their correspondent impressions. I believe it will readily be allow'd, that the several distinct ideas of colours, which enter by the eyes, or those of sounds, which are convey'd by the hearing, are really different from each other, tho' at the same time resembling. Now if this be true of different colours, it must be no less so of the different shades of the same colour, that each of them produces a distinct idea, independent of the rest. For if this shou'd be deny'd, 'tis possible, by the continual gradation of shades, to run a colour insensibly into what is most remote from it; and if you will not allow any of the means to be different, you cannot without absurdity deny the extremes to be the same. Suppose therefore a person to have enjoyed his sight for thirty years, and to have become perfectly well acquainted with colours of all kinds, excepting one particular shade of blue, for instance, which it never has

been his fortune to meet with. Let all the different shades of that colour, except that single one, be plac'd before him, descending gradually from the deepest to the lightest; 'tis plain, that he will perceive a blank, where that shade is wanting, and will be sensible, that there is a greater distance in that place betwixt the contiguous colours, than in any other. Now I ask, whether 'tis possible for him, from his own imagination, to supply this deficiency, and raise up to himself the idea of that particular shade, tho' it had never been conveyed to him by his senses? I believe there are few but will be of opinion that he can; and this may serve as a proof, that the simple ideas are not always derived from the correspondent impressions; tho' the instance is so particular and singular, that 'tis scarce worth our observing, and does not merit that for it alone we should alter our general maxim.

But besides this exception, it may not be amiss to remark on this head, that the principle of the priority of impressions to ideas must be understood with another limitation, *viz.* that as our ideas are images of our impressions, so we can form secondary ideas, which are images of the primary; as appears from this very reasoning concerning them. This is not, properly speaking, an exception to the rule so much as an explanation of it. Ideas produce the images of themselves in new ideas; but as the first ideas are supposed to be derived from impressions, it still remains true, that all our simple ideas proceed either mediately or immediately from their correspondent impressions.

This then is the first principle I establish in the science of human nature; nor ought we to despise it because of the simplicity of its appearance. For 'tis remarkable, that the present question concerning the precedency of our impressions or ideas, is the same with what has made so much noise in other terms, when it has been disputed whether there be any *innate ideas*, or whether all ideas be derived from sensation and reflexion. We may observe, that in order to prove the ideas of extension and colour not to be innate, philosophers do nothing but shew, that they are conveyed by our senses. To prove the ideas of passion and desire not to be innate, they observe that we have a preceding experience of these emotions in ourselves. Now if we carefully examine these arguments, we shall find that they prove nothing but that ideas are preceded by other more lively perceptions, from which they are derived, and which they represent. I hope this clear stating of the question will remove all disputes concerning it, and will render this principle of more use in our reasonings, than it seems hitherto to have been.

Section II: Division of the Subject

Since it appears, that our simple impressions are prior to their correspondent ideas, and that the exceptions are very rare, method seems to require we should examine our impressions, before we consider our ideas. Impressions may be divided into two kinds, those of SENSATION and those of REFLEXION. The first kind arises in the soul originally, from unknown causes. The second is derived in a great measure from our ideas, and that in the following order. An impression first strikes upon the senses, and makes us perceive heat or cold, thirst or hunger, pleasure or pain of some kind or other. Of this impression there is a copy taken by the mind, which remains after the impression ceases; and this we call an idea. This idea of pleasure or pain, when it returns upon the soul, produces the new impressions of desire and aversion, hope and fear, which may properly be called impressions of reflexion, because derived from it. These again are copied by the memory and imagination, and become ideas; which perhaps in their turn give rise to other impressions and ideas. So that the impressions of reflexion are only antecedent to their correspondent ideas; but posterior to those of sensation, and deriv'd from them. The examination of our sensations belongs more to anatomists and natural philosophers than to moral; and therefore shall not at present be enter'd upon. And as the impressions of reflexion, *viz.* passions, desires, and emotions, which principally deserve our attention, arise mostly from ideas, 'twill be necessary to reverse that method, which at first sight seems most natural; and in order to explain the nature and principles of the human mind, give a particular account of ideas, before we proceed to impressions. For this reason I have here chosen to begin with ideas.

Section III: Of the Ideas of the Memory and Imagination

We find by experience, that when any impression has been present with the mind, it again makes its appearance there as an idea; and this it may do after two different ways: either when in its new appearance it retains a considerable degree of its first vivacity, and is somewhat intermediate betwixt an impression and an idea; or when it entirely loses that vivacity, and is a perfect idea. The faculty, by which we repeat our impressions in the first manner, is called the MEMORY, and the other the IMAGINATION. 'Tis evident at first sight, that the ideas of the memory are much more lively and strong than those of the imagination, and that the former faculty paints its objects in more distinct colours, than any which are employ'd by the latter. When we remember any past event, the idea of it flows in upon the mind in a forcible manner; whereas in the imagination the perception is faint and languid, and cannot without difficulty be preserv'd by the mind steddy and uniform for any considerable time. Here then is a sensible difference betwixt one species of ideas and another. But of this more fully hereafter.[2]

There is another difference betwixt these two kinds of ideas, which is no less evident, namely that tho' neither the ideas of the memory nor imagination, neither the lively nor faint ideas can make their appearance in the mind, unless their correspondent impressions have gone before to prepare the way for them, yet the imagination is not restrain'd to the same order and form with the original impressions; while the memory is in a manner ty'd down in that respect, without any power of variation.

'Tis evident, that the memory preserves the original form, in which its objects were presented, and that where-ever we depart from it in recollecting any thing, it proceeds from some defect or imperfection in that faculty.

[2]Part III, sect. v.

An historian may, perhaps, for the more convenient carrying on of his narration, relate an event before another, to which it was in fact posterior; but then he takes notice of this disorder, if he be exact; and by that means replaces the idea in its due position. 'Tis the same case in our recollection of those places and persons, with which we were formerly acquainted. The chief exercise of the memory is not to preserve the simple ideas, but their order and position. In short, this principle is supported by such a number of common and vulgar phænomena, that we may spare ourselves the trouble of insisting on it any farther.

The same evidence follows us in our second principle, *of the liberty of the imagination to transpose and change its ideas*. The fables we meet with in poems and romances put this entirely out of question. Nature there is totally confounded, and nothing mentioned but winged horses, fiery dragons, and monstrous giants. Nor will this liberty of the fancy appear strange, when we consider, that all our ideas are copy'd from our impressions, and that there are not any two impressions which are perfectly inseparable. Not to mention, that this is an evident consequence of the division of ideas into simple and complex. Where-ever the imagination perceives a difference among ideas, it can easily produce a separation.

Section IV: Of the Connexion or Association of Ideas

As all simple ideas may be separated by the imagination, and may be united again in what form it pleases, nothing wou'd be more unaccountable than the operations of that faculty, were it not guided by some universal principles, which render it, in some measure, uniform with itself in all times and places. Were ideas entirely loose and unconnected, chance alone wou'd join them; and 'tis impossible the same simple ideas should fall regularly into complex ones (as they commonly do) without some bond of union among them, some associating quality, by which one idea naturally introduces another. This uniting principle among ideas is not to be consider'd as an inseparable connexion; for that has been already excluded from the imagination: nor

yet are we to conclude, that without it the mind cannot join two ideas; for nothing is more free than that faculty: but we are only to regard it as a gentle force, which commonly prevails, and is the cause why, among other things, languages so nearly correspond to each other; nature in a manner pointing out to every one those simple ideas, which are most proper to be united into a complex one. The qualities, from which this association arises, and by which the mind is after this manner convey'd from one idea to another, are three, *viz.* RESEMBLANCE, CONTIGUITY in time or place, and CAUSE and EFFECT.

I believe it will not be very necessary to prove, that these qualities produce an association among ideas, and upon the appearance of one idea naturally introduce another. 'Tis plain, that in the course of our thinking, and in the constant revolution of our ideas, our imagination runs easily from one idea to any other that *resembles* it, and that this quality alone is to the fancy a sufficient bond and association. 'Tis likewise evident, that as the senses, in changing their objects, are necessitated to change them regularly, and take them as they lie *contiguous* to each other, the imagination must by long custom acquire the same method of thinking, and run along the parts of space and time in conceiving its objects. As to the connexion, that is made by the relation of *cause and effect*, we shall have occasion afterwards to examine it to the bottom, and therefore shall not at present insist upon it. 'Tis sufficient to observe, that there is no relation, which produces a stronger connexion in the fancy, and makes one idea more readily recall another, than the relation of cause and effect betwixt their objects.

That we may understand the full extent of these relations, we must consider, that two objects are connected together in the imagination, not only when the one is immediately resembling, contiguous to, or the cause of the other, but also when there is interposed betwixt them a third object, which bears to both of them any of these relations. This may be carried on to a great length; tho' at the same time we may observe, that each remove considerably weakens the relation. Cousins in the fourth degree are connected by *causation*, if I may be allowed to use that term; but not so closely as brothers, much less as child and parent. In general we may observe, that all the relations of blood depend upon cause and effect, and are esteemed near or remote, according to the number of connecting causes interpos'd betwixt the persons.

Of the three relations above-mention'd this of causation is the most extensive. Two objects may be consider'd as plac'd in this relation, as well when one is the cause of any of the actions or motions of the other, as when the former is the cause of the existence of the latter. For as that action or motion is nothing but the object itself, consider'd in a certain light, and as the object continues the same in all its different situations, 'tis easy to imagine how such an influence of objects upon one another may connect them in the imagination.

We may carry this farther, and remark, not only that two objects are connected by the relation of cause and effect, when the one produces a motion or any action in the other, but also when it has a power of producing it. And this we may observe to be the source of all the relations of interest and duty, by which men influence each other in society, and are plac'd in the ties of government and subordination. A master is such-a-one as by his situation, arising either from force or agreement, has a power of directing in certain particulars the actions of another, whom we call servant. A judge is one, who in all disputed cases can fix by his opinion the possession or property of any thing betwixt any members of the society. When a person is possess'd of any power, there is no more required to convert it into action, but the exertion of the will; and *that* in every case is consider'd as possible, and in many as probable; especially in the case of authority, where the obedience of the subject is a pleasure and advantage to the superior.

These are therefore the principles of union or cohesion among our simple ideas, and in the imagination supply the place of that inseparable connexion, by which they are united in our memory. Here is a kind of ATTRACTION, which in the mental world will be found to have as extraordinary effects as in the natural, and to shew itself in as many and as various forms. Its effects are every where con-

spicuous; but as to its causes, they are mostly unknown, and must be resolv'd into *original* qualities of human nature, which I pretend not to explain. Nothing is more requisite for a true philosopher, than to restrain the intemperate desire of searching into causes, and having establish'd any doctrine upon a sufficient number of experiments, rest contented with that, when he sees a farther examination would lead him into obscure and uncertain speculations. In that case his enquiry wou'd be much better employ'd in examining the effects than the causes of his principle.

Amongst the effects of this union or association of ideas, there are none more remarkable, than those complex ideas, which are the common subjects of our thoughts and reasoning, and generally arise from some principle of union among our simple ideas. These complex ideas may be divided into *Relations, Modes,* and *Substances.* We shall briefly examine each of these in order, and shall subjoin some considerations concerning our *general* and *particular* ideas, before we leave the present subject, which may be consider'd as the elements of this philosophy.

Section V: Of Relations

The word RELATION is commonly used in two senses considerably different from each other. Either for that quality, by which two ideas are connected together in the imagination, and the one naturally introduces the other, after the manner above-explained; or for that particular circumstance, in which, even upon the arbitrary union of two ideas in the fancy, we may think proper to compare them. In common language the former is always the sense, in which we use the word, relation; and 'tis only in philosophy, that we extend it to mean any particular subject of comparison, without a connecting principle. Thus distance will be allowed by philosophers to be a true relation, because we acquire an idea of it by the comparing of objects: But in a common way we say, *that nothing can be more distant than such or such things from each other, nothing can have less relation;* as if distance and relation were incompatible.

It may perhaps be esteemed an endless task

to enumerate all those qualities, which make objects admit of comparison, and by which the ideas of *philosophical* relation are produced. But if we diligently consider them, we shall find that without difficulty they may be compriz'd under seven general heads, which may be considered as the sources of all *philosophical* relation.

1. The first is *resemblance:* And this is a relation, without which no philosophical relation can exist; since no objects will admit of comparison, but what have some degree of resemblance. But tho' resemblance be necessary to all philosophical relation, it does not follow, that it always produces a connexion or association of ideas. When a quality becomes very general, and is common to a great many individuals, it leads not the mind directly to any one of them; but by presenting at once too great a choice, does thereby prevent the imagination from fixing on any single object.

2. *Identity* may be esteem'd a second species of relation. This relation I here consider as apply'd in its strictest sense to constant and unchangeable objects; without examining the nature and foundation of personal identity, which shall find its place afterwards. Of all relations the most universal is that of identity, being common to every being, whose existence has any duration.

3. After identity the most universal and comprehensive relations are those of *Space* and *Time,* which are the sources of an infinite number of comparisons, such as *distant, contiguous, above, below, before, after,* &c.

4. All those objects, which admit of *quantity,* or *number,* may be compar'd in that particular; which is another very fertile source of relation.

5. When any two objects possess the same *quality* in common, the *degrees,* in which they possess it, form a fifth species of relation. Thus of two objects, which are both heavy, the one may be either of greater, or less weight than with the other. Two colours, that are of the same kind, may yet be of different shades, and in that respect admit of comparison.

6. The relation of *contrariety* may at first sight be regarded as an exception to the rule, *that no relation of any kind can subsist without some degree of resemblance.* But let us consider, that no two ideas are in themselves contrary, except those of existence and non-existence, which are plainly resembling, as implying both of them an idea of the object; tho' the latter excludes the object from all times and places, in which it is supposed not to exist.

7. All other objects, such as fire and water, heat, and cold, are only found to be contrary from experience, and from the contrariety of their *causes* or *effects;* which relation of cause and effect is a seventh philosophical relation, as well as a natural one. The resemblance implied in this relation, shall be explain'd afterwards.

It might naturally be expected, that I should join *difference* to the other relations. But that I consider rather as a negation of relation, than as any thing real or positive. Difference is of two kinds as oppos'd either to identity or resemblance. The first is called a difference of *number;* the other of *kind.*

Section VI: Of Modes and Substances

I wou'd fain ask those philosophers, who found so much of their reasonings on the distinction of substance and accident, and imagine we have clear ideas of each, whether the idea of *substance* be deriv'd from the impressions of sensation or reflexion? If it be convey'd to us by our senses, I ask, which of them; and after what manner? If it be perceiv'd by the eyes, it must be a colour; if by the ears, a sound; if by the palate, a taste; and so of the other senses. But I believe none will assert, that substance is either a colour, or sound, or a taste. The idea of substance must therefore be deriv'd from an impression of reflexion, if it really exist. But the impressions of reflexion resolve themselves into our passions and emotions; none of which can possibly represent a substance. We have therefore no idea of substance, distinct from that of a collection of particular qualities, nor have we any other meaning when we either talk or reason concerning it.

The idea of a substance as well as that of a mode, is nothing but a collection of simple ideas, that are united by the imagination, and have a particular name assigned them, by which we are able to recall, either to ourselves or others, that collection. But the difference betwixt these ideas consists in this, that the particular qualities, which form a substance, are commonly refer'd to an unknown *something,* in which they are supposed to inhere; or granting this fiction should not take place, are at least supposed to be closely and inseparably connected by the relations of contiguity and causation. The effect of this is, that whatever new simple quality we discover to have the same connexion with the rest, we immediately comprehend it among them, even tho' it did not enter into the first conception of the substance. Thus our idea of gold may at first be a yellow colour, weight, malleableness, fusibility; but upon the discovery of its dissolubility in *aqua regia,* we join that to the other qualities, and suppose it to belong to the substance as much as if its idea had from the beginning made a part of the compound one. The principle of union being regarded as the chief part of the complex idea, gives entrance to whatever quality afterwards occurs, and is equally comprehended by it, as are the others, which first presented themselves.

That this cannot take place in modes, is evident from considering their nature. The simple ideas of which modes are formed, either represent qualities, which are not united by contiguity and causation, but are dispers'd in different subjects; or if they be all united together, the uniting principle is not regarded as the foundation of the complex idea. The idea of a dance is an instance of the first kind of modes; that of beauty of the second. The reason is obvious, why such complex ideas cannot receive any new idea, without changing the name, which distinguishes the mode.

Section VII: Of Abstract Ideas

A very material question has been started concerning *abstract* or *general* ideas, *whether they be general or particular in the mind's conception of them.* A great philosopher[3] has disputed the receiv'd opinion in this particular, and has asserted, that all general ideas are nothing but particular ones, annexed to a certain term,

which gives them a more extensive signification, and makes them recall upon occasion other individuals, which are similar to them. As I look upon this to be one of the greatest and most valuable discoveries that has been made of late years in the republic of letters, I shall here endeavour to confirm it by some arguments, which I hope will put it beyond all doubt and controversy.

'Tis evident, that in forming most of our general ideas, if not all of them, we abstract from every particular degree of quantity and quality, and that an object ceases not to be of any particular species on account of every small alteration in its extension, duration and other properties. It may therefore be thought, that here is a plain dilemma, that decides concerning the nature of those abstract ideas, which have afforded so much speculation to philosophers. The abstract idea of a man represents men of all sizes and all qualities; which 'tis concluded it cannot do, but either by representing at once all possible sizes and all possible qualities, or by representing no particular one at all. Now it having been esteemed absurd to defend the former proposition, as implying an infinite capacity in the mind, it has been commonly infer'd in favour of the latter; and our abstract ideas have been suppos'd to represent no particular degree either of quantity or quality. But that this inference is erroneous, I shall endeavour to make appear, *first,* by proving, that 'tis utterly impossible to conceive any quantity or quality, without forming a precise notion of its degrees: And *secondly* by showing, that tho' the capacity of the mind be not infinite, yet we can at once form a notion of all possible degrees of quantity and quality, in such a manner at least, as, however imperfect, may serve all the purposes of reflexion and conversation.

To begin with the first proposition, *that the mind cannot form any notion of quantity or quality without forming a precise notion of degrees of each;* we may prove this by the three following arguments. First, We have observ'd, that whatever objects are different are distinguishable, and that whatever objects are distinguishable are separable by the thought and imagination. And we may here add, that these propositions are equally true in the *inverse,* and that whatev-

---

[3]Dr. *Berkeley.*

er objects are separable are also distinguishable, and that whatever objects are distinguishable are also different. For how is it possible we can separate what is not distinguishable, or distinguish what is not different? In order therefore to know, whether abstraction implies a separation, we need only consider it in this view, and examine, whether all the circumstances, which we abstract from in our general ideas, be such as are distinguishable and different from those, which we retain as essential parts of them. But 'tis evident at first sight, that the precise length of a line is not different nor distinguishable from the line itself; nor the precise degree of any quality from the quality. These ideas, therefore, admit no more of separation than they do of distinction and difference. They are consequently conjoined with each other in the conception; and the general idea of a line, notwithstanding all our abstractions and refinements, has in its appearance in the mind a precise degree of quantity and quality; however it may be made to represent others, which have different degrees of both.

Secondly, 'tis confest, that no object can appear to the senses; or in other words, that no impression can become present to the mind, without being determin'd in its degrees both of quantity and quality. The confusion, in which impressions are sometimes involv'd, proceeds only from their faintness and unsteadiness, not from any capacity in the mind to receive any impression, which in its real existence has no particular degree nor proportion. That is a contradiction in terms; and even implies the flattest of all contradictions, *viz.* that 'tis possible for the same thing both to be and not to be.

Now since all ideas are deriv'd from impressions, and are nothing but copies and representations of them, whatever is true of the one must be acknowledg'd concerning the other. Impressions and ideas differ only in their strength and vivacity. The foregoing conclusion is not founded on any particular degree of vivacity. It cannot therefore be affected by any variation in that particular. An idea is a weaker impression; and as a strong impression must necessarily have a determinate quantity and quality, the case must

be the same with its copy or representative.

Thirdly, 'tis a principle generally receiv'd in philosophy, that every thing in nature is individual, and that 'tis utterly absurd to suppose a triangle really existent, which has no precise proportion of sides and angles. If this therefore be absurd in *fact and reality*, it must also be absurd *in idea;* since nothing of which we can form a clear and distinct idea is absurd and impossible. But to form the idea of an object, and to form an idea simply is the same thing; the reference of the idea to an object being an extraneous denomination, of which in itself it bears no mark or character. Now as 'tis impossible to form an idea of an object, that is possest of quantity and quality, and yet is possest of no precise degree of either; it follows, that there is an equal impossibility of forming an idea, that is not limited and confin'd in both these particulars. Abstract ideas are therefore in themselves individual, however they may become general in their representation. The image in the mind is only that of a particular object, tho' the application of it in our reasoning be the same, as if it were universal.

This application of ideas beyond their nature proceeds from our collecting all their possible degrees of quantity and quality in such an imperfect manner as may serve the purposes of life, which is the second proposition I propos'd to explain. When we have found a resemblance among several objects, that often occur to us, we apply the same name to all of them, whatever differences we may observe in the degrees of their quantity and quality, and whatever other differences may appear among them. After we have acquired a custom of this kind, the hearing of that name revives the idea of one of these objects, and makes the imagination conceive it with all its particular circumstances and proportions. But as the same word is suppos'd to have been frequently applied to other individuals, that are different in many respects from that idea, which is immediately present to the mind; the word not being able to revive the idea of all these individuals, only touches the soul, if I may be allow'd so to speak, and revives that custom, which we have acquir'd by surveying them. They are not really and in fact present to the mind, but only in power; nor do we draw them all out distinctly in the imagination, but keep ourselves in a readiness to survey any of them, as we may be prompted by a present design or necessity. The word raises up an individual idea, along with a certain custom; and that custom produces any other individual one, for which we may have occasion. But as the production of all the ideas, to which the name may be apply'd, is in most cases impossible, we abridge that work by a more partial consideration, and find but few inconveniences to arise in our reasoning from that abridgment.

For this is one of the most extraordinary circumstances in the present affair, that after the mind has produc'd an individual idea, upon which we reason, the attendant custom, reviv'd by the general or abstract term, readily suggests any other individual, if by chance we form any reasoning, that agrees not with it. Thus shou'd we mention the word, triangle, and form the idea of a particular equilateral one to correspond to it, and shou'd we afterwards assert, *that the three angles of a triangle are equal to each other,* the other individuals of a scalenum and isoceles, which we overlook'd at first, immediately crowd in upon us, and make us perceive the falshood of this proposition, tho' it be true with relation to that idea, which we had form'd. If the mind suggests not always these ideas upon occasion, it proceeds from some imperfection in its faculties; and such a one as is often the source of false reasoning and sophistry. But this is principally the case with those ideas which are abstruse and compounded. On other occasions the custom is more entire, and 'tis seldom we run into such errors.

Nay so entire is the custom, that the very same idea may be annext to several different words, and may be employ'd in different reasonings, without any danger of mistake. Thus the idea of an equilateral triangle of an inch perpendicular may serve us in talking of a figure, of a rectilineal figure, of a regular figure, of a triangle, and of an equilateral triangle. All these terms, therefore, are in this case attended with the same idea; but as they are wont to be apply'd in a greater or lesser compass, they excite their particular habits, and

thereby keep the mind in a readiness to observe, that no conclusion be form'd contrary to any ideas, which are usually compriz'd under them.

Before those habits have become entirely perfect, perhaps the mind may not be content with forming the idea of only one individual, but may run over several, in order to make itself comprehend its own meaning, and the compass of that collection, which it intends to express by the general term. That we may fix the meaning of the word, figure, we may revolve in our mind the ideas of circles, squares, parallelograms, triangles of different sizes and proportions, and may not rest on one image or idea. However, this may be, 'tis certain *that* we form the idea of individuals, whenever we use any general term; *that* we seldom or never can exhaust these individuals; and *that* those, which remain, are only represented by means of that habit, by which we recall them, whenever any present occasion requires it. This then is the nature of our abstract ideas and general terms; and 'tis after this manner we account for the foregoing paradox, *that some ideas are particular in their nature, but general in their representation.* A particular idea becomes general by being annex'd to a general term; that is, to a term, which from a customary conjunction has a relation to many other particular ideas, and readily recalls them in the imagination.

The only difficulty, that can remain on this subject, must be with regard to that custom, which so readily recalls every particular idea, for which we may have occasion, and is excited by any word or sound, to which we commonly annex it. The most proper method, in my opinion, of giving a satisfactory explication of this act of the mind, is by producing other instances, which are analogous to it, and other principles, which facilitate its operation. To explain the ultimate causes of our mental actions is impossible. 'Tis sufficient, if we can give any satisfactory account of them from experience and analogy.

First then I observe, that when we mention any great number, such as a thousand, the mind has generally no adequate idea of it, but only a power of producing such an idea, by its adequate idea of the decimals, under which the number is comprehended. This imperfection, however in our ideas, is never felt in our reasonings; which seems to be an instance parallel to the present one of universal ideas.

Secondly, we have several instances of habits, which may be reviv'd by one single word; as when a person, who has by rote any periods of a discourse, or any number of verses, will be put in remembrance of the whole, which he is at a loss to recollect, by that single word or expression, with which they begin.

Thirdly, I believe every one, who examines the situation of his mind in reasoning, will agree with me, that we do not annex distinct and compleat ideas to every term we make use of, and that in talking of *government, church, negotiation, conquest,* we seldom spread out in our minds all the simple ideas, of which these complex ones are compos'd. 'Tis however observable, that notwithstanding this imperfection we may avoid talking nonsense on these subjects, and may perceive any repugnance among the ideas, as well as if we had a full comprehension of them. Thus if instead of saying, *that in war the weaker have always recourse to negotiation,* we shou'd say, *that they have always recourse to conquest,* the custom, which we have acquir'd of attributing certain relations to ideas, still follows the words, and makes us immediately perceive the absurdity of that proposition; in the same manner as one particular idea may serve us in reasoning concerning other ideas, however different from it in several circumstances.

Fourthly, As the individuals are collected together, and plac'd under a general term with a view to that resemblance, which they bear to each other, this relation must facilitate their entrance in the imagination, and make them be suggested more readily upon occasion. And indeed if we consider the common progress of the thought, either in reflexion or conversation, we shall find great reason to be satisfy'd in this particular. Nothing is more admirable, than the readiness, with which the imagination suggests its ideas, and presents them at the very instant, in which they become necessary or useful. The fancy runs from one end of the universe to the other in collecting those ideas, which belong to any subject. One would think the whole intellectual world of ideas was at once subjected to our view, and that we did

nothing but pick out such as were most proper for our purpose. There may not, however, be any present, beside those very ideas, that are thus collected by a kind of magical faculty in the soul, which, tho' it be always most perfect in the greatest geniuses, and is properly what we call a genius, is however inexplicable by the utmost efforts of human understanding.

Perhaps these four reflexions may help to remove all difficulties to the hypothesis I have propos'd concerning abstract ideas, so contrary to that, which has hitherto prevail'd in philosophy. But to tell the truth I place my chief confidence in what I have already prov'd concerning the impossibility of general ideas, according to the common method of explaining them. We must certainly seek some new system on this head, and there plainly is none beside what I have propos'd. If ideas be particular in their nature, and at the same time finite in their number, 'tis only by custom they can become general in their representation, and contain an infinite number of other ideas under them.

Before I leave this subject I shall employ the same principles to explain that *distinction of reason,* which is so much talk'd of, and is so little understood, in the schools. Of this kind is the distinction betwixt figure and the body figur'd; motion and the body mov'd. The difficulty of explaining this distinction arises from the principle above explain'd, *that all ideas, which are different, are separable.* For it follows from thence, that if the figure be different from the body, their ideas must be separable as well as distinguishable; if they be not different, their ideas can neither be separable nor distinguishable. What then is meant by a distinction of reason, since it implies neither a difference nor separation?

To remove this difficulty we must have recourse to the foregoing explication of abstract ideas. 'Tis certain that the mind wou'd never have dream'd of distinguishing a figure from the body figur'd, as being in reality neither distinguishable, nor different, nor separable; did it not observe, that even in this simplicity there might be contain'd many different resemblances and relations. Thus when a globe of white marble is presented, we receive only the impression of a white colour dispos'd in a certain form, nor are we able to separate and distinguish the colour from the form. But observing afterwards a globe of black marble and a cube of white, and comparing them with our former object, we find two separate resemblances, in what formerly seem'd, and really is, perfectly inseparable. After a little more practice of this kind, we begin to distinguish the figure from the colour by a *distinction of reason;* that is, we consider the figure and colour together, since they are in effect the same and undistinguishable; but still view them in different aspects, according to the resemblances, of which they are susceptible. When we wou'd consider only the figure of the globe of white marble, we form in reality an idea both of the figure and colour, but tacitly carry our eye to its resemblance with the globe of black marble: And in the same manner, when we wou'd consider its colour only, we turn our view to its resemblance with the cube of white marble. By this means we accompany our ideas with a kind of reflexion, of which custom renders us, in a great measure, insensible. A person, who desires us to consider the figure of a globe of white marble without thinking on its colour, desires an impossibility; but his meaning is, that we shou'd consider the colour and figure together, but still keep in our eye the resemblance to the globe of black marble, or that to any other globe of whatever colour or substance.

Part II:
Of the Ideas of Space
and Time

Section I:
Of the Infinite Divisibility of
Our Ideas of Space and Time

Whatever has the air of a paradox, and is contrary to the first and most unprejudic'd notions of mankind is often greedily embrac'd by philosophers, as shewing the superiority of their science, which cou'd discover opinions so remote from vulgar conception. On the other hand, any thing propos'd to us, which causes surprize and admiration, gives such a satisfaction to the mind, that it indulges itself in those agreeable emotions, and will never be perswaded that its pleasure is entirely without foundation. From these dispositions in philosophers and their disciples arises that mutual complaisance betwixt them; while the former furnish such plenty of strange and unaccountable opinions, and the latter so readily believe them. Of this mutual complaisance I cannot give a more evident instance than in the doctrine of infinite divisibility, with the examination of which I shall begin this subject of the ideas of space and time.

'Tis universally allow'd, that the capacity of the mind is limited, and can never attain a full and adequate conception of infinity: And tho' it were not allow'd, 'twou'd be sufficiently evident from the plainest observation and experience. 'Tis also obvious, that whatever is capable of being divided *in infinitum,* must consist of an infinite number of parts, and that 'tis impossible to set any bounds to the number of parts, without setting bounds at the same time to the division. It requires scarce any induction to conclude from hence, that the *idea,* which we form of any finite quality, is not infinitely divisible, but that by proper distinctions and separations we may run up this idea to inferior ones, which will be perfectly simple and indivisible. In rejecting the infinite capacity of the mind, we suppose it may arrive at an end in the division of its ideas; nor are there any possible means of evading the evidence of this conclusion.

'Tis therefore certain, that the imagination reaches a *minimum,* and may raise up to itself an idea, of which it cannot conceive any subdivision, and which cannot be diminished without a total annihilation. When you tell me of the thousandth and ten thousandth part of a grain of sand, I have a distinct idea of these numbers and of their different proportions; but the images, which I form in my mind to represent the things themselves, are nothing different from each other, nor inferior to that image, by which I represent the grain of sand itself, which is suppos'd so vastly to exceed them. What consists of parts is distinguishable into them, and what is distinguishable is separable. But whatever we may imagine of the thing, the idea of a grain of sand is not distinguishable, nor separable into twenty, much less into a thousand, ten thousand, or an infinite number of different ideas.

'Tis the same case with the impressions of the senses as with the ideas of the imagination. Put a spot of ink upon paper, fix your eye upon that spot, and retire to such a distance, that at last you lose sight of it; 'tis plain, that the moment before it vanish'd the image or impression was perfectly indivisible. 'Tis not for want of rays of light striking on our eyes, that the minute parts of distant bodies convey not any sensible impression; but because they are remov'd beyond that distance, at which their impressions were reduc'd to a *minimum*, and were incapable of any farther diminution. A microscope or telescope, which renders them visible, produces not any new rays of light, but only spreads those, which always flow'd from them; and by that means both gives parts to impressions, which to the naked eye appear simple and uncompounded, and advances to a *minimum*, what was formerly imperceptible.

We may hence discover the error of the common opinion, that the capacity of the mind is limited on both sides, and that 'tis impossible for the imagination to form an adequate idea, of what goes beyond a certain degree of minuteness as well as of greatness. Nothing can be more minute, than some ideas, which we form in the fancy; and images, which appear to the senses; since there are ideas and images perfectly simple and indivisible. The only defect of our senses is, that they give us disproportion'd images of things, and represent as minute and uncompounded what is really great and compos'd of a vast number of parts. This mistake we are not sensible of; but taking the impressions of those minute objects, which appear to the senses, to be equal or nearly equal to the objects, and finding by reason, that there are other objects vastly more minute, we too hastily conclude, that these are inferior to any idea of our imagination or impression of our senses. This however is certain, that we can form ideas, which shall be no greater than the smallest atom of the animal spirits of an insect a thousand times less than a mite: And we ought rather to conclude, that

the difficulty lies in enlarging our conceptions so much as to form a just notion of a mite, or even of an insect a thousand times less than a mite. For in order to form a just notion of these animals, we must have a distinct idea representing every part of them; which, according to the system of infinite divisibility, is utterly impossible, and according to that of indivisible parts or atoms, is extremely difficult, by reason of the vast number and multiplicity of these parts.

Section II: Of the Infinite Divisibility of Space and Time

Wherever ideas are adequate representations of objects, the relations, contradictions and agreements of the ideas are all applicable to the objects; and this we may in general observe to be the foundation of all human knowledge. But our ideas are adequate representations of the most minute parts of extension; and thro' whatever divisions and subdivisions we may suppose these parts to be arriv'd at, they can never become inferior to some ideas, which we form. The plain consequence is, that whatever *appears* impossible and contradictory upon the comparison of these ideas, must be *really* impossible and contradictory, without any farther excuse or evasion.

Every thing capable of being infinitely divided contains an infinite number of parts; otherwise the division would be stopt short by the indivisible parts, which we should immediately arrive at. If therefore any finite extension be infinitely divisible, it can be no contradiction to suppose, that a finite extension contains an infinite number of parts: And *vice versa*, if it be a contradiction to suppose, that a finite extension contains an infinite number of parts, no finite extension can be infinitely divisible. But that this latter supposition is absurd, I easily convince myself by the consideration of my clear ideas. I first take the least idea I can form of a part of extension, and being certain that there is nothing more minute than this idea, I conclude, that whatever I discover by its means must be a real quality of extension. I then repeat this idea once, twice, thrice, &c. and find the compound idea of extension, arising from its repetition, always to augment, and become double, triple, quadruple, &c. till at last it swells up to a considerable bulk, greater or smaller, in proportion as I repeat more or less the same idea. When I stop in the addition of parts, the idea of extension ceases to augment; and were I to carry on the addition *in infinitum,* I clearly perceive, that the idea of extension must also become infinite. Upon the whole, I conclude, that the idea of an infinite number of parts is individually the same idea with that of an infinite extension; that no finite extension is capable of containing an infinite number of parts; and consequently that no finite extension is infinitely divisible.[1]

I may subjoin another argument propos'd by a noted author,[2] which seems to me very strong and beautiful. 'Tis evident, that existence in itself belongs only to unity, and is never applicable to number, but on account of the unites, of which the number is compos'd. Twenty men may be said to exist; but 'tis only because one, two, three, four, &c. are existent; and if you deny the existence of the latter, that of the former falls of course. 'Tis therefore utterly absurd to suppose any number to exist, and yet deny the existence of unites; and as extension is always a number, according to the common sentiment of metaphysicians, and never resolves itself into any unite or indivisible quantity, it follows, that extension can never at all exist. 'Tis in vain to reply, that any determinate quantity of extension is an unite; but such-a-one as admits of an infinite number of fractions, and is inexhaustible in its subdivisions. For by the same rule these twenty men *may be consider'd as an unite.* The whole globe of the earth, nay the whole universe *may be consider'd as an unite.* That term of unity is merely a fictitious denomination, which the mind may apply to any quantity of objects it collects together; nor can such an unity any

more exist alone than number can, as being in reality a true number. But the unity, which can exist alone, and whose existence is necessary to that of all number, is of another kind, and must be perfectly indivisible, and incapable of being resolved into any lesser unity.

All this reasoning takes place with regard to time; along with an additional argument, which it may be proper to take notice of. 'Tis a property inseparable from time, and which in a manner constitutes its essence, that each of its parts succeeds another, and that none of them, however contiguous, can ever be co-existent. For the same reason, that the year 1737 cannot concur with the present year 1738, every moment must be distinct from, and posterior or antecedent to another. 'Tis certain then, that time, as it exists, must be compos'd of indivisible moments. For if in time we could never arrive at an end of division, and if each moment, as it succeeds another, were not perfectly single and indivisible, there would be an infinite number of coexistent moments, or parts of time; which I believe will be allow'd to be an arrant contradiction.

The infinite divisibility of space implies that of time, as is evident from the nature of motion. If the latter, therefore, be impossible, the former must be equally so.

I doubt not but it will readily be allow'd by the most obstinate defender of the doctrine of infinite divisibility, that these arguments are difficulties, and that 'tis impossible to give any answer to them which will be perfectly clear and satisfactory. But here we may observe, that nothing can be more absurd, than this custom of calling a *difficulty* what pretends to be a *demonstration,* and endeavouring by that means to elude its force and evidence. 'Tis not in demonstrations as in probabilities, that difficulties can take place, and one argument counter-ballance another, and diminish its authority. A demonstration, if just, admits of no opposite difficulty; and if not just, 'tis a mere sophism, and consequently can never be a difficulty. 'Tis either irresistible, or has no manner of force. To talk therefore of objections and replies, and ballancing of arguments in such a question as this, is to confess, either that human reason is nothing but a play of words,

---

[1]It has been objected to me, that infinite divisibility supposes only an infinite number of *proportional* not of *aliquot* parts, and that an infinite number of proportional parts does not form an infinite extension. But this distinction is entirely frivolous. Whether these parts be call'd *aliquot* or *proportional,* they cannot be inferior to those minute parts we conceive; and therefore cannot form a less extension by their conjunction.
[2]Mons. *Malezieu.*

or that the person himself, who talks so, has not a capacity equal to such subjects. Demonstrations may be difficult to be comprehended, because of the abstractedness of the subject; but can never have any such difficulties as will weaken their authority, when once they are comprehended.

'Tis true, mathematicians are wont to say, that there are here equally strong arguments on the other side of the question, and that the doctrine of indivisible points is also liable to unanswerable objections. Before I examine these arguments and objections in detail, I will here take them in a body, and endeavour by a short and decisive reason to prove at once, that 'tis utterly impossible they can have any just foundation.

'Tis an establish'd maxim in metaphysics, *That whatever the mind clearly conceives includes the idea of possible existence,* or in other words, *that nothing we imagine is absolutely impossible.* We can form the idea of a golden mountain, and from thence conclude that such a mountain may actually exist. We can form no idea of a mountain without a valley, and therefore regard it as impossible.

Now 'tis certain we have an idea of extension; for otherwise why do we talk and reason concerning it? 'Tis likewise certain, that this idea, as conceiv'd by the imagination, tho' divisible into parts or inferior ideas, is not infinitely divisible, nor consists of an infinite number of parts: For that exceeds the comprehension of our limited capacities. Here then is an idea of extension, which consists of parts or inferior ideas, that are perfectly indivisible: consequently this idea implies no contradiction: consequently 'tis possible for extension really to exist conformable to it: and consequently all the arguments employ'd against the possibility of mathematical points are mere scholastick quibbles, and unworthy of our attention.

These consequences we may carry one step farther, and conclude that all the pretended demonstrations for the infinite divisibility of extension are equally sophistical; since 'tis certain these demonstrations cannot be just without proving the impossibility of mathematical points; which 'tis an evident absurdity to pretend to.

Section III:
Of the Other Qualities of
Our Ideas of Space and Time

No discovery cou'd have been made more happily for deciding all controversies concerning ideas, than that above-mention'd, that impressions always take the precedency of them, and that every idea, with which the imagination is furnish'd, first makes its appearance in a correspondent impression. These latter perceptions are all so clear and evident, that they admit of no controversy; tho' many of our ideas are so obscure, that 'tis almost impossible even for the mind, which forms them, to tell exactly their nature and composition. Let us apply this principle, in order to discover farther the nature of our ideas of space and time.

Upon opening my eyes, and turning them to the surrounding objects, I perceive many visible bodies; and upon shutting them again, and considering the distance betwixt these bodies, I acquire the idea of extension. As every idea is deriv'd from some impression, which is exactly similar to it, the impressions similar to this idea of extension, must either be some sensations deriv'd from the sight, or some internal impressions arising from these sensations.

Our internal impressions are our passions, emotions, desires and aversions; none of which, I believe, will ever be asserted to be the model, from which the idea of space is deriv'd. There remains therefore nothing but the senses, which can convey to us this original impression. Now what impression do our senses here convey to us? This is the principal question, and decides without appeal concerning the nature of the idea.

The table before me is alone sufficient by its view to give me the idea of extension. This idea, then, is borrow'd from, and represents some impression, which this moment appears to the senses. But my senses convey to me only the impressions of colour'd points, dispos'd in a certain manner. If the eye is sensible of any thing farther, I desire it may be pointed out to me. But if it be impossible to shew any thing farther, we may conclude with certainty, that the idea of extension is nothing but a copy of these colour'd points, and of the manner of their appearance.

Suppose that in the extended object, or composition of colour'd points, from which we first receiv'd the idea of extension, the points were of a purple colour; it follows, that in every repetition of that idea we wou'd not only place the points in the same order with respect to each other, but also bestow on them that precise colour, with which alone we are acquainted. But afterwards having experience of the other colours of violet, green, red, white, black, and of all the different compositions of these, and finding a resemblance in the disposition of colour'd points, of which they are compos'd, we omit the peculiarities of colour, as far as possible, and found an abstract idea merely on that disposition of points, or manner of appearance, in which they agree. Nay even when the resemblance is carry'd beyond the objects of one sense, and the impressions of touch are found to be similar to those of sight in the disposition of their parts; this does not hinder the abstract idea from representing both, upon account of their resemblance. All abstract ideas are really nothing but particular ones, consider'd in a certain light; but being annexed to general terms, they are able to represent a vast variety, and to comprehend objects, which, as they are alike in some particulars, are in others vastly wide of each other.

The idea of time, being deriv'd from the succession of our perceptions of every kind, ideas as well as impressions, and impressions of reflection as well as of sensation, will afford us an instance of an abstract idea, which comprehends a still greater variety than that of space, and yet is represented in the fancy by some particular individual idea of a determinate quantity and quality.

As 'tis from the disposition of visible and tangible objects we receive the idea of space, so from the succession of ideas and impressions we form the idea of time, nor is it possible for time alone ever to make its appearance, or be taken notice of by the mind. A man in a sound sleep, or strongly occupy'd with one thought, is insensible of time; and according as his perceptions succeed each other with greater or less rapidity, the same duration appears longer or shorter to his imagination. It has been remark'd by a great philosopher,[3] that our perceptions have certain bounds in this particular which are fix'd by the original nature and constitution of the mind, and beyond which no influence of external objects on the senses is ever able to hasten or retard our thought. If you wheel about a burning coal with rapidity, it will present to the senses an image of a circle of fire; nor will there seem to be any interval of time betwixt its revolutions; meerly because 'tis impossible for our perceptions to succeed each other with the same rapidity, that motion may be communicated to external objects. Wherever we have no successive perceptions, we have no notion of time, even tho' there be a real succession in the objects. From these phænomena, as well as from many others, we may conclude, that time cannot make its appearance to the mind, either alone, or attended with a steady unchangeable object, but is always discover'd by some *perceivable* succession of changeable objects.

To confirm this we may add the following argument, which to me seems perfectly decisive and convincing. 'Tis evident, that time or duration consists of different parts: For otherwise we cou'd not conceive a longer or shorter duration. 'Tis also evident, that these parts are not co-existent: For that quality of the co-existence of parts belongs to extension, and is what distinguishes it from duration. Now as time is compos'd of parts, that are not co-existent; an unchangeable object, since it produces none but co-existent impressions, produces none that can give us the idea of time; and consequently that idea must be deriv'd from a succession of changeable objects, and time in its first appearance can never be sever'd from such a succession.

Having therefore found, that time in its first appearance to the mind is always conjoin'd with a succession of changeable objects, and that otherwise it can never fall under our notice, we must now examine whether it can be *conceiv'd* without our conceiving any succession of objects, and whether it can alone form a distinct idea in the imagination.

In order to know whether any objects,

[3]Mr. *Locke*.

which are join'd in impression, be separable in idea, we need only consider, if they be different from each other; in which case, 'tis plain they may be conceiv'd apart. Every thing, that is different, is distinguishable; and every thing, that is distinguishable, may be separated, according to the maxims above-explain'd. If on the contrary they be not different, they are not distinguishable; and if they be not distinguishable, they cannot be separated. But this is precisely the case with respect to time, compar'd with our successive perceptions. The idea of time is not deriv'd from a particular impression mix'd up with others, and plainly distinguishable from them; but arises altogether from the manner, in which impressions appear to the mind, without making one of the number. Five notes play'd on a flute give us the impression and idea of time; tho' time be not a sixth impression, which presents itself to the hearing or any other of the senses. Nor is it a sixth impression, which the mind by reflection finds in itself. These five sounds making their appearance in this particular manner, excite no emotion in the mind, nor produce an affection of any kind, which being observ'd by it can give rise to a new idea. For *that* is necessary to produce a new idea of reflection, nor can the mind, by revolving over a thousand times all its ideas of sensation, ever extract from them any new original idea, unless nature has so fram'd its faculties, that it feels some new original impression arise from such a contemplation. But here it only takes notice of the *manner*, in which the different sounds make their appearance; and that it may afterwards consider without considering these particular sounds, but may conjoin it with any other objects. The ideas of some objects it certainly must have, nor is it possible for it without these ideas ever to arrive at any conception of time; which since it appears not as any primary distinct impression, can plainly be nothing but different ideas, or impressions, or objects dispos'd in a certain manner, that is, succeeding each other.

I know there are some who pretend, that the idea of duration is applicable in a proper sense to objects, which are perfectly unchangeable; and this I take to be the common opinion of philosophers as well as of the vulgar. But to be convinc'd of its falsehood we need but reflect on the foregoing conclusion, that the idea of duration is always deriv'd from a succession of changeable objects, and can never be convey'd to the mind by any thing stedfast and unchangeable. For it inevitably follows from thence, that since the idea of duration cannot be deriv'd from such an object, it can never in any propriety or exactness be apply'd to it, nor can any thing unchangeable be ever said to have duration. Ideas always represent the objects or impressions, from which they are deriv'd, and can never without a fiction represent or be apply'd to any other. By what fiction we apply the idea of time, even to what is unchangeable, and suppose, as is common, that duration is a measure of rest as well as of motion, we shall consider[4] afterwards.

There is another very decisive argument, which establishes the present doctrine concerning our ideas of space and time, and is founded only on that simple principle, *that our ideas of them are compounded of parts, which are indivisible*. This argument may be worth the examining.

Every idea, that is distinguishable, being also separable, let us take one of those simple indivisible ideas, of which the compound one of *extension* is form'd, and separating it from all others, and considering it apart, let us form a judgment of its nature and qualities.

'Tis plain it is not the idea of extension. For the idea of extension consists of parts; and this idea, according to the supposition, is perfectly simple and indivisible. Is it therefore nothing? That is absolutely impossible. For as the compound idea of extension, which is real, is compos'd of such ideas; were these so many non-entities, there wou'd be a real existence compos'd of non-entities; which is absurd. Here therefore I must ask, *What is our idea of a simple and indivisible point?* No wonder if my answer appear somewhat new, since the question itself has scarce ever yet been thought of. We are wont to dispute concerning the nature of mathematical points, but seldom concerning the nature of their ideas.

[4]Sect. v (p. 288).

The idea of space is convey'd to the mind by two senses, the sight and touch; nor does any thing ever appear extended, that is not either visible or tangible. That compound impression, which represents extension, consists of several lesser impressions, that are indivisible to the eye or feeling, and may be call'd impressions of atoms or corpuscles endow'd with colour and solidity. But this is not all. 'Tis not only requisite, that these atoms shou'd be colour'd or tangible, in order to discover themselves to our senses; 'tis also necessary we shou'd preserve the idea of their colour or tangibility in order to comprehend them by our imagination. There is nothing but the idea of their colour or tangibility which can render them conceivable by the mind. Upon the removal of the ideas of these sensible qualities, they are utterly annihilated to the thought or imagination.

Now such as the parts are, such is the whole. If a point be not consider'd as colour'd or tangible, it can convey to us no idea; and consequently the idea of extension, which is compos'd of the ideas of these points, can never possibly exist. But if the idea of extension really can exist, as we are conscious it does, its parts must also exist; and in order to that, must be consider'd as colour'd or tangible. We have therefore no idea of space or extension, but when we regard it as an object either of our sight or feeling.

The same reasoning will prove, that the indivisible moments of time must be fill'd with some real object or existence, whose succession forms the duration, and makes it be conceivable by the mind.

Section IV: Objections Answered

Our system concerning space and time consists of two parts, which are intimately connected together. The first depends on this chain of reasoning. The capacity of the mind is not infinite; consequently no idea of extension or duration consists of an infinite number of parts or inferior ideas, but of a finite number, and these simple and indivisible: 'Tis therefore possible for space and time to exist conformable to this idea: And if it be possible, 'tis certain they actually do exist conformable to it;

since their infinite divisibility is utterly impossible and contradictory.

The other part of our system is a consequence of this. The parts, into which the ideas of space and time resolve themselves, become at last indivisible; and these indivisible parts, being nothing in themselves, are inconceivable when not fill'd with something real and existent. The ideas of space and time are therefore no separate or distinct ideas, but merely those of the manner or order, in which objects exist: Or, in other words, 'tis impossible to conceive either a vacuum and extension without matter, or a time, when there was no succession or change in any real existence. The intimate connexion betwixt these parts of our system is the reason why we shall examine together the objections, which have been urg'd against both of them, beginning with those against the finite divisibility of extension.

I. The first of these objections, which I shall take notice of, is more proper to prove this connexion and dependence of the one part upon the other, than to destroy either of them. It has often been maintain'd in the schools, that extension must be divisible, *in infinitum,* because the system of mathematical points is absurd; and that system is absurd, because a mathematical point is a non-entity, and consequently can never by its conjunction with others form a real existence. This wou'd be perfectly decisive, were there no medium betwixt the infinite divisibility of matter, and the non-entity of mathematical points. But there is evidently a medium, *vis.* the bestowing a colour or solidity on these points; and the absurdity of both the extremes is a demonstration of the truth and reality of this medium. The system of *physical* points, which is another medium, is too absurd to need a refutation. A real extension, such as a physical point is suppos'd to be, can never exist without parts, different from each other; and wherever objects are different, they are distinguishable and separable by the imagination.

II. The second objection is deriv'd from the necessity there wou'd be of *penetration,* if extension consisted of mathematical points. A simple and indivisible atom, that touches another, must necessarily penetrate it; for 'tis impossible it can touch it by its external parts, from the very supposition of its perfect simplicity, which excludes all parts. It must therefore touch it intimately, and in its whole essence, *secundum se, tota, & totaliter;* which is the very definition of penetration. But penetration is impossible: Mathematical points are of consequence equally impossible.

I answer this objection by substituting a juster idea of penetration. Suppose two bodies containing no void within their circumference, to approach each other, and to unite in such a manner that the body, which results from their union, is no more extended than either of them; 'tis this we must mean when we talk of penetration. But 'tis evident this penetration is nothing but the annihilation of one of these bodies, and the preservation of the other, without our being able to distinguish particularly which is preserv'd and which annihilated. Before the approach we have the idea of two bodies. After it we have the idea only of one. 'Tis impossible for the mind to preserve any notion of difference betwixt two bodies of the same nature existing in the same place at the same time.

Taking then penetration in this sense, for the annihilation of one body upon its approach to another, I ask any one, if he sees a necessity, that a colour'd or tangible point shou'd be annihilated upon the approach of another colour'd or tangible point? On the contrary, does he not evidently perceive, that from the union of these points there results an object, which is compounded and divisible, and may be distinguish'd into two parts, of which each preserves its existence distinct and separate, notwithstanding its contiguity to be other? Let him aid his fancy by conceiving these points to be of different colours, the better to prevent their coalition and confusion. A blue and a red point may surely lie contiguous without any penetration or annihilation. For if they cannot, what possibly can become of them? Whether shall the red or the blue be annihilated? Or if these colours unite into one, what new colour will they produce by their union?

What chiefly gives rise to these objections, and at the same time renders it so difficult to give a satisfactory answer to them, is the natural infirmity and unsteadiness both of our imagination and senses, when employ'd on such minute objects. Put a spot of ink upon paper, and retire to such a distance, that the spot becomes altogether invisible; you will find, that upon your return and nearer approach the spot first becomes visible by short intervals; and afterwards becomes always visible; and afterwards acquires only a new force in its colouring without augmenting its bulk; and afterwards, when it has encreas'd to such a degree as to be really extended, 'tis still difficult for the imagination to break it into its component parts, because of the uneasiness it finds in the conception of such a minute object as a single point. This infirmity affects most of our reasonings on the present subject, and makes it almost impossible to answer in an intelligible manner, and in proper expressions, many questions which may arise concerning it.

III. There have been many objections drawn from the *mathematics* against the indivisibility of the parts of extension; tho' at first sight that science seems rather favourable to the present doctrine; and if it be contrary in its *demonstrations,* 'tis perfectly conformable in its *definitions.* My present business then must be to defend the definitions, and refute the demonstrations.

A surface is *defin'd* to be length and breadth without depth: A line to be length without breadth or depth: A point to be what has neither length, breadth nor depth. 'Tis evident that all this is perfectly unintelligible upon any other supposition than that of the composition of extension by indivisible points or atoms. How else cou'd any thing exist without length, without breadth, or without depth?

Two different answers, I find, have been made to this argument; neither of which is in my opinion satisfactory. The first is, that the objects of geometry, those surfaces, lines and points, whose proportions and positions it examines, are mere ideas in the mind; and not only never did, but never can exist in nature. They never did exist; for no one will pretend to draw a line or make a surface entirely conformable to the definition: They never can exist; for we may produce demonstrations from these very ideas to prove that they are impossible.

But can any thing be imagin'd more absurd and contradictory than this reasoning? Whatever can be conceiv'd by a clear and distinct idea necessarily implies the possibility of existence; and he who pretends to prove the impossibility of its existence by any argument deriv'd from the clear idea, in reality asserts, that we have no clear idea of it, because we have a clear idea. 'Tis in vain to search for a contradiction in any thing that is distinctly conceiv'd by the mind. Did it imply any contradiction, 'tis impossible it cou'd ever be conceiv'd.

There is therefore no medium betwixt allowing at least the possibility of indivisible points, and denying their idea; and 'tis on this latter principle, that the second answer to the foregoing argument is founded. It has been[5] pretended, that tho' it be impossible to conceive a length without any breadth, yet by an abstraction without a separation, we can consider the one without regarding the other; in the same manner as we may think of the length of the way betwixt two towns, and overlook its breadth. The length is inseparable from the breadth both in nature and in our minds; but this excludes not a partial consideration, and a *distinction of reason,* after the manner above explain'd.

In refuting this answer I shall not insist on the argument, which I have already sufficiently explain'd, that if it be impossible for the mind to arrive at a *minimum* in its ideas, its capacity must be infinite, in order to comprehend the infinite number of parts, of which its idea of any extension wou'd be compos'd. I shall here endeavour to find some new absurdities in this reasoning.

A surface terminates a solid; a line terminates a surface; a point terminates a line; but I assert, that if the *ideas* of a point, line or surface were not indivisible, 'tis impossible we shou'd ever conceive these terminations. For let these ideas be suppos'd infinitely divisible; and then let the fancy endeavour to fix itself on the idea of the last surface, line or point; it immediately finds this idea to break into parts; and upon its seizing the last of these parts, it loses its hold by a new division, and so on *in*

[5]*L'Art de penser.*

infinitum, without any possibility of its arriving at a concluding idea. The number of fractions bring it no nearer the last division, than the first idea it form'd. Every particle eludes the grasp by a new fraction; like quicksilver, when we endeavour to seize it. But as in fact there must be something, which terminates the idea of every finite quantity; and as this terminating idea cannot itself consist of parts or inferior ideas; otherwise it wou'd be the last of its parts, which finish'd the idea, and so on; this is a clear proof, that the ideas of surfaces, lines and points admit not of any division; those of surfaces in depth; of lines in breadth and depth; and of points in any dimension.

The *schoolmen* were so sensible of the force of this argument, that some of them maintain'd, that nature has mix'd among those particles of matter, which are divisible *in infinitum,* a number of mathematical points, in order to give a termination to bodies; and others eluded the force of this reasoning by a heap of unintelligible cavils and distinctions. Both these adversaries equally yield the victory. A man who hides himself, confesses as evidently the superiority of his enemy, as another, who fairly delivers his arms.

Thus it appears, that the definitions of mathematics destroy the pretended demonstrations; and that if we have the idea of indivisible points, lines and surfaces conformable to the definition, their existence is certainly possible: but if we have no such idea, 'tis impossible we can ever conceive the termination of any figure; without which conception there can be no geometrical demonstration.

But I go farther, and maintain, that none of these demonstrations can have sufficient weight to establish such a principle, as this of infinite divisibility; and that because with regard to such minute objects, they are not properly demonstrations, being built on ideas, which are not exact, and maxims, which are not precisely true. When geometry decides any thing concerning the proportions of quantity, we ought not to look for the utmost *precision* and exactness. None of its proofs extend so far. It takes the dimensions and proportions of figures justly; but roughly, and with some liberty. Its errors are never considerable; nor wou'd it err at all, did it not aspire to such an absolute perfection.

I first ask mathematicians, what they mean when they say one line or surface is EQUAL to, or GREATER, or LESS than another? Let any of them give an answer, to whatever sect he belongs, and whether he maintains the composition of extension by indivisible points, or by quantities divisible *in infinitum*. This question will embarrass both of them.

There are few or no mathematicians who defend the hypothesis of indivisible points; and yet these have the readiest and justest answer to the present question. They need only reply, that lines or surfaces are equal, when the numbers of points in each are equal; and that as the proportion of the numbers varies, the proportion of the lines and surfaces is also vary'd. But tho' this answer be *just*, as well as obvious; yet I may affirm, that this standard of equality is entirely *useless*, and that it never is from such a comparison we determine objects to be equal or unequal with respect to each other. For as the points, which enter into the composition of any line or surface, whether perceiv'd by the sight or touch, are so minute and so confounded with each other, that 'tis utterly impossible for the mind to compute their number, such a computation will never afford us a standard, by which we may judge of proportions. No one will ever be able to determine by an exact numeration, that an inch has fewer points than a foot, or a foot fewer than an ell or any greater measure; for which reason we seldom or never consider this as the standard of equality or inequality.

As to those, who imagine, that extension is divisible *in infinitum*, 'tis impossible they can make use of this answer, or fix the equality of any line or surface by a numeration of its component parts. For since, according to their hypothesis, the least as well as greatest figures contain an infinite number of parts; and since infinite numbers, properly speaking, can neither be equal nor unequal with respect to each other; the equality or inequality of any portions of space can never depend on any proportion in the number of their parts. 'Tis true, it may be said, that the inequality of an ell and a yard consists in the different numbers of the feet, of which they are compos'd; and that

of a foot and a yard in the number of the inches. But as that quantity we call an inch in the one is suppos'd equal to what we call an inch in the other, and as 'tis impossible for the mind to find this equality by proceeding *in infinitum* with these references to inferior quantities; 'tis evident, that at last we must fix some standard of equality different from an enumeration of the parts.

There are some,[6] who pretend, that equality is best defin'd by *congruity*, and that any two figures are equal, when upon the placing of one upon the other, all their parts correspond to and touch each other. In order to judge of this definition let us consider, that since equality is a relation, it is not, strictly speaking, a property in the figures themselves, but arises merely from the comparison, which the mind makes betwixt them. If it consists, therefore, in this imaginary application and mutual contact of parts, we must at least have a distinct notion of these parts, and must conceive their contact. Now 'tis plain, that in this conception we wou'd run up these parts to the greatest minuteness, which can possibly be conceiv'd; since the contact of large parts wou'd never render the figures equal. But the minutest parts we can conceive are mathematical points; and consequently this standard of equality is the same with that deriv'd from the equality of the number of points; which we have already determin'd to be a just but a useless standard. We must therefore look to some other quarter for a solution of the present difficulty.

'Tis evident, that the eye, or rather the mind is often able at one view to determine the proportions of bodies, and pronounce them equal to, or greater or less than each other, without examining or comparing the number of their minute parts. Such judgments are not only common, but in many cases certain and infallible. When the measure of a yard and that of a foot are presented, the mind can no more question, that the first is longer than the second, than it can doubt of those principles, which are the most clear and self-evident.

There are therefore three proportions, which the mind distinguishes in the general appearance of its objects, and calls by the

6See Dr. *Barrow's* mathematical lectures.

names of *greater, less* and *equal*. But tho' its decisions concerning these proportions be sometimes infallible, they are not always so; nor are our judgments of this kind more exempt from doubt and error, than those on any other subject. We frequently correct our first opinion by a review and reflection; and pronounce those objects to be equal, which at first we esteem'd unequal; and regard an object as less, tho' before it appear'd greater than another. Nor is this the only correction, which these judgments of our senses undergo; but we often discover our error by a juxta-position of the objects; or where that is impracticable, by the use of some common and invariable measure, which being successively apply'd to each, informs us of their different proportions. And even this correction is susceptible of a new correction, and of different degrees of exactness, according to the nature of the instrument by which we measure the bodies, and the care which we employ in the comparison.

When therefore the mind is accustom'd to these judgments and their corrections, and finds that the same proportion which makes two figures have in the eye that appearance, which we call *equality*, makes them also correspond to each other, and to any common measure, with which they are compar'd, we form a mix'd notion of equality deriv'd both from the looser and stricter methods of comparison. But we are not content with this. For as sound reason convinces us that there are bodies *vastly* more minute than those, which appear to the senses; and as a false reason wou'd perswade us, that there are bodies *infinitely* more minute; we clearly perceive, that we are not possess'd of any instrument or art of measuring, which can secure us from all error and uncertainty. We are sensible, that the addition or removal of one of these minute parts, is not discernible either in the appearance or measuring; and as we imagine, that two figures, which were equal before, cannot be equal after this removal or addition, we therefore suppose some imaginary standard of equality, by which the appearances and measuring are exactly corrected, and the figures reduc'd entirely to that proportion. This standard is plainly imaginary. For as the very

idea of equality is that of such a particular appearance corrected by juxta-position or a common measure, the notion of any correction beyond what we have instruments and art to make, is a mere fiction of the mind, and useless as well as incomprehensible. But tho' this standard be only imaginary, the fiction however is very natural; nor is any thing more usual, than for the mind to proceed after this manner with any action, even after the reason has ceas'd, which first determin'd it to begin. This appears very conspicuously with regard to time; where tho' 'tis evident we have no exact method of determining the proportions of parts, not even so exact as in extension, yet the various corrections of our measures, and their different degrees of exactness, have given us an obscure and implicit notion of a perfect and entire equality. The case is the same in many other subjects. A musician finding his ear becomes every day more delicate, and correcting himself by reflection and attention, proceeds with the same act of the mind, even when the subject fails him, and entertains a notion of a compleat *tierce* or *octave*, without being able to tell whence he derives his standard. A painter forms the same fiction with regard to colours. A mechanic with regard to motion. To the one *light* and *shade;* to the other *swift* and *slow* are imagin'd to be capable of an exact comparison and equality beyond the judgments of the senses.

We may apply the same reasoning to CURVE and RIGHT lines. Nothing is more apparent to the senses, than the distinction betwixt a curve and a right line; nor are there any ideas we more easily form than the ideas of these objects. But however easily we may form these ideas, 'tis impossible to produce any definition of them, which will fix the precise boundaries betwixt them. When we draw lines upon paper or any continu'd surface, there is a certain order, by which the lines run along from one point to another, that they may produce the entire impression of a curve or right line; but this order is perfectly unknown, and nothing is observ'd but the united appearance. Thus even upon the system of indivisible points, we can only form a distant notion of some unknown standard to these objects. Upon that of infinite divisibility we cannot go even this length; but are reduc'd meerly to the general appearance, as the rule by which we determine lines to be either curve or right ones. But tho' we can give no perfect definition of these lines, nor produce any very exact method of distinguishing the one from the other; yet this hinders us not from correcting the first appearance by a more accurate consideration, and by a comparison with some rule, of whose rectitude from repeated trials we have a greater assurance. And 'tis from these corrections, and by carrying on the same action of the mind, even when its reason fails us, that we form the loose idea of a perfect standard to these figures, without being able to explain or comprehend it.

'Tis true, mathematicians pretend they give an exact definition of a right line, when they say, *it is the shortest way betwixt two points.* But in the first place, I observe, that this is more properly the discovery of one of the properties of a right line, than a just definition of it. For I ask any one, if upon mention of a right line he thinks not immediately on such a particular appearance, and if 'tis not by accident only that he considers this property? A right line can be comprehended alone; but this definition is unintelligible without a comparison with other lines, which we conceive to be more extended. In common life 'tis establish'd as a maxim, that the streightest way is always the shortest; which wou'd be as absurd as to say, the shortest way is always the shortest, if our idea of a right line was not different from that of the shortest way betwixt two points.

Secondly, I repeat what I have already establish'd, that we have no precise idea of equality and inequality, shorter and longer, more than of a right line or a curve; and consequently that the one can never afford us a perfect standard for the other. An exact idea can never be built on such as are loose and undeterminate.

The idea of a *plain surface* is as little susceptible of a precise standard as that of a right line; nor have we any other means of distinguishing such a surface, than its general appearance. 'Tis in vain, that mathematicians represent a plain surface as produc'd by the flowing of a right line. 'Twill immediately be objected, that our idea of a surface is as independent of this method of forming a surface, as our idea of an ellipse is of that of a cone; that the idea of a right line is no more precise than that of a plain surface; that a right line may flow irregularly, and by that means form a figure quite different from a plane; and that therefore we must suppose it to flow along two right lines, parallel to each other, and on the same plane; which is a description, that explains a thing by itself, and returns in a circle.

It appears, then, that the ideas which are most essential to geometry, *viz.* those of equality and inequality, of a right line and a plain surface, are far from being exact and determinate, according to our common method of conceiving them. Not only we are incapable of telling, if the case be in any degree doubtful, when such particular figures are equal; when such a line is a right one, and such a surface a plain one; but we can form no idea of that proportion, or of these figures, which is firm and invariable. Our appeal is still to the weak and fallible judgment, which we make from the appearance of the objects, and correct by a compass or common measure; and if we join the supposition of any farther correction, 'tis of such-a-one as is either useless or imaginary. In vain shou'd we have recourse to the common topic, and employ the supposition of a deity, whose omnipotence may enable him to form a perfect geometrical figure, and describe a right line without any curve or inflexion. As the ultimate standard of these figures is deriv'd from nothing but the senses and imagination, 'tis absurd to talk of any perfection beyond what these faculties can judge of; since the true perfection of any thing consists in its conformity to its standard.

Now since these ideas are so loose and uncertain, I wou'd fain ask any mathematician what infallible assurance he has, not only of the more intricate and obscure propositions of his science, but of the most vulgar and obvious principles? How can he prove to me, for instance, that two right lines cannot have one common segment? Or that 'tis impossible to draw more than one right line betwixt any two points? Shou'd he tell me, that these opinions are obviously absurd, and repugnant to our clear ideas; I wou'd answer, that I do not deny, where two right lines incline upon each other with a sensible angle, but 'tis absurd to imagine them to have a common segment. But supposing these two lines to approach at the rate of an inch in twenty leagues, I perceive no absurdity in asserting, that upon their contact they become one. For, I beseech you, by what rule or standard do you judge, when you assert, that the line, in which I have suppos'd them to concur, cannot make the same right line with those two, that form so small an angle betwixt them? You must surely have some idea of a right line, to which this line does not agree. Do you therefore mean, that it takes not the points in the same order and by the same rule, as is peculiar and essential to a right line? If so, I must inform you, that besides that in judging after this manner you allow, that extension is compos'd of indivisible points (which, perhaps, is more than you intend) besides this, I say, I must inform you, that neither is this the standard from which we form the idea of a right line; nor, if it were, is there any such firmness in our senses or imagination, as to determine when such an order is violated or preserv'd. The original standard of a right line is in reality nothing but a certain general appearance; and 'tis evident right lines may be made to concur with each other, and yet correspond to this standard, tho' corrected by all the means either practicable or imaginable.

This may open our eyes a little, and let us see, that no geometrical demonstration for the infinite divisibility of extension can have so much force as what we naturally attribute to every argument, which is supported by such magnificent pretensions. At the same time we may learn the reason, why geometry fails of evidence in this single point, while all its other reasonings command our fullest assent and approbation. And indeed it seems more requisite to give the reason of this exception, than to shew, that we really must make such an exception, and regard all the mathematical arguments for infinite divisibility as utterly sophistical. For 'tis evident, that as no idea of quantity is infinitely divisible, there cannot be imagin'd a more glaring absurdity, than to endeavour to prove, that quantity itself admits of such a division; and to prove this by means of ideas, which are directly opposite in that particular. And as this absurdity is very glaring in itself, so there is no argument founded on it, which is not attended with a new absurdity, and involves not an evident contradiction.

I might give as instances those arguments for infinite divisibility, which are deriv'd from the *point of contact*. I know there is no mathematician, who will not refuse to be judg'd by the diagrams he describes upon paper, these being loose draughts, as he will tell us, and serving only to convey with greater facility certain ideas, which are the true foundation of all our reasoning. This I am satisfy'd with, and am willing to rest the controversy merely upon these ideas. I desire therefore our mathematician to form, as accurately as possible, the ideas of a circle and a right line; and I then ask, if upon the conception of their contact he can conceive them as touching in a mathematical point, or if he must necessarily imagine them to concur for some space. Whichever side he chuses, he runs himself into equal difficulties. If he affirms, that in tracing these figures in his imagination, he can imagine them to touch only in a point, he allows the possibility of that idea, and consequently of the thing. If he says, that in his conception of the contact of those lines he must make them concur, he thereby acknowledges the fallacy of geometrical demonstrations, when carry'd beyond a certain degree of minuteness; since 'tis certain he has such demonstrations against the concurrence of a circle and a right line; that is, in other words, he can prove an idea, *viz.* that of concurrence, to be *incompatible* with two other ideas, *viz.* those of a circle and right line; tho' at the same time he acknowledges these ideas to be *inseparable*.

Section V: The Same Subject Continued

If the second part of my system be true, *that the idea of space or extension is nothing but the idea of visible or tangible points distributed in a certain order;* it follows, that we can form no idea of a vacuum, or space, where there is nothing visible or tangible. This gives rise to three objections, which I shall examine together, because the answer I shall give to one is a consequence of that which I shall make use of for the others.

First, It may be said, that men have disputed for many ages concerning a vacuum and a plenum, without being able to bring the affair to a final decision; and philosophers, even at this day, think themselves at liberty to take party on either side, as their fancy leads them. But whatever foundation there may be for a controversy concerning the things themselves, it may be pretended, that the very dispute is decisive concerning the idea, and that 'tis impossible men cou'd so long reason about a vacuum, and either refute or defend it, without having a notion of what they refuted or defended.

Secondly, If this argument shou'd be contested, the reality or at least possibility of the *idea* of a vacuum may be prov'd by the following reasoning. Every idea is possible, which is a necessary and infallible consequence of such as are possible. Now tho' we allow the world to be at present a plenum, we may easily conceive it to be depriv'd of motion; and this idea will certainly be allow'd possible. It must also be allow'd possible, to conceive the annihilation of any part of matter by the omnipotence of the deity, while the other parts remain at rest. For as every idea, that is distinguishable, is separable by the imagination; and as every idea, that is separable by the imagination, may be conceiv'd to be separately existent; 'tis evident, that the existence of one particle of matter, no more implies the existence of another, than a square figure in one body implies a square figure in every one. This being granted, I now demand what results from the concurrence of these two possible ideas of *rest* and *annihilation,* and what must we conceive to follow upon the annihilation of all the air and subtile matter in the chamber, supposing the walls to remain the same, without any motion or alteration? There are some metaphysicians, who answer, that since matter and extension are the same, the annihilation of one necessarily implies that of the other; and there being now no distance betwixt the walls of the chamber, they touch each other; in the same manner as my hand touches the paper, which is immediately before me. But tho' this answer be very common, I defy these metaphysicians to conceive the matter according to their hypothesis, or imagine the floor and roof, with all the opposite sides of the chamber, to touch each other, while they continue in rest, and preserve the same position. For how can the two walls, that run from south to north, touch each other, while they touch the opposite ends of two walls, that run from east to west? And how can the floor and roof ever meet, while they are separated by the four walls, that lie in a contrary position? If you change their position, you suppose a motion. If you conceive any thing betwixt them, you suppose a new creation. But keeping strictly to the two ideas of *rest* and *annihilation,* 'tis evident, that the idea, which results from them, is not that of a contact of parts, but something else; which is concluded to be the idea of a vacuum.

The third objection carries the matter still farther, and not only asserts, that the idea of a vacuum is real and possible, but also necessary and unavoidable. This assertion is founded on the motion we observe in bodies, which, 'tis maintain'd, wou'd be impossible and inconceivable without a vacuum, into which one body must move in order to make way for another. I shall not enlarge upon this objection, because it principally belongs to natural philosophy, which lies without our present sphere.

In order to answer these objections, we must take the matter pretty deep, and consider the nature and origin of several ideas, lest we dispute without understanding perfectly the subject of the controversy. 'Tis evident the idea of darkness is no positive idea, but merely the negation of light, or more properly speaking, of colour'd and visible objects. A man, who enjoys his sight, receives no other perception from turning his eyes on every side, when entirely depriv'd of light, than what is common to him with one born blind; and 'tis certain such-a-one has no idea either of light or darkness. The consequence of this is, that 'tis not from the mere removal of visible objects we receive the impression of extension without matter; and that the idea of utter darkness can never be the same with that of vacuum.

Suppose again a man to be supported in the air, and to be softly convey'd along by some invisible power; 'tis evident he is sensible of nothing, and never receives the idea of extension, nor indeed any idea, from this invariable motion. Even supposing he moves his limbs to and fro, this cannot convey to him that idea. He feels in that case a certain sensation or impression, the parts of which are successive to each other, and may give him the idea of time: But certainly are not dispos'd in such a manner, as is necessary to convey the idea of space or extension.

Since then it appears, that darkness and motion, with the utter removal of every thing visible and tangible, can never give us the idea of extension without matter, or of a vacuum; the next question is, whether they can convey this idea, when mix'd with something visible and tangible?

'Tis commonly allow'd by philosophers, that all bodies, which discover themselves to the eye, appear as if painted on a plain surface, and that their different degrees of remoteness from ourselves are discover'd more by reason than by the senses. When I hold up my hand before me, and spread my fingers, they are separated as perfectly by the blue colour of the firmament, as they cou'd be by any visible object, which I cou'd place betwixt them. In order, therefore, to know whether the sight can convey the impression and idea of a vacuum, we must suppose, that amidst an entire darkness, there are luminous bodies presented to us, whose light discovers only these bodies themselves, without giving us any impression of the surrounding objects.

We must form a parallel supposition concerning the objects of our feeling. 'Tis not proper to suppose a perfect removal of all tangible objects: we must allow something to be perceiv'd by the feeling; and after an interval and motion of the hand or other organ of sensation, another object of the touch to be met with; and upon leaving that, another; and so on, as often as we please. The question is, whether these intervals do not afford us the idea of extension without body?

To begin with the first case; 'tis evident, that when only two luminous bodies appear to the eye, we can perceive, whether they be conjoin'd or separate; whether they be separated by a great or small distance; and if this distance varies, we can perceive its increase or diminution, with the motion of the bodies. But as the distance is not in this case any thing

colour'd or visible, it may be thought that there is here a vacuum or pure extension, not only intelligible to the mind, but obvious to the very senses.

This is our natural and most familiar way of thinking; but which we shall learn to correct by a little reflexion. We may observe, that when two bodies present themselves, where there was formerly an entire darkness, the only change, that is discoverable, is in the appearance of these two objects, and that all the rest continues to be as before, a perfect negation of light, and of every colour'd or visible object. This is not only true of what may be said to be remote from these bodies, but also of the very distance; which is interpos'd betwixt them; *that* being nothing but darkness, or the negation of light; without parts, without composition, invariable and indivisible. Now since this distance causes no perception different from what a blind man receives from his eyes, or what is convey'd to us in the darkest night, it must partake of the same properties: And as blindness and darkness afford us no ideas of extension, 'tis impossible that the dark and undistinguishable distance betwixt two bodies can ever produce that idea.

The sole difference betwixt an absolute darkness and the appearance of two or more visible luminous objects consists, as I said, in the objects themselves, and in the manner they affect our senses. The angles, which the rays of light flowing from them, form with each other; the motion that is requir'd in the eye, in its passage from one to the other; and the different parts of the organs, which are affected by them; these produce the only perceptions, from which we can judge of the distance. But as these perceptions are each of them simple and indivisible, they can never give us the idea of extension.

We may illustrate this by considering the sense of feeling, and the imaginary distance or interval interpos'd betwixt tangible or solid objects. I suppose two cases, *viz.* that of a man supported in the air, and moving his limbs to and fro, without meeting any thing tangible; and that of a man, who feeling something tangible, leaves it, and after a motion, of which he is sensible, perceives another tangible object; and I then ask, wherein consists the difference betwixt these two cases? No one will make any scruple to affirm, that it consists meerly in the perceiving those objects, and that the sensation, which arises from the motion, is in both cases the same: And as that sensation is not capable of conveying to us an idea of extension, when unaccompany'd with some other perception, it can no more give us that idea, when mix'd with the impressions of tangible objects; since that mixture produces no alteration upon it.

But tho' motion and darkness, either alone, or attended with tangible and visible objects, convey no idea of a vacuum or extension without matter, yet they are the causes why we falsly imagine we can form such an idea. For there is a close relation betwixt that motion and darkness, and a real extension, or composition of visible and tangible objects.

First, We may observe, that two visible objects appearing in the midst of utter darkness, affect the senses in the same manner, and form the same angle by the rays, which flow from them, and meet in the eye, as if the distance betwixt them were fill'd with visible objects, that give us a true idea of extension. The sensation of motion is likewise the same, when there is nothing tangible interpos'd betwixt two bodies, as when we feel a compounded body, whose different parts are plac'd beyond each other.

Secondly, We find by experience, that two bodies, which are so plac'd as to affect the senses in the same manner with two others, that have a certain extent of visible objects interpos'd betwixt them, are capable of receiving the same extent, without any sensible impulse or penetration, and without any change on that angle, under which they appear to the sense. In like manner, where there is one object, which we cannot feel after another without an interval, and the perceiving of that sensation we call motion in our hand or organ of sensation; experience shews us, that 'tis possible the same object may be felt with the same sensation of motion, along with the interpos'd impression of solid and tangible objects, attending the sensation. That is, in other words, an invisible and intangible distance may be converted into a visible and tangible one, without any change on the distant objects.

Thirdly, We may observe, as another relation betwixt these two kinds of distance, that they have nearly the same effects on every natural phænomenon. For as all qualities, such as heat, cold, light, attraction, &c. diminish in proportion to the distance; there is but little difference observ'd, whether this distance be mark'd out by compounded and sensible objects, or be known only by the manner, in which the distant objects affect the senses.

Here then are three relations betwixt that distance, which conveys the idea of extension, and that other, which is not fill'd with any colour'd or solid object. The distant objects affect the senses in the same manner, whether separated by the one distance or the other; the second species of distance is found capable of receiving the first; and they both equally diminish the force of every quality.

These relations betwixt the two kinds of distance will afford us an easy reason, why the one has so often been taken for the other, and why we imagine we have an idea of extension without the idea of any object either of the sight or feeling. For we may establish it as a general maxim in this science of human nature, that wherever there is a close relation betwixt two ideas, the mind is very apt to mistake them, and in all its discourses and reasonings to use the one for the other. This phaenomenon occurs on so many occasions, and is of such consequence, that I cannot forbear stopping a moment to examine its causes. I shall only premise, that we must distinguish exactly betwixt the phænomenon itself, and the causes, which I shall assign for it; and must not imagine from any uncertainty in the latter, that the former is also uncertain. The phænomenon may be real, tho' my explication be chimerical. The falshood of the one is no consequence of that of the other; tho' at the same time we may observe, that 'tis very natural for us to draw such a consequence; which is an evident instance of that very principle, which I endeavor to explain.

When I receiv'd the relations of *resemblance, contiguity* and *causation,* as principles of union among ideas, without examining into their causes, 'twas more in prosecution of my first maxim, that we must in the end rest contented with experience, than for want of something specious and plausible, which I might have display'd on that subject. 'Twou'd have been easy to have made an imaginary dissection of the brain, and have shewn, why upon our conception of any idea, the animal spirits run into all the contiguous traces, and rouze up the other ideas, that are related to it. But tho' I have neglected any advantage, which I might have drawn from this topic in explaining the relations of ideas, I am afraid I must here have recourse to it, in order to account for the mistakes that arise from these relations. I shall therefore observe, that as the mind is endow'd with a power of exciting any idea it pleases; whenever it dispatches the spirits into that region of the brain, in which the idea is plac'd; these spirits always excite the idea, when they run precisely into the proper traces, and rummage that cell, which belongs to the idea. But as their motion is seldom direct, and naturally turns a little to the one side or the other; for this reason the animal spirits, falling into the contiguous traces, present other related ideas in lieu of that, which the mind desir'd at first to survey. This change we are not always sensible of; but continuing still the same train of thought, make use of the related idea, which is presented to us, and employ it in our reasoning, as if it were the same with what we demanded. This is the cause of many mistakes and sophisms in philosophy; as will naturally be imagin'd, and as it wou'd be easy to shew, if there was occasion.

Of the three relations above-mention'd that of resemblance is the most fertile source of error; and indeed there are few mistakes in reasoning, which do not borrow largely from that origin. Resembling ideas are not only related together, but the actions of the mind, which we employ in considering them, are so little different, that we are not able to distinguish them. This last circumstance is of great consequence; and we may in general observe, that wherever the actions of the mind in forming any two ideas are the same or resembling, we are very apt to confound these ideas, and take the one for the other. Of this we shall see many instances in the progress of this treatise. But tho' resemblance be the relation, which most readily produces a mistake in ideas, yet the others of causation and contiguity may also concur in the same influence. We might produce the figures of poets and orators, as sufficient proofs of this, were it as usual, as it is reasonable, in metaphysical subjects to draw our arguments from that quarter. But lest metaphysicians shou'd esteem this below their dignity, I shall borrow a proof from an observation, which may be made on most of their own discourses, viz. that 'tis usual for men to use words for ideas, and to talk instead of thinking in their reasonings. We use words for ideas, because they are commonly so closely connected, that the mind easily mistakes them. And this likewise is the reason, why we substitute the idea of a distance, which is not considered either as visible or tangible, in the room of extension, which is nothing but a composition of visible or tangible points dispos'd in a certain order. In causing this mistake there concur both the relations of *causation* and *resemblance*. As the first species of distance is found to be convertible into the second, 'tis in this respect a kind of cause; and the similarity of their manner of affecting the senses, and diminishing every quality, forms the relation of resemblance.

After this chain of reasoning and explication of my principles, I am now prepared to answer all the objections that have been offer'd, whether deriv'd from *metaphysics* or *mechanics*. The frequent disputes concerning a vacuum, or extension without matter, prove not the reality of the idea, upon which the dispute turns; there being nothing more common, than to see men deceive themselves in this particular; especially when by means of any close relation, there is another idea presented, which may be the occasion of their mistake.

We may make almost the same answer to the second objection, deriv'd from the conjunction of the ideas of rest and annihilation. When every thing is annihilated in the chamber, and the walls continue immoveable, the chamber must be conceiv'd much in the same manner as at present, when the air that fills it, is not an object of the senses. This annihilation leaves to the *eye,* that fictitious distance, which is discover'd by the different parts of the organ, that are affected, and by the degrees of light and shade; and to the *feeling,* that which consists in a sensation of motion in the hand, or other member of the body. In vain shou'd we search any farther. On whichever side we turn this subject, we shall find that these are the only impressions such an object can produce after the suppos'd annihilation; and it has already been remark'd, that impressions can give rise to no ideas, but to such as resemble them.

Since a body interpos'd betwixt two others may be suppos'd to be annihilated, without producing any change upon such as lie on each hand of it, 'tis easily conceiv'd, how it may be created anew, and yet produce as little alteration. Now the motion of a body has much the same effect as its creation. The distant bodies are no more affected in the one case, than in the other. This suffices to satisfy the imagination, and proves there is no repugnance in such a motion. Afterwards experience comes in play to persuade us that two bodies, situated in the manner above-describ'd, have really such a capacity of receiving body betwixt them, and that there is no obstacle to the conversion of the invisible and intangible distance into one that is visible and tangible. However natural that conversion may seem, we cannot be sure it is practicable, before we have had experience of it.

Thus I seem to have answer'd the three objections abovemention'd; tho' at the same time I am sensible, that few will be satisfy'd with these answers, but will immediately propose new objections and difficulties. 'Twil probably be said, that my reasoning makes nothing to the matter in hand, and that I explain only the manner in which objects affect the senses, without endeavoring to account for their real nature and operations. Tho' there be nothing visible or tangible interpos'd betwixt two bodies, yet we find *by experience,* that the bodies may be plac'd in the same manner, with regard to the eye, and require the same motion of the hand in passing from one to the other, as if divided by something visible and tangible. This invisible and intangible distance is also found *by experience* to contain a capacity of receiving body, or of becoming visible and tangible. Here is the whole of my system; and in no part of it have I endeavour'd to explain the cause, which separates bodies after this

manner, and gives them a capacity of receiving others betwixt them, without any impulse or penetration.

I answer this objection, by pleading guilty, and by confessing that my intention never was to penetrate into the nature of bodies, or explain the secret causes of their operations. For besides that this belongs not to my present purpose, I am afraid, that such an enterprise is beyond the reach of human understanding, and that we can never pretend to know body otherwise than by those external properties, which discover themselves to the senses. As to those who attempt any thing farther, I cannot approve of their ambition, till I see, in some one instance at least, that they have met with success. But at present I content myself with knowing perfectly the manner in which objects affect my senses, and their connections with each other, as far as experience informs me of them. This suffices for the conduct of life; and this also suffices for my philosophy, which pretends only to explain the nature and causes of our perceptions, or impressions and ideas.

I shall conclude this subject of extension with a paradox, which will easily be explain'd from the foregoing reasoning. This paradox is, that if you are pleas'd to give to the invisible and intangible distance, or in other words, to the capacity of becoming a visible and tangible distance, the name of a vacuum, extension and matter are the same, and yet there is a vacuum. If you will not give it that name, motion is possible in a plenum, without any impulse *in infinitum,* without returning in a circle, and without penetration. But however we may express ourselves, we must always confess, that we have no idea of any real extension without filling it with sensible objects and conceiving its parts as visible or tangible.

As to the doctrine, that time is nothing but the manner, in which some real objects exist; we may observe, that 'tis liable to the same objections as the similar doctrine with regard to extension. If it be a sufficient proof, that we have the idea of a vacuum, because we dispute and reason concerning it; we must for the same reason have the idea of time without any changeable existence; since there is no subject of dispute more frequent and common. But that we really have no such idea, is certain. For whence shou'd it be deriv'd? Does it arise from an impression of sensation or of reflexion? Point it out distinctly to us, that we may know its nature and qualities. But if you cannot point out *any such impression,* you may be certain you are mistaken, when you imagine you have *any such idea.*

But tho' it be impossible to shew the impression, from which the idea of time without a changeable existence is deriv'd; yet we can easily point out those appearances, which make us fancy we have that idea. For we may observe, that there is a continual succession of perceptions in our mind; so that the idea of time being for ever present with us; when we consider a stedfast object at five-a-clock, and regard the same at six; we are apt to apply to it that idea in the same manner as if every moment were distinguish'd by a different position, or an alteration of the object. The first and second appearances of the object, being compar'd with the succession of our perceptions, seem equally remov'd as if the object had really chang'd. To which we may add, what experience shews us, that the object was susceptible of such a number of changes betwixt these appearances; as also that the unchangeable or rather fictitious duration has the same effect upon every quality, by encreasing or diminishing it, as that succession, which is obvious to the senses. From these three relations we are apt to confound our ideas, and imagine we can form the idea of a time and duration, without any change or succession.

Section VI:
Of the Idea of Existence and of External Existence

It may not be amiss, before we leave this subject, to explain the ideas of *existence* and of *external existence;* which have their difficulties, as well as the ideas of space and time. By this means we shall be the better prepar'd for the examination of knowledge and probability, when we understand perfectly all those particular ideas, which may enter into our reasoning.

There is no impression nor idea of any kind, of which we have any consciousness or memory, that is not conceiv'd as existent; and 'tis evident, that from this consciousness the most perfect idea and assurance of *being* is deriv'd. From hence we may form a dilemma, the most clear and conclusive that can be imagin'd, *viz.* that since we never remember any idea or impression without attributing existence to it, the idea of existence must either be deriv'd from a distinct impression, conjoin'd with every perception or object of our thought, or must be the very same with the idea of the perception or object.

As this dilemma is an evident consequence of the principle, that every idea arises from a similar impression, so our decision betwixt the propositions of the dilemma is no more doubtful. So far from there being any distinct impression, attending every impression and every idea, that I do not think there are any two distinct impressions, which are inseparably conjoin'd. Tho' certain sensations may at one time be united, we quickly find they admit of a separation, and may be presented apart. And thus, tho' every impression and idea we remember be consider'd as existent, the idea of existence is not deriv'd from any particular impression.

The idea of existence, then, is the very same with the idea of what we conceive to be existent. To reflect on any thing simply, and to reflect on it as existent, are nothing different from each other. That idea, when conjoin'd with the idea of any object, makes no addition to it. Whatever we conceive, we conceive to be existent. Any idea we please to form is the idea of a being; and the idea of a being is any idea we please to form.

Whoever opposes this, must necessarily point out that distinct impression, from which the idea of entity is deriv'd, and must prove, that this impression is inseparable from every perception we believe to be existent. This we may without hesitation conclude to be impossible.

Our foregoing[7] reasoning concerning the *distinction* of ideas without any real *difference* will not here serve us in any stead. That kind of distinction is founded on the different resemblances, which the same simple idea may have to several different ideas. But no object

[7]Part I, sect. vii.

can be presented resembling some object with respect to its existence, and different from others in the same particular; since every object, that is presented, just necessarily be existent.

A like reasoning will account for the idea of *external existence*. We may observe, that 'tis universally allow'd by philosophers, and is besides pretty obvious of itself, that nothing is ever really present with the mind but its perceptions or impressions and ideas, and that external objects become known to us only by those perceptions they occasion. To hate, to love, to think, to feel, to see; all this is nothing but to perceive.

Now since nothing is every present to the mind but perceptions, and since all ideas are deriv'd from something antecedently present to the mind; it follows, that 'tis impossible for us so much as to conceive or form an idea of any thing specifically different from ideas and impressions. Let us fix our attention out of ourselves as much as possible: Let us chace our imagination to the heavens, or to the utmost limits of the universe; we never really advance a step beyond ourselves, nor can conceive any kind of existence, but those perceptions, which have appear'd in that narrow compass. This is the universe of the imagination, nor have we any idea but what is there produc'd.

The farthest we can go towards a conception of external objects, when suppos'd *specifically* different from our perceptions, is to form a relative idea of them, without pretending to comprehend the related objects. Generally speaking we do not suppose them specifically different; but only attribute to them different relations, connexions and durations. But of this more fully hereafter.[8]

Part IV: Of the Sceptical and Other Systems of Philosophy

Section V: of the Immateriality of the Soul

Having found such contradictions and difficulties in every system concerning external ob-

[8]Part IV, sect. ii.

jects, and in the idea of matter, which we fancy so clear and determinate, we shall naturally expect still greater difficulties and contradictions in every hypothesis concerning our internal perceptions, and the nature of the mind, which we are apt to imagine so much more obscure, and uncertain. But in this we shou'd deceive ourselves. The intellectual world, tho' involv'd in infinite obscurities, is not perplex'd with any such contradictions, as those we have discover'd in the natural. What is known concerning it, agrees with itself; and what is unknown, we must be contented to leave so.

'Tis true, wou'd we hearken to certain philosophers, they promise to diminish our ignorance; but I am afraid 'tis at the hazard of running us into contradictions, from which the subject is of itself exempted. These philosophers are the curious reasoners concerning the material or immaterial substances, in which they suppose our perceptions to inhere. In order to put a stop to these endless cavils on both sides, I know no better method, than to ask these philosophers in a few words, *What they mean by substance and inhesion?* And after they have answer'd this question, 'twill then be reasonable, and not till then, to enter seriously into the dispute.

This question we have found impossible to be answer'd with regard to matter and body: But besides that in the case of the mind, it labours under all the same difficulties, 'tis burthen'd with some additional ones, which are peculiar to that subject. As every idea is deriv'd from a precedent impression, had we any idea of the substance of our minds, we must also have an impression of it; which is very difficult, if not impossible, to be conceiv'd. For how can an impression represent a substance, otherwise than by resembling it? And how can an impression resemble a substance, since, according to this philosophy, it is not a substance, and has none of the peculiar qualities or characteristics of a substance?

But leaving the question *of what may or may not be,* for that other *what actually is,* I desire those philosophers, who pretend that we have an idea of the substance of our minds, to point out the impression that produces it, and tell distinctly after what manner that impression operates, and from what object it is deriv'd. Is it an impression of sensation or of reflection? Is it pleasant, or painful, or indifferent? Does it attend us at all times, or does it only return at intervals? If at intervals, at what times principally does it return, and by what causes is it produc'd?

If instead of answering these questions, any one shou'd evade the difficulty, by saying, that the definition of a substance is *something which may exist by itself;* and that this definition ought to satisfy us: Shou'd this be said, I shou'd observe, that this definition agrees to every thing, that can possibly be conceiv'd; and never will serve to distinguish substance from accident, or the soul from its perceptions. For thus I reason. Whatever is clearly conceiv'd may exist; and whatever is clearly conceiv'd, after any manner, may exist after the same manner. This is one principle, which has been already acknowledg'd. Again, every thing, which is different, is distinguishable, and every thing which is distinguishable, is separable by the imagination. This is another principle. My conclusion from both is, that since all our perceptions are different from each other, and from every thing else in the universe, they are also distinct and separable, and may be consider'd as separately existent, and may exist separately, and have no need of any thing else to support their existence. They are, therefore, substances, as far as this definition explains a substance.

Thus neither by considering the first origin of ideas, nor by means of a definition are we able to arrive at any satisfactory notion of substance; which seems to me a sufficient reason for abandoning utterly that dispute concerning the materiality and immateriality of the soul, and makes me absolutely condemn even the question itself. We have no perfect idea of any thing but of a perception. A substance is entirely different from a perception. We have, therefore, no idea of a substance. Inhesion in something is suppos'd to be requisite to support the existence of our perceptions. Nothing appears requisite to support the existence of a perception. We have, therefore, no idea of inhesion. What possibility then of answering that question, *Whether perceptions inhere in a material or immaterial substance,* when we do not so much as understand the meaning of the question?

There is one argument commonly employ'd for the immateriality of the soul, which seems to me remarkable. Whatever is extended consists of parts; and whatever consists of parts is divisible, if not in reality, at least in the imagination. But 'tis impossible any thing divisible can be *conjoin'd* to a thought or perception, which is a being altogether inseparable and indivisible. For supposing such a conjunction, wou'd the indivisible thought exist on the left or on the right hand of this extended divisible body? On the surface or in the middle? On the back- or fore-side of it? If it be conjoin'd with the extension, it must exist somewhere within its dimensions. If it exists within its dimensions, it must either exist in one particular part; and then that particular part is indivisible, and the perception is conjoin'd only with it, not with the extension: Or if the thought exists in every part, it must also be extended, and separable, and divisible, as well as the body; which is utterly absurd and contradictory. For can any one conceive a passion of yard in length, a foot in breadth, and an inch in thickness? Thought, therefore, and extension are qualities wholly incompatible, and never can incorporate together into one subject.

This argument affects not the question concerning the *substance* of the soul, but only that concerning its *local conjunction* with matter; and therefore it may not be improper to consider in general what objects are, or are not susceptible of a local conjunction. This is a curious question, and may lead us to some discoveries of considerable moment.

The first notion of space and extension is deriv'd solely from the senses of sight and feeling; nor is there any thing, but what is colour'd or tangible, that has parts dispos'd after such a manner, as to convey that idea. When we diminish or encrease a relish, 'tis not after the same manner that we diminish or increase any visible object; and when several sounds strike our hearing at once, custom and reflection alone make us form an idea of the degrees of the distance and contiguity of those bodies, from which they are deriv'd. Whatever marks the place of its existence either must be extended, or must be a mathematical point, without parts or composition. What is extended must have a particular figure, as square, round, triangular; none of which will agree to a desire, or indeed to any impression or idea, except of these two senses above-mention'd. Neither ought a desire, tho' indivisible, to be consider'd as a mathematical point. For in that case 'twou'd be possible, by the addition of others, to make two, three, four desires, and these dispos'd and situated in such a manner, as to have a determinate length, breadth and thickness; which is evidently absurd.

"Twill not be surprizing after this, if I deliver a maxim, which is condemn'd by several metaphysicians, and is esteem'd contrary to the most certain principles of human reason. This maxim is *that an object may exist, and yet be no where:* and I assert, that this is not only possible, but that the greatest part of beings do and must exist after this manner. An object may be said to be no where, when its parts are not so situated with respect to each other, as to form any figure or quantity; nor the whole with respect to other bodies so as to answer to our notions of contiguity or distance. Now this is evidently the case with all our perceptions and objects, except those of the sight and feeling. A moral reflection cannot be plac'd on the right or on the left hand of a passion, nor can a smell or sound be either of a circular or a square figure. These objects and perceptions, as far from requiring any particular place, are absolutely incompatible with it, and even the imagination cannot attribute it to them. And as to the absurdity of supposing them to be no where, we may consider, that if the passions and sentiments appear to the perception to have any particular place, the idea of extension might be deriv'd from them, as well as from the sight and touch; contrary to what we have already establish'd. If they *appear* not to have any particular place, they may possibly *exist* in the same manner; since whatever we conceive is possible.

'Twill not now be necessary to prove, that those perceptions, which are simple, and exist no where, are incapable of any conjunction in place with matter or body, which is extended and divisible; since 'tis impossible to found a relation[1] but on some common quality. It may be better worth our while to remark, that this question of the local conjunction of objects does not only occur in metaphysical disputes concerning the nature of the soul, but that even in common life we have every moment occasion to examine it. Thus supposing we consider a fig at one end of the table, and an olive at the other, 'tis evident, that in forming the complex ideas of these substances, one of the most obvious is that of their different relishes; and 'tis as evident, that we incorporate and conjoin these qualities with such as are colour'd and tangible. The bitter taste of the one, and sweet of the other are suppos'd to lie in the very visible body, and to be separated from each other by the whole length of the table. This is so notable and so natural an illusion, that it may be proper to consider the principles, from which it is deriv'd.

Tho' an extended object be incapable of a conjunction in place with another, that exists without any place or extension, yet are they susceptible of many other relations. Thus the taste and smell of any fruit are inseparable from its other qualities of colour and tangibility; and which-ever of them be the cause or effect, 'tis certain they are always co-existent. Nor are they only co-existent in general, but also co-temporary in their appearance in the mind; and 'tis upon the application of the extended body to our senses we perceive its particular taste and smell. These relations, then, of *causation, and contiguity in the time of their appearance*, betwixt the extended object and the quality, which exists without any particular place, must have such an effect on the mind, that upon the appearance of one it will immediately turn its thought to the conception of the other. Nor is this all. We not only turn our thought from one to the other upon account of their relation, but likewise endeavour to give them a new relation, viz. that of *a conjunction in place*, that we may render the transition more easy and natural. For 'tis a quality, which I shall often have occasion to remark in human nature, and shall explain more fully in its proper place, that when objects are united by any relation, we have a strong propensity to

[1]Part I, sect. v.

add some new relation to them, in order to compleat the union. In our arrangement of bodies we never fail to place such as are resembling, in contiguity to each other, or at least in correspondent points of view: Why? but because we feel a satisfaction in joining the relation of contiguity to that of resemblance, or the resemblance of situation to that of qualities. The effects of this propensity have been[2] already observ'd in that resemblance, which we so readily suppose betwixt particular impressions and their external causes. But we shall not find a more evident effect of it, than in the present instance, where from the relations of causation and contiguity in time betwixt two objects, we feign likewise that of a conjunction in place, in order to strengthen the connexion.

But whatever confus'd notions we may form of an union in place betwixt an extended body, as a fig, and its particular taste, 'tis certain that upon reflection we must observe in this union something altogether unintelligible and contradictory. For shou'd we ask ourselves one obvious question, *viz.* if the taste, which we conceive to be contain'd in the circumference of the body, is in every part of it or in one only, we must quickly find ourselves at a loss, and perceive the impossibility of ever giving a satisfactory answer. We cannot reply, that 'tis only in one part: For experience convinces us, that every part has the same relish. We can as little reply, that it exists in every part: For then we must suppose it figur'd and extended; which is absurd and incomprehensible. Here then we are influenc'd by two principles directly contrary to each other, *viz.* that *inclination* of our fancy by which we are determin'd to incorporate the taste with the extended object, and our *reason*, which shows us the impossibility of such an union. Being divided betwixt these opposite principles, we renounce neither one nor the other, but involve the subject in such confusion and obscurity, that we no longer perceive the opposition. We suppose, that the taste exists within the circumference of the body, but in such a manner, that it fills the whole without extension, and exists entire in every part without separation. In short, we use

in our most familiar way of thinking, that scholastic principle, which, when crudely propos'd, appears so shocking, of *totum in toto & totum in qualibet parte:* Which is much the same, as if we shou'd say, that a thing is in a certain place, and yet is not there.

All this absurdity proceeds from our endeavoring to bestow a place on what is utterly incapable of it; and that endeavour again arises from our inclination to compleat an union, which is founded on causation, and a contiguity of time, by attributing to the objects a conjunction in place. But if ever reason be of sufficient force to overcome prejudice, 'tis certain, that in the present case it must prevail. For we have only this choice left, either to suppose that some beings exist without any place; or that they are figur'd and extended; or that when they are incorporated with extended objects, the whole is in the whole, and the whole in every part. The absurdity of the two last suppositions proves sufficiently the veracity of the first. Nor is there any fourth opinion. For as to the supposition of their existence in the manner of mathematical points, it resolves itself into the second opinion, and supposes, that several passions may be plac'd in a circular figure, and that a certain number of smells, conjoin'd with a certain number of sounds, may make a body to twelve cubic inches; which appears ridiculous upon the bare mentioning of it.

But tho' in this view of things we cannot refuse to condemn the materialists, who conjoin all thought with extension; yet a little reflection will show us equal reason for blaming their antagonists, who conjoin all thought with a simple and indivisible substance. The most vulgar philosophy informs us, that no external object can make itself known to the mind immediately, and without the interposition of an image or perception. That table, which just now appears to me, is only a perception, and all it qualities are qualities of a perception. Now the most obvious of all its qualities is extension. The perception consists of parts. These parts are so situated, as to afford us the notion of distance and contiguity; of length, breadth, and thickness. The termination of these three dimensions is what we call figure. This figure is moveable, separable, and

[2]Sect ii, towards the end.

divisible. Mobility, and separability are the distinguishing properties of extended objects. And to cut short all disputes, the very idea of extension is copy'd from nothing but an impression, and consequently must perfectly agree to it. To say the idea of extension agrees to any thing, is to say it is extended.

The free-thinker may now triumph in his turn; and having found there are impressions and ideas really extended, may ask his antagonists, how they can incorporate a simple and indivisible subject with an extended perception? All the arguments of Theologians may here be retorted upon them. Is the indivisible subject, or immaterial substance, if you will, on the left or on the right hand of the perception? Is it in this particular part, or in that other? Is it in every part without being extended? Or is it entire in any one part without deserting the rest? 'Tis impossible to give any answer to these questions, but what will both be absurd in itself, and will account for the union of our indivisible perceptions with an extended substance.

This gives me an occasion to take a-new into consideration the question concerning the substance of the soul; and tho' I have condemn'd that question as utterly unintelligible, yet I cannot forbear proposing some farther reflections concerning it. I assert, that the doctrine of the immateriality, simplicity, and indivisibility of a thinking substance is a true atheism, and will serve to justify all those sentiments, for which *Spinoza* is so universally infamous. From this topic, I hope at least to reap one advantage, that my adversaries will not have any pretext to render the present doctrine odious by their declamations, when they see that they can be so easily retorted on them.

The fundamental principle of the atheism of *Spinoza* is the doctrine of the simplicity of the universe, and the unity of that substance, in which he supposes both thought and matter to inhere. There is only one substance, says he, in the world; and that substance is perfectly simple and indivisible, and exists every where, without any local presence. Whatever we discover externally by sensation; whatever we feel internally by reflection; all these are nothing but modifications of that one, simple, and necessarily existent being, and are not possest of any separate or distinct existence. Every passion of the soul; every configuration of matter, however different and various, inhere in the same substance, and preserve in themselves their characters of distinction, without communicating them to that subject, in which they inhere. The same *substratum,* if I may so speak, supports the most different modifications, without any difference in itself; and varies them, without any variation. Neither time, nor place, nor all the diversity of nature are able to produce any composition or change in its perfect simplicity and identity.

I believe this brief exposition of the principles of that famous atheist will be sufficient for the present purpose, and that without entering farther into these gloomy and obscure regions, I shall be able to shew, that this hideous hypothesis is almost the same with that of the immateriality of the soul, which has become so popular. To make this evident, let us[3] remember, that as every idea is deriv'd from a preceding perception, 'tis impossible our idea of a perception, and that of an object or external existence can ever represent what are specifically different from each other. Whatever difference we may suppose betwixt them, 'tis still incomprehensible to us; and we are oblig'd either to conceive an external object merely as a relation without a relative, or to make it the very same with a perception or impression.

The consequence I shall draw from this may, at first sight, appear a mere sophism; but upon the least examination will be found solid and satisfactory. I say then, that since we may suppose, but never can conceive a specific difference betwixt an object and impression; any conclusion we form concerning the connexion and repugnance of impressions, will not be known certainly to be applicable to objects; but that on the other hand, whatever conclusions of this kind we form concerning objects, will most certainly be applicable to impressions. The reason is not difficult. As an object is suppos'd to be different from an impression, we cannot be sure, that the circumstance, upon which we found our reasoning, is common to both, supposing we form the reasoning upon the impression. 'Tis still possible,

[3]Part II, sect. vi.

that the object may differ from it in that particular. But when we first form our reasoning concerning the object, 'tis beyond doubt, that the same reasoning must extend to the impression: And that because the quality of the object, upon which the argument is founded, must at least be conceiv'd by the mind; and cou'd not be conceiv'd, unless it were common to an impression; since we have no idea but what is deriv'd from that origin. Thus we may establish it as a certain maxim, that we can never, by any principle, but by an irregular kind[4] of reasoning from experience, discover a connexion or repugnance betwixt objects, which extends not to impressions; tho' the inverse proposition may not be equally true, that all the discoverable relations of impressions are common to objects.

To apply this to the present case; there are two different systems of beings presented, to which I suppose myself under a necessity of assigning some substance, or ground of inhesion. I observe first the universe of objects or of body: The sun, moon and stars; the earth, seas, plants, animals, men, ships, houses, and other productions either of art or nature. Here *Spinoza* appears, and tells me, that these are only modifications; and that the subject, in which they inhere, is simple, incompounded, and indivisible. After this I consider the other system of beings, *viz.* the universe of thought, or my impressions and ideas. There I observe another sun, moon and stars; an earth, and seas, cover'd and inhabited by plants and animals; towns, houses, mountains, rivers; and in short every thing I can discover or conceive in the first system. Upon my enquiring concerning these, Theologians present themselves, and tell me, that these also are modifications, and modifications of one simple, uncompounded, and indivisible substance. Immediately upon which I am deafen'd with the noise of a hundred voices, that treat the first hypothesis with detestation and scorn, and the second with applause and veneration. I turn my attention to these hypotheses to see what may be the reason of so great a partiality; and find that they have the same fault of being

unintelligible, and that as far as we can understand them, they are so much alike, that 'tis impossible to discover any absurdity in one, which is not common to both of them. We have no idea of any quality in an object, which does not agree to, and may not represent a quality in an impression; and that because all our ideas are deriv'd from our impressions. We can never, therefore, find any repugnance betwixt an extended object as a modification, and a simple uncompounded essence, as its substance, unless that repugnance takes place equally betwixt the perception or impression of that extended object, and the same uncompounded essence. Every idea of a quality of an object passes thro' an impression; and therefore every *perceivable* relation, whether of connexion or repugnance, must be common both to objects and impressions.

But tho' this argument, consider'd in general, seems evident beyond all doubt and contradiction, yet to make it more clear and sensible, let us survey it in detail; and see whether all the absurdities, which have been found in the system of *Spinoza*, may not likewise be discover'd in that of Theologians.[5]

First, It has been said against *Spinoza*, according to the scholastic way of talking, rather than thinking, that a mode, not being any distinct or separate existence, must be the very same with its substance, and consequently the extension of the universe, must be in a manner identify'd with that simple, uncompounded essence, in which the universe is suppos'd to inhere. But this, it may be pretended, is utterly impossible and inconceivable unless the indivisible substance expand itself, so as to correspond to the extension, or the extension contract itself, so as to answer to the indivisible substance. This argument seems just, as far as we can understand it; and 'tis plain nothing is requir'd, but a change in the terms, to apply the same argument to our extended perceptions, and the simple essence of the soul; the ideas of objects and perceptions being in every respect the same, only attended with the supposition of a difference, that is unknown and incomprehensible.

Secondly, It has been said, that we have no

---

[4]Such as that of sect. ii, from the coherence of our perceptions.

[5] See *Bayle's* dictionary, article of *Spinoza*.

idea of substance, which is not applicable to matter; nor any idea of a distinct substance, which is not applicable to every distinct portion of matter. Matter, therefore, is not a mode but a substance, and each part of matter is not a distinct mode, but a distinct substance. I have already prov'd, that we have no perfect idea of substance; but that taking it for *something, that can exist by itself,* 'tis evident every perception is a substance, and every distinct part of a perception a distinct substance: And consequently the one hypothesis labours under the same difficulties in this respect with the other.

Thirdly, It has been objected to the system of one simple substance in the universe, that this substance being the support or *substratum* of every thing, must at the very same instant by modify'd into forms, which are contrary and incompatible. The round and square figures are incompatible in the same substance at the same time. How then is it possible, that the same substance can at once be modify'd into that square table, and into this round one? I ask the same question concerning the impressions of these tables; and find that the answer is no more satisfactory in one case than in the other.

It appears, then, that to whatever side we turn, the same difficulties follow us, and that we cannot advance one step towards the establishing the simplicity and immateriality of the soul, without preparing the way for a dangerous and irrecoverable atheism. 'Tis the same case, if instead of calling thought a modification of the soul, we shou'd give it the more antient, and yet more modish name of an *action*. By an action we mean much the same thing, as what is commonly call'd an abstract mode; that is, something, which, properly speaking, is neither distinguishable, nor separable from its substance, and is only conceiv'd by a distinction of reason, or an abstraction. But nothing is gain'd by this change of the term of modification, for that of action; nor do we free ourselves from one single difficulty by its means; as will appear from the two following reflexions.

First, I observe, that the word, action, according to this explicaton of it, can never justly be apply'd to any perception, as deriv'd

from a mind or thinking substance. Our perceptions are all really different, and separable, and distinguishable from each other, and from every thing else, which we can imagine; and therefore 'tis impossible to conceive, how they can be the action or abstract mode of any substance. The instance of motion, which is commonly made use of to shew after what manner perception depends, as an action, upon its substance, rather confounds than instructs us. Motion to all appearance induces no real nor essential change on the body, but only varies its relation to other objects. But betwixt a person in the morning walking in a garden with company, agreeable to him; and a person in the afternoon inclos'd in a dungeon, and full of terror, despair, and resentment, there seems to be a radical difference, and of quite another kind, than what is produc'd on a body by the change of its situation. As we conclude from the distinction and separability of their ideas, that external objects have a separate existence from each other; so when we make these ideas themselves our objects, we must draw the same conclusion concerning *them,* according to the precedent reasoning. At least it must be confest, that having no idea of the substance of the soul, 'tis impossible for us to tell how it can admit of such differences, and even contrarieties of perception without any fundamental change; and consequently can never tell in what sense perceptions are actions of that substance. The use, therefore, of the word, *action,* unaccompany'd with any meaning, instead of that of modification, makes no addition to our knowledge, nor is of any advantage to the doctrine of the immateriality of the soul.

I add in the second place, that if it brings any advantage to that cause, it must bring an equal to the cause of atheism. For do our Theologians pretend to make a monopoly of the word, *action,* and may not the atheists likewise take possession of it, and affirm that plants, animals, men, &c. are nothing but particular actions of one simple universal substance, which exerts itself from a blind and absolute necessity? This you'll say is utterly absurd. I own 'tis unintelligible; but at the same time assert, according to the principles above-explain'd, that 'tis impossible to discover any absurdity in the supposition, that all the various objects in nature are actions of one simple substance, which absurdity will not be applicable to a like supposition concerning impressions and ideas.

From these hypotheses concerning the *substance and local conjunction* of our perceptions, we may pass to another, which is more intelligible than the former, and more important than the latter, *viz.* concerning the *cause* of our perceptions. Matter and motion, 'tis commonly said in the schools, however vary'd, are still matter and motion, and produce only a difference in the position and situation of objects. Divide a body as often as you please, 'tis still body. Place it in any figure, nothing ever results but figure, or the relation of parts. Move it in any manner, you still find motion or a change of relation. 'Tis absurd to imagine, that motion in a circle, for instance, shou'd be nothing but merely motion in a circle; while motion in another direction, as in an ellipse, shou'd also be a passion or moral reflexion: That the shocking of two globular particles shou'd become a sensation of pain, and that the meeting of two triangular ones shou'd afford a pleasure. Now as these different shocks, and variations, and mixtures are the only changes, of which matter is susceptible, and as these never afford us any idea of thought or perception, 'tis concluded to be impossible, that thought can ever be caus'd by matter.

Few have been able to withstand the seeming evidence of this argument; and yet nothing in the world is more easy than to refute it. We need only reflect on what has been prov'd at large, that we are never sensible of any connexion betwixt causes and effects, and that 'tis only by our experience of their constant conjunction, we can arrive at any knowledge of this relation. Now as all objects, which are not contrary, are susceptible of a constant conjunction, and as no real objects are contrary;[6] I have inferr'd from these principles, that to consider the matter *a priori*, any thing may produce any thing, and that we shall never discover a reason, why any object may or may not be the cause of any other, however great,

or however little the resemblance may be betwixt them. This evidently destroys the precedent reasoning concerning the cause of thought or perception. For tho' there appear no manner of connexion betwixt motion or thought, the case is the same with all other causes and effects. Place one body of a pound weight on one end of a lever, and another body of the same weight on another end; you will never find in these bodies any principle of motion dependent on their distances from the center, more than of thought and perception. If you pretend, therefore, to prove *a priori*, that such a position of bodies can never cause thought; because turn it which way you will, 'tis nothing but a position of bodies; you must by the same course of reasoning conclude, that it can never produce motion; since there is no more apparent connexion in the one case than in the other. But as this latter conclusion is contrary to evident experience, and as 'tis possible we may have a like experience in the operations of the mind, and may perceive a constant conjunction of thought and motion; you reason too hastily, when from the mere consideration of the ideas, you conclude that 'tis impossible motion can ever produce thought, or a different position of parts give rise to a different passion or reflexion. Nay 'tis not only possible we may have such an experience, but 'tis certain we have it; since every one may perceive, that the different dispositions of his body change his thoughts and sentiments. And shou'd it be said, that this depends on the union of soul and body; I wou'd answer, that we must separate the question concerning the substance of the mind from that concerning the cause of its thought; and that confining ourselves to the latter question we find by the comparing their ideas, that thought and motion are different from each other, and by experience, that they are constantly united; which being all the circumstances, that enter into the idea of cause and effect, when apply'd to the operations of matter, we may certainly conclude that motion may be, and actually is, the cause of thought and perception.

There seems only this dilemma left us in the present case; either to assert, that nothing can be the cause of another, but where the mind can perceive the connexion in its idea of the

---

[6] Part III, sect. xv.

objects: Or to maintain, that all objects, which we find constantly conjoin'd, are upon that account to be regarded as causes and effects. If we choose the first part of the dilemma, these are the consequences. *First,* We in reality affirm, that there is no such thing in the universe as a cause or productive principle, not even the deity himself; since our idea of that supreme Being is deriv'd from particular impressions, none of which contain any efficacy, nor seem to have *any* connexion with *any* other existence. As to what may be said, that the connexion betwixt the idea of an infinitely powerful being, and that of any effect, which he wills, is necessary and unavoidable; I answer, that we have no idea of a being endow'd with any power, much less of one endow'd with infinite power. But if we will change expressions, we can only define power by connexion; and then in saying, that the idea of an infinitely powerful being is connected with that of every effect, which he wills, we really do no more than assert, that a being, whose volition is connected with every effect, is connected with every effect; which is an identical proposition, and gives us no insight into the nature of this power or connexion. But, *secondly,* supposing, that the deity were the great and efficacious principle, which supplies the deficiency of all causes, this leads us into the grossest impieties and absurdities. For upon the same account, that we have recourse to him in natural operations, and assert that matter cannot of itself communicate motion, or produce thought, *viz.* because there is no apparent connexion betwixt these objects; I say, upon the very same account, we must acknowledge that the diety is the author of all our volitions and perceptions; since they have no more apparent connexion either with one another, or with the suppos'd but unknown substance of the soul. This agency of the supreme Being we know to have been asserted by[7] several philosophers with relation to all the actions of the mind, except volition, or rather an inconsiderable part of volition; tho' 'tis easy to perceive, that this exception is a mere pretext, to avoid the dangerous consequences of that doctrine. If nothing be active but what has

[7]As father *Malebranche* and other *Cartesians.*

an apparent power, thought is in no case any more active than matter; and if this inactivity must make us have recourse to a deity, the supreme being is the real cause of all our actions, bad as well as good, vicious as well as virtuous.

Thus we are necessarily reduc'd to the other side of the dilemma, *viz.* that all objects, which are found to be constantly conjoin'd, are upon that account only to be regarded as causes and effects. Now as all objects, which are not contrary, are susceptible of a constant conjunction, and as no real objects are contrary; it follows, that for ought we can determine by the mere ideas, any thing may be the cause or effect of any thing; which evidently gives the advantage to the materialists above their antagonists.

To pronounce, then, the final decision upon the whole; the question concerning the substance of the soul is absolutely unintelligible: All our perceptions are not susceptible of a local union, either with what is extended or unextended; there being some of them of the one kind, and some of the other: And as the constant conjunction of objects constitutes the very essence of cause and effect, matter and motion may often be regarded as the causes of thought, as far as we have any notion of that relation.

'Tis certainly a kind of indignity to philosophy, whose sovereign authority ought every where to be acknowledg'd, to oblige her on every occasion to make apologies for her conclusions, and justify herself to every particular art and science, which may be offended at her. This puts one in mind of a king arraign'd for high-treason against his subjects. There is only one occasion, when philosophy will think it necessary and even honourable to justify herself, and that is, when religion may seem to be in the least offended; whose rights are as dear to her as her own, and are indeed the same. If any one, therefore, shou'd imagine that the foregoing arguments are any ways dangerous to religion, I hope the following apology will remove his apprehensions.

There is no foundation for any conclusion *a priori,* either concerning the operations or duration of any object, of which 'tis possible for the human mind to form a conception.

Any object may be imagin'd to become entirely inactive, or to be annihilated in a moment; and 'tis an evident principle, *that whatever we can imagine, is possible.* Now this is no more true of matter, than of spirit; of an extended compounded substance, than of a simple and unextended. In both cases the metaphysical arguments for the immortality of the soul are equally inconclusive; and in both cases the moral arguments and those deriv'd from the analogy of nature are equally strong and convincing. If my philosophy, therefore, makes no addition to the arguments for religion, I have at least the satisfaction to think it takes nothing from them, but that every thing remains precisely as before.

Section VI: Of Personal Identity

There are some philosophers, who imagine we are every moment intimately conscious of what we call our SELF; that we feel its existence and its continuance in existence; and are certain, beyond the evidence of a demonstration, both of its perfect identity and simplicity. The strongest sensation, the most violent passion, say they, instead of distracting us from this view, only fix it the more intensely, and make us consider their influence on *self* either by their pain or pleasure. To attempt a farther proof of this were to weaken its evidence; since no proof can be deriv'd from any fact, of which we are so intimately conscious; nor is there any thing, of which we can be certain, if we doubt this.

Unluckily all these positive assertions are contrary to that very experience, which is pleaded for them, nor have we any idea of *self,* after the manner it is here explain'd. For from what impression cou'd this idea be deriv'd? This question 'tis impossible to answer without a manifest contradiction and absurdity; and yet 'tis a question, which must necessarily be answer'd, if we wou'd have the idea of self pass for clear and intelligible. It must be some one impression, that gives rise to every real idea. But self or person is not any one impression, but that to which our several impressions and ideas are suppos'd to have a reference. If any impression gives rise to the idea of self, that impression must continue invariably the same,

thro' the whole course of our lives; since self is suppos'd to exist after that manner. But there is no impression constant and invariable. Pain and pleasure, grief and joy, passions and sensations succeed each other, and never all exist at the same time. It cannot, therefore, be from any of these impressions, or from any other, that the idea of self is deriv'd; and consequently there is no such idea.

But farther, what must become of all our particular perceptions upon this hypothesis? All these are different, and distinguishable, and separable from each other, and may be separately consider'd, and may exist separately, and have no need of any thing to support their existence. After what manner, therefore, do they belong to self; and how are they connected with it? For my part, when I enter most intimately into what I call *myself*, I always stumble on some particular perception or other, of heat or cold, light or shade, love or hatred, pain or pleasure. I never can catch *myself* at any time without a perception, and never can observe any thing but the perception. When my perceptions are remov'd for any time, as by sound sleep; so long am I insensible of *myself*, and may truly be said not to exist. And were all my perceptions remov'd by death, and cou'd I neither think, nor feel, nor see, nor love, nor hate after the dissolution of my body, I shou'd be entirely annihilated, nor do I conceive what is farther requisite to make me a perfect non-entity. If any one upon serious and unprejudic'd reflexion, thinks he has a different notion of *himself*, I must confess I can reason no longer with him. All I can allow him is, that he may be in the right as well as I, and that we are essentially different in this particular. He may, perhaps, perceive something simple and continu'd, which he calls *himself;* tho' I am certain there is no such principle in me.

But setting aside some metaphysicians of this kind, I may venture to affirm of the rest of mankind, that they are nothing but a bundle or collection of different perceptions, which succeed each other with an inconceivable rapidity, and are in a perpetual flux and movement. Our eyes cannot turn in their sockets without varying our perceptions. Our thought is still more variable than our sight;

and all our other senses and faculties contribute to this change; nor is there any single power of the soul, which remains unalterably the same, perhaps for one moment. The mind is a kind of theatre, where several perceptions successively make their appearance; pass, re-pass, glide away, and mingle in an infinite variety of postures and situations. There is properly no *simplicity* in it at one time, nor *identity* in different; whatever natural propension we may have to imagine that simplicity and identity. The comparison of the theatre must not mislead us. They are the successive perceptions only, that constitute the mind; nor have we the most distant notion of the place, where these scenes are represented, or of the materials, of which it is compos'd.

What then gives us so great a propension to ascribe an identity to these successive perceptions, and to suppose ourselves possest of an invariable and uninterrupted existence thro' the whole course of our lives? In order to answer this question, we must distinguish betwixt personal identity, as it regards our thought or imagination, as it regards our passions or the concern we take in ourselves. The first is our present subject; and to explain it perfectly we must take the matter pretty deep, and account for that identity, which we attribute to plants and animals; there being a great analogy betwixt it, and the identity of a self or person.

We have a distinct idea of an object, that remains invariable and uninterrupted thro' a suppos'd variation of time; and this idea we call that of *identity* or *sameness*. We have also a distinct idea of several different objects existing in succession, and connected together by a close relation; and this to an accurate view affords as perfect a notion of *diversity,* as if there was no manner of relation among the objects. But tho' these two ideas of identity, and a succession of related objects be in themselves perfectly distinct, and even contrary, yet 'tis certain, that in our common way of thinking they are generally confounded with each other. That action of the imagination, by which we consider the uninterrupted and invariable object, and that by which we reflect on the succession of related objects, are almost the same to the feeling, nor is there much

more effort of thought requir'd in the latter case than in the former. The relation facilitates the transition of the mind from one object to another, and renders its passage as smooth as if it contemplated one continu'd object. This resemblance is the cause of the confusion and mistake, and makes us substitute the notion of identity, instead of that of related objects. However at one instant we may consider the related succession as variable or interrupted, we are sure the next to ascribe to it a perfect identity, and regard it as invariable and uninterrupted. Our propensity to this mistake is so great from the resemblance above-mention'd, that we fall into it before we are aware; and tho' we incessantly correct ourselves by reflexion, and return to a more accurate method of thinking, yet we cannot long sustain our philosophy, or take off this biass from the imagination. Our last resource is to yield to it, and boldly assert that these different related objects are in effect the same, however, interrupted and variable. In order to justify to ourselves this absurdity, we often feign some new and unintelligible principle, that connects the objects together, and prevents their interruption or variation. Thus we feign the continu'd existence of the perceptions of our senses, to remove the interruption; and run into the notion of a *soul,* and *self,* and *substance,* to disguise the variation. But we may farther observe, that where we do not give rise to such a fiction, our propension to confound identity with relation is so great, that we are apt to imagine[8] something unknown and mysterious, connecting the parts, beside their relation; and this I take to be the case with regard to the identity we ascribe to plants and vegetables. And even when this does not take place, we still feel a propensity to confound these ideas, tho' we are not able fully to satisfy ourselves in that particular, nor find any thing invariable and uninterrupted to justify our notion of identity.

Thus the controversy concerning identity is

[8]If the reader is desirous to see how a great genius may be influenc'd by these seemingly trivial principles of the imagination, as well as the mere vulgar, let him read my Lord *Shaftsbury*'s reasonings concerning the uniting principle of the universe, and the identity of plants and animals. See his *Moralists* or *Philosophical rhapsody.*

not merely a dispute of words. For when we attribute identity, in an improper sense, to variable or interrupted objects, our mistake is not confin'd to the expression, but is commonly attended with a fiction, either of something invariable and uninterrupted, or of something mysterious and inexplicable, or at least with a propensity to such fictions. What will suffice to prove this hypothesis to the satisfaction of every fair enquirer, is to shew from daily experience and observation, that the objects, which are variable or interrupted, and yet are suppos'd to continue the same, are such only as consist of a succession of parts, connected together by resemblance, contiguity, or causation. For as such a succession answers evidently to our notion of diversity, it can only be by mistake we ascribe to it an identity; and as the relation of parts, which leads us into this mistake, is really nothing but a quality, which produces an association of ideas, and an easy transition of the imagination from one to another, it can only be from the resemblance, which this act of the mind bears to that, by which we contemplate one continu'd object, that the error arises. Our chief business, then, must be to prove, that all objects, to which we ascribe identity, without observing their invariableness and uninterruptedness, are such as consist of a succession of related objects.

In order to this, suppose any mass of matter, of which the parts are contiguous and connected, to be plac'd before us; 'tis plain we must attribute a perfect identity to this mass, provided all the parts continue uninterruptedly and invariably the same, whatever motion or change of place we may observe either in the whole or in any of the parts. But supposing some very *small* or *inconsiderable* part to be added to the mass, or substracted from it; tho' this absolutely destroys the identity of the whole, strictly speaking; yet as we seldom think so accurately, we scruple not to pronounce a mass of matter the same, where we find so trivial an alteration. The passage of the thought from the object before the change to the object after it, is so smooth and easy, that we scarce perceive the transition, and are apt to imagine, that 'tis nothing but a continu'd survey of the same object.

There is a very remarkable circumstance, that attends this experiment; which is, that tho' the change of any considerable part in a mass of matter destroys the identity of the whole, yet we must measure the greatness of the part, not absolutely, but by its *proportion* to the whole. The addition or diminution of a mountain wou'd not be sufficient to produce a diversity in a planet; tho' the change of a very few inches wou'd be able to destroy the identity of some bodies. 'Twill be impossible to account for this, but by reflecting that objects operate upon the mind, and break or interrupt the continuity of its actions not according to their real greatness, but according to their proportion to each other: And therefore, since this interruption makes an object cease to appear the same, it must be the uninterrupted progress of the thought, which constitutes the imperfect identity.

This may be confirm'd by another phaenomenon. A change in any considerable part of a body destroys its identity; but 'tis remarkable, that where the change is produc'd *gradually* and *insensibly* we are less apt to ascribe to it the same effect. The reason can plainly be no other, than that the mind, in following the successive changes of the body, feels an easy passage from the surveying its condition in one moment to the viewing of it in another, and at no particular time perceives any interruption in its actions. From which continu'd perception, it ascribes a continu'd existence and identity to the object.

But whatever precaution we may use in introducing the changes gradually, and making them proportionable to the whole, 'tis certain, that where the changes are at last observ'd to become considerable, we make a scruple of ascribing identity to such different objects. There is, however, another artifice, by which we may induce the imagination to advance a step farther; and that is, by producing a reference of the parts to each other, and a combination to some *common end* or purpose. A ship, of which a considerable part has been chang'd by frequent reparations, is still consider'd as the same; nor does the difference of the materials hinder us from ascribing an identity to it. The common end, in which the parts conspire, is the same under all their variations, and affords an easy transition of the imagination from one situation of the body to another.

But this is still more remarkable, when we add a *sympathy* of parts to their *common end,* and suppose that they bear to each other, the reciprocal relation of cause and effect in all their actions and operations. This is the case with all animals and vegetables; where not only the several parts have a reference to some general purpose, but also a mutual dependance on, and connexion with each other. The effect of so strong a relation is, that tho' every one must allow, that in a very few years both vegetables and animals endure a *total* change, yet we still attribute identity to them, while their form, size, and substance are entirely alter'd. An oak, that grows from a small plant to a large tree, is still the same oak; tho' there be not one particle of matter, or figure of its parts the same. An infant becomes a man, and is sometimes fat, sometimes lean, without any change in his identity.

We may also consider the two following phænomena, which are remarkable in their kind. The first is, that tho' we commonly be able to distinguish pretty exactly betwixt numerical and specific identity, yet it sometimes happens, that we confound them, and in our thinking and reasoning employ the one for the other. Thus a man, who hears a noise, that is frequently interrupted and renew'd, says, it is still the same noise; tho' 'tis evident the sounds have only a specific identity or resemblance, and there is nothing numerically the same, but the cause, which produc'd them. In like manner it may be said without breach of the propriety of language, that such a church, which was formerly of brick, fell to ruin, and that the parish rebuilt the same church of free-stone, and according to modern architecture. Here neither the form nor materials are the same, nor is there any thing common to the two objects, but their relation to the inhabitants of the parish; and yet this alone is sufficient to make us denominate them the same. But we must observe, that in these cases the first object is in a manner annihilated before the second comes into existence; by which means, we are never presented in any one point of time with the idea of difference and multi-

plicity; and for that reason are less scrupulous in calling them the same.

Secondly, We may remark, that tho' in a succession of related objects, it be in a manner requisite, that the change of parts be not sudden nor entire, in order to preserve the identity, yet where the objects are in their nature changeable and inconstant, we admit of a more sudden transition, than wou'd otherwise be consistent with that relation. Thus as the nature of a river consists in the motion and change of parts; tho' in less than four and twenty hours these be totally alter'd; this hinders not the river from continuing the same during several ages. What is natural and essential to any thing is, in a manner, expected; and what is expected makes less impression, and appears of less moment, than what is unusual and extraordinary. A considerable change of the former kind seems really less to the imagination, than the most trivial alteration of the latter; and by breaking less the continuity of the thought, has less influence in destroying the identity.

We now proceed to explain the nature of *personal identity,* which has become so great a question in philosophy, especially of late years in *England,* where all the abstruser sciences are study'd with a peculiar ardour and application. And here 'tis evident, the same method of reasoning must be continu'd, which has so successfully explain'd the identity of plants, and animals, and ships, and houses, and of all the compounded and changeable productions either of art or nature. The identity, which we ascribe to the mind of man, is only a fictitious one, and of a like kind with that which we ascribe to vegetables and animal bodies. It cannot, therefore, have a different origin, but must proceed from a like operation of the imagination upon like objects.

But lest this argument shou'd not convince the reader; tho' in my opinion perfectly decisive; let him weigh the following reasoning, which is still closer and more immediate. 'Tis evident, that the identity, which we attribute to the human mind, however perfect we may imagine it to be, is not able to run the several different perceptions into one, and make them lose their characters of distinction and difference, which are essential to them. 'Tis still true, that every distinct perception, which enters into the composition of the mind, is a distinct existence, and is different, and distinguishable, and separable from every other perception, either contemporary or successive. But, as, notwithstanding this distinction and separability, we suppose the whole train of perceptions to be united by identity, a question naturally arises concerning this relation of identity; whether it be something that really binds our several perceptions together, or only associates their ideas in the imagination. That is, in other words, whether in pronouncing concerning the identity of a person, we observe some real bond among his perceptions, or only feel one among the ideas we form of them. This question we might easily decide, if we wou'd recollect what has been already prov'd at large, that the understanding never observes any real connexion among objects, and that even the union of cause and effect, when strictly examin'd, resolves itself into a customary association of ideas. For from thence it evidently follows, that identity is nothing really belonging to these different perceptions, and uniting them together; but is merely a quality, which we attribute to them, because of the union of their ideas in the imagination, when we reflect upon them. Now the only qualities, which can give ideas an union in the imagination, are these three relations above-mention'd. These are the uniting principles in the ideal world, and without them every distinct object is separable by the mind, and may be separately consider'd, and appears not to have any more connexion with any other object, than if disjoin'd by the greatest difference and remoteness. 'Tis, therefore, on some of these three relations of resemblance, contiguity and causation, that identity depends; and as the very essence of these relations consists in their producing an easy transition of ideas; it follows, that our notions of personal identity, proceed entirely from the smooth and uninterrupted progress of the thought along a train of connected ideas, according to the principles above-explain'd.

The only question, therefore, which remains, is, by what relations this uninterrupted progress of our thought is produc'd, when we consider the successive existence of a mind or thinking person. And here 'tis evident we must confine ourselves to resemblance and causation, and must drop contiguity, which has little or no influence in the present case.

To begin with *resemblance;* suppose we cou'd see clearly into the breast of another, and observe that succession of perceptions, which constitutes his mind or thinking principle, and suppose that he always preserves the memory of a considerable part of past perceptions; 'tis evident that nothing cou'd more contribute to the bestowing a relation on this succession amidst all its variations. For what is the memory but a faculty, by which we raise up the images of past perceptions? And as an image necessarily resembles its object, must not the frequent placing of these resembling perceptions in the chain of thought, convey the imagination more easily from one link to another, and make the whole seem like the continuance of one object? In this particular, then, the memory not only discovers the identity, but also contributes to its production, by producing the relation of resemblance among the perceptions. The case is the same whether we consider ourselves or others.

As to *causation;* we may observe, that the true idea of the human mind, is to consider it as a system of different perceptions or different existences, which are link'd together by the relation of cause and effect, and mutually produce, destroy, influence, and modify each other. Our impressions give rise to their correspondent ideas; and these ideas in their turn produce other impressions. One thought chaces another, and draws after it a third, by which it is expell'd in its turn. In this respect, I cannot compare the soul more properly to any thing than to a republic or commonwealth, in which the several members are united by the reciprocal ties of government and subordination, and give rise to other persons, who propagate the same republic in the incessant changes of its parts. And as the same individual republic may not only change its members, but also its laws and constitutions; in like manner the same person may vary his character and disposition, as well as his impressions and ideas, without losing his identity. Whatever changes he endures, his several parts are still connected by the relation of causation. And in this view our identity with regard to the passions serves to corroborate that with regard to the imagination, by the making our distant perceptions influence each other, and by giving us a present concern for our past or future pains or pleasures.

As memory alone acquaints us with the continuance and extent of this succession of perceptions, 'tis to be consider'd, upon that account chiefly, as the source of personal identity. Had we no memory, we never shou'd have any notion of causation, nor consequently of that chain of causes and effects, which constitute our self or person. But having once acquir'd this notion of causation from the memory, we can extend the same chain of causes, and consequently the identity of our persons beyond our memory, and can comprehend times, and circumstances, and actions, which we have entirely forgot, but suppose in general to have existed. For how few of our past actions are there, of which we have any memory? Who can tell me, for instance, what were his thoughts and actions on the first of *January* 1715, the 11th of *March* 1719, and the 3d of *August* 1733? Or will he affirm, because he has entirely forgot the incidents of these days, that the present self is not the same person with the self of that time; and by that means overturn all the most establish'd notions of personal identity? In this view, therefore, memory does not so much *produce* as *discover* personal identity, by shewing us the relation of cause and effect among our different perceptions. 'Twill be incumbent on those, who affirm that memory produces entirely our personal identity, to give a reason why we can thus extend our identity beyond our memory.

The whole of this doctrine leads us to a conclusion, which is of great importance in the present affair, *viz.* that all the nice and subtile questions concerning personal identity can never possibly be decided and are to be regarded rather as grammatical than as philosophical difficulties. Identity depends on the relations of ideas; and these relations produce identity, by means of that easy transition they occasion. But as the relations, and the easiness of the transition may diminish by insensible degrees, we have no just standard, by which

we can decide any dispute concerning the time, when they acquire or lose a title to the name of identity. All the disputes concerning the identity of connected objects are merely verbal, except so far as the relation of parts gives rise to some fiction or imaginary principle of union, as we have already observ'd.

What I have said concerning the first origin and uncertainty of our notion of identity, as apply'd to the human mind, may be extended with little or no variation to that of *simplicity*. An object, whose different co-existent parts are bound together by a close relation, operates upon the imagination after much the same manner as one perfectly simple and indivisible, and requires not a much greater stretch of thought in order to its conception. From this similarity of operation we attribute a simplicity to it, and feign a principle of union as the support of this simplicity, and the center of all the different parts and qualities of the object.

Thus we have finish'd our examination of the several systems of philosophy, both of the intellectual and moral world; and in our miscellaneous way of reasoning have been led into several topics; which will either illustrate and confirm some preceding part of this discourse, or prepare the way for our following opinions. 'Tis now time to return to a more close examination of our subject, and to proceed in the accurate anatomy of human nature, having fully explain'd the nature of our judgment and understanding.

Section VII:
Conclusion of This Book

But before I launch out into those immense depths of philosophy, which lie before me, I find myself inclin'd to stop a moment in my present station, and to ponder that voyage, which I have undertaken, and which undoubtedly requires the utmost art and industry to be brought to a happy conclusion. Methinks I am like a man, who having struck on many shoals, and having narrowly escap'd ship-wreck in passing a small frith, has yet the temerity to put out to sea in the same leaky weather-beaten vessel, and even carries his ambition so far as to think of compassing the globe under these disadvantageous circumstances. My memory of past errors and perplexities, makes me diffident for the future. The wretched condition, weakness, and disorder of the faculties, I must employ in my enquiries, encrease my apprehensions. And the impossibility of amending or correcting these faculties, reduces me almost to despair, and makes me resolve to perish on the barren rock, on which I am at present, rather than venture myself upon that boundless ocean, which runs out into immensity. This sudden view of my danger strikes me with melancholy; and as 'tis usual for that passion, above all others, to indulge itself; I cannot forbear feeding my despair, with all those desponding reflections, which the present subject furnishes me with in such abundance.

I am first affrighted and confounded with that forelorn solitude, in which I am plac'd in my philosophy, and fancy myself some strange uncouth monster, who not being able to mingle and unite in society, has been expell'd all human commerce, and left utterly abandon'd and disconsolate. Fain wou'd I run into the crowd for shelter and warmth; but cannot prevail with myself to mix with such deformity. I call upon others to join me, in order to make a company apart; but no one will hearken to me. Every one keeps at a distance, and dreads that storm, which beats upon me from every side. I have expos'd myself to the enmity of all metaphysicians, logicians, mathematicians, and even theologians; and can I wonder at the insults I must suffer? I have declar'd my disapprobation of their systems; and can I be surpriz'd, if they shou'd express a hatred of mine and of my person? When I look abroad, I foresee on every side, dispute, contradiction, anger, calumny and detraction. When I turn my eye inward, I find nothing but doubt and ignorance. All the world conspires to oppose and contradict me; tho' such is my weakness, that I feel all my opinions loosen and fall of themselves, when unsupported by the approbation of others. Every step I take is with hesitation, and every new reflection makes me dread an error and absurdity in my reasoning.

For with what confidence can I venture upon such bold enterprizes, when beside those numberless infirmities peculiar to myself, I find so many which are common to human nature? Can I be sure, that in leaving all establish'd opinions I am following truth; and by what criterion shall I distinguish her, even if fortune shou'd at last guide me on her footsteps? After the most accurate and exact of my reasonings, I can give no reason why I shou'd assent to it; and feel nothing but a *strong* propensity to consider objects *strongly* in that view, under which they appear to me. Experience is a principle, which instructs me in the several conjunctions of objects for the past. Habit is another principle, which determines me to expect the same for the future; and both of them conspiring to operate upon the imagination, make me form certain ideas in a more intense and lively manner, than others, which are not attended with the same advantages. Without this quality, by which the mind enlivens some ideas beyond others (which seemingly is so trivial, and so little founded on reason) we cou'd never assent to any argument, nor carry our view beyond those few objects, which are present to our senses. Nay, even to these objects we cou'd never attribute any existence, but what was dependent on the senses; and must comprehend them entirely in that succession of perceptions, which constitutes our self or person. Nay farther, even with relation to that succession, we cou'd only admit of those perceptions, which are immediately present to our consciousness, nor cou'd those lively images, with which the memory presents us, be ever receiv'd as true pictures of past perceptions. The memory, senses, and understanding are, therefore, all of them founded on the imagination, or the vivacity of our ideas.

No wonder a principle so inconstant and fallacious shou'd lead us into errors, when implicitely follow'd (as it must be) in all its variations. 'Tis this principle, which makes us reason from causes and effects; and 'tis the same principle, which convinces us of the continu'd existence of external objects, when absent from the senses. But tho' these two operations be equally natural and necessary in the human mind, yet in some circumstances they are directly contrary,[9] nor is it possible for us to

[9]Sect. iv (p. 282).

reason justly and regularly from causes and effects, and at the same time believe the continu'd existence of matter. How then shall we adjust those principles together? Which of them shall we prefer? Or in case we prefer neither of them, but successively assent to both, as is usual among philosophers, with what confidence can we afterwards usurp that glorious title, when we thus knowingly embrace a manifest contradiction?

This contradiction[10] wou'd be more excusable, were it compensated by any degree of solidity and satisfaction in the other parts of our reasoning. But the case is quite contrary. When we trace up the human understanding to its first principles, we find it to lead us into such sentiments, as seem to turn into ridicule all our past pains and industry, and to discourage us from future enquiries. Nothing is more curiously enquir'd after by the mind of man, than the causes of every phænomenon; nor are we content with knowing the immediate causes, but push on our enquiries, till we arrive at the original and ultimate principle. We wou'd not willingly stop before we are acquainted with that energy in the cause, by which it operates on its effect; that tie, which connects them together; and that efficacious quality, on which the tie depends. This is our aim in all our studies and reflections: And how must we be disappointed, when we learn, that this connexion, tie, or energy lies merely in ourselves, and is nothing but that determination of the mind, which is acquir'd by custom, and causes us to make a transition from an object to its usual attendant, and from the impression of one to the lively idea of the other? Such a discovery not only cuts off all hope of ever attaining satisfaction, but even prevents our very wishes; since it appears, that when we say we desire to know the ultimate and operating principle, as something, which resides in the external object, we either contradict ourselves, or talk without a meaning.

This deficiency in our ideas is not, indeed, perceiv'd in common life, nor are we sensible, that in the most usual conjunctions of cause and effect we are as ignorant of the ultimate principle, which binds them together, as in the most unusual and extraordinary. But this proceeds merely from an illusion of the imagination; and the question is, how far we ought to yield to these illusions. This question is very difficult, and reduces us to a very dangerous dilemma, whichever way we answer it. For if we assent to every trivial suggestion of the fancy; beside that these suggestions are often contrary to each other; they lead us into such errors, absurdities, and obscurities, that we must at last become asham'd of our credulity. Nothing is more dangerous to reason than the flights of the imagination, and nothing has been the occasion of more mistakes among philosophers. Men of bright fancies may in this respect be compar'd to those angels, whom the scripture represents as covering their eyes with their wings. This has already appear'd in so many instances, that we may spare ourselves the trouble of enlarging upon it any farther.

But on the other hand, if the consideration of these instances makes us take a resolution to reject all the trivial suggestions of the fancy, and adhere to the understanding, that is, to the general and more establish'd properties of the imagination; even this resolution, if steadily executed, wou'd be dangerous, and attended with the most fatal consequences. For I have already shewn,[11] that the understanding, when it acts alone, and according to its most general principles, entirely subverts itself, and leaves not the lowest degree of evidence in any proposition, either in philosophy or common life. We save ourselves from this total scepticism only by means of that singular and seemingly trivial property of the fancy, by which we enter with difficulty into remote views of things, and are not able to accompany them with so sensible an impression, as we do those, which are more easy and natural. Shall we, then, establish it for a general maxim, that no refin'd or elaborate reasoning is ever to be receiv'd? Consider well the consequences of such a principle. By this means you cut off entirely all science and philosophy: You proceed upon one singular quality of the imagination, and by a parity of reason must embrace all of them: And you expresly contradict

[10]Part III. sect. xiv

[11]Sect. I

yourself; since this maxim must be built on the preceding reasoning, which will be allow'd to be sufficiently refin'd and metaphysical. What party, then, shall we choose among these difficulties? If we embrace this principle, and condemn all refin'd reasoning, we run into the most manifest absurdities. If we reject it in favour of these reasonings, we subvert entirely the human understanding. We have, therefore, no choice left but betwixt a false reason and none at all. For my part, I know not what ought to be done in the present case. I can only observe what is commonly done; which is, that this difficulty is seldom or never thought of; and even where it has once been present to the mind, is quickly forgot, and leaves but a small impression behind it. Very refin'd reflections have little or no influence upon us; and yet we do not, and cannot establish it for a rule, that they ought not to have any influence; which implies a manifest contradiction.

But what have I here said, that reflections very refin'd and metaphysical have little or no influence upon us? This opinion I can scarce forbear retracting, and condemning from my present feeling and experience. The *intense* view of these manifold contradictions and imperfections in human reason has so wrought upon me, and heated my brain, that I am ready to reject all belief and reasoning, and can look upon no opinion even as more probable or likely than another. Where am I, or what? From what causes do I derive my existence, and to what condition shall I return? Whose favour shall I court, and whose anger must I dread? What beings surround me? and on whom have I any influence, or who have any influence on me? I am confounded with all these questions, and begin to fancy myself in the most deplorable condition imaginable, inviron'd with the deepest darkness, and utterly depriv'd of the use of every member and faculty.

Most fortunately it happens, that since reason is incapable of dispelling these clouds, nature herself suffices to that purpose, and cures me of this philosophical melancholy and delirium, either by relaxing this bent of mind, or by some avocation, and lively impression of my senses, which obliterate all these chimeras. I dine, I play a game of back-gammon, I converse, and am merry with my friends; and when after three or four hours' amusement, I wou'd return to these speculations, they appear so cold, and strain'd, and ridiculous, that I cannot find in my heart to enter into them any farther.

Here then I find myself absolutely and necessarily determin'd to live, and talk, and act like other people in the common affairs of life. But notwithstanding that my natural propensity, and the course of my animal spirits and passions reduce me to this indolent belief in the general maxims of the world, I still feel such remains of my former disposition, that I am ready to throw all my books and papers into the fire, and resolve never more to renounce the pleasures of life for the sake of reasoning and philosophy. For those are my sentiments in that splenetic humour, which governs me at present. I may, nay I must yield to the current of nature, in submitting to my senses and understanding; and in this blind submission I shew most perfectly my sceptical disposition and principles. But does it follow, that I must strive against the current of nature, which leads to indolence and pleasure; that I must seclude myself, in some measure, from the commerce and society of men, which is so agreeable; and that I must torture my brain with subtilities and sophistries, at the very time that I cannot satisfy myself concerning the reasonableness of so painful an application, nor have any tolerable prospect of arriving by its means at truth and certainty. Under what obligation do I lie of making such an abuse of time? And to what end can it serve either for the service of mankind, or for my own private interest? No: If I must be a fool, as all those who reason or believe anything *certainly* are, my follies shall at least be natural and agreeable. Where I strive against my inclination, I shall have a good reason for my resistance; and will no more be led a wandering into such dreary solitudes, and rough passages, as I have hitherto met with.

These are the sentiments of my spleen and indolence; and indeed I must confess, that philosophy has nothing to oppose to them, and expects a victory more from the returns of a serious good-humour'd disposition, than from the force of reason and conviction. In all the incidents of life we ought still to preserve our scepticism. If we believe, that fire warms, or water refreshes, 'tis only because it costs us too much pains to think otherwise. Nay if we are philosophers, it ought only to be upon sceptical principles, and from an inclination, which we feel to the employing ourselves after that manner. Where reason is lively, and mixes itself with some propensity, it ought to be assented to. Where it does not, it never can have any title to operate upon us.

At the time, therefore, that I am tir'd with amusement and company, and have indulg'd a *reverie* in my chamber, or in a solitary walk by a river-side, I feel my mind all collected within itself, and am naturally *inclin'd* to carry my view into all those subjects, about which I have met with so many disputes in the course of my reading and conversation. I cannot forbear having a curiosity to be acquainted with the principles of moral good and evil, the nature and foundation of government, and the cause of those several passions and inclinations, which actuate and govern me. I am uneasy to think I approve of one object, and disapprove of another; call one thing beautiful, and another deform'd; decide concerning truth and falshood, reason and folly, without knowing upon what principles I proceed. I am concern'd for the condition of the learned world, which lies under such a deplorable ignorance in all these particulars. I feel an ambition to arise in me of contributing to the instruction of mankind, and of acquiring a name by my inventions and discoveries. These sentiments spring up naturally in my present disposition; and shou'd I endeavour to banish them, by attaching myself to any other business or diversion, I *feel* I shou'd be a loser in point of pleasure; and this is the origin of my philosophy.

But even suppose this curiosity and ambition shou'd not transport me into speculations without the sphere of common life, it wou'd necessarily happen, that from my very weakness I must be led into such enquiries. 'Tis certain, that superstition is much more bold in its systems and hypotheses than philosophy; and while the latter contents itself with assigning new causes and principles to the phæ-

nomena, which appear in the visible world, the former opens a world of its own, and presents us with scenes, and beings, and objects, which are altogether new. Since therefore 'tis almost impossible for the mind of man to rest, like those of beasts, in that narrow circle of objects, which are the subject of daily conversation and action, we ought only to deliberate concerning the choice of our guide, and ought to prefer that which is safest and most agreeable. And in this respect I make bold to recommend philosophy, and shall not scruple to give it the preference to superstition of every kind or denomination. For as superstition arises naturally and easily from the popular opinions of mankind, it seizes more strongly on the mind, and is often able to disturb us in the conduct of our lives and actions. Philosophy on the contrary, if just, can present us only with mild and moderate sentiments; and if false and extravagant, its opinions are merely the objects of a cold and general speculation, and seldom go so far as to interrupt the course of our natural propensities. The CYNICS are an extraordinary instance of philosophers, who from reasonings purely philosophical ran into as great extravagancies of conduct as any *Monk* or *Dervise* that ever was in the world. Generally speaking, the errors in religion are dangerous; those in philosophy only ridiculous.

I am sensible, that these two cases of the strength and weakness of the mind will not comprehend all mankind, and that there are in *England,* in particular, many honest gentlemen, who being always employ'd in their domestic affairs, or amusing themselves in common recreations, have carried their thoughts very little beyond those objects, which are every day expos'd to their senses. And indeed, of such as these I pretend not to make philosophers, nor do I expect them either to be associates in these researches or auditors of these discoveries. They do well to keep themselves in their present situation; and instead of refining them into philosophers, I wish we cou'd communicate to our founders of systems, a share of this gross earthy mixture, as an ingredient, which they commonly stand much in need of, and which wou'd serve to temper those fiery particles, of which they are compos'd. While a warm imagination is allow'd to enter into philosophy, and hypotheses embrac'd merely for being specious and agreeable, we can never have any steady principles, nor any sentiments, which will suit with common practice and experience. But were these hypotheses once remov'd, we might hope to establish a system or set of opinions, which if not true (for that, perhaps, is too much to be hop'd for) might at least be satisfactory to the human mind, and might stand the test of the most critical examination. Nor shou'd we despair of attaining this end, because of the many chimerical systems, which have successively arisen and decay'd away among men, wou'd we consider the shortness of that period, wherein these questions have been the subjects of enquiry and reasoning. Two thousand years with such long interruptions, and under such mighty discouragements are a small space of time to give any tolerable perfection to the sciences; and perhaps we are still in too early an age of the world to discover any principles, which will bear the examination of the latest posterity. For my part, my only hope is, that I may contribute a little to the advancement of knowledge, by giving in some particulars a different turn to the speculations of philosophers, and pointing out to them more distinctly those subjects, where alone they can expect assurance and conviction. Human Nature is the only science of man; and yet has been hitherto the most neglected. 'Twill be sufficient for me, if I can bring it a little more into fashion; and the hope of this serves to compose my temper from that spleen, and invigorate it from that indolence, which sometimes prevail upon me. If the reader finds himself in the same easy disposition, let him follow me in my future speculations. If not, let him follow his inclination, and wait the returns of application and good humour. The conduct of a man, who studies philosophy in this careless manner, is more truly sceptical than that of one, who feeling in himself an inclination to it, is yet so over-whelm'd with doubts and scruples, as totally to reject it. A true sceptic will be diffident of his philosophical doubts, as well as of his philosophical conviction; and will never refuse any innocent satisfaction, which offers itself, upon account of either of them.

Nor is it only proper we shou'd in general indulge our inclination in the most elaborate philosophical researches, notwithstanding our sceptical principles, but also that we shou'd yield to that propensity, which inclines us to be positive and certain in *particular points,* according to the light, in which we survey them in any *particular instant.* 'Tis easier to forbear all examination and enquiry, than to check ourselves in so natural a propensity, and guard against that assurance, which always arises from an exact and full survey of an object. On such an occasion we are apt not only to forget our scepticism, but even our modesty too; and make use of such terms as these, *'tis evident, 'tis certain, 'tis undeniable;* which a due deference to the public ought, perhaps, to prevent. I may have fallen into this fault after the example of others; but I here enter a *caveat* against any objections, which may be offer'd on that head; and declare that such expressions were extorted from me by the present view of the object, and imply no dogmatical spirit, nor conceited idea of my own judgment, which are sentiments that I am sensible can become no body, and a sceptic still less than any other.

VIII

Gottfried Leibniz

GOTTFRIED WILHELM LEIBNIZ (1646–1716), philosopher, mathematician, logician, and historian, is one of the greatest systematic thinkers of modern times. He is perhaps most famous for independently developing differential and integral calculus. As a lifelong project, he sought to invent a universal language based on a logical calculus that would provide a common mathematical, philosophical, logical, and scientific foundation to all thought; all the deepest philosophical disagreements would, under Leibniz's sharpened pencil, end in a series of careful and rigorous calculations.

The son of a philosophy professor of Slavonic descent (the family name was originally Lubeniecz), young Leibniz could speak Latin and Greek before the age of 12. At 15 he entered the University of Leipzig to study law. There, under the tutelage of one of the greatest scientific German philosophers of the time, a neo-Aristotelian named Jakob Thomasius, Leibniz fell under the influence of Bacon, Kepler, Galileo, and Descartes. His undergraduate thesis, *De principio individui* (1663), written when he was only 20, presented a nominalistic view of individuation and identity, according to which individuality is constituted by the whole. After taking his doctorate in law, he worked for the Elector of Mainz in Frankfurt until 1672, when he went to Paris for five years. There he met and worked with Melebranche, Arnauld, and Huygens, on his way home he visited Spinoza at The Hague. He later traveled to Hanover to work as a librarian and historian at the House of Brunswick. In Berlin he directed the founding of the Academy and served as its first president. During his life he continued trying to apply philosophy and mathematics to everyday affairs, trying to demonstrate, using logic and mathematics, why a German candidate should succeed to the Polish throne and even using his calculus to try to make peace between Catholic and Protestant theologies.

The last years of his life were tormented by the controversy over whether he or Newton had first invented the calculus. By then he had already fallen out of favor with the princes of Brunswick, who viewed his philosophy and academic propaganda as no longer useful. Leibniz died in virtual obscurity. Unlike most prominent philosophers, he left no single great work, and his original and powerful writings cannot be found in his two principal books, *New Essays on the Human Understanding* (1705) and *Theodicy* (1710), but, rather, in his many shorter works. For this reason, I have chosen to supplement the main selection, his famous *Monadology*, with an overview of his work by one of the great American philosophers and leading exponent of pragmatism, John Dewey (1859–1952). Dewey gives some breadth and depth to Leibniz's overall views, especially about the fundamental role of mind in the nature of ultimate reality.

Leibniz and the Origin of the Modern Mind

John Dewey

I. The Sources of His Philosophy

What is true of all men is true of philosophers, and of Leibniz among them. Speaking generally, what they are unconsciously and fundamentally, they are through absorption of their antecedents and surroundings. What they are consciously and reflectively, they are through their reaction upon the influence of heredity and environment. But there is a spiritual line of descent and a spiritual atmosphere; and in speaking of a philosopher, it is with this intellectual heredity and environment, rather than with the physical, that we are concerned. Leibniz was born into a period of intellectual activity the most teeming with ideas, the most fruitful in results, of any, perhaps, since the age of Pericles. We pride ourselves justly upon the activity of our own century, and in diffusion of intellectual action and wide-spread application of ideas the age of Leibniz could not compare with it. But ours *is* the age of diffusion and application, while his was one of fermentation and birth.

Such a period in its earlier days is apt to be turbid and unsettled. There is more heat of friction than calm light. And such had been the case in the hundred years before Leibniz. But when he arrived at intellectual maturity much of the crudity had disappeared. The troubling of the waters of thought had ceased; they were becoming clarified. Bacon, Hobbes, Descartes, each had crystallized something out of that seething and chaotic mass of new ideas which had forced itself into European con-

From John Dewey, *Leibniz's New Essays Concerning Human Understanding: A Critical Exposition.* First published in 1888.

sciousness. Men had been introduced into a new world, and the natural result had been feelings of strangeness, and the vagaries of intellectual wanderings. But by the day of Leibniz the intellectual bearings had been made out anew, the new mental orientation had been secured.

The marks of this "new spiritual picture of the universe" are everywhere to be seen in Leibniz. His philosophy is the dawning consciousness of the modern world. In it we see the very conception and birth of the modern interpretation of the world. The history of thought is one continuous testimony to the ease with which we become hardened to ideas through custom. Ideas are constantly precipitating themselves out of the realm of ideas into that of ways of thinking and of viewing the universe. The problem of one century is the axiom of another. What one generation stakes its activity upon investigating is quietly taken for granted by the next. And so the highest reach of intellectual inspiration in the sixteenth century is to-day the ordinary food of thought, accepted without an inquiry as to its source, and almost without a suspicion that it has a recent historic origin. We have to go to Bacon or to Leibniz to see the genesis and growth of those ideas which to-day have become materialized into axiomatic points of view and into hard-and-fast categories of thought. In reading Leibniz the idea comes over us in all its freshness that there was a time when it was a discovery that the world is a universe, made after one plan and of one stuff. The ideas of inter-relation, of the harmony of law, of mutual dependence and correspondence, were not always the assumed starting-points of thought; they were once the crowning discoveries of a philosophy aglow and almost intoxicated with the splendor of its far-reaching generalizations. I take these examples of the unity of the world, the continu-

ity and interdependence of all within it, because these are the ideas which come to their
conscious and delighted birth in the philosophy of Leibniz. We do not put ourselves into
the right attitude for understanding his
thought until we remember that these ideas—
the commonest tools of our thinking—were
once new and fresh, and in their novelty and
transforming strangeness were the products
of a philosophic interpretation of experience.
Except in that later contemporary of Leibniz,
the young and enthusiastic Irish idealist,
Berkeley, I know of no historic thinker in
whom the birth-throes (joyous, however) of a
new conception of the world are so evident as
in Leibniz. But while in Berkeley what we see
is the young man carried away and astounded
by the grandeur and simplicity of a "new way
of ideas" which he has discovered, what we see
in Leibniz is the mature man penetrated
throughout his being with an idea which in its
unity answers to the unity of the world, and
which in its complexity answers, tone to tone,
to the complex harmony of the world.

The familiarity of the ideas which we use
hides their grandeur from us. The unity of the
world is a matter of course with us; the dependent order of all within it a mere starting-
point upon which to base our investigations.
But if we will put ourselves in the position of
Leibniz, and behold, not the new planet, but
the new universe, so one, so linked together,
swimming into our ken, we shall feel something of the same exultant thrill that Leibniz
felt,—an exultation not indeed personal in its
nature, but which arises from the expansion of
the human mind face to face with an expanding world. The spirit which is at the heart of
the philosophy of Leibniz is . . . a spirit which
feels that the secret of the universe has been
rendered up to it, and which breathes a
buoyant optimism. And if we of the nineteenth century have chosen to bewail the complexity of the problem of life, and to run
hither and thither multiplying "insights" and
points of view till this enthusiastic confidence
in reason seems to us the rashness of an ignorance which does not comprehend the problem, and the unity in which Leibniz rested
appears cold and abstract beside the manifold
richness of the world, we should not forget

that after all we have incorporated into our
very mental structure the fundamental
thoughts of Leibniz,—the thoughts of the rationality of the universe and of the "reign of
law."

What was the origin of these ideas in the
mind of Leibniz? What influences in the philosophic succession of thinkers led him in this
direction? What agencies acting in the intellectual world about him shaped his ideal
reproduction of reality? Two causes above all
others stand out with prominence,—one, the
discoveries and principles of modern physical
science; the other, that interpretation of experience which centuries before had been
formulated by Aristotle. Leibniz has a double
interest for those of to-day who reverence science and who hold to the historical method.
His philosophy was an attempt to set in order
the methods and principles of that growing
science of nature which even then was
transforming the emotional and mental life of
Europe; and the attempt was guided everywhere by a profound and wide-reaching
knowledge of the history of philosophy. On
the first point Leibniz was certainly not alone.
Bacon, Hobbes, Descartes, Spinoza, each felt
in his own way the fructifying touch of the
new-springing science, and had attempted under its guidance to interpret the facts of nature
and of man. But Leibniz stood alone in his
interest in the history of thought. He stands
alone indeed till he is greeted by his compeers
of the nineteenth century. To Bacon previous
philosophy—the Greek, the scholastic—was an
"eidol of the theatre." The human mind must
be freed from its benumbing influence. To
Descartes it was useless rubbish to be cleared
away, that we might get a *tabula rasa* upon
which to make a fresh start. And shall Locke
and the empirical English school, or Reid and
the Scotch school, or even Kant, be the first to
throw a stone at Bacon and Descartes? It was
reserved to Leibniz, with a genius almost two
centuries in advance of his times, to penetrate
the meaning of the previous development of
reflective thought. It would be going beyond
our brief to claim that Leibniz was interested
in this *as* a historical movement, or that he
specially concerned himself with the genetic
lines which connected the various schools of

thought. But we should come short of our duty to Leibniz if we did not recognize his conscious and largely successful attempt to apprehend the core of truth in all systems, however alien to his own, and to incorporate it into his own thinking.

Nothing could be more characteristic of Leibniz than his saying, "I find that most systems are right in a good share of that which they advance, but not so much in what they deny;" or than this other statement of his, "We must not hastily believe that which the mass of men, or even of authorities, advance, but each must demand for himself the proofs of the thesis sustained. Yet long research generally convinces that the old and received opinions are good, provided they be interpreted justly." It is in the profound union in Leibniz of the principles which these quotations image that his abiding worth lies. Leibniz was interested in affirmations, not in denials. He was interested in securing the union of the modern *method,* the spirit of original research and independent judgment, with the conserved *results* of previous thought. Leibniz was a man of his times; that is to say, he was a scientific man,—the contemporary, for example, of men as different as Bernouilli, Swammerdam, Huygens, and Newton, and was himself actively engaged in the prosecution of mathematics, mechanics, geology, comparative philology, and jurisprudence. But he was also a man of Aristotle's times,—that is to say, a philosopher, not satisfied until the facts, principles, and methods of science had received an interpretation which should explain and unify them.

Leibniz's acquaintance with the higher forms of mathematics was due, as we have seen, to his acquaintance with Huygens. As he made the acquaintance of the latter at the same time that he made the acquaintance of the followers of Descartes, it is likely that he received his introduction to the higher developments of the scientific interpretation of nature and of the philosophic interpretation of science at about the same time. For a while, then, Leibniz was a Cartesian; and he never ceased to call the doctrine of Descartes the antechamber of truth. What were the ideas which he received from Descartes? Fundamentally they were two,—one about the method of truth, the other about the substance of truth. He received the idea that the method of philosophy consists in the analysis of any complex group of ideas down to simple ideas which shall be perfectly clear and distinct; that all such clear and distinct ideas are true, and may then be used for the synthetic reconstruction of any body of truth. Concerning the substance of philosophic truth, he learned that nature is to be interpreted mechanically, and that the instrument of this mechanical interpretation is mathematics. I have used the term "received" in speaking of the relation of Leibniz to these ideas. Yet long before this time we might see him giving himself up to dreams about a vast art of combination which should reduce all the ideas concerned in any science to their simplest elements, and then combine them to any degree of complexity. We have already seen him giving us a picture of a boy of fifteen gravely disputing with himself whether he shall accept the doctrine of forms and final causes, or of physical causes, and as gravely deciding that he shall side with the "moderns;" and that boy was himself. In these facts we have renewed confirmation of the truth that one mind never receives from another anything expecting the stimulus, the reflex, the development of ideas which have already possessed it. But when Leibniz, with his isolated and somewhat ill-digested thoughts, came in contact with that systematized and connected body of doctrines which the Cartesians presented to him in Paris, his ideas were quickened, and he felt the necessity—that final mark of the philosophic mind—of putting them in order.

About the method of Descartes, which Leibniz adopted from him, or rather formulated for himself under the influence of Descartes, not much need be said. It was the method of Continental thought till the time of Kant. It was the mother of the philosophic systems of Descartes, Leibniz, and Spinoza. It was equally the mother of the German *Aufklärung* and the French *éclaircissement.* Its fundamental idea is the thought upon which Rationalism everywhere bases itself. It says: Reduce everything to simple notions. Get clearness; get distinctness. Analyze the complex. Shun the obscure. Discover axioms; employ these axioms in connection with the simple notions, and build up from them. Whatever can be treated in this way is capable of proof, and only this. Leibniz, I repeat, possessed this method in common with Descartes and Spinoza. The certainty and demonstrativeness of mathematics stood out in the clearest contrast to the uncertainty, the obscurity, of all other knowledge. And to them, as to all before the days of Kant, it seemed beyond doubt that the method of mathematics consists in the analysis of notions, and in their synthesis through the medium of axioms, which are true because identical statements; while the notions are true because clear and distinct.

And yet the method led Leibniz in a very different direction. One of the fundamental doctrines, for example, of Leibniz is the existence everywhere of minute and obscure perceptions,—which are of the greatest importance, but of which we, at least, can never have distinct consciousness. How is this factor of his thought, which almost approaches mysticism, to be reconciled with the statements just made? It is found in the different application which is made of the method. The object of Descartes is the *erection of a new structure of truth* upon a *tabula rasa* of all former doctrines. The object of Leibniz is the *interpretation of an old body of truth* by a method which shall reveal it in its clearest light. Descartes and Spinoza are "rationalists" both in their method and results. Leibniz is a "rationalist" in his method; but his application of the method is everywhere controlled by historic considerations. It is, I think, impossible to overemphasize this fact. Descartes was profoundly convinced that past thought had gone wrong, and that its results were worthless. Leibniz was as profoundly convinced that its instincts had been right, and that the general idea of the world which it gave was correct. Leibniz would have given the heartiest assent to Goethe's saying, "Das Wahre war schon längst gefunden." It was out of the question, then, that he should use the new method in any other than an interpreting way to bring out in a connected system and unity the true meaning of the subject-matter.

So much of generality for the method of Leibniz. The positive substance of doctrine which he developed under scientific influence affords matter for more discussion. Of the three influences which meet us here, two are still Cartesian; the third is from the new science of biology, although not yet answering to that name. These three influences are, in order: the idea that nature is to be explained mechanically; that this is to be brought about through the application of mathematics; and, from biology, the idea that all change is of the nature of continuous growth or unfolding. Let us consider each in this order.

What is meant by the mechanical explanation of nature? To answer a question thus baldly put, we must recall the kind of explanations which had satisfied the scholastic men of science. They had been explanations which, however true, Leibniz says, as general principles, do not touch the details of the matter. The explanations of natural facts had been found in general principles, in substantial forces, in occult essences, in native faculties. Now, the first contention of the founders of the modern scientific movement was that such general considerations are not verifiable, and that if they are, they are entirely aside from the point,—they fail to explain any given fact. Explanation must always consist in discovering an immediate connection between some fact and some co-existing or preceding fact. Explanation does not consist in referring a fact to a general power, it consists in referring it to an antecedent whose existence is its necessary condition. It was not left till the times of Mr. Huxley to poke fun at those who would explain some concrete phenomenon by reference to an abstract principle ending in —ity. Leibniz has his word to say about those who would account for the movements of a watch by reference to a principle of horology, and of mill-stones by a fractive principle.

Mechanical explanation consists, accordingly, in making out an actual connection between two existing facts. But this does not say very much. A connection of what kind? In the first place, a connection of the same order as the facts observed. If we are explaining corporeal phenomena, we must find a corporeal link; if we are explaining phenomena of motion, we must find a connection of motion. In one of his first philosophical works Leibniz, in taking the mechanical position, states what he means by it. In the "Confession of Nature against the Atheists" he says that it must be confessed to those who have revived the corpuscular theory of Democritus and Epicurus, to Galileo, Bacon, Gassendi, Hobbes, and Descartes, that in explaining material phenomena recourse is to be had neither to God nor to any other incorporeal thing, form, or quality, but that all things are to be explained from the nature of matter and its qualities, especially from their magnitude, figure, and motion. The physics of Descartes, to which was especially due the spread of mechanical notions, virtually postulated the problem: given a homogeneous quantity of matter, endowed only with extension and mobility, to account for all material phenomena. Liebniz accepts this mechanical view without reserve.

What has been said suggests the bearing of mathematics in this connection. Extension and mobility may be treated by mathematics. It is indeed the business of the geometer to give us an analysis of figured space, to set before us all possible combinations which can arise, assuming extension only. The higher analysis sets before us the results which inevitably follow if we suppose a moving point or any system of movements. Mathematics is thus the essential tool for treating physical phenomena as just defined. But it is more. The mechanical explanation of Nature not only requires such a development of mathematics as will make it applicable to the interpretation of physical facts, but the employment of mathematics is necessary for the very discovery of these facts. Exact observation was the necessity of the growing physical science; and exact observation means such as will answer the question, *How much?* Knowledge of nature depends upon our ability to *measure* her processes,— that is, to reduce distinctions of quality to those of quantity. The only assurance that we can finally have that two facts are connected in such a way as to fulfil the requirements of scientific research, is that there is a complete quantitative connection between them, so that one can be regarded as the other transformed. The advance of physical science from the days of Copernicus to the present has consisted,

therefore, on one hand, in a development of mathematics which has made it possible to apply it in greater and greater measure to the discussion and formulation of the results of experiment, and to deduce laws which, when interpreted physically, will give new knowledge of fact; and, on the other, to multiply, sharpen, and make precise all sorts of devices by which the processes of nature may be measured. The explanation of nature by natural processes; the complete application of mathematics to nature,—these are the two thoughts which, so far, we have seen to be fundamental to the development of the philosophy of Leibniz.

The third factor, and that which brings Leibniz nearer, perhaps, our own day than either of the others, is the growth of physiological science. Swammerdam, Malpighi, Leewenhoek,—these are names which occur and recur in the pages of Leibniz. Indeed, he appears to be the first of that now long line of modern philosophers to be profoundly influenced by the conception of life and the categories of organic growth. Descartes concerned himself indeed with physiological problems, but it was only with a view to applying mechanical principles. The idea of the vital unity of all organs of the body might seem to be attractive to one filled with the notion of the unity of all in God, and yet Spinoza shows no traces of the influence of the organic conception. Not until Kant's famous definition of organism do we see another philosopher moved by an attempt to comprehend the categories of living structure.

But it is the idea of organism, of life, which is radical to the thought of Leibniz. I do not think, however, that it can truly be said that he was led to the idea simply from the state of physiological investigation at that time. Rather, he had already learned to think of the world as organic through and through, and found in the results of biology confirmations, apt illustrations of a truth of which he was already thoroughly convinced. His writings show that there were two aspects of biological science which especially interested him. One was the simple fact of organism itself,—the fact of the various activities of different organs occurring in complete harmony for one end.

This presented three notions very dear to the mind of Leibniz, or rather three moments of the same idea,—the factors of activity, of unity brought about by co-ordinated action, and of an end which reveals the meaning of the activity and is the ideal expression of the unity. The physiologists of that day were also occupied with the problem of growth. The generalization that all is developed *ab ovo* was just receiving universal attention. The question which thrust itself upon science for solution was the mode by which ova, apparently homogeneous in structure, developed into the various forms of the organic kingdom. The answer given was "evolution." But evolution had not the meaning which the term has to-day. By evolution was meant that the whole complex structure of man, for example, was virtually contained in the germ, and that the apparent phenomenon of growth was not the addition of anything from without, but simply the unfolding and magnifying of that already existing. It was the doctrine which afterwards gave way to the epigenesis theory of Wolff, according to which growth is not mere unfolding or unwrapping, but progressive differentiation. The "evolution" theory was the scientific theory of the times, however, and was warmly espoused by Leibniz. To him, as we shall see hereafter, it seemed to give a key which would unlock one of the problems of the universe.

Such, then, were the three chief generalizations which Leibniz found current, and which most deeply affected him. But what use did he make of them? He did not become a philosopher by letting them lie dormant in his mind, nor by surrendering himself passively to them till he could mechanically apply them everywhere. He was a philosopher only in virtue of the active attitude which his mind took towards them. He could not simply accept them at their face-value; he must ask after the source of their value, the royal stamp of meaning which made them a circulatory medium. That is to say, he had to interpret these ideas, to see what they mean, and what is the basis of their validity.

Not many men have been so conscious of just the bearings of their own ideas and of their source as was he. He often allows us a direct glimpse into the method of his thinking, and nowhere more than when he says: "Those who give themselves up to the details of science usually despise abstract and general researchers. Those who go into universal principles rarely care for particular facts. But I equally esteem both." Leibniz, in other words, was equally interested in the application of scientific principles to the explanation of the details of natural phenomena, and in the bearing and meaning of the principles themselves,—a rare combination, indeed, but one, which existing, stamps the genuine philosopher. Leibniz substantially repeats this idea when he says: "Particular effects mut be explained mechanically; but the general principles of physics and mathematics depend upon metaphysics." And again: "All occurs mechanically; but the mechanical principle is not to be explained from material and mathematical considerations, but it flows from a higher and a metaphysical source."

As a man of science, Leibniz might have stopped short with the ideas of mechanical law, of the application of mathematics, and of the continuity of development. As a philosopher he could not. There are some scientific men to whom it always seems a perversion of their principles to attempt to carry them any beyond their application to the details of the subject. They look on in a bewildered and protesting attitude when there is suggested the necessity of any further inquiry. Or perhaps they dogmatically deny the possibility of any such investigation, and as dogmatically assure the sufficiency of their principles for the decision of all possible problems. But bewildered fear and dogmatic assertion are equally impotent to fix arbitrary limits to human thought. Wherever there is a subject that has meaning, there is a field which appeals to mind, and the mind will not cease its endeavors till it has made out what that meaning is, and has made it out in its entirety. So the three principles already spoken of were but the starting-points, the stepping-stones of Leibniz's philosophic thought. While to physical science they are solutions, to philosophy they are problems; and as such Leibniz recognized them. What solution did he give?

So far as the principle of mechanical explanation is concerned, the clew is given by considering the factor upon which he laid most emphasis, namely, motion. Descartes had said that the essence of the physical world is extension. "Not so," replied Leibniz; "it is motion." These answers mark two typical ways of regarding nature. According to one, nature is something essentially rigid and static; whatever change in it occurs, is a change of form, of arrangement, an external modification. According to the other, nature is something essentially dynamic and active. Change according to law is its very essence. Form, arrangement are only the results of this internal principle. And so to Leibniz, extension and the spatial aspects of physical existence were only secondary, they were phenomenal. The primary, the real fact was motion.

The considerations which led him to this conclusion are simple enough. It is the fact already mentioned, that explanation always consists in reducing phenomena to a law of motion which connects them. Descartes himself had not succeeded in writing his physics without everywhere using the conception of motion. But motion cannot be got out of the idea of extension. Geometry will not give us activity. What is this, except virtually to admit the insufficiency of purely statical conceptions? Leibniz found himself confirmed in this position by the fact that the more logical of the followers of Descartes had recognized that motion is a superfluous intruder, if extension be indeed the essence of matter, and therefore had been obliged to have recourse to the immediate activity of God as the cause of all changes. But this, as Leibniz said, was simply to give up the very idea of mechanical explanation, and to fall back into the purely general explanations of scholasticism.

This is not the place for a detailed exposition of the ideas of Leibniz regarding matter, motion, and extension. We need here only recognize that he saw in motion the final reality of the physical universe. But what about motion? To many, perhaps the majority, of minds to-day it seems useless or absurd, or both, to ask any question about motion. It is simply an ultimate *fact,* to which all other facts are to be reduced. We are so familiar with it as a solution of all physical problems that we are confused, and fail to recognize it when it

appears in the guise of a problem. But, I repeat, philosophy cannot stop with facts, however ultimate. It must also know something about the meaning, the significance, in short the ideal bearing, of facts. From the point of view of philosophy, motion has a certain function in the economy of the universe; it is, as Aristotle saw, something ideal.

The name of Aristotle suggests the principles which guided Leibniz in is interpretation of the fact of motion. The thought of Aristotle moves about the two poles of potentiality and actuality. Potentiality is not *mere* capacity; it is being in an undeveloped, imperfect stage. Actuality is, as the word suggests, activity. Anything is potential in so far as it does not manifest itself in action; it is actual so far as it does thus show forth its being. Now, movement, or change in its most general sense, is that by which the potential comes to the realization of its nature, and functions as an activity. Motion, then, is not an ultimate fact, but is subordinate. It exists for an end. It is that by which existence realizes its idea; that is, its proper type of action.

Now Leibniz does not formally build upon these distinctions; and yet he is not very far removed from Aristotle. Motion, he is never weary of repeating, means force, means energy, means activity. To say that the essence of nature is motion, is to say that the natural world finally introduces us to the supremacy of action. Reality is activity. *Substance c'est l'action.* That is the key-note and the battle-cry of the Leibnizian philosophy. Motion is that by which being expresses its nature, fulfils its purpose, reveals its idea. In short, the specific scientific conception of motion is by Leibniz transformed into the philosophic conception of force, of activity. In motion he sees evidence of the fact that the universe is radially dynamic.

In the applicability of mathematics to the interpretation of nature Leibniz finds witness to the continuity and order of the world. We have become so accustomed to the fact that mathematics may be directly employed for the discussion and formulation of physical investigations that we forget what is implied in it. It involves the huge assumption that the world answers to reason; so that whatever the mind finds to be ideally true may be taken for granted to be physically true also. But in those days, when the correlation of the laws of the world and the laws of mathematical reasoning was a fresh discovery, this aspect of the case could not be easily lost sight of.

In fact it was this correlation which filled the *Zeitgeist* of the sixteenth century with the idea that it had a new organ for the penetration of nature, a new sense for learning its meaning. Descartes gives the following as the origin of his philosophy: "The long chains of simple and easy reasons which geometers employ, even in their most complex demonstrations, made me fancy that all things which are the objects of human knowledge are *similarly interdependent.*" To Leibniz also mathematics seemed to give a clew to the order, the interdependence, the harmonious relations, of the world.

In this respect the feeling of Plato that God geometrizes found an echoing response in Leibniz. But the latter would hardly have expressed it in the same way. He would have preferred to say that God everywhere uses the infinitesimal calculus. In the applicability of the calculus in the discussion of physical facts, Leibniz saw two truths reflected,—that everything that occurs has its reason, its dependent connection upon something else, and that all is continuous and without breaks. While the formal principles of his logic are those of identity and contradiction, his real principles are those of sufficient reason and of continuity. Nature never makes leaps; everything in nature has a sufficient reason why it is as it is: these are the philosophic generalizations which Leibniz finds hidden in the applicability of mathematics to physical science. Reason finds itself everywhere expressed in nature; and the law of reason is unity in diversity, continuity.

Let us say, in a word, that the correlation between the laws of mathematics and of physics is the evidence of the rational character of nature. Nature may be reduced to motions; and motions can be understood only as force, activity. But the laws which connect motions are fundamentally mathematical laws,—laws of reason. Hence force, activity, can be understood only as rational, as spiritual. Nature is thus seen to mean Activity, and Activity is seen to mean Intelligence. Furthermore, as the fundamental law of intelligence is the production of difference in unity, the primary law of physical change must be the manifestation of this unity in difference,—or, as Leibniz interpreted it, continuity. In nature there are no breaks, neither of quantity nor of quality nor of relationship. The full force of this law we shall see later.

Such an idea can hardly be distinguished from the idea of growth or development; one passes naturally into the other. Thus it is equally proper to say that the third scientific influence, the conception of organism and growth, is dominant in the Leibnizian thought, or that this is swallowed up and absorbed in the grand idea of continuity. The law of animal and vegetable life and the law of the universe are identified. The substance of the universe is activity; the law of the universe is interdependence. What is this but to say that the universe is an organic whole? Its activity is the manifestation of life,—nay, it is life. The laws of its activity reveal that continuity of development, that harmony of inter-relation, which are everywhere the marks of Life. The final and fundamental notion, therefore, by which Leibniz interprets the laws of physics and mathematics is that of Life. This is his regnant category. It is "that higher and metaphysical source" from which the very existence and principles of mechanism flow. The perpetual and ubiquitous presence of motion reveals the pulsations of Life; the correlation, the rationality, of these motions indicate the guiding presence of Life. This idea is the alpha and omega of his philosophy.

II. The Fundamental Problem and Its Solution

Leibniz, like every great man, absorbed into himself the various thoughts of his time, and in absorbing transformed them. He brought into a focus of brilliancy the diffused lights of truth shining here and there. He summed up in a pregnant and comprehensive category the scattered principles of his age. Yet we are not to suppose that Leibniz considered these various ideas one by one, and then patched them into an artificial unity of thought. Philosophies are not manufactured piecemeal out of isolated and fragmentary thoughts; they grow from a single root, absorbing from their environment whatever of sustenance offers itself, and maturing in one splendid fruit of spiritual truth. It is convenient, indeed, to isolate various phases of truth, and consider them as distinct forces working to shape one final product, and as a convenient artifice it is legitimate. But it answers to no process actually occurring. Leibniz never surrendered his personal unity, and out of some one root-conception grew all his ideas. The principles of his times were not separate forces acting upon him, they were the foods of which he selected and assimilated such as were fitted to nourish his one great conception.

But it is more than a personal unity which holds together the thinking of a philosopher. There is the unity of the problem, which the philosopher has always before him, and in which all particular ideas find their unity. All else issues from this and merges into it. The various influences which we have seen affecting Leibniz, therefore, got their effectiveness from the relation which he saw them bear to the final problem of all thought. This is the inquiry after the unity of experience, if we look at it from the side of the subject; the unity of reality, if we put it from the objective side. Yet each age states this problem in its own way, because it sees it in the light of some difficulty which has recently arisen in consciousness. At one time, the question is as to the relation of the one to the many; at another, of the relation of the sensible to the intelligible world; at another, of the relation of the individual to the universal. And this last seems to have been the way in which it specifically presented itself to Leibniz. This way of stating it was developed, though apparently without adequate realization of its meaning, by the philosophy of scholasticism. It stated the problem as primarily a logical question,—the relation of genera, of species, of individuals to each other. And the school-boy, made after the stamp of literary tradition, knows that there were two parties among the Schoolmen,—the Realists, and the Nominalists; one asserting, the other denying, the objective reality of universals. To regard this discussion as useless, is to utter the condemnation of philosophy, and to relegate the foundation of science to the realm of things not to be inquired into. To say that it is an easy matter to decide, is to assume the decision with equal ease of all the problems that have vexed the thought of humanity. To us it seems easy because we have bodily incorporated into our thinking the results of both the realistic and the nominalistic doctrines, without attempting to reconcile them, or even being conscious of the necessity of reconciliation. We assert in one breath that the individual is alone real, and in the next assert that only those forms of consciousness which represent something in the universe are to be termed knowledge. At one moment we say that universals are creations of the individual mind, and at the next pass on to talk of laws of nature, or even of a reign of law. In other words, we have learned to regard both the individual and the universal as real, and thus ignoring the problem, think we have solved it.

But to Leibniz the problem presented itself neither as a logical question, nor yet as one whose solution might be taken for granted. On the contrary, it was just this question: How shall we conceive the individual to be related to the universe? which seemed to him to be the nerve of the philosophic problem, the question whose right answer would solve the problems of religion, of morals, of the basis of science, as well as of the nature of reality. The importance of just this way of putting the question had been rendered evident by the predecessors and contemporaries of Leibniz, especially by Descartes, Spinoza, and Locke. His more specific relations to the last-named will occupy us hereafter; at present we must notice how the question stood at the hands of Descartes and Spinoza.

Descartes had separated the individual from the universal. His philosophy began and ended with a dualism. I have just said that the problem of philosophy is the unity of experience. Yet we find that there have been thinkers, and those of the first rank, who have left the matter without discovering any ultimate unity, or rather who have made it the burden of their contention that we cannot explain the world without at least two disparate principles. But if we continue to look at the matter in this historical way, we shall see that this dualism has always been treated by the successors of such a philosopher, not as a solution, but as a deeper statement of the problem. It is the function of dualistic philosophies to re-state the question in a new and more significant way. There are times when the accepted unity of thought is seen to be inadequate and superficial. Men are thrashing old straw, and paying themselves with ideas which have lost their freshness and their timeliness. There then arises a philosopher who goes deep, beyond the superficial unity, and who discovers the untouched problem. His it is to assert the true meaning of the question, which has been unseen or evaded. The attitude of dualism is thus always necessary, but never final. Its value is not in any solution, but in the generality and depth of the problem which it proposes, and which incites thought to the discovery of a unity of equal depth and comprehensiveness.

Except for Descartes, then, we should not be conscious of the gulf that yawns between the individual mind and the universe in front of it. He presented the opposition as between mind and matter. The essence of the former is thought; of the latter, extension. The conceptions are disparate and opposed. No interaction is possible. His disciples, more consistent than their master, called in a *deus ex machina*,—the miraculous intervention of God,—in order to account for the appearance of reciprocal action between the universe of matter and the thinking individual. Thus they in substance admitted the relation between them to be scientifically inexplicable, and had recourse to the supernatural. The individual does not act upon the universe to produce, destroy, or alter the arrangement of anything. But upon the *occasion* of his volition God produces a corresponding material change. The world does not act upon the soul of the individual to produce thoughts or sensations. God, upon *occasion* of the external affection, brings them into being. With such thoroughness Descartes performed his task of separation. Yet the introduction of the *deus ex machi-*

na only complicated the problem; it introduced a third factor where two were already too many. What is the relation of God to Mind and to Matter? Is it simply a third somewhat, equally distinct from both, or does it contain both within itself?

Spinoza attempted to solve the problem in the latter sense. He conceived God to be the one substance of the universe, possessing the two known attributes of thought and matter. These attributes are one in God; indeed, he is their unity. This is the sole legitimate outcome of the Cartesian problem stated as Descartes would have it stated. It overcomes the absoluteness of the dualism by discovering a common and fundamental unity, and at the same time takes the subject out of the realm of the miraculous. For the solution works both ways. It affects the nature of God, as well as of extension and thought. It presents him to us, not as a supernatural being, but as the unity of thought and extension. In knowing these as they are, we know God as he is. Spinoza, in other words, uses the conception of God in a different way from the Cartesians. The latter had treated him as the God of theology,—a being supernatural; Spinoza uses the conception as a scientific one, and speaks of *Deus sive Natura*.

Leibniz recognized the unphilosophic character of the recourse to a *deus ex machina* as clearly as Spinoza, and yet did not accept his solution. To find out why he did not is the problem of the historian of thought. The one cause which stands out above all others is that in the unity of Spinoza all difference, all distinction, is lost. All particular existences, whether things or persons, are *modes* of extension and thought. Their *apparent* existence is due to the imagination, which is the source of belief in particular things. When considered as they really are,—that is, by the understanding,—they vanish. The one substance, with its two unchanging attributes of thought and extension, alone remains. If it is a philosophic error to give a solution which permits of no unity, is it not equally a philosophic error to give one which denies difference? So it seemed to Leibniz. The problem is to reconcile difference in unity, not to swallow up difference in a blank oneness,—to reconcile the individual with the universe, not to absorb him.

The unsatisfactoriness of the solution appears if we look at it from another side. Difference implies change, while a unity in which all variety is lost implies quiescence. Change is as much an illusion of imagination to Spinoza as is variety. The One Reality is permanent. How repugnant the conception of a static universe was to Leibniz we have already learned. Spinoza fails to satisfy Leibniz, therefore, because he does not allow the conceptions of individuality and of activity. He presents a unity in which all distinction of individuals is lost, and in which there is no room for change. But Spinoza certainly presented the problem more clearly to Leibniz, and revealed more definitely the conditions of its solution. The search is henceforth for a unity which shall avoid the irresolvable dualism of Descartes, and yet shall allow free play to the principles of individuality and of activity. There must be, in short, a universe to which the individual bears a real yet independent relation. What is this unity? The answer, in the phraseology of Leibniz, is the *monad*. Spinoza would be right, said Leibniz, were it not for the existence of monads. I know there are some who have done Leibniz the honor of supposing that this is his way of saying, "Spinoza is wrong because I am right;" but I cannot help thinking that the saying has a somewhat deeper meaning. What, then, is the nature of the monad? The answer to this question takes us back to the point where the discussion of the question was left at the end of chapter second. The nature of the monad is life. The monad is the spiritual activity which lives in absolute harmony with an infinite number of other monads.

Let us first consider the reasons of Leibniz for conceiving the principle of unity as spiritual. Primarily it is because it is impossible to conceive of a unity which is material. In the sensible world there is no unity. There are, indeed, aggregations, collections, which seem like unities; but the very fact that these are aggregations shows that the unity is factitious. It is the very nature of matter to be infinitely divisible: to say this is to deny the existence of any true principle of unity. The world of nature is the world of space and time; and where in space or time shall we find a unity where we

may rest? Every point in space, every moment in time, points beyond itself. It refers to a totality of which it is but a part, or, rather, a limitation. If we add resistance, we are not better situated. We have to think of something which resists; and to this something we must attribute extension,—that is to say, difference, plurality. Nor can we find any resistance which is absolute and final. There may be a body which is undivided, and which resists all energy now acting upon it; but we cannot frame an intelligible idea of a body which is absolutely indivisible. To do so is to think of a body out of all relation to existing forces, something absolutely isolated; while the forces of nature are always relative to one another. That which resists does so in comparison with some opposing energy. The absolutely indivisible, on the other hand, would be that which could not be brought into comparison with other forces; it would not have any of the attributes of force as we know it. In a word, whatever exists in nature is relative in space, in time, and in qualities to all else. It is made what it is by virtue of the totality of its relations to the universe; it has no ultimate principle of self-subsistent unity in it.

Nor do we fare better if we attempt to find unity in the world of nature as a whole. Nature has its existence as a whole in space and time. Indeed, it is only a way of expressing the totality of phenomena of space and time. It is a mere aggregate, a collection. Its very essence is plurality, difference. It is divisible without limit, and each of its divisions has as good a right to be called one as the whole from which it is broken off. We shall consider hereafter Leibniz's idea of infinity; but it is easy to see that he must deny any true infinity to nature. An ultimate whole made up of parts is a contradictory conception; and the idea of a quantitative infinite is equally so. Quantity means number, measure, limitation. We may not be able to assign number to the totality of occurrences in nature, nor to measure her every event. This shows that nature is indefinitely greater than any *assignable* quantity; but it does not remove her from the category of quantity. As long as the world is conceived as that existing in space and time, it is conceived as that which has to be measured. As we saw in the last chapter, the heart of the mechanical theory of the world is in the application of mathematics to it. Since quantity and mathematics are correlative terms, the natural world cannot be conceived as infinite or as an ultimate unity.

In short, Leibniz urges and suggests in one form and another those objections to the mechanical theory of reality which later German philosophers have made us so familiar with. The objections are indeed varied in statement, but they all come to the impossibility of finding any unity, any wholeness, anything except plurality and partiality in that which is externally conditioned,—as everything is in nature.

But the reasons as thus stated are rather negative than positive. They show why the ultimate unity cannot be conceived as material, rather than why it must be conceived as spiritual. The immediate evidence of its spiritual nature Leibniz finds in the perception of the one unity directly known to us,—the "me," the conscious principle within, which reveals itself as an active force, and as truly one, since not a spatial or temporal existence. And this evidence he finds confirmed by the fact that whatever unity material phenomena appear to have comes to them through their perception by the soul. Whatever the mind grasps in one act, is manifested as one.

But it is not in any immediate certainty of fact that Leibniz finds the best or completest demonstration of the spiritual nature of the ultimate unity. This is found in the use which can be made of the hypothesis. The truest witness to the spiritual character of reality is found in the capacity of this principle to comprehend and explain the facts of experience. With this conception the reason of things can be ascertained, and light introduced into what were otherwise a confused obscurity. And, indeed, this is the only sufficient proof of any doctrine. It is not what comes before the formulation of a theory which proves it; it is not the facts which suggest it, or the processes which lead up to it: it is what comes after the formation of the theory,—the uses that it can be put to; the facts which it will render significant. The whole philosophy of Leibniz in its simplicity, width, and depth, is the real evidence of the truth of his philosophical principle.

The monad, then, is a spiritual unity; it is individualized life. Unity, activity, individuality, are synonymous terms in the vocabulary of Leibniz. Every unity is a true substance, containing within itself the source and law of its own activity. It is that which is internally determined to action. It is to be conceived after the analogy of the soul. It is an indivisible unity, like "that particular something in us which thinks, apperceives and wills, and distinguishes us in a way of its own from whatever else thinks and wills." Against Descartes, therefore, Leibniz stands for the principle of unity; against Spinoza, he upholds the doctrine of individuality, of diversity, of multiplicity. And the latter principle is as important in his thought as the former. Indeed, they are inseparable. The individual is the true unity. There is an infinite number of these individuals, each distinct from every other. The law of specification, of distinction, runs through the universe. Two beings cannot be alike. They are not individualized merely by their different positions in space or time; duration and extension, on the contrary, are, as we have seen, principles of relativity, of connection. Monads are specified by an internal principle. Their distinct individuality is constituted by their distinct law of activity. Leibniz will not have a philosophy of abstract unity, representing the universe as simple only, he will have a philosophy equal to the diversity, the manifold wealth of variety, in the universe. This is only to say that he will be faithful to his fundamental notion,—that of Life. Life does not mean a simple unity like a mathematical one, it means a unity which is the harmony of the interplay of diverse organs, each following its own law and having its own function. When Leibniz says, God willed to have more monads rather than fewer, the expression is indeed one of *naïveté*, but the thought is one of unexplored depth. It is the thought that Leibniz repeats when he says, "Those who would reduce all things to modifications of one universal substance do not have sufficient regard to the *order*, the *harmony* of reality." Leibniz applies here, as everywhere, the principle of continuity, which is unity in and through diversity, not the principle of bare oneness. There is a kingdom of monads, a realm truly infinite, composed of individual unities or activities in an absolute continuity. Leibniz was one of the first, if not the first, to use just the expression "uniformity of nature;" but even here he explains that it means "uniform in variety, one in principle, but varied in manifestation." The world is to be as rich as possible. This is simply to say that distinct individuality as well as ultimate unity is a law of reality.

But has not Leibniz fallen into a perilous position? In avoiding the monotone of unity which characterizes the thought of Spinoza, has he not fallen into a lawless variety of multiplicity, infinitely less philosophic than even the dualism of Descartes, since it has an infinity of ultimate principles instead of only two? If Spinoza sacrificed the individual to the universe, has not Leibniz, in his desire to emphasize the individual, gone to the other extreme? Apparently we are introduced to a universe that is a mere aggregate of an infinite multiplicity of realities, each independent of every other. Such a universe would not be a universe. It would be a chaos of disorder and conflict. We come, therefore, to a consideration of the relation between these individual monads and the universe. We have to discover what lifts the monads out of their isolation and bestows upon them that stamp of universality which makes it possible for them to enter into the coherent structure of reality: in a word, what is the universal content which the monad in its formal individuality bears and manifests?

The way in which the question has just been stated suggests the Leibnizian answer. The monad, indeed, in its form is thoroughly individual, having its own unique mode of activity; but its content, that which this activity manifests, is not peculiar to it as an individual, but is the substance or law of the universe. It is the very nature of the monad to be representative. Its activity consists in picturing or reproducing those relations which make up the world of reality. In a conscious soul, the ability thus to represent the world is called "perception," and thus Leibniz attributes perception to all the monads. This is not to be understood as a conscious representation of reality to itself (for

this the term "apperception" is reserved), but it signifies that the very essence of the monad is to produce states which are not its own peculiar possessions, but which reflect the facts and relations of the universe. Leibniz never wearies in finding new ways to express this purely representative character of the monad. The monads are little souls; they are mirrors of the world; they are concentrations of the universe, each expressing it in its own way; borrowing a term from scholasticism, they are "substantial forms." They are substantial, for they are independent unities; they are forms, because the term "form" expresses, in Aristotelian phraseology, the type or law of some class of phenomena. The monad is an individual, but its whole content, its objectivity or reality, is the summation of the universe which it represents. It is individual, but whatever marks it as actual is some reproduction of the world. His reconciliation of the principles of individuality and universality is contained in the following words: "Each monad contains within itself an order corresponding to that of the universe,—indeed, the monads represent the universe in an infinity of ways, all different, and all true, thus multiplying the universe as many times as is possible, approaching the divine as near as may be, and giving the world all the perfection of which it is capable." The monad is individual, for it represents reality in its own way, from its own point of view. It is universal, for its whole content is the order of the universe.

New light is thus thrown upon the former statement that reality is activity, that the measure of a being is the action which it puts forth. That statement is purely formal. It leaves the kind of activity and its law wholly undetermined. But this relation of "representativeness" which we have discovered gives definiteness. It is the law of the monad's action to mirror, to reflect, the universe; its changes follow each other so as to bring about this reflection in the completest degree possible. The monad is literally the many in the one; it is the answer to the inquiry of Greek philosophy. The many are not present by way of participation in some underlying essence, not yet as statically possessed by the one, as attributes are sometimes supposed to inhere in a substratum. The "many" is the manifestation of the activity of the "one." The one and the many are related as form and content in an organic unity, which is activity. The essence of a substance, says Leibniz, consists in that regular tendency of action by which its phenomena follow one another in a certain order; and that order, as he repeatedly states, is the order in which the universe itself is arranged.

The activity of a monad may be advantageously compared to that of a supposed atom, granting, for the sake of the illustration, that there is such a thing. Each is in a state of change: the atom changes its place, the monad its representation, and each in the simplest and most uniform way that its conditions permit. How, then, is there such a similarity, such a monotony, in the change of an atom, and such variety and complexity in the change of a monad? It is because the atom has merely parts, or external variety, while the monad has an internal variety. Multiplicity is organically wrought into its very being. It has an *essential* relation to all things in the universe; and to say that this relation is essential, is to say that it is one which constitutes its very content, its being. Hence the cause of the changes of the monad, of their variety and complexity, is one with the cause of the richness, the profusion, the regulated variety of change in the universe itself. While we have employed a comparison with atoms, this very comparison may serve to show us the impossibility of atoms as they are generally defined by the physicist turned philosopher. Atoms have no internal and essential relation to the world; they have no internal connection with any one thing in the world: and what is this but to say that they do not enter anywhere into the structure of the world? By their very conception they are forever aliens, banished from any share or lot in the realm of reality. The idea which Leibniz never lets go, the idea which he always accentuates, is, then, the idea of an individual activity which in its continual change manifests as its own internal content and reality that reality and those laws of connection which make up the world itself.

We are thus introduced naturally to the conception which plays so large a part in the Leibnizian philosophy, that of pre-established harmony. This term simply names the fact, which we see to be fundamental with Leibniz,—the fact that, while the form of every monad is individuality, a unique principle of action, its content is universal, the very being and laws of the world. For we must now notice more explicitly what has been wrapped up in the idea all along. There is no direct influence of monads upon each other. One cannot affect another causally. There is no actual interaction of one upon another. Expressed in that figurative language which was ever natural to Leibniz, the monads have no windows by which anything can get in or out. This follows, of course, from the mutual independence and individuality of the monads. They are a true democracy, in which each citizen has sovereignty. To admit external influences acting upon them is to surrender their independence, to deny their sovereignty. But we must remember the other half. This democracy is not after the Platonic conception of democracy, in which each does as it pleases, and in which there is neither order nor law, but the extremest assertion of individuality. What each sovereign citizen of the realm of reality expresses is precisely law. Each is an embodiment in its own way of the harmony, the order, of the whole kingdom. Each is sovereign because it is dynamic law,—law which is no longer abstract, but has realized itself in life. Thus another way of stating the doctrine of pre-established harmony is the unity of freedom and necessity. Each monad is free because it is individual, because it follows the law of its own activity unhindered, unretarded, by others; it is self-determined. But it is self-determined to show forth the order, the harmony, of the universe. There is nothing of caprice, of peculiarity, in the content of the monad. It shows forth order; it is organized by law; it reveals the necessary connections which constitute the universe. The pre-established harmony is the unity of the individual and the universe; it is the organic oneness of freedom and necessity.

We see still further what it means when we learn that it is by this conception that Leibniz reconciles the conceptions of physical and final causation. There is no principle closer to the thought of Leibniz than that of the equal presence and efficiency everywhere of both physical and final causes. Every fact which occurs is susceptible of a mechanical and of a rational explanation. It is necessarily connected with preceding states, and it has a necessary end which it is fulfilling. The complete meaning of this principle will meet us hereafter; at present we must notice that it is one form of the doctrine of pre-established harmony. All things have an end because they form parts of one system; everything that occurs looks forward to something else and prepares the way for it, and yet it is itself mechanically conditioned by its antecedents. This is only another way of saying that there is complete harmony between all beings in the universe; so that each monad in fulfilling the law of its own existence contributes to the immanent significance of the universe. The monads are co-ordinated in such a way that they express a common idea. There is a plan common to all, in which each has its own place. All are making towards one goal, expressing one purpose. The universe is an organism; and Leibniz would have applied to it the words which Milne-Edwards applied to the human organism, as I find them quoted by Lewes: "In the organism everything seems to be calculated with one determined result in view; and the harmony of the parts does not result from the influence which they exert upon one another, but from their co-ordination under the rule of a common force, a preconceived plan, a pre-existent force." That is to say, the universe is teleological, both as a whole and in its parts; for there is a common idea animating it and expressed by it; it is mechanical, for this idea is realized and manifested by the outworking of forces.

It ought to be evident even from this imperfect sketch that the Leibnizian theory of pre-established harmony is not that utterly artificial and grotesque doctrine which it is sometimes represented to be. The phrase "pre-established harmony" is, strictly speaking, tautologous. The term "pre-established" is superfluous. It means "existent." There is no real harmony which is not existent or pre-

established. An accidental harmony is a contradiction in terms. It means a chaotic cosmos, an unordered order, a lawless law, or whatever else is nonsensical.

Harmony, in short, means relation, means connection, means subordination and co-ordination, means adjustment, means a variety, which yet is one. The Leibuizian doctrine is not a factitious product of his imagination, nor is it a mechanical scheme for reconciling a problem which has no existence outside of the bewildered brains of philosophers. It is an expression of the fact that the universe is one of order, of continuity, of unity; it is the accentuating of this doctrine so that the very essence of reality is found in this ordered combination; it is the special application of this principle to the solution of many of the problems which "the mind of man is apt to run into,"—the questions of the relation of the individual and the universal, of freedom and necessity, of the physical and material, of the teleological and mechanical. We may not be contented with the doctrine as he presents it, we may think it to be rather a summary and highly concentrated statement of the problem than its solution, or we may object to details in the carrying out of the doctrine. But we cannot deny that it is a genuine attempt to meet a genuine problem, and that it contains some, if not all, of the factors required for its adequate solution. To Leibniz must remain the glory of being the thinker to seize upon the perfect unity and order of the universe as its essential characteristic, and of arranging his thoughts with a view to discovering and expressing it.

We have but to notice one point more, and our task is done so far as it serves to make plain the standpoint from which Leibniz criticised Locke. There is, we have seen, the greatest possible continuity and complexity in the realm of monads. There is no break, quantitative nor qualitative. It follows that the human soul has no gulf set between it and what we call nature. It is only the highest, that is to say the most active and the most representative, of all monads. It stands, indeed, at the head of the scale, but not outside it. From the monad which reveals its presence in that stone which with blinded eyes we call dead, through that which acts in the plant, in the animal, up to that of man, there is no chasm, no interruption. Nay, man himself is but one link in the chain of spiritual beings which ends only in God. All monads are souls; the soul of man is a monad which represents the universe more distinctly and adequately. The law which is enfolded in the lower monads is developed in it and forms a part of its conscious activity. The universe, which is confusedly mirrored by the perception of the lower monad, is clearly brought out in the conscious apperception of man. The stone is representative of the whole world. An all-knowing intelligence might read in it relations to every other fact in the world, might see exemplified the past history of the world, and prefigured the events to come. For the stone is not an isolated existence, it is an inter-organic member of a system. Change the slightest fact in the world, and in some way it is affected. The law of the universe is one of completed reciprocity, and this law must be mirrored in every existence of the universe. Increase the activity, the representative power, until it becomes turned back, as it were, upon itself, until the monad not only is a mirror, but knows itself as one, and you have man. The soul of man is the world come to consciousness of itself. The realm of monads in what we call the inorganic world and the lower organic realm shows us the monad let and hindered in its development. These realms attempt to speak forth the law of their being, and reveal the immanent presence of the universe; but they do not hear their own voice, their utterance is only for others. In man the universe is manifested, and is manifested to man himself.

III. Locke and Leibniz— Innate Ideas

The reader, impatient of what may have seemed an over-long introduction, has perhaps been asking when he was to be brought to the subject under consideration,—the relations of Leibniz to Locke. But it has been impossible to come to this question until we had

formed for ourselves an outline of the philosophical position of Leibniz. Nowhere in the "Nouveaux Essais" does Leibniz give a connected and detailed exposition of his philosophy, either as to his standpoint, his fundamental principles, or his method.

Some preliminary view of his position is therefore a necessity. The demand for this preliminary exposition becomes more urgent as we recognize that Leibniz's remarks upon Locke are not a critique of Locke from the standpoint of the latter, but are the application of his own philosophical conclusions. Criticism from within, an examination of a system of thought with relation to the consistency and coherency of its results, the connection between these results and the method professedly employed, investigation which depends not at all upon the position of the critic, but occupies itself with the internal relations of the system under discussion,—such criticism is a product of the present century. What we find in the "Nouveaux Essais" is a comparison of the ideas of Locke with those of Leibniz himself, a testing of the former by the latter as a standard, their acceptance when they conform, their rejection when they are opposed, their completion when they are in partial harmony.

The value of this sort of criticism is likely to be small and evanescent. If the system used as a standard is meagre and narrow, if it is without comprehensiveness and flexibility, it does not repay after-examination. The fact that the "Nouveaux Essais" of Leibniz have escaped the oblivion of the philosophical criticism of his day is proof, if proof still be needed, of the reasoned basis, the width of grasp, the fertility of suggestion which characterize the thought of Leibniz. But the fact that the criticism is, after all, external and not internal has made necessary the foregoing extended account of his method and general results.

On the other hand, what of Locke? How about him who is the recipient of the criticism? I assume that no extended account of his ideas is here necessary, and conceive myself to be justified in this assumption by the fact that we are already better acquainted with Locke. This acquaintance, indeed, is not confined to those who have expressly studied Locke. His thought is an inheritance into which every English-speaking person at least is born. Only he who does not think escapes this inheritance. Locke did the work which he had to do so thoroughly that every Englishman who will philosophize must either build upon Locke's foundations, or, with conscious purpose, clear the ground before building for himself. And it would be difficult to say that the acceptance of Locke's views would influence one's thought more than their rejection. This must not, of course, be taken too literally. It may be that one who is a lineal descendant of Locke in the spiritual generations of thought would not state a single important truth as Locke stated it, or that those who seek their method and results elsewhere have not repudiated the thought of Locke as expressly belonging to him.

But the fundamental principles of empiricism: its conception of intelligence as an individual possession; its idea of reality as something over against and distinct from mind; its explanation of knowledge as a process of action and reaction between these separate things; its account of our inability to know things as they really are,—these principles are congenital with our thinking. They are so natural that we either accept them as axiomatic, and accuse those who reject them of metaphysical subtlety, or, staggered perchance by some of their results, give them up with an effort. But it is an effort, and a severe one; and there is none of us who can tell when some remnant of the conception of intelligence as purely particular and finite will catch him tripping. On the other hand, we realize much better than those who have behind them a Leibniz and a Kant, rather than a Locke and a Hume, the meaning and the thorough-going necessity of the universality of intelligence. Idealism must be in some ways arbitrary and superficial to him who has not had a pretty complete course of empiricism.

Leibniz seems to have been impressed with the Essay on the Human Understanding at its first appearance. As early as 1696 we find him writing a few pages of comment upon the book. Compared with his later critique, these early "reflections" seem colorless, and give the impression that Leibniz desired to minimize his differences from Locke rather than to set them forth in relief. Comparatively slight as were his expressions of dissent, they appear to have stung Locke when they reached him. Meantime Locke's book was translated into French, and made its way to a wider circle of readers. This seems to have suggested to Leibniz the advisability of pursuing his comments somewhat further; and in the summer of 1703 he produced the work which now occupies us. A letter which Leibniz wrote at about this time is worth quoting at large for the light which it throws upon the man, as well as for suggesting the chief points in which he differed from Locke. Leibniz writes:—

I have forgotten to tell you that my comments upon the work of Locke are nearly done. As he has spoken in a chapter of his second book about freedom, he has given me an opportunity to discuss that; and I hope that I may have done it in such a way as will please you. Above all, I have laid it upon myself to save the immateriality of the soul, which Locke leaves doubtful. I justify also the existence of innate ideas, and show that the soul produces their perception out of itself. Axioms, too, I approve, while Locke has a low opinion of them. In contradiction to him, I show that the individuality of man, through which he preserves his identity, consists in the duration of the simple or immaterial substance which animates him; that the soul is never without representations; that there is neither a vacuum nor atoms; that matter, or the passive principle, cannot be conscious, excepting as God unites with it a conscious substance. We disagree, indeed, in numerous other points, for I find that he rates too low the noble philosophy of the Platonic school (as Descartes did in part), and substitutes opinions which degrade us, and which may become hurtful to morals, though I am persuaded that Locke's intention was thoroughly good. I have made these comments in leisure hours, when I have been journeying or visiting, and could not occupy myself with investigations requiring great pains. The work has continued to grow under my hands, for in almost every chapter, and to a greater extent than I had thought possible, I have found matter for remark. You will be astonished when I tell you that I have worked upon this as upon something which requires no great pains. But the fact is, that I long ago established the general principles of philosophic subjects in my mind in a demonstrative way, or pretty nearly so, and that they do not require much new consideration from me.

Leibniz goes on to add that he has put these reflections in the form of a dialogue that they may be more attractive; has written them in the popular language, rather than in Latin, that they may reach as wide a circle as the work of Locke; and that he hopes to publish them soon, as Locke is already an old man, and he wishes to get them before the public while Locke may still reply.

But unfortunately this last hope was destined to remain unrealized. Before the work of revision was accomplished, Locke died. Leibniz, in a letter written in 1714, alludes to his controversy with Locke as follows: "I do not like the thought of publishing refutations of authors who are dead. These should appear during their life, and be communicated to them." Then, referring to his earlier comments, he says: "A few remarks escaped me, I hardly know how, and were taken to England. Mr. Locke, having seen them, spoke of them slightingly in a letter to Molineux. I am not astonished at it. We were somewhat too far apart in principle, and that which I suggested seemed paradoxical to him." Leibniz, according to his conviction here expressed, never published his "Nouveaux Essais sur l'Entendement Humain." Schaarschmidt remarks that another reason may have restrained him, in that he did not wish to carry on too many controversies at once with the English people. He had two on his hands then,—one with the Newtonians regarding the infinitesimal calculus; the other with Bishop Clarke regarding the nature of God, of time and space, of freedom, and cognate subjects. However, in 1765, almost fifty years after the death of Leibniz, his critique upon Locke finally appeared.

It is somewhat significant that one whose tendency was conciliatory, who was eminently what the Germans delight to call him, a "mediator," attempting to unite the varied truths which he found scattered in opposed systems, should have had so much of his work called forth by controversy. Aside from the cases just mentioned, his other chief work, the

Theodicy, is, in form, a reply to Bayle. Many of his minor pieces are replies to criticism or are developments of his own thought with critical reference to Descartes, Malebranche, and others. But Leibniz has a somewhat different attitude towards his British and towards his Continental opponents. With the latter he was always in sympathy, while they in turn gave whatever he uttered a respectful hearing. Their mutual critiques begin and end in compliments. But the Englishmen found the thought of Leibniz "paradoxical" and forced. It seemed to them wildly speculative, and indeed arbitrary guess-work, without any special reason for its production, and wholly unverifiable in its results. Such has been the fate of much of the best German thought since that time in the land of the descendants of Newton and Locke. But Leibniz, on the other hand, felt as if he were dealing, in philosophical matters at least, with foemen hardly worthy of his steel. Locke, he says, had subtlety and address, and a sort of *superficial* metaphysics; but he was ignorant of the method of mathematics,—that is to say, from the standpoint of Leibniz, of the method of all science. We have already seen that he thought the examination of a work which had been the result of the continued labor of Locke was a matter for he leisure hours of his courtly visits. Indeed, he would undoubtedly have felt about it what he actually expressed regarding his controversy with Clarke,—that he . . . regarded the English as superficial and without grasp of principles, as they thought him over-deep and over-theoretical.

From this knowledge of the external circumstances of the work of Leibniz and its relation to Locke, it is necessary that we turn to its internal content, to the thought of Leibniz as related to the ideas of Locke. The Essay on the Human Understanding is, as the name implies, an account of the nature of knowledge. Locke tells us that it originated in the fact that often, when he had been engaged in discussions with his friends, they found themselves landed in insoluble difficulties. This occurred so frequently that it seemed probable that they had been going at matters from the wrong side, and that before they attempted to come to conclusions about questions, they ought to examine the capacity of intelligence, and see whether it is fitted to deal with such questions. Locke, in a word, is another evidence of that truth which lies at the basis of all forms of philosophical thought, however opposed they may be to one another,—the truth that knowledge and reality are so organic to each other that to come to any conclusion about one, we must know something about the other. Reality equals objects known or knowable, and knowledge equals reality dissolved in ideas,—reality which has become translucent through its meaning.

Locke's Essay is, then, an account of the origin, nature, extent, and limitations of human knowledge. Such is its subject-matter, What is its method? Locke himself tells us that he uses the "plain historical method." We do not have to resort to the forcing of language to learn that this word "historical" contains the key to his work. Every page of the Essay is testimony to the fact that Locke always proceeds by inquiring into the way and circumstances by which knowledge of the subject under consideration came into existence and into the conditions by which it was developed. Origin means with Locke, not logical dependence, but temporal production; development means temporal succession. In the language of our day, Locke's Essay is an attempt to settle ontological questions by a psychological method. And as we have before noticed, Leibniz meets him, not by inquiry into the pertinence of the method or into the validity of results so reached, but by the more direct way of impugning his psychology, by substituting another theory of the nature of mind and of the way in which it works.

The questions with which the discussion begins are as to the existence of innate ideas, and as to whether the soul always thinks,—questions which upon their face will lead the experienced reader of to-day to heave a sigh in memory of hours wasted in barren dispute, and which will create a desire to turn elsewhere for matter more solid and more nutritive. But in this case, under the form which the discussion takes at the hands of Leibniz, the question which awaits answer under the meagre and worn-out formula of "innate ideas" is the function of intelligence in experience.

Locke denies, and denies with great vigor, the existence of innate ideas. His motives in so doing are practical and theoretical. He sees almost every old idea, every hereditary prejudice, every vested interest of thought, defended on the ground that it is an innate idea. Innate ideas were sacred, and everything which could find no defence before reason was an innate idea. Under such circumstances he takes as much interest in demolishing them as Bacon took in the destruction of the "eidols." But this is but a small portion of the object of Locke. He is a thorough-going empiricist; and the doctrine of innate ideas appears to offer the greatest obstacle to the acceptance of the truth that all the furnishing of the intellect comes from experience. Locke's metaphors for the mind are that it is a blank tablet, an empty closet, an unwritten book. The "innate idea" is only a sentence written by experience, but which, deified by a certain school of philosophers, has come to be regarded as eternally imprinted upon the soul.

Such, indeed, is Locke's understanding of the nature of innate ideas. He conceives of them as "characters *stamped*, as it were, upon the mind of man, which the soul has received in its first being and brings into the world with it;" or they are "constant *impressions* which the souls of men receive in their first beings." They are "truths *imprinted* upon the soul." Having this conception of what is meant by "innate ideas," Locke sets himself with great vigor, and, it must be confessed, with equal success, to their annihilation.

His argument is somewhat diffuse and scattered, but in substance it is as follows: Whatever is in the mind, the mind must be conscious of. "To be in the mind and not to be perceived, is all one as to say that anything is and is not in the mind." If there be anything in the mind which is innate, it must be present to the consciousness of all, and, it would seem, of all at all times, savages, infants, and idiots included. And as it requires little philosophical penetration to see that savages do not ponder upon the principle that whatever is, is; that infants do not dwell in their cradle upon the thought of contradiction, or idiots ruminate upon that of excluded middle,—it ought to be evident that such truths cannot be innate. Indeed, we must admit, with Locke, that probably few men ever come to the explicit consciousness of such ideas, and that these few are such as direct their minds to the matter with some pains. Locke's argument may be summed up in his words: If these are not notions naturally imprinted, how can they be innate? And if they are notions naturally imprinted, how can they be unknown?

But since it may be said that these truths are in the mind, but in such a way that it is only when they are proposed that men assent to them, Locke goes on to clinch his argument. If this be true, it shows that the ideas are not innate; for the same thing is true of a large number of scientific truths, those of mathematics and morals, as well as of purely sensible facts, as that red is not blue, sweet is not sour, etc.,—truths and facts which no one calls innate. Or if it be said that they are in the mind implicitly or potentially, Locke points out that this means either nothing at all, or else that the mind is *capable* of knowing them. If this is what is meant by innate ideas, then all ideas are innate; for certainly it cannot be denied that the mind is capable of knowing all that it ever does know, or, as Locke ingenuously remarks, "nobody ever denied that the mind was capable of knowing several truths."

It is evident that the force of Locke's contention against innate ideas rests upon a certain theory regarding the nature of innate ideas and of the relations of consciousness to intelligence. Besides this, there runs through his whole polemic the assertion that, after all, innate ideas are useless, as experience, in the sense of impressions received from without, and the formal action of intelligence upon them, is adequate to doing all they are supposed to do. It is hardly too much to say that the nerve of Locke's argument is rather in this positive assertion than in the negations which he brings against this existence. Leibniz takes issue with him on each of these three points. He has another conception of the very nature of innate ideas; he denies Locke's opinions about consciousness; he brings forward an opposed theory upon the relation of experience to reason. This last point we shall take up in a chapter by itself, as its importance extends far beyond the mere question as to the existence

of ideas which may properly be called innate. The other two questions, as to the real character of innate ideas and the relation of an idea to consciousness, afford material to occupy us for the present.

The metaphor which Locke constantly uses is the clew to his conception of innate ideas. They are characters stamped or imprinted upon the mind, they exist *in* the mind. The mind would be just what it is, even if they had no existence. It would not have quite so much "in" it, but its own nature would not be changed. Innate ideas he conceives as bearing a purely external relation to mind. They are not organic to it, nor necessary instruments through which it expresses itself; they are mechanically impressed upon it. But what the "intellectual" school had meant by innate ideas was precisely that the relation of ideas to intelligence is *not* that of passive holding or containing on the side of mind, and of impressions or stamps on the side of the ideas. Locke reads the fundamental category of empiricism—mechanical relation, or external action—into the nature of innate ideas, and hence easily infers their absurdity. But the object of the upholders of innate ideas had been precisely to deny that this category was applicable to the whole of intelligence. By an innate idea they meant an assertion of the dynamic relation of intelligence and some of its ideas. They meant to assert that intelligence has a structure, which necessarily functions in certain ways. While Locke's highest conception of an innate idea was that it must be something ready made, dwelling in the mind prior to experience, Leibniz everywhere asserts that it is a connection and relation which forms the logical prius and the psychological basis of experience. He finds no difficulty in admitting all there is of positive truth in Locke's doctrine; namely, that we are not conscious of these innate ideas until a period later than that in which we are conscious of sensible facts, or, in many cases, are not conscious of them at all. This priority in time of sensible experience to rational knowledge, however, can become a reason for denying the "innate" character of the latter only when we suppose that they are two entirely different orders of fact, one knowledge due to experience, the other knowledge already formed and existing in the mind prior to "experience."

Leibniz's conception of the matter is brought out when he says that it is indeed true that we begin with particular experiences rather than with general principles, but that the order of nature is the reverse, for the ground, the basis of the particular truths is in the general; the former being in reality only instances of the latter. General principles, he says, enter into *all* our thoughts, and form their soul and interconnection. They are as necessary for thought as muscles and tendons are for walking, although we may not be conscious of their existence. This side of the teaching of Leibniz consists, accordingly, in the assertion that "innate" knowledge and knowledge derived from experience are not two kinds of knowledge, but rather two ways of considering it. If we consider it as it comes to us, piecemeal and fragmentary, a succession of particular instances, to be gathered up at a future time into general principles, and stated in a rational form, it is seen as empirical. But, after all, this is only a superficial and external way of looking at it. If we examine into it we shall see that there are contained in these transitory and particular experiences certain truths more general and fundamental, which condition them, and at the same time constitute their meaning.

If we inquire into the propriety of calling these truths "innate," we find it is because they are native to intelligence, and are not acquisitions which it makes. Indeed, it may be said that they *are* intelligence, so close and organic is their relation, just as the muscles, the tendons, the skeleton, are the body. Thus it is that Leibniz accepts the statement, *Nihil est in intellectu quod non fuerit in sensu*, with the addition of the statement *nisi ipse intellectus*. The doctrine of the existence of innate ideas is thus shown to mean that intelligence exists with a real content which counts for something in the realm of experience. If we take intelligence and examine into its structure and ascertain its modes of expression, we find organically inherent in its activity certain conceptions like unity, power, substance, identity, etc., and these we call "innate." An idea, in short, is no longer conceived as something existing in the mind or in consciousness; it is an activity of intelligence. An innate idea is a necessary activity of intelligence; that is, such an activity as enters into the framework of all experience.

Leibniz thus succeeds in avoiding two errors into which philosophers whose general aims are much like his have fallen. One is dividing *a priori* and *a posteriori* truths from each other by a hard and fixed line, so that we are conceived to have some knowledge which comes wholly from experience, while there is another which comes wholly from reason. According to Leibniz, there is no thought so abstract that it does not have its connection with a sensible experience, or rather its embodiment in it. And, on the other hand, there is no experience so thoroughly sensuous that it does not bear in itself traces of its origin in reason. "*All* our thoughts come from the depths of the soul," says Leibniz; there are none that "come" to us from without. The other error is the interpretation of the existence of innate ideas or "intuitions" (as this school generally calls them) in a purely formal sense. They are thus considered as truths contained in and somehow expressed by intelligence, but yet not so connected with it that in knowing them we necessarily know intelligence itself. They are considered rather as arbitrary determinations of truths by a power whose own nature is conceivably foreign to truth, than as so many special developments of an activity which may indifferently be called "intelligence" or "truth." Leibniz, however, never fails to state that an innate truth is, after all, but one form or aspect of the activity of the mind in knowing.

In this way, by bringing to light a deeper and richer conception of what in reality constitutes an innate idea, Leibniz answers Locke. His reply is indirect; it consists rather in throwing a flood of new light upon the matter discussed, than in a ponderous response and counter attack. But when Leibniz touches upon the conception of a *tabula rasa*, of a mind which in itself is a mere blank, but has the capacity for knowing, he assumes the offensive. The idea of a bare capacity, a formal faculty, of power which does not already involve some actual content within itself, he repudiates as a relic of scholasticism. What is the soul, which has nothing until it gets it from without? The doctrine of a vacuum, an emptiness which is real, is always absurd; and it is doubly so when to this vacuum is ascribed powers of feeling and thinking, as Locke does. Accepting for the moment the metaphor of a *tabula rasa*, Leibniz asks where we shall find a tablet which yet does not have some quality, and which is not a co-operating cause, at least, in whatever effects are produced upon it? The notion of a soul without thought, an empty tablet of the soul, he says, is one of a thousand fictions of philosophers. He compares it with the idea of "space empty of matter, absolute uniformity or homogeneity, perfect spheres of the second element produced by primordial perfect cubes, abstractions pure and simple, to which our ignorance and inattention give birth, but of which reality does not admit." If Locke admits then (as he does) certain capacities inherent in the soul, he cannot mean the scholastic fiction of bare capacity or mere possibility; he must mean "real possibilities,"— that is, capacities accompanied with some actual tendency, an inclination, a disposition, an aptitude, a preformation which determines our soul in a certain direction, and which makes it necessary that the possibility becomes actual. And this tendency, this actual inclination of intelligence in one way rather than another, so that it is not a matter of indifference to intelligence what it produces, is precisely what constitutes an innate idea. So Leibniz feels certain that at bottom Locke must agree with him in this matter if the latter is really in earnest in rejecting the "faculties" of the scholastics and in wishing for a real explanation of knowledge.

But the argument of Locke rests upon yet another basis. He founds his denial of innate ideas not only upon a static conception of their ready made existence "in" the soul, but also upon an equally mechanical conception of consciousness. "Nothing can be in the mind which is not in consciousness." This statement appears axiomatic to Locke, and by it he would settle the whole discussion. Regarding it, Leibniz remarks that if Locke has such a prejudice as this, it is not surprising that he rejects innate ideas. But consciousness and mental activity are not thus identical. To go no farther, the mere empirical fact of memory is sufficient to show the falsity of such an idea. Memory reveals that we have an indefinite amount of knowledge of which we are not always conscious. Rather than that knowledge and consciousness are one, it is true that actual consciousness only lays hold of an infinitesimal fraction of knowledge. But Leibniz does not rely upon the fact of memory alone. We must constantly keep in mind that to Leibniz the soul is not a form of being wholly separate from nature, but is the culmination of the system of reality. The reality is everywhere the monad, and the soul is the monad with the power of feeling, remembering, and connecting its ideas. The activities of the monad, those representative changes which sum up and symbolize the universe, do not cease when we reach the soul. They are continued. If the soul has the power of attention, they are potentially conscious. Such as the soul actually attends to, thus giving them relief and making them distinct, are actually conscious. But all of them exist.

Thus it is that Leibniz not only denies the equivalence of soul and consciousness, but asserts that the fundamental error of the psychology of the Cartesians (and here, Locke is a Cartesian) is in identifying them. He asserts that "unconscious ideas" are of as great importance in psychology as molecules are in physics. They are the link between unconscious nature and the conscious soul. Nothing happens all at once; nature never makes jumps; these facts stated in the law of continuity necessitate the existence of activities, which may be called ideas, since they belong to the soul and yet are not in conciousness.

When, therefore, Locke asks how an innate idea can exist and the soul not be conscious of it, the answer is at hand. The "innate idea" exists as an activity of the soul by which it represents—that is, expresses—some relation of the universe, although we have not yet become conscious of what is contained or enveloped in this activity. To become conscious of the innate idea is to lift it from the sphere of nature to the conscious life of spirit. And thus it is, again, that Leibniz can assert that all ideas whatever proceed from the depths of the soul. It is because it is the very being of the soul as a monad to reflect "from its point of view" the world. In this way Leibniz brings the discussion regarding innate ideas out of the plane of examination into a matter of psychological fact into a consideration of the essential nature of spirit. An innate idea is now seen to be one of the relations by which the soul reproduces some relation which constitutes the universe of reality, and at the same time realizes its own individual nature. It is one reflection from that spiritual mirror, the soul. With this enlarged and transformed conception of an idea apt to be so meagre we may well leave the discussion. There has been one mind at least to which the phrase "innate idea" meant something worth contending for, because it meant something real.

IV. Sensation and Experience

A careful study of the various theories which have been held concerning sensation would be of as much interest and importance as an investigation of any one point in the range of philosophy. In the theory of a philosopher about sensation we have the reflex of his fundamental category and the clew to his further doctrine. Sensation stands on the border-line between the world of nature and the realm of soul; and every advance in science, every development of philosophy, leaves its impress in a change in the theory of sensation. Apparently one of the simplest and most superficial of questions, in reality it is one of the most difficult and far-reaching. At first sight it seems as if it were a sufficient account of sensation to say that an object affects the organ of sense, and thus impresses upon the mind the quality which it possesses. But this simple statement arouses a throng of further questions: How is it possible that one substance,—matter,—should affect another,—mind? How can a causal relation exist between them? Is the mind passive or active in this impression? How can an object convey unchanged to the mind a quality which it possesses? Or is the sensational *quale* itself a product of the mind's activity? If so, what is the nature of the object which ex-

cites the sensation? As known, it is only a collection of sensuous qualities; if these are purely mental, what becomes of the object? And if there is no object really there, what is it that excites the sensation? Such questionings might be continued almost indefinitely; but those given are enough to show that an examination of the nature and origin of sensation introduces us to the problems of the relation of intelligence and the world; to the problem of the ultimate constitution of an object which is set over against a subject and which affects it; and to the problem of the nature of mind, which as thus affected from without must be limited in its nature, but which as bearer of the whole known universe must be in some sense infinite. If we consider, not the mode of production of sensation, but its relation to knowledge, we find philosophical schools divided into two,—Sensationalists, and Rationalists. If we inquire into its functions, we find that the empiricist sees in it convincing evidence of the fact that all knowledge originates from a source *extra mentem;* that the intellectual idealist finds in it evidence of the gradual transition of nature into spirit; that the ethical idealist, like Kant and Fichte, sees in it the material of the phenomenal world, which is necessary in its opposition to the rational sphere in order that there may occur that conflict of pure law and sensuous impulse which alone makes morality possible. We thus realize that as we look at the various aspects of sensation, we are taken into the discussion of ontology, of the theory of knowledge and of ethics.

Locke virtually recognizes the extreme importance of the doctrine of sensation, and his second book might almost be entitled "Concerning the Nature and Products of Sensation." On the other hand, one of the most characteristic and valuable portions of the reply of Leibniz is in his development of a theory of sensation which is thoroughly new, except as we seek for its germs in its thoughts of Plato and Aristotle. According to Locke, knowledge originates from two sources,—sensation and reflection. Sensations are "the impressions made on our senses by outward objects that are extrinsic to the mind." When the mind "comes to reflect on its own operations about the ideas got by sensation, and thereby stores itself with a new set of ideas," it gets ideas of reflection.

If we leave out of account for the present the ideas of reflection, we find that the ideas which come through sensation have two main characteristics. First, in having sensations, the mind is passive; its part is purely receptive. The objects impress themselves upon the mind, they obtrude into consciousness, whether the mind will or not. There is a purely external relation existing between sensation and the understanding. The ideas are offered to the mind, and the understanding cannot refuse to have them, cannot change them, blot them out, nor create them, any more than a mirror can refuse, alter, or obliterate the images which objects produce in it. Sensation, in short, is a purely passive having of ideas. Secondly, every sensation is simple. Locke would say of sensations what Hume said of all ideas,—every distinct sensation is a separate existence. Every sensation is "uncompounded, containing nothing but one uniform appearance, not being distinguishable into different ideas." Knowledge is henceforth a process of compounding, of repeating, comparing, and uniting sensation. Man's understanding "reaches no further than to compound and divide the materials that are made to his hand."

It hardly need be said that Locke has great difficulty in keeping up this thoroughly atomic theory of mind. It is a theory which makes all relations external; they are, as Locke afterwards says, "superinduced" upon the facts. It makes it impossible to account for any appearance of unity and connection among ideas, and Locke quietly, and without any consciousness of the contradiction involved, introduces certain inherent relations into the structure of the ideas when he comes to his constructive work. "Existence and unity are two ideas," he says, "that are suggested to the understanding by every object without, and every idea within."

At other places he introduces the idea of quality of a substance, effect of a cause, continued permanence or identity into a sensation, as necessary constituents of it; thus making a sensation a unity of complex elements instead of an isolated bare notion. How far he could

have got on in his account of knowledge without this surreptitious qualifying of a professedly simple existence, may be seen by asking what would be the nature of a sensation which did not possess existence and unity, and which was not conceived as the quality of a thing or as the effect of an external reality.

This digression has been introduced at this point because the next character of a sensation which Locke discusses is its objective character,—its relation to the object which produces it. To discourse of our ideas intelligibly, he says, it will be convenient to distinguish them as they are ideas in our minds and as they are modifications of matter in the bodies that cause them. In other words, he gives up all thought of considering ideas as simply mental modifications, and finds it necessary to take them in their relations to objects.

Taking them in this way, he finds that they are to be divided into two classes, of which one contains those ideas that are copies and resemblances of qualities in the objects, ideas "which are really in the object, whether we take notice of them or no,"—in which case we have an idea of the thing as it is in itself; while the other class contains those which are in no way resemblances of the objects which produce them, "having no more similitude than the idea of pain and of a sword." The former are primary qualities, and are solidity, extension, figure, motion or rest, and number; while the secondary qualities are colors, smells, and tastes. The former ideas are produced by impulse of the bodies themselves, which simply effect a transference of their qualities over into the mind; while the secondary qualities are arbitrarily annexed by the power of God to the objects which excite them.

It will be noticed that there are two elements which make the sensation of Locke what it is. With reference to its *production*, it is the effect which one substance, matter, has upon another substance, mind, which is unlike it in nature, and between which whatever relations exist, are thoroughly incomprehensible, so that, indeed, their connections with each other can be understood only by recourse to a *tertium quid,* an omnipotent power which can arbitrarily produce such collocations as please it. With reference to its *function,* it is the isolated and "simple" (that is, non-relational) element out of which all actual forms of knowledge are made by compositions and re-arrangement.

Leibniz, without entering into explicit criticism of just these two points, develops his own theory with reference to them. To Leibniz, reality constitutes a system; that is, it is of such a nature that its various portions have an essential and not merely external relation to one another. Sensation is of course no exception. It is not a mere accident, nor yet a supernatural yoking of things naturally opposed. It has a meaning in that connection of things which constitute the universe. It contributes to the significance of the world. It is one way in which those activities which make the real express themselves. It has its place or reason in the totality of things, and this whether we consider its origin or its position with regard to knowledge. In a word, while the characteristic of Locke's theory is that he conceives sensation as in external relation both to reality, as mechanically produced by it, and to knowledge, as being merely one of the atomic elements which may enter into a compound, Leibniz regards reality as organic to sensation, and this in turn as organic to knowledge. We have here simply an illustration of the statement with which we set out; namely, that the treatment of sensation always reflects the fundamental philosophical category of the philosopher.

All reality exists in the form of monads; monads are simple substances whose nature is action; this action consists in representing, according to a certain law of succession, the universe. Various monads have various degrees of activity; that is, of the power of reflecting the world. So much of Leibniz's general philosophical attitude it is necessary to recall, to understand what he means by "sensation." The generic name which is applied to this mirroring activity of the monads is "perception," which, as Leibniz often says, is to be carefully distinguished from apperception, which is the representation become conscious. Perception may be defined, therefore, as the inclusion of the many or multiform (the world of objects) in a unity (the simple substance). It was the great defect of previous philosophy that it "considered only spirits or self-

conscious beings as souls," and had consequently recognized only conscious perceptions. It had been obliged, therefore, to make an impassable gulf between mind and matter, and sensations were thus rendered inexplicable. But Leibniz finds his function as a philosopher in showing that these problems, which seem insoluble, arise when we insist upon erecting into actual separations or differences of kind what really are only stages of development or differences of degree. A sensation is not an effect which one substance impresses upon another because God pleased that it should, or because of an incomprehensible incident in the original constitution of things. It is a higher development of that representative power which belongs to every real being.

Certain monads reach a state of development, or manifestation of activity, which is characterized by the possession of distinct organs. Such monads may be called, in a preeminent sense, "souls," and include all the higher animals as well as man. This possession of differentiated organs finds its analogue in the internal condition of the monad. What appears externally as an organ of sense appears ideally as a conscious representative state which we call "sensation." "When," Leibniz says, "the monad has its organs so developed that there is relief and differentiation in the impressions received, and consequently in the perceptions which represent them, we have feeling or sensation; that is, a perception accompanied by memory," to which at other times he adds "attention." Life, he says, "is a perceptive principle; the soul is sensitive life; mind is rational soul." And again he says in substance that when the soul begins to have interests, and to regard one representation as of more value than others, it introduces relief into its perceptions, and those which stand out are called "sensations."

This origin of sensations as higher developments of the representative activities of a monad conditions their relation to further processes of knowledge. The sensations are confused knowledge; they are ideas in their primitive and most undifferentiated form. They constitute, as Leibniz somewhere says, the vertigo of the conscious life. In every sentient organism multitudes of sensations are constantly thronging in and overpowering its distinct consciousness. The soul is so flooded with ideas of everything in the world which has any relation to its body that it has distinct ideas of nothing. Higher knowledge, then, does not consist in compounding these sensations; that would literally make confusion worse confounded. It consists in introducing distinctness into the previously confused sensations,—in finding out what they mean; that is, in finding out their bearings, what they point to, and how they are related. Knowledge is not an external process performed upon the sensations, it is the development of their internal content.

It follows, therefore, that sensation is organic to all forms of knowledge whatever. The monad, which is pure activity, that which culminates the scale of reality, has no confused ideas, and to it all knowledge is eternally rational, having no sensible traces about it. But every other monad, having its activity limited, has ideas which come to it at first in a confused way, and which its activity afterwards differentiates. Thus it is that Leibniz can agree so heartily with the motto of the Sensationalist school,—that there is nothing in the intellect which was not first in the sensory. But Leibniz uses this phrase as Aristotle would have done, having in mind the distinction between potentiality and actuality. *In posse*, sensation is all knowledge; but only *in posse*. And he, like Aristotle, interprets the relation between potentiality and actuality as one of a difference of activity. The potential is that which becomes real through a dynamic process. The actual is capacity plus action. Sensation, in short, is spiritual activity in an undeveloped and hence partial and limited condition. It is not, as Locke would have it, the real factor in all knowledge.

The marks of sensation which Locke lays down,—their passivity, their simplicity, their position as the real element in knowledge,—Leibniz either denies, therefore, or accepts in a sense different from that of Locke. Strictly speaking, sensation is an activity of the mind. There are no windows through which the soul receives impressions. Pure passivity of any kind is a myth, as scholastic fiction. Sensation

is developed from the soul within; it is the activity of reality made manifest to itself. It is a higher kind of action than anything we find in minerals or in plants. If we look at sensation ideally, however, that is, according to the position which it holds in the system of knowledge, it is properly regarded as passive. It represents the limitation, the unrealized (that is, the non-active) side of spiritual life.

"Efficient causality" is a term which has its rightful and legitimate use in physical science. Simply from the scientific point of view we are correct in speaking of objects as affecting the body, and the body, through its nervous system, as affecting the soul and producing sensations. But philosophy does not merely use categories, it explains them. And Leibniz contends that to explain the category of causality in a mechanical sense, to understand by it physical influence actually transferred from one thing to another, is to make the idea inexplicable and irrational. The true meaning of causality is ideal. It signifies the relative positions which the objects concerned have in the harmonious system of reality. The body that is higher in the scale impresses the other; that is to say, it dominates it or gives its law. There is no energy or quality which passes physically from one to the other. But one monad, as higher in the stage of development than another, makes an ideal demand upon that one. It places before the other its own more real condition. The less-developed monad, since its whole activity consists in representing the universe of reality, answers to this demand by developing the corresponding quality in itself. The category of harmonious or co-operative action is thus substituted for that of external and mechanical influence. Physical causality when given a philosophic interpretation means organic development. The reality of a higher stage is the more active: the more active has a greater content in that it mirrors the universe more fully; it manifests accordingly more of the law of the universe, and hence has an ideal domination over that which is lower in the scale. It is actually (that is, in activity) what the other is potentially. But as the entire existence of the latter is in representing or setting forth the relations which make the world, its activity is aroused to a corresponding production. Hence the former is called "cause," and the latter "effect."

This introduces us to the relation of soul and body, or, more generally stated, to the relation of mind and matter. It is the theory of co-operation, of harmonious activity, which Leibniz substitutes for the theory which Descartes had formulated, according to which there are two opposed substances which can affect each other only through the medium of a *deus ex machina*. Locke, on the other hand, took the Cartesian principle for granted, and thus enveloped himself in all the difficulties which surround the question of "mind and matter." Locke wavers between two positions, one of which is that there are two unknown substances,—the soul and the object in itself,—which, coming in contact, produce sensations; while the other takes the hypothetical attitude that there may be but one substance,—matter,—and that God, out of the plenitude of his omnipotence, has given matter a capacity which does not naturally belong to it,—that of producing sensations. In either case, however, the final recourse is to the arbitrary power of God. There is no natural—that is, intrinsic and explicable—connection between the sensation and that which produces it. Sensation occupied the hard position which the mechanical school of to-day still allots it. It is that "inexplicable," "mysterious," "unaccountable" link between the domains of matter and mind of which no rational account can be given, but which is yet the source of all that we know about matter, and the basis of all that is real in the mind!

Leibniz, recognizing that reality is an organic whole,—not two parts with a chasm between them,—says that "God does not arbitrarily give substances whatever qualities may happen, or that he may arbitrarily determine, but only such as are natual; that is, such as are related to one another in an *explicable* way as modifications of the substance." Leibniz feels sure that to introduce the idea of the inexplicable, the purely supernatural, into the natural is to give up all the advantages which the modern mechanical theory had introduced, and to relapse into the meaningless features of scholasticism. If the "supernatural"—that is, the essentially inexplicable—is introduced in

this one case, why should it not be in others; why should we not return outright to the "fanatic philosophy which explains all facts by simply attributing them to God immediately or by way of miracle, or to the barbarian philosophy, which explains phenomena by manufacturing, *ad hoc*, occult qualities or faculties, seemingly like little demons or spirits capable of performing, without ceremony, whatever is required,—as if watches marked time by their horodeictic power, without wheels, and mills ground grain, without grindstones, by their fractive power"? In fact, says Leibniz, by introducing the inexplicable into our *explanations* "we fall into something worse than occult qualities,—we give up philosophy and reason; we open asylums for ignorance and laziness, holding not only that there are qualities which we do not understand (there are, indeed, too many such), but qualities which the greatest intelligence, if God gave it all the insight possible, could not understand,—that is, such as are *in themselves* without rhyme or reason. And indeed it would be a thing without rhyme or reason that God should perform miracles in the ordinary course of nature." And regarding the whole matter of introducing the inconceivable and the inexplicable into science, he says that "while the conception of men is not the measure of God's power, their capacity of conception is the measure of *nature's* power, since everything occurring in the natural order is capable of being understood by the created intelligence." Such being the thought of Leibniz regarding the virtual attempt to introduce in his day the unknowable into philosophy, it is evident that he must reject, from the root up, all theories of sensation which, like Locke's, make it the product of the inexplicable intercourse of two substances.

For this doctrine, then, Leibniz substitutes that of an infinite number of substances, all of the same kind, all active, all developing from within, all conspiring to the same end, but of various stages of activity, or bearing various relations of completeness to the one end.

Indeed, one and the same monad has various degrees of activity in itself; that is, it represents more or less distinctly the universe according to its point of view. Its point of view requires of it, of course, primarily, a representation of that which is about it. Thus an infinity of states arises, each corresponding to some one of the multitude of objects surrounding the monad. The soul has no control, no mastery, over these states. It has to take them as they come; with regard to them, the soul appears passive. It appears so because it does not as yet clearly distinguish them. It does not react upon them and become conscious of their meaning or thoroughly rational character. We shall afterwards see that "matter" is, with Leibniz, simply this passive or confused side of monads. It is the monad so far as it has not brought to light the rational activity which is immanent in it. At present we need only notice that the body is simply the part of matter or of passivity which limits the complete activity of any monad. So Leibniz says, "in so far as the soul has perfection, it has distinct thoughts, and God has accommodated the body to the soul. So far as it is imperfect and its perceptions are confused, God has accommodated the soul to the body in such a way that the soul lets itself be inclined by the passions, which are born from corporeal representations. It is by its confused thoughts (sensations) that the soul represents the bodies about it," just as, we may add, its distinct thoughts represent the monads or souls about it, and, in the degree of their distinctness, God, the monad which is *purus actus*.

Following the matter into more detail, we may say that since God alone is pure energy, knowing no limitation, God alone is pure spirit. Every finite soul is joined to an organic body. "I do not admit," says Leibniz, "that there are souls entirely separate from matter, nor created spirits detached from body. . . . It is this body which the monad represents most distinctly; but since this body expresses the entire universe by the connection of all matter throughout it, the soul represents the entire universe in representing the body which belongs to it most particularly." But according to the principle of continuity there must be in the least apparent portion of matter still "a universe of creatures, of souls, of entelechies. There is nothing sterile, nothing dead in the universe. It is evident from these considerations that every living body has a dominant entelechy, which is the soul in that body,

but that the members of this living body are again full of other living beings and souls," which, however, since not of so high a grade, that is, not representing the universe so fully, appear to be wholly material and subject to the "dominant" entelechy; namely, to the one which gives the law to the others by expressing more adequately the idea at which they only confusedly aim. Owing to the constant change of activity, however, these particles do not remain in constant subordination to the same entelechy (that is, do not form parts of the same body), but pass on to higher or lower degrees of "evolution," and have their places taken by others undergoing similar processes of change. Thus "all bodies are in a perpetual flux, like rivers, with parts continually leaving and entering in." Or, interpreting this figurative language, each monad is continually, in its process of development, giving law to new and less developed monads, which therefore appear as its body. The nature of matter in itself, and of its phenomenal manifestation in the body, are, however, subjects which find no explanation here, and which will demand explanation in another chapter.

We may sum up Leibniz's theory of sensation by saying that it is a representative state developed by the self-activity of the soul; that in itself it is a confused or "involved" grade of activity, and in its relation to the world represents the confused or passive aspects of existence; that this limitation of the monad constitutes matter, and in its necessary connection with the monad constitutes the body which is always joined to the finite soul; that to this body are joined in all cases an immense number of monads, whose action is subordinate to that of this dominant monad, and that it is the collection of these which constitute the visible animal body. Thus if we look at sensation with regard to the monad which possesses it, it is a product of the body of the monad; if we look at it with reference to other monads, it represents or reflects their passive or material side. This is evidently one aspect again of the pre-established harmony,—an aspect in which some of the narrower of Leibniz's critics have seen the whole meaning of the doctrine exhausted. It is, however, simply one of the many forms in which the harmony, the union of spiritual and mechanical, ideal and material, meets us. In truth, while in other systems the fact of sensation is a fact demanding some artificial mode of reconciling "mind" and "matter," or is else to be accepted as an inexplicable fact, in the system of Leibniz it is itself evidence that the spiritual and the mechanical are not two opposed kinds of existence, but are organically united. It is itself the manifestation of the harmony of the ideal and the material, not something which requires that a factitious theory be invented for explaining their appearance of harmony. Sensation has within itself the ideal element, for it is the manifestation, in its most undeveloped form, of the spiritual meaning of the universe. It has a mechanical element, for it expresses the limitation, the passivity, of the monad.

It is from this standpoint that Leibniz criticises what Locke says about the relation of sensations to the objects which produce them. Leibniz holds that all our sensations have a definite and natural connection with the qualities of objects,—the "secondary" as well as the "primary." They all represent certain properties of the object. Even the pain which the thrust of a needle gives us, while it does not resemble anything in the needle, does in some way represent or resemble motions going on in our body. This resemblance is not necessarily one of exact form, but just as the ellipse, hyperbola, and parabola are projections of the circle in the sense that there is a natural and fixed law of connection between them, so that every point of one corresponds by a certain relation with every point of the other, so the resemblance between the sensation and the quality of the object is always in the form of a fixed law of order, which, however unknown to us it may now be, is capable of being found out. If we are to make any distinction between "secondary" and "primary" sensations, it should be not that one presents qualities that are in the objects, and the other affections which exist only in us, but that the primary sensations (of number, form, size, etc.) represent the qualities in a distinct way, appealing to the rational activity of intelligence, while the secondary represent the qualities in a confused way, a way not going beyond the effect

upon the mind into relations, that is, into distinct knowledge.

This brings regularly before us the question of the relation of sensations to knowledge. We have seen enough already to know that Leibniz does not believe that knowledge begins with the simple (that is, unrelated), and then proceeds by a process of compounding. The sensation is not simple to Leibniz, but thoroughly complex, involving confusedly within itself all possible relations. As relations are brought forth into distinct light out of this confusion, knowledge ends rather than begins with the simple. And again it is evident that Leibniz cannot believe that knowledge begins and ends in experience, in the sense in which both himself and Locke use the word; namely, as meaning the combination and succession of impressions.

"Experience," as they use the term, consists in sensations and their association,—"consecution" as Leibniz calls it. Experience is the stage of knowledge reached by animals, and in which the majority of men remain,—and indeed all men in the greater part of their knowledge. Leibniz takes just the same position regarding the larger part of our knowledge which Hume takes regarding it all. It consists simply in associations of such a nature that when one part recurs there is a tendency to expect the recurrence of the other member. It resembles reason, but it is based on the accidental experience of events in a consecutive order, and not on knowledge of their causal connection. We all expect the sun to rise to-morrow; but with all of us, excepting the astronomer, such expectation is purely "empirical," being based on the images of past experiences which recur. The astronomer, however, sees into the grounds, that is, the reasons, of the expectation, and hence his knowledge is rational.

Thus we have two grades of knowledge,—one empirical, consisting of knowledge of facts; the other rational, being of the truths of reason. The former is contingent and particular, the latter is necessary and universal. Leibniz insists, with a pertinacity which reminds us of Kant, that "experience" can give instances or examples only, and that the fact that anything has happened in a given way any num-

ber of times in the past, can give no assurance
that it will continue to do so in the future.
There is nothing in the nature of the case
which renders its exact opposite impossible.
But a rational truth is necessary, for its opposite is impossible, being irrational or
meaningless. This may not always be evident
in the case of a complex rational truth; but if it
be analyzed into simpler elements, as a
geometrical proposition into definitions, axioms, and postulates, the absurdity of its opposite becomes evident. Sensation, in conclusion, is the having of confused ideas,—ideas
corresponding to matter. Experience is the
association of these confused ideas, and their
association according to their accidental juxtaposition in the life of the soul. It therefore is
not only thoroughly sensible, but is also phenomenal. Its content is sensations; its form is
contingent and particular consecution. Both
form and content, accordingly, need to be re-
constructed if they are to be worthy of the
name of science or of knowledge. This is
the position which Leibniz assumes as against
the empiricist, Locke. The details of this
reconstruction, its method and result, we must
leave till we come in the course of the argument again to the subject of knowledge.

V. The Impulses
and The Will

Locke, after discussing the subject of innate
ideas in their relation to knowledge, goes on to
discuss their practical side, or connection with
will. We shall follow him in this as Leibniz
does; but we shall consider in connection with
this, Leibniz's general theory of will, which is
developed partially in this chapter, but more
completely in his critical remarks upon what
Locke has to say of the notion of "power."
Since the theory of morals is as closely connected with will as the theory of knowledge is
with the intellect, we shall supplement this discussion with what Leibniz says upon the ethical
question, drawing our material somewhat
freely from his other writings.

The doctrine of will which Leibniz pro-

pounds is in closest harmony with his conception of intelligence, and this not merely in the
way of empirical juxtaposition, but as the result of his fundamental principles. If we recall
what has been said concerning the monad, we
shall remember that it is an activity, but an
activity with a content. It is a force, but a force
which mirrors the universe. The content, that
portion of reality which is reflected in the action, is knowledge, or the idea; the activity
which brings this about is will, or the volition.
They are related to each other as form and
content. There is, strictly speaking, no "state"
of mind; there is only a tension, a pushing
forward of mind. There is no idea which is not
a volition. Will is thus used, in a very broad
sense, as equivalent to action. Since, however,
the activity of the monad is in no case aimless,
but has an end in view, the will is not *mere*
activity in general, it is action towards some
definite end. And since the end at which
the monad aims is always the development
of an idea, the reflection of some constituent
of the universe, the will is always directed
towards and determined by some idea of the
intellect.

We have seen, however, that there are various stages in the reflecting power of the soul,
or in the realization of intellect. Taking only
the broadest perception and apperception;
that is, there are division, there are the conscious and the unconscious mirroring of reality. We shall expect, then, to find two corresponding stages of volition. Leibniz calls these
stages "appetition" and "volition" in the narrower sense. The constant tendency in every
monad to go from one perception to another,—that is, the following of the law of development,—constitutes appetition. If joined
to feeling, it constitutes instinct. Since, again,
there are two degrees of apperception, one of
empirical, the other of rational, consciousness,
we shall expect to find two grades of volition
proper,—one corresponding to action for conscious particular ends; the other for ends
which are proposed by reason, and are hence
universal. In this chapter we shall simply expand and illustrate these various propositions.

Sensations, looked at not as to what they
represent, but in themselves, are impulses. As
such they constitute the lowest stage of will.

Impulsive action then includes all such as occurs for an end which is unknown, or at best but dimly felt. Such action may be called blind, not in the sense that it is without reason, but in the sense that reason is not consciously present. We are not to think of this instinctive action, however, as if it were found simply in the animals. Much of human action is also impulsive; probably, indeed, an impulsive factor is contained in our most rational willing. We are never able to take complete account of the agencies which are acting upon us. Along with the reasons of which we are conscious in choosing, there are mingled faint memories of past experience, subconscious solicitations of the present, dim expectations for the future. Such elements are decisive factors far more than we realize.

Indeed, it is because of the extent to which such unconscious influences bear upon us and move us that there arises the idea of indifferent or unmotivated choice. Were both motive and choice unconscious, the question as to whether choice were antecedently determined would not arise; and were our motives and their results wholly in consciousness, the solution of the question would be evident. But when we are conscious of our choice, but are not conscious of our impulses and motives, we get the impression that our choice is unmotivated, and hence come to believe in "indifferent freedom,"—the ability to choose as we will.

We shall shortly take up in more detail the theory of Leibniz regarding the freedom of will; and it is needful here to remark only that the conception which makes it consist in ability to choose without reason is in direct contradiction to his fundamental thought,—namely, that there can be no activity which does not aim at some reflection of the universe, by which, therefore, it is determined. From the psychological point of view, it is interesting also to notice how Leibniz's theory of unconscious ideas enables him to dispose of the strongest argument for indifferent choice,—that drawn from the immediate "testimony" of consciousness.

Upon the origin and nature of desires Leibniz has much more to say than about the impulses. His account of the transition from impulse to desire is based upon the conception of unconscious ideas. Slight and imperceptible impulses are working upon us all the time. Indeed, they are a necessity; for the actual state of a soul or monad at any time is, of course, one of incompleteness. Our nature must always work to free itself from its hindrances and obtain its goal of complete development. But it will not do this unless there is some stimulus, some solicitation to induce it to overcome its limitation. There is found accordingly in our every condition a feeling of dissatisfaction, or, using Locke's word, of "uneasiness;" and it is this which calls forth that activity which brings about a nearer approach to the soul's real good. But Leibniz differs from Locke in saying that this feeling of uneasiness is not a distinct, or even in most cases a conscious, one. It is not pain, although it differs from pain only in degree. Uneasiness and pain are related to each other as appetite for food is to hunger,—the first suffices to stimulate us to satisfaction, but if the want is not met, results in actual pain; if met, these "half pains" become tributary to pleasure itself. These unconscious stimuli to action result in actions which meet the want, and the aggregation of these satisfactions results in pleasure. In Leibniz's own words:—

> If these elements of pain were themselves true pains, we should always be in a state of misery, even in pursuing the good. But since there is always going on a summation of minute successes in overcoming these states of uneasiness, and these put us more and more at ease, there comes about a decided pleasure, which often has greater value even than the enjoyment of the good. Far, then, from regarding this uneasiness as a thing incompatible with happiness, I find that it is an essential condition of our happiness. For this does not consist in perfect possession, which would make is insensible and stupid, but in a constant progress towards greater results, which must always be accompanied, accordingly, by this element of desire or uneasiness.

And again he says that "we enjoy all the advantages of pain without any of its inconveniences. If the uneasiness should become too distinct, we should be miserable in our awaiting the good which relieves it; but as it is, there is a constant victory over these half-pains, which we always find in desire, and this gives us a quantity of half-pleasures, whose continuance and summation (for they acquire force like a moving body as it falls) result in a whole and true pleasure." In short, there is indeed an element of pain in all desire which stimulates us to action, and therefore to higher development. But ordinarily this element of pain is not present as such in consciousness, but is absorbed in the pleasure which accompanies the realization of the higher good. Thus Leibniz, accepting and emphasizing the very same fact that served Schopenhauer as a psychological base of pessimism, uses it as a foundation stone of optimism.

But desire, or the conscious tendency towards something required as a good, accompanied by the dim feeling of uneasiness at its absence, does not yet constitute the complete act of volition. "Several impulses and inclinations meet in forming the complete volition which is the result of their conflict." In the concrete act of will there are contained impulses which push us towards some end whose nature is not known; there is desire both in its inchoate stage, where pleasure and pain are not in consciousness, and in its formed state, where the pain and pleasure are definitely presented. Mixed with these desires and impulses are images of past experiences which call up the feelings which were formerly attached to them, and thus there are aroused indirectly additional impulses and desires. Out of this complicated mass of impulses, desires, and feelings, both original and reproduced, comes the "dominant effort" which constitutes complete will. But what governs the production of this prevailing or dominant effort, which we may interpret as the act of choice? The answer is simple: the result of the conflict of these various factors, the striking of the balance, *is* the choice. Some desire emerges from the confused complex, and that desire is the final determination of the will. This desire may not in all cases be the strongest in itself,—that is, the one whose satisfaction will allay the greatest "uneasiness," for the others, taken together, may outweigh it; it may, so to speak, have a plurality, but not a majority, of volitional forces on its side,—and in this case a fusion

of opposing factors may defeat it. But in any event the result will be the *algebraic* sum of the various desires and impulses.

It is not at all necessary, however, that the net outcome shall make itself apparent as a mechanical equivalent of the forces at work. The soul, Leibniz says, may use its skill in the formation of parties, so as to make this or that side the victor. How is this to be done, and still disallow the possibility of arbitrary choice? This problem is solved through action becoming deliberate. Deliberate action is impossible unless the soul has formed the habit of looking ahead and of arranging for modes of action which do not present themselves as immediate necessities. Only in this way can one look at the matter impartially and coolly; "at the moment of combat there is not time for discussion. Everything which then occurs throws its full force on the balance, and contributes to an outcome made up on the same way as in mechanics." The formation of certain habits beforehand, therefore, is the secret of translating impulsive action into the deliberate sphere.

Of these habits the simplest consists in thinking only occasionally and incidentally of certain things. Imagination is the mother of desire. If we do not allow the imagination to dwell upon certain lines of thought, the probability of such thoughts acquiring sufficient force to become motives of weight is small. A still more effective method of regulating action is "to accustom ourselves to forming a train of thoughts of which reason, and not chance (that is, association), is the basis. We must get out of the tumult of present impressions, beyond our immediate surroundings, and ask: *Dic cur hic? respice finem!*" In other words, we must cross-question our impulses and desires, we must ask whence they come, that we may see how valid are the credentials which they offer. We must ask whither they tend, that we may measure them, not by their immediate interest, but by their relation to an end. The desires are not to be taken at their face-value, but are to be weighed and compared.

Such a process will evidently result in arresting instantaneous action. There will be a pause between the presentation of the desires and the overt act. During this pause it may well occur that the examination to which the desires have been subject has awakened contrary desires. The thought of the ignoble origin of a desire or of its repulsive, though remote, result will bring into action desires of an opposed kind. Thus the soul regulates action, not as if, however, it had any direct influence over desires, but by its ability of bringing other desires into the field. The will, in short, is not opposed to desire, though rational desire may be opposed to sensuous desire. "By various artifices, then," Leibniz concludes, "we become masters of ourselves, and can make ourselves think and do that which we ought to will, and which reason ordains." Such is the summary of Leibniz's analysis of the elements and mechanism of volition. There was not much psychology existing at the time which could aid him in such an acute and subtle account; only in Aristotle could he have found much help. On the other hand, it has been so generally incorporated into current psychology that we may seem to have wasted space in repeating truisms.

Of moral action, however, we have as yet heard nothing. We have an account of a psychological mechanism; but for what ethical end does this work, and by what method? This question may best be answered by turning in more detail to the question of the "freedom of the will." Freedom in the sense of arbitrary choice Leibniz wholly rejects, as we have seen. It is inconsistent with at least two of his fundamental principles; those, namely, of sufficient reason, and of continuity. "Everything that occurs must have a sufficient reason for its occurrence." This oft-repeated dictum of Leibniz, the logical way of stating the complete rationality of experience, would be shattered into fragments by collision with groundless choice. It conflicts equally (indeed for the same reason) with the principle of continuity. "The present is pregnant with the future." "Nature never makes leaps." "An absolute equilibrium is a chimera." "The soul is never wholly at rest." These are only various ways of saying that the notion of arbitary or unmotivated choice rests upon the assumption that there is a complete break in the life of the soul, so that it is possible for something to

happen which bears no organic relation to anything that precedes. The notion of a state of the soul without motives, followed by the irruption of a certain line of conduct, the notion of an equilibrium broken by arbitrary choice, is simply the counterpart of the idea of a vacuum. All that makes Leibniz reject the latter conception makes it impossible for him to accept the former.

This should not be interpreted to mean that Leibniz denied the "freedom of the will." What he denied is a notion of freedom which seemed to him at once inverifiable, useless, and irrational. There is a conception of freedom which Leibniz not only accepts, but insists upon. Such a notion of freedom is indeed his ethical ideal. Its three traits are contingency, spontaneity, and rationality of action. How action can be at the same time contingent and determined is perhaps difficult to understand; but Leibniz takes the position that it is. His first step is to distinguish between physical, mathematical, metaphysical, and moral necessity. There are truths which are eternal, truths which are absolutely necessary, because their opposites involve contradiction. They cannot be violated without involving us in absurdity. There are other truths which are "positive," that is, ordained for good reason. These truths may be *a priori*, or rational, and not merely empirical; for they have been chosen for reasons of advantage. God always chooses and ordains the best of a number of possibilities; but he does it, not because the opposite is impossible, but because it is inferior. Truths whose opposites are impossible have metaphysical and mathematical necessity. Positive truths have moral necessity. The principle of causation *must* be true; the three interior angles of a triangle *must* be equal to two right angles. But that God shall choose the better of two courses is a moral necessity only. It involves no absolute logical contradiction to conceive him choosing some other way. Upon moral necessity depends the physical. The particular laws of nature are necessary, not because their opposites are logically absurd, but because these laws are most in accordance with the general principles of good and order, in agreement with which God chooses. Physical and moral action is therefore in all cases contingent. (Contingency does not of itself, of course, constitute freedom, but conjoined with the characteristics of rationality and spontaneity, does so.)

Necessity, in short, is based upon the principle of logical contradiction; contingency upon that of sufficient reason. Since our actions are in no case necessitated in such a way that their opposite is self-contradictory, or, put positively, since our actions are always determined by the choice of that which seems best, our actions are contingent. Occasionally Leibniz puts the matter in a much simpler way, and one which brings out the essential element more clearly than the foregoing distinction. Some facts are determined by the principle of physical causation; others by that of final causation. Some, in other words are necessary as the mechanical outcome of their antecedents; others are necessary as involved in the reaching of a given end. It is simply the Aristotelian distinction between efficient and teleological causation. Human action is determined, since it always has a motive or reason; it is contingent, because it springs from this reason and not from its temporal antecedents. It is, in short, determined, but it is also free.

It does not require much analysis, however, to see that this distinction, in whatever way it be put, really has no significance, except as it points to the other marks of freedom,—spontaneity and rationality. As we shall see, Leibniz makes and can make no absolute distinction between truths of reason and truths of fact. The contingent and the necessary are one at bottom. To us with our limited intelligence it does indeed often appear as if no contradiction were involved in the former,—as if, for example, a man could turn either to right or left without there being any logical contradiction in either case; but this is because of our defective insight. An intelligence cognizant of the whole matter could see that one action would contradict some truth involved in the constitution of the universe. The source of the contingent and changing is in the necessary and eternal. Thus it is that although Leibniz at one time says that "neither one's self nor any other spirit more enlightened could demonstrate that the opposite of a given action (like

going out in preference to staying in) involves contradiction," at another time he says that "a perfect knowledge of all the circumstances, internal and external, would enable any one to foresee" the decision in a given case. If that be so, any other action must be impossible; that is, according to Leibniz's invariable logic, imply contradiction.

We get the same result if we consider the relation of final and efficient causes. It is only when speaking in a very general way that Leibniz opposes action as determined by precedent activities to that directed towards the attainment of an end. He does not really mean that *some* action is physical, while *other* is teleological. He cannot suppose that some action has an antecedent cause, while other has a purpose. The very essence of his thought is that action is both mechanical and teleological; that all action follows in a law of order from precedent action, and that all fulfills a certain spiritual function. The distinction is not, with Leibniz, one between two kinds of action, but between two ways of looking at every action. The desire to go rather than to stay, has its efficient cause; the movements by which the desire is executed, have their final cause. The truth of the matter seems to be that Leibniz in his desire to guard against being thought a fatalist, or one denying all freedom, uses terms which are compatible only with a freedom of indifference. So in his statement that man's action is free because "contingent," he seems actuated rather by a wish to avoid the hateful term "necessity" than by considerations strictly in harmony with his own principles.

Had he confined his use of the term "contingent," however, simply to re-stating the fact that human action is spontaneous, no such apparent contradiction would have presented itself. Human actions may be called contingent, as physical actions are not, because the latter always seem to be externally determined, while the former are internally directed. Motions act from without; motives from within. The cause of the falling of a stone lies outside it; the source of a desire which moves to action is from the mind itself. We are thus introduced to contingency as a synonym of "spontaneity."

Kuno Fischer calls attention to the fact that

Spinoza and Leibniz both use the same sort of illustration to show the non-arbitrary character of human action. but the same illustration with a difference; and in the difference he finds the distinction between the two philosophies. Spinoza says that a stone falling to the ground, if endowed with consciousness, might imagine itself following its own will in falling. Leibniz says that a magnetic needle similarly endowed might imagine that it turned towards the north simply because it wished. Both examples are used to illustrate the folly of relying upon the immediate "testimony" of consciousness. But the example of Spinoza is that of an object, all whose movements are absolutely necessitated from without; the example of Leibniz is that of an object whose activity, though following law, and not caprice, is apparently initiated from within. Of course in reality the movements of the magnetic needle are just as much externally conditioned as those of the stone; but the appearance of self-action in the latter case may serve at least to exemplify what is meant by spontaneity as attributed to human action.

It must be noticed at the outset that spontaneity belongs to every simple substance. We have only to recall the doctrine of monads. These suffer nothing from without, all their activity is the expression, is the unfolding, of their own law. "By nature," Leibniz says, "every simple substance has perceptions, and its individuality consists in the permanent law which forms the succession of its perceptions, that are born naturally one of another. Hence it is not necessary for it to receive any physical influence from without; and therefore the soul has in itself a perfect spontaneity in such a way that its actions depend only upon God and itself." Or if we put the matter in its connection with his psychology rather than with his metaphysics, it is true that our actions are determined by our motives; but motives are not forces without the soul, they are forces of the soul. In acting according to motives the soul is simply acting according to its own laws. A desire is not an impulsion from an external cause; it is the expression of an inward tendency. To say that the soul acts from the strongest desire is simply to say, from this standpoint, that it manifests the most real part of itself, not

that it obeys a foreign force. Impulses, desires, motives, are all psychical; they admit of no description or explanation except in their relation to the soul itself. Thus when Leibniz compares, as he often does, motives to weights acting upon a balance, we are to remember that the balance is not to be conceived as the soul, and the weights as energies outside it, but that this is only a way of picturing what is going on *within* the soul itself. The soul may be a mechanism, but it is a self-directing and self-executing mechanism. To say that human action is free because it is spontaneous, is to say that it follows an immanent principle, that it is independent of foreign influences,—in a word, that it is self-determined.

But here again it seems as if Leibniz had stated a principle altogether too wide to throw any light upon the nature of moral freedom. Spontaneity is no more an attribute of human activity than it is of all real activity. Every monad, even the unconscious, as truly follows its own law without interference from without as does man himself. If the spontaneity of action constitutes its morality, we are not in a condition to ascribe morality to man any more than to any real thing. We are thus thrown back again upon the conception of rationality as the final and decisive trait of freedom and of ethical conduct. Just as "contingency" gets a moral import only in connection with conscious ends of action, so "spontaneity" comes within the moral realm only when conjoined to reason.

Why is there this close connection between reason and freedom? The reader has only to recall what was said of Leibniz's theory of causality to get a glimpse into their unity. Causality is not a matter of physical influence, but of affording the reason in virtue of which some fact is what it is. This applies of course to the relation of the soul and the body. "So far as the soul is perfect and has distinct ideas, God has accommodated the body to it; so far as the soul is imperfect and its ideas are confused, God has accommodated the soul to the body. In the former case the body always responds to the demands of the soul; in the latter the soul is moved by the passions which are born of the sensuous ideas. Each is thought to act upon the other in the measure of its perfection [that is, degree of activity], since God has adjusted one thing to another according to its perfection or imperfection. Activity and passivity are always reciprocal in created things, because a portion of the reasons which serve to explain what goes on is in one substance, and another portion in the other. This is what makes us call one active, the other passive."

If we translate these ideas out of their somewhat scholastic phraseology, the meaning is that the self-activity of any substance is accurately measured by the extent to which it contains the reasons for its own actions; and conversely, that it is dependent or enslaved just so far as it has its reasons beyond itself. Sensations, sensuous impulses, represent, as we have seen before, the universe only in a confused and inarticulate way. They are knowledge which cannot give an account of itself. They represent, in short, that side of mind which may be regarded as affected, or the limitation of mind,—its want of activity. So far as the mind acts from these sensations and the feelings which accompany them, it is ideally determined from without; it is a captive to its own states; it is in a condition of passivity. In all action, therefore, which occurs from a sensuous basis, the soul is rightly regarded as unfree.

On the other hand, just in the degree in which distinctness is introduced into the sensations, so that they are not simply experienced as they come, but are related to one another so that their reason for existence, their spiritual meaning, is ascertained, just in that degree is the soul master of itself. In Leibniz's own words: "Distinct knowledge or intelligence has its place in the true use of reason, while the senses furnish confused ideas. Hence we can say that we are free from slavery just in the degree that we act with distinct knowledge, but are subject to our passions in just the degree that our ideas are confused;" that is, not really representative of things as they are. "Intelligence is the soul of liberty."

This psychological explanation rests, of course, upon the foundation principle of the Leibnizian philosophy. Spirit is the sole reality, and spirit is activity. But there are various degrees of activity, and each grade lower than the *purus actus* may be rightfully regarded as in so far passive. This relative passivity or unreality constitutes the material and hence the sensuous world. One who has not insight into truth, lives and acts in this world of comparative unreality; he is in bondage to it. From this condition of slavery only reason, the understanding of things as they are, can lift one. The rational man is free because he acts, in the noble words of Spinoza, *sub specie æternitatis.* He acts in view of the eternal truth of things,—as God himself would act.

God alone, it further follows, is wholly free. In him alone are understanding and will wholly one. In him the true and the good are one; while every created intelligence is subject in some degree to sensuous affection, to passion. "In us, besides the judgment of the understanding, there is always mixed some unreal idea of the sensation which gives birth to passions and impulses, and these traverse the judgment of the practical understanding." Freedom, in fine, is not a ready made garment with which all men are clothed to do with as they will. It is the ethical ideal; it is something to be attained; it is action in conformity with reason, or insight into the spiritual nature of reality and into its laws; it is not the starting-point, it is the goal. Only with a great price do men purchase such freedom. It will be noticed at once that Leibniz comes very close to Plato in his fundamental ethical ideas. The unity of virtue and reason, of virtue and freedom,— these are thoroughly Platonic conceptions. To both Plato and Leibniz reason is the ethical ideal because it is the expression of, nay, rather *is* the reality of the universe; while all else is, as Leibniz says, imperfect or unreal, since it is not an activity, or, as Plato says, a mixture of Being and Non-Being. Again, to both man bears a similar relation to this spiritual reality. In Plato's words, he participates in the Ideas; in those of Leibniz he reflects, as a mirror, the universe. To both, in a word, the reality, the true-self of the individual, is the spiritual universe of which it is an organic member. To both, therefore, man obtains freedom or self-realization only as he realizes his larger and more comprehensive identity with the Reason of the universe. With both, knowledge is the good, ignorance is the evil.

No man is voluntarily bad, but only through lack of knowledge of the true Good. Leibniz, however, with a more developed psychology, supplements Plato in the point where the latter had the most difficulty,—the possibility of the feelings or of a love of pleasure overcoming knowledge of the good. This possibility Plato was compelled to deny, while Leibniz, by his subtle identifying of the passions with lack of knowledge, or with confused knowledge, can admit it. "It is an imperfection of our freedom," says Leibniz, "which causes us to choose evil rather than good,—a greater evil rather than the less, the less good rather than the greater. This comes from the *appearances* of good and evil which deceive us; but God, who is perfect knowledge, is always led to the true and to the best good, that is, to the true and absolute good."

It only remains briefly to apply these conceptions to some specific questions of moral actions. Locke asks whether there are practical innate ideas, and denies them, as he denies theoretical. Leibniz, in replying, recognizes two kinds of "innate" practical principles, one of which is to be referred to the class of instincts, the other to that of maxims. Primarily, and probably wholly in almost all men, moral truths take the rank of instincts alone. All men aim at the Good; it is impossible to think of man wilfully seeking his own evil. The methods, the means of reaching this Good, are implanted in men as instincts. These instincts, when brought to the light of reason and examined, become *maxims* of action; they lose their particular and impulsive character, and become universal and deliberate principles. Thus Leibniz is enabled to answer the various objections which are always brought against any "intuitive" theory of moral actions,—the variability of men's moral beliefs and conduct in different countries and at different times. Common instincts, but at first instincts only, are present in all men whenever and wherever they live. These instincts may readily be "resisted by men's passions, obscured by prejudice, and changed by custom." The moral instincts are always the basis of moral action, but "custom, tradition, education" become mixed with them. Even when so confounded, however, the instinct will generally prevail,

and custom is, upon the whole, on the side of right rather than wrong, so that Leibniz thinks there is a sense in which all men have one common morality.

But these moral instincts, even when pure, are not ethical science. This is innate, Leibniz says, only in the sense in which arithmetic is innate,—it depends upon demonstrations which reason furnishes. Leibniz does not, then, oppose intuitive and demonstrative, as sometimes happens. Morality is *practically* intuitive in the sense that all men tend to aim at the Good, and have an instinctive feeling of what makes towards the Good. It is *theoretically* demonstrative, since it does not become a science until Reason has an insight into the nature of the Good, and ascertains the fixed laws which are tributary to it. Moral principles are *not* intuitive in the sense that they are immediately discovered as separate principles by some one power of the soul called "conscience." Moral laws are intuitive, he says, "as the *consequences* of our own development and our true well-being." Here we may well leave the matter. What is to be said in detail of Leibniz's ethics will find its congenial home in what we have to say of his theology.

VI. Matter and Its Relation to Spirit

Locke's account of innate ideas and of sensation is only preparatory to a discussion of the ideas got by sensation. His explanation of the mode of knowledge leads up to an explanation of the things known. He remains true to his fundamental idea that before we come to conclusions about any matters we must "examine our own ability." He deals first with ideas got by the senses, whether by some one or by their conjoint action. Of these the ideas of solidity, of extension, and of duration are of most concern to us. They form as near an approach to a general philosophy of nature as may be found anywhere in Locke. They are, too, the germ from which grew the ideas of matter, of space, and of time, which, however more comprehensive in scope and more amply worked out in detail, characterize succeeding British thought, and which are reproduced to-day by Mr. Spencer.

"The idea of solidity we receive by our touch." "The ideas we get by more than one sense are of space or extension, figure, rest, and motion." These sentences contain the brief statement of the chief contention of the sensational school. Locke certainly was not conscious when he wrote them that they were the expression of ideas which should resolve the world of matter and of space into a dissolving series of accidentally associated sensations; but such was none the less the case. When he writes, "If any one asks me what solidity is, I send him to his senses to inform him," he is preparing the way for Berkeley, and for a denial of all reality beyond the feelings of the individual mind. When he says that "we get the idea of space both by sight and touch," this statement, although appearing truistic, is none the less the source of the contention of Hume that even geometry contains no necessary or universal elements, but is an account of sensible appearances, relative, as are all matters of sensation.

Locke's ideas may be synopsized as follows: It is a sufficient account of solidity to say that it is got by touch and that it arises from the resistance found in bodies to the entrance of any other body. "It is that which hinders the approach of two bodies when they are moved towards one another." If not identical with matter, it is at all events its most essential property. "This of all others seems the idea most intimately connected with and essential to body, so as nowhere else to be found or imagined, but only in matter." It is, moreover, the source of the other properties of matter. "Upon the solidity of bodies depend their mutual impulse, resistance, and protrusion." Solidity, again, "is so inseparable an idea from body that upon that depends its filling of space, its contact, impulse, and communication of motion upon impulse." It is to be distinguished, therefore, from hardness, for hardness is relative and derived, various bodies having various degrees of it; while solidity consists in utter exclusion of other bodies from the space possessed by any one, so that the hardest body has no more solidity than the softest.

The close connection between solidity and matter makes it not only possible, but necessary, to distinguish between matter and extension as against the Cartesians, who had identified them. In particular Locke notes three differences between these notions. Extension includes neither solidity nor resistance; its parts are inseparable from one another both really and mentally, and are immovable; while matter has solidity, its parts are mutually separable, and may be moved *in* space. From this distinction between space and matter it follows, according to Locke, that there is such a thing as a vacuum, or that space is not necessarily a plenum of matter. Matter is that which fills space; but it is entirely indifferent to space whether or not it is filled. Space is occupied by matter, but there is no eessential relation between them. Solidity is the essence of matter; emptiness is the characteristic of space. "The idea of space is as distinct from that of solidity as it is from that of scarlet color. It is true, solidity cannot exist without extension, neither can scarlet colar exist without extension; but this hinders not that they are *distinct ideas.*"

Thus there is fixed for us the idea of space as well as of matter. It is a distinct idea; that is, absolute or independent in itself, having no intrinsic connection with phenomena *in* space. Yet it is got through the senses. How that can be a matter of sensation which is not only not material, but has no connection in itself with matter, Locke does not explain. He thinks it sufficient to say that we see distance between bodies of different color just as plainly as we see the colors. Space is, therefore, a purely immediate idea, containing no more organic relation to intelligence than it has to objects. We get the notion of time as we do that of space, excepting that it is the observation of internal states and not of external objects which furnishes the material of the idea. Time has two elements,—succession and duration. "Observing what passes in the mind, how of our ideas there in train some constantly vanish, and others begin to appear, we come by the idea of succession, and by observing a distance in the parts of this succession we get the idea of duration." Whether, however, time is something essentially empty, having no relation to the events which fill it, as space is essentially empty, without necessary connection with the objects which fill it, is a question Locke does not consider. In fact, the gist of his ideas upon this point is as follows: there is actually an objective space or pure emptiness; employing our senses, we get the idea of this space. There is actually an objective time; employing reflection, we perceive it. There is not the slightest attempt to form a philosophy of them, or to show their function in the construction of an intelligible world, except in the one point of the absolute independence of matter and space.

It cannot be said that Leibniz criticises the minor points of Locke in such a way as to throw much light upon them, or that he very fully expresses his own ideas about them. He contents himself with declaring that while the senses may give instances of space, time, and matter, and may suggest to intelligence the stimuli upon which intelligence realizes these notions from itself, they cannot be the source of these notions themselves; finding the evidence of this in the sciences of geometry, arithmetic, and pure physics. For these sciences deal with the notions of space, time, and matter, giving necessary and demonstrative ideas concerning them, which the senses can never legitimate. He further denies the supposed absoluteness or independence of space, matter, and motion. Admitting, indeed, the distinction between extension and matter, he denies that this distinction suffices to prove the existence, or even the possibility, of a vacuum, and ends with a general reference to his doctrine of pre-established harmony, as serving to explain these matters more fully and more accurately.

Leibniz has, however, a complete philosophy of nature. In his other writing, he explains the ideas of matter and force in their dependence upon his metaphysic, or doctrine of spiritual entelechies. The task does not at first sight appear an easy one. The reality, according to Leibniz, is purely spiritual, does not exist in space nor time, and is a principle of activity following its own law,—that of reflecting the universe of spiritual relations. How from this world of ideal, unextended, and non-temporal dynamic realities we are to pass over to a material world of extension, with its static existence in space, and transitory passage in time, is a question challenging the whole Leibnizian system. It is a question, however, for which Leibniz himself has provided an answer. We may not regard it as adequate; we may think that he has not truly derived the material world from his spiritual principles: but at all events he asked himself the question, and gave an answer. We shall investigate this answer by arranging what Leibniz has said under the heads of: matter as a metaphysical principle; matter as a physical phenomenon; and the relation of phenomena to absolute reality, or of the physical to the metaphysical. In connection with the second head, particularly, we shall find it necessary to discuss what Leibniz has said about space, time, and motion.

Wolff, who put the ideas of Leibniz into systematic shape, did it at the expense of almost all their significance. He took away the air of paradox, of remoteness, that characterized Leibniz's thought, and gave it a popular form. But its depth and suggestiveness vanished in the process. Unfortunately, Wolff's presentations of the philosophy of Leibniz have been followed by others, to whom it seemed a dull task to follow out the intricacies of a thought nowhere systematically expressed. This has been especially the case as concerns the Leibnizian doctrine of matter. A superficial interpretation of certain passages in Leibniz has led to an almost universal misunderstanding about it. Leibniz frequently says that since matter is composite or complex, it follows that there must be something simple as its basis, and this simple something is the monad. The misinterpretation just spoken of consists in supposing that Leibniz meant that matter as composite is made up of monads as simple; that the monad and matter are facts of the same order, the latter being only an aggregate, or continued collection of the former. It interpreted the conception of Leibniz in strict analogy with the atomic theory of Lucretius, excepting that it granted that the former taught that the ultimate atom, the component of all complex forms of matter, has position only, not extension, its essence consisting in its exercise of force, not in its mere space occupancy. The monad was thus considered to be *in* space, or at least conditioned by space relations, as is a mathematical point, although not itself spatial in the sense of being extended. Monad and matter were thus represented as facts of the same kind or genus, having their difference only in their relative isolation or aggregation.

But Leibniz repudiated this idea, and that not only by the spirit of his teaching, but in express words. Monads "are not ingredients or constituents of matter," he says, "but only *conditions* of it." "Monads can no more be said to be parts of bodies, or to come in contact with them, or to compose them, than can souls or mathematical points." "Monads *per se* have *no* situation relative to one another." An increase in the number of created monads, he says again, if such a thing could be supposed, would no more increase the amount of matter in existence, than mathematical points added to a line would increase its length. And again: "There is no nearness or remoteness among monads; to say that they are gathered in a point or are scattered in space, is to employ mental fictions, *in trying to imagine what can only be thought.*" The italicized words give the clew to the whole discussion. To make monads of the same order as corporeal phenomena, is to make them sensible, or capable of being imaged, or conditioned by space and time,—three phases which are strictly correlative. But the monads can only be thought,—that is, their qualities are ideal, not sensible; they can be realized only by reason, not projected in forms having spatial outline and temporal habitation, that is, in images. Monads and material things, in other words, are facts of two distinct orders; they are related as the rational or spiritual and the physical or sensible. Matter is no more composed of monads than it is of thoughts or of logical principles. As Leibniz says over and over again: Matter, space, time, motion are only phenomena, although phenomena *bene fundata*,—phenomena, that is, having their rational basis and condition. The monads, on the other hand, are not appearances, they are realities.

Having freed our minds from the supposition that it is in any way possible to form an image or picture of the monad; having realized that it is wholly false to suppose that monads occupy position in space, and then by their continuity fill it, and make extended matter,—we must attempt to frame a correct theory of the nature of matter and its relation to the monad. We shall do this only as we realized that "matter," so far as it has any reality, or so far as it has any real *fundamentum*, must be something ideal, or, in Leibniz's language, "metaphysical." As he says over and over again, the only realities are the substances or spiritual units of activity, to which the name "monad" is given. In the inquiry, then, after such reality as matter may have, we must betake ourselves to this unit of living energy.

Although every monad is active, it is not entirely active. There is, as we have already seen, an infinite scale of substances; and since substance is equivalent to activity, this is saying that there is an infinite scale of activities. God alone is *purus actus*, absolute energy, untouched by passivity or receptivity. Every other being has the element of incompleteness, of inadequacy; it does not completely represent the universe. In this passivity consists its finitude, so that Leibniz says that not even God himself could deprive monads of it, for this would be to make them equal to himself. In this passivity, incompleteness, or finitude, consists what we call matter. Leibniz says that he can understand what Plato meant when he called matter something essentially imperfect and transitory. Every finite monad is a union of two principles,—those of activity and of passivity. "I do not admit," says Leibniz, "that there are souls existing simply by themselves, or that there are created spirits detached from all body. God alone is above all matter, since he is its author; creatures freed from matter would be at the same time detached from the universal connection of things, and, as it were, deserters from the general order." And again, "Beings have a nature which is both active and passive; *that is*, material and immaterial." And again, he says that every created monad requires both an entelechy, or principle of activity, and matter. "Matter is essential to any entelechy, and can never be separated from it, since matter *com-*

pletes it." In short, the term "monad" is equivalent to the term "entelechy" only when applied to God. In every other monad, the entelechy, or energy, is but one factor. "Matter, or primitive passive power, completes the entelechy, or primitive active power, so that it becomes a perfect substance, or monad." On the other hand, of course, matter, as the passive principle, is a mere potentiality or abstraction, considered in itself. It is real only in its union with the active principle. Matter, he says, "cannot exist without immaterial substances." "To every particular portion of matter belongs a particular *form*; that is, a soul, a spirit." To this element of matter, considered as an abstraction, in its distinction from soul, Leibniz, following the scholastics, and ultimately Aristotle, gives the name, "first" or "bare" matter. The same influence is seen in the fact that he opposes this element of matter to "form," or the active principle.

Our starting-point, therefore, for the consideration of matter is the statement that it is receptivity, the capacity for being affected, which always constitutes matter. But what is meant by "receptivity"? To answer this question we must return to what was said about the two activities of the monad,—representation, or perception, and appetition,—and to the difference between confused and distinct ideas. The monad has appetition so far as it determines itself from within to change, so far as it follows an internal principle of energy. It is representative so far as it is determined from without, so far as it receives impressions from the universe. Yet we have learned to know that in one sense everything occurs from the spontaneity of the monad itself; it receives no influence or influxus from without; everything comes from its own depths, or is appetition. But, on the other hand, all that which so comes forth is only a mirroring or copying of the universe. The whole content of the appetition is representation. Although the monad works spontaneously, it is none the less determined in its activities to produce only reflections or images of the world. In this way appetition and representation appear to be identical. The monad is determined from within, indeed, but it is determined to exactly the same results as if wholly determined from

without. What light, then, can be thrown from this distinction upon the nature of matter?

None, unless we follow Leibniz somewhat farther. If we do, we shall see that the soul is regarded as appetitive, or self-active, so far as it has clear and distinct ideas. If the monad reaches distinct consciousness, it has knowledge of self,—that is, of the nature of pure spirit,—or, what again is equivalent to this, of the nature of reality as it universally is. Such knowledge is knowledge of God, of substance, of unity, of pure activity, and of all the innate ideas which elevate the confused perceptions of sense into science. Distinct consciousness is therefore equivalent to self-activity, and this to recognition of God and the universal. But if knowledge is confused, it is not possible to see it in its relations to self; it cannot be analyzed; the rational or ideal element in it is concealed from view. In confused ideas, therefore, the soul appears to be passive; being passive, to be determined from without. This determination from without is equivalent to that which is opposed to spirit or reason, and hence appears as matter. Such is in outline the Leibnizian philosophy.

It thus is clear that merely stating that matter is passivity in the monad is not the ultimate way of stating its nature. For passivity means in reality nothing but confused representations,—representations, that is, whose significance is not perceived. The true significance of every representation is found in its relation to the ego, or pure self-activity, which, through its dependent relation upon God, the absolute self-activity and ego, produces the representation from its own ideal being. So far as the soul does not have distinct recognition of relation of all representations to self, it feels them as coming from without; as foreign to spirit; in short, as matter. Leibniz thus employs exactly the same language about confused ideas that he does about passivity, or matter. It is not possible that the monad should have distinct consciousness of itself as a mirror of the whole universe, he says, "for in that case every entelechy would be God." Again, "the soul would be God if it could enter at once and with distinctness into everything occuring within it." But it is necessary "that we should have passions which consist in confused ideas, in which there is something involuntary and unknown, and which represent the body and constitute our imperfection." Again, he speaks of matter as "the *mixture* (*mélange*) of the effects of the infinite environing us." In that expression is summed up his whole theory of matter. It is a mixture; it is, that is to say, confused, aggregated, irresolvable into simple ideas. But it is a mixture of "effects of the infinite about us;" that is, it takes its rise in the true, the real, the spiritual. It only fails to represent this as it actually is. Matter, in short, is a phenomenon dependent upon inability to realize the entire spiritual character of reality. It is spirit apprehended in a confused, hesitating, and passive manner.

It is none the less a necessary phenomenon, for it is involved in the idea of a continuous gradation of monads, in the distinction between the infinite and the finite, or, as Leibniz often prefers to put it, between the "creator" and the "created." There is involved everywhere in the idea of Leibniz the conception of subordination; of a hierarchy of forms, each of which receives the law of its action from the next higher, and gives the law to the next lower. We have previously considered the element of passivity or receptivity as relating only to the monad which manifests it. It is evident, however, that what is passive in one, implies something active in another. What one receives, is what another gives. The reciprocal influence of monads upon one another, therefore, as harmonious members of one system, requires matter. More strictly speaking, this reciprocal influence *is* matter. To take away all receptivity, all passivity, from monads would be to isolate them from all relations with others; it would be to deprive them of all power of affecting or being affected by others. That is what Leibniz meant by the expression already quoted, that if monads had not matter as an element in them, "they would be, as it were, deserters from the general order." The note of unity, of organic connection, which we found to be the essence of the Leibnizian philosophy, absolutely requires, therefore, matter, or passivity.

It must be remembered that this reciprocal influence is ideal. As Leibniz remarks, "When it is said that one monad is affected by another, this is to be understood concerning its *representation* of the other. For the Author of things has so accommodated them to one another that one is said to suffer (or receive from the other) when its relative value gives way to that of the other." Or again, "the modifications of one monad are the ideal causes of the modifications of another monad, so far as there appear in one the reasons on account of which God brought about in the beginning certain modifications in another." And most definitely of all: "A creature is called active so far as it has perfection; passive in so far as it is imperfect. One creature is more perfect than another so far as there is found in it that which serves to *render the reason, a priori,* for that occurring in the other; and it is in this way that it acts upon the other."

We are thus introduced, from a new point of view and in a more concrete way, to the conception of pre-established harmony. The activity of one, the energy which gives the law to the other and makes it subordinate in the hierarchy of monads, is conceived necessarily as spirit, as soul; that which receives, which is rendered subordinate by the activity of the other, is body. The pre-established harmony is the fact that they are so related that one can receive the law of its activity from the other. Leibniz is without doubt partially responsible for the ordinary misconception of his views upon this point by reason of the illustration which he was accustomed to use; namely, of two clocks so constructed that without any subsequent regulation each always kept perfect time with the other,—as much so as if there were some actual physical connection between them. This seems to put soul and body, spirit and matter, as two co-ordinate substances, on the same level, with such natural opposition between them that some external harmony must arrange some unity of action. In causing this common idea of his theory of pre-established harmony, Leibniz has paid the penalty for attempting to do what he often reproves in others,—imagining or presenting in sensible form what can only be thought. But his other explanations show clearly enough that the pre-established harmony expresses, not a relation between two parallel substances, but a condition of dependence of lower forms of activity upon the higher for the law of their existence and activity,—in modern terms, it expresses the fact that phenomena are conditioned upon noumena; that material facts get their significance and share of reality through their relation to spirit.

We may sum up what has been said about matter as an element in the monad, or as a metaphysical principle, as follows: The existence of matter is not only one opposed to the fundamental ideas of Leibniz, but is a necessary deduction from them. It is a necessity of the principle of continuity; for this requires an infinity of monads, alike indeed in the universal law of their being, but unlike, each to each, in the specific coloring or manifestation of this law. The principle of organic unity requires that there be as many real beings as possible participating in and contributing to it. It is necessary, again, in order that there may be reciprocal influence or connection among the monads. Were it not for the material element in the monad, each would be a God; if each were thus infinite and absolute, there would be so many principles wholly independent and isolated. The principle of harmony would be violated. So much for the necessity of the material factor. As to its nature, it is a principle of passivity; that is, of ideal receptivity, of conformity to a law apparently not self-imposed, but externally laid down. This makes matter equivalent to a phenomenon: that is to say, to the having of confused, imperfect, inadequate ideas. To say that matter is correlative to confused ideas is to say that there is no recognition of its relation to self or to spirit. As Leibniz sometimes puts it, since there is an infinity of beings in the universe, each one of which exercises an ideal influence upon every other one of the series, it is impossible that this other one should realize their full meaning; they appear only as confused ideas, or as matter. To use language which Leibniz indeed does not employ, but which seems to convey his thought, the spirit, not seeing them as they really are, does not *find* itself in them. But matter is thus not only the confused manifestation or phenomenon of spirit, it is also its potentiality. Passivity is always relative. It does not mean complete lack of activity; that, as Leibniz says, is nothingness, and matter is not

a form of nothingness. Leibniz even speaks of it as passive *power*. That is to say, there is an undeveloped or incomplete activity in what appears as matter, and this may be,—if we admit an infinity of time,—must be developed. When developed it manifests itself as it really is, as spirit. Confused ideas, as Leibniz takes pains to state, are not a genus of ideas antithetical to distinct; they differ only in degree or grade. They are on their way to become distinct, or else they are distinct ideas which have fallen back into an "involved" state of being. Matter, therefore, is not absolutely opposed to spirit,—on the one hand because it is the manifestation, the phenomenon, of spirit; on the other, because it is the potentiality of spirit, capable of sometime realizing the whole activity implied in it, but now latent.

Thus it is that Leibniz says that everything is "full" of souls or monads. What appears to be lifeless is in reality like a pond full of fishes, like a drop of water full of infusoria. Everything is organic down to the last element. More truly, there is no last element. There is a true infinity of organic beings wrapped up in the slightest speck of apparently lifeless matter. These illustrations, like many others which Leibniz uses, are apt to suggest that erroneous conception of the relation of monads to spirit which we were obliged, in Leibniz's name, to correct at the outset,—the idea, namely, that matter is composed, in a spatial or mechanical way, of monads. But after the foregoing explanations we can see that what Leibniz means when he says that every portion of matter is full of entelechies or souls, like a garden full of plants, is that there is an absolute continuity of spiritual principles, each having its ideal relation with every other. There is no point of matter which does not represent in a confused way the entire universe. It is therefore as infinite in its activities as the universe. In idea also it is capable of representing in distinct consciousness, or as a development of its own self-activity, each of these infinite activities.

In a word, every created or finite being may be regarded as matter or as spirit, according as it is accounted for by its external relations, as the reasons for what happen in it are to be found elsewhere than in its own explicit activity, or according as it shows clearly in itself the reasons for its own modifications, and also accounts for changes occurring in other beings. The externally conditioned is matter; the internally conditioned, the self-explanatory, is self-active, or spirit. Since all external relations are finally dependent on organic; since the ultimate source of all explanation must be that which is its own reason; since the ultimate source of all activity must be that which is self-active,—the final reason or source of matter is spirit.

The Monadology

Gottfried Wilhelm Leibniz

1. The Monad, of which we will speak here, is nothing else than a simple substance, which goes to make up composites; by simple, we mean without parts.

2. There must be simple substances because there are composites; for a composite is nothing else than a collection or *aggregatum* of simple substances.

3. Now, where there are no constituent parts there is possible neither extension, nor form, nor divisibility. These Monads are the true Atoms of nature, and, in fact, the Elements of things.

4. Their dissolution, therefore, is not to be feared and there is no way conceivable by which a simple substance can perish through natural means.

5. For the same reason there is no way conceivable by which a simple substance might, through natural means, come into existence, since it can not be formed by composition.

6. We may say then, that the existence of Monads can begin or end only all at once, that is to say, the Monad can begin only through creation and end only through annihilation. Composites, however, begin or end gradually.

7. There is also no way of explaining how a Monad can be altered or changed in its inner being by any other created thing, since there is no possibility of transposition within it, nor can we conceive of any internal movement which can be produced, directed, increased or diminished there within the substance, such as can take place in the case of composites where a change can occur among the parts. The Monads have no windows through which anything may come in or go out. The Attributes are not liable to detach themselves and make an excursion outside the substance, as could *sensible species* of the Schoolmen. In the same way neither substance nor attribute can enter from without into a Monad.

8. Still Monads must needs have some qualities, otherwise they would not even be existences. And if simple substances did not differ at all in their qualities, there would be no means of perceiving any change in things. Whatever is in a composite can come into it only through its simple elements and the Monads, if they were without qualities, since they do not differ at all in quantity, would be indistinguishable one from another. For instance, if we imagine *a plenum* or completely filled space, where each part receives only the equivalent of its own previous motion, one state of things would not be distinguishable from another.

9. Each Monad, indeed, must be different from every other. For there are never in nature two beings which are exactly alike, and in which it is not possible to find a difference either internal or based on an intrinsic property.

10. I assume it as admitted that every created being, and consequently the created

SOURCE: G. W. Leibniz, *The Monadology* translated by George Montgomery (Open Court, 1902).

Monad, is subject to change, and indeed that this change is continuous in each.

11. It follows from what has just been said, that the natural changes of the Monad come from an internal principle, because an external cause can have no influence upon its inner being.

12. Now besides this principle of change there must also be in the Monad a manifoldness which changes. This manifoldness constitutes, so to speak, the specific nature and the variety of the simple substances.

13. This manifoldness must involve a multiplicity in the unity or in that which is simple. For since every natural change takes place by degrees, there must be something which changes and something which remains unchanged, and consequently there must be in the simple substance a plurality of conditions and relations, even though it has no parts.

14. The passing condition which involves and represents a multiplicity in the unity, or in the simple substance, is nothing else than what is called Perception. This should be carefully distinguished from Apperception or Consciousness, as will appear in what follows. In this matter the Cartesians have fallen into a serious error, in that they treat as nonexistent those perceptions of which we are not conscious. It is this also which has led them to believe that spirits alone are Monads and that there are no souls of animals or other Entelechies, and it has led them to make the common confusion between a protracted period of unconsciousness and actual death. They have thus adopted the Scholastic error that souls can exist entirely separated from bodies, and have even confirmed ill-balanced minds in the belief that souls are mortal.

15. The action of the internal principle which brings about the change or the passing from one perception to another may be called Appetition. It is true that the desire (*l'appetit*) is not always able to attain to the whole of the perception which it strives for, but it always attains a portion of it and reaches new perceptions.

16. We, ourselves, experience a multiplicity in a simple substance, when we find that the most trifling thought of which we are conscious involves a variety in the object. Therefore, all those who acknowledge that the soul is a simple substance ought to grant this multiplicity in the Monad, and Monsieur Bayle should have found no difficulty in it, as he has done in his *Dictionary*, article "Rorarius."

17. It must be confessed, however, that Perception, and that which depends upon it, are inexplicable by mechanical causes, that is to say, by figures and motions. Supposing that there were a machine whose structure produced thought, sensation, and perception, we could conceive of it as increased in size with the same proportions until one was able to enter into its interior, as he would into a mill. Now, on going into it he would find only pieces working upon one another, but never would he find anything to explain Perception. It is accordingly in the simple substance, and not in the composite nor in a machine that the Perception is to be sought. Furthermore, there is nothing besides perceptions and their changes to be found in the simple substance. And it is in these alone that all the internal activities of the simple substance can consist.

18. All simple substances or created Monads may be called Entelechies, because they have in themselves a certain perfection. There is in them a sufficiency which makes them the source of their internal activities, and renders them, so to speak, incorporeal Automatons.

19. If we wish to designate as soul everything which has perceptions and desires in the general sense that I have just explained, all simple substances or created Monads could be called souls. But since feeling is something more than a mere perception I think that the general name of Monad or Entelechy should suffice for simple substances which have only perception, while we may reserve the term Soul for those whose perception is more distinct and is accompanied by memory.

20. We experience in ourselves a state where we remember nothing and where we have no distinct perception, as in periods of fainting, or when we are overcome by a profound, dreamless sleep. In such a state the soul does not sensibly differ at all from a simple Monad. As this state, however, is not per-

manent and the soul can recover from it, the soul is something more.

21. Nevertheless it does not follow at all that the simple substance is in such a state without perception. This is so because of the reasons given above; for it cannot perish, nor on the other hand would it exist without some affection and the affection is nothing else than its perception. When, however, there are a great number of weak perceptions where nothing stands out distinctively, we are stunned; as when one turns around and around in the same direction, a dizziness comes on, which makes him swoon and makes him able to distinguish nothing. Among animals, death can occasion this state for quite a period.

22. Every present state of a simple substance is a natural consequence of its preceding state, in such a way that its present is big with its future.

23. Therefore, since on awakening after a period of unconsciousness we become conscious of our perceptions, we must, without having been conscious of them, have had perceptions immediately before; for one perception can come in a natural way only from another perception, just as a motion can come in a natural way only from a motion.

24. It is evident from this that if we were to have nothing distinctive, or so to speak prominent, and of a higher flavor in our perceptions, we should be in a continual state of stupor. This is the condition of Monads which are wholly bare.

25. We see that nature has given to animals heightened perceptions, having provided them with organs which collect numerous rays of light or numerous waves of air and thus make them more effective in their combination. Something similar to this takes place in the case of smell, in that of taste and of touch, and perhaps in many other senses which are unknown to us. I shall have occasion very soon to explain how that which occurs in the soul represents that which goes on in the sense-organs.

26. The memory furnishes a sort of consecutiveness which imitates reason but is to be distinguished from it. We see that animals when they have the perception of something which they notice and of which they have had a similar previous perception, are led by the representation of their memory to expect that which was associated in the preceding perception, and they come to have feelings like those which they had before. For instance, if a stick be shown to a dog, he remembers the pain which it has caused him and he whines or runs away.

27. The vividness of the picture, which comes to him or moves him, is derived either from the magnitude or from the number of the previous perceptions. For, oftentimes, a strong impression brings about, all at once, the same effect as a long-continued habit or as a great many re-iterated, moderate perceptions.

28. Men act in like manner as animals, in so far as the sequence of their perceptions is determined only by the law of memory, resembling, the *empirical physicians* who practice simply, without any theory, and we are empiricists in three-fourths of our actions. For instance, when we expect that there will be day-light to-morrow, we do so empirically, because it has always happened so up to the present time. It is only the astronomer who uses his reason in making such an affirmation.

29. But the knowledge of eternal and necessary truths is that which distinguishes us from mere animals and gives us reason and the sciences, thus raising us to a knowledge of ourselves and of God. This is what is called in us the Rational Soul or the Mind.

30. It is also through the knowledge of necessary truths and through abstractions from them that we come to perform Reflective Acts, which cause us to think of what is called the I, and to decide that this or that is within us. It is thus, that in thinking upon ourselves we think of *being*, of *substance*, or the *simple* and *composite*, of a *material* thing and of *God* himself, conceiving that what is limited in us is in him without limits. These Reflective Acts furnish the principal objects of our reasonings.

31. Our reasoning is based upon two great principles: first, that of Contradiction, by means of which we decide that to be false which involves contradiction and that to be true which contradicts or is opposed to the false.

32. And second, the principle of Sufficient Reason, in virtue of which we believe that no

fact can be real or existing and no statement true unless it has a sufficient reason why it should be thus and not otherwise. Most frequently, however, these reasons cannot be known by us.

33. There are also two kinds of Truths: those of Reasoning and those of Fact. The Truths of Reasoning are necessary, and their opposite is impossible. Those of Fact, however, are contingent, and their opposite is possible. When a truth is necessary, the reason can be found by analysis in resolving it into simpler ideas and into simpler truths until we reach those which are primary.

34. It is thus that with mathematicians the Speculative Theorems and the practical Canons are reduced by analysis to Definitions, Axioms, and Postulates.

35. There are finally simple ideas of which no definition can be given. There are also the Axioms and Postulates or, in a word, the primary principles which cannot be proved and, indeed, have no need of proof. These are identical propositions whose opposites involve express contradictions.

36. But there must be also a sufficient reason for contingent truths or truths of fact; that is to say, for the sequence of the things which extend throughout the universe of created beings, where the analysis into more particular reasons can be continued into greater detail without limit because of the immense variety of the things in nature and because of the infinite division of bodies. There is an infinity of figures and of movements, present and past, which enter into the efficient cause of my present writing, and in its final cause there are an infinity of slight tendencies and dispositions of my soul, present and past.

37. And as all this detail again involves other and more detailed contingencies, each of which again has need of a similar analysis in order to find its explanation, no real advance has been made. Therefore, the sufficient or ultimate reason must needs be outside of the sequence or series of these details of contingencies, however infinite they may be.

38. It is thus that the ultimate reason for things must be a necesssary substance, in which the detail of the changes shall be present merely potentially as in the fountainhead, and this substance we call God.

39. Now, since this substance is a sufficient reason for all the above mentioned details, which are linked together throughout, *there is but one God, and this God is sufficient.*

40. We may hold that the supreme substance, which is unique, universal and necessary with nothing independent outside of it, which is further a pure sequence of possible being, must be incapable of limitation and must contain as much reality as possible.

41. Whence it follows that God is absolutely perfect, perfection being understood as the magnitude of positive reality in the strict sense, when the limitations or the bounds of those things which have them are removed. There where there are no limits, that is to say, in God, perfection is absolutely infinite.

42. It follows also that created things derive their perfections through the influence of God, but their imperfections come from their own natures, which cannot exist without limits. It is in this latter that they are distinguished from God. An example of this original imperfection of created things is to be found in the natural inertia of bodies.

43. It is true, furthermore, that in God is found not only the source of existences, but also that of essences, in so far as they are real. In other words, he is the source of whatever there is real in the possible. This is because the Understanding of God is in the region of eternal truths or of the ideas upon which they depend, and because without him there would be nothing real in the possibilities of things, and not only would nothing be existent, nothing would be even possible.

44. For it must needs be that if there is a reality in essences or in possibilities or indeed in the eternal truths, this reality is based upon something existent and actual, and, consequently, in the existence of the necessary Being in whom essence includes existence or in whom possibility is sufficient to produce actuality.

45. Therefore God alone (or the Necessary Being) has this prerogative that if he be possible he must necessarily exist, and, as nothing is able to prevent the possibility of that which involves no bounds, no negation, and con-

sequently, no contradiction, this alone is sufficient to establish *a priori* his existence. We have, therefore, proved his existence through the reality of eternal truths. But a little while ago we also proved it *a posteriori*, because contingent beings exist which can have their ultimate and sufficient reason only in the necessary being which, in turn, has the reason for existence in itself.

46. Yet we must not think that the eternal truths being dependent upon God are therefore arbitrary and depend upon his will, as Descartes seems to have held, and after him M. Poiret. This is the case only with contingent truths which depend upon fitness or the choice of the greatest good; necessarily truths on the other hand depend solely upon his understanding and are the inner objects of it.

47. God alone is the ultimate unity or the original simple substance, of which all created or derivative monads are the products, and arise, so to speak, through the continual out-flashings (fulgurations) of the divinity from moment to moment, limited by the receptivity of the creature to whom limitation is an essential.

48. In God are present: power, which is the source of everything; knowledge, which contains the details of the ideas; and, finally, will, which changes or produces things in accordance with the principle of the greatest good. To these correspond in the created monad, the subject or basis, the faculty of perception, and the faculty of appetition. In God these attributes are absolutely infinite or perfect, while in the created monads or in the entelechies (*perfectihabies,* as Hermolaus Barbarus translates this word), they are imitations approaching him in proportion to the perfection.

49. A created thing is said to act outwardly in so far as it has perfection, and to be acted upon by another in so far as it is imperfect. Thus action is attributed to the monad in so far as it has distinct perceptions, and passion or passivity is attributed in so far as it has confused perceptions.

50. One created thing is more perfect than another when we find in the first that which gives an *a priori* reason for what occurs in the second. This why we say that one acts upon the other.

51. In the case of simple substances, the influence which one monad has upon another is only ideal. It can have its effect only through the mediation of God, in so far as in the ideas of God each monad can rightly demand that God, in regulating the others from the beginning of things, should have regarded it also. For since one created monad cannot have a physical influence upon the inner being of another, it is only through the primal regulation that one can have dependence upon another.

52. It is thus that among created things action and passivity are reciprocal. For God, in comparing two simple substances, finds in each one reasons obliging him to adopt the other to it; and consequently what is active in certain respects is passive from another point of view, active in so far as what we distinctly know in it serves to give a reason for what occurs in another, and passive in so far as the reason for what occurs in it is found in what is distinctly known in another.

53. Now as there are an infinity of possible universes in the ideas of God, and but one of them can exist, there must be a sufficient reason for the choice of God which determines him to select one rather than another.

54. And this reason is to be found only in the fitness or in the degree of perfection which these worlds possess, each possible thing having the right to claim existence in proportion to the perfection which it involves.

55. This is the cause for the existence of the greatest good; namely, that the wisdom of God permits him to know it, his goodness causes him to choose it, and his power enables him to produce it.

56. Now this interconnection, relationship, or this adaptation of all things to each particular one, and of each one to all the rest, brings it about that every simple substance has relations which express all the others and that it is consequently a perpetual living mirror of the universe.

57. And as the same city regarded from different sides appears entirely different, and is, as it were, mutliplied respectively, so, because of the infinite number of simple substances, there are a similar infinite number of universes which are, nevertheless, only the

aspects of a single one as seen from the special point of view of each monad.

58. Through this means has been obtained the greatest possible variety, together with the greatest order that may be; that is to say, through this means has been obtained the greatest possible perfection.

59. This hypothesis, moreover, which I venture to call demonstrated, is the only one which fittingly gives proper prominence to the greatness of God. M. Bayle recognized this when in his dictionary (article "Rorarius") he raised objections to it; indeed, he was inclined to believe that I attributed too much to God, and more than it is possible to attribute to him: But he was unable to bring forward any reason why this universal harmony which causes every substance to express exactly all others through the relation which it has with them is impossible.

60. Besides, in what has just been said can be seen the *a priori* reasons why things cannot be otherwise than they are. It is because God, in ordering the whole, has had regard to every part and in particular to each monad; and since the monad is by its very nature *representative,* nothing can limit it to represent merely a part of things. It is nevertheless true that this representation is, as regards the details of the whole universe, only a confused representation, and is distinct only as regards a small part of them, that is to say, as regards those things which are nearest or greatest in relation to each monad. If the representation were distinct as to the details of the entire universe, each monad would be a Diety. It is not in the object represented that the monads are limited, but in the modifications of their knowledge of the object. In a confused way they reach out to infinity or to the whole, but are limited and differentiated in the degree of their distinct perceptions.

61. In this respect composites are like simple substances, for all space is filled up, therefore, all matter is connected. And in a plenum or filled space every movement has an effect upon bodies in proportion to this distance, so that not only is every body affected by those which are in contact with it and responds in some way to whatever happens to them, but also by means of them the body responds to those bodies adjoining them, and their intercommunication reaches in any distance whatsoever. Consequently every body responds to all that happens in the universe, so that he who saw all could read in each one what is happening everywhere, and even what has happened and what will happen. He can discover in the present what is distant both as regards space and as regards time; "All things conspire" as Hippocrates said. A soul can, however, read in itself only what is there represented distinctly. It cannot all at once open up all its folds, because they extend to infinity.

62. Thus although each created monad represents the whole universe, it represents more distinctly the body which specially pertains to it and of which it constitutes the entelechy. And as this body expresses all the universe through the interconnection of all matter in the plenum, the soul also represents the whole universe in representing this body, which belongs to it in a particular way.

63. The body belonging to a monad, which is its entelechy or soul, constitutes together with the entelechy what may be called a *living being,* and with a soul what is called an *animal.* Now this body of a living being or of an animal is always organic, because every monad is a mirror of the universe is regulated with perfect order there must needs be order also in what represents it, that is to say in the perceptions of the soul and consequently in the body through which the universe is represented in the soul.

64. Therefore every organic body of a living being is a kind of divine machine or natural automaton, infinitely surpassing all artificial automatons. Because a machine constructed by man's skill is not a machine in each of its parts; for instance, the teeth of a brass wheel have parts or bits which to us are not artificial products and contain nothing in themselves to show the use to which the wheel was destined in the machine. The machines of nature, however, that is to say, living bodies, are still machines in their smallest parts *ad infinitium.* Such is the difference between nature and art, that is to say, between divine art and ours.

65. The author of nature has been able to employ this divine and infinitely marvelous

artifice, because each portion of matter is not only, as the ancients recognized, infinitely divisible, but also because it is really divided without end, every part into other parts, each one of which has its own proper motion. Otherwise it would be impossible for each portion of matter to express all the universe.

66. Whence we see that there is a world of created things, of living beings, of animals, of entelechies, of souls, in the minutest particle of matter.

67. Every portion of matter may be conceived as like a garden full of plants and like a pond full of fish. But every branch of a plant, every member of an animal, and every drop of the fluids within it, is also such a garden or such a pond.

68. And although the ground and air which lies between the plants of the garden, and the water which is between the fish in the pond, are not themselves plants or fish, yet they nevertheless contain these, usually so small however as to be imperceptible to us.

69. There is, therefore, nothing uncultivated, or sterile or dead in the universe, no chaos, no confusion, save in appearance; somewhat as a pond would appear at a distance when we could see in it a confused movement, and so to speak, a swarming of the fish, without however discerning the fish themselves.

70. It is evident, then, that every living body has a dominating entelechy, which in animals is the soul. The parts, however, of this living body are full of other living beings, plants and animals, which in turn have each one its entelechy or dominating soul.

71. This does not mean, as some who have misunderstood my thought have imagined, that each soul has a quantity or portion of matter appropriated to it or attached to itself for ever, and that it consequently owns other inferior living beings destined to serve it always; because all bodies are in a state of perpetual flux like rivers, and the parts are continually entering in or passing out.

72. The soul, therefore, changes its body only gradually and by degrees, so that it is never deprived all at once of all its organs. There is frequently a metamorphosis in animals, but never metempsychosis or a transmigration of souls. Neither are there souls wholly separate from bodies, nor bodiless spirits. God alone is without body.

73. This is also why there is never absolute generation or perfect death in the strict sense, consisting in the separation of the soul from the body. What we call generation is development and growth, and what we call death is envelopment and diminution.

74. Philosophers have been much perplexed in accounting for the origin of forms, entelechies, or souls. To-day, however, when it has been learned through careful investigations made in plant, insect and animal life, that the organic bodies of nature are never the product of chaos or putrefaction, but always come from seeds in which there was without doubt some preformation, it has been decided that not only is the organic body already present before conception, but also a soul in this body, in a word, the animal itself; and it has been decided that, by means of conception the animal is merely made ready for a great transformation, so as to become an animal of another sort. We can see cases somewhat similar outside of generation when grubs become flies and caterpillers butterflies.

75. These little animals, some of which by conception become large animals, may be called spermatic. Those among them which remain in their species, that is to say, the greater part, are born, multiply, and are destroyed, like the larger animals. There are only a few chosen ones which come out upon a greater stage.

76. This, however, is only half the truth. I believe, therefore, that if the animal never actually commences by natural means, no more does it by natural means come to an end. Not only is there no generation, but also there is no entire destruction or absolute death. These reasonings, carried on *a posteriori* and drawn from experience, accord perfectly with the principles which I have above deduced *a priori*.

77. Therefore we may say that not only the soul (the mirror of the indestructible universe) is indestructible, but also the animal itself is, although its mechanism is frequently destroyed in parts and although it puts off and takes on organic coatings.

78. These principles have furnished me the means of explaining on natural grounds the union, or rather the conformity between the soul and the organic body. The soul follows its own laws, and the body likewise follows its own laws. They are fitted to each other in virtue of the preestablished harmony between all substances, since they are all representations of one and the same universe.

79. Souls act in accordance with the laws of final causes through their desires, ends and means. Bodies act in accordance with the laws of efficient causes or of motion. The two realms, that of efficient causes and that of final causes, are in harmony, each with the other.

80. Descartes saw that souls cannot at all impart force to bodies, because there is always the same quantity of force in matter. Yet he thought that the soul could change the direction of bodies. This was, however, because at that time the law of nature which affirms also that conservation of the same total direction in the motion of matter was not known. If he had known that law, he would have fallen upon my system of preestablished harmony.

81. According to this system bodies act as if (to suppose the impossible) there were no souls at all, and souls act as if there were no bodies, and yet both body and soul act as if the one were influencing the other.

82. Although I find that essentially the same thing is true of all living things and animals, which we have just said (namely, that animals and souls begin from the very commencement of the world and that they no more come to an end than does the world) nevertheless, rational animals have this peculiarity, that their little spermatic animals, as long as they remain such, have only ordinary or sensuous souls, but those of them which are, so to speak, elected, attain by actual conception to human nature, and their sensuous souls are raised to the rank of reason and to the prerogative of spirits.

83. Among the differences that there are between ordinary souls and spirits, some of which I have already instanced, there is also this, that while souls in general are living mirrors or images of the universe of created things, spirits are also images of the Deity himself or of the author of nature. They are capable of knowing the system of the universe, and of imitating some features of it by means of artificial models, each spirit like a small divinity in its own sphere.

84. Therefore, spirits are able to enter into a sort of social relationship with God, and with respect to them he is not only what an inventor is to his machine (as in his relation to the other created things), but he is also what a prince is to his subjects, and even what a father is to his children.

85. Whence it is easy to conclude that the totality of all spirits must compose the city of God, that is to say, the most perfect state that is possible under the most perfect monarch.

86. This city of God, this truly universal monarchy, is a moral world within the natural world. It is what is noblest and most divine among the works of God. And in it consists in reality the glory of God, because he would have no glory were not his greatness and goodness known and wondered at by spirits. It is also in relation to this divine city that God properly has goodness. His wisdom and his power are shown everywhere.

87. As we established above that there is a perfect harmony between the two natural realms of efficient and final causes, it will be in place here to point out another harmony which appears between the physical realm of nature and the moral realm of grace, that is to say, between God considered as the architect of the mechanism of the world and God considered as the monarch of the divine city of spirits.

88. This harmony brings it about that things progress of themselves toward grace along natural lines, and that this earth, for example, must be destroyed and restored by natural means at those times when the proper government of spirits demands it, for chastisement in the one case and for a reward in the other.

89. We can say also that God, the Architect, satisfies in all respects God the Law-Giver, that therefore sins will bring their own penalty with them through the order of nature, and because of the very structure of things, mechanical though it is. And in the same way the good actions will attain their rewards in mechanical way through their relation to bodies, although

this cannot and ought not always to take place without delay.

90. Finally, under this perfect government, there will be no good action unrewarded and no evil action unpunished; everything must turn out for the well-being of the good; that is to say, of those who are not disaffected in this great state, who, after having done their duty, trust in Providence and who love and imitate, as is meet, the Author of all Good, delighting in the contemplation of his perfections according to the nature of that genuine, pure love which finds pleasure in the happiness of those who are loved. It is for this reason that wise and virtuous persons work in behalf of everything which seems conformable to presumptive or antecedent will of God, and are, nevertheless, content with what God actually brings to pass through his secret, consequent and determining will, recognizing that if we were able to understand sufficiently well the order of the universe, we should find that it surpasses all the desires of the wisest of us, and that it is impossible to render it better than it is, not only for all in general, but also for each one of us in particular, provided that we have the proper attachment for the author of all, not only as the Architect and the efficient cause of our being, but also as our Lord and the Final Cause, who ought to be the whole goal of our will, and who alone can make us happy.

IX
Immanuel Kant

IMMANUEL KANT (1726–1806) was born in East Prussia, where his grandfather had emigrated from Scotland. He became the first of the great modern philosophers to earn his living as a university professor. He mainly taught logic and metaphysics. His salary, however, was paid not by an administration but directly by the students. Like many philosophers before him, he got in trouble with the authorities —for the "distortion of many leading and fundamental doctrines of holy writ and Christianity," in the words of the Prussian king, Frederick William II. The king ordered Kant not to lecture or write further on such topics. Kant dutifully obeyed until the day the king died, at which point Kant promptly resumed his writings and teachings.

Showing why space, time, and causality are not fully objective but, to a great extent, are the products of the human mind, was in Kant's view a philosophical revolution on a par with the Copernican scientific revolution. Indeed, Albert Einstein said that reading Kant had the greatest impact on him of all philosophical works and helped him directly in his development of relativity.

The 19th-century German philosopher Arthur Schopenhauer began his book *The World as Will and Representation* by writing:

> In endless space countless luminous spheres, round each of which some dozen smaller illuminated ones revolve, hot at the core and covered over with a hard cold crust; on this crust a mouldy film has produced living and knowing beings: this is empirical truth, the real, the world. . . . All that empirical science can teach is only the more precise

nature and rule of these events. But at last the philosophy of modern times, especially through Berkeley and Kant, has called to mind that all this in the first instance is only *phenomenon of the brain,* and is encumbered by so many great and different *subjective* conditions that its supposed absolute reality vanishes, and leaves room for an entirely different world-order that lies at the root of that phenomenon, in other words, is related to it as is the thing-in-itself to the mere appearance.

Many philosophers today consider Kant's monumental main work, *The Critique of Pure Reason,* one of the major achievements in philosophy. Antony Flew, for instance, refers to it as "one of the greatest masterpieces of philosophy, although also one of the most unreadable." Kant would not object. He himself called the *Critique* "dry, obscure, contrary to all ordinary ideas, and on top of that prolix." Consequently he wrote the *Prolegomena,* in which he stated: "[The *Critique*], which discusses the pure faculty of reason in its whole compass and bounds, will remain the foundation, to which the *Prolegomena,* as a preliminary exercise, refer; for critique as a science must first be established as complete and perfect before we can think of letting metaphysics appear on the scene or even have the most distant hope of attaining it."

Prolegomena to Any Future Metaphysics

Immanuel Kant

First Part of the Main Transcendental Problem

. . . Whatever is given us as object, must be given us in intuition. All our intuition however takes place by means of the senses only; the understanding intuites nothing, but only reflects. And . . . the senses never and in no manner enable us to know things in themselves, but only their phenomena, which are mere representations of the sensibility, we conclude that 'all bodies, together with the space in which they are, must be considered nothing but mere representations in us, and exist nowhere but in our thoughts.' You will say: Is not this manifest idealism?

Idealism consists in the assertion, that there are none but thinking beings, all other things, which we think are perceived in intuition, being nothing but representations in the thinking beings, to which no object external to them corresponds in fact. Whereas I say, that things as objects of our senses existing outside us are given, but we know nothing of what they may be in themselves, knowing only their phenomena, that is, the representations which they cause in us by affecting our senses. Consequently I grant by all means that there are bodies without us, that is, things which, though quite unknown to us as to what they are in themselves, we yet know by the representations which their influence on our sensibility procures us, and which we call bodies, a term signifying merely the appearance of the thing which is unknown to us, but not therefore less actual. Can this be termed idealism? It is the very contrary.

All this had been generally assumed and granted long before Locke's time, and still more generally ever since—that, without detriment to the actual existence of external things, many of their predicates may be said to belong not to the things in themselves, but to their phenomena, and to have no proper existence outside our representation. Heat, colour, and taste, for instance, are of this kind. But that I should go farther, and rank as mere phenomena, for weighty reasons, the remaining qualities of bodies also, which are called primary, such as extension, place, and in general space, with all which belongs to it (impenetrability or materiality, figure, etc.)—against this proceeding no one can contend with any reason that it is inadmissible. As little as the man who admits colours not to be properties of the object in itself, but only modifications of the sense of seeing, can on that account be named an idealist, so little can my system be named idealistic, merely because I find *that more, nay, that all the properties which constitute the intuition of a body* belong merely to its phenomenon; for the existence of the thing that appears is thereby not destroyed, as in true idealism, but it is only shown, that we cannot possibly know it by the senses as it is in itself.

I should be glad to know what my assertions must be in order to avoid all idealism. I suppose I must say, not only that the representation of space is perfectly conformable to the relation which our sensibility has to objects—for that I have said—but also that it is quite similar to them; an assertion in which I can find as little meaning as if I said that the sensation of red has a similarity to the property of vermilion, which excites this sensation in me.

Hence we may at once obviate an easily foreseen but worthless objection, 'that by admitting the ideality of space and of time the whole sensible world would be turned into mere illusion.' For men had at first spoiled all philosophical insight into the nature of sensuous cognition, by making the sensibility

SOURCE: Immanuel Kant, *Prolegomena to Any Future Metaphysics,* translated by G. J. Mahaffy (London, 1872).

merely a confused mode of representation, according to which we still know things as they are, but without being able to bring everything in this our representation to a clear consciousness; whereas we had proved, that sensibility consists not in this logical distinction of clearness and obscurity, but in the genetical one of the origin of cognition itself. For sensuous cognition represents things not at all as they are, but only the mode in which they affect our senses, and consequently by it phenomena only and not things themselves are given to the understanding for reflection. After this necessary correction, an objection is mooted arising from an unpardonable and almost intentional misconception, as if my system turned all the things of the world of sense into mere illusion.

When an appearance is given us, we are still quite free as to our judgment on the matter. The phenomenon depends upon the senses, but the judgment upon the understanding, and the only question is, whether in the determination of the object there is truth or not. But the difference between truth and dreaming is not ascertained by the nature of the representations, which are referred to objects (for they are the same in both cases), but by their connexion according to those rules, which determine the coherence of the representations in the concept of an object, and by ascertaining whether they can subsist together in experience or not. And it is not the fault of the phenomena if our cognition takes illusion for truth, that is, if the intuition, by which an object is given us, is considered a concept of the thing or if its existence also, which the understanding can only think. The senses represent to us the paths of the planets as now forward, now backward, and herein is neither falsehood nor truth, because as long as we hold this path to be nothing but appearance, we do not judge of the objective nature of their motion. But as a false judgment may easily arise when the understanding does not carefully guard against this subjective mode of representation being considered objective, we say they appear to move backward; it is not the senses however which are charged with the illusion, but the understanding, whose province alone it is to give an objective judgment on the phenomenon.

Thus, even if we did not at all reflect on the origin of our representations, and connect our intuitions of sense (whatever they may contain), in space and in time, according to the rules of the coherence of all cognition in experience, illusion or truth may arise according as we are negligent or careful; it is merely a question of the use of sensuous representations in the understanding, and not of their origin. Again—when I consider all the representations of the senses, together with their form, space and time, to be nothing but phenomena, and space and time to be a mere form of the sensibility, which is not to be met with in objects out of it, and when I make use of these representations in reference to possible experience only—there is nothing therein that can lead to error, nor is there any illusion implied in my holding them mere phenomena; for they can notwithstanding cohere rightly according to rules of truth in experience. Thus all the propositions of geometry hold good of space as well as of all the objects of the senses, consequently of all possible experience, whether I consider space as a mere form of the sensibility, or as something cleaving to the things themselves. It is only in the former case that I can comprehend how it is possible to know these propositions of all the objects of external intuition *a priori;* everything else which regards all possible experience remains just as if I had not seceded from the common opinion.

But if I venture to go beyond all possible experience with my notions of space and time, which I cannot avoid doing if I proclaim them qualities which adhere to things in themselves (for what can prevent my letting them hold good of the same things, however my senses might be changed, and whether they were suited to them or not?), then a grave error resting upon a illusion may arise. For I proclaim to be universally valid what is merely a subjective condition of the intuition of things and sure for all objects of sense, but therefore only valid for all possible experience; since in doing so, I refer this condition to things in themselves, and do not limit it to the conditions of experience.

My theory of the ideality of space and of time, therefore, so far from reducing the whole sensible world to mere illusion, is rather the only means of securing the application of one of the most important cognitions (that which mathematic propounds *a priori*) to actual objects, and of preventing its being regarded mere illusion. For without this observation it would be quite impossible to make out whether the intuitions of space and time, which we borrow from no experience, and which yet lie in our representation *a priori*, are not mere chimeras of our brain, to which no object whatever corresponds, at least adequately, and consequently, whether geometry itself is not a mere illusion, whereas we have been able to show its unquestionable validity with regard to all the objects of the sensible world because they are mere phenomena.

Secondly: These my principles, because they make phenomena of the representations of the senses, are so far from turning the truth of experience into mere illusion, that they are rather the only means of preventing the transcendental illusion, by which metaphysics has hitherto been deceived, and led to the childish endeavour of catching at bubbles, while phenomena, which are mere representations, were taken for things in themselves—an error which gave occasion to the remarkable antinomy of reason that I shall mention by and by, and which is destroyed by the single observation, that phenomenon, as long as it is used in experience, produces truth, but the moment it transgresses the bounds of experience, and consequently becomes transcendent, produces nothing but illusion.

As I therefore leave to things as we obtain them by the senses their actuality, and only limit our sensuous intuition of these things to this, that they represent in no respect, not even in the pure intuitions of space and of time, anything more than mere appearances of those things, but never their constitution in themselves, this is not a thoroughgoing illusion invented for nature by me. My protestation too against all charges of idealism is so valid and clear as even to seem superfluous, were there not incompetent judges, who, while they would have an old name for every deviation from their perverse though common opinion, and never judge of the spirit of philosophic nomenclature, but cling to the letter only, are ready to put their own conceits in the place of well-determined notions, and thereby deform and distort them. For my having given this my theory the name of transcendental idealism, can authorise no one to confound it with the empirical idealism of Descartes. (Indeed his was only an insoluble problem, owing to which he thought every one at liberty to deny the existence if the corporeal world, as it never could be proved satisfactorily.) Nor with the mystical and visionary idealism of Berkeley, against which and other similar chimeras our critique rather contains the proper antidote. For my idealism concerns not the existence of things (the doubting of which however constitutes idealism in the ordinary sense), since it never came into my head to doubt them, but it concerns the sensuous representation of things, to which space and time especially belong. Of these, consequently of all *phenomena* in general, I have only shown, that they are neither things (nor determinations belonging to things in themselves), but mere species of representation. But the word 'transcendental,' which with me means a reference of our cognition not to things, but only to the *cognitive faculty*, was meant to obviate this misconception. Yet rather than give further occasion to it by this word, I now retract it, and desire this idealism of mine to be called critical. But if it be really an objectionable idealism to convert actual things (not phenomena) into mere representations, by what denomination shall we distinguish that idealism which conversely makes things of mere representations? It may, I think, be called *dreaming* idealism, in contradistinction to the former, which may be called *visionary*, both of which are to be obviated by my transcendental, or, better, *critical* idealism.

Second Part of the General Transcendental Problem

. . . [W]e shall here be concerned with experience only, and the universal conditions given *a priori* of its possibility, and we shall thence determine nature as the whole object of all possible experience. I think it will be understood that I here do not mean the rules of the *observation* of a nature that is already given, for these already presuppose experience; that I do not therefore mean how we (by experience) can learn from nature her laws; for these would not then be laws *a priori*, and would yield us no pure science of nature; but [I mean to inquire] how the conditions *a priori* of the possibility of experience are at the same time the sources from which all the universal laws of nature must be derived.

We must then in the first place observe that, though all judgments of experience are empirical—that is, have their ground in the immediate perception of the senses—all empirical judgments are not therefore conversely judgments of experience, but that, besides the empirical, and in general besides what is given to the sensuous intuition, particular concepts must yet be superadded—concepts which have their origin quite *a priori* in the pure understanding, and under which every perception must be first of all subsumed and then by their means changed into experience.

Empirical judgments, so far as they have objective validity, are JUDGMENTS OF EXPERIENCE; but those which are *only subjectively valid*, I name mere JUDGMENTS OF PERCEPTION. The latter require no pure concept of the understanding, but only the logical connexion of perception in a thinking subject. But the former always require, besides the representation of the sensuous intuition, particular *concepts originally begotten in the understanding*, which produce the objective validity of the judgment of experience.

All our judgments are at first mere perceptive judgments; they hold good merely for us (that is, for our subject), and we do not till afterwards give them a new reference (to an object), and desire that they shall always hold good for us and alike for everybody else; for when a judgment agrees with an object, all judgments concerning the same object must likewise agree among themselves, and thus the objective validity of the judgment of experience signifies nothing else than its necessary universality of application. And conversely when we have reason to consider a judgment necessarily universal (which never depends upon perception, but upon the pure concept of the understanding, under which the perception is subsumed), we must consider it

objective also, that is, that it expresses not merely a reference of our perception to a subject, but a quality of the object. For there would be no reason for the judgments of other men necessarily agreeing with mine, if it were not the unity of the object to which they all refer, and with which they accord; hence they must all agree with one another.

Objective validity therefore and necessary universality (for everybody) are equivalent notions, and though we do not know the object in itself, yet when we consider a judgment as universal, and also necessary, we understand it to have objective validity. By this judgment we cognise the object (though it remains unknown as it is in itself) by the universal and necessary connexion of the perceptions given to us. As this is the case with all objects of sense, judgments of experience take their objective validity not from the immediate cognition of the object (which is impossible), but from the condition of universal validity in empirical judgments, which, as already said, never rests upon empirical, or, in short, sensuous conditions, but upon a pure concept of the understanding. The object always remains unknown in itself; but when by the concept of the understanding the connexion of the representations of the object, which are given to our sensibility, is determined as universally valid, it (the object) is determined by this relation, and the judgment is objective.

To illustrate the matter: that the room is warm,[1] sugar sweet, and wormwood bitter— these are merely subjectively valid judgments. I by no means require, that I or every other person shall always find them true as I now

---

[1] I concede at once that these examples do not represent such judgments of perception as ever could become judgments of experience, even though a concept of the understanding were superadded, because they refer merely to feeling, which everybody knows to be merely subjective, and which of course can never be attributed to the object, and consequently never become objective. I only wished at present to give an example of a judgment that is merely subjectively valid, and contains in itself no ground for universal validity, and thereby for a reference to the object. An example of the judgments of perception, which become judgments of experience by superadded concepts of the understanding, will be given in the next note.

do; they only express a reference of two sensations to the same subject, to myself, and that only in my present state of perception; consequently they are not valid of the object; such judgments I have named those of perception. Judgments of experience are of quite a different nature. What experience teaches me under certain circumstances, it must always teach me and everybody, and its validity I do not limit to the subject or to its state at a particular time. Hence I pronounce all such like judgments objectively valid. For instance, when I say the air is elastic, this judgment is as yet a judgment of perception only—I do nothing but refer two of my sensations to one another. But, if I would have it called a judgment of experience, I require this connexion to stand under a condition, which makes it universally valid. I desire therefore that I and everybody else should always conjoin necessarily the same perceptions under the same circumstances.

We must consequently analyse experience in general, in order to see what is contained in this product of the senses and of the understanding, and how the judgment of experience itself is possible. The foundation is conscious intuition, that is, perception which pertains merely to the senses. But in the next place, judging also (which belongs only to the understanding) pertains thereto. But this judging may be twofold—first, in that I merely compare perceptions and conjoin them in a consciousness of my state, or secondly, in that I conjoin them in consciousness generally. The former judgment is merely a judgment of perception, and so far of subjective validity only: it is merely a connexion of perceptions in my mental state, without reference to the object. Hence it is not, as is commonly imagined, enough for experience to compare perceptions and to connect them in consciousness through the judgment; there thus arises no universality and necessity of the judgment, by which alone it can be objectively valid and [become] experience.

Quite another judgment therefore is required before perception can become experience. The given intuition must be subsumed under a concept, which determines the form of judging in general relatively to intuition, connects its empirical consciousness in consciousness generally, and thereby procures universal validity for empirical judgments; a concept of this nature is a pure *a priori* concept of the understanding, which does nothing but determine for an intuition the general way in which it can serve for judging. Suppose the concept of cause to be such, then it determines the intuition which is subsumed under it, *e.g.* that of air, relative to judging in general, so that the concept of air serves with regard to expanding in the relation of the antecedent to the consequent in a hypothetical judgment. The concept of cause then is a pure concept of the understanding, which is totally distinct from all possible perception, and only serves to determine the representation contained under it, relatively to judging in general, and so to make a universally valid judgment possible.

Before, therefore, a judgment of perception can become a judgment of experience, it is requisite that the perception should be subsumed under such a concept of the understanding as we have been describing; for instance, air ranks under the concept of causes, which determines our judgment about it in regard to extending as hypothetical.[2] But this extension is thereby represented not as merely belonging to my perception of the air in my present state or in many of my states or in the state of perception of others, but as belonging to this perception *of necessity*. So this judgment, 'the air is elastic,' becomes universally valid, and a judgment of experience, only by certain judgments preceding it, which subsume the intuition of air under the concept of cause and effect: and they thereby determine the perceptions not merely as regards one another in me, but relatively to the form of judging in general (here the hypothetical), and in

---

[2]As an easier example, we may take the following: 'When the sun shines on the stone, it grows warm.' This judgment, however often I and others may have perceived it, is a mere judgment of perception, and contains no necessity; perceptions are only usually conjoined in this manner. But if I say, 'The sun *warms* the stone,' I add to the perception the understanding-concept of cause, which *necessarily* connects with the concept of sunshine that of heat, and the synthetical judgment becomes of necessity universally valid, consequently objective, and is converted from a perception into experience.

this way they render the empirical judgment universally valid.

If all our synthetical judgments are analysed so far as they are objectively valid, it will be found that they never consist of mere intuitions connected only (as is commonly believed) by comparison in a judgment; but that they would be impossible were not a pure concept of the understanding superadded to the concepts abstracted from intuition, under which concept these latter are subsumed, and in this manner only connected in an objectively valid judgment. Even the judgments of pure mathematics in their simplest axioms are not exempt from this condition. The principle, 'a straight line is the shortest between two points,' presupposes that the line is subsumed under the concept of quantity, which certainly is no mere intuition, but has its seat in the understanding alone, and serves to determine the intuition (of the line) with regard to the judgments which may be made about it, relatively to their quantity, that is, to plurality.[3] For under them it is understood that in a given intuition there is contained a plurality of homogeneous parts.

In order therefore to show the possibility of experience so far as it rests upon pure concepts of the understanding *a priori*, we must first represent what belongs to judging generally, and the various phases of the understanding in it, in a complete table. For the pure understanding-concepts must run parallel to these phases, as such concepts are nothing more than concepts of intuitions in general, so far as these are determined by one or other of these ways of judging, in themselves, that is, necessarily and universally. Hereby also the *a priori* principles of the possibility of all experience, as of an objectively valid empirical cognition, will be precisely determined. For they are

nothing but propositions by which all perception is (under certain universal conditions of intuition) subsumed under those pure concepts of the understanding.

Logical Table of Judgments

1.	2.
As to Quantity	*As to Quality*
Universal	Affirmative
Particular [plurative]	Negative
Singular	Infinite
3.	4.
As to Relation	*As to Modality*
Categorical	Problematical
Hypothetical	Assertorial
Disjunctive	Apodeictical

Transcendental Table of the Pure Concepts of the Understanding

1.	2.
As to Quantity	*As to Quality*
Unity (the Measure)	Reality
Plurality (the Quantity)	Negation
Totality (the Whole)	Limitation
3.	4.
As to Relation	*As to Modality*
Substance	Possibility
Cause	Existence
Community	Necessity

Pure Physiological Table of the Universal Principles of the Science of Nature

1.	2.
Axioms of Intuition	Anticipations of Perception
3.	4.
Analogies of Experience	Postulates of Empirical Thinking Generally

In order to comprise the whole matter in one notion, it is first necessary to remind the

---

[3]I prefer this name for the judgments, which are termed *particular* in logic. For the word particular seems to imply the notion that they are not universal. But when I begin from unity (in singular judgments) and so proceed to universality, I must not imply any reference to universality: I think of plurality merely without universality, not as its exception. This distinction is necessary, if logical distinctions are to afford the basis of the pure concepts of the understanding: in logical use the matter is not worth changing.

reader that we are discussing not the origin of experience, but of that which lies in experience. The former pertains to empirical psychology, and would even then never be adequately explained without the latter, which belongs to the critique of cognition, and particularly of the understanding.

Experience consists of intuitions, which pertain to the sensibility, and of judgments, which are entirely a work of the understanding. But the judgments, which the understanding forms entirely from sensuous intuitions, are far from being judgments of experience. For in the one case the judgment connects only the perceptions as they are given in the sensuous intuition, but in the other the judgments are to express what experience in general, and not what the mere perception, with its subjective validity, contains. The judgment of experience must therefore add to the sensuous intuition and its logical connexion in a judgment (after it has been made universal by comparison) something that determines the synthetical judgment as necessary and therefore as universally valid. This can be nothing else than that concept which represents the intuition as determined in itself with regard to one form of judgment rather than another, which is a concept of that synthetical unity of intuitions which can only be represented by a given logical function of judgments.

The sum of the matter is this: the business of the senses is to intuite—that of the understanding is to think. But thinking means uniting representations in one consciousness. This union is either merely relative to the subject, and is contingent and subjective, or is absolute, and is necessary or objective. The union of representations in one consciousness is judgment. Thinking therefore is the same as judging, or referring representations to judgments in general. Hence judgments are either merely subjective, when representations are referred to a consciousness in one subject only, and united in it, or objective, when they are united in a consciousness generally, that is, necessarily. The logical phases of all judgments are but various modes of uniting representations in consciousness. But if they serve for concepts, they are concepts of their *necessary* union in a consciousness, and so principles of objectively valid judgments. This union in a consciousness is either analytical, by identity, or synthetical, by the combination and addition of various representations one to another. Experience consists in the synthetical connexion of phenomena (perceptions) in consciousness, so far as this connexion is necessary. Hence the pure concepts of the understanding are those under which all perceptions must be subsumed ere they can serve for judgments of experience, in which the synthetical unity of the perceptions is represented as necessary and universally valid.[4]

So far as judgments are merely considered the condition of the union of given representations in a consciousness, they are rules. These rules, so far as they represent the union as necessary, are rules *a priori*, and so far as they cannot be deduced from higher rules, are fundamental principles. But in regard to the possibility of all experience, merely in relation to the form of thinking in it, no conditions of experience-judgments are higher than those which bring the phenomena, according to the various form of their intuition, under pure concepts of the understanding, and render the empirical judgment objectively valid. These concepts are therefore the *a priori* principles of possible experience.

The principles of possible experience are then at the same time universal laws of nature, which can be cognised *a priori*. And thus the problem in our second question, *How is the pure Science of Nature possible?* is solved. For

[4]But how does this proposition, 'that judgments of experience contain necessity in the synthesis of perceptions,' agree with my statement so often before inculcated, that 'experience as cognition *a posteriori* can afford contingent judgments only?' When I say that experience teaches me something, I mean only the perception that lies in it—for example, that heat always follows the shining of the sun on a stone; consequently the proposition of experience is always so far contingent. That this heat necessarily follows the shining of the sun is contained indeed in the judgment of experience (by means of the concept of cause), yet is a fact not learned by experience; for conversely, experience is first of all generated by this addition of the concept of the understanding (of cause) to perception. How perception attains this addition may be seen by referring in the *Critique* itself to the section on the Transcendental faculty of Judgment [vol. i. pp. 144 *sqq.*]

the system which is required for the form of a science is to be met with in perfection here, because, beyond the above-mentioned formal conditions of all judgments in general (viz. of all the general rules of logic), no others are possible, and these constitute a logical system. The concepts grounded thereupon, which contain the *a priori* conditions of all synthetical and necessary judgments, accordingly constitute a transcendental system. Finally the principles, by means of which all phenomena are subsumed under these concepts, constitute a physiological system, that is, a system of nature, which precedes all empirical cognition of nature, makes it even possible, and hence may in strictness be denominated the universal and pure science of nature.

The first[5] of the physiological principles subsumes all phenomena, as intuitions in space and time, under the concept of *quantity*, and is so far a principle of the application of mathematics to experience. By the second that which is empirical, or sensation, which denotes what is real in intuitions, is not indeed directly subsumed under the concept of *quantity*, because sensation is not an intuition that *contains* either space or time, though it places the object related to itself in both. But still there is between reality (sensible representation) and nothing, or the total void of intuition in time, a difference which has a quantity. For between every given degree of light and of darkness, between every degree of heat and of absolute cold, between every degree of weight and of absolute lightness, between every degree of occupied space and of totally void space, diminishing degrees can be conceived, in the same manner as between consciousness and total unconsciousness (psychological obscurity) ever diminishing degrees find their place. Hence there is no perception that can prove an absolute want; for instance, no psychological obscurity that cannot be considered as a [weaker] consciousness, which is only outbalanced by a stronger consciousness. This

occurs in all cases of sensation, and so the understanding can anticipate even sensations, which constitute the peculiar quality of empirical representations (phenomena), by means of this principle: that they all have (consequently that what is real in all phenomena has) a degree. Here is the second application of mathematics to the science of nature.

As to the relation of phenomena, and indeed merely with a view to their existence, the determination is not mathematical, but dynamical, and can never be objectively valid, consequently never fit for experience, if it does not come under *a priori* principles by which the cognition of experience relative to phenomena becomes even possible. Hence phenomena must be subsumed under the concept of substance, which is the foundation of all determination of existence, as a concept of the thing itself; or secondly—so far as a succession is found among phenomena, that is, an event—under the concept of an effect with reference to cause; or lastly—so far as coexistence is to be known objectively, that is, by a judgment of experience—under the concept of community (action and reaction). Thus *a priori* principles form the basis of objectively valid, though empirical judgments, that is, of the possibility of experience so far as it must connect objects as existing in nature. These principles are the proper laws of nature, which may be termed dynamical.

And finally the cognition of the agreement and connexion not only of phenomena among themselves in experience, but of their relation to experience in general, belongs to the judgments of experience. This relation [concerns] either their agreement with the formal conditions, which the understanding cognises, or their coherence with the materials of the senses and of perception, or combines both into one concept. Consequently it contains possibility, actuality, and necessity according to universal laws of nature; and this constitutes the physiological doctrine of method, or the distinction of truth and of hypotheses, and the bounds of the certainty of the latter.

Yet it is not by any means the greatest merit of this third table of principles drawn *from the nature of the understanding itself* after the critical method, that it shows an inherent perfection,

---

[5]Without referring to what the *Critique* itself says on the subject of the principles, the three following paragraphs will not be well understood; they may, however, be of service in giving a general view of the principles, and in fixing the attention on the main points.

which raises it far above every other, that has hitherto though in vain been tried or may yet be tried by analysing *things themselves* dogmatically. Nor is it that the table exhibits all synthetical *a priori* principles completely and on one principle, viz. the faculty of judging in general, which constitutes the essence of experience as regards the understanding, so that we can be certain that there are no more such like principles—a satisfaction which the dogmatical method never can afford.

The ground of proof must be carefully noticed, as it shows the possibility of this cognition *a priori*, and at the same time limits all such principles to a condition, which must never be forgotten, if we desire them not to be misunderstood, and extended in use beyond the original sense which the understanding attaches to them. This limit is, that they contain nothing but the conditions of possible experience in general so far as it is subjected to laws *a priori*. Consequently I do not say, that things *in themselves* possess a quantity, [that] their reality [has] a degree, their existence a connexion of accidents in a substance, etc.; for this nobody can prove, because such a synthetical connexion from mere concepts, without any reference to sensuous intuition on the one side, or connexion of it in a possible experience on the other, is absolutely impossible. The essential limitation of the concepts in these principles then is: That all things stand necessarily *a priori* under the afore-mentioned conditions, *as objects of experience only.*

Hence there follows secondly a specifically peculiar mode of proof of these principles: That they are not referred directly to phenomena and their relation, but to the possibility of experience, of which phenomena constitute the matter only, not the form. Thus they are referred to objectively and universally valid synthetical propositions, in which judgments of experience are distinguished from those of perception. This takes place because phenomena, as mere intuitions, *which occupy a part of space and time*, come under the concept of quantity, which unites their multiplicity *a priori* according to rules synthetically. Again, so far as the perception contains, besides intuition, sensation, between which and nothing, or its total disappearance, a transition by di-

minishing always occurs, what is real in phenomena must have a degree, so far as it does not itself *occupy any part of space or of time.*[6] Still the transition to it from empty time or space is only possible in time; consequently though sensation, as the quality of empirical intuition, can never be cognised *a priori*, by its specific difference from other sensations, yet it can, in a possible experience in general, as a quantity of perception be intensively distinguished from every other similar perception. Hence then the application of mathematics to nature is rendered possible and determined, as regards the sensuous intuition by which nature is given to us.

But the reader must above all pay attention to the mode of proof of the principles which occur under the title of analogies of experience. For these do not regard the generation of intuitions, like the principles of the application of mathematic to the science of nature generally, but regard the connexion of their existence in experience. This can be nothing but the determination of their existence in time according to necessary laws, under which alone the connexion is objectively valid, and consequently becomes experience. The proof therefore does not turn on the synthetical unity in the connexion of *things* in themselves, but of *perceptions*, and of these not in regard to their matter, but to the determination of time and of the relation of their existence in it, according to universal laws. These universal laws, therefore, if the empirical determination in relative time is to be objectively valid (*i.e.* to be experience), contain the necessary determination of existence in time generally

---

[6]Heat and light are in a small space just as large (as to degree) as in a large one; in like manner the internal representations, pain, consciousness in general, whether they last a short or a long time, need not vary as to the degree. Hence the quantity is here in a point and in a moment just as great as in any space or time however great. Degrees are therefore capable of increase, but not in intuition, rather in mere sensation (or the quantity of the degree of an intuition). Hence they can only be estimated quantitatively by the relation of 1 to 0—that is, by their capability of decreasing by infinite intermediate degrees to disappearance, or of increasing from nought through infinite gradations to a determinate sensation in a certain time. *Quantitas qualitatis est gradus.*

(consequently according to a rule of the understanding *a priori*). The reader has probably been long accustomed to consider experience a mere empirical synthesis of perceptions, and hence not to reflect that it goes much farther than these extend, as it gives empirical judgments universal validity, and for that purpose requires a pure unity of the understanding, which precedes *a priori*. In Prolegomena on this subject I can only recommend such readers to pay great attention to this distinction of experience from a mere aggregate of perceptions, and to judge the mode of proof from this point of view.

This is the proper place to remove Hume's difficulty. He justly maintains, that we can by no means see by reason the possibility of causality, that is, of the reference of the existence of one thing to the existence of another, which is necessitated by the former. I add, that we comprehend just as little the concept of subsistence, that is, the necessity that at the foundation of the existence of things there lies a subject which cannot itself be a predicate of any other thing; nay, we cannot even form a notion of the possibility of such a thing (though we can point out examples of its use in experience). The very same incomprehensibility affects the community of things, as we cannot comprehend how from the state of one thing an inference to the state of quite another thing beyond it, and *vice versa,* can be drawn, and how substances which have each their own separate existence should depend upon one another necessarily. But I am very far from holding these concepts to be derived merely from experience, and the necessity represented in them, to be imaginary and a mere illusion produced in us by long habit. On the contrary, I have amply shown, that they and the principles [derived] from them are firmly established *a priori*, or before all experience, and have their undoubted objective value, though only with regard to experience.

I have indeed no notion of such a connexion of things in themselves, that they can either exist as substances, or act as causes, or stand in community with others (as parts of a real whole), and I can just as little conceive such properties in phenomena as such, because those concepts contain nothing that lies

in the phenomena, but what the understanding alone must think. But we have a concept of such a connexion of representations in our understanding, and in judgments generally— a concept that representations appear in one sort of judgments as subject in relation to predicate, in another as reason in relation to consequence, and in a third as parts, which constitute together a total possible cognition. Besides we cognise *a priori* that without considering the representation of an object as determined in some of these respects, we can have no valid cognition of the object, and, if we should occupy ourselves about the object *per se,* there is no possible attribute, by which I could know that it is determined under any of these aspects, that is, under the concept either of substance, or of cause, or (in relation to other substances) of community, for I have no notion of the possibility of such a connexion of existence. But the question is not how things in themselves, but how the empirical cognition of things is determined, as regards the above aspects of judgments in general, that is, how things, as objects of experience, can and shall be subsumed under these concepts of the understanding. And then it is clear, that I completely comprehend not only the possibility, but also the necessity of subsuming all phenomena under these concepts, that is, of using them for principles of the possibility of experience.

Let us make an experiment with Hume's problematical concept (his *crux metaphysicorum*), the concept of cause. In the first place I am given *a priori*, by means of logic, the form of a conditional judgment in general, that is, one given cognition as antecedent and another as consequent. But it is possible, that in perception we may meet with a rule of relation, which runs thus: that a certain phenomenon is constantly followed by another (though not conversely), and this is a case for me to use the hypothetical judgment, and, for instance, to say, if the sun shines long enough upon a body, it grows warm. Here there is indeed as yet no necessity of connexion, or concept of cause. But I proceed and say, that if the [above] proposition, which is merely a subjective connexion of perceptions, is to be a judgment of experience, it must be considered as necessary and universally valid. Such a proposition would be, 'the sun is by its light the cause of heat.' The empirical rule is now considered as a law, and as valid not merely of phenomena, but valid of them for the purposes of a possible experience which requires thoroughly and therefore necessarily valid rules. I therefore easily comprehend the concept of cause, as a concept necessarily belonging to the mere form of experience, and its possibility as a synthetical union of perceptions in consciousness generally; but I do not at all comprehend the possibility of a thing generally as a cause, because the concept of cause denotes a condition not at all belonging to things, but to experience. It is nothing in fact but an objectively valid cognition of phenomena and of their succession, so far as the antecedent can be conjoined with the consequent according to the rule of hypothetical judgments.

Hence to the pure concepts of the understanding, if they quit objects of experience and would refer to things in themselves, (noumena) have no signification whatever. They serve, as it were, only to spell phenomena, that we may be able to read them as experience; the principles which arise from their reference to the sensible world, only serve our understanding for empirical use. Beyond this they are arbitrary combinations, without objective reality, and we can neither cognise their possibility a priori, nor verify their reference to objects or make it intelligible by any example; because examples can only be borrowed from some possible experience, consequently the objects of these concepts can be found nowhere but in a possible experience.

This complete (though to its originator unexpected) solution of Hume's problem preserves therefore to the pure concepts of the understanding their a priori origin, and to the universal laws of nature their validity, as laws of the understanding, yet so that their use is limited to experience, because their possibility depends solely on the reference of the understanding to experience; but not by deriving them from experience, but by deriving it from them, a completely reversed mode of connexion which never occurred to Hume.

This is therefore the result of all our foregoing inquiries: all synthetical principles a priori are nothing more than principles of possible experience, and can never be referred to things in themselves, but to phenomena as objects of experience. And hence pure mathematics as well as pure physics can never be referred to anything more than mere phenomena, and can only represent either that which makes experience generally possible, or else that which, as it is derived from these principles, must always be capable of being represented in some possible experience.

And thus we have at last something definite, upon which to depend in all metaphysical undertakings, which have hitherto attempted everything without distinction boldly enough but always at random. It never struck dogmatical thinkers, that the aim of their exertions should be so proximate. It never struck even those, who, confident in their supposed sound common sense, started with concepts and principles of pure reason (which were legitimate and natural, but destined for mere empirical use) in quest of fields of knowledge to which they neither knew nor could know any determinate bounds, because they had never reflected nor were able to reflect on the nature or even on the possibility of such a pure understanding.

Many a naturalist of pure reason (by which I mean the man who believes he can decide in matters of metaphysics without any science) may pretend, that he long ago by the prophetic spirit of his sound sense, not only suspected, but knew and comprehended, what is here propounded with so much ado, or, if he likes, with prolix and pedantic pomp: 'that with all our reason we can never reach beyond the field of experience.' But when he is questioned about his rational principles individually, he must grant, that there are many of them which he has not taken from experience, and which are therefore independent of it and valid a priori. How then and on what grounds will he restrain both himself and the dogmatist, who makes use of these concepts and principles beyond all possible experience, because they are recognised independent of it? And even he, this adept in sound sense, in spite of all the cheaply acquired wisdom he arrogates to himself, is not so secure from wandering insensibly beyond objects of experience into the field of chimeras. He too is often deeply enough involved in them, though he gives a colour to his groundless pretensions by his popular language, in which he announces everything as mere probability, rational conjecture, or analogy.

Since the oldest days of philosophy inquirers into pure reason have conceived, besides the things of sense, or appearances (phenomena), which make up the sensible world, certain objects of the understanding (noumena), which should constitute an intelligible world. And as appearance and illusion were by those men identified (a thing which we may well excuse in an undeveloped epoch), actuality was only conceded to the noumena.

And we indeed, when, as is reasonable, we consider objects of sense as mere appearances, hereby confess that they are based upon a thing in itself, though we know not this thing as to its internal constitution, but only know its phenomena, viz.: the way in which our senses are affected by this unknown something. The understanding therefore, by assuming phenomena, grants the existence of things in themselves also, and so far we may say, that the representation of such beings as form the basis of phenomena, consequently of mere beings of the understanding, is not only admissible, but unavoidable.

Our critical deduction by no means excludes beings of that sort (noumena), but rather limits the principles of the aesthetic to this, that they shall not extend to all things, as everything would then be turned into mere phenomenon, but that they shall only hold good of objects of possible experience. Hereby then objects of the understanding are granted, but with the inculcation of this rule which admits of no exception: 'that we neither know nor can know anything at all determinate of these pure objects of the understanding, because our pure concepts of the understanding as well as our pure intuitions extend to nothing but objects of possible experience, consequently to mere things of sense, and as soon as we leave this sphere these concepts retain no meaning whatever.'

There is indeed something seductive in our pure concepts of the understanding, which tempts us to a transcendent use; I mean the use which transcends all possible experience. Not only are our concepts of substance, of power, of action, of reality, and others, quite independent of experience, containing no phenomenon of sense, and so apparently applicable to things in themselves (noumena), but, what strengthens this presumption, they contain a necessity of determination in themselves, which experience never attains. The concept of cause implies a rule, according to which one state follows another necessarily; but experience can only show us, that one state of things often, or at most, commonly, follows another, and therefore affords neither strict universality, nor necessity.

Hence the categories seem to have a deeper meaning and import than can be exhausted by their empirical use, and so the understanding insensibly adds for itself to the house of experience a much more extensive wing, which it fills with nothing but creatures of thought, without ever observing that it has transgressed with its otherwise lawful concepts the bounds of their use.

I was obliged therefore to institute two important, and even indispensable, though very dry investigations. In the one (Critique, p. 107) it is shown, that the senses furnish not the pure concepts of the understanding in concreto, but only the schema for their use, and that the object conformable to it occurs only in experience (as the production of the understanding from materials of the sensibility). In the other (Critique, p. 178) it is shown, that, although our pure concepts of the understanding and our principles are independent of experience, and despite of the apparently greater sphere of their use, still nothing whatever can be thought by them beyond the field of experience, because they can do nothing but merely determine the logical form of the judgment relatively to given intuitions. But as there is no intuition at all beyond the field of the sensibility, these pure concepts, as they cannot possibly be exhibited in concreto, are totally without meaning; consequently all these noumena, together with their complex, the intelligible world,[7] are nothing but representation of a problem, of which the object in itself is possible, but the solution, from the nature of our understanding, totally impossible. For our understanding is not a faculty of intuition, but of the connexion of given intuitions in experience. Experience must therefore contain all the objects for our concepts; but beyond it no concepts have any signification, as there is no intuition for their basis.

The imagination may perhaps be forgiven for occasional extravagance, and for not keeping carefully within the limits of experience, since it at least gains life and vigour by such flights, and since it is always easier to moderate its boldness, than to stimulate its languor. But the understanding which ought to *think* can never be forgiven for substituting *extravagance;* for we depend upon it alone for assistance to set bounds, when necessary, to the extravagance of the imagination.

But the understanding begins its vagaries very innocently and modestly. It first separates the elementary cognitions, which inhere in it prior to all experience, but yet must always have their application in experience. It gradually drops these limits, and what is there to prevent it, as it has quite freely derived its principles from itself? And then it proceeds first to newly-imagined powers in nature, then to beings outside nature; in short to a world, for whose construction the materials cannot be wanting, because fertile fiction furnishes them abundantly, and though not confirmed, is never refuted, by experience. This is the reason that young thinkers are so partial to metaphysics of the truly dogmatical kind, and often sacrifice to it their time and their talents, which might be otherwise better employed.

But there is no use in trying to moderate these fruitless endeavours of pure reason by all manner of cautions as to the difficulties of solving questions so occult, by complaints of the limits of our reason, and by degrading our assertions into mere conjectures. For, if their *impossibility* is not distinctly shown, and the *self-knowledge* of reason does not become a true science, in which the field of its right use is distinguished, so to say, with mathematical certainty from that of its worthless and idle use, these fruitless efforts will never be fully abandoned.

How Is Nature Itself Possible?

This question—the highest point that transcendental philosophy can ever reach, and to which, as its boundary and completion, it must proceed—properly contains two questions.

FIRST: How is nature at all possible in the *material* sense, as to intuition, [I mean nature] considered as the complex of phenomena; how are space, time, and that which fills both—the object of sensation, in general possible? The answer is: By means of the constitution of our sensibility, according to which it is specifically affected by objects, which are in themselves unknown to it, and totally distinct from those phenomena. This answer is given in the *Critique* itself in the transcendental aesthetic, and in these *Prolegomena* by the solution of the first general problem.

SECONDLY: How is nature possible in the formal sense, nature as the complex of the rules, under which all phenomena must come, in order to be thought as connected in experience? The answer must be this: It is only possible by means of the constitution of our understanding, according to which all the above representations of the sensibility are necessarily referred to a consciousness, and by which the peculiar way in which we think (that is, by rules), and hence experience also, are possible, but must be clearly distinguished from an insight into the objects in themselves. This answer is given in the *Critique* itself in the transcendental logic, and in these *Prolegomena*, in the course of the solution of the second main problem.

But how this peculiar property of our sensibility itself is possible, or that of our un-

---

[7]Not (as the usual expression is) *intellectual* world. For *cognitions* are *intellectual* through the understanding, and refer to our world of sense also; but *objects,* so far as they can be represented *merely by the understanding,* and to which none of our sensible intuitions can refer, are termed *intelligible.* But as some possible intuition must correspond to every object, we must conceive an understanding that intuites things immediately; but of such we have not the least notion, nor have we of the *things of understanding,* to which it should be applied.

derstanding and of the apperception which is necessarily its basis and that of all thinking—this cannot be further resolved or answered, because we require these [faculties] for all our answers and for all our thinking about objects.

There are many laws of nature, which we can only know by means of experience; but conformity to law in the connexion of phenomena, that is, nature in general, we cannot discover by any experience, because experience itself requires laws, which are *a priori* at the basis of its possibility.

The possibility of experience in general is therefore at the same time the universal law of nature, and the principles of the former (experience) are the very laws of the latter (nature). For we do not know nature but as the complex of the phenomena, that is, of representations in us, and hence can only derive the laws of its connexion from the principles of their connexion in us, that is, from the conditions of their necessary union in consciousness, which union constitutes the possibility of experience.

Even the main proposition expounded throughout this section—that universal laws of nature can be distinctly cognised *a priori*—leads naturally to the proposition: that the highest legislation of nature must lie in ourselves (that is, in our understanding), and that we must not seek the universal laws of nature in nature by means of experience, but conversely must seek nature, as to its universal conformity to law, in the conditions of the possibility of experience, which lie in our sensibility and in our understanding. For how were it otherwise possible to know *a priori* these laws, as they are not rules of analytical cognition, but really synthetical extensions of it? Such a necessary agreement of the principles of possible experience with the laws of the possibility of nature, can only proceed from one of two reasons: either these laws are drawn from nature by means of experience, or conversely nature is derived from the laws of the possibility of experience in general, and is quite the same as the mere universal conformity to law of the latter. The former is self-contradictory, for the universal laws of nature can and must be cognised *a priori* (that is, independent of all experience), and be the

foundation of all empirical use of the understanding; the latter alternative therefore alone remains.[8]

But we must distinguish the empirical laws of nature, which always presuppose particular perceptions, from the pure or universal laws of nature, which, without being based on particular perceptions, contain merely the conditions of their necessary union in experience. In relation to the latter, nature and *possible* experience are quite the same, and as the conformity to law here depends upon the necessary connexion of phenomena in experience (without which we cannot cognise any object whatever in the sensible world), consequently upon the original laws of the understanding, it seems at first strange, but is not the less certain, to says as regards the latter: *The understanding does not draw its laws (a priori) from nature, but prescribes them to it.*

We shall illustrate this apparently daring proposition by an example, which will show, that laws, which we discover in objects of sensuous intuition (especially when these laws are cognised as necessary), are commonly held by us to be such as the understanding has placed in them, though they are similar in all points to the laws of nature, which we ascribe to experience.

If we consider the properties of the circle, by which this figure unites so many arbitrary determinations of space in itself, and therefore in a universal rule, we cannot avoid attributing a nature to this geometrical thing. Two right lines, for example, which intersect one another and the circle, however they may be drawn, are always divided so that the rectangle under the segments of the one is equal to that under the segments of the other. The question now is: Does this law lie in the circle or in the understanding, that is, Does this figure, independently of the understanding, con-

---

[8]Crusius alone thought of a compromise: that a spirit, who can neither err nor deceive, implanted these laws in us originally. But since false principles often intrude themselves, as indeed the very system of this man shows in not a few examples, we are involved in difficulties as to the use of such a principle in the absence of sure criteria to distinguish the genuine origin from the spurious, as we never can know certainly what the spirit of truth or the father of lies may have instilled into us.

tain in itself the ground of the law, or does the understanding, having constructed according to its concepts (according to the equality of the radii) the figure itself, introduce into it this law of the chords cutting one another in geometrical proportion? When we follow the proofs of this law, we soon perceive, that it can only be derived from the condition on which the understanding founds the construction of this figure, and which is that of the equality of the radii. But, if we enlarge this concept, to pursue further the unity of various properties of geometrical figures under common laws, and consider the circle as a conic section, which of course is subject to the same fundamental conditions of construction as other conic sections, we shall find, that all the chords, which intersect within the ellipse, parabola, and hyperbola, always intersect so that the rectangles under their segments are not indeed equal, but always bear a constant ratio to one another [the directions of the chords being fixed]. If we proceed still farther, to the fundamental laws of physical astronomy, we find a physical law of reciprocal attraction diffused over all material nature, the rule of which attraction is: 'that it decreases inversely as the square of the distance from each attracting point, that is, as the spherical surfaces, over which this power diffuses itself—increase,' which law seems to be necessarily inherent in the very nature of things, and hence is usually propounded as cognisable *a priori*. Simple as the sources of this law are, merely resting upon the relation of spherical surfaces of different radii, its consequences are so valuable with regard to the variety of their agreement and its regularity, that not only are all possible orbits of the celestial bodies conic sections, but such a relation of these orbits to each other results, that no other law of attraction, than that of the inverse square of the distance, can be imagined as fit for a cosmical system.

Here then is a nature that rests upon laws which the understanding cognises *a priori*, and chiefly from the universal principles of the determination of space. And the question now is: Do the laws of nature lie in space, and does the understanding learn them by merely endeavouring to find out the fruitful meaning that lies in space; or do they inhere in the understanding and in the way in which it determines space according to the conditions of the synthetical unity in which its concepts are all centered? Space is something so uniform and as to all particular properties so indeterminate, that we should certainly not seek a store of laws of nature in it. Whereas that which determines space to the form of a circle or to the figures of a cone and a sphere, is the understanding, so far as it contains the ground of the unity of their constructions. The mere universal form of intuition, called space, must therefore be the substratum of all intuitions determinable to particular objects, and in it of course the condition of the possibility and of the variety of these intuitions lies. But the unity of the objects is entirely determined by the understanding, and on conditions which lie in its own nature; and thus the understanding is the origin of the universal order of nature, in that it comprehends all appearances under its own laws, and thereby first constructs, *a priori*, experience (as to its form), by means of which whatever is to be cognised only by experience, is subjected to its laws necessarily. For we are not now concerned with the nature of things in themselves, which is independent of the conditions both of our sensibility and our understanding, but with nature, as an object of possible experience, and in this case the understanding, whilst it makes experience possible, thereby insists that the sensuous world is either not an object of experience at all, or must be nature.

Appendix to the Pure Science of Nature

Of the System of the Categories

There can be nothing more desirable to a philosopher, than to be able to derive the scattered multiplicity of the concepts or the principles, which had occurred to him in concrete use, from a principle *a priori*, and to unite everything in this way in one cognition. He formerly only believed that those things, which remained after a certain abstraction, and seemed by comparison among one another to constitute a particular kind of cognitions, were completely collected; but this was only an *aggregate*. Now he knows, that just so many, neither more nor less, can constitute the mode of cognition, and perceives the necessity of his division, which is a [mental] comprehension; and now only he has attained a *system*.

To search in common cognition for the concepts, which do not rest upon particular experience, and yet occur in all cognition of experience, in which they as it were constitute the mere form of connexion—to do this presupposes neither greater reflection nor deeper insight, than to detect in a language the rules of the actual use of words generally, and thus to collect elements for a grammar. In fact both researches are very nearly related, even though we are not able to give a reason why each language has just this and no other formal constitution, and still less why an exact number of such formal determinations in general are found in it.

Aristotle collected ten pure elementary concepts under the name of categories.[1] To these, which are also called predicaments, he found himself obliged afterwards to add five post-predicaments,[2] some of which however (*prius, simul,* and *motus*) are contained in the former; but this random collection must rather be considered (and commended) as a hint for future inquirers, than as a regularly developed idea, and hence it has, in the present more advanced state of philosophy, been rejected as quite useless.

After long reflection on the pure elements of human knowledge (those which contain nothing empirical), I at last succeeded in distinguishing with certainty and in separating the pure elementary notions of the sensibility (space and time) from those of the understanding. Thus the 7th, 8th and 9th categories are excluded from the old list. And the others were of no service to me; because there was [in Aristotle's mind] no principle, on

[1] 1. *Substantia.* 2. *Qualitas.* 3. *Quantitas.* 4. *Relatio.* 5. *Actio.* 6. *Passio.* 7. *Quando.* 8. *Ubi.* 9. *Situs.* 10. *Habitus.*
[2] *Oppositum. Prius. Simul. Motus. Habere.*

which the understanding could be fully investigated, and all the functions, whence its pure concepts arise, determined completely and with precision.

But in order to discover such a principle, I looked about for an act of the understanding which comprises all the rest, and is distinguished only by various modifications or phases, in reducing the multiplicity of representation to the unity of thinking in general: I found this act of the understanding to consist in judging. Here then the labours of the logicians were ready at hand, though not yet quite free from defects, and with this help I was enabled to exhibit a complete table of the pure functions of the understanding, which are however undetermined in regard to any object. I finally referred these functions of judging to objects in general, or rather to the condition of determining judgments as objectively valid, and so there arose the pure concepts of the understanding, concerning which I could make certain, that these, and this exact number only, constitute our whole cognition of things from pure understanding. I was justified in calling them by their old name, *categories;* while I reserved for myself the liberty of adding, under the title of *predicables*, a complete list of all the concepts deducible from them, by combinations whether among themselves, or with the pure form of the phenomenon (space or time), or with its matter, so far as it is not yet empirically determined (the object of sensation in general). This should be done as soon as a system of transcendental philosophy, towards which I am at present only contributing by the *Critique of Pure Reason* itself, comes to be constructed.

Now the essential point in this system of categories, which distinguishes it from the old random collection without principle, and for which alone it deserves to be considered as philosophy, consists in this: that by means of it the true signification of the pure concepts of the understanding and the condition of their use could be precisely determined. For here it became obvious that they are themselves nothing but logical functions, and as such do not produce the least concept of an object, but require sensuous intuition as a basis. They therefore only serve to determine empirical judgments, which are otherwise undetermined and indifferent as regards all functions of judging, relatively to these functions, thereby procuring them universal validity, and by means of them making *judgments of experience* in general possible.

Such an insight into the nature of the categories, which limits them at the same time to the mere use of experience, never occurred either to their first author, or to any of his successors; but without this insight (which immediately depends upon their derivation or deduction), they are quite useless and only a miserable list of names, without explanation or rule for their use. Had the ancients ever conceived such a notion, doubtless the whole study of the pure rational knowledge, which under the name of metaphysics has for centuries spoiled many a sound mind, would have reached us in quite another shape, and would have enlightened the human understanding, instead of actually exhausting it in obscure and vain subtilties, and rendering it unfit for true science.

Again: this system of categories makes all treatment of every object of pure reason itself systematic, and affords a direction or clue how and through what points of inquiry every metaphysical consideration must proceed, in order to be complete; for it exhausts all the momenta of the understanding, among which every concept must be classed. In like manner the table of principles found its origin, the completeness of which we can only vouch for by the system of the categories; and even in the division of the concepts, which must go beyond the physiological use of the understanding, it is the very same clue, which, as it must always be carried through the same fixed points determined *a priori* in the human understanding, always forms a closed circle; so that there is no doubt that the object of a pure understanding or of a rational-concept, so far as it is to be estimated philosophically and on *a priori* principles, can in this way be completely cognised. I could not therefore omit to make use of this clue with regard to one of the most abstract ontological divisions, the various distinctions of the *notions of something and of nothing*, and to construct accordingly a regular and necessary table of their divisions.[3]

And this system, like every other true one founded on a universal principle, shows its inestimable value in this, that it excludes all foreign concepts, which might otherwise intrude among the pure concepts of the understanding, and determines the place of every cognition. Those concepts, which under the name of *concepts of reflection* have been likewise arranged in a table, according to the clue of the categories, intrude themselves, without leave or right, among the pure concepts of the understanding in ontology, though these are concepts of connexion, and thereby of the objects themselves, whereas the former are only concepts of the mere comparison of concepts already given, and are hence of quite another nature and use; by my orderly divisior they are saved from this confusion. But the value of the separate table of the categories will be still more obviot when we presently separate the table of the transcendent concepts of reason, which are of quite another nature and origin, and hence must have quite *another* form from the concepts of the understanding. This so

---

[3]Many neat observations may be made on the table of the categories, for instance: (1) that the third arises from the first and the second joined in one concept; (2) that in those of quantity and of quality there is merely a progress from unity to totality or from something to nothing (for this purpose the categories of quality must stand thus: reality, limitation, total negation), without *correlates* or *opposita*, whereas those of relation and of modality carry such with them; (3) that, as in *logic* categorical judgments are the basis of all others, so the category of substance is the basis of all concepts of actual things; (4) that as modality in the judgment is not a particular predicate, so by the modal concepts a determination is not superadded to things, etc. etc. Such observations are of great use. If we besides enumerate all the *predicables*, which we can find pretty completely in any good ontology (for example, Baumgarten's), and arrange them in classes under the categories, in which operation we must not neglect to add as complete a dissection of all these concepts as possible, there will then arise a merely analytical part of metaphysics, which does not contain a single synthetical proposition, which might precede the second (the synthetical), and would by its precision and completeness be not only useful, but, in virtue of its system, be even to some extent elegant.

necessary separation has never yet been made in any system of metaphysics [where on the contrary] these rational Ideas live with the categories without separation, like the children of one family—a confusion not to be avoided in the absence of a definite system of categories.

Third Part of the Main Transcendental Problem

How Are Metaphysics, in General, Possible?

Pure mathematics and pure science of nature had no occasion for such a deduction, as we have made of both, *for their own safety* and certainty; for the former rests upon its own evidence; and the latter (though sprung from pure sources of the understanding) upon experience and its thorough confirmation, which latter testimony physics, cannot altogether refuse and dispense with; because with all its certainty, it can never, as philosophy, rival mathematics. Both sciences therefore stood in need of this inquiry, not for themselves, but for the sake of another science, metaphysics.

Metaphysics has to do not only with concepts of nature, which always find their application in experience, but with pure rational concepts, which never can be given in any possible experience, consequently with concepts whose objective reality (as different from mere chimeras), and with assertions whose truth or falsity, cannot be discovered or confirmed by any experience. This part of metaphysics is precisely what constitutes its essential end, to which the rest is only a means, and thus this science requires a similar deduction *for its own sake.* The third question now proposed relates therefore as it were to the root and essential difference of metaphysics that is, the occupation of reason with itself, and the supposed knowledge of objects arising immediately from this incubation of its own concepts, without requiring, or indeed being

able to reach that knowledge through, experience.[1]

Without resolving this question reason never does itself justice. The empirical use to which reason limits the pure understanding, does not satisfy its proper destination. Every single experience is only a part of the whole sphere of its domain, but *the absolute totality of all possible experience* is itself not experience. Yet it is a necessary problem for reason, the mere representation of which requires concepts quite different from the categories, whose use is only *immanent,* or refers to experience, so far as it can be given. Whereas the concepts of Reason extend to the completeness, that is, the collective unity of all possible experience, and thereby exceed every given experience, and become *transcendent.*

As the understanding stands in need of categories for experience, reason contains in itself the source of ideas, by which I mean necessary notions, whose object *cannot* be given in any experience. The latter are inherent in the nature of reason, as the former are in that of the understanding; and if the categories carry with them an illusion likely to mislead, in the ideas it is inevitable, though it certainly can be kept from misleading us.

As all illusion consists in holding the subjective ground of our judgments to be objective, a self-knowledge of pure reason in its transcendent (exaggerated) use is the sole preservative from the aberrations into which reason falls when it mistakes its destination, and refers that to the object transcendently, which only regards its own subject and its guidance in all immanent use.

The distinction of ideas, that is, of pure concepts of reason, from categories, or pure concepts of the understanding, as cognitions of a quite distinct species, origin and use, is so important a point in founding a science which is to contain the system of all these *a priori*

[1] If we can say, that a science is *actual,* at least in the idea of all men, as soon as it appears that the problems which lead to it are proposed to everybody by the nature of human reason, and that hence many (though faulty) essays in it are always unavoidable, then we are bound to say, that metaphysics is subjectively (and indeed necessarily) actual, and therefore we justly ask, how is it (objectively) possible.

cognitions, that without this distinction metaphysic is absolutely impossible, or is at best a random, bungling attempt to build a castle in the air without a knowledge of the materials or of their fitness for any purpose. Had the *Critique of Pure Reason* done nothing but first point out this distinction, it had thereby contributed more to clear up our notions and to guide our inquiry in the field of metaphysics, than all the vain efforts which have hitherto been made to satisfy the transcendent problems of pure reason, without ever surmising that we were in quite another field than that of the understanding, and hence classing concepts of the understanding and those of reason together, as if they were of the same kind.

All pure cognitions of the understanding have this feature, that their concepts present themselves in experience, and their principles can be confirmed by it; whereas the transcendent cognitions of reason cannot, either as *ideas,* appear in experience, or as *propositions* ever be confirmed or refuted by it. Hence whatever errors may slip in unawares, can only be discovered by pure reason itself—a discovery of much difficulty, because this very reason naturally becomes dialectical by means of its ideas, and this unavoidable illusion cannot be limited by any objective and dogmatical researches into things, but by a subjective investigation of reason itself as a source of ideas.

In the *Critique of Pure Reason* it was always my greatest care to endeavour not only carefully to distinguish the species of cognition, but to derive notions belonging to each one of them from their common source. I did this in order that by knowing whence they originated, I might determine their use with safety, and also have the very novel but incalculable advantage of knowing the completeness of my enumeration, classing, and specification of concepts *a priori,* and therefore according to principles. Without this metaphysics is mere rhapsody, in which no one knows whether he has enough, or whether and where something is still wanting. We can indeed have this advantage only in pure philosophy, but of this philosophy it constitutes the very essence.

As I had found the origin of the categories in the four logical functions of all the judg-ments of the understanding, it was quite natural to seek the origin of the ideas in the three functions of the syllogisms of reason; for as soon as these pure concepts of reason (the transcendental ideas) are given, they could hardly, except they be held innate, be found anywhere else, than in the same act of reason. This, so far as it regards mere form, constitutes the logical element of the syllogisms of reason; but, so far as it represents the judgments of the understanding as determined relatively to the one or to the other form *a priori,* constitutes transcendental concepts of pure reason.

The formal distinction of syllogisms renders their division into categorical, hypothetical, and disjunctive necessary. The concepts of reason founded on them contained therefore, first, the idea of the complete subject (the substantial); secondly, the idea of the complete series of conditions; thirdly, the determination of all concepts in the idea of a complete complex of [all] possible [being].[2] The first idea is psychological, the second cosmological, the third theological, and, as all three give occasion to dialectic, yet each in its own way, the division of the whole dialectic of pure reason into its paralogism, its antinomy, and its ideal, was arranged accordingly. Through this deduction we may feel assured that all the claims of pure reason are completely represented, and that none can be wanting; because the faculty of reason itself, whence they all take their origin, is thereby completely surveyed.

In these general considerations it is also remarkable that the idea of reason is not, like the categories, of any service to the use of our understanding in experience, but with respect

---

[2]In disjunctive judgments we consider all *possibility* as divided in relation to a particular concept. The ontological principle of the thorough determination of a thing in general (viz., one of all possible opposite predicates belongs to everything), which is at the same time the principle of all disjunctive judgments, presupposes the complex of all possibility, in which the possibility of everything in general is considered as determined [reading *bestimmt*]. This may serve as a slight explanation of the above proposition: that the act of reason in disjunctive syllogisms is formally the same as that by which it accomplishes the idea of a complex of all reality, which contains in itself the positive of all contradictory predicates.

to that use is quite dispensable, and even an impediment to the maxims of the rational cognition of nature, though necessary in another aspect still to be determined. Whether the soul is or is not a simple substance, is of no consequence to us in the explanation of its phenomena. For we cannot render the notion of a simple being intelligible by any possible experience sensuously or *in concreto*. The notion is therefore quite void as regards all hoped-for insight into the cause of phenomena, and cannot at all serve as a principle of the explanation of that which internal or external experience supplies. So the cosmological ideas of the beginning of the world or of its eternity *(a parte ante)* cannot be of any greater service to us for the explanation of any event in the world itself. And finally we must, according to a right maxim of the philosophy of nature, refrain from all explanations of the design of nature, drawn from the will of a supreme being; because this is not natural philosophy, but an acknowledgment that we have come to the end of it. The use of these ideas, therefore, is quite distinct from that of those categories by which (and by the principles built upon which) experience itself first becomes possible. But our laborious analytic of the understanding would be superfluous if we had nothing else in view than the mere cognition of nature as it can be given in experience; for reason does its work, both in mathematics and in the science of nature, quite safely and well without any of this subtle deduction; our critique of the understanding therefore combines with the ideas of pure reason for a purpose placed beyond the empirical use of the understanding, which we have already declared to be in this aspect totally impossible, and without any object or meaning. But yet there must be harmony between that which belongs to the nature of reason and to that of the understanding, and the former must contribute to the perfection of the latter, and cannot possibly confuse it.

The solution of this question is as follows: Pure reason does not in its ideas point to particular objects, which lie beyond the field of experience, but only requires completeness of the use of the understanding in the system of experience. But this completeness can be a completeness of principles only, not of intuitions and of objects. In order however to represent the ideas to itself determinately, reason conceives them as the cognition of an object which is as regards these rules completely determined (though the object is only an idea), for the purpose of bringing the cognition of the understanding as near as possible to the completeness which that Idea denotes.

Prefatory Remark to the Dialectic of Pure Reason

We have above shown that the purity of the categories from all admixture of sensuous determinations may mislead reason into extending their use, quite beyond all experience, to things *per se;* though as these categories themselves find no intuition which can give them meaning or sense *in concreto,* they (as mere logical functions) can represent a thing in general, but not give by themselves alone a determinate concept of anything. Such hyperbolical objects are distinguished by the appellation of *noümena,* or pure beings of the understanding (or better, beings of thought), such as, for example, *substance,* but conceived without *permanence* in time, or *cause,* but not *acting in time,* etc. Here predicates, that only serve to make the conformity-to-law of experience possible, are applied to these concepts, and yet they are deprived of all the conditions of intuition, on which alone experience is possible, and so these concepts lose all signification.

There is no danger of the understanding spontaneously making an excursion so very wantonly beyond its own bounds into the field of the mere creatures of thought, without being impelled by foreign laws. But when reason, which cannot be fully satisfied with any empirical use of the rules of the understanding, as being always conditioned, requires a completion of this chain of conditions, then the understanding is forced out of its sphere. And then it partly represents objects of experience in a series so extended as no experience can grasp, partly even (with a view to complete the series) it seeks entirely beyond it *noumena,* to which it can attach that chain, and so, having at last escaped from the conditions of experience, make its attitude as it were final. These are then the transcendental ideas, which, though according to the true but hidden ends of the natural determination of our reason, they may aim not at extravagant concepts, but at unbounded extension of empirical use, yet seduce the understanding by an unavoidable illusion to a *transcendent* use, which, though deceitful, cannot be restrained within the bounds of experience by any resolution, but only by scientific instruction and with much difficulty.

I. The Psychological Idea

It has been long since observed, that in all substances the proper subject, that which remains after all the accidents (as predicates) are abstracted, consequently that which is itself *substantial,* is unknown, and various complaints have been made concerning these limits to our knowledge. But we must take care to observe, that the human understanding is not to be blamed for its inability to know the substance of things, that is, to determine it by itself, but rather for requiring to cognise a mere idea determinately, like a given object. Pure reason requires us to seek for every predicate of a thing its proper subject, and for this subject, which is itself necessarily nothing but a predicate, *its* subject, and so on indefinitely (or as far as we can reach). But hence it follows, that we must not hold anything, at which we can arrive, to be an ultimate subject, and that substance itself never can be thought by our understanding, however deep we may penetrate, even if all nature were unveiled to us. For the specific nature of our understanding consists in thinking everything discursively, that is, representing it by concepts, and so by mere predicates, to which therefore the absolute subject must always be wanting. Hence all the real properties, by which we cognise bodies, are mere accidents, not excepting impenetrability, which we can only represent to ourselves as the effect of a power of which the subject is unknown to us.

Now we appear to have this substance in the consciousness of ourselves (in the thinking subject), and indeed in an immediate intuition; for all the predicates of an internal sense refer to the *ego,* as subject, and I cannot conceive myself as the predicate of any other subject. Hence completeness in the reference of the given concepts as predicates to a subject—not merely an idea, but an object—that is, the *absolute subject* itself, seems to be given in experience. But this expectation is disappointed. For the *ego* is not a concept,[3] but only the indication of the object of the internal sense, so far as we cognise it by no further predicate. Consequently it cannot be in itself a predicate of any other thing; but just as little can it be a determinate concept of an absolute subject, but is, as in all other cases, only the reference of the internal phenomena to their unknown subject. Yet this idea (which serves very well, as a regulative principle, totally to destroy all materialistic explanations of the internal phenomena of the soul) occasions by a very natural misunderstanding a very specious argument, which, from this supposed cognition of the substance of our thinking being, infers its nature, so far as the knowledge of it falls quite without the complex of experience.

But though this thinking self (the soul) should be termed substance, as being the ultimate subject of thinking which cannot be further represented as the predicate of another thing; yet this concept remains quite empty and without results, if permanence—the quality which renders the concept of substances in experience fruitful—cannot be deduced from it.

But permanence can never be proved from the concept of a substance, as a thing *per se,* but for the purposes of experience only. This is sufficiently shown by the first analogy of experience, and whoever will not yield to this proof may try for himself whether he can succeed in proving, from the concept of a subject which does not exist itself as the predicate of another thing, that its existence is thoroughly permanent, and that it cannot either in itself or by any natural cause originate or be annihilated.

[3] Were the representation of the apperception (the *ego*) a concept, by which anything could be thought, it could be used as a predicate of other things or contain predicates in itself. But it is nothing more than the feeling of an existence without the least definite notion and is only the representation of that, to which all thinking stands in relation *(relatione accidentis.)*

These synthetical *a priori* propositions can never be proved in themselves, but only in reference to things as objects of possible experience.

If therefore from the concept of the soul as a substance, we would infer its permanence, this can hold good as regards possible experience only, not as a thing in itself and beyond all possible experience. But life is the subjective condition of all our possible experience, consequently we can only infer the permanence of the soul in life; for the death of man is the end of all experience which concerns the soul as an object of experience, except the contrary be roved, which is the very question in hand. The permanence of the soul can therefore only be proved where everybody grants it, during the life of man. But we cannot [establish it], as we desire to do, after death; and for this general reason, that the concept of substance, so far as it is to be considered necessarily combined with the concept of permanence, can be so combined only according to principles of possible experience, and therefore for the purposes of experience only.[4]

[4]It is indeed very remarkable, how carelessly metaphysicians have always passed over the principle of the permanence of substances without ever attempting a proof of it; doubtless because they found themselves abandoned by all proofs as soon as they began to deal with the concept of substance. Common sense, which felt distinctly that without this presupposition no union of perceptions in experience is possible, supplied the want by a postulate; for from experience itself it never could derive such a principle, partly because substances cannot be so traced in all their alterations and dissolutions, that the matter can always be found undiminished, partly because the principle contains *necessity*, which is always the sign of an *a priori* principle. People then boldly applied this postulate to the concept of soul as a *substance*, and concluded a necessary continuance of the soul after the death of man (especially as the simplicity of this substance, which is inferred from the indivisibility of consciousness, secured it from destruction by dissolution). Had they found the genuine source of this principle—a discovery which requires deeper researches than they were ever inclined to make—they would have seen, that the law of the permanence of substances has place for the purposes of experience only, and hence can hold good of things, so far as they are to be cognised and conjoined with others in experience, but never independently of all possible experience, and consequently cannot hold good of the soul after death.

That something actual without us not only corresponds, but must correspond, to our external perceptions, can likewise be proved not as a connexion of things in themselves, but for the purpose of experience. This means:—that it certainly admits of proof that there is something empirical, *i.e.* [existing] as phenomenon in space without us; for we have nothing to do with other objects than those which belong to possible experience; because objects, which cannot be given us in any experience, are nothing to us. That which is intuited in space, is empirically without me, and space, together with all the phenomena which it contains, belongs to the representations, whose connexion according to laws of experience proves their objective truth, just as the connexion of the phenomena of the internal sense proves the actuality of my soul (as an object of the internal sense). I am therefore conscious by means of external experience of the actuality of bodies, as external phenomena in space, in the same manner as I am, by means of the internal experience, of the existence of my soul in time. For this (soul) I only cognise as an object of the internal sense by phenomena that constitute an internal state, and of which the being *per se,* which forms the basis of these phenomena, is unknown to me. Cartesian idealism therefore does nothing but distinguish external experience from dreaming; and the conformity to law (as a criterion of its truth) of the former, from the irregularity and the false illusion of the latter. In both it presupposes space and time as conditions of the existence of objects, and it only inquires whether the objects of the external senses, which we when awake put in space, are as actually to be found in it, as the object of the internal sense, the soul, is in time; that is, whether experience carries with it sure criteria to distinguish it from imagination. Now this doubt may easily be removed, and we always do remove it in common life by investigating the connexion of phenomena in both [space and time] according to universal laws of experience, and we cannot doubt, when the representation of external things thoroughly agrees therewith, that they constitute truthful experience. Material idealism, in which phenomena are considered as such only according to their connexion in experience, may accordingly be very easily refuted; and it is just as sure an experience, that bodies exist without us (in space), as that I myself exist according to the representation of the internal sense (in time): for the notion *without* us, only signifies existence in space. However as the *ego* in the proposition, *I am*, means not only the object of internal intuition (in time), but the subject of consciousness, just as body means not only external intuition (in space), but the thing *in itself*, which is the basis of this phenomenon; the question, whether bodies (as phenomena of the external sense) exist as bodies *apart from my thoughts*, may without any hesitation be denied in nature. But the question, whether I myself *as a phenomenon of the internal sense* (the soul according to empirical psychology) exist apart from my faculty of representation in time, is an exactly similar inquiry, and must likewise be answered in the negative. And in this manner everything, when it is reduced to its true meaning, is decided and certain. The formal (which I have also called transcendental) actually abolishes the material, or Cartesian, idealism. For if space be nothing but a form of my sensibility, it is as a representation in me just as actual as I myself am, and nothing but the empirical truth of the representations in it remains for consideration. But, if this is not the case, if space and the phenomena in it are something existing out of us, then all the criteria of experience beyond our perception can never prove the actuality of these objects without us.

II. The Cosmological Idea

This product of pure reason in its transcendent use is its most remarkable phenomenon, and the most powerful of all means of rousing philosophy from its dogmatic slumber, and of exciting it to undertake the arduous task of the *Critique of Pure Reason* itself

I term this idea cosmological, because it only takes its objects from the sensible world, and does not use any other than those whose object is given to sense, consequently is so far at home [immanent], not transcendent, and therefore so far not an idea; whereas, to conceive the soul as a simple substance, already

means to conceive such an object (the simple) as cannot be presented to the senses. Yet the cosmological idea extends the connexion of the conditioned with its condition (whether the connexion is mathematical or dynamical) so far, that experience never can keep up with it. It is therefore with regard to this point always an idea, whose object never can be adequately given any experience.

In the first place, the use of a system of categories becomes here so obvious and unmistakable, that even if there were not several other proofs of it, this alone would sufficiently prove it indispensable in the system of pure reason. There are only four such transcendent ideas, as there are so many classes of categories; in each of which, however, they refer only to the absolute completeless of the series of the conditions for a given conditioned. And conformably to these cosmological ideas there are only four kinds of dialectical assertions of pure reason, which, as they are dialectical, thereby prove, that to each of them, on equally specious principles of pure reason, a contradictory assertion stands opposed. As all the metaphysical art of the most subtile distinction cannot prevent this opposition, it compels the philosopher to recur to the first sources of pure reason itself. This antinomy, not arbitrarily invented, but founded in the nature of human reason, and hence unavoidable and never ceasing, contains the following four theses together with their antitheses:

1.

Thesis:

The world has, as to time and space, a beginning (bounds).

Antithesis:

The world is, as to time and space, infinite.

2.

Thesis:

Every thing in the world consists of *simple* [parts].

Antithesis:

There is nothing simple, but every thing is *composite*.

3.

Thesis:

There are in the world causes through *freedom*.

Antithesis:

There is no liberty, but all is *nature*.

4.

Thesis:

In the series of the world-causes there is some *necessary being.*

Antithesis:

There is nothing in the world, but in this series *all is contingent.*

Here we have the most singular phenomenon of human reason, no other instance of which can be shown in any other use. If we, as is commonly done, represent to ourselves the phenomena of the sensible world as things in themselves,—if we assume the principles of their combination as principles universally valid of things in themselves and not merely of experience (as is usually, nay without our critique, unavoidably done),—there arises an unexpected conflict, which never can be removed in the common dogmatical way; because the thesis, as well as the antithesis, can be shown by equally clear, evident, and irresistable proofs—for I pledg myself as to the correctness of all these proofs—and reason therefore perceives that it is divided with itself, a state at which the sceptic rejoices, but which must cause the critical philosopher reflection and uneasiness.

We may make divers blunders in metaphysics without any fear of being detected in falsehood. For we never can be refuted by experience if we but avoid self-contradiction, which in synthetical, though purely invented propositions, may be done whenever the concepts, which we connect, are mere ideas, that cannot be given (as to their whole content) in experience. For how can we make out by experience, whether the world is from eternity or had a beginning, whether matter is infinitely divisible or consists of simple parts? Such concepts cannot be given in any experience, however great, and consequently the falsehood either of the positive or the negative proposition cannot be discovered by this test.

The only possible case, in which reason re-

veals unintentionally its secret dialectic, which it falsely announces as dogmatic, is when it grounds an assertion upon a universally admitted principle, and from another equally admitted infers, with the greatest accuracy of inference, the exact contrary. This is actually here the case with regard to four natural ideas of reason, whence four assertions on the one side, and as many counter-assertions on the other arise, each strictly following from universally-acknowledged principles. Thus the dialectical illusion of pure reason appears in the use of these principles, which must otherwise be for ever concealed.

This is therefore a decisive experiment, which must necessarily expose any error lying hidden in the assumptions of reason.[5] Contradictory propositions cannot both be false, except the concept, which is the subject of both, is self-contradictory; for example, the propositions, 'a square circle is round, and a square circle is not round,' are both false. For, as to the former it is false, that the circle is round, because it is quadrangular; and it is likewise false, that it is not round, that is, angular, because it is a circle. For the logical mark of the impossibility of a concept consists in this, that if we presuppose it, two contradictory propositions both become false; consequently, as no middle between them is conceivable, *nothing at all* is thought by that concept.

The first two antinomies, which I call mathematical, because they are concerned with the addition or division of the homogeneous, are founded on such a self-contradictory concept; and hence I explain how it happens, that the thesis in both, as well as the antithesis is false.

When I speak of objects in time and in

[5] I therefore request the critical reader to make this antinomy his chief study, because nature itself seems to have established it with a view to stagger reason in its daring pretensions, and to force it to self-examination. For every proof, which I have given, as well of the thesis as of the antithesis, I undertake to be responsible, and thereby to show the certainty of the inevitable antinomy of reason. As soon as the reader is brought by this curious phenomenon to recur to the proof of the presumption upon which it rests, he will feel himself constrained to investigate the first foundation of all the cognition of pure reason with me more thoroughly.

space, it is not of things in themselves, of which I know nothing, but of things as phenomena, that is, of experience, as the particular way of cognising objects which is vouchsafed to man. Accordingly I must not say of what I think in time or in space, that in itself, and beyond these my thoughts, it exists in space and in time; for in that case I should contradict myself; because space and time, together with the phenomena in them, are nothing existing in themselves and without my representations, but are themselves only modes of representation, and it is palpably contradictory to say, that a mere mode of representation exists without our representation. Objects of the senses therefore exist only in experience; whereas to give them a self-subsisting existence apart from experience or before it, is merely to represent to ourselves, that experience actually exists apart from experience or before it.

Now if I inquire after the quantity of the world, as to space and time, it is equally impossible, as regards all my notions, to declare it infinite, or to declare it finite. For neither assertion can be contained in experience, because experience either of an *infinite* space, or of an infinite time elapsed, or again, of the *bounding* of the world by a void space or an antecedent void time, is impossible; these are only ideas. This quantity of the world, which is determined in either way, should therefore exist in the world *per se* apart from all experience. But this contradicts the notion of a world of sense, which is merely a complex of the phenomena whose existence and connexion occur only in our representations, that is, in experience, since this latter is not a thing *per se*, but is itself a mere mode of representation. Hence it follows, that as the concept of an absolutely existing world of sense is self-contradictory, the solution of the problem concerning its quantity, whether attempted affirmatively or negatively, is always false.

The same holds good of the second antinomy, which relates to the division of phenomena. For these are mere representations, and the parts exist merely in their representation, consequently in the division, or in a possible experience where they are given, and the division reaches only as far as this latter

reaches. To assume that a phenomenon, *e.g.* that of body, contains in itself before all experience all the parts, which any possible experience can ever reach, is to give a mere phenomenon, which can exist only in experience, withal an existence previous to experience; or to say, that mere representations exist before they occur in our faculty of representation, which assertion is self-contradictory, as also every solution of our misunderstood problem, whether we maintain, that bodies in themselves consist of an infinite number of parts, or of a finite number of simple parts.

In the first (the mathematical) class of antinomies the falsehood of the assumption consists in representing that what is self-contradictory (a phenomenon as a thing *per se*) can be united in one concept. But, as to the second (the dynamical) class of antinomies, the falsehood of the representation consists in representing as contradictory what can be united; so that, as in the former case, the opposed assertions are both false, in this case, on the other hand, where they are opposed to one another by mere misunderstanding, they may both be true.

For mathematical connexion necessarily presupposes homogeneity of what is connected (in the concept of quantity), but this is by no means requisite in the dynamical. When the quantum of what is extended is in question, all the parts must be homogeneous with one another and with the whole; whereas, in the connexion of cause and effect, homogeneity may indeed likewise be found, but is not necessary; for the concept of causality (by means of which something is posited through something else quite distinct from it), at all events, does not require it.

If the objects of the sensuous world are taken for things in themselves, and the above laws of nature for the laws of things in themselves, the contradiction would be unavoidable. So also, if the subject of freedom is, like other objects, represented as mere phenomenon, the contradiction is just as unavoidable, for the same predicate is at once affirmed and denied of the same kind of object in the same sense. But if natural necessity is referred merely to phenomena, and freedom merely to things in themselves, no contradiction arises, if we at once assume, or admit both kinds of causality, however difficult or impossible it may be to make the latter kind conceivable.

In the phenomenon every effect is an event, or something that happens in time; it must, according to the universal law of nature, be preceded by a determination of the causality (or state) of its cause, which follows according to a constant law. But this determination of the cause to [produce] causality must likewise be something that happens, or *takes place;* the cause must have *begun to act,* otherwise no succession between it and the effect could be conceived. Otherwise the effect, as well as the causality of the cause, would have always existed. Therefore *the determination* of the cause to act must also have originated among phenomena, and must consequently, as well as its effect, be an event, which must again have its cause, and so on; hence natural necessity must be the condition, on which effective causes are determined. Whereas if freedom is to be a property of certain causes of phenomena, it must, as regards these, which are events, be a faculty of beginning them *from itself (sponte),* that is, without the causality of the cause itself beginning, and hence without requiring any other ground to determine its beginning. But then the *cause,* as to its causality, must not rank under time-determinations of its state, that is, *not be a phenomenon,* and must be considered a thing *per se,* and its *effects* only as phenomena.[6]

[6]The idea of freedom occurs only in the relation of the *intellectual,* as cause, to the *phenomenon,* as effect. Hence we cannot attribute freedom to matter in regard to the incessant action by which it fills its space, though this action takes place from an internal principle. We can likewise find no notion of freedom suitable to pure rational beings, for instance, to God, so far as his action is immanent. For his action, though independent of external determining causes, is determined in his eternal reason, that is, in the divine *nature.* It is only, if *something is to begin* by an action, and so the effect occurs in the sequence of time, or in the world of sense (*e.g.* the beginning of the world), that we can put the question, whether the causality of the cause must likewise itself begin, or whether the cause can originate an effect without its causality itself beginning. In the former case the concept of this causality is a concept of natural necessity, in the latter, that of freedom. From this the reader will see, that, as I explained freedom to be the faculty of beginning an event spontaneously, I have exactly hit the notion which is the problem of metaphysics.

If we can think such an influence of the things of understanding on phenomena without contradiction, then natural necessity will attach to all connexion of cause and effect in the sensuous world, but, on the other hand, freedom can be granted to such cause, as is itself not a phenomenon (though the basis of appearance). Nature therefore and freedom can without contradiction be attributed to the very same thing, but in different relations—on one side as a phenomenon, on the other as a thing *per se.*

We have in us a faculty, which not only stands in connexion with its subjective determining grounds, that are the natural causes of its actions, and is so far the faculty of a being that itself belongs to phenomena: but is [also a faculty] referred to objective grounds, that are only ideas, so far as they can determine this faculty, a connexion which is expressed by the word *ought.* This faculty is called *reason,* and, so far as we consider a being (man) entirely according to this objectively determinable reason, he cannot be considered as a being of sense, but this property is that of a thing *per se,* of which we cannot comprehend the possibility—I mean how the *ought* (which however has never yet taken place) should determine its activity, and can become the cause of actions, whose effect is a phenomenon in the sensible world. Yet the causality of reason would be freedom with regard to the effects in the sensuous world, so far as we can consider *objective grounds,* which are themselves ideas, as determining in regard to it. For its action in that case would not depend upon subjective conditions, consequently not upon those of time, and of course not upon the law of nature, which serves to determine them, because grounds of reason give to actions the rule universally, according to principles, without the influence of the circumstances of either time or place.

What I adduce here is merely meant as an example to make the thing intelligible, and does not necessarily belong to our problem, which must be decided from mere concepts, independently of the properties which we meet in the actual world.

Not I may say without contradiction: that all the actions of rational beings, so far as they are phenomena (occuring in any experience), are subject to the necessity of nature; but the same actions, as regards merely the rational subject and its faculty of acting according to mere reason, are free. For what is required for the necessity of nature? Nothing farther than the determinability of every event in the world of sense according to constant laws, that is, a reference to cause in the phenomenon; in this process the thing in itself at its basis and its causality remain unknown. But I say, that *the law of nature remains*, whether the rational being is the cause of the effects in the sensuous world from reason, that is, through freedom, or whether it does not determine them on grounds of reason. For, if the former is the case, the action is performed according to maxims, the effect of which as phenomenon is always conformable to constant laws; if the latter is the case, and the action not performed on principles of reason, it is subjected to the empirical laws of the sensibility, and in both cases the effects are connected according to constant laws; more than this we do not require or know concerning natural necessity. But in the former case reason is the cause of these laws of nature, and therefore free; in the latter the effects follow according to mere natural laws of sensibility, because reason does not influence it; but reason itself is not determined on that account by the sensibility, and is therefore free in this case too. Freedom is therefore no hindrance to natural law in phenomena, neither does this law interfere with the freedom of the practical use of reason, which is connected with things in themselves, as determining grounds.

And thus we rescue practical freedom, or that in which reason has causality according to objectively determining grounds, and do not curtail natural necessity in the least with regard to the very same effects, as phenomena. The same remarks may be serviceable for the illustration of what we had to say concerning transcendental freedom and its union with natural necessity (in the same subject, but not taken in the same reference). For, as to this, every beginning of the action of a being from objective causes regarded as determining grounds, is always a *first beginning*, though the same action is in the series of phenomena only

a *subaltern beginning*, which must be preceded by a state of the cause, which determines it, and is itself determined in the same manner by another immediately preceding. Thus we are able, in rational beings, or in beings generally, so far as their causality is determined in them as things *per se*, to imagine a faculty of beginning from itself a series of states, without falling into contradiction with the laws of nature. For the relation of the action to objective grounds of reason is not a time-relation; in this case that which determines the causality does not precede in time the action, because such determining grounds represent not a reference to objects of sense, *e.g.* to causes in the phenomenon, but [they represent] determining causes, as things *per se*, which do not rank under conditions of time. And in this way the action, with regard to the causality of reason, can be considered as a first beginning in respect to the series of phenomena, and yet also as a merely subordinate beginning. We may therefore consider it (without contradiction) in the former aspect as free, but in the latter (as it is merely phenomenon) as subject to natural necessity.

As to the *fourth* antinomy, it is solved in the same way as the conflict of reason with itself in the third. For, provided the *cause in the phenomenon* is distinguished from the *cause of the phenomena* (so far as it can be thought as *a thing per se*), both propositions are perfectly reconcilable: the one, that there is nowhere in the sensuous world a cause (according to similar laws of causality), whose existence is absolutely necessary; the other, that this world is nevertheless connected with a necessary being as its cause (but of another kind and according to another law). The incompatibility of these propositions entirely rests upon the mistake of extending what is valid merely of phenomena to things in themselves, and in general confusing both in one concept.

This is the arrangement and this is the solution of the whole antinomy, in which reason finds itself involved in the application of its principles to the sensible world, the former of which alone (the mere arrangement) would be of considerable use in promoting the knowledge of human reason, even though the solution failed to fully satisfy the reader, who has here to combat a natural illusion, which has been but recently exposed to him, and which he had hitherto always regarded as true. For one result at least is unavoidable. As it is quite impossible to prevent this conflict of reason with itself—so long as the objects of the sensible world are taken for things in themselves, and not for mere phenomena, which they are in fact—the reader is thereby compelled to examine over again the deducton of all or *a priori* cognition and the proof which I have given of my deduction in order to come to a decision on the question. This is all I require at present; for when in this occupation he shall have thought himself far enough into the nature of pure reason, the only notions by which the solution of the conflict of reason is possible, will become sufficiently familiar to him. Without this preparation I cannot expect a hasty assent even from the most attentive reader.

III. *The Theological Idea*

The third transcendental idea, which affords matter for the most important, but, if pursued only speculatively, transcendent and thereby dialectical use of reason, is the ideal of pure reason. Reason in this case does not, as with the psychological and the cosmological ideas, begin from experience, and err by exaggerating its grounds, in striving to attain, if possible, the absolute completeness of their series. It rather breaks totally with experience, and from mere concepts of what constitutes the absolute completeness of a thing in general, consequently by means of the idea of a most perfect primal being, it proceeds to determine the possibility and therefore the actuality of all other things. And so the mere presupposition of a being, who is conceived not in the series of experience, yet for the purposes of experience—for the sake of comprehending its connexion, order, and unity—that is, the *idea,* is more easily distinguished from the concept of the understanding here, than in the former cases. Hence we can easily expose the dialectical illusion which arises from our making the subjective conditions of our thinking objective conditions of things themselves, and a necessary hypothesis for the satisfaction of

our reason to be a dogma. As the observations of the *Critique* on the pretensions of transcendental theology are intelligible, clear, and decisive, I have nothing more to add on the subject.

The objects, which are given us by experience, are in many respects incomprehensible, and many questions, to which the law of nature leads us, when carried beyond a certain point (though quite conformably to the laws of nature), admit of no answer; as for example the question: why substances attract one another? But if we entirely quit nature, or in pursuing its combinations, exceed all possible experience, and so involve ourselves in mere ideas, we cannot then say that the object is incomprehensible, and that the nature of things proposes to us insoluble problems. For we are not then concerned with nature or in general with given objects, but with concepts, which have their origin merely in our reason, and with mere creatures of thought. As regards these all the problems that arise from our notions of them must be solved, because of course reason can and must give a full account of its own procedure.[7] As the psychological, cosmological, and theological ideas are nothing but pure concepts of reason, which cannot be given in any experience, the questions which reason asks us about them are put to us not by the objects, but by mere maxims of our reason for the sake of its own satisfaction. They must collectively be capable of complete answers, which is done by showing that they are principles which bring our use of the understanding into thorough agreement, completeness, and synthetical unity, and that they

[7]And therefore Platner in his Aphorisms acutely says, 'If reason be a criterion, no concept, which is incomprehensible to human reason, can be possible. Incomprehensibility has place in what is actual only. Here incomprehensibility arises from the insufficiency of the acquired ideas.' It therefore only sounds paradoxical, but is otherwise not strange to say, that in nature there is much incomprehensible (*e.g.* the faculty of generation) but if we mount still higher, and even go beyond nature, everything again becomes comprehensible; for we then quit entirely the objects, which can be given us, and occupy ourselves merely about ideas, in which occupation we can easily comprehend the law that reason prescribes by them to the understanding for its use in experience, because the law is the reason's own production.

so far hold good of experience only, but of experience as a *whole*. But though an absolute whole of experience is impossible, yet the idea of a whole of cognition according to principles must above all things afford our knowledge a particular sort of unity, that of a system, without which it is nothing but patchwork, and cannot be used for the highest end (which can only be the system of all ends)—I do not here mean only the practical, but also the highest end of the speculative use of reason.

The transcendental ideas therefore express the peculiar destination of reason as a principle of systematic unity in the use of the understanding. Yet [we are apt to consider] this unity of the mode of cognition as attached to the object of cognition, if we regard that which is merely *regulative* to be *constitutive*, and if we persuade ourselves, that we can by means of these ideas enlarge our cognition transcendently, or far beyond all possible experience. But [if we do] so—as this unity only serves to render experience within itself as nearly complete as possible, that is, to limit its progress by nothing that cannot belong to experience—it is a mere misunderstanding in our estimate of the proper destination of our reason and of its principles, a dialectic, which both confuses the empirical use of reason, and also sets reason at variance with itself.

Conclusion: On the Determination of the Bounds of Pure Reason

After all the very cogent proofs already adduced, it were absurd for us to hope to know more of any object, than belongs to the possible experience of it, or to lay claim to the least atom of knowledge about anything not assumed to be an object of possible experience, which would determine it according to the constitution it has in itself. For how could we compass this determination, as time, space, and the categories, and still more all the concepts formed by empirical intuition or *perception* in the sensible world, have and can have no other use, than to make experience possible. And if this condition is not imposed on the pure concepts of the understanding, they do not determine any object, and have no meaning whatever.

But it would be on the other hand a still greater absurdity if we conceded no things *per se*, or set up our experience for the only possible mode of knowing things, our intuition in space and in time for the only possible intuition, and our discursive understanding for the archetype of every possible understanding; in fact if we wished to have the principles of the possibility of experience considered universal conditions of things in themselves.

Our principles, which limit the use of reason merely to possible experience, might in this way become *transcendent*, and the limits of our reason be set up as limits of the possibility of things themselves (as Hume's dialogues may illustrate), if a careful critique did not guard the bounds of our reason with respect to its empirical use, and set a limit to its pretensions. Scepticism originally arose from metaphysics and its licentious dialectic. At first it might, merely to favour the empirical use of reason, announce everything that transcends this use as worthless and deceitful; but by and by, when it was perceived that the very same principles that are used in experience, insensibly, and apparently with the same right, led still further than experience extends, then men began to doubt even the propositions of experience. But here there is no danger; for sound sense will doubtless always assert its rights. A certain confusion, however, arose in science which cannot determine how far reason is to be trusted, and why only so far and no further, and this confusion can only be cleared up and all future relapses obviated by a formal determination, on principle, of the boundary of the use of our reason.

We cannot indeed, beyond all possible experience, form a determinate notion of what things in themselves may be. Yet we are not at liberty to abstain entirely from inquiring into them; for experience never satisfies reason fully, but in answering questions, refers us further and further back and leaves us dissatisfied with regard to their complete solution. This any one may gather from the dialectic of pure reason, which therefore has its good subjective grounds. If we can advance, as regards the nature of our soul, as far as a clear consciousness of the subject, and the conviction, that its phenomena cannot be *materialisti-*

cally explained, who can refrain from asking what the soul really is, and, if no concept of experience suffices for the purpose, from accounting for it by a concept of reason (that of a simple immaterial being), though we cannot by any means prove its objective reality? Who can satisfy himself with mere empirical knowledge in all the cosmological questions of the duration and of the quantity of the world, of freedom or of natural necessity, as every answer given on principles of experience begets a fresh question, which likewise requires its answer, and thereby clearly shows the insufficiency of all physical modes of explanation to satisfy reason? Finally, who is there that does not see, in the thorough contingency and dependence of all his thoughts and assumptions on mere principles of experience, the impossibility of stopping there? And who does not feel himself compelled, notwithstanding all interdictions against losing himself in transcendent ideas, to seek tranquillity and contentment beyond all the concepts which he can vindicate by experience, in the concept of a single being? The possibility indeed of this idea in itself, we cannot conceive, but at the same time we cannot refute it, because it relates to a mere being of the understanding, and without it reason must needs remain for ever dissatisfied.

Bounds (in extended beings) always presuppose a space existing outside a certain determinate place, and inclosing it; limits do not require this, but are mere negations, which affect a quantity, so far as it is not absolutely complete. But our reason, as it were, sees a space around it for the cognition of things in themselves, though it never can have determinate notions of them, and is limited to phenomena only.

As long as the cognition of reason is homogeneous, determinate bounds to it are inconceivable. In mathematics and in natural philosophy human reason admits of limits, but not of bounds, viz. that something indeed lies without it, at which it can never arrive, but not that it will at any point find completion in its internal progress. The enlarging of our views in mathematics, and the possibility of new discoveries, are infinite; and the same is the case, with the discovery of new properties of nature, of new powers and laws, by continued experience and its rational combination. But limits cannot be mistaken here, for mathematics refers to *phenomena* only, and what cannot be an object of sensuous intuition, such as the concepts of metaphysics and of morals, lies entirely without its sphere, and it can never lead to them; neither does it require them. It is therefore not a continual progress and an approximation towards these sciences, and there is not, as it were, any point or line of contact. Natural philosophy will never discover to us the internal constitution of things, which is not phenomenon, yet can serve as the ultimate ground of explanation of phenomena; but that science does not require this for its physical explanations. Nay even if such grounds should be offered from other sources (for instance, the influence of immaterial beings), they must be rejected and not used in the progress of its explanations. For these explanations must only be grounded upon that which as an object of sense can belong to experience, and be brought into connexion with our actual perceptions and empirical laws.

But metaphysics leads us towards bounds in the dialectical attempts of pure reason (not undertaken arbitrarily or wantonly, but excited by the nature of reason itself). And the transcendental ideas, as they do not admit of evasion, and are never capable of realisation, serve to point out to us actually not only the bounds of the pure use of reason, but also the way to determine them. Such is the end and the use of this natural predisposition of our reason, which has brought forth metaphysics as its pet, whose generation, like every other in the world, is not to be ascribed to blind chance, but to an original germ, wisely organised for great ends. For metaphysics in its fundamental features, perhaps more than any other science, is placed in us by nature itself, and cannot be considered the production of a voluntary choice or a casual enlargement in the progress of experience from which it is quite distinct.

Reason finds of itself no satisfaction by all its concepts and laws of the understanding, which suffice for empirical use, or within the sensible world, as ever-recurring questions deprive us of all hope of their complete solution.

The transcendental ideas, which have that completion in view, are such problems of reason. But it sees clearly, that the sensuous world cannot contain this completion, neither consequently can all the concepts, which serve merely for understanding the world of sense, such as space and time, and whatever we have adduced under the name of pure concepts of the understanding. The sensuous world is nothing but a chain of phenomena connected according to universal laws; it has therefore no subsistence by itself; it is not the thing in itself, and consequently must point to that which contains the basis of this experience, to beings which cannot be cognised merely as phenomena, but as things *per se.* In the cognition of them alone reason can hope to satisfy its desire of completeness in proceeding from the conditioned to its conditions.

We have indicated the limits of reason with regard to all cognition of mere creatures of thought. Now only—since the transcendental ideas compel us to approach them, and so have led us, as it were, only to the contact of the full space (of experience) with the void (of which we can know nothing, *noumena*)—now only we can determine the bounds of pure reason. For in all bounds there is something positive (*e.g.,* a surface is the boundary of corporeal space, and is therefore itself a space, a line is a space, which is the boundary of the surface, a point the boundary of the line, but yet always a place in space), whereas limits contain mere negations. The limits pointed out in those paragraphs are not enough after we have discovered that beyond them there still lies something (though we can never cognise what it is in itself). For the question now is, What is the attitude of our reason in this connexion of what we know with what we do not, and never shall, know? This is an actual connexion of a known thing with one quite unknown (and which will always remain so), and though what is unknown should not become the least more known—which we cannot even hope—yet the notion of this connexion must be definite, and capable of being rendered distinct. . . .

At the beginning of this observation I made use of the metaphor of a *boundary,* in order to establish the limits of reason in regard to its suitable use. The world of sense contains merely phenomena, which are not things in themselves, which *(noumena)* therefore the understanding must assume. In our reason both are comprised, and the question is, How does reason proceed to bound the understanding as regards both these fields? Experience, which contains all that belongs to the sensuous world, does not bound itself; it only attains from every conditioned to some other equally conditioned object. Its boundary must lie quite without it, and this field is that of the pure beings of the understanding. But this field, so far as the *determination* of the nature of these beings is concerned, is an empty space for us, and if dogmatically-determined concepts alone are in question, we cannot pass out of the field of possible experience. But as a boundary itself is something positive, which belongs as well to that which lies within, as to the space that lies without the given complex, it is still an actual positive cognition, which reason only acquires by enlarging itself to this boundary, yet without attempting to pass it; because it there finds itself in presence of an empty space, in which it can conceive forms of things, but not things themselves. But the *bounding* of the field of the understanding by something, which is otherwise unknown to it, is still a cognition which remains to reason even at this standpoint, and by which it is neither shut up within the sensible, nor does it stray without it, but confines itself, as befits the knowledge of a boundary, to the relation between that which lies without it, and that which is contained within it.

Natural theology is a concept of that sort at the boundary of human reason, because we are obliged to look beyond this boundary to the idea of supreme being (and, in morals to that of an intelligible world also). [We do this] not in order to determine anything relatively to this mere being of the understanding, and consequently beyond the world of sense, but in order to guide the use of reason within it according to principles of the greatest possible (theoretical as well as practical) unity. For this purpose we make use of the reference of the world of sense to a self-sufficient reason, as the cause of all its connexions. But not in order merely to invent a being for ourselves, but, as beyond the sensible world there must be some-thing thought only by the pure understand-ing, to *determine* that something in this particu-lar way, though only of course according to analogy.

And thus there remains our original propo-sition, which is the result of the whole *Critique:* 'that reason by all its *a priori* principles never teaches us anything more than objects of possi-ble experience, and even of these nothing more than can be cognised in experience.' But this limitation does not prevent the reason leading us to the objective *boundary* of experi-ence, viz. to the *reference* to something which is not itself an object of experience, but is the ground of all experience. Reason does not however teach us anything concerning the thing in itself: it only instructs us as regards its own complete and noblest use in the field of possible experience. But this is all that can be reasonably desired in the present case, and with which we have cause to be satisfied.

Thus we have fully exhibited metaphysics as it is actually given in the *natural predisposition* of human reason, and in that which constitutes the essential end of its pursuit, according to its subjective possibility. Yet we have found, that this *merely natural* use of such a predisposition of our reason, if no discipline arising only from a scientific critique bridles and sets limits to it, involves us in transcendent, either apparently or really conflicting, *dialectical* syl-logisms. We here also found this fallacious metaphysics not only unnecessary as regards the promotion of our knowledge of nature, but even disadvantageous to it. There still therefore remains a problem worthy of solu-tion, to find out the *natural ends* intended by this disposition to transcendent concepts in our reason, because everything that lies in na-ture must be originally intended for some use-ful purpose.

Such an inquiry is here out of place; and I acknowledge, that what I can say about it is conjecture only, like every speculation about the first ends of nature. It may be allowed me in this case only, as the question does not con-cern the objective validity of metaphysical judgments, but our natural predisposition to them, and therefore belongs to anthropology, outside the system of metaphysics.

When I [consider] all the transcendental ideas, the complex of which constitutes the peculiar problem of natural pure reason, and compels it to quit the mere contemplation of nature, to transcend all possible experience, and in this endeavour to produce the thing (be it knowledge or nonsense) called metaphysics, I think I perceive that the aim of this natural tendency is, to free our notions from the fet-ters of experience and from the limits of the mere contemplation of nature so far as at least to open to us a field, which contains mere objects for the pure understanding, which no sensibility can reach. [We do this] not indeed with the view of speculatively occupying our-selves with them (because we can find no ground to stand on), but, in order that prac-tical principles [may be secured], which, with-out finding some such scope for their neces-sary expectation and hope, could not expand to the universality, which reason unavoidably requires from the moral point of view.

So I find that the *psychological idea* (however little it may reveal to me the nature of the human soul, which is pure and raised above all concepts of experience), yet shows the in-sufficiency of these concepts plainly enough, and thereby deters me from materialism, as a notion unfit for any explanation of nature, and besides confining reason [unduly] in the practical direction. The *cosmological ideas,* by the obvious insufficiency of all possible cogni-tion of nature to satisfy reason in its lawful inquiry, serve in the same manner to keep us from naturalism, which asserts nature to be sufficient for itself. Finally, all natural necessi-ty in the sensible world is conditional, as it always presupposes the dependence of things upon others, and unconditional necessity must be sought only in the unity of a cause dis-tinguished from the world of sense. But as the causality of this cause, in its turn, were it mere-ly nature, could never render the existence of the contingent (as its consequent) com-prehensible, reason frees itself by means of the *theological idea* from fatalism (both as a blind natural necessity in the coherence of nature itself, without a first principle, as well as a blind causality of this principle itself), and leads to the concept of a cause possessing free-dom, or of a supreme intelligence. Thus the transcendental ideas serve, if not to instruct us positively, at least to destroy the rash assertions of *materialism,* of *naturalism,* and of *fatalism,* and thus to afford scope for the moral ideas beyond the field of speculation. These considerations, I should think, explain in some measure the natural predisposition of which I spoke.

The practical value, which a merely speculative science may have, lies without the bounds of this science, and can therefore be considered as a *scholion* merely, and like all scholia does not form part of the science itself. This application however surely lies within the bounds of philosophy, especially of philosophy drawn from the pure sources of reason, where its speculative use in metaphysics must necessarily be at unity with its practical use in morals. Hence the unavoidable dialectic of pure reason, considered in metaphysics as a natural tendency, deserves to be explained not as an illusion merely, which is to be removed, but also, if possible, as a *natural provision* as regards its end, though this duty, a work of supererogation, cannot justly be assigned to metaphysics proper.

The solutions of the questions which occupy from page 410 of the *Critique* to page 432, should be considered a second *scholion,* which however has a greater affinity with the content of metaphysics. For there certain rational principles are expounded which determine *a priori* the order of nature or rather of the understanding, which seeks nature's laws through experience. They seem to be constitutive and legislative with regard to experience, though they spring from mere reason, which cannot be considered, like the understanding, as a principle of possible experience. Now does this harmony rest upon the fact, that just as nature does not inhere in phenomena or in their source (the sensibility) *per se,* but only in so far as the latter is in relation to the understanding, so thorough unity in applying the understanding to obtain a collective possible experience (in a system) can only belong to the understanding when in relation to reason? and is experience in this way mediately subordinate to the legislation of reason? The answer may be discussed by those who desire to trace the nature of reason even

beyond its use in metaphysics, into the general principles of systematising a history of nature; I have represented this problem as important, but not attempted its solution, in the book itself.[8]

And thus I conclude the analytical solution of the problem I had proposed: How is metaphysics in general possible? by ascending from the facts, where the use of the science is actually given, at least in its consequences, to the grounds of its possibility. . . .

Appendix A: Deduction of the Pure Concepts of the Understanding

---

Of the A Priori Grounds of the Possibility of Experience

That a concept should be generated completely *a priori,* and have relation to an object, without itself belonging to the [general] notion of possible experience, or being made up of the elements of possible experience—this is perfectly self-contradictory and impossible. For such a concept would have no content, because no intuition would correspond to it; since intuitions in general, by which objects are capable of being given to us, make up the field, or total object, of possible experience. A concept *a priori,* which did not refer to such intuitions, would be only the logical form for a concept, but not the very concept itself, through which something is thought.

If there be then pure concepts *a priori,* these indeed can of course contain nothing empirical; they must, nevertheless, be merely *a priori* conditions of possible experience, as upon this alone can their objective reality rest.

[8]It was my constant design through the *Critique* to neglect nothing, were it ever so dark, that could complete the inquiry into the nature of pure reason. Everybody may afterwards carry his researches as far as he pleases, when he has been merely shown what yet remains to be done, a duty reasonably to be expected from those who have made it their business to survey the whole of this field, in order to consign it to others for future allotment and cultivation. And to this branch both the *scholia* belong, which will hardly recommend themselves by their dryness to amateurs, and hence are added for competent judges only.

If we wish, then, to know how pure concepts of the understanding are possible, we must inquire what are the *a priori* conditions on which the possibility of experience depends, and which form its foundation, when we abstract from all that is empirical in phenomena. A concept which expresses this formal and objective condition of experience universally and adequately might be denominated a pure concept of the understanding. Having once obtained pure concepts of the understanding, I can, if I like, also excogitate objects, perhaps impossible, perhaps possible *per se*, but given in no experience; since I may omit in the connexion of these concepts something which still necessarily belongs to the conditions of possible experience (*e.g.* the notion of a spirit); or else I may extend pure concepts of the understanding further than experience can reach (*e.g.* the notion of the deity). But the *elements* of all *a priori* cognitions, even those of capricious and absurd chimeras, cannot indeed be borrowed from experience (or they would not be *a priori* cognitions), but must in every case contain the pure *a priori* conditions of possible experience, and of an object thereof; otherwise we should not only be thinking nothing by means of such chimeras, but they themselves, having no starting-point, could not even originate in thought.

Now these concepts, which contain *a priori* the pure thinking in each individual experience, we find in the categories; and it will be a sufficient deduction of them, and a justification of their objective validity, if we prove that through them alone can an object be thought. But, as in such a thought there is more than the mere faculty of thinking—that is, the understanding—concerned; and as this faculty, considered as a cognitive faculty, which must relate to objects, will also require some explanation, with regard to the possibility of such relation;—we must, accordingly, first discuss the subjective sources which constitute the *a priori* foundation of the possibility of experience, not according to their empirical, but according to their transcendental, nature.

If each individual representation were quite estranged from the rest, so as to be as it were isolated and separated from them, such a thing as knowledge never could come into existence; for knowledge means a totality of compared and connected representations. If then I add to sense, because it contains multiplicity in its intuition, a synopsis, to this synopsis must correspond in every case a synthesis; and it is only when combined with *spontaneity* that *receptivity* can make cognitions possible. This spontaneity, then, is the foundation of a threefold synthesis, which necessarily occurs in all knowledge: first, the *apprehension* of representations, as modifications of the mind in intuition; secondly, the *reproduction* of them in the imagination; and, thirdly, their *recognition* in the concept. These point to three subjective sources of cognition which render possible the understanding itself, and through it experience also, as an empirical product of the understanding.

The deduction of the categories is involved in such difficulties, and compels us to penetrate so deeply into the original causes and conditions of the possibility of our knowledge in general, that in order to avoid the diffuseness of a complete theory, and at the same time to omit nothing in so necessary an investigation, I have thought it better, in the four following paragraphs, rather to prepare than instruct the reader, and not to lay before him the systematic discussion of these elements of the understanding till the succeeding third section. I hope the reader will not permit the obscurity he at first meets to deter him, as such obscurity is unavoidable on entering upon a wholly untrodden path, but will, I hope, be perfectly removed in the section to which I have referred.

I. Of the Synthesis of Apprehension in Intuition. From whatsoever source our representations arise—whether through the influence of external things, or from internal causes—whether they originate *a priori*, or empirically, they must nevertheless belong as phenomena (being modifications of our minds) to the internal sense; and, as such, all our cognitions must ultimately be subject to the formal condition of our internal sense—time—as being that in which they are all ordered, connected, and brought into relation. This general remark must be above all things kept carefully in view throughout the following discussion.

Every intuition contains in itself a multiplicity, which nevertheless would not be represented as such, if the mind did not distinguish *time* in the sequence of impressions one upon another; for, so far *as it is contained in a single instant,* no representation could ever be anything but an absolute unity. In order, then, to make out of this manifold a unity of intuition (as, for example, in the representation of space), it is in the first instance necessary to run through the multiplicity, and then grasp it together—an action which I call *synthesis of apprehension,* as being directed immediately towards intuition, which indeed presents to us multiplicity, but which without a simultaneous synthesis cannot produce it as such, and also as contained in one representation.

Now this synthesis of apprehension must also be carried out *a priori,* that is to say, in the case of representations which are not empirical. For without it we could not have representations either of space or time *a priori,* as these can only be generated by means of the synthesis of the manifold, which the sensibility offers in its original receptivity. We have then a pure synthesis of apprehension.

2. *Of the Synthesis of Reproduction in the Imagination.* It is indeed only an empirical law, according to which representations which have often accompanied or followed one another at length become associated, and so form a connexion, according to which, even in the absence of the object, one of these representations produces a transition of the mind to another, by a fixed rule. But this law of reproduction presupposes that phenomena themselves are actually subject to such a rule, and that in the multiplicity of their representations there is a concomitance or sequence, according to a fixed rule; for otherwise our empirical imagination would never find anything to do suited to its nature, and would consequently remain hidden within the depths of the mind as a torpid faculty, not even known to ourselves. Supposing vermilion were at one time red, at another black—at one time heavy, at another light; were a man changed first into one, then into another animal—were

our fields covered on the longest day, at one time with corn, at another with ice and snow—then my empirical faculty of imagination would never have had even the opportunity of thinking of the heavy vermilion, when red colour was presented to it; or again, were a certain word applied first to one thing, then to another, or the same thing called by different names, without the control of a fixed law, to which the phenomena are already themselves subject, there could be no empirical synthesis of reproduction.

There must, then, be something which makes even the reproduction of phenomena possible, by being the *a priori* foundation of a necessary synthetical unity among them. But we very soon hit upon it when we reflect that phenomena are not things in themselves, but the mere play of our representations, which are, after all, only determinations of our internal sense. For if we can make it plain that even our purest *a priori* intuitions afford us no knowledge, except so far as they contain a combination of multiplicity only to be produced by a thoroughgoing synthesis of reproduction, then the synthesis of the imagination must also be founded *a priori* on a principle prior to all experience, and we must assume a pure transcendental synthesis of the imagination, which lies at the very foundation of even the possibility of any experience (as that which necessarily presupposes the possibility of reproducing phenomena). Now, it is plain that if I draw a line in thought, or think of the time from today at noon to tomorrow at the same hour, or even wish to represent to myself any definite number, first of all I must necessarily grasp in thought these manifold representations successively. But if I lost out of mind, and could not reproduce the earlier parts (the first part of the line, the prior portions of the time, or the successively represented unities), whilst I proceed to the succeeding ones, there never could arise a complete representation, nor any of the thoughts just named—nay, not even the first and purest fundamental representations of space and time.

The synthesis of apprehension, then, is inseparably connected with that of reproduction. And as the former is the transcendental foundation of the possibility of any cognitions at all (not only of the empirical, but of the pure *a priori* also), the reproductive synthesis of the imaginative faculty is one of the transcendental operations of the mind; and, in reference to these, we shall name this faculty the transcendental imagination.

3. *Of the Synthesis of Recognition in the Concept.* Without the consciousness that what we now think is identical with what we thought a moment ago, all reproductions in the series of representations would be useless. For what we now think would be a new representation at the present moment, not at all belonging to the act by which it should have been gradually produced; and the manifold thereof would never make up a totality, because it must want that unity which consciousness alone can give it. If in counting I were to forget that the units which are now pictured to my senses were added by me gradually to one another, I should not cognise the generation of quantity by the successive addition of unit to unit, nor, consequently, should I know number; for this concept consists essentially in the consciousness of the unity of the synthesis.

The very word concept might of itself lead us to this remark. For it is this *one* (single) consciousness which unites the manifold, gradually intuited, and then also reproduced into *one* representation. This consciousness, too, may often be weak, so that we perceive it only in the result and not in the act; that is to say, we do not join it immediately with the generating of the representation; but notwithstanding these distinctions, we must always have *one* single consciousness, even though it does not stand forth with striking clearness, and without it concepts (and consequently knowledge of objects) are quite impossible.

And here it is necessary to make it clear what we mean by the expression: object of representations. We have said above, that phenomena are nothing but sensuous representations, and these again must be considered in the very same way, viz., not to be objects (beyond the faculty of representation). What do we mean, then, when we speak of an object corresponding to cognition, and yet distinct from it? It is easy to see that this object must be

thought as something in general = *x*, because outside our cognition we surely possess nothing which we could place over against it, as corresponding to it.

But we find that our thought of the relation of cognition to its object carries with it some sort of necessity, since the object is considered to be that which prevents our cognitions from being determined at random or capriciously, but *a priori* in some certain way, because, by being referred to an object, they must also necessarily, in relation to that object, agree among themselves; that is to say, they must have that unity which constitutes the concept of an object.

But—since we are only concerned with the manifold of our representations, and the *x* which corresponds to them (the object), as it must be something different from our representations, can be to us nothing—it is clear that the unity which the object necessarily produces can be nothing else than the formal unity of consciousness in the synthesis of the multiplicity of representations. We say then: 'we cognise the object,' when we have produced in the manifold of intuition synthetical unity. But this unity would be impossible, unless we were able to produce the intuition by means of such a function of synthesis according to rule as renders necessary the reproduction of the manifold *a priori*, and also a concept in which it is united. We think, for example, of a triangle as an object, in that we are conscious of the combination of three right lines according to a rule by which such an intuition can at any time be brought before us. This unity of the rule determines all multiplicity, and limits it to conditions which make the unity of a perception possible; and the concept of this unity is the representation of object = *x*, which I think by means of the aforesaid predicates of a triangle.

All cognition requires a concept, however incomplete or obscure; and this, in its very form, is something universal, and which serves as a rule. So the concept of body according to the unity of the manifold, which is thought by means of it, serves as a rule for our cognition of external phenomena. But it can only become a rule of intuition by representing, along with given phenomena, the necessary reproduction of their multiplicity, and conjointly the synthetical unity in the consciousness thereof. So the concept of body, when we perceive anything without us, makes the representation of extension, and with it that of solidity, figure, etc., necessary.

There is always a transcendental condition at the foundation of any necessity. Hence, we must be able to find a transcendental ground of the unity of consciousness in the synthesis of the manifold in all our intuitions, and in all our concepts of objects generally—consequently, in all objects of experience. Without this it would be impossible to think any object as belonging to our intuitions; for such object is nothing else than that something, of which the concept expresses such a necessity of synthesis.

This original and transcendental condition is no other than transcendental apperception. The consciousness of self, according to the determination of our states in internal perception, is merely empirical—always changeable; there can be no fixed or permanent self in this flux of our internal phenomena; and this sort of consciousness is usually called the *internal sense,* or *empirical apperception.* That which is *necessarily* represented as numerically identical, cannot be thought as such by means of empirical data. There must be a condition, anticipating and rendering possible all experience. This condition only can render valid such a transcendental assumption.

Neither can cognitions take place in us, nor any conjunction or unity among them, without this unity of consciousness, which is prior to all the data of intuition, and by reference to which alone all representation of objects is rendered possible. This pure, original, unchangeable consciousness, I intend to call *transcendental apperception.* That it deserves this name is plain from the fact, that even the purest objective unity, namely, that of *a priori* concepts (space and time), is only possible by the reference of intuitions to such consciousness. The numerical unity, then, of this apperception is just as much the *a priori* basis of all concepts, as the multiplicity of space and time is the basis of the intuitions of sensibility.

But this very transcendental unity of apperception forms a connexion according to

laws of all the possible phenomena so far as they can come together in our experience. For this unity of consciousness would be impossible if the mind, in the cognition of the manifold, were not self-conscious of the identity of the function by means of which it connects this manifold synthetically in a cognition. Consequently, the original and necessary consciousness of the identity of self is at the same time a consciousness of just as necessary a unity of the synthesis of all phenomena according to concepts; that is, according to rules which not only make the phenomena necessarily reproducible, but *ipso facto* also determine an object for (their) intuition, and this object is a concept of something in which they are necessarily connected. For the mind could not possibly think its own identity in the multiplicity of representations, and this too *a priori,* if it had not before its eyes (so to speak) the identity of its own action, which subjects all the empirical synthesis of apprehension to a transcendental unity, and is the necessary condition of the connexion of this apprehension according to rules. We shall now be able to determine more correctly our notion of an *object.* All representations have, as such, their object, and may themselves also become the objects of other representations. Phenomena are the only objects which can be given us immediately, and that which in the phenomenon refers immediately to the object is called intuition. These phenomena are not things *per se,* but themselves only representations, which, again, have *their* object, and this we can no longer intuite; it may therefore be called the non-empirical, or transcendental object = *x.*

The pure concept of the transcendental object (which is really in all our cognitions of the same sort = *x*) is that which can obtain for all our empirical concepts in general reference to an object—that is, objective reality. Now this concept can contain no determinate intuition, and can therefore refer to nothing but that unity which must be found in the multiplicity of a cognition, so far as it stands in relation to an object. But this relation is merely the necessary unity of consciousness, and also of the synthesis of the manifold by a general function of the mind, which connects the manifold into one representation. Since this unity must be regarded as necessary *a priori* (otherwise the cognition would have no object) the relation to a transcendental object—that is, the objective reality of our empirical knowledge—depends on the transcendental law, that all phenomena (so far as objects are to be given us through them) must submit to the *a priori* rules of their synthetical unity, according to which their relation in empirical intuition is alone possible.

In short, phenomena must in experience stand under the conditions of the necessary unity of apperception, just as they must stand in mere intuition under the formal conditions of space and time; so that only through the former does any cognition become even possible.

4. Preliminary Explanation of the Possibility of the Categories as A Priori Cognitions.

There is only *one* experience, in which all perceptions are represented in thoroughgoing and regular connexion; just as there is only *one* space and one time in which all forms of phenomena, and all relations of existence or nonexistence, are found. When we speak of different experiences, they only mean so many perceptions, as far as they belong to one and the same universal experience. The thoroughgoing and synthetical unity of perceptions is exactly what constitutes the form of experience, and experience is nothing but the synthetical unity of phenomena according to concepts. Unity of synthesis according to empirical concepts would be quite contingent; and, were these not based on a transcendental ground of unity, it would be possible for a confused crowd of phenomena to fill our minds, without our ever forming experience from them. But then all reference of cognition to objects must vanish, because the connexion of experience according to universal and necessary laws would be wanting; we should then have thoughtless intuition, never amounting to knowledge, and so for us equivalent to nothing.

The *a priori* conditions of any possible experience are, at the same time, the conditions of the possibility of the objects of experience. Now I assert that the above-mentioned *categories* are nothing but the *conditions of thinking in possible experience*, just as *space and time are the conditions of the intuition* which is requisite for the same. The former, then, are likewise fundamental concepts which enable us to think objects in general for phenomena, and are, accordingly, objectively valid—the very point we wished to ascertain.

But the possibility, nay even the necessity, of these categories depends upon the relation in which the whole sensibility, and with it all possible phenomena, must stand to primitive apperception; in which apperception everything must necessarily accord with the conditions of the thoroughgoing unity of self-consciousness, which means that everything must be subject to universal functions of synthesis—synthesis according to concepts. By this means alone can apperception prove its thoroughgoing and necessary identity. For example, the concept of cause is nothing but a synthesis (of that which follows in the series of time with other phenomena) according to concepts, and without such a unity, which has its rule *a priori* and controls the phenomena, thoroughly universal and necessary unity of consciousness could not occur in the multiplicity of phenomena: in which case these phenomena would belong to no experience, and therefore be without any object, but only a random play of representations, less even than a dream.

All attempts, then, to deduce from experience these pure concepts of the understanding, and to give them a merely empirical origin, are perfectly idle and useless. I waive the point that the concept, for example, of cause carries with it the feature of necessity, which could not be given by any experience, for this indeed teaches us, that something usually follows a certain phenomenon, but never that it must follow necessarily; nor could it teach us that we may conclude *a priori*, and quite universally, from the cause as a condition, to the effect. But this empirical rule of association, which we must of course assume as universally applicable, when we say that everything in the series of events is so strictly obedient to law, that nothing happens without being preceded by something upon which it always follows—this rule I say, as a law of nature, upon what does it depend? How, I ask, is this association even possible? The foundation of the possibility of this association of the manifold, as far as it lies in the object, is called the *affinity* of the manifold. I ask, then, what makes this thoroughgoing affinity of phenomena conceivable to you (by which they stand under, and *must* be subject to permanent laws)?

Upon my principles it is easily understood. All possible phenomena belong, as representations, to the whole of possible self-consciousness. But this being a transcendental representation, its numerical identity is indivisible and certain *a priori,* because we cannot possibly know anything, except through this primitive apperception. Now, as this identity must necessarily be introduced into the synthesis of all the manifold of phenomena, which are ever to become empirical cognition, the phenomena must be subject to *a priori* conditions, to which their synthesis (in apprehension) must thoroughly conform. The representation of a general condition, according to which a certain multiplicity *can* be brought before us (that is to say, a definite way of doing it), is called *rule;* if it *must* be so brought before us, *law.* Consequently all phenomena stand in thorough connexion with one another according to necessary laws, and hence in a *transcendental affinity,* of which the *empirical* is merely the consequence.

That nature must conform to our subjective apperception—nay, even that its order must depend on this relation—probably sounds very absurd and strange. But if we reflect that this nature is nothing in itself but the sum-total of phenomena, consequently nothing *per se,* but merely a number of mental representations, we need not be surprised that we see it subject to the radical faculty of all our *knowledge;* that is to say, subject to transcendental apperception, and hence subject to that unity through which alone it can become the object of any possible experience; or, in other words, become nature. It is for the very same reason that we can cognise this unity *a priori,* and therefore necessarily, which would be impossible were it given *in itself,* independent of the highest sources of our thinking. In this latter case, I know not whence we could draw the synthetical propositions of such a universal unity of nature; for then we must borrow them from the objects of nature themselves.

As this could only be done empirically, nothing could be inferred but a contingent unity, which is very far from being the necessary connexion which we mean by the word nature.

Of the Relation of the Understanding to Objects in General, and of the Possibility of Cognising Them A Priori

The detached observations made in the previous section we shall here unite and present in a connected form. There are three subjective sources of cognition, upon which rest the possibility of experience in general, and the cognition of objects; these are *sense, imagination,* and *apperception.* Each of these can be considered empirically, that is, in its application to given phenomena; but all of them are also [original] elements [of the mind], and *a priori* conditions, which make even this empirical use possible. *Sense* represents phenomena empirically in *perception; imagination,* in *association* (and reproduction); *apperception,* in the *empirical consciousness* of the identity of these reproduced representations with the (original) phenomena, that is to say, in *recognition.* But at the *a priori* basis of the whole of our perceptions lie pure intuitions (or if we regard them as representations—the form of internal intuitions, time). At the basis of association lies the pure synthesis of the imagination; and at the basis of empirical consciousness, pure apperception, that is, the thoroughgoing identity of self in all possible representations. If we wish, then, to analyse the internal causes of this connexion of representations, till we reach the point where all representations must meet (in order to start with unity of cognition, which is the necessary condition of possible experience), we must begin from pure apperception. All intuitions are for us nothing, and do not the least concern us, if they cannot be taken up into consciousness, whether directly or indirectly, and only through this means is cognition at all possible. We are *a priori* conscious of our own complete identity in regard to all representations which can ever belong to our cognition; and this we regard as the necessary condition of the possibility of all representations. (For these only represent anything in me, by belonging, with all the rest, to one consciousness, in which they *can* at any rate be connected.) This principle is established *a priori,* and may be called the *transcendental principle of the unity* of all multiplicity in our representations (even in intuition). Now, the unity of multiplicity in one subject is synthetical. Pure apperception, then, gives us a principle of the synthetical unity of multiplicity in all possible intuition.[1]

But this synthetical unity presupposes or implies a synthesis; and if the former is to be necessary *a priori,* the latter must be an *a priori* synthesis. Consequently, the transcendental unity of apperception points to the pure synthesis of imagination, as an *a priori* condition of the possibility of any combination of the manifold into a single cognition. But it is only the *productive synthesis of the imagination* which can take place *a priori;* for the *reproductive* depends on empirical conditions. Consequently, before apperception, the principle of the necessary unity of the pure (productive) synthesis of the imagination is the foundation of

[1]Let us pay particular attention to this proposition, which is of the greatest importance. All representations have a necessary reference to a possible empirical consciousness; for if they had not this feature, and were it quite impossible to become conscious of them, this would mean that they do not exist. But all empirical consciousness has a necessary reference to a transcendental consciousness (preceding all particular experience), namely, the consciousness of self, as the primitive apperception. It is absolutely necessary that in my cognition all consciousness should belong to one consciousness (of myself). Now this is a synthetical unity of the manifold (of consciousness) which is cognised *a priori,* and which gives just the same basis for synthetical *a priori* propositions which relate to pure thinking, as space and time give to such propositions as relate to the form of mere intuition. The synthetical proposition, that the various empirical consciousnesses must be combined in one single self-consciousness, is absolutely the first and synthetical principle of our thinking in general. But we must never forget, that the bare representation *ego* is the transcendental consciousness in relation to all others (the collective unity of which it renders possible). This representation may then be clear (empirical consciousness) or obscure—a fact which is here of no importance; nay, not even the fact whether it have any actuality or not; but the possibility of the logical form of all knowledge rests necessarily on the relation to this apperception *as a faculty.*

the possibility of any knowledge, especially of experience.

We denominate the synthesis of multiplicity in the imagination transcendental, when, without distinguishing the intuitions, it aims at nothing but the combination of multiplicity *a priori:* and the unity of this synthesis is called transcendental, if, as referring to the original unity of apperception, it is represented as necessary *a priori.* Now, as this latter lies at the foundation of all cognitions, the transcendental unity of the synthesis of the imagination is the pure form of all possible cognition, by means of which all objects of possible experience must be represented *a priori.*

The unity of apperception in relation to the synthesis of the imagination is the *understanding;* and this very unity, in relation to the *transcendental* synthesis of the imagination, is the *pure* understanding. There are, then, in the understanding pure cognitions *a priori* which contain the necessary unity of the pure synthesis of the imagination, in reference to all possible phenomena. But these are the categories, or pure concepts of the understanding. Consequently, the empirical faculty of cognition which belongs to our nature contains an understanding which relates to all objects of the senses, but this only immediately, through intuition and its synthesis by means of the imagination, to which understanding all phenomena must consequently be subject, as data for a possible experience. But, as this relation of phenomena to possible experience is also necessary (because without this they would afford us no cognition, and not concern us at all) it follows, that the pure understanding, by means of the categories, is a formal and synthetical principle of all experiences, and phenomena have a *necessary relation to the understanding.*

We shall now expound the necessary connexion of the understanding with phenomena by means of the categories, by beginning from below—from the empirical extremity. The first thing given us is the phenomenon, which, if combined with consciousness, is called perception. (Without relation at least to a possible consciousness, the phenomenon could never be for us an object of cognition, and would hence be to us as nothing; having no objective reality, and only existing as known, it would be absolutely nothing at all.) But as every phenomenon contains a certain multiplicity—that is to say, as various perceptions are found within us, in themselves scattered and single—a connexion of them is necessary, and this they cannot have in mere sense. There is, then, within us an active faculty of the synthesis of this multiplicity, which we call the faculty of Imagination; and the action of which, when directed immediately upon the perceptions, I call apprehension.[2] The province of the imagination is to unite the manifold of intuition into an *image;* it must first, then, grasp the impressions actively, viz. *apprehend* them.

But it is clear that even this apprehension of the manifold by itself could produce no image, nor connexion of impressions, if there were not present a subjective condition for summoning a perception from which the mind had made a transition to the next, to join this next, and so produce whole series of these perceptions—in fact, if we did not possess a reproductive faculty of the imagination, which even then is only empirical. But representations, if they suggested one another just as they chanced to meet together originally, would have no determinate connexion, but be a mere confused crowd, from which could spring no cognition; their reproduction must therefore have a rule by which a representation enters into combination rather with this than with another representation in the imagination. The subjective and empirical ground of reproduction according to rules, we call the *association* of representations.

But if this unity of association had not also an objective basis, so as to make it impossible for phenomena to be apprehended by the imagination except under the condition of a possible synthetical unity of this apprehension, then it would also be quite contingent that phenomena, when combined, should be adapted to human cognitions. For although we had the faculty of associating perceptions, it would still be quite undetermined in itself, and accidental, whether they were also themselves capable of such association; and supposing they were not, a quantity of perceptions, and even a whole sensibility, would be possible, in which the mind might meet with a great deal of empirical consciousness, but disconnected, and without belonging to one *consciousness of myself,* which is nevertheless impossible. For it is only when I attribute all my perceptions to one consciousness (of pure apperception) that I can say I am conscious of them. There must, then, be an objective ground prior to any of the empirical laws of imagination, and *a priori,* on which depends the possibility—nay, even the necessity—of a law extending over all phenomena; which regards them universally to be such data of the senses as are in themselves associable, and subject to the general rules of a thoroughgoing connexion when reproduced. This objective basis of all association of representations I call *affinity.* We cannot meet it elsewhere than in the principle of the unity of apperception, as regards all cognitions which can belong to me. According to this principle, every phenomenon without exception must so enter the mind, or be apprehended, as to agree with the unity of apperception, which apperception would itself be impossible without synthetical unity in its connexion; this latter is, accordingly, also objectively necessary.

The objective unity of all (empirical) consciousness in one consciousness (of primitive apperception) is then the necessary condition even of all possible perception; and the affinity of all phenomena (proximate or remote) is the necessary consequence of a synthesis in the imagination, which is founded *a priori* upon rules.

The imagination is then also a faculty or *a priori* synthesis, for which reason we give it the name of the productive imagination; and since, as far as it relates to the multiplicity of phenomena, it has no further object than to produce the necessary unity in their synthesis, we may call it the transcendental function of the imagination. It is then sufficiently clear

[2]That the faculty of imagination is a necessary ingredient even in perception, has perhaps not as yet struck any psychologist. This arises partly from confining the faculty to mere reproductions; partly because it was thought that the senses not only gave us impressions, but even combined them, and so brought images of objects before us—a process which, nevertheless, most certainly requires somewhat besides the mere receptivity of impressions, namely, a function of their synthesis.

from what precedes, though it may sound rather strange, that only by means of the transcendental function of the imagination does even the affinity of phenomena, and with it their association, and through this, too, their reproduction in accordance with laws—in fact, does experience—become possible; because without it no concepts of objects would ever coalesce into one experience.

For the fixed and unchanging *ego* (of pure apperception) constitutes the correlatum of all our representations, so far as it is merely possible to become conscious of them; and all consciousness belongs just as much to an all-comprehensive pure apperception as all sensuous intuition (*qua* representation) belongs to a pure internal intuition—namely, that of time. It is, then, this apperception which must be added to the imagination, to render its function intellectual. For in itself the synthesis of imagination, though exercised *a priori*, is yet always sensuous, because it only combines the manifold as it appears in intuition—for example, the figure of a triangle. But it is only through the relation of the manifold to the unity of apperception that concepts can be formed, and this only by means of the imagination in relation to the sensuous intuition.

We have then the pure imagination, as an original faculty of the human soul, lying at the basis of all cognition *a priori*. By means of it we bring on the one side the multiplicity of intuition, and on the other the condition of the necessary unity of apperception, into mutual relation. Both extremities—sensibility and understanding—must be necessarily connected by means of this transcendental function of the imagination; otherwise, there might indeed be appearances, but no objects of empirical cognition, or experience. Actual experience, consisting of apprehension, association (of reproduction), and finally, of the recognition of phenomena, contains in this last and highest (merely empirical element of experience) concepts, which render possible the formal unity of experience, and with it all objective validity (truth) of empirical cognition. These fundamental causes of the recognition of multiplicity, so far as they concern merely

the *form of experience in general,* are the very categories of which we are speaking. On them is founded not only all formal unity of the synthesis of the imagination, but through it the unity even of all that belongs to its empirical use (in recognition, reproduction, association, apprehension) down to phenomena; because it is only by means of these elements of our knowledge that phenomena can belong to our consciousness, and hence to ourselves.

Thus the order and regularity in phenomena, which we call *nature*, we ourselves introduce, and should never find it there, if we, or the nature of our mind, had not originally placed it there. For this unity of nature must be a necessary unity of connexion, that is to say, certain *a priori*. But how could we possibly produce *a priori* a synthetical unity, if subjective foundations for such unity *a priori* were not contained in the original sources of knowledge in our mind, and if these subjective conditions were not at the same time objectively valid, by being the very basis of the possibility of cognising any object at all in experience?

We have already explained the *understanding* in various ways: by a spontaneity of cognition (as opposed to the receptivity of sensibility), or by a faculty of thinking, or of concepts, or even of judgments—all of which explanations, if properly understood, coincide. We may now characterise it as the *faculty of rules.* This attribute is more fruitful, and explains its nature better. Sensibility gives us forms (of intuition), but the understanding give us rules. This latter is always occupied in hunting through phenomena, in order to find any rule they may present. Rules, so far as they are objective (or belong necessarily to the cognition of the object) are called laws. Although we learn many laws from experience, yet are these only particular determinations of higher laws, among which the highest (to which the rest are subordinate) are derived from the understanding itself, and are not borrowed from experience, but rather render phenomena subject to law, and by this very means make experience itself possible. The understanding is, then, not merely a faculty of forming for itself rules by the comparison of phenomena; it is itself a code of laws for nature, that is to say, without the understanding there would be no nature at all, or synthetical unity of phenomena according to rules; for phenomena cannot, as such, find place without us, but exist only in our sensibility. But this, as an object of knowledge in experience, with all that it may contain, is only possible in the unity of apperception. This unity of apperception is the transcendental basis of the necessary regularity of all phenomena in experience. The same unity in relation to the multiplicity of representations (that is to say, determining it from a single representation) is the rule, and the faculty of these rules is the understanding. Thus all phenomena, as possible objects of experience, lie *a priori* in the understanding, and receive from it their possibility, just as mere intuitions lie in the sensibility, and, as to form, are only possible through it.

However exaggerated or absurd, then, it may seem to assert that the understanding itself is the source of the laws of nature, and of the formal unity thereof, such an assertion is nevertheless equally correct and applicable to the object, that is, to experience. Empirical laws, indeed, as such, can by no means deduce their origin from the pure understanding, just as the infinite variety of phenomena could not be adequately conceived from the pure form of sensuous intuition. But all empirical laws are only particular determinations of the pure laws of the understanding, under which, and according to the type of which, they first become possible; so that phenomena assume a fixed form, just as all phenomena, in spite of the variety of their empirical form, must nevertheless always accord with the conditions of the pure form of sensibility.

The pure understanding is, then, in the categories, the law of the synthetical unity of all phenomena; and hence it first renders experience possible as to form. But this was our whole aim throughout the transcendental deduction of the categories, namely, this relation of the understanding to sensibility, and through it to all objects of experience; in fact, to render intelligible the objective validity of the pure concepts of the understanding, and so to establish their origin and truth.

Summary Statement of the Correctness and Possibility of this and No Other Deduction of the Pure Concepts of the Understanding

Were the objects with which our knowledge is concerned things in themselves, we could not have any *a priori* concepts of them. For from whence could we obtain such concepts? Suppose we took them from the object (without pausing to investigate how this could become known to us at all), then our concepts would be merely empirical, and not *a priori*. Suppose we took them from ourselves, then that which is merely within us could not determine the nature of an object distinct from our representations; that is to say, it could not form a reason why there should exist a thing to which our thoughts should correspond, rather than that such representations should be totally void. On the contrary, if we are altogether concerned only with phenomena, it is not only possible, but even necessary, that certain *a priori* concepts should antecede the empirical cognition of objects. For, as phenomena, they produce an object which exists only in us, because a mere modification of our sensibility cannot exist without us. Now this very representation—that all these phenomena, and objects with which we can employ ourselves, are all in me, that is, are determinations of my identical self—this representation, I say, expresses their complete unity in one and the same apperception to be necessary. But in this unity of possible consciousness consists also the form of all cognition of objects (by which multiplicity is thought as belonging to *one* object). So that the way in which the manifold of sensuous representations (intuition) belongs to one consciousness, precedes all cognition of the object, as being its intellectual form, and even produces a formal cognition of all objects *a priori*, so far as they are thought (categories). Their synthesis through the pure imagination, and the unity of all representations in relation to primitive apperception, precede all empirical cognition. Consequently, all pure concepts of the understanding are only for this reason possible—nay, even in relation to experience, necessary—that our knowledge is concerned with nothing but phenomena, the possibility of which lies within ourselves, and the conjunction and unity of which (in the representation of an object) are to be found only in ourselves; so that these must precede all experience, and make it even possible as to form. It is then on this, the only possible basis, that our deduction of the categories has been constructed. . . .

Appendix C

The First Paralogism of Substantiality

That of which the representation is the absolute subject of our judgments, and which consequently cannot be used to determine anything else is *substance*.

I, as a thinking being, am the *absolute* subject of all my possible judgments, and this representation of myself cannot be used as the predicate of anything else.

Therefore I, as a thinking being (soul), am *substance*.

Critique of the First Paralogism of Pure Psychology

We have shown in the analytical part of the transcendental logic that pure categories (and among them that of substance) have in themselves no objective meaning at all, except when based on an intuition, to the diversity of which they can be applied, as functions of the synthetical unity. Without this, they are merely functions of judgment, without content. Of anything in general, I may say it is substance, so far as I distinguish it from the mere predicates and determinations of things. Now in all our thinking, the *ego* is the subject, in which thoughts inhere merely as determinations, and this *ego* cannot be used to determine anything else. Consequently, every one must necessarily consider himself as the substance, and his thoughts as the accidents, of his existence, and determinations of his condition. But what use can I make of this notion of a substance? That I, as a thinking being, exist permanently; that I cannot naturally either originate or pass away—this I cannot at all infer from it, and yet it is the only use of the concept of the substantiality of my thinking subject, with which I could otherwise very well dispense.

We are so far from being able to conclude these properties from the mere pure category of substance, that we are obliged to start from the permanence of an object derived from experience, if we wish to bring such an object under the empirically applicable concept of *substance*. Now, in the proposition we are discussing, we have not taken any experience for our basis, but have drawn our conclusion simply from the concept of the relation which all thought has to the *ego*, in which it inheres, as its common subject. Neither could we, supposing we desired to do it, establish such a permanence by any safe observation. For the *ego* is present indeed in all thoughts; but there is not the least intuition connected with this representation, to distinguish it from other objects of intuition. We may then indeed perceive that this representation is ever recurring in every act of thought, but not that it is the fixed and permanent intuition in which thoughts (being transient) alternate.

It follows, that the first syllogism of transcendental psychology only palms off upon us a pretended discovery, by setting up the constant logical subject of thinking as the cognition of the real subject of inherence. Of this latter we neither have, nor can have, the least knowledge, because consciousness is the only thing which makes all our representations thoughts, and wherein all our perceptions must be found, as their transcendental subject; and beyond this logical meaning of the *ego*, we have no knowledge of the subject in itself, which lies as *substratum* at the basis of this [representation of self], as well as of all other thoughts. The proposition, then, *the soul is a substance*, may be allowed to stand, provided we keep in mind that this notion leads us no further, and cannot teach us any of the usual conclusions of sophistical psychology; for example, its permanence through all changes, and even after death. It denotes then a substance only in idea, but not in reality.

The Second Paralogism, of Simplicity

A thing, of which the action cannot be regarded as the concurrence of the action of several things, is *simple*.

Now the soul, or thinking *ego*, is such a thing.

Therefore, etc.

Critique of the Second Paralogism of Transcendental Psychology

This is the Achilles of all the dialectical syllogisms of pure psychology; not merely a play of sophistry ingeniously contrived by the dogmatical philosopher, to produce some show of argument for his assertions, but a conclusion which seems to withstand the most acute investigation, and the most circumspect consideration. Here it is:—

Every *composite* substance is an aggregate of many; and the action of any composite, or that which inheres in it as such, is the aggregate of many actions or accidents, divided among a number of substances. Now, an effect which arises from the concurrence of several acting substances is possible when this effect is merely external (as, for instance, the motion of a body is the joint motion of all its parts). But the case is different with thoughts, which are accidents belonging internally to a thinking being. For supposing that this composite did think, each part of it would contain part of the thought; but all of them only when combined, the whole thought. Now this is contradictory. For since the representations which are contained under the different parts (suppose the individual words of a verse) are never a whole thought (a verse), so thought cannot be inherent in a composite as such. Thought, therefore, is only possible in a substance which is not an aggregate of many substances, but absolutely simple.[1]

The so-called *nervus probandi* of this argument lies in the proposition: that many representations must be contained in the absolute unity of the thinking subject, to make up one

[1] It is very easy to give this proof in the usual scholastic form. But it is sufficient for my purpose to present its ground of proof though merely in a popular form.

thought. But this proposition no one can prove *from concepts*. For how could he even commence his argument? The proposition: a thought can only be the effect of the absolute unity of the thinking being—cannot be treated analytically. For the unity of a thought which consists of many representations is collective, and, as far as pure concepts go, might just as well refer to the collective unity of the co-operating substances (like the motion of the body being the composite motion of its parts), as to the absolute unity of the subject. Proceeding then according to the rule of identity, we cannot see the necessity of presupposing a simple substance to account for a composite thought. But that this proposition should be recognised synthetically and perfectly *a priori* from pure concepts, no one will venture to assert, who understands the basis of the possibility of synthetical *a priori* judgments, as already set forth.

Now it is equally impossible to deduce from experience this necessary unity of the subject, as the condition of the possibility of each single thought. For experience could give no necessity, and besides the concept of absolute unity is far beyond its sphere. Whence then do we get this proposition, on which the whole psychological syllogism rests? ·

It is plain that, if we wish to represent a thinking being, we must put ourselves in its place, and so supply our own subject to the object which we wish to obtain (which is not the case in any other sort of investigation), and that we only demand the absolute unity of the subject, because otherwise we could not say: I think (the manifold of the representation). For, although the sum of the thought might be divided and distributed among many subjects, yet the subjective *ego* cannot be divided or distributed, and this we certainly presuppose in all thinking.

Here, then, as in the previous paralogism, the formal proposition of apperception, *I think*, is also the whole basis upon which rational psychology ventures to extend her cognitions—a proposition which is not experience, but merely the form of apperception, belonging to, and preceding, every experience. But with reference to possible cognition, this must be regarded merely as a *subjective condition*, which we have no right to exalt to a condition of the possibility of objects, that is, to a *concept* of a thinking being in general, because we cannot represent such a being to ourselves, without putting ourselves with the formula of our consciousness in the place of every other intelligent being.

The simplicity of myself (as a soul) is not actually inferred from the proposition, I think; for it already exists in every thought. The proposition, *I am simple,* must be regarded as an immediate expression of apperception, just as the supposed Cartesian conclusion, *cogito ergo sum,* is really tautological, as *cogito (= sum cogitans)* expressly asserts existence. *I am simple* means nothing but this—that the representation *I* does not contain the least multiplicity, and that it is an absolute (although merely logical) unity.

Consequently, this celebrated psychological demonstration is merely based upon the indivisible *unity* of a representation which only directs the verb [*cogitare*] to refer to a person. But it is plain that the subject of inherence is only indicated as transcendental by the *ego* attached to the thought, without noting in the least any of its properties, and without knowing or cognising anything at all about it. It means something in general (a transcendental subject), the representation of which must indeed be simple, for the obvious reason that nothing at all is determined in it, since we cannot represent a thing more simply than by the notion of a mere something. But the fact of the simplicity of the representation of a subject is not, for that reason, a cognition of the simplicity of the subject itself; total abstraction being made from its properties, when it is merely indicated by the perfectly contentless expression *ego* (which I can apply to every thinking subject).

So much is certain, that I represent to myself by *ego* always an absolute, though only a logical, unity of the subject (Simplicity), but do not cognise through it the actual simplicity of my subject. As the proposition, I am substance, means nothing but the pure category, of which I can make no concrete use (empirically), so I may also be allowed to say, I am a simple substance, that is, one whose represen-

tation never contains a synthesis of multiplicity; but this concept, or even this proposition, does not give us the least information with regard to myself as an object of experience, because the concept of substance itself is only used as a function of synthesis, without being based on intuition, that is, without any object; so that it only applies to the condition of our knowledge, not to any object which we could name. Let us make an experiment with regard to the supposed use of this proposition.

Every one must confess that the assertion of the simple nature of the soul is merely of value so far as I am able by it to separate this subject from all matter, and consequently exempt it from decay, to which matter is always liable. It is for this use that the above proposition is specially intended, and it is therefore often thus expressed: The soul is not corporeal. Now if I can show that, even conceding to this cardinal proposition of rational psychology all objective validity (that all which thinks is simple substance), in the pure meaning of a mere judgment of the reason (from pure categories)—even conceding this, I say—not the least use can be made of it with reference to its dissimilarity or relation to matter, then I may fairly claim to have relegated this pretended philosophical truth into the region of pure ideas, which are wanting in reality when objectively used.

We have proved irrefragably in our transcendental aesthetic that bodies are mere phenomena of our external sense, and not things in themselves. In accordance with this we may say justly, that our thinking subject is not corporeal, viz. that as it is represented to us as an object of the internal sense, it cannot, so far as it thinks, be an object of the external senses, or a phenomenon in space. This is equivalent to saying: Thinking beings, as such, can never be represented to us among external intuitions; or, we cannot intuite their thoughts, consciousness, desires, etc. externally; for all these must come before the internal sense. This argument indeed appears to be also the natural and popular one, which seems to have satisfied even the most ordinary understandings, so that from very early times they began to consider souls as totally distinct from bodies.

Now extension, incompressibility, connexion, and motion—in short, all that our external senses only can give us—are not, and indeed do not contain, thought, feeling, desire, or resolve, which are not at all objects of external intuition. Nevertheless, *that* something which lies at the basis of external phenomena—which so affects our sense as to give it the representations of space, matter, form, etc.—that something, I say, considered as a noumenon (or perhaps better as a transcendental object), might also at the same time be the subject of thoughts, although we may not be able to obtain any intuition of mental states (but only of space and its determinations), through the means by which our external sense is affected. But this something is not extended, impenetrable, or composite, because all these predicates only concern sensibility and its intuition, so far as we are affected by that sort of objects (otherwise unknown to us). Yet these expressions by no means declare to us what sort of an object it is, but only this, that the predicates of external phenomena cannot be applied to it, considered as an object in itself, and without reference to external senses. But the predicates of the internal sense—representation and thinking—do not contradict it. Consequently, even admitting the simplicity of its nature, the human soul is not at all proved to be distinct from matter, as regards their respective *substrata*, when considered (as it should be) merely as a phenomenon.

If matter were a thing *per se*, it would, as a composite being, be altogether different from the soul, as a simple being. But it is only an external phenomenon, of which the *substratum* is not cognised by any producible predicates. I might, then, be quite justified in assuming of this *substratum* that it was in itself simple, although in the way which it affects our senses it produces in us the intuition of extension, and, along with it, of composition It might follow that this substance, to which extension is added by reference to our external sense, is accompanied by thoughts in itself, which through its own peculiar internal sense can be represented with consciousness. In this way the very same thing which in one relation is

called corporeal, is at the same time in another called a thinking being, whose thoughts indeed we cannot intuite, but only their evidences, in phenomena. We should thus get rid of the expression, that souls only (as being a peculiar sort of substances) think; we should rather use the ordinary phrase, that men think; that is to say, that the very same thing which is extended as an external phenomenon, is internally (in itself) a subject not composite, but simple and thinking.

But, without admitting such hypotheses, we may observe in general, that if I mean by soul a thinking being *per se*, the very question is improper, if we mean to ask whether it is of the same kind, or not, as matter (which is not a thing *per se*, but only a sort of representation in us); for it is self-evident that a thing *per se* must be of a different nature from the determinations which merely constitute its states.

But, if we compare the thinking *ego*, not with matter, but with the intelligible something at the basis of the external phenomena, which we call matter, as we know nothing of this latter, we cannot assert that the soul differs from it in any way internally.

Accordingly, simple consciousness is not a cognition of the simple nature of our subject, so far as it is to be distinguished as such from matter as a composite existence.

But if this concept of simplicity is useless in the only case where it could be of service (that is, to determine the peculiar and distinguishing feature of our subject, when I compare myself with the objects of external experience), we may fairly despair of ever knowing that *I*, the soul (a name for the transcendental object of the internal sense), am simple. This expression has no application extending to actual objects, and cannot possibly, therefore, enlarge our knowledge.

If these remarks are true, the whole of rational psychology falls to the ground with its principal support; and we can as little here as elsewhere hope to extend our information by pure concepts (still less by consciousness, the mere subjective form of all our concepts). More especially, the fundamental notion of *a simple nature* is such that it cannot be found in any experience at all; so that there is no way of reaching it as an objectively valid concept.

The Third Paralogism, or Personality

That which is conscious of its own numerical identity at different times is, so far, a person.

Now, the soul has this consciousness.

Therefore, it is a person.

Critique of the Third Paralogism of Transcendental Psychology

If I desire to cognise the numerical identity of an external object by experience, I pay attention to the permanent [part] of the phenomenon, to which, as subject, all the rest refers as determination, and remark the identity of the former in time, while the latter changes. But I am an object of the internal sense, and all time is merely the form of the internal sense. Consequently, I refer my successive modifications, one and all, to the numerically identical self in all time, that is, in the form of the internal intuition of myself. Upon this ground the personality of the soul should be regarded, not as an inference, but as a perfectly identical assertion of self-consciousness in time; and this, too, is the reason why it is valid *a priori*. For it says nothing but this: In all the time in which I am conscious of myself, I am conscious of this time, belonging to the unity of myself; and it is indifferent whether I say, The whole of time is in me, who am an individual unity; or, I am, with my numerical identity, present in all this time.

Personal identity, then, must be always found in my own consciousness. But, if I consider myself from the point of view of another person (as an object of his external intuition), this observer external to me first of all considers *me in time;* for in apperception *time* is properly only represented *in me.* He will, consequently, not conclude the objective permanence of myself from the *ego,* which accompanies all representations at all times *in my consciousness,* and indeed with perfect identity, even though he concedes its presence. For, as the time in which the observer places me is not that which is met with in my sensibil-

ity, but in his, the identity which is necessarily bound up with my consciousness is not bound up with his, that is, with an external intuition of my subject.

The identity, then, of the consciousness of myself at different times is only a formal condition of my thoughts and their connexion, and does not demonstrate the numerical identity of my subject, in which, notwithstanding the logical identity of the *ego,* such a change might have taken place as to preclude its identity. We might nevertheless always attribute to it that *ego,* which never varies in name, and which in every different state, even were the subject changed, could yet always preserve the thought of the previous subject, and hand it over to the succeeding.[2]

Although the proposition of some ancient schools—that everything is in a flux, and nothing permanent—cannot stand if we assume substances, it is not refuted by the unity of self-consciousness; for we ourselves cannot decide from our own consciousness whether we, as souls, are permanent or not, because we only consider *that* to belong to our identical selves, of which we are conscious; and so, of course, we judge necessarily that we are the very same in the whole time of which we are conscious. But from the point of view of a stranger we cannot hold this to be a valid inference; because, as we meet in the soul no permanent phenomenon except the representation self, which accompanies and connects all the rest, we can never ascertain whether this *ego* (a mere thought) is not subject to the same flux as the remaining thoughts which are connected by it.

[2]An elastic ball which strikes full upon a similar one imparts to it all its motion, or all its state (if we merely regard places in space). Now, let us assume substances after the analogy of such bodies, where each [reading *je*] imparts representations to the next, along with a consciousness of them. We might thus conceive a whole series of them, the first of which imparted its state, and the consciousness thereof, to the second; this again its own state, along with that of the first, to the third; this again its own and the states of all the previous ones, etc. In such a case the last substance would be conscious of all the states of the previously changed substances as its own, since those states were transferred to it along with the consciousness of them; nevertheless, it would not have been the very same person in all these states.

But it is remarkable that the personality, and the permanence which it presupposes— that is, the substantiality of the soul—*must now be proved first;* for, could we presuppose it, there would follow, not indeed the permanence of consciousness, but the possibility of a lasting consciousness in a permanent subject; and this is sufficient for personality, which need not itself cease, even though its action be interrupted for a time. But this permanence is not given us at all before the numerical identity of ourselves, which we infer from the identity of apperception, but is rather inferred from the identity (and after this, to make the argument valid, should follow the concept of substance, which is the only one of them that is of empirical use). Now, as this identity of person by no means follows from the identity of the *ego* in all the time in which I cognise myself—so we already found that the substantiality of the soul could not be based upon it.

Nevertheless, the concept of personality (as well as that of substance and simplicity) may remain, so far as it is transcendental, and means a unity of the subject otherwise unknown to us, but in whose states there is thorough-going connexion through apperception. And so far indeed this concept is both necessary and sufficient for all practical uses; but we can never depend upon it to extend our self-cognition through pure reason (which mirrors to us a permanence of the subject), from the mere concept of the identical self, as this concept always revolves about it itself, and does not assist in solving a single question which aims at synthetical cognition. What sort of thing *per se* (transcendental object) matter may be is wholly unknown to us; nevertheless, its permanence as phenomenon may be observed when it is represented as something external. But when I wish to observe the mere *ego* in the alteration of all representations—as I have no other *correlatum* for my comparisons except the same identical self with the universal conditions of my consciousness—I can only give tautological answers to all questions by supplying my concept, and its unity, to those properties which I possess as an object, and so by assuming what was under investigation.

The Fourth Paralogism, of Ideality (of External Relations)

Whatsoever can only be inferred to exist, as the cause of given perceptions, has only a *doubtful existence.*

Now, all external phenomena are of such a kind that their present existence cannot be perceived immediately, but we infer them to exist as the cause of given perceptions.

Consequently, the existence of all the objects of the external senses is doubtful. This uncertainty I call the ideality of external phenomena; and the doctrine which holds this ideality is *idealism,* in contrast to which the assertion of a possible certainty of objects of the external senses is called *dualism.*

Critique of the Fourth Paralogism of Transcendental Psychology

We shall first analyse the premises. We may justly assert that only what is within us can be immediately perceived, and that my own existence alone is the object of a bare perception. Consequently, the existence of an actual object without me (if this word be used in an intellectual sense) is never given immediately in perception, but can only be added in thought to the perception (which is a modification of our internal sense) as its external cause, and so inferred from it. Consequently, Descartes justly restricted all perception in the strictest sense to the proposition, I (as a thinking being) exist; for it is clear that, as the external is not in me, it cannot possibly be found in my apperception, or in any perception, which is properly only a determination of apperception.

I cannot, then, properly perceive external things, but only infer their existence from my internal perception by regarding it as an effect, of which something external is the proximate cause. But the inference from a given effect to a determinate cause is always precarious, because the effect may have been produced by more than one cause.

Consequently, with regard to the relation of perception to its cause, it must ever remain doubtful whether such cause be internal or external—whether all so-called external perceptions are not a mere play of our internal sense, or whether they indeed refer to actual external objects as their causes. At all events, the existence of the latter is only an inference, and runs the risk of all inferences; while, on the contrary, the object of the internal sense (I myself, with all my representations) is perceived immediately, and its existence can be in no doubt.

By *idealist*, then, we must not understand the man who denies the existence of external objects, but only one who will not concede that it is known by immediate perception, and who concludes, accordingly, that we can never be absolutely certain of their actuality by any possible experience.

Now, before I propound our paralogism in its delusive form, I must observe that we must necessarily distinguish two sorts of idealism— transcendental and empirical. By the *transcendental idealism* of all phenomena, I mean the doctrine according to which we regard them all as mere representations, not as things *per se,* and according to which space and time are merely sensuous forms of our intuition, not determinations given *per se,* or conditions of objects as things *per se.* Opposed to this doctrine is *transcendental realism,* which regards space and time as something given *per se* (independent of our sensibility). The transcendental realist, then, represents to himself external phenomena (if we allow their actuality) as things *per se,* which exist independent of us and our sensibility, and should therefore also be without us according to pure concepts. This transcendental realist is the proper man to turn empirical idealist; and, after he has falsely assumed of objects of our senses, that if they are to be external, they must possess existence in themselves apart from the senses, he then finds all the representations of our senses insufficient to guarantee the actuality of these representations.

The transcendental idealist, on the contrary, can be an empirical realist, or, as he is called, a *dualist;* that is, he can concede the existence of matter without going beyond mere self-consciousness, or assuming anything beyond the certainty of the representations in me, or the *cogito ergo sum.* For since he considers this matter, and even its internal possibility, to be nothing but phenomenon, which

apart from our sensibility is nothing at all, he only considers it as a kind of representations (intuition) which are called external, *not as if they referred to objects external in themselves,* but because they refer perceptions to space, in which all things are reciprocally external, while space itself is within us.

We have declared ourselves in favour of this transcendental idealism throughout. Accepting our doctrine, all difficulty of admitting the existence of matter on the testimony of our mere consciousness vanishes, as well as of declaring it so proved, just as the existence of myself as a thinking being is so proved. For I am surely conscious of my representations; these then, and I who have them, exist. But external objects (bodies) are mere phenomena, and nothing at all but a species of my representations, the objects of which only exist through these representations, and apart from them are nothing. External things, therefore, exist just as much as I myself do, and both upon the immediate evidence of my self-consciousness; with this difference, that the representation of myself as a thinking subject is referred only to the internal sense, but the representations which denote extended existences are referred also to the external sense. With regard to the actuality of external objects, I have just as little need of inference as with regard to the actuality of the object of my internal sense (my thoughts); for they are both nothing but representations, the immediate perception (consciousness) of which is likewise a sufficient proof of their actuality.

The transcendental idealist is then an empirical realist, and allows matter, as phenomenon, an actuality which need not be inferred, but is immediately perceived. Transcendental realism, on the other hand, necessarily becomes perplexed, and is forced to make way for empirical idealism, because it regards the objects of external senses as something distinct from the senses themselves, and mere phenomena as independent beings existing without us. However perfectly we may be conscious of our representation of these things, this is far from proving that, if the representation exists, its corresponding object must also exist; while on our system, these external things (or matter, in all its forms and changes) are nothing but mere phenomena, or representations in us, of whose actuality we are immediately conscious.

As all the psychologists who subscribe to empirical idealism are, as far as I know, also transcendental realists, they have been perfectly consistent in attaching great weight to empirical idealism, as one of those problems which human reason can hardly solve. For, most assuredly, if we regard external phenomena as representations which are produced in us by their object—a thing *per se* existing without us—then how can its existence be known, except by interring the cause from the effect, in which case it must always remain doubtful whether this latter be within or without us. Now it may indeed be conceded that something is possibly the cause of our external intuitions, which is without us in the transcendental sense; but this is not the object which we understand by the representations of matter and corporeal things; for these are mere phenomena—mere species of representation—which are in all cases only within us; and their actuality rests upon immediate consciousness, just as the consciousness of my thoughts does. The transcendental object, as well of internal as of external intuition, is to use equally unknown. Not this however, but the empirical object, is in question, which is called *external* if *it is in space—internal*, if it is represented *in time-relations* only; but space and time are both only to be found *within us.*

But, as the expression *without us* is unavoidably ambiguous (meaning either that which exists as a thing *per se*, distinct from us, or merely that which belongs to *external phenomena*), in order to secure to this concept the latter meaning—being that in which the psychological question about the reality of our external intuition arises—we shall distinguish *empirically external* objects from those possibly so called in a transcendental sense, by denominating them simply things *which can be perceived in space.*

Space and time are indeed representations *a priori* present to us as forms of our sensuous intuition, before any actual object has determined us by sensation to represent it under these sensuous relations. But this material or real something, which is to be intuited in

space, necessarily presupposes perception, and cannot be in any way imagined or produced independently of this perception, which announces the actuality of something in space. It is then sensation which indicates actuality in space and time, as soon as this sensation has been referred to either species of sensuous intuition. Sensation, when applied to an object in general, without determining it, is called perception. This sensation being given, by means of its manifoldness we can imagine various objects which, beyond imagination have no empirical place in space or time. Whatever examples then of sensations we take, whether pleasure or pain, or external ones like colour and heat, this remains quite certain, that perception is that through which the material must be given, in order to supply objects to sensuous intuition. This perception then (to keep to external intuitions at present), represents something actual in space. For in the first place, perception is the representation actuality, as space is of the mere possibility, of simultaneous existence. Secondly, this actuality is represented for the external sense, that is, in space. Thirdly, space itself is nothing but mere representation. Nothing then can be considered as actual in space, except that which is represented in it,[3] and, *vice versa*, what is given in space (or represented through perception) is also actual in it; for, were it not actual in it—that is, were it not given immediately by empirical intuition—it could not be invented, because the real element in intuitions cannot at all be obtained by *a priori* thinking.

All external perception, then, proves immediately that there is something actual in space, or rather it is itself this very actuality, and so far empirical realism is beyond question; that is to say, there corresponds to ex-

[3]This paradoxical, but true, proposition should be carefully noted—viz., nothing is in space except what is represented in it. For space itself is nothing but representations; consequently, whatsoever is in space must be contained in the representation, and there is nothing at all in space except so far as it is actually represented in it. The assertion, no doubt, sounds strange—that a thing can only exist in its own representation; but the absurdity is here obviated since we are concerned not with things *per se*, but only with phenomena—*sc.* representations.

ternal intuitions something actual in space. It is true that space itself, with all its phenomena, only exists within me; but nevertheless in this space reality, or the material of all objects of external intuition, is given actually and independently of all invention. It is also impossible that in *this space* anything *without us* (in the transcendental sense) should be given, because space itself, apart from our sensibility, is nothing. The most extreme idealist cannot, then, call upon us to prove that the object without us (in the strict sense) corresponds to our perception. For is such a thing did exist, it could not be represented or intuited as without us, since this would presuppose space; and actuality in space, as of a mere representation, is nothing but the perception itself. That which is real in external phenomena is only actual in perception, nor can it be actual in any other sense.

From perception we can produce objects, either by the play of fancy, or through experience. And so, no doubt, illusive representations may arise, not corresponding with objects, and we must ascribe this illusion either to images of the fancy (dreams), or to a mistake of the faculty of judgment (in the case of the so-called deceptions of the senses). To avoid these illusions, we proceed according to the following rule: *that which is connected with a perception according to empirical laws is actual.* But this illusion, as well as the caution against it, affects idealism, as well as dualism, since it only concerns the form of experience. In order to refute empirical idealism, which falsely questions the objective reality of external perceptions, it is enough that external perception should immediately prove an actuality in space, which space, although it be the mere form of representations, nevertheless possesses objective reality with regard to all external phenomena, which are nothing but representations. It is enough to show that without perception even invention and dreaming would be impossible; so that our external senses, as far as the data for experience are concerned, must have their actual corresponding object in space.

The man who *denies* the existence of matter would be the *dogmatical idealist;* he who *doubts* it, because it cannot be proved, would be the *sceptical idealist.* The former theory results from believing that there are contradictions in the possibility of there being matter at all—a question with which we are not yet concerned. The following section, on dialectical syllogisms, which portrays the reason in internal conflict about the concepts which it has formed as regards the possibility of what belongs to connected experience, will help to solve that difficulty. But the sceptical idealist, who only attacks the grounds of our assertion, and declares our conviction of the existence of matter to be insufficient—which we believe we can found on immediate perception—such a man is a benefactor to human reason, since he compels us, even in the most trifling steps of ordinary experience, to keep wide awake, and not to annex as lawful property anything that we have obtained by foul means. The use of these idealistic objections is now quite clear. They force us, if we wish to avoid confusion in our most ordinary assertions, to consider all perceptions, whether internal or external, as merely the consciousness of what belongs to our sensibility; and their external objects not as things *per se,* but only representations, of which we are as immediately conscious as of any other representations. They are only called external because they belong to that sense which we call the external sense, of which the intuition is space; and this space is nothing but an internal species of representation, in which certain perceptions are connected with one another.

Supposing we allowed external objects to be things *per se,* it would be absolutely impossible to comprehend how we could obtain a knowledge of their actuality without us, since we rely merely on the representation which is within us. For, since no one can have a sensation without himself, but only within, the whole of self-consciousness gives us nothing but our own determinations. Consequently sceptical idealism compels us to take refuge in the only course still open, that is, in the ideality of all phenomena; and this we expounded in the transcendental aesthetic, independent of the consequences, which we could not have then foreseen. If it be now asked, whether dualism must consequently follow in psychology, we answer, certainly, but only in the empirical sense; that is to say, in the connected whole of experience, matter, as substance in phenomena, is actually given to the external sense, and the thinking *ego* is also given to the internal sense, as substance in the phenomenon; and in both cases phenomena must be connected according to the rules which this category [of substance] introduces into the connexion of our external as well as internal representations. But if we desire to widen, as is usual, the notion of dualism, and take it in its transcendental sense, then neither this doctrine, nor *pneumatism* nor *materialism*, which oppose it from different sides, have the least basis. We should then miss the proper determination of our concepts, and consider a difference in the mode of representation of objects (which remain unknown to us, as to what they are in themselves) to be a difference in these things themselves. *I*, who am represented through the internal sense as in time, and *objects* without me, are indeed phenomena totally distinct in kind, but need not therefore be thought as distinct things. The *transcendental object*, which lies at the basis of internal intuition as well as of external phenomena, is neither matter, nor a thinking being *per se*, but a basis of phenomena unknown to us, and these give us the empirical concept as well of the first as of the second.

If then, as the present *Critique* plainly compels us, we keep faithfully to the rule we have established, not to push our questions any further than possible experience has supplied us with objects for them, it will never even come into our heads to make investigations about the objects of our senses as to what they may be in themselves, out of relation to our senses. But if the psychologist takes phenomena for things in themselves, he may, as a materialist, accept for his doctrine nothing but matter; or, as a spiritualist, nothing but thinking beings (according to the form of our internal sense); or even, as a dualist, he may regard both to be things existing *per se*. In any case his misconception will condemn him to be ever speculating how that is to exist *per se* which is no thing *per se*, but only the phenomenon of a thing in general.

Reflection Concerning the Whole of Pure Psychology, as an Appendix to These Paralogisms

If we contrast the *doctrine of the soul*, as the physiology of the internal sense, with the *science of bodies*—as the physiology of the objects of the external senses—we shall find (in addition to the fact that in both we know a great deal empirically) this remarkable difference, that in the latter science much can be cognised *a priori* from the mere concept of an extended incompressible being; whereas in the former, from the concept of a thinking being, nothing can be cognised synthetically *a priori*. Because although both are phenomena, yet the phenomenon presented to the external sense has something permanent or fixed, which gives a *substratum* lying at the basis of changeable determinations, and so gives us a synthetical concept, namely, that of space and a phenomenon in it. Time, on the contrary, which is the only form of our internal intuition, has nothing permanent in it; so that it only lets us know the change of determinations, not the determinable object. For in that which we call the soul everything is in a continuous flux, and nothing is permanent except (if you *will* have it so) the *ego*, which is perfectly simple, merely because this representation has no content or multiplicity; for which reason it seems to represent or, I should rather say, indicate a simple object. In order to produce a pure rational cognition of the nature of a thinking being in general, this *ego* should be an intuition, which, being presupposed in all thinking (antecedent to any experience), should give us synthetical *a priori* propositions. But this *ego* is just as little an intuition as it is a concept of any object, being merely the form of consciousness which can accompany both kinds of representations, and raise them to cognitions, so far as something else is given in intuition which supplies the material for the representation of an object. Thus all rational psychology falls to the ground, being a science surpassing all the powers of the human reason; and there remains nothing for us except to study our souls according to the clue given by experience, and to keep within the limits of questions not exceeding the content which can possibly be given by internal experience.

But though this science gives us no ampliative knowledge, but is composed (when it attempts to do so) of nothing but paralogisms, yet we cannot deny it an important negative use, if we consider it as nothing but a critical treatment of our dialectical syllogisms, and indeed of the ordinary natural reason.

Why do we require a psychology founded upon pure principles of the reason only? Without doubt, for the particular object of securing our thinking self from the danger of materialism. This is done by the rational notion of our thinking self, which we have set forth; for, instead of there being any danger that if matter were taken away, all thinking— and even the existence of thinking beings— would consequently vanish, it is rather clearly shown that, if I take away the thinking subject, the whole world of matter must vanish, being only what appears in the sensibility of our subject, as a species of its representations.

Having proved this, I am of course not in the least better able to know this thinking self by its properties. Nay, I cannot even prove its existence to be independent of the transcendental *substratum* (whatever it is) of external phenomena; for both are to me unknown. Yet, as it is possible for me to find a reason in other than merely speculative grounds for hoping that my thinking nature will remain permanent in the midst of all possible changes of state—as this is possible, though I openly confess my own ignorance—an important point is gained, since I am able to repel the dogmatical attacks of speculative opponents, and show them that they can never know more of the nature of my thinking subject, to enable them to deny the possibility of my hopes, than I can, to enable me to maintain them.

On this transcendental illusion in our psychological concepts are based three additional dialectical questions, which form the proper object of rational psychology, and which can only be decided by the foregoing investigations. These are:—(α) The possibility of the community of the soul and an organic body, *i.e.* the animality and condition of the soul in this life; (β) The commencement of this community, *i.e.* the state of the soul at and

before birth; (γ) The end of this community, *i.e.* the state of the soul at and after death (the question of immortality).

Now I assert that all the difficulties with which these questions are supposed to be beset, and with which, used as dogmatical objections, men pretend to a deeper insight into the nature of things than can be obtained by plain common sense—I say that all such difficulties are based on a mere delusion, by which what only exists in our thoughts is hypostatised, and, without its quality being changed, assumed to be an actual object without the thinking subject: for example, extension, which is nothing but a phenomenon, is taken for a property of external things existing apart from our sensibility; and motion is regarded as their action, taking place actually in itself, even apart from our senses. For matter, the community of which with the soul raises such difficulties, is nothing but a mere form, or a certain species, of the representation of an unknown object through that intuition which is called the external sense. There may indeed, then, be something without us to which this phenomenon, which we call matter, corresponds; but in the same quality as phenomenon it is not without us [in the transcendental sense], but merely a thought within us, although this thought (through the sense just mentioned) represents it as to be found without us. Matter then signifies, not a species of substance, thus distinct and heterogeneous from the object of the internal sense (soul), but only the difference in kind of the phenomena of objects (in themselves unknown to us), whose representations we call external, as compared with those ascribed to the internal sense, even though the former belong just as much to the thinking subject as do all the rest of our thoughts. They have, however, this illusion about them, that as they represent objects in space, they as it were sever themselves from the soul, and seem to exist separate from it, although space itself, in which they are intuited, is nothing but a representation, the object of which, in the same quality, cannot be met at all without the soul. Accordingly, the question is no longer about the community of the soul with other known and heterogeneous substances without us, but merely concerning the connexion of the representations of the internal sense with the modifications of our external sensibility; and how it is that these are connected together according to constant laws, so as to form one systematic experience.

As long as we conjoin in experience internal and external phenomena as mere representations, we find nothing absurd or strange in the community of both species of sense. But as soon as we hypostatise external phenomena, and consider them no longer as representations, *but as things existing by themselves without us, in the same quality as they are in us,* and refer their activity, which they exhibit as phenomena in mutual relation, to our thinking subject—if we do this, the effective causes without us assume a character which will not tally with their effects in us, because the former refers merely to the external, the latter to the internal, sense; and, though these are united in one subject, they are still very different in kind. Here, then, we have no external effects, except changes of place, and no forces except tendencies which concern relations in space as their effects. But within us the effects are thoughts, among which no relation of place, motion, figure, or any space-determination takes place; and we lose the clue to the causes altogether in the effects, which they should manifest in the internal sense. But we ought to remember that bodies are not objects *per se,* present to us, but a mere appearance of nobody-knows-what-sort-of unknown object; that motion is not the effect of this unknown cause, but merely the appearance of its influence on our senses; consequently, that both are not anything without us, but mere representations within us. It follows, that it is not the motion of matter which produces representations in us, but that this motion itself (and matter also, which makes itself cognoscible by this means) is mere representation; and, finally, that the whole difficulty we have conjured up amounts to this: how, and through what cause, the representations of our sensibility are so related, that those which we call external intuitions can be represented as objects without us, according to empirical laws. This question by no means contains the supposed difficulty of explaining the origin of the representations of causes which exist without us,

and act in a foreign way—in that we take the appearances of an unknown cause to be a cause without us—a proceeding which can breed nothing but confusion. In those judgments where there occurs a misconception rooted in long habit, it is not possible to bring the correction within our grasp, in the same degree as in those other cases where no such unavoidable illusion confuses our concepts. Hence this our emancipation of the reason from sophistical theories, can hardly as yet have the clearness which alone produces perfect satisfaction.

I hope to make the matter plainer in the following way:—

All *objections* may be divided into *dogmatical, critical,* and *sceptical.* A dogmatical objection is directed against a *proposition;* a critical, against the *proof* of a proposition. The former presupposes an insight into the nature of an object, in order that we may be able to assert the reverse of what is stated concerning the object; such a proposition, then, is itself dogmatical, and professes to know more of the property in question than its opponent. The critical objection, as it never touches the truth or falsity of the proposition, and only attacks the proof, does not require, or pretend to, a better knowledge of the object than the opposed assertion; it only proves the assertion groundless—not that it is false. The sceptical objection opposes mutually the proposition and its contradictory, as objections of equal value, proposing each in turn as a dogma, and the other as the objection to it, and so appears to be from opposite sides dogmatical, in order to destroy completely any judgment about the object. Both the dogmatical and sceptical objections must pretend to so much insight into their objects as is necessary to assert something of them affirmatively or negatively. The critical alone differs from them, in that it overthrows the theory by showing that something worthless or merely imaginary has been assumed in its assertions, and by removing this supposed foundation, without wishing to assert anything concerning the nature of the object.

Now according to the ordinary notions of our reason as to the community in which our thinking subject stands with things without us, we are dogmatical, and regard them as true objects, existing independent of us, according to a transcendental dualism, which does not attribute these external phenomena, as representations, to the subject, but transports them, just as we get them from sensuous intuition, out of ourselves as objects, which this dualism separates completely from the thinking subject. This *subreptio* is the foundation of all theories as to the community between body and soul; and the question is never raised whether the objective reality of phenomena be certainly true: this is rather assumed as conceded, and fallacious reasonings started as to its explanation or conception. The three ordinary systems invented to meet this difficulty, and indeed the only possible ones, are those of *physical influence*, of *pre-established harmony*, and of *supernatural assistance*.

The two latter explanations of the community of the soul with matter are based upon objections to the first (which is the representation of common sense), namely, that what appears as matter cannot by immediate influence be the cause of representations, which are a perfectly heterogeneous sort of effect. But when men argue in this way they cannot unite with the 'object of the external sensibility' the notion of a matter which is only phenomenon, or in itself mere representation, produced by any sort of external objects; for it they held this, they would have said that the representations of external objects (phenomena) cannot be external causes of phenomena in our minds—a senseless objection, for it never could come into any man's head to consider that what he had already acknowledged to be mere representation was an external cause. According to our principles, their theory must rather attempt to show that the true (transcendental) object of our external senses cannot be the cause of those representations (phenomena) which we understand by the word matter. Now, as no one can pretend with any reason to know aught of the transcendental cause of the representations of our external senses, their assertion is quite groundless. But, if the pretended correctors of the doctrine of physical influence regard matter as such (after the usual manner of transcendental dualism) to be a thing *per se* (and not the mere phenomenon of an unknown thing), and direct their objections to prove that such an external object, which exhibits no other sort of causality except motions, can never be the efficient cause of representations, but that a third being must interfere to produce, if not reciprocal action, at least correspondence or harmony between both; then their refutation of their opponents must begin by assuming the [same] πρῶτον ψεῦδος [as the theory] of physical influence in their own dualism; and so by their objection they would not so much refute natural influence as refute their own dualistic assumption. For all difficulties which beset the connexion of thinking nature with matter arise, without exception, merely from the insinuation of the dualistic representation, that matter as such is not phenomenon, or a mere representation of the mind, to which an unknown object corresponds, but is that object in itself, as it exists without us, and apart from all sensibility.

There can, then, be no dogmatical objection made to the usually accepted physical influence; for, if our opponent assumes that matter and its motion are mere phenomena, and therefore themselves mere representations, he can only raise this difficulty, that the unknown object of our sensibility cannot be the cause of representations in us—a thing which he has not the least right to assert, because nobody can tell of an unknown object what it can or cannot do. He must, however, after the proofs given above, necessarily concede this transcendental idealism, so far as he does not openly hypostatise representations, and place them, as true things, without himself.

But a well-founded *critical objection* can still be made to the common doctrine of physical influence. Such a pretended community between two kinds of substances—the thinking and the extended—presupposes a gross dualism, and makes the latter, which are nothing but mere representations of the thinking subject, into things existing *per se*. Physical influence thus misconceived may then be completely overthrown by showing its grounds of proof to be idle, and surreptitiously obtained.

The notable question concerning the community of that which thinks and that which is extended—if we discard all fictions—would simply come to this: *How external intuition,* viz. that of space (the occupation of it, figure and motion) *can be at all possible in a thinking subject?* But to this question no man can ever find an answer; and we can never supply this gap in our knowledge, but only indicate it by ascribing external phenomena to a transcendental object (as the cause of this sort of phenomena), which however we do not know, and of which we can never obtain any notion. In all problems which may arise in the field of experience we treat these phenomena as objects *per se,* without concerning ourselves about the highest ground [or condition] of their possibility. But, if we transgress this boundary, the concept of a transcendental object becomes necessary.

From these considerations about the community between extended and thinking beings there follows, as an immediate consequence, the settlement of all disputes or objections which concern the condition of this thinking nature before the community (this life), or after its cessation (in death). The opinion that the thinking subject could think previous to any community with the body would be thus expressed: that before the commencement of this sort of sensibility, by which something appears to us in space, the same transcendental objects—which in our present condition appear as bodies—may have been intuited quite differently. The opinion that the soul, after the cessation of all community with the corporeal world, can still continue to think, would announce itself in this form: that when that sort of sensibility ceases by which transcendental—and now wholly unknown—objects appear to us, all intuition of them may not consequently vanish; and that it is quite possible for the same unknown objects to continue being cognised by the subject, though, of course, no longer in the quality of bodies.

Now it is true that no one can show the smallest foundation for such an assertion from speculative principles, or even explain its possibility, but only presuppose it; yet on the other hand no one can oppose it with any valid dogmatical objection. For, whoever he may be, he knows no more of the absolute and internal cause of external or corporeal phenomena

than I or anybody else. He cannot then reasonably pretend to know on what the actuality of external phenomena depends in the present state (in life), nor consequently, that the condition of all external intuition, or even that the thinking subject itself, must cease to exist after this state (in death).

The whole dispute, then, about the nature of our thinking being and its connexion with the world of matter, merely arises from our supplying the gaps in our knowledge by paralogisms of the reason, in that we make our thoughts to be things, and hypostatise them, whence arises an imaginary science, both as regards its affirmations and its negations. We either pretend to know something of objects, of which nobody has the least notion, or we consider our own representations to be objects, and so become involved in a perpetual circle of ambiguities and contradictions. Nothing but the sobriety of a severe but fair *Critique* can free us from this dogmatical illusion, which enslaves so many of us in fancied happiness under theories and systems, and can restrict all our speculative claims to the field of possible experience—not indeed by ill-natured ridicule of our many failures, nor by pious laments about the limits of our reason, but by determining these limits accurately according to fixed principles. By this means its 'thus far, and no farther,' is most securely fixed at those pillars of Hercules which nature herself has set up, in order to allow the voyage of our reason to extend only as far as the receding coasts of experience reach—coasts that we cannot leave without venturing into a boundless ocean, which, after constant illusions, ultimately compels us to give up as hopeless all our laborious and tedious efforts.

We still owe to our reader a distinct and general explanation of the transcendental and yet natural illusion in the paralogisms of the pure reason, as well as a justification of their systematic arrangement running parallel to the categories. This we could not undertake at the commencement of the section without the danger of becoming obscure, or awkwardly anticipating ourselves. We now desire to discharge this obligation.

We can consider all illusion to consist in

this—that the subjective condition of thinking is taken for the cognition of the object. We have further shown, in the introduction to the transcendental dialectic, that pure reason is merely concerned with the totality of the synthesis of the conditions of a given conditioned. Now, as the dialectical illusion of the pure reason cannot be an empirical illusion, occurring with determinate empirical cognition, it must concern the conditions of thinking generally, and there can be only three cases of dialectical use of the pure reason—

1. The synthesis of the conditions of a thought in general;
2. The synthesis of the conditions of empirical thinking;
3. The synthesis of the conditions of pure thinking.

In all these cases the pure reason merely employs itself upon the absolute totality of this synthesis; that is, upon that condition which is itself unconditioned. On this division also is founded the threefold transcendental illusion, which gives rise to the three divisions of the dialectic, and affords the idea to just as many apparent sciences arising out of pure reason—to transcendental psychology, cosmology, and theology. We are here only concerned with the first.

As in the case of thinking in general we abstract from all relation of our thought to any object (be it of the senses, or of the pure understanding), the synthesis of the conditions of a thought in general (No. 1) is not at all objective, but merely a synthesis of the thought with the subject, which synthesis is falsely held to be a synthetical representation of an object.

But it follows from this, that the dialectical inference to the condition of all thinking in general, which is itself unconditioned, does not make a mistake as to content (for it abstracts from all content or object), but that it is merely false as to form, and must be called a paralogism.

Furthermore, as the condition which accompanies all thinking is the *ego,* in the general proposition, 'I think,' reason must be concerned with this condition, so far as it is itself unconditioned. But this is only the for-

mal condition or logical unity of every thought, in which I abstract from all objects, and yet it is represented as an object which I think, that is, the *ego* and its unconditioned unity.

Suppose any one were to put me the general question: Of what sort of nature is a thinking being? I do not in the least know how to answer the question *a priori,* because the answer must be synthetical (for an analytical answer might, perhaps, explain thinking, but could not extend our knowledge of that upon which thinking depends as to its possibility). But for every synthetical solution intuition is necessary, a point which is wholly passed over in the vague problem proposed. It is equally impossible to answer, in all its generality, the question: Of what nature must a thing capable of motion be? For incompressible extension (matter) is not then given to us. Yet, although I know no answer in general to that sort of question, it appears to me that I might give one in the special case of the proposition, 'I think,' which expresses consciousness. For this *ego* is the first subject—that is, substance—it is simple, etc. But these must be mere empirical judgments, which, at the same time, could not contain any such predicates (which are not empirical), without a general rule to express the conditions of the possibility of thinking them in general, and this *a priori.* Thus, what I at first thought so feasible (viz. judgments concerning the nature of the thinking being, and this from pure concepts), becomes suspicious, even though I have not yet discovered my mistake.

But the further investigation into the origin of these properties, which I attribute to myself, as a thinking being in general, exposes the error. They are nothing more than pure categories, by which I can never think a determined object, but only the unity of representations, in order to determine them as an object. Without being founded on an intuition, the category alone can never provide me with a concept of an object; for only by intuition is the object given, which is afterwards thought in accordance with the category. If I assert a thing to be a substance in phenomenon, the predicates of its intuition must have been previously given to me, by which I distinguish the permanent from the changeable, and the *substratum* (thing in itself) from what is merely attached to it. If I call a thing *simple* in phenomenon, I mean by this that its intuition, indeed, is part of my phenomena, but is itself not divisible, etc. But if anything is known to be simple only in concept, and not in appearance, then I have actually no knowledge at all of the object, but only of my concept, which I frame about *something* in general, and which is not capable of being properly intuited. I only say that I think a thing to be quite simple, because I can actually say nothing more about it, except merely that it is something.

Now, mere apperception (*ego*) is in concept substance, is in concept simple, etc., and so far all these psychological dogmas have indisputable truth. Yet what we want to know about the soul is not at all discoverable in this way; for, since none of these predicates are valid of intuition, and since therefore they can have no consequence applicable to objects of experience, they are quite void. For the above mentioned concept of substance does not teach me that the soul continues to exist by itself, nor that it is a part of the external intuitions, which cannot itself be further divided, and which can, consequently, neither originate nor pass away by any changes of nature: all of which are properties which would make the soul cognoscible to me in the connexion of experience, and might throw some light upon its origin and future state. But when I assert by the mere category, that the soul is a simple substance, it is clear that as the mere concept of substance contains nothing but this, that a thing shall be represented as a subject *per se*, without also being the predicate of another, [it is clear, I say that] from this concept no permanence follows, and that the attribute of simplicity could certainly not add this permanence; so that we are not in the least informed of what might happen to the soul in the changes of the world. If we could be told that it is a *simple part of matter*, we might, owing to what experience tells us, infer permanence, and along with its simple nature indestructibility. But about this, the concept of the *ego* in the psychological first principle (I think) tells us not a word.

The following is the reason that the being which in us imagines it can cognise itself by pure categories, and indeed by those which express absolute unity under each of their classes. Apperception is itself the ground of the possibility of the categories, which on their side represent nothing but the synthesis of the manifold in intuition, so far as it has unity in apperception. Hence, self-consciousness in general is the representation of that which is the condition of all unity, and yet itself unconditioned. Of the thinking *ego*, then, or soul (which represents itself as substance, simple, numerically identical at all times, and the *correlatum* of all existence, from which all other existence must be inferred), we may say, that it does not cognise *itself through the categories*, but rather the categories, and through them all objects in the absolute unity of apperception, viz. *through itself*. It is indeed quite plain that what I must presuppose in order to cognise any object at all, I cannot also cognise as an object; and that the determining *self* (thinking) is distinguished from the determinable self (the thinking subject), as cognition is from objects. Still nothing is more natural or seductive than the illusion of considering the unity in the synthesis of thoughts to be a perceived unity in the subject of these thoughts. We might call it the subreption of hypostatised consciousness (*apperceptionis substantiatæ*).

If we wish to give its logical name to the paralogism in the dialectical syllogisms of rational psychology, so far as their premises are in themselves true, it may be called a *sophisma figuræ dictionis*, in which the major premiss makes merely a transcendental use of the category with reference to its condition, but the minor premiss and conclusion make of the same category an empirical use with reference to the soul, which has been subsumed under this condition. So, for example, in the paralogism of simplicity the concept of substance is a pure intellectual concept, which, without the condition of sensuous intuition, is merely of transcendental, that is, of no, use. But in the minor premiss the very same concept is applied to the object of all internal experience, yet without first establishing and laying down as a basis the condition of its application *in concreto*, that is, its permanence; hence, there is here an empirical, though illegitimate, application made of it. In order to show the systematic connexion of all these dialectical assertions in a fallacious psychology, as connected in the pure reason—that is, in order to show its completeness—observe that the apperception is carried through all the classes of the categories, but only applied to those concepts of the understanding which in each [class] supply to the rest the basis of unity in a possible perception, and these are—subsistence, reality, unity (not plurality), and existence; only that reason here represents them as the conditions of the possibility of a thinking being, which conditions are themselves conditioned. Consequently, the soul cognises itself as—

1. The unconditioned unity of *relation,* that is, not as inhering, but *subsisting;*

2. The unconditioned unity of *quality,* that is, not as a real whole, but *simple;*[4]

3. The unconditioned unity in *plurality in time,* that is, not in different times numerically different, but as *one* and the very *same subject;*

4. The unconditioned unity of *existence in space,* that is, not as the consciousness of several things without it, but *only of its own existence,* and of other things, on the contrary, merely as its *representations.*

Reason is the faculty of principles. The assertions of pure psychology do not contain empirical predicates of the soul, but those which, if they occur, should determine the object *per se* independent of experience, that is, through the pure reason. They must, then, be fairly based upon principles and universal notions of thinking natures in general. Instead of this, we find that the single representation, *I am,* governs the whole of it, which, because it expresses the pure formula of all my experience (indeterminately), announces itself as an universal proposition, valid for all thinking beings; and, as it is single from every point of view, assumes the appearance of an absolute unity in the conditions of thinking in general,

[4]How the simple here again corresponds to the category of reality, I am as yet unable to show; but it will be explained upon the occasion of another rational use of the very same concept.

and so extends itself further than possible experience can reach.

Appendix D

Possibility of Causality Through Freedom in Harmony with the Universal Law of Natural Necessity

That in an object of the senses which is not itself phenomenon, I term *intelligible.* If, accordingly, an object which must be regarded as a phenomenon in the sensuous world possesses in itself also a faculty which is not an object of sensuous intuition, but by means of which it is capable of being the cause of phenomena, the *causality* of this being may be regarded from two different points of view. The causality may be considered to be *intelligible,* as regards its *action*—the action of a thing in itself—and also *sensible,* as regards its *effects* as a phenomenon belonging to the sensuous world.

We should, accordingly, have to form both an empirical concept of the faculty of such a subject, as well as an intellectual concept of its causality, which both occur together in one and the same effect. This twofold manner of thinking the faculty of a sensuous object does not run counter to any of the concepts which we ought to form of phenomena, or of possible experience; for as phenomena—not being things in themselves—must have a transcendental object as a foundation, which determines them as mere representations, there seems to be no reason why we should not ascribe to this transcendental object, in addition to the property by means of which it appears, a *causality* which is not a phenomenon, although its *effects* are observed in the world of phenomena.

But every effective cause must possess a *character*—that is to say, a law of its causality—without which it would not be a cause at all. Accordingly, in a subject of the world of sense we should have an *empirical character,* which guaranteed that its actions, as phenomena, stand in complete and harmonious connexion, conformably to unvarying natural laws, with all other phenomena, and can be deduced from these as conditions; and that they do thus, in connexion with these, constitute members of a single series in the order of nature.

In the second place, we should be obliged to concede to it an *intelligible character* also, by means of which it is indeed the cause of those actions as phenomena, but which is not itself a phenomenon, nor subordinate to the conditions of the world of sense. The former may be termed the character of the thing as a phenomenon; the latter, the character of the thing as a thing *per se.*

Now this acting subject would, in its intelligible character, be subject to no conditions of time; for time is only a condition of phenomena, and not of things in themselves. No *action* would *begin* or *cease to be* in this subject; it would, consequently, be free from the law of all determination of time—of all change— namely, that everything *which happens* must have a cause in the *phenomena* (of the preceding state). In a word, the causality of the subject, in so far as it is intelligible, would not form a part of the series of empirical conditions which necessitated the event in the world of sense. Again, this intelligible character of a thing could indeed never be immediately cognised, because we can perceive nothing except so far as it appears, but it must still be thought in accordance with the empirical character; just as we find ourselves compelled in a general way, to place, in thought, a transcendental object at the basis of phenomena, although we know nothing of what it is in itself.

Accordingly, as to its empirical character, this subject, being a phenomenon, would be subject to the causal *nexus* in all the laws of its determination; and it would so far be nothing but a part of the world of sense, of which the effects would follow without fail from nature, like every other phenomenon. When influenced by external phenomena—when cognised through experience in its empirical character, *i.e.* in the law of its causality—all its actions must be explicable according to natural laws, and all the requisites for their complete

and necessary determination must occur in possible experience.

By virtue of its intelligible character, on the other hand (although we possess only the general notion of this character), the subject must be regarded as free from all sensuous influences, and from all phenomenal determination. Moreover, as nothing happens in this subject—as far as it is a *noumenon*—and there does not, consequently, exist in it any change demanding the dynamical determination of time, and for the same reason no connexion with phenomena as its causes—this active being must, in its actions, be so far free from and independent of natural necessity, for this necessity exists only in sensibility. It would be quite correct to say that it originates or begins its effects in the world of sense from itself without the action beginning in itself. We should not be in this case affirming that these sensuous effects began to exist of themselves, because they are always determined by prior empirical conditions, but only by virtue of the empirical character (which is the phenomenon of the intelligible character), and are possible only as constituting a continuation of the series of natural causes. And thus nature and freedom—each in its complete signification—can meet, without contradiciton or disagreement, in the same action, according as it is compared with its intelligible or sensible cause.

Further Elucidation of the Cosmological Idea of Freedom in Connection with the Universal Law of Natural Necessity

I have thought it advisable to lay before the reader at first a mere sketch of the solution of this transcendental problem, in order to enable him to form with greater ease a clear notion of the course which reason must adopt in the solution. I shall now proceed to exhibit the several *momenta* of this solution, and to consider them in their order. The natural law, that everything which happens must have a cause; that the causality of this cause, that is, *the action* (which cannot always have existed, but must be itself an *event*, for it precedes in time some effect which has then *originated*), must have its cause among phenomena by which it is determined; and consequently, that all events are empirically determined in an order of nature—this law, I say, which lies at the foundation of the possibility of experience and of a connected system of phenomena, or *nature,* is a law of the understanding, from which no departure, and to which no exception, can be admitted. For to except even a single phenomenon from its operation is to exclude it from the sphere of possible experience, and make it a mere fiction of thought, or phantom of the brain.

Thus we are obliged to acknowledge the existence of a chain of causes, in the regress of which, however, *absolute totality* cannot be found. But we need not detain ourselves with this difficulty; for it has already been removed in our general discussion of the antinomy of the reason, when it attempts to reach the unconditioned in the series of phenomena. If we permit ourselves ot be deceived by the deception of transcendental realism, we shall find that neither nature nor freedom remain. Here the only question is: Whether, recognising nothing but natural necessity in the whole series of events, it is possible to consider the same effect as on the one hand an effect of nature, and on the other an effect of freedom; or, whether these two species of causality are absolutely contradictory.

Among the causes in phenomena there can surely be nothing which could commence a series absolutely, and of itself. Every action, as phenomenon, so far as it produces an event, is itself an event or occurrence presupposing another state, in which its cause is to be found. Thus everything that happens is but a continuation of the series; and no commencement, starting of itself, is here possible. The actions of natural causes are accordingly themselves effects, and presuppose causes preceding them in time. An *original* action—an action by which something happens which was not previously—is beyond the causal connexion of phenomena.

Now, is it necessary that, granting all effects to be phenomena, the causality of their cause, which (cause) is itself a phenomenon, must belong to the empirical world? Is it not rather possible that, although for every effect in the phenomenon a connexion with its cause

according to the laws of empirical causality is required, this empirical causality may be itself an effect of a causality not empirical, but intelligible—its connexion with natural causes remaining, nevertheless, intact?

Such a causality would be considered, in reference to phenomena, as the original action of a cause which is in so far, therefore, not phenomenal, but, as regards this faculty, intelligible, although the cause must at the same time, as a link in the chain of nature, be regarded as belonging to the sensuous world.

A belief in the causality of phenomena among each other is necessary, if we are required to look for and give an account of the natural conditions of natural events; that is to say, their causes in phenomena. This being admitted as unexceptionally valid, the requirements of the understanding, which recognises nothing but nature, and is entitled to it, are satisfied; and our physical explanations may proceed in their regular course, without let or hindrance.

But it is no stumbling-block in the way, even assuming it to be a mere fiction, to admit that there are some natural causes which have a faculty that is only intelligible, inasmuch as it is not determined to action by empirical conditions, but solely upon grounds of the understanding; so, however, that the *action in the phenomenon* of this cause must be in accordance with all the laws of empirical causality.

Thus the acting subject, as a *causa phenomenon,* would continue to preserve a complete connexion with nature and natural conditions; and only the noumenon of this subject (with all its causality in the phenomenon) would contain certain conditions, which, if we ascend from the empirical to the *transcendental* object, must be regarded as merely intelligible. For if we attend, in our inquiries with regard to causes in the world of phenomena, to the directions of nature alone, we need not trouble ourselves about what sort of basis is conceived for these phenomena and their natural connexion in the transcendental subject (which is empirically unknown to us).

This intelligible ground of phenomena does not concern empirical questions. Perhaps it has only to do with thinking in the pure understanding; and, although the effects of this thinking and acting of the pure understanding are discoverable in phenomena, these phenomena must, nevertheless, be capable of a full and complete explanation, in accordance with natural laws. And in this case we attend solely to their empirical (as the highest ground of explanation), and omit all consideration of their intelligible, character (which is the transcendental cause of the former), as completely unknown, except in so far as it is indicated by the latter as its sensuous symbol.

Now let us apply this to experience. Man is one of the phenomena of the sensuous world, and so far also one of the natural causes, the causality of which must be regulated by empirical laws. As such, he must possess an empirical character, like all other objects of nature. We remark this empirical character in his effects, which reveal the presence of certain powers and faculties. If we consider inanimate or merely brute nature, we can discover no reason for conceiving any faculty to be determined otherwise than in a purely sensuous manner.

But man, to whom the rest of nature reveals herself only through sense, cognises himself (not only by his senses, but) also through mere apperception; and this in actions and internal determinings, which he cannot regard as sensuous impressions. He is thus to himself on the one hand indeed a phenomenon; but on the other, in respect of certain faculties, a purely intelligible object—intelligible, because its action cannot be ascribed to the receptivity of sensibility. We call these faculties understanding and reason.

The latter, especially, is in a peculiar manner distinct from all empirically-conditioned faculties; for it considers its objects merely in accordance with ideas, and by means of these determines the understanding, which then proceeds to make an empirical use of its concepts, which indeed are also pure.

X
William James

WILLIAM JAMES (1842–1910), brother of the novelist Henry James, was born in New York City. He studied science at Harvard University. Using the pragmatic theory of truth of another great American philosopher, Charles Sanders Pierce, he developed the philosophy of radical empiricism. One of the founders of psychology, James was the first president of the American Psychological Association. He published the first textbook on psychology, the monumental *Principles of Psychology*. After teaching physiology and psychology at Johns Hopkins University in Baltimore, in 1880 he became professor of philosophy at Harvard.

The following essays on the nature of mind and its relation to knowledge and reality begin with a denial that there even is such a thing as what, ordinarily, we call consciousness. What there is, instead, is "pure experience." In some ways, James' philosophy is a synthesis of previous developments in the philosophy of mind leading up to the revolution in 20th-century physics, pioneered by Einstein, Russell, and Bohr, in which the mind is seen not just as the observer of reality but as a pivotal factor in the structuring of reality. Indeed, the real world, according to James, is, ultimately, a world of pure experience. See page 489 for Bertrand Russell's comments regarding how the following essay "startled the world."

Essays in Philosophical Psychology

William James

Does 'Consciousness' Exist?

'Thoughts' and 'things' are names for two sorts of object, which common sense will always find contrasted and will always practically oppose to each other. Philosophy, reflecting on the contrast, has varied in the past in her explanations of it, and may be expected to vary in the future. At first, 'spirit and matter,' 'soul and body,' stood for a pair of equipollent substances quite on a par in weight and interest. But one day Kant undermined the soul and brought in the transcendental ego, and ever since then the bipolar relation has been very much off its balance. The transcendental ego seems nowadays in rationalist quarters to stand for everything, in empiricist quarters for almost nothing. In the hands of such writers as Schuppe, Rehmke, Natorp, Münsterberg—at any rate in his earlier writings, Schubert-Soldern and others, the spiritual principle attenuates itself to a thoroughly ghostly condition, being only a name for the fact that the 'content' of experience *is known*. It loses personal form and activity—these passing over to the content—and becomes a bare *Bewusstheit* or *Bewusstsein überhaupt*,* of which in its own right absolutely nothing can be said.

I believe that 'consciousness,' when once it has evaporated to this estate of pure diaphaneity, is on the point of disappearing altogether. It is the name of a nonentity, and has no right to a place among first principles. Those who still cling to it are clinging to a mere echo, the faint rumor left behind by the disappearing 'soul' upon the air of philosophy. During the

*['consciousness' or 'consciousness in general' (ed.)]

SOURCE: *Journal of Philosophy, Psychology and Scientific Methods*, Vol I, No. 18 (September 1904).

past year, I have read a number of articles whose authors seemed just on the point of abandoning the notion of consciousness, and substituting for it that of an absolute experience not due to two factors. But they were not quite radical enough, not quite daring enough in their negations. For twenty years past I have mistrusted 'consciousness' as an entity; for seven or eight years past I have suggested its non-existence to my students, and tried to give them its pragmatic equivalent in realities of experience. It seems to me that the hour is ripe for it to be openly and universally discarded.

To deny plumply that 'consciousness' exists seems so absurd on the face of it—for undeniably 'thoughts' do exist—that I fear some readers will follow me no farther. Let me then immediately explain that I mean only to deny that the word stands for an entity, but to insist most emphatically that it does stand for a function. There is, I mean, no aboriginal stuff or quality of being, contrasted with that of which material objects are made, out of which our thoughts of them are made; but there is a function in experience which thoughts perform, and for the performance of which this quality of being is invoked. That function is *knowing*. 'Consciousness' is supposed necessary to explain the fact that things not only are, but get reported, are known. Whoever blots out the notion of consciousness from his list of first principles must still provide in some way for that function's being carried on.

1.

My thesis is that if we start with the supposition that there is only one primal stuff or material in the world, a stuff of which everything is composed, and if we call that stuff 'pure experience,' then knowing can easily be explained as a particular sort of relation towards one another into which portions of pure experience may enter. The relation itself is a part of pure experience; one of its 'terms' becomes the subject or bearer of the knowledge, the knower,[1] the other becomes the object known. This will need much explanation before it can be understood. The best way to get it understood is to contrast it with the alternative view; and for that we may take the recentest alternative, that in which the evaporation of the definite soul-substance has proceeded as far as it can go without being yet complete. If neo-Kantism has expelled earlier forms of dualism, we shall have expelled all forms if we are able to expel neo-Kantism in its turn.

For the thinkers I call neo-Kantian, the word consciousness to-day does no more than signalize the fact that experience is indefeasibly dualistic in structure. It means that not subject, not object, but object-plus-subject is the minimum that can actually be. The subject-object distinction meanwhile is entirely different from that between mind and matter, from that between body and soul. Souls were detachable, had separate destinies; things could happen to them. To consciousness as such nothing can happen, for, timeless itself, it is only a witness of happenings in time, in which it plays no part. It is, in a word, but the logical correlative of 'content' in an Experience of which the peculiarity is that *fact comes to light* in it, that *awareness of content* takes place. Consciousness as such is entirely impersonal—'self' and its activities belong to the content. To say that I am self-conscious, or conscious of putting forth volition, means only that certain contents, for which 'self' and 'effort of will' are the names, are not without witness as they occur.

Thus, for these belated drinkers at the Kantian spring, we should have to admit consciousness as an 'epistemological' necessity, even if we had no direct evidence of its being there.

But in addition to this, we are supposed by almost every one to have an immediate consciousness of consciousness itself. When the world of outer fact ceases to be materially present, and we merely recall it in memory, or fancy it, the consciousness is believed to stand out and to be felt as a kind of impalpable inner flowing, which, once known in this sort of experience, may equally be detected in presentations of the outer world. "The moment we try to fix our attention upon consciousness and to see *what*, distinctly, it is," says a recent writer, "it seems to vanish. It seems as if we had before us a mere emptiness. When we try to introspect the sensation of blue, all we can see is the blue; the other element is as if it were diaphanous. Yet it *can* be distinguished, if we look attentively enough, and know that there is something to look for."[2] "Consciousness" (Bewusstheit), says another philosopher, "is inexplicable and hardly describable, yet all conscious experiences have this in common that what we call their content has this peculiar reference to a centre for which 'self' is the name, in virtue of which reference alone the content is subjectively given, or appears. . . . While in this way consciousness, or reference to a self, is the only thing which distinguishes a conscious content from any sort of being that might be there with no one conscious of it, yet this only ground of the distinction defies all closer explanations. The existence of consciousness, although it is the fundamental fact of psychology, can indeed be laid down as certain, can be brought out by analysis, but can neither be defined nor deduced from anything but itself."[3]

'Can be brought out by analysis,' this author says. This supposes that the consciousness is one element, moment, factor—call it what you like—of an experience of essentially dualistic inner constitution, from which, if you abstract the content, the consciousness will remain revealed to its own eye. Experience, at this rate, would be much like a paint of which the world pictures were made. Paint has a dual constitution, involving, as it does, a menstruum[4] (oil,

---

[1]In my *Psychology* I have tried to show that we need no knower other than the 'passing thought.' [*Principles of Psychology*, vol. I, pp. 338 ff.]

[2]G. E. Moore: *Mind*, vol. XII, N.S., [1903], p. 450.

[3]Paul Natorp: *Einleitung in die Psychologie*, 1888, pp. 14, 112.

[4]"Figuratively speaking, consciousness may be said to be the one universal solvent, or menstruum, in which the different concrete kinds of psychic acts and facts are contained, whether in concealed or in obvious form." G. T. Ladd: *Psychology, Descriptive and Explanatory*, 1894, p. 30.

size or what not) and a mass of content in the form of pigment suspended therein. We can get the pure menstruum by letting the pigment settle, and the pure pigment by pouring off the size or oil. We operate here by physical subtraction; and the usual view is, that by mental subtraction we can separate the two factors of experience in an analogous way—not isolating them entirely, but distinguishing them enough to know that they are two.

2.

Now my contention is exactly the reverse of this. *Experience, I believe, has no such inner duplicity; and the separation of it into consciousness and content comes, not by way of subtraction, but by way of addition*—the addition, to a given concrete piece of it, of other sets of experiences, in connection with which severally its use or function may be of two different kinds. The paint will also serve here as an illustration. In a pot in a paint-shop, along with other paints, it serves in its entirety as so much saleable matter. Spread on a canvas, with other paints around it, it represents, on the contrary, a feature in a picture and performs a spiritual function. Just so, I maintain, does a given undivided portion of experience, taken in one context of associates, play the part of a knower, of a state of mind, of 'consciousness;' while in a different context the same undivided bit of experience plays the part of a thing known, of an objective 'content.' In a word, in one group it figures as a thought, in another group as a thing. And, since it can figure in both groups simultaneously we have every right to speak of it as subjective and objective both at once. The dualism connoted by such double-barrelled terms as 'experience,' 'phenomenon,' 'datum,' '*Vorfindung*'—terms which, in philosophy at any rate, tend more and more to replace the single-barrelled terms of 'thought' and 'thing'—that dualism, I say, is still preserved in this account, but reinterpreted, so that, instead of being mysterious and elusive, it becomes verifiable and concrete. It is an affair of relations, it falls outside, not inside, the single experience considered, and can always be particularized and defined.

The entering wedge for this more concrete way of understanding the dualism was fashioned by Locke when he made the word 'idea' stand indifferently for thing and thought, and by Berkeley when he said that what common sense means by realities is exactly what the philosopher means by ideas. Neither Locke nor Berkeley thought his truth out into perfect clearness, but it seems to me that the conception I am defending does little more than consistently carry out the 'pragmatic' method which they were the first to use.

If the reader will take his own experiences, he will see what I mean. Let him begin with a perceptual experience, the 'presentation,' so called, of a physical object, his actual field of vision, the room he sits in, with the book he is reading as its centre; and let him for the present treat this complex object in the common-sense way as being 'really' what it seems to be, namely, a collection of physical things cut out from an environing world of other physical things with which these physical things have actual or potential relations. Now at the same time it is just *those self-same things* which his mind, as we say, perceives; and the whole philosophy of perception from Democritus's time downwards has been just one long wrangle over the paradox that what is evidently one reality should be in two places at once, both in outer space and in a person's mind. 'Representative' theories of perception avoid the logical paradox, but on the other hand they violate the reader's sense of life, which knows no intervening mental image but seems to see the room and the book immediately just as they physically exist.

The puzzle of how the one identical room can be in two places is at bottom just the puzzle of how one identical point can be on two lines. It can, if it be situated at their intersection; and similarly, if the 'pure experience' of the room were a place of intersection of two processes, which connected it with different groups of associates respectively, it could be counted twice over, as belonging to either group, and spoken of loosely as existing in two places, although it would remain all the time a numerically single thing.

Well, the experience is a member of diverse processes that can be followed away from it along entirely different lines. The one self-identical thing has so many relations to the rest of experience that you can take it in disparate systems of association, and treat it as belonging with opposite contexts. In one of these contexts it is your 'field of consciousness'; in another it is 'the room in which you sit,' and it enters both contexts in its wholeness, giving no pretext for being said to attach itself to consciousness by one of its parts or aspects, and to outer reality by another. What are the two processes, now, into which the room-experience simultaneously enters in this way?

One of them is the reader's personal biography, the other is the history of the house of which the room is part. The presentation, the experience, the *that* in short (for until we have decided *what* it is it must be a mere *that*) is the last term of a train of sensations, emotions, decisions, movements, classifications, expectations, etc., ending in the present, and the first term of a series of similar 'inner' operations extending into the future, on the reader's part. On the other hand, the very same *that* is the *terminus ad quem* of a lot of previous physical operations, carpentering, papering, furnishing, warming, etc., and the *terminus a quo* of a lot of future ones, in which it will be concerned when undergoing the destiny of a physical room. The physical and the mental operations form curiously incompatible groups. As a room, the experience has occupied that spot and had that environment for thirty years. As your field of consciousness it may never have existed until now. As a room, attention will go on to discover endless new details in it. As your mental state merely, few new ones will emerge under attention's eye. As a room, it will take an earthquake, or a gang of men, and in any case a certain amount of time, to destroy it. As your subjective state, the closing of your eyes, or any instantaneous play of your fancy will suffice. In the real world, fire will consume it. In your mind, you can let fire play over it without effect. As an outer object, you must pay so much a month to inhabit it. As an inner content, you may occupy it for any length of time rent-free. If, in short, you follow it in the mental direction, taking it along with events of personal biography solely, all sorts of things are true of it which are false, and false of it which are true if

you treat it as a real thing experienced, follow it in the physical direction, and relate it to associates in the outer world.

3.

So far, all seems plain sailing, but my thesis will probably grow less plausible to the reader when I pass from percepts to concepts, or from the case of things presented to that of things remote. I believe, nevertheless, that here also the same law holds good. If we take conceptual manifolds, or memories, or fancies, they also are in their first intention mere bits of pure experience, and, as such, are single *thats* which act in one context as objects, and in another context figure as mental states. By taking them in their first intention, I mean ignoring their relation to possible perceptual experiences with which they may be connected, which they may lead to and terminate in, and which then they may be supposed to 'represent.' Taking them in this way first, we confine the problem to a world merely 'though-of' and not directly felt or seen. This world, just like the world of percepts, comes to us at first as a chaos of experiences, but lines of order soon get traced. We find that any bit of it which we may cut out as an example is connected with distinct groups of associates, just as our perceptual experiences are, that these associates link themselves with it by different relations,[5] and that one forms the inner history of a person, while the other acts as an impersonal 'objective' world, either spatial and temporal, or else merely logical or mathematical, or otherwise 'ideal.'

The first obstacle on the part of the reader to seeing that these non-perceptual experiences have objectivity as well as subjectivity will probably be due to the intrusion into his mind of *percepts*, that third group of associates with which the non-perceptual experiences have relations, and which, as a whole, they 'represent,' standing to them as thoughts to things. This important function of the non-perceptual experiences complicates the ques-

[5]Here as elsewhere the relations are of course *experienced* relations, members of the same originally chaotic manifold of nonperceptual experience of which the related terms themselves are parts.

tion and confuses it; for, so used are we to treat percepts as the sole genuine realities that, unless we keep them out of the discussion, we tend altogether to overlook the objectivity that lies in non-perceptual experiences by themselves. We treat them, 'knowing' percepts as they do, as through and through subjective, and say that they are wholly constituted of the stuff called consciousness, using this term now for a kind of entity, after the fashion which I am seeking to refute.

Abstracting, then, from percepts altogether, what I maintain is, that any single non-perceptual experience tends to get counted twice over, just as a perceptual experience does, figuring in one context as an object or field of objects, in another as a state of mind: and all this without the least internal self-diremption on its own part into consciousness and content. It is all consciousness in one taking; and, in the other, all content.

I find this objectivity of non-perceptual experiences, this complete parallelism in point of reality between the presently felt and the remotely thought, so well set forth in a page of Münsterberg's *Grundzüge*, that I will quote it as it stands.

"I may only think of my objects," says Professor Münsterberg; "yet, in my living thought they stand before me exactly as perceived objects would do, no matter how different the two ways of apprehending them may be in their genesis. The book here lying on the table before me, and the book in the next room of which I think and which I mean to get, are both in the same sense given realities for me, realities which I acknowledge and of which I take account. If you agree that the perceptual object is not an idea within me, but that percept and thing, as indistinguishably one, are really experienced *there, outside*, you ought not to believe that the merely thought-of object is hid away inside of the thinking subject. The object of which I think, and of whose existence I take cognizance without letting it now work upon my senses, occupies its definite place in the outer world as much as does the object which I directly see."

"What is true of the here and the there, is also true of the now and the then. I know of the thing which is present and perceived, but I know also of the thing which yesterday was but is no more, and which I only remember. Both can determine my present conduct, both are parts of the reality of which I keep account. It is true that of much of the past I am uncertain, just as I am uncertain of much of what is present if it be but dimly perceived. But the interval of time does not in principle alter my relation to the object, does not transform it from an object known into a mental state. . . . The things in the room here which I survey, and those in my distant home of which I think, the things of this minute and those of my long-vanished boyhood, influence and decide me alike, with a reality which my experience of them directly feels. They both make up my real world, they make it directly, they do not have first to be introduced to me and mediated by ideas which now and here arise within me. . . . This not-me character of my recollections and expectations does not imply that the external objects of which I am aware in those experiences should necessarily be there also for others. The objects of dreamers and hallucinated persons are wholly without general validity. But even were they centaurs and golden mountains, they still would be 'off there,' in fairy land, and not 'inside' of ourselves."[6]

This certainly is the immediate, primary, naïf, or practical way of taking our thought-of world. Were there no perceptual world to serve as its 'reductive,' in Taine's sense, by being 'stronger' and more genuinely 'outer' (so that the whole merely thought-of world seems weak and inner in comparison), our world of thought would be the only world, and would enjoy complete reality in our belief. This actually happens in our dreams, and in our day-dreams so long as percepts do not interrupt them.

And yet, just as the seen room (to go back to our late example) is *also* a field of consciousness, so the conceived or recollected room is *also* a state of mind; and the doubling-up of the experience has in both cases similar grounds.

The room thought-of, namely, has many thought-of couplings with many thought-of

[6]Münsterberg: *Grundzüge der Psychologie*, vol. 1, p. 48.

things. Some of these couplings are inconstant, others are stable. In the reader's personal history the room occupies a single date—he saw it only once perhaps, a year ago. Of the house's history, on the other hand, it forms a permanent ingredient. Some couplings have the curious stubbornness, to borrow Royce's term, of fact; others show the fluidity of fancy—we let them come and go as we please. Grouped with the rest of its house, with the name of its town, of its owner, builder, value, decorative plan, the room maintains a definite foothold, to which, if we try to loosen it, it tends to return, and to reassert itself with force.[7] With these associates, in a word, it coheres, while to other houses, other towns, other owners, etc., it shows no tendency to cohere at all. The two collections, first of its cohesive, and, second, of its loose associates, inevitably come to be contrasted. We call the first collection the system of external realities, in the midst of which the room, as 'real,' exists; the other we call the stream of our internal thinking, in which, as a 'mental image,' it for a moment floats.[8] The room thus again gets counted twice over. It plays two different rôles, being *Gedanke* and *Gedachtes*, the thought-of-an-object, and the object-thought-of, both in one; and all this without paradox or mystery, just as the same material thing may be both low and high, or small and great, or bad and good, because of its relations to opposite parts of an environing world.

As 'subjective' we say that the experience represents; as 'objective' it is represented. What represents and what is represented is here numerically the same; but we must remember that no dualism of being represented and representing resides in the experience *per se.* In its pure state, or when isolated, there is no self-splitting of it into consciousness and what the consciousness is 'of.' Its subjectivity and objectivity are functional attributes solely, realized only when the experience is 'taken,' *i.e.*, talked-of, twice, considered along with its two differing contexts respectively, by a new retrospective experience, of which that whole past complication now forms the fresh content.

The instant field of the present is at all times what I call the 'pure' experience. It is only virtually or potentially either object or subject as yet. For the time being, it is plain, unqualified actuality, or existence, a simple *that.* In this *naïf* immediacy it is of course *valid;* it is *there,* we *act* upon it; and the doubling of it in retrospection into a state of mind and a reality intended thereby, is just one of the acts. The 'state of mind,' first treated explicitly as such in retrospection, will stand corrected or confirmed, and the retrospective experience in its turn will get a similar treatment; but the immediate experience in its passing is always 'truth,'[9] practical truth, *something to act on,* at its own movement. If the world were then and there to go out like a candle, it would remain truth absolute and objective, for it would be 'the last word,' would have no critic, and no one would ever oppose the thought in it to the reality intended.[10]

I think I may now claim to have made my thesis clear. Consciousness connotes a kind of external relation, and does not denote a special stuff or way of being. *The peculiarity of our experiences, that they not only are, but are known, which their 'conscious' quality is invoked to explain, is better explained by their relations—these relations themselves being experiences—to one another.*

---

[7]Cf. A. L. Hodder: *The Adversaries of the Sceptic,* pp 94–99.

[8]For simplicity's sake I confine my exposition to 'external' reality. But there is also the system of ideal reality in which the room plays its part. Relations of comparison, of classification, serial order, value, also are stubborn, assign a definite place to the room, unlike the incoherence of its places in the mere rhapsody of our successive thoughts.

[9]Note the ambiguity of this term, which is taken sometimes objectively and sometimes subjectively.

[10]In the *Psychological Review* for July [1904], Dr. R. B. Perry has published a view of Consciousness which comes nearer to mine than any other with which I am acquainted. At present, Dr. Perry thinks, every field of experience is so much 'fact.' It becomes 'opinion' or 'thought' only in retrospection, when a fresh experience, thinking the same object, alters and corrects it. But the corrective experience becomes itself in turn corrected, and thus experience as a whole is a process in which what is objective originally forever turns subjective, turns into our apprehension of the object. I strongly recommend Dr. Perry's admirable article to my readers.

4.

Were I now to go on to treat of the knowing of perceptual by conceptual experiences, it would again prove to be an affair of external relations. One experience would be the knower, the other the reality known; and I could perfectly well define, without the notion of 'consciousness,' what the knowing actually and practically amounts to—leading-towards, namely, and terminating-in percepts, through a series of transitional experiences which the world supplies. But I will not treat of this, space being insufficient. I will rather consider a few objections that are sure to be urged against the entire theory as it stands.

5.

First of all, this will be asked: "If experience has not 'conscious' existence, if it be not partly made of 'consciousness,' of what then is it made? Matter we know, and thought we know, and conscious content we know, but neutral and simple 'pure experience' is something we know not at all. Say *what* it consists of—for it must consist of something—or be willing to give it up!"

To this challenge the reply is easy. Although for fluency's sake I myself spoke early in this article of a stuff of pure experience, I have now to say that there is no *general* stuff of which experience at large is made. There are as many stuffs as there are 'natures' in the things experienced. If you ask what any one bit of pure experience is made of, the answer is always the same: "It is made of *that*, of just what appears, of space, of intensity, of flatness, brownness, heaviness, or what not." Shadworth Hodgson's analysis here leaves nothing to be desired. Experience is only a collective name for all these sensible natures, and save for time and space (and, if you like, for 'being') there appears no universal element of which all things are made.

6.

The next objection is more formidable, in fact it sounds quite crushing when one hears it first.

"If it be the self-same piece of pure experi-ence, taken twice over, that serves now as thought and now as thing"—so the objection runs—"how comes it that its attributes should differ so fundamentally in the two takings. As thing, the experience is extended; as thought, it occupies no space or place. As thing, it is red, hard, heavy; but who ever heard of a red, hard or heavy thought? Yet even now you said that an experience is made of just what appears, and what appears is just such adjectives. How can the one experience in its thing-function be made of them, consist of them, carry them as its own attributes, while in its thought-function it disowns them and attributes them elsewhere. There is a self-contradiction here from which the radical dualism of thought and thing is the only truth that can save us. Only if the thought is one kind of being can the adjectives exist in it 'intentionally' (to use the scholastic term); only if the thing is another kind, can they exist in it constitutively and energetically. No simple subject can take the same adjectives and at one time be qualified by it, and at another time be merely 'of' it, as of something only meant or known."

The solution insisted on by this objector, like many other common-sense solutions, grows the less satisfactory the more one turns it in one's mind. To begin with, *are* thought and thing as heterogeneous as is commonly said?

No one denies that they have some categories in common. Their relations to time are identical. Both, moreover, may have parts (for psychologists in general treat thoughts as having them); and both may be complex or simple. Both are of kinds, can be compared, added and subtracted and arranged in serial orders. All sorts of adjectives qualify our thoughts which appear in incompatible with consciousness, being as such a bare diaphaneity. For instance, they are natural and easy, or laborious. They are beautiful, happy, intense, interesting, wise idiotic, focal, marginal, insipid, confused, vague, precise, rational, casual, general, particular, and many things besides. Moreover, the chapters on 'Perception' in the psychology-books are full of facts that make for the essential homogeneity of thought with thing. How, if 'subject' and 'object' were separated 'by the whole diameter of being,' and had no attributes in common, could it be so hard to tell, in a presented and recognized material object, what part comes in through the sense-organs and what part comes 'out of one's own head'? Sensations and apperceptive ideas fuse here so intimately that you can no more tell where one begins and the other ends, than you can tell, in those cunning circular panoramas that have lately been exhibited, where the real foreground and the painted canvas join together.[11]

Descartes for the first time defined thought as the absolutely unextended, and later philosophers have accepted the description as correct. But what possible meaning has it to say that, when we think of a foot-rule or a square yard, extension is not attributable to our thought? Of every extended object the *adequate* mental picture must have all the extension of the object itself. The difference between objective and subjective extension is one of relation to a context solely. In the mind the various extents maintain no necessarily stubborn order relatively to each other, while in the physical world they bound each other stably, and, added together, make the great enveloping Unit which we believe in and call real Space. As 'outer,' they carry themselves adversely, so to speak, to one another, exclude one another and maintain their distances; while, as 'inner,' their order is loose, and they form a *durcheinander* in which unity is lost.[12] But to argue from this that inner experience is absolutely inextensive seems to me little short of absurd. The two worlds differ, not by the presence or absence of extension, but by the relations of the extensions which in both worlds exist.

Does not this case of extension now put us on the track of truth in the case of other quali-

ties? It does; and I am surprised that the facts should not have been noticed long ago. Why, for example, do we call a fire hot, and water wet, and yet refuse to say that our mental state, when it is 'of' these objects, is either wet or hot? 'Intentionally,' at any rate, and when the mental state is a vivid image, hotness and wetness are in it just as much as they are in the physical experience. The reason is this, that, as the general chaos of all our experiences gets sifted, we find that there are some fires that will always burn sticks and always warm our bodies, and that there are some waters that will always put out fires; while there are other fires and waters that will not act at all. The general group of experiences that *act*, that do not only possess their natures intrinsically, but wear them adjectively and energetically, turning them against one another, comes inevitably to be contrasted with the group whose members, having identically the same natures, fail to manifest them in the 'energetic' way. I make for myself now an experience of blazing fire; I place it near my body; but it does not warm me in the least. I lay a stick upon it, and the stick either burns or remains green, as I please. I call up water, and pour it on the fire, and absolutely no difference ensues. I account for all such facts by calling this whole train of experiences unreal, a mental train. Mental fire is what won't burn real sticks; mental water is what won't necessarily (though of course it may) put out even a mental fire. Mental knives may be sharp, but they won't cut real wood. Mental triangles are pointed, but their points won't wound. With 'real' objects, on the contrary, consequences always accrue; and thus the real experiences get sifted from the mental ones, the things from our thoughts of them, fanciful or true, and precipitated together as the stable part of the whole experience-chaos, under the name of the physical world. Of this our perceptual experiences are the nucleus, they being the originally *strong* experiences. We add a lot of conceptual experiences to them, making these strong also in imagination, and building out the remoter parts of the physical world by their means; and around this core of reality the world of laxly connected fancies and mere rhapsodical objects floats like a bank of clouds. In the clouds, all sorts of

[11]Spencer's proof of his 'Transfigured Realism' (his doctrine that there is an absolutely non-mental reality) comes to mind as a splendid instance of the impossibility of establishing radical heterogeneity between thought and thing. All his painfully accumulated points of difference run gradually into their opposites, and are full of exceptions. [Cf. Spencer: *Principles of Psychology*, part VII, ch. XIX.]

[12]I speak here of the complete inner life in which the mind plays freely with its materials. Of course the mind's free play is restricted when it seeks to copy real things in real space.

rules are violated which in the core are kept. Extensions there can be indefinitely located; motion there obeys no Newton's laws.

7.

There is a peculiar class of experiences to which, whether we take them as subjective or as objective, we *assign* their several natures as attributes, because in both contexts they affect their associates actively, though in neither quite as 'strongly' or as sharply as things affect one another by their physical energies. I refer here to *appreciations*, which form an ambiguous sphere of being, belonging with emotion on the one hand, and having objective 'value' on the other, yet seeming not quite inner nor quite outer, as if a diremption had begun but had not made itself complete.

Experiences of painful objects, for example, are usually also painful experiences; perceptions of loveliness, of ugliness, tend to pass muster as lovely or as ugly perceptions; intuitions of the morally lofty are lofty intuitions. Sometimes the adjective wanders as if uncertain where to fix itself. Shall we speak of seductive visions or of visions of seductive things? Of wicked desires or of desires for wickedness? Of healthly thoughts or of thoughts of healthy objects? Of good impulses, or of impulses towards the good? Of feelings of anger, or of angry feelings? Both in the mind and in the thing, these natures modify their context, exclude certain associates and determine others, have their mates and incompatibles. Yet not as stubbornly as in the case of physical qualities, for beauty and ugliness, love and hatred, pleasant and painful can, in certain complex experiences, coexist.

If one were to make an evolutionary construction of how a lot of originally chaotic pure experiences became gradually differentiated into an orderly inner and outer world, the whole theory would turn upon one's success in explaining how or why the quality of an experience, once active, could become less so, and, from being an energetic attribute in some cases, elsewhere lapse into the status of an inert or merely internal 'nature.' This would be the 'evolution' of the psychical from the bosom of the physical, in which the esthetic moral and otherwise emotional experiences would represent a halfway stage.

8.

But a last cry of *non possumus* will probably go up from many readers. "All very pretty as a piece of ingenuity," they will say, "but our consciousness itself intuitively contradicts you. We, for our part, *know* that we are conscious. We *feel* our thought, flowing as a life within us, in absolute contrast with the objects which it so unremittingly escorts. We can not be faithless to this immediate intuition. The dualism is a fundamental *datum:* Let no man join what God has put asunder."

My reply to this is my last word, and I greatly grieve that to many it will sound materialistic. I can not help that, however, for I, too, have my intuitions and I must obey them. Let the case be what it may in others, I am as confident as I am of anything that, in myself, the stream of thinking (which I recognize emphatically as a phenomenon) is only a careless name for what, when scrutinized, reveals itself to consist chiefly of the stream of my breathing. The 'I think' which Kant said must be able to accompany all my objects, is the 'I breathe' which actually does accompany them. There are other internal facts besides breathing (intracephalic muscular adjustments, etc., of which I have said a word in my larger Psychology), and these increase the assets of 'consciousness,' so far as the latter is subject to immediate perception; but breath, which was ever the original of 'spirit,' breath moving outwards, between the glottis and the nostrils, is, I am persuaded, the essence out of which philosophers have constructed the entity known to them as consciousness. *That entity is fictitious, while thoughts in the concrete are fully real. But thoughts in the concrete are made of the same stuff as things are.*

I wish I might believe myself to have made that plausible in this article. In another article I shall try to make the general notion of a world composed of pure experiences still more clear.

A World of Pure Experience

It is difficult not to notice a curious unrest in the philosophic atmosphere of the time, a loosening of old landmarks, a softening of oppositions, a mutual borrowing from one another on the part of systems anciently closed, and an interest in new suggestions, however vague, as if the one thing sure were the inadequacy of the extant school-solutions. The dissatisfaction with these seems due for the most part to a feeling that they are too abstract and academic. Life is confused and superabundant, and what the younger generation appears to crave is more of the temperament of life in its philosophy, even though it were at some cost of logical rigor and of formal purity. Transcendental idealism is inclining to let the world wag incomprehensibly, in spite of its Absolute Subject and his unity of purpose. Berkeleyan idealism is abandoning the principle of parsimony and dabbling in panpsychic speculations. Empiricism flirts with teleology; and, strangest of all, natural realism, so long decently buried, raises its head above the turf, and finds glad hands outstretched from the most unlikely quarters to help it to its feet again. We are all biased by our personal feelings, I know, and I am personally discontented with extant solutions; so I seem to read the signs of a great unsettlement, as if the upheaval of more real conceptions and more fruitful methods were imminent, as if a true landscape might result, less clipped, straight-edged and artificial.

If philosophy be really on the eve of any considerable rearrangement, the time should be propitious for any one who has suggestions of his own to bring forward. For many years past my mind has been growing into a certain type of *Weltanschauung*. Rightly or wrongly, I have got to the point where I can hardly see things in any other pattern. I propose, therefore, to describe the pattern as clearly as I can consistently with great brevity, and to throw my description into the bubbling vat of publicity where, jostled by rivals and torn by critics, it will eventually either disappear from notice, or else, if better luck befall it, quietly subside to the profundities, and serve as a possible ferment of new growths or a nucleus of new crystallization.

SOURCE: *Journal of Philosophy, Psychology and Scientific Methods*, Vol. I, No. 20 and No. 21 (1904).

1. Radical Empiricism

I give the name of 'radical empiricism' to my *Weltanschauung*. Empiricism is known as the opposite of rationalism. Rationalism tends to emphasize universals and to make wholes prior to parts in the order of logic as well as in that of being. Empiricism, on the contrary, lays the explanatory stress upon the part, the element, the individual, and treats the whole as a collection and the universal as an abstraction. My description of things, accordingly, starts with the parts and makes of the whole a being of the second order. It is essentially a mosaic philosophy, a philosophy of plural facts, like that of Hume and his descendants, who refer these facts neither to Substances in which they inhere nor to an Absolute Mind that creates them as its objects. But it differs from the Humian type of empiricism in one particular which makes me add the epithet radical.

To be radical, an empiricism must neither admit into its constructions any element that is not directly experienced, nor exclude from them any element that is directly experienced. For such a philosophy, *the relations that connect experiences must themselves be experienced relations, and any kind of relation experienced must be accounted as 'real' as anything else in the system.* Elements may indeed be redistributed, the original placing of things getting corrected, but a real place must be found for every kind of thing experienced, whether term or relation, in the final philosophic arrangement.

Now, ordinary empiricism, in spite of the fact that conjunctive and disjunctive relations present themselves as being fully co-ordinate parts of experience, has always shown a tendency to do away with the connections of things, and to insist most on the disjunctions. Berkeley's nominalism, Hume's statement that whatever things we distinguish are as 'loose and separate' as if they had 'no manner of connection,' James Mill's denial that similars have anything 'really' in common, the resolution of the causal tie into habitual sequence, John Mill's account of both physical things and selves as composed of discontinuous possibilities, and the general pulverization of all Experience by association and the mind-dust theory, are examples of what I mean.

The natural result of such a world-picture has been the efforts of rationalism to correct its incoherencies by the addition of trans-experiential agents of unification, substances, intellectual categories and powers, or Selves; whereas, if empiricism had only been radical and taken everything that comes without disfavor, conjunction as well as separation, each at its face value, the results would have called for no such artificial correction. *Radical empiricism,* as I understand it, *does full justice to conjunctive relations,* without, however, treating them as rationalism always tends to treat them, as being true in some supernal way, as if the unity of things and their variety belonged to different orders of truth and vitality altogether.

2. *Conjunctive Relations*

Relations are of different degrees of intimacy. Merely to be 'with' one another in a universe of discourse is the most external relation that terms can have, and seems to involve nothing whatever so to farther consequences. Simultaneity and time-interval come next, and then space-adjacency and distance. After them, similarity and difference, carrying the possibility of many inferences. Then relations of activity, tying terms into series involving change, tendency, resistance, and the causal order generally. Finally, the relation experienced between terms that form states of mind, and are immediately conscious of continuing each other. The organization of the Self as a system of memories, purposes, strivings, fulfilments or disappointments, is incidental to this most intimate of all relations, the terms of which seem in many cases actually to compenetrate and suffuse each other's being.

Philosophy has always turned on grammatical particles. With, near, next, like, from, towards, against, because, for, through, my—these words designate types of conjunctive relation arranged in a roughly ascending order of intimacy and inclusiveness. *A priori,* we can imagine a universe of withness but no nextness; or one of nextness but no likeness, or of likeness with no activity, or of activity with no purpose, or of purpose with no ego. These would be universes, each with its own grade of unity. The universe of human experience is, by one or another of its parts, of each and all these grades. Whether or not it possibly enjoys some still more absolute grade of union does not appear upon the surface.

Taken as it does appear, our universe is to a large extent chaotic. No one single type of connection runs through all the experiences that compose it. If we take space-relations, they fail to connect minds into any regular system. Causes and purposes obtain only among special series of facts. The self-relation seems extremely limited and does not link two different selves together. *Prima facie,* if you should liken the universe of absolute idealism to an aquarium, a crystal globe in which goldfish are swimming, you would have to compare the empiricist universe to something more like one of those dried human heads with which the Dyaks of Borneo deck their lodges. The skull forms a solid nucleus; but innumerable feathers, leaves, strings, beads, and loose appendices of every description float and dangle from it, and, save that they terminate in it, seem to have nothing to do with one another. Even so my experiences and yours float and dangle, terminating, it is true, in a nucleus of common perception, but for the most part out of sight and irrelevant and unimaginable to one another. This imperfect intimacy, this bare relation of *withness* between some parts of the sum total of experience and other parts, is the fact that ordinary empiricism over-emphasizes against rationalism, the latter always tending to ignore it unduly. Radical empiricism, on the contrary, is fair to both the unity and the disconnection. It finds no reason for treating either as illusory. It allots to each its definite sphere of description, and agrees that there appear to be actual forces at work which tend, as time goes on, to make the unity greater.

The conjunctive relation that has given most trouble to philosophy is *the co-conscious transition,* so to call it, by which one experience passes into another when both belong to the same self. About the facts there is no question. My experiences and your experiences are 'with' each other in various external ways, but mine pass into mine, and yours pass into yours in a way in which yours and mine never pass into one another. Within each of our personal histories, subject, object, interest and purpose *are continuous or may be continuous.* Personal histories are processes of change in time, and *the change itself is one of the things immediately experienced.* 'Change' in this case means continuous as opposed to discontinuous transition. But continuous transition is one sort of a conjunctive relation; and to be a radical empiricist means to hold fast to this conjunctive relation of all others, for this is the strategic point, the position through which, if a hole be made, all the corruptions of dialectics and all the metaphysical fictions pour into our philosophy. The holding fast to this relation means taking it at its face value, neither less nor more; and to take it at its face value means first of all to take it just as we feel it, and not to confuse ourselves with abstract talk *about* it, involving words that drive us to invent secondary conceptions in order to neutralize their suggestions and to make our actual experience again seem rationally possible.

What I do feel simply when a later moment of my experience succeeds an earlier one is that though they are two moments, the transition from the one to the other is *continuous.* Continuity here is a definite sort of experience; just as definite as is the *discontinuity-experience* which I find it impossible to avoid when I seek to make the transition from an experience of my own to one of yours. In this latter case I have to get on and off again, to pass from a thing lived to another thing only conceived, and the break is positively experienced and noted. Though the functions exerted by my experience and by yours may be the same (*e.g.,* the same objects known and the same purposes followed), yet the sameness has in this case to be ascertained expressly (and often with difficulty and uncertainty) after the break has been felt; whereas in passing from one of my own moments to another the sameness of object and interest is unbroken, and both the earlier and the later experience are of things directly lived.

There is no other *nature,* no other whatness than this absence of break and this sense of continuity in that most intimate of all conjunctive relations, the passing of one experience into another when they belong to the same self. And this whatness is real empirical 'content,' just as the whatness of separation and discontinuity is real content in the contrasted case. Practically to experience one's personal continuum in this living way is to know the originals of the ideas of continuity and of sameness, to know what the words stand for concretely, to own all that they can ever mean. But all experiences have their conditions; and over-subtle intellects, thinking about the facts here, and asking how they are possible, have ended by substituting a lot of static objects of conception for the direct perceptual experiences. "Sameness," they have said, "must be a stark numerical identity; it can't run on from next to next. Continuity can't mean mere absence of gap; for if you say two things are in immediate contact, *at* the contact how can they be two? If, on the other hand, you put a relation of transition between them, that itself is a third thing, and needs to be related or hitched to its terms. An infinite series is involved," and so on. The result is that from difficulty to difficulty, the plain conjunctive experience has been discredited by both schools, the empiricists leaving things permanently disjoined, and the rationalist remedying the looseness by their Absolutes or Substances, or whatever other fictitious agencies of union they may have employed. From all which artificiality we can be saved by a couple of simple reflections: first, that conjunctions and separations are, at all events, co-ordinate phenomena which, if we take experiences at their face value, must be accounted equally real; and second, that if we insist on treating things as really separate when they are given as continuously joined, invoking, when union is required, transcendental principles to overcome the separateness we have assumed, then we ought to stand ready to perform the converse act. We ought to invoke higher principles of *dis*union, also, to make our merely experienced *dis*junctions more truly real. Failing thus, we ought to let the originally given continuities stand on their own bottom. We have no right to be lopsided or to blow capriciously hot and cold.

3. *The Cognitive Relation*

The first great pitfall from which such a radical standing by experience will save us is an artificial conception of the *relations between knower and known*. Throughout the history of philosophy the subject and its object have been treated as absolutely discontinuous entities; and thereupon the presence of the latter to the former, or the 'apprehension' by the former of the latter, has assumed a paradoxical character which all sorts of theories had to be invented to overcome. Representative theories put a mental 'representation,' 'image,' or 'content' into the gap, as a sort of intermediary. Common-sense theories left the gap untouched, declaring our mind able to clear it by a self-transcending leap. Transcendentalist theories left it impossible to traverse by finite knowers, and brought an Absolute in to perform the saltatory act. All the while, in the very bosom of the finite experience, every conjunction required to make the relation intelligible is given in full. Either the knower and the known are:

(1) the self-same piece of experience taken twice over in different contexts; or they are

(2) two pieces of *actual* experience belonging to the same subject, with definite tracts of conjunctive transitional experience between them; or

(3) the known is a *possible* experience either of that subject or another, to which the said conjunctive transitions *would* lead, if sufficiently prolonged.

To discuss all the ways in which one experience may function as the knower of another, would be incompatible with the limits of this essay.[1] I have just treated of type 1, the kind of

knowledge called perception. This is the type of case in which the mind enjoys direct 'acquaintance' with a present object. In the other types the mind has 'knowledge-about' an object not immediately there. Of type 2, the simplest sort of conceptual knowledge, I have given some account in two [earlier] articles. Type 3 can always formally and hypothetically be reduced to type 2, so that a brief description of that type will put the present reader sufficiently at my point of view, and make him see what the actual meanings of the mysterious cognitive relation may be.

Suppose me to be sitting here in my library at Cambridge, at ten minutes' walk from 'Memorial Hall,' and to be thinking truly of the latter object. My mind may have before it only the name, or it may have a clear image, or it may have a very dim image of the hall, but such intrinsic differences in the image make no difference in its cognitive function. Certain *extrinsic* phenomena, special experiences of conjunction, are what impart to the image, be it what it may, its knowing office.

For instance, if you ask me what hall I mean by my image, and I can tell you nothing; or if I fail to point or lead you towards the Harvard Delta; or if, being led by you, I am uncertain whether the Hall I see be what I had in mind or not; you would rightly deny that I had 'meant' that particular hall at all, even though my mental image might to some degree have resembled it. The resemblance would count in that case as coincidental merely, for all sorts of things of a kind resemble one another in this world without being held for that reason to take cognizance of one another.

On the other hand, if I can lead you to the hall, and tell you of its history and present uses; if in its presence I feel my idea, however imperfect it may have been, to have led hither

---

[1] For brevity's sake I altogether omit mention of the type constituted by knowledge of the truth of general propositions. This type has been thoroughly and, so far as I can see, satisfactorily elucidated in Dewey's *Studies in Logical Theory*. Such propositions are reducible to the *S-is-P* form; and the 'terminus' that verifies and fulfils is the *SP* in combination. Of course percepts may be involved in the mediating experiences, or in the 'satisfactoriness' of the *P* in its new position.

and to be now *terminated;* if the associates of the image and of the felt hall run parallel, so that each term of the one context corresponds serially, as I walk, with an answering term of the others; why then my soul was prophetic, and my idea must be, and by common consent would be, called cognizant of reality. That percept was what I *meant,* for into it my idea has passed by conjunctive experiences of sameness and fulfilled intention. Nowhere is there jar, but every later moment continues and corroborates an earlier one.

In this continuing and corroborating, taken in no transcendental sense, but denoting definitely felt transitions, *lies all that the knowing of a percept by an idea can possibly contain or signify.* Wherever such transitions are felt, the first experience *knows* the last one. Where they do not, or where even as possibles they can not, intervene, there can be no pretence of knowing. In this latter case the extremes will be connected, if connected at all, by inferior relations—bare likeness or succession, or by 'withness' alone. Knowledge of sensible realities thus comes to life inside the tissue of experience. It is *made;* and made by relations that unroll themselves in time. Whenever certain intermediaries are given, such that, as they develop towards their terminus, there is experience from point to point of one direction followed, and finally of one process fulfilled, the result is that *their starting-point thereby becomes a knower and their terminus an object meant or known.* That is all that knowing (in the simple case considered) can be known-as, that is the whole of its nature, put into experiential terms. Whenever such is the sequence of our experiences we may freely say that we had the terminal object 'in mind' from the outset, even although *at* the outset nothing was there in us but a flat piece of substantive experience like any other, with no self-transcendency about it, and no mystery save the mystery of coming into existence and of being gradually followed by other pieces of substantive experience, with conjunctively transitional experiences between. That is what we *mean* here by the object's being 'in mind.' Of any deeper more real way of being in mind we have no positive conception, and we have no right to discredit our actual experience by talking of such a way at all.

I know that many a reader will rebel at this. "Mere intermediaries," he will say, "even though they be feelings of continuously growing fulfilment, only *separate* the knower from the known, whereas what we have in knowledge is a kind of immediate touch of the one by the other, an 'apprehension' in the etymological sense of the word, a leaping of the chasm as by lightning, an act by which two terms are smitten into one, over the head of their distinctness. All these dead intermediaries of yours are out of each other, and outside of their termini still."

But do not such dialectic difficulties remind us of the dog dropping his bone and snapping at its image in the water? If we knew any more real kind of union *aliunde,* we might be entitled to brand all our empirical unions as a sham. But unions by continuous transition are the only ones we know of, whether in this matter of a knowledge-about that terminates in an acquaintance, whether in personal identity, in logical predication through the copula 'is,' or elsewhere. If anywhere there were more absolute unions realized, they could only reveal themselves to us by just such conjunctive results. These are what the unions are *worth,* these are all that *we can ever practically mean* by union, by continuity. Is it not time to repeat what Lotze said of substances, that to *act like* one is to *be* one? Should we not say here that to be experienced as continuous is to be really continuous, in a world where experience and reality come to the same thing? In a picture gallery a painted hook will serve to hang a painted chain by, a painted cable will hold a painted ship. In a world where both the terms and their distinctions are affairs of experience, conjunctions that are experienced must be at least as real as anything else. They will be 'absolutely' real conjunctions, if we have no transphenomenal Absolute ready, to derealize the whole experienced world by, at a stroke. If, on the other hand, we had such an Absolute, not one of our opponents' theories of knowledge could remain standing any better than ours could; for the distinctions as well as the conjunctions of experience would impartially fall its prey. The whole question of how 'one' thing can know 'another' would cease to be a real one at all in a world where otherness itself was an illusion.[2]

So much for the essentials of the cognitive relation, where the knowledge is conceptual in type, or forms knowledge 'about' an object. It consists in intermediary experiences (possible, if not actual) of continuously developing progress, and, finally, of fulfilment, when the sensible percept, which is the object, is reached. The percept here not only *verifies* the concept, proves its function of knowing that percept to be true, but the percept's existence as the terminus of the chain of intermediaries *creates* the function. Whatever terminates that chain was, because it now proves itself to be, what the concept 'had in mind.'

The towering importance for human life of this kind of knowing lies in the fact that an experience that knows another can figure as its *representative*, not in any quasi-miraculous 'epistemological' sense, but in the definite practical sense of being its *substitute* in various operations, sometimes physical and sometimes mental, which lead us to its associates and results. By experimenting on our ideas of reality, we may save ourselves the trouble of experimenting on the real experiences which they severally mean. The ideas form related systems, corresponding point for point to the systems which the realities form; and by letting an ideal term call up its associates systematically, we may be led to a terminus which the corresponding real term would have led to in case we had operated on the real world. And this brings us to the general question of substitution.

4. Substitution

In Taine's brilliant book on 'Intelligence,' substitution was for the first time named as a cardinal logical function, though of course the facts had always been familiar enough. What,

exactly, in a system of experiences, does the 'substitution' of one of them for another mean?

According to my view, experience as a whole is a process in time, whereby innumerable particular terms lapse and are superseded by others that follow upon them by transitions which, whether disjunctive or conjunctive in content, are themselves experiences, and must in general be accounted at least as real as the terms which they relate. What the nature of the event called 'superseding' signifies, depends altogether on the kind of transition that obtains. Some experiences simply abolish their predecessors without continuing them in any way. Others are felt to increase or to enlarge their meaning, to carry out their purpose, or to bring us nearer to their goal. They 'represent' them, and may fulfil their function better than they fulfilled it themselves. But to 'fulfil a function' in a world of pure experience can be conceived and defined in only one possible way. In such a world transitions and arrivals (or terminations) are the only events that happen, though they happen by so many sorts of path. The only function that one experience can perform is to lead into another experience; and the only fulfilment we can speak of is the reaching of a certain experienced end. When one experience leads to (or can lead to) the same end as another, they agree in function. But the whole system of experiences as they are immediately given presents itself as a quasi-chaos through which one can pass out of an initial term in many directions and yet end in the same terminus, moving from next to next by a great many possible paths.

Either one of these paths might be a functional substitute for another, and to follow one rather than another might on occasion be an advantageous thing to do. As a matter of fact, and in a general way, the paths that run through conceptual experiences, that is, through 'thoughts' or 'ideas' that 'know' the things in which they terminate, are highly advantageous paths to follow. Not only do they yield inconceivably rapid transitions; but, owing to the 'universal' character[3] which they

---

[2]Mr. Bradley, not professing to know his absolute *aliunde*, nevertheless derealizes Experience by alleging it to be everywhere infected with self-contradiction. His arguments seem almost purely verbal, but this is no place for arguing that point out. [Cf. F. H. Bradley; *Appearance and Reality* . . .]

[3]Of which all that need be said in this essay is that it also can be conceived as functional, and defined in terms of transitions, or of the possibility of such.

frequently possess, and to their capacity for association with one another in great systems, they outstrip the tardy consecutions of the things themselves, and sweep us on towards our ultimate termini in a far more labor-saving way than the following of trains of sensible perception ever could. Wonderful are the new cuts and the short-circuits which the thought-paths make. Most thought-paths, it is true, are substitutes for nothing actual; they end outside the real world altogether, in wayward fancies, utopias, fictions or mistakes. But where they do re-enter reality and terminate therein, we substitute them always; and with these substitutes we pass the greater number of our hours.

This is why I called our experiences, taken all together, a quasi-chaos. There is vastly more discontinuity in the sum total of experiences than we commonly suppose. The objective nucleus of every man's experience, his own body, is, it is true, a continuous percept; and equally continuous as a percept (though we may be inattentive to it) is the material environment of that body, changing by gradual transition when the body moves. But the distant parts of the physical world are at all times absent from us, and form conceptual objects merely, into the perceptual reality of which our life inserts itself at points discrete and relatively rare. Round their several objective nuclei, partly shared and common and partly discrete, of the real physical world, innumerable thinkers, pursuing their several lines of physically true cogitation, trace paths that intersect one another only at discontinuous perceptual points, and the rest of the time are quite incongruent; and around all the nuclei of shared 'reality,' as around the Dyak's head of my late metaphor, floats the vast cloud of experiences that are wholly subjective, that are non-substitutional, that find not even an eventual ending for themselves in the perceptual world—the mere day-dreams and joys and sufferings and wishes of the individual minds. These exist *with* one another, indeed, and with the objective nuclei, but out of them it is probable that to all eternity no interrelated system of any kind will ever be made.

This notion of the purely substitutional or conceptual physical world brings us to the most critical of all the steps in the development of a philosophy of pure experience. The paradox of self-transcendency in knowledge comes back upon us here, but I think that our notions of pure experience and of substitution, and our radically empirical view of conjunctive transitions, are *Denkmittel** that will carry us safely through the pass.

5. *What Objective Reference Is*

Whosoever feels his experience to be something substitutional even while he has it, may be said to have an experience that reaches beyond itself. From inside of its own entity it says 'more,' and postulates reality existing elsewhere. For the transcendentalist, who holds knowing to consist in a *salto mortale* across an 'epistemological chasm,' such an idea presents no difficulty; but it seems at first sight as if it might be inconsistent with an empiricism like our own. Have we not explained that conceptual knowledge is made such wholly by the existence of things that fall outside of the knowing experience itself—by intermediary experiences and by a terminus that fulfils? Can the knowledge be there before these elements that constitute its being have come? And, if knowledge be not there, how can objective reference occur?

The key to this difficulty lies in the distinction between knowing as verified and completed, and the same knowing as in transit and on its way. To recur to the Memorial Hall example lately used, it is only when our idea of the Hall has actually terminated in the percept that we know 'for certain' that from the beginning it was truly cognitive of *that*. Until established by the end of the process, its quality of knowing that, or indeed of knowing anything, could still be doubted; and yet the knowing really was there, as the result now shows. We were *virtual* knowers of the Hall long before we were certified to have been its actual knowers, by the percept's retroactive validating power. Just so we are 'mortal' all the time, by reason of the virtuality of the inevitable event which will make us so when it shall have come.

*[tools of thought (ed.)]

Now the immensely greater part of all our knowing never gets beyond this virtual stage. It never is completed or nailed down. I speak not merely of our ideas of imperceptibles like ether-waves or dissociated 'ions,' or of 'ejects' like the contents of our neighbors' minds; I speak also of ideas which we might verify if we would take the trouble, but which we hold for true although unterminated perceptually, because nothing says 'no' to us, and there is no contradicting truth in sight. *To continue thinking unchallenged is, ninety-nine times out of a hundred, our practical substitute for knowing in the completed sense.* As each experience runs by cognitive transition into the next one, and we nowhere feel a collision with what we elsewhere count as truth or fact, we commit ourselves to the current as if the port were sure. We live, as it were, upon the front edge of an advancing wave-crest, and our sense of a determinate direction in falling forward is all we cover of the future of our path. It is as if a differential quotient should be conscious and treat itself as an adequate substitute for a traced-out curve. Our experience, *inter alia,* is of variations of rate and of direction, and lives in these transitions more than in the journey's end. The experiences of tendency are sufficient to act upon—what more could we have *done* at those moments even if the later verification comes complete?

This is what, as a radical empiricist, I say to the charge that the objective reference which is so flagrant a character of our experiences involves a chasm and a mortal leap. A positively conjunctive transition involves neither chasm nor leap. Being the very original of what we mean by continuity, it makes a continuum wherever it appears. I know full well that such brief words as these will leave the hardened transcendentalist unshaken. Conjunctive experiences *separate* their terms, he will still say: they are third things interposed, that have themselves to be conjoined by new links, and to invoke them makes our trouble infinitely worse. To 'feel' our motion forward is impossible. Motion implies terminus; and how can terminus be felt before we have arrived? The barest start and sally forwards, the barest tendency to leave the instant, involves the chasm and the leap. Conjunctive transi-

tions are the most superficial of appearances, illusions of our sensibility which philosophical reflection pulverizes at a touch. Conception is our only trust-worthy instrument, conception and the Absolute working hand in hand. Conception disintegrates experience utterly, but its disjunctions are easily overcome again when the Absolute takes up the task.

Such transcendentalists I must leave, provisionally at least, in full possession of their creed. I have no space for polemics in this article, so I shall simply formulate the empiricist doctrine as my hypothesis, leaving it to work or not work as it may.

Objective reference, I say then, is an incident of the fact that so much of our experience comes as an insufficient and consists of process and transition. Our fields of experience have no more definite boundaries than have our fields of view. Both are fringed forever by a *more* that continuously develops, and that continuously supersedes them as life proceeds. The relations, generally speaking, are as real here as the terms are, and the only complaint of the transcendentalist's with which I could at all sympathize would be his charge that, by first making knowledge to consist in external relations as I have done, and by then confessing that nine-tenths of the time these are not actually but only virtually there, I have knocked the solid bottom out of the whole business, and palmed off a substitute of knowledge for the genuine thing. Only the admission, such a critic might say, that our ideas are self-transcendent and 'true' already, in advance of the experiences that are to terminate them, can bring solidity back to knowledge in a world like this, in which transitions and terminations are only by exception fulfilled.

This seems to me an excellent place for applying the pragmatic method. When a dispute arises, that method consists in auguring what practical consequences would be different if one side rather than the other were true. If no difference can be thought of, the dispute is a quarrel over words. What then would the self-transcendency affirmed to exist in advance of all experiential mediation or termination, be *known-as*? What would it practically result in for *us,* were it true?

It could only result in our orientation, in the turning of our expectations and practical tendencies into the right path; and the right path here, so long as we and the object are not yet face to face (or can never get face to face, as in the case of ejects), would be the path that led us into the object's nearest neighborhood. Where direct acquaintance is lacking, 'knowledge about' is the next best thing, and an acquaintance with what actually lies about the object, and is most closely related to it, puts such knowledge within our grasp. Ether-waves and your anger, for example, are things in which my thoughts will never *perceptually* terminate, but my concepts of them lead me to their very brink, to the chromatic fringes and to the hurtful words and deeds which are their really next effects.

Even if our ideas did in themselves carry the postulated self-transcendency, it would still remain true that their putting us into possession of such effects *would be the sole cash-value of the self-transcendency for us.* And this cash-value, it is needless to say, is *verbatim et literatim* what our empiricist account pays in. On pragmatist principles therefore, a dispute over self-transcendency is a pure logomachy. Call our concepts of ejective things self-transcendent or the reverse, it makes no difference, so long as we don't differ about the nature of that exalted virtue's fruits—fruits for us, of course, humanistic fruits. If an Absolute were proved to exist for other reasons, it might well appear that *his* knowledge is terminated in innumerable cases where ours is still incomplete. That, however, would be a fact indifferent to our knowledge. The latter would grow neither worse nor better, whether we acknowledged such an Absolute or left him out.

So the notion of a knowledge still *in transitu* and on its way joins hands here with that notion of a 'pure experience' which I tried to explain in . . . 'Does Consciousness Exist?' The instant field of the present is always experience in its 'pure' state, plain unqualified actuality, a simple *that*, as yet undifferentiated into thing and thought, and only virtually classifiable as objective fact or as some one's opinion about fact. This is as true when the field is conceptual as when it is perceptual. 'Memorial

Hall' is 'there' in my idea as much as when I stand before it. I proceed to act on its account in either case. Only in the later experience that supersedes the present one is this *naïf* immediacy retrospectively split into two parts, a 'consciousness' and its 'content,' and the content corrected or confirmed. While still pure, or present, any experience—mine, for example, of what I write about in these very lines—passes for 'truth.' The morrow may reduce it to 'opinion.' The transcendentalist in all his particular knowledges is as liable to this reduction as I am: his Absolute does not save him. Why, then, need he quarrel with an account of knowing that merely leaves it liable to this inevitable condition? Why insist that knowing is a static relation out of time when it practically seems so much a function of our active life? For a thing to be valid, says Lotze, is the same as to make itself valid. When the whole universe seems only to be making itself valid and to be still incomplete (else why its ceaseless changing?) why, of all things, should knowing be exempt? Why should it not be making itself valid like everything else? That some parts of it may be already valid or verified beyond dispute, the empirical philosopher, of course, like any one else, may always hope.

6. How Can Two Minds Know the Same Thing?

With transition and prospect thus enthroned in pure experience, it is impossible to subscribe to the idealism of the English school. Radical empiricism has, in fact, more affinities with natural realism than with the views of Berkeley or of Mill, and this can be easily shown.

For the Berkeleyan school, ideas (the verbal equivalent of what I term experiences) are discontinuous. The content of each is wholly immanent, and there are no transitions with which they are consubstantial and through which their beings may unite. Your Memorial Hall and mine, even when both are percepts, are wholly out of connection with each other. Our lives are a congeries of solipsisms, out of which in strict logic only a God could compose a universe even of discourse. No dynamic currents run between my objects and your objects. Never can our minds meet in the *same*.

The incredibility of such a philosophy is flagrant. It is 'cold, strained, and unnatural' in a supreme degree; and it may be doubted whether even Berkeley himself, who took it so religiously, really believed, when walking through the streets of London, that his spirit and the spirits of his fellow wayfarers had absolutely different towns in view.

To me the decisive reason in favor of our minds meeting in *some* common objects at least is that, unless I make that supposition, I have no motive for assuming that your mind exists at all. Why do I postulate your mind? Because I see your body acting in a certain way. Its gestures, facial movements, words and conduct generally, are 'expressive,' so I deem it actuated as my own is, by an inner life like mine. This argument from analogy is my *reason,* whether an instinctive belief runs before it or not. But what is 'your body' here but a percept in *my* field? It is only as animating *that* object, *my* object, that I have any occasion to think of you at all. If the body that you actuate be not the very body that I see there, but some duplicate body of your own with which that has nothing to do, we belong to different universes, you and I, and for me to speak of you is folly. Myriads of such universes even now may coexist, irrelevant to one another; my concern is solely with the universe with which my own life is connected.

In that perceptual part of *my* universe which I call *your* body, your mind and my mind meet and may be called conterminous. Your mind actuates that body and mine sees it; my thoughts pass into it as into their harmonious cognitive fulfilment; your emotions and volitions pass into it as causes into their effects.

But that percept hangs together with all our other physical percepts. They are of one stuff with it; and if it be our common possession, they must be so likewise. For instance, your hand lays hold of one end of a rope and my hand lays hold of the other end. We pull against each other. Can our two hands be mutual objects in this experience, and the rope not be mutual also? What is true of the rope is true of any other percept. Your objects are

over and over again the same as mine. If I ask you *where* some object of yours is, our old Memorial Hall, for example, you point to *my* Memorial Hall with *your* hand which *I* see. If you alter an object in your world, put out a candle, for example, when I am present, *my* candle *ipso facto* goes out. It is only as altering my objects that I guess you to exist. If your objects do not coalesce with my objects, if they be not identically where mine are, they must be proved to be positively somewhere else. But no other location can be assigned for them, so their place must be what it seems to be, the same.[4]

Practically, then, our minds meet in a world of objects which they share in common, which would still be there, if one or several of the minds were destroyed. I can see no formal objection to this supposition's being literally true. On the principles which I am defending, a 'mind' or 'personal consciousness' is the name for a series of experiences run together by certain definite transitions, and an objective reality is a series of similar experiences knit by different transitions. If one and the same experience can figure twice, once in a mental and once in a physical context (as I have tried, in my article on 'Consciousness,' to show that it can), one does not see why it might not figure thrice, or four times, or any number of times, by running into as many different mental contexts, just as the same point, lying at their intersection, can be continued into many different lines. Abolishing any number of contexts would not destroy the experience itself or its other contexts, any more than abolishing some of the point's linear continuations would destroy the others, or destroy the point itself.

I well know the subtle dialectic which insists that a term taken in another relation must needs be an intrinsically different term. The crux is always the old Greek one, that the same man can't be tall in relation to one neighbor, and short in relation to another, for that would make him tall and short at once. In this essay I can not stop to refute this dialectic, so I pass on, leaving my flank for the time exposed. But if my reader will only allow that the

[4]The notion that our objects are inside of our respective heads is not seriously defensible, so I pass it by.

same '*now*' both ends his past and begins his future; or that, when he buys an acre of land from his neighbor, it is the same acre that successively figures in the two estates; or that when I pay him a dollar, the same dollar goes into his pocket that came out of mine; he will also in consistency have to allow that the same object may conceivably play a part in, as being related to the rest of, any number of otherwise entirely different minds. This is enough for my present point: the common-sense notion of minds sharing the same object offers no special logical or epistemological difficulties of its own; it stands or falls with the general possibility of things being in conjunctive relation with other things at all.

In principle, then, let natural realism pass for possible. Your mind and mine *may* terminate in the same percept, not merely against it, as if it were a third external thing, but by inserting themselves into it and coalescing with it, for such is the sort of conjunctive union that appears to be experienced when a perceptual terminus 'fulfils.' Even so, two hawsers may embrace the same pile, and yet neither one of them touch any other part except that pile, of what the other hawser is attached to.

It is therefore not a formal question, but a question of empirical fact solely, whether, when you and I are said to know the 'same' Memorial Hall, our minds do terminate at or in a numerically identical percept. Obviously, as a plain matter of fact, they do *not*. Apart from color-blindness and such possibilities, we see the Hall in different perspectives. You may be on one side of it and I on another. The percept of each of us, as he sees the surface of the Hall, is moreover only his provisional terminus. The next thing beyond my percept is not your mind, but more percepts of my own into which my first percept develops, the interior of the Hall, for instance, or the inner structure of its bricks and mortar. If our minds were in a literal sense *conterminous*, neither could get beyond the percept which they had in common, it would be an ultimate barrier between them—unless indeed they flowed over it and became 'co-conscious' over a still larger part of their content, which (thought-transference apart) is not supposed to be the case. In point of fact the ultimate

common barrier can always be pushed, by both minds, farther than any actual percept of either, until at last it resolves itself into the mere notion of imperceptibles like atoms or ether, so that, where we do terminate in percepts, our knowledge is only speciously completed, being, in theoretic strictness, only a virtual knowledge of those remoter objects which conception carries out.

Is natural realism, permissible in logic, refuted then by empirical fact? Do our minds have no object in common after all?

Yes, they certainly have *Space* in common. On pragmatic principles we are obliged to predicate sameness wherever we can predicate no assignable point of difference. If two named things have every quality and function indiscernible, and are at the same time in the same place, they must be written down as numerically one thing under two different names. But there is no test discoverable, so far as I know, by which it can be shown that the place occupied by your percept of Memorial Hall differs from the place occupied by mine. The percepts themselves may be shown to differ; but if each of us be asked to point out where his percept is, we point to an identical spot. All the relations, whether geometrical or causal, of the Hall originate or terminate in that spot wherein our hands meet, and where each of us begins to work if he wishes to make the Hall change before the other's eyes. Just so it is with our bodies. That body of yours which you actuate and feel from within must be in the same spot as the body of yours which I see or touch from without. 'There' for me means where I place my finger. If you do not feel my finger's contact to be 'there' in *my* sense, when I place it on your body, where then do you feel it? Your inner actuations of your body meet my finger *there*: it is *there* that you resist its push, or shrink back, or sweep the finger aside with your hand. Whatever farther knowledge either of us may acquire of the real constitution of the body which we thus feel, you from within and I from without, it is in that same place that the newly conceived or perceived constituents have to be located, and it is *through* that space that your and my mental intercourse with each other has always to be carried on, by the mediation of impressions which I convey thither, and of the reactions thence which those impressions may provoke from you.

In general terms, then, whatever differing contents our minds may eventually fill a place with, the place itself is a numerically identical content of the two minds, a piece of common property in which, through which, and over which they join. The receptacle of certain of our experiences being thus common, the experiences themselves might some day become common also. If that day ever did come, our thoughts would terminate in a complete empirical identity, there would be an end, so far as *those* experiences went, to our discussions about truth. No points of difference appearing, they would have to count as the same.

7. Conclusion

With this we have the outlines of a philosophy of pure experience before us. At the outset of my essay, I called it a mosaic philosophy. In actual mosaics the pieces are held together by their bedding, for which bedding the Substances, transcendental Egos, or Absolutes of other philosophies may be taken to stand. In radical empiricism there is no bedding; it is as if the pieces clung together by their edges, the transitions experienced between them forming their cement. Of course such a metaphor is misleading, for in actual experience the more substantive and the more transitive parts run into each other continuously, there is in general no separateness needing to be overcome by an external cement; and whatever separateness is actually experienced is not overcome, it stays and counts as separateness to the end. But the metaphor serves to symbolize the fact that Experience itself, taken at large, can grow by its edges. That one moment of it proliferates into the next by transitions which, whether conjunctive or disjunctive, continue the experiential tissue, can not, I contend, be denied. Life is in the transitions as much as in the terms connected; often, indeed, it seems to be there more emphatically, as if our spurts and sallies forward were the real firing-line of the battle, were like the thin line of flame advancing across the dry autumnal field which the farmer proceeds to burn. In this line we live prospectively as well as retrospectively. It

is 'of' the past, inasmuch as it comes expressly as the past's continuation; it is 'of' the future in so far as the future, when it comes, will have continued *it*.

These relations of continuous transition experienced are what make our experiences cognitive. In the simplest and completest cases the experiences are cognitive of one another. When one of them terminates a previous series of them with a sense of fulfilment, it, we say, is what those other experiences 'had in view.' The knowledge, in such a case, is verified; the truth is 'salted down.' Mainly, however, we live on speculative investments, or on our prospects only. But living on things *in posse* is as good as living in the actual, so long as our credit remains good. It is evident that for the most part it is good, and that the universe seldom protests our drafts.

In this sense we at every moment can continue to believe in an existing *beyond*. It is only in special cases that our confident rush forward gets rebuked. The beyond must, of course, always in our philosophy be itself of an experiential nature. If not a future experience of our own or a present one of our neighbor, it must be a thing in itself in Dr. Prince's and Professor Strong's sense of the term—that is, it must be an experience *for* itself whose relation to other things we translate into the action of molecules, ether-waves, or whatever else the physical symbols may be.[5] This opens the chapter of the relations of radical empiricism to panpsychism, into which I can not enter now.

The beyond can in any case exist simultaneously—for it can be experienced *to have existed* simultaneously—with the experience that practically postulates it by looking in its direction, or by turning or changing in the direction of which it is the goal. Pending that actuality of union, in the virtuality of which the 'truth,' even now, of the postulation consists, the beyond and its knower are entities split off from each other. The world is in so far

[5]Our minds and these ejective realities would still have space (or pseudo-space, as I believe Professor Strong calls the medium of interaction between 'things-in-themselves') in common. These would exist *where*, and begin to act *where*, we locate the molecules, etc., and *where* we perceive the sensible phenomena explained thereby.

forth a pluralism of which the unity is not fully experienced as yet. But, as fast as verifications come, trains of experience, once separate, run into one another; and that is why I said, earlier in my article, that the unity of the world is on the whole undergoing increase. The universe continually grows in quantity by new experiences that graft themselves upon the older mass; but these very new experiences often help the mass to a more consolidated form.

These are the main features of a philosophy of pure experience. It has innumerable other aspects and arouses innumerable questions, but the points I have touched on seem enough to make an entering wedge. In my own mind such a philosophy harmonizes best with a radical pluralism, with novelty and indeterminism, moralism and theism, and with the 'humanism' lately sprung upon us by the Oxford and the Chicago schools.[6] I can not, however, be sure that all these doctrines are its necessary and indispensable allies. It presents so many points of difference, both from the common sense and from the idealism that have made our philosophic language, that it is almost as difficult to state it as it is to think it out clearly, and if it is ever to grow into a respectable system, it will have to be built up by the contributions of many co-operating minds. It seems to me, as I said at the outset of this essay, that many minds are, in point of fact, now turning in a direction that points towards radical empiricism. If they are carried farther by my words, and if then they add their stronger voices to my feebler one, the publication of this essay will have been worth while.

The Thing and Its Relations

Experience in its immediacy seems perfectly fluent. The active sense of living which we all enjoy, before reflection shatters our instinctive world for us, is self-luminous and suggests no paradoxes. Its difficulties are disappointments

[6] I have said something of this latter alliance in an article entitled 'Humanism and Truth,' in *Mind,* October, 1904.

SOURCE: *Journal of Philosophy, Psychology and Scientific Methods,* Vol. II, No. 2 (January 1905).

and uncertainties. They are not intellectual contradictions.

When the relative intellect gets at work, however, it discovers incomprehensibilities in the flowing process. Distinguishing its elements and parts, it gives them separate names, and what it thus disjoins it can not easily put together. Pyrrhonism accepts the irrationality and revels in its dialectic elaboration. Other philosophies try, some by ignoring, some by resisting, and some by turning the dialectic procedure against itself, negating its first negations, to restore the fluent sense of life again, and let redemption take the place of innocence. The perfection with which any philosophy may do this is the measure of its human success and of its importance in philosophic history. In [the last essay], 'A World of Pure Experience,' I tried my own hand sketchily at the problem, resisting certain first steps of dialectics by insisting in a general way that the immediately experienced conjunctive relations are as real as anything else. If my sketch is not to appear too *naïf,* I must come closer to details, and in the present essay I propose to do so.

1.

'Pure experience,' is the name which I gave to the immediate flux of life which furnishes the material to our later reflection with its conceptual categories. Only new-born babes, or men in semi-coma from sleep, drugs, illnesses, or blows, may be assumed to have an experience pure in the literal sense of a *that* which is not yet any definite *what,* tho' ready to be all sorts of whats; full both of oneness and of manyness, but in respects that don't appear; changing throughout, yet so confusedly that its phases interpenetrate and no points, either of distinction or of identity, can be caught. Pure experience in this state is but another name for feeling or sensation. But the flux of it no sooner comes than it tends to fill itself with emphases, and these salient parts become identified and fixed and abstracted; so that experience now flows as if shot through with adjectives and nouns and prepositions and conjunctions. Its purity is only a relative term, meaning the proportional amount of unverbalized sensation which it still embodies.

Far back as we go, the flux, both as a whole and in its parts, is that of things conjunct and separated. The great continua of time, space, and the self envelope everything, betwixt them, and flow together without interfering. The things that they envelope come as separate in some ways and as continuous in others. Some sensations coalesce with some ideas, and others are irreconcilable. Qualities compenetrate one space, or exclude each other from it. They cling together persistently in groups that move as units, or else they separate. Their changes are abrupt or discontinuous; and their kinds resemble or differ; and, as they do so, they fall into either even or irregular series.

In all this the continuities and the discontinuities are absolutely co-ordinate matters of immediate feeling. The conjunctions are as primordial elements of 'fact' as are the distinctions and disjunctions. In the same act by which I feel that this passing minute is a new pulse of my life, I feel that the old life continues into it, and the feeling of continuance in no wise jars upon the simultaneous feeling of a novelty. They, too, compenetrate harmoniously. Prepositions, copulas, and conjunctions, 'is,' 'isn't,' 'then,' 'before,' 'in,' 'on,' 'beside,' 'between,' 'next,' 'like,' 'unlike,' 'as,' 'but,' flower out of the stream of pure experience, the stream of concretes or the sensational stream, as naturally as nouns and adjectives do, and they melt into it again as fluidly when we apply them to a new portion of the stream.

2.

If now we ask why we must thus translate experience from a more concrete or pure into a more intellectualized form, filling it with ever more abounding conceptual distinctions, rationalism and naturalism give different replies.

The rationalistic answer is that the theoretic life is absolute and its interests imperative; that to understand is simply the duty of man; and that who questions this need not be argued with, for by the fact of arguing he gives away his case.

The naturalist answer is that the environment kills as well as sustains us, and that the tendency of raw experience to extinguish the experient himself is lessened just in the degree in which the elements in it that have a practical bearing upon life are analyzed out of the continuum and verbally fixed and coupled together, so that we may know what is in the wind for us and get ready to react in time. Had pure experience, the naturalist says, been always perfectly healthy, there would never have arisen the necessity of isolating or verbalizing any of its terms. We should just have experienced inarticulately and unintellectually enjoyed. This leaning on 'reaction' in the naturalist account implies that, whenever we intellectualize a relatively pure experience, we ought to do so for the sake of redescending to the purer or more concrete level again; and that if an intellect stays aloft among its abstract terms and generalized relations, and does not reinsert itself with its conclusions into some particular point of the immediate stream of life, it fails to finish out its function and leaves its normal race unrun.

Most rationalists nowadays will agree that naturalism gives a true enough account of the way in which our intellect arose at first, but they will deny these latter implications. The case, they will say, resembles that of sexual love. Originating in the animal need of getting another generation born, this passion has developed secondarily such imperious spiritual needs that, if you ask why another generation ought to be born at all, the answer is: 'Chiefly that love may go on.' Just so with our intellect: it originated as a practical means of serving life; but it has developed incidentally the function of understanding absolute truth; and life itself now seems to be given chiefly as a means by which that function may be prosecuted. But truth and the understanding of it lie among the abstracts and universals, so the intellect now carries on its higher business wholly in this region, without any need of redescending into pure experience again.

If the contrasted tendencies which I thus designate as naturalistic and rationalistic are not recognized by the reader, perhaps an example will make them more concrete. Mr. Bradley, for instance, is an ultra-rationalist. He admits that our intellect is primarily practical, but says that, for philosophers, the practical need is simply Truth. Truth, moreover, must be assumed 'consistent.' Immediate experience has to be broken into subjects and qualities, terms and relations, to be understood as truth at all. Yet when so broken it is less consistent than ever. Taken raw, it is all undistinguished. Intellectualized, it is all distinction without oneness. 'Such an arrangement may *work*, but the theoretic problem is not solved.' The question is '*how* the diversity can exist in harmony with the oneness.' To go back to pure experience is unavailing. 'Mere feeling gives no answer to our riddle.' Even if your intuition is a fact, it is not an *understanding*. 'It is a mere experience, and furnishes no consistent view.' The experience offered as facts or truths 'I find that my intellect rejects because they contradict themselves. They offer a complex of diversities conjoined in a way which it feels is not its way and which it can not repeat as its own. . . . For to be satisfied, my intellect must understand, and it can not understand by taking a congeries in the lump.' So Mr. Bradley, in the sole interests of 'understanding' (as he conceives that function), turns his back on finite experience forever. Truth must lie in the opposite direction, the direction of the Absolute; and this kind of rationalism and naturalism, or (as I will now call it) pragmatism, walk thenceforward upon opposite paths. For the one, those intellectual products are most true which, turning their face towards the Absolute, come nearest to symbolizing its ways of uniting the many and the one. For the other, those are most true which most successfully dip back into the finite stream of feeling and grow most easily confluent with some particular wave or wavelet. Such confluence not only proves the intellectual operation to have been true (as an addition may 'prove' that a subtraction is already rightly performed), but it constitutes, according to pragmatism, all that we mean by calling it true. Only in so far as they lead us, successfully or unsuccessfully, back into sensi ble experience again, are our abstracts and universals true or false at all.

3.

In Section 6 of [the last essay], I adopted in a general way the common-sense belief that one and the same world is cognized by our different minds; but I left undiscussed the dialectical arguments which maintain that this is logically absurd. The usual reason given for its being absurd is that it assumes one object (to wit, the world) to stand in two relations at once; to my mind, namely, and again to yours; whereas a term taken in a second relation can not logically be the same term which it was at first.

I have heard this reason urged so often in discussing with absolutists, and it would destroy my radical empiricism so utterly, if it were valid, that I am bound to give it an attentive ear, and seriously to search its strength.

For instance, let the matter in dispute be term M, asserted to be on the one hand related to L, and on the other to $N;$ and let the two cases of relation be symbolized by $L - M$ and $M - N$ respectively. When, now, I assume that the experience may immediately come and be given in the shape $L - M - N$, with no trace of doubling or internal fission in the $M,$ I am told that this is all a popular delusion; that $L - M - N$ logically means two different experiences, $L - M$ and $M - N$, namely; and that although the Absolute may, and indeed must, from its superior point of view, read its own kind of unity into M's two editions, yet as elements in finite experience the two M's lie irretrievably asunder, and the world between them is broken and unbridged.

In arguing this dialectic thesis, one must avoid slipping from the logical into the physical point of view. It would be easy, in taking a concrete example to fix one's ideas by, to choose one in which the letter M should stand for a collective noun of some sort, which noun, being related to L by one of its parts and to N by another, would inwardly be two things when it stood outwardly in both relations. Thus, one might say: 'David Hume, who weighed so many stone by his body, influences posterity by his doctrine.' The body and the doctrine are two things, between which our finite minds can discover no real sameness, though the same name covers both of them. And then, one might continue: 'Only an Absolute is capable of uniting such a non-identity.' We must, I say, avoid this sort of example, for the dialectic insight, if true at all, must apply to terms and relations universally. It must be true of abstract units as well as of nouns collective; and if we prove it by concrete examples we must take the simplest, so as to avoid irrelevant material suggestions.

Taken thus in all its generality, the absolutist contention seems to use as its major premise Hume's notion 'that all our distinct perceptions are distinct existences, and that the mind never perceives any real connexion among distinct existences.' Undoubtedly, since we use two phrases in talking first about 'M's relation to L' and then about 'M's relation to N,' we must be having, or must have had, two distinct perceptions;—and the rest would then seem to follow duly. But the starting-point of the reasoning here seems to be the fact of the two *phrases;* and this suggests that the argument may be merely verbal. Can it be that the whole dialectic consists in attributing to the experience talked-about a constitution similar to that of the language in which we describe it? Must we assert the objective doubleness of the M merely because we have to name it twice over when we name its two relations?

Candidly, I can think of no other reason than this for the dialectic conclusion;[1] for, if we think, not of our words, but of any simple concrete matter which they may be held to signify, the experience itself belies the paradox asserted. We use indeed two separate concepts in analyzing our object, but we know them all the while to be but substitutional, and that the M in $L — M$ and the M in $M — N$ *mean* (*i.e.,* are capable of leading to and terminating in) one self-same piece, M, of sensible experience. This persistent identity of certain units (or emphases, or points, or objects, or members—call them what you will) of the experience-continuum, is just one of those conjunctive features of it, on which I am obliged to insist so emphatically. For samenesses are parts of experience's indefeasible structure. When I hear a bell-stroke and, as life flows on, its after image dies away, I still hark back to it as 'that same bell-stroke.' When I see a thing M, with L to the left of it and N to the right of

it, I see it *as* one $M;$ and if you tell me I have had to 'take' it twice, I reply that if I 'took' it a thousand times I should still *see* it as a unit.[2] Its unity is aboriginal, just as the multiplicity of my successive takings is aboriginal. It comes unbroken as *that* M, as a singular which I encounter; they come broken, as *those* takings, as my plurality of operations. The unity and the separateness are strictly co-ordinate. I do not easily fathom why my opponents should find the separateness so much more easily understandable that they must needs infect the whole of finite experience with it, and relegate the unity (now taken as a bare postulate and no longer as a thing positively perceivable) to the region of the Absolute's mysteries. I do not easily fathom this, I say, for the said opponents are above mere verbal quibbling; yet all that I can catch in their talk is the substitution of what is true of certain words for what is true of what they signify. They stay with the words,—not returning to the stream of life whence all the meaning of them came, and which is always ready to reabsorb them.

4.

For aught this argument proves, then, we may continue to believe that one thing can be known by many knowers. But the denial of one thing in many relations is but one application of a still profounder dialectic difficulty. Man can't be good, said the sophists, for man is *man* and *good* is good; and Hegel and Herbart in their day, more recently A. Spir, and most recently and elaborately of all, Mr. Bradley, informs us that a term can logically only be a punctiform unit, and that not one of the conjunctive relations between things, which experience seems to yield, is rationally possible.

Of course, if true, this cuts off radical empiricism without even a shilling. Radical

---

[1]Technically, it seems classable as a 'fallacy of composition.' A duality, predicable of the two wholes, $L — M$ and $M — N$, is forthwith predicated of one of their parts, M.

[2]I may perhaps refer here to my *Principles of Psychology*, vol. I, pp. 459 ff. It really seems 'weird' to have to argue (as I am forced now to do) for the notion that it is one sheet of paper (with its two surfaces and all that lies between) which is both under my pen and on the table while I write—the 'claim' that it is two sheets seems so brazen. Yet I sometimes suspect the absolutists of sincerity!

empiricism takes conjunctive relations at their face value, holding them to be as real as the terms united by them. The world it represents as a collection, some parts of which are conjunctively and others disjunctively related. Two parts, themselves disjoined, may nevertheless hang together by intermediaries with which they are severally connected, and the whole world eventually may hang together similarly, inasmuch as *some* path of conjunctive transition by which to pass from one of its parts to another may always be discernible. Such determinately various hanging-together may be called *concatenated union,* to distinguish it from the 'through-and-through' type of union, 'each in all and all in each' (union of *total conflux,* as one might call it), which monistic systems hold to obtain when things are taken in their absolute reality. In a concatenated world a partial conflux often is experienced. Our concepts and our sensations are confluent; successive states of the same ego, and feelings of the same body are confluent. Where the experience is not of conflux, it may be of conterminousness (things with but one thing between); or of contiguousness (nothing between); or of likeness; or of nearness; or of simultaneousness; or of inness; or of on-ness; or of for-ness; or of simple with-ness; or even of mere and-ness, which last relation would make of however disjointed a world otherwise, at any rate for that occasion a universe, at any rate for that occasion a universe 'of discourse.' Now Mr. Bradley tells us that none of these relations, as we actually experience them, can possibly be real.[3] My next duty, accordingly, must be to rescue radical empiricism from Mr. Bradley. Fortunately, as it seems to me, his general conten-

tion, that the very notion of relation is unthinkable clearly, has been successfully met by many critics.

It is a burden to the flesh, and an injustice both to readers and to the previous writers, to repeat good arguments already printed. So, in noticing Mr. Bradley, I will confine myself to the interests of radical empiricism solely.

5.

The first duty of radical empiricism, taking given conjunctions at their face-value, is to class some of them as more intimate and some as more external. When two terms are *similar,* their very natures enter into the relation. Being *what* they are, no matter where or when, the likeness never can be denied, if asserted. It continues predicable as long as the terms continue. Other relations, the *where* and the *when,* for example, seem adventitious. The sheet of paper may be 'off' or 'on' the table, for example; and in either case the relation involves only the outside of its terms. Having an outside, both of them, they contribute by it to the relation. It is external: the term's inner nature is irrelevant to it. Any book, any table, may fall into the relation, which is created *pro hac vice,* not by their existence, but by their casual situation. It is just because so many of the conjunctions of experience seem so external that a philosophy of pure experience must tend to pluralism in its ontology. So far as things have space-relations, for example, we are free to imagine them with different origins even. If they could get to *be,* and get into space at all, then they may have done so separately. Once there, however, they are *additives* to one another, and, with no prejudice to their natures, all sorts of space-relations may supervene between them. The question of how things could come to be anyhow, is wholly different from the question what their relations, once the being accomplished, may consist in.

Mr. Bradley now affirms that such external relations as the space-relations which we here talk of must hold of entirely different subjects from those of which the absence of such relations might a moment previously have been plausibly asserted. Not only is the *situation* different when the book is on the table, but the

---

[3]Here again the reader must beware of slipping from logical into phenomenal considerations. It may well be that we *attribute* a certain relation falsely, because the circumstances of the case, being complex, have deceived us. At a railway station we may take our own train, and not the one that fills our window, to be moving. We here put motion in the wrong place in the world, but in its original place the motion is a part of reality. What Mr. Bradley means is nothing like this, but rather that such things as motion are nowhere real, and that, even in their aboriginal and empirically incorrigible seats, relations are impossible of comprehension.

book itself is different as a book, from what it was when it was off the table.[4] He admits that "such external relations seem possible and even existing. . . . That you do not alter what you compare or rearrange in space seems to common sense quite obvious, and that on the other side there are as obvious difficulties does not occur to common sense at all. And I will begin by pointing out these difficulties. . . . There is a relation in the result, and this relation, we hear, is to make no difference in its terms. But, if so, to what does it make a difference? [*Doesn't it make a difference to us onlookers, at least?*] and what is the meaning and sense of qualifying the terms by it? [*Surely the meaning is to tell the truth about their relative position.*] If, in short, it is external to the terms, how can it possibly be true *of* them? [*Is it the 'intimacy' suggested by the little word 'of,' here, which I have underscored, that is the root of Mr. Bradley's trouble?*] . . . If the terms from their inner nature do not enter into the relation, then, so far as they are concerned, they seem related for no reason at all. . . . Things are spatially related, first in one way, and then become related in another way, and yet in no way themselves are altered; for the relations, it is said, are but external. But I reply that, if so, I can not *understand* the leaving by the terms of one set of relations and their adoption of another fresh set. The process and its result to the terms, if they contribute nothing to it [*Surely they contribute to it all there is 'of' it!*] seem irrational throughout. [*If 'irrational' here means simply 'non-rational,' or non-deducible from the essence of either term singly, it is no reproach; if it means 'contradicting' such essence, Mr. Bradley should show wherein and how.*] But, if they contribute

anything, they must surely be affected internally. [*Why so, if they contribute only their surface? In such relations as 'on,' 'a foot away,' 'between,' 'next,' etc., only surfaces are in question.*] . . . If the terms contribute anything whatever, then the terms are affected [*inwardly altered?*] by the arrangement. . . . That for working purposes we treat, and do well to treat, some relations as external merely I do not deny, and that of course is not the question at issue here. That question is . . . whether in the end and in principle a mere external relation [*i.e., a relation which can change without forcing its terms to change their nature simultaneously*] is possible and forced on us by the facts."[5]

Mr. Bradley next reverts to the antinomies of space, which, according to him, prove it to be unreal, although it appears as so prolific a medium of external relations; and he then concludes that "Irrationality and externality can not be the last truth about things. Somewhere there must be a reason why this and that appear together. And this reason and reality must reside in the whole from which terms and relations are abstractions, a whole in which their internal connection must lie, and out of which from the background appear those fresh results which never could have come from the premises." And he adds that "Where the whole is different, the terms that qualify and contribute to it must so far be different. . . . They are altered so far only [*How far? farther than externally, yet not through and through?*] but still they are altered. . . . I must insist that in each case the terms are qualified by their whole [*Qualified how?—Do their external relations, situations, dates, etc., changed as these are in the new whole, fail to qualify them 'far' enough?*], and that in the second case there is a whole which differs both logically and psychologically from the first whole; and I urge that in contributing to the change the terms so far are altered."

Not merely the relations, then, but the terms are altered: *und zwar* 'so far.' But just *how* far is the whole problem; and 'through-and-through' would seem (in spite of Mr.

---

[4]Once more, don't slip from logical into physical situations. Of course, if the table be wet, it will moisten the book, or if it be slight enough and the book heavy enough, the book will break it down. But such collateral phenomena are not the point at issue. The point is whether the successive relations 'on' and 'not-on' can rationally (not physically) hold of the same constant terms, abstractly taken. Professor A. E. Taylor drops from logical into material considerations when he instances color-contrast as a proof that *A*, 'as contradistinguished from *B*, is not the same thing as mere *A* not in any way affected' (*Elements of Metaphysics*, p. 145). Note the substitution, for 'related' of the word 'affected,' which begs the whole question.

[5][Bradley:] *Appearance and Reality*, second edition, pp. 575–576.

Bradley's somewhat undecided utterances[6]) to be the full Bradleyan answer. The 'whole' which he here treats as primary and determinative of each part's manner of 'contrasting,' simply *must*, when it alters, alter in its entirety. There *must* be total conflux of its parts, each into and through each other. The 'must' appears here as a *Machtspruch*, as an *ipse dixit* of Mr. Bradley's absolutistically tempered 'understanding,' for he candidly confesses that how the parts *do* differ as they contribute to different wholes, is unknown to him.

Although I have every wish to comprehend the authority by which Mr. Bradley's understanding speaks, his words leave me wholly unconverted. 'External relations' stand with their withers all unwrung, and remain, for aught he proves to the contrary, not only practically workable, but also perfectly intelligible factors of reality.

6.

Mr. Bradley's understanding shows the most extraordinary power of perceiving separations and the most extraordinary impotence in comprehending conjunctions. One would naturally say 'neither or both,' but not so Mr. Bradley. When a common man analyzes certain *whats* from out the stream of experience, he understands their distinctness *as thus isolated*. But this does not prevent him from equally well understanding their combination with each other *as originally experienced in the concrete*, or their confluence with new sensible experiences in which they recur as 'the same.' Returning into the stream of sensible presentation, nouns and adjectives, and *thats* and abstract *whats*, grow confluent again, and the word 'is' names all these experiences of conjunction. Mr. Bradley understands the isolation of the abstracts, but to understand the combination is to him impossible.[7] "To understand a complex *AB*," he says, "I must begin with *A* or *B*. And beginning, say with *A*, if I then merely find *B*, I have either lost *A*, or I have got beside *A*, [*the word 'beside' seems here vital, as meaning a conjunction 'external' and therefore unintelligible*] something else, and in neither case have I understood. For my intellect can not simply unite a diversity, nor has it in itself any form or way of togetherness, and you gain nothing if, beside *A* and *B*, you offer me their conjunction in fact. For to my intellect that is no more than another external element. And 'facts,' once for all, are for my intellect not true unless they satisfy it. . . . The intellect has in its nature no principle of mere togetherness."

Of course Mr. Bradley has a right to define 'intellect' as the power by which we perceive separations but not unions—provided he give

---

[6]I say 'undecided,' because, apart from the 'so far,' which sounds terribly half-hearted, there are passages in these very pages in which Mr. Bradley admits the pluralistic thesis. Read, for example, what he says, on p. 578, of a billiard ball keeping its 'character' unchanged, though, in its change of place, its 'existence' gets altered; or what he says, on p. 579, of the possibility that an abstract quality A, B, or C, in a thing, 'may throughout remain unchanged' although the thing be altered; or his admission that in red-hairedness, both as analyzed out of a man and when given with the rest of him, there may be 'no change' (p. 580). Why does he immediately add that for the pluralist to plead the non-mutation of such abstractions would be an *ignoratio elenchi*? It is impossible to admit it to be such. The entire *elenchus* and inquest is just as to whether parts which you can abstract from existing wholes can also contribute to other wholes without changing their inner nature. If they can thus mould various wholes into new *gestaltqualitäten*, then it follows that the same elements are logically able to exist in different wholes [whether physically able would depend on additional hypotheses]; that partial changes are thinkable, and through-and-through change not a dialectic necessity; that monism is only an hypothesis; and that an additively constituted universe is a rationally respectable hypothesis also. All the theses of radical empiricism, in short, follow.

[7]So far as I catch his state of mind, it is somewhat like this: 'Book,' 'table,' 'on'—how does the existence of these three abstract elements result in *this* book being livingly on *this* table. Why isn't the table on the book? Or why doesn't the 'on' connect itself with another book, or something that is not a table? Mustn't something *in* each of the three elements already determine the two others to *it*, so that they do not settle elsewhere or float vaguely? Mustn't the *whole fact be prefigured in each part*, and exist *de jure* before it can exist *de facto*? But, if so, in what can the jural existence consist, if not in a spiritual miniature of the whole fact's constitution actuating every partial factor as its purpose? But is this anything but the old metaphysical fallacy of looking behind a fact *in esse* for the ground of the fact, and finding it in the shape of the very same fact *in posse*? Somewhere we must leave off with a *constitution* behind which there is nothing.

due notice to the reader. But why then claim that such a maimed and amputated power must reign supreme in philosophy, and accuse on its behoof the whole empirical world of irrationality? It is true that he elsewhere attributes to the intellect a *proprius motus* of transition, but says that when he looks for *these* transitions in the detail of living experience, he 'is unable to verify such a solution.'

Yet he never explains what the intellectual transitions would be like in case we had them. He only defines them negatively—they are not spatial, temporal, predicative, or causal; or qualitatively or otherwise serial; or in any way relational as we naïvely trace relations, for relations *separate* terms, and need themselves to be hooked on *ad infinitum*. The nearest approach he makes to describing a truly intellectual transition is where he speaks of *A* and *B* as being 'united, each from its own nature, in a whole which is the nature of both alike.' But this (which, *pace* Mr. Bradley, seems exquisitely analogous to 'taking' a congeries in a 'lump,' if not to 'swamping') suggests nothing but that *conflux* which pure experience so abundantly offers, as when 'space,' 'white' and 'sweet' are confluent in a 'lump of sugar,' or kinesthetic, dermal, and optical sensations confluent in 'my hand.'[8] All that I can verify in the transitions which Mr. Bradley's intellect desiderates as its *proprius motus* is a reminiscence of these and other sensible conjunctions (especially space-conjunctions), but a reminiscence so vague that its originals are not recognized. Bradley in short repeats the fable of the dog, the bone, and its image in the water. With a world of particulars, given in loveliest union, in conjunction definitely various, and variously definite, the 'how' of which you 'understand' as soon as you see the fact of them,[9]

for there is no 'how' except the constitution of the fact as given; with all this given him, I say, in pure experience, he asks for some ineffable union in the abstract instead, which, if he gained it, would only be a duplicate of what he has already in his full possession. Surely he abuses the privilege which society grants to all us philosophers, of being puzzle-headed.

Polemic writing like this is odious; but with absolutism in possession in so many quarters, omission to defend my radical empiricism against its best known champion would count as either superficiality or inability. I have to conclude that its dialectic has not invalidated in the least degree the usual conjunctions by which the world, as experienced, hangs so variously together. In particular it leaves an empirical theory of knowledge intact, and lets us continue to believe with common sense that one object *may* be known, if we have any ground for thinking that it *is* known, to many knowers.

In [the next essay, "How Two Minds Can Know One Thing"] I shall return to this last supposition, which seems to me to offer other difficulties much harder for a philosophy of pure experience to deal with than any of absolutism's dialectic objections.

How Two Minds Can Know One Thing

In . . . 'Does Consciousness Exist?' I have tried to show that when we call an experience 'conscious,' that does not mean that it is suffused throughout with a peculiar modality of being ('psychic' being) as stained glass may be suffused with light, but rather that it stands in certain determinate relations to other portions of experience extraneous to itself. These form one peculiar 'context' for it; while, taken in another context of experiences, we class it as a fact in the physical world. This 'pen,' for example, is, in the first instance, a bald *that*, a

---

[8]How meaningless is the contention that in such wholes (or in 'book-on-table,' 'watch-in-pocket,' etc.) the relation is an additional entity *between* the terms, needing itself to be related again to each! Both Bradley (*op. cit.*, pp. 32–33) and Royce (*The World and the Individual*, vol. I, p. 128) lovingly repeat this piece of profundity.

[9]The 'why' and the 'whence' are entirely other questions, not under discussion, as I understand Mr. Bradley. Not how experience gets itself born, but how it can be what it is after it is born, is the puzzle.

SOURCE: *Journal of Philosophy, Psychology and Scientific Methods*, Vol. II, No. 7 (March 1905).

datum, fact, phenomenon, content, or whatever other neutral or ambiguous name you may prefer to apply. I called it in that article a 'pure experience.' To get classed either as a physical pen or as some one's percept of a pen, it must assume a *function,* and that can only happen in a more complicated world. So far as in that world it is a stable feature, holds ink, marks paper and obeys the guidance of a hand, it is a physical pen. That is what we mean by being 'physical,' in a pen. So far as it is instable, on the contrary, coming and going with the movements of my eyes, altering with what I call my fancy, continuous with subsequent experiences of its 'having been' (in the past tense), it is the percept of a pen in my mind. Those peculiarities are what we mean by being 'conscious,' in a pen.

In ["A World of Pure Experience"] I tried to show that the same *that,* the same numerically identical pen of pure experience, can enter simultaneously into many conscious contexts, or, in other words, be an object for many different minds. I admitted that I had not space to treat of certain possible objections in that article; but in [the last essay] I took some of the objections up. At the end of that [essay] I said that still more formidable-sounding objections remained; so, to leave my pure-experience theory in as strong a state as possible, I propose to consider those objections now.

1.

The objections I previously tried to dispose of were purely logical or dialectical. No one identical term, whether physical or psychical, it had been said, could be the subject of two relations at once. This thesis I sought to prove unfounded. The objections that now confront us arise from the nature supposed to inhere in psychic facts specifically. Whatever may be the case with physical objects, a fact of consciousness, it is alleged (and indeed very plausibly), can not, without self-contradiction, be treated as a portion of two different minds, and for the following reasons.

In the physical world we make with impu-

nity the assumption that one and the same material object can figure in an indefinitely large number of different processes at once. When, for instance, a sheet of rubber is pulled at its four corners, a unit of rubber in the middle of the sheet is affected by all four of the pulls. It *transmits* them each, as if it pulled in four different ways at once itself. So, an air-particle or an ether-particle 'compounds' the different directions of movement imprinted on it without obliterating their several individualities. It delivers them distinct, on the contrary, at as many several 'receivers' (ear, eye or what not) as may be 'tuned' to that effect. The apparent paradox of a distinctness like this surviving in the midst of compounding is a thing which, I fancy, the analyses made by physicists have by this time sufficiently cleared up.

But if, on the strength of these analogies, one should ask: "Why, if two or more lines can run through one and the same geometrical point, or if two or more distinct processes of activity can run through one and the same physical thing so that it simultaneously plays a rôle in each and every process, might not two or more streams of personal consciousness include one and the same unit of experience so that it would simultaneously be a part of the experience of all the different minds?" one would be checked by thinking of a certain peculiarity by which phenomena of consciousness differ from physical things.

While physical things, namely, are supposed to be permanent and to have their 'states,' a fact of consciousness exists but once and *is* a state. Its *esse* is *sentiri;* it is only so far as it is felt; and it is unambiguously and unequivocally exactly *what* is felt. The hypothesis under consideration would, however, oblige it to be felt equivocally, felt now as part of my mind and again at the same time *not* as a part of my mind, but of yours (for my mind is *not* yours), and this would seem impossible without doubling it into two distinct things, or, in other words, without reverting to the ordinary dualistic philosophy of insulated minds each knowing its object representatively as a third thing,—and that would be to give up the pure-experience scheme altogether.

Can we see, then, any way in which a unit of pure experience might enter into and figure in two diverse streams of consciousness without turning itself into the two units which, on our hypothesis, it must not be?

2.

There is a way; and the first step towards it is to see more precisely how the unit enters into either one of the streams of consciousness alone. Just what, from being 'pure,' does its becoming 'conscious' *once* mean?

It means, first, that new experiences have supervened; and, second, that they have borne a certain assignable relation to the unit supposed. Continue, if you please, to speak of the pure unit as 'the pen.' So far as the pen's successors do but repeat the pen or, being different from it, are 'energetically' related to it, it and they will form a group of stably existing physical things. So far, however, as its successors differ from it in another well-determined way, the pen will figure in their context, not as a physical, but as a mental fact. It will become a passing 'percept,' *my* percept of that pen. What now is that decisive well-determined way?

In the chapter on 'The Self,' in my *Principles of Psychology*, I explained the continuous identity of each personal consciousness as a name for the practical fact that new experiences[1] come which look back on the old ones, find them 'warm,' and greet and appropriate them as 'mine.' These operations mean, when analyzed empirically, several tolerably definite things, viz.:

1. That the new experience has past time for its 'content,' and in that time a pen that 'was';

2. That 'warmth' was also about the pen, in the sense of a group of feelings ('interest' aroused, 'attention' turned, 'eyes' employed, etc.) that were closely connected with it and that now recur and evermore recur with unbroken vividness, though from the pen of now, which may be only an image, all such vividness may have gone;

[1] I call them 'passing thoughts' in the book. . . .

3. That these feelings are the nucleus of 'me';

4. That whatever once was associated with them was, at least for that one moment, 'mine'—my implement if associated with hand-feelings, my 'percept' only, if only eye-feelings and attention-feelings were involved.

The pen, realized in this retrospective way as my percept, thus figures as a fact of 'conscious' life. But it does so only so far as 'appropriation' has occurred; and appropriation is *part of the content of a later experience* wholly additional to the originally 'pure' pen. *That* pen, virtually both objective and subjective, is at its own moment actually and intrinsically neither. It has to be looked back upon and *used,* in order to be classed in either distinctive way. But its use, so called, is in the hands of the other experience, while *it* stands, throughout the operation, passive and unchanged.

If this pass muster as an intelligible account of how an experience originally pure can enter into one consciousness, the next question is as to how it might conceivably enter into two.

3.

Obviously so new kind of condition would have to be supplied. All that we should have to postulate would be a second subsequent experience, collateral and contemporary with the first subsequent one, in which a similar act of appropriation should occur. The two acts would interfere neither with one another nor with the originally pure pen. It would sleep undisturbed in its own past, no matter how many such successors went through their several appropriative acts. Each would know it as 'my' percept, each would class it as a 'conscious' fact.

Nor need their so classing it interfere in the least with their classing it at the same time as a physical pen. Since the classing in both cases depends upon the taking of it in one group or another of associates, if the superseding experience were of wide enough 'span' it could think the pen in both groups simultaneously, and yet distinguish the two groups. It would then see the whole situation conformably to what we call 'the representative theory of cognition,' and that is what we all spontaneously do. As a man philosophizing 'popularly,' I believe that what I see myself writing with is double—I think it in its relations to physical nature, and also in its relations to my personal life; I see that it is in my mind, but that it also is a physical pen.

The paradox of the same experience figuring in two consciousnesses seems thus no paradox at all. To be 'conscious' means not simply to be, but to be reported, known, to have awareness of one's being added to that being; and this is just what happens when the appropriative experience supervenes. The pen-experience in its original immediacy is not aware of itself, it simply *is*, and the second experience is required for what we call awareness of it to occur.[2] The difficulty of understanding what happens here is, therefore, not a logical difficulty: there is no contradiction involved. It is an ontological difficulty rather. Experiences come on an enormous scale, and if we take them all together, they come in a chaos of incommensurable relations that we can not straighten out. We have to abstract different groups of them, and handle these separately if we are to talk of them at all. But how the experiences ever *get themselves made,* or *why* their characters and relations are just such as appear, we can not begin to understand. Granting, however, that, by hook or crook, they *can* get themselves made, and can appear in the successions that I have so schematically described, then we have to confess that even although (as I began by quoting from the adversary) 'a feeling only is as it is felt,' there is still nothing absurd in the notion of its being felt in two different ways at once, as yours, namely, and as mine. It is, indeed, 'mine' only as it is felt as mine, and 'yours' only as it is felt as yours. But it is felt as neither *by itself,* but only when 'owned' by our two several remembering experiences, just as one undivided estate is owned by several heirs.

[2]Shadworth Hodgson has laid great stress on the fact that the minimum of consciousness demands two sub-feelings, of which the second retrospects the first. . . . 'We live forward, but we understand backward' is a phrase of Kierkegaard's which Höffding quotes. . . .

4.

One word, now, before I close, about the corollaries of the views set forth. Since the acquisition of conscious quality on the part of an experience depends upon a context coming to it, it follows that the sum total of all experiences, having no context, can not strictly be called conscious at all. It is a *that,* an Absolute, a 'pure' experience on an enormous scale, undifferentiated and undifferentiable into thought and thing. This the post-Kantian idealists have always practically acknowledged by calling their doctrine an *Identitätsphilosophie.* The question of the *Beseelung* of the All of things ought not, then, even to be asked. No more ought the question of its *truth* to be asked, for truth is a relation inside of the sum total, obtaining between thoughts and something else, and thoughts, as we have seen, can only be contextual things. In these respects the pure experiences of our philosophy are, in themselves considered, so many little absolutes, the philosophy of pure experience being only a more comminuted *Identitätsphilosophie.*

Meanwhile, a pure experience can be postulated with any amount whatever of span or field. If it exert the retrospective and appropriative function on any other piece of experience, the latter thereby enters into its own conscious stream. And in this operation time intervals make no essential difference. After sleeping, my retrospection is as perfect as it is between two successive waking moments of my time. Accordingly if, millions of years later, a similarly retrospective experience should anyhow come to birth, my present thought would form a genuine portion of its long-span conscious life. 'Form a portion,' I say, but not in the sense that the two things could be entitatively or substantively one—they cannot, for they are numerically discrete facts—but only in the sense that the *functions* of my present thought, its knowledge, its purpose, its content and 'consciousness,' in short, being inherited, would be continued practically unchanged. Speculations like Fechner's, of an Earth-soul, of wider spans of consciousness enveloping narrower ones throughout the cosmos, are, therefore, philosophically quite in order, provided they distinguish the functional from the entitative point of view, and do not treat the minor consciousness under discussion as a kind of standing material of which the wider ones *consist*.

The Place of Affectional Facts in a World of Pure Experience

Common sense and popular philosophy are as dualistic as it is possible to be. Thoughts, we all naturally think, are made of one kind of substance, and things of another. Consciousness, flowing inside of us in the forms of conception or judgment, or concentrating itself in the shape of passion or emotion, can be directly felt as the spiritual activity which it is, and known in contrast with the space-filling objective 'content' which it envelopes and accompanies. In opposition to this dualistic philosophy, I tried . . . to show that thoughts and things are absolutely homogeneous as to their material, and that their opposition is only one of relation and of function. There is no thought-stuff different from thing-stuff, I said; but the same identical piece of 'pure experience' (which was the name I gave to the *materia prima* of everything) can stand alternately for a 'fact of consciousness' or for a physical reality, according as it is taken in one context or in another.

The commonest objection which the doctrine there laid down runs up against is drawn from the existence of our 'affections.' In our pleasures and pains, our loves and fears and angers, in the beauty, comicality, importance or preciousness of certain objects and situations, we have, I am told by many critics, a great realm of experience intuitively recognized as spiritual, made, and felt to be made, of consciousness exclusively, and different in nature from the space-filling kind of being which is enjoyed by physical objects. . . . I now return to the subject, because I believe that, so far from invalidating my general thesis, these

SOURCE: *Journal of Philosophy, Psychology and Scientific Methods*, Vol. II, No. 11 (May 1905).

phenomena, when properly analyzed, afford it powerful support.

The central point of the pure-experience theory is that 'outer' and 'inner' are names for two groups into which we sort experiences according to the way in which they act upon their neighbors. Any one 'content,' such as *hard*, let us say, can be assigned to either group. In the outer group it is 'strong,' it acts 'energetically' and aggressively. Here whatever is hard interferes with the space its neighbors occupy. It dents them; is impenetrable by them; and we call the hardness then a physical hardness. In the mind, on the contrary, the hard thing is nowhere in particular, it dents nothing, it suffuses through its mental neighbors, as it were, and interpenetrates them. Taken in this group we call both it and them 'ideas' or 'sensations;' and the basis of the two groups respectively is the different type of interrelation, the mutual impenetrability, on the one hand, and the lack of physical interference and interaction, on the other.

That what in itself is one and the same entity should be able to function thus differently in different contexts is a natural consequence of the extremely complex reticulations in which our experiences come. To her offspring a tigress is tender, but cruel to every other living thing—both cruel and tender, therefore, at once. A mass in movement resists every force that operates contrariwise to its own direction, but to forces that pursue the same direction, or come in at right angles, it is absolutely inert. It is thus both energetic and inert; and the same is true (if you vary the associates properly) of every other piece of experience. It is only towards certain specific groups of associates that the physical energies, as we call them, of a content are put forth. In another group it may be quite inert.

It is possible to imagine a universe of experiences in which the only alternative between neighbors would be either physical interaction or complete inertness. In such a world the mental or the physical *status* of any piece of experience would be unequivocal. When active, it would figure in the physical, and when inactive, in the mental group.

But the universe we live in is more chaotic than this, and there is room in it for the hybrid or ambiguous group of our affectional experiences, of our emotions and appreciative perceptions. In the paragraphs that follow I shall try to show:

(1) That the popular notion that these experiences are intuitively given as purely inner facts is hasty and erroneous; and

(2) That their ambiguity illustrates beautifully my central thesis that subjectivity and objectivity are affairs not of what an experience is aboriginally made of, but of its classification. Classifications depend on our temporary purposes. For certain purposes it is convenient to take things in one set of relations, for other purposes in another set. In the two cases their contexts are apt to be different. In the case of our affectional experiences we have no permanent and steadfast purpose that obliges us to be consistent, so we find it easy to let them float ambiguously, sometimes classing them with our feelings, sometimes with more physical realities, according to caprice or to the convenience of the moment. Thus would these experiences, so far from being an obstacle to the pure experience philosophy, serve as an excellent corroboration of its truth.

First of all, then, it is a mistake to say, with the objectors whom I began by citing, that anger, love and fear are affections purely of the mind. That, to a great extent at any rate, they are simultaneously affections of the body is proved by the whole literature of the James-Lange theory of emotion. All our pains, moreover, are local, and we are always free to speak of them in objective as well as in subjective terms. We can say that we are aware of a painful place, filling a certain bigness in our organism, or we can say that we are inwardly in a 'state' of pain. All our adjectives of worth are similarly ambiguous—I instanced some of the ambiguities [in the first essay]. Is the preciousness of a diamond a quality of the gem? or is it a feeling in our mind? Practically we treat it as both or as either, according to the temporary direction of our thought. 'Beauty,' says Professor Santayana, 'is pleasure objectified'; and in Sections 10 and 11 of his work, *The Sense of Beauty,* he treats in a masterly way of this equivocal realm. The various pleasures we receive from an object may count as 'feelings' when we take them singly, but when they combine in a total richness, we call the result the 'beauty' of the object, and treat it as an outer attribute which our mind perceives. We discover beauty just as we discover the physical properties of things. Training is needed to make us expert in either line. Single sensations also may be ambiguous. Shall we say an 'agreeable degree of heat,' or an 'agreeable feeling' occasioned by the degree of heat? Either will do; and language would lose most of its esthetic and rhetorical value were we forbidden to project words primarily connoting our affections upon the objects by which the affections are aroused. The man is really hateful; the action really mean; the situation really tragic—all in themselves and quite apart from our opinion. We even go so far as to talk of a weary road, a giddy height, a jocund morning or a sullen sky; and the term 'indefinite' while usually applied only to our apprehensions, functions as a fundamental physical qualification of things in Spencer's 'law of evolution,' and doubtless passes with most readers for all right.

Psychologists, studying our perceptions of movement, have unearthed experiences in which movement is felt in general but not ascribed correctly to the body that really moves. Thus in optical vertigo, caused by unconscious movements of our eyes, both we and the external universe appear to be in a whirl. When clouds float by the moon, it is as if both clouds and moon and we ourselves shared in the motion. In the extraordinary case of amnesia of the Rev. Mr. Hanna, published by Sidis and Goodhart in their important work on *Multiple Personality,* we read that when the patient first recovered consciousness and "noticed an attendant walk across the room, he identified the movement with that of his own. He did not yet discriminate between his own movements and those outside himself." Such experiences point to a primitive stage of perception in which discriminations afterwards needful have not yet been made. A piece of experience of a determinate sort is there, but there at first as a 'pure' fact. Motion originally simply *is;* only later is it confined to this thing or to that. Something like this is true of every experience, however complex, at the moment of its actual presence. Let the reader arrest himself in the act of reading this article now. *Now* this is a pure experience, a phenomenon, or datum, a mere *that* or content of fact. '*Reading*' *simply is, is there;* and whether there for some one's consciousness, or there for physical nature, is a question not yet put. At the moment, it is there for neither; later we shall probably judge it to have been there for both.

With the affectional experiences which we are considering, the relatively 'pure' condition lasts. In practical life no urgent need has yet arisen for deciding whether to treat them as rigorously mental or as rigorously physical facts. So they remain equivocal; and, as the world goes, their equivocality is one of their great conveniences.

The shifting place of 'secondary qualities' in the history of philosophy is another excellent proof of the fact that 'inner' and 'outer' are not coefficients with which experiences come to us aboriginally stamped, but are rather results of a later classification performed by us for particular needs. The common-sense stage of thought is a perfectly definite practical halting-place, the place where we ourselves can proceed to act unhesitatingly. On this stage of thought things act on each other as well as on us by means of their secondary qualities. Sound, as such, goes through the air and can be intercepted. The heat of the fire passes over, as such, into the water which it sets a-boiling. It is the very light of the arclamp which displaces the darkness of the midnight street, etc. By engendering and translocating just these qualities, actively efficacious as they seem to be, we ourselves succeed in altering nature so as to suit us; and until more purely intellectual, as distinguished from practical, needs had arisen, no one ever thought of calling these qualities subjective. When, however, Galileo, Descartes, and others found it best for philosophic purposes to class sound, heat, and light along with pain and pleasure as purely mental phenomena, they could do so with impunity.

Even the primary qualities are undergoing the same fate. Hardness and softness are effects on us of atomic interactions, and the atoms themselves are neither hard nor soft, nor solid nor liquid. Size and shape are deemed subjective by Kantians; time itself is subjective according to many philosophers; and even the activity and causal efficacy which lingered in physics long after secondary qualities were banished are now treated as illusory projections outwards of phenomena of our own consciousness. There are no activities or effects in nature, for the most intellectual contemporary school of physical speculation. Nature exhibits only *changes*, which habitually coincide with one another so that their habits are describable in simple 'laws.'

There is no original spirituality or materiality of being, intuitively discerned, then; but only a translocation of experiences from one world to another; a grouping of them with one set or another of associates for definitely practical or intellectual ends.

I will say nothing here of the persistent ambiguity of *relations*. They are undeniable parts of pure experience; yet, while common sense and what I call radical empiricism stand for their being objective, both rationalism and the usual empiricism claim that they are exclusively the 'work of the mind'—the finite mind or the absolute mind, as the case may be.

Turn now to those affective phenomena which more directly concern us.

We soon learn to separate the ways in which things appeal to our interests and emotions from the ways in which they act upon one another. It does not *work* to assume that physical objects are going to act outwardly by their sympathetic or antipathetic qualities. The beauty of a thing or its value is no force that can be plotted in a polygon of compositions, nor does its 'use' or 'significance' affect in the minutest degree its vicissitudes or destiny at the hands of physical nature. Chemical 'affinities' are a purely verbal metaphor; and, as I just said, even such things as forces, tensions, and activities can at a pinch be regarded as anthropomorphic projections. So far, then, as the physical world means the collection of contents that determine in each other certain regular changes, the whole collection of our appreciative attributes has to be treated as falling outside of it. If we mean by physical nature whatever lies beyond the surface of our bodies, these attributes are inert throughout the whole extent of physical nature.

Why then do men leave them as ambiguous

as they do, and not class them decisively as purely spiritual?

The reason would seem to be that, although they are inert as regards the rest of physical nature, they are not inert as regards that part of physical nature which our own skin covers. It is those very appreciative attributes of things, their dangerousness, beauty, rarity, utility, etc., that primarily appeal to our attention. In our commerce with nature these attributes are what give *emphasis* to objects; and for an object to be emphatic, whatever spiritual fact it may mean, means also that it produces immediate bodily effects upon us, alterations of tone and tension, of heart-beat and breathing, of vascular and visceral action. The 'interesting' aspects of things are thus not wholly inert physically, though they be active only in these small corners of physical nature which our bodies occupy. That, however, is enough to save them from being classed as absolutely non-objective.

The attempt, if any one should make it, to sort experiences into two absolutely discrete groups, with nothing but inertness in one of them and nothing but activities in the other, would thus receive one check. It would receive another as soon as we examined the more distinctively mental group; for though in that group it be true that things do not act on one another by their physical properties, do not dent each other or set fire to each other, they yet act on each other in the most energetic way by those very characters which are so inert extracorporeally. It is by the interest and importance that experiences have for us, by the emotions they excite, and the purposes they subserve, by their affective values, in short, that their consecution in our several conscious streams, as 'thoughts' of ours, is mainly ruled. Desire introduces them; interest holds them; fitness fixes their order and connection. I need only refer for this aspect of our mental life, to Wundt's article 'Ueber psychische Causalität,' which begins Volume X. of his *Philosophische Studien*.[1]

---

[1] It is enough for my present purpose if the appreciative characters but *seem* to act thus. Believers in an activity *an sich*, other than our mental experiences of activity, will find some farther reflections on the subject in my address on 'The Experience of Activity.'

It thus appears that the ambiguous or amphibious *status* which we find our epithets of value occupying is the most natural thing in the world. It would, however, be an unnatural status if the popular opinion which I cited at the outset were correct. If 'physical' and 'mental' meant two different kinds of intrinsic nature, immediately, intuitively, and infallibly discernible, and each fixed forever in whatever bit of experience it qualified, one does not see how there could ever have arisen any room for doubt or ambiguity. But if, on the contrary, these words are words of sorting, ambiguity is natural. For then, as soon as the relations of a thing are sufficiently various it can be sorted variously. Take a mass of carrion, for example, and the 'disgustingness' which for us is part of the experience. The sun caresses it, and the zephyr wooes it as if it were a bed of roses. So the disgustingness fails to *operate* within the realm of suns and breezes,— it does not function as a physical quality. But the carrion 'turns our stomach' by what seems a direct operation—it *does* function physically, therefore, in that limited part of physics. We can treat it as physical or as non-physical according as we take it in the narrower or in the wider context, and conversely, of course, we must treat it as non-mental or as mental.

Our body itself is the palmary instance of the ambiguous. Sometimes I treat my body purely as a part of outer nature. Sometimes, again, I think of it as 'mine,' I sort it with the 'me,' and then certain local changes and determinations in it pass for spiritual happenings. Its breathing is my 'thinking,' its sensorial adjustments are my 'attention,' its kinesthetic alterations are my 'efforts,' its visceral perturbations are my 'emotions.' The obstinate controversies that have arisen over such statements as these (which sound so paradoxical, and which can yet be made so seriously) prove how hard it is to decide by bare introspection what it is in experiences that shall make them either spiritual or material. It surely can be nothing intrinsic in the individual experience. It is their way of behaving towards each other, their system of relations, their function; and all these things vary with the context in which we find it opportune to consider them.

I think I may conclude, then (and I hope that my readers are now ready to conclude with me), that the pretended spirituality of our emotions and of our attributes of value, so far from proving an objection to the philosophy of pure experience, does, when rightly discussed and accounted for, serve as one of its best corroborations.

Percept and Concept

William James

1. The Import of Concepts

The problem convenient to take up next in order will be that of the difference between thoughts and things. 'Things' are known to us by our senses, and are called 'presentations' by some authors, to distinguish them from the ideas or 'representations' which we may have when our senses are closed. I myself have grown accustomed to the words 'percept' and 'concept' in treating of the contrast, but concepts flow out of percepts and into them again, they are so interlaced, and our life rests on them so interchangeably and undiscriminatingly, that it is often difficult to impart quickly to beginners a clear notion of the difference meant. Sensation and thought in man are mingled, but they vary independently. In our quadrupedal relatives thought proper is at a minimum, but we have no reason to suppose that their immediate life of feeling is either less or more copious than ours. Feeling must have been originally self-sufficing; and thought appears as a superadded function, adapting us to a wider environment than that of which brutes take account. Some parts of the stream of feeling must be more intense, emphatic, and exciting than others in animals as well as in ourselves; but whereas lower animals simply react upon these more salient sensations by appropriate movements, higher animals remember them, and men react on them intellectually, by using nouns, adjectives, and verbs to identify them when they meet them elsewhere.

The great difference between percepts and concepts[1] is that percepts are continuous and concepts are discrete. Not discrete in their *being*, for conception as an *act* is part of the flux of feeling, but discrete from each other in their several *meanings*. Each concept means just what it singly means, and nothing else; and if the conceiver does not know whether he means this or means that, it shows that his concept is imperfectly formed. The perceptual flux as such, on the contrary, *means* nothing, and is but what it immediately is. No matter how small a tract of it be taken, it is always a much-at-once, and contains innumerable aspects and characters which conception can pick out, isolate, and thereafter always intend. It shows duration, intensity, complexity or simplicity, interestingness, excitingness, pleasantness or their opposites. Data from all our senses enter into it, merged in a general extensiveness of which each occupies a big or little share. Yet all these parts leave its unity unbroken. Its boundaries are no more distinct than are those of the field of vision. Boundaries are things that intervene; but here noth-

SOURCE: William James, *Some Problems of Philosophy* (London: Longmans, Green and Co., 1911), Ch. IV, V.

---

[1] In what follows I shall freely use synonyms for these two terms. 'Idea,' 'thought,' and 'intellection' are synonymous with 'concept.' Instead of 'percept' I shall often speak of 'sensation,' 'feeling,' 'intuition,' and sometimes of 'sensible experience' or of the 'immediate flow' of conscious life. Since Hegel's time what is simply perceived has been called the 'immediate,' while the 'mediated' is synonymous with what is conceived.

ing intervenes save parts of the perceptual flux itself, and these are overflowed by what they separate, so that whatever we distinguish and isolate conceptually is found perceptually to telescope and compenetrate and diffuse into its neighbors. The cuts we make are purely ideal. It my reader can succeed in abstracting from all conceptual interpretation and lapse back into his immediate sensible life at this very moment, he will find it to be what someone has called a big blooming buzzing confusion, as free from contradiction in its 'much-at-onceness' as it is all alive and evidently there.[2]

Out of this aboriginal sensible muchness attention carves out objects, which conception then names and identifies forever—in the sky 'constellations,' on the earth 'beach,' 'sea,' 'cliff,' 'bushes,' 'grass.' Out of time we cut 'days' and 'nights,' 'summers' and 'winters.' We say *what* each part of the sensible continuum is, and all these abstracted *whats* are concepts.[3]

The intellectual life of man consists almost wholly in his substitution of a conceptual order for the perceptual order in which his experience originally comes. But before tracing the consequences of the substitution, I must say something about the conceptual order itself.[4]

Trains of concepts unmixed with percepts grow frequent in the adult mind; and parts of these conceptual trains arrest our attention just as parts of the perceptual flow did, giving rise to concepts of a higher order of abstractness. So subtle is the discernment of man, and so great the power of some men to single out the most fugitive elements of what passes before them, that these new formations have no

limit. Aspect within aspect, quality after quality, relation upon relation, absences and negations as well as present features, end by being noted and their names added to the store of nouns, verbs, adjectives, conjunctions, and prepositions by which the human mind interprets life. Every new book verbalizes some new concept, which becomes important in proportion to the use that can be made of it. Different universes of thought thus arise, with specific sorts of relation among their ingredients. The world of common-sense 'things'; the world of material tasks to be done; the mathematical world of pure forms; the world of ethical propositions; the worlds of logic, of music, etc., all abstracted and generalized from long forgotten perceptual instances, from which they have as it were flowered out, return and merge themselves again in the particulars of our present and future perception. By those *whats* we apperceive all our *thises*. Percepts and concepts interpenetrate and melt together, impregnate and fertilize each other. Neither, taken alone, knows reality in its completeness. We need them both, as we need both our legs to walk with.

From Aristotle downwards philosophers have frankly admitted the indispensability, for complete knowledge of fact, of both the sensational and the intellectual contribution.[5] For complete knowledge of fact, I say; but facts are particulars and connect themselves with practical necessities and the arts; and Greek philosophers soon formed the notion that a knowledge of so-called 'universals,' consisting of concepts of abstract forms, qualities, numbers, and relations was the only knowledge worthy of the truly philosophic mind. Particular facts decay and our perceptions of them vary. A concept never varies; and between such unvarying terms the relations must be constant and express eternal verities. Hence there arose a tendency, which has lasted all through philosophy, to contrast the knowledge of universals and intelligibles, as godlike, dignified, and honorable to the knower, with that of particulars and sensibles as some-

---

[2]Compare W. James: *A Pluralistic Universe*, pp. 282–288.

[3]The account I give directly contradicts that which Kant gave which has prevailed since Kant's time. Kant always speaks of the aboriginal sensible flux as a 'manifold' of which he considers the essential character to be its disconnectedness. To get any togetherness at all into it requires, he thinks, the agency of the 'transcendental ego of apperception,' and to get any definite connections requires the agency of the understanding, with its synthesizing concepts or 'categories.' The reader must decide which account agrees best with his own actual experience.

[4]The substitution was first described in these terms by S. H. Hodgson in his *Philosophy of Reflection*, i, 288–310.

[5]See, for example, book i, chap. ii, of Aristotle's *Metaphysics*.

thing relatively base which more allies us with the beasts.[6]

For rationalistic writers conceptual knowledge was not only the more noble knowledge, but it originated independently of all perceptual particulars. Such concepts as God, perfection, eternity, infinity, immutability, identity, absolute beauty, truth, justice, necessity, freedom, duty, worth, etc., and the part they play in our mind, are, it was supposed, impossible to explain as results of practical experience. The empiricist view, and probably the true view, is that they do result from practical experience.[7] But a more important question than that as to the origin of our concepts is that as to their functional use and value;—is *that* tied down to perceptual experience, or out of all relation to it? Is conceptual knowledge self-suffing and a revelation all by itself, quite apart from its uses in helping to a better understanding of the world of sense?

Rationalists say, Yes. For, as we shall see in later places, . . . the various conceptual universes . . . can be considered in complete abstraction from perceptual reality, and when they are so considered, all sorts of fixed relations can be discovered among their parts. From these the *a priori* sciences of logic, mathematics, ethics, and æsthetics (so far as the last two can be called sciences at all) result. Conceptual knowledge must thus be called a self-suffing revelation; and by rationalistic writers it has always been treated as admitting us to a diviner world, the world of universal rather than that of perishing facts, of essential qualities, immutable relations, eternal principles of truth and right. Emerson writes: 'Generalization is always a new influx of divinity into the mind: hence the thrill that attends it.' And a disciple of Hegel, after exalting the knowledge of 'the General, Unchangeable, and alone Valuable' above that of 'the Particular, Sensible and Transient,' adds that if you reproach philosophy with being unable to make a single grass-blade grow, or even to know how it does grow, the reply it that since such a particular 'how' stands not above but below knowledge, strictly so-called, such an ignorance argues no defect.[8]

To this ultra-rationalistic opinion the empiricist contention that *the significance of concepts consists always in their relation to perceptual particulars* has been opposed. Made of percepts, or distilled from parts of percepts, their essential office, it has been said, is to coalesce with percepts again, bringing the mind back into the perceptual world with a better command of the situation there. Certainly whenever we *can* do this with our concepts, we do *more* with them than when we leave them flocking with their abstract and motionless companions. It is possible therefore, to join the rationalists in allowing conceptual knowledge to be self-suffing, while at the same time one joins the empiricists in maintaining that the full *value* of such knowledge is got only by combining it with perceptual reality again. This mediating attitude is that which this book must adopt. But to understand the nature of concepts better we must now go on to distinguish their *function* from their *content*.

The concept 'man,' to take an example, is three things: 1, the word itself; 2, a vague picture of the human form which has its own value in the way of beauty or not; and 3, an instrument for symbolizing certain objects from which we may expect human treatment when occasion arrives. Similarly of 'triangle,' 'cosine,'—they have their substantive value both as words and as images suggested, but they also have a functional value whenever they lead us elsewhere in discourse.

There are concepts, however, the image-part of which is so faint that their whole value seems to be functional. 'God,' 'cause,' 'number,' 'substance,' 'soul,' for example, suggest no definite picture; and their significance seems to consist entirely in their *tendency*, in the further turn which they may give to our action or our thought. We cannot rest in the contemplation of their form, as we can in that of a 'circle' or a 'man'; we must pass beyond.

[6]Plato in numerous places, but chiefly in books 6 and 7 of the *Republic,* contrasts perceptual knowledge as 'opinion' with real knowledge, to the latter's glory. . . .

[7]John Locke, in his *Essay concerning Human Understanding,* books i, ii, was the great popularizer of this doctrine. . . .

[8]Michelet, Hegel's *Werke,* vii, 15, quoted by A. Gratry, *De la Connaissance de l'Âme,* i, 231.

Now however beautiful or otherwise worthy of stationary contemplation the substantive part of a concept may be, the more important part of its significance may naturally be held to be the consequences to which it leads. These may lie either in the way of making us think, or in the way of making us act. Whoever has a clear idea of these knows effectively what the concept practically signifies, whether its substantive content be interesting in its own right or not.

This consideration has led to a method of interpreting concepts to which I shall give the name of *the Pragmatic Rule*.[9]

The pragmatic rule is that the meaning of a concept may always be found, if not in some sensible particular which it directly designates, then in some particular difference in the course of human experience which its being true will make. Test every concept by the question 'What sensible difference to anybody will its truth make?' and you are in the best possible position for understanding what it means and for discussing its importance. If, questioning whether a certain concept be true or false, you can think of absolutely nothing that would practically differ in the two cases, you may assume that the alternative is meaningless and that your concept is no distinct idea. If two concepts lead you to infer the same particular consequence, then you may assume that they embody the same meaning under different names.

This rule applies to concepts of every order of complexity, from simple terms to propositions uniting many terms.

So many disputes in philosophy hinge upon ill-defined words and ideas, each side claiming its own word or idea to be true, that any accepted method of making meanings clear must be of great utility. No method can be handier of application than our pragmatic rule. If you claim that any idea is true, assign at the same time some difference that its being true will make in some possible person's history, and we shall know not only just what you are really claiming but also how important an issue it is, and how to go to work to verify the claim. In obeying this rule we neglect the substantive content of the concept, and follow its function only. This neglect might seem at first sight to need excuse, for the content often has a value of its own which might conceivably add lustre to reality, if it existed, apart from any modification wrought by it in the other parts of reality. Thus it is often supposed that 'Idealism' is a theory precious in itself, even though no definite change in the details of our experience can be deduced from it. Later discussion will show that this is a superficial view, and that particular consequences are the only criterion of a concept's meaning, and the only test of its truth.

Instances are hardly called for, they are so obvious. That A and B are 'equal,' for example, means either that 'you will find no difference' when you pass from one to the other, or that in substituting one for the other in certain operations 'you will get the same result both times.' 'Substance' means that 'a definite group of sensations will recur.' 'Incommensurable' means that 'you are always confronted with a remainder.' 'Infinite' means either that, or that 'you can count as many units in a part as you can in the whole.' 'More' and 'less' mean certain sensations, varying according to the matter. 'Freedom' means 'no feeling of sensible restraint.' 'Necessity' means that 'your way is blocked in all directions save one.' 'God' means that 'you can dismiss certain kinds of fear,' 'cause' that 'you may expect certain sequences,' etc. etc. We shall find plenty of examples in the rest of this book; so I go back now to the more general question of whether the whole import of the world of concepts lies in its relation to perceptual experience, or whether it be also an independent revelation of reality. Great ambiguity is possible in answering this question, so we must mind our Ps and Qs.

The first thing to notice is that in the earliest stages of human intelligence, so far as we can guess at them, thought proper must have had an exclusively practical use. Men classed their sensations, substituting concepts for them, in order to 'work them for what they were worth,' and to prepare for what might lie ahead. Class-names suggest consequences that have attached themselves on other occasions to

[9]Compare W. James, *Pragmatism,* chap. ii and *passim;* also Baldwin's *Dictionary of Philosophy,* article 'Pragmatism,' by C. S. Peirce.

other members of the class—consequences which the present percept will also probably or certainly show.[10] The present percept in its immediacy may thus often sink to the status of a bare sign of the consequences which the substituted concept suggests.

The substitution of concepts and their connections, of a whole conceptual order, in short, for the immediate perceptual flow, thus widens enormously our mental panorama. Had we no concepts we should live simply 'getting' each successive moment of experience, as the sessile sea-anemone on its rock receives whatever nourishment the wash of the waves may bring. With concepts we go in quest of the absent, meet the remote, actively turn this way or that, bend our experience, and make it tell us whither it is bound. We change its order, run it backwards, bring far bits together and separate near bits, jump about over its surface instead of plowing through its continuity, string its items on as many ideal diagrams as our mind can frame. All these are ways of *handling* the perceptual flux and *meeting* distant parts of it; and as far as this primary function of conception goes, we can only conclude it to be what I began by calling it, a faculty superadded to our barely perceptual consciousness for its use in practically adapting us to a larger environment than that of which brutes take account. We *harness* perceptual reality in concepts in order to drive it better to our ends.

Does our conceptual translation of the perceptual flux enable us also to understand the latter better? What do we mean by making us 'understand'? Applying our pragmatic rule to the interpretation of the word, we see that the better we understand anything the more we are able to *tell about it*. Judged by this test, concepts do make us understand our percepts better: knowing *what* these are, we can tell all sorts of farther truths about them, based on the relation of those whats to other whats. The whole system of relations, spatial, temporal, and logical, of our fact, gets plotted out. An ancient philosophical opinion, inherited from Aristotle, is that we do not understand a thing until we know it by its causes. When the maid-servant says that 'the cat' broke the tea-cup, she would have us conceive the fracture in a causally explanatory way. No otherwise when Clerk-Maxwell asks us to conceive of gas-electricity as due to molecular bombardment. An imaginary agent out of sight becomes in each case a part of the cosmic context in which we now place the percept to be explained; and the explanation is valid in so far as the new causal *that* is itself conceived in a context that makes its existence probable, and with a nature agreeable to the effects it is imagined to produce. All our scientific explanations would seem to conform to this simple type of the 'necessary cat.' The conceived order of nature built round the perceived order and explaining it theoretically, as we say, is only a system of hypothetically imagined *thats*, the *whats* of which harmoniously connect themselves with the *what* of any *that* which we immediately perceive.

The system is essentially a topographic system, a system of the distribution of things. It tells us what's what, and where's where. In so far forth it merely prolongs that opening up of the perspective of practical consequences which we found to be the primordial utility of the conceiving faculty: it adapts us to an immense environment. Working by the causes of things we gain advantages which we never should have compassed had we worked by the things alone.

But in order to reach such results the concepts in the explanatory system must, I said, 'harmoniously connect.' What does that mean? Is this also only a practical advantage, or is it something more? It seems something more, for it points to the fact that when concepts of various sorts are once abstracted or constructed, new relations are then found between them, connecting them in peculiarly intimate, 'rational,' and unchangeable ways. In another book[11] I have tried to show that these rational relations are all products of our faculty of comparison and of our sense of 'more.'

The sciences which exhibit these relations are the so-called *a priori* sciences of mathemat-

---

[10]For practical uses of conception compare W. James, *Principles of Psychology*, chap. xxii. . . .

[11]*Principles of Psychology*, 1890, chap. xxviii.

ics and logic. But these sciences express relations of comparison and identification exclusively. Geometry and algebra, for example, first define certain conceptual objects, and then establish equations between them, substituting equals for equals. Logic has been defined as the 'substitution of similars'; and in general one may say that the perception of likeness and unlikeness generates the whole of 'rational' or 'necessary' truth. Nothing *happens* in the worlds of logic, mathematics or moral and æsthetic preference. The static nature of the relations in these worlds is what gives to the propositions that express them their 'eternal' character: The binomial theorem, e. g., expresses the value of any power of any sum of two terms, to the end of time.

These vast unmoving systems of universal terms form the new worlds of thought of which I spoke [earlier]. The terms are elements (or are framed of elements) abstracted from the perceptual flux; but in their abstract shape we note relations between them (and again between these relations) which enable us to set up various schemes of fixed serial orders or of 'more and more.' The terms are indeed manmade, but the order, being established solely by comparison, is fixed by the nature of the terms on the one hand and by our power of perceiving relations on the other. Thus two abstract twos are always the same as an abstract four; what contains the container contains the contained of whatever material either be made; equals added to equals always give equal results, in the world in which abstract equality is the only property the terms are supposed to possess; the more than the more is more than the less, no matter in what direction of moreness we advance; if you dot off a term in one series every time you dot one off in another, the two series will either never end, or will come to an end together, or one will be exhausted first, etc. etc.; the result being those skeletons of 'rational' or 'necessary' truth in which our logic- and mathematics-books (sometimes our philosophy-books) arrange their universal terms.

The 'rationalization' of any mass of perceptual fact consists in assimilating its concrete terms, one by one, to so many terms of the conceptual series, and then in assuming that the relations intuitively found among the latter are what connect the former too. Thus we rationalize gas-pressure by identifying it with the blows of hypothetic molecules; then we see that the more closely the molecules are crowded the more frequent the blows upon the containing walls will become; then we discern the exact proportionality of the crowding with the number of blows; so that finally Mariotte's empirical law gets rationally explained. All our transformations of the sense-order into a more rational equivalent are similar to this one. We interrogate the beautiful apparition, as Emerson calls it, which our senses ceaselessly raise upon our path, and the items there refer us to their interpretants in the shape of ideal constructions in some static arrangement which our mind has already made out of its concepts alone. The interpretants are then substituted for the sensations, which thus get rationally conceived. To 'explain' means to coördinate, one to one, the *thises* of the perceptual flow with the *whats* of the ideal manifold, whichever it be.

We may well call this a theoretic conquest over the order in which nature originally comes. The conceptual order into which we translate our experience seems not only a means of practical adaptation, but the revelation of a deeper level of reality in things. Being more constant, it is *truer*, less illusory than the perceptual order, and ought to command our attention more.

There is still another reason why conception appears such an exalted function. Concepts not only guide us over the map of life, but we *revalue* life by their use. Their relation to percepts is like that of sight to touch. Sight indeed helps us by preparing us for contacts while they are yet far off, but it endows us in addition with a new world of optical splendor, interesting enough all by itself to occupy a busy life. Just so do concepts bring their proper splendor. The mere possession of such vast and simple pictures is an inspiring good: they arouse new feelings of sublimity, power, and admiration, new interests and motivations.

Ideality often clings to things only when they are taken thus abstractly. "Causes, as anti-slavery, democracy, etc., dwindle when realized in their sordid particulars. Abstractions will touch us when we are callous to the concrete instances in which they lie embodied. Loyal in our measure to particular ideals, we soon set up abstract loyalty as something of a superior order, to be infinitely loyal to; and truth at large becomes a 'momentous issue' compared with which truths in detail are 'poor scraps, mere crumbling successes.' "[12] So strongly do objects that come as universal and eternal arouse our sensibilities, so greatly do life's values deepen when we translate percepts into ideas! The translation appears as far more than the original's equivalent.

Concepts thus play three distinct parts in human life.

1. They steer us practically every day, and provide an immense map of relations among the elements of things, which, though not now, yet on some possible future occasion, may help to steer us practically;

2. They bring new values into our perceptual life, they reanimate our wills, and make our action turn upon new points of emphasis;

3. The map which the mind frames out of them is an object which possesses, when once it has been framed, an independent existence. It suffices all by itself for purposes of study. The 'eternal' truths it contains would have to be acknowledged even were the world of sense annihilated.

We thus see clearly what is gained and what is lost when percepts are translated into concepts. Perception is solely of the here and now; conception is of the like and unlike, of the future, of the past, and of the far away. But

[12]J. Royce: *The Philosophy of Loyalty*, 1908, particularly Lecture vii, § 5.

Emerson writes: 'Each man sees over his own experience a certain stain of error, whilst that of other men looks fair and ideal. Let any man go back to those delicious relations which make the beauty of his life, which have given him sincerest instruction and nourishment, he will shrink and moan. Alas! I know not why, but infinite compunctions embitter in mature life the remembrances of budding joy, and cover every beloved name. Everything is beautiful seen from the point of view of the intellect, or as truth, but all is sour, if seen as experience. Details are melancholy; the plan is seemly and noble. In the actual world—the painful kingdom of time and place—dwell care, and canker, and fear. With thought, with the ideal, is immortal hilarity, the rose of Joy. Round it all the muses sing. But grief clings to names and persons, and the partial interests of to-day and yesterday ' (*Essay on Love.*)

this map of what surrounds the present, like all maps, is only a surface; its features are but abstract signs and symbols of things that in themselves are concrete bits of sensible experience. We have but to weigh extent against content, thickness against spread, and we see that for some purposes the one, for other purposes the other, has the higher value. Who can decide offhand which is absolutely better to live or to understand life? We must do both alternately, and a man can no more limit himself to either than a pair of scissors can cut with a single one of its blades.

---

2. *The Abuse of Concepts*

In spite of this obvious need of holding our percepts fast if our conceptual powers are to mean anything distinct, there has always been a tendency among philosophers to treat conception as the more essential thing in knowledge.[13] The Platonizing persuasion has ever been that the intelligible order ought to supersede the senses rather than interpret them. The senses, according to this opinion, are organs of wavering illusion that stand in the way of 'knowledge,' in the unalterable sense of that term. They are an unfortunate complication on which philosophers may safely turn their backs.

'Your sensational modalities,' writes one of these, 'are but darkness, remember that. Mount higher, up to reason, and you will see light. Impose silence on your senses, your imagination, and your passions, and you will then hear the pure voice of interior truth, the clear and evident replies of our common mistress [reason]. Never confound that evidence which results from the comparison of ideas with the vivacity of those feelings which move and touch you. . . . We must follow reason despite the caresses, the threats and the insults of the body to which we are conjoined, despite

[13]The traditional rationalist view would have it that to understand life, without entering its turmoil, is the absolutely better part. Philosophy's 'special work,' writes William Wallace, 'is to comprehend the world, not try to make it better' (*Prolegomena to the Study of Hegel's Philosophy*, 2d edition, Oxford, 1894, p. 29).

the action of the objects that surround us. . . . I exhort you to recognize the difference there is between knowing and feeling, between our clear ideas, and our sensations always obscure and confused.'[14]

This is the traditional intellectualist creed. When Plato, its originator, first thought of concepts as forming an entirely separate world and treated this as the only object fit for the study of immortal minds, he lit up an entirely new sort of enthusiasm in the human breast. These objects were precious objects, concrete things were dross. Introduced by Dion, who had studied at Athens, to the corrupt and worldly court of the tyrant of Syracuse, Plato, as Plutarch tells us, 'was received with wonderful kindness and respect. . . . The citizens began to entertain marvellous hopes of a speedy reformation when they observed the modesty which now ruled the banquets, and the general decorum which reigned in all the court, their tyrant also behaving himself with gentleness and humanity. . . . There was a general passion for reasoning and philosophy, so much so that the very palace, it is reported, was filled with dust by the concourse of the students in mathematics who were working their problems there' in the sand. Some 'professed to be indignant that the Athenians, who formerly had come to Syracuse with a great fleet and numerous army, and perished miserably without being able to take the city, should now, by means of one sophister, overturn the sovereignty of Dionysius; inveigling him to cashier his guard of 10,000 lances, dismiss a navy of 400 galleys, disband an army of 10,000 horse and many times over that number of foot, and go seek in the schools an unknown and imaginary bliss and learn by the mathematics how to be happy.'

Having now set forth the merits of the conceptual translation, I must proceed to show its shortcomings. We extend our view when we insert our percepts into our conceptual map. We learn *about* them, and of some of them we transfigure the value; but the map remains superficial through the abstractness, and false through the discreteness of its elements; and the whole operation, so far from making things appear more rational, becomes the source of quite gratuitous unintelligibilities. Conceptual knowledge is forever inadequate to the fulness of the reality to be known. Reality consists of existential particulars as well as of essences and universals and class-names, and of existential particulars we become aware only in the perceptual flux. The flux can never be superseded. We must carry it with us to the bitter end of our cognitive business, keeping it in the midst of the translation even when the latter proves illuminating, and falling back on it alone when the translation gives out. 'The insuperability of sensation' would be a short expression of my thesis.

To prove it, I must show: 1. That concepts are secondary formations, inadequate, and only ministerial; and 2. That they falsify as well as omit, and make the flux impossible to understand.

1. Conception is a secondary process, not indispensible to life. It presupposes perception, which is self-sufficing, as all lower creatures, in whom conscious life goes on by reflex adaptations, show.

To understand a concept you must know what it *means*. It means always some *this,* or some abstract portion of a *this,* with which we first made acquaintance in the perceptual world, or else some grouping of such abstract portions. All conceptual content is borrowed: to know what the concept 'color' means you must have *seen* red or blue, or green. To know what 'resistance' means, you must have made some effort; to know what 'motion' means, you must have had some experience, active or passive, thereof. This applies as much to concepts of the most rarified order as to qualities like 'bright' and 'loud.' To know what the word 'illation' means one must once have sweated through some particular argument. To know what a 'proportion' means one must have compared ratios in some sensible case. You can create new concepts out of old elements, but the elements must have been perceptually given; and the famous world of universals would disappear like a soap-bubble if the definite contents of feeling, the *thises* and *thats,* which its terms severally denote, could be at once withdrawn. Whether our concepts live by returning to the perceptual world or not, they live by having come from it. It is the nourishing ground from which their sap is drawn.

[14]Malebranche: *Entretiens sur la Métaphysique,* 3me. Entretien, viii, 9.

2. Conceptual treatment of perceptual reality makes it seem paradoxical and incomprehensible; and when radically and consistently carried out, it leads to the opinion that perceptual experience is not reality at all, but an appearance or illusion.

Briefly, this is a consequence of two facts: First, that when we substitute concepts for percepts, we substitute their relations also. But since the relations of concepts are of static comparison only, it is impossible to substitute them for the dynamic relations with which the perceptual flux is filled. Secondly, the conceptual scheme, consisting as it does of discontinuous terms, can only cover the perceptual flux in spots and incompletely. The one is no full measure of the other, essential features of the flux escaping whenever we put concepts in its place.

This needs considerable explanation, for we have concepts not only of qualities and relations, but of happenings and actions; and it might seem as if these could make the conceptual order active.[15] But this would be a false interpretation. The concepts themselves are fixed, even though they designate parts that move in the flux; they do not act, even though they designate activities; and when we substitute them and their order, we substitute a scheme the intrinsically stationary nature of which is not altered by the fact that some of its terms symbolize changing originals. The concept of 'change,' for example, is always that fixed concept. If it changed, its original self would have to stay to mark what it had changed from; and even then the change would be a perceived continuous process, of which the translation into concepts could only consist in the judgment that later and earlier parts of it *differed*—such 'differences' being conceived as absolutely static relations.

Whenever we conceive a thing we *define* it; and if we still don't understand, we define our definition. Thus I define a certain percept by saying 'this is motion,' or 'I am moving'; and then I define motion by calling it the 'being in new positions at new moments of time.' This habit of telling what everything is becomes inveterate. The farther we push it, the more we learn *about* our subject of discourse, and we end by thinking that knowing the latter always consists in getting farther and farther away from the perceptual type of experience. This uncriticized habit, added to the intrinsic charm of the conceptual form, is the source of 'intellectualism' in philosophy.

But intellectualism quickly breaks down. When we try to exhaust motion by conceiving it as a summation of parts, *ad infinitum*, we find only insufficiency. Although, when you have a continuum given, you can make cuts and dots in it, *ad libitum*, enumerating the dots and cuts will not give you your continuum back. The rationalist mind admits this; but instead of seeing that the fault is with the concepts, it blames the perceptual flux. This, Kant contends, has no reality in itself, being a mere apparitional birth-place for concepts, to be substituted indefinitely. When these themselves are seen never to attain to a completed sum, reality is sought by such thinkers outside both of the perceptual flow and of the conceptual scheme. Kant lodges it before the flow, in the shape of

---

[15]Prof. Hibben, in an article in the *Philosophic Review*, vol. xix, pp. 125 ff. (1910), seeks to defend the conceptual order against attacks similar to those in the text, which, he thinks, come from misapprehensions of the true function of logic. 'The peculiar function of thought is to represent the continuous,' he says, and he proves it by the example of the calculus. I reply that the calculus, in substituting for certain perceptual continuities its peculiar symbols, lets us follow changes point by point, and is thus their *practical,* but not their *sensible* equivalent. It cannot *reveal* any change to one who never felt it, but it can lead him to where the change would lead him. It may practically replace the change, but it cannot *reproduce* it. What I am contending for is that the non-reproducible part of reality is an essential part of the content of philosophy, whilst Hibben and the logicists seem to believe that conception, if only adequately attained to, might be all-sufficient. 'It is the peculiar duty and privilege of philosophy,' Mr. Hibben writes, 'to exalt the prerogatives of intellect.' He claims that universals are able to deal adequately with particulars, and that concepts do not so exclude each other, as my text has accused them of doing. Of course 'synthetic' concepts abound, with subconcepts included in them, and the *a priori* world is full of them. But they are all designative; and I think that no careful reader of my text will accuse me of identifying 'knowledge' with either perception or conception absolutely or exclusively. Perception gives 'intension,' conception gives 'extension' to our knowledge.

so-called 'things in themselves';[16] others place it beyond perception, as an Absolute (Bradley), or represent it as a Mind whose ways of thinking transcend ours (Green, the Cairds, Royce). In either case, both our percepts and our concepts are held by such philosophers to falsify reality; but the concepts less than the percepts, for they are static, and by all rationalist authors the ultimate reality is supposed to be static also, while perceptual life fairly boils over with activity and change.

If we take a few examples, we can see how many of the troubles of philosophy come from assuming that to be understood (or 'known' in the only worthy sense of the word) our flowing life must be cut into discrete bits and pinned upon a fixed relational scheme.

Example 1. *Activity and causation are incomprehensible,* for the conceptual scheme yields nothing like them. Nothing happens therein: concepts are 'timeless,' and can only be juxtaposed and compared. The concept 'dog' does not bite; the concept 'cock' does not crow. So Hume and Kant translate the fact of causation into the crude juxtaposition of two phenomena. Later authors, wishing to mitigate the crudeness, resolve the adjacency, whenever they can, into identity: cause and effect must be the same reality in disguise, and our perception of difference in these successions thus becomes an illusion. Lotze elaborately establishes that the 'influencing' of one thing by another is inconceivable. 'Influence' is a concept, and, as such, a distinct third thing, to be identified neither with the agent nor the patient. What becomes of it on its way from the former to the latter? And when it finds the latter, how does it act upon it? By a second influence which it puts forth in turn?—But then again how? and so forth, and so forth till our whole intuition of activity gets branded as illusory because you cannot possibly reproduce its flowing substance by juxtaposing the discrete. Intellectualism draws the dynamic continuity out of nature as you draw the thread out of a string of beads.

[16]'We must suppose Noumena,' says Kant, 'in order to set bounds to the objective validity of sense-knowledge' [Critique of Pure Reason], 2d ed., p. 310). The old moral need of somehow rebuking 'Sinnlichkeit'!

Example 2. *Knowledge is impossible;* for knower is one concept, and known is another. Discrete, separated by a chasm, they are mutually 'transcendent' things, so that how an object can ever get into a subject, or a subject ever get at an object, has become the most unanswerable of philosophic riddles. An insincere riddle, too, for the most hardened 'epistemologist' never really doubts that knowledge somehow does come off.

Example 3. *Personal identity is conceptually impossible.* 'Ideas' and 'states of mind' are discrete concepts, and a series of them in time means a plurality of disconnected terms. To such an atomistic plurality the associationists reduce our mental life. Shocked at the discontinuous character of their scheme, the spiritualists assume a 'soul' or 'ego' to melt the separate ideas into one collective consciousness. But this ego itself is but another discrete concept; and the only way not to pile up more puzzles is to endow it with an incomprehensible power of producing that very character of manyness-in-oneness of which rationalists refuse the gift when offered in its immediate perceptual form.

Example 4. *Motion and change are impossible.* Perception changes pulsewise, but the pulses continue each other and melt their bounds. In conceptual translation, however, a continuum can only stand for elements with other elements between them *ad infinitum,* all separately conceived; and such an infinite series can never be exhausted by successive addition. From the time of Zeno the Eleatic, this intrinsic contradictoriness of continuous change has been one of the worst skulls at intellectualism's banquet.

Example 5. *Resemblance, in the way in which we naïvely perceive it, is an illusion.* Resemblance must be *defined;* and when defined it reduces to a mixture of identity with otherness. To know a likeness understandingly we must be able to abstract the identical point distinctly. If we fail of this, we remain in our perceptual limbo of 'confusion.'

Example 6. *Our immediate life is full of the sense of direction, but no concept of the direction of a process is possible until the process is completed.* Defined as it is by a beginning and an ending, a direction can never be prospectively but only retrospectively known. Our perceptual discernment beforehand of the way we are going, and all our dim foretastes of the future, have therefore to be treated as inexplicable or illusory features of experience.

Example 7. *No real thing can be in two relations at once;* the same moon, for example, cannot be seen both by you and by me. For the concept 'seen by you' is not the concept 'seen by me'; and if, taking the moon as a grammatical subject and, predicating one of these concepts of it, you then predicate the other also, you become guilty of the logical sin of saying that a thing can both be A and not-A at once. Learned trifling again; for clear though the conceptual contradictions be, nobody sincerely disbelieves that two men see the same thing.

Example 8. *No relation can be comprehended or held to be real in the form in which we innocently assume it.* A relation is a distinct concept; and when you try to make two other concepts continuous by putting a relation between them, you only increase the discontinuity. You have now conceived three things instead of two, and have two gaps instead of one to bridge over. Continuity is impossible in the conceptual world.

Example 9. *The very relation of subject to predicate in our judgments, the backbone of conceptual thinking itself, is unintelligible and self-contradictory.* Predicates are ready-made universal ideas by which we qualify perceptual singulars or other ideas. Sugar, for example, we say 'is' sweet. But if the sugar was *already* sweet, you have made no step in knowledge; whilst if not so already, you are identifying it with a concept, with which, in its universality, the particular sugar cannot be identical. Thus neither the sugar as described, nor your description, is comprehensible.[17]

[17]I have cited in the text only such conceptual puzzles as have become classic in philosophy, but the concepts eurrent in physical science have also developed mutual oppugnancies which (although not yet classic com-

These profundities of inconceivability, and many others like them, arise from the vain attempt to reconvert the manifold into which our conception has resolved things, back into the continuum out of which it came. The concept 'many' is not the concept 'one'; therefore the manyness-in-oneness which perception offers is impossible to construe intellectually. Youthful readers will find such difficulties too whimsical to be taken seriously; but since the days of the Greek sophists these dialectic puzzles have lain beneath the surface of all our thinking like the shoals and snags in the Mississippi river; and the more intellectually conscientious the thinkers have been, the less they have allowed themselves to disregard them. But most philosophers have noticed this or that puzzle only, and ignored the others. The pyrrhonian Sceptics first, then Hegel, then in our day Bradley and Bergson, are the only writers I know who have faced them collectively, and proposed a solution applicable to them all.

The sceptics gave up the whole notion of truth light-heartedly, and advised their pupils not to care about it. Hegel wrote so abominably that I cannot understand him, and will say nothing about him here.[18] Bradley and Bergson write with beautiful clearness and their arguments continue all that I have said.

Mr. Bradley agrees that immediate feeling possesses a native wholeness which conceptual

monplaces in philosophy) are beginning to make physicists doubt whether such notions develop unconditional 'truth.' Many physicists now think that the concepts of 'matter,' 'mass,' 'atom,' 'ether,' 'inertia,' 'force,' etc. are not so much duplicates of hidden realities in nature as mental instruments to handle nature by aftersubstitution of their scheme. They are considered, like the kilogram or the imperial yard, 'artefacts,' not revelations. . . .

[18]Hegel connects immediate perception with ideal truth by a ladder of intermediary concepts—at least, I suppose they are concepts. The best opinion among his interpreters seems to be that ideal truth does not abolish immediate perception, but preserves it as an indispensable 'moment.'. . . In other words Hegel does not pull up the ladder after him when he gets to the top, and may therefore be counted as a non-intellectualist, in spite of his desperately intellectualist *tone.*

treatment analyses into a many, but cannot unite again. In every 'this' as merely felt, Bradley says, we 'encounter' reality, but we encounter it only as a fragment, see it, as it were, only 'through a hole.'[19] Our sole practicable way of extending and completing this fragment is by using our intellect with its universal ideas. But with ideas, that harmonious compenetration of manyness-in-oneness which feeling originally gave is no longer possible. Concepts indeed extend our *this*, but lose the inner secret of its wholeness; when ideal 'truth' is substituted for 'reality' the very nature of 'reality' disappears.

The fault being due entirely to the conceptual form in which we have to think things, one might naturally expect that one who recognizes its inferiority to the perceptual form as clearly as Mr. Bradley does, would try to save both forms for philosophy, delimiting their scopes, and showing how, as our experience works, they supplement each other. This is M. Bergson's procedure; but Bradley, though a traitor to orthodox intellectualism in holding fast to feeling as a revealer of the inner oneness of reality, has yet remained orthodox enough to refuse to admit immediate feeling into 'philosophy' at all. 'For worse or for better,' he writes, the man who stays on particular feeling must remain outside philosophy.' The philosopher's business, according to Mr. Bradley, is to qualify the real 'ideally' (i.e. by concepts), and never to look back. The 'ideas' meanwhile yield nothing but a patchwork, and show no unity like that which the living perception gave. What shall one do in these perplexing circumstances? Unwilling to go back, Bradley only goes more desperately forward. He makes a flying leap ahead, and assumes, beyond the vanishing point of the whole conceptual perspective, an 'absolute' reality, in which the coherency of feeling and the completeness of the intellectual ideal shall unite in some indescribable way. Such an absolute totality in unity *can* be, it *must* be, it *shall* be, it *is* he says. Upon this incomprehensible metaphysical object the Bradleyan metaphysic establishes its domain.[20]

The sincerity of Bradley's criticisms has cleared the air of metaphysics and made havoc with old party lines. But, critical as he is, Mr. Bradley preserves one prejudice uncriticized. Perception 'untransmuted,' he believes, must not, cannot, shall not, enter into final 'truth.'

Such loyalty to a blank direction in thought, no matter where it leads you, is pathetic: concepts disintegrate—no matter, their way must be pursued; percepts are integral—no matter, they must be left behind. When antisensationalism has become an obstinacy like this, one feels that it draws near its end.

Since it is only the conceptual form which forces the dialectic contradictions upon the innocent sensible reality, the remedy would seem to be simple. Use concepts when they help, and drop them when they hinder understanding; and take reality bodily and integrally up into philosophy in exactly the perceptual shape in which it comes. The aboriginal flow of feeling sins only by a quantitative defect. There is always much-at-once of it, but there is never enough, and we desiderate the rest. The only way to get the rest without wading through all future time in the person of numberless perceivers, is to substitute our various conceptual systems which, monstrous abridgments though they be, are nevertheless each an equivalent, for some partial aspect of the full perceptual reality which we can never grasp.

This, essentially, is Bergson's view of the matter, and with it I think that we should rest content.

I will now sum up compendiously the result of what precedes. If the aim of philosophy were the taking full possession of all reality by the mind, then nothing short of the whole of immediate perceptual experience could be the subject-matter of philosophy, for only in such experience is reality intimately and concretely found. But the philosopher, although he is unable as a finite being to compass more than

---

[19]F. H. Bradley: *The Principles of Logic*, book i, chap. ii, pp. 29–32.

[20]Mr. Bradley has expressed himself most pregnantly in an article in volume xviii, N. S. of *Mind*, p. 489. See also his *Appearance and Reality, passim,* especially the Appendix to the second edition.

a few passing moments of such experience, is yet able to extend his knowledge beyond such moments by the ideal symbol of the other moments.[21] He thus commands vicariously innumerable perceptions that are out of range. But the concepts by which he does this, being thin extracts from perception, are always insufficient representatives thereof; and, although they yield wider information, must never be treated after the rationalistic fashion, as if they gave a deeper quality of truth. The deeper features of reality are found only in perceptual experience. Here alone do we acquaint ourselves with continuity, or the immersion of one thing in another, here alone with self, with substance, with qualities, with activity in its various modes, with time, with cause, with change, with novelty, with tendency, and with freedom. Against all such features of reality the method of conceptual translation, when candidly and critically followed out, can only raise its *non possumus*, and brand them as unreal or absurd.

---

3. Some Corollaries

The first corollary of the conclusions of the foregoing chapter is that *the tendency known in philosophy as empiricism, becomes confirmed*. Empiricism proceeds from parts to wholes, treating the parts as fundamental both in the order of being and in the order of our knowledge.[22] In human experience the parts are percepts, built out into wholes by our conceptual additions. The percepts are singulars that change

incessantly and never return exactly as they were before. This brings an element of concrete novelty into our experience. This novelty finds no representation in the conceptual method, for concepts are abstracted from experiences already seen or given, and he who uses them to divine the new can never do so but in ready-made and ancient terms. Whatever actual novelty the future may contain (and the singularity and individuality of each moment makes it novel) escapes conceptual treatment altogether. Properly speaking, concepts are post-mortem preparations, sufficient only for retrospective understanding; and when we use them to define the universe prospectively we ought to realize that they can give only a bare abstract outline or approximate sketch, in the filling out of which perception must be invoked.

Rationalistic philosophy has always aspired to a rounded-in view of the whole of things, a closed system of kinds, from which the notion of essential novelty being possible is ruled out in advance. For empiricism, on the other hand, reality cannot be thus confined by a conceptual ring-fence. It overflows, exceeds, and alters. It may turn into novelties, and can be known adequately only by following its singularities from moment to moment as our experience grows. Empiricist philosophy thus renounces the pretension to an all-inclusive vision. It ekes out the narrowness of personal experience by concepts which it finds useful but not sovereign; but it stays inside the flux of life expectantly, recording facts, not formulating laws, and never pretending that man's relation to the totality of things as a philosopher is essentially different from his relation to the parts of things as a daily patient or agent in the practical current of events. Philosophy, like life, must keep the doors and windows open.

In the remainder of this book we shall hold fast to this empiricist view. We shall insist that, as reality is created temporally day by day, concepts, although a magnificent sketchmap for showing us our bearings, can never fitly supersede perception, and that the 'eternal' systems which they form should least of all be regarded as realms of being to know which is a kind of knowing that casts the knowledge of

---

[21]It would seem that in 'mystical" ways, he may extend his vision to an even wider perceptual panorama than that usually open to the scientific mind. I understand Bergson to favor some such idea as this. See W. James: 'A Suggestion about Mysticism,' *Journal of Philosophy*, vii, 4. The subject of mystical knowledge, as yet very imperfectly understood, has been neglected both by philosophers and scientific men.

[22]Naturally this applies in the present place only to the greater whole which philosophy considers; the universe namely, and its parts, for there are plenty of minor wholes (animal and social organisms, for example) in which both the being of the parts and our understanding of the parts are founded.

particulars altogether into the shade. That rationalist assumption is quite beside the mark. Thus does philosophy prove again that essential identity with science which we argued for in our first chapter.[23]

The last paragraph does not mean that concepts and the relations between them are not just as 'real' in their 'eternal' way as percepts are in their temporal way. What is it to be 'real'? The best definition I know is that which the pragmatist rule gives: 'anything is real of which we find ourselves obliged to take account in any way.'[24] Concepts are thus as real as percepts, for we cannot live a moment without taking account of them. But the 'eternal' kind of being which they enjoy is inferior to the temporal kind, because it is so static and schematic and lacks so many characters which temporal reality possesses. Philosophy must thus recognize many realms of reality which mutually interpenetrate. The conceptual systems of mathematics, logic, aesthetics, ethics, are such realms, each strung upon some peculiar form of relation, and each differing from perceptual reality in that in no one of them is history or happening displayed. Perceptual reality involves and contains all these ideal systems, and vastly more besides.

A concept, it was said above, means always the same thing: Change means always change, white always white, a circle always a circle. On this self-sameness of conceptual objects the static and 'eternal' character of our systems of ideal truth is based; for a relation, once perceived to obtain, must obtain always, between terms that do not alter. But many persons find difficulty in admitting that a concept used in different contexts can be intrinsically the same. When we call both snow and paper 'white' it is supposed by these thinkers that there must be two predicates in the field. As James Mill says:[25] 'Every colour is an individual colour, every size is an individual size, every shape is an individual shape. But things have no individual colour in common, no individual shape in common; no individual size in common; that is to say, they have neither shape, colour, nor size in common. What, then, is it which they have in common which the mind can take into view? Those who affirmed that it was something, could by no means tell. They substituted words for things; using vague and mystical phrases, which, when examined, meant nothing.' The truth, according to this nominalist author, is that the only thing that can be possessed in common by two objects is the same *name*. Black in the coat and black in the shoe are the same in so far forth as both shoe and coat are called black—the fact that on this view the name can never twice be the 'same' being quite overlooked. What now does the concept 'same' signify? Applying, as usual, the pragmatic rule, we find that when we call two objects the same we mean either (a) that no difference can be found between them when compared, or (b) that we can substitute the one for the other in certain operations without changing the result. If we are to discuss sameness profitably we must bear these pragmatic meanings in mind.

Do then the snow and the paper show no difference in color? And can we use them indifferently in operations? They may certainly replace each other for reflecting light, or be used indifferently as backgrounds to set off anything dark, or serve as equally good samples of what the word 'white' signifies. But the snow may be dirty, and the paper pinkish or yellowish without ceasing to be called 'white'; or both snow and paper in one light may differ from their own selves in another and still be 'white,'—so the no-difference criterion seems to be at fault. This physical difficulty (which all house painters know) of matching two tints so exactly as to show no difference seems to be the sort of fact that nominalists have in mind when they say that our ideal meanings are never twice the same. Must we therefore admit that such a concept as 'white' can never keep exactly the same meaning?

It would be absurd to say so, for we know that under all the modifications wrought by changing light, dirt, impurity in pigment, etc.,

---

[23]One way of stating the empiricist contention is to say that the 'alogical' enters into philosophy on an equal footing with the 'logical.'. . .

[24]Prof. A. E. Taylor gives this pragmatist definition in his *Elements of Metaphysics* (1903), p. 51. On the nature of logical reality, cf. B. Russell: *Principles of Mathematics*.

[25]*Analysis of the Human Mind* (1869).

there is an element of color-quality, different from other color-qualities, which we mean that our word *shall* inalterably signify. The impossibility of isolating and fixing this quality physically is irrelevant, so long as we can isolate and fix it mentally, and decide that whenever we say 'white,' that identical quality, whether applied rightly or wrongly, is what we shall be held to mean. Our meanings can be the same as often as we intend to have them so, quite irrespective of whether what is meant be a physical possibility or not. Half the ideas we make use of are of impossible or problematic things,—zeros, infinites, fourth dimensions, limits of ideal perfection, forces, relations sundered from their terms, or terms defined only conceptually, by their relations to other terms which may be equally fictitious. 'White' means a color quality of which the mind appoints the standard, and which it can decree to be there under all physical disguises. *That* white is always the same white. What sense can there be in insisting that although we ourselves have fixed it as the same, it cannot be the same twice over? It works perfectly for us on the supposition that it is there self-identically; so the nominalist doctrine is false of things of that conceptual sort, and true only of things in the perceptual flux.

What I am affirming here is the platonic doctrine that concepts are singulars, that concept-stuff is inalterable, and that physical realities are constituted by the various concept-stuffs of which they 'partake.' It is known as 'logical realism' in the history of philosophy; and has usually been more favored by rationalistic than by empiricist minds. For rationalism, concept-stuff is primordial and perceptual things are secondary in nature. The present book, which treats concrete percepts as primordial and concepts as of secondary origin, may be regarded as somewhat eccentric in its attempt to conbine logical realism with an otherwise empiricist mode of thought.[26]

I mean by this that they are made of the same kind of stuff, and melt into each other when we handle them together. How could it be otherwise when the concepts are like evaporations out of the bosom of perception, into which they condense again whenever practical service summons them? No one can tell, of the things he now holds in his hand and reads, how much comes in through his eyes and fingers, and how much, from his apperceiving intellect, unites with that and makes of it this particular 'book'? The universal and the particular parts of the experience are literally immersed in each other, and both are indispensable. Conception is not like a painted hook, on which no real chain can be hung; for we hang concepts upon percepts, and percepts upon concepts interchangeably and indefinitely; and the relation of the two is much more like what we find in those cylindrical 'panoramas' in which a painted background continues a real foreground so cunningly that one fails to detect the joint. The world we practically live in is one in which it is impossible, except by theoretic retrospection, to disentangle the contributions of intellect from those of sense. They are wrapt and rolled together as a gunshot in the mountains is wrapt and rolled in fold on fold of echo and reverberative clamor. Even so do intellectual reverberations enlarge and prolong the perceptual experience which they envelop, associating it with remoter parts of existence. And the ideas of these in turn work like those resonators that pick out partial tones in complex sounds. They help us to decompose our percept into parts and to abstract and isolate its elements.

The two mental functions thus play into each other's hands. Perception prompts our thought, and thought in turn enriches our perception. The more we see, the more we think; while the more we think, the more we see in our immediate experiences, and the greater grows the detail and the more signifi-

[26]For additional remarks in favor of the sameness of conceptual objects, see W. James in *Mind,* vol. iv, 1879, pp. 331–335; F. H. Bradley: *Ethical Studies* (1876), pp. 151–154, and *Principles of Logic* (1883), pp. 260 ff., 282 ff. The nominalist view is presented by James Mill, as above, and by John Stuart Mill in his *System of Logic,* 8th ed. i, 77.

cant the articulateness of our perception.[27] Later, when we come to treat of causal activity, we shall see how practically momentous is this enlargement of the span of our knowledge through the wrapping of our percepts in ideas. It is the whole coil and compound of both by which effects are determined, and they may then be different effects from those to which the perceptual nucleus would by itself give rise. But the point is a difficult one and at the present stage of our argument this brief mention of it must suffice.

Readers who by this time agree that our conceptual systems are secondary and on the whole imperfect and ministerial forms of being, will now feel able to return and embrace the flux of their hourly experience with a hearty feeling that, however little of it at a time be given, what is given is absolutely real. Rationalistic thought, with its exclusive interest in the unchanging and the general, has

[27]Cf. F. C. S. Schiller: 'Thought and Immediacy,' in the *Journal of Philosophy*, etc., iii, 234. The interpretation goes so deep that we may even act as if experience consisted of nothing but the different kinds of concept-stuff into which we analyze it. Such concept-stuff may often be treated, for purposes of action and even of discussion, as if it were a full equivalent for reality. But it is needless to repeat, after what precedes, that no amount of it can ever be a *full* equivalent, and that in point of genesis it remains a secondary formation.

always de-realized the passing pulses of our life. It is no small service on empiricism's part to have exorcised rationalism's veto, and reflectively justified our instinctive feeling about immediate experience. 'Other world?' says Emerson, 'there is no other world,'—than this one, namely, in which our several biographies are founded. . . . The belief in the genuineness of each particular moment in which we feel the squeeze of this world's life, as we actually do work here, or work is done upon us, is an Eden from which rationalists seek in vain to expel us, now that we have criticized their state of mind.

But they still make one last attempt, and charge us with self-stultification.

'Your belief in the particular moments,' they insist, 'so far as it is based on reflective argument (and is not a mere omission to doubt, like that of cows and horses) is grounded in abstraction and conception. Only by using concepts have you established percepts in reality. The concepts are the vital things, then, and the percepts are dependent on them for the character of "reality" with which your reasoning endows them. You stand self-contradicted: concepts appear as the sole triumphant instruments of truth, for you have to employ their proper authority, even when seeking to install perception in authority above them.'

XI

Bertrand Russell

BERTRAND RUSSELL (1872–1970) was one of the most prolific and influential philosophers of the 20th century. He came from a distinguished family but both his parents died while he was young and he was raised by his grandmother and a governess. At 18 he went to Cambridge University to study mathematics and philosophy, becoming a fellow at Trinity College. During World War I he was fired for being a pacifist. When he came to the United States, he was denied a teaching job at City College of New York because of his liberal views on sex. He was jailed many times, up to the age of 89 when he was arrested for protesting against nuclear arms.

His early work, which focused on philosophy of logic and philosophy of mathematics, includes the ground-breaking *Principia Mathematica* (1910), which he wrote with Alfred North Whitehead. Russell contributed to virtually every area of philosophy. He was awarded the Nobel Prize in 1950.

Here is what Russell had to say about the first of the James selections in the previous section:

> Twenty-three years have elapsed since William James startled the world with his article entitled, "Does Consciousness Exist?" In this article . . . he set out the view that "there is only one primal stuff or material in the world," and that the word "consciousness" stands for a function, not an entity. He holds that there are "thoughts," which perform the function of "knowing," but that thoughts are not made of any different "stuff" from that of which material objects are made. He thus laid the foundations for what is called "neutral monism," a view advocated by most American realists.

Russell, too, was an advocate of neutral monism, in which the mind-body problem raised by Descartes is resolved through an analysis in which mind and physical matter are but different constructions out of the same basic elements that are neither mental nor physical. In taking such a functional approach, Russell helped pave the way toward a purely logico-mathematical model of the mind. In the *Principles of Mathematics,* from which the following selection is taken, we see the beginnings of a purely formal and functional analysis of the elements of thought that later in the 20th century would help make possible the invention of mechanical minds and artificial intelligence (computers) modeled after the human mind. Russell's detailed and precise analysis of logic, language, and mathematical reasoning, especially his attempts to reduce the concepts of mathematics to logic in his monumental *Principia Mathematica,* were instrumental in paving the way for today's revolutionary developments.

Mathematics and the Logic of Mind

Bertrand Russell

Philosophy asks of Mathematics: What does it mean? Mathematics in the past was unable to answer, and Philosophy answered by introducing the totally irrelevant notion of mind. But now Mathematics is able to answer, so far at least as to reduce the whole of its propositions to certain fundamental notions of logic. At this point, the discussion must be resumed by Philosophy.

Chapter I:
Definition of Pure Mathematics

1. Pure Mathematics is the class of all propositions of the form "*p* implies *q*," where *p* and *q* are propositions containing one or more variables, the same in the two propositions, and neither *p* nor *q* contains any constants except logical constants. And logical constants are all notions definable in terms of the following: Implication, the relation of a term to a class of which it is a member, the notion of *such that,* the notion of relation, and such further notions as may be involved in the general notion of propositions of the above form. In addition to these, mathematics *uses* a notion which is not a constituent of the propositions which it considers, namely the notion of truth.

2. The above definition of pure mathematics is, no doubt, somewhat unusual. Its various parts, nevertheless, appear to be capable of exact justification—a justification which it will be the object of the present work to provide. It will be shown that whatever has, in the past, been regarded as pure mathematics, is included in our definition, and that whatever else is included possesses those marks by which mathematics is commonly though vaguely distinguished from other studies. The definition professes to be, not an arbitrary decision to use a common word in an uncommon signification, but rather a precise analysis of the ideas which, more or less unconsciously, are implied in the ordinary employment of the term. Our method will therefore be one of analysis, and our problem may be called philosophical—in the sense, that is to say, that we seek to pass from the complex to the simple, from the demonstrable to its indemonstrable premisses. But in one respect not a few of our discussions will differ from those that are usually called philosophical. We shall be able, thanks to the labours of the mathematicians themselves, to arrive at certainty in regard to most of the questions with which we shall be concerned; and among those capable of an exact solution we shall find many of the problems which, in the past, have been involved in all the traditional uncertainty of philosophical strife. The nature of number, of infinity, of space, time and motion, and of mathematical inference itself, are all questions to which, in the present work, an answer professing itself demonstrable with mathematical certainty will be given—an answer which, however, consists in reducing the above problems to problems in pure logic, which last will not be found satisfactorily solved in what follows.

3. The Philosophy of Mathematics has been hitherto as controversial, obscure and unprogressive as the other branches of philosophy. Although it was generally agreed that mathematics is in some sense true, philosophers disputed as to what mathematical propositions really meant: although something was true, no two people were agreed as to what it was that was true, and if something was known, no one knew what it was that was known. So long, however, as this was doubtful, it could hardly be said that any certain and

SOURCE: Bertrand Russell, *Principles of Mathematics* (New York: W. W. Norton, 1903).

exact knowledge was to be obtained in mathematics. We find, accordingly, that idealists have tended more and more to regard all mathematics as dealing with mere appearance, while empiricists have held everything mathematical to be approximation to some exact truth about which they had nothing to tell us. This state of things, it must be confessed, was thoroughly unsatisfactory. Philosophy asks of Mathematics: What does it mean? Mathematics in the past was unable to answer, and Philosophy answered by introducing the totally irrelevant notion of mind. But now Mathematics is able to answer, so far at least as to reduce the whole of its propositions to certain fundamental notions of logic. At this point, the discussion must be resumed by Philosophy. I shall endeavour to indicate what are the fundamental notions involved, to prove at length that no others occur in mathematics, and to point out briefly the philosophical difficulties involved in the analysis of these notions. A complete treatment of these difficulties would involve a treatise on Logic, which will not be found in the following pages.

4. There was, until very lately, a special difficulty in the principles of mathematics. It seemed plain that mathematics consists of deductions, and yet the orthodox accounts of deduction were largely or wholly inapplicable to existing mathematics. Not only the Aristotelian syllogistic theory, but also the modern doctrines of Symbolic Logic, were either theoretically inadequate to mathematical reasoning, or at any rate required such artificial forms of statement that they could not be practically applied. In this fact lay the strength of the Kantian view, which asserted that mathematical reasoning is not strictly formal, but always uses intuitions, *i.e.* the *à priori* knowledge of space and time. Thanks to the progress of Symbolic Logic, especially as treated by Professor Peano, this part of the Kantian philosophy is now capable of a final and irrevocable refutation. By the help of ten principles of deduction and ten other premisses of a general logical nature (*e.g.* "implication is a relation"), all mathematics can be strictly and formally deduced; and all the entities that occur in mathematics can be defined in terms

of those that occur in the above twenty premisses. In this statement, Mathematics includes not only Arithmetic and Analysis, but also Geometry, Euclidean and non-Euclidean, rational Dynamics, and an indefinite number of other studies still unborn or in their infancy. The fact that all Mathematics is Symbolic Logic is one of the greatest discoveries of our age; and when this fact has been established, the remainder of the principles of mathematics consists in the analysis of Symbolic Logic itself.

5. The general doctrine that all mathematics is deduction by logical principles from logical principles was strongly advocated by Leibniz, who urged constantly that axioms ought to be proved and that all except a few fundamental notions ought to be defined. But owing partly to a faulty logic, partly to belief in the logical necessity of Euclidean Geometry, he was led into hopeless errors in the endeavour to carry out in detail a view which, in its general outline, is now known to be correct. The actual propositions of Euclid, for example, do not follow from the principles of logic alone; and the perception of this fact led Kant to his innovations in the theory of knowledge. But since the growth of non-Euclidean Geometry, it has appeared that pure mathematics has no concern with the question whether the axioms and propositions of Euclid hold of actual space or not: this is a question for applied mathematics, to be decided, so far as any decision is possible, by experiment and observation. What pure mathematics asserts is merely that the Euclidean propositions follow from the Euclidean axioms—*i.e.* it asserts an implication: any space which has such and such properties has also such and such other properties. Thus, as dealt with in pure mathematics, the Euclidean and non-Euclidean Geometries are equally true: in each nothing is affirmed except implications. All propositions as to what actually exists, like the space we live in, belong to experimental or empirical science, not to mathematics; when they belong to applied mathematics, they arise from giving to one or more of the variables in a proposition of pure mathematics some constant value satisfying the hypothesis, and thus enabling us, for that value of the variable, actually to assert

both hypothesis and consequent instead of asserting merely the implication. We assert always in mathematics that if a certain assertion p is true of any entity x, or of any set of entities $x, y, z, \ldots$, then some other assertion q is true of those entities; but we do not assert either p or q separately of our entities. We assert a relation between the assertions p and q, which I shall call *formal implication*.

6. Mathematical propositions are not only characterized by the fact that they assert implications, but also by the fact that they contain *variables*. The notion of the variable is one of the most difficult with which Logic has to deal, and in the present work a satisfactory theory. For the present, I only wish to make it plain that there are variables in all mathematical propositions, even where at first sight they might seem to be absent. Elementary Arithmetic might be thought to form an exception: $1 + 1 = 2$ appears neither to contain variables nor to assert an implication. But as a matter of fact, as will be shown in Part II, the true meaning of this proposition is: "If x is one and y is one, and x differs from y, then x and y are two." And this proposition both contains variables and asserts an implication. We shall find always, in all mathematical propositions, that the words *any* or *some* occur; and these words are the marks of a variable and a formal implication. Thus the above proposition may be expressed in the form: "Any unit and any other unit are two units." The typical proposition of mathematics is of the form "$\phi(x, y, z, \ldots)$ implies $\psi(x, y, z, \ldots)$, whatever values $x, y, z, \ldots$ may have"; where $\phi(x, y, z, \ldots)$ and $\psi(x, y, z, \ldots)$, for every set of values of $x, y, z, \ldots$, are propositions. It is not asserted that ϕ is always true, nor yet that ψ is always true, but merely that, in all cases, when ϕ is false as much as when ϕ is true, ψ follows from it.

The distinction between a variable and a constant is somewhat obscured by mathematical usage. It is customary, for example, to speak of parameters as in some sense constants, but this is a usage which we shall have to reject. A constant is to be something absolutely definite, concerning which there is no ambiguity whatever. Thus 1, 2, 3, e, π, Socrates, are constants; and so are *man*, and the human race, past, present and future, considered col-

lectively. Proposition, implication, class, etc. are constants; but a proposition, any proposition, some proposition, are not constants, for these phrases do not denote one definite object. And thus what are called parameters are simply variables. Take, for example, the equation $ax + by + c = 0$, considered as the equation to a straight line in a plane. Here we say that x and y are variables, while a, b, c are constants. But unless we are dealing with one absolutely particular line, say the line from a particular point in London to a particular point in Cambridge, our a, b, c are not definite numbers, but stand for *any* numbers, and are thus also variables. And in Geometry nobody does deal with actual particular lines; we always discuss *any* line. The point is that we collect the various couples x, y into classes of classes, each class being defined as those couples that have a certain fixed relation to one triad (a, b, c). But from class to class, a, b, c also vary, and are therefore properly variables.

7. It is customary in mathematics to regard our variables as restricted to certain classes: in Arithmetic, for instance, they are supposed to stand for numbers. But this only means that *if* they stand for numbers, they satisfy some formula, *i.e.* the hypothesis that they are numbers implies the formula. This, then, is what is really asserted, and in this proposition it is no longer necessary that our variables should be numbers: the implication holds equally when they are not so. Thus, for example, the proposition "x and y are numbers implies $(x^2 + y)^2 = x^2 + 2xy + y^2$" holds equally if for x and y we substitute Socrates and Plato[1]: both hypothesis and consequent, in this case, will be false, but the implication will still be true. Thus in every proposition of pure mathematics, when fully stated, the variables have an absolutely unrestricted field: any conceivable entity may be substituted for any one of our variables without impairing the truth of our proposition.

8. We can now understand why the constants in mathematics are to be restricted to logical constants in the sense defined above. The process of transforming constants in a

[1]It is necessary to suppose arithmetical addition and multiplication defined (as may be easily done) so that the above formula remains significant when x and y are not numbers.

proposition into variables leads to what is called generalization, and gives us, as it were, the formal essence of a proposition. Mathematics is interested exclusively in *types* of propositions; if a proposition *p* containing only constants be proposed, and for a certain one of its terms we imagine others to be successively substituted, the result will in general be sometimes true and sometimes false. Thus, for example, we have "Socrates is a man"; here we turn Socrates into a variable, and consider "*x* is a man." Some hypotheses as to *x*, for example, "*x* is a Greek," insure the truth of "*x* is a man"; thus "*x* is a Greek" implies "*x* is a man," and this holds for all values of *x*. But the statement is not one of pure mathematics, because it depends upon the particular nature of *Greek* and *man*. We may, however, vary these too, and obtain: If *a* and *b* are classes, and *a* is contained in *b*, then "*x* is an *a*" implies "*x* is a *b*." Here at last we have a proposition of pure mathematics, containing three variables and the constants *class, contained in,* and those involved in the notion of formal implications with variables. So long as any term in our proposition can be turned into a variable, our proposition can be generalized; and so long as this is possible, it is the business of mathematics to do it. If there are several chains of deduction which differ only as to the meaning of the symbols, so that propositions symbolically identical become capable of several interpretations, the proper course, mathematically, is to form the class of meanings which may attach to the symbols, and to assert that the formula in question follows from the hypothesis that the symbols belong to the class in question. In this way, symbols which stood for constants become transformed into variables, and new constants are substituted, consisting of classes to which the old constants belong. Cases of such generalization are so frequent that many will occur at once to every mathematician, and innumerable instances will be given in the present work. Whenever two sets of terms have mutual relations of the same type, the same form of deduction will apply to both. For example, the mutual relations of points in a Euclidean plane are of the same type as those of the complex numbers; hence plane geometry, considered as a branch of

pure mathematics, ought not to decide whether its variables are points or complex numbers or some other set of entities having the same type of mutual relations. Speaking generally, we ought to deal, in every branch of mathematics, with any class of entities whose mutual relations are of a specified type; thus the class, as well as the particular term considered, becomes a variable, and the only true constants are the types of relations and what they involve. Now a *type* of relation is to mean, in this discussion, a class of relations characterized by the above formal identity of the deductions possible in regard to the various members of the class; and hence a type of relations, as will appear more fully hereafter, if not already evident, is always a class definable in terms of logical constants.[2] We may therefore define a type of relations as a class of relations defined by some property definable in terms of logical constants alone.

9. Thus pure mathematics must contain no indefinables except logical constants, and consequently no premisses, or indemonstrable propositions, but such as are concerned exclusively with logical constants and with variables. It is precisely this that distinguishes pure from applied mathematics. In applied mathematics, results which have been shown by pure mathematics to follow from some hypothesis as to the variable are actually asserted of some constant satisfying the hypothesis in question. Thus terms which were variables become constant, and a new premiss is always required, namely: this particular entity satisfies the hypothesis in question. Thus for example Euclidean Geometry, as a branch of pure mathematics, consists wholly of propositions having the hypothesis "*S* is a Euclidean space." If we go on to: "The space that exists is Euclidean," this enables us to assert of the space that exists the consequents of all the hypotheticals constituting Euclidean Geometry, where now the variable *S* is replaced by the constant *actual space*. But by this step we pass from pure to applied mathematics.

10. The connection of mathematics with logic, according to the above account, is ex-

[2]One-one, many-one, transitive, symmetrical, are instances of types of relations with which we shall be often concerned.

ceedingly close. The fact that all mathematical constants are logical constants, and that all the premisses of mathematics are concerned with these, gives, I believe, the precise statement of what philosophers have meant in asserting that mathematics is *à priori*. The fact is that, when once the apparatus of logic has been accepted, all mathematics necessarily follows. The logical constants themselves are to be defined only by enumeration, for they are so fundamental that all the properties by which the class of them might be defined presuppose some terms of the class. But practically, the method of discovering the logical constants is the analysis of symbolic logic, which will be the business of the following chapters. The distinction of mathematics from logic is very arbitrary, but if a distinction is desired, it may be made as follows. Logic consists of the premisses of mathematics, together with all other propositions which are concerned exclusively with logical constants and with variables but do not fulfil the above definition of mathematics (§1). Mathematics consists of all the consequences of the above premisses which assert formal implications containing variables, together with such of the premisses themselves as have these marks. Thus some of the premisses of mathematics, *e.g.* the principle of the syllogism, "if p implies q and q implies r, then p implies r," will belong to mathematics, while others, such as "implication is a relation," will belong to logic but not to mathematics. But for the desire to adhere to usage, we might identify mathematics and logic, and define either as the class of propositions containing only variables and logical constants; but respect for tradition leads me rather to adhere to the above distinction, while recognizing that certain propositions belong to both sciences.

From what has now been said, the reader will perceive that the present work has to fulfil two objects, first, to show that all mathematics follows from symbolic logic, and secondly to discover, as far as possible, what are the principles of symbolic logic itself. The first of these objects will be pursued in the following Parts, while the second belongs to Part I. And first of all, as a preliminary to a critical analysis, it will be necessary to give an outline of Symbolic Logic considered simply as a branch of math-

ematics. This will occupy the following chapter.

Chapter II:
Symbolic Logic

11. Symbolic or Formal Logic—I shall use these terms as synonyms—is the study of the various general types of deduction. The word *symbolic* designates the subject by an accidental characteristic, for the employment of mathematical symbols, here as elsewhere, is merely a theoretically irrelevant convenience. The syllogism in all its figures belongs to Symbolic Logic, and would be the whole subject if all deduction were syllogistic, as the scholastic tradition supposed. It is from the recognition of asyllogistic inferences that modern Symbolic Logic, from Leibniz onward, has derived the motive to progress. Since the publication of Boole's *Laws of Thought* (1854), the subject has been pursued with a certain vigour, and has attained to a very considerable technical development. Nevertheless, the subject achieved almost nothing of utility either to philosophy or to other branches of mathematics, until it was transformed by the new methods of Professor Peano. Symbolic Logic has now become not only absolutely essential to every philosophical logician, but also necessary for the comprehension of mathematics generally, and even for the successful practice of certain branches of mathematics. How useful it is in practice can only be judged by those who have experienced the increase of power derived from acquiring it; its theoretical functions must be briefly set forth in the present chapter.[3]

12. Symbolic Logic is essentially concerned with inference in general,[4] and is distin-

[3] In what follows the main outlines are due to Professor Peano, except as regards relations; even in those cases where I depart from his views, the problems considered have been suggested to me by his works.
[4] I may as well say at once that I do not distinguish between inference and deduction. What is called induction appears to me to be either disguised deduction or a mere method of making plausible guesses.

guished from various special branches of mathematics mainly by its generality. Neither mathematics nor symbolic logic will study such special relations as (say) temporal priority, but mathematics will deal explicitly with the class of relations possessing the formal properties of temporal priority—properties which are summed up in the notion of continuity. And the formal properties of a relation may be defined as those that can be expressed in terms of logical constants, or again as those which, while they are preserved, permit our relation to be varied without invalidating any inference in which the said relation is regarded in the light of a variable. But symbolic logic, in the narrower sense which is convenient, will not investigate what inferences are possible in respect of continuous relations (*i.e.* relations generating continuous series); this investigation belongs to mathematics, but is still too special for symbolic logic. What symbolic logic does investigate is the general rules by which inferences are made, and it requires a classification of relations or propositions only in so far as these general rules introduce particular notions. The particular notions which appear in the propositions of symbolic logic, and all others definable in terms of these notions, are the logical constants. The number of indefinable logical constants is not great: it appears, in fact, to be eight or nine. These notions alone form the subject-matter of the whole of mathematics: no others, except such as are definable in terms of the original eight or nine, occur anywhere in Arithmetic, Geometry, or rational Dynamics. For the technical study of Symbolic Logic, it is convenient to take as a single indefinable the notion of a formal implication, *i.e.* of such propositions as "x is a man implies x is a mortal, for all values of x"—propositions whose general type is: "$\phi(x)$ implies $\psi(x)$ for all values of x," where $\phi(x)$, $\psi(x)$, for all values of x, are propositions. The analysis of this notion of formal implication belongs to the principles of the subject, but is not required for its formal development. In addition to this notion, we require as indefinables the following: Implication between propositions not containing variables, the relation of a term to a class of which it is a member, the notion of *such that*, the notion of rela-

tion, and truth. By means of these notions, all the propositions of symbolic logic can be stated.

13. The subject of Symbolic Logic consists of three parts, the calculus of propositions, the calculus of classes, and the calculus of relations. Between the first two, there is, within limits, a certain parallelism, which arises as follows: In any symbolic expression, the letters may be interpreted as classes or as propositions, and the relation of inclusion in the one case may be replaced by that of formal implication in the other. Thus, for example, in the principle of the syllogism, if a, b, c be classes, and a is contained in b, b in c, then a is contained in c; but if a, b, c be propositions, and a implies b, b implies c, then a implies c. A great deal has been made of this duality, and in the later editions of the *Formulaire*, Peano appears to have sacrificed logical precision to its preservation. But, as a matter of fact, there are many ways in which the calculus of propositions differs from that of classes. Consider, for example, the following: "If p, q, r are propositions, and p implies q or r, then p implies q or p implies r." This proposition is true; but its correlative is false, namely: "If a, b, c are classes, and a is contained in b or c, then a is contained in b or a is contained in c." For example, English people are all either men or women, but are not all men nor yet all women. The fact is that the duality holds for propositions asserting of a variable term that it belongs to a class, *i.e.* such propositions as "x is a man," provided that the implication involved be formal, *i.e.* one which holds for all values of x. But "x is a man" is itself not a proposition at all, being neither true nor false; and it is not with such entities that we are concerned in the propositional calculus, but with genuine propositions. To continue the above illustration: It is true that, for all values of x, "x is a man or a woman" either implies "x is a man" or implies "x is a woman." But it is false that "x is a man or woman" either implies "x is a man" for all values of x, or implies "x is a woman" for all values of x. Thus the implication involved, which is always one of the two, is not formal, since it does not hold for all values of x, being not always the same one of the two. The symbolic affinity of the propositional and the class

logic is, in fact, something of a snare, and we have to decide which of the two we are to make fundamental. Mr McColl, in an important series of papers,[5] has contended for the view that implication and propositions are more fundamental than inclusion and classes; and in this opinion I agree with him. But he does not appear to me to realize adequately the distinction between genuine propositions and such as contain a real variable: thus he is led to speak of propositions as sometimes true and sometimes false, which of course is impossible with a genuine proposition. As the distinction involved is of very great importance, I shall dwell on it before proceeding further. A proposition, we may say, is anything that is true or that is false. An expression such as "x is a man" is therefore not a proposition, for it is neither true nor false. If we give to x any constant value whatever, the expression becomes a proposition: it is thus as it were a schematic form standing for any one of a whole class of propositions. And when we say "x is a man implies x is a mortal for all values of x," we are not asserting a single implication, but a class of implications; we have now a genuine proposition, in which, though the letter x appears, there is no real variable: the variable is absorbed in the same kind of way as the x under the integral sign in a definite integral, so that the result is no longer a function of x. Peano distinguishes a variable which appears in this way as *apparent*, since the proposition does not depend upon the variable; whereas in "x is a man" there are different propositions for different values of the variable, and the variable is what Peano calls *real*.[6] I shall speak of propositions exclusively where there is no real variable: where there are one or more real variables, and for all values of the variables the expression involved is a proposition, I shall

call the expression a *propositional function*. The study of genuine propositions is, in my opinion, more fundamental than that of classes; but the study of propositional functions appears to be strictly on a par with that of classes, and indeed scarcely distinguishable therefrom. Peano, like McColl, at first regarded propositions as more fundamental than classes, but he, even more definitely, considered propositional functions rather than propositions. From this criticism, Schröder is exempt: his second volume deals with genuine propositions, and points out their formal differences from classes.

A. *The Propositional Calculus*

14. The propositional calculus is characterized by the fact that all its propositions have as hypothesis and as consequent the assertion of a material implication. Usually, the hypothesis is of the form "p implies p," etc., which (§ 16) is equivalent to the assertion that the letters which occur in the consequent are propositions. Thus the consequents consist of propositional functions which are true of all propositions. It is important to observe that, though the letters employed are symbols for variables, and the consequents are true when the variables are given values which are propositions, these values must be genuine propositions, not propositional functions. The hypothesis "p is a proposition" is not satisfied if for p we put "x is a man," but it is satisfied if we put "Socrates is a man" or if we put "x is a man implies x is a mortal for all values of x." Shortly, we may say that the propositions represented by single letters in this calculus are variables, but do not contain variables—in the case, that is to say, where the hypotheses of the propositions which the calculus asserts are satisfied.

15. Our calculus studies the relation of *implication* between propositions. This relation must be distinguished from the relation of *formal* implication, which holds between propositional functions when the one implies the other for all values of the variable. Formal implication is also involved in this calculus, but is not explicitly studied: we do not consider propositional functions in general, but only certain definite propositional functions which

[5]Cf. "The Calculus of Equivalent Statements," *Proceedings of the London Mathematical Society,* Vol. IX and subsequent volumes; "Symbolic Reasoning," *Mind,* Jan. 1880, Oct. 1897, and Jan. 1900; "La Logique Symbolique et ses Applications," *Bibliothèque du Congrès International de Philosophie,* Vol. III (Paris, 1901). I shall in future quote the proceedings of the above Congress by the title *Congrès.*
[6]*F.* 1901, p. 2.

occur in the propositions of our calculus. How far formal implication is definable in terms of implication simply, or material implication as it may be called, is a difficult question, which will be discussed in Chapter III. What the difference is between the two, an illustration will explain. The fifth proposition of Euclid follows from the fourth: if the fourth is true, so is the fifth, while if the fifth is false, so is the fourth. This is a case of material implication, for both propositions are absolute constants, not dependent for their meaning upon the assigning of a value to a variable. But each of them *states* a formal implication. The fourth states that if x and y be triangles fulfilling certain conditions, then x and y are triangles fulfilling certain other conditions, and that this implication holds for all values of x and y; and the fifth states that if x is an isosceles triangle, x has the angles at the base equal. The formal implication involved in each of these two propositions is quite a different thing from the material implication holding between the propositions as wholes; both notions are required in the propositional calculus, but it is the study of material implication which specially distinguishes this subject, for formal implication occurs throughout the whole of mathematics.

It has been customary, in treatises on logic, to confound the two kinds of implication, and often to be really considering the formal kind where the material kind only was apparently involved. For example, when it is said that "Socrates is a man, therefore Socrates is a mortal," Socrates is *felt* as a variable: he is a type of humanity, and one feels that any other man would have done as well. If, instead of *therefore*, which implies the truth of hypothesis and consequent, we put "Socrates is a man implies Socrates is a mortal," it appears at once that we may substitute not only another man, but any other entity whatever, in the place of Socrates. Thus although what is explicitly stated, in such a case, is a material implication, what is meant is a formal implication; and some effort is needed to confine our imagination to material implication.

16. A definition of implication is quite impossible. If p implies q, then if p is true q is true, *i.e.* p's truth implies q's truth; also if q is false p is false, *i.e.* q's falsehood implies p's falsehood.[7] Thus truth and falsehood give us merely new implications, not a definition of implication. If p implies q, then both are false or both true, or p is false and q true; it is impossible to have q false and p true, and it is necessary to have q true or p false.[8] In fact, the assertion that q is true or p false turns out to be strictly equivalent to "p implies q"; but as equivalence means mutual implication, this still leaves implication fundamental, and not definable in terms of disjunction. Disjunction, on the other hand, is definable in terms of implication, as we shall shortly see. It follows from the above equivalence that of any two propositions there must be one which implies the other, that false propositions imply all propositions, and true propositions are implied by all propositions. But these are results to be demonstrated; the premisses of our subject deal exclusively with rules of inference.

It may be observed that, although implication is indefinable, *proposition* can be defined. Every proposition implies itself, and whatever is not a proposition implies nothing. Hence to say "p is a proposition" is equivalent to saying "p implies p"; and this equivalence may be used to define propositions. As the mathematical sense of *definition* is widely different from that current among philosophers, it may be well to observe that, in the mathematical sense, a new propositional function is said to be defined when it is stated to be equivalent to (*i.e.* to imply and be implied by) a propositional function which has either been accepted as indefinable or has been defined in terms of indefinables. The definition of entities which are not propositional functions is derived from such as are in ways which will be explained in connection with classes and relations.

17. We require, then, in the propositional calculus, no indefinables except the two kinds of implication—remembering, however, that

---

[7]The reader is recommended to observe that the main implications in these statements are formal, *i.e.* "p implies q" *formally* implies "p's truth implies q's truth," while the subordinate implications are material.

[8]I may as well state once for all that the alternatives of a disjunction will never be considered as mutually exclusive unless expressly said to be so.

formal implication is a complex notion, whose analysis remains to be undertaken. As regards our two indefinables, we require certain indemonstrable propositions, which hitherto I have not succeeded in reducing to less than ten. Some indemonstrables there must be; and some propositions, such as the syllogism, must be of the number, since no demonstration is possible without them. But concerning others, it may be doubted whether they are indemonstrable or merely undemonstrated; and it should be observed that the method of supposing an axiom false, and deducing the consequences of this assumption, which has been found admirable in such cases as the axiom of parallels, is here not universally available. For all our axioms are principles of deduction; and if they are true, the consequences which appear to follow from the employment of an opposite principle will not really follow, so that arguments from the supposition of the falsity of an axiom are here subject to special fallacies. Thus the number of indemonstrable propositions may be capable of further reduction, and in regard to some of them I know of no grounds for regarding them as indemonstrable except that they have hitherto remained undemonstrated.

18. The ten axioms are the following. (1) If p implies q, then p implies q;[9] in other words, whatever p and q may be, "p implies q" is a proposition. (2) If p implies q, then p implies p; in other words, whatever implies anything is a proposition. (3) If p implies q, then q implies q; in other words, whatever is implied by anything is a proposition. (4) A true hypothesis in an implication may be dropped, and the consequent asserted. This is a principle incapable of formal symbolic statement, and illustrating the essential limitations of formalism—a point to which I shall return at a later stage. Before proceeding further, it is desirable to define the joint assertion of two propositions, or what is called their logical product. This definition is highly artificial, and illustrates the great distinction between mathematical and philosophical definitions. It is as follows: If p implies p, then, if q implies q, pq (the logical prod-

uct of p and q) means that if p implies that q implies r, then r is true. In other words, if p and q are propositions, their joint assertion is equivalent to saying that every proposition is true which is such that the first implies that the second implies it. We cannot, with formal correctness, state our definition in this shorter form, for the hypothesis "p and q are propositions" is already the logical product of "p is a proposition" and "q is a proposition." We can now state the six main principles of inference, to each of which, owing to its importance, a name is to be given; of these all except the last will be found in Peano's accounts of the subject. (5) If p implies p and q implies q, then pq implies p. This is called *simplification*, and asserts merely that the joint assertion of two propositions implies the assertion of the first of the two. (6) If p implies q and q implies r, then p implies r. This will be called the *syllogism*. (7) If q implies q and r implies r, and if p implies that q implies r, then pq implies r. This is the principle of *importation*. In the hypothesis, we have a product of three propositions; but this can of course be defined by means of the product of two. The principle states that if p implies that q implies r, then r follows from the joint assertion of p and q. For example: "If I call on so-and-so, then if she is at home I shall be admitted" implies "If I call on so-and-so and she is at home, I shall be admitted." (8) If p implies p and q implies q, then, if pq implies r, then p implies that q implies r. This is the converse of the preceding principle, and is called *exportation*.[10] The previous illustration reversed will illustrate this principle. (9) If p implies q and p implies r, then p implies qr: in other words, a proposition which implies each of two propositions implies them both. This is called the principle of *composition*. (10). If p implies p and q implies q, then "'p implies q' implies p" implies p. This is called the principle of *reduction;* it has less self-evidence than the previous principles, but is equivalent to many propositions that are self-evident. I prefer it to these, because it is explicitly concerned, like its

[9]Note that the implications denoted by *if* and *then*, in these axioms, are formal, while those denoted by *implies* are material.

[10](7) and (8) cannot (I think) be deduced from the definition of the logical product, because they are required for passing from "If p is a proposition, then 'q is a proposition' implies etc." to "If p and q are propositions, then etc."

predecessors, with implication, and has the same kind of logical character as they have. If we remember that "p implies q" is equivalent to "q or not-p," we can easily convince ourselves that the above principle is true; for " 'p implies q' implies p" is equivalent to "p or the denial of 'q or not-p,' " *i.e.* to "p or 'p and not q,' " *i.e.* to p. But this way of persuading ourselves that the principle of reduction is true involves many logical principles which have not yet been demonstrated, and cannot be demonstrated except by reduction or some equivalent. The principle is especially useful in connection with negation. Without its help, by means of the first nine principles, we can prove the law of contradiction; we can prove, if p and q be propositions, that p implies not-not-p; that "p implies not-q" is equivalent to "q implies not-p" and to not-pq; that "p implies q" implies "not-q implies not-p"; that p implies that not-p implies p; that not-p is equivalent to "p implies not-p"; and that "p implies not-q" is equivalent to "not-not-p implies not-q." But we cannot prove without reduction or some equivalent (so far at least as I have been able to discover) that p or not-p must be true (the law of excluded middle); that every proposition is equivalent to the negation of some other proposition; that not-not-p implies p; that "not-q implies not-p" implies "p implies q"; that "not-p implies p" implies p, or that "p implies q" implies "q or not-p." Each of these assumptions is equivalent to the principle of reduction, and may, if we choose, be substituted for it. Some of them—especially excluded middle and double negation—appear to have far more self-evidence. But when we have seen how to define disjunction and negation in terms of implication, we shall see that the supposed simplicity vanishes, and that, for formal purposes at any rate, reduction is simpler than any of the possible alternatives. For this reason I retain it among my premises in preference to more usual and more superficially obvious propositions.

19. Disjunction or logical addition is defined as follows: "p or q" is equivalent to " 'p implies q' implies q." It is easy to persuade ourselves of this equivalence, by remembering that a false proposition implies every other; for if p is false, p does imply q, and therefore, if "p implies q" implies q, it follows that q is true.

But this argument again uses principles which have not yet been demonstrated, and is merely designed to elucidate the definition by anticipation. From this definition, by the help of reduction, we can prove that "p or q" is equivalent to "q or p". An alternative definition, deducible from the above, is: "Any proposition implied by p and implied by q is true," or, in other words, " 'p implies s' and 'q implies s' together imply s, whatever s may be." Hence we proceed to the definition of negation: not-p is equivalent to the assertion that p implies all propositions, *i.e.* that "r implies r" implies "p implies r" whatever r may be.[11] From this point we can prove the laws of contradiction and excluded middle and double negation, and establish all the formal properties of logical multiplication and addition—the associative, commutative and distributive laws. Thus the logic of propositions is now complete.

Philosophers will object to the above definitions of disjunction and negation on the ground that what we *mean* by these notions is something quite distinct from what the definitions assign as their meanings, and that the equivalences stated in the definitions are, as a matter of fact, significant propositions, not mere indications as to the way in which symbols are going to be used. Such an objection is, I think, well-founded, if the above account is advocated as giving the true philosophic analysis of the matter. But where a purely formal purpose is to be served, any equivalence in which a certain notion appears on one side but not on the other will do for a definition. And the advantage of having before our minds a strictly formal development is that it provides

---

[11] The principle that false propositions imply all propositions solves Lewis Carroll's logical paradox in *Mind*, N. S. No. 11 (1894). The assertion made in that paradox is that, if p, q, r be propositions, and q implies r, while p implies that q implies not-r, then p must be false, on the supposed ground that "q implies r" and "q implies not-r" are incompatible. But in virtue of our definition of negation, if q be false both these implications will hold: the two together, in fact, whatever proposition r may be, are equivalent to not-q. Thus the only inference warranted by Lewis Carroll's premises is that if p be true, q must be false, *i.e.* that p implies not-q; and this is the conclusion, oddly enough, which common sense would have drawn in the particular case which he discusses.

the data for philosophical analysis in a more definite shape than would be otherwise possible. Criticism of the procedure of formal logic, therefore, will be best postponed until the present brief account has been brought to an end.

B. The Calculus of Classes

20. In this calculus there are very much fewer new primitive propositions—in fact, two seem sufficient—but there are much greater difficulties in the way of non-symbolic exposition of the ideas embedded in our symbolism. These difficulties, as far as possible, will be postponed to later chapters. For the present, I shall try to make an exposition which is to be as straightforward and simple as possible.

The calculus of classes may be developed by regarding as fundamental the notion of *class,* and also the relation of a member of a class to its class. This method is adopted by Professor Peano, and is perhaps more philosophically correct than a different method which, for formal purposes, I have found more convenient. In this method we still take as fundamental the relation (which, following Peano, I shall denote by ϵ) of an individual to a class to which it belongs, *i.e.* the relation of Socrates to the human race which is expressed by saying that Socrates is a man. In addition to this, we take as indefinables the notion of a propositional function and the notion of *such that.* It is these three notions that characterize the class-calculus. Something must be said in explanation of each of them.

21. The insistence on the distinction between ϵ and the relation of whole and part between classes is due to Peano, and is of very great importance to the whole technical development and the whole of the applications to mathematics. In the scholastic doctrine of the syllogism, and in all previous symbolic logic, the two relations are confounded, except in the work of Frege.[12] The distinction is the same as that between the relation of individual to species and that of species to genus, between the relation of Socrates to the class of Greeks and the relation of Greeks to men. On

the philosophical nature of this distinction I shall enlarge when I come to deal critically with the nature of classes; for the present it is enough to observe that the relation of whole and part is transitive, while ϵ is not so: we have Socrates is a man, and men are a class, but not Socrates is a class. It is to be observed that the class must be distinguished from the class-concept or predicate by which it is to be defined: thus men are a class, while *man* is a class-concept. The relation ϵ must be regarded as holding between Socrates and men considered collectively, not between Socrates and *man*. I shall return to this point in Chapter VI. Peano holds that all propositional functions containing only a single variable are capable of expression in the form "*x* is an *a*," where *a* is a constant class; but this view we shall find reason to doubt.

22. The next fundamental notion is that of a propositional function. Although propositional functions occur in the calculus of propositions, they are there each defined as it occurs, so that the general notion is not required. But in the class-calculus it is necessary to introduce the general notion explicitly. Peano does not require it, owing to his assumption that the form "*x* is an *a*" is general for one variable, and that extensions of the same form are available for any number of variables. But we must avoid this assumption, and must therefore introduce the notion of a propositional function. We may explain (but not define) this notion as follows: ϕx is a propositional function if, for every value of *x*, ϕx is a proposition, determinate when *x* is given. Thus "*x* is a man" is a propositional function. In any proposition, however complicated, which contains no real variables, we may imagine one of the terms, not a verb or adjective, to be replaced by other terms: instead of "Socrates is a man" we may put "Plato is a man," "the number 2 is a man," and so on.[13] Thus we get successive propositions all agreeing except as to the one variable term. Putting *x* for the variable term, "*x* is a man" expresses the type

[12] See his *Begriffsschrift,* Halle, 1879, and *Grundgesetze der Arithmetik,* Jena, 1893, p. 2.

[13] Verbs and adjectives occurring as such are distinguished by the fact that, if they be taken as variable, the resulting function is only a proposition for *some* values of the variable, *i.e.* for such as are verbs or adjectives respectively. See Chap. IV.

of all such propositions. A propositional function in general will be true for some values of the variable and false for others. The instances where it is true for *all* values of the variable, so far as they are known to me, all express implications, such as "*x* is a man implies *x* is a mortal"; but I know of no *à priori* reason for asserting that no other propositional functions are true for all values of the variable.

23. This brings me to the notion of *such that*. The values of *x* which render a propositional function *ϕx* true are like the roots of an equation—indeed the latter are a particular case of the former—and we may consider all the values of *x* which are *such that* *ϕx* is true. In general, these values form a *class*, and in fact a class may be defined as all the terms satisfying some propositional function. There is, however, some limitation required in this statement, though I have not been able to discover precisely what the limitation is. This results from a certain contradiction which I shall discuss at length at a later stage (Chap. X). The reasons for defining *class* in this way are, that we require to provide for the null-class, which prevents our defining a class as a term to which some other has the relation *ϵ*, and that we wish to be able to define classes by relations, *i.e.* all the terms which have to other terms the relation *R* are to form a class, and such cases require somewhat complicated propositional functions.

24. With regard to these three fundamental notions, we require two primitive propositions. The first asserts that if *x* belongs to the class of terms satisfying a propositional function *ϕx,* then *ϕx* is true. The second asserts that if *ϕx* and *ψx* are equivalent propositions for all values of *x*, then the class of *x*'s such that *ϕx* is true is identical with the class of *x*'s such that *ψx* is true. Identity, which occurs here, is defined as follows: *x* is identical with *y* if *y* belongs to every class to which *x* belongs, on other words, if "*x* is a *u*" implies "*y* is a *u*" for all values of *u*. With regard to the primitive proposition itself, it is to be observed that it decides in favour of an extensional view of classes. Two class concepts need not be identical when their extensions are so: *man* and *featherless biped* are by no means identical, and no more are *even prime* and *integer between* 1 *and*

3. These are class-*concepts*, and if our axiom is to hold, it must not be of these that we are to speak in dealing with classes. We must be concerned with the actual assemblage of terms, not with any concept denoting that assemblage. For mathematical purposes, this is quite essential. Consider, for example, the problem as to how many combinations can be formed of a given set of terms taken any number at a time, *i.e.* as to how many classes are contained in a given class. If distinct classes may have the same extension, this problem becomes utterly indeterminate. And certainly common usage would regard a class as determined when all its terms are given. The extensional view of classes, in some form, is thus essential to Symbolic Logic and to mathematics, and its necessity is expressed in the above axiom. But the axiom itself is not employed until we come to Arithmetic; at least it need not be employed, if we choose to distinguish the equality of classes, which is defined as mutual inclusion, from the identity of individuals. Formally, the two are totally distinct: identity is defined as above, equality of *a* and *b* is defined by the equivalence of "*x* is an *a*" and "*x* is a *b*" for all values of *x*.

25. Most of the propositions of the class-calculus are easily deduced from those of the propositional calculus. The logical product or common part of two classes *a* and *b* is the class of *x*'s such that the logical product of "*x* is an *a*" and "*x* is a *b*" is true. Similarly we define the logical sum of two classes (*a* or *b*), and the negation of a class (not-*a*). A new idea is introduced by the logical product and sum of a class of classes. If *k* is a class of classes, its logical product is the class of terms belonging to each of the classes of *k*, *i.e.* the class of terms *x* such that "*u* is a *k*" implies "*x* is a *u*" for all values of *u*. The logical sum is the class which is contained in every class in which every class of the class *k* is contained, *i.e.* the class of terms *x* such that, if "*u* is a *k*" implies "*u* is contained in *c*" for all values of *u*, then, for all values of *c*, *x* is a *c*. And we say that a class *a* is contained in a class *b* when "*x* is an *a*" implies "*x* is a *b*" for all values of *x*. In like manner with the above we may define the product and sum of a class of propositions. Another very important notion is what is called the *existence* of a class—a word

which must not be supposed to mean what existence means in philosophy. A class is said to exist when it has at least one term. A formal definition is as follows: a is an existent class when and only when any proposition is true provided "x is an a" always implies it whatever value we may give to x. It must be understood that the proposition implied must be a genuine proposition, not a propositional function of x. A class a exists when the logical sum of all propositions of the form "x is an a" is true, *i.e.* when not all such propositions are false.

It is important to understand clearly the manner in which propositions in the class-calculus are obtained from those in the propositional calculus. Consider, for example, the syllogism. We have "p implies q" and "q implies r" imply "p implies r." Now put "x is an a," "x is a b," "x is a c" for p, q, r, where x must have some definite value, but it is not necessary to decide what value. We then find that if, for the value of x in question, x is an a implies x is a b, and x is a b implies x is a c, then x is an a implies x is a c. Since the value of x is irrelevant, we may vary x, and thus we find that if a is contained in b, and b in c, then a is contained in c. This is the class-syllogism. But in applying this process it is necessary to employ the utmost caution, if fallacies are to be successfully avoided. In this connection it will be instructive to examine a point upon which a dispute has arisen between Schröder and Mr McColl.[14] Schröder asserts that if p, q, r are propositions, "pq implies r" is equivalent to the disjunction "p implies r or q implies r." Mr McColl admits that the disjunction implies the other, but denies the converse implication. The reason for the divergence is, that Schröder is thinking of propositions and material implication, while Mr McColl is thinking of propositional functions and formal implication. As regards propositions, the truth of the principle may be easily made plain by the following considerations. If pq implies r, then, if either p or q be false, the one of them which

is false implies r, because false propositions imply all propositions. But if both be true, pq is true, and therefore r is true, and therefore p implies r and q implies r, because true propositions are implied by every proposition. Thus in any case, one at least of the propositions p and q must imply r. (This is not a proof, but an elucidation.) But Mr McColl objects: Suppose p and q to be mutually contradictory, and r to be the null proposition, then pq implies r but neither p nor q implies r. Here we are dealing with propositional functions and formal implication. A propositional function is said to be null when it is false for all values of x; and the class of x's satisfying the function is called the null-class, being in fact a class of no terms. Either the function or the class, following Peano, I shall denote by Λ. Now let our r be replaced by Λ, our p by ϕx, and our q by not-ϕx, where ϕx is any propositional function. Then pq is false for all values of x, and therefore implies Λ. But it is not in general the case that ϕx is always false, nor yet that not-ϕx is always false; hence neither always implies Λ. Thus the above formula can only be truly interpreted in the propositional calculus: in the class-calculus it is false. This may be easily rendered obvious by the following considerations: Let ϕx, ψx, χx be three propositional functions. Then "$\phi x \cdot \psi x$ implies χx" implies, for all values of x, that either ϕx implies χx or ψx implies χx. But it does not imply that either ϕx implies χx for all values of x, or ψx implies χx for all values of x. The disjunction is what I shall call a *variable* disjunction, as opposed to a constant one: that is, in some cases one alternative is true, in others the other, whereas in a constant disjunction there is one of the alternatives (though it is not stated which) that is always true. Wherever disjunctions occur in regard to propositional functions, they will only be transformable into statements in the class-calculus in cases where the disjunction is constant. This is a point which is both important in itself and instructive in its bearings. Another way of stating the matter is this: In the proposition: If $\phi x \cdot \psi x$ implies χx, then either ϕx implies χx or ψx implies χx, the implication indicated by *if* and *then* is formal, while the subordinate implications are material; hence the subordinate implications do not

[14]McColl, "Calculus of Equivalent Statements," fifth paper, *Proc. Lond. Math. Soc.* Vol. XXVIII, p. 182.

lead to the inclusion of one class in another, which results only from formal implication.

The formal laws of addition, multiplication, tautology and negation are the same as regards classes and propositions. The law of tautology states that no change is made when a class or proposition is added to or multiplied by itself. A new feature of the class-calculus is the null-class, or class having no terms. This may be defined as the class of terms that belong to every class, as the class which does not exist (in the sense defined above), as the class which is contained in every class, as the class Λ which is such that the propositional function "x is a Λ" is false for all values of x, or as the class of x's satisfying any propositional function ϕx which is false for all values of x. All these definitions are easily shown to be equivalent.

26. Some important points arise in connection with the theory of identity. We have already defined two terms as identical when the second belongs to every class to which the first belongs. It is easy to show that this definition is symmetrical, and that identity is transitive and reflexive (*i.e.* if x and y, y and z are identical, so are x and z; and whatever x may be, x is identical with x). Diversity is defined as the negation of identity. If x be any term, it is necessary to distinguish from x the class whose only member is x: this may be defined as the class of terms which are identical with x. The necessity for this distinction, which results primarily from purely formal considerations, was discovered by Peano; I shall return to it at a later stage. Thus the class of even primes is not to be identified with the number 2, and the class of numbers which are the sum of 1 and 2 is not to be identified with 3. In what, philosophically speaking, the difference consists, is a point to be considered in Chapter VI.

C. The Calculus of Relations

27. The calculus of relations is a more modern subject than the calculus of classes. Although a few hints for it are to be found in De Morgan, the subject was first developed by C. S. Peirce. A careful analysis of mathematical reasoning shows (as we shall find in the course of the present work) that types of relations are the true subject-matter discussed, however a bad phraseology may disguise this fact; hence the logic of relations has a more immediate bearing on mathematics than that of classes or propositions, and any theoretically correct and adequate expression of mathematical truths is only possible by its means. Peirce and Schröder have realized the great importance of the subject, but unfortunately their methods, being based, not on Peano, but on the older Symbolic Logic derived (with modifications) from Boole, are so cumbrous and difficult that most of the applications which ought to be made are practically not feasible. In addition to the defects of the old Symbolic Logic, their method suffers technically (whether philosophically or not I do not at present discuss) from the fact that they regard a relation essentially as a class of couples, thus requiring elaborate formulae of summation for dealing with single relations. This view is derived, I think, probably unconsciously, from a philosophical error: it has always been customary to suppose relational propositions less ultimate than class-propositions (or subject-predicate propositions, with which class-propositions are habitually confounded), and this has led to a desire to treat relations as a kind of classes. However this may be, it was certainly from the opposite philosophical belief, which I derived from my friend Mr G. E. Moore, that I was led to a different formal treatment of relations. This treatment, whether more philosophically correct or not, is certainly far more convenient and far more powerful as an engine of discovery in actual mathematics.

28. If R be a relation, we express by xRy the propositional function "x has the relation R to y." We require a primitive (*i.e.* indemonstrable) proposition to the effect that xRy is a proposition for all values of x and y. We then have to consider the following classes: The class of terms which have the relation R to some term or other, which I call the class of *referents* with respect to R; and the class of terms to which some term has the relation R, which I call the class of *relata*. Thus if R be paternity, the referents will be fathers and the relata will be children. We have also to consider the corresponding classes with respect to particular terms or classes of terms: so-and-so's children,

or the children of Londoners, afford illustrations.

The intensional view of relations here advocated leads to the result that two relations may have the same extension without being identical. Two relations R, R' are said to be equal or equivalent, or to have the same extension, when xRy implies and is implied by $xR'y$ for all values of x and y. But there is no need here of a primitive proposition, as there was in the case of classes, in order to obtain a relation which is determinate when the extension is determinate. We may replace a relation R by the logical sum or product of the class of relations equivalent to R, i.e. by the assertion of some or of all such relations; and this is identical with the logical sum or product of the class of relations equivalent to R', if R' be equivalent to R. Here we use the identity of two classes, which results from the primitive proposition as to identity of classes, to establish the identity of two relations—a procedure which could not have been applied to classes themselves without a vicious circle.

A primitive proposition in regard to relations is that every relation has a converse, i.e. that, if R be any relation, there is a relation R' such that xRy is equivalent to $yR'x$ for all values of x and y. Following Schröder, I shall denote the converse of R by R. Greater and less, before and after, implying and implied by, are mutually converse relations. With some relations, such as identity, diversity, equality, inequality, the converse is the same as the original relation: such relations are called *symmetrical*. When the converse is incompatible with the original relation, as in such cases as greater and less, I call the relation *asymmetrical;* in intermediate cases, *not-symmetrical.*

The most important of the primitive propositions in this subject is that between any two terms there is a relation not holding between any two other terms. This is analogous to the principle that any term is the only member of some class; but whereas that could be proved, owing to the extensional view of classes, this principle, so far as I can discover, is incapable of proof. In this point, the extensional view of relations has an advantage; but the advantage appears to me to be outweighed by other considerations. When relations are considered in-

tensionally, it may seem possible to doubt whether the above principle is true at all. It will, however, be generally admitted that, of any two terms, some propositional function is true which is not true of a certain given different pair of terms. If this be admitted, the above principle follows by considering the logical product of all the relations that hold between our first pair of terms. Thus the above principle may be replaced by the following, which is equivalent to it: If xRy implies $x'Ry'$, whatever R may be, so long as R is a relation, then x ans x', y and y' are respectively identical. But this principle introduces a logical difficulty from which we have been hitherto exempt, namely a variable with a restricted field; for unless R is a relation, xRy is not a proposition at all, true or false, and thus R, it would seem, cannot take *all* values, but only such as are relations. I shall return to the discussion of this point at a later stage.

29. Other assumptions required are that the negation of a relation is a relation, and that the logical product of a class of relations (*i.e.* the assertion of all of them simultaneously) is a relation. Also the *relative product* of two relations must be a relation. The relative product of two relations R, S is the relation which holds between x and z whenever there is a term y to which x has the relation R and which has to z the relation S. Thus the relation of a maternal grandfather to his grandson is the relative product of father and mother; that of a paternal grandmother to her grandson is the relative product of mother and father; that of grandparent to grandchild is the relative product of parent and parent. The relative product, as these instances show, is not in general commutative, and does not in general obey the law of tautology. The relative product is a notion of very great importance. Since it does not obey the law of tautology, it leads to powers of relations: the square of the relation of parent and child is the relation of grandparent and grandchild, and so on. Peirce and Schröder consider also what they call the relative sum of two relations R and S, which holds between x and z, when, if y be any other term whatever, either x has to y the relation R, or y has to z the relation S. This is a complicated notion, which I have found no occasion to

employ, and which is introduced only in order to preserve the duality of addition and multiplication. This duality has a certain technical charm when the subject is considered as an independent branch of mathematics; but when it is considered solely in relation to the principles of mathematics, the duality in question appears devoid of all philosophical importance.

30. Mathematics requires, so far as I know, only two other primitive propositions, the one that material implication is a relation, the other that ϵ (the relation of a term to a class to which it belongs) is a relation.[15] We can now develop the whole of mathematics without further assumptions or indefinables. Certain propositions in the logic of relations deserve to be mentioned, since they are important, and it might be doubted whether they were capable of formal proof. If u, v be any two classes, there is a relation R the assertion of which between any two terms x and y is equivalent to the assertion that x belongs to u and y to v. If u be any class which is not null, there is a relation which all its terms have to it, and which holds for no other pairs of terms. If R be any relation, and u any class contained in the class of referents with respect to R, there is a relation which has u for the class of its referents, and is equivalent to R throughout that class; this relation is the same as R where it holds, but has a more restricted domain. (I use *domain* as synonymous with *class of referents*.) From this point onwards, the development of the subject is technical: special types of relations are considered, and special branches of mathematics result.

D. Peano's Symbolic Logic

31. So much of the above brief outline of Symbolic Logic is inspired by Peano, that it seems desirable to discuss his work explicitly, justifying by criticism the points in which I have departed from him.

The question as to which of the notions of symbolic logic are to be taken as indefinable, and which of the propositions as indemonstrable, is, as Professor Peano has insisted, to some

extent arbitrary. But it is important to establish all the mutual relations of the simpler notions of logic, and to examine the consequence of taking various notions as indefinable. It is necessary to realize that definition, in mathematics, does not mean, as in philosophy, an analysis of the idea to be defined into constituent ideas. This notion, in any case, is only applicable to concepts, whereas in mathematics it is possible to define terms which are not concepts.[16] Thus also many notions are defined by symbolic logic which are not capable of philosophical definition, since they are simple and unanalyzable. Mathematical definition consists in pointing out a fixed relation to a fixed term, of which one term only is capable: this term is then defined by means of the fixed relation and the fixed term. The point in which this differs from philosophical definition may be elucidated by the remark that the mathematical definition does not point out the term in question, and that only what may be called philosophical insight reveals which it is among all the terms there are. This is due to the fact that the term is defined by a concept which *denotes* it unambiguously, not by actually mentioning the term denoted. What is meant by *denoting*, as well as the different ways of denoting, must be accepted as primitive ideas in any symbolic logic:[17] in this respect, the order adopted seems not in any degree arbitrary.

32. For the sake of definiteness, let us now examine some one of Professor Peano's expositions of the subject. In his later expositions he has abandoned the attempt to distinguish clearly certain ideas and propositions as primitive, probably because of the realization that any such distinction is largely arbitrary. But the distinction appears useful, as introducing greater definiteness, and as showing that a certain set of primitive ideas and propositions are sufficient; so far from being abandoned, it ought rather to be made in every possible way. I shall, therefore, in what follows, expound one of his earlier expositions, that of 1897.

The primitive notions with which Peano starts are the following: Class, the relation of

---

[15]There is a difficulty in regard to this primitive proposition, discussed in §§ 53, 94 below.

[16]See Chap. IV.
[17]See Chap. V.

an individual to a class of which it is a member, the notion of a term, implication where both propositions contain the same variables, *i.e.* formal implication, the simultaneous affirmation of two propositions, the notion of definition, and the negation of a proposition. From these notions, together with the division of a complex proposition into parts, Peano professes to deduce all symbolic logic by means of certain primitive propositions. Let us examine the deduction in outline.

We may observe, to begin with, that the simultaneous affirmation of *two* propositions might seem, at first sight, not enough to take as a primitive idea. For although this can be extended, by successive steps, to the simultaneous affirmation of any finite number of propositions, yet this is not all that is wanted; we require to be able to affirm simultaneously all the propositions of any class, finite or infinite. But the simultaneous assertion of a class of propositions, oddly enough, is much easier to define than that of two propositions (see § 34, (3)). If k be a class of propositions, their simultaneous affirmation is the assertion that "p is a k" implies p. If this holds, all propositions of the class are true; if it fails, one at least must be false. We have seen that the logical product of two propositions can be defined in a highly artificial manner; but it might almost as well be taken as indefinable, since no further property can be proved by means of the definition. We may observe, also, that formal and material implication are combined by Peano into one primitive idea, whereas they ought to be kept separate.

33. Before giving any primitive propositions, Peano proceeds to some definitions. (1) If a is a class, "x and y are a's" is to mean "x is an a and y is an a." (2) If a and b are classes, "every a is a b" means "x is an a implies that x is a b." If we accept formal implication as a primitive notion, this definition seems unobjectionable; but it may well be held that the relation of inclusion between classes is simpler than formal implication, and should not be defined by its means. This is a difficult question, which I reserve for subsequent discussion. A formal implication appears to be the assertion of a whole class of material implications. The complication introduced at this point arises from the nature of the variable, a point which Peano, though he has done very much to show its importance, appears not to have himself sufficiently considered. The notion of one proposition containing a variable implying another such proposition, which he takes as primitive, is complex, and should therefore be separated into its constituents; from this separation arises the necessity of considering the simultaneous affirmation of a whole class of propositions before interpreting such a proposition as "x is an a implies that x is a b." (3) We come next to a perfectly worthless definition, which has been since abandoned. This is the definition of *such that*. The x's such that x is an a, we are told, are to mean the class a. But this only gives the meaning of *such that* when placed before a proposition of the type "x is an a." Now it is often necessary to consider an x such that some proposition is true of it, where this proposition is not of the form "x is an a." Peano holds (though he does not lay it down as an axiom) that every proposition containing only one variable is reducible to the form "x is an a." But we shall see (Chap. x) that at least one such proposition is not reducible to this form. And in any case, the only utility of *such that* is to effect the reduction, which cannot therefore be assumed to be already effected without it. The fact is that *such that* contains a primitive idea, but one which it is not easy clearly to disengage from other ideas.

In order to grasp the meaning of *such that*, it is necessary to observe, first of all, that what Peano and mathematicians generally call *one* proposition containing a variable is really, if the variable is apparent, the conjunction of a certain class of propositions defined by some constancy of form; while if the variable is real, so that we have a propositional function, there is not a proposition at all, but merely a kind of schematic representation of *any* proposition of a certain type. "The sum of the angles of a triangle is two right angles," for example, when stated by means of a variable, becomes: Let x be a triangle; then the sum of the angles of x is two right angles. This expresses the conjunction of all the propositions in which it is said of particular definite entities that if they are triangles, the sum of their angles is two right angles. But a propositional function, where the variable is real, represents *any* proposition of a certain form, not *all* such propositions (see §§ 59–62). There is, for each propositional function, an indefinable relation between propositions and entities, which may be expressed by saying that all the propositions have the same form, but different entities enter into them. It is this that gives rise to propositional functions. Given, for example, a constant relation and a constant term, there is a one-one correspondence between the propositions asserting that various terms have the said relation to the said term, and the various terms which occur in these propositions. It is this notion which is requisite for the comprehension of *such that*. Let x be a variable whose values form the class a, and let $f(x)$ be a one-valued function of x which is a true proposition for all values of x within the class a, and which is false for all other values of x. Then the terms of a are the class of terms *such that* $f(x)$ is a true proposition. This gives an explanation of *such that*. But it must always be remembered that the appearance of having *one* proposition $f(x)$ satisfied by a number of values of x is fallacious: $f(x)$ is not a proposition at all, but a propositional function. What is fundamental is the relation of various propositions of given form to the various terms entering severally into them as arguments or values of the variable; this relation is equally required for interpreting the propositional function $f(x)$ and the notion *such that,* but is itself ultimate and inexplicable. (4) We come next to the definition of the logical product, or common part, of two classes. If a and b be two classes, their common part consists of the class of terms x such that x is an a and x is a b. Here already, as Padoa points out (*loc. cit.*), it is necessary to extend the meaning of *such that* beyond the case where our proposition asserts membership of a class, since it is only by means of the definition that the common part is shown to be a class.

34. The remainder of the definitions preceding the primitive propositions are less important, and may be passed over. Of the primitive propositions, some appear to be merely concerned with the symbolism, and not to express any real properties of what is symbolized; others, on the contrary, are of high logical importance.

(1) The first of Peano's axioms is "every class is contained in itself." This is equivalent to "every proposition implies itself." There seems no way of evading this axiom, which is equivalent to the law of identity, except the method adopted above, of using self-implication to define propositions. (2) Next we have the axiom that the product of two classes is a class. This ought to have been stated, as ought also the definition of the logical product, for a class of classes; for when stated for only two classes, it cannot be extended to the logical product of an infinite class of classes. If *class* is taken as indefinable, it is a genuine axiom, which is very necessary to reasoning. But it might perhaps be somewhat generalized by an axiom concerning the terms satisfying propositions of a given form: *e.g.* "the terms having one or more given relations to one or more given terms form a class." In Section B, above, the axiom was wholly evaded by using a generalized form of the axiom as the definition of *class*. (3) We have next two axioms which are really only one, and appear distinct only because Peano defines the common part of two classes instead of the common part of a class of classes. These two axioms state that, if a, b be classes, their logical product, ab, is contained in a and is contained in b. These appear as different axioms, because, as far as the symbolism shows, ab might be different from ba. It is one of the defects of most symbolisms that they give an order to terms which intrinsically have none, or at least none that is relevant. So in this case: if K be a class of classes, the logical product of K consists of all terms belonging to *every* class that belongs to K. With this definition, it becomes at once evident that no order of the terms of K is involved. Hence if K has only two terms, a and b, it is indifferent whether we represent the logical product of K by ab or by ba, since the order exists only in the symbols, not in what is symbolized. It is to be observed that the corresponding axiom with regard to propositions is, that the simultaneous assertion of a class of propositions implies any proposition of the class; and this is perhaps the best form of the axiom. Neverthe-

less, though an axiom is not required, it is necessary, here as elsewhere, to have a means of connecting the case where we start from a class of classes or of propositions or of relations with the case where the class results from enumeration of its terms. Thus although no order is involved in the product of a *class* of propositions, there is an order in the product of two definite propositions p, q, and it is significant to assert that the products pq and qp are equivalent. But this can be proved by means of the axioms with which we began the calculus of propositions (§ 18). It is to be observed that this proof is prior to the proof that the class whose terms are p and q is identical with the class whose terms are q and p. (4) We have next two forms of syllogism, both primitive propositions. The first asserts that, if a, b, c be classes, and a is contained in b, and x is an a, then x is a b; the second asserts that if a, b, c be classes, and a is contained in b, b in c, then a is contained in c. It is one of the greatest of Peano's merits to have clearly distinguished the relation of the individual to its class from the relation of inclusion between classes. The difference is exceedingly fundamental: the former relation is the simplest and most essential of all relations, the latter a complicated relation derived from logical implication. It results from the distinction that the syllogism in Barbara has two forms, usually confounded: the one the time-honoured assertion that Socrates is a man, and therefore mortal, the other the assertion that Greeks are men, and therefore mortal. These two forms are stated by Peano's axioms. It is to be observed that, in virtue of the definition of what is meant by one class being contained in another, the first form results from the axiom that, if p, q, r be propositions, and p implies that q implies r, then the product of p and q implies r. This axiom is now substituted by Peano for the first form of the syllogism: it is more general and cannot be deduced from the said form. The second form of the syllogism, when applied to propositions instead of classes, asserts that implication is transitive. This principle is, of course, the very life of all chains of reasoning. (5) We have next a principle of reasoning which Peano calls *composition:* this asserts that

if a is contained in b and also in c, then it is contained in the common part of both. Stating this principle with regard to propositions, it asserts that if a proposition implies each of two others, then it implies their joint assertion or logical product; and this is the principle which was called *composition* above.

35. From this point, we advance successfully until we require the idea of *negation*. This is taken, in the edition of the *Formulaire* we are considering, as a new primitive idea, and disjunction is defined by its means. By means of the negation of a proposition, it is of course easy to define the negation of a class: for "x is a not-a" is equivalent to "x is not an a." But we require an axiom to the effect that *not-a* is a class, and another to the effect that not-not-a is a. Peano gives also a third axiom, namely: If a, b, c be classes, and ab is contained in c, and x is an a but not a c, then x is not a b. This is simpler in the form: If p, q, r be propositions, and p, q together imply r, and q is true while r is false, then q is false. This would be still further improved by being put in the form: If q, r are propositions, and q implies r, then not-r implies not-q; a form which Peano obtains as a deduction. By dealing with propositions before classes or propositional functions, it is possible, as we saw, to avoid treating negation as a primitive idea, and to replace all axioms respecting negation by the principle of reduction.

We come next to the definition of the disjunction or logical sum of two classes. On this subject Peano has many times changed his procedure. In the edition we are considering, "a or b" is defined as the negation of the logical product of not-a and not-b, *i.e.* as the class of terms which are not both not-a and not-b. In later editions (*e.g. F.* 1901, p. 19), we find a somewhat less artificial definition, namely: "a or b" consists of all terms which belong to any class which contains a and contains b. Either definition seems logically unobjectionable. It is to be observed that a and b are classes, and that it remains a question for philosophical logic whether there is not a quite different notion of the disjunction of individuals, as *e.g.* "Brown or Jones." I shall consider this question in Chapter V. It will be remembered that, when we begin by the calculus of propositions, disjunction is defined before negation; with the above definition (that of 1897), it is plainly necessary to take negation first.

36. The connected notions of the null-class and the existence of a class are next dealt with. In the edition of 1897, a class is defined as null when it is contained in every class. When we remember the definition of one class *a* being contained in another *b* ("*x* is an *a*" implies "*x* is a *b*" for all values of *x*), we see that we are to regard the implication as holding for *all* values, and not only for those values for which *x* really is an *a*. This is a point upon which Peano is not explicit, and I doubt whether he has made up his mind on it. If the implication were only to hold when *x* really is an *a*, it would not give a definition of the null-class, for which this hypothesis is false for all values of *x*. I do not know whether it is for this reason or for some other that Peano has since abandoned the definition of the inclusion of classes by means of formal implication between propositional functions: the inclusion of classes appears to be now regarded as indefinable. Another definition which Peano has sometimes favoured (*e.g. F.* 1895, Errata, p. 116) is, that the null-class is the product of any class into its negation—a definition to which similar remarks apply. In *R. d. M.* VII, No. 1 (§ 3, Prop. 1.0), the null-class is defined as the class of those terms that belong to every class, *i.e.* the class of terms *x* such that "*a* is a class" implies "*x* is an *a*" for all values of *a*. There are of course no such terms *x*; and there is a grave logical difficulty in trying to interpret extensionally a class which has no extension. This point is one to which I shall return in Chapter VI.

From this point onward, Peano's logic proceeds by a smooth development. But in one respect it is still defective: it does not recognize as ultimate relational propositions not asserting membership of a class. For this reason, the definitions of a function and of other essentially relational notions are defective. But this defect is easily remedied by applying, in the manner explained above, the principles of the *Formulaire* to the logic of relations.

Chapter III: Implication and Formal Implication

37. In the preceding chapter I endeavoured to present, briefly and uncritically, all the data, in the shape of formally fundamental ideas and propositions, that pure mathematics requires. In subsequent Parts I shall show that these are all the data by giving definitions of the various mathematical concepts—number, infinity, continuity, the various spaces of geometry, and motion. In the remainder of Part I, I shall give indications, as best I can, of the philosophical problems arising in the analysis of the data, and of the directions in which I imagine these problems to be probably soluble. Some logical notions will be elicited which, though they seem quite fundamental to logic, are not commonly discussed in works on the subject; and thus problems no longer clothed in mathematical symbolism will be presented for the consideration of philosophical logicians.

Two kinds of implication, the material and the formal, were found to be essential to every kind of deduction. In the present chapter I wish to examine and distinguish these two kinds, and to discuss some methods of attempting to analyze the second of them.

In the discussion of inference, it is common to permit the intrusion of a psychological element, and to consider our acquisition of new knowledge by its means. But it is plain that where we validly infer one proposition from another, we do so in virtue of a relation which holds between the two propositions whether we perceive it or not: the mind, in fact, is as purely receptive in inference as common sense supposes it to be in perception of sensible objects. The relation in virtue of which it is possible for us validly to infer is what I call material implication. We have already seen that it would be a vicious circle to define this relation as meaning that *if* one proposition is true, *then* another is true, for *if* and *then* already involve implication. The relation holds, in fact, when it does hold, without any reference to the truth or falsehood of the propositions involved.

But in developing the consequences of our assumptions as to implication, we were led to conclusions which do not by any means agree with what is commonly held concerning implication, for we found that any false proposition implies every proposition and any true proposition is implied by every proposition. Thus propositions are formally like a set of lengths each of which is one inch or two, and implication is like the relation "equal to or less than" among such lengths. It would certainly not be commonly maintained that "$2 + 2 = 4$" can be deduced from "Socrates is a man," or that both are implied by "Socrates is a triangle." But the reluctance to admit such implications is chiefly due, I think, to preoccupation with formal implication, which is a much more familiar notion, and is really before the mind, as a rule, even where material implication is what is explicitly mentioned. In inferences from "Socrates is a man," it is customary not to consider the philosopher who vexed the Athenians, but to regard Socrates merely as a symbol, capable of being replaced by any other man; and only a vulgar prejudice in favour of true propositions stands in the way of replacing Socrates by a number, a table, or a plum-pudding. Nevertheless, wherever, as in Euclid, one particular proposition is deduced from another, material implication is involved, though as a rule the material implication may be regarded as a particular instance of some formal implication, obtained by giving some constant value to the variable or variables involved in the said formal implication. And although, while relations are still regarded with the awe caused by unfamiliarity, it is natural to doubt whether any such relation as implication is to be found, yet, in virtue of the general principles laid down in Section C of the preceding chapter, there must be a relation holding betwen nothing except propositions, and holding between any two propositions of which either the first is false or the second true. Of the various equivalent relations satisfying these conditions, one is to be called *implication*, and if such a notion seems unfamiliar, that does not suffice to prove that it is illusory.

38. At this point, it is necessary to consider a very difficult logical problem, namely, the distinction between a proposition actually asserted, and a proposition considered merely as a complex concept. One of our indemonstrable principles was, it will be remembered, that if the hypothesis in an implication is true, it may be dropped, and the consequent asserted. This principle, it was observed, eludes formal statement, and points to a certain failure of formalism in general. The principle is employed whenever a proposition is said to be *proved;* for what happens is, in all such cases, that the proposition is shown to be implied by some true proposition. Another form in which the principle is constantly employed is the substitution of a constant, satisfying the hypothesis, in the consequent of a formal implication. If ϕx implies ψx for all values of x, and if a is a constant satisfying ϕx, we can assert ψa, dropping the true hypothesis ϕa. This occurs, for example, whenever any of those rules of inference which employ the hypothesis that the variables involved are propositions, are applied to particular propositions. The principle in question is, therefore, quite vital to any kind of demonstration.

The independence of this principle is brought out by a consideration of Lewis Carroll's puzzle, "What the Tortoise said to Achilles."[18] The principles of inference which we accepted lead to the proposition that, if p and q be propositions, then p together with "p implies q" implies q. At first sight, it might be thought that this would enable us to assert q provided p is true and implies q. But the puzzle in question shows that this is not the case, and that, until we have some new principle, we shall only be led into an endless regress of more and more complicated implications, without ever arriving at the assertion of q. We need, in fact, the notion of *therefore*, which is quite different from the notion of *implies*, and holds between different entities. In grammar, the distinction is that between a verb and a verbal noun, between, say, "A is greater than B" and "A's being greater than B." In the first of these, a proposition is actually asserted, whereas in the second it is merely considered. But these are psychological terms, whereas the difference which I desire to express is

[18]*Mind*, N. S. Vol. IV, p. 278.

genuinely logical. It is plain that, if I may be allowed to use the word *assertion* in a non-psychological sense, the proposition "*p* implies *q*" *asserts* an implication, though it does not *assert p* or *q*. The *p* and the *q* which enter into this proposition are not strictly the same as the *p* or the *q* which are separate propositions, at least, if they are true. The question is: How does a proposition differ by being actually true from what it would be as an entity if it were not true? It is plain that true and false propositions alike are entities of a kind, but that true propositions have a quality not belonging to false ones, a quality which, in a non-psychological sense, may be called being *asserted*. Yet there are grave difficulties in forming a consistent theory on this point, for if assertion in any way changed a proposition, no proposition which can possibly in any context be unasserted could be true, since when asserted it would become a different proposition. But this is plainly false; for in "*p* implies *q*," *p* and *q* are not asserted, and yet they may be true. Leaving this puzzle to logic, however, we must insist that there is a difference of some kind between an asserted and an unasserted proposition. When we say *therefore,* we state a relation which can only hold between asserted propositions, and which thus differs from implication. Wherever *therefore* occurs, the hypothesis may be dropped, and the conclusion asserted by itself. This seems to be the first step in answering Lewis Carroll's puzzle.

39. It is commonly said that an inference must have premisses and a conclusion, and it is held, apparently, that two or more premisses are necessary, if not to all inferences, yet to most. This view is borne out, at first sight, by obvious facts: every syllogism, for example, is held to have two premisses. Now such a theory greatly complicates the relation of implication, since it renders it a relation which may have any number of terms, and is symmetrical with respect to all but one of them, but not symmetrical with respect to that one (the conclusion). This complication is, however, unnecessary, first, because every simultaneous assertion of a number of propositions is itself a single proposition, and secondly, because, by the rule which we called *exportation*, it is always possible to exhibit an implication explicitly as

holding between single propositions. To take the first point first: if *k* be a class of propositions, all the propositions of the class *k* are asserted by the single proposition "for all values of *x*, if *x* implies *x*, then '*x* is a *k*' implies *x*," or, in more ordinary language, "every *k* is true." And as regards the second point, which assumes the number of premisses to be finite, "*pq* implies *r*" is equivalent, if *q* be a proposition, to "*p* implies that *q* implies *r*," in which latter form the implications hold explicitly between single propositions. Hence we may safely hold implication to be a relation between two propositions, not a relation of an arbitrary number of premisses to a single conclusion.

40. I come now to formal implication, which is a far more difficult notion than material implication. In order to avoid the general notion of propositional function, let us begin by the discussion of a particular instance, say "*x* is a man implies *x* is a mortal for all values of *x*." This proposition is equivalent to "all men are mortal" "every man is mortal" and "any man is mortal." But it seems highly doubtful whether it is the same proposition. It is also connected with a purely intensional proposition in which *man* is asserted to be a complex notion of which *mortal* is a constituent, but this proposition is quite distinct from the one we are discussing. Indeed, such intensional propositions are not always present where one class is included in another: in general, either class may be defined by various different predicates, and it is by no means necessary that every predicate of the smaller class should contain every predicate of the larger class as a factor. Indeed, it may very well happen that both predicates are philosophically simple: thus *colour* and *existent* appear to be both simple, yet the class of colours is part of the class of existents. The intensional view, derived from predicates, is in the main irrelevant to Symbolic Logic and to Mathematics, and I shall not consider it further at present.

41. It may be doubted, to begin with, whether "*x* is a man implies *x* is a mortal" is to be regarded as asserted strictly of all possible terms, or only of such terms as are men. Peano, though he is not explicit, appears to hold the latter view. But in this case, the hypothesis ceases to be significant, and becomes

a mere definition of x: x is to mean any man. The hypothesis then becomes a mere assertion concerning the meaning of the symbol x, and the whole of what is asserted concerning the matter dealt with by our symbol is put into the conclusion. The premiss says: x is to mean any man. The conclusion says: x is mortal. But the implication is merely concerning the symbolism: since any man is mortal, if x denotes any man, x is mortal. Thus formal implication, on this view, has wholly disappeared, leaving us the proposition "any man is mortal" as expressing the whole of what is relevant in the proposition with a variable. It would now only remain to examine the proposition "any man is mortal," and if possible to explain this proposition without reintroducing the variable and formal implication. It must be confessed that some grave difficulties are avoided by this view. Consider, for example, the simultaneous assertion of all the propositions of some class k: this is not expressed by " 'x is a k' implies x for all values of x." For as it stands, this proposition does not express what is meant, since, if x be not a proposition, "x is a k" cannot imply x; hence the range of variability of x must be confined to propositions, unless we prefix (as above, § 39) the hypothesis "x implies x." This remark applies generally, throughout the propositional calculus, to all cases where the conclusion is represented by a single letter: unless the letter does not actually represent a proposition, the implication asserted will be false, since only propositions can be implied. The point is that, if x be our variable, x itself is a proposition for all values of x which are propositions, but not for other values. This makes it plain what the limitations are to which our variable is subject: it must vary only within the range of values for which the two sides of the principal implication are propositions, in other words, the two sides, when the variable is not replaced by a constant, must be genuine propositional functions. If this restriction is not observed, fallacies quickly begin to appear. It should be noticed that there may be any number of subordinate implications which do not require that their terms should be propositions: it is only of the principal implication that this is required. Take, for example, the first principle of inference: If p implies q, then p

implies q. This holds equally whether p and q be propositions or not; for if either is not a proposition, "p implies q" becomes false, but does not cease to be a proposition. In fact, in virtue of the definition of a proposition, our principle states that "p implies q" is a propositional function, *i.e.* that it is a proposition for *all* values of p and q. But if we apply the principle of importation to this proposition, so as to obtain " 'p implies q,' together with p, implies q," we have a formula which is only true when p and q are propositions: in order to make it true universally, we must preface it by the hypothesis "p implies p and q implies q." In this way, in many cases, if not in all, the restriction on the variability of the variable can be removed; thus, in the assertion of the logical product of a class of propositions, the formula "if x implies x, then 'x is a k' implies x" appears unobjectionable, and allows x to vary without restriction. Here the subordinate implications in the premiss and the conclusion are material: only the principal implication is formal.

Returning now to "x is a man implies x is a mortal," it is plain that no restriction is required in order to insure our having a genuine proposition. And it is plain that, although we *might* restrict the values of x to men, and although this seems to be done in the proposition "all men are mortal," yet there is no reason, so far as the truth of our proposition is concerned, why we should so restrict our x. Whether x be a man or not, "x is a man" is always, when a constant is substituted for x, a proposition implying, for that value of x, the proposition "x is a mortal." And unless we admit the hypothesis equally in the cases where it is false, we shall find it impossible to deal satisfactorily with the null-class or with null propositional functions. We must, therefore, allow our x, wherever the truth of our formal implication is thereby unimpaired, to take *all* values without exception; and where any restriction on variability is required, the implication is not to be regarded as formal until the said restriction has been removed by being prefixed as hypothesis. (If ψx be a proposition whenever x satisfies ϕx, where ϕx is a propositional function, and if ψx, whenever it is a proposition, implies χx, then "ψx implies χ*x*" is not a formal implication, but "φ*x* implies that ψ*x* implies χ*x*" is a formal implication.)

42. It is to be observed that "*x* is a man implies *x* is a mortal" is not a relation of two propositional functions, but is itself a single propositional function having the elegant property of being always true. For "*x* is a man" is, as it stands, not a proposition at all, and does not imply anything; and we must not first vary our *x* in "*x* is a man," and then independently vary it in "*x* is a mortal," for this would lead to the proposition that "everything is a man" implies "everything is a mortal," which, though true, is not what was meant. This proposition would have to be expressed, if the language of variables were retained, by two variables, as "*x* is a man implies *y* is a mortal." But this formula too is unsatisfactory, for its natural meaning would be: "If anything is a man, then everything is a mortal." The point to be emphasized is, of course, that our *x*, though variable, must be the same on both sides of the implication, and this requires that we should not obtain our formal implication by first varying (say) Socrates in "Socrates is a man," and then in "Socrates is a mortal," but that we should start from the whole proposition "Socrates is a man implies Socrates is a mortal," and vary Socrates in this proposition as a whole. Thus our formal implication asserts a class of implications, not a single implication at all. We do not, in a word, have one implication containing a variable, but rather a variable implication. We have a class of implications, no one of which contains a variable, and we assert that every member of this class is true. This is a first step towards the analysis of the mathematical notion of the variable.

But, it may be asked, how comes it that Socrates may be varied in the proposition "Socrates is a man implies Socrates is mortal"? In virtue of the fact that true propositions are implied by all others, we have "Socrates is a man implies Socrates is a philosopher;" but in this proposition, alas, the variability of Socrates is sadly restricted. This seems to show that formal implication involves something over and above the relation of implication, and that some additional relation must hold where a term can be varied. In the case in question, it is natural to say that what is involved is the

relation of inclusion between the classes *men* and *mortals*—the very relation which was to be defined and explained by our formal implication. But this view is too simple to meet all cases, and is therefore not required in any case. A larger number of cases, though still not all cases, can be dealt with by the notion of what I shall call *assertions*. This notion must now be briefly explained, leaving its critical discussion to Chapter VII.

43. It has always been customary to divide propositions into subject and predicate; but this division has the defect of omitting the verb. It is true that a graceful concession is sometimes made by loose talk about the copula, but the verb deserves far more respect than is thus paid to it. We may say, broadly, that every proposition may be divided, some in only one way, some in several ways, into a term (the subject) and something which is said about the subject, which something I shall call the *assertion*. Thus "Socrates is a man" may be divided into *Socrates* and *is a man*. The verb, which is the distinguishing mark of propositions, remains with the assertion; but the assertion itself, being robbed of its subject, is neither true nor false. In logical discussions, the notion of assertion often occurs, but as the word *proposition* is used for it, it does not obtain separate consideration. Consider, for example; the best statement of the identity of indiscernibles: "If *x* and *y* be any two diverse entities, some assertion holds of *x* which does not hold of *y*." But for the word *assertion*, which would ordinarily be replaced by *proposition*, this statement is one which would commonly pass unchallenged. Again, it might be said: "Socrates was a philosopher, and the same is true of Plato." Such statements require the analysis of a proposition into an assertion and a subject, in order that there may be something identical which can be said to be affirmed of two subjects.

44. We can now see how, where the analysis into subject and assertion is legitimate, to distinguish implications in which there is a term which can be varied from others in which this is not the case. Two ways of making the distinction may be suggested, and we shall have to decide between them. It may be said that there is a relation between the two asser-

tions "is a man" and "is a mortal," in virtue of which, when the one holds, so does the other. Or again, we may analyze the whole proposition "Socrates is a man implies Socrates is a mortal" into Socrates and an assertion about him, and say that the assertion in question holds of all terms. Neither of these theories replaces the above analysis of "x is a man implies x is a mortal" into a class of material implications; but whichever of the two is true carries the analysis one step further. The first theory suffers from the difficulty that it is essential to the relation of assertions involved that both assertions should be made of the *same* subject, though it is otherwise irrelevant what subject we choose. The second theory appears objectionable on the ground that the suggested analysis of "Socrates is a man implies Socrates is a mortal" seems scarcely possible. The proposition in question consists of two terms and a relation, the terms being "Socrates is a man" and "Socrates is a mortal;" and it would seem that when a relational proposition is analyzed into a subject and an assertion, the subject must be one of the terms of the relation which is asserted. This objection seems graver than that against the former view; I shall therefore, at any rate for the present, adopt the former view, and regard formal implication as derived from a relation between assertions.

We remarked above that the relation of inclusion between classes is insufficient. This results from the irreducible nature of relational propositions. Take *e.g.* "Socrates is married implies Socrates had a father." Here it is affirmed that because Socrates has one relation, he must have another. Or better still, take "A is before B implies B is after A." This is a formal implication, in which the assertions are (superficially at least) concerning different subjects; the only way to avoid this is to say that both propositions have both A and B as subjects, which, by the way, is quite different from saying that they have the one subject "A and B." Such instances make it plain that the notion of a propositional function, and the notion of an assertion, are more fundamental than the notion of *class,* and that the latter is not adequate to explain all cases of formal implication. I shall not enlarge upon this point

now, as it will be abundantly illustrated in subsequent portions of the present work.

It is important to realize that, according to the above analysis of formal implication, the notion of *every term* is indefinable and ultimate. A formal implication is one which holds of every term, and therefore *every* cannot be explained by means of formal implication. If a and b be classes, we can explain "every a is a b" by means of "x is an a implies x is a b;" but the *every* which occurs here is a derivative and subsequent notion, presupposing the notion of *every term*. It seems to be the very essence of what may be called a *formal* truth, and of formal reasoning generally, that some assertion is affirmed to hold of every term; and unless the notion of *every term* is admitted, formal truths are impossible.

45. The fundamental importance of formal implication is brought out by the consideration that it is involved in all the rules of inference. This shows that we cannot hope wholly to define it in terms of material implication, but that some further element or elements must be involved. We may observe, however, that, in a particular inference, the rule according to which the inference proceeds is not required as a premiss. This point has been emphasized by Mr Bradley;[19] it is closely connected with the principle of dropping a true premiss, being again a respect in which formalism breaks down. In order to apply a rule of inference, it is formally necessary to have a premiss asserting that the present case is an instance of the rule; we shall then need to affirm the rule by which we can go from the rule to an instance, and also to affirm that here we have an instance of this rule, and so on into an endless process. The fact is, of course, that any implication warranted by a rule of inference does actually hold, and is not merely implied by the rule. This is simply an instance of the non-formal principle of dropping a true premiss: if our rule implies a certain implication, the rule may be dropped and the implication asserted. But it remains the case that the fact that our rule does imply the said implication, if introduced at all, must be simply perceived, and is not

[19]*Logic,* Book II, Part I, Chap. ii (p. 227).

guaranteed by any formal deduction; and often it is just as easy, and consequently just as legitimate, to perceive immediately the implication in question as to perceive that it is implied by one or more of the rules of inference.

To sum up our discussion of formal implication: a formal implication, we said, is the affirmation of *every* material implication of a certain class; and the class of material implications involved is, in simple cases, the class of all propositions in which a given fixed assertion, made concerning a certain subject or subjects, is affirmed to imply another given fixed assertion concerning the same subject or subjects. Where a formal implication holds, we agreed to regard it, wherever possible, as due to some relation between the assertions concerned. This theory raises many formidable logical problems, and requires, for its defence, a thorough analysis of the constituents of propositions. To this task we must now address ourselves.

Chapter IV: Proper Names, Adjectives, and Verbs

46. In the present chapter, certain questions are to be discussed belonging to what may be called philosophical grammar. The study of grammar, in my opinion, is capable of throwing far more light on philosophical questions than is commonly supposed by philosophers. Although a grammatical distinction cannot be uncritically assumed to correspond to a genuine philosophical difference, yet the one is *primâ facie* evidence of the other, and may often be most usefully employed as a source of discovery. Moreover, it must be admitted, I think, that every word occurring in a sentence must have *some* meaning: a perfectly meaningless sound could not be employed in the more or less fixed way in which language employs words. The correctness of our philosophical analysis of a proposition may therefore be usefully checked by the exercise of assigning the meaning of each word in the sentence expressing the proposition. On the whole, grammar

seems to me to bring us much nearer to a correct logic than the current opinions of philosophers; and in what follows, grammar, though not our master, will yet be taken as our guide.[20]

Of the parts of speech, three are specially important: substantives, adjectives, and verbs. Among substantives, some are derived from adjectives or verbs, as humanity from human, or sequence from *follows*. (I am not speaking of an etymological derivation, but of a logical one.) Others, such as proper names, or space, time, and matter, are not derivative, but appear primarily as substantives. What we wish to obtain is a classification, not of words, but of ideas; I shall therefore call adjectives or predicates all notions which are capable of being such, even in a form in which grammar would call them substantives. The fact is, as we shall see, that *human* and *humanity* denote precisely the same concept, these words being employed respectively according to the kind of relation in which this concept stands to the other constituents of a proposition in which it occurs. The distinction which we require is not identical with the grammatical distinction between substantive and adjective, since one single concept may, according to circumstances, be either substantive or adjective: it is the distinction between proper and general names that we require, or rather between the objects indicated by such names. In every proposition, as we saw in Chapter III, we may make an analysis into something asserted and something about which the assertion is made. A proper name, when it occurs in a proposition, is always, at least according to one of the possible ways of analysis (where there are several), the subject that the proposition or some subordinate constituent proposition is about, and not what is said about the subject. Adjectives and verbs, on the other hand, are capable of occurring in propositions in which they cannot be regarded as subject, but only as parts of the assertion. Adjectives are distinguished by capacity for *denoting*—a term which I intend to use in a technical sense to be discussed in Chapter V. Verbs are distin-

[20]The excellence of grammar as a guide is proportional to the paucity of inflexions, *i.e.* to the degree of analysis effected by the language considered.

guished by a special kind of connection, exceedingly hard to define, with truth and falsehood, in virtue of which they distinguish an asserted proposition from an unasserted one, *e.g.* "Caesar died" from "the death of Caesar." These distinctions must now be amplified, and I shall begin with the distinction between general and proper names.

47. Philosophy is familiar with a certain set of distinctions, all more or less equivalent: I mean, the distinctions of subject and predicate, substance and attribute, substantive and adjective, *this* and *what*.[21] I wish now to point out briefly what appears to me to be the truth concerning these cognate distinctions. The subject is important, since the issues between monism and monadism, between idealism and empiricism, and between those who maintain and those who deny that all truth is concerned with what exists, all depend, in whole or in part, upon the theory we adopt in regard to the present question. But the subject is treated here only because it is essential to any doctrine of number or of the nature of the variable. Its bearings on general philosophy, important as they are, will be left wholly out of account.

Whatever may be an object of thought, or may occur in any true or false proposition, or can be counted as *one*, I call a *term*. This, then, is the widest word in the philosophical vocabulary. I shall use as synonymous with it the words unit, individual, and entity. The first two emphasize the fact that every term is *one*, while the third is derived from the fact that every term has being, *i.e. is* in some sense. A man, a moment, a number, a class, a relation, a chimaera, or anything else that can be mentioned, is sure to be a term; and to deny that such and such a thing is a term must always be false.

It might perhaps be thought that a word of such extreme generality could not be of any great use. Such a view, however, owing to certain wide-spread philosophical doctrines, would be erroneous. A term is, in fact, possessed of all the properties commonly assigned to substances or substantives. Every term, to begin with, is a logical subject: it is, for example, the subject of the proposition that itself

is one. Again every term is immutable and indestructible. What a term is, it is, and no change can be conceived in it which would not destroy its identity and make it another term.[22] Another mark which belongs to terms is numerical identity with themselves and numerical diversity from all other terms.[23] Numerical identity and diversity are the source of unity and plurality; and thus the admission of many terms destroys monism. And it seems undeniable that every constituent of every proposition can be counted as one, and that no proposition contains less than two constituents. *Term* is, therefore, a useful word, since it marks dissent from various philosophies, as well as because, in many statements, we wish to speak of *any* term or *some* term.

48. Among terms, it is possible to distinguish two kinds, which I shall call respectively *things* and *concepts*. The former are the terms indicated by proper names, the latter those indicated by all other words. Here proper names are to be understood in a somewhat wider sense than is usual, and things also are to be understood as embracing all particular points and instants, and many other entities not commonly called things. Among concepts, again, two kinds at least must be distinguished, namely those indicated by adjectives and those indicated by verbs. The former kind will often be called predicates or class-concepts; the latter are always or almost always relations. (In intransitive verbs, the notion expressed by the verb is complex, and usually asserts a definite relation to an indefinite relatum, as in "Smith breathes.")

In a large class of propositions, we agreed, it is possible, in one or more ways, to distinguish a subject and an assertion about the subject. The assertion must always contain a verb, but except in this respect, assertions appear to have no universal properties. In a relational proposition, say "*A* is greater than *B*," we may regard *A* as the subject, and "is greater than *B*"

---

[21]This last pair of terms is due to Mr Bradley.

[22]The notion of a term here set forth is a modification of Mr G. E. Moore's notion of a *concept* in his article "On the Nature of Judgment," *Mind*, N. S. No. 30., from which notion, however, it differs in some important respects.

[23]On identity, see Mr G. E. Moore's article in the *Proceedings of the Aristotelian Society*, 1900–1901.

as the assertion, or *B* as the subject and "*A* is greater than" as the assertion. There are thus, in the case proposed, two ways of analyzing the proposition into subject and assertion. Where a relation has more than two terms, as in "*A* is here now,"[24] there will be more than two ways of making the analysis. But in some propositions, there is only a single way: these are the subject-predicate propositions, such as "Socrates is human." The proposition "humanity belongs to Socrates," which is equivalent to "Socrates is human," is an assertion about humanity: but it is a distinct proposition. In "Socrates is human," the notion expressed by *human* occurs in a different way from that in which it occurs when it is called *humanity*, the difference being that in the latter case, but not in the former, the proposition is *about* this notion. This indicates that humanity is a concept, not a thing. I shall speak of the *terms* of a proposition as those terms, however numerous, which occur in a proposition and may be regarded as subjects about which the proposition is. It is a characteristic of the terms of a proposition that any one of them may be replaced by any other entity without our ceasing to have a proposition. Thus we shall say that "Socrates is human" is a proposition having only one term; of the remaining components of the proposition, one is the verb, the other is a *predicate*. With the sense which *is* has in this proposition, we no longer have a proposition at all if we replace *human* by something other than a predicate. Predicates, then, are concepts, other than verbs, which occur in propositions having only one term or subject. Socrates is a thing, because Socrates can never occur otherwise than as term in a proposition: Socrates is not capable of that curious twofold use which is involved in *human* and *humanity*. Points, instants, bits of matter, particular states of mind, and particular existents generally, are things in the above sense, and so are many terms which do not exist, for example, the points in a non-Euclidean space and the pseudo-existents of a novel. All classes, it would seem, as numbers, men, spaces, etc.,

when taken as single terms, are things; but this is a point for Chapter VI.

Predicates are distinguished from other terms by a number of very interesting properties, chief among which is their connection with what I shall call *denoting*. One predicate always gives rise to a host of cognate notions: thus in addition to *human* and *humanity*, which only differ grammatically, we have *man, a man, some man, any man, every man, all men*,[25] all of which appear to be genuinely distinct one from another. The study of these various notions is absolutely vital to any philosophy of mathematics; and it is on account of them that the theory of predicates is important.

49. It might be thought that a distinction ought to be made between a concept as such and a concept used as a term, between, *e.g.*, such pairs as *is* and *being*, *human* and *humanity*, *one* in such a proposition as "this is one" and 1 in "1 is a number." But inextricable difficulties will envelop us if we allow such a view. There is, of course, a grammatical difference, and this corresponds to a difference as regards relations. In the first case, the concept in question is used as a concept, that is, it is actually predicated of a term or asserted to relate two or more terms; while in the second case, the concept is itself said to have a predicate or a relation. There is, therefore, no difficulty in accounting for the grammatical difference. But what I wish to urge is, that the difference lies solely in external relations, and not in the intrinsic nature of the terms. For suppose that *one* as adjective differed from 1 as term. In this statement, *one* as adjective has been made into a term; hence either it has become 1, in which case the supposition is self-contradictory; or there is some other difference between *one* and 1 in addition to the fact that the first denotes a concept not a term while the second denotes a concept which is a term. But in this latter hypothesis, there must be propositions concerning *one* as term, and we shall still

[24]This proposition means "*A* is in this place at this time." It will be shown in Part VII that the relation expressed is not reducible to a two-term relation.

[25]I use *all men* as collective, *i.e.* as nearly synonymous with *the human race*, but differing therefrom by being many and not one. I shall always use *all* collectively, confining myself to *every* for the distributive sense. Thus I shall say "every man is mortal," not "all men are mortal."

have to maintain propositions concerning *one* as adjective as opposed to *one* as term; yet all such propositions must be false, since a proposition about *one* as adjective makes *one* the subject, and is therefore really about *one* as term. In short, if there were any adjectives which could not be made into substantives without change of meaning, all propositions concerning such adjectives (since they would necessarily turn them into substantives) would be false, and so would the proposition that all such propositions are false, since this itself turns the adjectives into substantives. But this state of things is self-contradictory.

The above argument proves that we were right in saying that terms embrace everything that can occur in a proposition, with the possible exception of complexes of terms of the kind denoted by *any* and cognate words.[26] For if *A* occurs in a proposition, then, in this statement, *A* is the subject; and we have just seen that, if *A* is ever not the subject, it is exactly and numerically the same *A* which is not subject in one proposition and is subject in another. Thus the theory that there are adjectives or attributes or ideal things, or whatever they may be called, which are in some way less substantial, less self-subsistent, less self-identical, than true substantives, appears to be wholly erroneous, and to be easily reduced to a contradiction. Terms which are concepts differ from those which are not, not in respect of self-subsistence, but in virtue of the fact that, in certain true or false propositions, they occur in a manner which is different in an indefinable way from the manner in which subjects or terms of relations occur.

50. Two concepts have, in addition to the numerical diversity which belongs to them as terms, another special kind of diversity which may be called conceptual. This may be characterized by the fact that two propositions in which the concepts occur otherwise than as terms, even if, in all other respects, the two propositions are identical, yet differ in virtue of the fact that the concepts which occur in them are conceptually diverse. Conceptual diversity implies numerical diversity, but the converse implication does not hold, since not all terms are concepts. Numerical diversity, as

[26]See the next chapter.

its name implies, is the source of plurality, and conceptual diversity is less important to mathematics. But the whole possibility of making different assertions about a given term or set of terms depends upon conceptual diversity, which is therefore fundamental in general logic.

51. It is interesting and not unimportant to examine very briefly the connection of the above doctrine of adjectives with certain traditional views on the nature of propositions. It is customary to regard all propositions as having a subject and a predicate, *i.e.* as having an immediate *this*, and a general concept attached to it by way of description. This is, of course, an account of the theory in question which will strike its adherents as extremely crude; but it will serve for a general indication of the view to be discussed. This doctrine develops by internal logical necessity into the theory of Mr Bradley's Logic, that all words stand for ideas having what he calls *meaning*, and that in every judgment there is a something, the true subject of the judgment, which is not an idea and does not have meaning. To have meaning, it seems to me, is a notion confusedly compounded of logical and psychological elemens. *Words* all have meaning, in the simple sense that they are symbols which stand for something other than themselves. But a proposition, unless it happens to be linguistic, does not itself contain words: it contains the entities indicated by words. Thus meaning, in the sense in which words have meaning, is irrelevant to logic. But such concepts as *a man* have meaning in another sense: they are, so to speak, symbolic in their own logical nature, because they have the property which I call *denoting*. That is to say, when *a man* occurs in a proposition (*e.g.* "I met a man in the street"), the proposition is not about the concept *a man*, but about something quite different, some actual biped denoted by the concept. Thus concepts of this kind have meaning in a non-psychological sense. And in this sense, when we say "this is a man," we are making a proposition in which a concept is in some sense attached to what is not a concept. But when meaning is thus understood, the entity indicated by *John* does not have meaning, as Mr Bradley contends; and even among concepts,

it is only those that denote that have meaning. The confusion is largely due, I believe, to the notion that *words* occur in propositions, which in turn is due to the notion that propositions are essentially mental and are to be identified with cognitions. But these topics of general philosophy must be pursued no further in this work.

52. It remains to discuss the verb, and to find marks by which it is distinguished from the adjective. In regard to verbs also, there is a twofold grammatical form corresponding to a difference in merely external relations. There is the verb in the form which it has as verb (the various inflexions of this form may be left out of account), and there is the verbal noun, indicated by the infinitive or (in English) the present participle. The distinction is that between "Felton killed Buckingham" and "Killing no murder." By analyzing this difference, the nature and function of the verb will appear.

It is plain, to begin with, that the concept which occurs in the verbal noun is the very same as that which occurs as verb. This results from the previous argument, that every constituent of every proposition must, on pain of self-contradiction, be capable of being made a logical subject. If we say "*kills* does not mean the same as *to kill*," we have already made *kills* a subject, and we cannot say that the concept expressed by the word *kills* cannot be made a subject. Thus the very verb which occurs as verb can occur also as subject. The question is: What logical difference is expressed by the difference of grammatical form? And it is plain that the difference must be one in external relations. But in regard to verbs, there is a further point. By transforming the verb, as it occurs in a proposition, into a verbal noun, the whole proposition can be turned into a single logical subject, no longer asserted, and no longer containing in itself truth or falsehood. But here too, there seems to be no possibility of maintaining that the logical subject which results is a different entity from the proposition. "Caesar died" and "the death of Caesar" will illustrate this point. If we ask: What is asserted in the proposition "Caesar died"? the answer must be "the death of Caesar is asserted." In that case, it would seem, it is the death

of Caesar which is true or false; and yet neither truth nor falsity belongs to a mere logical subject. The answer here seems to be that the death of Caesar has an external relation to truth or falsehood (as the case may be), whereas "Caesar died" in some way or other contains its own truth or falsehood as an element. But if this is the correct analysis, it is difficult to see how "Caesar died" differs from "the truth of Caesar's death" in the case where it is true, or "the falsehood of Caesar's death" in the other case. Yet it is quite plain that the latter, at any rate, is never equivalent to "Caesar died." There appears to be an ultimate notion of assertion, given by the verb, which is lost as soon as we substitute a verbal noun, and is lost when the proposition in question is made the subject of some other proposition. This does not depend upon grammatical form; for if I say "*Caesar died* is a proposition," I do not assert that Caesar did die, and an element which is present in "Caesar died" has disappeared. Thus the contradiction which was to have been avoided, of an entity which cannot be made a logical subject, appears to have here become inevitable. This difficulty, which seems to be inherent in the very nature of truth and falsehood, is one with which I do not know how to deal satisfactorily. The most obvious course would be to say that the difference between an asserted and an unasserted proposition is not logical, but psychological. In the sense in which false propositions may be asserted, this is doubtless true. But there is another sense of assertion, very difficult to bring clearly before the mind, and yet quite undeniable, in which only true propositions are asserted. True and false propositions alike are in some sense entities, and are in some sense capable of being logical subjects; but when a proposition happens to be true, it has a further quality, over and above that which it shares with false propositions, and it is this further quality which is what I mean by assertion in a logical as opposed to a psychological sense. The nature of truth, however, belongs no more to the principles of mathematics than to the principles of everything else. I therefore leave this question to the logicians with the above brief indication of a difficulty.

53. It may be asked whether everything

that, in the logical sense we are concerned with, is a verb, expresses a relation or not. It seems plain that, if we were right in holding that "Socrates is human" is a proposition having only one term, the *is* in this proposition cannot express a relation in the ordinary sense. In fact, subject-predicate propositions are distinguished by just this non-relational character. Nevertheless, a relation between Socrates and humanity is certainly *implied*, and it is very difficult to conceive the proposition as expressing no relation at all. We may perhaps say that it is a relation, although it is distinguished from other relations in that it does not permit itself to be regarded as an assertion concerning either of its terms indifferently, but only as an assertion concerning the referent. A similar remark may apply to the proposition "*A* is," which holds of every term without exception. The *is* here is quite different from the *is* in "Socrates is human;" it may be regarded as complex, and as really predicating Being of *A*. In this way, the true logical verb in a proposition may be always regarded as asserting a relation. But it is so hard to know exactly what is meant by *relation* that the whole question is in danger of becoming purely verbal.

54. The twofold nature of the verb, as actual verb and as verbal noun, may be expressed, if all verbs are held to be relations, as the difference between a relation in itself and a relation actually relating. Consider, for example, the proposition "*A* differs from *B*." The constituents of this proposition, if we analyze it, appear to be only *A*, difference, *B*. Yet these constituents, thus placed side by side, do not reconstitute the proposition. The difference which occurs in the proposition actually relates *A* and *B*, whereas the difference after analysis is a notion which has no connection with *A* and *B*. It may be said that we ought, in the analysis, to mention the relations which difference has to *A* and *B*, relations which are expressed by *is* and *from* when we say "*A* is different from *B*." These relations consist in the fact that *A* is referent and *B* relatum with respect to difference. But "*A*, referent, difference, relatum, *B*" is still merely a list of terms, not a proposition. A proposition, in fact, is essentially a unity, and when analysis has de-

stroyed the unity, no enumeration of constituents will restore the proposition. The verb, when used as a verb, embodies the unity of the proposition, and is thus distinguishable from the verb considered as a term, though I do not know how to give a clear account of the precise nature of the distinction.

55. It may be doubted whether the general concept *difference* occurs at all in the proposition "*A* differs from *B*," or whether there is not rather a specific difference of *A* and *B*, and another specific difference of *C* and *D*, which are respectively affirmed in "*A* differs from *B*" and "*C* differs from *D*." In this way, *difference* becomes a class-concept of which there are as many instances as there are pairs of different terms; and the instances may be said, in Platonic phrase, to partake of the nature of difference. As this point is quite vital in the theory of relations, it may be well to dwell upon it. And first of all, I must point out that in "*A* differs from *B*" I intend to consider the bare numerical difference in virtue of which they are two, not difference in this or that respect.

Let us first try the hypothesis that *a* difference is a complex notion, compounded of difference together with some special quality distinguishing a particular difference from every other particular difference. So far as the relation of difference itself is concerned, we are to suppose that no distinction can be made between different cases; but there are to be different associated qualities in different cases. But since cases are distinguished by their terms, the quality must be primarily associated with the terms, not with difference. If the quality be not a relation, it can have no special connection with the difference of *A* and *B*, which it was to render distinguishable from bare difference, and if it fails in this it becomes irrelevant. On the other hand, if it be a new relation between *A* and *B*, over and above difference, we shall have to hold that any two terms have two relations, difference and a specific difference, the latter not holding between any other pair of terms. This view is a combination of two others, of which the first holds that the abstract general relation of difference itself holds between *A* and *B*, while the second holds that when two terms differ they have, corresponding to this fact, a specific relation of difference, unique and unanalyzable and not shared by any other pair of terms. Either of these views may be held with either the denial or the affirmation of the other. Let us see what is to be said for and against them.

Against the notion of specific differences, it may be urged that, if differences differ, their differences from each other must also differ, and thus we are led into an endless process. Those who object to endless processes will see in this a proof that differences do not differ. But in the present work, it will be maintained that there are no contradictions peculiar to the notion of infinity, and that an endless process is not to be objected to unless it arises in the analysis of the actual meaning of a proposition. In the present case, the process is one of implications, not one of analysis; it must therefore be regarded as harmless.

Against the notion that the abstract relation of difference holds between A and B, we have the argument derived from the analysis of "A differs from B," which gave rise to the present discussion. It is to be observed that the hypothesis which combines the general and the specific difference must suppose that there are two distinct propositions, the one affirming the general, the other the specific difference. Thus if there cannot be a general difference between A and B, this mediating hypothesis is also impossible. And we saw that the attempt to avoid the failure of analysis by including in the *meaning* of "A differs from B" the relations of difference to A and B was vain. This attempt, in fact, leads to an endless process of the inadmissible kind; for we shall have to include the relations of the said relations to A and B and difference, and so on, and in this continually increasing complexity we are supposed to be only analyzing the *meaning* of our original proposition. This argument establishes a point of very great importance, namely, that when a relation holds between two terms, the relations of the relation to the terms, and of these relations to the relation and the terms, and so on *ad infinitum*, though all implied by the proposition affirming the original relation, form no part of the *meaning* of this proposition.

But the above argument does not suffice to prove that the relation of A to B cannot be abstract difference: it remains tenable that, as was suggested to begin with, the true solution lies in regarding every proposition as having a kind of unity which analysis cannot preserve, and which is lost even though it be mentioned by analysis as an element in the proposition. This view has doubtless its own difficulties, but the view that no two pairs of terms can have the same relation both contains difficulties of its own and fails to solve the difficulty for the sake of which it was invented. For, even if the difference of A and B be absolutely peculiar to A and B, still the three terms, A, B, difference of A from B, do not reconstitute the proposition "A differs from B," any more than A and B and difference did. And it seems plain that, even if differences did differ, they would still have to have something in common. But the most general way in which two terms can have something in common is by both having a given relation to a given term. Hence if no two pairs of terms can have the same relation, it follows that no two terms can have anything in common, and hence different differences will not be in any definable sense *instances* of difference.[27] I conclude, then, that the relation affirmed between A and B in the proposition "A differs from B" is the general relation of difference, and is precisely and numerically the same as the relation affirmed between C and D in "C differs from D." And this doctrine must be held, for the same reasons, to be true of all other relations; relations do not have instances, but are strictly the same in all propositions in which they occur.

We may now sum up the main points elicited in our discussion of the verb. The verb, we saw, is a concept which, like the adjective, may occur in a proposition without being one of the terms of the proposition, though it may also be made into a logical subject. One verb, and one only, must occur as verb in every proposition; but every proposition, by turning

[27]The above argument appears to prove that Mr Moore's theory of universals with numerically diverse instances in his paper on Identity (*Proceedings of the Aristotelian Society*, 1900–1901) must not be applied to all concepts. The relation of an instance to its universal, at any rate, must be actually and numerically the same in all cases where it occurs.

its verb into a verbal noun, can be changed into a single logical subject, of a kind which I shall call in future a propositional concept. Every verb, in the logical sense of the word, may be regarded as a relation; when it occurs as verb, it actually relates, but when it occurs as verbal noun it is the bare relation considered independently of the terms which it relates. Verbs do not, like adjectives, have instances, but are identical in all the cases of their occurrence. Owing to the way in which the verb actually relates the terms of a proposition, every proposition has a unity which renders it distinct from the sum of its constituents. All these points lead to logical problems, which, in a treatise on logic, would deserve to be fully and thoroughly discussed.

Having now given a general sketch of the nature of verbs and adjectives, I shall proceed, in the next two chapters, to discussions arising out of the consideration of adjectives, and in Chapter VII to topics connected with verbs. Broadly speaking, classes are connected with adjectives, while propositional functions involve verbs. It is for this reason that it has been necessary to deal at such length with a subject which might seem, at first sight, to be somewhat remote from the principles of mathematics.

Chapter V: Denoting

56. The notion of denoting, like most of the notions of logic, has been obscured hitherto by an undue admixture of psychology. There is a sense in which *we* denote, when we point or describe, or employ words as symbols for concepts; this, however, is not the sense that I wish to discuss. But the fact that description is possible—that we are able, by the employment of concepts, to designate a thing which is not a concept—is due to a logical relation between some concepts and some terms, in virtue of which such concepts inherently and logically *denote* such terms. It is this sense of denoting which is here in question. This notion lies at the bottom (I think) of all theories of substance, of the subject-predicate logic, and

of the opposition between things and ideas, discursive thought and immediate perception. These various developments, in the main, appear to be mistaken, while the fundamental fact itself, out of which they have grown, is hardly ever discussed in its logical purity.

A concept *denotes* when, if it occurs in a proposition, the proposition is not *about* the concept, but about a term connected in a certain peculiar way with the concept. If I say "I met a man," the proposition is not about *a man*: this is a concept which does not walk the streets, but lives in the shadowy limbo of the logic-books. What I met was a thing, not a concept, an actual man with a tailor and a bank-account or a public-house and a drunken wife. Again, the proposition "any finite number is odd or even" is plainly true; yet the *concept* "any finite number" is neither odd nor even. It is only particular numbers that are odd or even; there is not, in addition to these, another entity, *any number*, which is either odd or even, and if there were, it is plain that it could not be odd and could not be even. Of the *concept* "any number," almost all the propositions that contain the *phrase* "any number" are false. If we wish to speak of the concept, we have to indicate the fact by italics or inverted commas. People often assert that man is mortal; but what is mortal will die, and yet we should be surprised to find in the "Times" such a notice as the following: "Died at his residence of Camelot, Gladstone Road, Upper Tooting, on the 18th of June 19—, Man, eldest son of Death and Sin." *Man*, in fact, does not die; hence if "man is mortal" were, as it appears to be, a proposition about *man*, it would be simply false. The fact is the proposition is about men; and here again, it is not about the concept *men*, but about what this concept denotes. The whole theory of definition, of identity, of classes, of symbolism, and of the variable is wrapped up in the theory of denoting. The notion is a fundamental notion of logic, and, in spite of its difficulties, it is quite essential to be as clear about it as possible.

57. The notion of denoting may be obtained by a kind of logical genesis from subject-predicate propositions, upon which it

seems more or less dependent. The simplest of propositions are those in which one predicate occurs otherwise than as a term, and there is only one term of which the predicate in question is asserted. Such propositions may be called subject-predicate propositions. Instances are: *A* is, *A* is one, *A* is human. Concepts which are predicates might also be called class-concepts, because they give rise to classes, but we shall find it necessary to distinguish between the words *predicate* and *class-concept*. Propositions of the subject-predicate type always imply and are implied by other propositions of the type which asserts that an individual belongs to a class. Thus the above instances are equivalent to: *A* is an entity, *A* is a unit, *A* is a man. These new propositions are not identical with the previous ones, since they have an entirely different form. To begin with, *is* is now the only concept not used as a term. *A man*, we shall find, is neither a concept nor a term, but a certain kind of combination of certain terms, namely of those which are human. And the relation of Socrates to *a man* is quite different from his relation to humanity; indeed "Socrates is human" must be held, if the above view is correct, to be not, in the most usual sense, a judgment of relation between Socrates and humanity, since this view would make *human* occur as term in "Socrats is human." It is, of course, undeniable that a relation to humanity is implied by "Socrates is human," namely the relation expressed by "Socrates has humanity;" and this relation conversely implies the subject-predicate proposition. But the two propositions can be clearly distinguished, and it is important to the theory of classes that this should be done. Thus we have, in the case of every predicate, three types of propositions which imply one another, namely, "Socrates is human," "Socrates has humanity," and "Socrates is a man." The first contains a term and a predicate, the second two terms and a relation (the second term being identical with the predicate of the first proposition),[28] while the third contains a term, a relation, and what I shall call a disjunc-

tion (a term which will be explained shortly).[29] The class-concept differs little, if at all, from the predicate, while the class, as opposed to the class-concept, is the sum or conjunction of all the terms which have the given predicate. The relation which occurs in the second type (Socrates has humanity) is characterized completely by the fact that it implies and is implied by a proposition with only one term, in which the other term of the relation has become a predicate. A class is a certain combination of terms, a class-concept is closely akin to a predicate, and the terms whose combination forms the class are determined by the class-concept. Predicates are, in a certain sense, the simplest type of concepts, since they occur in the simplest type of proposition.

58. There is, connected with every predicate, a great variety of closely allied concepts, which, in so far as they are distinct, it is important to distinguish. Starting, for example, with *human,* we have man, men, all men, every man, any man, the human race, of which all except the first are twofold, a denoting concept and an object denoted; we have also, less closely analogous, the notions "a man" and "some man," which again denote objects[30] other than themselves. This vast apparatus connected with every predicate must be borne in mind, and an endeavour must be made to give an analysis of all the above notions. But for the present, it is the property of denoting, rather than the various denoting concepts, that we are concerned with.

The combination of concepts as such to form new concepts, of greater complexity than their constituents, is a subject upon which writers on logic have said many things. But the

[29]There are two allied propositions expressed by the same words, namely "Socrates is a-man" and "Socrates is-a man." The above remarks apply to the former; but in future, unless the contrary is indicated by a hyphen or otherwise, the latter will always be in question. The former expresses the identity of Socrates with an ambiguous individual; the latter expresses a relation of Socrates to the class-concept *man.*

[30]I shall use the word *object* in a wider sense than *term,* to cover both singular and plural, and also cases of ambiguity, such as "a man." The fact that a word can be framed with a wider meaning than *term* raises grave logical problems. Cf. § 47.

[28]Cf. § 49.

combination of terms as such, to form what by analogy may be called complex terms, is a subject upon which logicians, old and new, give us only the scantiest discussion. Nevertheless, the subject is of vital importance to the philosophy of mathematics, since the nature both of number and of the variable turns upon just this point. Six words, of constant occurrence in daily life, are also characteristic of mathematics: these are the words *all, every, any, a, some* and *the*. For correctness of reasoning, it is essential that these words should be sharply distinguished one from another; but the subjects bristles with difficulties, and is almost wholly neglected by logicians.

It is plain, to begin with, that a phrase containing one of the above six words always denotes. It will be convenient, for the present discussion, to distinguish a class-concept from a predicate: I shall call *human* a predicate, and *man* a class-concept, though the distinction is perhaps only verbal. The characteristic of a class-concept, as distinguished from terms in general, is that "x is a u" is a propositional function when, and only when, u is a class-concept. It must be held that when u is not a class-concept, we do not have a false proposition, but simply no proposition at all, whatever value we may give to x. This enables us to distinguish a class-concept belonging to the null-class, for which all propositions of the above form are false, from a term which is not a class-concept at all, for which there are no propositions of the above form. Also it makes it plain that a class-concept is not a term in the proposition "x is a u," for u has a restricted variability if the formula is to remain a proposition. A denoting phrase, we may now say, consists always of a class-concept preceded by one of the above six words or some synonym of one of them.

59. The question which first meets us in regard to denoting is this: Is there one way of denoting six different kinds of objects, or are the ways of denoting different? And in the latter case, is the object denoted the same in all six cases, or does the object differ as well as the way of denoting it? In order to answer this question, it will be first necessary to explain the differences between the six words in question. Here it will be convenient to omit the word *the* to begin with, since this word is in a different position from the others, and is liable to limitations from which they are exempt.

In cases where the class defined by a class-concept has only a finite number of terms, it is possible to omit the class-concept wholly, and indicate the various objects denoted by enumerating the terms and connecting them by means of *and* or *or* as the case may be. It will help to isolate a part of our problem if we first consider this case, although the lack of subtlety in language renders it difficult to grasp the difference between objects indicated by the same form of words.

Let us begin by considering two terms only, say Brown and Jones. The objects denoted by *all, every, any, a* and *some*[31] are respectively involved in the following five propositions. (1) Brown and Jones are two of Miss Smith's suitors; (2) Brown and Jones are paying court to Miss Smith; (3) if it was Brown or Jones you met, it was a very ardent lover; (4) if it was one of Miss Smith's suitors, it must have been Brown or Jones; (5) Miss Smith will marry Brown or Jones. Although only two forms of words, *Brown and Jones* and *Brown or Jones*, are involved in these propositions, I maintain that five different combinations are involved. The distinctions, some of which are rather subtle, may be brought out by the following considerations. In the first proposition, it is Brown *and* Jones who are two, and this is not true of either separately; nevertheless it is not the whole composed of Brown and Jones which is two, for this is only one. The two are a genuine combination of Brown with Jones, the kind of combination which, as we shall see in the next chapter, is characteristic of classes. In the second proposition, on the contrary, what is asserted is true of Brown and Jones severally; the proposition is equivalent to, though not (I think) identical with, "Brown is paying court to Miss Smith and Jones is paying court to Miss Smith." Thus the combination indicated by *and* is not the same here as in the first case: the first case concerned *all* of them collectively, while the second concerns *all* distributively, *i.e.*

[31] I intend to distinguish between *a* and *some* in a way not warranted by language; the distinction of *all* and *every* is also a straining of usage. Both are necessary to avoid circumlocution.

each or every one of them. For the sake of distinction, we may call the first a *numerical* conjunction, since it gives rise to number, the second a *propositional* conjunction, since the proposition in which it occurs is equivalent to a conjunction of propositions. (It should be observed that the conjunction of propositions in question is of a wholly different kind from any of the combinations we are considering, being in fact of the kind which is called the logical product. The propositions are combined *quâ* propositions, not *quâ* terms.)

The third proposition gives the kind of conjunction by which *any* is defined. There is some difficulty about this notion, which seems half-way between a conjunction and a disjunction. This notion may be further explained as follows. Let *a* and *b* be two different propositions, each of which implies a third proposition *c*. Then the disjunction "*a* or *b*" implies *c*. Now let *a* and *b* be propositions assigning the same predicate to two different subjects, then there is a combination of the two subjects to which the given predicate may be assigned so that the resulting proposition is equivalent to the disjunction "*a* or *b*." Thus suppose we have "if you met Brown, you met a very ardent lover," and "if you met Jones, you met a very ardent lover." Hence we infer "if you met Brown or if you met Jones, you met a very ardent lover," and we regard this as equivalent to "if you met Brown or Jones, etc." The combination of Brown and Jones here indicated is the same as that indicated by *either* of them. It differs from a disjunction by the fact that it implies and is implied by a statement concerning *both*; but in some more complicated instances, this mutual implication fails. The method of combination is, in fact, different from that indicated by *both*, and is also different from both forms of disjunction. I shall call it the *variable* conjunction. The first form of disjunction is given by (4): this is the form which I shall denote by *a* suitor. Here, although it must have been Brown or Jones, it is not true that it must have been Brown, nor yet that it must have been Jones. Thus the proposition is not equivalent to the disjunction of propositions "it must have been Brown or it must have been Jones." The proposition, in fact, is not capable of statement either as a

disjunction or as a conjunction of propositions, except in the very roundabout form: "if it was not Brown, it was Jones, and if it was not Jones, it was Brown," a form which rapidly becomes intolerable when the number of terms is increased beyond two, and becomes theoretically inadmissible when the number of terms is infinite. Thus this form of disjunction denotes a variable term, that is, whichever of the two terms we fix upon, it does not denote this term, and yet it does denote one or other of them. This form accordingly I shall call the *variable* disjunction. Finally, the second form of disjunction is given by (5). This is what I shall call the *constant* disjunction, since here either Brown is denoted, or Jones is denoted, but the alternative is undecided. That is to say, our proposition is now equivalent to a disjunction of propositions, namely "Miss Smith will marry Brown, or she will marry Jones." She will marry *some* one of the two, and the disjunction denotes a particular one of them, though it may denote either particular one. Thus all the five combinations are distinct.

It is to be observed that these five combinations yield neither terms nor concepts, but strictly and only combinations of terms. The first yields many terms, while the others yield something absolutely peculiar, which is neither one nor many. The combinations are combinations of terms, effected without the use of relations. Corresponding to each combination there is, at least if the terms combined form a class, a perfectly definite concept, which *denotes* the various terms of the combination combined in the specified manner. To explain this, let us repeat our distinctions in a case where the terms to be combined are not enumerated, as above, but are defined as the terms of a certain class.

60. When a class-concept *a* is given, it must be held that the various terms belonging to the class are also given. That is to say, any term being proposed, it can be decided whether or not it belongs to the class. In this way, a collection of terms can be given otherwise than by enumeration. Whether a collection can be given otherwise than by enumeration or by a class-concept, is a question which, for the present, I leave undetermined. But the possibility of giving a collection by a class-concept is

highly important, since it enables us to deal with infinite collections, as we shall see in Part V. For the present, I wish to examine the meaning of such phrases as *all a's*, *every a*, *any a*, *an a*, and *some a*. All *a's*, to begin with, denotes a numerical conjunction; it is definite as soon as *a* is given. The concept *all a's* is a perfectly definite single concept, which denotes the terms of *a* taken all together. The terms so taken have a number, which may thus be regarded, if we choose, as a property of the class-concept, since it is determinate for any given class-concept. *Every a*, on the contrary, though it still denotes all the *a's*, denotes them in a different way, *i.e.* severally instead of collectively. *Any a* denotes only one *a*, but it is wholly irrelevant which it denotes, and what is said will be equally true whichever it may be. Moreover, *any a* denotes a variable *a*, that is, whatever particular *a* we may fasten upon, it is certain that *any a* does not denote that one; and yet of that one any proposition is true which is true of any *a*. *An a* denotes a variable disjunction: that is to say, a proposition which holds of *an a* may be false concerning each particular *a*, so that it is not reducible to a disjunction of propositions. For example, a point lies between any point and any other point; but it would not be true of any one particular point that it lay between any point and any other point, since there would be many pairs of points between which it did not lie. This brings us finally to *some a*, the constant disjunction. This denotes just one term of the class *a*, but the term it denotes may be any term of the class. Thus "some moment does not follow any moment" would mean that there was a first moment in time, while "a moment precedes any moment" means the exact opposite, namely, that every moment has predecessors.

61. In the case of a class *a* which has a finite number of terms—say $a_1, a_2, a_3, \ldots a_n$, we can illustrate these various notions as follows:

(1) *All a's* denotes a_1 and a_2 and ... and a_n.

(2) *Every a* denotes a_1 and denotes a_2 and ... and denotes a_n.

(3) *Any a* denotes a_1 or a_2 or ... a_n, where *or* has the meaning that it is irrelevant which we take.

(4) *An a* denotes a_1, or a_2, or ... or a_n, where *or* has the meaning that no one in particular must be taken, just as in *all a's* we must not take any one in particular.

(5) *Some a* denotes a_1 or denotes a_2 or ... or denotes a_n, where it is not irrelevant which is taken, but on the contrary some one particular *a* must be taken.

As the nature and properties of the various ways of combining terms are of vital importance to the principles of mathematics, it may be well to illustrate their properties by the following important examples.

(**α**) Let *a* be a class, and *b* a class of classes. We then obtain in all six possible relations of *a* to *b* from various combinations of *any*, *a* and *some*. *All* and *every* do not, in this case, introduce anything new. The six cases are as follows.

(1) Any *a* belongs to any class belonging to *b*, in other words, the class *a* is wholly contained in the common part or logical product of the various classes belonging to *b*.

(2) Any *a* belongs to a *b*, *i.e.* the class *a* is contained in any class which contains all the *b's*, or, is contained in the logical sum of all the *b's*.

(3) Any *a* belongs to some *b*, *i.e.* there is a class belonging to *b*, in which the class *a* is contained. The difference between this case and the second arises from the fact that here there is one *b* to which every *a* belongs, whereas before it was only decided that every *a* belonged to a *b*, and different *a's* might belong to different *b's*.

(4) An *a* belongs to any *b*, *i.e.* whatever *b* we take, it has a part in common with *a*.

(5) An *a* belongs to a *b*, *i.e.* there is a *b* which has a part in common with *a*. This is equivalent to "some (or an) *a* belongs to some *b*."

(6) Some *a* belongs to any *b*, *i.e.* there is an *a* which belongs to the common part of all the *b's*, or *a* and all the *b's* have a common part. These are all the cases that arise here.

(**β**) It is instructive, as showing the generality of the type of relations here considered, to compare the above case with the following. Let *a*, *b* be two series of real numbers; then six precisely analogous cases arise.

(1) Any *a* is less than any *b*, or, the series *a* is contained among numbers less than every *b*.

(2) Any *a* is less than a *b*, or, whatever *a* we

take, there is a *b* which is greater, or, the series *a* is contained among numbers less than a (variable) term of the series *b*. It does not follow that some term of the series *b* is greater than all the *a*'s.

(3) Any *a* is less than some *b*, or, there is a term of *b* which is greater than all the *a*'s. This case is not to be confounded with (2).

(4) An *a* is less than any *b*, *i.e.* whatever *b* we take, there is an *a* which is less than it.

(5) An *a* is less than a *b*, *i.e.* it is possible to find an *a* and a *b* such that the *a* is less than the *b*. This merely denies that any *a* is greater than any *b*.

(6) Some *a* is less than any *b*, *i.e.* there is an *a* which is less than all the *b*'s. This was not implied in (4), where the *a* was variable, whereas here it is constant.

In this case, actual mathematics have compelled the distinction between the variable and the constant disjunction. But in other cases, where mathematics have not obtained sway, the distinction has been neglected; and the mathematicians, as was natural, have not investigated the logical nature of the disjunctive notions which they employed.

(*γ*) I shall give one other instance, as it brings in the difference between *any* and *every*, which has not been relevant in the previous cases. Let *a* and *b* be two classes of classes; then twenty different relations between them arise from different combinations of the terms of their terms. The following technical terms will be useful. If *a* be a class of classes, its logical sum consists of all terms belonging to any *a*, *i.e.* all terms such that there is an *a* to which they belong, while its logical product consists of all terms belonging to every *a*, *i.e.* to the common part of all the *a*'s. We have then the following cases.

(1) Any term of any *a* belongs to every *b*, *i.e.* the logical sum of *a* is contained in the logical product of *b*.

(2) Any term of any *a* belongs to a *b*, *i.e.* the logical sum of *a* is contained in the logical sum of *b*.

(3) Any term of any *a* belongs to some *b*, *i.e.* there is a *b* which contains the logical sum of *a*.

(4) Any term of some (or an) *a* belongs to every *b*, *i.e.* there is an *a* which is contained in the product of *b*.

(5) Any term of some (or an) *a* belongs to a *b*, *i.e.* there is an *a* which is contained in the sum of *b*.

(6) Any term of some (or an) *a* belongs to some *b*, *i.e.* there is a *b* which contains one class belonging to *a*.

(7) A term of any *a* belongs to any *b*, *i.e.* any class of *a* and any class of *b* have a common part.

(8) A term of any *a* belongs to a *b*, *i.e.* any class of *a* has a part in common with the logical sum of *b*.

(9) A term of any *a* belongs to some *b*, *i.e.* there is a *b* with which any *a* has a part in common.

(10) A term of an *a* belongs to every *b*, *i.e.* the logical sum of *a* and the logical product of *b* have a common part.

(11) A term of an *a* belongs to any *b*, *i.e.* given any *b*, an *a* can be found with which it has a common part.

(12) A term of an *a* belongs to a *b*, *i.e.* the logical sums of *a* and of *b* have a common part.

(13) Any terms of every *a* belongs to every *b*, *i.e.* the logical product of *a* is contained in the logical product of *b*.

(14) Any term of every *a* belongs to a *b*, *i.e.* the logical product of *a* is contained in the logical sum of *b*.

(15) Any term of every *a* belongs to some *b*, *i.e.* there is a term of *b* in which the logical product of *a* is contained.

(16) A (or some) term of every *a* belongs to every *b*, *i.e.* the logical products of *a* and of *b* have a common part.

(17) A (or some) term of every *a* belongs to a *b*, *i.e.* the logical product of *a* and the logical sum of *b* have a common part.

(18) Some term of any *a* belongs to every *b*, *i.e.* any *a* has a part in common with the logical product of *b*.

(19) A term of some *a* belongs to any *b*, *i.e.* there is some term of *a* with which any *b* has a common part.

(20) A term of every *a* belongs to any *b*, *i.e.* any *b* has a part in common with the logical product of *a*.

The above examples show that, although it may often happen that there is a mutual implication (which has not always been stated) of corresponding propositions concerning *some* and *a*, or concerning *any* and *every*, yet in other cases there is no such mutual implication. Thus the five notions discussed in the present chapter are genuinely distinct, and to confound them may lead to perfectly definite fallacies.

62. It appears from the above discussion that, whether there are different ways of denoting or not, the objects denoted by *all men, every man*, etc. are certainly distinct. It seems therefore legitimate to say that the whole difference lies in the objects, and that denoting itself is the same in all cases. There are, however, many difficult problems connected with the subject, especially as regards the nature of the objects denoted. *All men*, which I shall identify with the class of men, seems to be an unambiguous object, although grammatically it is plural. But in the other cases the question is not so simple: we may doubt whether an ambiguous object is unambiguously denoted, or a definite object ambiguously denoted. Consider again the proposition "I met a man." It is quite certain, and is implied by this proposition, that what I met was an unambiguous perfectly definite man: in the technical language which is here adopted, the proposition is expressed by "I met some man." But the actual man whom I met forms no part of the proposition in question, and is not specially denoted by *some man*. Thus the concrete event which happened is not asserted in the proposition. What is asserted is merely that some one of a class of concrete events took place. The whole human race is involved in my assertion: if any man who ever existed or will exist had not existed or been going to exist, the purport of my proposition would have been different. Or, to put the same point in more intensional language, if I substitute for *man* any of the other class-concepts applicable to the individual whom I had the honour to meet, my proposition is changed, although the individual in question is just as much denoted as before. What this proves is, that *some man* must not be regarded as actually denoting Smith and actually denoting Brown, and so on: the whole procession of human beings throughout the ages is always relevant to every proposition in which *some man* occurs, and what is denoted is essentially not each separate man, but a kind of combination of all men. This is more evident in the case of *every, any*, and *a*. There is, then, a definite something, different in each of the five cases, which must, in a sense, be an object, but is characterized as a set of terms combined in a certain way, which something is denoted by *all men, every man, any man, a man* or *some man*; and it is with this very paradoxical object that propositions are concerned in which the corresponding concept is used as denoting.

63. It remains to discuss the notion of *the*. This notion has been symbolically emphasized by Peano, with very great advantage to his calculus; but here it is to be discussed philosophically. The use of identity and the theory of definition are dependent upon this notion, which has thus the very highest philosophical importance.

The word *the*, in the singular, is correctly employed only in relation to a class-concept of which there is only one instance. We speak of *the* King, *the* Prime Minister, and so on (understanding *at the present time*); and in such cases there is a method of denoting one single definite term by means of a concept, which is not given us by any of our other five words. It is owing to this notion that mathematics can give definitions of terms which are not concepts—a possibility which illustrates the difference between mathematical and philosophical definition. Every term is the only instance of *some* class-concept, and thus every term, theoretically, is capable of definition, provided we have not adopted a system in which the said term is one of our indefinables. It is a curious paradox, puzzling to the symbolic mind, that definitions, theoretically, are nothing but statements of symbolic abbreviations, irrelevant to the reasoning and inserted only for practical convenience, while yet, in the development of a subject, they always require a very large amount of thought, and often embody some of the greatest achievements of analysis. This fact seems to be explained by the theory of denoting. An object may be present to the mind, without our knowing any concept of which the said object is *the* instance; and the discovery of such a concept is not a mere improvement in notation. The reason why this appears to be the case is that, as soon as the definition is found, it becomes wholly unnecessary to the reasoning to remember the actual object defined, since only concepts are relevant to our deductions. In the moment of discovery, the definition is seen to be *true*, because the object to be defined was already in our thoughts; but as part of our reasoning it is not true, but merely symbolic, since what the reasoning requires is not that it should deal with *that* object, but merely that it should deal with the object denoted by the definition.

In most actual definitions of mathematics, what is defined is a *class* of entities, and the notion of *the* does not then explicitly appear. But even in this case, what is really defined is *the* class satisfying certain conditions; for a class, as we shall see in the next chapter, is always a term or conjunction of terms and never a concept. Thus the notion of *the* is always relevant in definitions; and we may observe generally that the adequacy of concepts to deal with things is wholly dependent upon the unambiguous denoting of a single term which this notion gives.

64. The connection of denoting with the nature of identity is important, and helps, I think, to solve some rather serious problems. The question whether identity is or is not a relation, and even whether there is such a concept at all, is not easy to answer. For, it may be said, identity cannot be a relation, since, where it is truly asserted, we have only one term, whereas two terms are required for a relation. And indeed identity, an objector may urge, cannot be anything at all: two terms plainly are not identical, and one term cannot be, for what is it identical with? Nevertheless identity must be something. We might attempt to remove identity from terms to relations, and say that two terms are identical in some respect when they have a given relation to a given term. But then we shall have to hold either that there is strict identity between the two cases of the given relation, or that the two cases have identity in the sense of having a given relation to a given term; but the latter view leads to an endless process of the illegitimate kind. Thus identity must be admitted, and the difficulty as to the two terms of a relation must be met by a sheer denial that two different terms are necessary. There must always be a referent and a relatum, but these need not be distinct; and where identity is affirmed, they are not so.[32]

But the question arises: Why is it ever worth while to affirm identity? This question is answered by the theory of denoting. If we say "Edward VII is the King," we assert an identity; the reason why this assertion is worth making is, that in the one case the actual term occurs, while in the other a denoting concept takes its place. (For purposes of discussion, I ignore the fact that Edwards form a class, and that seventh Edwards form a class having only one term. Edward VII is practically, though not formally, a proper name.) Often two denoting concepts occur, and the term itself is not mentioned, as in the proposition "the present Pope is the last survivor of his generation." When a term is given, the assertion of its identity with itself, though true, is perfectly futile, and is never made outside the logic-books; but where denoting concepts are introduced, identity is at once seen to be significant. In this case, of course, there is involved, though not asserted, a relation of the denoting concept to the term, or of the two denoting concepts to each other. But the *is* which occurs in such propositions does not itself state this further relation, but states pure identity.[33]

65. To sum up. When a class-concept, preceded by one of the six words *all, every, any, a, some, the,* occurs in a proposition, the proposition is, as a rule, not *about* the concept formed of the two words together, but about an object quite different from this, in general not a concept at all, but a term or complex of terms. This may be seen by the fact that propositions

[32]On relations of terms to themselves, *v. inf.* Chap. IX, § 95.

[33]The word *is* is terribly ambiguous, and great care is necessary in order not to confound its various meanings. We have (1) the sense in which it asserts Being, as in "*A* is"; (2) the sense of identity; (3) the sense of predication, in "*A* is human"; (4) the sense of "*A* is a-man" (cf. p. 54, note), which is very like identity. In addition to these there are less common uses, as "to be good is to be happy," where a relation of assertions is meant, that relation, in fact, which, where it exists, gives rise to formal implication. Doubtless there are further meanings which have not occurred to me. On the meanings of *is*, cf. De Morgan, *Formal Logic*, pp. 49, 50.

in which such concepts occur are in general false concerning the concepts themselves. At the same time, it is possible to consider and make propositions about the concepts themselves, but these are not the natural propositions to make in employing the concepts. "Any number is odd or even" is a perfectly natural proposition, whereas "*Any number* is a variable conjunction" is a proposition only to be made in a logical discussion. In such cases, we say that the concept in question *denotes*. We decided that denoting is a perfectly definite relation, the same in all six cases, and that it is the nature of the denoted object and the denoting concept which distinguishes the cases. We discussed at some length the nature and the differences of the denoted objects in the five cases in which these objects are combinations of terms. In a full discussion, it would be necessary also to discuss the denoting concepts: the actual meanings of these concepts, as opposed to the nature of the objects they denote, have not been discussed above. But I do not know that there would be anything further to say on this topic. Finally, we discussed *the*, and showed that this notion is essential to what mathematics calls definition, as well as to the possibility of uniquely determining a term by means of concepts; the actual use of identity, though not its meaning, was also found to depend upon this way of denoting a single term. From this point we can advance to the discussion of classes, thereby continuing the development of the topics connected with adjectives.

Chapter VI: Classes

66. To bring clearly before the mind what is meant by *class,* and to distinguish this notion from all the notions to which it is allied, is one of the most difficult and important problems of mathematical philosophy. Apart from the fact that *class* is a very fundamental concept, the utmost care and nicety is required in this subject on account of the contradiction to be discussed in Chapter X. I must ask the reader, therefore, not to regard as idle pedantry the apparatus of somewhat subtle discriminations to be found in what follows.

It has been customary, in works on logic, to distinguish two stand-points, that of extension and that of intension. Philosophers have usually regarded the latter as more fundamental, while Mathematics has been held to deal specially with the former. M. Couturat, in his admirable work on Leibniz, states roundly that Symbolic Logic can only be built up from the standpoint of extension; and if there really were only these two points of view, his statement would be justified. But as a matter of fact, there are positions intermediate between pure intension and pure extension, and it is in these intermediate regions that Symbolic Logic has its lair. It is essential that the classes with which we are concerned should be composed of terms, and should not be predicates or concepts, for a class must be definite when its terms are given, but in general there will be many predicates which attach to the given terms and to no others. We cannot of course attempt an intensional definition of a class as the class of predicates attaching to the terms in question and to no others, for this would involve a vicious circle; hence the point of view of extension is to some extent unavoidable. On the other hand, if we take extension pure, our class is defined by enumeration of its terms, and this method will not allow us to deal, as Symbolic Logic does, with infinite classes. Thus our classes must in general be regarded as objects denoted by concepts, and to this extent the point of view of intension is essential. It is owing to this consideration that the theory of denoting is of such great importance. In the present chapter we have to specify the precise degree in which extension and intension respectively enter into the definition and employment of classes; and throughout the discussion, I must ask the reader to remember that whatever is said has to be applicable to infinite as well as to finite classes.

67. When an object is unambiguously denoted by a concept, I shall speak of the concept as a concept (or sometimes, loosely, as *the* concept) of the object in question. Thus it will be necessary to distinguish the concept of a class from a class-concept. We agreed to call

man a class-concept, but *man* does not, in its usual employment, denote anything. On the other hand, *men* and *all men* (which I shall regard as synonyms) do denote, and I shall contend that what they denote is the class composed of all men. Thus *man* is the class-concept, *men* (the concept) is the concept of the class, and men (the object denoted by the concept *men*) are the class. It is no doubt confusing, at first, to use *class-concept* and *concept of a class* in different senses; but so many distinctions are required that some straining of language seems unavoidable. In the phraseology of the preceding chapter, we may say that a class is a numerical conjunction of terms. This is the thesis which is to be established.

68. In Chapter II we regarded classes as derived from assertions, *i.e.* as all the entities satisfying some assertion, whose form was left wholly vague. I shall discuss this view critically in the next chapter; for the present, we may confine ourselves to classes as they are derived from predicates, leaving open the question whether every assertion is equivalent to a predication. We may, then, imagine a kind of genesis of classes, through the successive stages indicated by the typical propositions "Socrates is human," "Socrates has humanity," "Socrates is a man," "Socrates is one among men." Of these propositions, the last only, we should say, explicitly contains the class as a constituent; but every subject-predicate proposition gives rise to the other three equivalent propositions, and thus every predicate (provided it can be sometimes truly predicated) gives rise to a class. This is the genesis of classes from the intensional standpoint.

On the other hand, when mathematicians deal with what they call a manifold, aggregate, *Menge, ensemble,* or some equivalent name, it is common, especially where the number of terms involved is finite, to regard the object in question (which is in fact a class) as defined by the enumeration of its terms, and as consisting possibly of a single term, which in that case *is* the class. Here it is not predicates and denoting that are relevant, but terms connected by the word *and,* in the sense in which this word stands for a *numerical* conjunction. Thus Brown and Jones are a class, and Brown singly is a class. This is the extensional genesis of classes.

69. The best formal treatment of classes in existence is that of Peano. But in this treatment a number of distinctions of great philosophical importance are overlooked. Peano, not I think quite consciously, identifies the class with the class-concept; thus the relation of an individual to its class is, for him, expressed by *is a.* For him, "2 is a number" is a proposition in which a term is said to belong to the class *number.* Nevertheless, he identifies the equality of classes, which consists in their having the same terms, with identity—a proceeding which is quite illegitimate when the class is regarded as the class-concept. In order to perceive that *man* and *featherless biped* are not identical, it is quite unnecessary to take a hen and deprive the poor bird of its feathers. Or, to take a less complex instance, it is plain that *even prime* is not identical with *integer next after* 1. Thus when we identify the class with the class-concept, we must admit that two classes may be equal without being identical. Nevertheless, it is plain that when two class-concepts are equal, some identity is involved, for we say that they have the *same* terms. Thus there is some object which is positively identical when two class-concepts are equal; and this object, it would seem, is more properly called the class. Neglecting the plucked hen, the class of featherless bipeds, every one would say, is the *same* as the class of men; the class of even primes is the *same* as the class of integers next after 1. Thus we must not identify the class with the class-concept, or regard "Socrates is a man" as expressing the relation of an individual to a class of which it is a member. This has two consequences (to be established presently) which prevent the philosophical acceptance of certain points in Peano's formalism. The first consequence is, that there is no such thing as the null-class, though there are null class-concepts. The second is, that a class having only one term is to be identified, contrary to Peano's usage, with that one term. I should not propose, however, to alter his practice or his notation in consequence of either of these points; rather I should regard them as proofs that Symbolic Logic ought to concern itself, as

far as notation goes, with class-concepts rather than with classes.

70. A class, we have seen, is neither a predicate nor a class-concept, for different predicates and different class-concepts may correspond to the same class. A class also, in one sense at least, is distinct from the whole composed of its terms, for the latter is only and essentially one, while the former, where it has many terms, is, as we shall see later, the very kind of object of which *many* is to be asserted. The distinction of a class as many from a class as a whole is often made by language: space and points, time and instants, the army and the soldiers, the navy and the sailors, the Cabinet and the Cabinet Ministers, all illustrate the distinction. The notion of a whole, in the sense of a pure aggregate which is here relevant, is, we shall find, not always applicable where the notion of the class as many applies (see Chapter X). In such cases, though terms may be said to belong to the class, the class must not be treated as itself a single logical subject.[34] But this case never arises where a class can be generated by a predicate. Thus we may for the present dismiss this complication from our minds. In a class as many, the component terms, though they have some kind of unity, have less than is required for a whole. They have, in fact, just so much unity as is required to make them many, and not enough to prevent them from remaining many. A further reason for distinguishing wholes from classes as many is that a class as one may be one of the terms of itself as many, as in "classes are one among classes" (the extensional equivalent of "class is a class-concept"), whereas a complex whole can never be one of its own constituents.

71. *Class* may be defined either extensionally or intensionally. That is to say, we may define the kind of object which is a class, or the kind of concept which denotes a class: this is the precise meaning of the opposition of extension and intension in this connection. But although the general notion can be defined in this two-fold manner, particular classes, ex-

cept when they happen to be finite, can only be defined intensionally, *i.e.* as the objects denoted by such and such concepts. I believe this distinction to be purely psychological: logically, the extensional definition appears to be equally applicable to infinite classes, but practically, if we were to attempt it, Death would cut short our laudable endeavour before it had attained its goal. Logically, therefore, extension and intension seem to be on a par. I will begin with the extensional view.

When a class is regarded as defined by the enumeration of its terms, it is more naturally called a *collection*. I shall for the moment adopt this name, as it will not prejudge the question whether the objects denoted by it are truly classes or not. By a collection I mean what is conveyed by "A and B" or "A and B and C," or any other enumeration of definite terms. The collection is defined by the actual mention of the terms, and the terms are connected by *and*. It would seem that *and* represents a fundamental way of combining terms, and that just this way of combination is essential if anything is to result of which a number other than 1 can be asserted. Collections do not presuppose numbers, since they result simply from the terms together with *and*: they could only presuppose numbers in the particular case where the terms of the collection themselves presupposed numbers. There is a grammatical difficulty which, since no method exists of avoiding it, must be pointed out and allowed for. A collection, grammatically, is singular, whereas A and B, A and B and C, etc. are essentially plural. This grammatical difficulty arises from the logical fact (to be discussed presently) that whatever is many in general forms a whole which is one; it is, therefore, not removable by a better choice of technical terms.

The notion of *and* was brought into prominence by Bolzano. In order to understand what infinity is, he says, "we must go back to one of the simplest conceptions of our understanding, in order to reach an agreement concerning the word that we are to use to denote it. This is the conception which underlies the conjunction *and,* which, however, if it is to stand out as clearly as is required, in many

---

[34] A plurality of terms is not the logical subject when a number is asserted of it: such propositions have not one subject, but many subjects. See end of § 74.

cases, both by the purposes of mathematics and by those of philosophy, I believe to be best expressed by the words: 'A system (*Inbegriff*) of certain things,' or 'a whole consisting of certain parts.' But we must add that every arbitrary object *A* can be combined in a system with any others *B, C, D, . . .* , or (speaking still more correctly) already forms a system by itself,[35] of which some more or less important truth can be enunciated, provided only that each of the presentations *A, B, C, D, . . .* in fact represents a *different* object, or in so far as none of the propositions '*A* is the same as *B*,' '*A* is the same as *C*,' '*A* is the same as *D*,' etc., is true. For if *e.g. A* is the same as *B*, then it is certainly unreasonable to speak of a system of the things *A* and *B*."

The above passage, good as it is, neglects several distinctions which we have found necessary. First and foremost, it does not distinguish the many from the whole which they form. Secondly, it does not appear to observe that the method of enumeration is not practically applicable to infinite systems. Thirdly, and this is connected with the second point, it does not make any mention of intensional definition nor of the notion of a class. What we have to consider is the difference, if any, of a class from a collection on the one hand, and from the whole formed of the collection on the other. But let us first examine further the notion of *and*.

Anything of which a finite number other than 0 or 1 can be asserted would be commonly said to be many, and many, it might be said, are always of the form "*A* and *B* and *C* and . . . ." Here *A, B, C, . . .* are each one and are all different. To say that *A* is one seems to amount to much the same as to say that *A* is not of the form "*A*₁ and *A*₂ and *A*₃ and . . . ." To say that *A, B, C, . . .* are all different seems to amount only to a condition as regards the symbols: it should be held that "*A* and *A*" is meaningless, so that diversity is implied by *and,* and need not be specially stated.

A term *A* which is one may be regarded as a particular case of a collection, namely as a collection of one term. Thus every collection which is many presupposes many collections

which are each one: *A and B* presupposes *A* and presupposes *B*. Conversely some collections of one term presuppose many, namely those which are complex: thus "*A* differs from *B*" is one, but presupposes *A and difference and B*. But there is not symmetry in this respect, for the ultimate presuppositions of anything are always simple terms.

Every pair of terms, without exception, can be combined in the manner indicated by *A and B*, and if neither *A* nor *B* be many, then *A* and *B* are two. *A* and *B* may be any conceivable entities, any possible objects of thought, they may be points or numbers or true or false propositions or events or people, in short anything that can be counted. A teaspoon and the number 3, or a chimaera and a four-dimensional space, are certainly two. Thus no restriction whatever is to be placed on *A* and *B*, except that neither is to be many. It should be observed that *A* and *B* need not exist, but must, like anything that can be mentioned, have Being. The distinction of Being and existence is important, and is well illustrated by the process of counting. What can be counted must be something, and must certainly *be*, though it need by no means be possessed of the further privilege of existence. Thus what we demand of the terms of our collection is merely that each should be an entity.

The question may now be asked: What is meant by *A and B*? Does this mean anything more than the juxtaposition of *A* with *B*? That is, does it contain any element over and above that of *A* and that of *B*? Is *and* a separate concept, which occurs besides *A, B*? To either answer there are objections. In the first place, *and,* we might suppose, cannot be a new concept, for if it were, it would have to be some kind of relation between *A* and *B*; *A and B* would then be a proposition, or at least a propositional concept, and would be one, not two. Moreover, if there are two concepts, there *are* two, and no third mediating concept seems necessary to make them two. Thus *and* would seem meaningless. But it is difficult to maintain this theory. To begin with, it seems rash to hold that any word is meaningless. When we use the word *and*, we do not seem to be uttering mere idle breath, but some idea seems to correspond to the word. Again some kind of

---

[35]*i.e.* the combination of *A* with *B, C, D, . . .* already forms a system.

combination seems to be implied by the fact that A and B are two, which is not true of either separately. When we say "A and B are yellow," we can replace the proposition by "A is yellow" and "B is yellow"; but this cannot be done for "A and B are two"; on the contrary, A is *one* and B is *one*. Thus it seems best to regard *and* as expressing a definite unique kind of combination, not a relation, and not combining A and B into a whole, which would be one. This unique kind of combination will in future be called *addition of individuals*. It is important to observe that it applies to terms, and only applies to numbers in consequence of their being terms. Thus for the present, 1 and 2 are two, and 1 and 1 is meaningless.

As regards what is meant by the combination indicated by *and*, it is indistinguishable from what we before called a numerical conjunction. That is, A and B is what is denoted by the concept of a class of which A and B are the only members. If u be a class-concept of which the propositions "A is a u" "B is a u" are true, but of which all other propositions of the same form are false, then "all u's" is the concept of a class whose only terms are A and B; this concept *denotes* the terms A, B combined in a certain way, and "A and B" *are* those terms combined in just that way. Thus "A and B" are the class, but are distinct from the class-concept and from the concept of the class.

The notion of *and*, however, does not enter into the *meaning* of a class, for a single term is a class, although it is not a numerical conjunction. If u be a class-concept, and only one proposition of the form "x is a u" be true, than "all u's" is a concept denoting a single term, and this term is the class of which "all u's" is a concept. Thus what seems essential to a class is not the notion of *and*, but the being denoted by some concept of a class. This brings us to the intensional view of classes.

72. We agreed in the preceding chapter that there are not different ways of denoting, but only different kinds of denoting concepts and correspondingly different kinds of denoted objects. We have discussed the kind of denoted object which constitutes a class; we have now to consider the kind of denoting concept.

The consideration of classes which results from denoting concepts is more general than the extensional consideration, and that in two respects. In the first place it allows, what the other *practically* excludes, the admission of infinite classes; in the second place it introduces the null concept of a class. But, before discussing these matters, there is a purely logical point of some importance to be examined.

If u be a class-concept, is the concept "all u's" analyzable into two constituents, *all* and *u*, or is it a new concept, defined by a certain relation to u, and no more complex than u itself? We may observe, to begin with, that "all u's" is synonymous with "u's," at least according to a very common use of the plural. Our question is, then, as to the meaning of the plural. The word *all* has certainly some definite meaning, but it seems highly doubtful whether it means more than the indication of a relation. "All men" and "all numbers" have in common the fact that they both have a certain relation to a class-concept, namely to *man* and *number* respectively. But it is very difficult to isolate any further element of *all-ness* which both share, unless we take as this element the mere fact that both are concepts of classes. It would seem, then, that "all u's" is not validly analyzable into *all* and *u*, and that language, in this case as in some others, is a misleading guide. The same remark will apply to *every, any, some, a,* and *the*.

It might perhaps be thought that a class ought to be considered, not merely as a numerical conjunction of terms, but as a numerical conjunction denoted by the concept of a class. This complication, however, would serve no useful purpose, except to preserve Peano's distinction between a single term and the class whose only term it is—a distinction which is easy to grasp when the class is identified with the class-concept, but which is inadmissible in our view of classes. It is evident that a numerical conjunction considered as denoted is either the same entity as when not so considered, or else is a complex of denoting together with the object denoted; and the object denoted is plainly what we mean by a class.

With regard to infinite classes, say the class of numbers, it is to be observed that the concept *all numbers*, though not itself infinitely complex, yet denotes an infinitely complex object. This is the inmost secret of our power to deal with infinity. An infinitely complex concept, though there may be such, can certainly not be manipulated by the human intelligence; but infinite collections, owing to the notion of denoting, can be manipulated without introducing any concepts of infinite complexity. Throughout the discussions of infinity in later Parts of the present work, this remark should be borne in mind: if it is forgotten, there is an air of magic which causes the results obtained to seem doubtful.

73. Great difficulties are associated with the null-class, and generally with the idea of *nothing*. It is plain that there is such a concept as *nothing*, and that in some sense nothing is something. In fact, the proposition "nothing is not nothing" is undoubtedly capable of an interpretation which makes it true—a point which gives rise to the contradictions discussed in Plato's *Sophist*. In Symbolic Logic the null-class is the class which has no terms at all; and symbolically it is quite necessary to introduce some such notion. We have to consider whether the contradictions which naturally arise can be avoided.

It is necessary to realize, in the first place, that a concept may denote although it does not denote anything. This occurs when there are propositions in which the said concept occurs, and which are not about the said concept, but all such propositions are false. Or rather, the above is a first step towards the explanation of a denoting concept which denotes nothing. It is not, however, an adequate explanation. Consider, for example, the proposition "chimaeras are animals" or "even primes other than 2 are numbers." These propositions appear to be true, and it would seem that they are not concerned with the denoting concepts, but with what these concepts denote; yet that is impossible, for the concepts in question do not denote anything. Symbolic Logic says that these concepts denote the null-class, and that the propositions in question assert that the null-class is contained in certain other classes. But with the strictly extensional view of classes propounded above, a class which has no terms fails to be anything at all: what is merely and solely a collection of terms cannot subsist when all the terms are removed. Thus we must

either find a different interpretation of classes, or else find a method of dispensing with the null-class.

The above imperfect definition of a concept which denotes, but does not denote anything, may be amended as follows. All denoting concepts, as we saw, are derived from class-concepts; and *a* is a class-concept when "*x* is an *a*" is a propositional function. The denoting concepts associated with *a* will not denote anything when and only when "*x* is an *a*" is false for all values of *x*. This is a complete definition of a denoting concept which does not denote anything; and in this case we shall say that *a* is a null class-concept, and that "all *a*'s" is a null concept of a class. Thus for a system such as Peano's, in which what are called classes are really class-concepts, technical difficulties need not arise; but for us a genuine logical problem remains.

The proposition "chimaeras are animals" may be easily interpreted by means of formal implication, as meaning "*x* is a chimaera implies *x* is an animal for all values of *x*." But in dealing with classes we have been assuming that propositions containing *all* or *any* or *every*, though equivalent to formal implications, were yet distinct from them, and involved ideas requiring independent treatment. Now in the case of chimaeras, it is easy to substitute the pure intensional view, according to which what is really stated is a relation of predicates: in the case in question the adjective *animal* is part of the definition of the adjective *chimerical* (if we allow ourselves to use this word, contrary to usage, to denote the defining predicate of chimaeras). But here again it is fairly plain that we are dealing with a proposition which implies that chimaeras are animals, but is not the same proposition—indeed, in the present case, the implication is not even reciprocal. By a negation we can give a kind of extensional interpretation: nothing is denoted by *a chimaera* which is not denoted by *an animal*. But this is a very roundabout interpretation. On the whole, it seems most correct to reject the proposition altogether, while retaining the various other propositions that would be equivalent to it if there were chimaeras. By symbolic logicians, who have experienced the utility of the null-class, this will be felt as a reactionary view. But I am not at present discussing what should be done in the logical calculus, where the established practice appears to me the best, but what is the philosophical truth concerning the null-class. We shall say, then, that, of the bundle of normally equivalent interpretations of logical symbolic formulae, the class of interpretations considered in the present chapter, which are dependent upon actual classes, fail where we are concerned with null class-concepts, on the ground that there is no actual null-class.

We may now reconsider the proposition "nothing is not nothing"—a proposition plainly true, and yet, unless carefully handled, a source of apparently hopeless antinomies. *Nothing* is a denoting concept, which denotes nothing. The concept which denotes is of course not nothing, *i.e.* it is not denoted by itself. The proposition which looks so paradoxical means no more than this: *Nothing*, the denoting concept, is not nothing, *i.e.* is not what itself denotes. But it by no means follows from this that there is an actual null-class: only the null class-concept and the null concept of a class are to be admitted.

But now a new difficulty has to be met. The equality of class-concepts, like all relations which are reflexive, symmetrical, and transitive, indicates an underlying identity, *i.e.* it indicates that every class-concept has to some term a relation which all equal class-concepts also have to that term—the term in question being different for different sets of equal class-concepts, but the same for the various members of a single set of equal class-concepts. Now for all class-concepts which are not null, this term is found in the corresponding class; but where are we to find it for null class-concepts? To this question several answers may be given, any of which may be adopted. For we now know what a class is, and we may therefore adopt as our term the class of all null class-concepts or of all null propositional functions. These are not null classes, but genuine classes, and to either of them all null class-concepts have the same relation. If we then wish to have an entity analogous to what is elsewhere to be called a class, but corresponding to null class-concepts, we shall be forced, wherever it is necessary (as in counting

classes) to introduce a term which is identical for equal class-concepts, to substitute everywhere the class of class-concepts equal to a given class-concept for the class corresponding to that class-concept. The class corresponding to the class-concept remains logically fundamental, but need not be actually employed in our symbolism. The null-class, in fact, is in some ways analogous to an irrational in Arithmetic: it cannot be interpreted on the same principles as other classes, and if we wish to give an analogous interpretation elsewhere, we must substitute for classes other more complicated entities—in the present case, certain correlated classes. The object of such a procedure will be mainly technical; but failure to understand the procedure will lead to inextricable difficulties in the interpretation of the symbolism. A very closely analogous procedure occurs constantly in Mathematics, for example with every generalization of number; and so far as I know, no single case in which it occurs has been rightly interpreted either by philosophers or by mathematicians. So many instances will meet us in the course of the present work that it is unnecessary to linger longer over the point at present. Only one possible misunderstanding must be guarded against. No vicious circle is involved in the above account of the null-class; for the general notion of *class* is first laid down, is found to involve what is called existence, is then symbolically, not philosophically, replaced by the notion of a class of equal class-concepts, and is found, in this new form, to be applicable to what corresponds to null class-concepts, since what corresponds is now a class which is not null. Between classes *simpliciter* and classes of equal class-concepts there is a one-one correlation, which breaks down in the sole case of the class of null class-concepts, to which no null-class corresponds; and this fact is the reason for the whole complication.

74. A question which is very fundamental in the philosophy of Arithmetic must now be discussed in a more or less preliminary fashion. Is a class which has many terms to be regarded as itself one or many? Taking the class as equivalent simply to the numerical conjunction "*A* and *B* and *C* and etc.," it seems plain that it is many; yet it is quite necessary

that we should be able to count classes as one each, and we do habitually speak of *a* class. Thus classes would seem to be one in one sense and many in another.

There is a certain temptation to identify the class as many and the class as one, *e.g., all men* and *the human race*. Nevertheless, wherever a class consists of more than one term, it can be proved that no such identification is permissible. A concept of a class, if it denotes a class as one, is not the same as any concept of the class which it denotes. That is to say, *classes of all rational animals,* which denotes the human race as one term, is different from *men*, which denotes men, *i.e.* the human race as many. But if the human race were identical with men, it would follow that whatever denotes the one must denote the other, and the above difference would be impossible. We might be tempted to infer that Peano's distinction, between a term and a class of which the said term is the only member, must be maintained, at least when the term in question is a class. But it is more correct, I think, to infer an ultimate distinction between a class as many and a class as one, to hold that the many are only many, and are not also one. The class as one may be identified with the whole composed of the terms of the class, *i.e.,* in the case of men, the class as one will be the human race.

But can we now avoid the contradiction always to be feared, where there is something that cannot be made a logical subject? I do not myself see any way of eliciting a precise contradiction in this case. In the case of concepts, we were dealing with what was plainly one entity; in the present case, we are dealing with a complex essentially capable of analysis into units. In such a proposition as "*A* and *B* are two," there is no logical subject: the assertion is not about *A*, nor about *B*, nor about the whole composed of both, but strictly and only about *A* and *B*. Thus it would seem that assertions are not necessarily *about* single subjects, but may be about many subjects; and this removes the contradiction which arose, in the case of concepts, from the impossibility of making assertions about them unless they were turned into subjects. This impossibility being here absent, the contradiction which was to be feared does not arise.

75. We may ask, as suggested by the above discussion, what is to be said of the objects denoted by *a man, every man, some man,* and *any man*. Are these objects one or many or neither? Grammar treats them all as one. But to this view, the natural objection is, which one? Certainly not Socrates, nor Plato, nor any other particular person. Can we conclude that no one is denoted? As well might we conclude that every one is denoted, which in fact is true of the concept *every man*. I think one is denoted in every case, but in an impartial distributive manner. *Any number* is neither 1 nor 2 nor any other particular number, whence it is easy to conclude that *any number* is not any one number, a proposition at first sight contradictory, but really resulting from an ambiguity in *any*, and more correctly expressed by "*any number* is not *some* one number." There are, however, puzzles in this subject which I do not yet know how to solve.

A logical difficulty remains in regard to the nature of the whole composed of all the terms of a class. Two propositions appear self-evident: (1) Two wholes composed of different terms must be different; (2) A whole composed of one term only is that one term. It follows that the whole composed of a class considered as one term is that class considered as one term, and is therefore identical with the whole composed of the terms of the class; but this result contradicts the first of our supposed self-evident principles. The answer in this case, however, is not difficult. The first of our principles is only universally true when all the terms composing our two wholes are simple. A given whole is capable, if it has more than two parts, of being analyzed in a plurality of ways; and the resulting constituents, so long as analysis is not pushed as far as possible, will be different for different ways of analyzing. This proves that different sets of constituents may constitute the same whole, and thus disposes of our difficulty.

76. Something must be said as to the relation of a term to a class of which it is a member, and as to the various allied relations. One of the allied relations is to be called ϵ, and is to be fundamental in Symbolic Logic. But it is to some extent optional which of them we take as symbolically fundamental.

Logically, the fundamental relation is that of subject and predicate, expressed in "Socrates is human"—a relation which, as we saw in Chapter IV, is peculiar in that the relatum cannot be regarded as a term in the proposition. The first relation that grows out of this is the one expressed by "Socrates has humanity," which is distinguished by the fact that here the relation is a term. Next comes "Socrates is a man." This proposition, considered as a relation between Socrates and the concept *man,* is the one which Peano regards as fundamental; and his ϵ expresses the relation *is a* between Socrates and *man.* So long as we use class-concepts for classes in our symbolism, this practice is unobjectionable; but if we give ϵ this meaning, we must not assume that two symbols representing equal class-concepts both represent one and the same entity. We may go on to the relation between Socrates and the human race, *i.e.* between a term and its class considered as a whole; this is expressed by "Socrates belongs to the human race." This relation might equally well be represented by ϵ. It is plain that, since a class, except when it has one term, is essentially many, it cannot be *as such* represented by a single letter: hence in any possible Symbolic Logic the letters which do duty for classes cannot represent the classes *as many*, but must represent either class-concepts, or the wholes composed of classes, or some other allied single entities. And thus ϵ cannot represent the relation of a term to its class as many; for this would be a relation of one term to many terms, not a two-term relation such as we want. This relation might be expressed by "Socrates is one among men"; but this, in any case, cannot be taken to be the meaning of ϵ.

77. A relation which, before Peano, was almost universally confounded with ϵ, is the relation of inclusion between classes, as *e.g.* between men and mortals. This is a time-honoured relation, since it occurs in the traditional form of the syllogism: it has been a battleground between intension and extension, and has been so much discussed that it is astonishing how much remains to be said about it. Empiricists hold that such propositions mean an actual enumeration of the terms of the contained class, with the assertion, in each case, of membership of the containing class. They must, it is to be inferred, regard it as doubtful whether all primes are integers, since they will scarcely have the face to say that they have examined all primes one by one. Their opponents have usually held, on the contrary, that what is meant is a relation of whole and part between the defining predicates, but turned in the opposite sense from the relation between the classes: *i.e.* the defining predicate of the larger class is part of that of the smaller. This view seems far more defensible than the other; and wherever such a relation does hold between the defining predicates, the relation of inclusion follows. But two objections may be made, first, that in some cases of inclusion there is no such relation between the defining predicates, and secondly, that in any case what is *meant* is a relation between the classes, not a relation of their defining predicates. The first point may be easily established by instances. The concept *even prime* does not contain as a constituent the concept *integer between* 1 *and* 10; the concept "English King whose head was cut off" does not contain the concept "people who died in 1649"; and so on through innumerable obvious cases. This might be met by saying that, though the relation of the defining predicates is not one of whole and part, it is one more or less analogous to implication, and is always what is really meant by propositions of inclusion. Such a view represents, I think, what is said by the better advocates of intension, and I am not concerned to deny that a relation of the kind in question does always subsist between defining predicates of classes one of which is contained in the other. But the second of the above points remains valid as against any intensional interpretation. When we say that men are mortals, it is evident that we are saying something about men, not about the concept *man* or the predicate *human.* The question is, then, what exactly are we saying?

Peano held, in earlier editions of his *Formulaire*, that what is asserted is the formal implication "*x* is a man implies *x* is a mortal." This is certainly implied, but I cannot persuade myself that it is the same proposition. For in this proposition, as we saw in Chapter III, it is essential that *x* should take *all* values, and not only such as are men. But when we say "all men are mortals," it seems plain that we are only speaking of men, and not of all other imaginable terms. We may, if we wish for a genuine relation of classes, regard the assertion as one of whole and part between the two classes each considered as a single term. Or we may give a still more purely extensional form to our proposition, by making it mean: Every (or any) man is a mortal. This proposition raises very interesting questions in the theory of denoting: for it appears to assert an identity, yet it is plain that what is denoted by *every man* is different from what is denoted by *a mortal*. These questions, however, interesting as they are, cannot be pursued here. It is only necessary to realize clearly what are the various equivalent propositions involved where one class is included in another. The form most relevant to Mathematics is certainly the one with formal implication, which will receive a fresh discussion in the following chapter.

Finally, we must remember that classes are to be derived, by means of the notion of *such that*, from other sources than subject-predicate propositions and their equivalents. Any propositional function in which a fixed assertion is made of a variable term is to be regarded, as was explained in Chapter II, as giving rise to a class of values satisfying it. This topic requires a discussion of assertions; but one strange contradiction, which necessitates the care in discrimination aimed at in the present chapter, may be mentioned at once.

78. Among predicates, most of the ordinary instances cannot be predicated of themselves, though, by introducing negative predicates, it will be found that there are just as many instances of predicates which are predicable of themselves. One at least of these, namely predicability, or the property of being a predicate, is not negative: predicability, as is evident, is predicable, *i.e.* it is a predicate of itself. But the most common instances are negative: thus non-humanity is non-human, and so on. The predicates which are not predicable of themselves are, therefore, only a selection from among predicates, and it is natural to suppose that they form a class having a defining predicate. But it so, let us examine whether this defining predicate belongs to the

class or not. If it belongs to the class, it is not predicable of itself, for that is the characteristic property of the class. But if it is not predicable of itself, then it does not belong to the class whose defining predicate it is, which is contrary to the hypothesis. On the other hand, if it does not belong to the class whose defining predicate it is, then it is not predicable of itself, *i.e.* it *is* one of those predicates that are not predicable of themselves, and therefore it does belong to the class whose defining predicate it is—again contrary to the hypothesis. Hence from either hypothesis we can deduce its contradictory. I shall return to this contradiction in Chapter X; for the present, I have introduced it merely as showing that no subtlety in distinguishing is likely to be excessive.

79. To sum up the above somewhat lengthy discussion. A class, we agreed, is essentially to be interpreted in extension; it is either a single term, or that kind of combination of terms which is indicated when terms are connected by the word *and*. But practically, though not theoretically, this purely extensional method can only be applied to finite classes. All classes, whether finite or infinite, can be obtained as the objects denoted by the plurals of class-concepts—men, numbers, points, etc. Starting with predicates, we distinguished two kinds of proposition, typified by "Socrates is human" and "Socrates has humanity," of which the first uses *human* as predicate, the second as a term of a relation. These two classes of propositions, though very important logically, are not so relevant to Mathematics as their derivatives. Starting from *human*, we distinguished (1) the class-concept *man*, which differs slightly, if at all, from *human*; (2) the various denoting concepts *all men, every man, any man, a man* and *some man*; (3) the objects denoted by these concepts, of which the one denoted by *all men* was called the *class as many*, so that *all men* (the concept) was called the *concept of the class*; (4) the class as one, *i.e.* the human race. We had also a classification of propositions about Socrates, dependent upon the above distinctions, and approximately parallel with them: (1) "Socrates is-a man" is nearly, if not quite, identical with "Socrates has humanity"; (2) "Socrates is a-man" expresses identity between Socrates

and one of the terms denoted by *a man;* (3) "Socrates is one among men," a proposition which raises difficulties owing to the plurality of men; (4) "Socrates belongs to the human race," which alone expresses a relation of an individual to its class, and, as the possibility of relation requires, takes the class as one, not as many. We agreed that the null-class, which has no terms, is a fiction, though there are null class-concepts. It appeared throughout that, although any symbolic treatment must work largely with class-concepts and intension, classes and extension are logically more fundamental for the principles of Mathematics; and this may be regarded as our main general conclusion in the present chapter.

Chapter VII:
Propositional Functions

80. In the preceding chapter an endeavour was made to indicate the kind of object that is to be called a class, and for purposes of discussion classes were considered as derived from subject-predicate propositions. This did not affect our view as to the notion of *class* itself; but if adhered to, it would greatly restrict the extension of the notion. It is often necessary to recognize as a class an object not defined by means of a subject-predicate proposition. The explanation of this necessity is to be sought in the theory of assertions and *such that.*

The general notion of an assertion has been already explained in connection with formal implication. In the present chapter its scope and legitimacy are to be critically examined, and its connection with classes and *such that* is to be investigated. The subject is full of difficulties, and the doctrines which I intend to advocate are put forward with a very limited confidence in their truth.

The notion of *such that* might be thought, at first sight, to be capable of definition; Peano used, in fact, to define the notion by the proposition "the *x*'s such that *x* is an *a* are the class *a*." Apart from further objections, to be noticed immediately, it is to be observed that the class as obtained from *such that* is the

genuine class, taken in extension and as many, whereas the *a* in "*x* is an *a*" is not the class, but the class-concept. Thus it is formally necessary, if Peano's procedure is to be permissible, that we should substitute for "*x*'s such that so-and-so" the genuine class-concept "*x* such that so-and-so," which may be regarded as obtained from the predicate "such that so-and-so" or rather, "being an *x* such that so-and-so," the latter form being necessary because so-and-so is a propositional function containing *x*. But when this purely formal emendation has been made the point remains that *such that* must often be put before such propositions as *xRa*, where *R* is a given relation and *a* a given term. We cannot reduce this proposition to the form "*x* is an *a'*" without using *such that;* for if we ask what a' must be, the answer is: a' must be such that each of its terms, and no other terms, have the relation *R* to *a*. To take examples from daily life: the children of Israel are a class defined by a certain relation to Israel, and the class can only be defined as the terms such that they have this relation. *Such that* is roughly equivalent to *who* or *which,* and represents the general notion of satisfying a propositional function. But we may go further: given a class *a,* we cannot define, in terms of *a,* the class of propositions "*x* is an *a*" for different values of *x*. It is plain that there is a relation which each of these propositions has to the *x* which occurs in it, and that the relation in question is determinate when *a* is given. Let us call the relation *R*. Then any entity which is a referent with respect to *R* is a proposition of the type "*x* is an *a*." But here the notion of *such that* is already employed. And the relation *R* itself can only be defined as the relation which holds between "*x* is an *a*" and *x* for all values of *x*, and does not hold between any other pairs of terms. Here *such that* again appears. The point which is chiefly important in these remarks is the indefinability of propositional functions. When these have been admitted, the general notion of one-valued functions is easily defined. Every relation which is many-one, *i.e.* every relation for which a given referent has only one relatum, defines a function: the relatum is that function of the referent which is defined by the relation in question. But where the function is a proposition, the notion involved is presupposed in the symbolism, and cannot be defined by means of it without a vicious circle: for in the above general definition of a function propositional functions already occur. In the case of propositions of the type "*x* is an *a*," if we ask *what* propositions are of this type, we can only answer "all propositions in which a term is said to be *a*;" and here the notion to be defined reappears.

81. Can the indefinable element involved in propositional functions be identified with assertion together with the notion of *every* proposition containing a given assertion, or an assertion made concerning *every* term? The only alternative, so far as I can see, is to accept the general notion of a propositional function itself as indefinable, and for formal purposes this course is certainly the best; but philosophically, the notion appears at first sight capable of analysis, and we have to examine whether or not this appearance is deceptive.

We saw in discussing verbs, in Chapter IV, that when a proposition is completely analyzed into its simple constituents, these constituents taken together do not reconstitute it. A less complete analysis of propositions into subject and assertion has also been considered; and this analysis does much less to destroy the proposition. A subject and an assertion, if simply juxtaposed, do not, it is true, constitute a proposition; but as soon as the assertion is actually asserted of the subject, the proposition reappears. The assertion is everything that remains of the proposition when the subject is omitted: the verb remains an asserted verb, and is not turned into a verbal noun; or at any rate the verb retains that curious indefinable intricate relation to the other terms of the proposition which distinguishes a relating relation from the same relation abstractly considered. It is the scope and legitimacy of this notion of assertion which is now to be examined. Can every proposition be regarded as an assertion concerning any term occurring in it, or are limitations necessary as to the form of the proposition and the way in which the term enters into it?

In some simple cases, it is obvious that the analysis into subject and assertion is legitimate. In "Socrates is a man," we can plainly distinguish Socrates and something that is asserted

about him; we should admit unhesitatingly that the *same* thing may be said about Plato or Aristotle. Thus we can consider a class of propositions containing this assertion, and this will be the class of which a typical number is represented by "*x* is a man." It is to be observed that the assertion must appear *as* assertion, not as term: thus "to be a man is to suffer" contains the same assertion, but used as term, and this proposition does not belong to the class considered. In the case of propositions asserting a fixed relation to a fixed term, the analysis seems equally undeniable. To be more than a yard long, for example, is a perfectly definite assertion, and we may consider the class of propositions in which this assertion is made, which will be represented by the propositional function "*x* is more than a yard long." In such phrases as "snakes which are more than a yard long," the assertion appears very plainly; for it is here explicitly referred to a variable subject, not asserted of any one definite subject. Thus if *R* be a fixed relation and *a* a fixed term, . . . *Ra* is a perfectly definite assertion. (I place dots before the *R*, to indicate the place where the subject must be inserted in order to make a proposition.) It may be doubted whether a relational proposition can be regarded as an assertion concerning the relatum. For my part, I hold that this can be done except in the case of subject-predicate propositions; but this question is better postponed until we have discussed relations.[36]

82. More difficult questions must now be considered. Is such a proposition as "Socrates is a man implies Socrates is a mortal," or "Socrates has a wife implies Socrates has a father," an assertion concerning Socrates or not? It is quite certain that, if we replace Socrates by a variable, we obtain a propositional function; in fact, the truth of this function for all values of the variable is what is asserted in the corresponding formal implication, which does not, as might be thought at first sight, assert a relation between two propositional functions. Now it was our intention, if possible, to explain propositional functions by means of assertions; hence, if our intention can be carried

[36]See § 96.

out, the above propositions must be assertions concerning Socrates. There is, however, a very great difficulty in so regarding them. An assertion was to be obtained from a proposition by simply omitting one of the terms occurring in the proposition. But when we omit Socrates, we obtain ". . . is a man implies . . . is a mortal." In this formula it is essential that, in restoring the proposition, the *same* term should be substituted in the two places where dots indicate the necessity of a term. It does not matter what term we choose, but it must be identical in both places. Of this requisite, however, no trace whatever appears in the would-be assertion, and no trace can appear, since all mention of the term to be inserted is necessarily omitted. When an x is inserted to stand for the variable, the identity of the term to be inserted is indicated by the repetition of the letter x; but in the assertional form no such method is available. And yet, at first sight, it seems very hard to deny that the proposition in question tells us a fact *about* Socrates, and that the *same* fact is true about Plato or a plum-pudding or the number 2. It is certainly undeniable that "Plato is a man implies Plato is a mortal" is, in some sense or other, the *same* function of Plato as our previous proposition is of Socrates. The natural interpretation of this statement would be that the one proposition has to Plato the same relation as the other has to Socrates. But this requires that we should regard the propositional function in question as definable by means of its relation to the variable. Such a view, however, requires a propositional function more complicated than the one we are considering. If we represent "x is a man implies x is a mortal" by ϕx, the view in question maintains that ϕx is the term having to x the relation R, where R is some definite relation. The formal statement of this view is as follows: For all values of x and y, "y is identical with ϕx" is equivalent to "y has the relation R to x." It is evident that this will not do as an explanation, since it has far greater complexity than what it was to explain. It would seem to follow that propositions may have a certain constancy of form, expressed in the fact that they are instances of a given propositional function, without its being possible to analyze the propositions into a constant and a variable factor. Such a view is curious and difficult: constancy of form, in all other cases, is reducible to constancy of relations, but the constancy involved here is presupposed in the notion of constancy of relation, and cannot therefore be explained in the usual way.

The same conclusion, I think, will result from the case of two variables. The simplest instance of this case is xRy, where R is a constant relation, while x and y are independently variable. It seems evident that this is a propositional function of two independent variables: there is no difficulty in the notion of the class of all propositions of the form xRy. This class is involved—or at least all those members of the class that are true are involved—in the notion of the classes of referents and relata with respect to R, and these classes are unhesitatingly admitted in such words as parents and children, masters and servants, husbands and wives, and innumerable other instances from daily life, as also in logical notions such as premisses and conclusions, causes and effects, and so on. All such notions depend upon the class of propositions typified by xRy, where R is constant while x and y are variable. Yet it is very difficult to regard xRy as analyzable into the assertion R concerning x and y, for the very sufficient reason that this view destroys the *sense* of the relation, *i.e.* its direction from x to y, leaving us with some assertion which is symmetrical with respect to x and y, such as "the relation R holds between x and y." Given a relation and its terms, in fact, two distinct propositions are possible. Thus if we take R itself to be an assertion, it becomes an ambiguous assertion: in supplying the terms, if we are to avoid ambiguity, we must decide which is referent and which relatum. We may quite legitimately regard . . . Ry as an assertion, as was explained before; but here y has become constant. We may then go on to vary y, considering the class of assertions . . . Ry for different values of y; but this process does not seem to be identical with that which is indicated by the independent variability of x and y in the propositional function xRy. Moreover, the suggested process requires the variation of an element in an assertion, namely of y in . . . Ry, and this is in itself a new and difficult notion.

A curious point arises, in this connection, from the consideration, often essential in actual Mathematics, of a relation of a term to itself. Consider the propositional function xRx, where R is a constant relation. Such functions are required in considering, *e.g.*, the class of suicides or of self-made men; or again, in considering the values of the variable for which it is equal to a certain function of itself, which may often be necessary in ordinary Mathematics. It seems exceedingly evident, in this case, that the proposition contains an element which is lost when it is analyzed into a term x and an assertion R. Thus here again, the propositional function must be admitted as fundamental.

83. A difficult point arises as to the variation of the concept in a proposition. Consider, for example, all propositions of the type aRb, where a and b are fixed terms, and R is a variable relation. There seems no reason to doubt that the class-concept "relation between a and b" is legitimate, and that there is a corresponding class; but this requires the admission of such propositional functions as aRb, which, moreover, are frequently required in actual Mathematics, as, for example, in counting the number of many-one relations whose referents and relata are given classes. But if our variable is to have, as we normally require, an unrestricted field, it is necessary to substitute the propositional function "R is a relation implies aRb." In this proposition the implication involved is material, not formal. If the implication were formal, the proposition would not be a function of R, but would be equivalent to the (necessarily false) proposition: "All relations hold between a and b." Generally we have some such proposition as "aRb implies $\phi(R)$ provided R is a relation," and we wish to turn this into a formal implication. If $\phi(R)$ is a proposition for all values of R, our object is effected by substituting "If 'R is a relation' implies 'aRb,' then $\phi(R)$." Here R can take all values,[37] and the *if* and *then* is a formal implication, while the *implies* is a material implication. If $\phi(R)$ is not a propositional function, but is a proposition only when R satisfies $\psi(R)$,

where $\psi(R)$ is a propositional function implied by "R is a relation" for all values of R, then our formal implication can be put in the form "If 'R is a relation' implies aRb, then, for all values of R, $\psi(R)$ implies $\phi(R)$," where both the subordinate implications are material. As regards the material implication "'R is a relation' implies aRb," this is always a proposition, whereas aRb is only a proposition when R is a relation. The new propositional function will only be true when R is a relation which does hold between a and b: when R is not a relation, the antecedent is false and the consequent is not a proposition, so that the implication is false; when R is a relation which does not hold between a and b, the antecedent is true and the consequent false, so that again the implication is false; only when both are true is the implication true. Thus in defining the class of relations holding between a and b, the formally correct course is to define them as the values satisfying "R is a relation implies aRb"—an implication which, though it contains a variable, is not formal, but material, being satisfied by some only of the possible values of R. The variable R in it is, in Peano's language, real and not apparent.

The general principle involved is: If ϕx is only a proposition for some values of x, then "'ϕx implies ϕx' implies ϕx" is a proposition for *all* values of x, and is true when and only when ϕx is true. (The implications involved are both material.) In some cases, "ϕx implies ϕx" will be equivalent to some simpler propositional function ψx (such as "R is a relation" in the above instance), which may then be substituted for it.[38]

Such a propositional function as "R is a relation implies aRb" appears even less capable than previous instances of analysis into R and an assertion about R, since we should have to assign a meaning to "$a \ldots b$," where the blank space may be filled by anything, not necessarily by a relation. There is here, however, a suggestion of an entity which has not yet been considered, namely the couple with sense. It may be doubted whether there is any such

---

[37]It is necessary to assign some meaning (other than a proposition) to aRb when R is not a relation.

[38]A propositional function, though for every value of the variable it is true or false, is not itself true or false, being what is denoted by "any proposition of the type in question," which is not itself a proposition.

entity, and yet such phrases as "R is a relation holding from a to b" seem to show that its rejection would lead to paradoxes. This point, however, belongs to the theory of relations, and will be resumed in Chapter IX (§ 98).

From what has been said, it appears that propositional functions must be accepted as ultimate data. It follows that formal implication and the inclusion of classes cannot be generally explained by means of a relation between assertions, although, where a propositional function asserts a fixed relation to a fixed term, the analysis into subject and assertion is legitimate and not unimportant.

84. It only remains to say a few words concerning the derivation of classes from propositional functions. When we consider the x's *such that* ϕx, where ϕx is a propositional function, we are introducing a notion of which, in the calculus of propositions, only a very shadowy use is made—I mean the notion of *truth*. We are considering, among all the propositions of the type ϕx, those that are true: the corresponding values of x give the class defined by the function ϕx. It must be held, I think, that every propositional function which is not null defines a class, which is denoted by "x's such that ϕx." There is thus always a concept of the class, and the class-concept corresponding will be the singular, "x such that ϕx." But it may be doubted—indeed the contradiction with which I ended the preceding chapter gives reason for doubting—whether there is always a defining predicate of such classes. Apart from the contradiction in question, this point might appear to be merely verbal: "being an x such that ϕx," it might be said, may always be taken to be a predicate. But in view of our contradiction, all remarks on this subject must be viewed with caution. This subject, however, will be resumed in Chapter X.

85. It is to be observed that, according to the theory of propositional functions here advocated, the ϕ in ϕx is not a separate and distinguishable entity: it lives in the propositions of the form ϕx, and cannot survive analysis. I am highly doubtful whether such a view does not lead to a contradiction, but it appears to be forced upon us, and it has the merit of enabling us to avoid a contradiction arising from the opposite view. If ϕ were a

distinguishable entity, there would be a proposition asserting ϕ of itself, which we may denote by $\phi(\phi)$; there would also be a proposition not-$\phi(\phi)$, denying $\phi(\phi)$. In this proposition we may regard ϕ as variable; we thus obtain a propositional function. The question arises: Can the assertion in this propositional function be asserted of itself? The assertion is non-assertibility of self, hence if it can be asserted of itself, it cannot, and if it cannot, it can. This contradiction is avoided by the recognition that the functional part of a propositional function is not an independent entity. As the contradiction in question is closely analogous to the other, concerning predicates not predicable of themselves, we may hope that a similar solution will apply there also.

Chapter VIII: The Variable

86. The discussions of the preceding chapter elicited the fundamental nature of the variable; no apparatus of assertions enables us to dispense with the consideration of the varying of one or more elements in a proposition while the other elements remain unchanged. The variable is perhaps the most distinctively mathematical of all notions; it is certainly also one of the most difficult to understand. The attempt, if not the deed, belongs to the present chapter.

The theory as to the nature of the variable, which results from our previous discussions, is in outline the following. When a given term occurs as term in a proposition, that term may be replaced by any other while the remaining terms are unchanged. The class of propositions so obtained have what may be called constancy of form, and this constancy of form must be taken as a primitive idea. The notion of a class of propositions of constant form is more fundamental than the general notion of *class*, for the latter can be defined in terms of the former, but not the former in terms of the latter. Taking *any* term, a certain member of any class of propositions of constant form will contain that term. Thus x, the variable, is what is denoted by *any term*, and ϕx, the propositional function, is what is denoted by *the* proposition of the form ϕ in which x occurs. We may say that x is *the x* is *any* ϕx, where ϕx denotes the class of propositions resulting from different values of x. Thus in addition to propositional functions, the notions of *any* and of denoting are presupposed in the notion of the variable. This theory, which, I admit, is full of difficulties, is the least objectionable that I have been able to imagine. I shall now set it forth more in detail.

87. Let us observe, to begin with, that the explicit mention of *any, some,* etc., need not occur in Mathematics: formal implication will express all that is required. Let us recur to an instance already discussed in connection with denoting, where a is a class and b a class of classes. We have

"Any a belongs to any b" is equivalent to " 'x is an a' implies that 'u is a b' implies 'x is a u' "

"Any a belongs to a b" is equivalent to " 'x is an a' implies 'there is a b, say u, such that x is a u' "[39]

"Any a belongs to some b" is equivalent to "there is a b, say u, such that 'x is an a' implies 'x is a u' "

and so on for the remaining relations considered in Chapter V. The question arises: How far do these equivalences constitute definitions of *any, a, some,* and how far are these notions involved in the symbolism itself?

The variable is, from the formal standpoint, *the* characteristic notion of Mathematics. Moreover it is *the* method of stating general theorems, which always *mean* something different from the intensional propositions to which such logicians as Mr Bradley endeavour to reduce them. That the meaning of an assertion about all men or any man is different from the meaning of an equivalent assertion about the concept *man*, appears to me, I must confess, to be a self-evident truth—as evident as the fact that propositions about John are not about the *name* John. This point, there-

fore, I shall not argue further. That the variable characterizes Mathematics will be generally admitted, though it is not generally perceived to be present in elementary Arithmetic. Elementary Arithmetic, as taught to children, is characterized by the fact that the *numbers* occurring in it are constants; the answer to any schoolboy's sum is obtainable without propositions concerning *any* number. But the fact that this is the case can only be proved by the help of propositions about *any* number, and thus we are led from schoolboy's Arithmetic to the Arithmetic which uses letters for numbers and proves general theorems. How very different this subject is from childhood's enemy may be seen at once in such works as those of Dedekind and Stolz. Now the difference consists simply in this, that our numbers have now become variables instead of being constants. We now prove theorems concerning n, not concerning 3 or 4 or any other particular number. Thus it is absolutely essential to any theory of Mathematics to understand the nature of the variable.

Originally, no doubt, the variable was conceived dynamically, as something which changed with the lapse of time, or, as is said, as something which successively assumed all values of a certain class. This view cannot be too soon dismissed. If a theorem is proved concerning n, it must not be supposed that n is a kind of arithmetical Proteus, which is 1 on Sundays and 2 on Mondays, and so on. Nor must it be supposed that n simultaneously assumes all its values. If n stands for any integer, we cannot say that n is 1, nor yet that it is 2, nor yet that it is any other particular number. In fact, n just denotes *any* number, and this is something quite distinct from each and all of the numbers. It is not true that 1 is any number, though it is true that whatever holds of any number holds of 1. The variable, in short, requires the indefinable notion of *any* which was explained in Chapter V.

88. We may distinguish what may be called the true or formal variable from the restricted variable. *Any term* is a concept denoting the true variable; if u be a class not containing all terms, *any u* denotes a restricted variable. The terms included in the object denoted by the defining concept of a variable are called the

---

[39] Here "there is a c," where c is any class, is defined as equivalent to "If p implies p, and 'x is a c' implies p for all values of x, then p is true."

values of the variable: thus every value of a variable is a constant. There is a certain difficulty about such propositions as "any number is a number." Interpreted by formal implication, they offer no difficulty, for they assert merely that the propositional function "*x* is a number implies *x* is a number" holds for all values of *x*. But if "any number" be taken to be a definite object, it is plain that it is not identical with 1 or 2 or 3 or any number that may be mentioned. Yet these are all the numbers there are, so that "any number" cannot be a number at all. The fact is that the concept "any number" does denote one number, but not a particular one. This is just the distinctive point about *any*, that it denotes a term of a class, but in an impartial distributive manner, with no preference for one term over another. Thus although *x* is a number, and no one number is *x*, yet there is here no contradiction, so soon as it is recognized that *x* is not one definite term.

The notion of the restricted variable can be avoided, except in regard to propositional functions, by the introduction of a suitable hypothesis, namely the hypothesis expressing the restriction itself. But in respect of propositional functions this is not possible. The *x* in ϕx, where ϕx is a propositional function, is an unrestricted variable; but the ϕx itself is restricted to the class which we may call ϕ. (It is to be remembered that the *class* is here fundamental, for we found it impossible, without a vicious circle, to discover any common characteristic by which the class could be defined, since the statement of any common characteristic is itself a propositional function.) By making our *x* always an unrestricted variable, we can speak of *the* variable, which is conceptually identical in Logic, Arithmetic, Geometry, and all other formal subjects. The *terms* dealt with are always *all* terms; only the complex concepts that occur distinguish the various branches of Mathematics.

89. We may now return to the apparent definability of *any*, *some*, and *a*, in terms of formal implication. Let *a* and *b* be class-concepts, and consider the proposition "any *a* is a *b*." This is to be interpreted as meaning "*x* is an *a* implies *x* is a *b*." It is plain that, to begin with, the two propositions do not *mean* the same thing: for *any a* is a concept denoting

only *a*'s, whereas in the formal implication *x* need not be an *a*. But we might, in Mathematics, dispense altogether with "any *a* is a *b*," and content ourselves with the formal implication: this is, in fact, symbolically the best course. The question to be examined, therefore, is: How far, if at all, do *any* and *some* and *a* enter into the formal implication? (The fact that the indefinite article appears in "*x* is an *a*" and "*x* is a *b*" is irrelevant, for these are merely taken as typical propositional functions.) We have, to begin with, a class of true propositions, each asserting of some constant term that if it is an *a* it is a *b*. We then consider the restricted variable, "any proposition of this class." We assert the truth of any term included among the values of this restricted variable. But in order to obtain the suggested formula, it is necessary to transfer the variability from the proposition as a whole to its variable term. In this way we obtain "*x* is an *a* implies *x* is a *b*." But the genesis remains essential, for we are not here expressing a relation of two propositional functions "*x* is an *a*" and "*x* is a *b*." If this were expressed, we should not require the *same x* both times. Only one propositional function is involved, namely the whole formula. Each proposition of the class expresses a relation of one term of the propositional function "*x* is an *a*" to one of "*x* is a *b*"; and we may say, if we choose, that the whole formula expresses a relation of *any* term of "*x* is an *a*" to *some* term of "*x* is a *b*." We do not so much have an implication containing a variable as a variable implication. Or again, we may say that the first *x* is *any* term, but the second is *some* term, namely the first *x*. We have a class of implications not containing variables, and we consider *any* member of this class. If *any* member is true, the fact is indicated by introducing a typical implication containing a variable. This typical implication is what is called a *formal* implication: it is *any* member of a class of material implications. Thus it would seem that *any* is presupposed in mathematical formalism, but that *some* and *a* may be legitimately replaced by their equivalents in terms of formal implications.

90. Although *some may* be replaced by its equivalent in terms of *any*, it is plain that this does not give the meaning of *some*. There is, in fact, a kind of duality of *any* and *some:* given a

certain propositional function, if *all* terms belonging to the propositional function are asserted, we have *any*, while if one at least is asserted (which gives what is called an existence-theorem), we get *some*. The proposition ϕx asserted without comment, as in "*x* is a man implies *x* is a mortal," is to be taken to mean that ϕx is true for *all* values of *x* (or for *any* value), but it might equally well have been taken to mean that ϕx is true for *some* value of *x*. In this way we might construct a calculus with two kinds of variable, the conjunctive and the disjunctive, in which the latter would occur wherever an existence-theorem was to be stated. But this method does not appear to possess any practical advantages.

91. It is to be observed that what is fundamental is not particular propositional functions, but the class-concept *propositional function*. A propositional function is the class of all propositions which arise from the variation of a single term, but this is not be considered as a definition, for reasons explained in the preceding chapter.

92. From propositional functions all other classes can be derived by definition, with the help of the notion of *such that*. Given a propositional function ϕx, the terms such that, when *x* is identified with any one of them, ϕx is true, are the class defined by ϕx. This is the class as many, the class in extension. It is not to be assumed that every class so obtained has a defining predicate: this subject will be discussed afresh in Chapter X. But it must be assumed, I think, that a class in extension is defined by any propositional function, and in particular that *all* terms form a class, since many propositional functions (*e.g.* all formal implications) are true of *all* terms. Here, as with formal implications, it is necessary that the whole propositional function whose truth defines the class should be kept intact, and not, even where this is possible for every value of *x*, divided into separate propositional functions. For example, if *a* and *b* be two classes, defined by ϕx and ψx respectively, their common part is defined by the product $\phi x \cdot \psi x$, where the product has to be made for every value of *x*, and then *x* varied afterwards. If this is not done, we do not necessarily have the *same x* in ϕx and ψx. Thus we do not multiply

propositional functions, but propositions: the new propositional function is the class of products of corresponding propositions belonging to the previous functions, and is by no means the product of ϕx and ψx. It is only in virtue of a definition that the logical product of the classes defined by ϕx and ψx is the class defined by $\phi x \cdot \psi x$. And wherever a proposition containing an apparent variable is asserted, what is asserted is the truth, for all values of the variable or variables, of the propositional function corresponding to the whole proposition, and is never a relation of propositional functions.

93. It appears from the above discussion that the variable is a very complicated logical entity, by no means easy to analyze correctly. The following appears to be as nearly correct as any analysis I can make. Given any proposition (not a propositional function), let *a* be one of its terms, and let us call the proposition $\phi(a)$. Then in virtue of the primitive idea of a propositional function, if *x* be any term, we can consider the proposition $\phi(x)$, which arises from the substitution of *x* in place of *a*. We thus arrive at the class of all propositions $\phi(x)$. If all are true, $\phi(x)$ is asserted simply: $\phi(x)$ may then be called a *formal* truth. In a formal implication, $\phi(x)$ *for every value of x*, states an implication, and the assertion of $\phi(x)$ is the assertion of a *class* of implications, not of a single implication. If $\phi(x)$ is sometimes true, the values of *x* which make it true form a class, which is the class defined by $\phi(x)$: the class is said to *exist* in this case. If $\phi(x)$ is false for all values of *x*, the class defined by $\phi(x)$ is said not to exist, and as a matter of fact, as we saw in Chapter VI, there is no such class, if classes are taken in extension. Thus *x* is, in some sense, the object denoted by *any term;* yet this can hardly be strictly maintained, for different variables may occur in a proposition, yet the object denoted by *any term*, one would suppose, is unique. This, however, elicits a new point in the theory of denoting, namely that *any term* does not denote, properly speaking, an assemblage of terms, but denotes one term, only not one particular definite term. Thus *any term* may denote different terms in different places. We may say: any term has some relation to any term; and this is quite a differ-

ent proposition from: any term has some relation to itself. Thus variables have a kind of individuality. This arises, as I have tried to show, from propositional functions. When a propositional function has two variables, it must be regarded as obtained by successive steps. If the propositional function $\phi(x, y)$ is to be asserted for all values of x and y, we must consider the assertion, for all values of y, of the propositional function $\phi(a, y)$, where a is a constant. This does not involve y, and may be represented by $\psi(a)$. We then vary a, and assert $\psi(x)$ for all values of x. The process is analogous to double integration; and it is necessary to prove formally that the order in which the variations are made makes no difference to the result. The individuality of variables appears to be thus explained. A variable is not *any term* simply, but any term as entering into a propositional function. We may say, if ϕx be a propositional function, that x is *the* term in *any* proposition of the class of propositions whose type is ϕx. It thus appears that, as regards propositional functions, the notions of class, of denoting, and of *any*, are fundamental, being presupposed in the symbolism employed. With this conclusion, the analysis of formal implication, which has been one of the principal problems of Part I, is carried as far as I am able to carry it. May some reader succeed in rendering it more complete, and in answering the many questions which I have had to leave unanswered.

Chapter IX:
 Relations

---

94. Next after subject-predicate propositions come two types of propositions which appear equally simple. These are the propositions in which a relation is asserted between two terms, and those in which two terms are said to be two. The latter class of propositions will be considered hereafter; the former must be considered at once. It has often been held that every proposition can be reduced to one of the subject-predicate type, but this view we shall, throughout the present work, find abundant

reason for rejecting. It might be held, however, that all propositions not of the subject-predicate type, and not asserting numbers, could be reduced to propositions containing two terms and a relation. This opinion would be more difficult to refute, but this too, we shall find, has no good grounds in its favour. We may therefore allow that there are relations having more than two terms; but as these are more complex, it will be well to consider first such as have two terms only.

A relation between two terms is a concept which occurs in a proposition in which there are two terms not occurring as concepts,[40] and in which the interchange of the two terms gives a different proposition. This last mark is required to distinguish a relational proposition from one of the type "*a* and *b* are two," which is identical with "*b* and *a* are two." A relational proposition may be symbolized by *aRb*, where R is the relation and a and b are the terms; and *aRb* will then always, provided a and b are not identical, denote a different proposition from *bRa*. That is to say, it is characteristic of a relation of two terms that it proceeds, so to speak, *from* one *to* the other. This is what may be called the *sense* of the relation, and is, as we shall find, the source of order and series. It must be held as an axiom that *aRb* implies and is implied by a relational proposition $bR'a$, in which the relation R' proceeds from b to a, and may or may not be the same relation as R. But even when *aRb* implies and is implied by *bRa*, it must be strictly maintained that these are different propositions. We may distinguish the term *from* which the relation proceeds as the *referent*, and the term *to* which it proceeds as the *relatum*. The sense of a relation is a fundamental notion, which is not capable of definition. The relation which holds between b and a whenever R holds between a and b will be called the *converse* of R, and will be denoted (following Schröder) by $\breve{R}$. The relation of R to $\breve{R}$ is the relation of oppositeness, or difference of sense; and this must not be defined (as would seem at first sight legitimate) by the above mutual implication in any single case, but only by the fact of

---

[40]This description, as we saw above (§ 48), excludes the pseudo-relation of subject to predicate.

its holding for all cases in which the given relation occurs. The grounds for this view are derived from certain propositions in which terms are related to themselves not-symmetrically, *i.e.* by a relation whose converse is not identical with itself. These propositions must now be examined.

95. There is a certain temptation to affirm that no term can be related to itself; and there is a still stronger temptation to affirm that, if a term can be related to itself, the relation must be symmetrical, *i.e.* identical with its converse. But both these temptations must be resisted. In the first place, if no term were related to itself, we should never be able to assert self-identity, since this is plainly a relation. But since there is such a notion as identity, and since it seems undeniable that every term is identical with itself, we must allow that a term may be related to itself. Identity, however, is still a symmetrical relation, and may be admitted without any great qualms. The matter becomes far worse when we have to admit not-symmetrical relations of terms to themselves. Nevertheless the following propositions seem undeniable; Being is, or has being; 1 is one, or has unity; concept is conceptual: term is a term; class-concept is a class-concept. All these are of one of the three equivalent types which we distinguished at the beginning of Chapter V, which may be called respectively subject-predicate propositions, propositions asserting the relation of predication, and propositions asserting membership of a class. What we have to consider is, then, the fact that a predicate may be predicable of itself. It is necessary, for our present purpose, to take our propositions in the second form (Socrates has humanity), since the subject-predicate form is not in the above sense relational. We may take, as the type of such propositions, "unity has unity." Now it is certainly undeniable that the relation of predication is asymmetrical, since subjects cannot in general be predicated of their predicates. Thus "unity has unity" asserts one relation of unity to itself, and implies another, namely the converse relation: unity has to itself both the relation of subject to predicate, and the relation of predicate to subject. Now if the referent and the relatum are identical, it is

plain that the relatum has to the referent the same relation as the referent has to the relatum. Hence if the converse of a relation in a particular case were defined by mutual implication in that particular case, it would appear that, in the present case, our relation has two converses, since two different relations of relatum to referent are implied by "unity has unity." We must therefore define the converse of a relation by the fact that aRb implies and is implied by $b\breve{R}a$ *whatever* a and b may be, and whether or not the relation R holds between them. That is to say, a and b are here essentially variables, and if we give them any constant value, we may find that aRb implies and is implied by $bR'a$, where R' is some relation other than $\breve{R}$.

Thus three points must be noted with regard to relations of two terms: (1) they all have sense, so that, provided a and b are not identical, we can distinguish aRb from bRa: (2) they all have a converse, *i.e.* a relation $\breve{R}$ such that aRb implies and is implied by $b\breve{R}a$, whatever a and b may be; (3) some relations hold between a term and itself, and such relations are not necessarily symmetrical, *i.e.* there may be two different relations, which are each other's converses, and which both hold between a term and itself.

96. For the general theory of relations, especially in its mathematical developments, certain axioms relating classes and relations are of great importance. It is to be held that to have a given relation to a given term is a predicate, so that all terms having this relation to this term form a class. It is to be held further that to have a given relation at all is a predicate, so that all referents with respect to a given relation form a class. It follows, by considering the converse relation, that all relata also form a class. These two classes I shall call respectively the *domain* and the *converse domain* of the relation; the logical sum of the two I shall call the *field* of the relation.

The axiom that all referents with respect to a given relation form a class seems, however, to require some limitation, and that on account of the contradiction mentioned at the end of Chapter VI. This contradiction may be stated as follows. We saw that some predicates can be predicated of themselves. Consider now those of which this is not the case. These are the referents (and also the relata) in what seems like a complex relation, namely the combination of non-predicability with identity. But there is no predicate which attaches to all of them and to no other terms. For this predicate will either be predicable or not predicable of itself. If it is predicable of itself, it is one of those referents by relation to which it was defined, and therefore, in virtue of their definition, it is not predicable of itself. Conversely, if it is not predicable of itself, then again it is one of the said referents, of all of which (by hypothesis) it is predicable, and therefore again it is predicable of itself. This is a contradiction, which shows that all the referents considered have no exclusive common predicate, and therefore, if defining predicates are essential to classes, do not form a class.

The matter may be put otherwise. In defining the would-be class of predicates, all those not predicable of themselves have been used up. The common predicate of all these predicates cannot be one of them, since for each of them there is at least one predicate (namely itself) of which it is not predicable. But again, the supposed common predicate cannot be any other predicate, for if it were, it would be predicable of itself, *i.e.* it would be a member of the supposed class of predicates, since these were defined as those of which it is predicable. Thus no predicate is left over which could attach to all the predicates considered.

It follows from the above that not every definable collection of terms forms a class defined by a common predicate. This fact must be borne in mind, and we must endeavour to discover what properties a collection must have in order to form such a class. The exact point established by the above contradiction may be stated as follows: A proposition apparently containing only one variable may not be equivalent to any proposition asserting that the variable in question has a certain predicate. It remains an open question whether every class must have a defining predicate.

That all terms having a given relation to a given term form a class defined by an exclusive common predicate results from the doctrine of Chapter VII, that the proposition aRb can be analyzed into the subject a and the assertion Rb. To be a term of which Rb can be asserted appears to be plainly a predicate. But it does not follow, I think, that to be a term of which, for some value of y, Ry can be asserted, is a predicate. The doctrine of propositional functions requires, however, that all terms having the latter property should form a class. This class I shall call the *domain* of the relation R as well as the class of referents. The domain of the converse relation will be also called the converse domain, as well as the class of relata. The two domains together will be called the *field* of the relation—a notion chiefly important as regards series. Thus if paternity be the relation, fathers form its domain, children its converse domain, and fathers and children together its field.

It may be doubted whether a proposition aRb can be regarded as asserting aR of b, or whether only $\check{R}a$ can be asserted of b. In other words, is a relational proposition only an assertion concerning the referent, or also an assertion concerning the relatum? If we take the latter view, we shall have connected with (say) "a is greater than b," four assertions, namely "is greater than b," "a is greater than," "is less than a" and "b is less than." I am inclined myself to adopt this view, but I know of no argument on either side.

97. We can form the logical sum and product of two relations or of a class of relations exactly as in the case of classes, except that here we have to deal with double variability. In addition to these ways of combination, we have also the relative product, which is in general noncommutative, and therefore requires that the number of factors should be finite. If R, S be two relations, to say that their relative product RS holds between two terms x, z is to say that there is a term y to which x has the relation R, and which itself has the relation S to z. Thus brother-in-law is the relative product of wife and brother or of sister and husband: father-in-law is the relative product of wife and father, whereas the relative product of father and wife is mother or step-mother.

98. There is a temptation to regard a rela-

tion as definable in extension as a class of couples. This has the formal advantage that it avoids the necessity for the primitive proposition asserting that every couple has a relation holding between no other pair of terms. But it is necessary to give sense to the couple, to distinguish the referent from the relatum: thus a couple becomes essentially distinct from a class of two terms, and must itself be introduced as a primitive idea. It would seem, viewing the matter philosophically, that sense can only be derived from some relational proposition, and that the assertion that *a* is referent and *b* relatum already involves a purely relational proposition in which *a* and *b* are terms, though the relation asserted is only the general one of referent to relatum. There are, in fact, concepts such as *greater,* which occur otherwise than as terms in propositions having two terms (§§ 48, 54); and no doctrine of couples can evade such propositions. It seems therefore more correct to take an intensional view of relations, and to identify them rather with class-concepts than with classes. This procedure is formally more convenient, and seems also nearer to the logical facts. Throughout Mathematics there is the same rather curious relation of intensional and extensional points of view: the symbols other than variable terms (*i.e.* the variable class-concepts and relations) stand for intensions, while the actual objects dealt with are always extensions. Thus in the calculus of relations, it is classes of couples that are relevant, but the symbolism deals with them by means of relations. This is precisely similar to the state of things explained in relation to classes, and it seems unnecessary to repeat the explanations at length.

99. Mr Bradley, in *Appearance and Reality,* Chapter III, has based an argument against the reality of relations upon the endless regress arising from the fact that a relation which relates two terms must be related to each of them. The endless regress is undeniable, if relational propositions are taken to be ultimate, but it is very doubtful whether it forms any logical difficulty. We have already had occasion (§ 55) to distinguish two kinds of regress, the one proceeding merely to perpetually new implied propositions, the other in the meaning of a proposition itself; of these two kinds, we agreed that the former, since the solution of the problem of infinity, has ceased to be objectionable, while the latter remains inadmissible. We have to inquire which kind of regress occurs in the present instance. It may be urged that it is part of the very meaning of a relational proposition that the relation involved should have to the terms the relation expressed in saying that it relates them, and that this is what makes the distinction, which we formerly (§ 54) left unexplained, between a relating relation and a relation in itself. It may be urged, however, against this view, that the assertion of a relation between the relation and the terms, though implied, is no part of the original proposition, and that a relating relation is distinguished from a relation in itself by the indefinable element of assertion which distinguishes a proposition from a concept. Against this it might be retorted that, in the concept "difference of *a* and *b*," difference relates *a* and *b* just as much as in the proposition "*a* and *b* differ"; but to this it may be rejoined that we found the difference of *a* and *b*, except in so far as some specific point of difference may be in question, to be indistinguishable from bare difference. Thus it seems impossible to prove that the endless regress involved is of the objectionable kind. We may distinguish, I think, between "*a* exceeds *b*" and "*a* is greater than *b*," though it would be absurd to deny that people usually mean the same thing by these two propositions. On the principle, from which I can see no escape, that every genuine word must have some meaning, the *is* and *than* must form part of "*a* is greater than *b*," which thus contains more than two terms and a relation. The *is* seems to state that *a* has to *greater* the relation of referent, while the *than* states similarly that *b* has to *greater* the relation of relatum. But "*a* exceeds *b*" may be held to express solely the relation of *a* to *b*, without including any of the implications of further relations. Hence we shall have to conclude that a relational proposition *aRb* does not include in its *meaning* any relation of *a* or *b* to *R*, and that the endless regress, though undeniable, is logically quite harmless. With

these remarks, we may leave the further theory of relations to later Parts of the present work.

Chapter X:
The Contradiction

---

100. Before taking leave of fundamental questions, it is necessary to examine more in detail the singular contradiction, already mentioned, with regard to predicates not predicable of themselves. Before attempting to solve this puzzle, it will be well to make some deductions connected with it, and to state it in various different forms. I may mention that I was led to it in the endeavour to reconcile Cantor's proof that there can be no greatest cardinal number with the very plausible supposition that the class of all terms (which we have seen to be essential to all formal propositions) has necessarily the greatest possible number of members.

Let w be a class-concept which can be asserted of itself, i.e. such that "w is a w." Instances are *class-concept*, and the negations of ordinary class-concepts, e.g. not-man. Then (α) if w be contained in another class v, since w is a w, w is a v; consequently there is a term of v which is a class-concept that can be asserted of itself. Hence by contraposition, (β) if u be a class-concept none of whose members are class-concepts that can be asserted of themselves, no class-concept contained in u can be asserted of itself. Hence further, (γ) if u be any class-concept whatever, and u' the class-concept of those members of u which are not predicable of themselves, this class-concept is contained in itself, and none of its members are predicable of themselves; hence by (β) u' is not predicable of itself. Thus u' is not a u', and is therefore not a u; for the terms of u that are not terms of u' are all predicable of themselves, which u' is not. Thus (δ) if u be any class-concept whatever, there is a class-concept contained in u which is not a member of u, and is also one of those class-concepts that are not predicable of themselves. So far, our deductions seem scarcely open to question. But if

we now take the last of them, and admit the class of those class-concepts that cannot be asserted of themselves, we find that this class must contain a classs-concept not a member of itself and yet not belonging to the class in question.

We may observe also that, in virtue of what we have proved in (β), the class of class-concepts which cannot be asserted of themselves, which we will call w, contains as members of itself all its sub-classes, although it is easy to prove that every class has more sub-classes than terms. Again, if y be any term of w, and w' be the whole of w except y, then w', being a sub-class of w, is not a w' but is a w, and therefore is y. Hence each class-concept which is a term of w has all other terms of w as its extension. It follows that the concept *bicycle* is a teaspoon, and *teaspoon* is a bicycle. This is plainly absurd, and any number of similar absurdities can be proved.

101. Let us leave these paradoxical consequences, and attempt the exact statement of the contradiction itself. We have first the statement in terms of predicates, which has been given already. If x be a predicate, x may or may not be predicable of itself. Let us assume that "not-predicable of oneself" is a predicate. Then to suppose either that this predicate is, or that it is not, predicable of itself, is self-contradictory. The conclusion, in this case, seems obvious: "not-predicable of oneself" is not a predicate.

Let us now state the same contradiction in terms of class-concepts. A class-concept may or may not be a term of its own extension. "Class-concept which is not a term of its own extension" appears to be a class-concept. But if it is a term of its own extension, it is a class-concept which is not a term of its own extension, and *vice versa*. Thus we must conclude, against appearances, that "class-concept which is not a term of its own extension" is not a class-concept.

In terms of classes the contradiction appears even more extraordinary. A class as one may be a term of itself as many. Thus the class of all classes is a class; the class of all the terms that are not men is not a man, and so on. Do all the classes that have this property form a class? If so, is it as one a member of itself as many or not? If it is, then it is one of the classes which, as ones, are not members of themselves as many, and *vice versa.* Thus we must conclude again that the classes which as ones are not members of themselves as many do not form a class—or rather, that they do not form a class as one, for the argument cannot show that they do not form a class as many.

102. A similar result, which, however, does not lead to a contradiction, may be proved concerning any relation. Let R be a relation, and consider the class w of terms which do not have the relation R to themselves. Then it is impossible that there should be any term a to which all of them and no other terms have the relation R. For, if there were such a term, the propositional function "x does not have the relation R to x" would be equivalent to "x has the relation R to a." Substituting a for x throughout, which is legitimate since the equivalence is formal, we find a contradiction. When in place of R we put ϵ, the relation of a term to a class-concept which can be asserted of it, we get the above contradiction. The reason that a contradiction emerges here is that we have taken it as an axiom that any propositional function containing only one variable is equivalent to asserting membership of a class defined by the propositional function. Either this axiom, or the principle that every class can be taken as one term, is plainly false, and there is no fundamental objection to dropping either. But having dropped the former, the question arises: Which propositional functions define classes which are single terms as well as many, and which do not? And with this question our real difficulties begin.

Any method by which we attempt to establish a one-one or many-one correlation of all terms and all propositional functions must omit at least one propositional function. Such a method would exist if all propositional functions could be expressed in the form $\ldots \epsilon u$, since this form correlates u with $\ldots \epsilon u$. But the impossibility of any such correlation is proved as follows. Let ϕ_x be a propositional function correlated with x; then, if the correlation covers all terms, the denial of $\phi_x(x)$ will be a propositional function, since it is a proposition for all values of x. But it cannot be included in the correlation; for if it were correlated with a, $\phi_a(x)$ would be equivalent, for all values of x, to the denial of $\phi_x(x)$; but this equivalence is impossible for the value a, since it makes $\phi_a(a)$ equivalent to its own denial. It follows that there are more propositional functions than terms—a result which seems plainly impossible, although the proof is as convincing as any in Mathematics. We shall shortly see how the impossibility is removed by the doctrine of logical types.

103. The first method which suggests itself is to seek an ambiguity in the notion of ϵ. But in Chapter VI we distinguished the various meanings as far as any distinction seemed possible, and we have just seen that with each meaning the same contradiction emerges. Let us, however, attempt to state the contradiction throughout in terms of propositional functions. Every propositional function which is not null, we supposed, defines a class, and every class can certainly be defined by a propositional function. Thus to say that a class as one is not a member of itself as many is to say that the class as one does not satisfy the function by which itself as many is defined. Since all propositional functions except such as are null define classes, all will be used up, in considering all classes having the above property, except such as do not have the above property. If any propositional function were satisfied by every class having the above property, it would therefore necessarily be one satisfied also by the class w of all such classes considered as a single term. Hence the class w does not itself belong to the class w, and therefore there must be some propositional function satisfied by the terms of w but not by w itself. Thus the contradiction re-emerges, and we must suppose, either that there is no such entity as w, or that there is no propositional function satisfied by its terms and by no others.

It might be thought that a solution could be found by denying the legitimacy of variable propositional functions. If we denote by k_ϕ, for the moment, the class of values satisfying ϕ, our propositional function is the denial of $\phi(k_\phi)$, where ϕ is the variable. The doctrine of Chapter VII, that ϕ is not a separable entity, might make such a variable seem illegitimate; but this objection can be overcome by substituting for ϕ the class of propositions ϕx, or the relation of ϕx to x. Moreover it is impossible to exclude variable propositional functions altogether. Wherever a variable class or a variable relation occurs, we have admitted a variable propositional function, which is thus essential to assertions about every class or about every relation. The definition of the domain of a relation, for example, and all the general propositions which constitute the calculus of relations, would be swept away by the refusal to allow this type of variation. Thus we require some further characteristic by which to distinguish two kinds of variation. This characteristic is to be found, I think, in the independent variability of the function and the argument. In general, ϕx is itself a function of two variables, ϕ and x; of these, either may be given a constant value, and either may be varied without reference to the other. But in the type of propositional functions we are considering in this Chapter, the argument is itself a function of the propositional function: instead of ϕx, we have $\phi \{f(\phi)\}$, where $f(\phi)$ is defined as a function of ϕ. Thus when ϕ is varied, the argument of which ϕ is asserted is varied too. Thus "x is an x" is equivalent to: "ϕ can be asserted of the class of terms satisfying ϕ," this class of terms being x. If here ϕ is varied, the argument is varied at the same time in a manner dependent upon the variation of ϕ. For this reason, $\phi \{f(\phi)\}$, though it is a definite proposition when x is assigned, is not a propositional function, in the ordinary sense, when x is variable. Propositional functions of this doubtful type may be called *quadratic forms*, because the variable enters into them in a way somewhat analogous to that in which, in Algebra, a variable appears in an expression of the second degree.

104. Perhaps the best way to state the suggested solution is to say that, if a collection of terms can only be defined by a variable propositional function, then, though a class as many may be admitted, a class as one must be denied. When so stated, it appears that propositional functions may be varied, provided the resulting collection is never itself made into the subject in the original propositional function. In such cases there is only a class as many, not a class as one. We took it as axiomatic that

the class as one is to be found wherever there is a class as many; but this axiom need not be universally admitted, and appears to have been the source of the contradiction. By denying it, therefore, the whole difficulty will be overcome.

A class as one, we shall say, is an object of the same *type* as its terms; *i.e.* any propositional function $\phi(x)$ which is significant when one of the terms is substituted for x is also significant when the class as one is substituted. But the class as one does not always exist, and the class as many is of a different type from the terms of the class, even when the class has only one term, *i.e.* there are propositional functions $\phi(u)$ in which u may be the class as many, which are meaningless if, for u, we substitute one of the terms of the class. And so "x is one among x's" is not a proposition at all if the relation involved is that of a term to its class as many; and this is the only relation of whose presence a propositional function always assures us. In this view, a class as many may be a logical subject, but in propositions of a different kind from those in which its terms are subjects; of any object other than a single term, the question whether it is one or many will have different answers according to the proposition in which it occurs. Thus we have "Socrates is one among men," in which men are plural; but "men are one among species of animals," in which men are singular. It is the distinction of logical types that is the key to the whole mystery.

105. Other ways of evading the contradiction, which might be suggested, appear undesirable, on the ground that they destroy too many quite necessary kinds of propositions. It might be suggested that identity is introduced in "x is not an x" in a way which is not permissible. But it has been already shown that relations of terms to themselves are unavoidable, and it may be observed that suicides or selfmade men or the heroes of Smiles's *Self-Help* are all defined by relations to themselves. And generally, identity enters in a very similar way into formal implication, so that it is quite impossible to reject it.

A natural suggestion for escaping from the contradiction would be to demur to the notion of *all* terms or of *all* classes. It might be urged that no such sum-total is conceivable; and if *all* indicates a whole, our escape from the contradiction requires us to admit this. But we have already abundantly seen that if this view were maintained against *any* term, all formal truth would be impossible, and Mathematics, whose characteristic is the statement of truths concerning *any* term, would be abolished at one stroke. Thus the correct statement of formal truths requires the notion of *any* term or *every* term, but not the collective notion of *all* terms.

It should be observed, finally, that no peculiar philosophy is involved in the above contradiction, which springs directly from common sense, and can only be solved by abandoning some common-sense assumption. Only the Hegelian philosophy, which nourishes itself on contradictions, can remain indifferent, because it finds similar problems everywhere. In any other doctrine, so direct a challenge demands an answer, on pain of a confession of impotence. Fortunately, no other similar difficulty, so far as I know, occurs in any other portion of the Principles of Mathematics.

106. We may now briefly review the conclusions arrived at in Part I. Pure Mathematics was defined as the class of propositions asserting formal implications and containing no constants except logical constants. And logical constants are: Implication, the relation of a term to a class of which it is a member, the notion of *such that*, the notion of relation, and such further notions as are involved in formal implication, which we found (§ 93) to be the following: propositional function, class,[41] denoting, and *any* or *every term*. This definition brought Mathematics into very close relation to Logic, and made it practically identical with Symbolic Logic. An examination of Symbolic Logic justified the above enumeration of mathematical indefinables. In Chapter III we distinguished implication and formal implication. The former holds between any two propositions provided the first be false or the second true. The latter is not a relation, but the assertion, for every value of the variable or

variables, of a propositional function which, for every value of the variable or variables, asserts an implication. Chapter IV distinguished what may be called *things* from predicates and relations (including the *is* of predications among relations for this purpose). It was shown that this distinction is connected with the doctrine of substance and attributes, but does not lead to the traditional results. Chapters V and VI developed the theory of predicates. In the former of these chapters it was shown that certain concepts, derived from predicates, occur in propositions not *about* themselves, but about combinations of terms, such as are indicated by *all, every, any, a, some,* and *the*. Concepts of this kind, we found, are fundamental in Mathematics, and enable us to deal with infinite classes by means of propositions of finite complexity. In Chapter VI we distinguished predicates, class-concepts, concepts of classes, classes as many, and classes as one. We agreed that single terms, or such combinations as result from *and*, are classes, the latter being classes as many; and that classes as many are the objects denoted by concepts of classes, which are the plurals of class-concepts. But in the present chapter we decided that it is necessary to distinguish a single term from the class whose only member it is, and that consequently the null-class may be admitted.

In Chapter VII we resumed the study of the verb. Subject-predicate propositions, and such as express a fixed relation to a fixed term, could be analyzed, we found, into a subject and an assertion; but this analysis becomes impossible when a given term enters into a proposition in a more complicated manner than as referent of a relation. Hence it became necessary to take *propositional function* as a primitive notion. A propositional function of one variable is any proposition of a set defined by the variation of a single term, while the other terms remain constant. But in general it is impossible to define or isolate the constant element in a propositional function, since what remains, when a certain term, wherever it occurs, is left out of a proposition, is in general no discoverable kind of entity. Thus the term in question must be not simply omitted, but replaced by a *variable*.

[41]The notion of *class* in general, we decided, could be replaced, as an indefinable, by that of the class of propositions defined by a propositional function.

The notion of the variable, we found, is exceedingly complicated. The x is not simply *any* term, but any term with a certain individuality; for if not, any two variables would be indistinguishable. We agreed that a variable is any term *quâ* term in a certain propositional function, and that variables are distinguished by the propositional functions in which they occur, or, in the case of several variables, by the place they occupy in a given multiply variable propositional function. A variable, we said, is *the* term in *any* proposition of the set denoted by a given propositional function.

Chapter IX pointed out that relational propositions are ultimate, and that they all have *sense: i.e.* the relation being the concept as such in a proposition with two terms, there is another proposition containing the same terms and the same concept as such, as in "*A* is greater than *B*" and "*B* is greater than *A*." These two propositions, though different, contain precisely the same constituents. This is a characteristic of relations, and an instance of the loss resulting from analysis. Relations, we agreed, are to be taken intensionally, not as classes of couples.

Finally, in the present chapter, we examined the contradiction resulting from the apparent fact that, if w be the class of all classes which as single terms are not members of themselves as many, then w as one can be proved both to be and not to be a member of itself as many. The solution suggested was that it is necessary to distinguish various types of objects, namely terms, classes of terms, classes of classes, classes of couples of terms, and so on; and that a propositonal function ϕx in general requires, if it is to have any meaning, that x should belong to some one type. Thus $x \epsilon x$ was held to be meaningless, because ϵ requires that the relatum should be a class composed of objects which are of the type of the referent. The class as one, where it exists, is, we said, of the same type as its constituents; but a quadratic propositional function in general appears to define only a class as many, and the contradiction proves that the class as one, if it ever exists, is certainly sometimes absent.

XII

Ludwig Wittgenstein

LUDWIG WITTGENSTEIN (1889–1951) was born to one of the wealthiest families in Vienna. After studying engineering, mathematics, and the physical sciences, he went to England to do research in aeronautical engineering (the forerunner of aerospace engineering), making possible the fateful meeting of two of the greatest minds of the 20th century. Bertrand Russell, in his autobiography, describes how he came to meet Wittgenstein at Cambridge before World War I. Apparently, while doing his engineering mathematics, Wittgenstein began to ponder what it was about the world and the mind that made mathematics possible. Not finding an answer in any of his mathematics books, he asked whom he should consult. Russell says:

> Somebody mentioned my name, and he took up his residence at Trinity. He was perhaps the most perfect example I have ever known of genius as traditionally conceived, passionate, profound, intense, and dominating. He had a kind of purity which I have never known equalled except by G. E. Moore. I remember taking him once to a meeting of the Aristotelian Society, at which there were various fools whom I treated politely. When we came away he raged and stormed against my [moral] degradation in not telling these men what fools they were. His life was turbulent and troubled, and his personal force was extraordinary. . . . He used to come to see me every evening at midnight, and pace up and down my room like a wild beast for three hours in agitated silence. Once I said to him: "Are you thinking about logic or about your sins?" "Both," he replied, and continued his pacing. I did not like to suggest that it was time for bed, as it seemed probable both to him and me that on leaving me he would commit suicide.

At the end of his first term at Trinity, he came to me and said: "Do you think I am an absolute idiot?" I said: "Why do you want to know?" He replied: "Because if I am I shall become an aeronaut, but if I am not I shall become a philosopher." I said to him: "My dear fellow, I don't know whether you are an absolute idiot or not, but if you will write me an essay during the vacation upon any philosophical topic that interests you, I will read it and tell you." He did so, and brought it to me at the beginning of the next term. As soon as I read the first sentence, I became persuaded that he was a man of genius, and assured him that he should on no account become an aeronaut.*

When Russell asked the great G. E. Moore, another legendary Cambridge philosopher, what he thought of Wittgenstein, Moore replied that he thought very well of him "because at my lectures he looks puzzled, and nobody else ever looks puzzled."

World War I interrupted Wittgenstein's studies with Russell and he became an officer in the Austrian army—completing his doctoral dissertation in the trenches! The work, *Tractatus Logico-Philosophicus*, which you are about to read, was the only one published in his lifetime but it helped create the revolution in modern philosophy that led to the development of logical positivism, linguistic analysis, and semantics. The noted Oxford philosopher P. F. Strawson called Wittgenstein "the preeminent philosopher of this century." The profound effect he has had on philosophy cannot be overstated. In an intimate letter to a woman friend, Russell describes hauntingly the influence his student had on him:

> Do you remember that at the time when you were seeing Vittoz I wrote a lot of stuff about Theory of Knowledge, which Wittgenstein criticized with the greatest severity? His criticism, though I don't think you realized it at the time, was an event of first-rate importance in my life, and affected everything I have done since. I saw he was right, and I saw that I could not hope ever again to do fundamental work in philosophy. My impluse was shattered, like a wave dashed to pieces against a breakwater. I became filled with utter despair. . . .†

In the following reading, Wittgenstein makes clear the relationship between language and thought and shows how through them the mind is able to hook onto reality. He warns, in the preface, that probably the book won't be understood unless the reader "has himself already had the thoughts that are expressed in it—or at least similar thoughts."

*From *The Autobiography of Bertrand Russell* (Boston: Little, Brown, 1951), pp. 142–143.
†Ibid., p. 68.

Tractatus Logico-Philosophicus

Ludwig Wittgenstein

1   The world is all that is the case.

1.1   The world is the totality of facts, not of things.

1.11   The world is determined by the facts, and by their being *all* the facts.

1.12   For the totality of facts determines what is the case, and also whatever is not the case.

1.13   The facts in logical space are the world.

1.2   The world divides into facts.

1.21   Each item can be the case or not the case while everything else remains the same.

2   What is the case—a fact—is the existence of states of affairs.

2.01   A state of affairs (a state of things) is a combination of objects (things).

. . . .

2.02   Objects are simple.

. . . .

2.03   In a state of affairs objects fit into one another like the links of a chain.

. . . .

2.04   The totality of existing states of affairs is the world.

2.05   The totality of existing states of affairs also determines which states of affairs do not exist.

2.06   The existence and non-existence of states of affairs is reality.

(We also call the existence of states of affairs a positive fact, and their non-existence a negative fact.)

. . . .

2.1   We picture facts to ourselves.

SOURCE: Ludwig Wittgenstein, *Tractatus Logico-Philosophicus*, translated by D. F. Pears and E. F. McGuinness (New Jersey: Humanities Press International, Inc., 1961).

2.11   A picture presents a situation in logical space, the existence and non-existence of states of affairs.

2.12   A picture is a model of reality.

2.13   In a picture objects have the elements of the picture corresponding to them.

. . . .

2.14   What constitutes a picture is that its elements are related to one another in a determinate way.

. . . .

2.15   The fact that the elements of a picture are related to one another in a determinate way represents that things are related to one another in the same way.

Let us call this connexion of its elements the structure of the picture, and let us call the possibility of this structure the pictorial form of the picture.

. . . .

2.16   If a fact is to be a picture, it must have something in common with what it depicts.

. . . .

2.17   What a picture must have in common with reality, in order to be able to depict it—correctly or incorrectly—in the way it does, is its pictorial form.

. . . .

2.18   What any picture, of whatever form, must have in common with reality, in order to be able to depict it—correctly or incorrectly—in any way at all, is logical form, i.e. the form of reality.

. . . .

2.19   Logical pictures can depict the world.

2.2   A picture has logico-pictorial form in common with what it depicts.

. . . .

2.21   A picture agrees with reality or fails to agree; it is correct or incorrect, true or false.

2.22   What a picture represents it represents independently of its truth or falsity, by means of its pictorial form.

. . . .

3   A logical picture of facts is a thought.

. . . .

3.01   The totality of true thoughts is a picture of the world.

3.02   A thought contains the possibility of the situation of which it is the thought. What is thinkable is possible too.

3.03   Thought can never be of anything illogical, since, if it were, we should have to think illogically.

. . . .

3.04   If a thought were correct a priori, it would be a thought whose possibility ensured its truth.

3.05   A priori knowledge that a thought was true would be possible only if its truth were recognizable from the thought itself (without anything to compare it with).

3.1   In a proposition a thought finds an expression that can be perceived by the senses.

3.11   We use the perceptible sign of a proposition (spoken or written, etc.) as a projection of a possible situation.

The method of projection is to think of the sense of the proposition.

3.12   I call the sign with which we express a thought a propositional sign.—And a proposition is a propositional sign in its projective relation to the world.

3.13   A proposition includes all that the projection includes, but not what is projected.

Therefore, though what is projected is not itself included, its possibility is.

A proposition, therefore, does not actually contain its sense, but does contain the possibility of expressing it.

('The content of a proposition' means the content of a proposition that has sense.)

A proposition contains the form, but not the content, of its sense.

3.14   What constitutes a propositional sign is that in it its elements (the words) stand in a determinate relation to one another.

. . . .

3.2   In a proposition a thought can be expressed in such a way that elements of the propositional sign correspond to the objects of the thought.

. . . .

3.21   The configuration of objects in a situation corresponds to the configuration of simple signs in the propositional sign.

3.22   In a proposition a name is the representative of an object.

. . . .

3.23   The requirement that simple signs be possible is the requirement that sense be determinate.

3.24   A proposition about a complex stands in an internal relation to a proposition about a constituent of the complex.

A complex can be given only by its description, which will be right or wrong. A proposition that mentions a complex will not be nonsensical, if the complex does not exist, but simply false.

When a propositional element signifies a complex, this can be seen from an indeterminateness in the propositions in which it occurs. In such cases we *know* that the proposition leaves something undetermined. (In fact the notation for generality *contains* a prototype.)

The contraction of a symbol for a complex into a simple symbol can be expressed in a definition.

3.25   A proposition has one and only one complete analysis.

. . . .

3.26   A name cannot be dissected any further by means of a definition: it is a primitive sign.

. . . .

3.3   Only propositions have sense; only in the nexus of a proposition does a name have meaning.

3.31   I call any part of a proposition that characterizes its sense an expression (or a symbol).

(A proposition is itself an expression.)

Everything essential to their sense that propositions can have in common with one another is an expression.

An expression is the mark of a form and a content.

. . . .

3.32   A sign is what can be perceived of a symbol.

. . . .

3.33   In logical syntax the meaning of a sign should never play a rôle. It must be possible to establish logical syntax without mentioning the *meaning* of a sign: *only* the description of expressions may be presupposed.

. . . .

3.34   A proposition possesses essential and accidental features.

Accidental features are those that result from the particular way in which the propositional sign is produced. Essential features are those without which the proposition could not express its sense.

. . . .

3.4   A proposition determines a place in logical space. The existence of this logical place is guaranteed by the mere existence of the constituents—by the existence of the proposition with a sense.

3.41   The propositional sign with logical co-ordinates—that is the logical place.

. . . .

3.42   A proposition can determine only one place in logical space: nevertheless the whole of logical space must already be given by it.

(Otherwise negation, logical sum, logical product, etc., would introduce more and more new elements—in coordination.)

(The logical scaffolding surrounding a picture determines logical space. The force of a proposition reaches through the whole of logical space.)

3.5   A propositional sign, applied and thought out, is a thought.

4   A thought is a proposition with a sense.

. . . .

4.01   A proposition is a picture of reality.

A proposition is a model of reality as we imagine it.

. . . .

4.02   We can see this from the fact that we understand the sense of a propositional sign without its having been explained to us.

. . . .

4.03   A proposition must use old expressions to communicate a new sense.

A proposition communicates a situation to us, and so it must be *essentially* connected with the situation.

And the connexion is precisely that it is its logical picture.

A proposition states something only in so far as it is a picture.

. . . .

4.04   In a proposition there must be exactly as many distinguishable parts as in the situation that it represents.

The two must possess the same logical (mathematical) multiplicity. (Compare Hertz's *Mechanics* on dynamical models.)

. . . .

4.05   Reality is compared with propositions.

4.06   A proposition can be true or false only in virtue of being a picture of reality.

. . . .

4.1   Propositions represent the existence and non-existence of states of affairs.

4.11   The totality of true propositions is the whole of natural science (or the whole corpus of the natural sciences).

. . . .

4.12   Propositions can represent the whole of reality, but they cannot represent what they must have in common with reality in order to be able to represent it—logical form.

In order to be able to represent logical form, we should have to be able to station ourselves with propositions somewhere outside logic, that is to say outside the world.

. . . .

4.2   The sense of a proposition is its agreement and disagreement with possibilities of existence and non-existence of states of affairs.

4.21   The simplest kind of proposition, an elementary proposition, asserts the existence of a state of affairs.

4.211   It is a sign of a proposition's being elementary that there can be no elementary proposition contradicting it.

4.22   An elementary proposition consists of names. It is a nexus, a concatenation, of names.

. . . .

4.23   It is only in the nexus of an elementary proposition that a name occurs in a proposition.

4.24   Names are the simple symbols: I indicate them by single letters ('x', 'y', 'z').

I write elementary propositions as functions of names, so that they have the form 'fx', '$\phi(x,y)$', etc.

Or I indicate them by the letters 'p', 'q', 'r'.

4.25   If an elementary proposition is true, the state of affairs exists: if an elementary proposition is false, the state of affairs does not exist.

4.26   If all true elementary propositions are given, the result is a complete description of the world. The world is completely described by giving all elementary propositions, and adding which of them are true and which false.

4.27   For n states of affairs, there are

$$K_n = \sum_{v=0}^{n} \binom{n}{v}$$

possibilities of existence and non-existence.

Of these states of affairs any combination can exist and the remainder not exist.

4.28   There correspond to these combinations the same number of possibilities of truth—and falsity—for n elementary propositions.

4.3   Truth-possibilities of elementary propositions mean possibilities of existence and non-existence of states of affairs.

4.31   We can represent truth-possibilities by schemata of the following kind ('T' means 'true', 'F' means 'false'; the rows of 'T's' and 'F's' under the row of elementary propositions symbolize their truth-possibilities in a way that can easily be understood):

p	q	r
T	T	T
F	T	T
T	F	T
T	T	F
F	F	T
F	T	F
T	F	F
F	F	F

p	q
T	T
F	T
T	F
F	F

p
T
F

4.4   A proposition is an expression of agreement and disagreement with truth-possibilities of elementary propositions.

4.41   Truth-possibilities of elementary propositions are the conditions of the truth and falsity of propositions.

. . . .

4.42   For *n* elementary propositions there are

$$\sum_{\kappa=0}^{K_n} \binom{K_n}{\kappa} = L_n$$

ways in which a proposition can agree and disagree with their truth-possibilities.

4.43   We can express agreement with truth-possibilities by correlating the mark '*T*' (true) with them in the schema.

The absence of this mark means disagreement.

. . . .

4.44   The sign that results from correlating the mark '*T*' with truth-possibilities is a propositional sign.

. . . .

4.45   For *n* elementary propositions there are L_n possible groups of truth-conditions.

The groups of truth-conditions that are obtainable from the truth-possibilities of a given number of elementary propositions can be arranged in a series.

4.46   Among the possible groups of truth-conditions there are two extreme cases.

In one of these cases the proposition is true for all the truth-possibilities of the elementary propositions. We say that the truth-conditions are *tautological*.

In the second case the proposition is false for all the truth-possibilities: the truth-conditions are *contradictory*.

In the first case we call the proposition a tautology; in the second, a contradiction.

4.5   It now seems possible to give the most general propositional form: that is, to give a description of the propositions of *any* sign-language *whatsoever* in such a way that every possible sense can be expressed by a symbol satisfying the description, and every symbol satisfying the description can express a sense, provided that the meanings of the names are suitably chosen.

It is clear that *only* what is essential to the most general propositional form may be included in its description—for otherwise it would not be the most general form.

The existence of a general propositional form is proved by the fact that there cannot be a proposition whose form could not have been foreseen (i.e. constructed). The general form of a proposition is: This is how things stand.

4.51   Suppose that I am given *all* elementary propositions: then I can simply ask what propositions I can construct out of them. And there I have *all* propositions, and *that* fixes their limits.

4.52   Propositions comprise all that follows from the totality of all elementary propositions (and, of course, from its being the *totality* of them all). (Thus, in a certain sense, it could be said that *all* propositions were generalizations of elementary propositions.)

4.53   The general propositional form is a variable.

5   A proposition is a truth-function of elementary propositions.

(An elementary proposition is a truth-function of itself.)

5.01   Elementary propositions are the truth-arguments of propositions.

5.02   The arguments of functions are readily confused with the affixes of names. For both arguments and affixes enable me to recognize the meaning of the signs containing them.

For example, when Russell writes '$+_c$', the '$_c$' is an affix which indicates that the sign as a whole is the addition-sign for cardinal numbers. But the use of this sign is the result of arbitrary convention and it would be quite possible to choose a simple sign instead of '$+_c$'; in '$\sim p$', however, 'p' is not an affix but an argument: the sense of '$\sim p$' *cannot* be understood unless the sense of 'p' has been understood already. (In the name Julius Caesar 'Julius' is an affix. An affix is always part of a description of the object to whose name we attach it: e.g. *the* Caesar of the Julian gens.)

If I am not mistaken, Frege's theory about the meaning of propositions and functions is based on the confusion between an argument and an affix. Frege regarded the propositions of logic as names, and their arguments as the affixes of those names.

5.1   Truth-functions can be arranged in series.

That is the foundation of the theory of probability.

. . . .

5.11   If all the truth-grounds that are common to a number of propositions are at the same time truth-grounds of a certain proposition, then we say that the truth of that proposition follows from the truth of the others.

5.12   In particular, the truth of a proposition 'p' follows from the truth of another proposition 'q' if all the truth-grounds of the latter are truth-grounds of the former.

. . . .

5.13   When the truth of one proposition follows from the truth of others, we can see this from the structure of the propositions.

. . . .

5.14   If one proposition follows from another, then the latter says more than the former, and the former less than the latter.

. . . .

5.15   If T_r is the number of the truth-grounds of a proposition 'r', and if T_{rs} is the number of the truth-grounds of a

proposition 's' that are at the same time truth-grounds of 'r', then we call the ratio $T_{rs} : T_r$ the degree of *probability* that the proposition 'r' gives to the proposition 's'.

. . . .

5.2   The structures of propositions stand in internal relations to one another.

5.21   In order to give prominence to these internal relations we can adopt the following mode of expression: we can represent a proposition as the result of an operation that produces it out of other propositions (which are the bases of the operation).

5.22   An operation is the expression of a relation between the structures of its result and of its bases.

5.23   The operation is what has to be done to the one proposition in order to make the other out of it.

. . . .

5.24   An operation manifests itself in a variable; it shows how we can get from one form of proposition to another.

It gives expression to the difference between the forms.

(And what the bases of an operation and its result have in common is just the bases themselves.)

. . . .

5.25   The occurrence of an operation does not characterize the sense of a proposition.

Indeed, no statement is made by an operation, but only by its result, and this depends on the bases of the operation.

(Operations and functions must not be confused with each other.)

5.3   All propositions are results of truth-operations on elementary propositions.

A truth-operation is the way in which a truth-function is produced out of elementary propositions.

It is of the essence of truth-operations that, just as elementary propositions yield a truth-function of themselves, so too in the same way truth-functions yield a further truth-function. When a truth-operation is applied to truth-functions of elementary propositions, it always generates another truth-function of elementary propositions, another proposition. When a truth-operation is applied to the results of truth-operations on elementary propositions, there is always a *single* operation on elementary propositions that has the same result.

Every proposition is the result of truth-operations on elementary propositions.

. . . .

5.31   The schemata in 4.31 have a meaning even when '*p*', '*q*', '*r*', etc. are not elementary propositions.

And it is easy to see that the propositional sign . . . 4.442 expresses a single truth-function of elementary propositions even when '*p*' and '*q*' are truth-functions of elementary propositions.

5.32   All truth-functions are results of successive applications to elementary propositions of a finite number of truth-operations.

5.4   At this point it becomes manifest that there are no 'logical objects' or 'logical constants' (in Frege's and Russell's sense).

5.41   The reason is that the result of truth-operations on truth-functions are always identical whenever they are one and the same truth-function of elementary propositions.

5.42   It is self-evident that v, ⊃, etc. are not relations in the sense in which right and left etc. are relations.

The interdefinability of Frege's and Russell's 'primitive signs' of logic is enough to show that they are not primitive signs, still less signs for relations.

And it is obvious that the '⊃' defined by means of '~' and 'v' is identical with the one that figures with '~' in the definition of 'v'; and that the second 'v' is identical with the first one; and so on.

5.43   Even at first sight it seems scarcely credible that there should follow from one fact *p* infinitely many *others*, namely ~~*p*, ~~~~*p*, etc. And it is no less remarkable that the infinite number of propositions of logic (mathematics) follow from half a dozen 'primitive propositions'.

But in fact all the propositions of logic say the same thing, to wit nothing.

5.44   Truth-functions are not material functions.

For example, an affirmation can be produced by double negation; in such a case does it follow that in some sense negation is contained in affirmation? Does '~~*p*' negate ~*p*, or does it affirm *p*—or both?

The proposition '~~*p*' is not about negation, as if negation were an object: on the other hand, the possibility of negation is already written into affirmation.

And if there were an object called '~', it would follow that '~~*p*' said something different from what '*p*' said, just because the one proposition would then be about ~ and the other would not.

. . . .

5.45   If there are primitive logical signs, then any logic that fails to show clearly how they are placed relatively to one another and to justify their existence will be incorrect. The construction of logic *out of* its primitive signs must be made clear.

. . . .

5.46   If we introduced logical signs properly, then we should also have introduced at the same time the sense of all combinations of them; i.e. not only '*p* v *q*' but '~(*p* v ~*q*)' as well, etc. etc. We should also have introduced at the same time the effect of all possible combinations of brackets. And thus it would have been made clear that the real general primitive signs are not '*p* v *q*', '(∃*x*).*fx*', etc. but the most general form of their combinations.

. . . .

5.47   It is clear that whatever we can say *in advance* about the form of all propositions, we must be able to say *all at once*.

An elementary proposition really contains all logical operations in itself. For '*fa*' says the same thing as

$$(\exists x) . fx . x = a'.$$

Wherever there is compositeness, argument and function are present, and where these are present, we already have all the logical constants.

One could say that the sole logical constant was what *all* propositions, by their very nature, had in common with one another.

But that is the general propositional form.

. . . .

5.5   Every truth-function is a result of successive applications to elementary propositions of the operation

$$(-----T)(\xi, \ldots .)'.$$

This operation negates all the propositions in the right-hand pair of brackets, and I call it the negation of those propositions.

. . . .

5.51   If ξ has only one value, then $N(\bar\xi) = \sim p$ (not p); if it has two values, then $N(\bar\xi) = \sim p . \sim q$ (neither p nor q).

. . . .

5.52   If ξ has as its values all the values of a function fx for all values of x, then $N(\bar\xi) = \sim(\exists x).fx$.

. . . .

5.53   Identity of object I express by identity of sign, and not by using a sign for identity. Difference of objects I express by difference of signs.

. . . .

5.54   In the general propositional form propositions occur in other propositions only as bases of truth-operations.

. . . .

5.55   We now have to answer a priori the question about all the possible forms of elementary propositions.

Elementary propositions consist of names. Since, however, we are unable to give the number of names with different meanings, we are also unable to give the composition of elementary propositions.

. . . .

5.6   *The limits of my language* mean the limits of my world.

5.61   Logic pervades the world; the limits of the world are also its limits.

So we cannot say in logic, 'The world has this in it, and this, but not that.'

For that would appear to presuppose that we were excluding certain possibilities, and this cannot be the case, since it would require that logic should go beyond the limits of the world; for only in that way could it view those limits from the other side as well.

We cannot think what we cannot think; so what we cannot think we cannot *say* either.

5.62   This remark provides the key to the problem, how much truth there is in solipsism.

For what the solipsist *means* is quite correct; only it cannot be *said*, but makes itself manifest.

The world is *my* world: this is manifest in the fact that the limits of *language* (of that language which alone I understand) mean the limits of *my* world.

5.63   I am my world. (The microcosm.)

. . . .

5.64   Here it can be seen that solipsism, when its implications are followed out strictly, coincides with pure realism. The self of solipsism shrinks to a point without extension, and there remains the reality co-ordinated with it.

. . . .

6   The general form of a truth-function is $[\bar p, \bar\xi, N(\bar\xi)]$. This is the general form of a proposition.

. . . .

6.01 Therefore the general form of an operation $\Omega'(\bar{\eta})$ is

$$[\bar{\xi}, N(\bar{\xi})]'(\bar{\eta}) \ (= [\bar{\eta}, \bar{\xi}, N(\bar{\xi})]).$$

This is the most general form of transition from one proposition to another.

6.02 And *this* is how we arrive at numbers. I give the following definitions

$$x = \Omega^{0\prime}x \ \text{Def.},$$
$$\Omega'\Omega^{v\prime}x = \Omega^{v+1\prime}x \ \text{Def.}$$

So, in accordance with these rules, which deal with signs, we write the series

$$x, \ \Omega'x, \ \Omega'\Omega'x, \ \Omega'\Omega'\Omega'x, \ \dots ,$$

in the following way

$$\Omega^{0\prime}x, \ \Omega^{0+1\prime}x, \ \Omega^{0+1+1\prime}x, \ \Omega^{0+1+1+1\prime}x, \ \dots .$$

Therefore, instead of '$[x, \ \xi, \ \Omega'\xi]$', I write '$[\Omega^{0\prime}x, \ \Omega^{v\prime}x, \ \Omega^{v+1\prime}x]$'.

And I give the following definitions

$$0+1 = 1 \ \text{Def.},$$
$$0+1+1 = 2 \ \text{Def.},$$
$$0+1+1+1 = 3 \ \text{Def.},$$
$$(\text{and so on}).$$

. . . .

6.03 The general form of an integer is $[0, \xi, \xi+1]$.

. . . .

6.1 The propositions of logic are tautologies.

6.11 Therefore the propositions of logic say nothing. (They are the analytic propositions.)

. . . .

6.12 The fact that the propositions of logic are tautologies *shows* the formal—logical—properties of language and the world.

The fact that a tautology is yielded by *this particular way* of connecting its constituents characterizes the logic of its constituents.

If propositions are to yield a tautology when they are connected in a certain way, they must have certain structural properties. So their yielding a tautology when combined *in this way* shows that they possess these structural properties.

. . . .

6.13 Logic is not a body of doctrine, but a mirror-image of the world.

Logic is transcendental.

6.2 Mathematics is a logical method.

The propositions of mathematics are equations, and therefore pseudo-propositions.

6.21 A proposition of mathematics does not express a thought.

. . . .

6.22 The logic of the world, which is shown in tautologies by the propositions of logic, is shown in equations by mathematics.

6.23 If two expressions are combined by means of the sign of equality, that means that they can be substituted for one another. But it must be manifest in the two expressions themselves whether this is the case or not.

When two expressions can be substituted for one another, that characterizes their logical form.

. . . .

6.24 The method by which mathematics arrives at its equations is the method of substitution.

For equations express the substitutability of two expressions and, starting from a number of equations, we advance to new equations by substituting different expressions in accordance with the equations.

. . . .

6.3 The exploration of logic means the exploration of *everything that is subject to law*. And outside logic everything is accidental.

6.31 The so-called law of induction cannot possibly be a law of logic, since it is obviously a proposition with sense,—Nor, therefore, can it be an a priori law.

6.32 The law of causality is not a law but the form of a law.

. . . .

6.33   We do not have an a priori *belief* in a law of conservation, but rather a priori *knowledge* of the possibility of a logical form.

6.34   All such propositions, including the principle of sufficient reason, the laws of continuity in nature and of least effort in nature, etc. etc.—all these are a priori insights about the forms in which the propositions of science can be cast.

. . . .

6.35   Although the spots in our picture are geometrical figures, nevertheless geometry can obviously say nothing at all about their actual form and position. The network, however, is *purely* geometrical; all its properties can be given a priori.

Laws like the principle of sufficient reason, etc. are about the net and not about what the net describes.

6.36   If there were a law of causality, it might be put in the following way: There are laws of nature.

But of course that cannot be said: it makes itself manifest.

. . . .

6.37   There is no compulsion making one thing happen because another has happened. The only necessity that exists is *logical* necessity.

. . . .

6.4   All propositions are of equal value.

6.41   The sense of the world must lie outside the world. In the world everything is as it is, and everything happens as it does happen: *in* it no value exists—and if it did exist, it would have no value.

If there is any value that does have value, it must lie outside the whole sphere of what happens and is the case. For all that happens and is the case is accidental.

What makes it non-accidental cannot lie *within* the world, since if it did it would itself be accidental.

It must lie outside the world.

6.42   So too it is impossible for there to be propositions of ethics.

Propositions can express nothing that is higher.

. . . .

6.43   If the good or bad exercise of the will does alter the world, it can alter only the limits of the world, not the facts—not what can be expressed by means of language.

In short the effect must be that it becomes an altogether different world. It must, so to speak, wax and wane as a whole.

The world of the man is a different one from that of the unhappy man.

. . . .

6.44   It is not *how* things are in the world that is mystical, but *that* it exists.

6.45   To view the world sub specie aeterni is to view it as a whole—a limited whole.

Feeling the world as a limited whole—it is this that is mystical.

6.5   When the answer cannot be put into words, neither can the question be put into words.

The riddle does not exist.

If a question can be framed at all, it is also *possible* to answer it.

6.51   Scepticism is *not* irrefutable, but obviously nonsensical, when it tries to raise doubts where no questions can be asked.

For doubt can exist only where a question exists, a question only where an answer exists, and an answer only where something *can be said*.

6.52   We feel that even when all *possible* scientific questions have been answered, the problems of life remain completely untouched. Of course there are then no questions left, and this itself is the answer.

. . . .

6.53   The correct method in philosophy would really be the following: to say nothing except what can be said, i.e. propositions of natural science—i.e. something that has nothing to do with philosophy—and then, whenever someone else wanted to say something metaphysical, to demonstrate to him that he had failed to give a meaning to certain signs in his propositions. Although it would not be satisfying to the other person—he would not have the feeling that we were teaching him philosophy—*this* method would be the only strictly correct one.

6.54   My propositions serve as elucidations in the following way: anyone who understands me eventually recognizes them as nonsensical, when he has used them—as steps—to climb up beyond them. (He must, so to speak, throw away the ladder after he has climbed up it.)

He must transcend these propositions, and then he will see the world aright.

7   What we cannot speak about we must pass over in silence.